THE REPUBLIC OF LETTERS

*The Correspondence between Thomas Jefferson
and James Madison 1776–1826*

EDITED BY

James Morton Smith

VOLUME THREE

1804–1836

W · W · Norton & Company · New York · London

Copyright © 1995 by James Morton Smith. *All rights reserved.* Printed in the United States of America.

THE TEXT OF THIS BOOK *is composed in Galliard with Janson Alternate and Avanta. The display type is set in Garamond and Naomi Script. Composition and manufacturing by The Haddon Craftsmen. Book design by Marjorie J. Flock.*

Library of Congress Cataloging-in-Publication Data

Jefferson, Thomas, 1743–1826.
    The republic of letters: the correspondence between Thomas Jefferson and James Madison, 1776–1826.
        p.   cm.
    Includes bibliographical references (v.3, p.   ) and index.
     Contents: v.1. 1776–1790 — v.2. 1790–1804 — v.3. 1804–1836
    1. Jefferson, Thomas, 1743–1826 — Correspondence.   2. Madison, James, 1751–1836 — Correspondence.   3. Presidents — United States — Correspondence.   I. Madison, James, 1751–1836.   II. Smith, James Morton.   III. Title.
E332.88.M33   1995
973.4′092′2–dc20   94-22924

ISBN 0-393-03691-X
(for the set of three volumes)

W. W. Norton & Company, Inc.
500 Fifth Avenue, New York, N.Y. 10110
www.wwnorton.com

W. W. Norton & Company Ltd.
Castle House, 75/76 Wells Street, London W1T 3QT

4 5 6 7 8 9 0

To
Scott David and Carolyn Ann Thompson,
the "busy bees,"
who, as John Adams observed to Thomas Jefferson
about Grandchildren,
have "been cheering to have . . . hovering about Us,"
and to the memory of my brother,
Vergil Earl Smith, Jr.

Contents

VOLUME THREE
1804–1836

	Abbreviations	ix
31.	Foreign-Policy Priorities, 1804–1805	1352
32.	The Perils of Neutrality, 1805–1806	1404
33.	A Conspiracy at Home and a Bad Treaty Abroad, 1806–1807	1442
34.	Embargo: The Rights of Neutrals and "the Wrongs of the Belligerents," 1807–1808	1503
35.	The End of the Embargo, 1808–1809	1548
36.	Madison Takes Over, 1809	1561
37.	The Macon Bills, 1810: "Better Than Nothing"	1614
38.	The Politics of Neutrality, 1811	1650
39.	War or Submission: 1812	1674
40.	The War of 1812: A Few Victories but More Defeats, 1812–1813	1708
41.	The Critical Year: 1814	1729
42.	Mr. Madison's War Ends: 1815	1753
43.	A Joint Retirement Project: The Origins of the University of Virginia, 1816–1817	1771
44.	Founding the University of Virginia, 1818–1819	1791
45.	Liberty and Learning, 1820–1822	1817
46.	Reminiscing about the Revolution and the Republic, 1823	1842
47.	Recruiting a Faculty, 1824	1883

48. The University Opens, 1825	*1915*
49. Jefferson's Last Year, 1826	*1952*
50. "Take Care of Me When Dead": Madison's Final Years, 1826–1836	*1972*
Bibliographical Essay	*2003*
Index	*2019*

ABBREVIATIONS

AHA American Historical Association.
AHR *American Historical Review.*
Amer. Phil. Soc. American Philosophical Society.
ASP Walter Lowrie and Matthew St. Clair Clarke, eds., *American State Papers: Documents, Legislative and Executive,* 38 vols. (Washington, 1832–61): *FR* (Foreign Relations); *M* (Miscellaneous).
Brant Irving Brant, *The Life of James Madison,* 6 vols. (Indianapolis, 1941–61): I, *James Madison: The Virginia Revolutionist* (1941); II, *James Madison: The Nationalist* (1948); III, *James Madison: Father of the Constitution* (1950); IV, *James Madison: Secretary of State* (1953); V, *James Madison: The President* (1956); VI, *James Madison: Commander in Chief* (1961).
Cappon Lester J. Cappon, ed., *The Adams-Jefferson Letters: The Complete Correspondence between Thomas Jefferson and Abigail and John Adams,* 2 vols. (Chapel Hill, 1959).
Fitzpatrick John C. Fitzpatrick, ed., *The Writings of George Washington . . . , 1745–1799,* 39 vols. (Washington, 1931–44).
Ford Paul Leicester Ford, ed., *The Writings of Thomas Jefferson,* 10 vols. (New York, 1892–99).
Hamilton, *Writings of Monroe* Stanislaus Murray Hamilton, ed., *The Writings of James Monroe . . . ,* 7 vols. (New York, 1898–1903).
Hening William Waller Hening, ed., *The Statutes at Large; Being a Collection of All the Laws of Virginia, from the First Session of the Legislature, in the Year 1619,* 13 vols. (Richmond and Philadelphia, 1819–23).
Hunt Gaillard Hunt, ed., *The Writings of James Madison,* 9 vols. (New York, 1900–10).
JAH *Journal of American History.*
JER *Journal of the Early Republic.*
JM James Madison.
J. So. Hist. *Journal of Southern History.*
Ketcham Ralph Ketcham, *James Madison: A Biography* (New York, 1971).
L. and B. A. A. Lipscomb and A. E. Bergh, eds., *The Writings of Thomas Jefferson,* 20 vols. (New York, 1903).
Malone Dumas Malone, *Jefferson and His Time,* 6 vols. (Boston, 1948–81): I, *Jefferson the Virginian* (1948); II, *Jefferson and the Rights of Man* (1951); III, *Jefferson and the Ordeal of Liberty* (1962); IV, *Jefferson the President: First Term, 1801–1805* (1970); V, *Jefferson the President: Second Term, 1805–1809* (1974): VI, *The Sage of Monticello* (1981).
MVHR *Mississippi Valley Historical Review.*
Peterson Merrill D. Peterson, *Thomas Jefferson and the New Nation: A Biography* (New York, 1970).
PJM William T. Hutchinson, William M. E. Rachal, Robert A. Rutland, J. C. A. Stagg, *et al.,* eds., *The Papers of James Madison,* 22 vols. to date (Chicago and Charlottesville, 1962–93): **(SS ser.)** is Secretary of State series; **(Pres. ser.)** is Presidential series.
PMHB *Pennsylvania Magazine of History and Biography.*
PTJ Julian P. Boyd, Charles Cullen, John Catanzariti, *et al.,* eds., *The Papers of Thomas Jefferson,* 28 vols. to date (Princeton, 1950–92).
Richardson James D. Richardson, ed., *A Compilation of the Messages and Papers of the Presidents, 1789–1897,* 10 vols. (Washington, 1907).
Syrett Harold C. Syrett and Jacob E. Cooke, eds., *The Papers of Alexander Hamilton,* 26 vols. (New York, 1961–79).
TJ Thomas Jefferson.
VMHB *Virginia Magazine of History and Biography.*
WMQ *William and Mary Quarterly.*

THE REPUBLIC OF LETTERS

31

FOREIGN-POLICY PRIORITIES, 1804–1805

AS THE ELECTION of 1804 approached, Congress proposed the Twelfth Amendment to the Constitution, which provided that presidential electors cast separate ballots for president and vice president, thus eliminating the possibility of a repetition of the tie vote that threw the Jefferson-Burr deadlock into the House of Representatives in 1800. Both the president and the secretary of state followed the ratification process carefully, hopeful that three-quarters of the states would approve the amendment before the presidential election took place. In that case, Jefferson counseled, "no time should be lost in publishing officially the final ratification."[1]

"Before I left Washington," Madison replied from Montpellier, "a circular letter was prepared and the requisite provisional steps taken for giving effect to the proposed amendment as soon as the ratification of Tennessee should be notified. As that has come to me thro' this office I take for granted that no time was lost in issuing the documents lying ready for the event."[2] Although there was a momentary hitch when the ratifying act of Georgia miscarried,[3] the Twelfth Amendment was proclaimed as ratified on September 25, 1804, well in advance of the fall elections.

Earlier in the year a congressional caucus had nominated Jefferson unanimously for a second term but had dropped Burr and substituted George Clinton of New York as his running mate. In a landslide victory, they defeated Charles Cotesworth Pinckney and Rufus King, the Federalist candidates, by a margin of 162 to 14, losing only the states of Connecticut and Delaware and two electoral districts in Maryland.

1. TJ to JM, Aug. 3, 1804, above.
2. JM to TJ, Aug. 13, 1804, above.
3. JM to TJ, Aug. 21, 1804, above.

In his inaugural address, Jefferson stressed the achievements of his first administration: the elimination of internal taxes; the shrinking of the national debt; the expansion of the Union. "Who," he asked, recurring to Madison's *Federalist* Number 10, "can limit the extent to which the federative principle may operate effectively? The larger our association, the less it will be shaken by local passions; and in any view, is it not better that the opposite bank of the Mississippi should be settled by our own brethren and children, than by strangers of another family?"[4]

The extension of the federative principle was built upon the expansion of free government, which depended essentially on the relationship of government to the people. Since the government was meant to be the servant of the people, whatever merit the measures of the administration had, the second-term president insisted, was due to "the reflecting character of our citizens at large, who, by the weight of public opinion, influence and strengthen the public measures." It was due to the sound discretion with which the people chose their representatives "from among themselves" that beneficial laws were made. It was the freely elected representatives of the people who laid "the foundations of public happiness in wholesome laws." Under the Constitution, the execution of the laws was left to the executive branch, where he as president was associated with "able and faithful auxiliaries," his left-handed tribute to Madison and his cabinet colleagues.

Because such a government depended upon public opinion and popular elections, Jefferson viewed his first term as an experiment to determine "whether freedom of discussion, unaided by power, is not sufficient for the propagation and protection of truth," testing "whether a government, conducting itself in the spirit of its constitution, with zeal and purity, and doing no act which it would be unwilling the whole world should witness, can be written down by falsehood and defamation."

The experiment has been tried; you have witnessed the scene; our fellow-citizens looked on, cool and collected; they saw the latent source from which these outrages proceeded; they gathered around their public functionaries, and when the Constitution called them to the decision by suffrage, they pronounced their verdict, honorable to those who had served them, and consolatory to the friend of man, who believes he may be intrusted with his own affairs.

But Jefferson still smarted from the vilification by opposition critics during his first term. "The artillery of the press has been levelled against us," loaded with licentious abuse that might "have been corrected by the wholesome punishments reserved and provided by the laws of the several States against falsehood and defamation." But urgent public duties precluded prosecutions of an abusive press, "and the offenders have therefore been left to find their punishment in the public indignation."

4. For TJ's second inaugural address, see Ford, VIII, pp. 341–48. For JM's suggestions, see JM to TJ, Feb. 8, 1805, below, and Feb. 21, 1805, below.

Thus, the experiment in popular government, founded on freedom of discussion, had prevailed, proving that "the public judgment will correct false reasonings and opinions, on a full hearing of all parties; and no other definite line can be drawn between the inestimable liberty of the press and its demoralizing licentiousness. If there still be improprieties which this rule would not restrain," he concluded, "its supplement must be sought in the censorship of public opinion."

After this brilliant exposition of the meaning of a free press in a free society, however, Jefferson added a caveat: "No inference is here intended, that the laws, provided by the States against false and defamatory publications should not be enforced; he who has time, renders a service to public morals and public tranquility, in reforming these abuses by the salutary coercions of the law."[5]

On foreign affairs, Jefferson said little in his inaugural address. But in the months between his inauguration in March and his message to Congress in December 1805, his administration gradually formulated its foreign-policy priorities as it tried to capitalize on American neutrality to force concessions from the British, French, and Spanish.

During most of the summer and fall, James and Dolley Madison were in Philadelphia, where Dr. Philip Physick treated an ulcerated tumor on Dolley's knee, while her husband served as her "unremitting nurse."[6] For the longest period in Jefferson's presidency, he and Madison were separated by such a great distance that they could not visit to discuss critical issues. Between July and November, therefore, there was a constant flow of letters between Monticello and Philadelphia as the president and the secretary of state formulated public policy and debated the issues of peace and war.

On the way from Washington, the Madisons had unknowingly passed the diplomatic courier carrying Monroe's announcement that negotiations with Spain had come to "an awkward termination," which Madison considered an affront "to the honor and sensibility of this Country."[7] Monroe, who had succeeded Rufus King as minister to Great Britain, had been appointed to a special mission to join Charles Pinckney at Madrid in trying to resolve smoldering issues raised by the unexpected acquisition of Louisiana from France. The Spanish, Madison observed, had bluntly rejected all American "overtures in a haughty tone": American claims to West Florida; the offer to purchase East Florida; recognition of the Rio Bravo as the western boundary of Louisiana; and the settlement of spoliation claims, estimated at $5 million to $8 million.[8] Spain and the United States had negotiated a spoliations convention

5. For differing interpretations of TJ's second inaugural address, see Frank Luther Mott, *Jefferson and the Press* (Baton Rouge, 1943), pp. 38–46, and Leonard W. Levy, *Jefferson and Civil Liberties: The Darker Side* (Cambridge, Mass., 1963), pp. 60–69.

6. Dolley Madison to Anna Cutts, July 29, 1805, in Brant, IV, p. 280.

7. JM to TJ, Aug. 2, 1805, below.

8. For the administration's position of these issues, see Brant, IV, pp. 280–81.

in 1802 to settle these claims, and the United States had dispatched its ratification to Madrid. But Spain was so outraged by the Mobile Act of 1804 that her foreign minister, Don Pedro de Cevallos, refused to discuss any issue until that act was revoked. Unless negotiations could be reopened, Madison wrote, "the question with the Legislature must be whether or not resort is to be had to force, to what extent and in what mode."[9]

As in the Louisiana crisis, Jefferson again thought about an alliance with Great Britain. He hoped for an agreement to preserve the status quo in West Florida, if the Perdido could not be confirmed as the eastern boundary of Louisiana, and perhaps for ratification of the spoliation convention of 1802. But he also thought that "the refusal to settle a limit is not of itself a sufficient cause of war, nor is the withholding a ratification worthy of such a redress. Yet these acts," he told Madison, "shew a purpose both in Spain and France against which we ought to provide before the conclusion of a peace. I think therefore we should take into consideration whether we ought not immediately to propose to England an eventual treaty of alliance, to come into force whenever (within   years) a war shall take place with Spain or France."[10] "I infer a confident reliance on the part of Spain," he added the next day, "on the omnipotence of Bonaparte" or perhaps on "a desire of procrastination till peace in Europe shall leave us without an ally."[11]

Anxious to avoid being isolated in either war or peace, the president pressed his view on Madison a fortnight later, suggesting that "should negotiations with England be advisable they should not be postponed a day unnecessarily, that we may lay their results before Congress before they rise next spring. Were the question only about the bounds of Louisiana" or even of Spanish spoliations, he confessed, "I should be for delay. . . . But I do not view peace as within our choice. I consider the cavalier conduct of Spain as evidence that France is to settle with us for her; and the language of France confirms it." For that reason, he concluded, "we should not permit ourselves to be found off our guard and friendless."[12] One week later, he expressed his fear of "hostile and treacherous intentions against us on the part of France" and urged that "we should lose no time in securing something more than a neutral friendship from England."[13]

In his diplomatic way, Madison tactfully noted some difficulties with the idea of an alliance with the British. "An eventual alliance with G. B.," he conceded, "if obtainable from her without inadmissable conditions, would be for us the best of all possible measures; but," he added, "I do not see the least

9. *Ibid.* The Spanish objected to Article 11 of the act, which vested discretionary power in the president to extend the U.S. revenue laws to the disputed territory; see Brant, IV, pp. 193–99.
10. TJ to JM, Aug. 4, 1805, below.
11. TJ to JM, Aug. 7, 1805, below.
12. TJ to JM, Aug. 17, 1805, below.
13. TJ to JM, Aug. 25, 1805, below. I think that Ford, VIII, p. 376, misread this as "something more than a *mutual* friendship with England."

chance of laying her under obligations to be called into force at our will without correspondent obligations on our part."[14] What worried him was the difficulty of obtaining "some eventual security for the active friendship of G. B." when one considered "the difficulty of obtaining it without a like security to her for ours. If she is to be *bound*, we must be *so too*, either to the same thing, that is, to join her in the war or to do what she will accept as equivalent to such an obligation. What can we offer her?" he asked.

Madison thought that a mutual guarantee of each country's objectives would be unsatisfactory to Great Britain unless it were "to involve us pretty certainly in her war." The United States might offer commercial privileges "or concessions on points in the Law of nations," but he thought these would have to be made in advance, a down payment "for aids which might never be recd. or required," the sort of bargain that seemed to him "liable to obvious objections of the most serious kind."[15]

Still anxious to explore a British alliance, Jefferson suggested that Madison might have "misconcieved the nature of the treaty I thought we should propose to England." Instead of an immediate commitment to enter the war, his proposed treaty "should be provisional only, to come into force on the event of our being engaged in war with either France or Spain during the present war in Europe. In that event we should make common cause, and England should stipulate not to make peace without our obtaining the objects for which we go to war to wit, the acknolegment by Spain of the rightful boundaries of Louisiana . . . and 2, indemnification for spoliations, for which purpose we should be allowed to make reprisal on the Floridas and *retain them* as an indemnification."

After justifying the proposed treaty as a war measure, the president backed off and suggested that war might not be necessary. "Our co-operation in the war (if we should actually enter into it) would be a sufficient consideration for Great Britain to engage for it's object." Once France and Spain learned of the treaty, they would probably agree to "a peaceable and immediate settlement of both points" before the United States became a belligerent.

Shifting his arguments back to war as an instrument of national policy, Jefferson argued that "the first wish of every Englishman's heart is to see us once more fighting by their sides against France; nor could the king or his ministers do an act so popular as to enter into alliance with us. The nation would not weigh the consideration by grains and scruples. They would consider it as the price and pledge of an indissoluble course of friendship. I think it possible that for such a provisional treaty they would give us their general guarantee of Louisiana and the Floridas. At any rate," he concluded on a nothing-ventured, nothing-gained note, "we might try them. A failure would not make our situation any worse."[16]

14. JM to TJ, Aug. 20, 1805, below.
15. JM to TJ, Sept. 1, 1805, below.
16. TJ to JM, Aug. 27, 1805, below.

These arguments must have struck Madison as wishful thinking, for he made no reference to an alliance in his response, endorsing instead suggestions he had just received from Monroe and John Armstrong, Livingston's successor as minister to France. They advised that the United States maintain the status quo in West Florida, seize Texas, and lay an embargo on trade with Spain and its colonies.[17]

If force should be necessary on our part, it can in no way be so justly or usefully employed as in maintaining the status quo. The efficacy of an imbargo also cannot be doubted. Indeed, if a commercial weapon can be properly shaped for the Executive hand, it is more and more apparent to me that it can force all the nations having colonies in this quarter of the globe, to respect our rights.[18]

Jefferson also found General Armstrong's recommendations worth consideration, especially since Spain was strengthening its posts in San Antonio, Nacogdoches, and Matagorda. But, ever tenacious of his proposals until dissuaded by contervailing arguments, he was still reluctant to give up his idea of an alliance with Great Britain and wove it into a proposed program for congressional action, if the secretary of state agreed:

Supposing then a previous alliance with England to guard us in the worst event, I should propose that Congress should pass acts, 1, authorising the Exve. to suspend intercourse with Spain at discretion; 2. to dislodge the new establishments of Spain between the Missipi and Bravo; and 3. to appoint Comm[issione]rs. to examine and ascertain all claims for spoliation that they might be preserved for future indemnification.[19]

The president hoped that the secretary of state would be able to attend a cabinet meeting on October 4, but Dolley Madison's slow recovery made that impossible. Instead, Madison sent along his views for the cabinet discussion. Although he was willing to explore an alliance with England, he preferred independent action in order to reach "an intermediate adjustment if attainable, with Spain." Indeed, he still doubted that Great Britain "will positively bind herself not to make peace whilst we refuse to bind ourselves positively to make war." At the same time, he agreed that the threat of such an alliance might be useful in discussions with France: "At Paris, I think Armstrong ought to recieve instructions to extinguish in the French Govt. every hope of turning our controversy with Spain into a French job public or private, to leave them under apprehensions of an eventual connexion between the U. S. and G. B. and to take advantage of any change in the French Cabinet favorable to our objects with Spain."

Taking a hard-nosed stance, the secretary of state said that there should be no direct negotiations with Spain, nor should the new minister, James Bow-

---

17. Armstrong, who had served as a general during the Revolution, predicted that Napoleon would intercede to prevent the quarrel from going further; see Brant, IV, p. 285.
18. JM to TJ, Sept. 14, 1805, below.
19. TJ to JM, Sept. 16, 1805, below.

doin, proceed to Madrid "untill occurrences shall invite him to Spain." Madison, therefore, opposed "any step whatever other than such as may fall within the path to be marked out for Armstrong" in Paris or for Governor Claiborne in his dealings with the Marquis de Casa Calvo in New Orleans. Claiborne should use "pretty strong language" in all such discussions and should "go every length the law will warrant agst. Morales and his project of selling lands" in the controverted area of West Florida.[20]

Madison's arguments prevented any premature action by the president and the cabinet, who considered the question of a provisional treaty with England as "too important and too difficult to be decided but on the fullest consideration," Jefferson wrote, "in which your aid and counsel should be waited for."[21]

Before Madison could return to Washington, events in Europe led him to urge "a little delay with respect to . . . England." After Napoleon crowned himself emperor in 1804, he had begun assembling boats and moving troops to the Channel for an invasion of England. Great Britain scrambled for allies to form a Third Coalition against France, signing an alliance with Austria early in 1805 and with Russia in April, after agreeing to pay £1,250,000 for every 100,000 troops raised by the Russians. Madison had just learned that Russian and Austrian armies had marched towards France in the summer of 1805, forcing Napoleon to move his army from the Channel to Bavaria. The maneuvers, he said, suggested "the probability of an extension of the war agst. France," thus making it uncertain that the United States could effect "with England such a shape for an arrangement as alone would be admissable." Under these circumstances, he emphasized, "I think it very questionable whether a little delay may not be expedient."[22]

It was a persuasive argument, Jefferson agreed, since "an extensive war on the continent of Europe" would give the United States "our great desideratum, time." Unembarrassed by any alliance, he said, "it gives us time . . . to make another effort for peaceable settlement" with Spain. "Where should this be done?" he asked Madison rhetorically, then answered: "Not at Madrid certainly. At Paris; through Armstrong, or Armstrong and Monroe as negotiators, France as the Mediator, the price of the Floridas as the means."[23]

Thus, after months of debate, events overtook plans, and Jefferson's administration adopted a new policy towards Spain, one that turned not on an alliance with England, but on French interest in Spanish affairs. After Madison returned to Washington, the cabinet formalized the new approach to Spain: purchase of the Floridas for $5 million; American cession of Texas territory

---

20. JM to TJ, Sept. 30, 1805, below. Moralès was the former Spanish intendant in Louisiana, and Calvo had been one of the Spanish commissioners.
21. TJ to JM, Oct. 11, 1805, below.
22. JM to TJ, Oct. 16, 1805, below.
23. TJ to JM, Oct. 23, 1805, below.

between the Rio Bravo and the Guadalupe in mid-Texas; Spanish payment of $4 million in spoliation claims; and, until payment was made, continued holding by the United States of the Texas territory.[24]

"An enlargement of the sum we had thought of," Jefferson told his secretary of state, "may be the bait to France," "to whom Spain is in arrears for subsidies and who will be glad also to secure us from going into the scale of England."[25] The concession on the Texas boundary "may be the soother of Spain." As for France, the president said that country could be informed that the United States was "determined not to ask justice of Spain again, yet desirous of making one other effort to preserve peace, we are willing to see whether her interposition can obtain it on terms which we think just."[26] Miraculously, Armstrong notified Madison that Talleyrand had volunteered the good offices of France in any negotiations with Spain, first suggesting $10 million for the Floridas before coming down to $7 million.[27] The cabinet reconvened, agreed to adopt the French connection, but kept $5 million as the top price.[28]

"This new state of things," Jefferson told Senator Wilson Cary Nicholas, "is the more fortunate in proportion as it would have been disagreeable to have proposed closer connections with England at a moment when so much just clamour exists against her for her new encroachments on neutral rights."[29] When the United States had been toying with the idea of an alliance with England, Madison had approved of Monroe's "winking at . . . [Britain's] dilatory policy, and keeping the way open for a fair and friendly experiment on your return from Madrid," where Monroe was to negotiate for the Floridas.[30] At the same time, however, Congress passed retaliatory legislation authorizing punitive action against foreign officers for "any trespass or tort or any spoliation, on board any vessel of the United States."[31]

Before Monroe returned empty-handed from Madrid to England, British admiralty courts had handed down a decision in the *Essex* case that abruptly altered British policy towards neutral shipping. In enforcing the Rule of

---

24. See TJ, JM, and the Cabinet's Decision on Spain, [Nov. 14, 1805], below.

25. Memorandum of cabinet meeting, Nov. 12, 1805, in Ford, I, pp. 308-9. The shipment of gold and silver from Mexico and Peru to Spain had been halted for fear of capture by the British navy, causing Spain to default on her subsidy to France.

26. TJ to JM, Oct. 23, 1805, below.

27. Cabinet memorandum of Nov. 19, 1805, in Ford, I, p. 309. Talleyrand, who had been involved in the XYZ shakedown, may have hoped for a cut. He had made over 10 million francs in assisting German rulers, whose dominions had been annexed to the French Republic by the Treaty of Campo Formio, to obtain compensatory territories on the right bank of the Rhine; see R. R. Palmer, *A History of the Modern World* (New York, 1952), p. 390.

28. Cabinet memorandum, Nov. 19, 1805, in Ford, I, p. 309. See also Malone, V, pp. 55-64, and Brant, IV, pp. 280-92.

29. TJ to Wilson Cary Nicholas, Oct. 25, 1805, in Ford, VIII, p. 383.

30. JM to James Monroe, Mar. 6, 1805, in Hunt, VII, p. 168.

31. Bradford Perkins, *The First Rapprochement: England and the United States, 1795-1805* (Philadelphia, 1955), p. 177.

1756—a unilateral pronouncement that held that trade forbidden in time of peace might not be opened up in time of war—Great Britain tried to prevent neutrals from carrying produce from the Caribbean colonies of France and Spain to Europe. American shippers had quickly perfected the principle of the "broken voyage," landing the forbidden cargoes in the United States, thus neutralizing them by paying duties, then reexporting them as neutral goods. In the case of the *Polly* in 1800, the British admiralty courts accepted this practice, ruling that enemy produce became neutral property if imported into the United States before being reexported. But in 1805, the courts began a stricter interpretation of the Rule of 1756, deciding that mere payment of duties in America did not break what amounted to a "continuous voyage" between the Caribbean islands and France or Spain; shippers had to furnish additional proof of their intent not to evade the British rule. In effect, Great Britain withdrew the permission previously extended, thus ending the rapprochement ushered in a decade earlier with Jay's treaty.[32]

To complicate matters, the *Essex* decision was not published, nor were new orders-in-council adopted. Instead, news of the new doctrine spread only as the Royal Navy began seizing scores of American ships engaged in the previously allowed trade. As early as August, Madison complained about "the provoking insults from British Commanders."[33] By the end of September, he reported from Philadelphia that "the merchts. are much alarmed at the late decisions in G. B. agst. their trade. It is conjectured that several millions of property are afloat, subject to capture under the doctrine now enforced."[34]

Even before he learned of the *Essex* decision, Madison had begun extensive research on the Rule of 1756, initiating his investigation in Washington by borrowing from the Library of Congress books on international law and admiralty proceedings by Grotius, Pufendorf, Sir William Temple, and Sir William Scott, the leading jurist in the British admiralty courts and generally recognized as the author of both the *Polly* and *Essex* decisions.[35] When Madison and his wife went to Philadelphia, Madison took his books and notes with him, he told Jefferson, so that he could continue his investigation. There he could pursue his research "with the greater success, as some books not at Washington would be within my reach," and he predicted that he would compile "a very considerable mass of matter." His preliminary findings convinced him of "the illegality of this mischevous innovation," which "threatens more loss and vexation to neutrals than all the other belligirent claims put together."[36]

As Dolley Madison's knee improved, Madison found more time in Phila-

32. Perkins, pp. 177–80, 218, notes the conflicting evidence about the date of the *Essex* decision but gives May 22, 1805, as the most likely one.
33. JM to TJ, Aug. 2, 1805, below.
34. JM to TJ, Sept. 30, 1805, below.
35. Brant, IV, p. 296. Perkins, pp. 178–79, notes that Scott was present on the bench in the *Essex* case but that the verdict was read by Sir William Grant.
36. JM to TJ, Sept. 14, 1805, below.

FOREIGN-POLICY PRIORITIES, 1804–1805   1361

delphia to pursue his "task of examining disproving and exposing the British principle which threatens to spread wide the havoc of our neutral commerce, and which has already by its effects thrown our merchants into general consternation. I have found it impossible," he told Jefferson, "to do what seemed to me any thing like justice to a question so new, and so important, and involving so many points, with^t. going thro' a wide field, and drawing together a large volume of matter. The result, however, fairly viewed, will I think fully establish the heresy of the British doctrine, and present her selfishness and inconsistences in a light, which it would be prudent in her to retreat from."

Madison was especially critical of Sir William Scott, calling him the "Colossal champion of Belligerent usurpations." Scott's decisions were often "at variance with each other and the arguments some times shamefully sophistical, at others grossly absurd." What worried Madison especially was Scott's stature in the United States, where his misguided "decisions and even dicta . . . are in a manner laws already in our Courts; and his authority if not checked will be as despotic here as it is in England." He hoped that some legal critic would undertake to overturn Scott's rulings, a task that Madison thought "absolutely necessary in order to save our admiralty jurisprudence from the misguidance which threatens it."[37]

One bright light peeked out of this "mass of matter," however. When Madison informed Anthony Merry, the British minister, that the British navy had seized the *New Orleans,* an American ship carrying a consignment of French wine for the president, the secretary of state, and Senator Pierce Butler of South Carolina, Merry requested the admiralty judge in Nova Scotia and the captain of the naval vessel to exempt "the Marseilles cargo," as Jefferson called it, from confiscation. That they did, and a British ship bound from Halifax to Trinidad sailed into New York to drop off what could now only be called neutral spirits. Thus, Merry could inform the secretary of state in June that "the effects belonging to the President and Mr. Madison have been liberated."[38]

Madison's concern for his wife was threaded through all of his correspondence from late July until late October, while he and Dolley were in Philadelphia. At first, the doctors in Washington had proposed an operation on the abscess on her knee.[39] But in Philadelphia, Dr. Physick thought a cure possible "without the use of the knife." When the knee did not respond, however, Mrs. Madison had to have "a small operation," which confined her to bed for

37. JM to TJ, Oct. 5, 1805, below. JM took on this task himself; see Ch. 32, below.
38. See TJ to JM, Aug. 27, 1805, below, and Oct. 11, 1805, below, and JM to TJ, Oct. 16, 1805, below, for their discussion of "our hermitage," "the Marseilles cargo." See also Brant, IV, p. 258. For TJ's preference for Hermitage as "the first wine in the world without a single exception," see *Jefferson and Wine: Model of Moderation,* ed. R. de Treville Lawrence III, 2d ed. (The Plains, Va., 1989), pp. 104–5. For a superb summary of TJ as America's first wine connoisseur, see Lisa King, "America's First Wine Connoisseur," *The Wine Spectator* 15 (Mar. 15, 1991): 24–33. This article was called to my attention by Melissa Jane Thompson.
39. JM to TJ, July 24, 1805, below.

weeks.[40] After yellow fever broke out in Philadelphia, the Madisons moved to the outskirts of the city for more than a month, where Madison alternately fretted about his wife's slow recovery and his continuing absence from cabinet deliberations, a situation that he found "peculiarly painful and perplexing. She will be infinitely distressed at my leaving her, with a gloomy prospect as to her relapse, and in a place which solitude would not be the only circumstance to render [it] disagreeable. On the other hand, I feel the obligations which call me to my post at this particular moment. In this dilemma, I shall wait a few days, to see whether my hopes of a favorable turn are justified: and if I should be disappointed shall wait a few more, in order to be decided by a letter from you," he told the president early in October. "If the business of the [cabinet] consultation should have been carried into execution, or can be so conveniently, without my share of service, or if what belongs to my duty can be executed under your instructions sent hither, I shall avail myself of your indulgence by remaining with my wife. If this indulgence be found improper, I shall do the best I can for her accomodation and comfort during my absence, and set out for Washington."[41]

The president sent his "fervent wishes for the speedy recovery of Mrs. Madison" in every letter he wrote to the secretary of state during the summer and fall of 1805. And when the war in Europe eased the pressure for a decision about a provisional alliance with England, Jefferson told his friend that "the present state of things does not so far press as to render it necessary for you to do violence to your feelings by prematurely leaving Mrs. Madison."[42] By late October, Dolley's leg was almost healed, the yellow fever had abated, and the Madisons moved back to Philadelphia, where she was "detained several weeks longer." But she had "advanced towards her recovery beyond the occasion of particular anxiety," so Madison reluctantly relinquished his role as nurse and returned to Washington alone.[43]

By the middle of November, Dolley was well enough to shop for a fashionable wig requested by the president for his daughter.[44] Learning that she would be joined later that month by her sister Anna and Congressman Richard Cutts of Massachusetts for the trip from Philadelphia to the nation's capital, Madison wrote with delight that the news "gives me much happiness." But, he added, "it cannot be complete till I have you again with me."[45]

40. JM to TJ, Aug. 2, 1805, below, and Sept. 1, 1805, below.
41. JM to TJ, Sept. 14, 1805, below, Oct. 5, 1805, below, and Oct. 20, 1805, below.
42. TJ to JM, Oct. 23, 1805, below.
43. JM to TJ, Oct. 20, 1805, below.
44. TJ to Dolley Madison, Nov. 1, 1805, cited in Brant, IV, p. 289.
45. *Ibid.,* pp. 288–89. Anna married Cutts in 1804; see *ibid.,* p. 242.

The Letters

Madison to Jefferson

[Washington Jan. 1, 1805]

Mr. Levy
Mr. Pinkney
Judge Livingston
Duvall
Granger
Rodney
J. T. Mason
Dallas

Madison to Jefferson

Washington Jan. 31, 1805

The Secretary of State, to whom the President of the United States has been pleased to refer the Resolution of the Senate of the 28th instant, requesting that there may be laid before the Senate such documents and papers, or other information, as the President should judge proper relative to complaints against arming the Merchant Ships or Vessels of the United States; or the conduct of the Captains and Crews of such as have been armed,—has the honor to annex hereto:—

1st A copy of a letter addressed to the Secretary of State by the Envoy of Great Britain, Dated on the 31st of August last.

2nd An extract of a letter to the same, from the late Charge d'Affaires of France Dated 6th May last, which was preceded and followed by other letters and conversations of the same Gentleman, urging the subject upon the attention of the Government. It has been also urged, by the present Minister of France, in his interviews with the Secretary of State.

Of the instances alluded to in the aforesaid letter and extract, the only authenticated statement, relative to the conduct of American Private armed Vessels, which has been received at this Department is contained in the annexed letter from Mr. George Barnwell of New York and the document accompanying it.[1] All which is respectfully submitted

JAMES MADISON

---

1. As a consequence of protests from Merry, Pichon, and Turreau, Congress enacted legislation

Madison to Jefferson

Washington Feb. 8, 1805

Notes for the second inaugural speech.

---

insert
"that the transactions of a portion of our Citizens whose intelligence and arrangements best shield them agst. the abuses, as well as inconveniences incident to the collection"[2]
substitute

Religion substitute "as religious exercises, could therefore be neither controuled nor prescribed by us. They have accordingly been left as the Constitution found them, under the direction and discipline acknowledged within the several States"[3]

Indians "no desire" instead of "nothing to desire"
substitute
"who feeling themselves in the present order of things and fearing to become nothing in any other, inculcate a blind attachment to the customs of their fathers in opposition to every light and example which wd. conduct them into a more improved state of existence. But the day I hope is not far distant when their prejudices will yield to their true interests and they will take their stand etc.[4]

press—strike out from "their own affairs"
last page—alter to—"views become manifest to them["]

---

that required armed merchantmen to post bond against unlawful use of their weapons; see Brant, IV, pp. 181–85, 273–75, 293.

2. This suggestion was based on TJ's statement about revenue from import duties "on the consumption of foreign articles [which] is paid chiefly by those who can afford to add foreign luxuries to domestic comforts"; see Richardson, I, p. 379.

3. This suggestion, which the president accepted, was an elaboration of TJ's statement that the free exercise of religion "is placed by the Constitution independent of the powers of the General Government"; see *ibid.*, pp. 379–80.

4. The president, who accepted several of these suggestions, devoted two paragraphs to Indian affairs, stressing the need for the aboriginal inhabitants, who were "endowed with the faculties and the rights of men," to move from "the hunter's state" to "agriculture and the domestic arts to . . . prepare them in time for that state of society, which to bodily comforts adds the improvement of the mind and morals"; see *ibid.*, p. 380. For TJ's position on the civilizing process for Indians, see Bernard W. Sheehan, *Seeds of Extinction: Jeffersonian Philanthropy and the American Indian* (Chapel Hill, 1973; rpt. New York, 1974), pp. 119–25 and *passim*. For an interpretation of these paragraphs—and the reluctance of the Indians to change—as a satiric assault on the Federalists, who were responsible for "the hue and cry raised against philosophy and the rights of man," see Noble E. Cunningham, Jr., *In Pursuit of Reason: The Life of Thomas Jefferson* (Baton Rouge, 1987), pp. 276–77, and Brant, IV, pp. 250–52.

Madison to Jefferson

Washington Feb. 21, 1805

Notes for the inaugural speech.

Is the fact certain that the am^t. of the internal taxes not objectionable in their nature would not have paid the collectors?[5]

What is the ammendment alluded to as necessary to a repartition of liberated revenues am^g. the states in time of peace?[6]

page 3—"in any vein" may be better than "in any event" that phrase having but just preceeded.[7]

Instead of "acts of religious exercise suited to it (religion)["] "exercises suited to it" or some equivalent variation, is suggested[8]

Jefferson to Madison

Washington Mar. 11, 1805

James Wilkinson of Maryland, Governor of the territory of Louisiana from and after the 3rd of July next for the term of 3. years then next ensuing, unless sooner etc.
Joseph Browne of N. York, Secretary of ditto from and after etc.
*Return Jonathan Meigs of Louisiana ⎫
*John B. C. Lucas of Pennsylvania ⎬ to be judges of the court of the territory of Louisiana from and after etc.
Rufus Easton of New York ⎭
George Duffield of Tennessee to be a judge of the Superior court of the territory of Orleans. [He lives at Greenville Greene county. Tennessee]
James Brown late of Kentucky, now of Orleans, Attorney of the U.S. for the district of Orleans

---

5. TJ retained his statement justifying the abolition of some minor internal taxes, which, though not inconvenient or the cause of "domiciliary vexation," cost more to collect than "would have paid the officers who collected them"; see Richardson, I, p. 379.

6. TJ looked forward to the day when federal revenues, after retiring the national debt, could be allocated to the states for internal improvements, "arts, manufactures, education, and other great objects." But he thought that such use of federal funds would require "a corresponding amendment of the Constitution"; see *ibid.*

7. TJ accepted this stylistic suggestion, although he changed it to "in any view," leading into his rhetorical question about the western bank of the Mississippi being settled by "our own brethern and children"; see *ibid.*

8. TJ retained his original phraseology on this point; see *ibid.*, pp. 379–80.

Henry Hill jun.^r of N. York Consul for the island of Cuba.
Edward Carrington of R. Island Consul at Canton.
James M. Henry of Virginia Agent at Jamaica.

*I am not sure these christian names are right

TH^s JEFFERSON

John Thompson of Kentucky Register of the land office in the Western part of the territory of Orleans
John W. Gurley, of Orleans Register etc. in the Eastern part of the territory of Orleans.
James Tremble of Tennissee Recorder of the territory of Louisiana

TH^s JEFFERSON

Madison to Jefferson

Washington Mar. 17, 1805

DEAR SIR

I inclose two letters from Monroe recd. since your departure. The intermediate ones referred to, of the 16 and 18 of Decr are not yet recd. I inclose also a letter of Decr 24. from Armstrong; who I am pleased to find understands the language in which the honorable and honest policy of this country ought to be expressed. You will find that I obey the wish of Govr Claiborne in taxing you with a lengthy communication from him rendered necessary by the persevering and elaborate attacks of his political adversaries. Fowler of Kentucky shewed me yesterday two letters one from James Brown, the other from Bradford the Editor of the newspapers. Brown without indicating any personal ill will agst. the Govr. appears to concur fully in denouncing his want of talents and weight of Character. He confirms the views given by others of the quiescent disposition of the Louisianans.

Bradford is bitter, wishes it to be inferred from circumstances which necessarily mean nothing unusual, that the Govr endeavored to give him a sop, in the job of public printing, and declares that if no removal takes place, the federal party will gain the upper hand of those attached to the administration, among whom he classes himself as one of the most zealous. His letter intimates that he had in a previous one mentioned two persons whom he dare not name as fit successors to Claiborne; but that he would name as preferable to all others, Chancellor Livingston in whose character he finds all the desirable qualifications.

Cathalan having been attacked very unjustly I dare say, because the accuser is notoriously of a worthless character, and sent a voluminous justification of himself. I do not trouble you with more of it, than the inclosed letter from Barnes, which is worth your perusal as it throws light on his own character. Lee has also written a long letter for a like purpose, which I inclose on account of some intelligence contained in it. With respectful attachment I remain Y.rs

JAMES MADISON

Jefferson to Madison

Monticello Mar. 23, 1805

SIR

Yours of the 17th was received on the 21st. I consider Armstrong's letter as giving us the result of the two inte[r]mediate letters of Monroe not received and that we may anticipate the effect of his mission. On it's failure as to the main object, I wish he may settle the right of navigating the Mobile, as every thing else may await further peaceable proceedings. But even then we shall have a difficult question to decide, to wit, whether we let the present crisis in Europe pass away without a settlement.[9]

Barnes letter strengthens the intimations we have received that he is but a wandering adventurer. His perpetual absence from his post offers just cause of superseding him whenever a good subject offers. Lee and Claiborne seem both pestered with intriguants, but as far as we see the conduct of both is without blame. In the case of Claiborne we must show that however thankfully we recieve personal information as to our officers, we will not permit them to be written down by newspaper defamation

The use of an 8 vo. Polygraph obliges me to write on paper of that size.[10] Affectionate salutations

TH.s JEFFERSON

Madison to Jefferson

Washington Mar. 27, 1805

DEAR SIR

I recd. on monday evening your favor of Mar. 23 with the return of Armstrong's and Monroe's letters first sent you. I cannot entirely dispair that Spain notwithstanding the support given by France to her claim to W. F. may yield to our proposed arrangement, partly from its intrinsic value to her, partly from an apprehension of the interference of G. B., and that this latter con-

---

9. See Malone, V, pp. 45-52.
10. For TJ's love affair with the polygraph, or portable copying machine, invented by Charles Willson Peale, see Silvio A. Bedini, *Thomas Jefferson and His Copying Machines* (Charlottesville, 1984).

sider[ation] may, as soon as France despairs of her pecuniary object, transfer her weight into our scale. If she should persist in disavowing her right to sell W. F. to the U. S. and above all can prove it to have been the initial understanding with Spain that W. F. was no part of Louisiana, it will place our claim on very different ground, such probably as could not be approved by the world, and such certainly as could not with that approbation be maintained by force.[11]

If our right be good agst. Spain at all, it must be supported by those rigid maxims of technical law, which have little weight in national questions generally, and none at all when opposed to the principles of universal equity. The world would decide that France having sold us the territory of a third party which she had no right to sell, that party having even remonstrated agst. the whole transaction, the right of the U. S. was limited to a sum and on France to procure and convey the territory, or to remit [part of?] the price, or to disown the bargain altogether. I am pleased to find that Talleyrand's letter is silent as to the W. Boundary. This circumstance is the more important as Monroe's letter to which Talleyrand's is an answer, expressly names the Rio Bravo as the W. limit of our claim.

The importance of some arrangement with Spain opening the Mobiles to our trade is sufficiently urged as in every event to be seriously pressed, in the instructions already in the hands of Monroe.

Inclosed are the letters from Cathalan which were sent on for perusal—a paper not before recd. from Monroe—a letter from C. Pinkney—and two from Jarvis with their inclosures, except the letters from the forger of draughts in Preble's name which have been put into the hands of the Sec^y. of the Navy; and a letter from D^r. Lattimore Y^{rs}. with respectful attachment

JAMES MADISON

Jefferson to Madison

Monticello Mar. 29, 1805

DEAR SIR

Your packet came to hand yesterday with the letters of Monroe, Armstrong, Coburn, Zeigler and Baldwin. Altho' I presume the appointment of Baldwin would be proper, yet as Zeigler continues to act it may lie awhile. I inclose you a letter from a Mr Thomas of Indiana inclosing a proclamation of Govr. Harrison and the names of 10. persons out of whom 5 are to be named as Counsellors. Who he is I know not, nor does he say. Whether he is in any office and whether his communication is official or private, whether this is the formal communication on which I am to act, is the question. Perhaps this may

---

11. See Malone, V, pp. 45–52.

be found out at Washington. If it is official and requires immediate action, be so good as to consult with the other gentlemen and name the 5. who are to be commissioned.[12]

Armstrong's stile of correspondence is satisfactory, but he is already forgetful of the temper of his country, and proves how readily we catch the hue of those around us.[13]

I have recieved a short letter from Fayette saying only that he had committed along one to Livingston explaining his purposes and situation, and covering the power of Attorney which I now inclose. I had thought the 600 acres on the canal of Carondelet too valuable to await this instrument, and had desired Claiborne to have it located and surveyed immediately and to draw on me for the expence. What has passed shall be communicated to you on my return. Dupont writes me that he will be over in the spring and probably La fayette with him.[14] Accept affectionate salutations

Th^s Jefferson

Madison to Jefferson

Washington Apr. 1, 1805

Dear Sir

I find by a letter just recd. from Mr. Tomkins that he declines the appointment lately made him, so that it will be necessary for you to think of another successor to Judge Hobart.[15] Writing at present without having the letter with me I can not inclose it.

A decree of Genl. Ferrand commanding at St. Domingo dated the 5th. of Feby. has just been forwarded from N. York, which transcends every former instance of barbarous misconduct towards neutrals. It subjects to death all persons aboard vessels allied as well as neutrals bound *to* or *from* ports occupied by the blacks, *or* found within two leagues of any such port, and the trial in these cases is to be by *military commission*. The decree is to operate after the 21. of April. Turreau is on an excursion to Baltimore. On his return which will

---

12. Jesse B. Thomas was an antislavery representative in the Indiana territorial legislature who later led the campaign to divide Illinois from Indiana as a separate territory. In 1808, he was elected to Congress as a representative from Indiana Territory, serving there when TJ signed the law of Feb. 3, 1809, creating Illinois Territory; see R. Carlyle Buley, *The Old Northwest: Pioneer Period, 1815–1840*, 2 vols. (Bloomington, Ind., 1951), I, p. 7, II, p. 60.

13. For an excellent biography, see C. Edward Skeen, *John Armstrong, Jr., 1758–1843: A Biography* (Syracuse, 1981).

14. In 1803, Congress voted a large land grant to Lafayette, who empowered TJ and JM to locate his claim; see Brant, IV, pp. 244–46.

15. For Daniel Tompkins's letter to JM declining his appointment as judge of the U.S. District Court in New York, Mar. 27, 1805, see Ray W. Irwin, *Daniel D. Tompkins: Governor of New York and Vice President of the United States* (New York, 1968), p. 50.

probably be in a day or two, I shall make this atrocious proceeding the subject of a conference with him, and shall urge his interposition immediately with Ferrand. It will of course be a subject of proper representation to the French Govt; but a remedy thro' that circuit can not be waited for. Will it be proper for this Dept. to address directly to Ferrand warning agst. the execution of the decree on citizens of the U. States? The conversation with Turreau may perhaps decide the question.[16] With respectful attachment Yrs truly

JAMES MADISON

Jefferson to Madison

Monticello Apr. 1, 1805

DEAR SIR

Yours of the 27th. is recieved. I put Lattimore's letter into my bundle of Agenda to be acted on in due time. Monroe's, Pinckney's and Jarvis's are now returned. I suspect that Pinckney gives us the true design of G. B. to be to oust the French and Dutch from our quarter and leave the Spaniards and Portuguese. It is possible she would rather see these two last in possession of the Southern continent than any other nation.

It is really of good augery that Taleyrand should have been silent about the Western boundary of Louisiana, and I have no doubt Monroe will make the most of it.[17] Should it end in our getting the navigation of the Mobile, only we must make our protestation to Spain that we reserve our right which neither time nor silence is to lessen and shall assert it when circumstances call for it. In the meantime propose the keeping it in status quo, unsettled.

I shall be glad that nothing be forwarded to me here after the mail which leaves Washington on Friday the 5th. Accept my affectionate salutations and assurances of constant esteem and respect.

TH. JEFFERSON

Madison to Jefferson

Washington Apr. 5, 1805

DEAR SIR

Yours of the 1st instant has been recd. with the letters of Jarvis Monroe and Pinkney. I had a conversation yesterday with Turreau on the subject of

16. General Marie-Louis Ferrand was captain general of French forces in the Caribbean; see Brant, IV, p. 271.
17. See Thomas M. Marshall, *A History of the Western Boundary of the Louisiana Purchase* (Berkeley, 1914).

Ferrand decree. He was perfectly rational and accomodating, expressed a wish to receive without delay a note from us on the subject, and promised to interpose as requested.[18] He regretted that Logan's motion to prohibit the trade with S^r. Domingo had not succeeded; observing that the Blacks had lately been enabled by American supplies to advance agst. Ferrand, and that the violence of his proclamation had been probably inspired by that circumstance. The Baltimore paper of yesterday seems to confirm this circumstance, and with the addition, that the French are likely to be driven out of the Island. Inclosed is a copy of Ferrand's Edict, and of the letter I sent to Turreau. His answer has not yet been rec^d. Y^{rs}. with respectful attachment

JAMES MADISON

Jefferson to Madison

Monticello Apr. 11, 1805

DEAR SIR

Yours of the 5th came to hand on the 8th and I now return the papers it covered. Ferrand's decree is serious and I have more hope of it's being corrected by Tureau than by Buonaparte. I shall be with you by the middle of the next week, and therefore defer to verbal explanation everything public. I shall leave my daughter in a state not immediately threatening nor yet clear of serious anxiety. A weakened stomach is the basis of her complaint, and great debility the consequence. She goes about however, is cheerful, and keeping her sufferings to herself, her friends know their extent incidentally only. We have had two very fine rains within the last fortnight. The trees are all leaved here, but in the neighborhood generally only the poplar. Our first asparagus was Mar 27. The 1st Whippoorwill Apr. 2. the 1st tick and the Dogwood blossoms on the 6th. My affectionate salutations to Mrs Madison and yourself and assurances of cordial esteem and respect.

TH^s JEFFERSON

Madison to Jefferson

Washington July 22, 1805

DEAR SIR

By this mail you will recieve the letters last recieved from Mr. Erving. No others have come to hand from any quarter worth troubling you with.

---

18. Turreau agreed that Ferrand's conduct violated the laws of humanity and the law of nations; see Brant, IV, p. 271.

Mr. Gallatin left Washington the day I beleive you did. I am still detained here by the situation of Mrs. M's complaint. The Doctr. does not claim less than seven or 8 days from this time, at least, in order to render the journey safe; and her recovery has been so much more slow than he calculated that I dare not be sanguine as to the time of my departure. I am not without apprehensions that the case may be of a very serious kind. Her appearance has changed for the better, during the state of absolute rest prescribed, but does not yet resemble that denoting the ordinary course of healing. With respectful attachment I remain always yours

JAMES MADISON

We had a fine shower yesterday, and a slight one a few days ago.

Jefferson to Madison

Monticello July 23, 1805

Th^s Jefferson presents his affectionate salutations to M$\bar{\text{r}}$ Madison and incloses him the extract of a letter from Mr Granger,[19] giving information of constant trespasses committing on a certain species of timber growing on the public lands on lake Erie of great value, and which he presumes should be the subject of a charge from the secretary of state to Governor Hull.[20] He presumes the governor should first warn all persons by proclamation from the commission of such trespass, and be afterwards watchful to have trespassers punished by indictment according to law.

P. S. Th J sets out on the 26th for Bedford and will be absent 10. days.

Madison to Jefferson

Washington July 24, 1805

DEAR SIR

At the date of my last I hoped by this time to be making ready for my journey on your track. A consultation of the Doctors Winn and Elzey on the situation of my wife's knee has ended in the joint opinion that an operation is indispinsable which can best be performed at Philadelphia and that it is prudent to avoid delay as much as possible. We shall accordingly set off tomor-

---

19. Gideon Granger was postmaster general.
20. William Hull was governor of Michigan Territory.

row, in order to put her under the care of Docr. Physic. No cause less urgent could have diverted me from my trip home, which had become very peculiarly desirable on several accounts. It is now altogether uncertain when I shall have that pleasure. If every thing goes well it is possible that the detention at Philada. may not exceed two or three weeks. I shall shorten it as much as can properly be done and then hasten to Virginia. In the mean time be pleased to address your public commands, which can not be fulfilled in the office, to me at Philada. till otherwise advised, and freely add any private ones when I can be of service. With respectful attachment I remain always yrs.

JAMES MADISON

Jefferson to Madison

Monticello July 25, 1805

DEAR SIR

Your letter of July 22. finds me in the hurry of my departure for Bedford. I return you Erving's letter and inclose Rankins' petition for a pardon; as also a correspondence sent me by Lee of Bordeaux, which tho' a little long, is entitled to a reading, as it throws light on subjects we ought to understand. I sincerely regret that Mrs Madison's situation confines her and yourself so long at Washington. I think it very unsafe for both. The climate of our quarter is really like that of another country. I have not felt one moment of disagreeable warmth since I have been at home. The thermom. has generally been, at it's maximum from 86 down to 81. In hopes that on my return I shall learn that Mrs Madison is much better and safely moored in Orange I tender you my affectionate salutations.

TH^S. JEFFERSON

P. S. I inclose you the list of the members appointed to the legislative council of Indiana, to be recorded

Madison to Jefferson

Philadelphia Aug. 2, 1805

DEAR SIR

Having passed Dalton on the road, I have received the dispatches from M. and Pinkney under the delay of their coming hither from Washington. You will have recd. copies from Washington, according to instructions I left there. The business at Madrid has had an awkward termination, and if nothing, as may be expected, particularly in the absence of the Emperor, sho^d. alleviate it at Paris, involves some serious questions[.] After the parade of a Mission extraordinary, a refusal of all our overtures in a haughty tone, without any offer of other terms, and a perserverance in withdrawing a stipulated provision for claims admitted to be just, without ex post facto conditions manifestly unreasonable and inadmissible, form a strong appeal to the honor and sensibility of this Country.[21] I find that, as was apprehended from the tenor of former communications, the military status quo in the controverted districts, the navigation of the rivers runing thro' W. Florida, and the spoliations subsequent to the Convention of 1802, have never had a place in the discussions. Bowdoin may perhaps be instructed, consistently with what has passed, to propose a suspension of the Territorial questions, the deposit, and the French spoliations, on condition that those points be yielded, with an incorporation of the Convention of 1802 with a provision for the subsequent claims. This is the utmost within the Executive purview. If this experiment should fail, the question with the Legislature must be whether or not resort is to be had to force, to what extent and in what mode. Perhaps the instructions to B. would be improved by including the idea of transfering the sequal of the business hither. This would have the appearance of an advance on the part of Spain, the more so as it would be attended with a new Mission to this Country, and would be most convenient for us also, if not made by Spain a pretext for delay. It will be important to hear from Monroe, after his interviews at Paris. It is not impossible if he should make an impression there, that without some remedy a rupture will be unavoidable, that an offer of mediation, or a promise of less formal interposition, may be given; And it will merit consideration, in which way, either should be met. Monroe talks as if he might take a trip from London home. If he comes, with a proper option to remain or return as may be thought proper, and so as not too much to commit the Govt. or himself, the trip may perhaps produce political speculations abroad, that may do no harm.

Inclosed are several letters from C.P. also a communication adding another instance to the provoking insults from British Commanders. I am not able to say how far the insult was aggravated by a violation of our territorial rights.

We arrived here on monday last; and have fixt ourselves in a pleasant, and as is believed a very safe part of the City [between 7 and 8 Streets, and Walnut and Chesnut.] Docr. Physic has no doubt of effecting the cure for which his assistance was acquired; and without the use of the knife. But this, if his patient could be reconciled to it, would greatly save time. Yrs. with respectful attachment

JAMES MADISON

---

21. Spain rejected American claims to West Florida and Texas, refused to discuss the sale of the Floridas, and withheld ratification of the claims convention negotiated in 1802; see Brant, IV, p. 281.

Jefferson to Madison

Monticello, Aug. 4, 1805

DEAR SIR:

On my return from Bedford two days ago I received your favor of July 24 and learnt with sincere regret that Mrs. Madison's situation required her going to Philadelphia. I suppose the choice between Physic and Baynham was well weighed. I hope the result will be speedy and salutary, and that we shall see you in this quarter before the season passes over.

A letter from Charles Pinckney of May 22. informs me that Spain refuses to settle a limit, and perseveres in withholding the ratification of the convention. He says not a word of the status quo, from which I conclude it has not been proposed. I observe by the papers that Dalton is arrived with the public dispatches, from which we shall know the particulars. I think the status quo, if not already proposed, should be immediately offered through Bowdoin. Should it even be refused, the refusal to settle a limit is not of itself a sufficient cause of war, nor is the withholding a ratification worthy of such a redress. Yet these acts shew a purpose both in Spain and France against which we ought to provide before the conclusion of a peace. I think therefore we should take into consideration whether we ought not immediately to propose to England an eventual treaty of alliance, to come into force whenever (within   years) a war shall take place with Spain or France. It may be proper for the ensuing Congress to make some preparations for such an event, and it should be in our power to shew we have done the same. This for your consideration.[22]

Mr. Wagner writes me that two black convicts from Surinam are landed at Philadelphia. Being on the spot you will have a better opportunity of judging what should be done with them. To me it seems best that we should send them to England with a proper representation against such a measure. If the transportation is not within any of the regular appropriations, it will come properly on the contingent fund. If the law does not stand in the way of such an act, and you think as I do, it may be immediately carried into execution. Accept for Mrs. Madison and yourself my affectionate salutations and assurances of constant esteem and respect.

TH. JEFFERSON

Jefferson to Madison

Monticello Aug. 7, 1805

DEAR SIR,

On a view of our affairs with Spain, presented me in a letter from C. Pinckney, I wrote you on the 23d of July, that I thought that we should offer

---

22. See *ibid.,* p. 283, and Malone, V, pp. 55-58.

them the status quo, but immediately propose provisional alliance with England. I have not yet received the whole correspondence. But the portion of the papers now enclosed to you, confirm me in the opinion of the expediency of a treaty with England, but make the offer of the status quo more doubtful. The correspondence will probably throw light on that question. From the papers already received I infer a confident reliance on the part of Spain on the omnipotence of Bonaparte, but a desire of procrastination till peace in Europe shall leave us without an ally. General Dearborn has seen all the papers. I will ask the favor of you to communicate them to Mr. Gallatin and Mr. Smith. From Mr. Gallatin I shall ask his first opinion, preparatory to the stating formal questions for our ultimate decision. I am in hopes you can make it convenient on your return to see and consult with Mr. Smith and Gen. Dearborn, unless the latter should he come on here where I can do it myself. On the receipt of your own ideas, Mr. Smith's and the other gentlemen, I shall be able to form points for our final consideration and determination.

I enclose you some communications from the Mediterranean. They shew Barron's understanding in a very favorable view. When you shall have perused them, be so good as to enclose them to the Secretary of the Navy. Accept my fervent wishes for the speedy recovery of Mrs. Madison, and your speedy visit to this quarter.

TH. JEFFERSON

Madison to Jefferson

Philadelphia Aug. 9, 1805

DEAR SIR

I select the inclosed papers relating [to] the ship New Jersey from a mass of which this is but a certain portion. They will enable you to decide on the question to which alone the case is reduced. This is whether in the claims under the French Convention Insurers stand in the shoes of the insured. The printed memoire by Dupont (de Nemours) deserves to be read as a Chef d'ouvre of the kind. Whatever the merits of the question in the abstract may be, I should suppose that in relation to the present case it must have been decided by the decisions in many preceeding ones, a great proportion of the claims, probably the greater part, having been in the hands of Insurers. It is surmised that Swann in connection with a corrupt member of the Council of liquidation has created the difficulty in order to secure his own claims out of a fund that might not be equal to the aggregate of claims. It is more easy to suppose this than to account for the opinion of Armstrong as stated by Dupont, which if just ought to have been applied to all claims of the like sort, and whether just or not, can scarcely be proper in its application to one as an exception to similar claims. I understand from the parties interested that in fact a considerable part of the indemnication [indemnification] in the case of the N.J. is due and claimed not by Insurers, but by the owners themselves in their own right.[23] And they are very urgent that something should pass from the Executive which may possibly be in time to save them from the erroneous interposition of the agent of the U. States. I have explained to them the principles on which the Ex. has proceeded, and the little chance there is that the whole business will not have been closed before any communication can reach Genl. Armstrong. I have suggested also the repugnance to any communication previous to intelligence from himself on the subject. In reply they urge considerations which are as obvious as they are plausible. I shall do nothing in the case til I recieve your sentiments. If these do not forbid, I shall transmit the case to Armstrong in a form which will merely glance at the point on which it is understood to turn, and will imply our confidence that he will do what is right on it.

I find by a postscript from Cadiz of June 28. that Bowdoin[24] had arrived at Santander. The time is not mentioned.

The wine etc. carried into Halifax was sent by Govr. Wentworth with polite instructions, by a vessel going to N. Y. which had no occasion to enter on her own acct. The consequence has been that she was entered on ours, and the foreign tonnage advanced, amounting to $168. including Majr. Butlers share. The duties and other charges will add not less than $50 more. This being a debt of honor admits of no hesitation. I shall pay your part, and if necessary write to Barnes to replace it. The articles are to go round to Washington.[25]

Mrs. M. is in a course of recovery, according to appearances and the opinion of Docr. Physic. Unfortunately an essential part of the remedy, the splinter and bandage, must it seems be continued til the cure is compleated. I fear therefore that our detention here will be protracted several weeks at least.

The drouht here is intense. The pastures have entirely failed, so as to drive the grazing [?] to the Hay Stacks: and the soil is troubled by the failure of the 2nd. crops of Hay. Yrs. respectfully and faithfully

JAMES MADISON

---

23. The ship *New Jersey* had been captured by the French during the quasi war, and its owners and underwriters claimed indemnification under the Convention of 1800 with France. The American minister to France, John Armstrong, at first argued that the benefits of the convention applied only to the owners, not the insurers. Du Pont, who served as agent for the insurers of the *New Jersey*, argued that the convention extended to insurers. See Skeen, pp. 64–68; Brant, IV, pp. 361–62; and Malone, V, p. 89.

24. James Bowdoin had been appointed Charles Pinckney's successor as minister to Spain on Nov. 28, 1804, but he did not sail until the next spring. He went first to London, then to Paris, before going to Madrid.

25. For the freeing of TJ and JM's French wine cargo, which had been seized by the British navy, see Brant, IV, p. 258.

Jefferson to Madison

Monticello Aug. 17, 1805

DEAR SIR

Yours of the 9th has been duly received, and I now return the papers it covered, and particularly those respecting the ship New Jersey, on which I have bestowed due attention. I think the error of General Armstrong a very palpable and unfortunate one, but one not at all chargeable on our government. By the French Convention the council of Liquidation has certain functions assigned to them of a judiciary nature. They are appointed by that government and over their nominations or opinions we have no control. Embarrassed to come to a conclusion in a particular case they transfer their functions to two other persons. These persons then stand in their place as the agents of the French government deriving their authorities from them and responsible to them alone, not to us. It is true that to command our confidence they have appointed one of these, a person who holds our commission of Minister Plenipotentiary but he does not act in this case under that commission. He is merely a French agent.[26] Messrs. Nicklin and Griffith[27] therefore may just as well suppose this government liable for all the errors of the council of liquidation, as for this; and that they are individually liable in their private fortunes for all their errors of judgment as General Armstrong for his. This renders it more delicate than usual to enter into explanations with Armstrong. Yet I think we may properly state to him our opinion. Honest men may justly be influenced by the opinion of those whose judgment they respect, especially where they are doubtful themselves. I have said these things to you, not as decisions but for your consideration and decision.

The conduct of Captain Drummond of the Fox in running away from Martinique without clearing or paying duties, is that of a rogue. But every government must contrive means within itself to enforce its own revenue laws; others cannot do it for them. I suppose Drummond might be sued here as other fugitive debtors, these actions being what the lawyers call transitory; and that it would be well for the French Consul at Boston or wherever he can be caught, to institute a suit.

I am anxious to receive opinions respecting our procedure with Spain: as should negociations with England be advisable they should not be postponed a day unnecessarily, that we may lay their results before Congress before they rise next spring. Were the question only about the bounds of Louisiana, I should be for delay. Were it only for spoliations, just as this is not cause of war, we might consider if no other expedient were more eligible for us. But I do not

---

26. For the role of Livingston and Armstrong in settling claims under the Louisiana Purchase Treaty, see George Dangerfield, *Chancellor Robert R. Livingston of New York, 1746–1813* (New York, 1960), p. 380.

27. Philip Nicklin and Robert E. Griffith were owners of the ship *New Jersey;* see Skeen, p. 64. TJ sent two messages to the Senate relative to the ship; see Richardson, I, p. 399.

view peace as within our choice. I consider the cavalier conduct of Spain as evidence that France is to settle with us for her; and the language of France confirms it: and that if she can keep us insulated till peace, she means to enforce by arms her will, to which she foresees we will not truckle and therefore does not venture on the mandate now. We should not permit ourselves to be found off our guard and friendless.[28]

I hear with great pleasure that Mrs Madison is on the recovery but fear we shall not have the pleasure of having you in our neighborhood this season, as cases like hers are slow. We are extremely seasonable in this quarter. Better crops were never seen. I have bought my provisions of corn @ 12/6. Accept for Mrs. Madison and yourself affectionate salutations.

TH. JEFFERSON

Madison to Jefferson

Philadelphia Aug. 20, 1805

DEAR SIR

Your two favors of the 4 and 7th. instant have come duly to hand. Letters from C. Pinckney to the 10th. of June have been forwarded to you thro' Washington. They confirm the idea that Spain emboldened by France, is speculating on the presumed aversion of this Country to war and to the military connection with G. B. They shew at the same time that Spain herself not only does not aim at war, but wishes to cover the unfriendly posture of things, with the appearances of an undiminished harmony. This idea is confirmed by the behaviour of the Spanish functionaries here. Yrujo particularly has multiplied his attentions, and with an air of cordiality which I should have thought it not easy for him to assume. By associating me with the Govr. in an invitation to dinner, and by the manner of it, a refusal was rendered unavoidable without giving it a point and the occasion an importance not due to it. I inclose the copy of a letter which I have since been obliged to write to him, the tone of which he will probably regard as too hard for that of our late intercourse. He has not yet answered it; and I have not seen him since he recd. it. I inclose also a letter from Turreau. Shall it be answered or not, and if answered, in what point of view.

I shall endeavor to see Mr. Smith on my return; and have sent him the dispatches from Madrid. My present view of our affairs with Spain suggests the expediency of such provisional measures as are within the Ex. authy., and when Cong. meets, of such an extension of them as will prevent or meet an actual rupture. It deserves consideration also whether with a view to all the Belligerent powers, the supply of their Colonies from the U. States ought not

28. For relations with Spain and France, see Malone, V, pp. 55-64.

to be made to depend on commercial justice. Bowdoin I think should be instructed to let Spain understand the absolute necessity of a status quo and the use of the Mobille, if not of an arbitration of acknowledged spoliations: but without any formal proposition or negociation, which if rejected would be the more mortifying to this Country, and would not leave the ultimate question as free [?] to the Congress as it ought to be. The conduct towards G. B. is delicate as it is important. No engagement can be expected from her if not reciprocal; and if reciprocal would put us at once into the war. She would certainly not stipulate to continue the war for a given period, without a stipulation on our part that within that period we would join in it. I think therefore that no formal proposition ought to be made on the subject. If the war goes on, the time will always be suitable for it. If peace is within her reach, her deliberations can let the state of things between this Country and Spain have their natural influence on her councils. For this purpose frank but informal explanations ought to be made; without commitments on our side, but with every preparation for a hostile event short of them. This course will have the further advantage of an appeal in a new forum to the policy of Spain and France, from whom the growing communications with G. B. would not be concealed. An eventual alliance with G. B. if attainable from her without inadmissible conditions, would be for us the best of all possible measures; but I do not see the least chance of laying her under obligations to be called into force at our will without correspondent obligations on our part.

I have kept so much from conversation on the politics of this state, that I can not give any very precise acct. of them. It is much to be feared that the mutual repulsion between the two immediate parties, will drive them both into extremes of doctrines as well as animosity.[29] Symptoms of these are showing themselves in the reasonings and language they oppose to each other. The federal party are not as yet settled in their plan of operations. Some are ready to support McKean as a barrier agst. the tendency they apprehend in the views of his adversaries. Others are disposed to withhold their votes from him, thro' personal and political dislike. And others taking a middle course are willing to join the Govrs. party on condition of obtaining some share of the Legislative election. The event [outcome] of the contest is uncertain. Both sides seem to be equally confident. Those most capable of a cool estimate seem to think that at this moment the Govrs. party is the stronger, but that the other is gaining ground.

We have now been here three weeks, without being able to fix the time of departure. I have every reason to believe that Mrs. M. is in the sure road to perfect recovery; but it proceeds as yet slowly.

The Aurora of this date gives the true state of the yellow fever. Yrs. as ever

JAMES MADISON

---

29. See Sanford W. Higginbotham, *The Keystone in the Democratic Arch: Pennsylvania Politics, 1800–1816* (Harrisburg, 1952), pp. 103–19.

Jefferson to Madison

Monticello Aug. 25, 1805

DEAR SIR,

I confess that the enclosed letter from General Turreau excites in me both jealousy and offence in undertaking, and without apology, to say in what manner we are to receive and treat Moreau within our own country. Had Turreau been here longer he would have known that the national authority pays honors to no foreigners, that the State authorities, municipalities and individuals, are free to render whatever they please, voluntarily, and free from restraint by us; and he ought to know that no part of the criminal sentence of another country can have any effect here. The style of that government in the Spanish business, was calculated to excite indignation; but it was a case in which that might have done injury. But the present is a case which would justify some notice in order to let them understand we are not of those powers who will recieve and execute mandates. I think the answer should shew independence as well as friendship.[30]

I am anxious to receive the opinions of our brethren after their view and consideration of the Spanish papers. I am strongly impressed with a belief of hostile and treacherous intentions against us on the part of France, and that we should lose no time in securing something more than a neutral friendship with England.[31]

Not having heard from you for some posts, I have had a hope you were on the road, and consequently that Mrs. Madison was re-established. We are now in want of rain, having had none within the last ten days. In your quarter I am afraid they have been much longer without it. We hear great complaints from F. Walker's, Lindsay's, Maury's etc. of drought. Accept affectionate salutations, and assurances of constant friendship.

P. S. I suppose Kuhn at Genoa should have new credentials.

TH. JEFFERSON

Jefferson to Madison

Monticello Aug. 27, 1805

DEAR SIR,

Yours of the 20th has been received, and in that a letter from Casinove, and another from Mrs. Ciracchi; but those from Turreau and to Yrujo were not enclosed. Probably the former was what came to me by the preceding post respecting Moreau: if so, you have my opinion on it in my last. Considering

---

30. General Jean-Victor-Marie Moreau, a French war hero who had been banished by Bonaparte, planned to visit the United States. The French minister to the United States conveyed the emperor's wish that no public reception be given to Moreau; see Brant, IV, pp. 272–73.
31. See Malone, V, pp. 57–58.

the character of Bonaparte, I think it material at once to let him see that we are not one of the powers who will receive his orders.

I think you have misconcieved the nature of the treaty I thought we should propose to England. I have no idea of committing ourselves immediately or independantly of our further will to the war. The treaty should be provisional only, to come into force on the event of our being engaged in war with either France or Spain during the present war in Europe. In that event we should make common cause, and England should stipulate not to make peace without our obtaining the objects for which we go to war to wit, the acknolegment by Spain of the rightful boundaries of Louisiana (which we should reduce to our minimum by a secret article) and 2, indemnification for spoliations, for which purpose we should be allowed to make reprisal on the Floridas and *retain them* as an indemnification. Our co-operation in the war (if we should actually enter into it) would be a sufficient consideration for Great Britain to engage for it's object; and it being generally known to France and Spain that we had entered into treaty with England would probably ensure us a peaceable and immediate settlement of both points. But another motive much more powerful would indubitably induce England to go much further. Whatever ill humor may at times have been expressed against us by individuals of that country the first wish of every Englishman's heart is to see us once more fighting by their sides against France; nor could the king or his ministers do an act so popular as to enter into alliance with us. The nation would not weigh the consideration by grains and scruples. They would consider it as the price and pledge of an indissoluble course of friendship. I think it possible that for such a provisional treaty they would give us their general guarantee of Louisiana and the Floridas. At any rate we might try them. A failure would not make our situation worse. If such a one could be obtained we might await our own convenience for calling up the *casus fœderis*. I think it important that England should recieve an overture as early as possible as it might prevent her listening to terms of peace. If I recollect rightly we had instructed Monroe, when he went to Paris to settle the deposit, if he failed in that object to propose a treaty to England immediately. We could not be more engaged to secure the deposit then, than we are the country now after paying 15. millions for it. I do expect therefore that considering the present state of things as analogous to that, and virtually within his instructions, he will very likely make the proposition to England. I write my thoughts freely, wishing the same from the other gentlemen that seeing and considering the ground of each other's opinions we may come as soon as possible to a result. I propose to be in Washington on the 2d of October. By that time I hope we shall be ripe for some conclusion.[32]

I have desired Mr. Barnes to pay my quota of expenses relating [to] the Marseilles cargo, whatever you will be so good as to notify him that it is.[33] I

---

32. See *ibid.*, pp. 58–59.
33. The "Marseilles cargo" refers to TJ and JM's French wine that had been seized by the British navy; see Brant, IV, p. 258.

wish I could have heard that Mrs. Madison's course of recovery were more speedy. I now fear we shall not see you but in Washington. Accept for her and yourself my affectionate salutations, and assurances of constant esteem and respect.

Madison to Jefferson

Philadelphia Sept. 1, 1805

DEAR SIR

I recd. yesterday yours of the 25th. The letter from Turreau appeared to me as to you, in the light of a reprehensible intrusion in a case where this Govt. ought to be guided by its own sense of propriety alone. Whether it be the effect of an habitual air of superiority in his Govt. or be meant as a particular disrespect to us is questionable. The former cause will explain it, and the latter does not seem to be a probable cause. Be it as it may, an answer breathing independence as well as friendship seems to be proper. And I inclose one to which that character was meant to be given. Just as I had finished it I was called on by Genl Smith, and considering him both in a public and personal view entitled to such a confidence, I communicated the letter and answer in order to have the benefit of the impressions made on his mind by both. He was not insensible to the improper tone of the former but regarded it as a misjudged precaution agst. proceedings which might be offensive to France and injurious to the harmony of the two countries rather than any thing positively disrespectful to the U. S. With respect to Turreau's part in the communication, he is entirely of that opinion. He says that Turreau speaks with the greatest respect and even affection towards the Administration; and such are the dispositions which it is certain he has been uniformly manifested to me. With this impression as to the letter, he thought the answer tho' due to its manner, was rather harder than was required by its intention.[34] I suggested for consideration whether it ought to be softened; and if so whether it will be sufficiently and properly done by substituting (in line 8th / for "the proper", "a sufficient" before "motive," and by inserting before "left" (in line 12) the words "of course" or by some other equivalent changes. If these alterations be approved, and the answer be otherwise so, you can have them made and the letter forewarded thro' Washington to Baltimore. For this purpose the date is left blank, that you may fill it suitably. If the letter should not appear proper without material alterations which can not be made with the copy sent, you will please to send it back with the requisite instructions for a new one. You will observe that I have not expressed or particularly implied the non responsibility of the nation for the proceedings of the State or other local authorities. Whilst it can

---

34. Brant, IV, pp. 272-73, observed that Senator Samuel Smith's reaction was not surprising. He was the uncle of Elizabeth Patterson, whose marriage to Jerome Bonaparte the emperor was trying to dissolve; Smith, therefore, "wanted no addition to the imperial anger."

not be on one hand necessary to admit it, I think it would not be expedient, and might not even be correct to deny it. Altho the Govt. of the U. S. may have no authority to restrain in such cases, the Foreign Govt. will not be satisfied with a reference to that feature in our Constitution, unless a real insult be offered to it; and such an insult seems possible. A State Legislature or City Corporation, might resolve and publish that Moreau had been barbarously treated, or that Bonaparte was a usurper and Tyrant etc.

The more I reflect on the papers from Madrid, the more I feel the value of some eventual security for the active friendship of G. B. but the more I see at the same time the difficulty of obtaining it without a like security to her for ours. If she is to be *bound,* we must be *so too,* either to the same thing, that is, to join her in the war or to do what she will accept as equivalent to such an obligation. What can we offer her? A mutual guaranty, unless so shaped as to involve us pretty certainly in her war would not be satisfactory. To offer commercial regulations, or concessions on points in the Law of nations, as a certain payment for aids which might never be recd. or required, would be a bargain liable to obvious objections of the most serious kind. Unless therefore some arrangement which has not occurred to me, can be devised, I see no other course than such an one as is suggested in my last letters. I have heard nothing from either of my colleagues on the subject. Mr. Gallatin in returning the Spanish papers merely remarked that the business had not ended quite so badly as he had previously supposed, concuring in a remark I had made to him, that the instructions to Bowdoin would involved much delicacy.

Moreau was visited by a crowd here; and it is said declined a public dinner with a promise to accept one on his return which w^d. be about October. He did not call on me, and I did not see him. The fever is still limited but very deadly in its attacks. The present rainy weather is giving it more activity. Mrs. M. is still on her bed, the apparatus of cure fixing her there. We hoped a few days ago that she would quickly be well; towards which great progress is made, but a small operation which could not be a avoided, will detain us a little longer. Yrs. always

J. MADISON

Madison to Jefferson

Gray's near Philadelphia Sept. 14, 1805

DEAR SIR

I inclose herewith sundry communications which I recd. yesterday. One of them is from Monroe at Paris,[35] who appears by a letter from Erving to have arrived at London the latter end of July. A letter from Armstrong went for you

---

35. Monroe had been instructed to join Pinckney in Madrid to try to settle differences with Spain aroused by the Louisiana Purchase. Their mission failed, and Monroe returned to his post as minister to Great Britain after stopping off in Paris; see Malone, V, pp. 45–52.

by the last mail. He seems to have moderated the scope of his former advice as to Spain. In that now given, there is in my judgment, great solidity. If force should be necessary on our part, it can in no way be so justly or usefully employed as in maintaining the status quo. The efficacy of an imbargo also cannot be doubted. Indeed, if a commercial weapon can be properly shaped for the Executive hand, it is more and more apparent to me that it can force all the nations having colonies in this quarter of the globe, to respect our rights. You will find in Erving's letters new marks of his talents.[36]

I inclose also a sample of wheat from Buenuos Ayres, another from Chile, and a sample of Barley from Galicia in Spain. The Wheat from B. A. I observe is weavel-eaten, and the paper when opened contained a number of the insects. If these are not known at Buenuos Ayres, and the wheat, as I presume, was in this sample immediately from that province, it is a proof that the egg, if laid in the green state of the wheat, is also laid after it has been gathered. This fact however has been otherwise established, I believe. The whole was sent me by the Marquis D'Yrujo to be forwarded to you. I have sent what he marked for myself to a careful gentleman in Orange; so that there will be two chances for the experiment. The Marquis recd. dispatches by the vessel which brought Moreau. I did not doubt that they communicated his recall and the demand of it; till I was told by Merry a few days ago, that the Marquis signified to him that he should pass the next winter in Washington. Perhaps this may be a finesse, tho' I see no object for it.[37] Mr. and Mrs Merry left Bush hill a few days ago, and are now at the Buck tavern about 11 miles on the Lancaster road, where she is sick with an intermittent [fever], with which she was seized at Bush hill. Her maid was so ill that it was suspected hers was a case of yellow fever. It turned out to have been a violent bilious fever only, and she is on the recovery. Merry himself is at length discharged by Dr. Physic as *fundamentally* cured.

The fever began to show itself in so many parts of the City, and so far westwardly, that we thought it prudent to retire from the scene; the more so as it was probable that a removal would be forced, before my wife would be ready to depart altogether, and it was becoming very difficult to find in the neighborhood quarters unoccupied by fugitives from the City. We were so lucky as to get rooms at this place. A day later and we should have been anticipated by others. How long we shall be detained here is uncertain. Mrs. M's complaint has varied its aspect so often, that altho' it seems now to be superficial and slight, it is not subject to an exact computation of time. If there be no retro-

---

36. George W. Erving of Boston had been appointed secretary to James Bowdoin, the new minister to Spain. When Bowdoin remained in Paris, Erving went to Madrid as chargé d'affaires and Pinckney returned home.

37. TJ and JM had urged Yrujo's recall but had not demanded it. In Nov. 1805, the cabinet agreed that he should be notified that he was unwelcome in Washington. When he remained, JM opposed expelling him by force but added that Yrujo had no diplomatic standing and could act only through the French minister; see Brant, IV, pp. 205-6, 210-11, 291, 324-25.

grade perverseness hereafter, we are promised by appearances that she will be entirely well in a few days.

The fever rages severely in Southwark, and is very deadly. The cases in the city are as yet not perhaps very numerous. But no reliance is to be put in the accuracy of the statements published. There were certainly cases in 8th Street two weeks ago which were never published. In the mean time the Medical corps continues split into opposite and obstinate opinions on the question whether it be or be not contagious. Each side puzzles itself with its own theory, and the other side with facts which the theory of the other does not explain. There is little probability therefore that the discord is near its term. The facts, indeed, which alone can decide the theory, are often so equivocal as to be construed into proofs on both sides.

I brought with me from Washington, the subject I had undertaken before you left it; I mean the new principle that a trade not open in peace, can not be opened by a nation at war to neutral nations; a principle that threatens more loss and vexation to neutrals than all the other belligirent claims put together. I had hoped that I should find leisure in Philada. to pursue the subject and with the greater success, as some books not at Washington would be within my reach. In the latter particular I have not been entirely disappointed. But such were the interruptions of visits of civility and of business, that with the heat of the weather, and the necessary correspondence from day to day with the office, I could make but little progress, particularly during the first three of four weeks after my arrival. I find my situation here now favorable, and am endeavoring to take advantage of it. I shall in fact before I leave it, have a very considerable mass of matter, but it will be truly a rudis indigestaque moles [a rude and unarranged mass]. From the authorities of the best Jurists, from a pretty thorough examination of Treaties, especially British Treaties, from the principles and practise of all other maritime nations, from the example of G. B. herself, in her laws and colonial regulations, and from a view of the arbitrary and contradictory decisions of the Admy. Courts, whether tested by the law of N[ations], the principles assumed by her, or the miscalled relaxations from time to time issued by the Cabinet, the illegality of this mischevous innovation, seems to admit the fullest demonstration. Be assured of the respectful attachment with which I remain Y^{rs}

JAMES MADISON

Jefferson to Madison

Monticello Sept. 16, 1805

DEAR SIR,

The enclosed letter from General Armstrong furnishes matter for consideration. You know the French considered themselves entitled to the Rio

Bravo, and that Laussat declared his orders to be to recieve possession to that limit, but not to the Perdido; and that France has to us been always silent as to the Western boundary, while she spoke decisively as to the Eastern. You know Turreau agreed with us that neither party should strengthen themselves in the disputed country during negociation; and Armstrong, who says Monroe concurs with him, is of opinion from the character of the Emperor that were we to restrict ourselves to taking the posts on the West side of the Missipi. and threaten a cessation of intercourse with Spain, Bonaparte would interpose efficiently to prevent the quarrel going further. Add to these things the fact that Spain has sent 500. colonists to St. Antonio, and 100 troops to Nacogdoches, and probably has fixed or prepared a post at the Bay of St. Bernard at Matagordo. Supposing then a previous alliance with England to guard us in the worst event, I should propose that Congress should pass acts, 1, authorising the Exve. to suspend intercourse with Spain at discretion; 2. to dislodge the new establishments of Spain between the Missipi. and Bravo; and 3. to appoint Commrs. to examine and ascertain all claims for spoliation that they might be preserved for future indemnification. I commit these ideas merely for consideration and that the subject may be matured by the time of our meeting at Washington, where I shall be myself on the 2d of October. I have for some time feared I should not have the pleasure of seeing you either in Albemarle or Orange, from a general observation of the slowness of surgical cases. However should Mrs. Madison be well enough for you to come to Orange I will call on you on my way to Washington if I learn you are at home. Genl. Dearborne is here. His motions depend on the stage. Accept for Mrs. M. and yourself affectionate salutations.

P. S. I am afraid Bowdoin's journey to England will furnish a ground for Pinckney's remaining at Madrid. I think he should be instructed to leave it immediately, and Bowdoin might as well perhaps delay going there till circumstances render it more necessary.

Jefferson to Madison

Monticello Sept. 18, 1805

DEAR SIR

I return you Monroe's letters most of the views of which appear to me very sound, and especially that which shews a measure which would engage France to compromise our difference rather than to take part in it and correct the dangerous error that we are a people whom no injuries can provoke to war. No further intelligence being nor expected on this subject, and some measures growing out of it requiring as early consideration as possible, I have asked of our collegues a cabinet meeting at Washington on the 4th. of Oct. at 12. o clock, where I hope Mrs Madison's situation will permit you to be, altho I despair of it's admitting your visit to Orange. It is most unfortunate that Monroe should be coming home so precipitately. I cannot but hope that Bonaparte's return to Paris about the 13th. of July would find and detain him there till it would be too late to get to England and wind up there in time to arrive here before winter. Accept for Mrs Madison and yourself affectionate salutations.

Th^s Jefferson

Madison to Jefferson

Gray's near Philadelphia Sept. 30, 1805

Dear Sir

I duly recd. your favor of [Sept. 18] from which I learn your purpose of meeting the Heads of Depts. in consultation on the 4th of Oct. It is no little mortification that it will not be in my power to obey the summons. Mrs. M's afflicted knee which has already detained us so long, tho' I trust perfectly healed, is in so tender a state and the whole limb so extremely feeble, that she could not be put on the journey for some days to come without a manifest risk, the more to be avoided on the road, as she would be out of reach of the necessary aid. If it were possible to place her in such a situation here as would justify my leaving her, I shd. not hesitate to set out without her, and either return or send for her. But no such situation can be found out of the City, and there the attempt is forbidden by the existing fever, which is understood too, to be growing considerably worse. There is another obstacle in my way which will oblige me to wait a few days longer. On the whole, I shall not be able to set out before Thursday or friday. I shall make it the first of those days if possible and shall be as expeditious on the journey as circumstances will permit.

Since I recd. your letter I have turned in my thoughts the several subjects which at the present moment press on the attention of the Executive.

With respect to G. B. I think we ought to go as far into an understanding on the subject of an eventual coalition in the war, as will not preclude us from an intermediate adjustment if attainable, with Spain. I see not however much chance that she will positively bind herself not to make peace whilst we refuse to bind ourselves positively to make war; unless indeed some positive advantage were yielded on our part in lieu of an engagement to enter into the war. No such advantage as yet occurs, as would be admissible to us and satisfactory to her.

At Paris, I think Armstrong ought to recieve instructions to extinguish in the French Govt. every hope of turning our controversy with Spain into a French job public or private, to leave them under apprehensions of an eventual connexion between the U. S. and G. B. and to take advantage of any change in the French Cabinet favorable to our objects with Spain.

As to Spain herself one question is whether Bowdoin ought to proceed or not to Madrid. My opinion is that his trip to G. B. was fortunate, and that the effect of it will be aided by his keeping aloof untill occurrences shall invite him to Spain. I think it will be expedient not even to order Erving thither for the present. The nicest question however is whether any or what step should be taken for a communication with the Spanish Govt. on the points not embraced by the late negociation. On this question my reflections disapprove of any step whatever other than such as may fall within the path to be marked out for Armstrong; or as may lie within the sphere of Claiborne's intercourse with the Marquis de Casa Calvo.

Perhaps the last may be the best opportunity of all for conveying to Spain the impressions we wish, without committing the Govt. in any respect more than may be adviseable. In general it seems to me proper that Claiborne should hold a pretty strong language in all cases, and particularly that he should go every length the law will warrant agst. Morales and his project of selling lands. If Congs. should be not indisposed, proceedings may be authorized that will be perfectly effectual, on that as well as other points. But before their meeting there will [be] time to consider more fully what ought to be suggested for their consideration.

The merchts. are much alarmed at the late decisions in G. B. agst. their trade. It is conjectured that several millions of property are afloat, subject to capture under the doctrine now enforced.[38] Accept assurances of my constant and most respectful attacht.

JAMES MADISON

Madison to Jefferson

Gray's near Philadelphia Oct. 5, 1805

DEAR SIR

At the date of my last I entertained hopes of being at this time half way to Washington. Instead of that I am unable to say when I shall be able to commence the journey. The ride which we took in order to train Mrs. M. for it has been succeeded by sensations and appearances which threaten a revival of her complaint in some degree and in some form or other. I flatter myself that as the appearances are rather in the vicinity than on the spot before affected, the cause may not be of a nature to re-open the part healed. Perhaps it may be very superficial and be quickly removed. My situation is nevertheless rendered peculiarly painful and perplexing. She will be infinitely distressed at my leaving her, with a gloomy prospect as to her relapse, and in a place which solitude would not be the only circumstance to render disagreeable. On the other hand, I feel the obligations which call me to my post at this particular moment. In this dilemma, I shall wait a few days, to see whether my hopes of a favorable turn

---

38. For a full discussion of JM's activities while he was in Philadelphia, see *ibid.*, pp. 280–92, and Malone, V, pp. 45–59.

are justified: and if I should be disappointed shall wait a few more, in order to be decided by a letter from you. If the business of the consultation should have been carried into execution, or can be so conveniently, without my share of service, or if what belongs to my duty can be executed under your instructions sent hither, I shall avail myself of your indulgence by remaining with my wife. If this indulgence be found improper, I shall do the best I can for her accomodation and comfort during my absence, and set out for Washington.

Should my continuance here be the result, I shall make it subservient to the task of examining disproving and exposing the British principle which threatens to spread wide the havoc on our neutral commerce, and which has already by its effects thrown our merchants into general consternation. I have found it impossible to do what seemed to me any thing like justice to a question so new, and so important, and involving so many points, with^t. going thro' a wide field, and drawing together a large volume of matter. The result, however, fairly viewed, will I think fully establish the heresy of the British doctrine, and present her selfishness and inconsistences in a light, which it would be prudent in her to retreat from. I have been for several days engaged in reviewing the judgments of Sr W. Scott in cases involving that doctrine. I find them more vulnerable than I had supposed. The decisions are often at variance with each other and the arguments some times shamefully sophistical, at others grossly absurd. It were to be wished that some Legal critic of leisure and talents would undertake to overturn this Colossal champion of Belligerent usurpations. He could not fail to succeed, and the task is becoming absolutely necessary in order to save our admiralty jurisprudence from the misguidance which threatens it. The decisions and even dicta of Sr. W. Scott are in a manner laws already in our Courts; and his authority if not checked will be as despotic here as it is in England.[39]

Cathcart I find is a candidate for a factorship among the Indians. He has written to me on the subject. You know him so well that I can give no information that could aid your estimate of his pretensions. I believe him honest and capable, and can not but think his knowledge of French and Spanish may balance in some measure the defect of his temper. It has been doubted I understand, whether his habits wd. descend to the functions to which he would be subjected. I am not so intimately acquainted with him as to be a judge on that point.[40] Perhaps an idea of dignity would have less effect in the wilderness, than in scenes of fashion. I hazard these remarks without knowing the competitions which probably exist, and cheifly under the influence of a sensibility to his need and expectation of some appt. which will testify the favorable opinion of the Govt. and give subsistance to his family. With respectful and constant attach^t. I remain y^{rs}.

JAMES MADISON

39. For JM's examination of the Rule of 1756, see Brant, IV, pp. 293–304.

40. James Leander Cathcart had previously served as American consul at Tripoli; see *PJM* (SS ser.), I, p. 3.

Jefferson to Madison

Washington Oct. 11, 1805

DEAR SIR.

The only questions which press on the Executive for decision are whether we shall enter into a provisional alliance with England to come into force only in the event that *during the present war* we become engaged in war *with France?*[41] leaving the declaration of the casus federis ultimately to us. Whether we shall send away Yrujo, Casacalvo, Morales? Whether we shall instruct Bowdoin not to go to Madrid until further orders? But we are all of opinion that the first of these questions is too important and too difficult to be decided but on the fullest consideration, in which your aid and counsel should be waited for. I sincerely regret the cause of your absence from this place and hope it will soon be removed; but it is one of those contingencies from the effects of which even the march of public affairs cannot be exempt. Perhaps it would not be amiss to instruct Bowdoin to await at London further orders; because if we conclude afterwards that he should proceed, this may follow the other instruction without delay.

I am glad we did not intermeddle with Armstrong's decision against the insurance companies. I am told these companies have a great mixture of English subscribers. If so, the question becomes affected by the partnership.

What is become of our hermitage?[42] As you are in the neighborhood of Butler I presume the claim upon us could be easily settled and apportioned. Present my respects to Mrs. Madison and my prayers for her speedy and perfect re-establishment and accept yourself affectionate salutations.

Madison to Jefferson

Gray's near Philadelphia Oct. 16, 1805

DEAR SIR

I recd. duly your favor of the 11th at this place where I am still very painfully detained by the situation of Mrs. M. The appearance of her knee is still equivocal; I am afraid discouraging as to a very prompt and compleat cure. I am the less able however to pronounce on this point, as the Dr. has been prevented by indisposition from seeing his patient for several days, and I can not be guided by her judgment. We expect he will visit her tomorrow. I am not the less distressed by this uncertainty, in consequence of the indulgent manner in which you regard my absence, but it would have been a great alleviation to me if my absence had not suspended important questions, on which my aid would have been so inconsiderable. The suspension however I

---

41. TJ's italics.

42. "Our hermitage" refers to TJ and JM's wine cargo from Marseilles, which had been seized by the British navy, then "liberated" for delivery to the president and Secretary of state; see JM to TJ, Aug. 9, 1805, above, and TJ to JM, Aug. 27, 1805, above.

hope will not be continued if circumstances should press for early decisions. The latest accounts from Europe may perhaps suggest a little delay with respect to any provisional arrangements with England. Considering the probability of an extension of the war agst. France, and the influence that may have on her temper towards the U. S. the uncertainty of effecting with England such a shape for an arrangement as alone would be admissible, and the possible effects elsewhere of abortive overtures to her, I think it very questionable whether a little delay may not be expedient, especially as in the mean time the English pulse will be somewhat felt by the discussions now on foot by Mr. Monroe. With respect to Morales, my idea is that he should be instantly ordered off, if Claiborne has the legal power necessary; to which ought to be added perhaps some public admonition agst. the purchase of lands from him. Casa Calvo has more of personal claim to indulgence. I lean to the opinion nevertheless that he should receive notice also to depart; unless Claiborne should be very decided in thinking his stay useful. The stronger his personal claim to indulgence may be, the stronger would be the manifestation of the public sentiment producing his dismission. Yrujo's case involves some delicate considerations. The harshness of his recall, as made by our Ministers, and then the footing of a voluntary return on which his leaving the U. S. was put, seem to suggest a degree of forbearance. On the other hand the necessity of some marked displeasure at the Spanish conduct, a necessity produced as is believed by his own mischeivous agency, and the indelicacy of his obtruding his functions here, if that should be the case, plead strongly for peremptory measures towards him. As it is not yet formally known, that he has heard from his Govt. in consequence of the letter of recall, altho' rendered pretty certain by a recurrence to dates, it may be well perhaps to see whether he manifests a purpose of remaining here. If he should the question will arise whether he shall receive notice that his departure was expected, or that he can no longer be received as the organ of communication with his Govt. Thro' private channels I collect that he proposes to be at Washington the ensuing winter. The idea is also given out by his family that they are to go to Spain. It can not be long before some occasion will arise for knowing his real intentions. and—therefore for expressing those of the Excutive. As to Bowdoin I think it clear he ought to remain in England for the present and if Erving should have not proceeded to Madrid, I think he also should remain there. Pinkney if, as is to be wished and his last letter promised, he should have left Spain, will have named Young or some one else, to be the shadow of a representation and if [he] shd. have named no one, perhaps so much the better.

    If you think it proper that Mr. Wagner should write to Bowdoin or Claiborne or both, he will on an intimation of what you wish to be said, write letters of which he is very capable, either in his own name refering to my absence, or to be sent hither for my signature.

    I find it necessary to mention, what I thought I had done before, that on receiving your sanction, I intimated to Armstrong the opinion here that Insurers stood in the shoes of the insured, under the Convention. I was particularly careful however to use terms that would not commit the Govt. on the question of a mixture of British subjects in the transactions. The question had occurred to me on reading the papers concerning the N Jersey and I suggested it [to] Mr. Dallas, who confirmed the fact of such a mixture. It appeared to me however, that it was best not to bring the matter into view by countenancing a different decision in a particular case, from what had taken place in similar cases. Probably ⅘ of the payments under the Convention involve the question.

I wrote long ago to Gelston to send me the precise amount of what is due on the Hermitage, with a promise to remit the money. I have not yet recd. an answer, which I ascribe to the confusion produced in N. Y. by the fever. In the same manner I explain his not having forwarded the wine to Washington.

I inclose a letter etc. from Truxton which explains itself. Also one from Frousant, with a recommendation of him for consul at Martinique. I explained the obstacle to the appt. of a Consul. He was not altogether unaware of it, but seemed to think that an informal agency at least would not be offensive, but otherwise, and would be very useful. I believe he wd. suit very well for such a purpose, probably better than any other to be had; and it is possible that Turreau might give some sort of sanction. Prudent guardians of our affairs in the W. Indies would probably prevent much loss to individuals, and much perplexity to the Govt. If you think the proposition in this case admissible, and that it ought to depend on Turreau, Wagner could communicate with Petry on the subject, unless any other mode of ascertaining the disposition in that quarter be thought better.[43]

I put under the same cover with this the last letters from Monroe, which you will please to send to the office when you think proper. I am sorry he did not transmit copies of the law opinions given him by Lord Mulgrave. With constant and respectful attacht. I remain Y^{rs}.

JAMES MADISON

Madison to Jefferson

Philadelphia Oct. 19, 1805

DEAR SIR

Doctor Park of this City is setting out with his daughter, on a trip Southwards, and proposes to be in Washington before he returns. He is an old acquaintance in the family of Mrs. Madison, and is truly an amiable and respectable man. That he may present his respects with the greater facility I have

---

43. Jean Baptiste Petry was secretary of the French legation in Washington; see Brant, IV, p. 267. For his earlier career in the United States, see Peter P. Hill, *French Perceptions of the Early American Republic* (Philadelphia, 1988), pp. 6–7, 62, 66.

asked him to accept a few lines making him known to you. With sentiments of respectful attachment I am Your mo: Obedt. hble Servt

JAMES MADISON

Madison to Jefferson

Philadelphia Oct. 20, 1805

DEAR SIR

The decrease of the fever in the City has induced us to return with Mrs. M. to it, with a view to place her in a situation that would justify me in leaving her for a while. She is likely to be detained several weeks longer, before the Doct. will approve of her entering on a journey; but I hope she is now or will be in a day or two advanced towards her recovery beyond the occasion of particular anxiety. I propose therefore to set out with little delay for Washington. Perhaps I may reach Washington by the last of the week. I have nothing to add but the respectful attachment with which I remain Y^{rs}.

JAMES MADISON

I took the liberty of giving yesterday a line of introduction to Dr. Parks of this City who is on a visit with a daughter to Washington. He is in his political convictions of the Old School I presume. But he is at least candid in his judgmt. of executive measures, and sincere in his personal esteem and respect. I am not sure that he will make use of the letter; but I think it probable. If he should not it will happen from circumstances incident to his movemts. His daughter is of the demi-Quaker manners—but sensible and accomplished

Jefferson to Madison

Washington Oct. 23, 1805

DEAR SIR,

Yours of the 20th came to hand last night. I sincerely regret that Mrs. Madison is not likely to be able to come on so soon as had been hoped. The probability of an extensive war on the continent of Europe strengthening every day for some time past, is now almost certain. This gives us our great desideratum, time. In truth it places us quite at our ease. We are certain of one year of campaigning at least, and one other year of negotiation for their peace arrangements. Should we be now forced into war, it is become much more questionable than it was whether we should not pursue it unembarrassed by any alliance and free to retire from it whenever we can obtain our separate terms. It gives us time too to make another effort for peaceable settlement. Where should this be done? Not at Madrid certainly. At Paris through Armstrong, or Armstrong and Monroe as negotiators, France as the Mediator, the price of the Floridas as the means. We need not care who gets that: and an enlargement of the sum we had thought of may be the bait to France, while the Guadaloupe as the western boundary may be the soother of Spain, providing for our spoliated citizens in some effectual way. We may announce to France that determined not to ask justice of Spain again, yet desirous of making one other effort to preserve peace, we are willing to see whether her interposition can obtain it on terms which we think just; that no delay however can be admitted, and that in the meantime should Spain attempt to change the status quo, we shall repel force by force, without undertaking other active hostilities till we see what may be the issue of her interference.[44] I hazard my own ideas merely for your consideration. The present state of things does not so far press as to render it necessary for you to do violence to your feelings by prematurely leaving Mrs. Madison. Accept for her and yourself my affectionate salutations.

P. S. Let Mr. Smith know as you pass thro' Baltimore, and he will come on.

Madison to Jefferson

[Washington Oct. 25, 1805][45]

(*a*) And which have been increased by peculiar circumstances in the W. Indn. seas, yet in the more distant channels, at least of our trade.

(*b*) The act authorizes etc. provisionally at least—a port etc. without the limits of the U. S. the words in (   ) may be left out.

(*c*) (On the part of Spain).

(*d*) (Proper to suspend) will accord better with the case—as the 6th. atr. is also made a ground of suspension.

(*e*) May reasonably be expected to replace the Spanish govt. in the disposition which originally concurred in the Convention.

(*f*) (Manifestations).

(*g*) (On proper) quer. if the last circumstance may not be omitted in so general a paragraph and left to be included in some particular message or taken up on informal suggestion.

(*h*) Quer here as above.

(*i*) (Effectual) is it not too strong?

---

44. For TJ's decision to open negotiations with Spain in Paris, see Malone, V, pp. 60-64. It was confirmed on Nov. 12, 1805, at the first cabinet meeting that JM attended after returning from Philadelphia; see Ford, I, pp. 308-9.

45. JM left Philadelphia on Oct. 23, 1805; see Brant, IV, p. 288. These notes are his first suggestions for alterations to TJ's draft of his fifth annual message to Congress, which the president delivered on Dec. 3. TJ's draft is in Ford, VIII, pp. 384-96. Also see Richardson, I, pp. 382-88.

Jefferson, Madison, and the Cabinet's Decision on Spain

[Washington Nov. 14, 1805]

1. Spain shall cede and confirm to the US. East and West Florida with the islands and waters thereon depending and shall deliver possn. immedly.

2. The US. shall pay to Spain in the city of Madrid on delivery of possn. 5. M. D. within   Months after the treaty shall have been ratified by Spain.

3. Spain and France to have the same privileges respecting trade in the Floridas as [illegible] in Louisa.

4. The boundary between the territories of Orleans and Louisiana on the one side and the domns. of Spain on the other shall be the river Colorado from its mouth to it's source thence due N. to the highlands inclosing the waters which run directly or indirectly into the Missouri or Misipi rivers, and along those highlands as far as they border on the Span. domns.

5. The country between the Western boundary of the territories of Orleans on the one side—and Louis^a on the other (the Rio Bravo and Eastern or Salt river branch thereof Rio Colorado) from its main source and by the shortest coast to the highlands before ment^d as the sd. Western bound^y shall remain unsettled for 30 years from the date of this treaty.

6. Spain shall pay to the US. in the city of Wash^n on or before the last day of Dec. 1807. 4. M^s D. as an indemnific^n and acquittance for all Spolians comm^d under her flag on the citizens of the US. prior to the 1st day of Nov. 1805. with interest thereon from the date of this treaty, and for the faithful perform^{ce} thereof she hypothecates to the US. the country described in the 5th article.

7. The US. in the mean time undertake to advance to their citizens the interest on their respective claims for such spolitns. to be settled by authority of the US. and in the event of a failure by Spain to pay the sd. 4. M. and inst. as before stipulated, the country described in the 5th Art. shall stand ipso facto vested in the US. who shall be ansable. to their citizens for their just demands as settled by the 7th Art., and all interest past and to come, so that Spain by the forfeiture of the sd. country shall stand liberated from all demands of principal or interest past or to come for the sd. spolians. but the US. shall permit no settlemt. with in the sd. country for the term of 30. years before mentioned.

Jefferson to Madison

[Washington] Nov. 22, 1805

Will you be so good as to give this a severe correction both as to state and matter, and as early a one as you can, because there remains little enough time to submit it to our brethern successively, to have copies made. Think also what documents it requires, and especially as to Spanish affairs. Before we promise a subsequent communication on that subject, it would be well to agree on it's substance, form, and accompaniments, that we may not be embarrassed by promising too much.[46]

Madison to Jefferson

[Washington Nov. 24, 1805][47]

(*a*) After "others" the insertion of "with commissions," seems necessary, as others refer to the armed vessels, not to commissns.

(*b*) Instead of "under the controul" it may be well to insert some such phrase as "unreached by any controul" in order not to sanction a plea agst. indemnification, drawn from an acknowledgment on our part that the enormities were uncontroullable.[48]

(*c*) "As unprofitable as immoral." Seems to be applicable to both parties. Some such substitute as the following is suggested. "As painful on one side as immoral on the other."[49]

(*a*) It is suggested whether naming the ages, particularly that of 18 years may not be too specific, and perhaps incur premature objections. It might be generalized in some such manner as this, "From the last Census it may be deduced that upwards of 300,000 able-bodied men will be found within the ages answering that character. These will give time for raising regular forces after the necessity of them shall become certain, and the reducing to the early period of life all its active service, cannot but be desirable to our younger citizens of all times, inasmuch as it engages to them in more advanced stages an undisturbed repose in the bosom of their families."[50]

---

46. For a succinct discussion of TJ's control of information to Congress and his "systematic implementation of a dual system of diplomatic correspondence," see Abraham D. Sofaer, *War, Foreign Affairs and Constitutional Power: The Origins* (Cambridge, Mass., 1976), pp. 176-88.

47. These are JM's second set of suggestions for alterations to TJ's fifth annual message to Congress.

48. Suggestions (a) and (b) related to TJ's discussion of private armed vessels, "some of them without commissions, some with illegal commissions, others with those of legal form," that were "committing piratical acts beyond the authority of their commissions"; see Ford, VIII, p. 389.

49. TJ deleted this passage; see *ibid.*, p. 391.

50. In his discussion of defense preparations "for a state of peace as well as of war," TJ called for the reorganization of the militia to include a classification of men between the ages of eighteen and twenty-six, using JM's words almost verbatim; see *ibid.*, p. 392. For his draft of a bill for classifying the militia, see *ibid.*, pp. 409-12.

Jefferson to Madison

[Washington] Nov. 24, 1805[51]

TH. J. TO J. M.

How will it do to amend the passage respecting England to read as follows?[52]

'New principles too have been interpolated into the Law of Nations, founded neither in justice, nor the usage or acknolegement of nations. According to these a belligerent takes to itself a commerce with it's own enemy, which it denies to a neutral on the ground of it's aiding that enemy. But reason revolts at such an inconsistency. And the neutral having equal right with the belligerent to decide the question, the interests of our constituents and the duty of maintaining the authority of reason, the only umpire between just nations, impose on us the obligation of providing an effectual and determined opposition to a doctrine' so injurious to peaceable nations.

Will you give me your opinion on the above immediately, as I wish to send the paper to Mr. Gallatin? Should we not lay before Congress the act of parl. proving the British take the trade to themselves, and the order of council proving they deny it to neutrals?

Madison to Jefferson

[Washington] Nov. 24, 1805

Although it is strictly true as here applied that reason is the sole umpire, yet as G. B. abuses the idea, in order to get rid of the instituted L. of nations, and as it may not be amiss to invite the attention of other neutrals, suppose there be added after a doctrine "as alarming to all peaceable nations as it is illegal (against all law) in itself," or some similar expression. This however is merely for consideration. The passage as it stands has a good countenance and is made of good stuff.[53]

---

51. These are TJ's questions relating to his annual message to Congress.

52. This passage refers to the Rule of 1756 and the new interpretation given in the *Essex* case, which JM had researched so carefully in Philadelphia. Brant, IV, p. 302, argues—correctly, I think—that TJ amended the paragraph respecting England because of JM's verbal suggestion that the enormity of England's violations was greater than those of Spain.

53. In his third set of suggested alterations for TJ's annual message to Congress, JM scribbled this note at the bottom of TJ's query of Nov. 24 about the passage respecting England. TJ then added a sentence to his strictures on Britain, expressing his hope that every belligerent would take a sounder view of the rights of neutral nations; see Ford, VIII, p. 390.

Jefferson to Madison

[Washington Nov. —, 1805]

Additions proposed on some subjects
suggested by Mr Gallatin submitted to Mr Madison by
Th. Jefferson

The object of the first addition is to give a practical or ostensible object to the Observations on the yellow fever: the true one however being to present facts to the governments of Europe, which in the ordinary course of things, would not otherwise reach them in half a century.

Madison to Jefferson

[Washington Nov. 27, 1805][54]

(a) "will become more able to regulate with effect their respective functions in their Departments." instead of what is between the first [ ][55]

(b) omit what is between the 2d. [ ]

(a) The first alteration is suggested on the ground that an Executive definition of the constitutional power of an Independent Branch of Government may be liable to criticism.

(b) The 2d. on the ground that it takes, apparently, side with the sect of Infectionists. If "really infected" be struck out after vessels and "in a state dangerous to health" were substituted, or some other neutral phrase, the objection would be taken away.[56]

The pencilled words have reference to the idea and anxiety of some that the State laws should be revised.

Jefferson to Madison

Washington Nov. 27, 1805[57]

will become able to regulate with effect their respective functions in these departments. The burthen of Quarantine's is felt at home as well as abroad.

54. This is JM's fourth set of suggestions for TJ's annual message to Congress.

55. In his discussion of the yellow-fever epidemic, TJ said that he had directed customs officials "to certify with exact truth for every vessel sailing for a foreign port the state of health respecting this fever which prevails at the place from which she sails." JM's suggestions related to the respective functions of public-health measures taken by state authorities and to commercial regulations taken by Congress under its power to regulate commerce; see Ford, VIII, pp. 386–89.

56. TJ changed "infectious" to "contagious."

57. After reading both of JM's suggestions labeled (a), TJ made this notation on JM's memorandum of Nov. 27, 1805, and later incorporated it into his message to Congress.

Their efficacy merits examination. Although the health laws of the states should not at this moment be found to require a particular revisal by Congress, yet Commerce claims that their attention be ever awake to them.

Jefferson to Madison

[Washington Nov. 28, 1805]

For consideration and correction. Th. J.[58]

1. Resolved, that no armed men, not being citizens of the United States ought to be permitted to enter or remain, nor any authority to be exercised but under the laws of the United States, within the former colony or province of Louisiana in the extent in which it was in the hands of Spain.

2. Resolved, that as to the residue of the said "former colony or province of Louisiana, in the extent it had when France possessed it," a peaceable adjustment of that extent is most reasonable and desirable, so far as it can be effected consistently with the honor of the United States.

3. Resolved, that pending measures for such peaceable adjustment, neither party ought to take new posts therein, nor to strengthen those they held before the 1st day of October, 1800, and that any proceeding to the contrary on the part of Spain ought to be opposed by force, and by taking possession of such posts as may be necessary to maintain the rights of the United States.

4. Resolved, that the subjects of Spain still on the Mississippi and its waters ought to be allowed an innocent passage, free from all imposts, along that part of the river which passes through the territory of the United States. And the citizens of the United States on the Mobile and its waters ought to be allowed an innocent passage, free from all imposts, along that part of the river below them which passes through the territory still held by Spain, but claimed by both parties;

Or that imposts should be levied for and by the United States on the

---

58. TJ's proposed resolutions respecting Spain. In his annual message to Congress on Dec. 3, 1805, TJ discussed the failure to settle differences with Spain and promised to send a more detailed communication. On Dec. 6, he sent a confidential message to both houses of Congress and, without mentioning the Floridas, made a plea for an appropriation whose only purpose could be in negotiations for their purchase. He also prepared these resolutions for submission to Congress, but they were not presented for fear that the executive branch might be encroaching on the legislature's prerogative. The message of Dec. 6 was referred to a House committee chaired by John Randolph, who broke with TJ on Dec. 8. Declaring that "most of the evils which the United States now suffered proceeded from the measures of the Executive," Randolph opposed the congressional appropriation as an effort to bribe France to persuade Spain to cede West Florida. Despite Randolph's opposition, Congress appropriated $2 million for use in acquiring Spanish territory and authorized the president to mobilize up to 100,000 militia; see Malone, V, pp. 70–77.

navigation of the Mississippi by Spanish subjects, countervailing those which may be levied for and by Spain on the navigation of the Mobile by citizens of the United States.

And that the navigation of the Mississippi by Spanish subjects should be prohibited whensoever that of the Mobile by citizens of the United States shall be prohibited.

5. Resolved, that in support of these resolutions, and of the consequences which may proceed from them, the citizens of the United States, by their Senate and Representatives in Congress assembled, do pledge their lives and fortunes; and that the execution of these resolutions be vested with the President of the United States.

6. Resolved, that for carrying these resolutions into effect, whether amicably or by the use of force, the President be authorized to apply any moneys in the Treasury of the United States not otherwise appropriated.

7. Resolved, that the President of the United States ought to be authorized by law to employ the armed vessels of the United States which may be in commission, for restraining the irregularities and oppressions of our commerce, other than those which amount to piracy, by privateers cruising within the Gulf Stream, in the Gulf itself, or among the islands bordering on it, and that a bill be brought in for that purpose.

Madison to Jefferson

[Washington Nov. 28, 1805]

Resolutions on Spain[59]

Resoln. 1. [substitute within any part of the former Louisiana comprehended in the delivery of possession thereof to the U.S.]

2. [omit] [substitute as may consist with the honor of the U. States) this change will look less towards advances by the U. S. *to effect* the adjustment.

4. [omit, as embarrassing and inefficacious]

5. quer. if not unnecessary and provided for by the succedg. Resol.]

6. [omit, on the idea that without this specification—amicable expence of adjustment will be in fact authorized, with an apparent reference to the use of force previously authorized]

The difficulty lies in covering an application of money to *a new purchase* of territory. As a means of adjustment it will be covered; but by a construction probably not entering into the views of Congs.

---

59. JM's suggested alterations for TJ's proposed resolutions on Spain.

Jefferson to Madison

[Washington Dec. 6-10, 1805]

TH J. TO MR MADISON

As we omit in the 2d. message to enumerate the aggressions of Spain, and refer for them to the documents, we must furnish the documents for every act, particularly[60]

— 1. the capture of the Huntress
— 2. the carrying our gunboats into Algersiras.
— 3. the late depredations on our commerce in Europe. Extracts from Pinckney's letters.
— 4. oppressions on our commerce on Mobille.
— 5. the delays of the evacuation of N. Orleans. Estimate from some of Govr. Claiborne's letters.
— 6. the dissemination of rumors of the probable restoration of Louisiana to Spain.
— 7. the new post taken on the bay of St. Bernard.
— 8. the reinforcement of Nacogdoches.
— 9. the robbery near Apelausa
— 10. that at Bayou Pierre
— 11. the patrols established on this side the Sabine.
— 12. the aggression on the Misipi territory in the case of the Kempers.
— 13. the subsequent one in the case of Flanagan and his wife.
— 14. the negociation at Madrid.
No. 1. 2. will come from the Navy department
7. 8. 9. 10. 11. from the War office.
4. 5. 6. from the offices of War and State both.
3. 12. 13. [14.] from the office of State.

Jefferson to Madison

[Washington] Dec. 22, 1805

TH:J. TO MR MADISON

The Tunisian Ambassador[61] put into my hands the packet now sent, and at his request I promised it should be safely returned to him before he went

60. Although TJ did not submit his resolutions on Spain to Congress, he did follow up his confidential message of Dec. 6 with a set of documents on Dec. 10, 1805, that summarized the festering relationship with Spain; see Ford, VIII, p. 397, and Malone, V, p. 70. The fourteen documents listed here are printed in *ASP, FR,* II, pp. 669-95.

61. For the unsuccessful mission of Sidi Suliman Mellimelli to Washington in quest of an annual tribute, see Brant, IV, pp. 305-8. For TJ's explanation of the mission to Congress, see his special message of Apr. 14, 1806, in Richardson, I, pp. 400-1.

away, as it contains the originals of letters. It presents a chronological view of the Bey's correspondence with our officers, with explanatory statements of facts connecting them. I found the whole worth reading, tho' I had read the letters hastily before. He appears to feel deep indignation against Davis, whom he considers as having alimented the whole by an unfaithful mediation, and by misrepresentations from the one to the other.

The Perils of Neutrality, 1805–1806

*A*FTER RUSSIA AND AUSTRIA JOINED GREAT BRITAIN in the Third Coalition against Napoleon, the European conflict engulfed the Old World in 1805. In October, the British navy under Admiral Nelson defeated the combined fleets of France and Spain at Cape Trafalgar, guaranteeing British supremacy of the seas. Before the year ended, Napoleon had defeated an Austrian army at Austerlitz, ensuring the collapse of the Third Coalition. When Jefferson heard the news, he quickly recognized the consequences for the United States, the last neutral of significance: "What an awful spectacle does the world exhibit at this instant, one man bestriding the continent of Europe like a Colossus, and another roaming unbridled on the ocean. But even this is better than that one should rule both elements. Our wish ought to be that he who has armies may not have the Dominion of the sea, and that he who has Dominion of the sea may be one who has no armies. In this way we may be quiet; at home at least."[1]

But it was not easy to remain quiet at home. A month earlier, Jefferson had sent Congress his most energetic and warlike annual message, calling for fortification of seaport towns, a sizable increase in the number of gunboats, construction of six 74-gun warships, creation of a naval militia reserve, and reorganization of the militia in order to protect American neutral rights and prepare the stage for negotiations with Spain over the continuing disputes involving boundaries, spoliations, and military movements along the Sabine riverfront. Although he considered the violation of neutral rights by Britain a greater concern than grievances against Spain, Jefferson did not distinguish between British seizures on the seas and Spanish action on the borders when

1. TJ to Thomas Lomax, Jan. 11, 1806, cited in Malone, V, p. 95.

he discussed "injuries" that were "of a nature to be met by force only."[2]

On December 5, 1805, Jefferson sent a secret message to Congress confirming the collapse of Monroe's negotiations with Spain. But in sharp contrast with his belligerent public message only three days earlier, the president predicted that the Florida question could be settled by new negotiations, observing that France would intervene to help resolve the disputes with Spain "on a plan analogous to what our ministers had proposed, and so comprehensive as to remove as far as possible the grounds of future collision and controversy on the eastern as well as western side of the Mississippi." Money, not war, was the key to the new diplomatic initiative. But Jefferson neither specified the amount needed nor the purpose for which it would be used, saying only that "the course to be pursued will require the command of means which it belongs to Congress exclusively to yield or to deny."[3]

That approach seemed to puzzle John Randolph, the eccentric Virginian who had managed administration policy in the House under similar circumstances at the time of the Louisiana Purchase. He, therefore, requested and received a private presidential briefing and learned that Jefferson wanted $2 million towards the purchase of the Floridas. The money, Jefferson had told the cabinet earlier, would be "the exciting motive with France, to whom Spain is in arrears for subsidies, and who will be glad also to secure us from going into the scale with England."

The doctrinaire Randolph, who had almost broken with Jefferson in 1804 over the Yazoo land compromise recommended by Madison, Gallatin, and Lincoln, refused to cooperate with the administration, declaring "it a prostration of the national character, to excite one nation by money to bully another out of its property." Despite Randolph's "attempts to assassinate" the plan,[4] Congress passed the Two Million Dollar Act for extraordinary—and undefined—expenses of diplomatic intercourse, and Madison sent instructions to Armstrong to meet the secret proposal made by Talleyrand the previous fall.[5]

Randolph's break with the administration was irreparable, but his followers were few, a handful of disgruntled Republicans whom he called "the *old* republican party" of 1798 but which became known as the Quids.[6] Nevertheless, the split in Republican ranks, the only schism of significance during Jefferson's presidency, created a crisis of discontent among the president's followers. Randolph's animosity against Madison in particular reached fever

2. For TJ's plan for the defense of New Orleans, see TJ to JM, Feb. 28, 1806, below. Also see Malone, V, pp. 69–72, and Peterson, pp. 815–16, 832–39.

3. Richardson, I, p. 390.

4. JM uses this phrase in his letter to TJ, May 26, 1806, below.

5. For Gallatin's plan to finance the purchase of the Floridas, see TJ to JM, Mar. 5, 1806, below. For Randolph's break with TJ and JM, see Malone, V, pp. 72–77.

6. For an excellent study, see Norman K. Risjord, *The Old Republicans: Southern Conservatism in the Age of Jefferson* (New York, 1965), pp. 40–71.

pitch in March 1806 during debate on a motion by Congressman Andrew Gregg to suspend the importation of British goods until England modified its policy of ship seizures and impressment. Randolph denounced the measure, which did not have administration backing, as though it were a Jefferson-Madison warlike plot to promote Madison to the presidency: "All eyes were in fact fixed on the half-way house [the President's House] between this [Capitol] and Georgetown, that the question was not what we should do with France, or Spain, or England, but who should be the next President. And at this moment, every motion that is made . . . is made with a view to the occupation of that House."[7]

To carry on negotiations for the Floridas under the auspices of France, Jefferson paired Armstrong, the American minister in Paris, and James Bowdoin, Pinckney's successor in Madrid.[8] Although he opposed the Florida policy of the administration, the Quaker senator from Pennsylvania, George Logan, introduced a bill that smoothed the path of negotiations by prohibiting trade with Santo Domingo, which was held by black rebels who defied Napoleon's efforts to regain control. Madison, who observed that the bill was not an administration measure, argued that it went "beyond our legal obligations" and denounced "the false ground that the act of Cong. was due to the rights of France." Moreover, he was convinced that the Santo Domingo trade would "certainly go on indirectly thro' other merchants, if not thro' ours" and concluded that "it may seem not unfair that ours should reap the harvest." Even so, he opposed the appointment of a consul at St. Thomas, for it might "seem to favor the trade to St. Domingo thro' a Danish Island."[9] Jefferson agreed. "We must not risk great things for small," he told Madison. "A Consul merely to patronize a commerce which the laws forbid, would be a measure in opposition to the law, and not for it's execution."[10] In choosing between commerce and diplomacy, the president preferred to abide by the law stopping American trade in order to aid negotiations with Spain under the auspices of French pressure. Indeed, Bonaparte persuaded the Spanish foreign minister to send a negotiator to Paris, but no agreement was reached with Spain during Jefferson's remaining years in office.[11]

Relations with Spain were complicated by a filibustering expedition launched from New York by Francisco de Miranda to liberate South America from Spanish rule. Although Miranda had conferred in general terms with Madison and dined with Jefferson, neither endorsed his venture, warning

---

7. Noble E. Cunningham, *The Jeffersonian Republicans in Power: Party Operations, 1801–1809* (Chapel Hill, 1963), p. 85.

8. See TJ to JM, May 11, 1806, below.

9. JM to TJ, Aug. 4, 1806, below.

10. TJ to JM, Aug. 8, 1806, below.

11. See Brant, IV, pp. 274–79, 365–66, and Peterson, pp. 825–26.

instead that "it would be incumbent on the United States to punish any transactions within their jurisdiction which might according to the law of nations involve an hostility against Spain, and that a statute of Congress had made express provision for such a case."[12] Unfortunately, neither the president nor the secretary of state alerted New York authorities to watch Miranda's movements, and the Venezuelan's ship left New York in February 1806 under a false clearance given by Colonel William Stephens Smith, surveyor of the port of New York, whom Miranda had convinced that the administration secretly sanctioned his project.[13]

Even before the Spanish minister lodged a protest, Jefferson and Madison ordered criminal prosecutions against Smith and other accomplices within the jurisdiction of the United States. Smith was dismissed from his federal post and brought to trial. In an effort to implicate the administration in the violation of neutrality policy, Federalist defense lawyers subpoenaed members of the Republican cabinet as witnesses. To Jefferson, who was at Monticello, Madison reported that "subpoenas have this day been served on Genl. Dearborn, Mr. Smith, and myself. The absence of Mr. Gallatin postpones the service on him. . . . It is perhaps not unfortunate," he added, "that so aggregate a blow has been aimed at the administration, as it places in a stronger view the malice of the proceeding and the inconvenience to the public business which would result from an attendance of all the heads of Dept. Still," he confessed, "I find a strong impression existing that the attendance is inevitable."[14]

When the three subpoenaed cabinet members informed the court that the president had, with regret, found that their public duties made attendance in New York impossible, Supreme Court Justice Paterson, who sat with the federal district judge, agreed that affidavits would be acceptable. But these were never called for, even though Madison delayed his departure for Montpellier for several days in case a request was made. "Altho' I have reason to believe that my departure will be the signal for opening the federal batteries agst- our letter to the Court, I shall postpone it for a few days only."[15]

While he was waiting, Madison learned that Smith had been acquitted. He promptly asked the federal prosecutor for "such a statement as will shew

12. JM to John Armstrong, Mar. 15, 1806, cited in Brant, IV, p. 327. See also William Spence Robertson, "Francisco de Miranda and the Revolutionizing of Spanish America," in *AHA: Report for 1907* (Washington, 1908).

13. Smith, who was the son-in-law of John and Abigail Adams, had once traveled with Miranda in Prussia. He became a partner in Miranda's expedition, and his son served as an aide to Miranda; see Brant, IV, pp. 325, 328.

14. JM to TJ, May 28, 1806, below. "Mr. Smith" was Secretary of the Navy Robert Smith.

15. JM to TJ, July 28, 1806, below. For an account of the trials of Smith and Samuel G. Ogden, see Dwight F. Henderson, *Congress, Courts, and Criminals: The Development of Federal Criminal Law, 1801–1829* (Westport, Conn., 1985), pp. 56–66.

the grounds on which the jury is understood to have given their verdict, with a view to the aid it may furnish in explaining the transaction to our foreign Ministers."[16] Even before the trial was over, Jefferson and his cabinet colleagues had decided to remove the federal marshal, John Swartout, a follower of Aaron Burr and a close friend of William Stephens Smith, who had allegedly packed the grand and trial juries with Federalists.[17] But the president, who had traveled from Paris to London with Smith when the latter was secretary to the American embassy in Great Britain, was not too upset by the jury's decision. "I had no wish to see Smith imprisoned," he wrote Gallatin; "he has been a man of integrity and honor, led astray by distress."[18]

Although the Miranda expedition was a discomforting diplomatic distraction for the administration, it did not cause the president and the secretary of state to take their eyes off their two main goals: acquisition of the Floridas and a treaty with Great Britain on neutral trade and neutral rights. In both cases, Jefferson created an extraordinary dual diplomatic mission, appointing Monroe and William Pinkney to negotiate in London with British representatives just as he had paired Armstrong and Bowdoin to negotiate in Paris with Spanish and French ministers. Pinkney, a Baltimore lawyer of Federalist leanings, had served in London for eight years as American claims commissioner under the Jay Treaty and had just written a lengthy memorial against the Rule of 1756 on behalf of Maryland merchants.[19]

On the day after the House passed the Two Million Dollar Act, the pamphlet that Madison had researched in Philadelphia, entitled *Examination of the British Doctrine, which Subjects to Capture a Neutral Trade Not Open in Time of Peace,* was distributed in Congress. A 204-page denunciation of the Rule of 1756, it boldly and baldly declared that British policy rested on British might, not legal right, and was based on mercantile jealousy of America's growing commerce. Jefferson thought that it "pulverized" the Rule of 1756 by "a logic not to be controverted,"[20] and John Quincy Adams later praised it as "a standard Treatise on the Law of Nations, not inferior to the works of any writer upon those subjects since the days of Grotius, and every way worthy of the author of Publius and Helvidius."[21] But John Randolph, now Madison's

---

16. JM to TJ, Aug. 4, 1806, below. For a brief summary of the Miranda venture and Smith's involvement, see Brant, IV, pp. 323-39.

17. For TJ's reference to Swartout, see TJ to JM, May 23 and 24, 1806, below. The cabinet decision was made on May 1, 1806; see Ford, I, pp. 315-16. For TJ's reference to Swartout's replacement, see TJ to JM, Aug. 8, 1806, below.

18. TJ to Albert Gallatin, Aug. 15, 1806, in Ford, VIII, p. 464.

19. Malone, V, p. 113.

20. See Noble E. Cunningham, *In Pursuit of Reason: The Life of Thomas Jefferson* (Baton Rouge, 1987), p. 283.

21. John Quincy Adams, *The Lives of James Madison and James Monroe* (Buffalo, 1850), pp. 66-68, 86-92, cited in *The Selected Writings of John and John Quincy Adams,* ed. Adrienne Koch and William Peden (New York, 1946), pp. 384-85. JM's pamphlet *A Memoir Containing an Examination of the British Doctrine, which Subjects to Capture a Neutral Trade Not Open in Time of Peace* (1806)

inveterate enemy, sneered that it was "a shilling pamphlet hurled against eight hundred ships of war."[22]

A little later Madison officially reported that 2,273 Americans had been recorded as impressed by the British between the renewal of the European war in 1803 and March 1806, with uncounted hundreds more lost without a trace.[23] As British captures of American shipping increased and violations of neutral rights multiplied, Congress retaliated with a selective Nonimportation Act against Great Britain's terrorism. But the act was to be suspended until November in order to give the Monroe-Pinkney mission time to seek redress and indemnification by negotiating an understanding to replace Jay's treaty, which had expired in 1803.[24] In broad outline, the nonimportaation policy was a return to the Madisonian doctrine of commercial retaliations, which Jefferson had subsequently endorsed in his final report as secretary of state and Madison had introduced in his commercial resolutions of 1794.

Monroe and Pinkney's primary tasks were to seek modification of the British system of impressment and to define blockade properly. Following the example of the Anglo-Russian treaty of 1801, the United States was willing to forgo, during the present conflict, the principle that "free ships make free goods," if Great Britain would ease the *Essex* rule on the colonial reexport trade, allowing neutral trade with any ports not under actual physical blockade and in all articles except military supplies.

But the administration, intent on pushing negotiations with Spain, did not take a hard line with Great Britain, especially after the death of William Pitt brought into power the Ministry of All-the-Talents, which included Charles James Fox as foreign minister. Fox, who was regarded as more friendly to the United States than Pitt, promptly recalled Anthony Merry as British minister to the United States and sent assurances "of the good will of the King towards the U. S. and his sincere desire that arrangements removing all causes of dispute might lay the foundation for permanent friendship and harmony between the two countries; and further that not a day would be unnecessarily lost in preparing to enter into Treaty with Mr. Monroe."[25] In a move designed to punish Prussia for joining France and, at the same time, calm the United States by substituting a blockade for the harsh *Essex* rule, the new

---

is in *Letters and Other Writings of James Madison,* ed. William C. Rives and Philip R. Fendall, 4 vols. (Philadelphia, 1865), II, pp. 227–391.

22. See Merrill D. Peterson, *James Madison: A Biography in His Own Words* (New York, 1974), p. 255.

23. Brant, IV, pp. 296–98; Peterson, pp. 807–8, 827; and Malone, V, pp. 99–101.

24. TJ to James Monroe, Mar. 5, 1804, cited in Donald R. Hickey, "The Monroe-Pinkney Treaty of 1806: A Reappraisal," *WMQ* 44 (1987): 66. Jay's treaty was to expire twelve years after the exchange of ratifications or two years after the preliminaries of peace were signed in Europe. The Peace of Amiens between England and France was signed on Oct. 1, 1801; hence, Jay's treaty expired two years later.

25. JM to TJ, May 26, 1806, below.

ministry issued an order-in-council proclaiming a blockade from the Elbe River to Brest.[26]

Madison attributed Fox's conciliatory moves to two factors: "the loss of the German Market" and the Nonimportation Act, which fanned "the fear that the temper of this country if not soothed by some such friendly assurances might shut the door now also agst. British manufactures."[27] Madison instructed Monroe and Pinkney to inform the British government that the administration's retaliatory legislation, which Congress had passed during Pitt's ministry, implied no distrust of the Ministry of All-the-Talents. In form, it was an act to encourage American manufacturers, and its discriminatory features imitated examples in British practice.[28]

Pinkney reached England in June, and although Fox became ill and turned negotiations over to Lords Holland and Auckland, the American negotiators were so optimistic in September that their negotiations would be successful that they requested the postponement of the Nonimportation Act from November 15, 1806, until the middle of the next year to allow negotiations to proceed without the pressure of an impending deadline.[29]

While friendly negotiations were under way in London, an explosive incident, sparked by the British navy, "renewed [the navy's] violent and lawless proceedings" in American waters. Lurking off New York harbor to search American merchant ships within territorial waters of the United States, His Majesty's warship *Leander* fired a warning shot across the bow of one vessel and killed an American seaman on another. Public indignation ran high, and New Yorkers rioted, following the public funeral of the sailor. Jefferson banned the *Leander* and two sister ships from American ports and issued a proclamation charging the captain with murder.

Merry apologized for the incident, and Fox promised an investigation of the "melancholy transaction" as well as the court martial of the captain.[30] When the *Cambrian,* one of the vessels barred from American ports, ventured into Chesapeake Bay in December, the president took measures for forcing her off "and for preventing her entering any other port of the U. S."[31]

26. The ministry did not disavow the *Essex* rule, however.

27. JM to TJ, May 26, 1806, below.

28. Brant, IV, pp. 366–67. Merry informed his government that the administration and the majority of Republicans believed that the selective Nonimportation Act was a mild measure that would not be "resented in a hostile manner" by His Majesty's government; see Malone, V, p. 110.

29. *Ibid.,* p. 397. Congress extended the effective date to July 1, 1807, and authorized the president to make further extensions until Congress met in December.

30. Bradford Perkins, *Prologue to War: England and the United States, 1805–1812* (Berkeley, 1963), pp. 106–8; Malone, V, pp. 114–17; and Brant, IV, pp. 367–70. For references to the incident, see JM to TJ, July 25, 1806, below, Aug. 30, 1806, below; and TJ to JM, Aug. 28, 1806, below, Sept. 2, 1806, below.

31. TJ to JM, Dec. 19, 1806, below. He also drafted a proclamation but did not issue it because the ship left on its own accord; see Proclamation Concerning H.M.S. Cambrian, enclosure, *ibid.*

Despite the British navy's "atrocious violation of our territorial rights," Jefferson stressed "forbearance at St. James's" and remained hopeful of a settlement of issues between the United States and Great Britain.[32] Indeed, he rejected Madison's suggestion that British frigates should be barred from using the Norfolk navy yard for repairs. Such aid, Madison thought, might "be resolved into an aid equivalent to money" and, therefore, appear unneutral; if so, it could lead to a French complaint of partiality. But Jefferson did not think "the loan of our navy yard any more contrary to neutrality than that of our ports. It is merely admitting a ship to a proper station in our waters."[33]

Compared to the diplomatic difficulties with Spain and England, the trouble with Tunis took on the air of an Arabian Nights' tale. When the American commander in the Mediterranean refused to restore a Tunisian vessel that was seized after it had tried to run the American blockade of Tripoli, the bey of Tunis dispatched Ambassador Sidi Suliman Mellimelli and his party of eleven to the United States to negotiate the matter or to obtain an annual tribute in lieu of the ship. Madison refused to discuss any tribute, but he showered the ambassador with presents so that he "should go away personally favorable to us."[34]

When Mellimelli went to Boston to arrange passage home, three members of his entourage rebelled against him, refusing to leave New York, where they were maintained at government expense. Madison asked Mayor DeWitt Clinton to send them on to Boston "by any means which he may be able to apply," and the mayor replied that "coercion alone will rid us of the Tunisians in revolt agst. Mellimelli."[35] Although the ambassador felt "little concern if the seceding part of his suite should be left behind," both Jefferson and Madison favored the use of legal force, if necessary.[36]

Early in September, Madison learned that an unhappy Mellimelli might exceed "all the preceding vexations" by coming to Montpellier and Monticello. "I have written to Wagner," the chief clerk in the State Department, "to save us from the persecution of a visit from him," Madison told the president, and new shipping arrangements for Mellimelli's speculative investment in American goods placated the Tunisian diplomat, who sailed for home.[37]

---

32. TJ to Jacob Crowninshield, May 13, 1806, in Ford, VIII, pp. 451–53.

33. JM to TJ, Sept. 22, 1806, below, and TJ to JM, Sept. 23, 1806, below.

34. See JM to TJ, May [17], 1806, below, and TJ to JM, May 19, 1806, below. For Mellimelli's mission, see Brant, IV, pp. 305–10. The standard study is Ray W. Irwin, *The Diplomatic Relations of the United States with the Barbary Powers* (Chapel Hill, 1931).

35. JM to TJ, July 25, 1806 (two letters), below.

36. TJ to JM, July 30, 1806, below, Aug. 8, 1806, below; and JM to TJ, July 28, 1806, below, Aug. 4, 1806, below, Aug. 15, 1806, below.

37. JM to TJ, Sept. 4, 1806, below. For a reference to Mellimelli's speculations, see JM to TJ, July 28, 1806, below.

"As to the refractory Tunisians," Jefferson wrote, "I think we should pay their passage [to England] and get rid of them."[38]

Despite the difficulties of the "squally" session of Congress—Jefferson called it "long and uneasy"[39]—the president had the pleasure of the company of his daughter Martha and her husband, Congressman Thomas Mann Randolph, and their six children from December 1805 until May 1806. In January, Martha delivered a new grandson in the President's House, the first child born in the executive mansion. She and her husband named their new son James Madison Randolph, no doubt pleasing both the grandfather and the namesake.[40] When Margaret Bayard Smith and her husband, Samuel Harrison Smith, editor of the *National Intelligencer,* visited the presidential family in May, they found Jefferson romping with his grandchildren, a role that the president played so effectively Mrs. Smith "could scarcely realize that he was one of the most celebrated men now living."[41]

THE LETTERS

Madison to Jefferson

Washington Jan. 25, 1806

The Secretary of State, to whom the President
has been pleased to refer the resolution
of the Senate, dated on the 10th instant,
has the honor to make the following report:

The most important of the principles interpolated into the law of nations, is that which appears to be maintained by the British Government and its prize courts, that a trade opened to neutrals by a nation at war, on account of the war, is unlawful.

This principle has been relaxed, from time to time, by orders, allowing, as favors to neutrals, particular branches of trade, disallowed by the general principle; which orders have, also, in some instances, extended the modifications of the principle beyond its avowed import.

In like manner, the last of these orders, bearing date the 24th of June 1803, has incorporated, with the relaxation, a collateral principle, which is

---

38. TJ to JM, Sept. 16, 1806, below. For the episode, see Irwin, pp. 161–67.
39. TJ to John Tyler, Apr. 26, 1806, in Ford, VIII, pp. 441–42, and Malone, V, p. 121.
40. Malone, V, pp. 65–66, 75.
41. *Ibid.,* p. 121.

itself an interpolation, namely, that a vessel on a return voyage is liable to capture by the circumstance of her having, on the outward voyage, conveyed contraband articles to an enemy's port. How far a like penalty, attached, by the same order, to the circumstance of a previous communication with a blockaded port, would likewise be an interpolation, may depend upon the construction under which that part of the order has been, or is to be, carried into execution.

The general principle, first above stated, as lately applied to re-exportations of articles imported into neutral countries from hostile colonies, or *vice versa,* by considering the re-exportation, in many cases, as a continuation of the original voyage, forms another interpolation, deeply affecting the trade of neutrals. For a fuller view of this and some other interpolations, reference may be had to the documents communicated with the message to Congress of the 17th instant.[1]

The British principle which makes a notification to foreign Governments of an intended blockade equivalent to the notice required by the law of nations, before the penalty can be incurred; and that which subjects to capture vessels, arriving at a port, in the interval between a removal and return of the blockading force, are other important deviations from the code of public law.

Another unjustifiable measure is the mode of search practised by British ships, which, instead of remaining at a proper distance from the vessel to be searched, and sending their own boat with a few men for the purpose, compel the vessel to send her papers in her own boat, and sometimes with great danger from the condition of the boat and the state of the weather.

To these instances, without adverting to others of an inferior or less definite character, in the practice of Great Britain, must be added the assumed right to impress persons from American vessels, sailing under the American flag on the high seas. An explanation of this practice will be found in the extract from the instructions to Mr. Monroe, communicated with the message of the President above referred to.

Among the interpolations introduced by the French Government, is a decree dated June 6, 1805, (18th Prairial, 13th year,) importing that every privateer of which two-thirds of the crew should not be natives of England, or subjects of a Power the enemy of France, shall be considered as pirates.

Another is evidenced by the result of an application made by the deputy consul of the United States, at Cadiz, through the French consul, to Admiral

---

1. On Jan. 17, 1806, TJ had sent Congress a special message on British violations of neutral rights following the *Essex* decision, including memorials from American merchants and shippers as well as correspondence between JM and Monroe. For the message, see Richardson, I, p. 395. In a separate and confidential transmittal, he sent Monroe's letter, which claimed that Great Britain meant "to check if not to crush" American commerce. After the letter was read to the Senate, it was returned to the president. When the Senate asked to see it again, TJ asked JM to prepare fuller documentation, which TJ conveyed in this letter. TJ then sent Monroe's letter to the Senate on Jan. 26, 1806; see Malone, V, pp. 99–101. He sent JM's letter of Jan. 25, along with supporting documents, on Jan. 27, 1806; see *ASP, FR,* II, pp. 727–73.

Villeneuve, for the liberation of some seamen of the United States, who were on board the French fleet under his command. The answer of the Admiral, dated 29th August last, (11th Fructidor, 13th year,) states that "a decision of His Imperial and Royal Majesty provides that every foreigner found on board the vessels of war or of commerce of the enemy, is to be treated as a prisoner of war, and can have no right to the protection of the diplomatic and commercial agents of his nation."

Other unjustifiable innovations on the law of nations are exemplified in the decree of General Ferrand, lately passed at the city of St. Domingo, a translation of which is annexed.

The irregular mode of search above described is also practised by the cruisers of France and Spain.

The cruisers of the two latter Powers have harassed the commerce of the United States in various other forms, but as it is not known or believed that their conduct has been prescribed or santioned by the public authority of their respective nations, they are not considered as falling within the purview of the resolution of the Senate.

All which is respectfully submitted.

JAMES MADISON.

Madison to Jefferson

[Washington Jan. 26, 1806]

The Secretary of State supposes, that the within abstract in the form of a report to the President, with the decree annexed to it, and the documents and correspondence communicated to Congress between the date of the Senate's resolution and that of the report, will be an ample compliance with the requisition of the former.

The favor is requested that the packet enclosed herewith for Mr. Randolph may be left with or for him at the time of the President's communication being made to the Senate, as the one is made to depend upon the other.[2]

JAMES MADISON

2. The portions of TJ's annual message of Dec. 3, 1805, dealing with neutral rights had been referred by the House to the Committee on Ways and Means, chaired by John Randolph. On Dec. 11, Randolph asked JM "what new principles, or constructions, of the laws of nations have been adopted by the belligerent powers of Europe, to the prejudice of neutral rights?" Before JM replied, TJ's special message of Jan. 17, 1806, was also referred to Randolph's committee. On Jan. 25, JM wrote Randolph that he was enclosing his report to the president (see the preceding letter), which TJ transmitted to the Senate and the House on Jan. 26, 1806; see Noble E. Cunningham, Jr., *The Process of Government under Jefferson* (Princeton, 1978), pp. 225–26, and Malone, V, pp. 101–3.

Madison to Jefferson

[Washington Jan. 27, 1806]

J. M. with respectful complts. to the Presidt. suggests an attention to the last paragraph in the Rept. to him concerning interpolations, lest it should not square with what was represented in the first Message agst. Spanish outrages on the high seas. The report was to go to the Presidt. on saturday or yesterday. A Baltimore paper has published Yrujo's letter to the Dept. of State commenting on the Message, with a circular to the Diplomatic corps here; and further appeals to the public may be expected.³ The section in Cobbett on the Amern. dispute is worth perusal. The P. will please to return the letter from Gen. Gates.
Monday

Jefferson to Madison

[Washington] Feb. 5, 1806

I think the District atty of N. Y. should be immediately instructed to investigate the expedition of the Leander, and of every person concerned in it;⁴ and to learn how it has happened that the officers of the government at that place should have paid no attention and given no information of it while going on. On the report of the Atty to us we may decide what shall be done.

Th: J.

Jefferson to Madison

[Washington Feb. 8, 1806]

Should not Claiborne be instructed to enter into a correspondence with Casa-Calvo, to insist on keeping things in their present state, and to let him

---

3. Although the administration had requested Yrujo's recall and no longer recognized his diplomatic status, they allowed him to live in Philadelphia and depart voluntarily at a later date. When he appeared in Washington on Jan. 15, 1806, JM notified him that his residence there was "dissatisfactory" to the president and ordered him to depart from the United States as soon as the inclement season ended. Yrujo exchanged insults with JM, sent the correspondence to the diplomats in Washington, and then published it in the Federalist press; see Brant, IV, pp. 323–25, and Henry Adams, *History of the United States of America during the Second Administration of Thomas Jefferson,* 9 vols. (New York, 1890), III, pp. 184–89.

4. In the fall of 1805 and the early winter months of 1806, H.M.S. *Leander* hovered off New York harbor, searching American ships for British deserters and/or impressing American seamen, often detaining a score or more ships simultaneously.

understand that if any new settlement is made in the disputed territory, and particularly the one meditated on Trinity we shall back it up.[5]

Jefferson to Madison

[Washington] Feb. 28, 1806

What would you think of raising a force for the defence of New Orleans in this manner? Give a bounty of 50 acres of land, to be delivered immediately, to every able bodied man who will immediately settle on it, and hold himself in readiness to perform 2 years military service (on the usual pay) if called on within the first seven years of his residence. The lands to be chosen by himself of any of those in the Orleans territory, on the West side of the Mississipi, actually surveyed and unsold, each to have his choice in the order of their arrival on the spot, a proclamation to be issued to this effect to engage as many as will to go on and present themselves to the officer there, and moreover recruiting officers to be sent into different parts of the Union to raise and conduct settlers at the public expence. When settled there, to be well trained as militia by officers living among them.[6]

A similar provision for Tombigbee.

Jefferson to Madison

[Washington] Mar. 5, 1806

TH. J. TO MR MADISON

I think the several modifications in Mr. Gallatin's paper may be reduced to simple instructions in some such form as follows:

The sum to be paid will consist I. of 2. millions ready money. II. of a residuary sum, not exceeding 3 millions, to be paid afterwards as shall be agreed.[7]

I. The ready money (as a 1st proposition) not to be paid till possession of the whole country ceded is delivered and evacuated.

5. Spanish forces in Texas had crossed the Sabine River in Oct. 1805, and Secretary of War Henry Dearborn ordered American troops to dislodge them in Nov. If border clashes led to war, TJ wanted to raise an armed force to defend New Orleans; see Thomas P. Abernethy, *The Burr Conspiracy* (New York, 1954), pp. 47–49.

6. TJ labeled this document "Submitting a plan for defense of New Orleans" and also sent it to Secretary of the Treasury Albert Gallatin and Secretary of War Henry Dearborn. TJ thought that "we ought to have 30,000 men at least there. That territory will never be invaded by an army of less than 15, or 20,000 men"; see Ford, VIII, p. 427. For succinct discussions, see Richard A. Erney, *The Public Life of Henry Dearborn* (New York, 1979), pp. 159–61, and Everett Somerville Brown, "Jefferson's Plan for a Military Colony in Orleans Territory," *MVHR* 8 (1922): 373–76.

7. For the cabinet decision to pay $5 million for the Floridas, see TJ's notes of Nov. 14, 1805, in Ford, VIII, pp. 383–84.

But, in ultimato, to be paid on putting into our hands orders for an absolute delivery of the government to us, on sight of the order, an evacuation of the country by all troops in the same instant, and the departure of all officers and agents within 3 months after.

II. The residuary sum to be a fund for paying claimants under the convention;[8] either to be settled by a commission, in which case any surplus will belong to Spain and any defect be supplied by her; or, which would be far preferable, that residuum to be left with us for the sufferers, we exonerating Spain from all further demands on their part.

But, in ultimato, the residuary sum to be paid to Spain by bills on the treasury in annual instalments, if that can be obtained, or by stock to be created, if insisted on: and a fixed sum of 2, 3, or 4 millions to be immediately paid by colonial bills to the U. S. who, on reciept of the money, exonerate Spain from all further demand from the claimants under the Convention.

If the sum to be allowed by Spain for spoliations, be retained by us out of the residuary price, and be less than that residuum, the difference to be paid to her by bills on our treasury at the end of one year.

Perhaps the above ideas may aid you in framing your instructions. They are hazarded with that view only.[9]

Jefferson to Madison

[Washington] Mar. 16, 1806

Th. Jefferson submits to the heads of departments the papers in the case of the Louisiana Commissioners with the Attorney General's opinion. He prays them to give him their separate opinions on the subject, and to hand on the papers with this note, from one to the other, to be finally returned to Th. J.

Madison to Jefferson

Washington Mar. 16, 1806

The reasons given by the Attorney General against the decision of the Louisiana Commissioners referred to in the Presidents note of this date, appear to establish conclusively the illegality of that decision. Still as there are no

---

8. This provision referred to spoliation claims by American merchants for ships seized by Spain prior to Nov. 1, 1805.

9. For JM's instructions to Armstrong and Bowdoin, Mar. 13, 1806, see Hunt, VII, pp. 192-200, and Brant, IV, pp. 362-63.

circumstances justifying a presumption that the error had a corrupt source, and as it is sufficiently presumeable in my view that it would be corrected by the transmission of the reasons and opinion of the Attorney General, with the sanction of the President thereto, I deem that course preferable to an immediate removal of the Commissioners. Respectfully by

JAMES MADISON

Jefferson to Madison

[Washington] Mar. 20, 1806

TH. J. TO MR. MADISON

My list tells me I signed commissions for the following persons, which being omitted from the list now recieved from the office renders it desirable that the office be again reminded to ascertain whether the error is in their list or mine.

- Mar. 9. Julian Poydras of Orleans a member of the legislative council of Orleans
- 20. Samuel Trescott of Massach Collectr. and Inspector of Mass. The blank commission of Marshal of N. Carolina was filled up by the Governor with the name of John S. West (who held it before)

Madison to Jefferson

[Washington Mar. 20, 1806]

Julian Poydras had been submitted to the Senate, where the President signed the Commission as above.
Samuel Trescott was accidentally submitted in the list furnished the President. The commission is dated 14 March last.

Jefferson to Madison

Washington Apr. 11, 1806

As the letter proposed to the Emperor of Russia may lead to something of importance, I wish to communicate it to the other gentlemen of the administration. Will you therefore be so good as to *correct it severely*, and return it to me as you would approve it?

Jefferson to Madison

[Washington] Apr. 14, 1806

Th: Jefferson recieved last night an advice of Senate to ratify the treaty with Tripoli, which of course determines the Mediterranean fund. He therefore asks a meeting of the heads of departments at 11. oclock to-day to consult on laying before Congress the state of affairs with Tunis.

Jefferson to Madison

[Washington] Apr. 17, 1806

I presume the correspondce between the Ambassador of Tunis and Secretary of State, must be considd. as exhibiting the only causes of difference, and that that correspondence alone need be sent to the Senate. Want of time for copies must authorize sending the originals, to be returned.

It will be necessary to copy the letters to Mellimelli.[10]

Jefferson to Madison

Monticello May 11, 1806

DEAR SIR

I have recieved, signed and forwarded Poydrass's commission, and have forwarded the letter to Prevost. I inclose for your perusal a letter from Armstrong. The fact therein stated changes considerably the idea we had formed of Bowdoin's caution and prudence.[11] That mentioned in Bowdoin's letter is comfortable tho' it be little more than a repetition of what Armstrong had communicated. Some additional details give additional hopes.

The drought here is distressing, the crop of oats irretrievably lost; the May's wheat little better. Common wheat tho' backward is healthy, and may yet do well. Peaches and cherries are almost wholly destroyed and the few remaining are too much injured to come to perfection. As this was the effect of

---

10. Sidi Suliman Mellimelli was the Tunisian ambassador who requested a present of naval supplies in return for which the United States would be assured of three years of peace in the Mediterranean, "after which the inference is obvious that a renewal of the presents is to be expected to renew the prolongation of peace for another term"; see TJ to the Senate, Apr. 18, 1806, in Richardson, I, pp. 401–2.

11. Armstrong reported that Bowdoin favored notifying France that if France would persuade Spain to sell the Florida, the United States might "take part in the war" against Great Britain; see C. Edward Skeen, *John Armstrong, Jr., 1758–1843: A Biography* (Syracuse, 1981), pp. 78–79.

a cold wind, the mountain situations have suffered equally with the plains. Apples have escaped. I presume you will have heard of the death of Frank Walker, and that he died drunk in his carriage unknown to the driver. It was discovered only when the carriage stopped at the next house. Accept affectionate salutns

Th^s Jefferson

Madison to Jefferson

Washington May 12, 1806

Dear Sir

Mr. Pinkney is now with us collecting his outfit of information, and is to sail from Baltimore on sunday the 18th instant. This being an earlier day than was anticipated, it has become necessary to hasten the conclusion of all the Documents he is to take with him, the provisional as well as the positive. With this view they are now forwarded for your signature by an Express who we hope will be back by friday evening.[12]

We have recd. nothing new from any quarter since the last mail for Charlottesville. With respectful attachment I remain yours

James Madison

Jefferson to Madison

Monticello May 14, 1806

ThJ to J. Madison

Your express arrived at 12 oclock this day and I dispatch him in half an hour with the papers for Mr. Pinckney signed. I inclose another letter to Monroe, to be forwarded by him. Affectionate salutations.

Madison to Jefferson

Washington May [17], 1806

Dear Sir

The communications which will be forwarded by Mr. Smith seem to render it certain that the frigates from the Medn. cannot be expected till the

---

12. For William Pinkney's joint mission with Monroe, see Hickey, 65–88. Pinkney arrived in London on June 19, 1806.

fall, and consequently that the plan of sending Mellimelli in the Chesapeake is frustrated.[13] It also appears that the Xebeck for which we are pledged has been sold at Malta. Will it not be best in this state of things to equip a small vessel here which the navy Dept. can spare and which Mr. Smith will describe to you, as a substitute for the Xebeck and for the return of Mellimelli? The greater value of the substitute will be outweighed by shortening the period of Mellimelli's stay, or the expence of chartering a vessel. In every other respect the arrangements concerning him may remain the same; so also those relating to Mr. Lear. I inclose a letter from Barlow suggesting ideas, some of which may be of importance. I can add nothing on the head of news. With respectful attacht. yours

JAMES MADISON

Jefferson to Madison

Monticello May 19, 1806

TH JEFFERSON TO MR MADISON.

My letter to Mr Smith takes up the whole of the subject of his and your letters by the last post, and as he informs me he has a vessel on demurrage till he recieves my answer, I hire an express which will deliver it 5. days sooner that the post would. Not to detain him I must refer you to my letter to Mr Smith for answer to yours. I return you Mr Barlows letter. His anxiety makes me more anxious that Mellimelli should go away personally favorable to us.

We had a pretty good rain on the 15th. But the earth is already dry. Indeed such is the drought as to threaten the loss of every thing. Affectionate salutations.

Jefferson to Madison

[Washington May 20, 1806]

I observe also that I signed the following commission omitted in the list from the office.
May 20. John Broadbent of Sicily Counsul for Messina [?]; yet I seem to have a faint recollection that the appointment had been approved by the Senate

---

13. The *Chesapeake*, which was destined for the Mediterranean because of the Tunisian threats, was being repaired; see TJ to Jacob Crowninshield, May 13, 1806, in Ford, VIII, pp. 451-53.

Madison to Jefferson

[Washington May 20, 1806]

John Broadbent was submitted to and approved by the Senate the 14 [?] Jany. 1806 but not having received the commission a duplicate was sent to the President for signature at the above date, and hence it has been noted as a new apptment.

Madison to Jefferson

Washington May [22, 1806]

DEAR SIR

The express returned with the documents for London the night before the last, and the despatches arrived in Baltimore yesterday morning in due time for the intended embarkation of Mr. Pinkney.

Herewith are letters from Mr. Monroe of Mar 31. and Apl. 3. with their accompaniments.

I observe in an English paper of Mar. 31. a paragraph under the "Hague" Mar. 25. (I believe), saying that Mr. Armstrong with his suite had arrived from Paris, and was going to Amsterdam to embark for America. It is difficult to question the fact, and not less so to explain it. If the state of his health or the attack on his character should have been the motive he may have been led to yield to it, by the consideration that Mr. Bowdoin's continuance at Paris would lessen the inconvenience of his leaving it. I find that the precaution was not omitted of making their Commission Exty. several as well as joint.

Mr. Gallatin sets out this afternoon on his western trip. Mr. Smith and Genl. Dearborn continue on the ground. With respectful attachment I am Sir

JAMES MADISON

It just occurs that Armstrong's trip to the Hague may refer to a claim with which he was charged agst. the Batavian Govt. for French spoliations within its responsibility, and that his purpose of embarking for America may have been the mistake of the Editor. In a letter of Decr. to this Dept. he signified that he preferred a direct correspondence with that Govt. to a negociation with its minister at Paris.

Jefferson to Madison

Monticello May 23 and 24, 1806

DEAR SIR,

Your's by the last post was recieved yesterday, and I now return Monroe's letters. That Armstrong should be returning so suddenly and without notice is quite an impossibility. Any other hypothesis for his journey to Amsterdam would be more probable. I send you a letter from Pierpoint Edwards respecting Swartwout. His testimony against him cannot be suspected, considering their mutual relation to a common center, Burr.[14] I send you also a letter from Mr. Gallatin on account of the last paragraph, tho' as far as I can trust my memory, every article suggested has been provided for. These two letters to be returned. I have desired the Postmasters of Washington and Richmd. to send nothing here after the 28th, proposing to leave this on the 4th and be in Washington the 7th of June. It occurred to me yesterday that a letter is necessary from me to the Bashaw of Tripoli, and I have hastily prepared a draught which will need much correction. I pray you to give it freely, and submit it to Mr. Smith also. If you can return the fair draught by the post leaving Washington the 28th. I may sign and send it by the return of the same post, so that you may recieve it the 3d. of June. Or if not wanting sooner, it may lie with you till the 7th. when I can sign it at Washington.

At length we have had a copious rain. It continued with slight remissions two days (Wed. and Thursday) falling moderately so that the earth is saturated without raising the streams. It was from the N. E. and has cleared up cold, the wind at N. and thermometer 50°. Mr. Burwell is here. He understands well the occurrences at Washington but had not so well understood Clarke.[15] Accept affectionate salutations.

P.S. The above was written yesterday morning. In the evening it recommenced raining, continued steadily tho' moderately thro' the night, and still continues this morning, with the wind at N. W. The earth has enough, but more is wanting for the springs and streams. May 24. 7.o'clock a.m.

Madison to Jefferson

Washington May 26, 1806

DEAR SIR

Your letter of the 19th. by express, was duly recd. For the result of the consultation among us on the mediterranean arrangements, I refer to what you will doubtless learn from Mr. Smith.

I inclose letters from Armstrong, Bowdoin Lee and Forbes. That from A. is particularly interesting. Altho there is a tint in it which is not agreeable, it

---

14. John Swartwout was the federal marshal in New York who TJ suspected of packing the jury that acquitted William S. Smith of conspiring with Miranda to violate America's neutrality laws. TJ later removed Swartwout from office. Pierpont Edwards was special government counsel in this case. See Adams, III, pp. 189-96; Brant, IV, pp. 323-39; and Malone, V, pp. 87-88.

15. William A. Burwell had served as TJ's private secretary during Jefferson's first term as president. When John Randolph, writing as "Decius," publicized his break with the administration in the Richmond *Enquirer* in the fall of 1806, TJ furnished Burwell with information for a rebuttal. Burwell was subsequently elected to Congress from the district that included Poplar Forest, succeeding Christopher Clark, a supporter of Randolph; see Cunningham, *The Jeffersonian Republicans*, pp. 257-58, and Malone, V, pp. 161-63.

seems a further proof that the plan laid would have been in the nick of time, and sure of success if the attempts to assassinate it here had not taken place. I am particularly glad to find that the idea of indemnities had taken such root, and that there was not more repugnance to a disincumbrance of W[est] F[lorida] of post nati grants.[16] I forgot to mention in my last that the letter from A. to you referred to in yours before the last was not inclosed.

I inclose also a communication from Mr. Merry, on the intended blockade of the German rivers, with such an answer as I have thought a proper guard agst. misconceptions.[17]

Mr. Merry communicated at the same time a letter from Mr. Fox of Apl. 7, observing that notwithstanding the impatience for an answer to Mr. Monroe's complaints, and the heats which seemed to be rising in the U. S. an answer had been prevented by the importance of the necessary investigations, and by the pressure of other affairs; instructing Mr. Merry at the same time to assure the Amn. Govt. of the good will of the King towards the U. S. and his sincere desire that arrangements removing all causes of dispute might lay the foundation for permanent friendship and harmony between the two countries; and further that not a day would be unnecessarily lost in preparing to enter into Treaty with Mr. Monroe. As no written communication was made by Mr. M. I give the substance of it from memory which I believe I can rely on, as I was permitted to peruse the letter of Mr. Fox.[18]

From the moment and manner of this step by Mr. Fox, there is no doubt that it has been stimulated by the loss of the German Market, and the fear that the temper of this country if not soothed by some such friendly assurances might shut the door now also agst. British manufactures. The English papers were beginning to republish the propositions of Gregg, Genrl. Smith etc.

We have had a fine but not a sufficient rain, but with a degree of cold and wind since till yesterday, that lessens the binefit of it With respectful attachment. Y^{rs}.

JAMES MADISON

Madison to Jefferson

Washington May 28, 1806

DEAR SIR

The last mail brought me yours inclosing the letters to you from P. Edwards and Mr. Gallatin, which I retain for your return. The supplemental

16. JM referred to John Randolph's opposition to the Two Million Dollar Act for the purchase of West Florida.

17. JM's answer to the "paper blockade" stated that American ships would enter any European port unless a British blockading fleet actually closed it; see Brant, IV, pp. 367–68.

18. For an excellent discussion of the efforts of the Grenville-Fox Ministry of All-the-Talents to replace the *Essex* decision and regularize American trade, see Perkins, pp. 103–6.

instruction to A. and Bowdoin had not escaped attention.

Subpoenas have this day been served on Genl. Dearborn, Mr. Smith and myself. The absence of Mr. Gallatin postpones the service on him. Mr. Wesson, Doct. Thornton, and Mr. Duncansern and Mr. Bradley of Vermont, are also on the list of Witnesses, brought by the Messenger, and either have been or will be summoned. It is perhaps not unfortunate that so aggregate a blow has been aimed at the administration, as it places in a stronger view the malice of the proceeding and the inconvenience to the public business which would result from an attendance of all the heads of Dept. Still I find a strong impression existing that the attendance is inevitable.[19] Yrs. etc.

J. MADISON

Jefferson to Madison

Monticello May 30, 1806

THJ TO MR MADISON

Yours of the 26th came to hand yesterday. I now return you the letters recieved from you of Shrader, Bowdoin, Armstrong, Milner, Lee, Forbes, Merry, your's to him, and Duplantier's.

I inclose a letter to me from Brudenhem to be filed and not otherwise noticed, and one from Vettenhort, on which we are bound by courtesy to do what can be done without inconvenience.

In another package I inclose for your perusal, letters I have recieved from Armstrong, Bowdoin and Coxe.

Ryland Randolph, asks a Consulship in the Mediterranean, and his health obliges him to request an early answer. I think him so honest a man, as to be worthy the best vacancy we have on the Northern coast of that sea.[20] But this may be a subject of consideration, as well as those above mentioned, on my return. The present is probably the last letter I shall write you before I leave this place which will be on Wednesday the 4th prox.

Our late rain did not prove to have been as abundant as at first believed. It is supposed to have wet the earth about 6.f. deep.

A caterpillar is devouring the crops of latter wheat Southwestwardly of us, and as far as this river. I have not heard of it farther N.Eastwardly. It eats off the whole foliage, it also attacks the corn and tobacco and indeed the weeds of various kinds. Affectte. salutations

---

19. For discussion of these subpoenas in the trial of William S. Smith in the Miranda episode, see Brant, IV, pp. 335–37.

20. Ryland Randolph owned lands in Goochland and Amelia counties; see Edwin M. Betts, ed., *Thomas Jefferson's Farm Book* . . . (Princeton, 1953), p. 522.

Madison to Jefferson

[Washington] June 14, 1806

The vessel for the Bey of Tunis is a small one purchased by Capt. Preble in the Mediterranean. The final cost can not be ascertained in the absence of the Upper Clerks of the Navy Dept. It is supposed not to have exceeded a very few thousand dollars.[21]

Madison to Jefferson

[Washington] July 8, 1806

The H. of R. refused approprns for the Convention with the Cherokees made at Washn.[,] the Chickasaw Treaty[,] the last Piankesha Treaty for the country between the Vincennes and Kaskaskia country

Jefferson to Madison

[Washington] July 9, 1806

Propositions for consideration
and consultation respecting Yrujo

That a letter be written to him requiring him to leave the US. for which as much time will be allowed him as will be necessary for the arrangement of his affairs and accomodation of his family; and notifying him that if this requisition be not complied with within the time which the Executive shall think reasonable, he will be seized and sent off without a moment's further warning: and that a communication of this is now made to his court.

That a letter be written to Mr Erving, to be communicated to the government of Spain, stating the time when we first instructed our Minister there first to complain of Yrujo, then to desire his recall; the time when they promised to recall him, his continued insults to this government, his intrigues, his bribes, his seditious writings in the papers; that we have now required him to leave the US. that should he fail to obey this requisition, we shall still wait a short time expecting that in consequence of the reiterated request through our ministers at Paris and Madrid he will be peaceably withdrawn by the authority

---

21. The bey of Tunis finally accepted $10,000 as indemnification for losses he claimed to have sustained by the confiscation of his vessels; see Irwin, p. 166.

of his government: but that if this does not take place after a certain further delay (say Octbr. 1) he will then be seized by this government and sent out of its limits.

That a copy of the letter to Irvine [Erving] be sent to General Armstrong to be communicated to the government of France.

TH. JEFFERSON

On consultation July 19. we concluded to let this matter lie till October.

Jefferson to Madison

[Monticello] July 17, 1806

TH. J. TO MR MADISON

I return the Commission made out for Mr Briscoe as Commn. of the Western road, his residence at or near Fort-Cumberland being thought to make him liable to an influence which might affect the direction of the road. Baltimore being peculiarly interested in having that road conducted along the best rout without regard for the local interests of the neighborhood. I have thought it best to ask of Mr Smith, when he goes to Baltimore to consult with Mr. M^{c}radie and Mr Moore, the delegates of that neighborhood, who probably know some proper characters, and will be present to inform the Senate of the grounds of appointment. Whenever Mr Smith therefore shall name a person to the department of State, I would wish the commission to issue, without farther consulting me.[22]

Madison to Jefferson

Washington July 25, 1806

DEAR SIR

The inclosed letter from the Mayor of N. York shews that coercion alone will rid us of the Tunisians in revolt agst. Mellimelli. I have written to the Mayor that it is desirable that he should have them sent on to Boston, by any means which he may be able to apply. I believe it will be found necessary to take the course thought of before your departure for conveying the presents etc. to Tunis; that is by a chartered vessel. The articles for the Bey with the merchandize of the Ambassador are stated to be so bulky that it would be extremely inconvenient to encumber a public ship with them. In one of the

---

22. For a brief discussion of the first commissioners of the Cumberland Road—Thomas Moore of Maryland, Eli Williams of Maryland (replacing Briscoe), and Joseph Kerr of Ohio—see Philip Jordan, *The National Road* (Indianapolis, 1948), pp. 75-81.

inclosed Moniteur's you will find the paragraph referred to in Armstrong's letter, on the subject of Miranda, as it was drawn up under Talleyrand's direction. I have not yet fixt the day for setting out; but have in view a short one. It would be agreeable to get Lear's before I leave the City, but I shall not make that a sine qua non. It is just reported that the Essex is in the river, and I hope truly. Yrs. with respectful attachment

JAMES MADISON

The letter from Fox to Merry on the subject of Peirce[23] was dated June 6th. and marks the strongest desire to repress the hostile spirit here, which the British Govt. apprehended might result from the murder. Fox speaks of the affair as having taken place in the *Harbour* of N. York.

Madison to Jefferson

Washington July 25, 1806

DEAR SIR

I have thought it not amiss to add to the letter written yesterday to the Mayor of N. York the suggestions of which a copy is inclosed. In the liberty of giving your sanction to the use of legal force, I was governed by my recollection that you considered nothing wanted to authorize force here in sending the Tunisians on board the Franklin but the requisition of the Ambassador which was supplied by Cathcart's letter to Mr. Clinton Yrs. with respectful attacht

JAMES MADISON

Jefferson to Madison

Monticello July 26, 1806

I left at Washington a great coat of which I shall have great need. Should this reach you before your departure I will thank you to bring it and it will be in time if I recieve it when you come to Monticello yourself, as it will be on my return only that it will be wanting. I have written to Mr Lemaire to deliver it to you. The drought in this quarter is successive. It begins about the Rapidan, at Mr Strode's and some distance on each side they are abundantly wet. Corn

23. John Pierce was the American sailor who was killed on Apr. 25, 1806, when H.M.S. *Leander* fired a warning shot across the bow of another ship; see Adams, III, pp. 199, 206, and Perkins, pp. 107-9. For Charles Fox to Anthony Merry, June 6, 1806, see Bernard Mayo, ed., "Instructions to the British Ministers to the United States, 1791-1812," in *AHA Annual Report for 1936* (Washington, 1941), p. 223.

however still has a healthy look. The crop of wheat has been large, and of the first quality. I found Mr [Thomas Mann] Randolph's white family all recovered. But there is a good deal of sickness generally, proceeding from the abundance of stagnant pools into which all the rivers, creeks, and branches are now converted. Even the Rivanna, after taking out the water for my little toll mill, has not as much left as would turn another. The shallows in the river are all dry, and the deep parts covered with a green coat. All Charlottesville drinks out of one scanty spring which is constantly muddy, and more and more springs are failing daily. People come for bread from Amherst and Hanover to the three river mills we have in this neighborhood, to wit, mine, Wood's 5 miles and Magruder's 10 miles below. We grind each about 40 barrels a day. I informed you erroneously that our home post leaves Milton on Monday. It leaves it on Tuesdays. I salute you with affection and respect

TH^S JEFFERSON

Madison to Jefferson

Washington July 28, 1806

DEAR SIR

The Essex arrived yesterday morning, and I recd from Commodore Rodgers the inclosed letter from Mr. Lear. The Acct current to which it refers happened not to be put up with the inclosures. The general view of Mediterranean affairs given by Rodgers strengthens the favorable one presented by Lear.

Cathcart writes that Mellimelli had accepted a reimbursement of the cost of the supernumerary articles, and had been restored by the measure to good humour, which had been strongly affected by the change in the arrangement for transporting the articles, and his suspicions that he should either never receive them or receive them at a day too distant for his speculations. Mellimelli it seems had also signified that he should feel little concern if the seceding part of his suite should be left behind. But as there is reason to believe that his indifference proceeded from a fear that he might have to pay their debts, and as such a disposition of the seceders might do no harm at Tunis, as well as give us trouble here, it has been thought best not to recall the request made to the Mayor of N. York.

The Newspapers tell us that Col.Smith has been returned by the Jury not guilty. I do not learn the ground on which the verdict was understood to be formed, or on which it was pressed by the Counsel. If it was not a mere sic volo, sic jubeo [wish and order], it probably is to be charged to the want of irresistable proof of the intent, or to the success of the Counsel in presenting the intermediate destinations, as breaking the continuity of the expedition.

Altho' I have reason to believe that my departure will be the signal for opening the federal batteries agst- our letter to the Court, I shall postpone it for a few days only. We are still without rain. The fields have lost entirely their verdure. The corn looks better than could be expected. The crops of Tobo. in Maryland are likely to fail at least to the amount of a half. With respectful attachment Yrs.

JAMES MADISON

Jefferson to Madison

Monticello July 30, 1806

DEAR SIR

I return you the letter of DeWitt Clinton and your answer. I think that if he can deliver or send to Mellimelli the refractory members of his family under the ordinary laws of N. Y. it will be better; but that force should be employed if other resources fail. Airth's letter and the anonymous one from Havanna are also returned. I send you a letter from the new King of Wirtemburg, one from some detained sailors, and one from Henry Banks informing us of the abuses in the St. Domingo trade. This last should perhaps be sent to Mr Gallatin. I inclose also the sketch of an answer to the King of Wirtemburg, which when you shall have made it what it should be, have the goodness to have copied fair and returned to me for signature. Accept affectionate salutations.

TH JEFFERSON

Jefferson to Madison

[Monticello, July 31?, 1806][24]

Notes on Mr. Eaton's accounts, additional
to those of the Secretary of State.

When we consider that this is the first of the Barbary accounts which come to us for settlement, and that every article now allowed will be a precedent for futurity we ought to reduce it to what is rigorously right. The rules of settlement of the accounts of our foreign ministers are generally applicable to those of the Barbary Consuls.

1st Head. No outfit can be allowed.

The office of Consul is determined by the receipt of their recall, or by their departure, in the case of recall, a quarter's salary for their return is just:

---

24. Undated but placed between July 31 and Aug. 1, 1806, in Presidential Papers Microfilm, James Madison papers, reel 9.

and it seems a good enough measure when they come away by order of the Bey.

2d. The article of 382.52 is inadmissible.

House rent. This is not allowed our foreign ministers. It therefore will be proper to consider what are the circumstances which give these consuls a better right to it. Repairs, alterations and additions to the house, outhouses etc. In my opinion totally inadmissible. As to external repairs the landlord does them everywhere, and the tenant internal. As to alterations from time to time at the caprice or particular taste of the tenant, the next one will perhaps undo them, and there is no bottom to such an article of indulgence. See articles 51.28/10.92/4.12/9.89/7.93/60.68/14.57

The present in return for a present is inadmissible. Carriages, mules and attendants to Bardo. Are not these the ordinary expences, as are carriages etc. to Versailles, to Pardo, San Il defonso etc. See articles 3.60/7./1.56/.86/3.43

Horse and mule hire monthly. Forage for horses. barley field for etc. These are ordinary expences, as much as those of the table. The salary is to be employed in them.

Contingencies. A very heavy article. They should be detailed and sifted.

4th. Charities. No such article is allowed ministers, or any other public servant in a single instance. States never allow charities at the public expense, but on a special act of their legislature. Charity is the duty of the indivicual and should be out of his own funds, as a portion of his ordinary expence. If it be allowed to give charities out of the pocket of another, the greatest abuses would follow.

7th The houses of ministers are not furnished. They buy their own furniture, sell it as they can, and never bring it into the public account. The paiments for furniture were misapplications of the public monies, and ought to be disallowed.

8th head. A particular explanation of every article should be given so as to enable us to have it enquired into by the successor.

Jefferson to Madison

Monticello Aug. 2, 1806

DEAR SIR

I return you Mr Lear's letters, in which I am sorry to find he says not a word about the Tripoline family. I presume the family has chosen not to be given up.[25] I inclose you a letter from Salvatore Bosutti at Malta, which may

25. The peace treaty that ended the war between the United States and Tripoli contained a complicated provision relating to the ruling pasha, Yusuf, and his brother, Hamet Caramalli, the former ruler who had been exiled but whose wife and family were held hostage by Yusuf. Although Hamet's family was supposed to be released, Yusuf negotiated a four-year delay in a secret agree-

be filed in the office I presume without answer. Noble's letter and sample should I suppose be filed in the patent-office. It may be a charity tho' it is not a duty to inform him of the steps he ought to take. The letters from Rogers, after perusal, I will ask the favor of you to return to the Navy office. The case of the Ketch Gheretti is not a pleasant one to form the commencement of our correspondence with the Ottoman government. Shall we let it pass without an answer? Or give them a solid one? She had joined our enemies in war against us. We took her. Had we considered her crew as Ottoman subjects, we must have hung them up as pirates and perhaps complained to that government. We thought it a proof of moderation to identify them, as they had done themselves with the Tripolines, to confiscate the vessel, and, on the peace, to discharge them. But through whom can we answer? My journey to Bedford is still to be made; but I have not yet fixed a day. I have retained the papers now sent in expectation you would recieve them in Orange. Accept affectionate salutations and continued respect.

Th. Jefferson

Madison to Jefferson

Washington Aug. 4, 1806

Dear Sir

The inclosed letters from Cathcart and Mellimelli explain the unexpected and perplexing determination of the latter with respect to the Franklin. The least evil left to our choice has been thought to be that of chartering a vessel at Boston. Cathcart has accordingly been instructed to do so. It has been thought proper also to take advantage of a vessel going from Alexa. to Boston, for sending the   and other articles excluded from the Franklin, wch. may now accompany the other presents for the Bey. I have not yet heard from the Mayor of N. York on the subject of the refractory members of the Tunisian suite. I wish there may not be some serious difficulty in the use of compulsion, or some room for criticizing the legality of it.

I inclose also two letters from P. Edwards which throw much light on the state of things at N. York as connected with the late trials of S[mith] and O[gden]. They give a very favorable idea at the same time of his own honest and stedfast attachment to the administration. These letters on their return will find me in Orange. I have recd. from Sanford a short letter stating the result of the trials, without adding any explanations.[26] I have requested of him

---

ment that TJ finally learned about the next year. See Gardner W. Allen, *Our Navy and the Barbary Corsairs* (Boston, 1905), pp. 263–65; Malone, V, pp. 40–42; and Brant, IV, pp. 308–10.

26. Nathan Sanford was the U.S. attorney for New York who prosecuted the case against William S. Smith and Samuel G. Ogden for their roles in the Miranda affair; see Brant, IV, p. 331.

such a statement as will shew the grounds on which the jury is understood to have given their verdict, with a view to the aid it may furnish in explaining the transaction to our foreign Ministers. I should have been glad to receive it for that purpose before my departure, but cannot now expect it.

I have been detained here several days longer than I apprehended, by an unavoidable delay in some private arrangements. I calculate on being enabled by the mail of this evening to start tomorrow, or at furthest the morning after; beyond which nothing will detain me but some obstacle wholly unforeseen.

The inclosed reccommendations of G. Taylor to be Consul at St. Thomas, have just been handed to me. One question to be decided in the case is whether it be expedient to make any appt. at this time, which may seem to favor the trade to St. Domingo thro' a Danish Island. On one hand, as the law agst. a direct trade has gone beyond our legal obligations, and the trade will certainly go on indirectly thro' other merchants, if not thro' ours, it may seem not unfair that ours should reap the harvest. On the other, France is ready to espy every variance not congenial with the law part, and may unseasonably be soured by that of appointing a Consul as proposed. Turreau as you will see by his letter inclosed has already, tho' probably out of mere diplomatic activity, interposed a representation agst. the supposed trade circuitously carried on with St. Domingo. I have not answered his letter because I think it questionable whether it ought to be answered, as the letter proceeds on the false ground that the act of Cong. was due to the rights of France. It will be observed also that he specifies no particular instance of our evasion of the law, nor even of the mode or channel used for the purpose.

I have recd yours of [July 26] and shall bring your cloak. The drouth here continues with at least equal severity as with you. Yours most respectfully

JAMES MADISON

Jefferson to Madison

Monticello Aug. 8, 1806

DEAR SIR,

Yours of the 4th is received. I think the course which has been taken for sending Mellimeni home is the best; and I concur with you in the expediency of giving no answer to Turreau. Indeed his letter does not seem to call for one. In the present state of our affairs it will certainly be better not to appoint a Consul at St. Thomas's. We must not risk great things for small. A Consul merely to patronize a commerce which the laws forbid, would be a measure in opposition to the law, and not for it's execution.

I have recieved an impression from some cause or other that we had a convention with Spain for the mutual surrender of fugitives from justice in cases of murder and forgery: but on examining my collection of the laws here (which however is imperfect) I do not find such an one.[27] If we have such a Convention the murderer of his negro must certainly be given up. If we have not, he as certainly cannot. Of this I imagine you can satisfy yourself. If he is to be given up our constitution secures to him a previous trial by jury. He should be regularly indicted for having committed a certain crime within the territories of Spain, and the jury finding him guilty, the judgment of the court should be that he be delivered up to the Spanish authority. The case is of new creation by the convention, and should therefore take the course of analogous cases already known to the law.

The fact mentioned by Govr. Lewis, that the British have a fort on the Isthmus near Carleton or Buck Island is equally unknown and astonishing to me. Certainly we are bound to look into it immediately. The first step to be taken I think is to ascertain the fact, for which purpose I should suppose it best that Genl. Dearborne should send a discreet judicious officer to the place, with orders to do nothing more than to satisfy himself of the fact and report it to him.

I think a new marshall should now be appointed for N. York and will thank you to order a blank commission for this purpose to be forwarded to Mr. Gallatin, as was settled before we parted.

I now return you the letters of P. Edwards, Cathcart, Govr. Lewis, Turreau and Govr. Claiborne; and I inclose to you for your office Mellimenni's letter to me, Brown's with an official report, Jones's petn for a pardon, Govr. Claiborne's and Judge Hall's recommendation in Perryman's case, on which two last, pardons are to be issued; and Phelp's letter to be lodged in the patent office.

I am likely to be detained here a week more before I can set out for Bedford. My absence will be of about 10 days. If you can have my great coat put into the hands of the stage driver as he passes on Wednesday afternoon, I shall get it in time for my journey, and be very thankful to you for the accommodation. My affectionate salutations are tendered to yourself and Mrs. Madison.

Th. Jefferson

Jefferson to Madison

Monticello Aug. 15, 1806

Th Jefferson to Mr Madison.

I send you some papers from the Secretary of Louisiana for your office; also a letter from Sandford to Mr Gallatin for your perusal and then to be

---

27. Jacob Wagner, State Department clerk, quickly informed the president that there was no such convention between the United States and Spain, "though the Spaniards have often urged us to make one"; see Jacob Wagner to TJ, Aug. 12, 1806, Presidential Papers Microfilm, James Madison Papers, reel 9. TJ probably recalled his proposal in Mar. 1792 of a convention with Spain to deal with reciprocal extradition of fugitives; if so, he forgot that no agreement was reached. See *PTJ*, XXIII, pp. 327-32.

reinclosed to Mr Gallatin. Altho' I have not heard of your arrival at home, yet I trust that you are there. I expect to set out for Bedford tomorrow or very shortly after, and shall be absent 10. days. This may account for delays of answers to your communications should any occur. After my return I shall hope to have the pleasure of seeing Mrs Madison and yourself here. Accept my affectionate salutations and assurances of constant esteem.

Madison to Jefferson

Orange Aug. 15, 1806

DEAR SIR

I left Washington on the morning of the 6th. and ended my journey on Saturday evening. Having received no communications from the Office before the mail which arrived the day before yesterday, and concluding that your trip to Bedford was probably undertaken about this time I have been the less in a hurry to trouble you with a letter. I now inclose several papers transmitted by Mr. Wagner. Among them is a letter from Cathcart and another from the Mayor of N. Y. explaining the situation of the refractory Tunisians. If the answer to that of the Mayor which is inclosed, be approved, I must beg the favor of you to forward it as addressed to Mr. Wagner.

I found at the post office your favor of the 2d. instant. In the answer to the King of Wirtemberg, I have taken the liberty to pencil an alteration relieving it from the appearance of admitting in every *Govt* to new model itself, independently of the nation. If the change of idea be thought for the better, you will be able to improve the expression, and will either send it back to me, or forward it directly to the office to be prepared for your signature, as you may chuse. Just as I was starting from Washington I received the inclosed letter from Dr. Thornton disclosing the perturbation excited in his mind, by some of the operations of Mr. laTrobe. With perfect respect and attachment I remain Yrs.

JAMES MADISON

The drouth here continues with a severity truly distressing

Jefferson to Madison

Monticello Aug. 17, 1806

TH J. TO J. M.

The death of Meriwether Jones having taken place, I have written to Mr Wagner *directly* to forward to Mr Page a Commission for the loan office, in order to save a post and shorten the term of sollicitations. I shall set out this morning for Bedford and be back about the 25th. Affectionate salutations.

Jefferson to Madison

Monticello Aug. 28, 1806

DEAR SIR

On my return the day before yesterday I found here your's of the 15th. As the Russian ships are expected at Philadelphia are connected with the Imperial family, and their report will certainly be made to the emperor, would it not be well for you to write either to Mr. Gallatin, or at shorter hand, to Muhlenberg to recommend them to his particular attention good offices and indulgence, and those of the other officers of the customs. The case of the Indostan on which we complained to Turreau, and some of the groundless cases on which he has complained to us, shew that we ought on neither side to act on any complaint until the facts are supported by affidavits. After we shall have begun to observe this rule ourselves, we may require from the foreign ministers to be furnished with affidavits of the facts on which they complain, and it will save to both parties a great deal of useless trouble. I think Fitzsimmons should be told we can do nothing on general surmises. The cases of wrong by privateers should be specified and supported by affidavits, and then we will act according to our means. The instructions asked by Simpson on ransoming from the Arabs are very difficult. They had better lie till we meet. If Dr. Thornton's complaint of Latrobe's having built inconsistently with his plan of the middle part of the capitol be correct, it is without my knolege and against my instructions. For altho' I consider that plan as incapable of execution, yet I determined that nothing should be done which would not leave the question of it's execution free.[28] I have sent to Mr Wagner your letter to Dewitt Clinton and mine to the K. of Wirtemberg amended as you proposed. Meade's conduct towards Yznardi excited real indignation.[29] I will write to Mr Smith to revoke Campbell's unauthorised nomination of him as Navy agent, and to instruct the officers when they are in a port where there is no agent, to apply to the Consuls for the port.

I inclose you a letter from Monroe. Capt Lewis of the Leander I see is returned. I think we had better have his motions watched and arrest him in Jersey, Pensylvania or Columbia, or Norfolk should he be found in either.[30]

All the papers recieved from you are now returned, except recommendations to office which I retain as usual. Accept affectionate salutations.

TH. JEFFERSON

28. For TJ's relations with Latrobe, the architect who was surveyor of public buildings, and Dr. William Thornton, the designer of the Capitol whose criticism led Latrobe to sue him for libel, see Malone, V, pp. 532–38.

29. Richard Worsam Meade, the U.S. naval agent at Cadiz, and Josef Yznardi, the American consul there, accused each other of misconduct in office; see *PJM* (Pres. ser.), I, p. 46.

30. Thomas Lewis was captain of the *Leander,* the vessel owned by Samuel G. Ogden and chartered by General Miranda for his voyage to South America; see Brant, IV, pp. 325, 328, who calls him Jacob Lewis. In his letter to TJ, Aug. 30, 1806, below, JM identifies him as Thomas Lewis.

Madison to Jefferson

[Orange] Aug. 30, 1806

DEAR SIR

Among the papers inclosed is a letter from the District Attorney of N. Y. enquiring whether Ths. Lewis of the Leander is to be brought to trial. I have put under an unsealed cover to Mr. Wagner. an answer in the affirmative, which if approved may be forwarded from Monticello. I see no reason for discussing the indictment in this case more than there was for doing so in the case of Ogden, after the acquittal of Smith. The only circumstance for consideration seems to be the apparent preposterousness of punishing a subordinate offender, after a formal verdict in favor of the principals.

I have signed an amended letter prepared by Mr. Wagner, for the case of Morales. The conduct of this man presents so many marks of the adventurer if not the Impostor, that it is a fair question whether a suspension of his exequator ought not to be substituted, for the proposed admonition. The idea of a circular call for a statement of the fees required of Citizens by foreign Consuls, appears to be proper and well timed.

The complaint of Mr. Merry involving important topics now under discussion and negociation, and on which the sentiments of the Govt. here have been repeatedly expressed, it does not seem necessary to give it a formal answer. The suggestion however seems not amiss, that the enquiry necessary to vindicate the Collectors should be undertaken; if indeed a vindication can be necessary agst. testimony which convicts the witnesses of the most hardened disregard of truth.[31]

We propose to ourselves the pleasure of seeing Monticello, the latter part of this, or the early part of the following week; if nothing should interfere, and we should in the mean time hear of your return from Bedford. Yrs. with respectful attacht.

JAMES MADISON

Jefferson to Madison

Monticello Sept. 2, 1806

DEAR SIR

Yours of the 30th. I recieved yesterday, and now return the papers from Cathcart, Sullivan, De Ponceau, Ramage, Barnet, Merry, and that concerning Lewis. In a former letter I had suggested to you the waiting to arrest Lewis in some other state (for I believe that such an offence may be tried any where) but

---

31. Merry's complaints involved the alleged issuance of American certificates of citizenship to British sailors; see Brant, IV, p. 370.

considering the change of the Marshall it is possible a fair jury may be obtained now in N. York. I think it would be proper to send to Gelston, Purviance and Ohms a copy of the papers respectively concerning them, as well to ask explanations, as to admonish them to be scrupulously exact in their issuing certificates of citizenship, as the contrary conduct disgraces us. Perhaps it would be well to write a circular to bring all the Collectors to a sense of the exactness with which we wish that duty to be observed.[32]

As we shall have the pleasure of seeing you in a few days I retain the papers respecting Morales and the Indefatigable, to be a subject of conversation. You will of course come along the lower side of the mountain. You had better not come through Mr Randolph's farm, but keep the public road till you get to his gate opposite Milton, and there take the Charlottesville road, and half a mile further, at Johnson's, take the left hand by the Shadwell mills. The whole road after that is fine, and the ford made perfectly smooth. The road by Milton is very hilly and doubles the distance. The one by the mill is along the river bank to the foot of the mountain, where a new road gives an easy ascent. We have had a divine rain yesterday afternoon and in the night. Affectionate salutations.

TH. JEFFERSON

P. S. If you can set off at eight, you will be easily here to dinner.

Madison to Jefferson

[Orange] Sept. 4, 1806

DEAR SIR

I recd. by last mail your favor of the 28. and now forward such communications from Washington as have been recd. since my last. The freak of Mellimelli exceeds all the preceding vexations. I have written to Wagner to save us from the persecution of a visit from him, in case he should not be faced about at Baltimore; and to give Lear and the functionary at Tunis an explanation of the adventure. I can not yet decide whether our trip to Monticello is to be this or the ensuing week. We have just had a pretty shower, that is to say, last evening. The three preceding ones, though inconsiderable, have produced a general verdure, have aided materially the Tobo. and been of some little service to the corn. This last article however must be far short of half a crop. In many instances it will not amount to a fourth. Yrs. with respectl. affecn

JAMES MADISON

---

32. TJ was responding to JM's proposal of an inquiry to vindicate the collectors against charges by Merry; see *ibid*.

Jefferson to Madison

Monticello Sept. 16, 1806

DEAR SIR

I inclose you a letter and sundry papers recieved from Mr Gallatin of which I will ask the return. 1. As to the refractory Tunisians I think we should pay their passage and get rid of them. If they would stipulate to deliver themselves to any Tunisian or other Barbary Agent in England, it would excuse us to the Bey of Tunis.

The case of an American citizen impressed on board the Chichester, and information regularly given to you, as Colo. Newton says, requires I think a specific demand of him, and will not admit of our taking only the general step agreed on, yesterday. Still I think the general recommendation to Mr Merry should accompany the specific demand. Accept affectionate salutations.

TH JEFFERSON

P.S. Mr Gallatin leaves N. York on his return the 22d. inst.

Madison to Jefferson

[Orange] Sept. 22, 1806

DEAR SIR.

Among the inclosures is a letter from Turreau requesting a loan, to be applied to the equipment of the damaged ships of war now in our ports. I have sketched an answer for your consideration and correction. It is the more necessary to be explicit in the refusal, as the case may be followed by others of greater extent, and resulting from combat as well as casualties. I have proceeded on the ground that nothing but *humanity,* or a regard to our *own* advantage or conveniency, would reconcile public aids, with our neutral duties. I have taken for granted also that any such expenditure would not be within the contemplation of our appropriation laws.

I observe by the letters from Norfolk to Mr Gallatin, that the use of the public navy yard there has been offered for the repair of a British Frigate. As this may be resolved into an aid equivalent to money, would it not be well for the Navy Agent to be instructed not to repeat such civilities, and to have this for an answer to any complaint of partiality, which may come from a French Quarter?

I had a conversation with Mr. —— on my way home, and was glad to find him in every disposition which could be desired. He will be here on the 1st. of Octr., when I hope for the pleasure of seeing you, if not otherwise advised by you in the mean time. Permit me to suggest, what I really think will in every view be most suitable, that as in personal interviews the advances can not well be absolutely simultaneous, the [path?] should be smoothed by an unhesitating manifestation of your part, which I am sure will be duly met. Yrs. always with respectful attachment

JAMES MADISON

Jefferson to Madison

Monticello Sept. 23, 1806

DEAR SIR,

Yours by yesterday's post has been recieved, and I now return you the letters of Yznardi, Wilkinson, Cathcart, Clinton, Toulman and Turreau. In the answer to the latter I think it would be better to lay more stress on the constitutional bar to our furnishing the money, because it would apply in an occasion of peace as well as war. I submit to you therefore the striking out the words 'it is not etc.' within crotchets [ ] in your draught and inserting "but in indulging these dispositions the President is bound to stop at the limits prescribed by our constitution and law to the authorities placed in his hands. One of these limits is that 'no money shall be drawn from the treasury but in consequence of appropriations made by law' and no law having made any appropriation of money for any purpose similar to that expressed in your letter it lies of course beyond his constitutional powers. This insuperable bar renders it unnecessary to enquire whether the aid you request could be reconciled to" etc. But both as to the matter and form of this alteration, you will decide. I do not think the loan of our navy yard any more contrary to neutrality than that of our ports. It is merely admitting a ship to a proper station in our waters. But this may be a subject of future consultation. I send for your perusal two letters from Yznardi, and an anonymous one. The postmark on this last was Philadelphia, and you will be at no loss to conjecture it's Spanish source.

I still count on being with you on the 1st of Oct. and certainly feel no dispositions to be punctilious in the case you allude to. Doctr. Thornton and his family are here, and will be with you the first fair day. I salute you with affection and respect.

P. S. The death of Judge Patterson requires the nomination of a successor.[33]

Jefferson to Madison

Monticello Sept. 26, 1806

DEAR SIR

I now return you the papers recieved by yesterday's post. The letter to Monroe and one to Merry are forwarded [to] Mr Wagner. that to Merry

33. William Paterson was an associate justice of the Supreme Court.

respecting a murder committed on the high seas by a British subject, on board a British vessel, and on a British subject, is returned for consideration, as not being as explicit as amity to that government and the clear principle of right requires. I think he might be assured that we will immediately enquire into these facts alone, and that being found true he may be assured that measures shall be taken for the *liberation* of the prisoner, altho' he cannot be given up. Should the judge finally retain cognisance of the cause we ought to liberate by a pardon. The facts stated by Mr Williams to you are corroborated by other information communicated to me. It will be necessary, at our first meeting, to take this matter into serious consideration.

I think it would be better to return Haumont's letter to the writer. We are not the judges what communications should be handed to the emperor of France. If the minister of marine thinks that Haumont's work is of the nature of those things which the emperor does not chuse to be troubled with, we have no right to step between them. The communications of Irving are very interesting. They give hope as to the disposition to accomodate with us, but terror as to the price. I salute you with affection.

TH JEFFERSON

Madison to Jefferson

Orange Sept. 27, 1806

DEAR SIR

Yours of the 23. with accompaniments came duly to hand. I have adopted your amendment to the letter to Turreau. He may fairly be told that no appropriation has such an object as he presents, because the Legislature can not be presumed to have contemplated it; particularly taking into view the line of neutrality hitherto pursued. At the same time it is not amiss to avoid narrowing too much the scope of the *appropriations to foreign intercourse,* which are terms of great latitude, and may be drawn on by any urgent and unforeseen occurrences.[34] Will it not deserve attention, whether the vice-consul at Cadiz, or the Consulate at St. Lucar be not a more eligible berth for Mr. Hackly. than St. Tanders [Santander].[35] Yrs. with respectful attacht

JAMES MADISON

---

34. JM's italics. Several months earlier, JM had met Mellimelli's request for concubines and charged the cost to the State Department's "appropriations to foreign intercourse"; see Brant, IV, p. 306.

35. Richard Hackley was a relative of Thomas Mann Randolph, TJ's son-in-law. TJ appointed him U.S. consul at Sanlúcar (St. Lucar) later in the year; see *PJM* (Pres. ser.), I, p. 124.

33

A CONSPIRACY AT HOME AND A BAD TREATY ABROAD, 1806–1807

*O*N ONE OF HIS TWO VISITS to Monticello during the long, hot summer of 1806, Jefferson lamented the distressing drought that "threaten[ed] the loss of every thing"—oats and wheat, peaches and cherries.[1] By the end of July, he wrote that "all Charlottesville drinks out of one scanty spring which is constantly muddy, and more and more springs are failing daily."[2] Not until the first of September did "a divine rain" bring relief.[3] James and Dolley Madison roasted in Washington until August, then boiled in Virginia until October, where they welcomed any rainfall as "a pretty shower."[4] The Madisons scheduled a visit to Monticello in September, and Jefferson stopped overnight at Montpellier on October 1.[5]

The summer idyll ended when the president and the secretary of state returned to Washington in the fall. Although there was no news of significance on the foreign front, reports of a growing conspiracy in the West, headed by Aaron Burr, led Jefferson to convene the cabinet on October 22 to meet the domestic crisis. For months, rumors and warnings about the former vice president's movements had reached the nation's capital. No one yet knew that Vice President Burr, shortly after killing Hamilton in the duel that doomed his political career, had made a secret offer to Anthony Merry, the British minister in Washington, "to lend his assistance to His Majesty's Gov-

1. TJ to JM, May 11, 1806, above, and May 19, 1806, above.
2. TJ to JM, July 26, 1806, above.
3. TJ to JM, Sept. 2, 1806, above.
4. JM to TJ, Sept. 4, 1806, above.
5. See TJ to JM, Aug. 15, 1806, above, Sept. 2, 1806, above, Sept. 16, 1806, above, and Sept. 23, 1806, above; and JM to TJ, Aug. 30, 1806, above, Sept. 4, 1806, above, and Sept. 22, 1806, above.

ernment in any Manner in which they may think fit to employ him, particularly in endeavouring to effect a Separation of the Western Part of the United States from that which lies between the Atlantick and the Mountains."[6] But news of his trip through the West after he left office had raised questions about his motives in 1805, when widely published reports suggested that he might be plotting the formation of a separate government in the West or the conquest of Mexico. Although Jefferson received both anonymous and private reports about Burr's mysterious activities and his visits with General James Wilkinson, governor of Upper Louisiana and commander of the United States Army in the West, he took no action until October 1806, when Gideon Granger, the postmaster general, informed him that Burr had offered a military command to General William Eaton, back from his campaign against Tripoli, for an expedition to separate the western states from the Union.[7]

Jefferson laid this letter before the cabinet along with earlier reports that he and Madison had received on Burr's actions.[8] The cabinet agreed to send a naval force to New Orleans and to dispatch John Graham, secretary of the Orleans Territory who was then in Washington, to alert military and civil authorities in the West to the conspiracy and to arrest Burr if he committed any overt act. Madison's research persuaded Jefferson to conclude that regular troops could not be used against insurrections but could be used against expeditions against a foreign country.[9] It was also discovered that the navy lacked the funds and authority to send gunboats.

While Burr was moving west, his co-conspirator, General Wilkinson, got cold feet and, without naming Burr, warned the president of the conspiracy. On November 27, 1806, Jefferson, also not naming Burr, issued a presidential proclamation warning against the "criminal enterprise" to launch an attack on the dominions of Spain. But in a special message to Congress on January 22, 1807, with new information furnished by Wilkinson, Jefferson did name Burr as the leader and announced that Burr's guilt was beyond question, an imprudent pronouncement more worthy of a prosecutor than a president.[10]

By that time, Burr had surrendered in Mississippi Territory. But he then jumped bail and fled, only to be arrested and made a military prisoner in February. Since Burr's expedition had been fitted out on Blennerhassett Island in the Ohio River, which lay within the jurisdiction of Virginia (now West

---

6. Anthony Merry to Lord Harrowby, Aug. 6, 1804, cited in Noble E. Cunningham, *In Pursuit of Reason: The Life of Thomas Jefferson* (Baton Rouge, 1987), p. 285.

7. Thomas P. Abernethy, *The Burr Conspiracy* (New York, 1954), is the standard study. The documentary record is in Aaron Burr, *Political Correspondence and Public Papers of Aaron Burr,* ed. Mary-Jo Kline and Joanne Wood Ryan, 2 vols. (Princeton, 1983), II, *passim.*

8. See Malone, V, p. 239, and Brant, IV, pp. 344-45.

9. JM to TJ, [Oct. 30, 1806,] below, with TJ's endorsement.

10. See Richardson, I, pp. 392-93, 400-5.

Virginia), he was brought under guard for trial to Richmond, where Chief Justice John Marshall presided on circuit. On All Fools' Day, Marshall committed Burr on a charge of misdemeanor for mounting an unauthorized expedition against Spanish territories in the West. He refused to indict Burr on a treason charge for assembling an armed force to be used for separating the western states from the Union, claiming that there was insufficient evidence to support that count.

But the chief justice also noted that the federal prosecutor could seek an indictment whenever he had evidence of a treasonable assemblage. When Marshall lectured the prosecution on its failure to produce affidavits and made an injudicious remark about the executive "hand of malignity" that had "capriciously" seized Burr, an outraged president denounced "the tricks of the judges to force trials before it is possible to collect the evidence, dispersed through a line of 2000 miles from Maine to Orleans."[11]

To obtain evidence, Jefferson directed Madison, in the absence of the attorney general, to expedite the movement of witnesses from the West, particularly "the witnesses proving White's enlistment of men for Burr." Since most witnesses would "be brought from great distances, and carried from one scene of trial to another," he suggested payment of "a reasonable allowance . . . for their expenses."[12] On April 25, the president sent Madison a warrant for $5,000 to cover allowances authorized by the attorney general.[13] When Madison received a report that "the proposition for separating the western country" had also been made in Paris, the president asked if "our Ministers at Paris, London, and Madrid, could find out Burr's propositions and agents there." The secretary of state then instructed Armstrong to ascertain the agents and intrigues of Burr at Paris.[14]

In June, a grand jury indicted Burr and others for treason, and he was held for trial in August. Since a defendant in a treason trial is not eligible for bail, Burr obtained an order from Marshall allowing him to live under guard in the house of one of his lawyers. Jonathan Dayton, Burr's co-conspirator who had not yet been brought to trial, then asked the president and the secretary of state to support similar treatment for him. Both agreed that "after a proceeding has been judicially instituted in such a case, it is so purely a matter to which the law and the accused are alone parties, and the authority to decide on it so exclusive in the Court, that neither the consent of the prosecuting officer, nor of the Ex. ought to be admitted into the question." But Madison cautioned Jefferson, who was critical of Marshall's handling of Burr's case, to omit one

11. TJ to William B. Giles, Apr. 20, 1807, in Ford, IX, pp. 42–46.
12. TJ to JM, Apr. 14, 1807, below, and JM to TJ, Apr. 17, 1807, below.
13. TJ to JM, Apr. 25, 1807, below.
14. TJ to JM, May 1, 1807, below, and JM to John Armstrong, May 22, 1807, in Hunt, VII, pp. 448–49. For Burr's later activities in Paris during Madison's presidency, see Brant, IV, pp. 358–59.

A CONSPIRACY AND A BAD TREATY, 1806-1807 *1445*

sentence, "which might be regarded as either an approbation of the conduct of the Court if made indiscriminate, or a covered animadversion on its indulgence to Col. Burr."[15] Jefferson thought Madison's letter to Dayton, a fellow delegate to the Constitutional Convention and most recently a senator from New Jersey, was "perfectly right, unless perhaps the expression of personal sympathy . . . might be misconstrued."[16]

By the time the Madisons visited Jefferson at Monticello in September, Burr had been acquitted of treason, but the misdemeanor indictment for setting on foot an expedition against Spanish territory was still pending. Acting on Jefferson's view that "a short conference saves a long letter,"[17] the two friends conferred, and the president sent the district attorney the following instruction: "I am happy in having the benefit of Mr. Madison's counsel on this occasion, he happening to be now with me. We are both strongly of opinion that the prosecution against Burr for misdemeanor should proceed at Richmond. If defeated, it will heap coals of fire on the head of the Judge; if convicted, it will give time to see whether a prosecution for treason against him can be instituted in any, and what other court."[18] For a second time, Burr was acquitted, but Marshall committed him for trial on another misdemeanor charge in Ohio, where acts against Spain had been more overt, and granted bail. For a second time, Burr jumped bail and this time escaped to England.

Long before Burr's ignominious exit from American history, Jefferson and Madison had turned their attention to England. On June 22, 1807, two days before the grand jury in Richmond indicted Burr for treason, His Majesty's warship *Leopard* precipitated a major Anglo-American crisis by attacking the American frigate *Chesapeake* off Norfolk when the frigate refused to be searched for British deserters. Deadly cannonades killed three and wounded eighteen American sailors in a brutal attack that amounted to an act of war. After the battered *Chesapeake* struck its colors, the British boarded the ship and dragged off four alleged deserters, pushing the smoldering issue of impressment to the center of the diplomatic stage.

In their instructions to Monroe and Pinkney the previous year, Jefferson and Madison had issued an ultimatum demanding the abolition of impressment. When the American ministers reported that the British negotiators would not incorporate such a provision in the treaty although they would agree informally to use caution in exercising the practice, the envoys accepted this assurance and continued their negotiations. "The more I consider the letter of our ministers in London," a surprised Jefferson told

15. JM to TJ, Aug. 16, 1807, below.
16. JM to TJ, Aug. 19, 1807, below, and TJ to JM, Aug. 20, 1807, below.
17. TJ to JM, Sept. 1, 1807, below.
18. TJ to George Hay, Sept. 4, 1807, cited in Brant, IV, pp. 356-57.

Madison in February 1807, "the more seriously it impresses me. I believe the sine quâ non we made is that of the nation, and that they would rather go on without a treaty than with one which does not settle this article."[19] Madison promptly instructed the envoys that the president would not accept a treaty that was silent on impressment, but as evidence of its friendly attitude the cabinet recommended the renewal of the suspension of the Nonimportation Act.[20]

When the Monroe-Pinkney Treaty arrived in Washington in March 1807, it contained no reference to impressment, although an accompanying note contained the informal assurances that the British negotiators had signed. But it also included a British note, added after London learned of Napoleon's Berlin Decree proclaiming a blockade of Britain and barring British products from Europe. The second note announced that the king would not ratify the treaty unless the United States agreed that it would not submit to the French system, a last-minute precondition that would have rendered the country a virtual satellite to Great Britain.[21]

Jefferson quickly repudiated the treaty package, refusing to submit it to the Senate for consideration. Two days later, he told the British minister that "the influence of Washington himself would not have been sufficient to restrain the Impatience of the People of the United States at the Idea" of England making a demand for assurances about "what they would do in the event of a grave Insult or Injury" by France or any other power.[22]

After rejecting the treaty, the president and the cabinet worked on a strategy for renewing negotiations, including a new way to deal with the impressment issue. Madison proposed that the United States exclude British seamen, whom the Royal Navy often seized as deserters, from American ships on the high seas. When Gallatin's estimates indicated that more than one-third of the sailors on American vessels in the foreign trade were British, a number that he thought "would materially injure our navigation,"[23] Madison came up with another proposition to demonstrate America's "accomodating disposition," suggesting that the United States follow the British example, "which claims all alien seamen serving two years on British ships, as British seamen."

19. TJ to JM, Feb. 1, 1807, below.

20. JM to James Monroe and William Pinkney, Feb. 3, 1807, cited in Malone, V, p. 406.

21. The Monroe-Pinkney Treaty had been signed on Dec. 31, 1806. The French had assured Armstrong that the Berlin Decree would have no effect on neutral ships except when they entered French ports.

22. David Erskine to Lord Howick, Mar. 6, 1807, cited in Malone, V, p. 409.

23. By examining the federal hospital tax withheld from seamen's wages, Gallatin estimated that the United States had a total of 67,000 men in the the merchant marine, with 24,000 engaged in the overseas trade. Of this group, about 9,000 were British; see Brant, IV, p. 379, and Donald R. Hickey, "The Monroe-Pinkney Treaty of 1806: A Reappraisal," *WMQ* 44 (1987): 86. Both TJ and JM thought this estimate too high; see JM to TJ, Apr. 13, 1807, below, and TJ to JM, Apr. 21, 1807, below.

A Conspiracy and a Bad Treaty, 1806–1807 1447

Thus, "all British seamen who shall prior to the exchange of Ratifications, have been two years out of British service, and in no other than ours," would be considered American seamen.[24]

While seeking new ways to reopen negotiations, the president and the secretary of state took turns listing the faults of what Jefferson called the "bad" treaty.[25] It "clearly squinted at the expectation that we would join in resistance to France," Jefferson said, "or they [Great Britain] would not regard the treaty."[26] After "looking critically" at the article on colonial trade, which had been viewed as a retreat from the *Essex* decision since it allowed the reexport trade on the landing of colonial cargo and the payment of duties in an American port, Madison found it more damaging to American commerce "than was at first noticed." The provisions permitted the United States "to be a channel merely between the *Colonies,* and *Europe,*" Madison concluded, restricting American trade to the transshipment of the produce of Europe to enemy colonies in the Caribbean and the reexport of enemy colonial goods to Europe. This put the colonies in the Far East—"beyond the C[ape] of G[ood] Hope"—on the same footing with those in the Western Hemisphere, which meant that "nothing from India, China, or the French Dutch or Spanish Eastern Colonies, can be sent to Spanish America, or the Enemy Islands in the W. Indies: nor can the productions of the latter be sent to Smirna, etc., or the Coast of Barbary etc., or elsewhere than to Europe." It followed that any American trade between European colonies in the Far East and such countries as China, "to which G. B. has not applied her principle at all, or with restrictions, (the trade having been open, or pressured to be so in time of peace), will be abolished by the Article."[27]

When Madison sought expert corroboration of his interpretation and referred the article to Senator Samuel Smith, a Baltimore shipping magnate who had criticized the president for not sending the treaty to the Senate, Smith agreed that it would "completely prostrate our commerce at the foot of Great Britain." War would be preferable to such submission, the senator declared.[28]

In some ways, the Republican reaction was reminiscent of their response to Jay's treaty a decade earlier. Like that treaty, which this one was designed to

24. JM to TJ, Apr. 17, 1807, below.

25. See JM to TJ, Apr. 13, 1807, below, Apr. 20, 1807, below, Apr. 27, 1807, below, and May 4, 1807, below; and TJ to JM, Apr. 21, 1807, below, Apr. 25, 1807, below, May 1, 1807, below, and May 8, 1807, below. For JM's full list of objections, see JM to James Monroe and William Pinkney, May 20, 1807, in Hunt, VII, pp. 407–45; for a summary of TJ's objections, see Peterson, p. 862.

26. Peterson, p. 862.

27. JM to TJ, Apr. 13, 1807, below.

28. Samuel Smith to JM, Apr. 18, 1807, cited in Brant, IV, p. 379; Peterson, p. 864; and JM to TJ, Apr. 13, 1807, below, and Apr. 20, 1807, below.

replace, the new one contained a provision that barred the United States from passing retaliatory commercial legislation against Great Britain for ten years. With the list of complaints against its commercial articles growing, with the informal assurances against impressment unacceptable, with the note on the Berlin Decree intolerable, this provision was the final straw. "We will never tie our hands by treaty," the president declared, "from the right of passing a non-importation or non-intercourse act, to make it in her interest to become just."[29]

As the criticisms of the treaty piled up, Madison concluded that it might be necessary to limit any new negotiations to the subject of impressment, "leaving the Colonial trade with other objects to their own courses" and to the influence that the application of the Nonimportation Acts "may have to that course.... The case of impressments," however, "is more urgent. Something seems essential to be done" on that score, while delaying further negotiations on a general treaty.[30]

Jefferson agreed that procrastination had its virtues. "Our best course," he told Madison, "is to let the negociation take a friendly nap and endeavor in the mean time to practice on such of it's principles as are mutually acceptable." To Secretary of the Treasury Gallatin, he wrote that "time strengthens my belief that no equal treaty will be obtained." Tinkering with the Monroe-Pinkney draft, therefore, would only be making a bad treaty worse. Indeed, his final conclusion about that treaty was "the more it is developed the worse it appears."[31]

But the treaty was not the worst news. Towards the end of April, Madison received word of "a very unexpected scene at St. James's" reporting an "unfriendly change in the British Cabinet" that brought into power a new Tory ministry under the duke of Portland. The only bright spot was that "the new Cabinet will be less averse to a tabula rasa for a new adjustment, than those who framed the instrument to be superseded."[32] Jefferson was even more pessimistic about "the explosion in the British ministry." "I know few of the characters of the new British administration," he conceded, but "the few I know are true Pittites, and Anti-American. From them we have nothing to hope, but that they will readily let us back out."[33]

There matters stood when the *Chesapeake* outrage erupted in June. Jefferson learned of the attack on June 25 and immediately recalled vacationing cabinet members for an emergency meeting. While waiting for them to assemble, he watched as public demands for war mounted in case satisfaction was not

29. Peterson, pp. 863–64.
30. JM to TJ, Apr. 20, 1807, below.
31. TJ to JM, Apr. 21, 1807, below, and April 25, 1807, below, and Peterson, p. 865. For a revisionist view of the treaty as a step "to substitute peace and prosperity for commercial sanctions and war," see Hickey, 65–88.
32. JM to TJ, Apr. 24, 1807, below, and May 4, 1807, below.
33. TJ to JM, May 1, 1807, below, and May 8, 1807, below.

A Conspiracy and a Bad Treaty, 1806-1807

given for the insult to American sovereignty. "This country," he wrote, "has never been in such a state of excitement since the battle of Lexington."[34] Spurred by the war mood, he pushed decisive actions, hunting an honorable way to settle the act of aggression peaceably but at the same time pursuing preparations for war, if bad came to worse. He and Madison drafted a proclamation barring all British warships from American ports unless the ships were on diplomatic business or in distress. Madison took a harder line than the president, inserting phrases such as "that bloody aggression," "a serious crisis by an act transcending all former outrages," "a pretext the more flagrant," "insults as gross as language could offer," "the avowed and insulting purpose of violating a ship of war under the American flag," and "her lawless and bloody purpose."[35]

Early in July, Jefferson and his cabinet agreed to issue the presidential proclamation, recall the Mediterranean squadron (the *Chesapeake* had been on its way to the Mediterranean), implement preparedness plans ranging from harbor defenses to a projected invasion of Canada, request state governors to mobilize 100,000 militia for federal service, dispatch the appropriately named frigate *Revenge* to England with instructions to the American ministers, and convene a special session of Congress on October 26, giving time for the *Revenge* to return with the response of the British ministry to the demands for redress. These included disavowal of the attack—Madison instructed Monroe that "this enormity is not a subject for discussion"; return of the four seamen seized; recall of Vice Admiral G. C. Berkeley, commander of the British fleet in North American waters who had authorized the attack; security against future attacks on American warships in time of peace; and "honorable reparation" for "the indignity offered to the sovereignty and flag of the nation, and the blood of citizens so wantonly and wickedly shed."

To this demand for reparations, Jefferson added the old ultimatum about the abolition of impressment, thus converting the negotiation from the single goal of seeking redress for the naval outrage to the larger diplomatic objective of altering Britain's basic policy. If the ministry refused, Madison instructed Monroe, all American ships in British ports were to be recalled prior to the probable resort "to measures constituting or leading to war."[36]

Indeed, Jefferson informed the secretary of state that "the *interdicted* ships" that had been ordered out of American waters "are *enemies*. Should they be forced by stress of weather to run up into safer harbors, we are to act towards them as we would towards enemies in regular war in a like case. Permit no intercourse, no supplies, and if they land[,] kill or capture them as enemies. If they lie still," he added, Captain Stephen Decatur, whose valor in the

---

34. Peterson, p. 876.
35. All of these phrases were omitted or softened in the official proclamation; see JM to TJ, [June 29, 1807,] below, and TJ's proclamation of July 2, 1807, below.
36. Brant, IV, pp. 382-83, and Malone, V, pp. 425-29.

Tripolitanian war had led to his appointment as commander of the Norfolk navy yard, "has orders not to attack them without stating the case to me and awaiting instructions. But if they attempt to enter Elizabeth river, he is to attack them without waiting for instructions."[37]

The president also pointed out that all "other armed vessels putting in from sea in distress," including those of France, "are *friends*. They must report themselves to the collector, he assigns them their station, and regulates their repairs, supplies, intercourse and stay. Not needing flags [of truce], they are under the direction of the Collector alone, who should be reasonably liberal as to their repairs and supplies, furnishing them for a voyage to any of their American ports: but I think with him their crews should be kept on board, and that they should not enter Elizabeth river."[38]

Defiant British commanders remained in American waters, however, dispatching landing parties for supplies and water. When five sailors were captured by Virginia militiamen, Governor William H. Cabell asked the president for advice. Citing legislation that he had signed two years earlier for the preservation of peace in American harbors that authorized a "qualified war" against such violators, Jefferson ruled that the sailors could be held as prisoners of war. Until the British government had responded to American demands for redress, however, he wished to avoid any act that might convert a qualified war into a general war and, therefore, ordered their return as "an act of favor."[39]

Communication with the warships, even by David Erskine, the British minister, was allowed only under flags of truce, and it took some time to decide that both "the commanding officer by land, as well as the one by water have equal authority to send and recieve flags."[40] When Erskine complained about having to communicate under flags with British warships "*in the* Chesapeake, or *off* the coast," Jefferson made it clear that the presidential proclamation applied to the first but not the second. "If, by *off* the coast he means those which being generally in our waters, go occasionally out of them to cruize or to acquire a title to communicate with their Consul it is too poor an evasion for him to expect us to be the dupes of. If vessels *off* the coast, and having never violated the proclamation wish to communicate with their Consul, they may send in by any vessel, without a flag."[41]

The president had one problem of his own in communicating with the British minister when Erskine demanded reparations for water kegs brought ashore by a landing party and smashed by Americans after they learned of the

---

37. TJ to JM, Aug. 26, 1807, below.
38. *Ibid.*
39. Malone, V, pp. 433–34.
40. TJ to JM, Aug. 7, 1807, below, Aug. 9, 1807, below, and Aug. 18, 1807, below; and JM to TJ, [Aug. 8, 1807,] below.
41. TJ to JM, Aug. 18, 1807, below.

British attack on the *Chesapeake*. It reminded him of the story of "one who having broke his cane over the head of another, demanded paiment for his cane. This demand," he added sarcastically, "might well enough have [been] made part of an offer to pay the damages done to the Chesapeake and to deliver up the authors of the murders committed on board her."[42]

Although hopeful of a peaceful settlement, Jefferson made energetic military preparations throughout the summer, approving a war establishment of 15,000 regulars for garrison duty and 32,000 volunteers for expeditionary services.[43] He also contemplated an order to "all the militia and volunteers destined for the Canadas to be embodied on the 26th of Octr, and to march immediately to such points on the way to their destination as shall be pointed out, there to await the decision of Congress," which alone could declare war.[44]

Earlier in the year, Jefferson and Madison had discussed the need for militia reform that would create a mobile force "for distant service." Madison's roving eye had spotted, in an unlikely source, a superior analysis of Napoleon's use of militia. In a pamphlet by his British antagonist, James Stephen, author of *War in Disguise; or, The Fraud of the Neutral Flags*, the author's discussion of Napoleon's use of the militia, Madison suggested, revealed "the true secret of the omnipotence of the French arms." When Madison called the analysis to Jefferson's attention as "a good lesson on the organization of our Militia,"[45] the president thought so well of it that he urged its publication in the *National Intelligencer* "to bring the public mind to this great point." He was "convinced that a militia of all ages promiscuously are entirely useless for distant service" and concluded that Napoleon's plan had merit over his own proposal to Congress in 1805 for a classification system.

"The idea is not new," he added; "as you may remember we adopted it once in Virginia during the revolution but abandoned it too soon." But he agreed that "Bonaparte's plan of making a class for every year between certain periods" was the real secret of his success.[46] And he was sure "that we never

---

42. TJ to JM, Aug. 19, 1807, below.
43. TJ to JM, Aug. 9, 1807, below.
44. TJ to JM, Sept. 20, 1807, below. Citing Mary P. Adams, "Jefferson's Military Policy . . . , 1805–1809" (Ph.D. diss., University of Virginia, 1958), Marshall Smelser notes that she "has confounded the conventional wisdom on the subject by troubling to read military archives instead of drawing deductions from Jefferson's reputation for military idiocy"; see Marshall Smelser, *The Democratic Republic, 1801–1815* (New York, 1968), p. 161. For a recent confirmation of TJ's military buildup, see Theodore J. Crackel, *Mr. Jefferson's Army: Political and Social Reform of the Military Establishment, 1801–1809* (New York, 1987).
45. JM to TJ, Apr. 24, 1807, below. The best study of Napoleon's army is Jean-Paul Bertaud's *The Army of the French Revolution: From Citizen-Soldiers to Instrument of Power*, trans. R. R. Palmer (Princeton, 1988).
46. See Isser Woloch, "Napoleonic Conscription: State Power and Civil Society," *Past and Present* 3 (1986): 101–29.

shall be safe until we have a selected corps for a year's distant service at least." Indeed, "the classification of our militia is now the most essential thing the U S have to do."[47]

Madison also instructed Armstrong and Bowdoin to drop negotiations for the purchase of the Floridas since the money earmarked for that purpose would be needed to finance the war, if it came. "I had rather have war against Spain than not," Jefferson told Madison, "if we go to war against England. Our southern defensive force can take the Floridas, volunteers for a Mexican army will flock to our standard, and rich pabulum will be offered to our privateers in the plunder of their commerce and coasts. Probably Cuba would add itself to our confederation."[48]

Two weeks later, the president returned to the possibility of war. As long as it was probable, "every thing leading to it with any other nation should be avoided, except with Spain. As to her," he told Madison, "I think it the precise moment when we should declare to the French government that we will instantly seise on the Floridas as reprisal for the spoliations denied us, and that if by a given day they are paid to us, we will restore all East of the Perdido and hold the rest subject to amicable decision. Otherwise we will hold them forever as compensation for the spoliations."[49]

At that moment, it looked as though the fortunes of the European war might pressure Great Britain into being conciliatory. To Madison, the president relayed the news "that Bonaparte has annihilated the allied armies," detaching Russia from the Third Coalition by the Treaty of Tilsit and leaving the Continent under French control. "The result will doubtless be peace on the continent," he thought, "an army despatched through Persia to India, and the main army brought back to their former position on the channel" as a prelude to a French invasion of England. "This will oblige England to withdraw everything home, and leave us an open field."[50]

The next day, Jefferson confessed that he had never "expected to be under the necessity of wishing success to Buonaparte. But the English being equally tyrannical at sea as he is on land, and that tyranny bearing on us in every point of either honor or interest, I say, 'down with England' and as for what Buonaparte is then to do to us, let us trust to the chapter of accidents. I cannot, with the Anglomen, prefer a certain present evil to a future hypothetical one."[51]

---

47. TJ to JM, May 5, 1807, below. For a brief discussion of TJ's unsuccessful efforts to obtain a militia classification system, see Crackel, pp. 162–63; Richard A. Erney, *The Public Life of Henry Dearborn* (New York, 1979), pp. 155–59, 231–34; and Malone, V, pp. 513–14.

48. TJ to JM, Aug. 16, 1807, below.

49. TJ to JM, Sept. 1, 1807, below.

50. TJ to JM, Aug. 20, 1807, below.

51. TJ to Thomas Leiper, Aug. 21, 1807, in Ford, IX, p. 130. For TJ's shifting attitudes towards Bonaparte, see Joseph I. Shulim, "Thomas Jefferson Views Napoleon," *VMHB* 60 (1960): 288–304.

Madison's hopes for a settlement jumped in September, when he put together "the late scraps of intelligence from England" from news accounts and parliamentary reports. He concluded hopefully "that the adjustment taking place with the U. S. would put an end to the Non-importation act." This could not be the case, Madison told the president, unless the British had made concessions on "security for our seamen, and for the colonial trade too," since impressment had been linked with the other American demands in instructions to Monroe.[52] But the usually optimistic Jefferson disagreed. "I do not give to the newspaper and Parliamentary scraps the same importance you do. I think they all refer to the Convention of limits sent us in the form of a project, brought forward only as a sop of the moment for Parliament and the public."[53]

Shortly thereafter, both men learned that Admiral Berkeley had tried all four seamen taken from the *Chesapeake* and had hanged one of them instead of restoring them to the United States as demanded. At almost the same time, they also learned that George Canning, the new foreign minister, had disavowed "the pretension to search ships of war for deserters." But Madison informed the president that Canning had employed "words which may possibly be meant to qualify the renunciation, or at least to quibble away the promised atonement.... The execution of the 4th. seaman, and the insulting trial at Halifax show that Berkley is in little dread of resentment in his superiors." He suspected that the seaman had been hanged to avoid "the humiliation of restoring" "this man, who was probably a British subject, with the other three." But he also thought "the rash step" had been taken in order to deter desertions. The whole distasteful episode, Madison informed the president, was additional proof "of the absolute necessity of a radical cure for the evils inflicted by British ships of war frequenting our waters."[54]

After a day's reflection, Madison had cooled down enough to suggest that Canning's "disavowal of the pretension to search ships of war" and his promise of "satisfaction for the attack on the Chesapeake" should be leaked to the *National Intelligencer* without quoting him directly. "This will enable the public," he told Jefferson, "to appreciate the chances of peace." The president promptly agreed to publication, warning only that "it should not appear to have been furnished by us."[55]

---

52. JM to TJ, Sept. 3, 1807, below.
53. TJ to JM, Sept. 4, 1807, below.
54. JM to TJ, Sept. 20, 1807, below.
55. JM to TJ, [Sept. 21, 1807,] below, and TJ to JM, Sept. 22, 1807, below. Canning's remarks appeared, without quotation marks, in the *National Intelligencer* on Sept. 28, 1807.

The Letters

Madison to Jefferson

[Washington Oct. 30, 1806]

Respecting Insurrections

See Act 2 May 1792 — Repealed
See ditto 20 Feby. 1795 — S. 1.
Militia may be used to repel invasions
——————————— to suppress an insurrection against a State, on the application of the Legislature, or, if it cannot be convened, of the Executive of the State

S. 2. They may be employed to suppress insurrections against the U. S. [the Act of 2 May above mentioned made a certificate of a Judge of the U. S. necessary previously to the use of the militia, which this Act does not][1]

See Act of 2 March 1799   Volunteers of the provisional army might be used as above [They were chiefly used to suppress the tumult in Northampton: but the Act is now not in force]

Enterprises against Foreign countries

See Act of June 5th. 1794
S. 7. 3. vol. p. 93.
The land and naval forces may be used

Thus It does not appear that regular troops can be employed, under any legal provision agst *insurrections*— but only agst expeditions having foreign Countries for the object.[2]

---

1. These brackets and those in the next passage were made by JM. TJ endorsed this memorandum "military in cases of insurrection." Since Attorney General John Breckinridge was ill, TJ asked JM to look into federal laws on the use of the military in the case of insurrection such as the rumored Burr conspiracy might become; see Malone, IV, pp. 252–53. In the next passage, "the tumult in Northampton" County, Pennsylvania, refers to Fries's Rebellion; see W. W. H. Davis, *The Fries Rebellion, 1798–99* (Doylestown, Pa., 1899).

2. This note is in TJ's handwriting.

A Conspiracy and a Bad Treaty, 1806-1807

Madison to Jefferson

[Washington 1806?]

Both of the Statistical Works on France referred to by Mr. C. are in the office of State. No order of Aug. 26, 1793, has been found. Mr. C. probably mistakes for it, that of June 8, 1793, which has been generally considered as the first sweeping order. There was an order of Aug. 6, 1794, which was of minor importance.

Jefferson to Madison

[Washington] Nov. 8, 1806

Represent to Genl Wilkerson

That the great probability of an amicable and early settlement of our differences with Spain at Paris had rendered the Executive extemely desirous of avoiding actual hostilities, because it would be a mere destruction of human life without effecting in the smallest degree the settlement, or its conditions. That therefore they had determined to assume the Sabine as a temporary line of separation between the troops of the two nations, including no place actually held by Spain, but Bayou Pierre, which was therefore excepted in the orders of May 6; and that without any restriction as to the force the Spaniards might chuse to place there. That we yielded to their retaining it's possession because they had it, and the temporary ground we thought it best to take was the status quo. The Executive hopes that Genl. Wilkinson has done no more than take the position hinted at in a former letter of his between Bayou Pierre and Nacogdoches; but still on our side of the Sabine, in order, by putting them in fear for Nacogodoches, to induce them to retire from Bayou Pierre. If this had taken place, and without any actual hostility, it will be deemed fortunate: but if hostilities have actually taken place in order to drive the Spaniards by force from Bayou Pierre, the Executive regret it as contrary to their intentions, and as an useless sacrifice of the lives it may have lost. But whether hostilities have been actually committed or not, Genl. Wilkerson is instructed immediately to propose to the Spanish Commandant a written Convention of the tenour of the one now inclosed; and if it is agreed to, let him leave at Natchitoches only [blank] companies and withdraw the rest of his forces to Fort Adams.[3]

(a) But if the convention cannot be obtained you may agree to such

---

3. Even before TJ sent these instructions to Wilkinson, the general had negotiated the Neutral Ground Agreement with the Spanish. For discussions of the agreement and its relation to Wilkinson's involvement in the Burr conspiracy, see Malone, V, pp. 245-47; Abernethy, pp. 154-56; and Walter F. McCaleb, *The Aaron Burr Conspiracy* (New York, 1903), pp. 153-57.

temporary line of partition between the positions then occupied by the troops of the two nations as will prevent or suppress hostilities till further orders; and if you should have at that time possession of Bayou Pierre, you may even agree if it is insisted on to withdraw the American troops from that settlement, provided that it shall not be occupied by the Spanish troops.

If every proposition either of convention or temporary line shall be rejected; take the best measures for the protection and defense of the settlements in our actual possession: still observing that if no hostilities shall have begun, you must remain, till attacked, strictly on the defensive; and that you must not, in any event whatever, cross the Sabine river.

If either a convention or a suspension of hostilities shall be agreed on, any Spanish post East of the Mississippi which might (as seems to have been contemplated by Genl. Wilkinson) have been previously occupied by the Americans must be evacuated. Nor is any such post to be occupied, even in case of hostilities on the west of the Mississippi, unless the safety of New Orleans should in the joint opinion of Govr. Claiborne and Gen. Wilkinson render it necessary to take possession of the country between the Misissippi and Pearl river. No part of the country east of the Pearl river must in any event be occupied.

Heads of a Convention to be proposed
between the Commanding officers of
the American and Spanish troops Westward
of the Misipi and Southward of the Red river.

I. There shall be an immediate suspension of hostilities between the American and Spanish troops Westward of the Misipi and Southward of the Red river; and the Sabine river and highlands including the Southern waters of the Red river shall be assumed as a temporary line of separation between the troops of the two nations; those of America not passing to the Westward or Southward of that line nor those of Spain to the Eastward or Northward of it.
II. The intercourse between the citizens and subjects of the two powers heretofore permitted, shall be restored. [or]
II. No intercourse shall be allowed between the citizens and subjects of the two nations dwelling on either side of the sd. line, and any such person passing to the other side thereof may be imprisoned at pleasure at the nearest post of the party arresting him.
III. Neither party shall establish any new military post between the meridians of Natchitoches and Nagodoches, but the increasing the strength of the military posts now held by them shall be no breach of this convention.
IV. Neither party shall excite the Indians to take up arms, or to take any part in the dispute between the two nations: on the contrary their right [of self-government in their own towns and territories, and] of passing freely and

amicably into the territories of these parties shall remain as heretofore.

V. The citizens or subjects of either party who have been arrested by the troops of the other and are in confinement shall be immediately liberated and passports given them to return home.

VI. The supreme authority of either nation shall be free to refuse it's ratification of this convention; and after ratifying it, shall be free to revoke it at pleasure; but no act shall be done in controvention of it by either party during six months from the date of this convention, nor thereafter, with one month's notice shall have been given the other party of such a refusal to ratify or of such revocation.

Madison to Jefferson

[Washington] Nov. 8, 1806

Substitute this instead of the first article

There shall be an immediate suspension of hostilities between the American and Spanish troops westward of the Mississippi.

The Sabine river shall be assumed as a temporary line of separation between the troops of the two nations, and the troops of neither party shall occupy any post on Red river or any of its waters above Natchitoches.

1st Note It may however be agreed as an ultimatum that the Spaniards may keep possession of Bayou Pierre but the garrison not to exceed the number it consisted of before the 1st day of June last.

2d Note If the Spaniards agree to withdraw their troops to St. Antonio, having no more than a given number say 300. at Nagodoches, it may be agreed that the Americans will withdraw their troops from Red river leaving no more than a given number say 300 at [the] banks of the Natchitoches, and in the other settlements west of the Misisippi.

II and III agreed

IV. Words between [ ] may be omitted

Vth. Not to be considered an ultimatum

Should the convention be refused, with an offer to concur in a suspension of hostilities, the suspension is to be agreed to, provided Spanish troops or patrols neither advance nor remain on the Eastn. side of the Sabine, except in the Bayou Pierre where the Spanish troops may remain if in possession; but it is desirable tho' not a sine qua non that they remove the troops across the Sabine, and leave the Bayou Pierre in its previous state.

Should Bayou Pierre have been taken into our possession, the possession in case of a convention or suspension may be restored on condition of its being put by the Spanish [authorities?] in its previous state.

Madison to Jefferson

[Washington Nov. 16, 1806]⁴

Foreign Relations. Insert "since" before "taken place" at the beginning of line 11. The preceding delay did not altogether proceed from events independent of the will of one of the parties, and those who are chargeable with it, ought not to be acquitted of the consequences. Perhaps the following change of the whole sentence might answer. "The delays which have since taken place in our negociations with the British govt appear to have proceeded from causes which leave me in expectation that etc."⁵

Spain. Instead of Spain has "consented" etc., it might be better to say Spain has taken steps preparatory to the negociation at Paris in which our ministers are authorized to meet her. The term used may seem to imply a proposition from the U. S. wch was consented to.

In the penult line of p. 1. For "hope of friendly settlement" perhaps "course of friendly negociation" might be a more suitable expression. Such a change however cannot be material if proper.⁶

The last instructions to Wilkinson do not assume the Sabine as the essential line of separation for the troops. They authorize him to settle a provisional line, and in no event to pass himself beyond that river. It may be well therefore to vary the sentence on that point so as to run "in that quarter to maintain a temporary line, separating the troops of the two nations and to permit no new settlement or post to be taken eastward of the Sabine river."

Would it not be well to allude to a continuance of our friendly standing with France, and the other belligerent nations, or generally with other nations of Europe.

New Orleans. Instead of "to secure that point by *all the means in our power*"—"to provide for that point a more adequate security."⁷

Insurrections. This paragraph suggests several legal questions; such as whether in strictness any *preventive* measures are consistent with our principles except security for the peace and good behavior. Whether this remedy is not already applicable to the case in question, where a preparation of force justifies a suspicion of criminal intention, and whether the existing provision for the case of an enterprise meditated vs. a foreign nation is not rather penal agst a crime actually committed by the preparation of means with such an intention,

---

4. JM headed this memorandum "Suggested revisions for President's annual message. Dec. 2, 1806." For TJ's message, see Ford, VIII, pp. 482–95.

5. TJ incorporated these suggestions in his message; see *ibid.*, p. 483.

6. TJ deleted specific references to negotiations with Spain and substituted a general statement that "nothing had taken place" that allowed any announcement about "the negotiations for settling our differences with Spain"; see *ibid.*

7. TJ accepted this suggestion about the defense of New Orleans; see *ibid.*, p. 490.

than *preventive* of the actual commission of a crime. To guard agst the criticisms which may be founded on these questions, some such change as the following is suggested for consideration:

"For those crimes when actually committed the laws make provision. Would it not moreover be salutary to provide for cases where the means of force are prepared only for a meditated enterprise agst the U. S. as has been done for cases where the enterprise is meditated by private individuals against a foreign nation? It merits consideration also, whether the preventive process of binding to the observance of the peace and good behaviour ought not to be expressly extended to acts without the limits of the U. S. in cases where the acts are contrary to law, and there is sufficient ground for suspecting the intention to commit them."[8]

This change is suggested on the supposition that the occasion requires a paragraph should be addressed to Congress; manifestly alluding to the late information etc. Perhaps the question may be decided with the advantage of new lights from the westward in time for the message.

Barbary. "The late mission" may be equivocal or obscure. "With Tunis alone some uncertainty remains" would perhaps be sufficient.[9]

Missouri. The tenor of this paragraph ought to be such as to give as little topic as possible for foreign jealousy or complaint; especially as we are not prepared to say that the expedition did not enter limits within which Spain has real or plausible claims. It is *certain* that it will be presented to Spain as a measure at which she has a right to take offence. The paragraph might better parry the inconvenience, by being made less particular and by avoiding any allusion to the uses to which the *Pacific country* may be applied.[10]

Red River. "Nearly as far as the French establishments etc." has the advantage of suggesting a plausible reason for not going on: but may it not also imply that those establishments were the limit to our claim?[11]

Mississippi. The survey of the Mississippi furnished, certainly, a very apt occasion for bringing into view our legitimate boundaries in the latitude 49; but as the mere assertion by ourselves will not strengthen our title, and may excite British sensations unseasonably, it may be doubted whether that much of the paragraph had not as well be omitted.[12]

University etc. The denunciation of standing armies, navies, and fortifications cannot be better expressed, if there be no room to apprehend that so emphatic a one may not at the present juncture embolden the presumption in

---

8. TJ utilized this suggestion in revising his message; see *ibid.*, p. 491.

9. TJ incorporated this suggestion verbatim; see *ibid.*

10. TJ accepted this advice, stressed the new geographical information gained by Lewis and Clark, and praised their "arduous service"; see *ibid.*, p. 492.

11. TJ rejected this suggestion; see *ibid.*

12. TJ omitted any reference to boundaries; see *ibid.*

foreign nations that an insuperable aversion to those objects guarantees the impunity of their insults and aggressions.[13]

"Arts, Manufactures and other objects of public improvement," seem to give a latitude nearly equivalent to "general welfare" afterwards suggested to be too dangerous to remain a part of the Constitution. "and other objects of public improvement which it may be thought proper to specify" would avoid the inconsistency.[14]

After "the present state of our country" might be added "and with the aid of the sale of public lands would be adequate to Roads and Canals also."

Instead of "sweep away all restraints etc."—"demolish the essential barriers between the General and the State Govts."[15]

Conclusion "as far as they are capable of defence" suggests a disagreeable and impolitic idea. "Preparations for the defence etc." without that expression, will suffice. This member of the sentence ought to be separated from the succeeding ones, which do not [illegible] etc., not being like these without expense till called into actual use.

It does not seem correct to say that war is forced on us by vain appeals to the justice of other nations. In spite of appeals etc., or some such turn to the expression would obviate the criticism.[16]

Madison to Jefferson

[Washington Nov. 27, 1806][17]

Draft of Presidential Proclamation Warning of a Military Conspiracy Against Spain

Whereas Information has been received that sundry persons, citizens of the U S or residents within the same, are conspiring and confederating together to begin and set on foot, provide and prepare the means for a military

---

13. TJ deleted all references to standing armies, navies, and fortifications; see *ibid.*, pp. 493–94.

14. In proposing a constitutional amendment to support education and internal improvements, TJ followed JM's suggestion; see *ibid.*, p. 494.

15. TJ's only reference to the public lands suggested the donation of lands to endow "a national establishment for education"; see *ibid.*

16. In his conclusion, TJ adopted JM's language but did not separate defense expenditures, which were immediate, from the mobilization of the militia, where expenditures would be prospective; see *ibid.*, p. 495. In JM's final suggestion, TJ also adopted JM's language: "in spite of our long and vain appeals"; see *ibid.*

17. This draft of TJ's presidential proclamation is in the handwriting of JM, who was substituting for Attorney General Breckinridge, who was ill. TJ issued it verbatim; see Richardson, I, pp. 404–5.

expedition or enterprise against the dominions of Spain, that for this purpose they are fitting out and arming vessels in the western waters of the U S, collecting provisions, arms, military stores, and means, are deceiving and seducing honest and well meaning citizens under various pretenses, to engage in their criminal enterprises; are organizing, officering, and arming themselves for the same, contrary to the laws in such cases made and provided: I have therefore thought proper to issue this my proclamation warning and enjoining all faithful citizens who have been led without due knowledge or consideration to participate in the said unlawful enterprizes, to withdraw from the same without delay; and commanding all persons whatsoever, engaged or concerned in the same, to cease all further proceedings therein, as they will answer the contrary at their peril, and incur prosecution with all the rigors of the law. And I hereby enjoin and require all officers civil and military of the U States, or of any of the States or Territories, and especially all governs. and other executive authorities, all judges, justices and other officers of the peace, all military officers of the army or Navy of the U States, and officers of the militia, to be vigilant each within his respective department and according to his functions, in searching out and bringing to condign punishment all persons engaged or concerned in such enterprizes, in seizing and detaining, subject to the disposition of the law, all vessels, arms, military stores, or other means provided or providing for the same, and in general, in preventing the carrying on such expedition or enterprize, by all lawful means within their power; and I require all good and faithful citizens, and others within the U S, to be aiding and assisting herein, and especially in the discovery, apprehension and bringing to justice of all such offenders, in preventing the execution of their unlawful designs, and in giving information against them to the proper authorities.

Given etc. 27 Nov 1806.

Madison to Jefferson

[Washington Nov. 29, 1806]

that whilst the public force was acting strictly on the defensive, and merely to protect our citizens from aggression, the criminal attempts of private individuals to decide for their country the question of peace or war, by commencing active and unauthorized hostilities, ought to be promptly and effectually suppressed[18]

---

18. These notes for the president's annual message of Dec. 2, 1806, were incorporated verbatim by TJ in the section on the Burr conspiracy; see *ibid.*, pp. 489-90. They are printed out of chronological order because they relate to the preceding item.

Madison to Jefferson

[Washington Nov. 27, 1806][19]

I have the satisfaction to inform you that the negotiation on foot between the U. States and the govt of G. B. is proceeding in a spirit of friendship and accommodation which promises a result of mutual advantage. The delays which have taken place are to be regretted; but as they were occasioned by the long illness which ended in the death of the British Minister charged with that duty, they could not have been foreseen nor taken into calculation: and it appears that the commissioners appointed to resume the negotiation, have shown every disposition to hasten its progress. Under these circumstances our special ministers recommend a suspension of the acts prohibiting certain importations the commencement of which was postponed till the 15th of last month when it went into operation, and assured us that such a mark of candor and confidence in the temper and views with which they have been met in the negotiation will have a happy effect on the course of it; whilst a disregard of that friendly consideration may have a different tendency. Considering that justice and conciliation have been the real objects of all our measures, and that whatever will promote them will be most conformable to our wishes and our interests, I cannot but join in the recommendation that the operation of the act be suspended for such additional term as may be deemed reasonable. It is not known here etc.

Jefferson to Madison

[Washington] Dec. 19, 1806

TH. J. TO MR MADISON.

I send you the draught of a proclamation dated for tomorrow.[20] I think all the letters and orders, to the effect already agreed on, should be instantaneously got ready; and I ask the heads of departments to meet here tomorrow at 11. oclock to consider what additional measures can be taken for forcing the Cambrian off, and for preventing her entering any other port of the U. S. Would it not be proper to ask Mr Erskine to see you immediately, to shew him

---

19. TJ labeled these "Madison's Notes" on the Monroe-Pinkney negotiations with Great Britain. His special message to Congress on Dec. 3, 1806, followed this draft closely and recommended the postponement of the Nonimportation Act in order to allow time to complete the negotiations. For the message, see Ford, VIII, pp. 496–97. Congress moved the date of the act back to July 1, 1807, and authorized the president to suspend the act until the next session of Congress in December, if he thought it desirable.

20. After H.M.S. *Leander* fired the warning shot that killed John Pierce in American waters, TJ issued a presidential proclamation in May 1806 charging the captain of that ship with murder and ordered it and two other British navy vessels, the *Cambrian* and the *Driver,* out of American ports, barring their return forever. When the *Cambrian* returned in December, he prepared the proclamation of Dec. 20, 1806, below.

the letter of Newton and report of the officer, and to let him know the measures we *will* take tomorrow. He may by tonight's post reinforce his advice to those officers.

ENCLOSURE
Proclamation Concerning H.M.S. Cambrian

[Dec. 20, 1806]

Whereas by a proclamation bearing date the 3d day of May last, for reasons therein stated, the British vessels of war called the Leander, the Cambrian and the Driver, were forever interdicted the entrance of the harbors and the waters under the jurisdiction of the U. S. and in case of any of them reentering the harbors or waters aforesaid, all intercourse with them was forbidden, all supplies and aid prohibited from being furnished them under the penalties of law provided: And whereas one of the said armed vessels, the Cambrian, has lately entered into the waters of the Chesapeake, within which, with certain other British armed vessels, she still remains: I have therefore thought fit to issue this my Proclamation, forbidding, so long as the said Cambrian shall be within the waters of the Chesapeake all intercourse, not only with the said armed vessel the Cambrian, but with every armed vessel of the same nation, their officers, and crews now in the sd bay of Chesapeake, or it's waters, or which may enter the same. And I do declare and make known, that if any person from, or within, the jurisdictional limits of the U. S. shall afford any aid to any of the said armed vessels, contrary to the prohibition contained in this proclamation, either in repairing any of them, or in furnishing them, their officers or crews, with supplies of any kind, or in any manner whatsoever, or if any pilot shall assist in navigating any of the said armed vessels, unless it be for the purpose of carrying them, in the first instance, beyond the limits and jurisdiction of the U. S. such person or persons shall, on conviction, suffer all the pains and penalties by the laws provided for such offences. And I do hereby enjoin and require all persons bearing office civil or military within the U. S., and all others, citizens or inhabitants thereof, or being within the same, with vigilance and promptitude, to exert their respective authorities, and to be aiding and assisting to the carrying this proclamation and every part thereof into full effect.

In testimony whereof I have caused the seal of the U. S. to be affixed to these presents, and have signed the same with my hand. Given at the city of Washington the 20th day of December in the year of our Lord 1806 and of the sovereignty and independence of the United States the 31st.[21]

Madison to Jefferson

[Washington Jan. 4, 1807]

A counter post to Kingston if it can be sufficiently safe, seems to be a natural provision for the case. But ought not the State of N. Y. to turn its attention to such a call from its Citizens, and to co-operate at least in arming them? Few states are probably more able to do it.

21. TJ endorsed the proclamation "This was not issued, the Cambrian having gone off."

Jefferson to Madison

[Washington] Sunday Feb. 1, 1807

The more I consider the letter of our ministers in London the more seriously it impresses me. I believe the sine quâ non we made is that of the nation, and that they would rather go on without a treaty than with one which does not settle this article.[22] Under this dilemma, and at this stage of the business, had we not better take the advice of the Senate? I ask a meeting at eleven o'clock tomorrow to consult on this question.

Jefferson to Madison

[Washington] Mar. 14, 1807

the following commissions to be made out

Lemuel Trescott of Massachusets Collector of the district, and Inspector of the revenue for the port of Machias

Jonathan Palmer of Connecticut Surveyor of the port of Stonington, and Inspector of the revenue for the same.[23]

John Vernon junr. Surveyor of the port of Albany and Inspector of the revenue for the same.

Robert Cochran of N. Carolina Collector for the district of Wilmington N. C.

Abraham Bissent of Georgia Collector for the district of St. Mary's in Georgia

George M. Bibb Attorney for the U S. for the district of Kentucky.

Th Jefferson

Jefferson to Madison

[Washington] Mar. 14, 1807

On further enquiry and examination, I find it necessary to correct the list of justices before given in for Alexandria county. Commissions are therefore

---

22. For the sine qua non relating to impressments, see Bradford Perkins, *Prologue to War: England and the United States, 1805–1812* (Berkeley, 1963), pp. 134–35, and Brant, IV, p. 372.

23. TJ later withdrew his nomination of Palmer when the Treasury Department discovered that Congress had not authorized a surveyor and inspector of revenue for Stonington; see Richardson, I, pp. 431–32.

desired for Washington and Alexandria counties according to the subjoined lists, giving to all those who were in the former commissions the order in which they were therein placed, and adding the new names to the end.

Justices for Washington County	*Justices for Alexandria County*
Robert Brent	George Gilpin
Thomas Peter	Charles Alexander junr.
William Thornton	Jonah Thompson
Joseph Sprigg Belt	Abraham Taw
Thomas Corcoran	Cuthbert Powell
Samuel N. Smallwood	Alexander Smith
Robert Alexander	Jacob Hoffman
Richard Parrott	George Slacum
Thomas Fenwick	Elisha Cullen Dick
John B. Kirby	John McKinney
John Alt	Robert Young
Samuel Harrison Smith	Joseph Dean
Daniel Rapine	Richard Dinmore
Nicholas Young	Amos Alexander
John Threilkidd	Clement Sewell
	Richard Libby
	John Richards
	Henry O'Reily

TH JEFFERSON.

Jefferson to Madison

[Washington Mar. ?, 1807]

The article against impressment to be a sine qua non. So also the withdrawing or modifying the declaration

Endeavor to alter the E. India article by restoring Jay's Art 8. Avoid if possible the express abandoning of free ships free goods.

10. Define Blockade according to the British note formerly rec'd.

17. Expunge stipulation to recieve their vessels of war and treat officers with respect.

Reserve the right to indemnification

Agree not to employ their seamen.

Madison to Jefferson

Washington Apr. 13, 1807

DEAR SIR

I inclose a letter from Messrs. Monroe and Pinkney with the communications recd. with it.

Also a letter from Turreau. As the scope of it is manifestly improper, and the more so as the letter can not have been founded on instructions from his Govt. will it not be best to leave it unanswered, unless he should renew the subject, and then to be the more explicit in the answer?

On looking critically into the Colonial Art. of the Treaty, I find it will have a more defalcating operation on our commerce, than was at first noticed. As it admits the U. S. to be a channel merely between the *Colonies,* and *Europe,* and puts the Colonies beyond the C. of G. Hope on the same footing with the American, nothing from India, China, or the French Dutch or Spanish Eastern Colonies, can be sent to Spanish America, or the Enemy Islands in the W. Indies: nor can the productions of the latter be sent to Smirna etc., or the Coast of Barbary etc., or elsewhere than to Europe. It follows also that the trade between the Eastern Colonies, and certain Eastern countries and ports as China, Mocha etc. etc. to which G. B. has not applied her principle at all, or with restrictions, (the trade having been open, or pressured to be so in time of peace), will be abolished by the Article. That the subject may be more fully understood, I have thought it prudent to inclose this Art: also to Genl. Smith, and request his ideas as to its operation in its present form, with a hint of any meliorations proper to be attempted, particularly any not adverse to the policy of G. B. herself.[24]

I fear that the No. of B. seamen may prove to be rather beyond our first estimate. I inclose such information as the enqueries of Mr. Gallatin have obtained, with his own remarks on the subject; which I beg the favor of you to return. Yrs. faithfully and affectly

JAMES MADISON

Jefferson to Madison

Monticello Apr. 14, 1807

DEAR SIR,

Mr. Rodney not being at Washington I send you the inclosed because it requires to be acted on immediately. I remember it was concluded that wit-

---

24. Samuel Smith, a Republican senator from Maryland, was a leading Baltimore merchant. He agreed that the article would ruin the trade to India, China, Turkey, and South America, putting American commerce at the mercy of British admiralty courts. He preferred war to such a treaty; see John S. Pancake, *Samuel Smith and the Politics of Business, 1752–1839* (University, Ala., 1972), pp. 77–78. On p. 79 of his article, Hickey notes that this provision "offered the United States less rather than more" when compared with the terms of the Jay Treaty.

nesses who should be brought from great distances, and carried from one scene of trial to another must have a reasonable allowance made for their expences and the money advanced. I expect it will be thought proper that the witnesses proving White's enlistment of men for Burr should be at his trial in Richmond. Be so good as to take the necessary measures to enable these men to come on.

I omitted to bring with me the laws of the last session which Mr Brent had collected for me from the newspapers, and therefore must ask the favor of you as you pass to step into my cabinet (which Mr Lemaire will open for you) and you will find them on a table in a window at the West end of the Cabinet, and to be so good as to inclose them to me with any additional ones Mr Brent may have for me.[25]

We are deluged with rain, wheat generally mean, great mortality among cattle. Affecte. salutations

TH JEFFERSON

Madison to Jefferson

Washington Apr. 17, 1807

DEAR SIR

I recd. this morning your favor of the 14th. and inclose the printed copies of the Acts of Congs. obtained from your Cabinet as pointed out. I inclose also a list of all the Acts, that you may direct a supply of any deficiency.

The letter to you from Clarke Mead etc. relating to the witnesses agst. White proceeds on a mistake of the legal allowance. This was originally 50 cents perday; but an act of Congs. of 28 Feby. 1799. raised it to 5 cents a mile, equal at this season of the year to 2 dollrs. a day, and 1 ¼ drs. a day during the attendance on the Court. I shall therefore hint this to Mr. Rodney who will apprize the attending witnesses of their right. It is too late now to produce the attendance of any who may not have already undertaken the journey.

The objection arising from Mr. Gallatin's estimate of British Seamen in our service, to the idea of forbearing altogether the use of them, has led us to think of some modification short of that concession that might invite G. B. into an adjustment. And it has occurred that in allusion to the British case which claims all alien seamen serving two years on British ships, as British seamen, we may except from the contemplated proposition, all British seamen who shall prior to the exchange of Ratifications, have been two years out of British service, and in no other than ours. Mr. G. I find acquiesies in this Ultimatum. I submit it for consideration whether, in case of its rejection it would be inadmissible to exclude from future service in our ships, all seamen

---

25. Daniel Brent was a senior clerk in the State Department; see Noble E. Cunningham, Jr., *The Process of Government under Jefferson* (Princeton, 1978), p. 328. Étienne Le Maire was TJ's maître d'hôtel; see Peterson, p. 729.

who did not enter our service prior to the commencement of the existing war. This would allude to the principle, that there is a greater right in the members of a state to transfer themselves into foreign service in time of peace than in time of war. These allusions tho not un-exceptionable as legal criteria, are better than assumptions absolutely naked, and may at least be adapted by an accomodating disposition. Should this last proposition be also rejected, it will remain to be decided whether the disuse of B. Seamen altogether, be a sacrifice too great, if essential, for the object in view. Genl. D. and Mr. G. seem disposed to go great lengths on this subject. Much however must depend on the proportion of B. Seamen in our trade, and Mr. Gallatin's data and deductions [?] command just attention. Still my impression is that the proportion cannot be as great as he estimates. I believe that of Genl. D. and Mr. S. leans the same way. Yrs. faithfully and affecy.

JAMES MADISON

This letter was actually recd. at Monto. in due time but by an accident escaped notice, and was not discovd. nor opened till May 30.[26]

Madison to Jefferson

Washington Apr. 20, 1807

DEAR SIR

Inclosed are a Letter from Consul Harris, another from the Consul at Santiago de Cuba. and an answer from Genl. Smith to my enquiry as to the operation of the Colonial art. of the Treaty of Decr. 31. Harris writes more like a Russian than an American; and forgetting that he is but a Consul, takes the tone of a Minister Plenipo: or rather goes beyond it in his answer to the communication of the Russian Minister of F. Affairs. The letter from Maurice suggests anew the value and the vacancy of a Consular Agency at Santo Domingo. It gives a favorable acct. of the disposition of the Spanish Authorities in Cuba. I hope Turreau's letter to Ferrand will be a remedy to the abuse in that quarter, of the Decree of Novr. 21.

The developments of Genl. Smith are precisely such as a critical attention to the scope of the 21 Art: had led me to anticipate. The shape to be given to the instructions to our Comissnrs. becomes more and more perplexing. I begin to suspect that it may eventually be necessary to limit the Treaty to the subject of impressments, leaving the Colonial trade with other objects to their own courses, and to the influence which the reserved power over our imports, may have to that course. In practice, the colonial trade and every thing else would probly be more favored, than they are by the articles forwarded, or would be by any remodifications to be expected. The case of impressments is

26. This endorsement is in TJ's handwriting.

more urgent. Something seems essential to be done, nor is any thing likely to be done without carrying fresh matter into the negociation. I am preparing the overture to disuse British Seamen, in the form of an ultimatum, graduated from an exception of those who have been two years in our navigation, to no exception at all, other than of such as have been naturalized. I shall take however no final step, till your determination arrives. Yrs. with the highest respect and attachment

JAMES MADISON

Jefferson to Madison

Monticello Apr. 21, 1807

DEAR SIR,

Yours of the 13th came to hand only yesterday and I now return you the letters of Turreau, Yrujo, and Woodward, and Mr. Gallatin's paper on foreign seamen. I retain Monroe and Pinckney's letters, to give them a more deliberate perusal than I can now before the departure of the post. By the next they shall be returned. I should think it best to answer Turreau at once, as he will ascribe delay to a supposed difficulty and will be sure to force an answer at last. I take the true principle to be that 'for violations of jurisdiction with the consent of the sovereign, or his voluntary sufferance, indemnification is due: but that for others he is bound only to use all *reasonable* means to obtain indemnification from the aggressor, which must be calculated on his circumstances, and these endeavors *bonâ fide* made, and failing, he is no further responsible.' It would be extraordinary indeed if we were to be answerable for the conduct of belligerents through our whole coast, whether inhabited or not.

Will you be so good as to send a passport to Julian V. Neimcewicz, an American citizen of New Jersey going to Europe on his private affairs. I have known him intimately for 20. years, the last 12. of which he has resided in the U S, of which he has a certificate of citizenship. He was the companion of Kosciusko. Be so good as to direct it to him at Elizabethtown, and without delay, as he is on his departure.[27]

Mr. Gallatin's estimate of the number of foreign seamen in our employ, renders it prudent I think to suspend all propositions respecting our nonemploiment of them. As, on a consultation when we were all together, we had

27. Julian U. Niemcewicz was a Polish patriot and literary figure when TJ first met him in Paris in 1787. He married Mrs. Susan Livingston Kean in 1800 and settled in Elizabethtown, New Jersey. In 1807, he left the United States to become secretary of state under the Grand Duchy of Warsaw. See Julian Ursyn Niemcewicz, *Under Their Vine and Fig Tree: Travels through America in 1797–1799, 1805, with some further account of life in New Jersey, by Julian Ursyn Niemcewicz,* ed. Metchie J. E. Budka (Elizabeth, N.J., 1965), pp. xxvii–xxxii; also see R. R. Palmer, *The Age of the Democratic Revolution: A Political History of Europe and America, 1760–1800,* 2 vols. (Princeton, 1959–64), II, pp. 152–55.

made up our minds on every article of the British treaty and this of not employing their seamen was only mentioned for further enquiry and consideration, we had better let the negociations go on on the ground then agreed on, and take time to consider this supplementary proposition. Such an addition as this to a treaty already so bad would fill up the measure of public condemnation. It would indeed be making bad worse. I am more and more convinced that our best course is to let the negociation take a friendly nap and endeavor in the mean time to practice on such of it's principles as are mutually acceptable. Perhaps we may hereafter barter the stipulation not to employ their seamen for some equivalent to our flag, by way of convention, or perhaps the general treaty of peace may do better for us, if we shall not, in the mean time, have done worse for ourselves. At any rate, it will not be the worse for lying three weeks longer. I salute you with sincere affection.

P. S. Will you be so good as to have me furnished with a copy of Mr. Gallatin's estimate of the number of foreign seamen? I think he overrates the number of officers greatly.

Madison to Jefferson

Washington Apr. 24, 1807

DEAR SIR

Your favor of the 21. with the letters returned under the same cover was recd. last night. As you had not then recd. the last letters from Mr. G. and myself on the modified proposal to disuse B. Seamen, I shall wait the arrival of your next before I conclude on the instructions which are to go by the Wasp. I find by the accts. from Bermuda, that the mere difficulty which suspends the Treaty is becoming a motive or pretext with both Courts [?] and Cruisers for worrying our commerce.

A late arrival from London presents a very unexpected scene at St. James's.[28] Should the revolution stated actually take place in the Cabinet, it will subject our affairs there to new calculations. On one hand the principles and dispositions of the new Ministry portend the most unfriendly course. On the other hand their feeble and tottering situation, and the force of their ousted rivals, who will probably be more explicit in maintaining the value of a good understanding with this Country, can not fail to inspire caution. It may happen also that the new Cabinet will be less averse to a tabula rasa for a new adjustment, than those who framed the instrument to be superseded; and if the intruders should be driven out as soon as is possible the exiles may return

28. The duke of Portland's ministry brought the mercurial George Canning to the foreign office and the influential Spencer Perceval as chancellor of the exchequer. Both were dedicated to vigorous prosecution of the war against Napoleon and tighter orders-in-council against neutrals; see Perkins, pp. 184–90.

into the negociation with us, more committed in favor of the policy from which its success must proceed.

I send herewith a copy of a pamphlet by the Author of war in disguise.[29] I have read a part of it only, which does not altogether support the reputation of his pen. The work must nevertheless be interesting. He has seized the true secret of the omnipotence of the French arms, and so far enforces a good lesson on the organization of our Militia. I inclose also the Trial of Sr. H. Popham, which discloses some political secrets, which will reward your perusal of it. The passport for Niemciwicz will go by the mail of this evening. Yrs. always with respectful attachment

JAMES MADISON

Jefferson to Madison

Monticello Apr. 25, 1807

DEAR SIR,

Yours of the 20th came to hand on the 23d, and I now return all the papers it covered, to wit Harris's, Maurice's, and Genl. Smith's letters, as also some papers respecting Burr's case, for circulation. Under another cover is a letter from Govr. Williams, confidential and for yourself alone as yet. I expect we shall have to remove Meade.[30] Under still a different cover you will recieve Monroe's and Pinckney's letters detained at the last post. I wrote you then on the subject of the British treaty, which the more it is developed the worse it appears. Mr. Rodney being supposed absent I enclose you a letter from Mr. Reed advising the summoning Rufus Easton as a witness; but if he is at St. Louis, he cannot be here by the 22d of May. You will observe that Govr. Williams asks immediate instructions what he shall do with Blennerhasset, Tyler, Floyd, and Ralston.[31] I do not know that we can do anything but direct Genl. Wilkerson to receive and send them to any place where the judge shall decide they ought to be tried. I suppose Blennerhasset should come to Richmond. On consulting with the other gentlemen, be so good as to write to Williams immediately, as a letter will barely get there by the 4th Monday of May. I inclose you a warrant for 5000 D. for Mr. Rodney in the form advised by Mr. Gallatin.

29. James Stephen's pamphlet *War in Disguise* (London, 1805) defended the Rule of 1756 and called for an aggressive policy towards neutrals. After JM published his attack on the rule, Stephen replied in a pamphlet that reprinted *The Speech of the Honorable John Randolph . . . with an Introduction by the Author of "War in Disguise"*; see Perkins pp. 77-79, and Brant, IV, p. 368.

30. Robert Williams was governor of Mississippi Territory, and Cowles Mead was territorial secretary; see Abernethy, p. 201. TJ removed Mead and appointed Thomas H. Williams; see TJ to JM, June 1, 1807, below.

31. For the roles of Harman Blennerhassett, Comfort Tyler, Major Davis Floyd, and Ralston in the Burr conspiracy, see Abernethy.

We have had three great rains within the last 13. days. It is just now clearing off after 36. hours of rain with little intermission. Yet it is thought not too much. I salute you with sincere affection.

TH. JEFFERSON

Madison to Jefferson

Washington Apr. 27, 1807

DEAR SIR

Your favor of the 21st. was recd. by the last mail. The passport for Niemcewicz went by the first succeeding opportunity.

Mr. Petry arrived two days ago with the inclosed letter from Genl. Turreau. The request it makes is not very consistent with the understanding which regulated the former compliances; but necessity is pleaded, with assurances that these shall be the last; and that the bills being in the form inclosed will be at shorter sight, and drawn on funds lying at Paris in the name of Beaujoin. I presume it will not be easy or gracious to cancel what has been done by a refusal in this case, however disagreeable such repetitions may be felt. Mr. Gallatin drops you a line on the subject by the present mail.

Several letters are herewith inclosed. That from the Consul at Curozoa aids in explaining the policy of the B. Govt. in shutting America agst. oriental manufactures passing thro' our ports. The object in taking possession of that Island is to secure the market to their own trade in those articles. The Document referred to in the letter shows the exports thither from the U. S consisted a good deal of China and India goods mixt with cargoes of our own produce. It appears as you will probably see, that on the 22d. of March, the revolution in the British [Cabinet?] was taking effect; and that Ld. Melville was to be at the head of the admiralty. Yrs. with respectful attachment

JAMES MADISON

Jefferson to Madison

Monticello May 1, 1807

DEAR SIR,

I return you Monroe's, Armstrong's, Harris's, and Anderson's letters, and add a letter and act from Gov. McKean, to be filed in your office. The proposition for separating the western country mentioned by Armstrong to have been made at Paris, is important. But what is the declaration he speaks of? for none accompanies his letter, unless he means Harry Grant's proposition. I wish our Ministers at Paris, London, and Madrid, could find out Burr's propositions and agents there. I know few of the characters of the new British administration. The few I know are true Pittites, and Anti-American. From them we have nothing to hope, but that they will readily let us back out. Whether they can hold their places will depend on the question whether the Irish propositions be popular or unpopular in England.

Dr. Sibley, in a letter to Gen. Dearborne, corrects an error of fact in my message to Congress of December. He says the Spaniards never had a single soldier at Bayou Pierre till Apr. 1805. Consequently it was not a keeping, but a taking of a military possession of that post. I think Gen. Dearborne would do well to desire Sibley to send us affidavits of that fact.

Our weather continues extremely seasonable and favorable for vegetation. I salute you with sincere affection.

TH. JEFFERSON

P. S. The pamphlet and papers shall be returned by next post.

Madison to Jefferson

Washington May 4, 1807

DEAR SIR

I recd by the last mail your note fixing the time for your return.[32]

The Wasp has put herself into a situation denoting a departure, but it is probable that a further delay is convenient for her compleat preparation. The dispatches could have [been] made ready for her some time since, but the lights thrown on the Treaty by the gentlemen consulted,[33] and the flaws which have successively disclosed themselves to a nearer inspection, have rendered the task more tedious as well as more difficult than was at first supposed. In several instances, particularly, the colonial article, the definition of our ultimatum presents questions which the authority pressed did [?] not presume to decide. Add to this, that there is found to be some variance in our impressions as to one or two articles, to which your memorandum refers, whether they were included or not in the ultimatum. Lastly, all of us are so apprehensive that nothing will be done on the subject of impressments, if the negociation be renewed with a recall even of concessions already made in the Treaty, as well as without any fresh concessions on that point, and that a final failure of the negociation must lead to a very serious posture of things, that it is thought best on the whole, to await your return, and your ultimate determination, how far it may be admissible to authorize an agreement, within certain limits not to employ British Seamen. Mr. Gallatin seems to join decidedly with the

32. Letter not found.
33. Senator Samuel Smith was consulted, among others.

other gentlemen, in thinking the crisis calls for the concession in the degree of not employing any who have been less than two years in our navigation. It is perhaps the more necessary that the concession which may be ultimately offered by us, or forced upon us by an offer from the other party, should accompany the present instructions, as the intermediate hazards may otherwise be a source of very specius censure; and as these hazards may be increased by the unfriendly change in the British Cabinet. At all events the delay of a few days seems to be far outweighed by the advantage of being guided by a more precise knowledge of your view of the whole subject: and the delay will be abridged as much as possible, by leaving nothing to be done that can be put in readiness, before your fiat shall be signified. I remain alway yours with respectful attachment.

JAMES MADISON

Jefferson to Madison

Monticello May 5, 1807

DEAR SIR

I recieved yesterday only yours of Apr. 27. with the letters of Armstrong, Turreau, Hull, Depeyster, Lee and the resolutions of Nelson county, all of which are now returned, with the pamphlet of the author of War in disguise, and a letter of Genl. Wilkinson's for circulation and to remain with the Attorney Genl.

I recieved no letter from Mr Gallatin on the subject of Turreau's application for 25,000 D. It is indeed a painful and perplexing thing. As the former advance was determined on consultation, I would ask the favor of you to consult the other gentlemen on the subject, and if you agree to the further advance on an assurance that it will be the last, I will approve of it, and say more, that, without the benefit here of hearing the sentiments of others I am, primâ facie, disposed to believe it expedient in the present state of our affairs with Spain and England. I salute you with constant and cordial affection.

TH JEFFERSON

Jefferson to Madison

Monticello May 5, 1807

I return you the pamphlet of the author of War in Disguise. Of its first half the topics and the treatment of them are very commonplace. But from page 118 to 130 it is most interesting to all nations, and especially to us.

Convinced that a militia of all ages promiscuously are entirely useless for distant service, and that we never shall be safe until we have a selected corps for a year's distant service at least, the classification of our militia is now the most essential thing the U S have to do. Whether on Bonaparte's plan of making a class for every year between certain periods, or that recommended in my message, I do not know, but I rather incline to his. The idea is not new, as you may remember we adopted it once in Virginia during the revolution but abandoned it too soon. It is the real secret of Bonaparte's success. Could S. H. Smith put better matter into his paper than the 12. pages above mentioned, and will you suggest it to him?[34] No effort should be spared to bring the public mind to this great point. I salute you with sincere affection.

Jefferson to Madison

Monticello May 8, 1807

TH.J TO MR MADISON

I return you Monroe's letter of Mar. 5. As the explosion in the British ministry took place about the 15th. I hope we shall be spared the additional embarrassment of his convention. I inclose you a letter of Michael Jones for circulation and to rest with the Atty Genl. It contains new instances of Burr's enlistments. I recieved this from Mr. Gallatin, so you can hand it to Genl Dearborn direct.

I expect to leave this on the 13th. but there is a possible occurrence which may prevent it till the 19th. which however is not probable. Accept affectionate salutations.

Jefferson to Madison

[Washington] June 1, 1807

Commissions are desired for the following persons.

Alexander Moore of Columbia as Register of wills for the county of Alexandria.
Thomas H. Williams of Misipi territory as Secretary of the sd. territory.
Jacob Descamps of Virginia as Surveyor of the port of Charlestown in the district of Misipi
Joseph Buell of Ohio as Surveyor of the port of Marietta in the district of Misipi

---

34. Samuel Harrison Smith was publisher of the *National Intelligencer*.

James W. Moss of Kentucky as Surveyor of the port of Limestone in the district of Misipi

Gideon D. Cobb of Indiana as Surveyor of the port of Massac in the district of Misipi

Jonathan Davis of Misipi a Surveyor of the port of Natchez in the district of Misipi

Thomas Nelson of York in Virginia as Collector of the district of Yorktown in Virginia. and Inspector of the revenue for the district of Yorktown.

TH JEFFERSON

Madison to Jefferson

[Washington June 29, 1807][35]

a free use of their harbors and waters, the means of refitting and refreshment, of succour to their sick and suffering have at all times and on equal principles, been extended to all; and this too while the officers of one of the belligerents recd. among us were in a continued course of insubordination to the laws, of violence to the persons of our Citizens, and of trespasses on their property. These abuses of the laws of hospitality have become habitual to commanders of British armed ships hovering on our coasts and frequenting our harbours. They have been the subject of repeated representations to their Govt.: assurances have been given that proper orders should restrain them within the limit of the rights and the respect due to a friendly nation: but these assurances have been without effect; nor has a single instance of punishment of past wrongs taken place. Even the murder of a Citizen peaceably pursuing his occupation within the limits of our jurisdiction remains unpunished; and omitting late insults as gross as language could offer,[36] the public sensibility has at length been brought to a serious crisis by an act transcending all former outrages. A frigate of the U. S. which had just left her port on a distant service, trusting to a state of peace *and therefore unprepared for defence,*[37] has been surprized and attacked by a vessel of superior force, being one of a squadron then lying on our waters to cover the transaction and has been disabled for service with the loss of a number of men killed and wounded. This enormity was not merely without provocation or any justifiable cause; it was committed with the avowed and insulting purpose of violating a ship of war under the American flag, and taking from her by force a part of her crew; a pretext the more flagrant as the British Commander was not unapprized that the seamen

35. JM's draft of a presidential proclamation following the British attack on the *Chesapeake*. TJ issued the proclamation on July 2, 1807; see Richardson, I, pp. 422–24.

36. TJ deleted this reference to the killing of John Pierce.

37. TJ deleted the italicized words.

in question were even native Citizens of the U. States. Having effected her lawless and bloody purpose, the British vessel returned immediately to anchor with her squadron within our jurisdiction. Hospitality under such circumstances ceases to be a duty; and a continuance of it with such uncontrouled abuses, would tend only by multiplying injuries and irritations, to bring on a rupture which it is the interest, and it is hoped the inclination of both nations to avoid. In this light the subject can not but present itself to the British Govt; and strengthen the motives to an honorable reparation for the wrong which has been done, and to that effectual controul of its naval commanders, which alone can justify the Govt. of the U. S. in the exercise of those hospitalities which it is constrained to discontinue, and maintain undiminished all the existing relations between the two nations.[38]

Jefferson's Proclamation about the Chesapeake *Affair*

Washington July 2, 1807

During the wars which for some time have unhappily prevailed among the powers of Europe the United States of America, firm in their principles of peace, have endeavored, by justice, by a regular discharge of all their national and social duties, and by every friendly office their situation has admitted, to maintain with all the belligerents their accustomed relations of friendship, hospitality, and commercial intercourse. Taking no part in the questions which animate these powers against each other, nor permitting themselves to entertain a wish but for the restoration of general peace, they have observed with good faith the neutrality they assumed, and they believe that no instance of a departure from its duties can be justly imputed to them by any nation. A free use of their harbors and waters, the means of refitting and of refreshment, of succor to their sick and suffering, have at all times and on equal principles been extended to all, and this, too, amidst a constant recurrence of acts of insubordination to the laws, of violence to the persons, and of trespasses on the property of our citizens committed by officers of one of the belligerent parties received among us. In truth, these abuses of the laws of hospitality have, with few exceptions, become habitual to the commanders of the British armed vessels hovering on our coasts and frequenting our harbors. They have been the subject of repeated representations to their Government. Assurances have been given that proper orders should restrain them within the limits of the rights and of the respect due to a friendly nation; but those orders and

---

38. TJ incorporated most of JM's draft in his proclamation. For a discussion, see Malone, V, pp. 427–28; Brant, IV, pp. 381–82; and Henry Adams, *History of the United States of America during the Second Administration of Thomas Jefferson,* 9 vols. (New York, 1890), IV, pp. 29–30.

assurances have been without effect—no instance of punishment for past wrongs has taken place. At length a deed transcending all we have hitherto seen or suffered brings the public sensibility to a serious crisis and our forbearance to a necessary pause. A frigate of the United States, trusting to a state of peace, and leaving her harbor on a distant service, has been surprised and attacked by a British vessel of superior force—one of a squadron then lying in our waters and covering the transaction—and has been disabled from service, with the loss of a number of men killed and wounded. This enormity was not only without provocation or justifiable cause, but was committed with the avowed purpose of taking by force from a ship of war of the United States a part of her crew; and that no circumstance might be wanting to mark its character, it had been previously ascertained that the seamen demanded were native citizens of the United States. Having effected her purpose, she returned to anchor with her squadron within our jurisdiction. Hospitality under such circumstances ceases to be a duty, and a continuance of it with such uncontrolled abuses would tend only, by multiplying injuries and irritations, to bring on a rupture between the two nations. This extreme resort is equally opposed to the interests of both, as it is to assurances of the most friendly dispositions on the part of the British Government, in the midst of which this outrage has been committed. In this light the subject can not but present itself to that Government and strengthen the motives to an honorable reparation of the wrong which has been done, and to that effectual control of its naval commanders which alone can justify the Government of the United States in the exercise of those hospitalities it is now constrained to discontinue.

In consideration of these circumstances and of the right of every nation to regulate its own police, to provide for its peace and for the safety of its citizens, and consequently to refuse the admission of armed vessels into its harbors or waters, either in such numbers or of such descriptions as are inconsistent with these or with the maintenance of the authority of the laws, I have thought proper, in pursuance of the authorities specially given by law, to issue this my proclamation, hereby requiring all armed vessels bearing commissions under the Government of Great Britain now within the harbors or waters of the United States immediately and without any delay to depart from the same, and interdicting the entrance of all the said harbors and waters to the said armed vessels and to all others bearing commissions under the authority of the British Government.

And if the said vessels, or any of them, shall fail to depart as aforesaid, or if they or any others so interdicted shall hereafter enter the harbors or waters aforesaid, I do in that case forbid all intercourse with them, or any of them, their officers or crews, and do prohibit all supplies and aid from being furnished to them, or any of them.

And I do declare and make known that if any person from or within the jurisdictional limits of the United States shall afford any aid to any such vessel contrary to the prohibition contained in this proclamation, either in repairing any such vessel or in furnishing her, her officers or crew, with supplies of any kind or in any manner whatsoever; or if any pilot shall assist in navigating any of the said armed vessels, unless it be for the purpose of carrying them in the first instance beyond the limits and jurisdiction of the United States, or unless it be in the case of a vessel forced by distress or charged with public dispatches, as hereinafter provided for, such person or persons shall on conviction suffer all the pains and penalties by the laws provided for such offenses.

And I do hereby enjoin and require all persons bearing office, civil or military, within or under the authority of the United States, and all others citizens or inhabitants thereof, or being within the same, with vigilance and promptitude to exert their respective authorities and to be aiding and assisting to the carrying this proclamation and every part thereof into full effect.

Provided, nevertheless, that if any such vessel shall be forced into the harbors or waters of the United States by distress, by the dangers of the sea, or by the pursuit of an enemy, or shall enter them charged with dispatches or business from their Government, or shall be a public packet for the conveyance of letters and dispatches, the commanding officer, immediately reporting his vessel to the collector of the district, stating the object or causes of entering the said harbors or waters, and conforming himself to the regulations in that case prescribed under the authority of the laws, shall be allowed the benefit of such regulations respecting repairs, supplies, stay, intercourse, and departure as shall be permitted under the same authority.

In testimony whereof I have caused the seal of the United States to be affixed to these presents, and signed the same.

[SEAL]   Given at the city of Washington, the 2d day of July, A. D. 1807, and of the Sovereignty and Independence of the United States the thirty-first.

TH: JEFFERSON.

By the President:
James Madison,
    Secretary of State.

Jefferson to Madison

[New Haven] July 29, 1807

The President of the United States of America—
To James Madison—Esqr—of Orange County in
the State of Virginia—Greeting——[39]

---

[39] Although this subpoena is not a part of the correspondence between TJ and JM, it is in the Madison Papers in the Library of Congress with the heading, from "The President of the United States of America," and the Witness, by "the Honorable John Marshall esq—Chief Justice of the

You are hereby commanded to appear before the Judges of the Court of the United States for the 2nd Circuit at the City of Hartford in the district of Connecticut, within said circuit on the Seventeenth day of September—next to testify and the truth to Say on behalf of Azel Backus of the town of Bethlehem and County of Litchfield in the State of Connecticut—in a Certain Matter of Controversy in the said Court empending and undetermined between the United States and said Backus—

and this you Shall in no wise omit under the penalty of the Law———

Witness the Honble. John Marshall Esq—Chief Justice of the Supreme Court of the United States At New Haven this 29th. day of July 1807. H: W: Edwards Clk *(Copy W Clark)*

Madison to Jefferson

Washington July 30, 1807

The Secretary of State, has the honor to state to the President, on the subject of the communication made to him by the Governor of Massachusetts, on the 18th. Ultimo, that negociations were in due time instituted for adjusting with Great Britain the limits between her territories on this Continent and those of the United States, that no serious difficulty has arisen in providing for an adjustment of the limits which are the subject of the said communication, but that the British Government not being willing to conclude a partial adjustment and difficulties having occurred in effecting a general demarcation a del[ay] has been unavoidable; that in consequence of late communications

---

Supreme Court of the United States." Both the heading and the witness were pro forma parts of the subpoena. Azel Backus, a Connecticut clergyman, was indicted in fedeal court in 1806 for a seditious libel against the government and President Jefferson, whom he called "a liar, whoremaster, debaucher, drunkard, gambler, and infidel" who kept black females in his family to supply "a wench as his whore." To support his charges of immorality, Backus subpoenaed JM, General Henry Lee, and other Virginians, including John Walker, with whose wife TJ had admitted some impropriety of conduct as a young man; see Malone, V, pp. 371–91, esp. pp. 386–87. For a harsher analysis, see Leonard W. Levy, *Jefferson and Civil Liberties: The Darker Side* (Cambridge, Mass., 1963), pp. 61–66. For the controversy about TJ's alleged affair with Sally Hemings, see Fawn M. Brodie, *Thomas Jefferson: An Intimate History* (New York, 1974), pp. 29–32, 228–34, 323, 349–53, 494–98; Brodie believes that the story of TJ's liaison with Sally Hemings is true, an account that I find unconvincing. For rebuttals, see Malone's long note in IV, pp. 494–98; Douglass Adair, "The Jefferson Scandals," in Douglass Adair, *Fame and the Founding Fathers: Essays by Douglass Adair*, ed. H. Trevor Colbourn (New York, 1974), pp. 160–91; and Clifford Dowdey, *The Jefferson Scandals: A Rebuttal* (New York, 1981). For a balanced appraisal of Sally Hemings, see Joel Williamson, *New People: Miscegenation and Mulattoes in the United States* (New York, 1980), pp. 42–48. For the racial context, see the perceptive analysis in Winthrop D. Jordan, *White over Black: American Attitudes toward the Negro, 1550–1812* (Chapel Hill, 1968; rpt. New York, 1977), pp. 429–81.

from our Plenipotentiary at London, fresh instructions have been transmitted, the result of which cannot be known, but which are calculated to narrow the difference between the parties, and may possibly close the negociation on terms answering the views of the State of Massachusetts. All which is respectfully submitted.

JAMES MADISON.

Jefferson to Madison

[Monticello] Aug. 7, 1807

These papers from Governor Cabell are inclosed for your perusal; I am about to answer the Governor's letter but whether I shall be able in time for this day's post, I do not know. If not, I will send you his letter and my answer by tomorrow's post, with which answer I will pray you to send him the papers now inclosed, returning to me his letter[40]

Will you be so good as to direct a commission to be sent to you from your office ready sealed, for Bolling Robertson of Virginia as Secretary for the Territory of Orleans, and to forward it to me with your signature.

TH:J.

Jefferson to Madison

[Monticello] Aug. 7, 1807

TH:J. TO J. M.

I have finished my letter alluded to in the cover of Govr. Cabell's papers, and no post is yet arrived. It therefore goes with those papers. Be so good as to examine it deliberately, and make in it any corrections it may need, noting them to me that I may make correspondent changes in the copy retained. If the corrections do not deface the letter, seal and send it on, returning me the Gov's letters. If they should render a new copy requisite, be so good as to return it with all the papers to me.

Shall we see Mrs Madison and yourself here this season? It will give great pleasure to us all. Affectionate salutations

---

40. At the request of TJ, Governor William H. Cabell reported regularly on the movement of the British naval squadron in the Chesapeake area; see Malone, V, pp. 432-35.

Madison to Jefferson

[Orange Aug. 8, 1807]

DEAR SIR

I reached home last evening a little before sunset. About ½ after eleven the post arrived under a misconception of the arrangement; and I dispatched him a letter before 2 oc. I was obliged to decide on your letter to the Govr. therefore without consulting the law or the Proclamation, and of course with but little reflection. It appeared however in all respects proper, as to the permanent course to be observed in the intercourse with the British Squadron. Perhaps it would have been as well for the officers at Norfolk etc. to have been less rigid with respect to dispatches irregularly sent previous to a notification of the needs [?]. The dispaches for Mr. E.[41] may be of a nature to render the delay disagreeable. In the letter which I wrote to the Mayor's enquiries, I had in view such a distinction, and Genl. Dearborne in one to the officer Commanding, expressly stated that dispatches on hand for Mr. E. were to be forwarded. By the way, both of those letters were written without our knowing that Decatur was to superintend the flag of truce; and I fear that Genl. Dearborn's letter may produce collision.

I observe that you have not particularly alluded to the case stated in the Govr's communications, of a ship going out of our limits, and thence sending letters otherwise than by a flag. This ought I shoud suppose, and will be regarded, as a mere evasion and frustrated as such.

I write in haste for the post who is just arrived (8 oc) having been retarded by the lateness of his departure hence for the Green Spring (about 10 or 12 miles below), where instead of here the riders met. Yrs. with respect and attachment

JAMES MADISON

Jefferson to Madison

Monticello Aug. 9, 1807

DEAR SIR,

Yours of yesterday was recieved in the course of the day. Our post-rider has not yet got to be punctual, arriving here from 2. to 4. hours later than he should do, that is to say from 3 to 5 o'clock instead of 1. I mean to propose to him that being rigorously punctual in his arrival, I will always discharge him the moment he arrives, instead of keeping him till 7 o'clock as the Postmaster proposes, taking for myself the forenoon of the succeeding day to answer every mail.

I do not exactly recollect who of the heads of departments were present,

---

41. David Erskine was British minister in Washington.

(but I think every one except Mr. Gallatin,) when, conversing on the bungling conduct of our officers with respect to Erskine's letters, and the more bungling conduct to be expected when the command should devolve on a militia Major, Mr. Smith proposed that the whole regulation of flags should be confided to Decatur, which appeared to obtain the immediate assent of all. However, the remedy is easy and perhaps more proper on the whole. That is, to let the commanding officer by land, as well as the one by water have equal authority to send and recieve flags. I will write accordingly to Govr. Cabell. This is the safer, as I believe T. Newton (of Congress) is the Major.[42]

Genl. Dearborne has sent me a plan of a war establishment for 15,000 regulars for garrisons and instead of 15,000 others, as a disposable force, to substitute 32,000 twelve-month volunteers, to be exercised and paid 3. months in the year, and consequently costing no more than 8000 permanent, giving us the benefit of 32,000 for any expedition, who would be themselves nearly equal to regulars, but could on occasion be put into the garrisons and the regulars employed in the expedition *primâ facie*. I like it well. I salute you affectionately.

P. S. The record of the blank commission for marshal of N. Carolina, sent to Govr. Alexander, must be filled up with the name of John S. West, the former marshal, who has agreed to continue.

Jefferson to Madison

Monticello Aug. 11, 1807

DEAR SIR

I pray you to peruse and consider the inclosed letters of Governor Cabell and my answer, and to exercise over the latter the same discretion I have confided to Genl. Dearborne, returning it to me for any material correction, or forwarding it to the General if you think it will do, and by the same post, as it goes so circuitously.

I suspect your difficulty with the mail lock proceeded as it did at first with me, from not understanding the lock.[43] I tried very long with both my keys and was about giving it up on the belief they had given me wrong keys, when I discovered by accident that it was a spring bolt, and therefore it was not necessary for the key to pass the bolt. I then found that both keys opened the locks readily. I salute you affectionately

TH JEFFERSON

42. Thomas Newton, Jr., was elected a member of Congress from Norfolk. He became chairman of the House Committee on Commerce and Manufactures when Congress convened in Oct.; see Cunningham, *Process of Government under Jefferson,* pp. 225–233, and Daniel P. Jordan, *Political Leadership in Jefferson's Virginia* (Charlottesville, 1983), pp. 63, 101, 174.

43. JM's letter about the mail lock has not been found.

Madison to Jefferson

[Orange Aug. 15, 1807]

DEAR SIR

The gentleman [a Mr. Cocke] also brings the inclosed letters recommending him for a public agency at Martinique. [He] had thoughts of proceeding to Monticello. He declines it in consequence of his conversation with us on the subject. I have apprized him, that it was not thought proper to give a formal commission in such a case without some formal or positive sanction from the French Govt. He readily enters into the nature of the proceeding, and is willing to go with credentials such as have been given to the agent for Guadalupe. The letters in his favor are simply sufficient as vouchers for his personal character, in case you should think proper to cloath him with a public one. On this point I have autho[rized][44] [missing words at frayed bottom of the page] owing probably to obstructions from the rain which has been excessive. In thirty six hours there fell upwards of 8 inches at least. How much more is uncertain, the vessel measuring it, running over each morning when examined. All the mills in this neighborhood have lost their dams. I learn that my little one, which I am about to visit, is among the sufferers.[45] Yrs. with respectful attacht

JAMES MADISON

Madison to Jefferson

[Orange Aug. 15, 1807]

DEAR SIR

The Post not arriving yesterday morning till between 7 and 8 oc. it was impossible for me to comply with your request as to the letters to Govr. C. and Genl. D. even so far as to peruse and reword them without risking a breach in the chain of rides. The letters therefore await the downward mail of this morning. The only remark I have to make on that to Govr. C. is that in commenting on the rule of expounding laws and on the means implied by the authority and contemplated, rather more latitude results from the strain of your expressions than I should my self have assumed. Still I do not think it proper to detain the letter on that consideration, inasmuch as I could not well suggest any particular changes of expression that would answer the purpose, and I am not sure that I could offer any general substitute that might not be liable equally to objections. Criticism appeared also the less to be indulged, as the general principles on which your observations turn are clearly sound, and no inconveniency is likely to arise from your deductions even if these should be a little too broad.

44. One or more lines are missing at the bottom of the first page.
45. JM lost his milldam on Blue Run; see Brant, IV, p. 387, and Ketcham, p. 455.

I inclose a letter from a Mr. Detourt, on the subject of a consul at Magadore. I know not who he is, but he writes like a well informed sensible man. It is probable he aspires to the appointment himself. I believe there is weight in his remarks, and that if a trade is to go on at that port, either a Consul, or an agent of Simpson will be useful there.

I have written to the office of State for a precise account of the obstruction complained of by Foronda.[46] With respect to his remembrance as to Miranda it is a question whether it be worth while at this moment to bring into view the history of the Spanish manoeuvres in the Western Country, or a very stunning answer might be given.[47]

This moment the rider for Monticello is returned from his unsuccessful attempt to get there Having been misled from the route I prescribed on S. side of the mountain, to the North route, he has been stopped at Blue run, and has wasted his time in misjudged efforts to get forwards. I have thought it best to take out the letters for you, which will be put into the mail momently expected from Fredg. and let him go downward as he wd. have done, if no disappointment had happened.

Jefferson to Madison

Monticello Aug. 16, 1807

DEAR SIR

I recieved yesterday your two letters without date on the subjects now to be answered. I do not see any objection to the appointment of Mr Cocke as Agent at Martinique. That of a Consul at Magadore is on more difficult ground. A Consul in Barbary is a diplomatic character, altho' the title does not imply that. He recieves a salary fixed by the legislature; being independant of Simpson we should have two ministers to the same sovereign. I should therefore think it better to leave the port of Magadore to an Agent of Simpson's appointment and under his controul.

If any thing Thrasonic and foolish from Spain could add to my contempt of that government it would be the demand of satisfaction now made by Foronda. However, respect to ourselves requires that the answer should be decent, and I think it fortunate that this opportunity is given to make a strong declaration of facts, to wit, how far our knolege of Miranda's objects went, what measures we took to prevent any thing further, the negligence of the Spanish agents to give us earlier notice, the measures we took for punishing those guilty, and our quiet abandonment of those taken by the Spaniards. But I would not say a word in recrimination as to the Western intrigues of Spain. I

---

46. Valentin de Foronda was Spanish chargé d'affaires in Philadelphia; see Isaac Joslin Cox, *The West Florida Controversy, 1798–1813* (Baltimore, 1918), p. 219, and Abernethy, p. 268.

47. For Miranda's purported role in Burr's western venture, see Abernethy, pp. 38, 40–49, 269–70.

think that is the snare intended by this Protest, to make it a set-off for the other. As soon as we have all the proofs of the Western intrigues, let us make a remonstrance and demand of satisfaction, and, if Congress approves, we may in the same instant make reprisals on the Floridas, until satisfaction for that and for spoliations, and until a settlemt of boundary. I had rather have war against Spain than not, if we go to war against England. Our southern defensive force can take the Floridas, volunteers for a Mexican army will flock to our standard, and rich pabulum will be offered to our privateers in the plunder of their commerce and coasts. Probably Cuba would add itself to our confederation. The paper in answer to Foronda should I think be drawn with a view to its being laid before Congress, and published to the world as our justification against the imputation of participation in Miranda's projects.

The late flood has swept all the mills in our neighborhood. About one half of my mill dam is gone. Great losses on the low grounds as well of the severed as the growing crop. Mr. Sam Carr tells me there was a trough at his house used for feeding his mules, 12. inches deep, standing in an open place. The mules had been fed in it in the evening of Wednesday the 12th. which proves there was no water in it then. With rain which fell that night only, it was running over the next morning, altho' it is presumed the mules had drunk out of it in the mean time. Wood's mill on the river has stood tolerably well. Macgruder's dam has stood, but the lock is gone, which interrupts our navigation.

We are flattering ourselves with the hope of a visit from Mrs. Madison and yourself some time this season. I tender her my friendly respects and salute yourself affectionately.

TH JEFFERSON

Madison to Jefferson

[Orange Aug. 16, 1807]

The mail has just brought me Daytons letter which is inclosed, with a letter from Foronda, and a Commission for Robinson.

J. M.
10 OC

Madison to Jefferson

[Orange Aug. 16, 1807]

DEAR SIR

The post having arrived last night after Eleven OC and the one from below being expected early this morning, I have had but little room for bestowing thought on Dayton's letter and your drafted answer.

It would be an advantage to know the precise answer given by Mr. Rodney to the application which was made to him on the same subject. I heard this read by Mr. R. but can not sufficiently rely on my recollection of its tenor or its implications, so far as related to the validity of his consent in justifying the Court in departing from a rule otherwise binding on it. On the supposition that his interference might not be irregular, the question would remain whether your interference with him would be equally so. These are points, depending too much on the course of practice to allow any value to my opinion. Judging from the principles which are generally impressed on my mind, I should infer that after a proceeding has been judicially instituted in such a case, it is so purely a matter to which the law and the accused are alone parties, and the authority to decide on it so exclusive in the Court, that neither the consent of the prosecuting officer, nor of the Ex. ought to be admitted into the question. This however may be mere theory, as it may be understood in practice, that the consent of the Executive in favor of the accused, is the consent of the law.

On the supposition that the theory is not controuled by the practice, I think you are not only right in declining to interfere but that the ground for it could not be better explained; and considering the stile and temper of D's letter, and the possibility that the cyphered [?] testimony agst. him, may be a forgery I think such an answer, no improper condescention. I am disposed to think however that it would be better to omit the last sentence of the first paragraph, which might be regarded as either an approbation of the conduct of the Court if made indiscriminate, or a covered animadversion on its indulgence to Col. Burr, and to vary at least the last paragraph, which might not be favorably construed by Wilkinson, tho' it certainly admits the most unexceptionable construction.[48]

I know not what is meant by the passage which says that the Secy. of State has been applied to for an acct. of the communication made by Genl. Wilkinson. No such application has been made, nor indeed if it had, could any answer have been given other than a reference to the documents, which I suppose to be already in the hands of the Attorney for the U. S. Yrs. with affecte. attachment

JAMES MADISON

Jefferson to Madison

Monticello Aug. 18, 1807

DEAR SIR,

I return you the papers received yesterday. Mr. Erskine complains of a want of communication between the British armed vessels *in the* Chesapeake, or *off* the coast. If, by *off* the coast he means those which being generally in our

---

48. For a brief discussion of TJ and JM's response to Dayton, see Brant, IV, p. 354.

waters, go occasionally out of them to cruize or to acquire a title to communicate with their Consul it is too poor an evasion for him to expect us to be the dupes of. If vessels *off* the coast, and having never violated the proclamation wish to communicate with their Consul, they may send in by any vessel, without a flag. He gives a proof of their readiness to restore deserters, from an instance of the Chichester lying along-side a wharf at Norfolk. It would have been as applicable if Capt Stopfield and his men had been in a tavern at Norfolk. All this too a British sergeant *is ready* to swear to, and further, that he saw British deserters enlisted in their British uniform by our officer. As this fact is probably false, and can easily be inquired into, names being given, and as the story of the Chichester can be ascertained by Capt Saunders, suppose you send a copy of the paper to the Secy. of the Navy and recommend to him having an enquiry made.

We ought gladly to procure evidence to hang the pirates, if no objection or difficulty occur from the place of trial. If the Driver is the scene of trial, where is she? If in our waters, we can have no communication with her, if out of them, it may be inconvenient to send the witnesses. Altho' there is neither candour nor dignity in solliciting the victualling the Columbine for 4. months for a voyage of 10 days, yet I think you had better give the permission. It is not by these huckstering maneuvres that the great national question is to be settled. I salute you affectionately.

Jefferson to Madison

[Monticello] Aug. 19, 1807

TH. J. TO MR MADISON

I suppose Mr. Gamble should be told that his opinion in favor of the appointment of a Consul General for the Danish islands being founded on the supposition of a war with England, the Executive cannot at present act on that ground. It would seem indeed that in the event of war, our agent or agents in those islands would be very important persons, and should therefore be chosen with care. I presume it would become the best office in the gift of the U. S.

It will be very difficult to answer Mr. Erskine's demand respecting the water casks in the tone proper for such a demand. I have heard of one who having broke his cane over the head of another, demanded paiment for his cane. This demand might well enough have made part of an offer to pay the damages done to the Chesapeake and to deliver up the authors of the murders committed on board her.

I return you the papers recieved yesterday. The Governor has inclosed me a letter from Genl. Matthews of August 13.th, mentioning the recent arrival of a ship in the Chesapeake bearing the flag of a Vice-Admiral; from whence he concludes that Barclay is arrived. I salute you affectionately.

Madison to Jefferson

[Orange] Aug. 19, 1807

DEAR SIR

I received last night your letter of the 18th. with a return of the letters sent with it.

Capt. Saunders who is alluded to in Mr. Erskine's communications, being in the land service, and the alledged enlistment of British diserters, being into the same service, I shall address the information to Genl. Dearborn, and shall intimate to Mr. E. that foreign deserters will not be permitted to enlist into the land more than into the sea service. I shall not forward the letter however till I know that you approve the intimation and will signify to the Secy. of War that his recruiting officers are to be instructed accordingly. To enlist deserters is a very different thing from merely leaving the Country open to them. It is a positive act of the Govt. amounting to an invitation and bounty to desertion, and consequently giving just umbrage to the foreign nation as well as staining the reputation of our own.

To avoid the danger of varying in my answer to Dayton's letter from the course taken by yours, I inclose the one I have prepared, with a request that it may be returned with whatever suggestions you may think proper.

Mrs. M and myself always include a visit to Monticello among the pleasures of the autumnal retreat from Washington; and we are not without hopes that the present season will not be an exception. It is far from certain however that we may not be disappointed; many circumstances uniting to render my continued presence here peculiarly requisite.

Jefferson to Madison

Monticello Aug. 20, 1807

TH.J. TO J MADISON

Your letter to Dayton I think perfectly right, unless perhaps the expression of personal sympathy in the 1st page might be misconstrued, and coupled with the circumstance that we had not yet instituted a prosecution against him, altho' possessed of evidence. Poor Yznardi seems to have been worked up into distraction by the persecutions of Meade. I inclose you a letter I have recieved from him. Also one from Warden, attested by Armstrong, by which you will see that the feuds there are not subsiding.[49]

By yesterday's or this day's mails you will have recieved the information that Bonaparte has annihilated the allied armies. The result will doubtless be

---

[49]. For the festering relationship between John Armstrong and David Bailie Warden, Armstrong's private secretary who sought the positions of consul in Paris and agent for prize cases in 1807, see C. Edward Skeen, *John Armstrong, Jr., 1758–1843: A Biography* (Syracuse, 1981), pp. 53, 113–16.

peace on the continent, an army despatched through Persia to India, and the main army brought back to their former position on the channel. This will oblige England to withdraw everything home, and leave us an open field. An account, apparently worthy of credit, in the Albany paper is that the British authorities are withdrawing all their cannon and magazines from Upper Canada to Quebec, considering the former not tenable, and the latter their only fast-hold. I salute you with sincere affection.

P. S. I had forgotten to express my opinion that deserters ought never to be enlisted but I think you may go further and say to Erskine that if ever such a practise has prevailed, it has been without the knolege of the Government, and would have been forbidden if known, and if any examples of it have existed (which is doubted,) they must have been few or they would have become known. The case presented from the Chichester, if true, does not prove the contrary, as the persons there said to have been enlisted are believed to have been American citizens, who whether impressed or enlisted into the British service, were equally right in returning to the duties they owed to their own country.

Jefferson to Madison

Monticello Aug. 24, 1807

I presume the two commissions of militia officers in the District of Columbia which you enclosed yesterday, were meant as resignations. I have sent them as such to the War office.

I was misinformed as to the name of the person appointed Secretary of Orleans. Altho always called Bolling Robertson it seems his name is Thomas Bolling Robertson. Will you be so good as to order a new commission, and that the record of the other be cancelled. Affte salutns

Jefferson to Madison

Monticello Aug. 25, 1807

DEAR SIR

Yours without date arrived yesterday. About 3. or 4 days ago,[50] Mr. Nelson called on me with a letter from General Lee informing me he was summoned in the case which is the subject of your letter and expressing his difficulties. I had never had any information of the case, its parties or subject,

50. JM to TJ, undated but received on Aug. 24, 1807, has not been found. It must have discussed JM's being summoned to testify in the prosecution of Azel Backus for seditious libel of TJ; see the court summons commanding JM's appearance, July 29, 1807, above.

A Conspiracy and a Bad Treaty, 1806-1807

until that I had read in the newspapers some time ago. That prosecution was commenced in Connecticut against a clergyman for either preaching or praying defamation against myself. My opinion to Mr Nelson was that General Lee could be under no difficulty because he was detained in Richmond by the authority of that court as a witness in Burr's case, which of course was cause sufficient for not attending another; that I perceived the cause would be continued on account of his absence, which would give me time to endeavor through a friend in Connecticut to have done what might properly be done. I accordingly wrote to Mr. Granger, who is at home, recommending in general an endeavor to have the whole prosecution dropped if it could be done. That if the tenor of my life did not support my character, the verdict of a jury would hardly do it, and that as to punishing a poor devil of a calumniator, the enmity and malignity were too extensive to be stopped in that way: but that at any event the charge against the defendant which might relate to the subject of General Lee's letter must be withdrawn, as those interviewed in that matter had agreed mutually to endeavor that it should be forever buried in oblivion, and that the dragging it into a court of justice was harrowing all our feelings. On this ground it rests at present. The papers inclosed in your letter give me the first information of the particular facts charged, of which none give me any concern but the one above alluded to. Time is necessary to have that at least disposed of. You remember that we received it from the attorney general in Burr's case as a confident opinion that the law had not as yet made any provision for enabling the judge of one district court to have compulsory process served on a witness in another. Any person may serve a subpoena any where but the attachment to compel attendance or to punish non-attendance must be served by a marshal. It cannot be by the marshal of the district court, because his authority is local and is nothing after crossing the limits of his district. It cannot be by the marshal of the district where the witness lives, because no law has authorised him to obey such a precept, and his attempting it would be false imprisonment and as such liable to action or prosecution. So if a commission issues to take a deposition and the witnesses do not choose to attend, they cannot be compelled, for want of authority to issue or serve an attachment. Unless therefore they volunteer themselves in the case, the party cannot have their testimony in any way. Whether he deserves their voluntary efforts in this case is not for me to determine. But if they do not attend, the cause will certainly be laid over till the spring term, which will give time to do what is proper. I had not supposed there was a being in human shape such a savage as to have summoned Mr. W. in such a case.[51] On account of the

---

51. For TJ's alleged attempt to seduce John Walker's wife, Betsey, in 1768 before he was married, see Malone, I, pp. 155–57, 447–51; IV, pp. 216–23; V, pp. 14–15, 386–87, 391; and Brodie, pp. 73–79, 366–69, 374–75. TJ confessed that "when young and single I offered love to a handsome lady. I acknolege its incorrectness"; see TJ to Robert Smith, July 1, 1805, in Thomas Jefferson, *Thomas Jefferson's Correspondence . . . in the Collection of William K. Bixby,* ed. W. C. Ford (Boston, 1916), pp. 114–15.

feelings of that family I shall spare nothing to have this article withdrawn. Were it not for them, I would rather the whole should be gone into that the world might judge for themselves and the scoundrel parson recieve his punishment.[52]

I think I shall go to Bedford about the 8th or 9th of September and shall be about a week, which I mention as it may govern the time of our having the pleasure of seeing Mrs Madison and yourself here. I salute you with affection and respect.

Th. Jefferson

Madison to Jefferson

[Orange] Aug. 26, 1807

Dear Sir

I recd. yours on the subject of the prosecution in Connecticut last night. Inclosed is a letter from Mr. Crowninshield, and one for Mr. Foster who went last evening to Gordon's in order to reach Monticello for dinner. It may not be amiss to let him have the envelope in which Mr. Brent explains the appearance of the seal. Yrs. with respectful attacht

J Madison

Jefferson to Madison

Monticello Aug. 26, 1807

Dear Sir,

Colo. Newton's enquiries are easily solved I think by application of the principles we have assumed. 1. The *interdicted* ships are *enemies*. Should they be forced by stress of weather to run up into safer harbors, we are to act towards them as we would towards enemies in regular war in a like case. Permit no intercourse, no supplies, and if they land kill or capture them as enemies. If they lie still, Decatur has orders not to attack them without stating the case to me and awaiting instructions. But if they attempt to enter Elizabeth river, he is to attack them without waiting for instructions. 2. Other armed vessels putting in from sea in distress, are *friends*. They must report themselves to the collector, he assigns them their station, and regulates their repairs, supplies, intercourse and stay. Not needing flags, they are under the direction of the Collector alone, who should be reasonably liberal as to their repairs and supplies, furnishing them for a voyage to any of their American ports: but I think

---

52. JM responded to this letter the same day or the next in a letter, now missing, that TJ received on Aug. 26, 1807. For JM's role, see Brant, IV, pp. 354–55, who notes that "Madison's two letters to Jefferson" on the libel prosecution of Backus "(received Aug. 24 and 26, 1807) have disappeared."

with him their crews should be kept on board, and that they should not enter Elizabeth river.

I remember Mr. Gallatin expressed an opinion that our negociations with England should not be laid before Congress at their meeting, but reserved to be communicated all together with the answer they shall send us, whenever received. I am not of this opinion. I think on the meeting of Congress we should lay before them everything that has passed to that day, and place them on the same ground of information we are on ourselves. They will thus have time to bring their minds to the same state of things with ours, and when the answer arrives, we shall all view it from the same position. I think therefore you should order the whole of the negociation to be prepared in two copies. I salute you affectionately.

Jefferson to Madison

Monticello Aug. 30, 1807

DEAR SIR

There can be no doubt that Foronda's claim for the money advanced to Lt. Pike should be repaid, and while his application to yourself is the proper one, we must attend to the money's being drawn from the proper fund, which is that of the war department. I presume therefore it will be necessary for you to apply to Genl. Dearborne to furnish the money. Will it not be proper to rebut Foronda's charge of this government sending a spy to Santa Fé by saying that this government has never employed a spy in any case: and that Pike's mission was to ascend the Arkansas and descend the Red river for the purpose of ascertaining their geography; that as far as we are yet informed, he entered the waters of the North river, believing them to be those of the Red river: and that, however certain we are of a right extending to the North river, and participating of it's navigation with Spain, yet Pike's voyage was not intended as an exercise of that right, which we notice here merely because he has chosen to deny it, a question to be settled in another way.[53]

From the present state of the tranquillity in the Chesapeake and the probability of its continuance, I begin to think the daily mail may soon be discontinued and an extra mail once a week substituted, to leave Fredericksburg Sunday morning, and Milton Wednesday morning. This will give us 2 mails a week. I should propose this change for Sep. 9., which is the day I set out for Bedford and will exactly close one month of daily mail. What do you think of it? Affectionate salutations.

TH: JEFFERSON

53. For the western exploration of Lt. Zebulon M. Pike and its relation to the Burr conspiracy, see Abernethy, pp. 119-37. For the loan of 1,000 pesos to Pike by Captain General Salcedo at Chihuahua, see p. 135, which cites JM to Valentin de Foronda, Sept. 1, 1807. Also see W. Eugene Hollon, *The Lost Pathfinder: Zebulon Montgomery Pike* (Norman, Okla., 1949).

Madison to Jefferson

[Orange] Aug. 31, 1807

DEAR SIR

Havg. written to the office for a statement of our affairs with Algiers, I have recd. the inclosed letter and documents from Mr. Brent. Will it not be prudent at the present crisis as well on the Coast of Barbary as elsewhere, to soothe the Dey with a part of the articles agreeable to him, say 20. or 30 dollrs. worth; or shall we wait for further information from Lear?

The tranquility in the Chesapeake would justify a discontinuance of the daily mail. The objection to it would arise from the probability that the contract extends thro' the recess of the Ex. and the chance that occurrences succeeding the discontinuance, might give an unfavorable aspect to the measure. Perhaps the abstract objection to change may balance the small saving that would be made by it. Yrs. with affecte. attacht.

JAMES MADISON

Jefferson to Madison

Monticello Sept. 1, 1807

DEAR SIR,

I think with you we had better send to Algiers some of the losing articles in order to secure peace there while it is uncertain elsewhere. While war with England is probable every thing leading to it with any other nation should be avoided, except with Spain. As to her, I think it the precise moment when we should declare to the French government that we will instantly seise on the Floridas as reprisal for the spoliations denied us, and that if by a given day they are paid to us we will restore all East of the Perdido and hold the rest subject to amicable decision: otherwise we will hold them for ever as compensation for the spoliations. This to be a subject of consideration when we assemble.

One reason for suggesting a discontinuance of the daily post was that it is not kept up by contract, but at the expence of the U. S. But the principal reason was to avoid giving ground for clamor. The general idea is that those who recieve annual compensations should be constantly at their posts. Our constituents might not in the first moment consider 1. that we all have property to take care of, which we cannot abandon for temporary salaries. 2. that we have health to take care of, which at this season cannot be preserved at Washington. 3. that while at our separate homes our public duties are fully executed, and at much greater personal labour than while we are together when a short conference saves a long letter. I am aware that in the present crisis some incident might turn up where a day's delay might infinitely overweigh a month's expence of the daily post. Affectte salutns.

TH. JEFFERSON

Jefferson to Madison

Monticello Sept. 2, 1807

DEAR SIR

The extract of a letter to Bishop Carroll I have inclosed to Genl. Dearborne. I return you Judge Davis's letter.[54] If we meddle in the case at all, should it not be by sending the letter to the Attorney General who will know best how to prevent a conflict of jurisdictions.

I inclose you the copy of a letter from Genl. Smith to Mr Gallatin, communicated by the General to P. Carr and by him to me. It is worth your perusal. Be so good as to return it when read. Affectionate salutations.

TH. JEFFERSON

Jefferson to Madison

Monticello Sept. 3, 1807

DEAR SIR,

Mr. Smith's letter of Aug. 29. and the papers it inclosed and which are now re-inclosed, will explain to you the necessity of my confirming his proposition as to the means of apprising our East India commerce of their danger, without waiting for further opinions on the subject. You will see that it throws on you the immediate burthen of giving the necessary instructions with as little delay as possible, lest the occasion by the vessels now sailing should be lost. Be so good as to return me his two letters, and to seal and forward on to him, mine, and the other papers. Affectionate salutations.

Madison to Jefferson

[Orange] Sept. 3, 1807

DEAR SIR

I recd. last night or rather this morning yours of yesterday, and return the remarks of Genl. S. inclosed in it. They strengthen the opinion as to the extent

---

54. John Davis was a federal judge in Massachusetts; see Levy, p. 133.

of his information on certain important subjects, and the vigor of his understanding.

The late scraps of intelligence from England put together make it probable that something towards an arrangement had taken place early in July. and before Purviance appears to have arrived.[55] Whether it has been an informal, or a provisional, or a positive convention, is uncertain. But it must, in either mode, have included our object with respect to impressments, since we know that the instruction of Mar. 18. given after the rect. of the Treaty, was in the hands of our Ministers. This inference is confirmed by the reply of Rose to Ld. Howick, on the subject of the Bill depending, that the adjustment taking place with the U. S. would put an end to the Non-importation act, which our Ministers wd. never undertake to do, without a security for our seamen, and for the colonial trade too.[56] It is to be wished however that Purviance may have delivered his budget before putting the last hand to the work. It is not improbable that appearances or apprehensions of an approximation of France towards the U. S. may have reenforced the impulse given to the British Cabinet by the events on the Continent. If Armstrong, as has been sd. and as he intended, should have proceeded to the French Camp, the effect of such apprehensions is the more probable.

We propose to be at Monticello on Saturday evening, if no obstacle intervenes. Yrs. with respectful attachment

JAMES MADISON

Jefferson to Madison

Monticello Sept. 4, 1807[57]

DEAR SIR

After writing to Mr Smith my letter of yesterday by the post of the day, I received one from him now inclosed, and covering a letter from Mr Crownenshield on the subject of notifying our E. India trade. To this I have written the answer herein, which I have left open for your perusal with Crownenshield's letter, praying you will seal and forward them immediately with any considerations of your own addressed to Mr Smith which may aid him in the decision I refer to him.

---

55. JM had returned the Monroe-Pinkney Treaty in May 1807 for renogtiation; see Hickey, 86.

56. George H. Rose was a member of the House of Commons who favored strong measures to bar American commerce with the British West Indies. For his report, which called for harsher measures than JM realized, see Perkins, p. 198. Canning subsequently appointed Rose as special British envoy to resolve difficulties related to the *Chesapeake* attack; see Ch. 34.

57. The first paragraph of this letter was published in L. and B., XI, p. 358, and dated Sept. 3, 1807.

I do not give to the newspaper and Parliamentary scraps the same importance you do. I think they all refer to the Convention of limits sent us in the form of a projet, brought forward only as a sop of the moment for Parliament and the public. Nothing but an exclusion of G. B. from the Baltic will dispose her to peace with us, and to defer her policy of subsisting her navy by the general plunder of nations.

We shall be happy to see Mrs Madison and yourself tomorrow, and shall wait dinner for you till half after four, believing you will easily reach this before that hour. My ford has been a little injured by the fresh, but is perfectly safe. It has a hollow of about 9 I. deep and 6 f. wide washed in one place exactly in the middle of the river, but even in that it will not be to the belly of the horse. I salute you with great affection and respect.

TH: JEFFERSON

Return Mr Smith's letter.

Jefferson to Madison

Monticello Sept. 18, 1807

TH.J. TO MR MADISON

I returned here yesterday afternoon and found, as I might expect, an immense mass of business.[58] With the papers recieved from you I enclose you some others which will need no explanation. I am desired by the Secy of the Navy to say what must be the conduct of Com Rodgers at New York on the late or any similar entry of that harbor by British armed vessels. I refer him to the orders to Decatur as to what he was to do if the vessels in the Chesapeake. 1. remain quiet in the Bay. 2. come to Hampton road. 3. Enter Eliz river: and recommend an application of the same rules to N York, accommodated to the localities of the place. Should the British government give us reparation of the past, and security for the future, yet the continuance of their vessels in our harbors in defiance constitutes a new injury, which will not be included in any settlement with our ministers, and will furnish good ground for declaring their future exclusion from our waters, in addition with the other reasonable ground before existing. Our Indian affairs in the N. W. on the Missouri, and at the Natchitoches, wear a very unpleasant aspect. As to the first all I think is done which is necessary. But for this and other causes, I am anxious to be again assembled. I have a letter from Connecticut. The prosecution there will be dismissed this term on the ground that the case is not cognisable by the courts of the U. S. Perhaps you can

---

58. TJ had returned from Poplar Forest, his farm in Bedford County, where he had spent eight days; see Malone, V, p. 451.

intimate this where it will give tranquillity.⁵⁹ Affectionate salutations.

The commission to the Secy of Orleans having another mistake, Robinson instead of Robertson, has been returned to me for correction. I have corrected it; but it will be necessary the record should also be set to rights.

Madison to Jefferson

[Orange] Sept. 18 and 19, 1807

DEAR SIR

With the other papers herewith inclosed is an answer to Mr. Erskine's letter of the 1st. instant. I have thought it proper not to forward it without previously submitting it to your perusal and corrections.

Sepr. 19

The mail for the 1st. time has arrived this morning. The rider now here, who carried up the first says he did not call because he did not know that I was at home as he went, and because the mail was empty as he returned. The rider who went down this morning, having not called, your communications, if any for me, have proceeding [proceeded] to Fredg. I add in haste his papers put up for yesterday, a letter from Erskine, and one from Madrid.

Jefferson to Madison

[Monticello] Sept. 20, 1807

I return all the papers recieved in yours of the 18. and 19th. except one solliciting office, and Judge Woodward's letters to be communicated to the Secretary at War. Should not Claiborne be instructed to say at once to Govr Folch that as we never did prohibit any articles (except slaves) from being carried up the Mississippi to Baton Rouge, so we do not mean to prohibit them, and that we only ask a perfect and equal reciprocity to be observed on the rivers which pass thro' the territories of both nations. Must we not denounce to Congress the Spanish decree as well as the British regulation pretending to be the countervail of the French? One of our first consultations, on meeting, must be on the Question whether we shall not order all the militia

59. The Backus indictment for seditious libel of the president had been brought under a presumed federal-law jurisdiction. TJ instructed Postmaster General Gideon Granger to consult with the federal district attorney in Hartford about dropping the case, which was done in 1808; see *ibid.*, pp. 386–91.

and volunteers destined for the Canadas to be embodied on the 26th of Octr, and to march immediately to such points on the way to their destination as shall be pointed out, there to await the decision of Congress?

I approve of the letter to Erskine. In answering his last should he not be reminded how strange it is he should consider as a hostility our refusing to recieve but under a flag, persons from vessels remaining and acting in our waters in defiance of the authority of the country? The post-rider of the day before yesterday has behaved much amiss in not calling on you. When I found your mail in the Valise and that they had not called on you, I replaced the mail in it and expressly directed him to return by you. Affectionate salutations.

Madison to Jefferson

[Orange] Sept. 20, 1807

DEAR SIR

The Post who neglected to call on me, as noticed in my letter of yesterday, met with one at the Gum spring who brought his mail back to me. I should have sent him on to Monticello with the letters etc. now inclosed, but that he signified he was to go down for the ensuing mail to Fredg. To prevent a break in the whole chain, and avoid delay to your packets for Washington and Richmond, I allowed him to pursue his own intentions. I regret that you did not open the letters for me returned from Monticello. I hope you will use more authority over them hereafter. The Letter from The Legation at London particularly should not have been treated with reserve.[60] You will find that the British Govt. renounces the pretension to search ships of war for deserters; but employs words which may possibly be meant to qualify the renunciation, or at least to quibble away the promised atonement. The irritation betrayed in Cannings note of Aug. 3. and the ground for believing that he was then possessed of Berkley's account of the matter, give force to this apprehension. The execution of the 4th. seaman, and the insulting trial at Halifax show that Berkley is in little dread of resentment in his superiors.[61] I think it possible that the step may have been the result of an anxiety to elude the return of this man, who was probably a British subject, with the other three, to the situation from which he was taken; or the obstacle to an adjustment which a refusal might produce. Besides the humiliation of restoring a British subject in such a case, the dreaded effect on the seamen generally, must have entered into the calculation, whereas the rash step taken, reverses the example. It gives us however additional ground for resisting any deficient arrangement, into which our

60. For a discussion of the vicissitudes of communication in that era, see *ibid.*, pp. 454–55.
61. For references to Admiral Berkeley's trial of the four seamen taken from the *Chesapeake* and the execution of Jenkin Ratford, see *ibid.*, p. 455; Perkins, p. 142; and Brant, IV, p. 388.

negociators may be led, by an ignorance of the accumulating proofs witnessed here, of the absolute necessity of a radical cure for the evils inflicted by British ships of war frequenting our waters. Yrs. most respectfully and affecty.

JAMES MADISON

Madison to Jefferson

[Orange Sept. 21, 1807]

Yours without date[62] was recd. last night by the rider who went up and came down without a valize. I presume he explained the cause of this which explained the failure of the mail due from Fredg.

Whether the B. Decree is to be renounced to Congs. must depend on intermediate accts. from London. If nothing changes the posture of things with Spain, very serious questions must arise with respect to that silly and arrogant power. I am glad to find Erving's conjectures to be such with respect to the feelings and intentions of Bonaparte towards it.

Would it not be proper to let Smith publish in the words of Canning, without quoting them, the disavowal of the pretension to search ships of war, and promising satisfaction for the attack on the Chesapeake. This will enable the public to appreciate the chances of peace and put all on an equal footing?[63]

I send a large bundle from the Collector at Passonugady [Passamaquoddy?]. You will understand the case from his letter and the memorial of the sufferer: but you will be able to abridge so much as you proceed, that it may be worth while to read at least some parts of some of the testimony, which you will select by their own indications, and the decision of the Court. The topograpy of the scene aided by a draft testified to be correct, the spirit of the British in that quarter, and the manner of intercourse between the traders in Planter and smuggled goods, will be distinctly seen. The iniquity of the Decree in throwing the Costs, enormous as they are on the Claimant, is so apparent, on the face of the proceedings, that I am persuaded the decree would be no bar to a remedy agst. the British officer or Collector, in case they should be caught within the jurisdiction of our Courts unless the neglect to appeal should operate agst. the Claimant. If I mistake not the Supreme Court of N. Y. has decided, and I think justly, that a foreign judgment, illegal on the face of it, is no bar to justice elsewhere. At any rate, I think it would not be amiss for Hewes to carry his case before Congs. and thus make the British proceedings known to the world. I could wish that Congs. might find it a safe precedent to

---

62. Letter not found.
63. Canning's words were published without quotation marks in the *National Intelligencer*, Sept. 28, 1807; see Malone, V, pp. 455–56, and Brant, IV, p. 389.

indemnify the sufferer, and refer to the Ex. a demand of reimbursement from the B. Govt. Yrs. always etc.

JAMES MADISON

Jefferson to Madison

Monticello Sept. 22, 1807

DEAR SIR

I return you the papers which accompanied yours of yesterday. I think the case of Capt. Hewes is merely a case for a demand of indemnification from Gr. Br. and a proper acknolegement of the violation of jurisdiction. It would be a very dangerous precedent for Congress to indemnify the individual.

I think it would be well for Smith to be furnished with the declaration of Mr Canning only taking care that it should not appear to have been furnished by us. Affectionate salutations.

TH JEFFERSON

Madison to Jefferson

[Orange] Sept. 22, 1807

DEAR SIR

I have forwarded your notes to the several Postmasters. The inclosed letter from Pleasanton[64] which mentions the terms on which the missionary to Batavia is engaged. I understand the $3000 to be in full of all expences etc. I directed payment out of the Foreign intercourse fund. The case of the Indefatigable and crew may be laid before Congs. either for their decision on the individual cases or for a definite provision for such cases. But I presume it is within the general fund for foreign [and?] Barbary intercourse, as it has [been] hitherto expounded and acted upon. Yrs. always

JAMES MADISON

Jefferson to Madison

Monticello Sept. 26, 1807

DEAR SIR:

Health and weather permitting I shall set out on Wednesday without fail. If I can get off early enough I will be with you by half after three, supposed

---

64. Stephen Pleasanton was a senior clerk in the State Department; see Cunningham, *Process of Government under Jefferson,* p. 328.

your dining hour, but knowing how difficult it is to clear out from home at any given hour, if I find I cannot be with you at half past three I shall dine at Gordon's. I beg not to be waited for. Receive for yourself and Mrs. Madison my affectionate salutations.

Th. Jefferson

34

EMBARGO: THE RIGHTS OF NEUTRALS AND "THE WRONGS OF THE BELLIGERENTS," 1807–1808

WHEN CONGRESS CONVENED in October 1807, the *Revenge* had not yet returned with Britain's answer to American demands for redress of the explosive *Chesapeake* affair. Jefferson urged a policy of watchful waiting while negotiations were under way, but he also pressed hard for additional preparedness measures, obtaining an appropriation of $850,000 for 188 gunboats and the recommissioning of three of the navy's largest ships.

In less than a month, he learned that Monroe's negotiations had failed, and he promptly labeled Canning's response as "unfriendly, proud, and harsh," offering little more than a disavowal of having ordered the attack on the *Chesapeake*. Moreover, Canning had flatly rejected any attempt to link impressment with reparations, then had added injury to insult by charging that the president's proclamation made the United States the aggressor. He also dispatched George Rose as special envoy to the United States to press the British view but doomed the mission to failure by issuing instructions that not only barred any discussion of impressment, but also demanded that Jefferson recall his presidential proclamation before negotiations could begin on reparations. As Madison observed, such conditions left "the insult offered in the attack on the American frigate . . . unexpiated."[1]

More bad news arrived in November and December. From Armstrong came word that France would apply Napoleon's Berlin Decree, which closed the Continent to British products, to the vessels of all nations.[2] Like the

---

1. Brant, IV, pp. 404–18, gives a full account of the Rose mission, showing the inflexibility of Canning's instructions. For TJ's comments on Canning, see Malone, V, p. 464.
2. Ships of the United States had been previously exempted; see Ch. 33, above.

English, the French would recognize no neutrals. "This a mortal blow to the American commerce," a merchant wrote, "and we fear will lead to a rupture between America and France."[3]

At the same time, the British press reliably reported "that our government had resolved to retaliate on France by a proclamation, exactly on the model of the French decree of blockade," settling once and for all "the clamors of the Americans respecting their right to trade with the British colonies."[4] From Pinkney (Monroe was on his way home) came the text of an October proclamation by George III for tightening the practice of impressment by "recalling and prohibiting British seamen from serving foreign Princes and States."[5] William Cobbett, the virulent "Porcupine" who had returned to England as a critic of the United States, translated the aggressive, unyielding Pittite policy of Canning into hard-nosed, journalistic language: "Our power upon the waves enables us to dictate the terms, upon which ships of all nations shall navigate. . . . Not a sail should be hoisted, except by stealth, without paying us a tribute."[6]

As the international situation deteriorated, Jefferson, Madison, and the cabinet deliberated in late November and acted in December.[7] On December 8, the president sent to Congress the Monroe-Canning correspondence chronicling the breakdown of the *Chesapeake* negotiations. Six days later, the twice-postponed Nonimportation Act of 1806 went into effect. And on December 18, 1807, Jefferson notified Congress of the king's proclamation on impressment and Napoleon's order authorizing seizure of American ships. He also sent a deceptively brief message announcing a bold new policy of economic retaliation. Utilizing Madison's draft, he recommended an embargo to protect the United States' "essential resources" of "our merchandise, our vessels and our seamen," which were threatened by "great and increasing danger . . . on the high seas and elsewhere from the belligerent powers of Europe."[8]

Congress took instant action, with the Senate passing the Embargo Act on the day it received the president's message and the House approving the

---

3. Brant, IV, p. 393.

4. *Ibid*. The official text of the British order-in-council of Nov. 11, 1807, did not arrive in Dec., but TJ knew its general content; see Bradford Perkins, *Prologue to War: England and the United States, 1805–1812* (Berkeley, 1963), p. 149.

5. Malone, V, p. 481.

6. Perkins, p. 187.

7. Malone, V, pp. 475–76, notes that "the extant records of the deliberations of the high executive officials regarding the international problems they faced in the critical month of December are scanty. Jefferson and Madison do not appear to have communicated with each other by letters or memoranda at this time or to have reduced their conversations to writing."

8. See JM's notes on TJ's draft of embargo message to Congress, [Dec. 17, 1807], below. For a discussion, see Brant, IV, pp. 394–95; Noble E. Cunningham, *In Pursuit of Reason: The Life of Thomas Jefferson* (Baton Rouge, 1987), pp. 311–12; Burton Spivak, *Jefferson's English Crisis: Commerce, Embargo, and the Republican Revolution* (Charlottesville, 1979), pp. 103–4; and Perkins, p. 153. For TJ's message to Congress, Dec. 18, 1807, see Richardson, I, p. 433. TJ recalled the use of JM's draft in his letter to JM, July 14, 1824, ch. 47, below.

legislation three days later. On December 22, Jefferson signed the measure that prohibited the departure of all American ships in the foreign trade. Although it did not bar imports in foreign vessels except for certain specified articles of British manufacture, it forbade foreign vessels in American ports from loading export cargo, forcing them to return home in ballast.

The imposition of economic sanctions was a drastic step whose consequences could not be foreseen, as Secretary of the Treasury Albert Gallatin observed in a prophetic warning: "Governmental prohibitions do always more mischief than had been calculated; and it is not without much hesitation that a statesman should hazard to regulate the concerns of individuals as if he could do it better than themselves."[9]

But Jefferson and Madison, the architects of the embargo, were convinced that the moment for hesitation had passed. The *Chesapeake* insult; the royal proclamation reaffirming Britain's right of impressment; the hanging of the seaman taken from the *Chesapeake;* France's enforcement of the Berlin Decree against American ships; the retaliatory British orders, which threatened to sweep American ships and sailors from the seas; and "the colonizing aspect of the British Orders"—all these made drastic action necessary.[10] Even so, Jefferson's cryptic message to Congress omitted any reference to the latest orders-in-council, which closed European ports to neutral carriers unless they cleared through British ports and paid a tax, a requirement that would have returned the United States to colonial status.[11] His first draft had described this British measure on the basis of confirmed reports and, linking it with the French decree, declared that "the whole world is thus laid under interdict by these two nations." Since the official text had not yet arrived, however, the cautious Madison persuaded the president to omit both his description of the British measure and his dramatic declaration against both British and French actions, leaving the administration with a popular program in terms of votes but without a clear public statement of justification for its draconic policy.[12]

Nor did the president ever inform the public of the administration's objectives in imposing the embargo. According to Merrill Peterson, "He betrayed his own principles of leadership, which underscored official openness and public trust, and contributed to the bewilderment and confusion surrounding the embargo."[13] In a series of articles attributed to Madison, however, the *National Intelligencer* argued that the embargo, while guarding the nation's essential resources, would "have the collateral effect of making it the

---

9. Albert Gallatin to TJ, Dec. 18, 1807, cited in Malone, V, p. 482.

10. For JM's observation on "the colonizing aspect of the British orders," see Ketcham, p. 459.

11. Henry Adams, *History of the United States of America during the Second Administration of Thomas Jefferson,* 9 vols. (New York, 1890), IV, p. 103, concluded: "In other words, American commerce was made English."

12. See TJ to JM, July 14, 1824, ch. 47, below. See also Spivak, pp. 103–4; Perkins, pp. 148–49; and Peterson, pp. 882–84.

13. *Ibid.,* p. 886.

interest of all nation's to change the system which has driven our commerce from the ocean." It was "a measure of peace and precaution," without "a shadow of a pretext to make it a cause of war." But its chief virtues were its rejection of "the insulting opinion in Europe that submission to wrongs of every sort" was preferable to nonintercourse and its affirmation of a new national character: "Let the example teach the world that our firmness equals our moderation; that having resorted to a measure just in itself, and adequate to its object, we will flinch from no sacrifices which the honor and good of the nation demand from virtuous and faithful citizens."[14]

But an article attributed to the secretary of state did not have the standing of a presidential proclamation as an explanation of administration policy. Was the embargo prudential and precautionary, a temporary defensive shield against foreign aggressions designed to gain time for preparedness measures and further negotiations? Or was it a long-range weapon of economic coercion against the aggressors that called for coercive enforcement at home in order to be totally effective abroad?

In the beginning, Jefferson stressed the defensive and temporary nature of the measure. "The great objects of the embargo," he told the governor of Virginia in March, "are keeping our ships and seamen out of harm's way."[15] "I take it to be an universal opinion," he had written Madison two days earlier, "that war will become preferable to a continuance of the embargo after a certain time. Should we not then avail ourselves of the intervening period to procure a retraction of the obnoxious decrees peaceably if possible?"

The president then suggested a new diplomatic initiative to be completed before Congress met in November 1808 and asked Madison "to instruct our ministers at Paris and London, by the next packet, to propose immediately to both those powers a declaration on both sides that these decrees and orders shall no longer be extended to vessels of the United States, in which case we shall remain faithfully neutral: but, without assuming the air of menace, to let them both percieve that if they do not withdraw these orders and decrees, there will arrive a time when our interests will render war preferable to a continuance of the embargo; that when that time arrives, if one has withdrawn and the other not, we must declare war against that other; if neither shall have withdrawn, we must take our choice of enemies between them."[16]

To prepare for this eventuality, Congress appropriated $4 million for eight new regiments, militia weapons, gunboats, and fortifications.[17] To plug loopholes in the embargo legislation, Congress passed supplementary acts applicable to coasting craft as well as oceangoing vessels, then extended the law

14. Brant, IV, pp. 402–3.
15. TJ to William Cabell, Mar. 13, 1808, in Spivak, p. 105.
16. TJ to JM, Mar. 11, 1808, below.
17. Marshall Smelser, *The Democratic Republic, 1801–1815* (New York, 1968), p. 165. See also H. N. Muller, "Smuggling into Canada: How the Champlain Valley Defied Jefferson's Embargo," *Vermont History* 38 (1970): 5–21.

to prohibit exports by land and inland waterways as well as by sea. Massachusetts, which included Maine, and the Lake Champlain frontier with Canada became critical areas for leaks in the embargo system, and the president finally proclaimed the Lake Champlain region in a state of insurrection. Ultimately, the Treasury Department, which administered the embargo system, was authorized to search and detain vessels suspected of fraudulent trading or the intention of violating the embargo.[18]

But the most important action came in April 1808, when Congress authorized the president to remove the embargo against one or both belligerents if his requirements were met during the congressional recess.[19] During the summer and fall, the embargo became such an obsession with Jefferson that he viewed it less as a temporary and prudential measure and more as a system of economic coercion. A program of permits allowed anyone with property abroad at the time the embargo was enacted to send a ship to fetch it home. Another law allowed the president to authorize governors of states where flour supplies were low to issue import licenses to states where there were surpluses. After allowing nearly 600 vessels to sail to foreign ports on authorized missions and then learning that many violated their permits, Jefferson ended the system.[20]

New England Federalists, constant critics of the embargo from the beginning, belittled the measure, arguing that it was comparable to "cutting one's throat to cure the nosebleed." Scrambling the letters in the word "embargo," they came up with anagrams such as "go-bar-em," "o-grab-me," and (best of all) "mob-rage," which, they claimed, had become the result of a measure that destroyed the trade it allegedly protected. To make this point, one New Hampshire Federalist composed an ode to the president and the president's favorite legislation:

> Our ships all in motion,
> Once whiten'd the ocean
>   They sail'd and return'd with a Cargo;
> Now doom'd to decay
>   They are fallen a prey,
> To Jefferson, worms, and EMBARGO.[21]

As other violations increased, more stringent methods of enforcement were initiated, especially in Federalist New England, where smuggling flourished. Madison suggested "that gun boats and other naval precautions should without the loss of a moment be displayed in the suspicious situations along the New England Coast. . . . I do not see why all our naval force other than

---

18. Smelser, pp. 165–69.

19. JM called this the most important action of the session; see Spivak, p. 119.

20. Malone, V, pp. 561–621, traces "the grievous task of enforcement." For references to the permit system, see TJ to JM, June 3, 1808, below, July 29, 1808, below, Aug. 9, 1808, below, and Aug. 12, 1808, below; and JM to TJ, Aug. 3, 1808, below, and Aug. 10, 1808, below.

21. Thomas A. Bailey, *A Diplomatic History of the American People* (New York, 1969), p. 126.

gunboats, actually equipped, might not patrol the coast suspected to be in collusion with British smugglers."[22] In exercising his role as czar over the nation's economy, Jefferson, with Madison's enthusiastic backing, played an unlikely role, as Dumas Malone has observed, one that made him appear "to be unmindful of republican theory and also of certain basic facts of human nature."[23]

Just as he became obsessed with the embargo during his final year as president, so, too, did Jefferson remain infatuated with Florida. When he learned that Pinkney was to confer with Canning on the cluster of current issues—the *Chesapeake* affair, impressments, and the orders-in-council—he optimistically linked a settlement with England with renewed pressure on Spain. "Should the conference . . . settle friendship between England and us," he told Madison, "and Bonaparte continue at war with Spain, a moment may occur favorable, without compromitting us with either France or England, for seizing our own from the Rio Bravo to Perdido as of right, and the residue of Florida as a reprisal for spoliations." Accordingly, he directed the secretary of war and the secretary of the navy to station "the new southern recruits and gunboats, so that we may strike in a moment when Congress says so."[24]

Madison was much more pessimistic about the outcome of any Pinkney-Canning conference. "I am the less inclined to hope much from it," he told the president. The failure of the Rose mission had made "little impression" in London since the papers there had passed "over the whole subject with little further notice." Moreover, the revolt in Spain against French dominance "will have had the usual effect on such a Cabinet, of raising its tone." Just when the embargo was being felt in Britain, the Spanish revolt had opened up a new market there to replace the American market. "Considering the narrow and selfish policy of the present Cabinet," the secretary of state concluded, "it is possible that it may be tempted to continue its orders[-in-council], lest a removal of our Embargo should interfere with her in the new commercial prospect. But I suspect," he added, referring to the coming presidential election, "that she is still more swayed by the hope of producing a revolution in the pub[lic] councils here, which might be followed by a coalition with her in the war" against France.[25]

Nonetheless, Jefferson remained more optimistic of Pinkney's negotiations than did Madison, although the president moderated his view to include three options. "If they repeal their orders," he wrote after reading a letter from the American minister, "we must repeal our embargo. If they make satisfaction

---

22. JM to TJ, Aug. 10, 1808, below.

23. Malone, V, p. 591. For differing views of the administration of the embargo, see Leonard D. White, *The Jeffersonians: A Study in Administrative History, 1801–1829* (New York, 1951), pp. 423–73, and Leonard W. Levy, *Jefferson and Civil Liberties: The Darker Side* (Cambridge, Mass., 1963), pp. 93–141.

24. TJ to JM, Aug. 12, 1808, below.

25. JM to TJ, Aug. 14, 1808, below, and Aug. 17, 1808, below.

for the Chesapeake, we must revoke our proclamation, and generalize its operation by a law. If they keep up impressments, we must adhere to nonintercourse, manufactures and a navigation act."²⁶

During the summer, however, Napoleon's policy confirmed Madison in his pessimistic view. In July, the secretary of state learned of the Bayonne Decree, Bonaparte's gratuitous announcement that he would help enforce the Embargo Act by capturing American vessels on the high seas or in European ports. Since they were supposed to be locked up in their home ports, American ships would be presumed to be British vessels sailing under false colors. An outraged Madison condemned the measure as "a sweeping stroke at all American vessels on the high seas."²⁷

Writing to the president later that summer, Madison confessed that the "difficulty springing from the French Decrees" had persuaded him that "we must therefore look to England alone for the chances of disembarrassment; and look with the greater solicitude, as it seems probable that nothing but some striking proof of the success of the Embargo, can arrest the successful perversion of it, by its enemies, or," he added, switching from the foreign to the domestic scene, "rather the enemies of their Country," the Federalist critics of strict enforcement. "Among the artifices used," he lamented, "the petitions from N. England have probably had a great effect; being so managed as to have received [?] critical circulation, before the answers to them could reach the public." That meant that they had imposed on "superficial minds" a belief that keeping ships "out of the way of plunder and insult" amounted to a "sacrifice of independence," even though the critics urged compliance with British regulations, thus "submitting to be insulted, and paying a tribute to encourage the practice."²⁸

As the fall congressional session approached, Jefferson's optimism faded, and his commitment to the embargo increased. "A letter from Mr. Pinkney," he wrote his son-in-law, "expresses a hope that the British government will repeal their orders on his engagement that we will repeal our embargo. He *infers* this from a conversation with Pinkney [Canning?], but I have little faith in diplomatic *inferences,* and less in Canning's good faith."²⁹ On the same day, he blasted Canning in a note to Madison, claiming that it would be difficult "to find a proper persifflage in return for the haughty stile of his government."³⁰ Faced with an unyielding Britain, taunted by the Bayonne Decree, stung by the continuing criticism—even disloyalty—of the New England Federalists, Jefferson held ever more tightly to the embargo as the ultimate

---

26. TJ to JM, Sept. 6, 1808, below.

27. JM to John Armstrong, July 22, 1808, cited in Malone, V, p. 601. See also JM to TJ, July 29, 1808, below.

28. JM to TJ, Sept. 14, 1808, below.

29. TJ to John Wayles Eppes, Sept. 20, 1808, cited in Spivak, p. 128.

30. TJ to JM, Sept. 20, 1808, below.

weapon of economic coercion and decided to pursue his policy well beyond his original time limit of November 1808.

During the summer, Jefferson and Madison made one other effort to protect neutral rights. But just as Jefferson had not explained to the public his rationale for the embargo system, neither did he explain to Congress his secret diplomatic mission to Russia, a well-intentioned attempt to enlist Czar Alexander's support for the rights of neutral nations when both England and France were attacking them. In his letter of credence to the czar, Jefferson stated that the purpose of the mission was to assure Alexander "of the sincere friendship of the United States, . . . to explain to your Majesty the position of the United States, and the considerations flowing from that which should keep them aloof from the contests of Europe, to assure your Majesty of their desire to observe a faithful and impartial neutrality, if not forced from that line by the wrongs of the belligerents, and to express their reliance that they will be befriended in these endeavors by your Majesty's powerful influence and friendship towards these States."

The president and the secretary of state agreed that the secrecy of the mission was essential and that the chosen emissary, William Short, who had been Jefferson's secretary while Jefferson was in Paris twenty years earlier, should sail "while the Senate is not sitting, in order that it may be kept secret."[31] Short sailed in September, but Jefferson did not notify the Senate until February 1809, on the eve of his departure from the presidency. In a surprising slap at the lame-duck magistrate, the Senate unanimously rejected the nomination as an unnecessary extension of the diplomatic service.[32]

THE LETTERS

Jefferson to Madison

[Washington] Oct. 21, 1807

TH. J. TO MR MADISON

I send you a letter from the Ex-basha of Tripoli. Had we not better be done with this man by giving him a plain answer stating the truth and sending him the extracts from our instructions, by which he will see that if our agent engaged any thing beyond that he went beyond his powers, and could not bind us. Nothing short of this can clear us of his sollicitations.[1] We might go

---

31. TJ to JM, July 29, 1808, below, and JM to TJ, July 31, 1808, below.

32. For references to Short's mission, see TJ to JM, Sept. 6, 1808, below, and JM to TJ, Aug. 17, 1808, below, Sept. 7, 1808, below, Sept. 14, 1808, below, and Sept. 26, 1808, below. For a succinct discussion, see Malone, V, pp. 661–64.

1. In Apr. 1806, the Senate had ratified a treaty that Tobias Lear had negotiated with Tripoli for the release of American prisoners. The Senate did not know of a secret agreement that allowed the bashaw four years to implement a provision promising that he would release the wife and children

further and promise to use all friendly means with his brother to procure the delivery of such of his family as chose to go with him; and also to transport him and them to any port in the Mediterranean he would wish to be placed in. Affectte. salutations

Madison to Jefferson

[Washington Nov. 10, 1807]

There appears only in a journalized acct. of the transaction [by Mr. Lear] a passage under date of June 3. intimating that he sd. be disposed to give time rather than suffer the business [of the negotiation] to be broken off—and our countrymen left in slavery—with a preceeding intimation that he had consented to the condition, of allowing time for the delivery of the family of the Ex Bashaw. This consent however not appearing in the article of public Treaty on that subject, Mr. Davis was directed to insist on its execution. An extract etc.; unless indeed he should have in considering unguardedly relied on the above information that he had been led by a humane regard to our Citizens in captivity to consent to a suspension of the sd. delivery of the Ex. B's family, as sufficient notice of a mutual understanding that the delivery was not immediately demandable under the Treaty.[2]

The date of Lear's letter of July 5. and the minute acct. of the Treaty the sole and professed subject of it, make it impossible that he could have omitted the notice of his declaration there, and have communicated [it] in any other letter; especially as there appears no chain in his correspondence. Will it not be better then not to presume a miscarriage, particularly in such strong terms. I am persuaded that the importance of the communication was lost in the magnitude of the general objects as viewed by Lear, and that he did no more than what appears in his Journal

In place of what is between [ ] something like the following is suggested

"How it has happened that the Declaration of June 5, has never before come to our knowledge, can not with certainty be said. But whether there has been a miscarriage of it, on the way, or a failure of the ordinary attention and correctness of that Functionary in making his communications I have thought it due to the Senate etc.

---

of his elder brother, whom he had ousted, if the ex-bashaw ceased his efforts to supplant the reigning bashaw; see Ray Brighton, *The Checkered Career of Tobias Lear* (Portsmouth, N.H., 1985), p. 256.

2. JM labeled this document "Notes for the Tripoline treaty." When the new consul (Davis) arrived in Tripoli in May 1807, he learned that Lear had made a secret agreement with the bashaw. TJ informed the Senate of the secret provision on Nov. 11, 1807, utilizing phraseology from the beginning and end of this memorandum. See Richardson, I, pp. 430-31; Malone, V, pp. 40-43; and Brighton, p. 256.

Jefferson to Madison

[Washington] Dec. 6, 1807

TH: J. TO MR MADISON.

I return you the papers on Clarke's claim, which indeed I have not considered with all the attention which should be done were this an ultimate decision, but my first impression is that the claim ought to be rejected.

It is clearly a claim for money, not for land.

The Commrs. of N. Y. were constituted a special court of justice to distribute the 30,000 D. of Vermont according to right, and they have determined against Clarke, which must be presumed right. To ground a right of applying to the government, their decision should be shewn to be palpably unjust.

This claim for mere money has laid 18 years since he came of age. All witnesses are probably dead, and so little now known or capable of being discovered as to his right, that it is barred by time.

If he has any claim, Great Britain is liable for it by treaty.

But the case merits the careful consideration of the Atty. Gen. and an opinion in form to be handed to Mr Erskine. Affectionate salutations.

Jefferson to Madison

[Washington Dec. 17, 1807]

[Draft of Embargo Message to Congress]

Although the decree of the French govnt. of Nov. 21 [Nov. 11] comprehended in its liberal terms the commerce of the US, yet the prompt explanation by one of the Ministers of that government that it was not so understood and that our treaty would be respected, the practice which had a place in the French ports conformably with that explanation and the recent interference of that government to procure in Spain a similar construction of a similar decree there had given well founded expectation that it would not be extended to it and this was much strengthened by the consideration of their obvious interests. But this information from our minister at Paris now communicated to Congress is that it is determined to extend the effect of that decree to us and the other neutrals [?] and it is probable that Spain and the other Atlantic and Mediterranean states of Europe will cooperate in the same measures.

The British regulations had before reduced us to a direct voyage to a single port of their enemies and it is now believed that they will interdict all commerce whatever with them. A proclamation too of that government of [date] (not officially indeed communicated to us, yet so given out to the public as to become a rule of action with them) seems to have shut the door on all negociation with us, except as to the single aggression on the Chesapeak.

The sum of these mutual enterprises on our national rights is that France and her allies, reserving for further considern the prohibiting our carrying any thing to the British territories, have virtually done it by prohibiting our bringing a return cargo from them: and Gr Britain after prohibiting a great proportion of our commerce with France and her allies, is now believed to have prohibited the whole. The whole world is thus laid under interdict by these two nations, and our vessels, their cargoes and crews are to be taken by the one or the other, for whatever place they may be destined, out of our own limits.

If therefore on leaving our harbors we are certain to lose them, is it not better, as to vessels cargoes and seamen, to keep them at home? This is submitted to the wisdom of Congress who alone are competent to provide a remedy.

Madison to Jefferson

[Washington Dec. 17, 1807]³

[Notes on Jefferson's Draft of Embargo Message to Congress]

The communications now made shewing the great and increasing danger with which our merchandise, our vessels and our seamen are threatened on the high seas and elsewhere from the belligerent powers of Europe, and it being of the greatest importance to keep in safety these essential resources, I deem it my duty to recommend the subject to the consideration of Congress, who will doubtless perceive all the advantage which may be expected from an immediate inhibition of the departure of our vessels from the ports of the U. States.

Their wisdom will also see the necessity of making every preparation for whatever events may grow out of the present crisis.

Madison to Jefferson

Washington Jan. 7, 1808

The Secretary of State, in compliance with the note of the President, relating to the public property at New Orleans, as reported by Governor Claiborne to the Secretary of the Treasury, begs leave to state that no part of that property appears to fall in any respect under the purview of the Department of State, unless it be the Government House, and the lot on which it stands. This, it is inferred from the representation given by Governor Claiborne, might be disposed of for a greater sum than would provide accommodations

---

3. On Dec. 17, 1807, TJ substituted JM's first paragraph for his earlier draft and added the second paragraph, sending it to Congress on Dec. 18; see Richardson, I, p. 433, and Brant, IV, pp. 394–95. TJ also asked JM to return "the letters of Messrs. Armstrong and Champagny which it would be improper to make public."

for the Governor of the Orleans territory, in a part of the city more eligible for his residence. It would require however further knowledge of the local circumstances, to enable the Secretary of State, to judge of the expediency of such a proceeding. And it is presumable, from the character given of the lot in question, that delay will not be attended with less advance in its value than will be incident to the spot which might be substituted; so that the proposed sale and substitution may probably at any time be carried into effect, without loss to the public.

Jefferson to Madison

[Washington] Jan. 8, 1808

TH. J. TO MR. MADISON

The inclosed act of Michigan, tho' dated Jan. 30. 07. did not get here till the last Congress had risen. It seems merely occasional, and the occasion passed over. I think therefore it is not worth communicating singly to Congress. Perhaps they will send their collection to be communicated, which will embrace this. In the mean time this may be filed in your office.

Madison to Jefferson

Washington Feb. 25, 1808

DEAR SIR

I think the grounds of a message communicating Pinkney's and Armstrong's letters should be those of aiding Congs. in appreciating our foreign relations, and in judging of the influence these ought to have on their measures of precaution.[4] The Private letter of P. would perhaps have some good effects; but besides the objection to taking such a liberty with it, the communication might be ascribed to an undue anxiety to make certain impressions, and in that view have counter effects more than equivalent. Yrs. most respectfully

JAMES MADISON

Armstrong's letter is in the hands of General Dearborn.

Jefferson to Madison

[Washington] Mar. 11, 1808

TH. J. TO MR MADISON

I suppose we must dispatch another packet, by the 1st of Apr. at farthest. I take it to be an universal opinion that war will become preferable to a continuance of the embargo after a certain time. Should we not then avail ourselves

---

4. TJ sent the letters to Congress on Feb. 26, 1808; see Richardson, I, pp. 441–42.

of the intervening period to procure a retraction of the obnoxious decrees peaceably if possible? An opening is given us by both parties sufficient to form a basis for such a proposition. I wish you to consider therefore the following course of proceeding, to wit

To instruct our ministers at Paris and London, by the next packet, to propose immediately to both those powers a declaration on both sides that these decrees and orders shall no longer be extended to vessels of the United States, in which case we shall remain faithfully neutral: but, without assuming the air of menace, to let them both percieve that if they do not withdraw these orders and decrees, there will arrive a time when our interests will render war preferable to a continuance of the embargo; that when that time arrives, if one has withdrawn and the other not, we must declare war against that other; if neither shall have withdrawn, we must take our choice of enemies between them. This it will certainly be our duty to have ascertained by the time Congress shall meet in the fall or beginning of winter, so that, taking off the embargo, they may decide whether war must be declared and against whom. Affectionate salutations.

Madison to Jefferson

[Washington Mar. 15, 1808]

It appears that Skipwith did not communicate the Milan Decree;[5] nor is it otherwise authenticated to us than in the Madrid Gazette and the reference in the Spanish decree.

It can not be said, that all ports are forbidden to neutrals except their own. The British decrees permit a trade with Enemy colonies, not forbidden by the mother Countries. The ports of neutrals are also open to each other, as from the U. S to China and some other ports of Asia and Africa.

Madison to Jefferson

[Washington Mar. 24, 1808][6]

incapable of giving a valid consent to their alienation[;] in others belong to persons who may refuse altogether to alienate, or demand a compensation

---

5. Napoleon issued the Milan Decree on Dec. 17, 1807.

6. JM did not date his memorandum, but TJ's endorsement gives the date and place. JM labeled this document "Notes for the message on sites for defenses of rivers and harbors." TJ incorporated this text almost verbatim in his message to Congress on Mar. 25, 1808 (Richardson, I, p. 447), prefacing it with the following observation: "In proceeding to carry into execution the act for fortifying our forts and harbors it is found that the sites most advantageous for their defense . . . are in some cases the property of minors."

far beyond the liberal justice allowable in such cases. From these causes the defence of our seaboard, so necessary to be pressed during the present season, will in various parts be defeated, unless a remedy can be applied. With a view to this I submit the case to the consideration of Congress, who estimating its importance and reviewing the powers vested in them by the Constitution combined with the amendment providing that private property shall not be taken for public use, without just compensation, will decide on the course most proper to be pursued.

I am aware etc.

(for consideration) As the constitutionality will be much agitated, it is doubted whether a precise opinion on that or the legal process be eligible[7]

Madison to Jefferson

Washington Apr. 1, 1808

The Secretary of State has the honor to report to the President, in conformity to the resolution of the House of Representatives, of the thirtieth of March, that the only information which has been received respecting the letter from which the extract inserted in General Armstrong's letter to the Secretary of State, of January the twenty-second, one thousand eight hundred and eight, was taken, is in the extract itself, to which no date is given; and that no copy of any letter from the French Ministry to him is subjoined to, or known to be referred to, in his said letter of January twenty-second, except that a copy of which was communicated to Congress by the President on the twenty-ninth of March, and which bears date the fifteenth January, one thousand eight hundred and eight. It does not appear from any information received by the Department of State at what date either this letter of January fifteenth, or the letter from which the inserted extract was taken, were received by the Minister of the United States at Paris. Respectfully submitted,

JAMES MADISON.

Jefferson to Madison

[Washington] Apr. 23, 1808

Notes on the British claims in the Mississippi territory.

1803. Mar. 3. act of Congress gave to Mar. 31, 1804. to exhibit their claims or grants.

---

7. For TJ's proposed resolution of constitutional issues involving federal-state relations in locating forts, see Brant, IV, pp. 394–95. For a discussion of the fortification of harbor defenses in 1808, see Richard A. Erney, *The Public Life of Henry Dearborn* (New York, 1979), pp. 216–24.

Embargo: 1807–1808

1804. Mar. 27 ditto gave to Nov. 30, 1804. and allowed transcripts instead of originals, etc.

1805. Mar. 2. ditto gave to Dec. 1, 1805. to file their grants. And in fact to Jan. 1, 1807. time when the sale might begin.

1807. Dec. 15. the British claimants memorialize again.

On no one of the acts did the British claimant take any step towards specifying his claim or it's location, but remained inactive till the time was expired and then remonstrated to his government that we had not given them time sufficient. And on the last of 1805. instead of having come forward with his claims, ready to avail himself of the 3d. term which was then to be asked, and which was granted nominally to Dec. 1, 1805. but in effect to Jan. 1, 1807. he stays at home inactive, and on the 15th. of Dec., 1807. again gives in a memorial that we have not given time enough, but still takes no step to inform us what and where his claim is.

Although these titles may have been confirmed by treaty, yet they could not thereby be intended to be withdrawn from the jurisdiction or conditions on which lands are held even by citizens. It is evident that these claimants are speculators whose object is to make what profit they can out of the patronage of their government, but to make no sacrifice of themselves either of money or trouble. They are entitled therefore, to no further notice from either government. However, Mr. Erskine may be informed *verbally*,[8] that as the day of commencing sales of lands there is now put off to Jan. 1. 1809. if any of these claimants will before that day file their claim, with its *precise location,* the executive is authorized to suspend the sale of any particular parcels, and will as to that, till the proper authority can decide on the title. but that the settlement of that country in general is too pressing, to be delayed one day by claims under the circumstances of these.

Jefferson to Madison

Washington Apr. 30, 1808

Notes on such parts of Foronda's letter of Apr. 26, 1808. as are worth answering

I. I know of no recent orders to Governor Claiborne as to the navigation of the Mississippi, Uberville and Pontchartrain. He should specify them, but he may be told that no order has ever been given contrary to the rights of Spain. These rights are 1. a treaty right that the ships of Spain coming directly from Spain or her colonies, loaded only *with the produce* or manufactures of Spain or her colonies, shall be admitted during the space of 12. years in the

---

8. TJ's italics here and below.

ports of N. Orleans, and in all other legal ports of entry within the ceded territory, in the same manner as the ships of the United States, etc.' 2. A right of innocent passage from the mouth of the Mississippi to 31° of Lat. exactly commensurate with our right of innocent passage up the rivers of Florida to 31° of latitude.

II. In answer to his question whether we consider Mobile among the ports of the United States, he may be told that so long as we consider the question whether the Perdido is not the Eastern boundary of Louisiana as continuing in a train of amicable proceedings for adjustment, so long that part only of the river Mobile which is above 31° of Lat. will be considered among the ports of the U. S., withholding the exercise of jurisdiction on our part within the disputed territory, on the general principle of letting things remain *in statu quo pendente lite.*

There is nothing else in his letter worth answering.

Madison to Jefferson

Capt. Winston's [Va.] May 11, 1808

DEAR SIR

Shortly after you set out from Washington, I was called on by Mr. E. Livingston, and requested to be the channel of a representation to the Executive on the subject of the Batture. Without adverting to the nature of the question involved, which connects it rather with the Dept. of Treasury than of State, I did not refuse the request; and recd. from him afterwards the letter and documents herewith inclosed, to be forwarded to you. I had an oppy. however of letting him know that the communication ought to have been made thro' Mr. Gallatin, and that I presumed it wd. be thro' him that the result of his supplication would be learned. He put into my hands also the newspaper containing his appeal to the public some time ago, which I believe we both saw soon after its appearance.[9]

I have not had time to do more than skim over his printed argument. I observe he labors more to establish the identity of the French with the Roman and Spanish law, than to shew that the proceeding on which his title depends, was under the Spanish, not the French law. At the time this took place France retained the possession, after having executed a Treaty of alienation. If France had a right to do what was done, it would seem that the French not the Spanish law, wd. be the rule in that as in all other transactions during the inteval of nondelivery of the ceded country: If the proceeding was not of right,

---

9. For Edward Livingston's claim to the batture, the beach between low and high water near New Orleans, see William B. Hatcher, *Edward Livingston: Jeffersonian Republican and Jacksonian Democrat* (Baton Rouge, 1940), pp. 139–89; Malone, VI, pp. 55–73; and Edward Dumbauld, *Thomas Jefferson and the Law* (Norman, Okla., 1978), pp. 36–74. For TJ's message to Congress, see Richardson, I, pp. 442–43; for his detailed account, see L. and B., XVIII, pp. 1–132.

the title derived from it must be a nullity also; unless made good by some subsequent sanction under the Spanish authority. To consider France as the Trustee of Spain, would make the Spanish code her guide, and viciate all proceedings under the French code. To consider France as the sovereign de facto, not de jure, wd. make the French law equally the law de facto, tho' not de jure, and exclude the Spanish law as the criterion in the case. Unless therefore the French law of alluvion be in reality the same with that of Spain, the title of Mr. E. will depend on the course of things relating to it, after the possessory transfer to Spain. These are very hasty ideas, and wd. not be hazarded without a knowledge that if incorrect they will be superseded by your better view of the subject.

I arrived here on monday morning, having been stopped on sunday night by the high waters of the North river; which I passed in a boat a little above Norman's ford, the morning after. I left Washington on saturday abt. 10 OC. the wind so high that I was obliged to go up to the Bridges. This prevented my getting farther than Elluots Mills. The next day notwithstanding occasional obstructions in the road, I should have reached this, but for the impassable state of Normans ford. At present I continue rain-bound, and how I am to cross the Waters before me I know not. I see no certainty but in pulling down to G man, where there is a good boat; but it will add 14 or 15 miles to the distance. Yrs. with constant attachment and the highest respect

JAMES MADISON

Madison to Jefferson

Orange May 15, 1808

DEAR SIR

I got home on friday night, by taking my carriage to pieces and making three trips with it over Porter's mill pond in something like a boat, and swimming my horses. I found the roads over the flat lands much better than I had hoped. Having been once dry and smoothed, the rains did not penetrate and left them very passable even where slightly covered with water. I was glad to learn that you had been not more detained on the way. A person who resides near Barretts Ford told me that you crossed it at the only moment that admitted it; the river having risen immediately after.

I send letters from Armstrong, Pinkney and Harris; with others of minor consequence. I have noted the proposed answer to that of Turreau. Smith and B.[10] I suppose may be told that as Dispatches for the Mediterranean will find a conveyance in the vessel for Algiers their request cd. not be complied with, without a mala fide request of passports from the foreign Ministers, and a

---

10. Smith and Buchanan was the Baltimore commercial firm of Senator Samuel Smith; see John S. Pancake, *Samuel Smith and the Politics of Business, 1750–1839* (University, Ala., 1972), pp. 37–38, 93–94.

special favor, having the appearance of partiality to individuals. As the trade to St. Domingo has been contrary to law, property lying there must be presumed to be an evidence of transgression in the owner. This consideration supplies an answer to Louis. Yrs. most affectly and respectfully

JAMES MADISON

The undecyphered letter from it. was probably misaddressed to the Secretary of State. No such cypher is in the office, and must be one connected with another correspondent.

Madison to Jefferson

[Orange May 16, 1808]

DEAR SIR
Finding on my return from a little ride, that the post was here without my having recd a key to the mail, I thought it best to have a link of the chain taken off, rather than take the alternative. It means the mail goes open, but I am enabled to send the letters addressed to me for your perusal. There are letters from Erving but old and not worth forwarding. In fact I take all of them to be duplicates. The rider having been much delayed, I do not detain him a moment longer than necessary. Yrs. as always

JAMES MADISON

Monday 3 OC

Jefferson to Madison

Monticello May 17, 1808

DEAR SIR
Your favors of the 11. 15. and 16. came to hand last night. The request of Turreau to be allowed a vessel to carry home another cargo of French citizens is admissible according to our former practice, only observing that the size of the vessel be proportioned to the number of passengers. I think also that Michaux, the botanist, may be allowed to go in our vessel, on the known usage of civilized nations to consider scientific voyagers as belonging to every country, and under the protection of every one. The characters of Bronatd [?] and Doury justify the Executive in instituting a prosecution against Mecklen by the District attorney, but the pretension to any *sacredness* of character should be repelled. It appears to me that the passage of Rademaker's secretary with Hill may be advantageous to us, and therefore quite admissible. Would it not be well, by way of answer to Lewis to call on him for a declaration of the property he has in St. Domingo, in whose hands, how it came there etc. supported by vouchers. This is required in all cases before a vessel is allowed. We cannot with good faith comply with the request of Smith and Buchanan.

Govr. Hislop's application is inadmissible in point of precedent, and because of the flagrant violations of the same laws by and for the same nation. He has let the object of his assiduities appear by asking to be the bearer of dispatches etc. All his letters prove him an intriguant. Yet I believe most of his facts, and particularly what he says of the Clintons. The old man is unquestionably hostile in his heart and it is the doings of that family, and not the embargo that has affected the elections in New York. I salute you with constant and great affection.

Th Jefferson

P.S. I retain till another post Pinckney's Armstrong's Livingston's and Mr Gallatin's letters. All the other papers are returned.

Jefferson to Madison

Monticello May 19, 1808

Dear Sir,

I now return you the papers reserved from the last post. Our regular answer to Mr. Livingston may well be that the Attorney General having given an official opinion that the right to the batture is in the United States, and the matter being now referred to Congress, it is our duty to keep the grounds clear of any adversary possession, until the legislature shall decide on it.[11] I have carefully read Mr. Livingston's printed memoir. He has shaken my opinion as to the line within the road having been intended as a line of *boundary,* instead of its being a line of *admeasurement* only. But he establishes another fact by the testimony of Trudeau very fatal to his claim, to wit that the high water mark, *batture, ou viennent battre les eaux lorsqu elles sont dans leurs plus grandes croissances,* is the universal boundary of private grants on the river.

Your observations on his allegations that Gravier's grant must be under the Spanish law, because after the cession of the province by France to Spain, though before delivery of possession, are conclusive. To which may be added that Louis XIV having established the Constumes de Paris as the law of Louisiana, this was not changed by the mere act of transfer; on the contrary, the Laws of France continued and continues to be the law of the land except where specially altered by some subsequent edict of Spain or act of Congress. He has not in the least shaken the doctrine that the bed of the river, and all the atterrissements or banks which arise on it by the depositions of the river, are the property of the King by a peculiarity in the law of France, so that nothing quoted from those of Spain or the Roman law is of authority on that point. Affectionate salutations.

Th. Jefferson

11. After Attorney General Caesar A. Rodney ruled that the batture was the property of the United States, JM sent instructions that trespassers should be ejected. When the president learned that these orders had been executed, he referred the question to Congress; see Malone, VI, pp. 57–58.

Jefferson to Madison

Monticello May 24, 1808

Dear Sir

Of the papers I recieved from you yesterday I sent Mr Graham's letter (in favor of R. Brent as paymaster) to Genl. Dearborne, and that of the Loune's to Mr Gallatin for information. All the rest are now returned. On some of them I will make short observations merely for your consideration and determination.

Rademaker's and Hills. I really think the good which may result from permitting Rademaker's clerk to go in our vessel greatly overweighs the evil of the risk of capture on that account. But I am sorry to see Hill postponing his departure. It is the less reasonable as he means to return for his family. Dr. Rush's application in favr. of Doctr. Clarke, can only be viewed as a proof of friendship, the measure proposed cannot be. Sr. J. Jay's. Do we not stand too much engaged for the Connecticut vessel to change on slight grounds.

Erving and Cevallos. What has been already said on the subject of Casa Calvo, Yrujo, Miranda is sufficient, and that these should be seriously brought up again argues extreme weakness in Cevallos, or a plan to keep things unsettled with us. But I think it would not be amiss to take him down from his high airs as to the right of the sovereign to hinder the upper inhabitants from the use of the Mobile, by observing, 1. that we claim to be the sovereign, although we give time for discussion. But 2. that the upper inhabitants of a navigable water have always a right of *innocent passage* along it. I think Cevallos will not probably be the minister when the letter arrives at Madrid, and that an eye to that circumstance may perhaps have some proper influence on the style of the letter, in which, if meant for himself, his hyperbolic airs might merit less respect. I think too that the truth as to Pike's mission might be so simply stated as to need no argument to show that (even during the suspension of our claims to the Eastern border of the Rio Norte) his getting on it was mere error, which ought to have called for the setting him right, instead of forcing him through the interior country.

Sullivan's letter. His view of things for some time past has been entirely distempered.

Cathcart's, Ridgeley's, Navoni's, Degen's, Appleton's, Lee's, and Baker's letters are all returned. I salute you with great affection and respect.

Th Jefferson

Jefferson to Madison

Monticello May 27, 1808

Dear Sir

I suppose the object of the inclosed information was to obtain a pardon; but as Judge Potter's means of information respecting the opinion of the

Supreme court in a like case may be imperfect, I think it would be best that the Attorney General should inquire into the case, and say whether a pardon ought to go on the ground of the illegality of the judgment.

I propose to leave this for Washington from the 6th. to the 8th. of June, and therefore shall direct the express rider, when he arrives on Monday not to come thus far again, and to take your orders as to his continuing to ride to Montpelier. I salute you with constant affection and respect.

TH JEFFERSON

Jefferson to Madison

Monticello May 31, 1808

DEAR SIR,

I return you all the papers received from you by yesterday's mail, except Mr. Burnley's, which I shall send to the Secretary at war. Although all the appointments below field-officers are made, it is possible some may decline, and open a way for new competition. I have observed that Turreau's letters have for some time past changed their style unfavorably. I believe this is the first occasion he has had to complain of French deserters being enlisted by us, and if so, the tone of his application is improper. The answer to him however is obvious as to our laws and instructions and the *discharge* not *delivery* of the men, for which purpose I presume you will write a line to the Secretary at war. Woodward's scruples are perplexing. And they are unfounded because, on his own principle, if a law requires an oath to be administered, and does not say by whom, he admits it may be by any judges. If therefore it names a person no longer in existence, it is as if it named nobody.[12] On this construction all the territories have practised, and all the authorities of the national government, even the legislature. It was wrong on a second ground; no judge ever refusing to administer an oath in any useful case, although he may not consider it as strictly judicial. If it may be valid or useful, he administers *ut valeat quantum valer potest.* But what is to be done? Would it not be well for you to send the case to the Attorney General, and get him to enclose his opinion to Governor Hull, who will use it with Judge Witherall, or some territorial judge or justice?[13]

With the quarrel of Judge Vandeberg and his bar we cannot intermeddle.[14] Mercer's querulous letter is an unreasonable one. How could his offer of

12. For Judge Augustus Woodward's refusal to administer the oath of office to William Hull, whom TJ had reappointed as governor of Michigan Territory in 1808, see Alec R. Gilpin, *The Territory of Michigan, 1805–1837* (East Lansing, 1970), pp. 29–30.
13. Hull was sworn in by Judge George McDougall of the district court; see *ibid.*
14. For Judge Henry Vanderburgh, see F. Clever Bald, *Detroit's First American Decade, 1796 to 1805* (Ann Arbor, 1948), pp. 222, 232.

service be acted on but by putting it in the hands of those who were to act on all others?

I shall to-day direct the Post-rider not to continue his route to this place after to-day, and to take your orders as to the time you would wish him to continue coming to you. I salute you with affectionate esteem and respect.

Madison to Jefferson

[Orange] May 31, 1808

DEAR SIR

I have just recd. by the Bearer, the inclosed letter. As I understand that the writer Mr. V[owles] and Mr. Dunbar, are both of them acquainted with the established course, in such cases, I fulfill their expectations as well as keep within the rule of propriety, in merely saying that I believe both to be men of respectable characters; and consequently not excluded from the ordinary indulgence grantable under general regulations. With perfect respect and attachment I remain yrs

JAMES MADISON

Madison to Jefferson

[Orange June 2, 1808]

DEAR SIR

Yours of yesterday was only delivered by the Rider. I have informed him that I do not wish him to make any additional trips on my account. It is my purpose to set out for Washington a day or two after you do. I shall be able to fix the day by the time you call on us, which I hope you will find it not inconvenient to do on your way. If you should return in the course you came, it will be an easy ride from this stage over to Fauquier's Court House. The best way from this to our Court House is now the short one, not more than 3½ or 4 miles: and I shall inquire whether a direct road to Bernards ford be not in a good state; in which case it will reduce the distance to Culpeper Ct. House to about 22 miles.

Your view of the Detroit case is precisely that which occurred to me. I was surprized that it escaped Woodwards sagacity. I shall refer it as you suggest to the Attorney General. Turreau's letter is exceptionable in several respects: and manifests a spirit different from his general one. I am not without apprehensions that the change is to be ascribed to communications from his Govt. which I have reason to believe he recd. some time before we left Washington, by the return of a Consul from France. It is possible however that he may be actuated by that misjudged zeal which often but explains such diplomatic aberrations.

The crops of wheat in this neighborhood and particularly my own on the red land make a wretched figure. The Hessian fly is certainly the chief cause. I do not calculate on a third of the usual product in some fields. The coolness and wetness of the season may reduce it still lower. Yrs. most respectfully and affecty.

JAMES MADISON

I write this before the arrival of the post from W. whose stay is too short for any other purpose, than merely to select from my budget the papers proper to go on to you, and sometimes scarcely for that.

Jefferson to Madison

Monticello June 3, 1808

DEAR SIR

Yours by yesterday's mail is recieved and I now return Pinckney's and Graham's letters. I thought it best to forward the passport for Hill's vessel to Mr Graham direct lest it should lose a post by going in to Montpelier. With Mr Grymes's request of a vessel I can do nothing till further advised. The application is new, and I think unnecessary, as I presume the trade to N. O. [New Orleans] is sufficiently open to furnish vessels, under Mr Gallatin's circular orders of May 20. allowing vessels to depart with provisions not exceeding ⅛ of the amount of their bond. The honest merchant has no objection to enlarge his bond in proportion as the temptation of foreign prices is enlarged.

I shall be with you possibly on Tuesday, but more probably on Wednesday, if not before 3. oclock, then certainly not till the evening. I salute you with constant affection and respect.

TH JEFFERSON

Jefferson to Madison

[Washington ca. June 16, 1808]

I retain Mr. Wilson's letter, and return you his two certificates, as he may wish to keep them. If I ever heard his name before it has entirely escaped me. I do not believe he has been misrepresented to me, and doubt if he has been represented in any way.

Jefferson to Madison

[Monticello] June 28, 1808

Robert H. Jones of N. Carolina to be District attorney for N. Carolina. He resides at Warrenton.

Jefferson to Madison

Monticello July 29, 1808

DEAR SIR,

The passport for the Leonidas goes by this post to the Collector of Norfolk. I return you Jarvis', Hackley's, and Montgomery's letters, and send you Hull's, Hunt's, Clarke's, and Mr. Short's for perusal and to be returned. On this last the following questions arise, When exactly shall the next vessel go? Whence? Is not the secrecy of the mission essential? Is it not the very ground of sending it while the Senate is not sitting, in order that it may be kept secret? I doubt the expediency of sending one of our regular armed vessels. If we do, she should go to Petersburg direct. And yet may there not be advantage in conferences between S. [Short] and A. [Armstrong]? I have signed the commission and letter of credence and now inclose them. Yet I must say I think the latter is very questionable indeed in point of propriety. It says that the minister is to *reside* near his person, but whether we should establish it at once into a permanent legation is much to be doubted, and especially in a recess of the Senate. I should think it better to express purposes something like the following 'to bear to your Imperial Majesty the assurances of the sincere friendship of the United States, and of their desire to maintain with your Majesty and your subjects the strictest relations of intercourse and commerce, to explain to your Majesty the position of the United States, and the considerations flowing from that which should keep them aloof from the contests of Europe, to assure your Majesty of their desire to observe a faithful and impartial neutrality, if not forced from that line by the wrongs of the belligerents, and to express their reliance that they will be befriended in these endeavors by your Majesty's powerful influence and friendship towards these States.' This is hasty,—it is too long, and neither the expressions nor thoughts sufficiently accurate; but something of this kind, more concise and correct, may be formed, leaving the permanency of the mission still in our power.[15]

There is no doubt but that the transaction at New Orleans, between Ortega and the British officer with the prize sloop Guadaloupe, has been a mere fraud to evade our regulation against the sale of prizes in our harbors, and his insolent letter intended merely to cover the fraud. His ready abandonment of the vessel and Ortega's resumption of her are clear proofs. Should not, or could not process be ordered against Ortega, and the vessel? I think a copy of Reeve's letter to Governor Claiborne, and of the proceedings of the court might be sent to Mr. Erskine with proper observations on this double outrage, and an intimation that the habitual insolence of their officers may force us to refuse them an asylum even when seeking it in real distress if the boon is to be abused as it has been by this insolent and dishonest officer. And as it is very

---

15. For TJ's letter to Czar Alexander, Aug. 29, 1808, see Ford, IX, pp. 206–7. For William Short's proposed mission to Russia, see Malone, V, pp. 450, 661–64.

possible the rascal may push his impostures to the making complaint to his government, this step with Mr. Erskine may anticipate it. I salute you with sincere and constant affection.

Madison to Jefferson

[Orange] July 29, 1808

DEAR SIR

The Bearer Mr. Dade has just handed me the inclosed which he wishes to support with your's; this object it explains. In addition to the testimony of Mr. Taylor etc. etc. I have a letter from my brother which speaks the same language, as justifiable by his personal knowledge. I am but slightly acquainted myself with Mr. Dade, but his character as I have always viewed it thro' his standing in the neighborhood corresponds with the outlines given in the inclosed. I have apprized him that the vacancy produced by the resignation of Capt. Maury, immediately in his age [?], had been filled. He is so bent however on military service, that he wishes to take the chance of any other that may be unfilled, or that may offer. I have apprized him also that the Sect. of War is in the District of Maine.

If nothing has happened to the mail, you will have seen the acct. of the farce at Bayonne. How will the result affect us? The transfer of Spanish America to Bonaparte, and the stipulation agst. *dismemberment,* wear a bad countenance on our side.[16] On another, the more South Ama. becomes the bone of contention as is implied by the transaction; the more the parties ought in common prudence, to see the importance of the U. States. I should feel great confidence in this reasoning if a like one had not been so little verified by what has passed.

We did not reach home till last night, having been delayed in our preparations at Washington so much that we did not set out till tuesday morning. We were as much favored by the weather on the journey as you were. Yrs. with respectful attacht

JAMES MADISON

---

16. In Mar. 1808, Charles IV of Spain abdicated, and his son Ferdinand succeeded him. When the latter met Napoleon at Bayonne in May to discuss French recognition and marriage to a Bonapartist princess, the emperor forced him to abdicate and installed his brother Joseph Bonaparte as king of Spain; see Georges Lefebvre, *Napoleon: From Tilsit to Waterloo, 1807–1815* (New York, 1969), pp. 16–17, and Steven T. Ross, *European Diplomatic History, 1789–1815: France against Europe* (New York, 1969), pp. 278–79. The French then informed Armstrong of the transfer of Spanish America to King Joseph and warned the United States that it had no right to occupy the Floridas without the consent of the king of Spain; see C. Edward Skeen, *John Armstrong, Jr., 1758–1843: A Biography* (Syracuse, 1981), p. 96.

Madison to Jefferson

Montpellier July 31, 1808[17]

DEAR SIR

I have just recd. yours of the 29. and inclose the papers noted "to be returned."

I think the best, and probably not the most expensive conveyance of Mr. S[hort] will be in a small public vessel, whether she go directly to his destination, or deliver him in France and, unless, previous to his departure, collateral reasons should urge an early communication to France or England, it appears to be eligible that he should proceed directly to St. P. If he take Paris in his way, concealment will be difficult, and is exposed moreover to the objections suggested by Mr. S. By going direct, the advantage without the inconvenience is assured; and outweighs the opportunity of conferring with A. who probably would say but little which wd. not be speedily learned at St. P. and whose present feelings might moreover tincture his communications and opinions. I concur in the suggested remodification of the letter of credence, which, as the Seal of the U. S. is not necessary to that document, may be made without resorting to the office of State. The Commission also, which was made out in the usual form, might perhaps be amended, but as it will be retained by himself, will be less an index to the Empr. of the intentions of this Govt. than the letter delivered to him. As to the time of sending the vessel, it would seem adviseable, to await further information from Engd. and France, such as may be expected very soon by the return of the St. Michail. and still sooner by a British Packet. The temper and views of those nations subsequent to the receipt of our Comunications by the Apl.[?] Packet and the St. Michael, may be such as to have a just influence on the instructions to Mr. S. Further accts. from Spain also may be useful. I recollect that Richd. Rush (son of the Docr.) was desirous of going with Mr. Pinkney to London, as his Secy. and that he was well recommended. It might not be amiss for you to hint him for the consideration of Mr. S. who probably has a personal knowledge of him, or can easily learn his dispositions and qualifications. I will attend to your hint as to Reeve's letter to Govr. C: and will have a copy of the case sent to Mr. Gallatin, who will judge of the steps proper to be taken as respects both the past and the future. Yrs. with affecte. respects

JAMES MADISON

---

17. This is JM's first use of "Montpellier" in these letters. He usually spelled it with two l's, a usage that I have followed in this work. See Brant, IV, p. 45. For TJ's first use, see TJ to JM, May 27, 1808, above.

Madison to Jefferson

[Montpellier] Aug. 3, 1808

DEAR SIR

The letter from me respecting the Leonidas was with the papers returned. I considered it as a mistake. But the letter was of so little acct. that I have not preserved it. Can you tell me any thing of the Randolph who has written one of the inclosed letters?

We have had fine rains since my arrival, and as this neighborhood had not previously suffered from drouth, our fields are very promising. The crops of Hay have been greater than ever known. and generally saved in favorable weather. The Wheat crop is scanty, and in some instances the quality very indifferent. I write this for the stage mail, and can therefore say nothing as to the budget expected by it. Yrs. with respectful attacht

JAMES MADISON

Jefferson to Madison

Monticello Aug. 5, 1808

DEAR SIR

Yours of the 3d. is recieved. I also have recieved a letter from B. R. Randolph. Who he is I know not. He may be of a family of Randalls of the neighborhood of Petersburg, who have lately begun to spell their names *Randolph,* tho' totally unconnected with those of that name. One of them was not long since convicted of the murder of his father, and the family is generally in very ill estimation. Yet they are in good circumstances, and perfectly equal to the care of the distressed of their own family, and the neighborhood being wealthy and knowing this man, are the proper judges whether he is an object, and the proper resources for his application. On us, strangers, and with objects of charity within our own knolege sufficient to claim what we can spare to those calls, he can have no claim. I shall therefore not answer his letter.

I inclose you 1. a letter from one Riddle of Pittsburg, merely for information. I know nothing of him.

2. Papers in the case of Richard Q. Hoskins whereon a pardon is to be issued.

3. The anonymous letter from New York. This is one of the wretched, and dastardly productions, to which the cowards dare not put their names, of which I have recieved, and you will recieve thousands. Of all the anonymous letters which have been constantly pouring in upon me, not more than half a dozen have been written with good views, and worthy of being read. They are almost universally the productions of the most ill-tempered and rascally part of

our country, often evidently written from tavern scenes of drunkenness. They never merit one moment's attention. Affectte. salutns

Th Jefferson

Madison to Jefferson

Montpellier Aug. 7, 1807 [1808]

Dear Sir

I return the letters of [B. R.] Randolph and Riddle. The complaint in that of the latter has been the subject of mail from others as he intimates. I was not aware that any of them except McKinley were as respectable as he describes them. But answers to such letters are always to be avoided farther than they may be given by the result itself. McKinley was answered verbally thro' his friend Mr. Jackson, but not as is stated. The case of Printers of the laws alone were referred to, and the special reason mentioned agst turning the discretion vested in the Dept. of State into a source of influence over the press, instead of guarding agst the abuse real or apparent to which it is liable, by subjecting it to general and fixed rules. One of these rules has been to make no change during the Congressional period for which the printers are from time to time appointed to publish the laws. The applications agst the Tree of Liberty have generally been made too at seasons which afforded particular objections agst an interposition: and made in favor of another press charged perhaps unjustly, with tendencies equally heretical.[18]

As you may not have recd. the Enquirer of Tuesday last I inclose one handed me by Mr. Venable who is now here on his way over the Mountains. It gives the news from Spain more fully than I have elsewhere seen it. If half of it be true, Bonaparte may find the tide at length beginning to turn agst. him. I suspect that if he finds serious difficulties in effecting his purpose by the Land [?], he will get over them for the present at least, by designating Ferdinand himself for the Throne.[19] The English will probably suspend their schemes with respect to So. America, till it be seen how the Spanish affairs will terminate; resuming them in the event of Bonaparte's success, and in a contrary event exchanging them for commercial arrangements with the reestablished Sovereign. This new scene ought not, according to ordinary calculations, to lessen the importance of the U.S. in the eyes of the contending parties; and in case Spanish America should become the bone of contention, there would seem to be new [?] powerful motives with both for cultivating peace at least with us. Yrs. with respectful attachment

James Madison

18. The Pittsburgh *Tree of Liberty* was published between 1800 and 1810; see Clarence S. Brigham, *History and Bibliography of American Newspapers, 1690–1820*, 2 vols. (Worcester, Mass., 1947), II, pp. 967–68.

19. After residing in Madrid for eleven days, Joseph Bonaparte was driven out by a Spanish insurrection; see Lefebvre, pp. 17–24. JM thought that Napoleon might return Ferdinand to the throne to quiet the rebellion.

Jefferson to Madison

Monticello Aug. 9, 1808

DEAR SIR

Yours of the 7th. was recieved yesterday, but the post was so late, and arriving with his portmanteau open threw me into great alarm, as I expected a large sum of money in the mail. I was relieved by finding it safe. I return you Pinckney's Joy's, Claiborne's, Foronda's and Bailey's letters. Would it not be worthwhile to send Erskine a copy of Bailey's letter, to observe to him that this disrespect by the officers of his government, and evidently with their connivance, if not corrected, may urge us by way of retaliation to take the same liberty with his correspondence.

Will you be so good as to have Michaux furnished with the papers he desires in the inclosed letter. His passage being merely scientific, I should be for imitating the liberal courtesy of nations, and allowing his botanical packages to go free of freight.

I send you a letter recieved from Govr. Sullivan, with my draught of an answer to it. You will percieve that this ought to be written with good consideration, and I will therefore pray you to suggest any alterations you would advise.[20] I send you at the same time a letter to Mr Smith, the last paragraph of which will shew you the spirit of the Boston tories. Be so good as to return these by the first post that the answer may be forwarded without delay.

I rejoice that Spain is likely to remove her Ne plus ultra to the Pyrenees, and that Bonaparte finds at length a limit to his power. Altho' the Spanish government is a wretched one, the people there have not, like the Germans, been rendered by oppression indifferent to the master they serve.[21] I salute you with affection.

TH JEFFERSON

Madison to Jefferson

Montpellier Aug. 10, 1808

DEAR SIR

I recd last evening yours of the 9th. with the papers to which it refers; and now return as desired Sullivan's and Ishomel's letters with your proposed answer to the former. The questions arising on them are not without difficulty, and this is not a little increased by the spirit which seems to haunt the Governor. His letter furnishes agst. his own statements the inference which is

---

20. For Governor James Sullivan's reports on political sentiment in Massachusetts, where the Federalists regained control of the legislature and launched an attack on the embargo, see Malone, V, pp. 569–74, 592–98, 602.

21. For a brief account of the Spanish uprising against Napoleon's troops, see Ross, pp. 279–82.

confirmed by the positive violations of the Embargo asserted and specified by Ishomel; and carries other inconsistencies on the face of it. Still it is much to be apprehended as is suggested that avarice and anglicism may be excited in that quarter to acts which would be as unfortunate at the present moment, as they would be shameful at all times. At home the evil would be tempered by opening the eyes of Honest Citizens every where to the real sources of our embarrassment. But the effect abroad could not fail to be of the worst kind, and ought particularly to be dreaded at this precise moment. It becomes questionable therefore whether it might not be as well to tolerate the indiscreet grant of permits a little longer, and substitute for their suspension, more invigorated means of another sort for enforcing the Embargo laws.[22] Indeed it seems requisite in every view that gun boats and other naval precautions should without the loss of a moment be displayed in the suspicious situations along the New England Coast; the more so as lumber and other articles produced in that quarter are smuggled as well as flour, and are perhaps still more wanted in the W. India markets. I do not see why all our naval force other than gunboats, actually equipped, might not patrol the coast suspected to be in collusion with British smugglers. It is more than probable, from what is stated, that they would if suddenly brought into that service, soon bring to light eno' of frauds to explain and justify the measure.[23]

I am the more apprehensive of some mischievous turn in case of an immediate discontinuance of the permits, as from the advice Sullivan has given, and the temper he is in, there is danger that his aim would be more to justify himself, than to carry thro' your measures. This is indicated by the use he calculates on making of your letter, tho' I think he wd. be a little staggared in this, by your recital of a passage from his.

After all, the laws must be enforced, and if it be thought the other means can not be made effectual, the consequences of suspending the permits, must be risked. The grounds on which your proposed letter places the question appear to be well chosen, and well presented. I have pencilled however an alteration or two with a view to avoid the appearance of charging the Govr. with flinching from his duty, and of sacrificing his popularity to that of the Ex. of the U. S. in Massachusets.[24] The literal recital from his letter may strengthen also the foreign policy which counts on the factious spirit agst. the Embargo.

If you approve of any alterations, you will make mine what they ought to be. Yrs. respectfully and affecy
JAMES MADISON

---

22. For Sullivan's use of permits, see Brant, IV, p. 460.

23. For the use of gunboats from Passamaquoddy Bay to Newport and of naval vessels from Block Island to Portland, see Malone, V, pp. 601–2.

24. For TJ's letter to James Sullivan, Aug. 12, 1808, see L. and B., XII, pp. 127–30.

Jefferson to Madison

Monticello Aug. 12, 1808

DEAR SIR,

Yours of the 10th came to hand yesterday and I return you Foronda's, Tuft's, Soderstrom's, and Turreau's letters. I think it is become necessary to let Turreau understand explicitly that the vessels we permit foreign ministers to send away are merely transports for the conveyance of such of their subjects as were here at the time of the embargo, that the numbers must be proportioned to the vessels as is usual with transports, and that all who meant to go away must be presumed to have gone before now, at any rate that none will be accommodated after the present vessel. We never can allow one belligerent to buy and fit out vessels here to be manned with his own people and probably act against the other.

You did not return my answer to Sullivan. But fortunately I have received another letter, which will enable me to give the matter an easier turn, and let it down more softly. Should the conference announced in Mr. Pinckney's letter of June 5, settle friendship between England and us, and Bonaparte continue at war with Spain, a moment may occur favorable, without compromitting us with either France or England, for seizing our own from the Rio Bravo to Perdido as of right, and the residue of Florida as a reprisal for spoliations. I have thought it proper to suggest this possibility to Genl Dearborne and Mr. Smith, and to recommend an eye to it in their rendezvousing and stationing the new southern recruits and gunboats, so that we may strike in a moment when Congress says so.

I have appointed Genl Steele successor to Shee.

Mr. and Mrs. Barlow and Mrs. Blagden will be here about the 25th. May we hope to see Mrs. Madison and yourself then, or when? I shall go to Bedford about the 10th of September. I salute you with constant affection and respect.

TH. JEFFERSON

Madison to Jefferson

Montpellier Aug. 14, 1808

DEAR SIR

Yours of the 12th. with the papers it refers to came duly to hand.

Among the letters now forwarded is one from Turreau inclosing a copy of one to him from Mr. Gallatin. He appears to have drawn conclusions from his conference with Mr. G. not warranted by it. Mine with him merely referred him to Mr. G. I think it will be not amiss, as he has acted and incurred expence in the case, to sanction this purpose. Whilst one belligerent has so many means for getting its subjects away, besides the Periodical Packets, it seems hard to restrict others from expedients which expose neither our property nor mariners: provided abuses of other sorts be sufficiently guarded agst. It is probable that the whole or very many, of the Frenchmen now in the U. S. were here before the Embargo took place. With this letter and copy, I send also those from Turreau just returned by you, that you may have an entire view of what has passed. Whatever your decision may be, it will be most convenient to send it direct to Mr. Gallatin.

As the interview with Canning held out by Pinkney, was probably sought by the latter, I am the less inclined to hope much from it, especially as the news from Spain will have had the usual effect on such a Cabinet, of raising its tone. It appears also from the English gazettes, that little impression was made by the arrival of what passed with Rose. The Morning Chronicle, you will observe, merely refers to the list of papers; whilst it re-publishes Erskines letter which combats its own party, with observations flattering to the writer. The Courier has republished Rose's ultimatum only, that is, his last letter, passing over the whole subject with little further notice. Nor does it appear that any allusion to these topics was made in Parliament, altho' not less than 10 days had elapsed. It is true the setts of papers I have are without a few links, and the hearing of the St. Michael may have contributed to suspense. But the appearance on the whole does not correspond with the anticipation of Erskine himself, as to the interest that wd. be excited.

Mr. P. has been drawn into an error by the importunity of Halsey and the pliability of the Portuguese Ambassador. It is not dishonorable for our Citizens to take licences from a foreign Govt. where their own acknowledges the right to refuse. But there is an obvious disadvantage in opening that door of foreign influence, and it is improper, were it otherwise, for the Govt. to patronize particular Citizens in pursuit of such favors. I see that it was a fact, that Percival rejected a request made in behalf of the W. Indies, to draw corn from G. B. so that but for the evasions of the Embargo, there must have been an uproar in the W. I. far more operative than the disturbance among the Weavers.

I think it can not fail to happen from the new turn in the belligerent state of things, that advantage will accrue to the U. S. and it is certainly our duty to make use of any occasions that may be presented for obtaining by honorable and prudent means, the justise that is witheld from us. I observe that Bonaparte is aware of the policy of augmenting his force in Germany, during the crisis with Spain, well knowing the latent dispositions in that quarter. Hence it may be inferred as well as from his character and past conduct, that if he relies on the sword in Spain, his operations will be as rapid and decisive as he can make them.[25] A protracted check even may produce a general reflex of the tide agst. him.

25. Before Napoleon transferred the Grande Armée from Prussia to Spain in his effort to quell the insurrection against Joseph, he met with Alexander at Erfurt to secure his position in northern and eastern Europe; see Ross, pp. 284–85.

I have done nothing yet as to Micheaux, not knowing whether the next vessel is to be a pub. or private one, nor whether if the former she will touch at a French port. If indeed he proceeds in a natl. vessel nothing will be necessary but instructions from the Secy. of the Navy to the Commander.

The Rider from Washington does not call here as his predecessor did, either going to or returning from his trip to Charlottesville. I presume this is not a part of the plan and that it was a courtesy only heretofore. I think however it wd. be an important improvement of the plan, for him to take both Monticello and me in his route, as it wd. quicken so much the communication between us. The delay now experienced, may be important. It has already been in some instances inconvenient. The end might be easily attained without expence to the public; by simply permitting him to leave W. at 12 or 1. instead of 3 OC. on tuesday, and substituting 11 or 12 instead of 9 for his return on Sunday. This wd. give 2 or 3 hours for your and my use: at the time that it wd. save us from sending to the post-office. The difference made at Washington wd. be of no consideration in the absence of the Ex., and wd. be over-balanced if it were less the case, by the accomadations afforded to what at present is the most important purpose answered by the regulation.

We have in view, if possible to make a visit to Monticello, and shall be gratified in making it coincide with the expected one which you mention. Our prospects of company however do not allow us to form any precise determinations. Yrs. with respectful attachment

JAMES MADISON

I think you will find your answer to Sullivan inclosed between the leaves of yours to me. I am confident it was sent.

Jefferson to Madison

Monticello Aug. 16, 1808

DEAR SIR

Yours of the 14th. is recieved and I now return the papers which accompanied it. I must cry peccavi as to the answer to Sullivan's letter. I found it in the letter itself. I now inclose you two letters from Mr Short. I fancy he is right in supposing that by the time he could arrive at the Baltic, it's navigation would be uncertain, if not impracticable; but certainly it would be closed before the vessel could return. I confess I do not like the idea of risking one of our armed vessels on such a voyage. If war takes place we should be certain of losing her. I wish you may find it convenient to come about the time proposed as that would be in time to prepare the papers for this mission, and we could consult together more easily, on all the details.

I presume we must permit Turreau to send his two vessels, but on the condition that they be filled with passengers, as transports could be. He seems to consider our indulgence as not granted on any particular principle and therefore indefinite in it's extent. But he should understand it as limited to the tonnage necessary to carry to France or the West Indies (and not to more distant seas) the French subjects who were here at the time of the embargo. And that this is not of right, but comity: inasmuch as foreigners who come into a country submit themselves to the effect of any measures which the situation of the country calls for. If he has 1500. sailors here, he will need more than two vessels.

I am astonished to learn that the Washington rider has not regularly called on you. Now as well as heretofore it was an express point in his establishment. The proof is the key delivered you from the Post office. I will speak to him on the subject to day. I salute you with affection and respect.

TH JEFFERSON

Madison to Jefferson

Montpellier Aug. 17, 1808

DEAR SIR

Yours of the 16 with the papers sent with it, were recd. last evening. Mr. Short did not seize exactly my ideas as to the concealment of his mission. If this could be made effectual, and freed from the appearance of being studied, by a direct voyage to St. P., I think it would be best. But if he is to pass thro' France, a frank but general disclosure of his destination wd. be preferable to an attempt at concealment which would certainly fail, and be more likely to excite jealousy and latent counteraction than a more open course. He mistakes also in supposing me to have had in view one of the smallest of the armed vessels. The trip made by the Revenge proved the unfitness of that size for a shorter voyage than into the Baltic. The Wasp or the Hornet is as small an armed vessel as ought to be put on such a service.

On the whole I yield to the objections agst. a passage into the Baltic, particularly at so late a season, and see no question remaining but between a public and private vessel for a voyage to France and England. On this question I still lean in favor of a public vessel, for reasons suggested by the trials made of private vessels. A public vessel wd. have avoided the delay experienced by the Osage, and which will probably have happened at a more critical moment to the St. Michail. What the fortune of the Hope may be is uncertain, but the expedient for avoiding the delays in her case is liable to casualties and difficulties which may have the matter not mended by it. You do not say whether you had signified to Mr. Gallatin your view of Turreau's requests. The Rider who does not call on me is the one from *Washington,* not *Fredg.* I will endeavor to be with you at the time you wish, and for the reason suggested, as well as others.

I see that the B. Parlt. is about opening a trade between her Cols. and Europe S. of Cape Finistere, making a return cargo of Provisions, a condition;

but principally I suspect to get the new market on the Cont. for Sugar and Coffee. Should Spain under her Temporary Govt. revoke her Decrees, or our Embargo be on other grounds removed, that market wd. be instantly supplied by the carriers of the U. S. without being even exposed to the British rule of '56. which applies only to an *Enemy* of G. B. Considering the narrow and selfish policy of the present Cabinet, it is possible that it may be tempted to continue its orders, lest a removal of our Embargo should interfere with her in the new commercial prospect. But I suspect that she is still more swayed by the hope of producing a revolution in the pub. councils here, which might be followed by a coalition with her in the war. Yrs. with affecte. and high respect

JAMES MADISON

Jefferson to Madison

Monticello Aug. 19, 1808

DEAR SIR

Yours of the 17th. came to hand yesterday. I wrote to Mr. Gallatin that the principle to govern our indulgencies of vessels to foreign ministers, was that it was fair to let them send home all their subjects caught here by the embargo and having no other means of getting home, proportioning the tonnage permitted to the number of persons according to the rules in the transport services, and that you would so explain it to Turreau for his government.

I mistook the rider meant in your letter, believing it to be that from Fredericksburg. The Washington rider never called on me either during my present or any former visit here. I suppose in fact he is so pressed for time as not to admit it.

I inclose you a petition from the Shipmasters of Philadelphia, to deliver which a member of their body was sent on to this place. However disagreeable, an answer is necessary. I send you the rough draught of one, which I pray you to amend as you think best.

I shall hope to see Mrs Madison and yourself as early next week as your convenience will admit, that the St. Petersburg mission may not be delayed disadvantageously. I salute you with affectionate respect.

TH JEFFERSON

Madison to Jefferson

Montpellier Aug. 20, 1808

DEAR SIR

Yours of yesterday reached me this morning, and I acknowledge it now, for the mail of tomorrow.

I return your draft of an answer to the memorials from Philada. with a few small alterations pencilled. One of them is intended to avoid the implication that no [illegible] had reached us on the Continent, where certainly we have suffered much, altho' not in a way to justify belligerent charges agst. our neutrality; another, to avoid an apparent exclusion of the care taken by local authorities, of seafaring persons having no recourse of their own. The word *crisis* is inserted, as bearing a *temporary* import. And *"Plunderers,"* necessarily to be applied to the agents of G. B. and the other belligerents, appeared to be harsher than may be becoming. I wd. have suggested a better substitute, than spoilers if one had occurred. Perhaps some general change of the phrase, may occur to yourself, if you approve of any change.

We shall make an effort to be at Monticello the ensuing week, but it can not be sooner than thursday, more probably friday. Yours with respecftful attacht

JAMES MADISON

Madison to Jefferson

[Montpellier Aug. 21, 1808]

DEAR SIR

Unwilling to detain the Rider I send the letters recd. by him witht. remark. It is possible we may be able to set out for Monticello on Wednesday next. This will however depend on circumstances Yrs etc. etc.

JAMES MADISON

Sunday afternoon

Madison to Jefferson

[Monticello ca. Aug. 26, 1808][26]

all regard to the rights of others having been thrown aside the Belligerent powers have beset the highway of commercial intercourse with edicts which taken together expose our commerce and mariners, under almost every desti-

---

26. This is JM's draft of TJ's response to a Federalist petition against the embargo from "the Inhabitants of the Towns of Boston, Newburyport and Providence, in Legal Town Meeting Assembled," Monticello, Aug. 26, 1808. The petitions arrived at Monticello on Aug. 22, and the Madisons arrived for their late summer visit to Monticello on or about Aug. 24, where JM wrote this draft. TJ followed it almost verbatim; see L and B., XVI, pp. 312–14. For the Federalist petitioning campaign, see James M. Banner, Jr., *To the Hartford Convention: The Federalists and the Origins of Party Politics in Massachusetts, 1789–1815* (New York, 1970), pp. 294–304. For the Madison's visit to Monticello, see Dolley Madison to Anna Cutts, Aug. 28, 1808, in Dolley Madison, *Memoirs and Letters of Dolly Madison,* ed. Lucia B. Cutts (Boston, 1886), pp. 65–66, and Ketcham, p. 460. See also Malone, V, pp. 608–11.

nation, to prey to their fleet and cruisers. Each party indeed would admit our commerce with themselves: with the view of associating us in their war agst. the other. But we have wished war with neither.

Under these circumstances were passed the laws of which you complain by those delegated to exercise the powers of legislation for you and having every sympathy of a common interest in exercising them faithfully.

had they not been passed our commerce and mariners must either have remained where they now are, in our own harbours, or incurred a risk of capture which few would have escaped

In reviewing the measures in the present occasion, we should advert to the difficulties out of which a choice was of necessity to be made.

To have submitted to the pretensions of any foreign nations whatever, to subject our lawful commerce with other foreign nations, to prohibitions, to restrictions, or to tributary exactions under any form, would have been to surrender our national independence, an idea at which the honorable pride and virtuous patriotism of every Citizen at once revolts.

To have resisted these attempts, these pretensions by Arms, would have been in effect an instant commencement of war, which there is no reason to believe was the choice of the nation any more than it was the dictate of prudence.

The only remaining course was that preferred by the Legislature, of suspending a commerce placed under such unexampled difficulties, and it is surely worthy of candid consideration, that whilst it has avoided the alternative of descending from the ground of an independent nation, or of rushing into a state of war with one or more powerful nations, it has equally afforded to those nations an oppy. of reflecting on their unjustifiable and impolitic conduct towards us, under the influence of the serious disadvantages resulting from it to themselves

Madison to Jefferson

[Montpellier] Sept. 4, 1808

DEAR SIR

The packet brought me by the mail of friday from Milton, was strangely delayed somewhere; more than by the mistake which carried it to Monticello. It contained the inclosed letter from Pinkney, which has a much better flavour than his preceding one of the 22d. June.[27] Should any future packets or letters from the office of State, get to Monticello in the first instance, I beg you to open them. In some cases it may be of real importance to do so. Yrs. with respectful attacht.

JAMES MADISON

---

27. Pinkney had offered to suspend the embargo as it affected Great Britain if the orders-in-council were revoked. Canning stalled throughout the summer, then rejected the overture; see *ibid.*, pp. 617–19, and Perkins, pp. 175–76.

Jefferson to Madison

Monticello Sept. 5, 1808

DEAR SIR,

The last post brought me the counter addresses now inclosed. That from Ipswich is signed by 40. persons; the town meeting which voted the petition consisted of 30. There are 500. voters in the place. The Counter address of Boston has 700. signatures. The town meeting voting the petition is said to have consisted of 500. In the draught of an answer inclosed, I have taken the occasion of making some supplementary observations which could not with propriety have been inserted in the answers to the petitions. The object is that the two together may present to our own people the strongest points in favor of the embargo in a short and clear view. An eye is also kept on foreign nations, in some of the observations.[28] Be so good as to make it what it should be and return it by the first post.

Mr. Dinsmore informs me you wish to employ Hugh Chisolm, a bricklayer now working for me in Bedford, if I have no occasion for him. He will probably finish for me this month; after which I shall have nothing more for him the present year. I will write to him on the subject of your desire. He is a very good humored man, works as well as most of our bricklayers, and has had the benefit of becoming familiar with many things, with which they are unacquainted.

Having found occasion in my last letters to Mr Gallatin and Genl. Dearborn to say to them when I should be in Washington, I have mentioned the 1st. day of October. I salute you with constant and sincere affection.

TH. JEFFERSON

Jefferson to Madison

Monticello Sept. 6, 1808

DEAR SIR,

I return you Pinckney's letter, the complection of which I like. If they repeal their orders, we must repeal our embargo. If they make satisfaction for the Chesapeake, we must revoke our proclamation, and generalize its operation by a law. If they keep up impressments, we must adhere to nonintercourse, manufactures and a navigation act.

I enclose for your perusal a letter of Mr. Short's. I inform him that any one of the persons he names would be approved, the government never recognizing a difference between the two parties of republicans in Pennsylvania.

---

28. For TJ's replies to addresses by supporters of the embargo, see L. and B., XVI, pp. 314–17. As the protest petitions and counteraddresses multiplied, TJ ordered 150 printed copies of his standard reply to the protesters and 50 copies of his reply to the supporters; see Malone, V, pp. 608–9.

I do not think the anonymous rhapsody is Cheatham's. Tho' mere declamation, it is of too high an order for him. I think it quite in Gouv. Morris's dictorial manner. It's matter is miserable sophistry. I salute you with constant affection.

Madison to Jefferson

Montpellier Sept. 7, 1808

DEAR SIR

Your favors of the 5th. and 6th. were duly recd. last evening. I return Mr. S.s letter; with the Addresses from Boston etc. and the proposed answer. The few changes which I have suggested, if proper will speak for themselves. It is a nice task to speak of war, so as to impress our own people with a dislike to it, and not impress foreign Govts. with the idea that they may take advantage of the dislike.

I inclose also, for Mr. Graham, draughts of instructions to Mr. S. and of a letter to Harris. If no other corrections be necessary than such as you can conveniently make with your own pen, it will be best to send the letter direct from Monticello, committed to the *Horse mail,* which will give Graham more time for his preparations. The letters for Armstrong and Pinkney, I will try to have ready for the mail as it returns by our Ct. House. As they will be mere letters of information, it is not material that you should previously see them, and time now is becoming urgent. Yrs. with respectful attacht

JAMES MADISON

Jefferson to Madison

Monticello Sept. 13, 1808

DEAR SIR,

I send you a letter of Short's for perusal, and one of Edgar Patterson, asking what is already I presume provided for, [and] one of General Armstrong, which I do not well understand, because I do not recollect the particular letter which came by Haley.[29] I presume the counsel he refers to is to take possession of the Floridas. This letter of June 15 is written after the cession by Carlos to Bonaparte of all his dominions, when he supposed England would at once pounce on the Floridas as a prey, or Bonaparte occupy it as a neighbor. His next will be written after the people of Spain will have annihilated the cession, England become the protector of Florida, and Bonaparte without title or means to plant himself there as our neighbor.[30]

29. Captain Nathan Haley was in Paris carrying messages from TJ and JM to Armstrong; see Skeen, p. 98.
30. See *ibid.,* p. 96.

Ought I to answer such a petition as that of Rowley? The people have a right to petition, but not to use that right to cover calumniating insinuations.

Turreau writes like Armstrong so much in the buskin, that he cannot give a naked fact in an intelligible form. I do not know what it is he asks for. If a transport or transports to convey sailors, there has been no refusal; and if any delay of answer, I presume it can be explained. If he wishes to buy vessels here, man them with French seamen, and send them elsewhere, the breach of neutrality would be in permitting, not in refusing it. But have we permitted this to England? His remedy is easy in every case. Repeal the decrees. I presume our Fredericksburg rider need not come after his next trip. I salute you affectionately.

TH. JEFFERSON

Madison to Jefferson

Montpellier Sept. 14, 1808

DEAR SIR

Yours of yesterday was duly recd. by the rider. I return Shorts and A's letters. Your observations on the latter place the subject of it in its true point of view. Perhaps the mail of today may bring me a letter of the same date, that may have lost the last mail, by passing thro' the office of State. If the letter to you be the sole communication it is another example from that quarter, of obscurity resulting from a labored brevity. The occupation of the Floridas is however certainly the advice alluded to. The advice, you may recollect, was given on a ground which failed according to the circumstances stated. The ground was that it would involve us with none; and certainly not with France, yet the occupancy was to be expressly agst. the occupancy of England, in order to be admissable to France. Writing from memory, I may not be absolutely exact, but I am sure that the advice was contravened by the fact on which it depended. I dislike much the prospect which the date and tenor of this letter give on the side of France. It forbids a hope of any information by Baker who must have left Paris 8 or 10 days after, that can lessen the difficulty springing from the French Decrees.[31] We must therefore look to England alone for the chances of disembarrassment; and look with the greater solicitude, as it seems probable that nothing but some striking proof of the success of the Embargo, can arrest the successful perversion of it, by its enemies, or rather the enemies of their Country. Among the artifices used, the petitions from N. England have probably had a great effect; being so managed as to have received [?] critical circulation, before the answers to them could reach the public.[32] The

---

31. John Martin Baker had been dispatched to England and France to bring back messages from Pinkney and Armstrong before Congress convened on Nov. 7, 1808; see *ibid.*, p. 95.

32. TJ later wrote that he "felt the foundations of the government shaken under my feet by the New England townships"; see L. and B., XIV, p. 422.

Petition from Rowley merits the chastisement of silent contempt at least. I observe a late one from N. Haven, elaborated more than any I have seen, and in some of its features, imposing on superficial minds. Yet what more absurd, than to charge the keeping out of the way of plunder and insult, with a sacrifice of independence, and advise at the same time, the submitting to be insulted, and paying a tribute to encourage the practice.

I was at a loss what to do with respect to pecuniary arrangements in the case of Mr. S. As they might lead to disclosure, I said nothing more to him, therefore than that he would from the *usual* allowances, with a *berth* only in the Aviso, which is due to his care of the dispatches. I concluded also that no advance wd. be necessary as he probably could make it out of his own means; and it could not be made well from the Treasy. without notice to every body. I ventured to conclude even that his own means wd. suffice after his arrival in Europe, till provision could be made without any premature disclosure. Finding from his letter that he looks for something more, I wrote a line yesterday evening to Mr. Graham, desiring him to make arrangemts if not too late, for a fund in Europe, (in concert with the Treasy. Dept. if necessary) covering its object by a *general* designation. I said nothing to Mr. S. as to allowing an outfit, leaving by the term *usual,* the way open for a distinction between a permanent, and occasional mission.

There have been several applications for the carriage of the dispatches to England. A letter in behalf of Suter has been sent to me also. I have authorized Mr. Graham to make a choice.

Turreau's letter is meant I presume for his own Gvt. more than for this. There is no pretext for complaint. He has had fair measure. He can not be so silly as to expect a neutral exercising its own rights, in pursuit of its own objects, to equalize the condition of belligerents of unequal power whether on water or land. As to delay, it has been owing to the distance of Mr. Gallatin and myself, and the share he has had in the business. But how impertinent are such complts. from the Rept. of Govts. which to important and reiterated letters from our Ministers delay answers for months and years, and sometimes do not vouchsafe them at all.

I shall give the rider notice on his return on sunday, not to make another trip to Fredg. unless directed by you. I submit for consideration however, whether, as he would return hither, in case of another trip, on the 25th. which will be before you pass on your way to Washington, it may not be expedient for him to make it, leaving your packets here, or carrying them to Monticello as you may direct. At the present crisis it may happen to be of use, that we should see the latest intelligence before your return to Washington, and that this may be hurried on my part, more than otherwise might take place. I barely suggest the point for consideration. Yrs. with respectful attachmt.

JAMES MADISON

Madison to Jefferson

Montpellier Sept. 18, 1808

DEAR SIR

Inclosed herewith are Letters from Armstrong and Erving recd. by the Mail of wednesday, and which could not of course be sooner forwarded. I add also sundry others of minor importance.

Armstrong's letters leave me wholly at a loss as to the time and plan of the St. Michael's return. From the permission of her return to France from Falmouth I fear that is to be her course; and what almost confirms it is that I have a letter from Baker dated Bordeaux *June 25,* which gives no information of a public nature, not even the occasion of his being there. If the St. Michail arrived July 7th. in Engd. as reported, Baker could not have been on board, and must have awaited her return to France. All this delay is truly mortifying. A. must at length have been convinced by Champagny's letter, that his advice to seize the Floridas was not founded as he supposed, tho' I suspect the tone of the explanation had reference to the guaranty by Joseph, of the Spanish Colonies, which is one of the *popular* appeals to the Spanish action. You will notice the terms in which A. explains the rejection of the attempt to engage us in the War, which weakens much the demand of redress for *passed* aggressions.[33] I do not recollect any such view of the subject to have been furnished to him; certainly not in his instructions, to be literally pursued. I am sorry to find that Marat's dispatches to Turreau were in reality put under Erving's cover to the Dept. of State. The official seal of a neutral ought not to conceal belligerent property, especially of a sort of contraband, any more than the flag of a national ship. I suspect he became a little aware of his error, and therefore stated the circumstance in his private not his public letter. Mr. Barlow got here yesterday, and proceeds to Monticello tomorrow morning. Yours with respectful attachment

JAMES MADISON

Jefferson to Madison

Monticello Sept. 20, 1808

DEAR SIR

I return you all your papers except Irvine's[34] which I have not yet entirely read. As far as I have gone they abate much of the hopes which Montgomery's letter might have excited. It is true that Irvine's opinions must be influenced by the French versions at Madrid, and Montgomery's by the popular rumors always afloat in such scenes.

---

33. For Armstrong's presentation of the administration's views, see Skeen, pp. 92–95.
34. TJ habitually misspelled the name of George W. Erving, chargé d'affaires in Madrid.

No answer surely shd. be given to Bollman, nor should government so far be instrumental to his withdrawing from future enquiry, as to permit him to go in a vessel of theirs, much less to give him a passport. The difficulty in answering Erskine's letter will be to find a proper persifflage in return for the haughty stile of his government. This will be a case for consultation at Washington. I send you some papers recd. from Mr Gallatin, to consider whether Soderstrom should not be seriously reprimanded. For a foreign agent, accredited to the Executive, to embody himself with the lawyers of a factious opposition to influence the opinions of the government is what no country ever before saw. Surely the government will chuse for itself the counsel for fixing the construction of the laws they are to execute. I think he might be told that we will not see a second act of that kind with indifference, and that the occasion is a good one for letting foreign agents know that they are not to combine with the factions in opposition. Be pleased to return the law opinions and Soderstrom's threatening letter to Mr Gallatin. I send you Fayette's letter for perusal. I will direct the rider to make another trip as far as Montpelier. I salute you with affection.

TH JEFFERSON

Madison to Jefferson

Montpellier Sept. 20, 1808

DEAR SIR

If you gave attention to Turreaus letter of Aug. 31 you will have seen in its stile and some of its remarks an arrogance which ought not to pass wholly unnoticed. That I may commit no error in the answer, I inclose the draft of one under an unsealed cover to Mr. Graham. You will either forward it directly to him, with your own corrections, or return it to me to be corrected according to your directions, as you may find most convenient. Yours' with respectful attacht.

JAMES MADISON

Madison to Jefferson

Montpellier Sept. 21, 1808

DEAR SIR

I return the letter of Mr. G. with that of Soderstrom and the opinions of the Lawyers. From a hasty perusal of these, I think the construction of Mr. Gallatin is clearly established. The exception in the Proviso to the Embargo law, ought to be taken strictly according to a general rule, unless the obvious policy of the law admit a latitude. Here the policy, notwithstanding the views taken of it by Martin etc., would be opposed by making it the interest of a wrong-doing nation to prolong the causes of the Embargo, in order to purchase for a trifle all our navigation, employ it for the present, in alleviation of the loss of neutral carriage, and finally destroy our rivalship. The course taken by Soderstrom is to the last degree impertinent, and merits any animadversion which pity for his stupidity and distresses will permit.

I am extremely gratified with the letter of Fayette which I also return. Yrs. with respectful attachment

JAMES MADISON

Jefferson to Madison

Monticello Sept. 23, 1808

DEAR SIR

Yours of the 20. and 21. were recieved yesterday. I have sent on the letter to Turreau without alteration. It was as little as either the stile or matter of his letter deserved. I shall be with you probably on Wednesday. Mr Barlow stays with us till then, and returns at the same time.

The bearer is Mr Chisolm the bricklayer who wished to see you before your departure. Dinsmore has suggested a very handsome improvement of your house, and I think the easiest by which you can make a fine room. It is to throw the middle room between your two passages out into a bow on the South side, taking a little from the passages to give it breadth, and with or without a portico there as you please. It will be somewhat in the manner of my parlour.[35] Affectionate salutations.

TH JEFFERSON

Madison to Jefferson

Montpellier Sept. 25, 1808

DEAR SIR

Yours by Mr. Chisolm was duly handed to me. I shall look for you and Mr. Barlow on wednesday, and for the pleasure of your company at dinner.

Among the papers herewith inclosed are a letter from Mr. Hackley of late date, and a Spanish documt. confirming the victory over Dupont.[36] The letter

---

35. For references to Hugh Chisholm's and James Dinsmore's work for TJ and JM, see Jack McLaughlin, *Jefferson and Monticello: The Biography of a Builder* (New York, 1988), pp. 334–36.

36. During the insurrection that followed Napoleon's installation of Joseph as king of Spain, a Spanish force defeated a French army under General Pierre-Antoine Dupont de l'Étang, who surrendered his entire command at Bailén, the first major capitulation of a French army since Napoleon had assumed command; see Lefebvre, pp. 22–23, and Ross, pp. 281–82.

from Graham mentions the disaster at the Capitol, of which it is probable you will have had a more particular account from another source.[37] Yrs. with respectful attacht.

JAMES MADISON

Madison to Jefferson

Montpellier Sept. 26, 1808

DEAR SIR

The rider reached me this morning only. His mail contains nothing particularly interesting, unless it be in Newspapers not yet looked into. I inclose the Natl. Gazette of friday, which gives the state of the election in Vermont as far as known, and La Trobe's explanation of the accident in the Capitol.[38]

The letters from Graham and Mr. S. shew the dilatory footing on which the arrangemts for the Ship Union rests. I shall write immediately, authorizing the discretion wished by Mr. S. as well in compliance with his anxiety, as in consideration of the season of the year, and of the importance of Mr. S's object which requires that landing in France should be hastened and secured as much as may be. An eventual delay in the return of the Union is also of the less consequence, as the return of the St. Michael and of the Hope will have lessened, probably, the importance of that of the Union. I shall endeavor to get a letter to Fredg from our Court to day, so as to reach Philada. a little sooner than by the next mail, or even by your return to Washington. The blank passport may be either taken on with you, or put into the mail as you chuse. It is not relied on, and will not be in time, unless new delays shall have arisen. Yrs. with respectful attacht

JAMES MADISON

---

37. During the construction of the Senate wing of the Capitol, a vault on the ground floor collapsed, killing John Lenthall, assistant to Benjamin H. Latrobe, surveyor of public buildings; see Malone, V, pp. 539–40.

38. For Latrobe's letter of Sept. 23, 1808, see *Thomas Jefferson and the National Capital, 1783–1818,* ed. Saul K. Padover (New York, 1946), pp. 436–39.

35

THE END OF THE EMBARGO, 1808–1809

THE CRISIS OVER NEUTRAL RIGHTS coincided with the presidential campaign of 1808. As Jefferson's second term moved into its third year, a spontaneous grass-roots campaign urged the president to seek a third term. Nine state legislatures and one territorial body joined Republican rallies in adopting resolutions proposing that Jefferson remain in office. But in December 1807, just as the embargo became the law of the land, Jefferson announced that he would willingly follow George Washington's sound precedent and retire after two terms.[1]

Madison had the strongest claim to the Republican nomination, but he was by no means the unanimous choice of the party. Vice President George Clinton of New York was supported by a New York–New England faction as a more logical successor, and Clinton agreed. He was Madison's senior, had a record of more prominent service during the Revolution, and came from a rapidly growing northern state that was ready to challenge Virginia's leading role in the Union and the Republican party. Moreover, John Randolph and a few southern Quids, who had broken with Jefferson and Madison several years earlier, supported James Monroe, who had returned from England resentful of the president and secretary of state for repudiating the treaty that he and Pinkney had negotiated with Great Britain in 1806.

Despite these challenges, Madison easily won the nomination of the Republican congressional caucus, which also endorsed Clinton for vice president. A secret Federalist caucus met in New York and named Charles Cotesworth Pinckney and Rufus King to head their ticket. The key issue was the embargo, and the election returns roughly reflected the popularity of that

---

1. Noble E. Cunningham, *The Jeffersonian Republicans in Power: Party Operations, 1801–1809* (Chapel Hill, 1963), pp. 108–24, and Brant, IV, pp. 419–40, 462–68, have the fullest discussions, but also see Robert K. Gooch, "Jeffersonianism and the Third Term Issue: A Retrospect," *Southern Review* 5 (1940–41): 736–39.

The End of the Embargo, 1808-1809 *1549*

measure throughout the country. Madison won only Vermont in New England, but he tallied 13 of 19 votes in New York, 7 of 9 in Maryland, 8 of 11 in North Carolina, and swept New Jersey, Pennsylvania, and the South and West for 122 electoral votes. Pinckney carried New England (except for Vermont) and Delaware plus 2 votes in Maryland and 3 in North Carolina, for 47 votes. Clinton received 6 votes in New York, while Monroe failed to receive any electoral votes. Despite serious schisms among the Republicans and the revival of the Federalist party as a result of the embargo, Madison became Jefferson's successor with solid public support.[2]

Given the long friendship and cordial working relationship between Jefferson and Madison, the political transition should have been smooth and well coordinated, but it was neither. In August 1808, Jefferson had assured Gallatin, the chief enforcement officer of the embargo, "that if orders and decrees are not repealed" by Britain and France, "and a continuance of the embargo is preferred to war, (which sentiment is universal here), Congress should legalize all *means* which may be necessary to obtain it's *end.*"[3] But three months later, while drafting his final annual message to Congress, he "declined expressing any opinion on its continuance."[4] Jefferson rationalized his decision by arguing that "it is fair to leave to those who are to act on them, the decisions they prefer, being to be myself a spectator."[5]

Jefferson's abdication came as a surprise to Madison and Gallatin, Madison's designated successor as secretary of state, who detected "a tone of complaint and despondency" in the president's draft of his message to Congress; together they rewrote important portions of Jefferson's farewell message.[6] Both found it difficult to understand the president's refusal to recommend policy in his final months of office, and both pressed him to assert leadership in the face of congressional confusion during the lame-duck session. In a joint letter written on behalf of the incoming president, who was suffering from a brief spell of sickness, Gallatin informed Jefferson that "both Mr. Madison and myself concur in opinion that, considering the temper of the Legislature, or rather of its members, it would be eligible to point out to them some precise and distinct course. As to what that should be," he confessed, "we may not all perfectly agree," and he conceded that he was "nearly as undetermined between enforcing the embargo or war as I was on our last [cabinet] meetings. But I think that we must"—and here Gallatin and Madison placed the respon-

---

2. Electors chosen by popular vote gave Madison 98 votes, Pinckney 16; see Marshall Smelser, *The Democratic Republic, 1801-1815* (New York, 1968), pp. 185-86.

3. TJ to Albert Gallatin, Aug. 11, 1808, in Ford, IX, p. 202.

4. TJ to Albert Gallatin, Oct. 30, 1808, *ibid.*, p. 215.

5. TJ to Levi Lincoln, Nov. 13, 1808, *ibid.*, pp. 227-28. For a harsh appraisal of TJ's abdication of executive responsibility for enforcing the embargo, see Richard Mannix, "Gallatin, Jefferson, and the Embargo of 1808," *Diplomatic History* 3 (1979): 151-72.

6. For Gallatin's reference to TJ's despondency, see Brant, IV, p. 465; for JM's notes for TJ's message, [Oct. 30, 1808], see below.

sibility squarely on the president's shoulders—"(or rather you must) decide the question absolutely, so that we may point out a decisive course either way to our friends."[7]

But Jefferson persisted in his refusal to make policy decisions, preferring instead "that my successor should now originate those measures of which he will be charged with the execution and responsibility, and that it is my duty to cloath them with the forms of authority."[8] Accordingly, Madison and Gallatin met with congressional leaders throughout the transition period between November 1808 and March 1809 to consider public policy. Madison had already outlined his views in dispatches to Pinkney in London, making it clear that he favored "an invigoration of the embargo, a prohibition of imports, *permanent* duties for encouraging manufacturers, and a *permanent* navigation act: with an extension of preparations and arrangements for the event of war." In addition to increased military spending, he wanted to encourage "a spirit of independence and indignation," which he thought necessary to reinforce the past measures. He also thought that Congress should supplement the embargo by extending nonintercourse to France as it had to Great Britain, thus giving a new "severity to the contest of privations."[9]

As a result of the consultations, Madison and Gallatin prepared a report on the embargo that was presented to the House by George Washington Campbell of Tennessee, chairman of the committee on foreign affairs.[10] There were only three options: abject and degrading submission, war with both nations, or a continuance and enforcement of the embargo.[11] The Campbell-Gallatin-Madison report of November 22, 1808, concluded that the aggressions of England and France were "to all intents and purposes, a maritime war waged by both nations against the United States":

There is no other alternative, but war with both nations, or a continuance of the present system. For war with one of the belligerents only, would be submission to the edicts or will of the other; and a repeal in whole or in part of the embargo must necessarily be war or submission.

A general repeal without arming, would be submission to both nations.

A general repeal and arming of our merchant vessels, would be war with both, and war of the worst kind; suffering our enemies to plunder us without retaliation upon them.

A partial repeal must, from the situation of Europe, necessarily be actual submission to one of the aggressors, and war with the other.[12]

---

7. JM and Albert Gallatin to TJ, Nov. 15, 1808, below.

8. TJ to James Monroe, Jan. 28, 1809, in Ford, IX, pp. 243-44.

9. JM to William Pinkney, Nov. 9, 1808, cited in J. C. A. Stagg, *Mr. Madison's War: Politics, Diplomacy, and Warfare in the Early American Republic, 1783–1830* (Princeton, 1983), pp. 23-34; Brant, IV, p. 469; and Burton Spivak, *Jefferson's English Crisis: Commerce, Embargo, and the Republican Revolution* (Charlottesville, 1979), p. 153.

10. Brant, IV, pp. 469-71.

11. Malone, V, pp. 629-30.

12. Brant, IV, pp. 471-72.

After three weeks of debate, Congress pledged not to submit to the edicts of the British and the French, and supported continuation of the embargo to protect the "rights, honor and independence" of the United States. To equalize treatment for the twin offenders, Congress supported the extension of nonimportation to France and the barring of French armed vessels from American ports, putting France on the same footing with Great Britain. The third resolution called for increased military preparations.[13]

While these measures were being debated in the House in December, a move by New England Federalists to repeal the embargo was decisively defeated in the Senate by a straight party vote—25 to 6.[14] Instead, Congress passed a draconic enforcement act, tightening provisions of the Embargo Act by vesting the president "with the most arbitrary powers,"[15] some of them clearly violating individual rights such as the search-and-seizure provisions of the Fourth Amendment.[16]

The enforcement measure, which was signed by the president on January 9, 1809, after the House passed it by the lopsided vote of 71 to 32, seemed a decisive test of public support. But things began to fall apart almost immediately. The Enforcement Act pushed New England Federalists from resistance to the edge of revolt. Imitating the Virginia Resolutions of 1798, the Massachusetts legislature adopted resolutions denouncing the law as "unconstitutional, and not legally binding" and called on the states to "interpose for arresting the progress" of such laws. The Connecticut General Assembly responded by voting "to abstain from any agency in the execution of [Embargo] measures, which are unconstitutional and despotic."[17]

With Jefferson on the sidelines and Madison lacking the authority of presidential power, Gallatin reported that "great confusion and perplexity reign in Congress."[18] Even before the Massachusetts and Connecticut resolutions reached Washington, New England Republicans were getting hard to hold to the party line, when one could be defined. On January 20, 1809, the lame-duck House tried to define one, coupling the proposal of a special session of the newly elected Congress in May with another to repeal the embargo as a prelude to war in the summer of 1809. Congress quickly set the special session for May 22. Four days later, Wilson Cary Nicholas presented a motion, labeled "Mr. Madison's proposed resolution" on Gallatin's copy, which moved that on a specific date the new Congress would repeal the embargo. Nicholas filled

---

13. *Ibid.;* Malone, V, p. 631; and Spivak, pp. 177-80.
14. Malone, V, p. 628.
15. Albert Gallatin to TJ, July 29, 1808, cited *ibid.,* p. 636.
16. For a harsh indictment of TJ's enforcement of the embargo, see Leonard W. Levy, *Jefferson and Civil Liberties: The Darker Side* (Cambridge, Mass., 1963), pp. 93-141. For an argument that "Jefferson's enforcement policies did not reveal a dark side to his encounter with civil liberties," see Spivak, p. 225, who says that "they merely combated the enemies of the Republic in proper eighteenth-century fashion."
17. Malone, V, pp. 651-55.
18. Brant, IV, p. 473.

the blank date with June 1, at which time the United States would "resume, maintain, and defend its navigation of the high seas, against any nation or nations having in force edicts, orders or decrees violating the lawful commerce and neutral rights of the United States."[19]

The plan also called for issuing letters of marque and reprisal against either or both of the belligerents, making it clear that repeal was not submission but a step towards war—the only course, Nicholas argued, that "can extricate [the country] from its difficulties."[20] In the interim between passage of the Nicholas-Madison resolution and June 1, the belligerents would have one last chance to modify their policies while the United States used the time for military preparations. The move would also make it possible for Jefferson to end his forty-year public career with the embargo in place and the nation still at peace.

Unfortunately, the proposal came after three months of procrastination and rudderless drifting by the Republicans and growing Federalist denunciations of the president as "a dish of skim milk."[21] After the motion for repeal had been separated from the motion for preparedness measures for purposes of debate, Nicholas suggested June 1 as the date for the repeal of the Embargo Act. But John Randolph and some Quiddish allies, all southern Republicans, promptly proposed three other dates—"forthwith" by Randolph, February 15 by David R. Williams of South Carolina, and March 4 by John Rhea of Tennessee.[22] During the week between the Nicholas-Madison motion and the vote on February 1, the weary Republican majority, which would have welcomed the Nicholas-Madison plan at the beginning of the session, could no longer restrain the New England wing, rocked by antiembargo petitions from home. "It has been our misfortune," Nicholas told Madison, "that the various expedients have been offered too late."[23] Instead, the New Englanders revolted and joined the Randolph and Clinton followers, other disenchanted Republicans who were fearful of the double threat of war and disunion, and the Federalist bloc in rejecting the Nicholas-Madison date of June 1 by a vote of 73 to 40. The House then filled in the blank with March 4, Madison's inaugural date.

On the eve of his inauguration, Madison concluded that "on no occasion were the ideas so unstable and so scattered."[24] The "sudden and unaccountable revolution of opinion," Jefferson thought, started with the antiembargo forces in the East, then kindled "a kind of panic" that spread to New England

19. *Ibid.*, pp. 477–78, and Malone, V, p. 644.
20. Spivak, p. 188.
21. Spivak entitles his chapter on policy and the presidential succession "A Rudderless Ship" and cites Josiah Quincy, Jr., to John Quincy Adams, Dec. 14, 1808, for this denunciation of TJ; see *ibid.*, p. 137.
22. *Ibid.*, pp. 188–90.
23. Wilson Cary Nicholas to JM, Feb. 6, 1809, cited in Brant, IV, p. 478.
24. JM to William Pinkney, Feb. 11, 1809, cited in Ketcham, p. 466.

and New York congressmen.[25] Madison agreed that "the Eastern seaboard is become so impatient under privations of activity and gain . . . that it becomes necessary for the sake of the Union that the spirit not be too much opposed."[26]

After the House rejected June 1 as the date for the repeal of the embargo, Nicholas tried to salvage something for the new administration, suggesting to Madison that "we must submit to the plan least disgraceful in which we can unite the greatest number of votes."[27] At the president-elect's request, the House added nonintercourse with Britain and France to repeal. As the end of the session—and of Jefferson's presidency—neared, the House substituted a Senate bill that linked letters of marque and reprisal with nonintercourse. The House quickly rejected the first, thus rejecting war, but accepted the second, establishing a new form of economic coercion but authorizing the president to resume trade with either belligerent upon the repeal of its illegal edicts.

The passage of the Nonintercourse Act, complained one disgruntled Republican, was "a novelty in legislation, for . . . it has not a friend in the House, nor did it represent the views of the incoming administration."[28] Patched together from various plans, it repealed the embargo, allowing the resumption of American commerce in general but imposing the nonintercourse legislation, which closed trade with both the British Empire and France, including the Continental areas controlled by Napoleon; extended to France the prohibitions barring armed ships from American ports; and authorized the incoming president to reopen trade with whichever power ceased its violations of America's neutral rights.

In the final analysis, it was the collapse of party discipline among the befuddled Republicans, not the opposition of the reviving Federalists, that defeated the embargo. As a New England Republican observed on the party split, "The South say embargo or war, and the North and East say, no embargo, no war. . . . I lament that this difference of opinion exists; yet, as it does exist, we must take things as they are, and legislate accordingly. The genius and duty of Republican Government is to make laws to suit the people, and not attempt to make the people suit the laws."[29]

Jefferson had entered the presidency at the head of a party devoted to him and had carried the party and the people in support of the embargo principle, which he never explained fully to the public. In his final months in office, he remained committed to the embargo personally but forfeited his role of leadership until it was too late to reclaim it from a turbulent and expiring Congress. Madison was also "inclined to hug the embargo, and die in its

25. TJ to Thomas Mann Randolph, Feb. 7, 1809, in Ford, IX, p. 244.
26. JM to William Pinkney, Jan. 3, 1809, cited in Ketcham, p. 465.
27. Wilson Cary Nicholas to JM, Feb. 6, 1809, cited in Brant, IV, p. 478.
28. Bradford Perkins, *Prologue to War: England and the United States, 1805–1812* (Berkeley, 1963), pp. 226–32.
29. Speech of Orchard Cook in Congress, Jan. 31, 1809, cited in Malone, V, pp. 646–47.

embrace,"[30] a captive of a policy that was as much his as it was Jefferson's. As a consequence, he inherited a demoralized and disunited party that had rejected his favorite policy after it appeared to require more sacrifices from its domestic supporters than it wrung from its targeted victims.

Jefferson signed the repeal measure on March 1, 1809, anxious at long last to return to Monticello. On the next day, he wrote an old friend: "Within a few days I retire to my family, my books and farms. . . . Never did a prisoner, released from his chains, feel such relief as I shall on shaking off the shackles of power."[31]

—————————— THE LETTERS ——————————

Madison to Jefferson

[Washington Oct. 30, 1808]

J. M. is obliged to send back the papers wanted by the P. witht. having executed the task of remodelling the 1st. and 2d. paragraphs. He was prevented last night by company, and has but just got up for breakfast. If the P. can spare it he will immediately go to work; or if he can send the rough original of that part, it will do as well. The notes of Mr. G. are retained.[1]
Sunday

Madison to Jefferson

[Washington Oct. 30, 1808][2]

(1)[3]to exercise the authority in such manner as would withdraw the pretext on which the aggressions were originally founded, and open the way for a

30. Orchard Cook to John Quincy Adams, Jan. 1, 1809, cited in Spivak, p. 189.
31. TJ to Pierre-Samuel du Pont de Nemours, Mar. 2, 1809, in L. and B., XII, pp. 259–60.
1. TJ's draft of his final annual message to Congress was written before the *Hope* arrived with dispatches from London and Paris rejecting American overtures to withdraw the embargo if either or both would repeal its orders or edicts. The ship pulled into New York on Oct. 26, 1808, and couriers delivered the dispatches in Washington on Oct. 29; see Malone, V, pp. 614–15, and Brant, IV, p. 465. JM was then asked to revise the first two paragraphs of TJ's message.
2. JM labeled this undated document "Notes for the message," and TJ endorsed it Nov. 8, the date of his message, which is in Ford, IX, pp. 213–25. But both Malone, V, p. 619, and Brant, IV, pp. 464, 518, date it Oct. 30, 1808. It is clear that JM made his revisions after reviewing the dispatches from the *Hope,* which he received on Oct. 29.
3. The first portion of TJ's message dealt with his authority to suspend the embargo in an effort to get the belligerents to revoke "their unrighteous edicts." The introductory part of TJ's sentence preceding JM's suggestions ran as follows: "Our ministers at London and Paris were instructed to explain to the respective governments there, our disposition."

renewal of that commercial intercourse which it was alledged on all sides had been reluctantly obstructed. As each of those Govts. had pledged its readiness to concur in renouncing a measure which reached its adversary thro' the incontestable rights of neutrals only, and as the measure had been assumed by each as a retaliation for an asserted acquiescence in the aggressions of the other, it was reasonably expected that the occasion would have been seized by both for evincing the sincerity of their professions, and for restoring to the commerce of the U. S. its legitimate freedom.

This course so clearly dictated by justice has been taken by neither. By France no answer has been given; nor is there any indication that a favorable change in her Decrees is contemplated. To that Govt. instead of a pledge for suspending our Embargo as to France whilst left in operation as to G. Britain, it was thought most consistent with the condition annexed to the authority vested in the Executive, requiring a sufficient safety to our commerce, to hold out the obvious change resulting from such an act of justice by one belligerent, and refusal of it by another, in the relations between the U. S. and the latter. To G. B. whose power on the ocean is so ascendant, it was deemed not inconsistent with that condition, to state explicitly, that on her rescinding her orders in relation to the U. S. their trade would be opened with her, and remain shut to her enemy, in case of his failure to rescind his decrees also. The unexceptionable nature of this proposition seemed to ensure its being received in the spirit in which it was made; and this was the less to be doubted as the British orders in Council, had not only been referred for their vindication to an acquiescence on the part of the U. S. no longer to be pretended; but as the arrangement proposed, whilst it resisted the illegal Decrees of France, involved moreover substantially, the precise advantages professedly aimed at by the B. Orders. The arrangement has, nevertheless, been explicitly rejected, the controverted fact being assumed, that the Enemy of G. B. was the original aggressor, and the extraordinary doctrine maintained, that without regard to any just interpositions of the neutral, agst. the aggressor not specifically effecting a revocation of his acts, the injured belligerent has a right to pursue[4] his retaliations against the neutral and is to be inferred from the practice witht. regard to the measure of injury sustained thro' the neutral.

This candid and liberal experiment having thus failed, and no other event having occurred, on which a suspension of the Embargo by the Executive, was authorized it necessarily remains in the extent originally given to it. We have the satisfaction however to reflect, that in return for the privations imposed by the measure, and which our fellow Citizens in general have borne with patriotism, it has had the important effects of saving our vast mercantile property and our mariners; as well as of affording time for prosecuting the defensive and provisional measures required on the part of the U. S. Whilst on another hand, the course pursued by them will have demonstrated to foreign nations the moderation and firmness which govern their Counsels and have confirmed

4. JM gave "continue" as an alternative word for "pursue."

in all their Citizens the motives which ought to unite them in support of the laws and the rights of their Country. To these considerations may be added, that the measure has thus long frustrated those usurpations and spoliations which if resisted involved war; if submitted to, sacrificed a vital principle of our national Independance.

Under a continuance of the belligerent measures which have overspread the ocean with danger, it will be with the wisdom of Congs. to decide on the course best adapted to such a state of things; and bringing with them as they do from every part of the Union the sentiments of our Constituents, my confidence is strengthened that in forming this decision, they will, with an unerring regard to the essential rights and interests of the nation, weigh and compare the painful alternatives out of which a choice is to be made. Nor should I do justice to the virtues which on other occasions have marked the character of the American people, if I did not cherish an equal confidence, that the alternative chosen, whatever it may be, will be maintained with all the fortitude and patriotism which the crisis ought to inspire.

The Documents containing the correspondences on the subject of the foreign Edicts agst. our commerce, with the instructions given to our ministers at London and Paris are laid before you.

(2) The Communications made to Congs. at their last session explained the posture in which the close of the discussions relating to the attack by a B. Ship of war, on the Frigate Chesapeake left a subject on which the nation had manifested so honorable a sensibility. Every view of what had passed, authorized a belief that immediate steps would be taken by the B. Govt. for redressing a wrong; which the more it was investigated, appeared the more clearly to require what had not been provided for in the special Mission. It is found that no steps have been taken for the purpose. On the contrary it will be seen in the documents laid before you, that the inadmissible preliminary which obstructed the adjustment, is still adhered to; and, moreover, that it is now brought into connexion with the distinct and irrelative case of the Orders in Council. The instruction which had been given to our Minister at London, with a view to facilitate if necessary, the reparation claimed by the U. S. are included in the documents communicated.[5]

The instructions given to our Ministers with respect to the different belligerents were necessarily modified with a reference to their different circumstances and to the condition annexed by law to the Excv power of suspension which was to be exercised only under a degree of security to our commerce as would not result from a repeal of the Edicts of France.[6] Instead of a pledge for a suspension of the Embargo as to her, in case of such a repeal, it was presumed that a sufficient inducement might be found in other considerations and particularly, in the change produced by a compliance with our just demands by

---

5. The preceding portions of JM's suggestions were incorporated into TJ's message. Ford, IX, pp. 213–15, prints "Madison's Draft, Nov. 08," but ends at this point.

6. TJ inserted this sentence in JM's first paragraph at the end of the second sentence, which concluded with the words "legitimate freedom."

one belligerent, and a refusal by the other in the relations between this other and the U. S.[7]

1. manner for *way:* this word following so nearly

(2) substitute "it will rest with the Congress to decide on the course best adapted to such a state of things; and bringing as they do from every part of the Union, the sentiments of our Constituents, my confidence is the stronger that they will, in forming this decision, weigh and compare with an unerring regard to the essential rights and interests of the nation, the painful alternatives out of which a choice is to be made.[8]

(3) it is worthy of consideration that a portion of the industry and capital spared from those pursuits, has been converted to internal manufactures and improvements.[9] The extent of this conversion is far beyond expectation, and little doubt remains that the establishts. formed and forming, will, under the auspices of cheap materials and subsistence, the freedom of labor from taxation with us, and the protection given by our commercial laws become permanent, and that with the aid of household fabrics, which needed a trial only to prove the durable advantage of excluding them,[10] the mass of our future wants from foreign sources will be materially diminished, and the nation consequently liberated in an equal degree from that species of dependence, as well as from the dangers and expence incident to the Element traversed in pursuit of foreign supplies.

(4) or shall the revenue be reduced   or shall it not   rather be appropriated etc. etc.

Madison and Gallatin to Jefferson

[Washington] Nov. 15, 1808[11]

DEAR SIR,

Both Mr. Madison and myself concur in opinion that, considering the temper of the Legislature, or rather of its members, it would be eligible to point out to them some precise and distinct course.

As to what that should be, we may not all perfectly agree; and perhaps the knowledge of the various feelings of the members and of the apparent public opinion may on consideration induce a revision of our own. I feel myself nearly as undetermined between enforcing the embargo or war as I was on our

---

7. This is an alternative wording for the third sentence in JM's second paragraph, above.
8. This is an alternative wording for the first sentence in JM's fourth paragraph, above.
9. JM's observations relate to the shift in investments from shipping to manufacturing as a result of the embargo. For Gallatin's criticism that any praise of benefits flowing from the suspension of commerce might "furnish a powerful weapon to the disaffected," see Brant, IV, p. 465.
10. JM meant that the brief trial of excluding foreign textiles under the Embargo Act had lessened reliance on foreign sources by stimulating domestic manufacturing; see *ibid.,* p. 464.
11. This letter is reproduced from Albert Gallatin, *The Writings of Albert Gallatin,* ed. Henry Adams, 3 vols. (Philadelphia, 1879), I, p. 428.

last meetings. But I think that we must (or rather you must) decide the question absolutely, so that we may point out a decisive course either way to our friends. Mr. Madison, being unwell, proposed that I should call on you and suggest our wish that we might, with the other gentlemen, be called by you on that subject. Should you think that course proper, the sooner the better. The current business has prevented my waiting on you personally in the course of the morning. Respectfully, your obedient servant.

[ALBERT GALLATIN]

Madison to Jefferson
                                             Washington Dec. 21, 1808

The Secretary of State, in pursuance of the Resolution of the House of Representatives of the 11th of Novr respectfully reports to the President of the United States, a copy of an Act of the British Parliament regulating the trade between the United States and Great Britain, and also copies of such belligerent Acts, Decrees, Orders, and Proclamations as affect neutral rights of commerce, and as have been attainable in the Department of State; with the exception however, of sundry acts, particularly blockades, of doubtful import or inferior importance, which it was supposed would have inconveniently extended the delay and the size of the Report.[12]

JAMES MADISON

Jefferson to Madison
                                                          [1808][13]

1796   June   19. was the last letter I ever wrote to Genl. Washington.
        July   6. he answered it partially.
        Augt.   28. his ultimate answer, and the last letter I ever received from him.
1797.   May.   the mutilated letter from me to Mazzei appeared here.

12. In the debates concerning the British orders-in-council and the French decrees affecting American commerce, the House requested the president to send "copies of all acts, decrees, orders, and proclamations, affecting the commercial rights of neutral nations, issued or enacted by Great Britain, and France, or any other belligerent Power, since the year 1791" along with any acts placing American commerce in foreign ports upon the footing of the most favored nations. For JM's enclosures, see *ASP, FR,* III, pp. 262–94.

13. This undated memorandum relating to TJ's correspondence with George Washington has the following undated notation in Dolley Madison's handwriting: "The following is a copy of a paper in Mr Jefferson's hand writing, among his letters to Mr. Madison, in the years 1807 and 1808."

Madison to Jefferson

[Washington Jan. 13, 1809]¹⁴

(1) placed us under that national Govt. which constitutes the safety of every part, by uniting for its protection the strength of the whole
(2) with indifference
(3) and to enervate a resistance to their oppressor
(4) propagated
(5) into any course that would eventually make them subservient to foreign views equally adverse to the political strength and commercial importance of their own Country
(6) of transporting and exchanging it
(7) as sacrifices in so peculiar a situation can be made to do so, and that a greater insult could not have been offered to an honorable State, than by propositions so unworthy of the tenor of its former history, so subversive of its essential interests and future prosperity

Madison to Jefferson

[Washington] Jan. 17, 1809

I communicate to Congs. certain letters, which passed between the B. Secy. of State Mr. Canning and Mr. P. our Minister Plenipotentiary at London. When the Documents concerning the relations between the U. S. and G. B. were laid before Congs. at the commencement of the Session, the answer of Mr. P. to the letter of Mr. Canning had not been received; and a communication of the latter alone would have accorded, neither with propriety, nor with the wishes of Mr. Pinkney. When that answer, afterwards arrived, it was considered that as what had passed in conversation, had been superceded by the written and formal correspondence on the subject, the variance in the statements of what had verbally passed, was not of sufficient importance to be made the matter of a distinct and special communication. The Letter of Mr. C. however, having lately appeared in print, unaccompanied by that of Mr. P. in reply and having a tendency to make impressions

---

14. JM did not date this memorandum, but TJ's endorsement lists the date he received it and the subject matter. These are JM's suggested alterations to the draft of TJ's letter of Jan. 14, 1809, to Dr. William Eustis, who had transmitted resolutions adopted by the Republican citizens of Boston on Dec. 19, 1808, supporting the embargo. In his reply to Eustis, TJ utilized the first and last suggestions by JM to defend the temporary restriction of American commerce in order to "make further preparation for enforcing the redress of its wrongs, and restoring it to its rightful freedom." "To save permanent rights," he argued, "temporary sacrifices were necessary"; see L. and B., XII, pp. 227–29.

not warranted by the statements of Mr. P. it has become proper that the whole of this correspondence should be brought into public view.[15]

Jefferson to Madison

[Washington] Jan. 23, 1809

TH:J. TO J. MADISON

In the wild range which Tatham's head takes, he often hits on good ideas.[16] Those explained in the within letter merit real attention. He knows the localities of that quarter; and should the idea of an artificial bason on the Middle grounds be found impracticable (for want of foundation) Lynhaven bay, deepened at it's entrance becomes the sole resource for defending the Chesapeake; and the connection proposed between that and the Eastern branch is easy and indispensable: that also with Curratuck would be highly important. Affectte. salutns

15. JM drafted this statement, which TJ signed and submitted verbatim to the Senate and House on the same day. See Richardson, I, p. 460; Malone, V, pp. 616–19; and Perkins, pp. 175–77, 203–6.

16. William Tatham, the father of topographical and coastal surveys, was appointed state geographer of Virginia in 1789; see *PTJ,* XXII, p. xxxviii. For Tatham's correspondence with TJ and JM, see Elizabeth McPherson, ed., "Letters of William Tatham," *WMQ* 2d ser., 16 (1936): 169–91, 362–98.

MADISON TAKES OVER, 1809

JAMES MADISON WAS INAUGURATED president of the United States three days after Jefferson signed the repeal of the Embargo Act. The two friends sat together at the front of the newly completed hall of the House of Representatives, which was jammed with an audience of "the high and the low . . . promiscuously blended on the floor and in the galleries." As one observer noted, "Mr. Jefferson appeared one of the most happy among this concourse of people."[1]

In his inaugural address, Madison paid tribute to the "illustrious services" of his predecessors, singling out Jefferson in particular by expressing "the sympathy with which my heart is full in the rich reward he enjoys in the benedictions of a beloved country, gratefully bestowed for exalted talents zealously devoted through a long career to the advancement of its highest interest and happiness."

The new president rehearsed the difficulties of a neutral nation in a world situation "without a parallel." "In their rage against each other," the belligerents had established principles of retaliation "equally contrary to universal reason and acknowledged law," resorting to arbitrary edicts whose revocation the United States had sought with "fair and liberal attempt." Since his inauguration followed four months of debate on the embargo and nonintercourse, however, Madison did not elaborate on foreign policy but instead summarized, in a single sentence of extraordinary length, his principles and purposes as president:

To cherish peace and friendly intercourse with all nations having correspondent dispositions; to maintain sincere neutrality toward belligerent nations; to prefer in all cases amicable discussion and reasonable accommodation of differences to a decision of them by an appeal to arms; to exclude foreign intrigues and foreign partialities, so degrading to all countries and so baneful to free ones; to foster a spirit of independence too just to invade the rights of others, too proud to surrender our own, too liberal to indulge

---

1. Noble E. Cunningham, *In Pursuit of Reason: The Life of Thomas Jefferson* (Baton Rouge, 1987), p. 319.

unworthy prejudices ourselves and too elevated not to look down upon them in others; to hold the union of the States as the basis of their peace and happiness; to support the Constitution, which is the cement of the Union, as well in its limitations as in its authorities; to respect the rights and authorities reserved to the States and to the people as equally incorporated with and essential to the success of the general system; to avoid the slightest interference with the rights of conscience or the functions of religion, so wisely exempted from civil jurisdiction; to preserve in their full energy the other salutary provisions in behalf of private and personal rights, and of the freedom of the press; to observe economy in public expenditures; to liberate the public resources by an honorable discharge of the public debts; to keep within the requisite limits a standing military force, always remembering that an armed and trained militia is the firmest bulwark of republics—that without standing armies their liberty can never be in danger, nor with large ones safe; to promote by authorized means improvements friendly to agriculture, to manufactures, and to external as well as internal commerce; to favor in like manner the advancement of science and the diffusion of information as the best aliment to true liberty; to carry on the benevolent plans which have been so meritoriously applied to the conversion of our aboriginal neighbors from the degradation and wretchedness of savage life to a participation of the improvements of which the human mind and manners are susceptible in a civilized state—as far as sentiments and intentions such as these can aid the fulfillment of my duty, they will be a resource which can not fail me.[2]

After the inauguration, the Madisons held open house at their residence on F Street, where they "stood to receive their company. She looked extremely beautiful," wrote Margaret Bayard Smith, "was drest in a plain cambrick-dress with a very long train, plain around the neck without any handkerchief, and beautiful bonnet of purple velvet, and white satin with white plumes. She was all dignity, grace, and affability."

The president was "dressed in a full suit of American manufacture, made of the wool of Merinos raised in this country." Jefferson wore a new blue suit from the same Connecticut manufacturer. Madison's was black but "not a bit smarter than Mr. Jefferson's."[3]

One observer told the retiring president, "You have now resigned a heavy burden."

"Yes, indeed," he responded, "and I am much happier at this moment than my friend."

Jefferson "seemed in high spirits," according to Mrs. Smith, "and his countenance beamed with a benevolent joy. I do believe," she added, "father never loved son more than he loves Mr. Madison."[4]

At the inaugural ball, Jefferson attended as "a plain, unassuming citizen." But all eyes were again on Dolley Madison, who "looked a queen" and dis-

2. Richardson, I, pp. 467–68. See Robert Allen Rutland's *The Presidency of James Madison* (Lawrence, Kans., 1990) for a lively account.
3. Ketcham, pp. 475–76, and Brant, V, p. 13.
4. *Ibid.*, pp. 13–14, and Ketcham, p. 475.

played charm enough to "conciliate even enemies." Indeed, she sat between General Louis Marie Turreau, the French minister, and David Montagu Erskine, the British minister, whose countries were at war; and the new president sat across the table from the first lady. Unfortunately, John Quincy Adams grumbled, "the crowd was excessive—the heat oppressive, and the entertainment bad."

Adams's wife, Louisa Catherine Adams, later left an incisive description of the new president and his wife:

Mr. Madison was a *very* small man in his *person,* with a *very* large *head*—his manners were peculiarly unassuming; and his conversation lively, often playful. . . . His language was chaste, well suited to [the] occasion, and the simple expression of the passing thought . . . in harmony with the taste of his hearers.

Mrs. Madison [on the other hand] was tall, large and rather masculine in personal dimensions; her complexion was so fair and brilliant as to redeem this objection, in its perfectly feminine beauty. . . . There was a frankness and ease in her deportment, that won golden opinions from all, and she possessed an influence so decided with her little Man.[5]

It took Jefferson a week to pack his belongings, vacate the White House, and leave for Monticello. He had already replied to an address from his neighbors in what he now called the "national metropolis," toasting "this solitary republic of the world, the only monument of human rights, and the sole depository of the sacred fire of freedom and self-government, from hence it is to be lighted up in other regions of the earth, if other regions of the earth ever become susceptible of its benign influence."[6] He left Washington on March 11 and had "a very fatiguing journey, having found the roads excessive bad, altho'," the veteran traveler added, "I have seen them worse. The last three days I found it better to be on horseback, and travelled 8. hours through as disagreeable a snow storm as I was ever in."[7]

The retired president quickly established his routine at Monticello, concentrating on his duties as an enterprising farmer: "From sunrise till breakfast only I allot for my pen and ink work," he told his grandson. "From breakfast [at 9] till dinner [about 4] I am in my garden, shops or on horseback in the farms, and after dinner I devote entirely to relaxation or light reading."[8]

Although the Federalists fostered the idea that Jefferson secretly dictated the direction of Madison's administration from Monticello, they were doubly mistaken. Madison seldom solicited advice, nor did Jefferson often offer it. Even before he left Washington for Monticello, Jefferson laid down a self-imposed law, announcing his intention never to interfere with Madison or the

---

5. For Adams's remark, see *ibid.,* pp. 475–76; for Mrs. Adams's appraisal, see Rutland, p. 21.

6. Cunningham, p. 321.

7. TJ to JM, Mar. 17, 1809, below.

8. TJ to Thomas Jefferson Randolph, Dec. 30, 1809, cited in Cunningham, p. 326.

heads of departments in supporting applicants for public office, fearing that it would transform him "from the character of a friend to that of an unreasonable and troublesome solicitor."[9]

After Jefferson retired, he and Madison continued their correspondence with the same sort of candor that had always marked it, writing as peers and partners who respected each other's views. The president kept Jefferson informed about the conduct of foreign policy, once lamenting the loss of the embargo as an instrument of national policy, but he usually cited newspaper accounts to keep his friend on his isolated mountaintop posted on political developments. On the few occasions when Jefferson's suggestions did not square with Madison's views, the president felt free to disregard them without fear of resentment. As Smelser has observed, Madison "was no junior Jefferson."[10]

Back home again at Monticello, Jefferson laced his letters to Madison with weather reports—"the spring is remarkably backward"; crop predictions—"the crop of corn turns out worse than was expected"; concern about his debts—"it is my duty to write to you on the subject of the Note you were so kind as to endorse for me at the bank of the US."; and local news of importance—James Monroe planned to move from Richmond "to his residence here" in Albemarle County.[11]

Jefferson was especially anxious to restore amicable relations between the president and Monroe, who had been Madison's rival in the election of 1808. Less than two weeks after he returned home, the peacemaker reported that Monroe had "dined and passed an evening with me. . . . He is sincerely cordial: and I learn from several that he has quite separated himself from the junto which had got possession of him." Indeed, he reported that Monroe and John Randolph "now avoid seeing one another, mutually dissatisfied," and he predicted that Monroe's "strong and candid mind will bring him to a cordial return to his old friends after he shall have been separated a while from his present circle" in Richmond.[12]

When Madison heard from another source that Monroe might be willing to accept an appointment as governor of Louisiana Territory, he asked Jefferson "to give a turn to conversation with Col. M. which may feel the disposition of his mind, without indicating any particular object."[13] Anxious to re-

---

9. TJ's circular letter of Mar. 1809, below.

10. Marshall Smelser, *The Democratic Republic, 1801–1815* (New York, 1968), p. 187. See also Brant, V, pp. 202–6, and Malone, VI, pp. 20–21. For a more extensive analysis of the relations between TJ and JM, see Roy J. Honeywell, "President Jefferson and His Successor" *AHR* 46 (1940): 64–75.

11. See TJ to JM, Mar. 17, 1809, below, Oct. 9, 1809, below, May 22, 1809, below, and Mar. 30, 1809, below.

12. TJ to JM, Mar. 30, 1809, below.

13. JM to TJ, Nov. 27, 1809, below.

Madison Takes Over, 1809

move "the curtain which seemed to be drawn between him and his best friends," Jefferson immediately rode over for "an hour or two's frank conversation" with Monroe, arguing that his acceptance of "any post would be a signal of reconciliation, on which the body of republicans, who lamented his absence from the public service, would again rally to him." Despite his wish "for the success of the administration," Monroe flatly rejected "any office where he should be subordinate to any body but the President himself, or which did not place his responsibility substantially with the President and the nation," such as a cabinet post. When Jefferson mentioned a military command under General James Wilkinson, Monroe wisely said that "he would sooner be shot than take [such] a command."[14]

Jefferson concluded his report on Monroe by observing that "everything from him breathed the purest patriotism, involving however, a close attention to his own honour and grade. He expressed himself with the utmost devotion to the interests of our own country." Madison replied that "Monroe's mind is very nearly what I had supposed," except for his surprising "willingness to have taken a seat in the Cabinet," a post that the president was to offer him later.[15]

The Madisons moved into the President's House the day that Jefferson moved out, and there were frequent housekeeping questions from the new president to his predecessor. "I forget," Madison confessed, "whether the time piece in the sitting room be *monthly* or weekly? Will you please when you inform me," he continued, " . . . add a memorandum of the Newspapers retained by you out of the list sent you whilst here, that I may know how to dispose of them."[16] But the new president turned over to Mrs. Madison most of the housekeeping questions. Dolley collaborated happily with Benjamin Henry Latrobe, surveyor of public buildings who doubled as purchasing agent and interior designer for a complete refurnishing of the presidential quarters.[17]

Although Mrs. Madison and the architect-decorator usually cooperated, they occasionally quarreled. But the first lady won most of the arguments, especially when it came to bright colors for curtains and textiles.[18] Together they spent $2,205 for knives, forks, bottle stands, and andirons; $458 for a pianoforte; and $28 for a guitar.[19] Jefferson, who considered Latrobe "a mas-

---

14. TJ to JM, Nov. 30, 1809, below.

15. JM to TJ, Dec. 11, 1809, below. For a discussion of the reconciliation, see Harry Ammon, *James Monroe: The Quest for National Identity* (New York, 1971), pp. 279–88.

16. JM to TJ, Mar. 27, 1809, below.

17. On Mar. 2 and 3, 1809, Congress appropriated $14,000 for new furnishings for the President's House and an additional $12,000 for improvements, repairs, and landscaping; see *The Statutes at Large of the United States, 1789–1873*, 17 vols. (Boston, 1845–73), II, pp. 533, 537.

18. For their correspondence, see *PJM* (Pres. ser.), I, *passim*. For color photographs of some of Latrobe's sketches of furniture for the Madisons, see Jack L. Lindsey, "An Early LaTrobe Furniture Commission," *Antiques* 129 (Jan. 1991): 208–19.

19. *Ibid.*, 212. For first-rate accounts of the redecorating, see Conover Hunt-Jones, *Dolley and the "Great Little Madison"* (Washington, 1977); Margaret Brown Klapthor, "Benjamin Henry La

terly agent in the line of his emploiment," had warned Madison that he might also be extravagant, suggesting that "the reins must be held with a firmness that never relaxes."[20] The president, therefore, apportioned $5,000 as the first advance for furnishing, a sum that was quickly expended between March 10 and May 29.[21] On May 31, 1809, Dolley Madison and the president opened the redecorated White House for the first of their soon-to-be-famous "drawing room" receptions. "The court dress for the men," wrote one observer, "appears to be a black or blue coat with vest, black breeches and black stockings. The ladies," he added in a chauvinistic put-down, "were not remarkable for anything so much as for the exposure of their swelling breasts and bare backs."[22]

On the domestic front, Madison's presidency got off to a dismal start, when Republican senators, spearheaded by William B. Giles, who wanted to be secretary of state, notified the new president that they would oppose Gallatin's appointment in the State Department. Since Madison owed his nomination to the party caucus, he decided not to start his presidency with a bruising intraparty fight. Instead, he retained Gallatin in the treasury post and promoted Robert Smith, a brother of Giles's colleague, Senator Samuel Smith of Maryland, from the Navy Department to secretary of state. John Randolph approved the move, noting sarcastically that since Smith "can spell he ought to be preferred to Giles."[23]

On the diplomatic front, Madison got off to a spectacular start when he and the British minister exchanged notes embodying the Erskine Agreement, which restored commerce with Great Britain. On April 19, 1809, Madison issued a presidential proclamation announcing that trade with Britain would begin on June 10, when the obnoxious orders-in-council would no longer be enforced against the United States.[24] Bells rang, cannons reverberated, grand illuminations lit the skies from Maine to Georgia, and ships began loading cargo for the reopened trade with England as Americans greeted news of the agreement. Even John Randolph, Madison's harshest critic, endorsed the president's "promptitude and frankness" in the negotiations.[25]

Madison happily notified Jefferson that the British cabinet "must have

---

Trobe and Dolley Madison Decorate the White House, 1809-1811," *Bulletin* (U.S. National Museum) 241 (1965): Paper 49, 153-64; and Robert L. Raley, "Interior Designs by . . . La Trobe for the President's House," *Antiques* 75 (1959): 568-69.

20. TJ to JM, Mar. 30, 1809, below.

21. The total came to $5,038.75; see *PJM* (Pres. ser.), I, pp. 212-13.

22. Ketcham, p. 478; the quotation is from William Seale, *The President's House: A History*, 2 vols. (Washington, 1986), I, p. 129.

23. For JM's problems in naming his cabinet, see Brant, V, pp. 22-33; Ketcham, pp. 481-83; Rutland, pp. 205-7.

24. The fullest discussions are in Brant, IV, pp. 34-50, and Bradford Perkins, *Prologue to War: England and the United States, 1805-1812* (Berkeley, 1963), pp. 206-22, 234.

25. Ketcham, p. 494, and Brant, V, pp. 49-50.

changed its course under a full conviction that an adjustment with this Country, had become essential." He suspected that they also hoped to "embroil us with France," but he planned to "give the proceeding a contrary turn." Indeed, he hoped that France would "follow the example of G. B." and revoke its decrees. Its allies, particularly Russia, were war-weary, and France "must be equally aware of the importance of our relations to Spanish America," the "great object of Napoleon's pride and Ambition." He thought it probable that Bonaparte might offer to cede the Floridas to the United States in exchange for a provision prohibiting American trade with the Spanish colonies, "which would present a dilemma not very pleasant."[26]

Like Madison's undemonstrative letter announcing the Erskine Agreement, Jefferson's reply, which was three times as long as Madison's note, seemed studiously restrained, though decidedly upbeat. "I sincerely congratulate you on the change it has produced in our situation," and he added: "It is the source of very general joy here." Warming to the almost incredible news, however, he finally confessed, "I rejoice in it as the triumph of our forbearing and yet persevering system. It will lighten your anxieties, take from cabal it's most fertile ground of war, will give us peace during your time, and by the compleat extinguishment of our public debt, open upon us the noblest application of revenue that has ever been exhibited by any nation."

Jefferson was convinced that "the British ministry has been driven from it's Algerine system, not by any remaining morality in the people but by their unsteadiness under severe trial." The embargo had worked belatedly, and "we never can have them more in our power." His chief worry was the dispatch of a new minister to negotiate a commercial treaty to replace the expired Jay Treaty, whose name and provisions, he said, should never again be "quoted, or looked at, or even mentioned." The British had "never made an equal commercial treaty with any nation," he added, "and we have no right to expect to be the first." But if Madison stood by "the principles we dictated to Monroe" and avoided any departure from them, the United States was in a "highly favorable" position to obtain an acceptable treaty, which rejected the form of the Jay treaty, a form that would "for ever be a millstone round our necks unless we now rid ourselves of it, once [and] for all."

Jefferson was much less hopeful of any reasonable action by France than was Madison. If Napoleon were governed by reason, he would "not doubt the revocation of his edicts. . . . But his policy is so crooked that it eludes conjecture. I fear his first object now is to dry up the sources of British prosperity by excluding her manufactures from the continent," he continued, but "he ought to be satisfied with having forced her to revoke the orders on which he pretended to retaliate, and to be particularly satisfied with us by whose unyielding adherence to principle she has been forced into the revocation."

If that were the case, Napoleon "ought the more to conciliate our good

---

26. JM to TJ, Apr. 24, 1809, below.

will, as we can be such an obstacle to the new career opening on him in the Spanish colonies. That he would give us the Floridas," he said, as he thought of his southern obsession, in order "to withold intercourse with the residue of those colonies cannot be doubted. But that is no price, because they are ours in the first moment of the first war, and until a war they are of no particular necessity to us." What Napoleon might do if he took over the colonies of Spain in his conquest of Europe would be to consent "to our recieving Cuba into our union" in order to "prevent our aid to Mexico and the other provinces." That would be a difficult decision for Bonaparte, but he would probably agree. "That," Jefferson conceded, "would be a price."

Almost as an afterthought, he added: "It will be objected to our recieving Cuba, that no limit can then be drawn for our future acquisitions." But he had a ready answer, though a peculiar one, for that charge, based on sound Republican doctrine: "Cuba can be defended by us without a navy. and this developes the principle which ought to limit our views. Nothing should ever be accepted which would require a navy to defend it." And if it should come to pass that the United States should obtain Cuba, he had an easy way to demonstrate to the world that there were limits to the southern extension of the Union: "I would immediately erect a column on the Southernmost limit of Cuba and inscribe on it a Ne plus ultra as to us in that direction."

After looking at Spanish territory that might be gained if France took over the Spanish colonies in the Western Hemisphere, the former president turned his possessive gaze towards Canada. "We should then have only to include the North in our confederacy, which would be of course in the first war, and we should have such an empire for liberty as she has never surveyed since the creation: and I am persuaded no constitution was ever before so well calculated as ours for extensive empire and self government."[27]

Against Jefferson's expansive dreams, Madison posed some sober considerations. He agreed that the French decrees would be repealed as a consequence of Britain's withdrawal of the orders-in-council, but he doubted that Napoleon would hand over Cuba. Conversations between Gallatin and Turreau, the French minister to the United States, indicated that "the difficulty most likely to threaten our relations with France, lies in the effort she may make to render us in some way subservient to the reduction of Span: America; particularly by witholding our commerce. This apprehension is corroborated by the language of Turreau. He alluded to his conversations with you relating to Cuba on which he builds jealousies which he did not conceal. Cuba will without doubt be a cardinal object with Napoleon."[28]

However, Madison remained hopeful of further progress with Great Brit-

27. TJ to JM, Apr. 27, 1809, below.

28. For a brief discussion of TJ's remarks to Turreau "in the unconstraint of confidential talk," see Brant, V, pp. 57–65. Gallatin told Turreau that TJ's remarks on Cuba "was a new idea of Mr. Jefferson which has not been approved by the [Madison] cabinet, and I protest to you in its name that even if they wished to give Cuba to us, we would not accept it"; see *ibid.*, p. 59.

ain. "The Spirit which England will bring into the ulterior negociations must differ much from that which influenced former Treaties"—Madison could hardly persuade himself to even utter the words "Jay's treaty"—"if it can be moulded to our just views; and we must be prepared to meet it with a prudent adherence to our essential interests. It is possible however that the school of adversity may have taught her the policy of substituting for her arrogant pretensions, somewhat of a conciliating moderation towards the US." Confirming that hope was a recent change in England's tone, which suggested that "she can be brought to a fair estimate of her real interest." If that were so, he concluded, "it seems very practicable to surmount the obstacles which have hitherto kept us at variance, and untill surmounted must continue to do so. The case of impressments, hitherto the greatest obstacle, seems to admit most easily of adjustment, on grounds mutually advantageous."[29]

The dream of resolving the differences with England turned into a midsummer's nightmare, much to Madison's mortification, when Canning disavowed the Erskine Agreement and recalled the minister for exceeding his instructions. After learning of the Nonintercourse Act, the Portland ministry had authorized Erskine to settle the *Chesapeake* imbroglio and promise to repeal the odious orders if the United States met three conditions: American ports were to be open to British trade but were to remain closed to French commerce; the Rule of 1756 was to be accepted; and the United States was to allow the Royal Navy to seize American ships violating the ban on trade with France, thus enforcing America's maritime laws from England's point of view but reducing the country to a colonial status from the American point of view.[30]

Knowing that Madison would never accept Canning's conditions, Erskine had abandoned some of them voluntarily and accepted informal explanations outside the agreement on others, violating the letter of his instructions but insisting that he had complied with their conciliatory spirit in negotiating the first significant executive agreement in American history.[31]

Two days after 600 American ships had sailed for England, Madison got his first hint that Erskine might have overplayed his hand when a ship brought news accounts from Britain of a new order-in-council, a "crooked proceeding" that shook Madison's faith in the Erskine Agreement.[32] Jefferson also showed "great anxiety," wondering whether "we have most to fear" from "the folly or

---

29. JM to TJ, May 1, 1809, below. As secretary of state, JM had suggested that if England would agree to stop impressing American sailors at sea, the United States would agree to exclude British seamen from American ships and to return deserters.

30. Perkins, pp. 210–12. Rufus King, the Federalist who served both the Adams and Jefferson administrations as minister to Great Britain, observed that should the United States consent to these conditions, America "would appear to have voluntarily submitted to Terms of Humiliation and Dishonor."

31. *Ibid.*

32. JM to TJ, June 12, 1809, below.

the faithlesness of the Cannings and Castlereaghs of the British ministry. Is it possible," he asked Madison, "that to get themselves out of a former hobble they should have involved themselves in another so much more difficult?" Whatever the explanation, he confessed that "my joy on our supposed settlement is extremely damped by the occurrence of a trick, so strange." He especially feared "a return of our difficulties" and offered the president his sincere wish for "a happy issue from them, for your own sake as well as for that of us all."[33]

Four days later, Madison reported that Erskine had given new assurances that resulted in "re-animating confidence in the pledge of the B. Govt. . . . in his arrangemt. with this Govt." Although the president thought that Erskine's explanation was extraordinary—the British government was convinced that the United States would not meet its overtures and, therefore, issued the new order as a "seasonable mitigation" of the expected failure—he sent it to Congress, where it quieted distrust but did not eliminate "the ill grace stamped on the British retreat." He nonetheless hoped "that the B. Govt. will fulfil what its Minister has stipulated; and that if it means to be trickish, it will frustrate the proposed [commercial] negociation, and then say, their orders were not permanently repealed, but only withdrawn, *in the mean time*."[34]

After the special session of Congress adjourned in July, the Madisons hastened to Montpellier, still under the impression that the Erskine Agreement had cemented Anglo-American reconciliation. There they found a remodeling program in full swing, supervised by three craftsmen sent from Monticello by Jefferson. In addition to rebuilding the foundations and stabilizing the central block of the house, the Madisons had approved the addition of one-story wings on each side of the house, designed by William Thornton, architect of the Capitol, aided by Benjamin Henry Latrobe. The carpenters also built a colonnade over the sunken icehouse, one of the first in Virginia.[35]

The Madisons had been home less than two weeks when the president learned officially that the Portland ministry had, "by the mixture of fraud and folly," repudiated the Erskine Agreement and created "the mortifying necessity" of his return to Washington.[36] He made a quick trip to meet with the cabinet, spending three days on the trip down, three days on deliberations, and three days on the return trip. A presidential proclamation of August 9, 1809, revoked the proclamation of April 19 and reimposed the Nonintercourse Act suspending trade with Great Britain. Since the British disavowal permitted American ships sailing under the Erskine Agreement to sell their

33. TJ to JM, June 16, 1809, below.
34. JM to TJ, June 20, 1809, below.
35. TJ to JM, Apr. 19, 1809, below, mentions architect and carpenter James Dinsmore, who supervised the renovation, and John Neilson, "a gardener by nature." Hugh Chisholm, a brickmaker and mason, was already on the job; see Hunt-Jones, pp. 67–72. Also see Brant, IV, pp. 69–70, and Ketcham, pp. 479–80.
36. JM to TJ, Aug. 3, 1809, below.

cargoes and depart without penalty, Madison's proclamation reciprocated by allowing a similar arrangement for British ships arriving under the impression that trade had been legalized.³⁷ Otherwise, the Erskine Agreement, like the embargo, ended in a debacle, although in this case the humiliated Madison administration was blameless. But the price of failure was high, as Gallatin pointed out, especially if war came:

> We are not so well prepared for resistance as we were one year ago. All or almost all our mercantile wealth was safe at home, our resources entire, and our finances sufficient to carry us through the first year of the contest. Our property is now afloat; England relieved by our relaxations might stand two years of privation with ease; we have wasted our resources without any national utility; and, our treasury being exhausted, we must begin any plan of resistance with considerable and therefore unpopular loans.³⁸

As for Erskine, Madison thought that he was "in a ticklish situation with his Govt. I suspect he will not be able to defend himself agst. the charge of exceeding his instructions," Madison observed to Jefferson. "But he will make out a strong case agst. Canning, and be able to avail himself much of the absurdity and evident inadmissibility of the articles disregarded by him." Madison thought that the difference between the Erskine arrangement and the British orders-in-council of April 26 "is too slight to justify the disavowal of him." The latter allowed indirect trade with Holland through Prussian ports while Erskine's allowed direct trade. If that distinction was the basis for the disavowal, it meant that their object was not to injure France, but was aimed at American competition. "Their ob[ject] is not to retaliate injury to an Enemy; but to prevent the legitimate trade of the U. S. from interfering with the London smugglers of Sugar and Coffee."³⁹

The sympathetic Jefferson blasted the Portland ministry "as the most shameless ministry which ever disgraced England. Copenhagen will immortalize their infamy. In general their administrations are so changeable, and they are obliged to descend to such tricks to keep themselves in place, that nothing like honor or morality can ever be counted on in transactions with them." He hoped that Erskine could justify his negotiations since he was a man of integrity who stood in stark contrast with Canning, a man of "unprincipled rascality."⁴⁰

To Federalist complaints about the legality of both of Madison's proclamations—the one announcing the Erskine Agreement and the one revoking it—Jefferson replied that both were sound exercises of presidential power. "The first has been sanctioned by universal approbation," he wrote reassuringly. "It proved to the whole world our desire of accomodation, and must have satisfied every candid federalist on that head. It was not only proper on

37. Brant, IV, pp. 78-79.
38. Perkins, pp. 219-20.
39. JM to TJ, Aug. 16, 1809, below.
40. TJ to JM, Aug. 17, 1809, below.

the well grounded confidence that the arrangement would be honestly executed, but ought to have taken place even had the perfidy of England been foreseen. Their dirty gain is richly remunerated to us, by our placing them so shamefully in the wrong, and by the union it must produce among ourselves. The last proclamation admits of quibbles," he conceded, "of which advantage will doubtless be endeavored to be taken by those to whom gain is their god, and their country nothing. But it is soundly defensible."

On the larger question of international consequences, Jefferson thought that if Napoleon had "the wisdom to correct his injustice towards us," trade with France would be restored, leading to British attacks on American ships. "This will be war on their part," he observed, and would make war with England inevitable. "The moment that open war shall be apprehended from them," he continued, "we should take possession of Baton rouge. If we do not, they will, and New Orleans becomes irrecoverable and the Western country blockaded during the war. It would be justifiable towards Spain on this ground, and equally so on that of title to W. Florida and reprisal extended to E. Florida. Whatever turn our present difficulty may take, I look upon all cordial conciliation with England as desperate during the life of the present king."[41]

Despite the full exchange of views between Madison and Jefferson on foreign affairs, the president reserved some of his thoughts for his summer visit to Monticello, when he could "say more than I cou'd well put on paper."[42] Several days after Madison's return from Washington, Mr. and Mrs. Gallatin arrived at Montpellier and joined the Madisons on their annual pilgrimage to Monticello on August 24. The three political leaders must have had serious discussions on foreign affairs, but none of their views was "put on paper." In turn, Jefferson visited the Madisons in September before they returned to Washington, after spending "two months on our mountain."[43]

When Madison arrived in the nation's capital in October, he met the new British minister, Francis James "Copenhagen" Jackson, who had replaced Erskine. Jackson's nickname came from his role two years earlier of delivering the threat of the British navy to destroy the Danish capital, making him, according to the leading diplomatic historian of the period, "a bad choice for a mission of tranquilization."[44] Madison hoped that he "comes with a real olive in his hand," but he feared that "the general slipperiness of his superior" and "some ideas [which] fell from him in his conversation with P[inkney]" in

---

41. *Ibid.*

42. JM to TJ, Aug. 16, 1809, below.

43. Ketcham, pp. 480–81, and Malone, VI, pp. 12–14. For references to the exchange of visits, see TJ to JM, July 12, 1809, below, Aug. 17, 1809, below, Sept. 12, 1809, below, and Sept. 18, 1809, below; and JM to TJ, July 23, 1809, below, Aug. 16, 1809, below, and Sept. 11, 1809, below.

44. Perkins, p. 222.

London provided grounds for "distrust of his views."[45] Jefferson agreed more with Madison's fears than his hopes, observing that "Canning's equivocations degrade his government as well as himself. I despair of accomodation with them," he confessed, "because I believe they are weak enough to intend seriously to claim the ocean as their conquest, and think to amuse us with embassies and negociations until the claim shall have been strengthened by time and exercise, and the moment arrive when they may boldly avow what hitherto they have only squinted at."[46]

Madison's and Jefferson's fears were quickly confirmed after the president returned to Washington. Madison suspected that Jackson had nothing to offer. "He is not deficient in the diplomatic professions," he confided to Jefferson, "but nothing appears to contradict the presumption that he is so in the requisite instructions."[47] Jefferson replied laconically: "Jackson's mountain will, I think produce but a mouse."[48] The fruitless exchange of correspondence between the British minister and the president and secretary of state lasted a little over a month before Madison demanded Jackson's recall for persistently stating or implying that the president had connived with Erskine in exceeding the latter's instructions.[49]

Even before Jackson was dismissed, "his patron, Canning," by his intrigues in the cabinet, had engineered the downfall of the Portland ministry and was forced from office.[50] From the new ministry, headed by Spencer Perceval, Madison expected little, fearing that its "quackeries and corruptions" seemed "likely to make bad worse." For that reason, he told Jefferson, "we shall proceed with a circumspect attention to all the circumstances mingled in our affairs, but with a confidence, at the same time, in a just sensibility of the nation to the respect due to it."[51] Jefferson replied that "the infatuation of the British government and nation is beyond everything immaginable. A thousand circumstances announce that they are on the point of being blown up, and they still proceed with the same madness and increased wickedness."[52]

---

45. JM to TJ, Sept. 11, 1809, below.
46. TJ to JM, Sept. 12, 1809, below.
47. JM to TJ, Oct. 6, 1809, below, and Oct. 30, 1809, below.
48. TJ to JM, Oct. 9, 1809, below.
49. For the short but stormy story of these negotiations, see Brant, V, pp. 83–101.
50. JM uses the "patron" phrase in his letter to TJ, Nov. 6, 1809, below. Also see Perkins, pp. 221–22, 235.
51. JM to TJ, Nov. 6, 1809, below.
52. TJ to JM, Nov. 26, 1809, below.

———————— THE LETTERS ————————

Jefferson's Circular Letter about His Relations with President Madison

[Washington] Mar. 1809

The friendship which has long subsisted between the President of the United States and myself gave me reason to expect, on my retirement from office, that I might often receive applications to interpose with him on behalf of persons desiring appointments. Such an abuse of his dispositions towards me would necessarily lead to the loss of them, and to the transforming me from the character of a friend to that of an unreasonable and troublesome solicitor. It therefore became necessary for me to lay down as a law for my future conduct never to interpose in any case, either with him or the heads of departments (from whom it must go to him) in any application whatever for office. To this rule I must scrupulously adhere, for were I to depart from it in a single instance I could no longer plead it with truth to my friends in excuse for my not complying with their requests. I hope therefore that the declining it in the present, as in every other case, will be ascribed to its true cause, the obligation of this general law, and not to any disinclination existing in this particular case; and still less to an unwillingness to be useful to my friends on all occasions not forbidden by a special impropriety.[1]

Jefferson to Madison

[Washington Mar. 1809]

Memoranda for the President

Information having been recieved in October last that many intruders had settled on the lands of the Cherokees and Chickasaws; the letter from Genl. Dearborn to Colo. Meigs[2] was written to have them ordered off, and to

---

1. Because of his friendship with President-elect Monroe, JM issued an identical letter when he retired in 1817; see Hunt, VIII, p. 389.

2. Return Jonathan Meigs was federal Indian commissioner to the Cherokee, who favored their removal beyond the Mississippi as the means of preserving the Cherokee nation rather than TJ's policy of civilization and incorporation as "fee-simple farmer-citizens"; see William G. McLoughlin, "Thomas Jefferson and the Beginning of Cherokee Nationalism, 1806 to 1809," *WMQ* 32 (1975): 556, 566, 575.

inform them they would be removed by military force in the spring if still on the lands. These orders remain still to be given, and they should go to the officer commanding at Highwassee. A very discreet officer should be selected. On the Cherokee lands, Wafford's settlement should not be disturbed as the Indians themselves expect to arrange that with us, and the exchange for lands beyond the Misipi will furnish a good opportunity.[3] From the lands of the Chickasaws all should be removed except those who settled on Doublehead's reserve under titles from him;[4] and they should be notified that those lands having been claimed by the Chickasaws as well as the Cherokees, we purchased the Cherokee right with an exception of Doublehead's reserve, which we did not guarantee to him, but left it as it stood under the claims of both nations; that consequently they are not under our protection. That whenever we purchase the Chickasaw right, all their titles under Doublehead will become void; as our laws do not permit individuals to purchase lands from the Indians: that they should therefore look out for themselves in time.

At Detroit, Genl. Dearborne and myself had concluded to purchase for the War-departmt [5] farm, near Detroit, now held by the Treasury office in satisfaction of a delinquency, provided it could be bought at it's real value supposed about 1000. or 1200. D. to employ the dwelling house and appurtenances for a school for the instruction of the Indian boys and girls in reading Etc learning English and houshold and mechanical arts under the care of Pere Richard, to place in the farm house a farmer (a labourer) of proper character to cultivate the farm with the aid of the Indian lads for the support of the institution, and to place on the same land the blacksmith and carpenter, who would have Indian apprentices under them. The advantages of assembling the whole at one place are obvious. Father Richard goes to France in the Mentor to procure an aid. If, when he brings him, he could exchange him with Bishop Carroll for an American, it would be infinitely more desirable.[6]

3. For the fullest discussion of TJ's Indian policy, see Bernard W. Sheehan, *Seeds of Extinction: Jeffersonian Philanthropy and the American Indian* (Chapel Hill, 1973; rpt. New York, 1974). For brief discussions of his dealings with the Cherokee, see Malone, V, pp. 273–76, and Grace S. Woodward, *The Cherokees* (Norman, Okla., 1963), pp. 127–31.

4. Meigs had secretly promised Chief Doublehead two tracts of land if the chief persuaded recalcitrant tribesmen to accept two treaties in 1805 and 1806; see *PJM* (Pres. ser.), I, p. 2. An anti-Doublehead group of chiefs later repudiated the treaties and assassinated Doublehead; see McLoughlin, 559–60.

5. TJ's blank.

6. Father Gabriel Richard was a French-born member of the Sulpician order who served as a missionary to the Indians at Detroit; see *PJM* (Pres. ser.), I, p. 2, and Sheehan, pp. 7, 122. He later served one term in Congress; see Allen Johnson and Dumas Malone, eds., *Dictionary of American Biography*, 22 vols. (New York, 1928–44), VIII, pp. 549–51. Also see TJ to JM, Dec. 7, 1809, below.

Jefferson to Madison

Monticello Mar. 17, 1809

DEAR SIR

On opening my letters from France in the moment of my departure from Washington, I found from their signatures that they were all from literary characters except one from Mr. Short, which mentioned in the outset that it was private, and that his public communications were in the letter to the Secretary of State, which I sent you. I find however on reading his letter to me (which I did not do till I got home) a passage of some length proper to be communicated to you and which I have therefore extracted.[7]

I had a very fatiguing journey, having found the roads excessive bad, altho' I have seen them worse. The last three days I found it better to be on horseback, and travelled 8. hours through as disagreeable a snow storm as I was ever in. Feeling no inconvenience from the expedition but fatigue, I have more confidence in my vis vitae than I had before entertained. The spring is remarkably backward. No oats sown, not much tobacco seed, and little done in the gardens. Wheat has suffered considerably. No vegetation visible yet but the red maple, weeping willow and Lilac. Flour is said to be at 8. D. at Richmond, and all produce is hurrying down.

I feel great anxiety for the occurrences of the ensuing 4. or 5. months. If peace can be preserved, I hope and trust you will have a smooth administration. I know no government which would be so embarrassing in war as ours. This would proceed very much from the lying and licentious character of our papers; but much also from the wonderful credulity of the members of Congress in the floating lies of the day. And in this no experience seems to correct them. I have never seen a Congress during the last 8. years a great majority of which I would not implicitly rely on in any question, could their minds have been purged of all errors of fact. The evil too increases greatly with the protraction of the session, and I apprehend, in case of war their sessions would have a tendency to become permanent. It is much therefore to be desired that war may be avoided if circumstances will admit. Nor in the present Maniac state of Europe should I estimate the point of honour by the ordinary scale. I believe we shall on the contrary have credit with the world for having made the avoidance of being engaged in the present unexampled war, our first object. War however may become a less losing business than unresisted depredation. With every wish that events may be propitious to your administration, I salute you with sincere affection and every sympathy of the heart.

TH: JEFFERSON

---

7. In a letter to TJ on Nov. 25, 1808, William Short expressed concern about being reimbursed for his expenses as minister to Russia, an appointment by TJ that the Senate later rejected on Feb. 27, 1809; see *PJM* (Pres. ser.), I, p. 60.

Madison to Jefferson

Washington Mar. 19, 1809

DEAR SIR

Altho' I feel reluctance in trespassing for a moment on the repose to which you have just retired, I can not well avoid inclosing a letter from Mr. La Trobe which he wishes may be seen by you before it be decided on, because he thinks you have already acquiesc'd in the reasonableness of its object: and which I wish you to see, because I am so raw on the whole subject, as to need any intimations you may find it convenient to give. You will observe that his proposal includes $700 for *past* services.[8]

Mr. Coles left us this morning.[9] The mail of yesterday brought a letter from Armstrong of Decr. 25. and Paris papers of the 27th. No change had taken place in our affairs. The occurrences and prospects in Spain will appear in the Natl. Intelligencer. No letter from Short, nor is he named by A. I conclude he had set out for St. P. Health and happiness.

JAMES MADISON

Jefferson to Madison

Monticello Mar. 24, 1809

DEAR SIR

I inclose you several letters which must have been intended for the office, and not the person named on the back. They belong therefore to your files, and I will pray you particularly as to those asking office on this and all other occasions to consider me merely as the channel of conveyance, and not as meaning to add an atom of weight to the sollicitations they convey, unless indeed I know any thing on the subject and mention it particularly. As in the case of Francis Page, being acquainted with him it is my duty to say that he is a most amiable young man, educated to the bar, perfectly correct in his conduct, and, as the son of our late friend, of good standing. I do not presume that York can present a more worthy or unexceptionable subject.[10]

Among these letters is one from Ray author of the War of Tripoli. He sent me one of his books, and in answering him with thanks I used the complimentary phrase he quotes. He lays hold of it to beg 100. D. of which I shall

---

8. John Lenthall, Latrobe's assistant as surveyor of public buildings, had been killed in an accident during construction of the Capitol building, and Latrobe claimed additional compensation because of duties that he assumed following Lenthall's death; see TJ to JM, Mar. 30, 1809, below.

9. Isaac Coles was TJ's private secretary; see Malone, V, pp. 140, 529.

10. Francis Page of Hanover County was the son of John Page, TJ's oldest friend and JM's colleague on Governor Jefferson's Executive Council. JM appointed young Page as collector of customs at Yorktown; see *PJM* (Pres. ser.), I, p. 78.

not be the dupe. I inclose it to you, as I think he has too much genius for the low station in which he was in the navy, and to place him in your recollection, if any occasion should arise wherein such a man can be useful in the navy or elsewhere. I send Mazzei's letter for your perusal. The part for your attention is in [ ][11] altho' no part of it is secret. I intended, but forgot to mention to you Genl. Dearborne's son for a military commission. I should have named him; but Mr. Smith of the W. O.[12] told me Pickering had been collecting some stories to oppose his nomination, which might have weight if not answered. I desired him therefore to write to the General and in the mean time to hold up the nomination. God bless you and prosper you.

TH: JEFFERSON

Mazzei's letter to be returned, but not the others.

Madison to Jefferson

Washington Mar. 27, 1809

DEAR SIR

Altho' the letter from Mr. Brown was probably intended for you, I could not hesitate in carrying it into effect; and finding that the Bill on the Navy Dept. will be paid, I inclose, in order to avoid the delay of a week, the sum drawn for in Bank notes. I send them to you rather than directly to Mrs. T.[13] first because I do not know what the direct address ought to be, and 2dly. because it is possible, that you may be possessed of authority from her to give them a particular destination.

Your letter of the 17th. was safely delivered by Shorter. I wish your exemption from ill effects from the snow storm may be permanent.

Mr. Short complains without reason on the subject of his allowances. Nothing was said as to an outfit, because it was more than possible that the Senate might reject him, and not certain that the Mission would be made permanent. And as to his expences of travelling, his running salary was as adequate at least to them, as to his stationery expences.

I forget whether the time piece in the sitting room be *monthly* or weekly? Will you please when you inform me, to add a memorandum of the Newspapers retained by you out of the list sent you whilst here, that I may know how to dispose of them. Yrs. with the highest esteem and truest affection.

JAMES MADISON

11. TJ's brackets.
12. John Smith was chief clerk in the War Department; see *PJM* (Pres. ser.), I, p. 78.
13. The enclosure was $500 for Mrs. Elizabeth Trist; see *ibid.*, p. 82.

Madison to Jefferson

[Washington] Mar. 28, 1809

DEAR SIR

I have yours of the 24. The enquiry as to Franzoni will be made as soon as an oppy. offers. F. Page had been appd. before your letter was recd. and his Commission forwarded.

We have letters from Erving to Jany. 28. He was at Cadiz, intending it appears to adhere to the Junta Suprema, till the drama should close, and then leave Spain, by way of Gibralter, Tangier, or England, if no other course offered itself.[14] I fear he has run from one Extreme to another, under the influence of the Existing Atmosphere. His news is pretty much like that in the paper inclosed. Yrujo was at Cadiz, going on with his Mills, which involving a Monopoly, were odious and not likely to survive popular fury in the only turn of things that cd. preserve his patent. He says he has sacrificed his fortune in promoting the patriotic cause. Adieu. Yrs

JAMES MADISON

Jefferson to Madison

Monticello Mar. 30, 1809

DEAR SIR

Yours of the 19th. came to hand by the last post; but that allows us so little time that I could not answer by it's return. I had not before heard of Mr. Latrobe's claim of Lenthall's salary in addition to his own.[15] That some of Lenthall's duties must have fallen on him I have no doubt; but that he could have performed them all in addition to his own so as to entitle himself to his whole salary, was impossible. Lenthall superintended directly the manual labors of the workmen, saw that they were in their places every working hour, that they executed their work with skill and fidelity, kept their accounts, laid off the work, measured it, laid off the centers and other moulds Etc. If the leisure of Mr. Latrobe's own duties allowed him to give one half or one third of his time to these objects, it is more than I had supposed. The whole of them we know occupied every moment of Lenthall, as laborious, as faithful, and as able in his line as man could be. This claim is subject to another consideration. It would be a bad precedent to allow the principal to discontinue offices indefinitely and absorb all the salaries on the presumption of his fulfilling the duties. It may sometimes happen that a place cannot be immediately and properly filled, or that the arrangements for suppressing it cannot be immedi-

---

14. As chargé d'affaires in Madrid, Erving followed the junta supporting Ferdinand instead of recognizing Joseph Bonaparte as king.

15. For Latrobe's claim for additional compensation, see JM to TJ, Mar. 19, 1809, above.

ately taken; and as some extra service may in the mean time fall on others, some extra allowance may be just. But this interval should be reasonably limited and accounted for. On weighing these considerations with Mr. Latrobe's explanations you will be able to judge what proportion of Lenthall's salary should be allowed him. I must add that tho he is a masterly agent in the line of his emploiment, you will find that the reins must be held with a firmness that never relaxes.

Colo. Monroe dined and passed an evening with me since I came home. He is sincerely cordial: and I learn from several that he has quite separated himself from the junto which had got possession of him, and is sensible that they had used him for purposes not respecting himself always. He and J. R. now avoid seeing one another, mutually dissatisfied. He solemnly disclaims all connection with the anomalous paper of the place and disapproves it.[16] His only tie remaining is a natural one, and that is said to be loosened.[17] I did not enter into any material political conversation with him, and still less as to the present course of things because I shall have better opportunities on his return with his family, whom he is gone to bring permanently to his residence here, and I think the daughter is expected to make a part of his family during the summer at least. On the whole I have no doubt that his strong and candid mind will bring him to a cordial return to his old friends after he shall have been separated a while from his present circle, which separation I think is one of the objects of his removal from Richmond, with which place he expressed to me much disgust.

On the 27th. 28th. 29th. the thermometer was at 23. 21. 32. attended by a piercing N. W. wind, which rendered it as cold to our sensations as any day in winter had been. The peach trees whose buds were so forward as to shew the colour of the blossom, have generally lost their fruit. Those less forward are safe. For this fruit therefore all will depend on the forwardness or backwardness of the situation this year. Altho' my situation is much forwarder than others, I have lost scarcely any thing. Fears of injury to the wheat are entertained. I salute you with constant affection.

TH: JEFFERSON

Jefferson to Madison

Monticello Mar. 31, 1809

DEAR SIR

Since my letter of yesterday I have recieved yours of the 27th. and 28th. and in the former the 500. D. for Mrs. Trist. The bronze time piece men-

---

16. John Randolph and the Old Republicans founded the newspaper *Spirit of '76* in Richmond in 1808 to support Monroe's bid for the presidency; see Ammon, p. 275.

17. Eliza Monroe married George Hay, a Richmond lawyer, in Sept. 1808; see *ibid.*, p. 279.

tioned will run a fortnight, but I found it better to wind it up once a week, as during the 2d. week the greater expansion of the spring occasioned her to lose time. With respect to newspapers, none can now come to Washington for me. Of those which, while there, I ordered and paid for, I directed a discontinuance except 3. or 4. which will come on to me here. Many others were sent gratis (which I rarely opened) to me as President of the US. They probably will be continued to you on the same principle.

I inclose a letter from the Speaker of Indiana on the election of two persons for the legislative council.[18] Such an one was forwarded to me in Oct. by Mr. Thomas then Speaker, as he told me; but I never recieved it. He therefore wrote back for another copy which is but now recieved. You will find among the papers I left you, a letter from Govr. Harrison advising as to the choice to be made.[19] Erving seems to have erred in principle, by not taking his stand with the government of Spain de facto. It is the more unlucky as Joseph Bonaparte has been said to be well disposed towards us. Affectionately yours

TH: JEFFERSON

Madison to Jefferson

[Washington] Apr. 9, 1809

DEAR SIR

I return the letter of Mazzei, without however having ascertained the fact as to the remittance by the Sculptor. Latrobe I presume, will give the information in his answer to the letter which I have forwarded to him. He is now in Philada.

A Secretary of Legation with a sort of *Extra* establishment has just arrived from England, with despatches for Erskine.[20] I have a private letter only from Pinkney. The Ministry of G. B. are pretty certainly shaken with respect to this Country. The Catastrophe in Spain, and the new policy to which it leads, have doubtless contributed towards it. But it is unquestionable that the documents communicated to Congs. and the countenance presented by their earlier resolutions, afford the true explanation. Erskine has not yet opened much of his budget to Mr. Smith. The contents of it were not disclosed to Pinkney; perhaps from an unwillingness to risk a discovery by France, or a use of them by Armstrong. Private letters from individuals in England, leave no doubt that a great dread prevailed of our perseverence in the Embargo.

---

18. Jesse B. Thomas wrote TJ on Oct. 12, 1808; see *PJM* (Pres. ser.), I, p. 93.
19. JM nominated Hugh McCally in May; see *ibid*.
20. Charles Oakley, new secretary of the British legation, brought instructions from Canning to Erskine about conditions for the repeal of the orders-in-council; see *ibid.*, p. 124.

Among the faux pas of Erving, he has brought about an arrangement between Iznardi, and Hackley, much to be regretted on acct. of the latter.[21] It is a sort of simoniacal contract, by which H. gives Iz 600 dolrs. a year, and receives from him the appt. of vice Consul; Iz: retaining the title without the responsibility of Consul. The contract, with sundry details, apportioning the functions and formalities, is executed in due form, with the sanction of Erving as a witness, and transmitted hither for that of the Govt. Erving (who appears to have become a little aware of the folly committed) was to have applied to the Spanish Authorities, for an exequatur to the Vice Consulate; but has suspended the application till he hears from us. In the mean time, the contract is in operation. No time was lost by the Dept. of State, in giving notice of the nullity and impropriety of such a transaction. I am persuaded from what appears that Mr. H. has been betrayed into it by his confidence in the judgmt. and experience of others. Erving remarks particularly that his conduct was unexceptionably delicate. It becomes a serious question nevertheless whether the contemplated appointment of him at Cadiz, would not leave suspicions that the bargain with Iznardi, was secretly in fulfilment, and of course furnish a handle to a disappd. Candidate for injurious attacks on the Govt. as well as Mr. H. If it were certain that Jarvis wd. not remain at Lisbon, it wd. mitigate the difficulty by transferring H. thither. It is not probable that Jarvis wd. be willing to remove to Cadiz, which I believe is not rated as high as Lisbon, as a Consular birth. I recollect no other vacancy that would bear a comparison with Cadiz. Yrs. Affectly.

JAMES MADISON

Jefferson to Madison

Monticello Apr. 19, 1809

DEAR SIR

I have to acknolege your favor of the 9th. and to thank you for the political information it contained. Reading the newspapers but little and that little but as the romance of the day, a word of truth now and then comes like the drop of water on the tongue of Dives. If the British ministry are changing their policy towards us, it is because their nation, or rather the city of London which is the nation to them, is shaken, as usual, by the late reverses in Spain. I have for some time been persuaded that the government of England was systematically decided to claim a dominion of the sea by conquest, and to levy contributions on all nations, by their licenses to navigate, in order to maintain

---

21. Erving was chargé d'affaires of the American legation in Madrid, and Josef Yznardi was consul at Cadiz. Richard Hackley, who was related to TJ's son-in-law Thomas Mann Randolph, had been appointed by TJ as consul at Sanlucar in 1806, but he had privately negotiated a deal with Yznardi to become vice-consul at Cadiz; see *ibid.*, pp. 124–25.

that dominion to which their own resources are inadequate. The mobs of their cities are unprincipled enough to support this policy in prosperous times, but change with the tide of fortune, and the ministers, to keep their places, change with them. I wish Mr. Oakley may not embarras you with his conditions of revoking the orders of council. Enough of the non importation law should be reserved 1. to pinch them into a relinquishment of impressments, and 2. to support those manufacturing establishments which their orders, and our interests, forced us to make.

I suppose the conquest of Spain will soon force a delicate question on you as to the Floridas and Cuba which will offer themselves to you. Napoleon will certainly give his consent without difficulty to our recieving the Floridas, and with some difficulty possibly Cuba. And tho' he will disregard the obligation whenever he thinks he can break it with success, yet it has a great effect on the opinion of our people and the world to have the moral right on our side, of his agreement as well as that of the people of those countries.

Mr. Hackley's affair is really unfortunate. He has been driven into this arrangement by his distresses which are great. He is a perfectly honest man, as is well known here where he was born; but unaccustomed to political subjects he has not seen it in that view. But a respect for the innocence of his views cannot authorize the sanction of government to such an example. If Jarvis continues to wish to go to Rio Janeiro, Lisbon would become vacant, and would suit Hackley. Ought the lying, malicious, and impudent conduct of Meade to force him on the government for Cadiz?[22] I know that the present Secretary of State has not seen his conduct in that light, or he would have removed him as Navy agent: but such has been his conduct in truth; and I have no doubt he will bring forward the transaction between Hackley and Yznardi, in new appeals to the public through the newspapers. Rather than he should obtain what he has so little merited, I would suggest Mr. Jefferson as a competitor, altho' I do not know that he has ever thought of a Consulship, nor would I suggest him, if Yznardi remains in the way. But as to all this do what circumstances will best permit; I shall be satisfied that whatever you do will be right.

I now inclose you the statement which I promised, with Le Maire's note of the articles within his department. If they were not found to be what he has stated, be so good as to make the necessary corrections, and whatever the amount is may be paid, entirely at your own convenience into the bank of the US. in diminution of my note.[23]

Dinsmore and Neilson set out yesterday for Montpelier.[24] If Mrs. Madison has any thing there which interests her in the gardening way, she cannot confide it better than to Neilson. He is a gardener by nature, and extremely

---

22. Richard W. Meade was U.S. naval agent at Cadiz; see *ibid.*, p. 46.
23. Étienne Le Maire served as maître d'hôtel during TJ's presidency.
24. John Neilson and James Dinsmore were craftsmen from Monticello who helped Madison remodel Montpellier; see Hunt-Jones, pp. 66–67.

attached to it. Be so good as to assure her of my most friendly respects, and to accept the same for yourself.

Th: Jefferson

ENCLOSURE NO. 1

		cents	D
392.	bushels of coal @ 25		98.
100.	bottles of Madeira		100.
36.	do. Noyau		36.
	expences filling the ice-house		77.205
	a horse		200.

	months	months	D
John Freeman.	76½ out of	132 @ 400.	231.81
			743.015

the deed for John is inclosed.[25]

ENCLOSURE NO. 2

I hereby assign and convey to James Madison President of the United States, the withinnamed servant, John, otherwise called John Freeman, during the remaining term of his service from the 11th. day of March last past when he was delivered to the said James [Madison] for the consideration of two hundred and thirty one Dollars 81. cents. Witness my hand this 19th. day of April 1809. at Monticello in Virginia.

Th. Jefferso[n]

Madison to Jefferson

Washington Apr. 24, 1809

Dear Sir

I have recd. your favor of the 19th. You will see in the newspapers the result of the Advances made by G. B. Attempts were made to give shapes to the arrangement implying inconsistency and blame on our part. They were however met in a proper manner and readily abandoned; leaving these charges in their full force, as they now bear on the other side. The B. Cabinet must have changed its course under a full conviction that an adjustment with this Country, had become essential; and it is not improbable that this policy may direct the ensuing negociation; mingling with it, at the same time, the hope that it may embroil us with France. To this use it may be expected the Federalists will endeavor to turn what is already done, at the coming session of Congs. The steps deemed proper to give the proceeding a contrary turn will not be omit-

25. John Freeman, who had accompanied TJ from Monticello when he became president, remained in Washington as JM's servant; see *PJM* (Pres. ser.), I, p. 125.

ted. And if France be not bereft of common sense, or be not predetermined on war with us, she will certainly not play into the hand of her Enemy. Besides the general motive to follow the example of G. B. she cannot be insensible of the dangerous tendency of prolonging the commercial sufferings of her Allies, particularly Russia, all of them already weary of such a state of things, after the pretext for enforcing it shall have ceased. She must be equally aware of the importance of our relations to Spanish America, which must now become the great object of Napoleon's pride and Ambition. Should he repeal his decrees with a view to this object, the most probable source of conflict will be in his extending the principle on which he required a *prohibition*[26] of the Trade with St. Domingo, to the case of the Spanish Colonies. Nor is it improbable that he may couple such a requisition with an offer to cede the Floridas, which would present a dilemma not very pleasant. Accept my sincerest affection and highest esteem.

JAMES MADISON

Jefferson to Madison

Monticello Apr. 27, 1809

DEAR SIR

Yours of the 24th. came to hand last night. The correspondence between Mr. Smith and Mr. Erskine had been recieved three days before. I sincerely congratulate you on the change it has produced in our situation. It is the source of very general joy here, and could it have arrived one month sooner would have had important effects not only on the elections of other states, but of this also, from which it would seem that wherever there was any considerable portion of federalism it has been so much reinforced by those of whose politics the price of wheat is the sole principle, that federalists will be returned from many districts of this state.[27] The British ministry has been driven from it's Algerine system, not by any remaining morality in the people but by their unsteadiness under severe trial. But whencesoever it comes, I rejoice in it as the triumph of our forbearing and yet persevering system. It will lighten your anxieties, take from cabal it's most fertile ground of war, will give us peace during your time, and by the compleat extinguishment of our public debt, open upon us the noblest application of revenue that has ever been exhibited by any nation. I am sorry they are sending a minister to attempt a treaty. They never made an equal commercial treaty with any nation, and we have no right to expect to be the first. It will place you between the injunctions of true patriotism and the clamors of a faction devoted to a foreign interest in preference to that of their own country. It will confirm the English too in their

---

26. JM's italics.

27. In Virginia, the Federalists picked up 3 seats. Nationally, the Republicans lost 24 seats in the House, retaining 94 to the Federalists' 48; see *PJM* (Pres. ser.), I, p. 140.

practice of whipping us into a treaty. They did it in Jay's case; were near it in Monroe's, and on failure of that, have applied the scourge with tenfold vigour, and now come on to try it's effect. But it is the moment when we should prove our consistence, by recurring to the principles we dictated to Monroe, the departure from which occasioned our rejection of his treaty, and by protesting against Jay's treaty being ever quoted, or looked at, or even mentioned. That form will for ever be a millstone round our necks unless we now rid ourselves of it, once for all. The occasion is highly favorable, as we never can have them more in our power. As to Bonaparte, I should not doubt the revocation of his edicts, were he governed by reason. But his policy is so crooked that it eludes conjecture. I fear his first object now is to dry up the sources of British prosperity by excluding her manufactures from the continent. He may fear that opening the ports of Europe to our vessels will open them to an inundation of British wares. He ought to be satisfied with having forced her to revoke the orders on which he pretended to retaliate, and to be particularly satisfied with us by whose unyielding adherence to principle she has been forced into the revocation. He ought the more to conciliate our good will, as we can be such an obstacle to the new career opening on him in the Spanish colonies. That he would give us the Floridas to withold intercourse with the residue of those colonies cannot be doubted. But that is no price, because they are ours in the first moment of the first war, and until a war they are of no particular necessity to us. But, altho' with difficulty, he will consent to our recieving Cuba into our union to prevent our aid to Mexico and the other provinces. That would be a price, and I would immediately erect a column on the Southernmost limit of Cuba and inscribe on it a Ne plus ultra as to us in that direction. We should then have only to include the North in our confederacy, which would be of course in the first war, and we should have such an empire for liberty as she has never surveyed since the creation: and I am persuaded no constitution was ever before so well calculated as ours for extensive empire and self government. As the Mentor went away before this change, and will leave France probably while it is still a secret in that hemisphere, I presume the expediency of pursuing her by a swift sailing dispatch was considered. It will be objected to our recieving Cuba, that no limit can then be drawn for our future acquisitions. Cuba can be defended by us without a navy. and this developes the principle which ought to limit our views. Nothing should ever be accepted which would require a navy to defend it.

Our spring continues cold and backward. Rarely one growing day without two or three cold ones following. Wheat is of very various complexions from very good to very bad. Fruit has not suffered as much as was expected except in peculiar situations. Gardens are nearly a month behind their usual state. I thank you for the Squashes from Maine. They shall be planted to day. I salute you with sincere and constant affection.

Th: Jefferson

Madison to Jefferson

Washington May 1, 1809

DEAR SIR

I am just favored with yours of the 27th. Young Gelston is here preparing to take his passage for France as bearer and expositor of dispatches, in the Syren sloop of war which is waiting for him at Baltimore.[28] He leaves this tomorrow morning. Mr. Gallatin has had a conversation with Turreau at his residence near Baltimore. He professes to be confident that his Govt. will consider England as broken down by the example she has given in repealing her orders, and that the F. Decrees will be repealed as a matter of course. His communications by the Syren will, if he be sincere, press the policy of an immediate repeal. No official accts. have been recd. from the French letter of Marque arrived at Boston. The difficulty most likely to threaten our relations with France, lies in the effort she may make to render us in some way subservient to the reduction of Span: America; particularly by witholding our commerce. This apprehension is corroborated by the language of Turreau. He alluded to his conversations with you relating to Cuba on which he builds jealousies which he did not conceal.[29] Cuba will without doubt be a cardinal object with Napoleon.

The Spirit which England will bring into the ulterior negociations must differ much from that which influenced former Treaties, if it can be moulded to our just views; and we must be prepared to meet it with a prudent adherence to our essential interests. It is possible however that the school of adversity may have taught her the policy of substituting for her arrogant pretensions, somewhat of a conciliating moderation towards the US. Judging from the tone lately used, a change of that sort would be the less wonderful. If she can be brought to a fair estimate of her real interest, it seems very practicable to surmount the obstacles which have hitherto kept us at variance, and untill surmounted must continue to do so. The case of impressments, hitherto the greatest obstacle, seems to admit most easily of adjustment, on grounds mutually advantageous. Yrs. with affectionate respects

JAMES MADISON

It is understood that the Election in the State of New York has issued very favorably.

---

28. Maltby Gelston was to carry State Department dispatches informing France about the Erskine Agreement; see *ibid.*, p. 150.

29. For TJ's indiscreet observation to Turreau that the United States "must have the Floridas and Cuba," see Brant, V, pp. 57–58.

Jefferson to Madison

Monticello May 22, 1809

DEAR SIR

It is my duty to write to you on the subject of the Note you were so kind as to endorse for me at the bank of the US. and I do it willingly altho' painfully. Notwithstanding a fixed determination to take care that at the termination of my duties at Washington my pecuniary matters should at least be square, and my confidence that they would be so, I found, by an estimate made in December last, that there would be a deficit in them of several thousand dollars. I took immediate measures for transferring that debt to Virginia, and did it the more easily as I was enabled to pledge certain resources which I had in possession, or not very distant. However after this liquidation effected, other demands, which had not come under my view, came upon me, one after another, and required to answer them the amount of the Note you indorsed for me. The forms of the bank requiring two Indorsers, for an absentee, I asked of Mr. Barnes to be the second,[30] which he very readily assented to, the cashier previously assuring me that it would have no effect on their transactions with Mr. Barnes on his private account, and so I assured him. But by a letter I have recieved from the old gentleman, I find that he is made uneasy by some circumstance in the execution of the note, which makes him liable in the first instance, were the bank, contrary to expectation, to make a sudden demand of the money. It would add much to my affliction to give him uneasy nights at his age, which obliges me to ask you to satisfy him by interposing yourself between him and the first liability to the bank, which I believe is done by your subscribing the words 'credit the drawer' instead of his doing it. He however can best say how this may be done. I might, without much delay, have relieved you from this unpleasant responsibility had I not engaged my earliest resources on my first estimate, which I then thought would discharge all demands. It is this circumstance which renders me unable to fix any time with confidence. I limit my expences here to my income here, leaving that of my Bedford estate free, which is about 2500. D. clear one year with another. But as this would take an improper course of time I am endeavoring to sell several detached parcels of land, unconnected with my possessions either here or in Bedford, and which I can spare without diminution of revenue or other inconvenience. They amount to between two and three thousand acres, and at the market prices would bring the double of these deficits. I trust that the bank, will find no interest in calling for a reimbursement before I shall have been able to avail myself of all my resources.

I had seen with much pleasure that the dispute with Pensylvania was likely to go off so smoothly; but am much mortified to see the spirit manifested by the prisoners themselves as well as by those who participated in the parade of

---

30. John Barnes was a factor who had resided in Philadelphia before moving to Georgetown. For TJ's dealings with the debt he incurred while he was president, see Malone, VI, pp. 39–40.

their liberation.[31] One circumstance in it struck my attention disagreeably, but it admitted a different explanation. I trust that no section of republicans will countenance the suggestions of the Federalists that there has ever been any difference at all in our political principles, or any sensible one in our views of the public interests.

After a most distressing drought of 5. or 6. weeks we had on the 18th. instant a very fine rain, followed by calm and tolerably warm weather, and yesterday and last night a plentiful rain has fallen again. The coldness and backwardness of the spring however had not advanced plants sufficiently to enable the planters to avail themselves of them as seasons. I tender always to Mrs. Madison my affectionate respects and to your self the assurances of my constant and cordial attachment.

TH: JEFFERSON

Jefferson to Madison and John Barnes

[Monticello] May 24, 1809

Sixty days after date I promise to pay to James Madison and John Barnes, or [on] order (without offset) Three thousand Seven hundred and forty six dollars 68/100 value recieved. Washington May 24th. 1809. payable at the Office of Discount and Deposit Credit the Drawer.

TH. JEFFERSON

Madison to Jefferson

Washington May 30, 1809

DEAR SIR

Your favor of the 22d. did not come to hand till the day before yesterday. It will give me pleasure to take the place of Mr. Barnes in the note to the Bank;

---

31. TJ referred to the aftermath of the complicated *Olmstead* case, which pitted the state militia of Pennsylvania against a federal process server and led to a historic Supreme Court decision on federal/state relations, with Chief Justice John Marshall upholding federal supremacy. Brigadier General Michael Bright and 14 state militiamen were convicted of forceable resistance to federal law and sentenced to 1 to 3 months in federal prison. JM, who supported the decision, quickly pardoned them within a week, and the prisoners then paraded through Philadelphia. Three days after TJ wrote this letter, a public dinner for General Bright attracted 300 supporters, including both factions of Pennsylvania Republicans. For a concise account, see Sanford W. Higginbotham, *The Keystone in the Democratic Arch: Pennsylvania Politics, 1800–1816* (Harrisburg, 1952), pp. 179-200, and George Lee Haskins and Herbert A. Johnson, *Foundations of Power: John Marshall, 1801–1815,* History of the Supreme Court of the United States Series, II (New York, 1981), pp. 322-31.

the more so as it will, it seems, be a relief to the Old Gentleman's pecuniary anxieties. I will have an early communication with him on the subject. I wish the original arrangement had taken the shape now proposed, and hope that you will make free use of my services if they can at any time or in any way be made convenient to your arrangements of money or other matters.

The newfangled policy of the federal party, you will have noticed, has made a considerable figure in the Newspapers. Some of the Editors are resuming the Old cant, and the others will doubtless soon follow the example. Nothing could exceed the folly of supposing that the principles and opinions manifested in our foreign discussions, were not, in the main at least, common to us; unless it be the folly of supposing that such shallow hypocrisy could deceive any one. The truth is, the sudden and unlooked for turn of the B. Cabinet, has thrown the party entirely off the Center. They have at present no settled plan. There is reason to believe that the leaders are [soured?] towards England, and much less disposed than heretofore to render our interests subservient to hers. Expressions have been used by one at least of the Essex Cabinet,[32] whether sincerely or insidiously may not be absolutely certain, from which it is inferred that a disposition exists in that quarter not even to continue the non-intercourse Act agst. France. Certain it is, that the desire of war with her is no longer manifested; that the deficiency of the English markets, excites a keen appetite for a trade with the Continent; and that a real uneasiness is felt lest the negociations with G. B. should end in sacrifices on our part, which they have been reproaching the Administration for not being ready to make. As one proof of their present feelings, the federal leaders shew a marked alienation from Erskine. The Elections in Massts. as well as in N. H. and N. Y. have issued unfavorably. But the smallness of the majority, and the overstrained exertions it has required, seem to depress rather than flatter the successful party. No confidence is felt in the permanency of the triumph.

Not a line has been recd. of late from any of our foreign Agents. All that is known is therefore to be gathered from the ordinary and fallacious channels. Accept my sincerest respects and attachment.

JAMES MADISON

Madison to Jefferson

Washington June 12, 1809

DR. SIR

The Pacific has just returned from G. B. bringing the accts. to be seen in the Newspapers. The communications from Pinkney add little to them. The new orders, considering the time, and that the act was known on the passage

---

32. JM preferred this expression to the more widely used "Essex Junto."

of which the instructions lately executed by Erskine, were predicated, present a curious feature in the conduct of the B Cabinet.[33] It is explained by some at the expence of its sincerity. It is more probably ascribed, I think to an awkwardness in getting out of an awkward situation, and to the policy of witholding as long as possible from France, the motive of its example, to advances on her part towards adjustment with us. The crooked proceeding seems to be operating as a check to the extravagance of credit given to G. B. for her late arrangement with us; and so far may be salutary. Be assured of my constant affection.

JAMES MADISON

Jefferson to Madison

Monticello June 16, 1809

DEAR SIR

I inclose you three letters from detained seamen which came to hand by the last post. Your favor of the 12th. was recieved at the same time. The intelligence by the Pacific gives me great anxiety. When I consider the tenor of the new order of council and the official exposition of it by the Lords of trade to the London American merchants (in the inclosed paper) and compare it with the engagement of Erskine under instructions given two months before, I am at a loss from which we have most to fear, the folly or the faithlesness of the Cannings and Castlereaghs of the British ministry. Is it possible that to get themselves out of a former hobble they should have involved themselves in another so much more difficult? And yet if they mean to adhere to the new order, their instructions to Erskine to enter into engagements in direct opposition to it, would be such a wanton abandonment of all pretensions to common honesty as one would suppose no men could deliberately intend. Et cui bono? Merely to catch a partial supply by a temporary relaxation of our measures? It seems impossible to believe either alternative, and yet the one or the other must be true. I presume it will produce some caution and hesitation in the proceedings of Congress. My joy on our supposed settlement is extremely damped by the occurrence of a trick, so strange, whatever solution may be given of it, and I fear a return of our difficulties, and it will be with increased force if they do recur. I sincerely wish a happy issue from them, for your own sake as well as for that of us all.

I am very happy in being enabled to relieve you from the disagreeable situation into which my improvidence had drawn your kind friendship. I felt

33. The *Pacific* brought news of the order-in-council of Apr. 26, 1809, which reopened some European trade but excluded neutral ships from the Netherlands, a restriction clearly not anticipated in the Erskine Agreement, which promised repeal of all the orders by June 10; see Perkins, p. 217.

severely the impropriety of dragging your name into the bank, as I had often been mortified with my own being there. But a too late attention to the state of my affairs at Washington had rendered it unavoidable. Mr. Barnes is now enabled to discharge my note at the bank, as well as a balance due to himself, and the separate account between you and myself may await your own entire convenience without in the least incommoding me, and I pray you to be assured of the sensibility with which I have experienced your kind accomodation to my difficulties.

For the last three days we have had fine and plentiful showers of rain, and were willing they should cease as appearances promised last night. But it commenced raining in the night and now continues with the wind at North East. This may become dangerous to the wheat which at best can only be a midling crop. That of tobacco cannot become great if the observation of the planters is correct that there never was a great crop of tobacco which was not pitched before the last of May. This year not a plant was in the ground till June: but the rains have been so favorable since that the whole crop is now standing and growing. I salute you with sincere affection and respect.

TH: JEFFERSON

Madison to Jefferson

Washington June 20, 1809

DEAR SIR

Yours of the 16th. came to hand yesterday. I hope you have not made any sacrifice of any sort to the scruple which has superseded my arrangemt. with Mr. Barnes. The execution of it would have equally accorded with my disposition and my conveniency.

The Gazette of yesterday contains the mode pursued for re-animating confidence in the pledge of the B. Govt. given by Mr. Erskine in his arrangemt. with this Govt. The puzzle created by the order of April struck every one. E. assures us that his Govt. was under such impressions as to the views of this, that not the slightest expectation existed, of our fairly meeting its overtures, and that the last order was considered as a seasonable mitigation of the tendency of a failure of the experiment.[34] This explanation seems as extraordinary as the alternatives it shews. The fresh declarations of Mr. E. seem to have quieted the distrust which was becoming pretty strong; but has not destroyed the effect of the ill grace stamped on the British retreat, and of the commercial rigor evinced by the new and insidious duties stated in the newspapers. It may

---

34. Erskine transmitted the order-in-council of Apr. 26, 1809, but explained that "it has no Connection whatever" with the agreement he had negotiated; that agreement "will be strictly fulfilled on the part of His Majesty"; see David Erskine to Robert Smith, June 15, 1809, in Hunt, VIII, p. 62.

be expected, I think that the B. Govt. will fulfil what its Minister has Stipulated; and that if it means to be trickish, it will frustrate the proposed negociation, and then say, their orders were not permanently repealed, but only withdrawn, *in the mean time.*

The only question likely now to agitate Congs. will be on the Bill which opens our ports to *French,* as well as B. *ships of war.* The Senate have passed it *unanimously.* Whether the Feds were sincere, or wished the debate etc. to take place in the H. of R. remains to be seen. Yrs. truly.

JAMES MADISON

Madison to Jefferson

Washington June 27, 1809

DR. SIR

I have recd. a private letter of Mar. 30. from Genl. Armstrong, in which he desires me "to present him most respectfully and cordially to you, and inform you that by the next public ship that goes to America, he shall have the pleasure to send you, an alteration of Mr. Guillaumes' plough, which in light soils, is a great improvement upon the old one."

To me he adds, "By the same vessel I propose consigning etc. a machine of prodigious consequence under present circumstances, combining great usefulness and little expence, and meant to take the place of the common small spinning Wheel in the manufacture of flax tow and hemp. It occupies little more room than the old spinning wheel, is put and kept in motion by any old or young negro wench, gives you twelve threads instead of one, and those of better texture and (if you chuse it) of greater fineness than can be given by fingers. The maker, who is an American, will probably accompany it."

On public affairs, he says, that the French Govt. had made several favorable regulations, among them, one for restoring the Cargoes sequestered under the municipal operation of the Berlin Decree; all of which had been arrested by a belief founded on language used in the British Parlt. that the U. S. were about to make war on France. The Mentor which is said to have arrived the latter end of Apl. will have given more correct, tho' possibly not satisfactory information of the policy prevailing here. Nothing more is known of the late Battle in Germany than you will see in the newspapers. The Senate passed, unanimously the Bill of non-intercourse with France, with a paragraph admitting French Ships of war, in common with British into our waters. The House of Reps. rejected yesterday by a large Majority, a motion to discriminate in favor of the British Ships. Be always assured of my affectionate and high respects.

JAMES MADISON

Madison to Jefferson

[Washington] July 4, 1809

DEAR SIR

The inclosed letter accompanied the skin of an Animal, not named by the writer, which belongs to the Region of the Rocky Mountains. The bundle being too large for the Mail, I shall forward it by some other oppy; perhaps as far as Orange, by a waggon I shall soon have on the return thither.

You will have seen that a re-nomination of J. Q. A. for Russia, has succeeded with the Senate.[35] In framing his Credence, it will be proper to adapt it to that given to Mr. Short, which deviated from the beaten form; and it appears that the original in that case passed on to Mr. Short, without being opened at the Office of State. No copy therefore exists but the one retained by yourself. Will you be so good as to lend me that, sending it to Orange Ct. House to await my arrival there; which will probably be at an early day next week. We continue without news from Europe later than the rumour from Holland of a defeat of the Austrians. Yrs. truly and respectfully

JAMES MADISON

Madison to Jefferson

Washington July 7, 1809

DEAR SIR

The inclosed letter from Mr. S. came under cover to me. It was brought by the vessel lately arrived at Phila. from Dunkirk. It appears that he had not left Paris, for Petersbg: nor meant to do so, untill he shd. hear further from the U. S.; as he has probably explained to you. Mr. Coles had rea[c]hed Paris; but in the absence of the French Court, nothing could be said very interesting on the subject of his errand.[36] From a paragraph in a letter from Genl. Armstrong to Mr. Gallatin, it would seem that the French Ministers were disposed to patronize a relaxation of the commercial policy of the Emperor, and that he was disposed to listen to any expedient that would save him from the appearance of inconsistency and retreat from his stand agst. G. B. There is some ground therefore to hope that the previous retreat of the latter may have a

---

35. For Adams's appointment, see Samuel Flagg Bemis, *John Quincy Adams and the Foundations of American Foreign Policy* (New York, 1949), pp. 151–52. Between the Senate's rejection of Adams on Mar. 7, 1807, and its confirmation of his appointment on June 27, news arrived of Czar Alexander's appointment of Andre de Daschkoff as consul general and chargé d'affaires to the United States; see *PJM* (Pres. ser.), I, pp. 87, 110–11.

36. The little-known mission of Isaac Coles, who had been TJ's private secretary, to France is briefly noted in Clifford L. Egan, *Neither Peace nor War: Franco-American Relations, 1803–1812* (Baton Rouge, 1983), pp. 106–10. He carried a proposal that promised hostility against Great Britain if France revoked or modified the decrees that affected the United States.

good effect; unless his new successes should inspire a pertinacity in his old projects. It is certain that great inconveniencies are felt in France, from the want of external commerce; and that the opening presented by the repeal of the B. orders, not only for a reasonable trade with the U. S. but thro' that between the different parts of the Continent itself, must render a continuance of the blockading system, peculiarly grating every where. The arrival of Dashkoff, makes it proper that I should not leave Washington before he reaches it; which I fear will not be for some days.[37] My purpose was to have set out tomorrow, or on Monday at farthest. Yrs. Affectly.

JAMES MADISON

Jefferson to Madison

Monticello July 12, 1809

DEAR SIR

Your two letters of the 4th. and 7th. were recieved by the last mail. I now inclose you the rough draught of the letter to the emperor of Russia. I think there must be an exact facsimile of it in the office, from which Mr. Short's must have been copied; because that the one now inclosed has never been out of my hands appears by there being no fold in the paper till now, and it is evidently a polygraphical copy.[38] I send for your perusal letters of W. Short and of Warden; because, tho private, they contain some things and views perhaps not in the public letters. Bonaparte's successes have been what we expected, altho' Warden appears to have supposed the contrary possible. It is fortunate for Bonaparte that he has not caught his brother emperor; that he has left an ostensible head to the government who may sell it to him to secure a mess of pottage for himself. Had the government devolved on the people as it did in Spain, they would resist his conquest as those of Spain do.[39]

I expect, within a week or 10. days to visit Bedford. My absence will be of about a fortnight.[40] I know too well the pressure of business which will be on

---

37. Andre de Daschkoff was chargé d'affaires for Russia; see Brant, V, pp. 68-69, and C. Edward Skeen, *John Armstrong, Jr., 1758–1843: A Biography* (Syracuse, 1981), p. 100.

38. For TJ's letter to Alexander, Aug. 29, 1808, see Ford, IX, pp. 206-7. For TJ's personal correspondence with the czar, see Malone, V, pp. 439-50.

39. With Napoleon occupied in his campaign in Spain, Archduke Charles of Austria decided that Bonaparte could not prosecute a war on two fronts and invaded Bavaria in Apr. 1809. But French units entered Vienna on May 12, forcing Emperor Francis Joseph to sue for peace; see Georges Lefebvre, *Napoleon: From Tilsit to Waterloo, 1807–1815* (New York, 1969), pp. 55-70, and Steven T. Ross, *European Diplomatic History, 1789–1815: France against Europe* (New York, 1969), pp. 294-96.

40. TJ had begun construction of his summer home in Bedford County in 1806. He was able to live at Poplar Forest for the first time in 1809; see Malone, VI, pp. 14-15. For the plans of the house, an early octagon design, see Frederick D. Nichols, *Thomas Jefferson's Architectural Drawings* (Boston, 1961), pp. 7-8, and Fiske Kimball, *Thomas Jefferson, Architect, with a New Introduction by*

you at Montpelier to count with certainty on the pleasure of seeing Mrs. Madison and yourself here; yet my wishes do not permit me to omit the expression of them. In any event I shall certainly intrude a flying visit on you during your stay in Orange. With my respectful devoirs to Mrs. Madison, I salute you with constant friendship and respect.

TH: JEFFERSON

Madison to Jefferson

Montpellier July 23, 1809

DEAR SIR

On my arrival at O[range] C[ourt] House on thursday I found your favor of the 12th. inst: with the document expected, and the letters from Short and Warden inclosed. The whole are now returned. No copy of the document was in the Office of State, as you suppose must have been the case. This was owing to the letter being written by your own hand at Monticello, and being sent on to Mr. S. without being opened at Washington. Mr. Shorts idea of leaving commerce to shift for itself, is not as new as he seems to think; and is liable to greater objections; in the case stated at least. A decisive objection wd. have been that the expedient would have given all the trade wanted to the power commanding the sea, whilst this would have cut off the commerce with its enemy; and thus have found an adequate motive to keep in force its obnoxious orders, as answering all its purposes. It was to be considered also as a further objection, that such an expedient would have involved our ignorant and credulous mariners, in the penalties incurred by the mercantile adventurers, without the indemnifying advantages which the latter would secure to themselves. It may be added that so formal an abandonment of the national rights, would not have borne an honorable appearance; tho' the discredit would have been mitigated by examples of powerful nations, and still more by the peculiarities of the actual state of the world.

I have not recd a line from any quarter, nor even a Newspaper since I left Washington. I can say nothing therefore on the score of news. I was detained at Washington some days, by an unwillingness to leave it at the Moment Daschkoff was to be expected. Altho' not more than titulary even a Chargè, he brought a letter of Credence from the Emperor himself. His conversation was in the spirit of this evidence of the respect and good will of his Sovereign

---

Frederick D. Nichols (New York, 1968), pp. 70–72. For a brief history, see Norma Cuthbert, "Poplar Forest: Jefferson's Legacy to His Grandson," *Huntington Library Quarterly* 6 (1943): 333–56. The house, which is in the village of Forest south of Lynchburg, is now open to the public. See the carefully researched book by S. Allen Chambers, Jr., *Poplar Forest and Thomas Jefferson* (Forest, Va., 1993).

towards the U. S. Adams has accepted his appt. and will embark as soon as practicable. Daschkoff was extremely anxious for an interview with him before his departure; and had proposed one at N. Y. if consistent with Mr. A's arrangements.

It is a part of our plan to pay our respects to Monticello; but we can say nothing as yet of the time. It will afford us much gratification to welcome you here, and with all of your family, that can accompany you. Be assured of my most affectionate respects

JAMES MADISON

Madison to Jefferson

Montpellier Aug. 3, 1809

DEAR SIR

Herewith you will receive a packet, which being wrapt up in a large one for me, from the Dept. of State, was taken out of the mail of yesterday, and not observed before the rider had set out.

I find myself under the mortifying necessity of setting out tomorrow morning for Washington. The intricate state of our affairs with England produced by the mixture of fraud and folly in her late conduct, and the important questions to be decided as to the legal effect of the failure of the arrangement of Apl. on our commercial relations with her, are thought by the Heads of Dept. to require that I should join them.[41] The main question is whether the non-intercourse act as continued at the last Session comes into force agst. England, thereby putting her on the same footing with France.

You will see by the instructions to Erskine as published by Canning, that the latter was as much determined that there should be no adjustment, as the former was that there should be one. There must however have been other instructions comprehending the case of the Chesapeak, and other communications from Canning accompanying the B. Orders of Apl. 26. as referred to in Erskines Quieting declaration last made to Mr. Smith. I believe also that Erskine's letter to Canning not disclosed by the latter, will not warrant his ascribing to Erskine, the statement of conversations with Mr. G. Mr. S. and myself. Pinkney will also disavow what Canning has put into his mouth.

I presume, from letters which reached me yesterday, that Mr. Smith has communications from Paris as late as the 10 or 12 of June; whether by the return of Mr Coles or another conveyance is uncertain. The disavowal in England reached Paris the day after the arrival of the arrangemt., transmitted by Mr. Gelston. Our affairs with France had taken no decided turn; owing as *alledged,* to the absence and occupation of the Emperor. The return of Gel-

---

41. For JM's reaction to Canning's disavowal of the Erskine Agreement, see Brant, V, pp. 71-82.

ston will probably put us in possession of a final estimate.[42] Accept my sincerest respect and attacht.

JAMES MADISON

Madison to Jefferson

Montpellier Aug. 16, 1809

DEAR SIR

I got home from my trip to Washington on Saturday last; having remained there three days only. You will have seen in the Procln. issued, the result of our consultations on the effect of what has passed on our commercial relations with G. B. The enforcement of the non-intercourse act agst. her, will probably be criticized by some friends and generally assailed by our adversaries, on the ground that the power given to the Ex. being special, was exhausted by the first exercise of it; and that the power having put out of force the laws to which it related, could under no possible construction restore their operation. In opposition to this reasoning, it was considered that the Act of the last Session continuing the non-intercourse, no otherwise excepted G. B. than by a proviso that it should not affect any trade which had been, or might be permitted, in conformity with the section of the original act authorizing a proclamation in favor of the nation revoking its Edicts; and that the proclamation in favor of G. B. was not conformable to that section. It was not so in substance, because the indispensable pre-requisite, a repeal of the Orders in Council, did not take place. It was not so even in form; the law requiring a past and not a future fact to be proclaimed, and the proclamation on its face pointing to a future, not to a past fact. This difficulty was felt at the time of issuing the first proclamation; but it yielded to the impossibility of otherwise obtaining without great delay the coveted trade with G. B. and an example that might be followed by France; to the idea that the mode in which the repeal tho' future, of the orders and of the law was coupled by the proclamn. might on the occurrence of the former, give a constructive validity to the latter; and to the opportunity afforded by an intervening session of Congs. for curing any defect in the proceeding. In one respect, it would have been clearly proper for Congress to have interposed its Authority, as was frequently intimated to members; that is, to provide for the contingency, not so much of a disavowal by G. B. which was never suspected, as of her not receiving the Act of her Minister, till after the 10th. of June. Congress however never could be brought to attend to the subject, altho' it was pressed by several members I believe, certainly by Gardenier,[43] on the general ground, that the Procln. however acceptable, was not in a form or under the circumstances, contem-

---

42. For French reaction to England's disavowal of the Erskine Agreement, see Egan, pp. 108–10.
43. Barent Gardenier was a Federalist congressman from New York.

plated by law. In some of the instructions given by Mr Gallatins circular, a liberty has been taken having no plea but manifest necessity, and as such will be before Congress.

Erskine is in a ticklish situation with his Govt. I suspect he will not be able to defend himself agst. the charge of exceeding his instructions, notwithstanding the appeal he makes to sundry others not published. But he will make out a strong case agst. Canning, and be able to avail himself much of the absurdity and evident inadmissibility of the articles disregarded by him. He can plead also that the difference between his arrangemt. and the spontaneous orders of Apl. 26. is too slight to justify the disavowal of him. This difference, seems indeed to limit its importance to the case of Holland, and to consist in the direct trade admitted by the arrangement, and an indirect one, thro' the adjoining ports, required by the orders. To give importance to this distinction, the Ministry must avow, what if they were not shameless they never wd. avow, that their ob[ject] is not to retaliate injury to an Enemy; but to prevent the legitimate trade of the U. S. from interfering with the London smugglers of Sugar and Coffee.

We are looking out for Mr. and Mrs. Gallatin every day. Untill they arrive, and we learn also the periods of your being at and absent from Home, we do not venture to fix a time for our proposed visit to Monticello. Accept my most affectionate respects

JAMES MADISON

Capt: Coles has been with us since sunday. I refer to him for the state of our foreign affairs with which he is sufficiently acquainted, to say more than I cou'd well put on paper.

Jefferson to Madison

Monticello Aug. 17, 1809

DEAR SIR

I recieved your's of yesterday by Mr. Coles. My journey to Bedford has been delayed by sickness among my laboring people. No new case having arisen for some time, I am in hopes it is at an end. Still no particular object fixing my departure to any precise time, it lies over for convenience, and should I fix a time before we have the pleasure of seeing yourself and Mrs. Madison here I shall certainly inform you of it for my own sake, that I may not, by absence, lose what will be a great gratification to me. An antient promise from Mr. and Mrs. Gallatin entitles me to hope they will extend their journey thus far, and give us a portion of the time they have to spare.

I never doubted the chicanery of the Anglomen on whatsoever measures you should take in consequence of the disavowal of Erskine. Yet I am satisfied that both the proclamations have been sound. The first has been sanctioned by universal approbation. Altho' it was not literally the case foreseen by the legislature, yet it was a proper extension of their provision to a case similar tho' not the same. It proved to the whole world our desire of accomodation, and must have satisfied every candid federalist on that head. It was not only proper on the well grounded confidence that the arrangement would be honestly executed, but ought to have taken place even had the perfidy of England been foreseen. Their dirty gain is richly remunerated to us,[44] by our placing them so shamefully in the wrong, and by the union it must produce among ourselves.

The last proclamation admits of quibbles of which advantage will doubtless be endeavored to be taken by those to whom gain is their god, and their country nothing. But it is soundly defensible. The British minister assured that the orders of council would be revoked before the 10th. of June. The Executive, trusting in that assurance, declared by proclamation that the revocation was to take place, and that on that event the law was to be suspended. But the event did not take place, and the consequence, of course, could not follow. This view is derived from the former non-intercourse law only, having never read the latter one.

I had doubted whether Congress must not be called; but that arose from another doubt whether their 2d. law had not changed the ground so as to require their agency to give operation to the law. Should Bonaparte have the wisdom to correct his injustice towards us, I consider war with England as inevitable. Our ships will go to France and it's dependancies, and they will take them. This will be war on their part, and leaves no alternative but reprisal. I have no doubt you will think it safe to act on this hypothesis, and with energy. The moment that open war shall be apprehended from them, we should take possession of Baton rouge. If we do not, they will, and New Orleans becomes irrecoverable and the Western country blockaded during the war. It would be justifiable towards Spain on this ground, and equally so on that of title to W. Florida and reprisal extended to E. Florida. Whatever turn our present difficulty may take, I look upon all cordial conciliation with England as desperate during the life of the present king. I hope and doubt not that Erskine will justify himself. My confidence is founded in a belief of his integrity, and in the unprincipled rascality of Canning. I consider the present as the most shameless ministry which ever disgraced England. Copenhagen will immortalize their infamy.[45] In general their administrations are so changeable, and they are obliged to descend to such tricks to keep themselves in place, that nothing like honor or morality can ever be counted on in transactions with them. I salute you with all possible affection.

TH: JEFFERSON

44. Two-thirds of the usual amount of British exports went to the United States in 1809 as a result of the temporary opening of trade under the Erskine Agreement; see Perkins, p. 219.

45. The British fleet bombarded Copenhagen, then forced Denmark to surrender its fleet to Great Britain as a temporary security for the safety of England.

Madison to Jefferson

Montpellier Aug. 23, 1809

DEAR SIR

Mr. and Mrs. Gallatin reached us on saturday last; and in fulfilment of their promise to you propose to set out for Monticello, tomorrow morning. We are preparing to accompany them. I see by the papers that Mr Smith has probably recd. dispatches from Mr. Pinkney, by a late arrival; but being in Baltimore, I have not yet heard from him on the subject. The newspaper dates from London were not later than the 3d. July; of course give nothing from the Continent. It appears only, in confirmation of late accts. that Russia as well as Holland adhere with rigor to the means of excluding B. Trade. Colonial produce, even Dutch in neutral vessels, is to be warehoused in Holland. Yrs. with truest affection

JAMES MADISON

Madison to Jefferson

Montpellier Sept. 11, 1809

DEAR SIR

I send herewith a few papers which have come to my hands along with those addressed to myself.

Jackson according to a note sent from Annapolis to Mr. Smith was to be in Washington on friday evening last.[46] The letters from Mr. Pinkney brought by him, were dated June 23. and merely rehearsed a conversation with Canning; from which it would seem, that C. readily admitted that his second condition (colonial trade) had no connection with the subject, and that it was not to be expected the U. S. would accede to the 3d (G. B. to execute our laws).[47] Why then make them Ultimata; or if not Ultimata, why reject the arrangemt. of E. for not including them; For as to the 1st. art: if he does not fly from his language to P. the continuance of the non-intercourse vs France, cannot be denied to be a substantial fulfilment of it. From this view of the matter, it might be inferred that Jackson comes with a real olive in his hand. But besides the general slipperiness of his superior, some ideas fell from him in his conversation with P. justifying distrust of his views.

The bearer of this is Mr. Palmer, a young man, respectable I believe, of

---

46. To replace Erskine, who was recalled in disgrace after Canning disavowed his agreement, the ministry sent Francis James Jackson, nicknamed "Copenhagen" for his role in the bombardment of the Danish capital and the seizure of the Danish fleet by the British; see Perkins, pp. 220-21, and Brant, V, pp. 83-101.

47. For Pinkney's letter to Secretary of State Robert Smith, see Hunt, VIII, pp. 70-72.

New York. He is very remarkable as a linguist, and for the most part self-taught. He is perhaps the only American, never out of his own Country, who has dipt as much into the Chinese.

The letter herewith for Capt: Coles,[48] was to have gone by the last mail. If no earlier conveyance shd. offer I beg the favor of its being sent to the post office in time for the next. Be assured always of my affectionate respects

JAMES MADISON

As we wish not to be from home, in case any of our friends from Monticello should indulge us with a visit, be so good as to drop us notice of the time.

I have mustered up the Weather Journals,[49] and wd send them by the present oppy. but that they wd. encumber too much. The fall of water I find has been noted, for not more than 7 or 8 years. The other items much longer.

Jefferson to Madison

Monticello Sept. 12, 1809

DEAR SIR

I had intended to have been with you before this, but my daughter, who wishes to pay her respects to Mrs. Madison and yourself at the same time, has been confined by the illness of her youngest child. He has been mending for some days, but slowly, and from the nature of his complaint (visceral) it will be some days yet before she can leave him. I think therefore, on the departure of our present company to take my journey to Bedford, from which I shall be returned in time to see you. I certainly shall not fail to be with you before your departure.

I have another letter from Daschkoff. He is just recovering from a serious illness. I judge from his letter that he means to visit our quarter as soon as he is well enough to travel.

Canning's equivocations degrade his government as well as himself. I despair of accomodation with them, because I believe they are weak enough to intend seriously to claim the ocean as their conquest, and think to amuse us with embassies and negociations until the claim shall have been strengthened by time and exercise, and the moment arrive when they may boldly avow what hitherto they have only squinted at. Always Your's with sincere affection

TH: JEFFERSON

---

48. Letter not found.
49. For the weather records kept by JM and his family, see *PJM,* VIII, pp. 514-15.

Jefferson to Madison

Monticello Sept. 18, 1809

DEAR SIR

Mr Coles, whom I saw yesterday, informs me you propose to set out for Washington this day week. I have been waiting in the hope that little Benjamin would so far recover as that his mother might leave him. But his recovery, tho' steady, is very slow. We barely discover every day some little additional proof of his getting better. I shall wait till the day after tomorrow in the hope of Mrs Randolph's accompanying me; but should the little boy be still too unwell to be left I will be with you on Thursday or Friday. Affectionately yours

TH. JEFFERSON

Madison to Jefferson

Washington Oct. 6, 1809

DEAR SIR,

I inclose, for perusal, a letter from Mr. Dupont D. N. What does he mean by his desire "to contribute" to the execution of his project of Education?[50] You will observe that he has sent for you a copy of the works of Turgot, as far as edited. Be so good as to point out the mode in which you wish them to be transmitted. I expect a wagon here next month which can take them to Orange, if you prefer that conveyance to a water one to Richmond.

The late news from Europe will be found in the newspapers. Jackson has been presented, and is on the threshold of business. He is not deficient in the diplomatic professions, but nothing appears to contradict the presumption that he is so in the requisite instructions.

We left Montpellier on Friday last and reached Washington on Sunday about 3 oclock. The heat was very oppressive on the road and has so continued since our arrival, notwithstanding a fair shower of rain the evening before the last. Be assured always of my affectionate and high respect.

JAMES MADISON

---

50. Du Pont congratulated JM on becoming TJ's successor as president and referred to his (du Pont's) correspondence with TJ in 1800 about a national plan for education in the United States; see *ibid.*, p. 286.

Jefferson to Madison

Monticello Oct. 9, 1809

DEAR SIR

I recieved last night yours of the 6th. and now return Mr Dupont's letter. At a time when I had a hope that Virginia would establish an University I asked of Mr Dupont and Dr. Priestly to give me their ideas on the best division of the useful sciences into Professorships. The latter did it concisely; but Dupont wrote an elaborate treatise on education which I still possess.[51] After I saw that establishment to be desperate, and with it, gave up the view of making it the legatary of my library,[52] I conceived the hope, and so mentioned to Dupont, that Congress might establish one at Washington. I think it possible that the willingness he expresses to contribute to the execution of his *plan,* may be by becoming President, or a professor. But this is conjecture only. The copy of Turgot's works he has sent me will come best by the mailstage, if put into the care of any passenger of your acquaintance who may be coming as far as Fredericksburg, and will there get Benson to transfer the packet to the Milton stage. Jackson's mountain will, I think produce but a mouse. The affairs of Walcheren and Spain may perhaps give him a little courage.[53] The crop of corn turns out worse than was expected. There certainly will not be half a common crop. It's scarcity and price will produce infinite distress. I set out in three days for Richmond, where I am summoned to be on the 20th.[54] With my best respects to Mrs Madison I am ever affectionately yours

TH JEFFERSON

Jefferson to Madison

Eppington Oct. 25, 1809

DEAR SIR

I recieved at Richmond your favor covering a check on the bank of Norfolk for 743. Doll. 15. cents the balance in full of our accounts. I have learnt from P. Carr that under an idea that Rodney was about to resign, and on a

---

51. For TJ's correspondense with Pierre-Samuel du Pont de Nemours in 1800, see Malone, III, pp. 450–51.

52. For TJ's offer of his library to a university in Virginia, if one were established by the state legislature, see his letter to Littleton W. Tazewell, Jan. 5, 1805, cited *ibid.,* V, p. 22.

53. British forces under Sir Arthur Wellesley, the future duke of Wellington, had pushed into Spain as far as Talavera in 1809. Another British expedition had captured Flushing as a preliminary step on an advance towards Antwerp, before taking up defensive positions on Walcheren Island; see Lefebvre, pp. 93–94, 97–102, and Ross, pp. 292–94, 298.

54. For an account of TJ's only visit to Richmond during his seventeen-year retirement, see Malone, VI, p. 14.

desire expressed by Mr R. Smith to him or some other person that Wirt should be sounded, it had been found that he would accept.[55] I do not know whether it was communicated to me in expectation that I should write it to you, or whether it may have [been] communicated to you more directly.

Altho' I repel all applications generally to recommend candidates for office yet there may be occasions where information of my own knolege of them may be useful and acceptable, and others where particular delicacies of situation may constrain me to say something. Of the latter description is the application of John Monroe (cousin of the Colonel) who in expectation that the Governor of Illinois means to resign, has sollicited my saying to you he would accept that office. I had formerly appointed him Atty of the West district of Virginia. He resided at Staunton and there lost the respect of many by some irregularities which his subsequent marriage has probably put an end to. His talents I believe are respectable, without being prominent: but I really believe you know as much of him as I do, having seen him myself once or twice only, and then for short intervals. Particular circumstances oblige me to mention him, without feeling a single wish on the subject, other than that it should be given to the fittest subject, which you will do of your own notion. Ever affectionately yours

TH JEFFERSON

Madison to Jefferson

Washington Oct. 30, 1809

DEAR SIR

In the operation of removing from my former quarters, the Digest of the City Code and business, which you had been so good as to furnish me, has, by some unaccountable accident, been either lost, or possibly so thrown out of place, as not to be found. I have written to Capt: Coles to take Monticello in his way, and ask the favor of you to permit him to take another copy, from your Original. As that letter however may not reach him, I must beg you to signify my wishes to him, in case he should call on you as he probably will.[56]

The Works of Turgot, remain on hand for want of some person to take charge of them to Fredg. They fill a Box abt. 15 inchs. by 12. and 8 inchs deep; too large therefore for the Mail. I shall avail myself of the 1st. oppy. for sending it on by the Stage. I was in hope, that the Race-field would have furnished some known person, returning by way of Fredg: but I was disappointed; there being very few Virginians there, and none from the Southern districts.

---

55. For Wirt, see Joseph C. Robert, "William Wirt, Virginian," *VMHB* 80 (1972): 387–441.
56. Isaac Coles returned from his mission to France late in July; see Egan, p. 108.

We just learn the melancholy fate of Govr. Lewis which possibly may not have travelled so quickly into your neighbourhood. He had, it seems betrayed latterly repeated symtoms of a disordered mind; and had set out under the care of a friend on a visit to Washington. His first intention was, to make the trip by water; but changing it, at the Chickasaw Bluffs, he struck across towards Nashville. As soon as he had passed the Tennessee, he took advantage of the neglect of his Companion, who had not secured his arms, to put an end to himself. He first fired a pistol, at his head, the ball of which glancing, was ineffectual. With the 2d. he passed a Ball thro' his body, wch. being also without immediate effect, he had recourse to his Dirk with wch he mangled himself considerably. After all he lived till the next morning, with the utmost impatience for death.

I inclose the latest accts. from Europe. Onis has returned to Philada. The reality or degree of his disappt. is not easily ascertained. His last conversation with Mr. Smith, did not manifest ill humour. How could he expect a different result, in the actual State of things? And what motive Can Spain or the Colonies have, in any State of things, to make enemies of the U. S? I see nothing to change the view of Jackson, which I formerly hinted to you.[57]

Jefferson to Madison

Monticello Nov. 6, 1809

DEAR SIR

Yours of Oct. 30. came to hand last night. Capt. Coles passed this place on the 31st. to Washington. I gave a copy of the paper you desire to Thomas Monroe for his government; and through him another to Mayor Brent, that the city magistracy might understand what I considered as the limits separating our rights and duties. Capt Coles can borrow either of these probably for copying. Should they be lost, on my return from Bedford, for which place I set out tomorrow, I will send you mine to be copied.

On the 3d. and 4th. we had a fall of 3. I. rain, more than had fallen in the 3. months following the 14th. of July. This morning the thermometer is at 33½. A few spiculae of white frost are visible here; but I expect it is severe in the neighborhood, and that there is ice.

I recieved a note from the Chevalr. de Onis which I answered. Perhaps he may make this the occasion of expressing his mind unofficially to me. Affectionately yours

TH JEFFERSON

---

57. Chevalier Luis de Onís sought recognition as minister of Ferdinand VII of Spain and the Supreme Junta. Having broken with Yrujo, JM decided that he would not receive a minister from the junta, backed by Great Britain, nor from Joseph Bonaparte. For the intervention by "Copenhagen" Jackson on Onís's behalf, see Brant, V, pp. 98–99.

Madison to Jefferson

Washington Nov. 6, 1809

DEAR SIR,

I received your letter from Eppington. I had not heard that either the Attorney General or the Governor of Illinois meant to resign.

Inclosed are several letters for you, received from France by the return of the Wasp. You will see the propriety of my adding one to myself from M!̣ Short, to be returned after perusal. Our information from Paris, of the 19th of September, gives no countenance to the rumoured renewal of hostilities in Austria. The delay of peace in form alone keeps alive such rumours. But why should such an event flatter the hopes of G. Britain? According to all the lessons of experience, it would quickly be followed by a more compleat prostration of her Ally. Armstrong had forwarded to the French Court the measure taken here in consequence of the disavowal of Erskine's arrangement, but there had not been time for an answer. The answer to the previous communication had been, let England annul her illegal blockade of France, and the Berlin decree will be revoked; let her then revoke her orders of November, and the Milan decree falls, of course. This state of the question between the two powers would promise some good, if it were ascertained that by the blockade of France previous to the Berlin decree was meant that of May, extending from the Elbe to Brest, or any other specific act. It is to be feared that there is an intentional obscurity, or that an *express* and general renunciation of the British practice is made the condition. From G. Britain we have only newspaper intelligence. The change in the Ministry seems likely to make bad worse, unless we are to look for some favorable change in the extremity to which things must rapidly proceed under the quackeries and corruptions of an administration headed by such a being as Perceval.[58] Jackson is proving himself a worthy instrument of his patron, Canning. We shall proceed with a circumspect attention to all the circumstances mingled in our affairs, but with a confidence, at the same time, in a just sensibility of the nation to the respect due to it.

Jefferson to Madison

Monticello Nov. 26, 1809

DEAR SIR,

Your letter of the 6th. was recieved from our post office on the 24th, after my return from Bedford. I now re-inclose the letters of Mr. Short and Ro-

---

58. The failure of the British to budge from Walcheren Island later led to the withdrawal of the invading army from Holland and caused the collapse of the duke of Portland's ministry. Canning and Castlereagh left office (and subsequently fought a duel), leaving Spencer Perceval to head the new ministry; see Perkins, p. 235.

manzoff, and with them a letter from Armstrong for your perusal, as there may be some matters in it not otherwise communicated. The infatuation of the British government and nation is beyond everything immaginable. A thousand circumstances announce that they are on the point of being blown up, and they still proceed with the same madness and increased wickedness. With respect to Jackson I hear of but one sentiment, except that some think he should have been sent off. The more moderate step was certainly more advisable.[59] There seems to be a perfect acquiescence in the opinion of the Government respecting Onis. The public interest certainly made his rejection expedient; and as that is a motive which it is not pleasant always to avow, I think it fortunate that the contending claims of Charles and Ferdinand furnished such plausible embarrassment to the question of right; for, on our principles, I presume the right of the Junta to send a Minister could not be denied.

La Fayette, in a letter to me expresses great anxiety to recieve his formal titles to the lands in Louisiana. Indeed I know not why the proper officers have not sooner sent on the papers on which the grants might issue. It will be in your power to forward the grants or copies of them by some safe conveyance, as La Fayette says that no negociation can be effected with out them.

I inclose you a letter from Maj. Neely, Chickasaw agent, stating that he is in possession of 2 trunks of the unfortunate Governor Lewis,[60] containing public vouchers, the manuscripts of his Western journey, and probably some private papers. As he desired they should be sent *to the president,* as the public vouchers render it interesting to the public that they should be safely recieved, and they would probably come most safely if addressed to you, would it not be advisable that Maj. Neely should recieve an order on your part to forward them to Washington addressed to you, by the stage, and if possible under the care of some person coming on?[61] When at Washington, I presume, the papers may be opened and distributed; that is to say, the Vouchers to the proper offices where they are cognisable; the Manuscript voyage, etc., to Genl. Clarke, who is interested in it, and is believed to be now on his way to Washington; and his private papers if any to his administrator, who is John Marks, his half brother. It is impossible you should have time to examine and distrib-

---

59. For the failure of Jackson's mission and JM's demand that he be recalled, see *ibid.*, pp. 220–21, 236–39, and Brant, V, pp. 83–101.

60. Meriwether Lewis, whom TJ had appointed governor of Louisiana Territory in 1807, committed suicide on Oct. 11, 1809; see Dawson A. Phelps, "The Tragic Death of Meriwether Lewis," *WMQ* 13 (1956): 305–18. TJ explained the tragic story in a letter of Aug. 18, 1813, which was printed as a preface to Nicholas Biddle and Paul Allen's *History of the Expedition under the Command of Captains Lewis and Clark* (Philadelphia, 1814). Although some historians dispute Dawson's view that Lewis committed suicide, leaning instead to a murder theory, the careful psychoanalytical appraisal by Howard I. Kushner confirms Dawson's findings; see his "The Suicide of Meriwether Lewis: A Psychoanalytical Inquiry," *WMQ* 38 (1981): 464–81, and his larger study, *Self-Destruction in the Promised Land: A Psychocultural Biology of American Suicide* (New Brunswick, N.J., 1989), pp. 119–32.

61. Major James Neelly accompanied Governor Lewis, who was en route from St. Louis to Washington, from Memphis to Nashville; see Phelps, 313–14.

ute them; but if Mr. Coles could find time to do it the family would have entire confidence in his distribution. The other two trunks, which are in the care of Capt. Russel at the Chickasaw bluffs,[62] and which Pernier (Governor Lewis's servant) says contain his private property,[63] I write to Capt. Russel, at the request of Mr. Marks, to forward [it] to Mr. Brown at New Orleans to be sent on to Richmond under my address. Pernier says that Governor Lewis owes him 240 D. for his wages. He has recieved money from Neely to bring him on here, and I furnish him to Washington, where he will arrive pennyless, and will ask for some money to be placed to the Governor's account. He rides a horse of the Governor's, which, with the approbation of the administrator, I tell him to dispose of and give credit for the amount in his account against the Governor. He is the bearer of this letter, and of my assurances of constant and affectionate esteem and respect.

TH. JEFFERSON

Madison to Jefferson

Washington Nov. 27, 1809

DEAR SIR

A gentleman of intelligence and good standing in Kentuckey lately signified to a friend here, that he was much in conversation with Col. Monroe during his trip to that Country, and that sentiments which were repeatedly dropped by him, left no doubt that altho' he declined a more important station at N. O. he would not object to the vacancy produced by the death of Govr. Lewis, which would place him in a more eligible climate. I can not bring myself to believe, that the Gentn. has not drawn a conclusion entirely erroneous, and that any step taken on a contrary supposition would not be otherwise than offensive. Still it may be my duty in a way that can not have such an effect, to acquire certainty on the subject. Will you permit me, with that view to ask of you to give a turn to conversation with Col. M. which may feel the disposition of his mind, without indicating any particular object. I need not suggest, that it will be desireable that the first opportunity occurring should be made use of.

I understand there is likely to be a Quorum in both Houses today notwithstanding the late bad weather.

It seems that Turreau has dispatches by a French sloop of war which left Bayonne Early in Octr. He is but just arrived from Baltimore, and there has not yet been any communication with him. From the date of the opportunity, it is not probable that any thing is recd. as to our Affairs either more recent or

---

62. Captain Gilbert C. Russell was stationed at Fort Pickering, now Memphis; see *ibid.*, 312.
63. For John Pernier, a free mulatto, see *ibid.*, 313.

important than the information from Genl. A. by the Wasp,[64] which will be laid before Congs. Yrs. always with affect. respects

JAMES MADISON

Jefferson to Madison

Monticello Nov. 30, 1809

DEAR SIR,

I recieved last night yours of the 27th, and rode this morning to Col. Monroe's. I found him preparing to set out tomorrow morning for Loudon [County], from whence he will not return till Christmas. I had an hour or two's frank conversation with him. The catastrophe of poor Lewis served to lead us to the point intended. I reminded him that in the letter I wrote to him while in Europe proposing the Government of Orleans, I also suggested that of Louisiana, if fears for health should be opposed to the other. I said something on the importance of the post, its advantages, etc. expressed my regret at the curtain which seemed to be drawn between him and his best friends, and my wish to see his talents and integrity engaged in the service of his country again, and that his going into any post would be a signal of reconciliation, on which the body of republicans, who lamented his absence from the public service, would again rally to him. These are the general heads of what I said to him in the course of our conversation. The sum of his answers was, that to accept of that office was incompatible with the respect he owed himself, that he never would act in any office where he should be subordinate to any body but the President himself, or which did not place his responsibility substantially with the President and the nation: that at your accession to the chair, he would have accepted a place in the cabinet, and would have exerted his endeavors most faithfully in support of your fame and measures; that he is not unready to serve the public and especially in the case of any difficult crisis in our affairs; that he is satisfied that such is the deadly hatred of both France and England, and such their self reproach and dread at the spectacle of such a government as ours, that they will spare nothing to destroy it; that nothing but a firm union among the whole body of republicans can save it, and therefore that no schism should be indulged on any ground; that in his present situation he is sincere in his anxieties for the success of the administration, and in his support of it as far as the limited sphere of his action or influence extends; that his influence to this end had been used with those with whom the world had ascribed to him an influence he did not possess, until, whatever it was, it was lost, (he particularly named J. Randolph who he said had plans of his own, on which he took no advice) and that he was now pursuing what he

---

64. For Armstrong's views, see Skeen, pp. 102–4.

Madison Takes Over, 1809 *1611*

believed his properest occupation, devoting his whole time and faculties to the liberation of his pecuniary embarrasments, which, 3. years of close attention he hoped would effect. In order to know more exactly what were the kinds of employ he would accept, I adverted to the information of the papers which came yesterday that Genl. Hampton was dead, but observed that the military life in our present state, offered nothing which could operate on the principle of patriotism; he said he would sooner be shot than take a command under Wilkinson.

In this sketch I have given truly the substance of his ideas, but not always his own words. On the whole I conclude he would accept a place in the Cabinet, or a military command dependent on the Executive alone, and I rather suppose a diplomatic mission, because it would fall within the scope of his views, and not because he said so, for no allusion was made to any thing of that kind in our conversation. Everything from him breathed the purest patriotism, involving however, a close attention to his own honour and grade. He expressed himself with the utmost devotion to the interests of our own country, and I am satisfied he will pursue them with honor and zeal in any character in which he shall be willing to act.[65]

I have thus gone far beyond the single view of your letter that you may, under any circumstances, form a just estimate of what he would be disposed to do. God bless you, and carry you safely through all your difficulties.

Th. Jefferson

Jefferson to Madison

Monticello Dec. 7, 1809

Dear Sir,

The inclosed letter is from Father Richard, the Director of a school at Detroit; and being on a subject in which the departments both of the Treasury and War are concerned, I take the liberty of inclosing it to yourself as the center which may unite these two agencies. The transactions which it alludes to took place in the months of Dec. and Jan. preceding my retirement from office, and as I think it probable they may not have been fully placed on the records of the War office, because they were conducted verbally for the most part, I will give a general statement of them as well as my recollection will enable me.

In the neighborhood of Detroit (2. or 3. miles from the town) is a farm, formerly the property of one Ernest, a bankrupt Collector. It is now in possession of the Treasury department, as a pledge for a sum in which he is in default to the government, much beyond the value of the farm. As it is a good one,

---

65. See Malone, VI, pp. 27–29; Brant, V, pp. 27–28; and Ammon, pp. 279–81.

has proper buildings, in a proper position for the purpose contemplated, General Dearborne proposed to purchase it for the War department, at its real value. Mr. Gallatin thought he should ask the sum for which it was hypothecated. I do not remember the last idea in which we all concurred, but I believe it was that, as the Treasury must, in the end, sell it for what it could get, the War department would become a bidder as far as it's real value, and in the meantime would rent it.

On this farm we proposed to assemble the following establishments:

1. Father Richard's school. He teaches the children of the inhabitants of Detroit. But the part of the school within our view was that of the young Indian girls instructed by two French females, natives of the place, who devote their whole time, and their own property which was not inconsiderable, to the care and instruction of Indian girls in carding, spinning, weaving, sowing, and the other household arts suited to the condition of the poor, and as practiced by the white women of that condition. Reading and writing were an incidental part of their education. We proposed that the war department should furnish the farm and houses for the use of the school, gratis, and add 400 D. a year to the funds, and that the benefits of the Institution should be extended to the boys also of the neighboring tribes, who were to be lodged, fed, and instructed there.

2. To establish there the farmer at present employed by the United States, to instruct those Indians in the use of the plough and other implements and practices of Agriculture, and in the general management of the farm. This man was to labour the farm himself, and to have the aid of the boys through a principal portion of the day, by which they would contract habits of industry, learn the business of farming, and provide subsistence for the whole institution. Reading and writing were to be a secondary object.

3. To remove thither the Carpenter and Smith at present employed by the United States among the same Indians; with whom such of the boys as had a turn for it should work and learn their trades.

This establishment was recommended by the further circumstance that whenever the Indians come to Detroit on trade or other business, they encamp on or about this farm. This would give them opportunities of seeing their sons and daughters, and their advancement in the useful arts, of seeing and learning from example all the operations and process of a farm, and of always carrying home themselves some additional knolege of these things. It was thought more important to extend the civilised arts, and to introduce a separation of property among the Indians of the country around Detroit than elsewhere, because learning to set a high value on their property and losing by degrees all other dependance for subsistence, they would deprecate war with us as bringing certain destruction on their property, and would become a barrier for that distant and insulated post against the Indians beyond them. There are, beyond them, some strong tribes, as the Sacs, Foxes, etc. with whom we have as yet had little connection, and slender opportunities of extending to them our benefits and influence. They are therefore ready instruments to be brought into operation on us by a powerful neighbor which still cultivates it's influence over them by nourishing the savage habits, which waste them, rather than by encouraging the civilized arts which would soften, conciliate and preserve them. The whole additional expense to the United States was to be the price of the farm, and an increase of 400 D. in the annual expenditures for these tribes.

This is the sum of my recollections. I cannot answer for their exactitude in all details; but General Dearborne could supply and correct the particulars of my statement. Mr. Gallatin too was so often in consultation on the subject that he must have been informed of the whole plan; and his memory is so much better than mine, that he will be able to make my statement what it should be. Add to this that, I think, I generally informed yourself of our policy and proceedings in the case as we went along; and, if I am not mistaken it was one of the articles of a memorandum I left with you of things still *in fieri* [pending], and which would merit your attention.

I have thought it necessary to put you in possession of these facts that you might understand the grounds of Father Richard's application, and be enabled to judge for yourself of the expediency of pursuing the plan, or of the means of withdrawing from it with justice to the individuals employed in it's execution. How far we are committed with the Indians themselves in this business will be seen in a speech of mine to them, of Jan. 31., filed in the war office, and perhaps something more may have passed to them from the Secretary at War. Always affectionately yours.

TH. JEFFERSON

THE MACON BILLS, 1810: "BETTER THAN NOTHING"

As PRESIDENT, Madison seldom sought Jefferson's advice but often received his approval. With respect to the presidential demand for the recall of "Copenhagen" Jackson, Jefferson said that he heard "of but one sentiment, except that some think he should have been sent off. The more moderate step [of dismissal] was certainly more advisable."[1] Indeed, Madison's move won almost universal approval not only by Republicans, but also by most Federalists, according to a Massachusetts Republican, except for " 'the mouthpiece of the British faction' at Baltimore under Timothy Pickering's auspices."[2] "In truth," the New England congressman continued, "I think that James Madison's administration is now as strongly entrenched in the public confidence as Thomas Jefferson's ever was at its fullest tide and I do think that it will be quite as likely not to ebb as much as that did towards its close."[3]

In his first annual message to Congress, Madison reviewed the "wrongs and vexations experienced from external causes" that "overclouded" the prospect of "this rising nation." Defending the Erskine Agreement as a proper "adjustment with one of the principal belligerent nations," he stressed the good faith with which it had "been carried into immediate execution on the part of the United States" and his surprise that the British government had refused "to abide by the act of its minister plenipotentiary" who had negotiated the Erskine Agreement.

Equally surprising was that government's "ensuing policy toward the United States" under his successor. Despite Jackson's obnoxious actions,

---

1. TJ to JM, Nov. 26, 1809, above.
2. Jacob Wagner, a protégé of Secretary of State Timothy Pickering in John Adams's administration, was retained as chief clerk in the State Department by JM for six years, but he became a harsh critic of his former mentor as the Federalist editor of the Baltimore *North American*.
3. Ezekiel Bacon to Joseph Story, Nov. 27, 1809, cited in Brant, V, p. 108.

which had led to his dismissal, Madison hoped that a new British envoy would bring "a favorable revision of the unfriendly policy which has been so long pursued toward the United States." As for "the other belligerent," he noted that France continued her "trespasses on our commercial rights," disregarding "our just remonstrances" and "measures taken on the part of the United States to effect a favorable change."[4]

Caught up in the Republican ideology of legislative leadership, Madison deferred to the wisdom of Congress for a policy to replace the Nonintercourse Act, which would expire at the end of the session. But he confessed to Jefferson that there was no way that the course of Congress could be predicted. "The Republicans as usual are either not decided, or have different leanings. The Federalists are lying in wait to spring on any opportunity of checking or diverting the tide now setting so strongly against them."[5] As if to confirm Madison's appraisal, the Republicans in the Senate promptly adopted resolutions written by Giles lauding Madison's handling of Erskine and Jackson, denouncing Jackson's insults, and promising forceful action to support the nation's rights. But the House spent three weeks of divisive debate before a nineteen-hour session ended at 5:30 A.M. with 72 congressmen voting for, and 41 voting against, the resolution supporting their own government.[6]

The House debate seemed to corroborate the view of Congressman William A. Burwell of Virginia, Jefferson's former secretary, who thought that "the spirit of the nation is evaporated"; he confessed that he despaired of Congress passing any measure "which would not meet with such opposition as to make it useless."[7] Since the Nonintercourse Act had not forced either belligerent to modify its obnoxious regulations, and since renewal of the embargo was impossible, Gallatin drafted an old-fashioned navigation act that allowed American ships to go anywhere, including Great Britain and France, but banned British and French merchant vessels and warships from American ports. The bill also authorized the president, in case either power revoked its decrees violating neutral commerce, to declare by proclamation that this ban would no longer apply to the commerce of that nation.

Although drafted by the administration, the bill took its name from its sponsor, Nathaniel Macon, former Speaker of the House and then chairman of the Committee on Foreign Affairs, and was supported by Madison and the cabinet as "better than nothing, which seemed to be the alternative."[8] Macon's Bill passed the House 73 to 52, but even its warmest supporters could

---

4. Richardson, I, pp. 473-77.

5. JM to TJ, Dec. 11, 1809, below. See Reginald C. Stuart, "James Madison and the Militants: Republican Disunity and Replacing the Embargo," *Diplomatic History* 6 (1982): 145-67, for an analysis.

6. Brant, V, pp. 120-22, and Bradford Perkins, *Prologue to War: England and the United States, 1805-1812* (Berkeley, 1963), pp. 238-39.

7. *Ibid.*, p. 238.

8. JM, "Memorandum as to Robert Smith," Apr. 1811, in Hunt, VIII, p. 141.

only recommend it as "a sort of Protestation against the infringements of our rights."[9] Recalcitrant Republicans in the Senate then joined obstructionist Federalists to defeat the bill.

Early in April, Macon introduced a second bill, dubbed Macon's Bill No. 2, offering a diametrically opposite approach. It proposed to end nonintercourse with both Britain and France on May 1, 1810, thus removing all restrictions on American commerce. But if either belligerent revoked its restrictions before March 5, 1811, and the other failed to follow suit within three months, the United States would reimpose the Nonintercourse Act of 1809 against it. The new bill led to an interminable debate but finally skinned through on May 1, 1810, without a roll-call vote, in the final hours of the last day of the session, when the Nonintercourse Act was scheduled to terminate automatically.[10]

While Congress floundered between Macon's Bills No. 1 and No. 2, the president told Jefferson that it remained "in the unhinged state which has latterly marked their proceedings; with the exception only that a majority in the H. of R. have stuck together so far as to pass a Bill providing for a conditional repeal by either of the Bellig^{ts} of their Edicts; laying in the mean time, an addition[al] 50 Per C^t to the present duties on imports from G. B. and France. What the Senate will do with the Bill is rendered utterly uncertain by the policy which seems to prevail in that Branch."[11] Madison doubted that the merchants advocating open trade with the belligerents would rush their ships and goods across the ocean. "The certainty of a glutted Market in England," he observed to Jefferson, "and the apprehension of Brit Blockades, and French confiscations" had led to "a voluntary Embargo." The mere mention of that word reminded him of the Embargo Act, whose repeal he regretted: "The experiment about to be made will probably open too late the eyes of the people, to the expediency and efficacy of the means which they have suffered to be taken out of the hands of the Gov^t and to be incapacitated for future use."[12]

Although Madison may not have agreed with a Republican congressman who condemned Macon's Bill for combining surrender with bribery—it "held up the honor and character of this nation to the highest bidder"[13]—he thought that it amounted to submission to both belligerents, although it tilted towards Britain. The congressional debates, he informed Jefferson, demonstrated that the Federalist party "prefers submission of our trade to British regulation" while the Republican majority "confesses the impossibility of resisting it."[14] The new measure gave Great Britain "the full enjoyment of

9. Ezekiel Bacon to Joseph Story, Nov. 27, 1809, cited in Perkins, p. 239.

10. Brant, V, pp. 126–40.

11. JM to TJ, Apr. 23, 1810, below. The Senate rejected the discriminatory duties, which would have been suspended in favor of whichever nation repealed its edicts.

12. *Ibid.*

13. For the quotation by Thomas Gholson, Jr., a Virginia Democratic-Republican, see Perkins, p. 241.

14. JM to TJ, Apr. 23, 1810, below.

our trade" while putting it "on the worst possible footing for France."[15] Under these circumstances, there was little reason for Richard C. Wellesley, Canning's successor, "to drag his Anti-American Colleagues into a change of policy."[16] "Unless G. Britain should apprehend an attempt from France to revive our non-intercourse against her, she has every earthly motive to continue her restrictions against us. She has our trade, in spite of France, as far as she can make it suit her interest, and our acquiescence in [her use of naval force for] cutting it off from the rest of the world, as far as she may wish to distress her adversaries, to cramp our growth as rivals, or to prevent our interference with her smuggling monopoly."[17]

That France had no intention of slackening its arbitrary system was demonstrated by a wave of confiscations of previously sequestered American ships. "The late confiscations by Bonaparte," Madison exploded, "comprise robbery, theft, and breach of trust, and exceed in turpitude any of his enormities not wasting human blood. This scene on the continent," he told Jefferson, "and the effect of the English monopoly on the value of our produce, are breaking the charm attached to what is called free trade, foolishly by some, and wickedly by others."[18]

Despite Madison's denunciation of "the atrocity of the French Government," he thought that "the original sin agst Neutrals lies with G. B."[19] Jefferson agreed that "at length Gr. Br. has been forced to pull off her mask and shew that her real object is the exclusive use of the ocean. Her good sense is overruled by her avarice," he concluded. But he balanced this view with a withering blast at French policy: Napoleon's good sense was overruled "by his own haughty and tyrannical temper."

To another correspondent, he summarized the scenes of "tumult and outrage" created by the twin tyrants of Europe: "Every government but one on the continent of Europe demolished, a conqueror roaming over the earth with havoc and destruction, a pirate spreading misery and ruin over the face of the ocean." Like Madison, he lamented the loss of the embargo as an economic and diplomatic weapon: "A return to embargo could alone save us."[20]

While the Madisons made their way from Washington to Montpellier in mid-July, news arrived of the Rambouillet Decree of March 23, 1810, which illustrated Napoleon's tyrannical temper. A belated reaction to the now defunct Nonintercourse Act, the decree was made retroactive to May 1809 and barred American shipping from Continental ports controlled by France and ordered the seizure and sale of any proscribed vessels that entered these

---

15. JM to William Pinkney, May 23, 1810, cited in Brant, V, p. 146, and JM to TJ, May 25, 1810, below.
16. JM to TJ, Apr. 23, 1810, below.
17. JM to TJ, May 7, 1810, below.
18. JM to TJ, May 25, 1810, below.
19. JM to TJ, June 15, 1810, below, and June 22, 1810, below.
20. TJ to JM, June 27, 1810, below, and TJ to Walter Jones, Mar. 5, 1810, in Ford, IX, p. 274.

ports.[21] At almost the same moment that news of the decree reached Washington, Armstrong notified the French minister, the duke of Cadore, that Macon's Bill had replaced the Nonintercourse Act.[22]

In a perceptive analysis of Macon's Bill, Madison had stressed the "*possibility* that the negotiations on foot at Paris" might be strengthened by the bill, since the measure "puts it in the option of her to revive the non-intercourse against England."[23] Although Macon's Bill might appear to be feeble, he wrote to William Pinkney in London, "it is possible that one or other of those powers may allow it more effect than was produced by overtures heretofore tried" since it could be viewed by Britain or France "not as a coercion or threat to itself, but a promise of attack on the other." He doubted that Britain would alter its policy since "the actual state of things" favored her. But this very inequality, he suggested, might become a motive with France "to turn the tables on Great Britain, by compelling her either to revoke her orders, or to lose the commerce of this country."[24]

On August 5, 1810, Cadore handed Armstrong a letter announcing that as a result of Macon's Bill, "the decrees of Berlin and Milan are revoked, and that after the 1st of November they will cease to have effect; it being understood that, in consequence of this declaration, the English shall revoke their orders in council, and renounce the new principles of blockade, which they have undertaken to establish; or that the United States, conformably to the act you have just communicated, shall cause their rights to be respected by the English."[25]

When the Cadore letter was published in American newspapers, Jefferson sent Madison congratulations "on the revocation of the French decrees, and Congress still more, for without something new from the belligerents, I know not what ground they could have taken for their next move." As for Great Britain, he predicted that she would "revoke her orders of council, but continue their effect by new paper blockades, doing in detail what the orders did in the lump. The exclusive right to the sea by conquest," he continued, "is the principle she has acted on in petto, tho' she dares not yet avow it. . . . I rejoice however that one power has got out of our way, and left us a clear field with the other."[26]

While weighing the ambiguous nature of the French offer as well as Napo-

21. Brant, V, pp. 154–56.
22. Perkins, p. 245.
23. He also thought that the Federalist losses in recent elections in New England might weaken the British ministry's "fallacious reliance on the British party here"; see JM to TJ, May 25, 1809, below.
24. JM to William Pinkney, May 23, 1810, cited in Abraham D. Sofaer, *War, Foreign Affairs and Constitutional Power: The Origins* (Cambridge, Mass., 1976), pp. 282–83. This is a superior study that covers the early national period to 1829.
25. Brant, V, p. 195.
26. TJ to JM, Oct. 15, 1810, below.

leon's reputation for chicanery, Madison explained that "all we know of the step taken by France towards a reconciliation with us, is thro the English papers sent by Mr. Pinkney, who had not himself rec^d any information on the subject from Genl A[rmstrong] nor held any conversation with the B. Ministry on it, at the date of his last letters. We hope from the step, the advantage at least of having but one contest on our hands at a time. If G. B. repeals her orders, without discontinuing her mock-blockades, we shall be at issue with her on ground strong in law, in the opinion of the world, and even in her own concessions. And," he concluded, "I do not believe that Cong^s will be disposed, or permitted by the Nation, to a tame submission; the less so as it would be not only perfidious to the other belligerent, but irreconcilable with an honorable neutrality."[27]

On the day that Madison dispatched his letter to Jefferson, news arrived from London that Armstrong had sent Pinkney official notice that France had revoked the Berlin and Milan decrees. Although the Cadore letter had not yet arrived from Paris, and despite some reservations about the phraseology of the letter, Madison and the cabinet decided to consider Armstrong's letter to Pinkney as official notification. On November 2, 1810, the day after Napoleon's promise was to become effective, Madison issued a proclamation announcing that France had met the requirements of Macon's Bill and that the Nonintercourse Act would be reimposed on Great Britain on February 2, 1811, unless the King-in-Council revoked their orders. On the same day, he informed the French that he accepted the Cadore letter as a statement of policy, not a conditional proposal. In case Great Britain continued its interference with American commerce, the United States would take measures that "necessarily lead to war."[28]

Four other topics—two political and two agricultural—dominated the letters that Madison and Jefferson exchanged in 1810. In his letter of May 25, Jefferson mentioned the political issues, both related to the federal judiciary and Jefferson's distant kinsman, John Marshall. The first involved the ownership of the Batture St. Marie, an extended beach near New Orleans built by silt from the Mississippi River. Submerged part of the year, it was used as a shoal anchorage by boats descending the river; when the river receded, it was used as a landing as well as a public source of sand and soil by local inhabitants. The governor of Orleans Territory claimed that the strip belonged to the United States, but a territorial court awarded it to Edward Livingston, the principal abutting owner. Jefferson and his cabinet denied the jurisdiction of the territorial court, ordered Livingston evicted from the national domain under provisions of the Squatters Act of 1807, and restored the batture to its previous condition, pending action by Congress. After attempts at negotiation, Livingston slapped a personal lawsuit for trespass against Jeffer-

27. JM to TJ, Oct. 19, 1810, below.
28. Brant, V, pp. 194–221, and Perkins, pp. 244–55.

son in the federal circuit court in Richmond, seeking personal damages of $100,000.[29]

Livingston's lawsuit was a shocking surprise to the former president, especially the demand for damages of $100,000. Jefferson agreed to prepare a statement of the controversy for use by his lawyers, and he asked Madison and his other cabinet members for assistance since "much of our proceedings was never committed to writing, and my memory cannot be trusted." He was sure, however, that what he had done in the case "was in harmony with the opinions of all the members of the administration, verbally expressed."

His distrust of John Marshall also surfaced quickly. He was convinced that Livingston's "knolege of Marshall's character has induced him to bring this action" of *Livingston* v. *Jefferson* in Richmond. The chief justice's "twistifications"—a wonderful word coined by Jefferson for the occasion—"in the case of Marbury [v. Madison], in that of Burr, and the late Yazoo case shew how dexterously he can reconcile law to his personal biasses: and nobody seems to doubt that he is ready prepared to decide that Livingston's right to the batture is unquestionable, and that I am bound to pay for it with my private fortune."[30]

In the same letter, Jefferson took a second slap at Marshall when he recommended Governor John Tyler of Virginia as a successor to the ailing district judge, Cyrus Griffin, who sat with the chief justice when he rode the federal circuit in the South. Virginia had suffered too long "by having such a cypher" as Griffin "in so important an office." Such "a milk and water character" should be replaced by a judge of "incorruptible integrity," one with "firmness enough to preserve his independance on the same bench with Marshall." A man of Tyler's character would serve as a "counterpoise to the rancorous hatred which Marshal bears to the government of his country, and from the cunning and sophistry within which he is able to enshroud himself."[31]

When the death of Associate Justice William Cushing created a vacancy on the Supreme Court, Jefferson congratulated Madison on his opportunity of appointing "a successor of unquestionable republican principles." Referring to the "Revolution of 1800," Jefferson observed that "the nation ten years ago declared it's will for a change in the principles of the administration of their affairs. They then changed the two branches depending on their will, and have steadily maintained the reformation in those branches. The third, not dependent on them, has so long bid defiance to their will, erecting themselves into a

---

29. Malone, VI, pp. 55–73. Livingston had defaulted to the Treasury for about half this amount in 1803 and had moved from New York to New Orleans in order to restore his fortune.

30. TJ to JM, May 25, 1810, below. For other references to the batture case, see TJ to JM, May 30, 1810, below, July 13, 1810, below, July 26, 1810, below, and Aug. 20, 1810, below; and JM to TJ, June 4, 1810, below.

31. TJ to JM, May 25, 1810, below, June 27, 1810, below, and JM to TJ, June 22, 1810, below. For Tyler's and Marshall's roles in deciding that Livingston could not bring action in the Virginia district court, see John Marshall, *The Papers of John Marshall*, ed. Charles F. Hobson *et al.* (Chapel Hill, 1993), VII, pp. 276–88.

political body to correct what they deem the errors of the nation." But the appointment of a New Englander of "firm republicanism" gave Madison "an opportunity of closing the reformation" of the judiciary. Back-sliding Republicans like Joseph Story, a young Massachusetts Republican who had treacherously "deserted us" on the embargo, should not be considered. Besides, Story was a tory and much "too young."[32]

Madison had earlier agreed that the judiciary needed reforming, particularly if it pressed Livingston's batture suit against the former president. "If the Judiciary should lend itself for such a purpose," he assured Jefferson, "it cannot fail I think, to draw down on itself the unbounded indignation of the Nation, and a change of the Constitution, under that feeling, carried perhaps too far in the opposite direction. In a Government whose vital principle is responsibility, it never will be allowed that the Legislative and Executive Departments should be compleatly subjected to the Judiciary, in which that characteristic feature is so faintly seen."[33] Now that there was a vacancy on the Supreme Court, he confessed that New England presented something of "a puzzle in supplying it."[34] After trying Levi Lincoln, Jefferson's first choice, and John Quincy Adams, both of whom rejected the appointment, Madison disregarded Jefferson's objections and picked the person his predecessor most opposed, Joseph Story.[35]

With Jefferson actively engaged in farming again, it was perhaps inevitable that he often wrote about questions of interest to his fellow farmer, President Madison. Indeed, the longest discussions in 1810 by both friends concerned merino sheep and plows (so spelled by Madison but spelled "ploughs" by Jefferson). The embargo had spurred a domestic manufacturing craze, followed by the quest for quality wool. As one of Jefferson's friends said, he was like everyone else, "sheepishly inclined."[36]

So were Jefferson and Madison, especially after the former reported that William Jarvis, American consul in Lisbon since 1802, had "sent us a pair of Merino sheep, each," as gifts.[37] Since these valuable animals were liable to accidents, Jefferson proposed "that we make them a common stock not to be divided till there be a pair for each, should any have died."[38] That made sense to Madison, who agreed that if "a loss be sustained by either of us, that it be repaired by the first increase from the pair of the other."[39] A month later, the

32. TJ to JM, Oct. 15, 1810, below.
33. JM to TJ, June 4, 1810, below.
34. JM to TJ, Oct. 19, 1810, below.
35. Malone, VI, p. 67, and Brant, V, pp. 167-72. See also Henry J. Abraham, *Justices and Presidents: A Political History of Appointments to the Supreme Court* (New York, 1985), pp. 87-90.
36. Malone, VI, p. 77, quotes Dr. William Thornton, who served as superintendent of the Patent Office after being appointed by TJ in 1802.
37. TJ to JM, Mar. 25, 1810, below.
38. *Ibid.*
39. JM to TJ, Apr. 2, 1810, below.

president expained that he would arrange transportation for both pairs of sheep, making it "unnecessary for you to attend to the matter till you hear of their arrival in Orange."[40]

Looking to the proliferation of the breed in the future, Jefferson asked, "What shall we do with them? I have been so disgusted with the scandalous extortions lately practised in the sale of these animals, and with the ascription of patriotism and praise to the sellers, as if the thousands of Dollars apiece they have not been ashamed to recieve were not reward enough, that I am disposed to consider, as right, whatever is the reverse of what they have done." Accordingly, he proposed to share their good fortune with "the farmers of our country" in order to shame the profiteers "of the shaving art, and to excite, by a better example, the condemnation due to theirs." He thought that "the few who can afford it should incur the risk and expense of all new improvements, and give the benefit freely to the many of more restricted circumstances." He then outlined an elaborate seven-year program to distribute rams to each county in the state, followed by the distribution of "an ewe also to every county if it be thought necessary." Jefferson confessed that "there will be danger that what is here proposed, tho' but an act of ordinary duty, may be perverted into one of ostentation. But malice will always find bad motives for good actions. Shall we therefore never do good?" queried the philosopher qua farmer.[41]

Jefferson also wrote the president about a French plow sent to him by the Paris Society of Agriculture, one "which they supposed the best ever made in Europe. They at the same time requested me to send them one of ours with my mould board. I have made one for them," he continued without false modesty, "which every body agrees to be the handsomest and of the most promising appearance they have ever seen." He reminded his fellow farmer that he had taken as a model "the ploughs we got through Dr. Logan (you and myself) a dozen years ago, and fixed my mould board to it." He now asked the president's assistance in getting it through the English blockade and the French Continental system "in some public vessel" since it was neither merchandise nor contraband, but instead a scientific present to the Paris society.[42]

Given the uncertainties of American relations with both France and Great Britain, Madison could only promise that "a conveyance of your plow . . . will be favored as much as possible." But he wondered whether the plow could till wet ground as well as it did dry soil. "My apprehension," wrote the Orange County farmer, "was, that the obtuseness of the Angles made by the Mould Board, and the line of draught, might too much increase the resistance and subject the plow moreover to be clogged, by a degree of moisture not having

---

40. JM to TJ, May 7, 1810, below.

41. TJ to JM, May 13, 1810, below. See also JM to TJ, May 25, 1810, below, June 8, 1810, below, June 22, 1810, below, July 2, 1810, below; and TJ to JM, June 27, 1810, below, and July 13, 1810, below.

42. TJ to JM, Mar. 25, 1810, below.

the same effect with the ordinary plows." But he thought that Jefferson's forthcoming experiments would soon answer his question.[43]

Jefferson reported that Robert Fulton, the inventor, had promised "to lend me his dynamometer, mine having been lost," so he could measure the "comparative merit" of his plow. "The mould-board which I first made, with a square toe," he confessed, "was liable to the objection you make of accumulating too much earth on it when in a damp state"; it also made the plow too long. But "by making it, on the same principles, with a sharp toe," the plow was shortened and "the great hollow on which the earth made it's lodgment" was eliminated. The sharp-toed plow was "as short and light" as Dr. Logan's plow. "I have certainly never seen a plough do better work or move so easily. Still," he concluded with scientific caution, Fulton's "instrument alone can ascertain it's merit mathematically."[44]

THE LETTERS

Madison to Jefferson

Washington Dec. 11, 1809

DEAR SIR,

I duly received your two letters of the 26 and 30 ult. The state of Col. Monroe's mind is very nearly what I had supposed. His willingness to have taken a seat in the Cabinet is what I had not supposed. I have written to Major Neely, according to your suggestion, and shall follow it also as to the distribution of Govr Lewis' papers when they arrive. Fayette in a letter to me has been equally urgent on the subject of his land titles, which are required as the basis of a loan. Owing to delays incident to the distance and the nature of the proceedings in consummating land titles, and more particularly to the miscarriage of a mail containing instructions from Mr. Gallatin, which was long unknown to him, the business has never been compleated. I have renewed my efforts to accelerate it, and have so written to Fayette, by the Ship John Adams, which carries a remittance from the Treasury to Holland, and will touch at France and England for collateral purposes. It was found cheaper to make the remittance in this way than by Bills of Exchange, at their present rate. The papers will tell you what Congress are about. There is not as yet any appearance by which their course can be foretold. The Republicans as usual are either not decided, or have different leanings. The Federalists are lying in wait to spring on any opportunity of checking or diverting the tide now setting so strongly against them. The wound received by Mr. J. G. Jackson is thought at

---

43. JM to TJ, Apr. 2, 1810, below.

44. TJ to JM, Apr. 16, 1810, below. For shipping arrangements, see JM to TJ, Apr. 23, 1810, below.

present to wear a very favorable appearance. As the Ball however remains in him, and the Hip bone is much broken, it is not certain that he may not be left somewhat of a cripple.[1] Be assured always of my high and affectionate esteem.

JAMES MADISON

I return the letter from Armstrong and Major Neely.

Jefferson to Madison

Monticello Mar. 25, 1810

DEAR SIR

You knew, I believe that the society of Agriculture of Paris had sent me a plough which they supposed the best ever made in Europe. They at the same time requested me to send them one of ours with my mould board. I have made one for them which every body agrees to be the handsomest and of the most promising appearance they have ever seen, and I have five on my own farms, than which we have never seen ploughs work better or easier. I have taken as a model the ploughs we got through Dr. Logan (you and myself) a dozen years ago, and fixed my mould board to it. But how to get it to Paris I know not, unless you can favor it with a passage in some public vessel. It is a present, and therefore no matter of merchandise. Can you encourage me for this purpose to send it to Washington, Baltimore, Philadelphia or New York? taking into account that I set out for Bedford tomorrow, not to return under two or three weeks, and consequently that your answer will have to lie here unopened to that time.

Jarvis writes me he has sent us a pair of Merino sheep, each, to arrive at Alexandria. Whether he has designated them individually I do not know; but as they are so liable to accidents by the way I propose that we make them a common stock not to be divided till there be a pair for each, should any have died. We are suffering by drought, and our river is so low as to be scarcely boatable. It would take very unusual quantities of rain to ensure it's usual state through the ensuing summer. Wheat looks well generally. It is believed the fruit has been all killed in the bud by the late extraordinary cold weather. Mine is untouched, tho I apprehend that a very heavy white frost which reached the top of the hill last night may have killed the blossoms of an Apricot which has been in bloom about a week. A very few peach blossoms are yet open. Always affectionately yours.

TH JEFFERSON

---

1. Congressman John G. Jackson was JM's brother-in-law, who had fought a duel after challenging a slur on the Republican leadership; see Ketcham, p. 499.

Madison to Jefferson

Washington Apr. 2, 1810

DEAR SIR

Yours of 25th. Mar: has been duly recd. Every thing is so uncertain at this moment with respect to our approaching relations to France and G. B; that I can only say that a conveyance of your plow to the Former will be favored as much as possible, and that I will endeavor to have more definite information on the subject ready at Monticello for your return from Bedford. I am glad to learn that your plow succeeds so well in practice. I always supposed that wd. be the case, when the soil was sufficiently dry. My apprehension was, that the obtuseness of the Angles made by the Mould Board, and the line of draught, might too much increase the resistance and subject the plow moreover to be clogged, by a degree of moisture not having the same effect with the ordinary plows. Your experiments will soon have decided this point. Your proposal as to the Merinos expected from Jarvis accords precisely with my ideas. I submit as a supplement, in case the pairs shd. be designated and a loss be sustained by either of us, that it be repaired by the first increase from the pair of the other. Be assured always of my high and affecte. respects

JAMES MADISON

Jefferson to Madison

Monticello Apr. 16, 1810

DEAR SIR

On my return from Bedford I found in our post office your favor of the 2d. inst. as also the inclosed letter from Mr Martin, formerly of N. C. recommended to us by Mr Blackledge. I dare say you will recollect more of him than I do. I remember that his being a native French man, educated I believe to the law there, very long a resident of this country and become a respectable lawyer with us, were circumstances which made us wish we could have then employed him at N. O. I know nothing of him however but what you learned from the same source, and I inclose his letter that you may see that emploiment would be agreed to on his part.

I have at the same time recieved an offer from Mr Fulton to lend me his dynamometer, mine having been lost.[2] I have concluded therefore to keep the plough till I can determine it's comparative merit by that instrument. The mould-board which I first made, with a square toe, was liable to the objection

---

2. TJ had shipped his dynamometer, which he described as "an instrument for measuring the exertions of draught animals," from Washington to Monticello by water. The trunk containing it and his thirty-year collection of Indian vocabularies was stolen from a boat on the James River; see Malone, VI, pp. 4–5.

you make of accumulating too much earth on it when in a damp state, and of making the plough too long. By making it, on the same principles, with a sharp toe, it has shortened the plough 9. I. and got rid of the great hollow on which the earth made it's lodgment. It is now as short and light as the plough we got from Philadelphia, which indeed was my model, with only the substitution of a much superior mould board. I have certainly never seen a plough do better work or move so easily. Still the instrument alone can ascertain it's merit mathematically. Our spring is wonderfully backward. We have had asparagus only two days. The fruit has escaped better than was believed. It is killed only in low places. We easily agree as to the Merinos: but had nothing happened would they not have been here? Ever your's affectionately

Th Jeff

Madison to Jefferson

Washington Apr. 23, 1810

Dear Sir

Yours of the 16th, has been rec^d. It is not improbable that there will be an early occasion to send for public purposes, a ship to G. B. and France: and that Norfolk will be the port of Departure. I recommend therefore that your plow be lodged there as soon as may be, with the proper instructions to your Agent. It may not be amiss to include in those a discretion to forward the plow to any other port if he sh^d learn in time, that another is substituted for Norfolk. Cong^s remain in the unhinged state which has latterly marked their proceedings; with the exception only that a majority in the H. of R. have stuck together so far as to pass a Bill providing for a conditional repeal by either of the Bellig^{rs} of their Edicts; laying in the mean time, an addition[al] 50 Per C^t to the present duties on imports from G. B. and France. What the Senate will do with the Bill is rendered utterly uncertain by the policy which seems to prevail in that Branch. Our last authentic information from G. B. is of the 28. Feb^y, and from France of the 2d of Feby. The information in both cases, has an aspect rather promising; but far from being definite; and subsequent acc^{ts}, thro. the ordinary channels, do not favor a reliance on general professions or appearances. Bonaparte, seems not to have yet attended to the distinction between the external and internal character of his Decrees; and to be bending his augmented faculties for annihilating British Commerce with the Cont^t with which our corrupt traders have confounded the Am^n flag. And it will be a hard matter for Wellesley, sh^d he be well disposed, to drag his Anti-American Colleagues into a change of policy; supported as they will be by the speeches and proceedings of Cong^s From those the inference will be that one party prefers submission of our trade to British regulation, and the other confesses the impossibility of resisting it. Without a change of Ministry, of which there is some prospect, it w^d be imprudent to count on any radical change of policy. For the moment, I understand that the Merch^{ts} will not avail themselves of the unshackled trade they have been contending for; a voluntary Embargo being produced by the certainty of a glutted Market in England, and the apprehension of Brit Blockades, and French confiscations. The experiment about to be made will probably open too late the eyes of the people, to the expediency and efficacy of the means which they have suffered to be taken out of the hands of the Gov^t and to be incapacitated for future use. The Merinos are not yet heard of. Be assured of my constant and aff^e respects.

JAMES MADISON

Madison to Jefferson

Washington May 7, 1810

DEAR SIR,

The inclosed letter from Jarvis accompanied one to me, on the subject of the Merinos. I learn that they have arrived safe, but the vessel is aground a few miles below Alexandria. Jo^s Doherty is gone to bring them up, making the selections warranted by Mr. Jarvis.[3] As the means I shall employ to have my pair conveyed to Virginia will suffice for yours, it will be unnecessary for you to attend to the matter till you hear of their arrival in Orange. Although there have been several late arrivals from England, we remain in the dark as to what has passed between Wellesley and Pinkney. The same as to the French Government and Armstrong. You will notice the footing on which Congress has left our relations with these powers. Unless G. Britain should apprehend an attempt from France to revive our non-intercourse against her, she has every earthly motive to continue her restrictions against us. She has our trade, in spite of France, as far as she can make it suit her interest, and our acquiescence in cutting it off from the rest of the world, as far as she may wish to distress her adversaries, to cramp our growth as rivals, or to prevent our interference with her smuggling monopoly. New England and New York are rallying to the Republican ranks. In New York every branch of the Government is again sound. The election in Massachusetts, now going on, will probably have a like issue with their late one. There is some danger, however, from the federal

---

3. Joseph Daugherty, who had served as TJ's coachman in Washington, carried on an animated correspondence with TJ about sheep; see Edwin M. Betts, ed., *Thomas Jefferson's Farm Book*... (Princeton, 1953), pp. 118–20.

artifice of pushing the federal towns to their maximum of Representation. Boston is to send forty. Yours always most affectly.

JAMES MADISON

Jefferson to Madison

Monticello May 13, 1810

DEAR SIR,

I thank you for your promised attention to my portion of the Merinos, and if there be any expences of transportation etc., and you will be so good as to advance my portion of them with yours and notify the amount it shall be promptly remitted. What shall we do with them? I have been so disgusted with the scandalous extortions lately practised in the sale of these animals, and with the ascription of patriotism and praise to the sellers, as if the thousands of Dollars apiece they have not been ashamed to recieve were not reward enough, that I am disposed to consider, as right, whatever is the reverse of what they have done. Since fortune has put the occasion upon us, is it not incumbent on us so to dispense this benefit to the farmers of our country, as to put to shame those who, forgetting their own wealth and the honest simplicity of the farmers, have thought them fit objects of the shaving art, and to excite, by a better example, the condemnation due to theirs? No sentiment is more acknoleged in the family of Agricolists than that the few who can afford it should incur the risk and expense of all new improvements, and give the benefit freely to the many of more restricted circumstances. The question then recurs, What are we to do with them? I shall be willing to concur with you in any plan you shall approve, and in order that we may have some proposition to begin upon, I will throw out a first idea, to be modified or postponed to whatever you shall think better.

Give all the full blooded males we can raise to the different counties of our state, one to each, as fast as we can furnish them. And as there must be some rule of priority, for the distribution, let us begin with our own counties, which are contiguous and nearly central to the state, and proceed, circle after circle, till we have given a ram to every county. This will take about 7. years, if we add to the full descendants those which will have past to the 4th. generation from common ewes. To make the benefit of a single male as general as practicable to the county, we may ask some known character in each county to have a small society formed which shall recieve the animal and prescribe rules for his care and government. We should retain ourselves all the full-blooded ewes, that they may enable us the sooner to furnish a male to every county. When all shall have been provided with rams, we may, in a year or two more, be in a condition to give an ewe also to every county if it be thought necessary. But I suppose it will not, as four generations from their full-blooded ram will give them the pure race from common ewes.

In the mean time we shall not be without a profit indemnifying our trouble and expense. For if, of our present stock of common ewes, we place with the ram as many as he may be competent to, suppose 50 we may sell the male lambs of every year for such reasonable price as, in addition to the wool, will pay for the maintenance of the flock. The 1st year they will be ½-bloods, the 2d. ¾, the 3d. ⅞, and the 4th. full-blooded, if we take care, in selling annually half the ewes also, to keep those of highest blood, this will be a fund for kindnesses to our friends, as well as for indemnification to ourselves; and our whole state may thus, from this small stock, so dispersed, be filled in a very few years with this valuable race, and more satisfaction result to ourselves than money ever administered to the bosom of a shaver.

There will be danger that what is here proposed, tho' but an act of ordinary duty, may be perverted into one of ostentation. But malice will always find bad motives for good actions. Shall we therefore never do good? It may also be used to commit us with those on whose example it will truly be a reproof. We may guard against this perhaps by a proper reserve, developing our purpose only by its execution.

> Vive, vale, et siquid novisti rectius istis
> Candidus imperti sinon, his ulere mecum.[4]

ENCLOSURE
Chart about merinos

From 2. full blooded ewes and their female descendants will proceed the following numbers either of rams or ewes separately, or the double in the aggregate.

1st. year	1	
2d.	2	
3d.	2	Being 34. rams for distribution
4th.	4	34. ewes + the 2. originals to be retained
5th.	5	
6th.	8	
7th.	12	

From 100. common ewes and their female descendants will proceed annually the following number of either rams or ewes separately, or the double in the aggregate of ½ breeds, ¾, ⅞, and full

---

4. "Live long, farewell. If you know something better than these precepts, pass it on, my good fellow. If not, join me in following these"; see Horace's *Epistles,* cited in *PJM* (Pres. ser.), II, p. 340.

	Half breeds	¾ blood	⅞ blood	Full blood
1st. year	50			
2d.	50	25		
3d.	50	25	13	
4th.	50	25	12+	6
5th.	50	25	13+	6+3
6th.	50	25	12+	6+3+2
7th.	50	25	13+	6+3+2+1
	350+	150+	63+	24+9+4+1 = 601

To wit 38. rams. full blooded for distribution
        38. ewes. full blooded to be retained
        63. rams ⎫
        63. ewes ⎭ ⅞ blood ⎫
       150. rams ⎫   ⎬ for our friends
       150. ewes ⎭ ¾ blood   ⎬ for sale or
       350. rams ⎫   ⎭ for the table
       350. ewes ⎭ ½ blood ⎭

Madison to Jefferson

Washington May 25, 1810

DEAR SIR,

I have duly received your favor of the 13th. The general idea of disposing of the supernumerary Merino Rams for the public benefit had occurred to me. The mode you propose for the purpose seems well calculated for it. But as it will be most proper, as you suggest, to let our views be developed to the public by the execution of them, there will be time for further consideration. When the sheep came into my hands, they were so infected with the scab that I found it necessary, in order to quicken and ensure their cure, to apply the mercurial ointment. I hope they are already well. One of the ewes has just dropt a ewe lamb, which is also doing well. I expect my overseer every day to conduct them to Orange. As he will have a wagon with him, the trip I hope may be so managed as to avoid injury to his charge.

A former National Intelligencer will have given you our last communications from G. Britain. That of this morning exhibits our prospects on the side of France. The late confiscations by Bonaparte comprise robbery, theft, and breach of trust, and exceed in turpitude any of his enormities not wasting human blood. This scene on the continent, and the effect of English monopoly on the value of our produce, are breaking the charm attached to what is called free trade, foolishly by some, and wickedly by others. We are hourly looking for the "John Adams." There is a *possibility* that the negotiations on foot at Paris may vary our prospects there. The chance would be better perhaps, if the last act of Congress were in the hands of Armstrong; which puts our trade on the worst possible footing for France but, at the same time, puts it in the option of her to revive the non-intercourse against England. There is a *possibility* also that the views of the latter may be somewhat affected by the recent elections; it being pretty certain that the change in the tone of Wellesley from that first manifested to Pinkney was in part at least, produced by the intermediate intelligence from the United States, which flattered a fallacious reliance on the British party here.

You receive by this mail a letter from Fayette, an open one from him to Duplantier, shews equally, the enormity of his debts (800,000 frs.) and the extravagance of his expectations. I have forwarded him deeds for 9,000 acres located near Pt. Coupe, and stated by Duplantier, as worth about $50,000, at an immediate cash price; of course intrinsically worth much more. I learn with much concern, that some difficulty not yet explained is likely to defeat altogether the location near the City of Orleans, which was the main dependence of Fayette.[5] Yrs. always and affecly.

Jefferson to Madison

Monticello May 25, 1810

DEAR SIR,

I inclose you the extract of a letter from Govr. Tyler which will explain itself, and I do it on the same principle on which I have sometimes done the same thing before, that whenever you are called on to select, you may have under consideration all those who may properly be thought of and the grounds of their pretensions. From what I can learn Griffin cannot stand it long, and really the state has suffered long enough by having such a cypher in so important an office, and infinitely the more from the want of any counterpoise to the rancorous hatred which Marshal bears to the government of his country, and from the cunning and sophistry within which he is able to enshroud himself. It will be difficult to find a character of firmess enough to preserve his independance on the same bench with Marshall. Tyler, I am certain, would do it. He is an able and well read lawyer about 59. years of age: he was popular as a judge, and is remarkably so as a governor, for his incorruptible integrity, which no circumstances have ever been able to turn from it's course. Indeed I think there is scarcely a person in the state so solidly popular, or who would be so much approved for that place. A milk and water character in that office would be seen as a calamity. Tyler having been the former state judge of that court too, and removed to make way for so wretched a fool as Griffin has a kind of right of reclamation, with the advantage of repeated

---

5. For a summary of "Madison and Lafayette's Louisiana Lands," see *ibid.*, pp. 35–38.

elections by the legislature, as Admiralty judge, circuit judge, and Governor. But of all these things you will judge fairly between him and his competitors.[6]

You have seen in the papers that Livingston has served a writ on me, stating damages at 100,000. D. The ground is not yet explained, but it is understood to be the batture. I have engaged Wirt, Hay, and Wickham as counsel. I shall soon look into my papers to make a state of the case to enable them to plead: and as much of our proceedings was never committed to writing, and my memory cannot be trusted, it is probable I shall have to appeal to that of my associates in the proceedings. I believe that what I did was in harmony with the opinions of all the members of the administration, verbally expressed altho' not in writing.[7]

I have been delighted to see the effect of Monroe's late visit to Washington on his mind.[8] There appears to be the most perfect reconciliation and cordiality established towards yourself. I think him now inclined to rejoin us with zeal. The only embarrasment will be from his late friends. But I think he has firmness of mind enough to act independently as to them. The next session of our legislature will shew.

We are suffering under a most severe drought of now 3. weeks continuance. Late sown wheat is yellow but the oats suffer especially. In speaking of Livingston's suit, I omitted to observe that it is little doubted that his knolege of Marshall's character has induced him to bring this action. His twistifications in the case of Marbury, in that of Burr, and the late Yazoo case shew how dexterously he can reconcile law to his personal biasses: and nobody seems to doubt that he is ready prepared to decide that Livingston's right to the batture is unquestionable, and that I am bound to pay for it with my private fortune. Ever affectionately your's.

ENCLOSURE
[John Tyler to Jefferson]

[Richmond May 12, 1810]

'My present station is a tedious insignificant one, and has but one good trait in it, and that is this, it gives me not power enough to do mischief in any other way than by the sin of neglect, which I avoid as much as possible by a constant attendance on the duties of my office; and if I retire without exciting envy or ill nature, tho' with a shattered fortune, I shall be content. Long have I neglected my private concerns in the engagement of those of the public, and also those of a social kind. Having had 21. children to bring up, besides my own, which took away so much of my life from a fair chance of encreasing my estate, so that I am much the worse, having got behind hand.

6. For the extract from Tyler's letter to TJ, see the enclosure to this letter, below. Cyrus Griffin died on Dec. 14, 1810. JM subsequently appointed Tyler as federal district judge. After Tyler resigned as governor, the legislature elected James Monroe in his place; see Harry Ammon, *James Monroe: The Quest for National Identity* (New York, 1971), p. 285, and Malone, VI, p. 29.

7. For the batture controversy, see William B. Hatcher, *Edward Livingston: Jeffersonian Republican and Jacksonian Democrat* (Baton Rouge, 1940), pp. 155 ff.

8. For Monroe's visit to Washington in May 1810, see Ammon, p. 283, and Brant, V, pp. 164–65.

However my eldest son has graduated as a Doctor of medecine, my 2d is now commencing the practice of law, leaving a son and daughter to promote as well as I can; and my object is to fall into some little public emploiment, if I live my time out here (or sooner) which may enable me to divide my estate among my children, after paying what I owe, and so glide off this scene of trouble as quiet as I can. Judge Griffin is in a low state of health and holds *my old office*, which Genl. Washington gave him because I was not for the new federal government without previous amendments, and of course could not be trusted in the British debt cases. This kind of conduct began the strong distinction which has embittered the cup of life, and in a great measure produced a spirit of retaliation when the republicans prevailed. But the British influence had the best share of the above policy in the beginning. I never did apply for an office, but I really hope the President will chance to think of me, now and then, in case of accidents, and if any opportunity offers, lay me down softly on a bed of roses, in my latter days, for I have been on thorns long enough.'

Jefferson to Madison

Monticello May 30, 1810

DEAR SIR

In the action brought against me by Edward Livingston, the counsel employed, Wirt and Hay (Wickham declining) desire me to furnish them with the grounds of defence, with as little delay as possible. The papers relating to the batture in the offices of State, the Treasury and war, will undoubtedly be needed to exhibit facts. I am now engaged on this subject, and not to give you unnecessary trouble I write to the Secretaries of State, Treasury and War directly, not doubting you will approve of their communicating what is necessary on the assurance of the papers being faithfully and promptly returnd, after extracting material parts. One article I am obliged to trouble yourself for; to wit Moreau de l'Isle's[9] Memoir which I have never read; and yet am sure it is too able not to be the most important I can consult. Will you be so good as to furnish me a printed copy if it has been printed or to lend the M. S. if not printed. I have copies of all the opinions printed before 1809. Poydras shewed me an argument of his in which I recollect that I thought there was one sound and *new* view.[10] I have now forgotten it, and have no copy. Your's affectionately

TH JEFFERSON

P. S. No rain since the 3d. inst. Every thing getting desperate.

9. Louis Moreau-Lislet was a New Orleans attorney; see Hatcher, p. 145. His "Mémoire au soutien des droits des États-unis à la Batture du Faubourg Ste. Marie" was never published, but the manuscript copy was finally forwarded to TJ in Oct. 1810.

10. TJ had appointed Julien Poydras to the Legislative Council in 1804, and he later served as territorial delegate to Congress. He consistently opposed Livingston's claim to the batture; see *ibid.*, pp. 114, 148.

Madison to Jefferson

Washington June 4, 1810

DEAR SIR,

I have received your two letters of the 25 and 30 ultimo. I have not yet seen any of the Secretaries to whom you have written on the subject of the papers relating to the Batture. I take for granted they will readily comply with your request. Mr. Gallatin is absent on a visit to his Farm in the western part of Pennsylvania. But his chief Clerk will, I presume, be able to furnish the papers, if any, lying in that Department. The argument of Moreau de Lislet has never been printed, nor, as I believe, fully translated. The original manuscript, if not in the hands of Mr. Rodney, will be forwarded from the Department of State. What Poydras has said on the subject is herewith inclosed. Although the ground to be taken in the suit against you is not disclosed, I think it not difficult to conjecture it. The act of Congress will be represented as unconstitutional, and the case of the Batture as not within its scope; and misconstructions as too obvious to be resolvible into official error of judgment. In any event there will be the chance of an obiter opinion of the Court on the merits of the case, strengthening the cause of Livingston. Till I received your letter, I had scarcely yielded my belief that a suit had been really instituted. If the Judiciary should lend itself for such a purpose, it cannot fail I think, to draw down on itself the unbounded indignation of the Nation, and a change of the Constitution, under that feeling, carried perhaps too far in the opposite direction. In a Government whose vital principle is responsibility, it never will be allowed that the Legislative and Executive Departments should be compleatly subjected to the Judiciary, in which that characteristic feature is so faintly seen.

My overseer left this on Friday at noon with our Merinoes under his charge. He will write to you on his arrival, that *when you chuse,* you may send to have them divided and your share removed. He will concur in any mode of division that may be preferred. That the result may be as equal as possible, I propose, that the owner of the Ewe with a lamb, should furnish the other party, with the first Ewe lamb that may follow from the same Ewe. I suggest this on the supposition that the other Ewe is not without lamb, a point which is not absolutely certain.

The John Adams still keeps us in suspense; and when she arrives will probably increase, rather than remove the perplexity of our situation.

The drought here is equal to what you experience, and I find by newspaper paragraphs, that it is nearly universal. We had a slight shower on Wednesday evening, and as much this morning as lays the dust, but the effect of both together will not be sensible. Yrs. always and most affectly

Madison to Jefferson

Washington June 8, 1810

DEAR SIR

Since I rendered the account of our Merinos sent on by My Overseer, I have learnt, that Mr. Hooe of Alexanda. considers the lamb yeaned after their arrival, as allotted to him by the intention of Mr. Jarvis.[11] I have not yet investigated the merits of his claim, by comparing what he may have recd. from Mr. J. with the language of Mr. J's letter to me; but I think it very possible that the claim will be entitled to attention. Mr. J. mentions in a postcript to me, that the Capt: had refused to take charge of the Sheep without a promise of two lambs in case they should drop on the passage, and that as a proof of his regard to Mr. Hooe and his partner, he wished him a like advantage, desiring that I would contribute to fulfil the engagemts. in case the Ewe chosen by me *should have yeaned.* It is probable that his letter to you contained a similar clause, or that he relied on a communication of the one in mine. According to the strict expression, Mr. Hooe, is evidently barred of a claim to the lamb in question, as it had not been yeaned at the time the Ewe came into my possession. But as it seems to have been the general intention of Mr. J. that his Alexa. friends should have the benefit of the actual pregnancies, leaving us the future increase only, and that he took for granted as he might well do, from the season of the voyage, that the lambs, if any, would drop before it was over, I do not think we ought to avail ourselves of the letter of the donation. Another question occurs between the Capt of the Vessel and Messrs. Hooe etc., and if the meaning of the postscript to me be not controuled by other explanations, the Capt: seems to have in strictness a priority of claim. But as the promise to him seems to have been extorted, and to be unsupported by strict construction, I should be disposed to favor the title of the others, which rests on the same friendly intentions with our own. As soon as I come to an understanding on the matter with the other parties I will write you more definitely. I have thought it proper to say this much at present, in order that the division between us may be suspended, or so made as to be consistent with the pending question. Always and affectly Yours

JAMES MADISON

---

11. Jarvis had promised J. H. Hooe, his consignee in Alexandria, two lambs in case any were born on shipboard en route to the United States. The one that JM mentioned was dropped on shore. For the complicated negotiations as to who could claim it, see Brant, V, p. 203, and Malone, VI, pp. 78-79.

Jefferson to Madison

Monticello June 14, 1810

DEAR SIR

Mr. Thweatt[12] my particular friend and connection expecting that an excursion he is to make will put it in his power to pay his respects to you personally, en passant, and being desirous to do so, I with pleasure present him to you as a gentleman of perfect worth, and of sincere zeal in those political principles which you and I have so steadily cultivated. His energy in their support has been often felt by our friends as well as opponents in Petersburg and it's vicinity. I pray you to accept with favor his and my devoirs and to be assured of my constant affection and respect.

TH: JEFFERSON

Madison to Jefferson

Washington June 15, 1810

DEAR SIR,

The inclosed letters were brought, together with the separate packet now forwarded, by the John Adams. The official communications received by her from France and G. Britain you will find in the National Intelligencer of this date. The Editor I perceive passes over the obnoxious refusal of G. Britain to comply with the reasonable course of putting an end to the predatory Edicts of both Nations; and it is not improbable that a like sensibility to the atrocity of the French Government may direct the public attention from what would otherwise strike it with due force.[13]

Madison to Jefferson

Washington June 22, 1810

DEAR SIR,

I enclose an authentication of the blood of our Merinos, as translated from the Original by Mr Graham: also a state of the charges incident to their

---

12. Archibald Thweatt married Lucy Eppes, TJ's niece and John Wayles Eppes's sister; see *PJM* (Pres. ser.), II, p. 380.
13. This is all that remains of this fragment of a letter.

passage, etc. The half falling to your share, of course, may be left for any convenient occasion of being replaced. You need not trouble yourself to remit it hither.

On the first publication of the despatches by the John Adams, so strong a feeling was produced by Armstrong's picture of the French robbery, that the attitude in which England was placed by the correspondence between P. and Wellesley was overlooked. The public attention is beginning to fix itself on the proof it affords that the original sin agst Neutrals lies with G. B. and that whilst she acknowledges it, she persists in it.

I am preparing for a departure from this place immediately after the 4th July. Having been deprived of the Spring visit to my Farm, I wish to commence the sooner the full recess. Be assured of my highest and most affec^{e} esteem.

JAMES MADISON

Have you rec^d a copy of Coopers (the Pen^a Judge) masterly opinion on the question whether the sentence of a foreign Admiralty Court in a prize Cause be conclusive evidence in a suit here between the Underwriter and Insured? It is a most *thorough,* investigation, and irrefragable disproof of the B. Doctrine on the subject, as adopted by a decision of the Supreme Court of the U. S.[14] If you are without a copy, I will provide and forward one.

ENCLOSURE
Bill for Shipping Merino Sheep

May 7, 1810

Four Spanish Merino sheep to Dougherty Dr
May 7th. – 10

	D	Cts
To freight from Lisbon to Alexa. Va.	24	-00
To 5 per cent primage	1	-20
To freight from below Alexa, to Washington	2	-50
To custom house permits	0	-40
To one Dollar for each sheep classed by the person that had the care of them on the passage	4	-00
To tavern expenses two and half Days at Alexa	4	-25
Doll	36	-35

Received the above from Mr. Madison

Jos. Dougherty

14. Thomas Cooper sat as a member of the Pennsylvania Court of Errors and Appeals in an admiralty case in 1808, but his dissenting opinion was not published until 1810. He denied that a decision in a foreign court of admiralty was conclusive proof of a breach of blockade, thus precluding recovery of insurance upon a vessel condemned by the British; see Dumas Malone, *The Public Life of Thomas Cooper, 1783–1839* (New Haven, 1926), pp. 194–97. The Supreme Court of the United States adopted the British rule; see Charles Warren, *The Supreme Court in United States History,* 2 vols. (Boston, 1923), I, pp. 319–20.

Jefferson to Madison

Monticello June 27, 1810

DEAR SIR

Your letters of the 8th. 15th. and 22d. are now to be acknoleged. I should consider the debt to Mr Hooe as made incumbent on us by the wish of our Donor, and shall chearfully acquiesce in any arrangement you make on that subject. I have accordingly suspended sending for my portion till further information from you. Dougherty's bill shall be duly attended to. I have recieved a copy of Judge Cooper's opinion but have not yet read it. I shall do it with pleasure because I am sure it is able. There is not a stronger head in the U. S. than his.

I hardly know whether I ought to trouble you with reading such a letter as the inclosed. The last half page is all that is material for you. The rest is an account of the country of Oppelousa. I know nothing of the writer, and take no interest in his application. Our sufferings from drought have been extreme. The rains of the last month were but 2. I. and of this month the same, till the one now falling which has already given us $6/10$ and promises more, perhaps too much, for we had just begun our harvest. If not injured by rain it will generally be as fine a one as we have ever seen. Corn, tho' lower than ever known, has still time to yield a good crop. This rain will enable every one to pitch his tobo. crop. It's result must depend on the length of the fall as well as the intermediate seasons. It is very unpromising at present. The present rain is too late for the oats. Very little will be high enough to cut. At length Gr. Br. has been forced to pull off her mask and shew that her real object is the exclusive use of the ocean. Her good sense is overruled by her avarice, and that of Bonaparte by his own haughty and tyrannical temper. A return to embargo could alone save us. Always yours affectionately

TH JEFFERSON

Be so good as to return the inclosed.

Madison to Jefferson

Washington July 2, 1810

DEAR SIR

I have recd. your favor of the 27th. by which I find you have suspended the sending for your portion of the Merinos. I have not yet come to an eclairissmnt. with Mr. Hooe. I learn however that a re examination of the tenor of Mr. J's. letter to him, has induced an abandonment of his pretensions to the Lamb. Still I am rather inclined to think that they are not altogether without foundation; and have written to Mr Jarvis in terms not inconsistent with that idea. As the Lamb whether it remain with us, or fall to the lot of

Mr. H. must be kept with the Ewe for a considerable time, would it not be best for a division to be made at once, as doubling the security of the germ agst. casualties. A single day, whilst they are all together, might put an end to it. To whichever of us the Ewe having the lamb might fall the lamb might remain a common property, if not finally delivered over to Mr. H. As it has not been proved that the other Ewe may not be barren, it may be understood if you do not object, that in that event, the first Ewe lamb from the other, shall make up for this defect. We have had latterly favorable rains here. They are too late however for oats not in moist or rich lands. The Wheat harvest will be good in this quarter. In N. Y. it will be very scanty: not very moderate in Pena. and on the Eastern Shore of Maryland the drought and H. fly, have in a manner destroyed the crop. Yrs. as always

JAMES MADISON

The return of Guarrants letter in my next.

Madison to Jefferson

Washington July 7, 1810

DEAR SIR

Not knowing where I could be enabled to answer the inclosed, with so much confidence in the fact as in your acquaintance with the historical antiquities of Virginia, I take the liberty of asking whether I may not say to Mr. Bassette, that no such accounts as he enquires after, are known to exist. As he seems desirous of an early answer you will oblige me by a few lines as soon as convenient.

Jefferson to Madison

Monticello July 13, 1810

DEAR SIR

I return you Mr Bassette's letter and think you may safely tell him we possess no Dutch accounts of Virginia. We have De Laët, but it is a folio volume of Latin, and I have no doubt a good translation will sell well. I have not examined De Bry's collection to see if that contains any Dutch account. That is in 3. folio volumes of Latin, and certainly will not take off one single reader from Mr Bassette's work. I have not sent for my Merinos till you should have settled the claims of others on them. If the lamb is to remain ours, it will be at your choice to keep it or not, returning the first ewe lamb in exchange. I come perfectly into your idea that if any accident shall put either of us out of the breed, the other shall put him in again with either a male or female of full blood or both if necessary; and this to be indefinite in point of time, because even after we have a tolerable stock, a total loss is not unexampled. In the mean time I am inclosing a lot of 5. or 6. acres with a fence dog-proof, on a plan of Mr Randolph's taking only half the rails a common fence does, with some more labour, so as to be on the whole about equal in expence.

I have recieved every thing I could desire in Livingston's case except Moreau's Memoire. Wirt, Hay and Tazewell are engaged in the defence. They desired of me to furnish them the grounds of defence. This has obliged me to study the case thoroughly, to place all the points on paper, with my own views of them and the authorities in their support. This is the more tedious, as the authorities being in few hands, and being in Latin, French, and Spanish entirely, are obliged to be copied in the body of the work. It has raised my rough draught to 8. sheets of letter paper. It is cruel to propose to you to read this, and yet I have three reasons of doing so. 1. The suit is an attack on the administration, and in a delicate point. I do not think myself free therefore to urge or omit any point of defence they would disapprove, and therefore I think to submit it also to Mr Smith and Mr Gallatin. 2. I know how much it will gain by such views as you will suggest. 3. I think it will be a great satisfaction to you to see how clear a case it is. A clearer never came before a court.[15]

I have a trip to Bedford on hand, but shall defer it till I have copied this, which will take me 8. or 10. days, at 2. or 3. hours a day given to it, shall have sent it to you for perusal and followed it myself to pay my respects to you. My absence will be of a month.

I have a pair of Shepherd's dogs for Dr. Thornton.[16] He desired me to send them to Mr Gooch's, your overseer who would keep them till Mr Barry or your waggon would be going to Washington. But as you will probably have a rider coming weekly to Montpelier, and the dogs lead well both, I should think he might carry them conveniently for a small premium from the doctor. I shall send them when I send for the sheep. They are most valuable dogs. Their sagacity is almost human, and qualifies them to be taught any thing you please.[17] Accept my affectionate salutations for Mrs Madison and yourself.

TH JEFFERSON

Madison to Jefferson

Montpellier July 17, 1810

DEAR SIR,

Among the papers relating to the Convention of 1787, communicated to you, that copies in your hands might double the security agst destructive casualties, was a delineation of Hamilton's plan of a Constitution in his writing.

---

15. For TJ's preparation of his brief of "revolting length" during the summer of 1810, see Malone, VI, pp. 60–63. It runs to 132 pages in L. and B., XVIII.
16. Dr. William Thornton was head of the U.S. Patent Office.
17. For TJ's interest in shepherd dogs, see Malone, VI, pp. 79–80.

On looking for it among the Debates etc., which were returned to me, this particular paper does not appear.[18] I conclude therefore that it had not then been copied, or was at the time in some separate situation. I am very sorry to trouble you on such a subject, but being under an engagement to furnish a Copy of that project, I must ask the favor of you to see whether it be not among your papers, and if so, to forward it by the mail.

I reached home on Wednesday last, and have since been somewhat indisposed. My fever has left me, and if as I hope, it was the effect of fatigue only, I consider myself as again well. I am not however, without sensations which make me apprehensive that if bile was not the sole cause, it was a partial one, and that it has not yet been entirely removed. Be assured of my affectionate respects and best wishes.

JAMES MADISON

Madison to Jefferson

[Montpellier ca. July 24, 1810]

DEAR SIR

Yours of the 13th. was duly recd. I have answered Bassette's Enquiry on the ground you have been so good as to furnish. Whether the lamb from the Merino Ewe is to remain ours or not, I think no time should now be lost in sending for your share, the season being at hand when the Ewes will be in heat; and as care will be taken of the lambs whenever they may drop, it will be best that they should drop early. It may make a year's difference in the maturity for breeding. I cannot account for your not getting Moreau's Memoir. I have given a hint for it now to be sent from the Dept. of State. His view of the case ought certainly to be comprized in your examination of it. I shall peruse this when recd. with pleasure; tho' not for all the reasons you enumerate, and for some which you do not; and I shall be particularly happy in the visit with which you flatter me. I see no convenient oppy. of sending on the Dogs to Dr. T. till my waggon goes in Novr. In the mean time they will be duly attended to by G. Gooch if committed to his custody. Be assured of my constant and affectionate attacht.

JAMES MADISON

Jefferson to Madison

Monticello July 26, 1810

DEAR SIR

Yours of the 17th. and that by the last mail are recieved. I have carefully searched among my papers for that of Hamilton which is the subject of your

---

18. At a later date, JM added this note: "Afterwards found."

letter, but certainly have it not. If I ever had it (which I should doubt) I must have returned it. I say I doubt having had it because I find it in your Conventional debates under date of June 18. where it is copied at full length, being so entered I presume in your Original manuscript. Having it in that, I do not suppose I should have wanted his original. I presume you have your MS. of the debates with you. If you have not, drop me a line and I will copy it from my copy.

    I hope I shall be ready to send you my statement of the case of the batture by Tuesday's post, and shall follow it myself within two or three days. I am obliged to send a copy also to my counsel the moment I can finish it, being ruled to plead before the 15th. prox. and Wirt being to leave Richmd. the 28th. inst. But our plea will be amendable should your own suggestions or those of Mr. Gallatin, Smith or Rodney render it adviseable. I extremely lament the not having been able to see Moreau's Memoir. I wrote to Mr Graham for it, and he to Mr Rodney: the latter wrote me in reply that he supposed it was among his papers at Washington and would send it to me on his return to that place, but that may be distant. I am afraid of taking false or untenable ground; tho my investigation of the subject gives me confidence that a stronger case never came before a court. I shall finish in a day or two the dog-proof inclosure for my sheep and will then send for them if I find my prospect of seeing you at Montpelier retarded. One of the dogs, the male, intended for Washington, died on the very day I wrote to you. The other shall be sent to Mr Gooch. Affectionately your's

Th Jefferson

Jefferson to Madison

Monticello Aug. 9, 1810

Th: J. to J. M.

    I have just time before closing the mail to send you the Memoir on the Batture.[19] It is long; but it takes a more particular view of the legal system of Orleans and the peculiar river on which it lies, than may have before presented itself. However you can readily skip over uninteresting heads. My visit to you depends on the getting a new threshing machine to work: which I expect will permit me to depart the last of this week or early in the next. Affectionate salutns.

19. TJ enclosed his manuscript "A Statement of the Usurpation of Edward Livingston on the Batture, or public Beach at New Orleans, and of the laws requiring his removal by the late Executive of the United States"; see *PJM* (Pres. ser.), II, p. 473.

Madison to Jefferson

[Montpellier ca. Aug. 12, 1810]

[Notes on Jefferson's Memoir on the Batture]

p. 16. form of stating the consultation seems to imply a more elaborate inquiry into the law than was then made: better to give a summary of the grounds; and appeal to the full view of the argts. in support of the opinion given.[20]

Id. too unqualified pre-eminence ascribed to Civil Law.

17. quer. the advantage of the note which seems rather erudite and curious, than strictly within the scope of the reasoning which is sufficiently voluminous of necessity.[21]

22. Tho' true that a mere change of Govt. does not change laws, is it not probable, that by usage, or some other mode, the Spanish law had come into operation; since Thierry on the spot speaks so confidently?[22] This remark applicable to the enquiry into the state of the F. and Civil Law previously in force.

27. comments on definition of Alluvion too strict. They destroy the idea of Alln: altogether. Alluvion, when real and legal, is found not like plastering a Wall, but coating a floor.

30. In the Etemologies, that of Platin, at least, far fetched.[23] It is more probably derived from Plat—flat.

35–36. characteristic features distinguishing the cases of the lands back of the river and the batture seem to be 1: (the appendix to the argument supersedes the attempt here intended)[24]

37 et seq. Is not the point superfluously proved by so many quotations?[25]

49 etc. trop recherchè peut être.[26]

---

20. TJ followed JM's suggestion and substituted for his description of the cabinet meeting on Nov. 27, 1807, the statement "we took of the whole case such views as the state of our information at that time presented"; see L. and B., XVIII, p. 30.

21. TJ rejected JM's suggestion, retaining his note on Roman law as a sort of natural law, arguing that it supplemented French feudal law in Louisiana; see *ibid.*, p. 35.

22. J. B. S. Thierry of New Orleans generally supported TJ's position in the batture controversy, but TJ disagreed with his contention that Spanish law in Louisiana had given alluvions to the riparian proprietor; see *ibid.*, p. 49, and *PJM* (Pres. ser.), I, p. 359.

23. JM was critical of TJ's arguments based on linguistic analysis of Greek and Roman law; see L. and B., XVIII, pp. 61–71.

24. See TJ's arguments comparing the Mississippi and the Nile rivers in terms of free navigation "by all the individuals of the nation"; *ibid.*, pp. 79–85.

25. TJ retained his multiple authorities about the right of the public to navigate the Mississippi; see *ibid.*, pp. 85–92.

26. TJ defended the "natural right" of both men and governments to repossess property taken by force or fraud as, he argued, Livingston had done; see *ibid.*, pp. 104–10.

51. et seq: distinction between fedl and state—Ex. and Legis: auths. not observd. in the reasoning
55. conveys idea of spontaneous advice, and *concurrence* of the P[resident].[27]
56. Well to be sure that the local law or usage did not confer the Chancery power exercised by the Court in this case.[28] Moreau's Memoir must be important on this as on some other points depending on the law of usage and the Civil law.

The rationale of the doctrine of Alluvion appears to be first, that the Claimant may lose as well as gain: secondly, that the space loses its fitness for common use, and takes a fitness for individual use: hence the doctrine does not apply to Towns where the gain would be disproporti[o]nate; and where the fitness of the space for public use, may be changed only, not lost.

The Batture would to Livingston be gain without possibility of loss; and retains its fitness for Pub: Use, as occasionally, a port, a Quay, and a quarry.[29]

Madison to Jefferson

Montpellier Aug. 15, 1810

DEAR SIR

I am offered the services of a Mr. Magee, now living with Mr. Randolph, as an overseer. I have discountenanced his offer, partly from an ignorance of his character, but particularly from the uncertainty whether Mr. R. means to part with him. Will you be kind eno' by a line, merely to say whether it is decided that he is not to remain where he is, the only condition on which I wd. listen to a negociation. 2. whether his conduct as an overseer recommends him to attention.

Jefferson to Madison

Monticello Aug. 16, 1810

DEAR SIR

Yours of yesterday was recieved last night. The McGehee who is the subject of it, is an overseer of mine at a place, which on account of it's impor-

---

27. TJ accepted JM's suggestion, altering his statement that he had concurred with his cabinet's unanimous opinion to indicate that "we were all unanimously of Opinion . . ."; see *PJM* (Pres. ser.), II, pp. 475–76.

28. TJ claimed that the injunction that Livingston obtained against eviction from the batture was a chancery process and denied that a chancery jurisdiction had been established by any law for the Louisiana Territory; see L. and B., XVIII, pp. 117–18.

29. TJ denied that the right of alluvion applied in Livingston's case; see *ibid.*, p. 67.

tance to me, Mr Randolph takes care of. He employed McGehee, and solely superintends him. We consider him as extremely industrious, active, attentive, and skilful in the old practices, but prejudiced against any thing he is not used to. We have obliged him to adopt the level ploughing, but he would get rid of it if he could. As far as we know or believe he is honest. So far good; but there are great set-offs, all proceeding from an unfortunate temper. To those under him he is harsh, severe and tyrannical, to those above him, insubordinate, self-willed, capable of insolence if not personally afraid, dictatorial and unbending: with this he is the most discontented mortal under all circumstances I have ever known. He has been overseer at three different places in our neighborhood, but not more than a year in either. Mr Randolph had intended however to try him another year, and thought he had agreed with him the day before he went to you. Finding however that Mcgehee thinks otherwise, he feels himself at liberty to look out for another, and if he would suit you we would both wish you to take him, and should part with him without reluctance, and whether you take him or not, I think Mr Randolph, loosened from what he thought an engagement, will try to get another. He was to have for the present year £ 50. certain and more if his management was approved; and on the late negociation Mr R. had agreed to £ 125. for this and the next year. I called at Mr Lindsay's the day I left you, and enquired of him respecting McGehee as I knew he had been his overseer. He gave exactly the above character of him and added the fact that his insults were so intolerable that he wished to have got rid of him in the middle of the year, and offered him 200. D. instead of his share to go off. McGehee asked 250. which were refused. He was overseer for Mrs Walker his neighbor, and carried a gun ordinarily for fear of an attack from the negroes. I have thus given you all the good and the bad I know of him that you may weigh and judge for yourself, which do freely as there is no attachment to him here. Always affectiony, yours

TH JEFFERSON

Jefferson to Madison

Monticello Aug. 20, 1810

DEAR SIR

Mr. Wirt having suggested to me that he thought the explanations in my case of the Batture, respecting the Nile and Mississipi not sufficiently clear, and that the authority cited respecting the Nile might be urged against me, I have endeavored, by a Note, to state their analogies more clearly. Being a shred of the argument I put into your hands I inclose it to you with a request, after perusal, to put it under cover to Mr Gallatin, the argument itself having, I presume, gone on. Mr Irving will be with you tomorrow. I shall set out for Bedford the next day, to be absent probably about three weeks. You shall know when I return in the hope of having the pleasure of seeing you here. Affectionate salutations to Mrs Madison and yourself.

TH JEFFERSON

Jefferson to Madison

Monticello Sept. 10, 1810

DEAR SIR

I returned yesterday from Bedford, and according to my letter written just before my departure, I take the liberty of informing you of it in the hope of seeing Mrs Madison and yourself here. And I do it with the less delay as I shall ere long be obliged to return to that place.

By a letter of Aug. 15. from Genl. Dearborn he sais in a P. S. that he has just recieved information that Bidwell had fled on account of fraud committed by him in his office of county treasurer.[30] These are mortifying and distressing incidents. Present my friendly respects to Mrs Madison and be assured of my constant affection

TH JEFFERSON

Jefferson to Madison

Monticello Oct. 15, 1810

DEAR SIR,

Tho' late, I congratulate you on the revocation of the French decrees, and Congress still more; for without something new from the belligerents, I know not what ground they could have taken for their next move. Britain will revoke her orders of council, but continue their effect by new paper blockades, doing in detail what the orders did in the lump. The exclusive right to the sea by conquest is the principle she has acted on in petto, tho' she dares not yet avow it. This was to depend on the events of the war. I rejoice however that one power has got out of our way, and left us a clear field with the other.

Another circumstance of congratulation is the death of Cushing. The Nation ten years ago declared it's will for a change in the principles of the administration of their affairs. They then changed the two branches depending on their will, and have steadily maintained the reformation in those branches. The third, not dependent on them, has so long bid defiance to their will, erecting themselves into a political body to correct what they deem the errors of the nation. The death of Cushing gives an opportunity of closing the

---

30. Former Congressman Barnabas Bidwell fled to Canada when a shortage in his accounts was discovered; see Malone, VI, pp. 66–67, and Brant, V, p. 167.

reformation by a successor of unquestionable republican principles. Our friend Lincoln has of course presented himself to your recollection. I know you think lightly of him as a lawyer; and I do not consider him as a correct common lawyer, yet as much so as any one which ever came, or ever can come from one of the Eastern states. Their system of Jurisprudence, made up from the Jewish law, a little dash of Common law, etc. a great mass of original notions of their own, is a thing sui generis, and one educated in that system can never so far eradicate early impressions as to imbibe thoroughly the principles of another system. It is so in the case of other systems, of which Ld. Mansfield is a splendid example. Lincoln's firm republicanism, and known integrity, will give compleat confidence to the public in the long desired reformation of their judiciary.[31] Were he out of the way, I should think Granger prominent for the place. His abilities are great, I have entire confidence in his integrity, tho' I am sensible that J. R. has been able to lessen the confidence of many in him.[32] But that I believe he would soon reconcile to him, if placed in a situation to shew himself to the public, as he is, and not as an enemy has represented him. As the choice must be of a New Englander, to exercise his functions for New England men, I confess I know of none but these two characters. Morton is really a republican, but inferior to both the others in every point of view. Blake calls himself republican, but never was one at heart. His treachery to us under the embargo should put him by for ever. Story and Bacon are exactly the men who deserted us on that measure and carried off the majority. The former is unquestionably a tory, and both are too young.[33] I say nothing of professing federalists. Granger and Morton have both been interested in Yazooism. The former however has long been clear of it.

I have said thus much because I know you must wish to learn the sentiments of others, to hear all, and then do what on the whole you percieve to be best.

Does Mr. Lee go back to Bordeaux? If he does, I have not a wish to the contrary. If he does not, permit me to place my friend and kinsman G. J. on the list of candidates. No appointment can fall on an honester man and his talents, tho' not of the first order, are fully adequate to the station. His judgment is very sound, and his prudence consummate.[34] Ever affectionately yours.

TH. JEFFERSON

---

31. JM offered the Supreme Court seat to Lincoln, who declined because of failing eyesight; see *ibid.*, p. 167.

32. Randolph had opposed Gideon Granger's involvement in the Yazoo land case.

33. JM offered the post to Alexander Wolcott, who was rejected by the Senate; then to John Quincy Adams, who turned it down; and finally to Joseph Story, who was confirmed by the Senate. For a first-rate biography, see R. Kent Newmyer, *Supreme Court Justice Joseph Story: Statesman of the Old Republic* (Chapel Hill, 1983).

34. George Jefferson, TJ's cousin, had been his agent in Richmond before being appointed consul at Lisbon; see Malone, VI, p. 82.

Madison to Jefferson

Washington Oct. 19, 1810

DEAR SIR

I have rec^d your favor of the 15th. All we know of the step taken by France towards a reconciliation with us, is thro the English papers sent by Mr. Pinkney, who had not himself rec^d any information on the subject from Genl A. nor held any conversation with the B. Ministry on it, at the date of his last letters. We hope from the step, the advantage at least of having but one contest on our hands at a time. If G. B. repeals her orders, without discontinuing her mock-blockades, we shall be at issue with her on ground strong in law, in the opinion of the world, and even in her own concessions. And I do not believe that Cong^s will be disposed, or permitted by the Nation, to a tame submission; the less so as it would be not only perfidious to the other belligerent, but irreconcilable with an honorable neutrality. The Crisis in W. Florida, as you will see, has come home to our feelings and our interests.[35] It presents at the same time serious questions, as to the Authority of the Executive, and the adequacy of the existing laws of the U. S. for territorial administration. And the near approach of Cong^s might subject any intermediate interposition of the Ex. to the charge of being premature and disrespectful, if not of being illegal. Still there is great weight in the considerations, that the Country to the Perdido, being our own, may be fairly taken possession of, if it can be done without violence, above all if there be danger of its passing into the hands of a third and dangerous party. The successful party at Baton Rouge have not yet made any communication or invitation to this Gov^t They certainly will call in either our Aid or that of G. B., whose conduct at the Caraccas gives notice of her propensity to fish in troubled waters.[36] From present appearances, our occupancy of W. F. would be resented by Spain, by England, and by France, and bring on not a triangular, but quadrangular contest. The Vacancy in the Judiciary is not without a puzzle in supplying it. Lincoln, obviously, is the first presented to our choice, but I believe he will be inflexible in declining it. Granger is *working hard* for it. His talents are as you state, a strong recommendation; but it is unfortunate that the only legal evidence of them known to the public, displays his Yazooism; and on this as well as some other acc^ts the more particularly offensive to the Southern half of the Nation. His bodily infirmity with its effect on his mental stability is an unfavorable circumstance also. On the other hand, it may be difficult to find a successor free from objections, of equal force. Neither Morton, nor Bacon, nor Story have yet been brought

---

35. For JM's role in the revolt in the Baton Rouge district against Spanish authority, see Brant, V, pp. 173–83. Also see Sofaer, pp. 291–303, and *PJM* (Pres. ser.), II, pp. 305–20.

36. On Oct. 25, 1810, JM learned that the West Florida convention had declared independence and requested annexation to the United States. On Oct. 27, he issued a presidential proclamation taking possession of the territory and added it to Orleans Territory; see Brant, V, pp. 183–89, and *PJM* (Pres. ser.), II, pp. 595–96.

forward, And I believe Blake will not be a candidate. I have never lost sight of Mr. Jefferson of Richmond. Lee I presume returns to Bourdeaux. Jarvis is making a visit to the U. S. but apparently with an intention to return to Lisbon. All the other consulships worthy of him are held by persons who manifest no disposition to part with their berths.

 My overseer G. Gooch is just setting out with the Algerine Rams. Two of them, I have directed him to forward to Monticello. I beg you to accept whichever of them you may prefer, and let Capt: Isaac Coles have the other. Of the 8 sent from Algiers, one was slaughtered on the passage, and a Wether substituted. Another was not of the large tail family; but a very large handsome sheep with 4 horns. His fleece is heavy, but like the others coarse. I send him to Virg[a] with the others, tho' at a loss what to have done with him there. Two of the large tails I have disposed of here, one to Claiborne for the benefit of the Orleans meat Market. I send home also by this opp[y] six Marino Ewes, two of them rec[d] from Jarvis, and the rest purchased here out of his late shipment. I have purchased also the Ewe lamb, which had been destined for Hooe of Alexand[a] Finding that the arrangements necessary for the original pair, would provide for a small flock, I have been tempted to make this addition to them, as a fund of pure Marino blood, worth attending to. The Ewes will stand me in at $175 a piece. Accept my affectionate respects

         JAMES MADISON

The Politics of Neutrality, 1811

While Madison wrestled with foreign-policy problems presented by French deceit and British insults, he had to face a rising tide of criticism not only from Federalists, but also from Republican factions. He owed his presidency to the Republican congressional caucus, and he had difficulty dominating his creators. At the beginning of his administration, the Senate, led by William Branch Giles of Virginia and Samuel Smith of Maryland, had blocked his efforts to make Albert Gallatin, his ablest ally, secretary of state, and they remained critics of Gallatin and, increasingly, of Madison even though the president, in an effort to preserve party unity, had elevated Smith's brother to the post of secretary of state, a move that he lived to regret. Madison also worried about James Monroe staying outside the inner circle, but he ignored Vice President George Clinton of New York, who remained estranged after challenging him for the presidency in the election of 1808.

The president tried to remain aloof from Republican factionalism within state parties, particularly the "Philadelphia Junto" of Pennsylvania Republicans headed by Senator Michael Leib and William Duane, editor of the Philadelphia *Aurora* and the harshest critic of his fellow Pennsylvanian, Gallatin. When Duane failed to receive government printing contracts after Madison's election, he compared Gallatin to his predecessor, Alexander Hamilton, labeling Gallatin "the evil genius of this nation, more pernicious and corrupt than Hamilton."[1] As his dislike for Gallatin hardened into hatred, Duane accused him of manipulating Madison to avoid a clash with Britain in order to fill the Treasury from the growing customs receipts. Most of the Clintonians in New York and Pennsylvania also supported more forcible resistance to the British than commercial retaliation. But John Randolph and a few "Old Republicans"

1. William Duane to Joseph C. Cabell, June 16, 1811, cited in J. C. A. Stagg, *Mr. Madison's War: Politics, Diplomacy, and Warfare in the Early American Republic, 1783–1830* (Princeton, 1983), p. 51.

from the South agreed with Monroe that the United States might yet negotiate an arrangement similar to his treaty of 1806 and eliminate economic coercion. As his term progressed, Madison realized that he would have to deal with his party's internal problems before he could deal effectively with the nation's external disputes.

In his second annual message to Congress on December 5, 1810, the chief executive made straightforward presentations defending two presidential proclamations. The first, that of November 1810, reinstated the Nonintercourse Act against Great Britain on February 2, 1811, unless the orders-in-council were withdrawn. The second was a direct outgrowth of the conflict between Britain and France in Spain, where the threatened collapse of the Spanish Empire offered the United States an opportunity to annex West Florida. In a proclamation issued on October 27, 1810, but not previously announced, the president explained the occupation of West Florida by U.S. forces as a move to forestall possession by Great Britain or France during the wartime upheavals in Spain, which had subverted Spanish authority in America and might threaten the national security of the Union. "Though of right appertaining to the United States" as part of the Louisiana Purchase, the president told Congress, West Florida "had remained in the possession of Spain awaiting the result of negotiations for its actual delivery to them." But he had authorized American occupation to protect "the tranquility and security of our adjoining territories," knowing that "the legality and necessity of the course pursued assure me of the favorable light in which it will present itself to the Legislature, and of the promptitude with which they will supply whatever provisions may be due to the essential rights and equitable interests of the people thus brought into the bosom of the American family."[2]

One domestic issue that Madison did not lay before Congress but should have was the rechartering of the Bank of the United States, whose twenty-year authorization would expire on March 4, 1811. Although Madison had opposed the establishment of the bank in 1791, he had concluded that it had proved its usefulness and even its constitutionality during its existence. But instead of sending a presidential message to Congress, a move that might have supplied enough votes to overcome its loss by one vote in each house, he assigned Gallatin as the administration spokesman to present the recharter bill since he was the most knowledgeable man in the nation about "the degree of necessity which exists at the present time for a national bank." The opposition to the bank was spearheaded by the senators who had stymied Gallatin's appointment as secretary of state—Giles of Virginia, Smith of Maryland, and Leib of Pennsylvania—and the deciding vote against it was cast by Vice President Clinton.[3]

2. The proclamations are printed in Richardson, I, pp. 480–82. For Madison's message, see *ibid.*, pp. 482–87. Brant, V, pp. 222–38, discusses the West Florida project. For JM's views on West Florida on the eve of this proclamation, see JM to TJ, Oct. 19, 1810, above.

3. Brant, V, pp. 265–70, blames JM for lack of leadership in this instance. The quotation is from Senator William H. Crawford of Georgia, administration spokesman.

Madison's problems with dissident Republicans was not confined to Congress and the press. It extended into the cabinet, where Robert Smith often sided with his brother in the Senate, who had led the fight against Macon's Bill No. 1. Even on foreign-policy issues, the secretary of state was indiscreet in his observations to foreign diplomats, if not disloyal to the president, admitting to the British chargé d'affaires on one occasion that Great Britain had a right to complain against the renewal of nonintercourse and suggesting that "the whole of the restrictive commercial system" ought to be repealed by Congress. Like his brother, Smith was also opposed to Gallatin, as John Randolph noted: "Our Cabinet presents a novel spectacle in the world; divided against itself, and the most deadly animosity raging between its principal members."[4]

The conflict in the cabinet, intensified by the defeat of the move to recharter the Bank of the United States and the open warfare between Smith and Gallatin, came to a head in March 1811 after Congress had adjourned. Duane's attacks in the *Aurora* were directed at Gallatin, but increasingly they ricocheted off Madison:

In the personal virtues, talents, and integrity of Mr. Madison, every man reposes implicit confidence; but the impression prevails throughout the country that Mr. Gallatin manages everything. . . . The retirement of that man only is wanting to restore what he has shaken.[5]

As soon as Congress left town, Gallatin, in a move that may have been orchestrated by Madison,[6] submitted his resignation to the president, citing "new subdivisions and personal factions" in the cabinet, "equally hostile to yourself and to the general welfare." Madison promptly rejected the resignation, called in Smith and demanded his resignation, at the same time offering him a face-saving appointment as minister to Russia. He also asked Gallatin to initiate an inquiry to find out if Monroe would join the administration. When Madison received assurances that Monroe would accept appointment as secretary of state, the president made a recess appointment, which did not require Senate confirmation until Congress met in the fall, and Monroe accepted immediately.[7]

Throughout the winter session of Congress, neither Madison nor Jefferson had written the other about substantive issues, although Jefferson had wished his successor "an easy and prosperous campaign" with Congress.[8] After Congress adjourned, Jefferson sent congratulations "on the close of your campaign." He did not yet know of Monroe's appointment, but he had kept up with news accounts of foreign difficulties, learning that the London govern-

---

4. Ketcham, pp. 484–85; Brant, V, 270–77; and Bradford Perkins, *Prologue to War: England and the United States, 1805–1812* (Berkeley, 1963), pp. 267–68.

5. Philadelphia *Aurora,* Feb. 11, 1811, cited in Brant, V, p. 276.

6. Brant, V, pp. 282, 292–93; Ketcham, p. 486; and Perkins, p. 268.

7. Brant, V, p. 282; Harry Ammon, *James Monroe: The Quest for National Identity* (New York, 1971), pp. 286–88; and Perkins, pp. 269–71.

8. TJ to JM, Dec. 8, 1810, below.

ment was in disarray after George III's illness forced the organization of a regency under the playboy Prince of Wales. "Our only chance as to England," he observed, "is the accession of the Prince of Wales to the throne," even though "he has much more understanding and good humor than principle or application." If he simply headed the regency, Jefferson thought, he would inherit the present ministry instead of replacing it, a move that would make him "less bold and strong to make a thorough change of system."⁹

Madison reported the mistaken news that the prince regent had appointed a new cabinet with Lord Holland as prime minister and Lord Grenville as foreign minister. He hoped that this would mean "some material change in the general policy of the Government, in relation to this Country," perhaps even "a repeal of the Orders in Council." But he suspected that "the attachment to maritime usurpations on public law, and the jealousy of our growing commerce, are sources from which serious difficulties must continue to flow, unless controuled by the distress of the Nation, or by a magnanimity not to be expected even from the personification of Fox in Lord Holland."

As for Napoleon, the president continued, he seemed to distrust "the stability and efficacy of our pledge to renew the non-intercourse agst G. B. and has wished to execute his [decrees] in a manner that would keep pace only with the execution of ours; and at the same time leave no interval for the operation of the British orders, without a counter operation in either his or our measures. In all this," Madison complained, "his folly is obvious," and he noted that Napoleon's "ignorance of commerce" was a major factor in his misguided policies. "Distrust on one side produces and authorizes it on the other; and must defeat every arrangement between parties at a distance from each other or which is to have a future or a continued execution. On the whole," he concluded, "our prospects are far from being very flattering; yet a better chance seems to exist than, with the exception of the adjustment with Erskine, has presented itself, for closing the scene of rivalship in plundering and insulting us, and turning it into a competition for our commerce and friendship."¹⁰

Even before news of Smith's dismissal was made public, Madison hinted about the cabinet upheaval to Jefferson. "In the midst of other perplexities, foreign and internal," he wrote on March 18, 1811, "a source has been opened very near me, and where co-operation agst them was to have been rightfully expected, from personal obligations, as well as public duty." Two weeks later, he could be specific about "the change which is taking place in the Department of State. Col. Monroe agrees to succeed Mr. Smith, who declines, however, the mission to Russia, at first not unfavorably looked at.¹¹ I was willing, notwithstanding many trying circumstances," he explained to the man who had introduced Smith to the cabinet, "to have smoothed the transaction as much

---

9. TJ to JM, Mar. 8, 1811, below.
10. JM to TJ, Mar. 18, 1811, below.
11. JM to TJ, Apr. 1, 1811, below. For Smith's vacillation, see Brant, V, pp. 283–90.

as possible, but it will be pretty sure to end in secret hostility, if not open warfare," an event that would be "truly painful for me." Nonetheless, Madison felt himself "on firm ground, as well in the public opinion as in my own consciousness."[12]

Jefferson sympathized with Madison, replying that the dismissal of Smith would probably trigger "the secret workings of an insatiable family. They may sow discontent," he added, "but [it] will neither benefit themselves nor injure you by it. The confidence of the public is too solid to be shaken by personal incidents." Moreover, he was ecstatic "that Monroe is added to your councils. He will need only to perceive that you are without reserve towards him, to meet it with the cordiality of earlier times. He will feel himself to be again at home in our bosoms, and happy in a separation from those who led him astray. I learn," he added for emphasis, "that John Randolph is now open-mouthed against him and Hay," Monroe's son-in-law who was representing Jefferson in the batture case.[13]

After Smith's ouster from the cabinet, Duane redoubled his attacks on Gallatin, arguing that Madison must abandon his secretary of the treasury before the people abandoned the president. Only his financial embarrassment, which he claimed was caused by Gallatin's banking friends, kept Duane silent temporarily as he scrambled for new backing. He turned first to Jefferson, who had pardoned him from his Sedition Act sentence, asking that he rally eighty Virginians to pledge $100 apiece. Jefferson launched the fund-raising campaign because of Duane's "past services to the cause of republicanism," but he informed the editor that his support was not "an approbation of his late attacks on Mr Gallatin, of which we unequivocally disapproved." When Duane expanded his slashing attacks from Gallatin to Madison, Jefferson and his contributors quickly withdrew their pledges, considering Duane "as unequivocally joining the banners of the opposition, federal or factious."

In an attempt to buck up Madison's spirits, Jefferson downplayed the loss of Duane as a proadministration editor. His "flying off from the government, may, for a little while, throw confusion into our ranks," just as the loss of John Randolph had done in his own presidency. "But, after a moment of time to reflect and rally, and to see where he is, we shall stand our ground with firmness. A few malcontents will follow him, as they did John Randolph." And the Federalists would, of course, "sing Hosannas," but "the world will thus know of a truth what they are." In the coming election of 1812, "this new minority will perhaps bring forward their new favorite, who seems already to have betrayed symptoms of consent."[14] But he predicted that "they will blast

12. JM to TJ, Apr. 1, 1811, below.

13. TJ to JM, Apr. 7, 1811, below. In a conciliatory move, JM had visited Monroe at his home near TJ's in Sept. 1810; see Brant, V, pp. 165–67, and Ammon, p. 284.

14. TJ to JM, Apr. 24, 1811, below. When General Armstrong resigned as minister to France, William Lee, a consular officer there, alleged that Armstrong had presidential ambitions; see Stagg, pp. 58–59.

him in the bud, which will be no misfortune. They will sound the tocsin against the antient dominion," which had furnished three of the nation's first four presidents, "and anti-dominionism may become their rallying point. And it is better that all this should happen," he concluded happily, "two, than six years hence," when Madison's second term would end.[15]

Jefferson made one last effort to reclaim Duane from "the dominion of his passions," eulogizing Madison, Gallatin, and the Republican party, and reminding him that "the last hope of human liberty in this world rests on us." "Our Executive and legislative authorities are the choice of the nation, and possess the nation's confidence. . . . It is the duty of the minority," he concluded, "to acquiesce and conform." He sent both of his letters to Madison, who thought that his "expostulations with Duane could not be improved," even though Duane remained incorrigible.[16]

Robert Smith fed material to Duane[17] before finally publishing a pamphlet justifying his conduct and attacking Madison. Jefferson thought "he has been very ill advised, both personally and publicly. As far as I can judge from what I hear," he told his friend in the President's House, "the impression made is entirely unfavorable to him." He deplored the fact that "the Chief Magistrate cannot enter the arena of the newspapers," but he hoped that "a short and simple statement of the case" would set the record right.[18] Joel Barlow, recently appointed minister to France as Armstrong's successor, and William Lee, former consul at Bordeaux, promptly published a reply in the *National Intelligencer* to Smith's "wicked publication," as Madison called it. "It is impossible however that the whole turpitude of his conduct can be understood," he told Jefferson, "without disclosures to be made by myself alone, and of course as he knows not to be made at all. Without these his infamy is daily fastening itself upon him; leaving no other consolation than the malignant hope of revenging his own ingratitude and guilt on others." Indeed, a fellow Virginian, former Congressman James Garnett, reported that Smith's pamphlet furnished "one of the rare instances of a man's giving the finishing stroke to his own character, in his eagerness to ruin his enemy."[19]

James Monroe became secretary of state on April 6, 1811, hopeful that he could negotiate a "fair and reasonable arrangement" with Great Britain, as he had attempted to do in 1806. If honorable terms were impossible, however, he

---

15. TJ to JM, Apr. 24, 1811, below.
16. TJ to JM, May 26, 1811, below, and JM to TJ, May 3, 1811, below, and June 7, 1811, below. See also TJ to William Duane, Mar. 28, 1811, and Apr. 30, 1811, in Ford, IX, pp. 313, 315–16, and Kim T. Phillips, "William Duane, Philadelphia's Democratic Republicans, and the Origins of Modern Politics," *PMHB* 101 (1977): 365–87.
17. JM to TJ, May 3, 1811, below, and Stagg, pp. 66–67.
18. TJ to JM, July 3, 1811, below.
19. JM to TJ, July 8, 1811, below. See also Brant, V, pp. 307–9. Garnett is quoted in Perkins, p. 269. For a recent attempt to rehabilitate Smith's reputation, see Thom M. Armstrong, *Politics, Diplomacy, and Intrigue in the Early Republic: The Cabinet Career of Robert Smith, 1801–1811* (Dubuque, 1991).

thought it would be necessary to abandon economic coercion, which he called "dealing in the small way of embargoes, non-intercourse, and non-importation with menaces of war" for more forceful measures.[20]

When Monroe took office, neither the United States nor Great Britain had a minister in the other's capital, each being represented only by chargés d'affaires. The British foreign secretary, the indolent marquess of Wellesley, had not replaced "Copenhagen" Jackson, and William Pinkney, noting that Britain had no minister in Washington, resigned his post and left London in May 1811. Before he sailed, however, he learned that Sir Augustus John Foster, who had served as secretary to the British legation during Jefferson's presidency, had been appointed minister to the United States. But he also learned from Wellesley that Great Britain's maritime policy under the prince regent would remain unchanged. Indeed, Madison suspected that "the mission of Foster, like that of Rose, plays the same game" of "folly and depravity," "modified for the purposes of plunder."[21]

As for France, "the jumble" of contradictory accounts emanating from Paris seemed to "indicate a renewal of trade" one moment and "a continuance of the Iron policy" at another. But by early May, Madison concluded that "the repeal of the Decrees is professedly adhered to; and that an exchange of the productions of the U. S. and F[rance] with an exception of certain articles, is permitted by the Municipal laws, under vexatious precautions agst British forgeries and American collusions; and perhaps under some distrust of the views of this Government."[22]

Even before Foster arrived in America, another international incident erupted, pitting the American warship the *President* against His Majesty's sloop of war *Little Belt*. After trade with France was reopened by Madison's proclamation of November 2, 1810, British cruisers returned to coastal waters, renewing their provocative policy of impressment. Although the orders of Commodore John Rodgers did not direct him to use force to recover impressed seamen, they did take into account the *Chesepeake* attack and authorized him to use force to protect American ships and "at every hazard to vindicate the injured honor of our navy, and revive the drooping spirits of the nation."[23] At twilight on May 16, 1811, the *President* overtook the *Little Belt*, and, after a confusing exchange of signals, a brief exchange of cannon fire forced the *Little Belt* to strike her colors. Both commanders claimed the other had fired the first shot, and both governments backed their commanding officers. To Jefferson, Madison wrote about "the new shapes our foreign relations are taking. The occurrence between Rogers and the British ship of war,

20. Ammon, p. 292.
21. JM to TJ, Apr. 19, 1811, below. Perkins, pp. 274–80, discusses Foster's instructions, which he thinks "precluded any real mutuality."
22. JM to TJ, Apr. 19, 1811, below, and May 3, 1811, below.
23. Perkins, p. 272, and Brant, V, p. 317.

not unlikely to bring on repetitions, will probably end in an open rupture, or a better understanding, as the calculations of the B. Gov.^{t} may prompt or dissuade from war."[24]

Madison was worried about "the protracted delay" of the return of the USS *Essex,* which had been dispatched to France carrying the recently revived Nonimportation Act against England. The long hiatus in news from Europe "leaves us a prey to the ignorance and interested falsehoods which fill our newspapers." In the absence of official news, however, "it would seem that G. B. is determined ag.st repealing her orders, and that Bonaparte is equally so on the destruction" of British commerce, so much so that "he readily sacrifices his own commerce with the U. S."

As for the French blockade of England announced by the Berlin Decree, "the decree to which alone the Act of Cong.^{s} and the [presidential] Proclamation have reference," there was no evidence that it was still in force. "All the Official evidence," he reported, "is on the other side," thus meeting the requirements on which he had based his nonimportation proclamation against Great Britain. "And yet," he grumbled, "by a confusion of ideas or artifice of language, the appearance is kept up that the ground of the non-importation has failed, and that it is consequently a wrong to G. B." To Jefferson, he confessed that the new policy of nonimportation with Britain, like the discarded embargo, was causing protests from New England.[25]

On June 29, the *Essex* finally arrived at Annapolis with Pinkney on board, shortly after Foster and his staff had landed. Neither brought news of consequence, as Madison observed a fortnight later. "Pinkney brings, of course, nothing, Foster being the channel of English news," he told Jefferson. "From the conciliatory disposition of the Prince Regent, and the contrary one of his Cabinet, still deriving an ascendency from the convalescense of the King, you will be very able to dive into the character of the mission." From other sources, the president detected "an increasing rigor towards this Country."[26]

The new British minister demanded that the United States prove that the French decrees had been revoked, arguing that the orders-in-council would be continued until Napoleon permitted British goods, as well as neutral trade, to enter the Continent. He then threatened retaliation against the United States if it continued its nonimportation policy against Great Britain, a demand, Monroe wrote to the English negotiator with whom he had cooperated in 1806, "so entirely inconsistent with the rights of the U States, and degrading to them as an independent nation," that it was viewed as "evidence of a determined hostility in your government against this country."[27]

In less than a month after Foster's arrival, a deadlock in negotiations

24. JM to TJ, June 7, 1811, below.
25. *Ibid.*
26. JM to TJ, July 8, 1811, below.
27. James Monroe to Lord Holland, [Sept. 1811], cited in Perkins, pp. 281–82.

forced Madison to issue a proclamation on July 24 calling Congress into an early session on November 4 to prepare the country for war with Great Britain. "This proclamation," according to Stagg, ". . . was the most critical act of Madison's first term," far more important than his acceptance of the Cadore letter in October 1810, "for it amounted to . . . a decision to prepare the United States for war with Britain."[28] At the same time, Madison dispatched Joel Barlow, already confirmed by the Senate, as minister to France but refused to replace Pinkney in London, explaining to Foster that an appointment could not be made until Congress convened.[29]

The president and the secretary of state then retreated to Virginia for the summer break, carrying on their Orange-Albemarle correspondence by courier as Jefferson and Madison had done. Monroe also paid Madison a visit late in August, and Jefferson made his annual trip to Montpellier early in September. When the president laid plans for the reciprocal call at Monticello, however, Monroe suggested "a doubt of the propriety of your making a visit at this time to this neighborhood," fearing that it would open the president to the criticism of being his predecessor's puppet.

But friendship prevailed over politics. "If tested by prudential considerations," Madison observed, the omission of a visit would probably attract greater attention. "I shall therefore yield to the feelings of personal esteem and friendship; and abide whatever may issue." The Madisons, therefore, visited Monticello in mid-September, where they joined Jefferson in watching an eclipse of the sun but missed the moment of contact because Jefferson's watch was slow.[30]

──────────────── THE LETTERS ────────────────

Madison to Jefferson

Washington Dec. 7, 1810

DEAR SIR

The letter inclosed came to me as you see it; and though probably meant more for me than you, is forwarded according to its ostensible destination.

We have nothing from abroad more than has been made public. The latest date from Pinkney is the 3d of October. The arrival of November will have been some test, positive or negative, of the views of England. Her party here seems puzzled more than usual. If they espouse her Blockades, they must

---

28. Stagg, p. 78.
29. He cited the example of TJ's appointee, William Short, who was rejected as minister to Russia after he had started on his mission with a recess appointment.
30. Brant, V, pp. 347–48.

sink under the odium. And this course is the more desperate, as it is possible that she may abandon them herself, under the duress of events.

Lincoln does not yield to the call I made in a private and pressing letter. Still, some wish him to be appointed, hoping he may serve for a time. Granger has stirred up recommendations throughout the Eastern States. The means by which this has been done are easily conjectured, and outweigh the recommendations themselves. The soundest republicans of N. England are working hard against him, as infected with Yazooism, and intrigue. They wish for J. Q. Adams as honest, able, independent and untainted with such objections. There are others however in the view of Southern Republicans, tho' perhaps less formidable to them, than Yazooism on the Supreme Court. If there be other Candidates, they are disqualified either politically, morally, or intellectually. Such is a prospect before me, which your experience will make you readily understand.

Rodney has not yet joined us; and of course draws on himself the blame even of his best friends. And I just learn that his plan of bringing his family here, for which he has a House engaged, is broken up by the loss of his furniture, which was coming round by sea, share the fate and a wreck on the Eastern Shore. The loss is increased by the addition of his Law Books and valuable papers. He has hopes however, of saving such articles as have been able to bear a compleat steeping in salt water. Be assured always of my sincerest affection

Jefferson to Madison

Monticello Dec. 8, 1810

DEAR SIR

I found among my papers the inclosed survey of La Fayette's lands adjacent to N. Orleans. Whether it be the legal survey or not I do not know. If it is, it gives a prospect of something considerable after the 600. yards laid off round the ramparts. I inclose it to you as it may possibly be of use. With me it can be of none.

I inclose you also a piece in the M S. from Dupont on the subject of our system of finance when the progress of manufacture shall have dried up the present source of our revenue. He is, as you know, a vigorous economist, and altho the system be not new, yet he always gives something new, and places his subject in strong lights. The application of the system to our situation also is new. On the whole it is well worth your reading, however oppressed with reading. When done with it I will thank you to hand it to Mr Gallatin with a request to return it to me when he shall have read it.

I have had a visit from Mr Warden. A failure in the stage detained him here 10. days. I suppose you had hardly as good an opportunity of becoming acquainted with him. He is a perfectly good humored, inoffensive man, a man of science and I observe a great favorite of those of Paris, and much more a man of business than Armstrong had represented him. His memoirs and proceedings in the cases of vessels seised shew this. I observed he had a great longing for his late office in Paris. I explained to him distinctly the impossibility of his succeeding in a competition before the Senate with such a man as Russell, a native, and of high standing. That failing, I endeavored to find out what other views and prospects he might have.[1] I find he is poor, and looks ultimately to the practice of physic for an independant livelihood; that he wishes to find some means of living while he should be pursuing that study. He spoke of a secretaryship in one of the territories as desirable in that view, and I believe he would suit that office. However any appointment which would give him present subsistence. The consulships which rely on mercantile business he does not much relish, having no turn to shillings and pence. Having left Paris very hastily, he would be glad to go back there as the bearer of public dispatches, to settle his affairs there, if there should be occasion for a messenger. I collected these things from him indirectly, believing you would wish to know his views. He is an interesting man, perfectly modest and good, and of a delicate mind. His principal seems to have thrown him first on the hands of the Executive and then off of his own.[2] We have not yet recieved your message, from which we expect to learn our situation, as well with our neighbors as beyond the Atlantic. Wishing you an easy and prosperous campaign for the winter I renew the assurances of my constant affection and respect.

TH JEFFERSON

Jefferson to Madison

Monticello Mar. 8, 1811

DEAR SIR

On my return from a journey of 5 weeks to Bedford I found here the two letters now inclosed which tho' directed to me belong in their matter to you. I never before heard of either writer and therefore leave them to stand on their own ground.

I congratulate you on the close of your campaign. Altho it has not conquered your difficulties, it leaves you more at leisure to consider and provide against them. Our only chance as to England is the accession of the Prince of Wales to the throne. If only to the regency, himself and his ministers may be less bold and strong to make a thorough change of system. It will leave them

1. David B. Warden had gone to Paris as Armstrong's secretary, then became temporary consul, replacing Fulwar Skipwith. But Armstrong opposed his permanent appointment as consul, and he was succeeded by Jonathan Russell, who had been chargé d'affaires in London; see C. Edward Skeen, *John Armstrong, Jr., 1758–1843: A Biography* (Syracuse, 1981), pp. 111–15.
2. JM reinstated Warden as consul in Paris; see *ibid.*, pp. 118–19.

too a pretext for doing less than right if so disposed. He has much more understanding and good humor than principle or application.³ But it seems difficult to understand what Bonaparte means towards us. I have been in hopes the consultations with[in] closed doors were for taking possession of E. Florida.⁴ It would give no more offence anywhere than taking the Western province, and I am much afraid the Percival ministry may have given orders for taking possession of it, before they were put out of power.

We have had a wretched winter for the farmer. Great consumption of food by the cattle and little weather for preparing the ensuing crop. During my stay in Bedford we had seven snows that of Feb. 22 which was of 15. I. about Richmond was of 6. I here, and only 3½ in Bedford. Ever affectionately yours

Th Jefferson

Madison to Jefferson

Washington Mar. 18, 1811

Dear Sir,

I have rec^d yours inclosing two letters improperly addressed to you.

A sketch, in manuscript was brought by yesterday's mail from N. York, saying that a vessel just arrived, stated that the Prince Regent had appointed his Cabinet; that Lord Holland was prime Minister, Grenville Secretary of State, Moira Commander in Chief etc. and that a new Parliament was to be called. Whether these details be correct or not, it is highly probable that some material change in the general policy of the Government, in relation to this Country as well as in other respects, will result from the change of the men in power.⁵ Nor is it improbable that a repeal of the Orders in Council will be accompanied by a removal in some form or other, of the other condition required by the Act of May last. Still the attachment to maritime usurpations on public law, and the jealousy of our growing commerce, are sources from which serious difficulties must continue to flow, unless controuled by the distress of the Nation, or by a magnanimity not to be expected even from the personification of Fox in Lord Holland. Grenville is known to be very high in his notions of British rights on the ocean; but he has never contended for more, on the subject of blockades than that cruising squadrons, creating a

3. As early as Dec. 1810, Pinkney had predicted that the Prince of Wales would assume the Regency since George III had suffered another siege of insanity; see Stagg, p. 64. Also see Perkins, pp. 11–12, 322.

4. Meeting in secret sessions in Jan. 1811, Congress authorized the president to take temporary possession of East Florida, if it were offered by local Spanish officials or if he thought it necessary to forestall occupancy by any other foreign power; see Brant, V, pp. 239–46.

5. On Mar. 19, 1811, the *National Intelligencer* mistakenly reported that there had been a change of ministry, but the prince regent made no changes in the Perceval ministry; see Stagg, pp. 64–65, and Perkins, p. 322.

manifest danger in entering particular ports, was equivalent to a stationary force, having the same effect. His principle however tho' construable into an important restriction of that modern practice, may be expanded so as to cover this abuse. It is, as you remark difficult to understand the meaning of Bonaparte towards us.[6] There is little doubt, that his want of money, and his ignorance of commerce have had a material influence. He has also distrusted the stability and efficacy of our pledge to renew the non-intercourse agst G. B. and has wished to execute his in a manner that would keep pace only with the execution of ours; and at the same time leave no interval for the operation of the British orders, without a counter operation in either his or our measures. In all this, his folly is obvious. Distrust on one side produces and authorizes it on the other; and must defeat every arrangement between parties at a distance from each other or which is to have a future or a continued execution. On the whole our prospects are far from being very flattering; yet a better chance seems to exist than, with the exception of the adjustment with Erskine, has presented itself, for closing the scene of rivalship in plundering and insulting us, and turning it into a competition for our commerce and friendship.

In the midst of other perplexities, foreign and internal, a source has been opened very near me, and where co-operation agst them was to have been rightfully expected, from personal obligations, as well as public duty.[7] I find also that the appointment of Warden is to draw forth the keenest resentments of Armstrong.[8] I have no doubt however that the ground on which we stand is sufficiently firm to support us with the Nation, agst individual efforts of any sort, or from any quarter. Be assured always of my highest esteem and sincerest attachment.

JAMES MADISON

Madison to Jefferson

Washington Apr. 1, 1811

DEAR SIR,

I intimated to you the offence taken by Armstrong at the reinstatement of Warden. It is not improbable that it will be the ground of an open hostility. This will call into view his present denunciations of Warden, which are pointed against him as an adventurer and Impostor, from the commencement to the end of his career, in comparison with the patronage so long continued

---

6. For a brief discussion of the "maze of French decrees, announced and unannounced, enforced and unenforced, all of which together spelled uncertainty and confusion," see Clifford L. Egan, *Neither Peace nor War: Franco-American Relations, 1803–1812* (Baton Rouge, 1983), pp. 118–24, 133.

7. This is an oblique reference to JM's demand for the resignation of Robert Smith as secretary of state on Mar. 19 or 20, 1811; see Brant, V, p. 283.

8. Armstrong had fired Warden as consul at Paris, but JM reappointed him on Mar. 3, 1811. For Armstrong's cooperation with the dissident Republican factions in New York and Pennsylvania, see Stagg, p. 66.

to him, and the sentiments heretofore expressed of him. Will you be so good as to send me the extract from Armstrong's letter, written in the Summer or Fall of 1808, which notifies the appointment of Warden as Consul, and gives the favorable side of his character, as well as the objections to a confirmation of the appointment? That letter was the only communication made on the subject.[9]

You will have inferred the change which is taking place in the Department of State. Col. Monroe agrees to succeed Mr. Smith,[10] who declines, however, the mission to Russia, at first not unfavorably looked at.[11] I was willing, notwithstanding many trying circumstances, to have smoothed the transaction as much as possible, but it will be pretty sure to end in secret hostility, if not open warfare. On account of my great esteem and regard for common friends, such a result is truly painful to me. For the rest, I feel myself on firm ground, as well in the public opinion as in my own consciousness.

Wilkinson, I find, has lately received a letter from you, which he has shewn to his friends with much apparent gratification. I understand, at the same time, that the letter is cautious, and limited to the charge of privity with Burr. Did he disown to you the anonymous letter printed in Clark's Book, or say any thing relative to that subject?

The latest information from Europe will be found in the inclosed papers. The indications from France are rather favorable. Should the old King displace the Regent in England, little is to be hoped from that quarter, unless forced on the Cabinet by national distress. In the last correspondence of Pinkney with Wellesley, the latter sufficiently shewed his teeth; and received the severest scourging that was ever diplomatically inflicted.[12] Be assured always of my great esteem and affection.

JAMES MADISON

Jefferson to Madison

Monticello Apr. 7, 1811

DEAR SIR,

Your favors of Mar. 18 and April 1 have been duly received. The extract from Armstrong's letter of July 28, '08, which you desire is in these words. 'My poor friend Warden writes to you, and asks from you the appointment of

---

9. For the Armstrong-Warden controversy, see Skeen, pp. 113–20.

10. For JM's offer to Monroe, see Brant, V, pp. 282–87, and Ammon, pp. 286–88.

11. To help ease Robert Smith out of the cabinet, JM had offered him the post of minister to Russia since John Quincy Adams, who held that position, had been confirmed as an associate justice to the Supreme Court. Smith first accepted, then rejected the offer. Adams also turned down the Supreme Court appointment; see Brant, V, pp. 283, 288.

12. See Perkins, pp. 310–11. Pinkney ended his mission to England in Feb. 1811, convinced "that, if the present Government continues, we cannot be friends with England."

consul for this place. I could not promise to do more than send his letter. He is an honest and amiable man, with as much Greek and Latin, and chemistry and theology as would do for the whole corps of consuls, but, after all, not well qualified for business. You have seen an order of scavans, really well informed, who, notwithstanding, scarcely knew how to escape from a shower of rain when it happened to beset them. He is of that family. No—the man for this place ought to be a man of business, as well as a gentleman.' He then goes on to put Leavenworth's pretensions out of the way, should he have proposed himself. The letter is headed 'private,' although relating as much to public as private transactions. What I saw of Warden during the ten days or fortnight he staid here, satisfied me that he merited all the good which Armstrong says of him, and that he was by no means the helpless and ineffective man in business which he represents him to be.[13] I knew, when I received the letter, that Armstrong's fondness for point, and pith, rendered it unsafe to take what he said literally. He is cynical and irritable, and implacable. Whether his temper or his views induced his dismission of Warden, his persecution of him now, will render public benefit by the development of his character. I have never heard a single person speak of Warden who did not rejoice in his appointment, and express disapprobation of Armstrong's conduct respecting him; and I am perfectly satisfied that, if the appointment is made to attract public attention it will be approved.

The other subject of uneasiness which you express must, I know, be afflicting.[14] You will probably see its effect in the secret workings of an insatiable family. They may sow discontent, but will neither benefit themselves nor injure you by it. The confidence of the public is too solid to be shaken by personal incidents. I do sincerely rejoice that Monroe is added to your councils. He will need only to perceive that you are without reserve towards him, to meet it with the cordiality of earlier times. He will feel himself to be again at home in our bosoms, and happy in a separation from those who led him astray. I learn that John Randolph is now open-mouthed against him and Hay.[15]

The letter which I wrote lately to Wilkinson was one of necessity written to thank him for his book which he sent me. He says nothing in his letter of the anonymous letter in Clarke's book to which you allude. I have never seen Clarke's book, and know nothing of its contents.[16] The only part of my letter which regards Wilkinson himself is in these words. 'I look back with commiser-

13. For Warden's visit with TJ, see Malone, VI, p. 83.
14. TJ referred to the firing of Secretary of State Robert Smith.
15. George Hay, who had prosecuted Aaron Burr, was Monroe's son-in-law.
16. Daniel Clark wrote *Proofs of the Corruption of Gen. James Wilkinson, and of his Connexion with Aaron Burr, with a Full Refutation of his Slanderous Allegations in Relation to the Character of the Principal Witnesses Against Him* (Philadelphia, 1809). Thomas P. Abernethy entitled his final chapter in *The Burr Conspiracy* (New York, 1954) "Whitewash for Wilkinson" and concluded that the general occupied "a niche of infamy unique in American history."

ation on those still buffeting the storm, and sincerely wish your Argosy may ride out, unhurt, that in which it is engaged. My belief is that it will; and I found that belief on my own knolege of Burr's transactions, on my view of your conduct in encountering them, and on the candor of your judges.' These are truths which I express without reserve whenever any occasion calls for them. Whatever previous communications might have passed between Burr and Wilkinson on the subject of Mexico, I believe that on the part of the latter it was on the hypothesis of the approbation of the government. I never believed Wilkinson would give up a dependance on the government under whom he was the first, to become a secondary and dependant on Burr. I enclose you a letter from Père Gabriel. In a Note of unfinished business which I left with you, you will see exactly how far he had a right to expect the government would go in aid of his establishment.[17]

I fear the glimmering of hope that England might return to reason has past off with the return of her mad king to power. Present me affectionately to Mrs. Madison, and be assured of my best wishes for your health and happiness, and that your labours for the public may be crowned with their love.

TH. JEFFERSON

Madison to Jefferson

Washington Apr. 19, 1811

DEAR SIR,

I have received your favor of [April 7], containing the requested extract from Armstrong's letter relating to Warden. Armstrong has entangled himself in such gross inconsistencies, that he may perhaps not execute his threat to vindicate his removal of Warden against my reinstatement of him. This consideration alone will restrain his enmity against both of us.[18] You will see the conflict in which he is engaged with Fulton. Pinkney is weekly expected by the return of the Essex. Previous to his taking leave of the Prince Regent, he ascertained by a correspondence with Wellesley, that his stay was wished for the mere purpose of delay and delusion. The mission of Foster, like that of Rose, plays the same game.[19] The convalescence of the King renders the Prince a cypher, and his Cabinet is inflexible in its folly and depravity.[20] The inclosed paper of Poulson publishes from the "Courier," a Cabinet paper, the

17. For Father Gabriel Richard, see TJ's "Memoranda for the President," [Mar. 1809], above.

18. For Armstrong's decision not to engage in a pamphlet war with the administration, see Skeen, p. 119.

19. Augustus John Foster succeeded Francis "Copenhagen" Jackson after a long delay; see Perkins, pp. 273–75.

20. Although the report of the king's recovery was incorrect, JM's conclusions about Perceval's ministry and the regent's role were close to the mark; see Stagg, p. 66.

doctrine which is to be maintained and modified for the purposes of plunder. We have been long without official intelligence from France. The last was not unfavorable. Appearances and reports have of late engendered suspicions of foul play. The arrival of two vessels from Bayonne, in the Delaware, with the notice of others to follow, indicate a renewal of trade. On the other hand extracts of letters seem to imply a continuance of the Iron policy in that quarter. The symptoms of approaching war between France and Russia seem to multiply. I am sorry to trouble you with a recurrence to your dormant files, but as I know the facility afforded by the method of them, I will ask the favor of you to look under the "Anonymous" head for a long letter or letters, written from London, in the beginning of 1809, in a disguised hand, and signed "A Man." If received at all, it probably was forwarded by Lyman. Affectionately and respectfully

JAMES MADISON

Jefferson to Madison

Monticello Apr. 24, 1811

DEAR SIR

Yours of the 19th. is recieved. I have carefully examined my letter files from July 1808, to'this day, and find among them no such Anonymous letter as you mention. Indeed the stong impression on my memory is that I never recieved an Anonymous letter from England, or from any other country than our own.

Certain newspapers are taking a turn which gives me uneasiness. Before I was aware of it, I was led to an interference, which tho' from just motives, I should not, at a later moment, have shaped exactly as I did. I cannot therefore repress the desire to communicate it fully to you. On the 24th. of March I recieved a friendly letter from Duane, informing me of the distress into which he had been thrown by his former friends, Lieper and Clay, withdrawing their endorsements for him at the banks; the latter expressly for his attacks on John Randolph, the former without assigning any particular cause; and he concluded by asking whether, in Virginia, where he had been flattered by the support of his paper, 80. gentlemen could not be found, who would advance him their hundred Dollars apiece, to be repaid at short periods. I immediately engaged Mr Peter Carr here, and Mr Wirt in Richmond to set the experiment afoot, and one of these engaged a friend in Baltimore to do the same. But I mentioned to these gentlemen that, to apprise Duane of the grounds on which we interested ourselves for him, to wit, his past services to the cause of republicanism, and that he might not mistake it as an approbation of his late attacks on Mr Gallatin, of which we unequivocally disapproved, I would write him a letter. I accordingly wrote him the one now inclosed, which I previously communicated to Messrs. Carr and Wirt. It did not leave this till the 1st. of April. The thing was going on hopefully enough, when his papers of the 4th.

and 8th. arrived here, the latter written probably after he had recieved my letter. The effect at Baltimore I have not learned but every person who had offered, here or at Richmond to join in aiding him, immediately withdrew, considering him as unequivocally joining the banners of the opposition, federal or factious. I have to give an account of this to Duane, but am waiting, in expectation of an answer to mine of March 26. In that I shall make one effort more to reclaim him from the dominion of his passions, but I expect it will be the last, and as unavailing as the former.[21]

I could not be satisfied until I informed you of this transaction, and must even request you to communicate it to Mr Gallatin: for altho the just tribute rendered him in the letter was certainly never meant to meet his eye, yet as it is there, among other things, it must go to him. Ritchie has been under hesitation. His paper of the 16th. decides his course as to yourself. And I propose to set him to rights, as to Mr Gallatin, through a letter to Wirt in which I shall expose the falsehood or futility of the facts they have harped upon.[22] All this however is confidential to yourself and Mr Gallatin, because, while I wish to do justice to truth, I wish also to avoid newspaper observation.

With respect to the opposition threatened, altho it may give some pain, no injury of consequence is to be apprehended. Duane flying off from the government, may, for a little while, throw confusion into our ranks, as John Randolph did. But, after a moment of time to reflect and rally and to see where he is, we shall stand our ground with firmness. A few malcontents will follow him, as they did John Randolph, and perhaps he may carry off some well meaning Anti-Snyderites of Pensylvania. The federalists will sing Hosannas, and the world will thus know of a truth what they are. This new minority will perhaps bring forward their new favorite, who seems already to have betrayed symptoms of consent.[23] They will blast him in the bud, which will be no misfortune. They will sound the tocsin against the antient dominion, and anti-dominionism may become their rallying point. And it is better that all this should happen two, than six years hence.

Disregarding all this, I am sure you will pursue steadily your own wise plans, that peace, with the great belligerents at least, will be preserved, until it becomes more losing than war, and that the total extinction of the national debt, and liberation of our revenues, for defence in war and improvement in peace, will seal your retirement with the blessings of your country. For all this, and for your health and happiness I pray to god fervently.

TH: JEFFERSON

P. S. Be so good as to return the inclosed as I have no other copy.

---

21. For the Duane episode, see *ibid.*, pp. 66-67; Malone, VI, pp. 32-33; Raymond Walters, Jr., *Albert Gallatin: Jeffersonian Financier and Diplomat* (New York, 1957), pp. 241-43.

22. TJ wrote to William Wirt about Duane on Mar. 30 and May 3, 1811; see Ford, IX, pp. 316-19.

23. For references to Armstrong, recently returned from France, as a presidential possibility, see Skeen, p. 117; Brant, V, pp. 272, 305; and Stagg, pp. 59-60.

Madison to Jefferson

Washington May 3, 1811

DEAR SIR

I have rec^d yours of the 24 Ap^l and return the letter inclosed in it; after having made the communication intended for Mr. Gallatin. Your expostulations with Duane could not be improved; but he gives proofs of a want of candor, as well as of temperance, that will probably repel advice, however rational or friendly. The great fulcrum of his attacks on Mr. Gallatin is Erskine's statement of his favorable dispositions toward England; and these attacks he obstinately reiterates and amplifies, notwithstanding the public and solemn denial of Mr. G: whilst Mr. Smith and myself, tho' included in a like statement, and in which we have both remained silent, have not been reproached on that account, and Mr. S. is become an object even of favor. A like want of candor is seen in the comments of the Aurora, on the putative explanation of the rupture between Mr. S. and myself.[24] Of the alledged points of difference, the main one, viz: the non-intercourse, it appears that his opinion is on my side; yet he takes the other side generally without alluding to the exception; and of late, restricts his comments to Macon's bills, or smothers the "non-intercourse" under an etc. or confounds the measure with the manner of its execution. Again, Whilst he admits occasionally that the non-intercourse, or rather non-importation now in force, is the best and the only adequate resort agst the aggressions of G. B. he continues his abuse on the Government, for abandoning the interests and rights of the Nation. I have always regarded Duane, and still regard him as a sincere friend of liberty, and as ready to make every sacrifice to its cause, but that of his passions. Of these he appears to be compleatly a slave.

Our expected frigate is not yet arrived from Europe; nor is there any acc^t of the departure either of Pinkney or Foster from G. B. The last account from P. was of Mar. 13, when he was packing up for his passage in the Frigate. Whether the delays, proceed from the approach of the Equinox, the posture of the Regency, or a wish to learn the result of things in Congress, or from some other cause, is unknown. From the jumble of acc^{ts} from France, it is probable that the repeal of the Decrees is professedly adhered to; and that an exchange of the productions of the U. S. and F. with an exception of certain articles, is permitted by the Municipal laws, under vexatious precautions agst British forgeries and American collusions; and perhaps under some distrust of the views of this Government. Accept my high esteem and best affections.

JAMES MADISON

---

24. For Smith's "authorized" version of his dismissal in the *Aurora*, see Stagg, pp. 66–67.

Jefferson to Madison

Monticello May 26, 1811

DEAR SIR

As I sent you my first effort to keep Duane right, so I communicate the second, which the failure of our measures to help him obliged me to write.[25] It probably closes our correspondence as I have not heard a word from him on the subject. Ritchie is correct as to the administration generally. I have written to a friend there what I am in hopes will put him right as to Mr Gallatin, altho, as my friend thinks, it is not certain.[26]

We have had much alarm as to the fly in our wheat. Some friendly rains however have enabled much of it to outgrow that danger. Good lands and husbandry have recieved little injury from it. But the indifferent present as yet rather a meagre appearance. You will be so good as to return me the inclosed after perusal and to accept the assurances of my constant affection.

TH JEFFERSON

Madison to Jefferson

Washington June 7, 1811

DEAR SIR

I return the letter from you to Duane, on the subject of Mr. Gallatin he seems to be incorrigible. If I am not misinformed, his eyes are opening to the conduct and character of Mr. S. with respect to both of which he has suffered himself to be misled partly by his own passions, partly by those who took advantage of them. You see the new shapes our foreign relations are taking.[27] The occurrence between Rogers and the British ship of war, not unlikely to bring on repetitions, will probably end in an open rupture, or a better understanding, as the calculations of the B. Gov^t may prompt or dissuade from war.[28] Among the items in these will be the temper here, as reported by its partizans. The state of parties in Mass^{ts} is in this view important, especially as it will attract particular notice by its effects in degrading Pickering, who has

---

25. For TJ's letters to William Duane, Mar. 28 and Apr. 30, 1811, see Ford, IX, pp. 310–14, 314–16.

26. For TJ's letter to "a friend" in Richmond about Ritchie's *Enquirer*, see TJ to William Wirt, May 3, 1811, *ibid.*, pp. 317–19.

27. Just before leaving London after resigning as minister to England, Pinkney learned of Foster's instructions and concluded that the Perceval ministry was incapable of "authorizing such an arrangement as ought to content us"; see William Pinkney to Robert Smith, Mar. 13, 1811, cited in Stagg, p. 71. JM referred to this account in his letter to TJ, May 3, 1811, above. "The new shapes our foreign relations are taking" date from the receipt of Pinkney's letter.

28. For the battle between the *President* under Commodore John Rodgers and the *Little Belt*, a British sloop of war, on May 16, 1811, see Brant, V, pp. 319–20, and Perkins, pp. 272–73.

made himself so conspicuous in the British service.[29] On the other hand much impatience is shewing itself in the East^n States, under the non-importation. The little embarrassment which occurs in procuring returns for the apples and onions sent from Connecticut to the W. Indies, is generating remonstrances as in the case of the Embargo. I have been obliged to answer one from N. Haven headed by Hillhouse, which they have not yet published.[30] The protracted delay of the Essex still leaves us a prey to the ignorance and interested falsehoods which fill our newspapers. It would seem that G. B. is determined agst repealing her orders, and that Bonaparte is equally so on the destruction of her commerce, to which he readily sacrifices his own commerce with the U. S. As to the blockade of England, the decree to which alone the Act of Cong^s and the Proclamation have reference, there is no evidence of its being continued in force. All the Official evidence is on the other side. And yet by a confusion of ideas or artifice of language, the appearance is kept up that the ground of the non-importation has failed, and that it is consequently a wrong to G. B. After all, we must remain somewhat in the dark till we hear more on the subject; probably till the return of the vessel that carried to France the Act of Cong^s putting in force the non-importation, for wch Bonap^e seems to be waiting. After a severe drought, we have had a copious rain. I hope you have shared it and that it will have aided the Wheatfields in their conflict with the Hessian fly. Be assured of my constant and truest affection.

JAMES MADISON

Jefferson to Madison

Monticello July 3, 1811

DEAR SIR,

I have seen with very great concern the late address of Mr. Smith to the public.[31] He has been very ill advised both personally and publicly. As far as I can judge from what I hear, the impression made is entirely unfavorable to him. Every man's own understanding readily answers all the facts and insinuations, one only excepted, and for that they look for explanations without any doubt that they will be satisfactory. That is Erving's case.[32] I have answered,

---

29. Senator Timothy Pickering was replaced by the former Speaker of the House, Joseph B. Varnum.

30. For the New Haven remonstrance written by Senator James Hillhouse, see Brant, V, p. 324.

31. The ousted secretary of state published his *Address to the People of the United States* late in June 1811; see *ibid.*, pp. 302–3. It was published in the *National Intelligencer* on July 12, 1811; see Stagg, p. 72.

32. About one-fourth of Smith's pamphlet dealt with the settlement of George W. Erving's account as claims agent under Jay's treaty, with Smith citing a letter from JM to Erving as evidence of a conspiracy to overpay the agent and defraud American claimants; see Brant, V, p. 304.

the enquiries of several on this head, telling them at the same time, what was really the truth, that the failure of my memory enabled me to give them rather conjectures than recollections. For in truth I have but indistinct recollections of the case. I know that what was done was on a joint consultation between us, and I have no fear that what we did will not have been correct and cautious. What I retain of the case, on being reminded of some particulars will reinstate the whole firmly in my remembrance, and enable me to state them to inquirers with correctness, which is the more important from the part I bore in them. I must therefore ask the favor of you to give me a short outline of the facts which may correct as well as supply my own recollections. But who is to give an explanation to the public? not yourself certainly. The chief magistrate cannot enter the arena of the newspapers. At least the occasion should be of a much higher order. I imagine there is some pen at Washington competent to it.[33] Perhaps the best form would be that of some one personating the friend of Erving, some one apparently from the North. Nothing laboured is requisite. A short and simple statement of the case will, I am sure, satisfy the public.

We are in the midst of a so-so harvest; probably one third short of the last. We had a very fine rain on Saturday last. Ever affectionately yours.

Madison to Jefferson

Washington July 8, 1811

DEAR SIR,

Your favor of the 3d came duly to hand. You will have noticed in the National Intelligencer that the wicked publication of Mr. Smith is not to escape with impunity. It is impossible however that the whole turpitude of his conduct can be understood without disclosures to be made by myself alone, and of course as he knows not to be made at all. Without these his infamy is daily fastening itself upon him; leaving no other consolation than the malignant hope of revenging his own ingratitude and guilt on others. The case of Erving will probably be better explained in the newspaper than I can here do it. The general facts of it I believe are, that the three offices at London were centered in him, with one of the salaries only, it being understood at the time that he would be made assessor to the Board under Jay's Treaty, in which case

---

33. For a discussion of the "Review of Robert Smith's Address," which was subsequently published in the *National Intelligencer,* see *ibid.,* pp. 307–8. Brant says it was written by William Lee, consul designate for Bordeaux, and corrected by Joel Barlow, minister designate to France. Stagg, p. 73, credits it to Barlow and lists Lee as collaborator. See also Mary Lee Mann, *A Yankee Jeffersonian: Selections from the Diary and Letters of William Lee of Massachusetts, Written from 1796 to 1840* (Cambridge, Mass., 1958), pp. 139–40, where Lee claims credit.

he would be well recompensed. The Board declined to appoint him, giving preference to Cabot. Still however a certain portion of business passed through his hands. On this he charged the usual commission of 2½ per cent., accruing from the individuals, and not from a public fund. Having paid over the whole of the money of individuals in his hands to the public, instead of retaining his commission, a resort to Congress became necessary. Whilst the subject was before them, doubts were excited as to the merits of the case, and a call made on Mr. Gallatin for information. His report put an end to the difficulty; the appropriation was immediately made; and, but for the perverted view of the matter now before the public, would never more have been thought of. The Treasury officers, though politically adverse to Mr. Erving, do him much justice on the occasion, declaring that his official transactions throughout, as presented in his accounts, are models of clearness and exactness; that he appears to have saved or gained to the public by his vigilance and assiduity 60. or 70,000 dollars; that there remains a surplus of unclaimed monies to a considerable amount, the greater part of which will probably never be claimed; and finally that the only error committed by Mr. Erving was his not avoiding the necessity of asking Congress to give back the amount of his commission, by deducting it himself from the sums paid into the public coffers.

It has been thought best, whilst Mr. Monroe is in communication with the British and French Ministers here, to be silent on the subject. As the latest information from Russell, is prior to the arrival of the non-importation act, the state of our affairs at Paris may be conjectured.[34] Pinkney brings, of course, nothing, Foster being the channel of English news. I do not know that he has yet opened himself compleatly to Mr. Monroe; but from the conciliatory disposition of the Prince Regent, and the contrary one of his Cabinet, still deriving an ascendency from the convalescence of the King, you will be very able to dive into the character of the mission. You will perceive in the printed paper inclosed a step by the British Minister, which, very unseasonably it would seem, denotes an increasing rigor towards this Country. According to a preceding interposition with the Court of Admiralty, cases under the orders in Council had been suspended.[35]

I have promised myself a release from position immediately after the 4th July. It will be some days yet before I shall be able to set out. Considering the excessive heat for some days past, no time has yet been lost. The weather has been as dry as hot. In general the drought has been so severe as to ruin almost the oats and flax. The crop of wheat, tho' shortened, will be tolerable, in tolerable land, where the Hessians have not committed their ravages. Be assured of my most affectionate esteem.

---

34. Jonathan Russell was chargé d'affaires at Paris; see Skeen, pp. 126–27.

35. For the tightening of British orders-in-council under Perceval's instructions to Foster, which "precluded any real mutuality," see Perkins, pp. 276–82.

Jefferson to Madison

Monticello Oct. 10, 1811

DEAR SIR

Mrs Lewis, the widow of Colo. Nich Lewis, has requested me to mention to yourself the name of a Mr Wood, an applicant for a commission in the army. On recieving the request I rode to her house to ask something about him, observing to her that something more than his name would be necessary. She candidly told me at once that he was a very capable young man, connected with her only as being a brother to one of her sons in law, that he had married a respectable girl in Louisa, but became so dissipated and disorderly in his conduct that his father in law drove him off and procured an act of divorce from his wife, who is now married to another husband. This affected him so that he went off to the Western country, and, as she has been informed, became quite a new man: but had no knolege of it herself. She was inclined to suppose it true as her son Nicholas had written to her pressingly on his behalf and had particularly urged her to get me to mention him to you. To this neighbor I can refuse nothing, and I therefore comply with her request, stating the grounds on which we are both put into motion, and adding some information which perhaps may not be conveyed by others.

The old king dies hard, but he will die.[36] I wish we were as sure that his successor would give us justice and peace. I think it a little more than barely possible, relying on his former habits of connection, not on his principles, for he has none worthy of reliance. Ever affectionately your's

TH JEFFERSON

---

36. The New York *Evening Post* had erroneously announced the death of George III early in 1811; in February the Prince of Wales became regent; see Brant, V, p. 310.

39

WAR OR SUBMISSION: 1812

JEFFERSON BELIEVED that the repeal of the embargo left little choice between war or submission to England and/or France. "From that moment, I have seen no system which could keep us entirely aloof from these agents of destruction." The "scenes of tumult and outrage" pitted "a conqueror roaming over the earth with havoc and destruction" against "a pirate spreading misery and ruin over the face of the ocean." "But happily for us," he observed from his mountaintop in rural Virginia, "the Mammoth cannot swim, nor the Leviathan move on dry land; and if we will keep out of their way, they cannot get at us." In that case, "the system of government which shall keep us afloat amidst the wreck of the world, will be immortalized in history."[1]

If the world had been governed by logic, Madison and Congress might have been able to keep out of the way of the battling belligerents. If the orders-in-council, which were admittedly illegal except as retaliation,[2] were defenses against the Napoleonic decrees, and if the decrees had been revoked, as the Cadore letter announced, then it followed that the orders should be repealed. But Great Britain refused to alter her unilateral revision of international law, denying that the decrees had been revoked in practice.

Both Secretary of State Monroe and President Madison contended that the decrees had been rescinded for American ships, which were now hampered only by "municipal" regulations. Indeed, Monroe had indicated that the administration still hoped for accommodation with Britain, even at the risk of outraging France. The new secretary of state, who had been minister to Great Britain when Fox's blockade had been established in 1806, informed Foster that the president accepted it as satisfactory, following assurances that future blockades would be maintained effectively; the United States, therefore, would not join France in demanding its revocation.

---

1. TJ to Walter Jones, Mar. 5, 1810, in Ford, IX, p. 274.
2. Bradford Perkins, *Prologue to War: England and the United States, 1805–1812* (Berkeley, 1963), p. 277.

Monroe also hinted to Foster that England might withdraw its orders-in-council as the French had withdrawn its decrees in the duke of Cadore's letters—that is, in an equally ambiguous way—and the United States would withdraw the Nonimportation Act against British commerce.³ But Foster rejected this solid approach to common ground, maintaining a hard-line explanation that permitted the policing of neutral ships through a trade-licensing system that, in fact if not in theory, reduced the United States to a colonial dependency.⁴

On the eve of the convening of Congress in November 1811, called into extraordinary session one month early by the president to discuss "great and weighty matters,"⁵ the *National Intelligencer* predicted that further forbearance towards Great Britain would expose the country "to the imputation of pusillanimity."⁶ In his message to Congress, Madison stressed "my deep sense of the crisis in which you are assembled," reviewed the increasingly rigorous execution of the British orders-in-council, and denounced the attack by the *Little Belt*, "hovering on our coasts," which had once again led to bloodshed "in maintaining the honor of the American flag."

As for France, the president contrasted American justice and fairness, "both before and since the revocation of her decrees," with her failure to follow up that measure with other amicable steps "to repair other wrongs done to the United States." Napoleon had yet to restore American property seized and condemned under internal regulations that, "though not affecting our neutral relations, and therefore not entering into questions between the United States and other belligerents," nonetheless deserved prompt reparations.

Turning again to that other belligerent, he referred to the long-festering *Chesapeake* affair without mentioning it directly, noting that "the British cabinet perseveres not only in withholding a remedy of other wrongs, so long and so loudly calling for it, but in the execution, brought home to the threshold of our territory, of measures which under existing circumstances have the character as well as the effect of war on our lawful commerce." Madison cited these incidents as "evidence of hostile inflexibility in trampling on rights which no independent nation can relinquish" and concluded that the time had now arrived to put "the United States into an armor and an attitude demanded by the crisis."

To implement this major change in foreign policy, the president then recommended national defense measures that would extend enlistments in the regular army, raise an auxiliary force for a shorter term, create a volunteers

---

3. *Ibid.*, pp. 280–81.
4. A. L. Burt, *The United States, Great Britain, and British North America from the Revolution to the Establishment of Peace after the War of 1812* (New Haven, 1940), pp. 207–25.
5. JM's Presidential Proclamation, July 24, 1811, in Richardson, I, p. 491.
6. Brant, V, p. 355.

corps of "patriotic ardor," prepare the militia for service, develop military academies, and strengthen the navy.[7]

Madison's message went to a receptive Congress, the first to be elected since the repeal of the embargo. One-third of the members were new, the largest turnover since the founding of the federal government. The younger generation of Republicans, which included Henry Clay from Kentucky, John C. Calhoun from South Carolina, and Felix Grundy from Tennessee, were disenchanted with half measures in foreign policy. Clay, who had served briefly in the Senate, was elected Speaker on his first day in the House of Representatives because his views on war reflected the growing consensus in the new Congress. In the Senate, he had argued that unless Americans defend their rights, "we forfeit the respect of the world, and what is infinitely worse, of ourselves." If war came, it would be backed by "the combined energies of a free people . . . wreaking a noble and manful vengeance upon a foreign foe."

Shortly after Congress met, Indian warfare broke out in Indiana Territory. Madison had mentioned sending troops to the northwestern frontier to meet "menacing preparations" by Indians directed by "a fanatic of the Shawanese tribe." The Prophet was a brother of Tecumseh, a remarkable leader and organizer of western tribes being pressured by expanding frontier settlements. When Governor William Henry Harrison, who considered Tecumseh a British agent, marched troops to disperse Indians settled at Prophetstown, the battle of Tippecanoe erupted, the settlement was destroyed, and an uneasy peace was restored.[8]

News that the British were behind Tecumseh's confederacy swept from the West to the nation's capital, where British intrigue on the frontier was viewed as an inland insult to national sovereignty comparable to British injuries to American pride on the high seas. But Madison's message to the warhawk Congress was a plea for preparedness, not a war message, although one historian has said that it "fell upon the surface of a rising tide and was borne with it."[9] It also represented the first basic change in American foreign policy since Jefferson had launched the embargo. Madison believed that as long as the Perceval ministry followed its "mad policy" of rigorous enforcement of the orders, there was little or no chance of getting concessions strong enough to rationalize the continuation of American neutrality.[10]

Working with Monroe, who had won a belated but unanimous confir-

---

7. Richardson, I, pp. 491–97.

8. See Norman K. Risjord, *Jefferson's America, 1760–1815* (Madison, Wis., 1991), pp. 270–73, 281–82. J. C. A. Stagg, *Mr. Madison's War: Politics, Diplomacy, and Warfare in the Early American Republic, 1783–1830* (Princeton, 1983), pp. 177–87. There are two excellent studies of the Shawnee leaders by R. David Edmunds: *The Shawnee Prophet* (Lincoln, Neb., 1983) and *Tecumseh and the Quest for Indian Leadership* (Boston, 1984). See also Allan W. Eckert, *A Sorrow in Our Heart: The Life of Tecumseh* (New York, 1992).

9. Perkins, p. 299.

10. JM to TJ, Feb. 7, 1812, below. See also Stagg, pp. 78–80.

mation as secretary of state, the House Committee on Foreign Affairs, headed by John C. Calhoun, supported preparedness measures, including an addition of 10,000 regular army enlistments for three years, a volunteer force of 50,000, and an invasion of Canada, now the principal source of naval supplies following Napoleon's closing of the Baltic. The Senate jumped the additional regular army to 25,000 and increased the period of enlistment to five years, causing a deadlock between the two houses of Congress.

"With a view to enable the Executive to step at once into Canada," Madison informed Jefferson with more than a touch of sarcasm, Congress had finally broken the deadlock and "provided after two months delay, for a regular force requiring 12 to raise it, and after 3 months for a volunteer force, on terms not likely to raise it at all for that object.[11] The mixture of good and bad, avowed and disguised motives accounting for these things is curious eno'," he complained, "but not to be explained in the compass of a letter."[12]

Jefferson commiserated with his friend, confessing his doubts "whether, in case of a war, Congress would find it practicable to do their part of the business. That a body containing 100. lawyers in it, should direct the measures of a war, is, I fear, impossible; and that thus that member of our constitution, which is it's bulwark, will prove to be an impracticable one from it's cacoethes loquendi [mania for talking]." But as a suggestion, he proposed cloture: "It may be doubted how far it has the power, but I am sure it has not the resolution, to reduce the right of talking to practicable limits."[13]

The real congressional test came on taxation to support preparedness measures. Because of the Republican party's philosophical reluctance to tax and the Federalists' opposition to war with England, it was touch and go, as a Federalist senator observed, as to whether "the war [would] float the taxes or the taxes sink the war."[14] "You will see that Cong^s, or rather the H. of R^s, have got down the dose of taxes," Madison told Jefferson. "It is the strongest proof they could give that they do not mean to flinch from the contest to which the mad conduct of G. B. drives them."[15]

The adoption of the dose of taxes convinced Jefferson that war was now inevitable. "Every body in this quarter expects the declarance of war as soon as the season will permit the entrance of militia into Canada and altho' peace may

11. JM thought that a regular force of 10,000 enlisted for three years could be more quickly recruited than a force of 25,000 enlisted for five years, "a difficult thing in this country," as Monroe pointed out. He also wanted the volunteer army subject to federal authority; but the Senate, reflecting state fears of any measure threatening state control over the militia, amended the administration bill and authorized state governments to recruit the volunteers and commission their officers. Stagg, pp. 84-92, discusses the preparedness legislation.

12. JM to TJ, Feb. 7, 1812, below. As JM recalled late in life, "It was not the suddenness of war as an executive policy but the tardiness of the legislative provisions" that left the United States so poorly prepared for combat; see JM to Henry Wheaton, Feb. 26, 1827, cited in Stagg, p. 92.

13. TJ to JM, Feb. 19, 1812, below.

14. James A. Bayard of Delaware; see Stagg, p. 91.

15. JM to TJ, Mar. 6, 1812, below.

be their personal interest and wish they would, I think, disapprove of it's longer continuance under the wrongs inflicted and unredressed by England. God bless you," he concluded, "and send you a prosperous course through your difficulties."[16]

The road to war was downhill all the way after war taxes were approved. Late news from Great Britain corroborated the belief that the prince regent would retain Perceval's ministry, strengthened by the duke of Wellington's success in the Peninsular campaign in Spain and Portugal. "It appears that Percival, etc. are to retain their places," Madison wrote, "and that they prefer war with us, to a repeal of their Orders in Council. We have nothing left therefore, but to make ready for it. As a step to it," he emphasized, he had recommended an embargo for 60 days on April 1. It was "agreed to in the H. of Rep^s by about 70 to 40" on the same day, and on April 3 he reported that "the Embargo will pass the Senate to-day, and possibly with an extension of the period to 75 or 90 days."

Although the president viewed the move as "a rational and provident measure," he would have preferred that Congress had acted earlier, before the success of the Peninsular campaign had become clear, and had established the embargo "for a period of 3 or 4 months." In that case, "it might have enlisted an alarm of the B[ritish] Cabinet, for their Peninsular System on the side of Concessions to us; and w^d have shaken their obstinacy, if to be shaken at all." Instead, the later timing, plus "the successes on that Theatre," had riveted the hold of the ministry on the regent "and the hold of both on the vanity and prejudices of the Nation." Indeed, Madison thought that only reverses in Spain and Portugal would "cut up the Percival ascendency by the roots."[17]

The timing of the embargo, Jefferson thought, caught farmers and planters by surprise, but "they appear at present to receive the embargo with perfect acquiescence and without a murmur, seeing the necessity of taking care of our vessels and seamen. Yet," he informed the president, with an eye to the market, "they would be glad to dispose of their produce in any way not endangering them" or the nation. He even went so far as to suggest trading indirectly with the enemy "by letting it go from a neutral place in British vessels. In this way we lose the carriage only; but better that than both carriage and cargo."[18]

Madison had meant the embargo as a sixty-day prelude to war, allowing time for the USS *Hornet* to return home with the latest news from Europe. "You will have noticed," he wrote Jefferson, "that the Embargo as recommended to Cong^s was limited to 60 days. Its extension to 90 proceeded from the united votes of those who wished to make it a negotiating instead of a war measure, of those who wished to put off the day of war as long as possible, if ultimately to be met, and of those whose mercantile constituents had ships

16. TJ to JM, Mar. 26, 1812, below.
17. JM to TJ, Apr. 3, 1812, below.
18. TJ to JM, Apr. 17, 1812, below.

abroad, which would be favored in their chance of getting safely home. Some also who wished and hoped to anticipate the expiration of the terms, calculated on the ostensible postponement of the war question as a ruse agst the Enemy. At present great differences of opinion exist, as to the time and form of entering into hostilities; whether at a very early or later day, or not before the end of the 90 days, and whether by a general declaration, or by a commencement with letters of M[arque] and Reprisal." He understood that "the question is also to be brought forward for an adjournment for 15 or 18 days," presumably to allow congressmen to consult their constituents.[19]

There was to be no adjournment. Instead, Madison and Congress marked time, awaiting the return of the *Hornet,* which was held in France by Barlow, who hoped to send a commercial treaty he was negotiating.[20] From Monticello came news that each of the Virginia counties on which Jefferson had information had "furnished its quota of volunteers. Your declaration of war," he reported, "is expected with perfect calmness, and if those in the North mean systematically to govern the majority it is as good a time for trying them as we can expect."[21]

After the *Hornet* returned on May 22, Madison concluded that "the grounds of our complaints remain the same," with the British orders still in place. But he also told his friend that "France has done nothing towards adjusting our differences with her," making the business of declaring war "more than ever puzzling."[22] War with Great Britain was certain. But "to go to war with Eng^d and not with France arms the federalists with new matter, and divides the Republicans some of whom with the Quids make a display of impartiality. To go to war agst both, presents a thousand difficulties, above all, that of shutting all the ports of the Continent of Europe agst our Cruisers who can do little without the use of them. It is pretty certain also, that it would not gain over the Federalists, who w^d turn all those difficulties agst the administration." The only thing in favor of "this triangular war" was the long-shot chance that it might hasten Great Britain or France to settle existing controversies and make peace. But the opposite might happen, and "a prolongation of such a war might be viewed by both Bellig^{ts} as desirable, with as little reason for the opinion, as has prevailed in the past conduct of both."[23]

Although the president did not take the threat of a "triangular war" seriously, Jefferson was astounded that it was discussed at all. He concluded that it "must be the idea of the Anglomen and malcontents, in other words the federalists and quids. Yet it would reconcile neither. It would only change the

19. JM to TJ, Apr. 24, 1812, below.
20. For references to Barlow's delays, see *ibid.* and JM to TJ, May 25, 1812, below.
21. TJ to JM, May 25, 1812, below.
22. French frigates had recently burned two American merchantmen bound for Spain, which implied that France may not have repealed its decrees against neutrals; see Stagg, p. 99.
23. JM to TJ, May 25, 1812, below.

topic of abuse with the former, and not cure the mental disease of the latter." In fact, it "would exhibit a solecism worthy of Don Quixot[e] only, that of a choice to fight two enemies at a time, rather than to take them by succession."[24]

After a deputation of congressional Republicans met with the president, Speaker Henry Clay summarized their views succinctly: "As to France we have no complaint . . . but to the past. Of England we have to complain in all the tenses."[25] The administration newspaper, the *National Intelligencer,* asserted that England was the greater enemy and pointed out that the sixty-day embargo that Madison had sought was about to expire.[26] On June 1, precisely sixty days after he had recommended the embargo, the president sent his war message to Congress, citing five major grievances against Great Britain: impressment, Indian incitement, illegal or "pretended blockades," plundering at sea and in American territorial waters, and orders-in-council. These actions constituted "a series of acts hostile to the United States as an independent and neutral nation." In truth, these progressive usurpations amounted to an undeclared "state of war against the United States," which had maintained until now "a state of peace toward Great Britain." "Such is the spectacle of injuries and indignities which have been heaped on our country," Madison declared, "and such the crisis which its unexampled forbearance and conciliatory efforts have not been able to avert."[27]

Madison's message was a forceful indictment of British wrongs and a vigorous defense of neutral rights.[28] Meeting behind closed doors in executive session, thus barring all visitors including newspaper reporters, the House, under the leadership of Speaker Henry Clay and the war hawks, quickly voted for a declaration of war, 79 to 49, on June 4. Two days later, the *National Intelligencer* informed the public that "some measure of a decisive character has passed the House, and has been sent to the Senate for concurrence." But the faction-ridden Senate, also meeting in secret session, argued for two weeks, before adopting the declaration of war, 19 to 13, on June 18. It was not until June 20, however, that the *National Intelligencer* reported that "the veil is at length removed from the Secret Proceedings of Congress" and announced Madison's presidential proclamation declaring war.[29]

24. TJ to JM, May 30, 1812, below.
25. Marshall Smelser, *The Democratic Republic, 1801–1815* (New York, 1968), p. 223.
26. Stagg, p. 109.
27. Richardson, I, pp. 499–505. As Smelser, p. 219, has observed, "The causes of the War of 1812 have been argued ever since late 1811." For recent reviews, see Norman K. Risjord, "1812: Conservatives, War Hawks, and the Nation's Honor," *WMQ* 18 (1961): 196–210; Reginald Horsman, *The Causes of the War of 1812* (Philadelphia, 1962); Roger H. Brown, *The Republic in Peril: 1812* (New York, 1964); and Stagg, pp. 3–119.
28. Perkins, p. 405, and Horsman, pp. 260–61.
29. For the executive sessions of the House and Senate, see Robert Allen Rutland, *The Presidency of James Madison* (Lawrence, Kans., 1990), pp. 102–3. For the vote in the House, see Ronald L. Hatzenbuehler, "Party Unity and the Decision for War in the House of Representatives, 1812,"

The only republic in the world had finally been sucked into the great Anglo-French war, "the first genuine democracy," as Richard Rush pointed out, "engaged in a war since the ancients."[30] There was "no alternative left," John Quincy Adams wrote from his post as minister to Russia, "but war or the abandonment of our right as an independent nation." Or as Madison phrased it in his war message, what was at stake were "the rights, the interests, and the honor" of "a virtuous, a free, and a powerful nation."[31]

The declaration of war was Madison's ultimate response to the external and internal, the diplomatic and the political, problems that had plagued him and his administration ever since he had assumed office on March 4, 1809, swearing "to foster a spirit of independence too just to invade the rights of others, too proud to surrender our own, too liberal to indulge unworthy prejudices ourselves and too elevated not to look down upon them in others."

Jefferson viewed the war against Great Britain as the Second War for American Independence: "the second weaning from British principles, British attachments, British manners and manufactures will be salutary, and will form an epoch of the spirit of nationalism and of consequent prosperity, which would never have resulted from a continued subordination to the interests and influence of England."[32]

It is one of the ironies of history that as the administration and Congress moved towards war, the British moved towards suspending the orders-in-council. On the day after the declaration of war, Madison learned that Perceval had been assassinated in May and that mercantile interests in Britain had launched a campaign against the orders-in-council. In the cabinet reorganization, Baron Hawkesbury, now the earl of Liverpool, with whom Monroe had begun his negotiations in 1803–1804, succeeded Perceval, but Britain's economic problems and political reorganization pushed American affairs into the background briefly. When action came, however, it was bloated manufacturing inventories coupled with a continuing depression, more than American complaints, that finally led Viscount Castlereagh, who had succeeded Wellesley in the Foreign Office, to suspend the orders-in-council on June 23, less than a week after Congress declared war. The decision, which reached Washington in August, was not only too late, it was also too little, a temporary suspension of the orders that could be restored at any time circumstances permitted.[33]

WMQ 29 (1972): 367–90. For the Senate, see Leland R. Johnson, "The Suspense Was Hell: The Senate Vote for War in 1812," *Indiana Magazine of History* 65 (1969): 247–67.

30. Ketcham, p. 530.

31. John Quincy Adams to John Adams, July 13, 1812, cited in Smelser, p. 225, and Richardson, I, p. 505. The best discussion of this theme is in Brown (n. 27, above).

32. Peterson, p. 932.

33. The best discussion of the repeal of the orders is Perkins, pp. 300–41. For JM's reaction, see JM to TJ, Aug. 17, 1812, below.

Madison signed the war declaration on June 18 and called on all Americans to unite in the war effort. But every Federalist in the House and Senate had voted against war, and Madison predicted that their congressional delegation would "put all the strength of their talents into a protest against the war, and that the party at large are to be brought out in all their force."[34] Jefferson assured the president that the war "is entirely popular here," the only adverse opinion being that the declaration "should have been issued the moment the season admitted the militia to enter Canada." But he confessed that even in Virginia the Federalists were "open mouthed against the declaration," adding that "they are poor devils here, not worthy of notice." Nonetheless, he had a ready remedy to propose: "A barrel of tar to each state South of the Potomac will keep all in order, and that will be freely contributed without troubling government" with naval shortages. As for New England Federalists, "they will give you more trouble," which might call for more draconian measures: "You may there have to apply the rougher drastics of Govr Wright, hemp and confiscation."[35]

To keep the war popular required two policies, according to Jefferson: "1. to stop Indian barbarities. The conquest of Canada will do this. 2. to furnish markets for our produce," which would involve ingenious ways for "carrying our produce to foreign markets." In addition to using "our own ships, [and] neutral ships," Jefferson was willing to consider, if necessary, the use of "even enemy ships under neutral flags, which I would wink at."[36]

Running true to form, the Federalists in Congress issued a minority report, defending their votes against the war, repeating British arguments on neutral rights, and calling for opposition to the prosecution of the war by all means short of forcible opposition. When General Dearborn requested the governors of the New England states to mobilize their militias, the Republican governors of Vermont and New Hampshire complied, but the Federalist governors of Massachusetts, Rhode Island, and Connecticut refused.[37] Less than a month after the declaration of war, former Senator Timothy Pickering of Massachusetts, who as secretary of state during the quasi war with France had rigorously enforced the Sedition Act against Republican critics, declared that there was no longer any "magic in the sound of Union. If the great objects of union are utterly abandoned—much more if they are wantonly, corruptly, and treacherously sacrificed by the Southern and Western States—let the Union be severed."[38]

---

34. JM to TJ, June 22, 1812, below. See Lawrence D. Cress, "'Cool and Serious Reflection': Federalist Attitudes toward War in 1812," *JER* 7 (1987): 123–45.

35. TJ to JM, June 29, 1812, below. This portion of TJ's letter was omitted from Ford, IX, pp. 364–65.

36. *Ibid.*

37. Ketcham, p. 537, and Stagg, pp. 257–61.

38. Timothy Pickering to E. Pennington, July 12, 1812, cited in Ketcham, p. 537. For a discussion of Federalist opposition, see Samuel Eliot Morison, in *Dissent in Three American Wars,* ed. Samuel Eliot Morison, Frederick Merk, and Frank Freidel (Cambridge, Mass., 1970), pp. 1–14.

The campaign against Canada, particularly the move towards Montreal, was thwarted by "the seditious opposition in Mass and Con[necticu]t," Madison complained to Jefferson in August. Federalist foot dragging, coupled "with the intrigues elsewhere insidiously co-operating with it, have so clogged the wheels of the war that I fear the campaign will not accomplish the object of it. With the most united efforts, in stimulating volunteers," he explained, "they would have probably fallen much short of the number required by the deficiency of regular enlistments. But under the discouragements substituted, and the little attraction contained in the volunteer Act, the two classes together, leave us dependent for every primary operation, on militia, either as volunteers or draughts for six months."[39]

Nature dictated that the military theaters for the Canadian campaign would be Lake Erie, Lake Ontario, and the Montreal/Lake Champlain valleys. "It would probably have been best, if it had been practicable in time," Madison told his predecessor, "to have concentrated a force which could have seized on Montreal, and thus at one stroke, have secured the upper Province, and cut off the sap that nourished Indian hostilities." But General Henry Dearborn, who had been Jefferson's secretary of war, could not rally enough troops in New England to raise such a force.

Instead, when Governor-General George Prevost sent word to Dearborn that the repeal of the orders-in-council was a prelude to peace, Dearborn agreed to a temporary truce on the New York frontier, hoping to beef up his army for a belated strike after the armistice terminated. Madison had insuperable objections to the truce and promptly ended it, knowing that a quick strike at Montreal would force the British to concentrate all their power in the East and allow western troops to invade Canada from Detroit and make a triumphal sweep north of Lake Erie to Niagara "for the purpose of occupying the central part of Upper Canada. In the mean time," Madison continued, "the preparations agst Montreal are going on, and perhaps may furnish a feint towards it, that may conspire with the other plan." The war spirit of the West stood in sharp contrast with the obstructionism of New England, particularly "the unanimity and ardor of Kentucky and Ohio, [which] promised the requisite force at once for that service, whilst it was too distant from the other points to be assailed."[40]

While Dearborn dallied at Albany, however, General Isaac Brock rallied his troops on the Canadian side of the Niagara frontier, moved them across Lake Erie quickly, and trapped General William Hull and his army at Detroit, making Hull's position, as Madison observed in a classic understatement, "very ineligible." After Hull surrendered his army without firing a shot, the British established a firm hold on the northern part of the Old Northwest, assuring that the Indians, as Madison lamented, "w^{d} continue to be active agst our frontiers." Knowing that the command of the Great Lakes was of funda-

39. JM to TJ, Aug. 17, 1812, below.
40. *Ibid.*

mental importance, he told Jefferson that "nothing but triumphant operations on the Theatre, which forms their connection with the Enemy, will controul their bloody inroads."[41]

Hull's surrender created a military crisis in the West, and Madison appointed William Henry Harrison, governor of Indiana Territory and the victor at Tippecanoe, the new commanding general for the district. "Our best hopes for the campaign rest on Harrison," he told Jefferson, "and if no disaster, always to be feared from Indian combats, befall him, there is a probability that he will regain Detroit, and perhaps do more. He has a force of 8 or 10,000 men at least, enthusiastically confiding in him, and a prospect of adequate supplies of every sort, unless it be Cannon, which tho' on the way, may possibly encounter fatal delays. This article however he appears not to make a sine qua non; nor will it be needed for Detroit, if it be true as is reported that every piece has been withdrawn by the British."[42] After relieving tiny Fort Wayne, which was besieged by "about 300 British troops with some field pieces and a body of Indians stated at 2000 or 2500," Harrison devised a fortified frontier in northern Ohio. As the year ended, however, the British held the northwestern half of the Old Northwest on a line running from St. Louis to Sandusky.[43]

To replace Dearborn's move against Montreal, an invasion of the Niagara peninsula had been scheduled to keep British troops nailed down, thus easing Hull's work in the West. But American troops were slow to assemble due to the absence of New England forces, which allowed Brock to dash to Detroit and defeat Hull. By the end of Dearborn's truce, Brock was back east and ready to defend the Niagara frontier. When Stephen Van Rensselaer launched the invasion with army regulars at Queenston, the New York militia refused to cross the state boundary to support them, and the British won an easy victory, which saved Upper Canada. In the fierce fighting, however, they lost the brave Brock, who was succeeded by Sir Gordon Drummond. Late in the year, Dearborn finally moved up Lake Champlain towards Montreal, but when he discovered that his militia would not cross the state line, he marched back to winter quarters at Plattsburgh.

The whole American campaign in 1812 had been a dismal disaster. "The seeing whether our untried Generals will stand proof is a very dear operation," Jefferson wrote in a sympathetic letter to Madison. In the barnyard, wrote the Albemarle farmer, "we can tell by his plumage whether a cock is dunghill or game." But in picking generals, "cowardice and courage wear the same plume." "Two of them have cost us a great many men.... Hull will of course be shot for cowardice and treachery. And will not Van Renslaer be broke for

---

41. *Ibid.* See also Robert S. Allen, "His Majesty's Indian Allies: Native Peoples, the British Crown and the War of 1812," *Michigan Historical Review* 14 (1988): 1–24.

42. JM to TJ, Oct. 14, 1812, below.

43. The best brief account of the war is Harry L. Coles, *The War of 1812* (Chicago, 1965). See also John R. Elting, *Amateurs, to Arms!: A Military History of the War of 1812* (Chapel Hill, 1991), and Donald R. Hickey, *The War of 1812: A Forgotten Conflict* (Urbana, 1989).

cowardice and incapacity?"[44] Jefferson thought that "Dearborne and Harrison have both courage and understanding, and having no longer a Brock to encounter, I hope we shall ere long hear something good from them. If we could but get Canada to Trois rivieres in our hands we should have a set off against spoliations to be treated of, and in the mean time separate the Indians from them and set the friendly to attack the hostile part with our aid."[45]

In 1812, the abortive army record was offset in part by the accomplishments of the small American navy. The *Constitution,* under the command of Captain Isaac Hull, nephew of the general, sank the *Guerrière* in August; the *United States,* under Captain Stephen Decatur, took the *Macedonian;* and the *Constitution,* this time under Captain William Bainbridge, battered and burned the *Java* in December. In addition to their brilliant record against the Royal Navy, a navy fleet of five ships under Captain John Rodgers captured eight merchantmen in a transatlantic cruise.

In the midst of the Canadian and sea campaigns, Madison faced a presidential campaign in 1812, this time teamed with Elbridge Gerry of Massachusetts, replacing Vice President George Clinton, who had died in May.[46] The Federalists, realizing that no antiwar regular could win, turned to Clinton's nephew, DeWitt Clinton, as a dissident Republican who differed from Madison enough to win their votes.[47]

"The current Elections," Madison informed Jefferson, "bring the popularity of the War or of the Administration, or both, to the Experimentum crucis. In this State [Maryland] the issue is not favorable, tho' less otherwise than would appear. In the Congressional Districts the Republicans I believe, have not lost ground at all, notwithstanding the auxiliaries to federalism. In the State Legislature, they will be in a minority on a joint vote. Penn^a, altho' admitted to be shaken, is represented to be safe. New Jersey is doubtful at least. The same is the case with New Hampshire. North Carolina is also reported to be in considerable vibration. The other States," he reported laconically, "remain pretty decided on one hand or on the other."[48] Clinton won all of New England, except Vermont, along with New York and New Jersey, plus 5 out of 11 votes in Maryland. Madison won the rest, including shaky Pennsylvania and vibrating North Carolina, receiving 128 electoral votes to Clinton's 89.

---

44. After he was exchanged as a prisoner of war, Hull was court-martialed and condemned to death, but JM pardoned him; see Milo Quaife, "General William Hull and His Critics," *Ohio Archeological and Historical Quarterly* 47 (1938): 168–82. Van Rensselaer's resignation was promptly accepted.

45. TJ to JM, Nov. 6, 1812, below.

46. See George A. Billias, *Elbridge Gerry: Founding Father and Republican Statesman* (New York, 1976).

47. The best account of the Young Federalist movement is David Hackett Fisher, *The Revolution of American Conservatism: The Federalist Party in the Era of Jeffersonian Democracy* (New York, 1965).

48. JM to TJ, Oct. 14, 1812, below.

Throughout the military and political campaigns of 1812, the president retained his sly sense of humor. "You will be amused," he predicted to Jefferson, "with the little work of the Author of several humorous publications," wrongly attributing James Kirke Paulding's *The Diverting History of John Bull and Brother Jonathan* to Washington Irving. "It sinks occasionally into low and local phrases, and some times forgets Allegorical character," wrote the presidential critic. "But [it] is in general good painting on substantial Canvas."[49]

―――――――――― THE LETTERS ――――――――――

Jefferson to Madison

Monticello Dec. 31, 1811

It is long since I have had occasion to address a line to you, and the present is an irksome one. With all the discouragements I can oppose to those who wish to make me the channel of their wishes for office, some will force themselves on me. I inclose you the letters of several merely to be placed on the file of candidates and to stand on their own ground, for I do not know one of them personally. Gerna indeed, the recommender of Arata, I once saw at Paris. He was a bookseller from Dublin, and I got him to send me some books from thence, and that is all I know of him. Le Compte Desprinville I never saw nor heard of before; nor have I ever seen de Neufville his recommender, but he wrote me a letter of introduction from the Countess d'Houdeton, an old lady from whom I recieved many civilities and much hospitality while in France. She was the intimate friend of Dr. Franklin, and I should feel myself obliged to render any civilities or personal services in my power to one of her recommendation. De la Croix I never saw. But he is a very able military man as far as I can judge from many excellent pamphlets and essays in the newspapers written by him, and Genl. Dearborne thought him a valuable man. I write to him and to de Neufville that they must send certificates of character to the Secretary at war, and I pray you to consider me only as the postrider bearing their letters to you.[1]

The prospect of the death of George III. still keeps up a hope of avoiding war. We have had a bad fall for our wheat. I never saw it look worse. We have had but ¾ I. of rain in the last 8. weeks. Your message had all the qualities it should possess, firm, rational and dignified, and the report of the commee of

---

49. *Ibid.*

1. Anthony Gerna was a bookseller in Dublin; see *PTJ*, XIII, p. 177. Jean de Neufville was a merchant in Amsterdam who later moved to Charleston, South Carolina; see *ibid.*, III, p. 91, X, p. 588, and XVII, p. 598. Jacques Vincent De la Croix served as a friendly courier for TJ's letters while TJ was in France; see *ibid.*, IX, pp. 444, 452, 499, 554. Arata and Count Despineville are not mentioned in TJ's earlier letters.

foreign relations was excellent. They carry conviction to every mind. Heaven help you through all your difficulties.

TH: JEFFERSON

Madison to Jefferson

Washington Feb. 7, 1812

DEAR SIR

I have rec^d several letters from you which not requiring special answers, I now beg leave to acknowledge in the lump. I have delayed it in the hope that I might add something on our public affairs not uninteresting. If there be any thing at present of this character it will be found in the inclosed paper from N. York. We have no late official information from Europe; but all that we see from G. B. indicates an adherence to her mad policy towards the U. S. The Newspapers give you a sufficient insight into the measures of Congress. With a view to enable the Executive to step at once into Canada they have provided after two months delay, for a regular force requiring 12 to raise it, and after 3 months for a volunteer force, on terms not likely to raise it at all for that object.[2] The mixture of good and bad, avowed and disguised motives accounting for these things is curious eno' but not to be explained in the compass of a letter. Among other jobbs on my hands is the case of Wilkinson. His defence fills 6 or 700 pages of the most collossal paper. The minutes of the Court, oral written and printed testimony, are all in proportion. A month has not yet carried me thro' the whole.[3]

We have had of late a hard winter and much Ice which still lies on the water in view. The reiteration of Earthquakes continues to be reported from various quarters. They have slightly reached the State of N. Y. and been severely felt W. and S. Westwardly. There was one here this morning at 5 or 6 minutes after 4 o'C. It was rather stronger than any preceding one, and lasted several minutes; with sensible tho' very slight repetitions throughout the succeeding hour.[4] Be assured of my best affections.

JAMES MADISON

2. For the war legislation, see Stagg, pp. 144-55.

3. For the court-martial of the general for being a pensioner of Spain and engaging in treasonable projects to dismember the United States, see James R. Jacobs, *Tarnished Warrior: Major General James Wilkinson* (New York, 1938), p. 274. Wilkinson was acquitted because there was not sufficient evidence to convict. JM approved the finding and returned Wilkinson's sword on Feb. 14, 1812, although he noted "with regret, that there are instances in the conduct ... of the officer on trial, which are evidently and justly objectionable." Rutland, p. 59, called JM's handling of the Wilkinson case "damaging to his presidency and ... probably the worst mistake he made while in the White House."

4. From Dec. 1811 through Feb. 1812, there were three major earthquakes in the area of New Madrid, Missouri. The one of Feb. 7 was the most severe, the quake and its largest aftershocks felt as far away as Washington and Quebec; see James Lal Penick, Jr., *The New Madrid Earthquakes* (Columbia, Mo., 1981).

Jefferson to Madison

Monticello Feb. 19, 1812

DEAR SIR,

Yours of the 12th. has been duly recieved. I have much doubted whether, in case of a war, Congress would find it practicable to do their part of the business. That a body containing 100. lawyers in it, should direct the measures of a war, is, I fear, impossible; and that thus that member of our constitution, which is it's bulwark, will prove to be an impracticable one from it's cacoethes loquendi. It may be doubted how far it has the power, but I am sure it has not the resolution, to reduce the right of talking to practicable limits.

I inclose you a letter from Foronda. You may be willing to see what part he takes in the proceedings in Spain. If you have time and inclination to read his folletos, papelles, and papelitos, I will send them to you. I have not yet looked into them.

Altho' I reject many applications to communicate petitions for office, yet some lay hold of the heart, or from other circumstances cannot be declined. But in the crowd of military appointments perhaps there may be less objection to communicate them. The inclosed letter from old Doctr. Gantt is one of these cases. You knew him personally and his merit. His letter will inform you of his misfortunes and his virtuous anxieties for his family. As I can add nothing to your knolege of his case and the information of the letter, I shall leave his application on these grounds and conclude with the tribute of my constant affection and respect

TH: JEFFERSON

Madison to Jefferson

Washington Mar. 6, 1812

DEAR SIR,

I return the letter from Foronda inclosed in yours of the 19^r Feby I find I shall not be able to read his lucubrations in print. The letter from Dr. Guantt is in the hands of the Sec^y of war, and will not be unheeded; but the course the nominations have taken makes it doubtful whether the wishes in behalf of his son can be fulfilled.

You will see that Cong^s, or rather the H. of R^s, have got down the dose of taxes.[5] It is the strongest proof they could give that they do not mean to flinch from the contest to which the mad conduct of G. B. drives them. Her perseverance in this seems to be sufficiently attested by the language of Ld Liverpoole and Mr. Perceval in their parliamentary comments on the Regent's

---

5. For resolutions approving taxes on items such as stills, bank notes, and carriages but postponing all new taxes and duties until after war had been declared, see Stagg, pp. 151–52.

message.⁶ The information from F. is pretty justly described in the paragraph inserted in the Nat!̲ Intelligencer after the arrival of the Constitution. The prints herewith inclosed are forwarded to you at the request of Thom^s Gimbrede, (of N. York,) the author. Be assured of my great and affectionate esteem.

JAMES MADISON

Jefferson to Madison

Monticello Mar. 8, 1812

DEAR SIR

On my return from a journey of 5 weeks to Bedford I found here the two letters now inclosed, which tho' directed to me, belong in their matter to you. I never before heard of either writer and therefore leave them to stand on their own ground.

I congratulate you on the close of your campaign. Altho it has not conquered your difficulties, it leaves you more at leisure to consider and provide against them. Our only chance as to England is the accession of the Prince of Wales to the throne. If only to the regency, himself and his ministers may be less bold and strong to make a thorough change of system. It will leave them too a pretext for doing less than right if so disposed. He has much more understanding and good humor than principle or application. But it seems difficult to understand what Bonaparte means towards us. I have been in hopes the consultations with closed doors were for the possession of E. Florida. It would give no more offence any where than taking the Western province, and I am much afraid the Percival ministry may have given orders for taking possession of it before they were out of power.

We have had a wretched winter for the farmer. Great consumption of food by the cattle and little weather for preparing the ensuing crop. During my stay at Bedford we had seven snows. That of Feb. 22. which was of 15. I. about Richmond was of 6 I. here, and only 3½ in Bedford. Ever affectionately yours

Madison to Jefferson

[Washington] Mar. 9, 1812

DEAR SIR,

As the Intelligencer will not publish the Message and documents just laid before Congress for the present mail, I send you a copy of the former. It is justified by the Documents, among which are the original credential and in-

---

6. William Pinkney became so discouraged that he resigned as minister to England and left for the United States at the end of Feb.; see Perkins, pp. 310–11.

structions from the Governor of Canada, and an original dispatch from the Earl of Liverpool to him approving the conduct of the secret agent. This discovery, or rather formal proof, of the cooperation between the Eastern Junto and the British Cabinet will, it is to be hoped, not only prevent future evils from that source, but extract good out of the past.[7]

Jefferson to Madison

Monticello Mar. 26, 1812

DEAR SIR

Your favor of the 6th. was recieved. The double treachery of Henry will do lasting good both here and in England. It prostrates the party here, and will prove to the people of England, beyond the power of palliation by the ministry, that the war is caused by the wrongs of their own nation.

The case of the Batture having been explained by a trial at bar as had been expected I have thought it necessary to do it by publishing what I had prepared for the use of my counsel.[8] This has been done at New York, and the printer informs me by a letter of the 21st. that he had forwarded by mail some copies to myself, and would send by the stage, under the care of a passenger those I had ordered for the members of both houses. But those sent to me are not yet arrived. From this parcel I shall send some to yourself and the members of the Cabinet, which I have thought it necessary to mention in anticipation that you may understand how it happens, if it does happen, that others get copies before yourself.

Every body in this quarter expects the declarance of war as soon as the season will permit the entrance of militia into Canada and altho' peace may be their personal interest and wish they would, I think, disapprove of it's longer continuance under the wrongs inflicted and unredressed by England. God bless you and send you a prosperous course through your difficulties

TH JEFFERSON

P. S. I had reason to expect that M Destutt Tracy, had, by the last vessel from France sent me some works of his thro' Mr Warden, and he thro' yourself.[9]

---

7. JM transmitted the John Henry letters, which revealed that Henry had been sent as a secret agent into the United States during the embargo crisis of 1808–9 by Sir James Craig, governor of Lower Canada, to evaluate the prospects for the secession of the New England states; see Brant, V, pp. 412–20, and Stagg, pp. 93–98. For detailed discussions, see Samuel Eliot Morison, "The Henry-Crillon Affair of 1812," *Massachusetts Historical Society Proceedings* 69 (1950): 207–31, and E. A. Cruikshank, *The Political Adventures of John Henry: The Record of an International Imbroglio* (Toronto, 1936).

8. The pamphlet was entitled *The Proceedings of the Government of the United States, in Maintaining the Public Right to the Beach of the Mississippi, Adjacent to New Orleans, Against the Intrusion of Edward Livingston* (New York, 1812).

9. TJ had arranged for the publication of A.-L.-C. Destutt de Tracy's *Commentary and Review of Montesquieu's Spirit of Laws* (Philadelphia, 1811). The manuscript that he was expecting, *A Treatise*

Madison to Jefferson

Washington Apr. 3, 1812

DEAR SIR,

I have rec^d your favor of the 26th, and have made to the members of the Cabinet the communication you suggest with respect to your printed Memoir on the Batture. I learn from the Department of State that some books were rec^d for you, and duly forwarded. What they were was not ascertained or remembered. If they do not on their arrival correspond with your expectation, let me know, and further enquiry will be made. Meantime there is in my possession, a very large packet, addressed to you, which is probably a Continuation of Humboldts draughts, or other Maps. It was accompanied by no letter to me, and being unfit for the mail, waits for the patronage of some trusty traveller, bound in the stage towards Monticello. A late arrival from G. B. brings dates subsequent to the maturity of the Prince Regent's authority. It appears that Percival, etc. are to retain their places, and that they prefer war with us, to a repeal of their Orders in Council. We have nothing left therefore, but to make ready for it. As a step to it an embargo for 60 days was recommended to Cong^s on Wednesday and agreed to in the H. of Rep^s by about 70 to 40. The Bill was before the Senate yesterday, who adjourned about 4 or 5 o'Clock without a decision. Whether this result was produced by the rule which arms a single member with a veto agst a decision in one day on a bill, or foretells a rejection of the Bill I have not yet heard. The temper of that body is known to be equivocal. Such a measure, even for a limited and short time, is always liable to adverse as well as favorable considerations; and its operations at this moment, will add fuel to party discontent, and interested clamor. But it is a rational and provident measure, and will be relished by a greater portion of the Nation, than an omission of it. If it could have been taken sooner and for a period of 3 or 4 months, it might have enlisted an alarm of the B. Cabinet, for their Peninsular System on the side of Concessions to us; and w^d have shaken their obstinacy, if to be shaken at all; the successes on that Theatre being evidently their hold on the P. Reg^t and the hold of both on the vanity and prejudices of the Nation. Whether if adopted for 60 days, it may beget apprehensions of a protraction, and thence lead to admissible overtures, before the sword is stained with blood, cannot be foreknown with certainty. Such an effect is not to be counted upon. You will observe that Liverpool was Sec^y for the Foreign Dep^t ad interim, and that Castlereagh is the definitive successor of Wellesley.[10] The resignation of this last, who has rec^d no other app^t is a little mysterious. There is some reason for believing that he is at variance with

---

on Political Economy, arrived later in 1812. He revised the translation, wrote an introduction, and arranged for its publication in 1818; see Malone, VI, pp. 207–10, 305–8.

10. On the day before, the *National Intelligencer* had described Castlereagh as a "decided enemy" of the United States; see Stagg, p. 97.

Percival, or that he distrusts the stability of the existing Cabinet, and courts an alliance with the Grenville party, as likely to overset it. If none of that party desert their colours, the calculation cannot be a very bad one; especially in case of war with the U. S., in addition to the distress of Br trade and manufactures, and the inflammation in Ireland, to say nothing of possible reverses in Spain and Portugal, which alone would cut up the Percival ascendency by the roots. From France we hear nothing. The delay of the Hornet is inexplicable, but on the reproachful supposition that the F. Gov.^t is waiting for the final turn of things at London, before it takes its course, which justice alone ought to prescribe towards us. If this be found to be its game, it will impair the value of concessions if made, and give to a refusal of them, consequences it may little dream of. Be assured of my constant and sincerest attachment.

I understand the Embargo will pass the Senate to-day, and possibly with an extension of the period to 75 or 90 days.[11]

Jefferson to Madison

Monticello Apr. 17, 1812

DEAR SIR,

The inclosed papers will explain themselves. Their coming to me is the only thing not sufficiently explained.

Your favor of the 3d. came duly to hand. Although something of the kind had been apprehended, the embargo found the farmers and planters only getting their produce to market and selling as fast as they could get it there. I think it caught them in this part of the State with one-third of their flour or wheat, and ¾ of their tobacco undisposed of. If we may suppose the rest of the middle country in the same situation, and that the upper and lower country may be judged by that as a mean, these will perhaps be the proportions of produce remaining in the hands of the producers. Supposing the objects of the government were merely to keep our vessels and men out of harm's way, and that there is no idea that the want of our flour will starve Great Britain, the sale of the remaining produce will be rather desirable, and what would be desired even in war, and even to our enemies. For I am favorable to the opinion which has been urged by others, sometimes acted on, and now partly so by France and Great Britain, that commerce under certain restrictions and licences may be indulged between enemies, mutually advantageous to the individuals, and not to their injury as belligerents. The capitulation of Amelia Island, if confirmed, might favor this object, and at any rate get off our produce now on hand.[12] I think a people would go thro' a war with much less impatience if they

---

11. The Senate extended the embargo to 90 days, or until July 4, 1812; see *ibid.*, p. 102.

12. General George Mathews had seized Amelia Island in East Florida; see Brant, V, pp. 442–45, and Stagg, pp. 98–99.

could dispose of their produce, and that unless a vent can be provided for them, they will soon become querulous and clamor for peace. They appear at present to receive the embargo with perfect aquiescence and without a murmur, seeing the necessity of taking care of our vessels and seamen. Yet they would be glad to dispose of their produce in any way not endangering them, as by letting it go from a neutral place in British vessels. In this way we lose the carriage only; but better that than both carriage and cargo. The rising of the price of flour, since the first panic is passed away, indicates some prospects in the merchants of disposing of it.

Our wheat had greatly suffered by the winter, but is as remarkably recovered by the favorable weather of the spring. Ever affectionately yours.

Th. Jefferson

Madison to Jefferson

Washington Apr. 24, 1812

Dear Sir,

I have just rec^d your favor of the 17th. The same mail brings me the "Proceedings of the Gov^t of the U. S. relative to the Batture," for which you will accept my thanks.

I had not supposed that so great a proportion of produce, particularly of Wheat and flour, was still in the hands of the farmers. In Penn^a it was known to be the case. In N. Y. almost the whole of the last crop, is in the Country, though chiefly in the hands of the merchants and millers. The measure of the Embargo was made a difficult one, both as to its duration and its date, by the conflict of opinions here, and of local interests elsewhere; and to these causes are to be added, that invariable opposition, open with some and covert with others, which have perplexed and impeded the whole course of our public measures. You will have noticed that the Embargo as recommended to Cong^s was limited to 60 days. Its extension to 90 proceeded from the united votes of those who wished to make it a negotiating instead of a war measure, of those who wished to put off the day of war as long as possible, if ultimately to be met, and of those whose mercantile constituents had ships abroad, which would be favored in their chance of getting safely home. Some also who wished and hoped to anticipate the expiration of the terms, calculated on the ostensible postponement of the war question as a ruse agst the Enemy. At present great differences of opinion exist, as to the time and form of entering into hostilities; whether at a very early or later day, or not before the end of the 90 days, and whether by a general declaration, or by a commencement with letters of M. and Reprisal. The question is also to be brought forward for an adjournment for 15 or 18 days.[13] Whatever may be the decision on all these

13. The Senate twice voted for a recess, but the House rejected the idea; see Brant, V, pp. 441–42.

points, it can scarcely be doubted that patience in the holders of Wheat and flour at least, will secure them good prices. Such is the scarcity all over Europe, and the dependence of the W. Indies on our supplies. Mr. Maury writes me, on the 21st of March, that flour had suddenly risen to 16½ dollars, and a further rise looked for. And it is foreseen, that in a State of War, the Spanish and Portuguese flags and papers real or counterfeit, will afford a neutral cover to our produce as far as wanted, in ports in the favor of G. B. Licences therefore on our part will not be necessary; which tho' in some respects mitigating the evils of war, are so pregnant with abuses of the worst sort, as to be liable in others to strong objections. As managed by the belligerents of Europe they are sources of the most iniquitous and detestable practices.

The Hornet still loiters. A letter from Barlow to Granger, fills us with serious apprehensions, that he is burning his fingers with matters which will work great embarrassment and mischief here; and which his instructions could not have suggested.[14] In E. Florida, Mathews has been playing a tragi-comedy, in the face of common sense, as well as of his instructions. His extravagances place us in the most distressing dilemma.[15] Always and affe.^y Yrs.

JAMES MADISON

Jefferson to Madison

Monticello May 2, 1812

DEAR SIR

It is a grievous thing to be pressed, as I am, into the service of those who want to get into service themselves. The great mass of those sollicitations I decline: but some come forward on such grounds as controul compliance. Mr Archibald C. Randolph, an applicant for command in the new army, is my near relation, which in his own eye and that of our common friends gives him a claim to my good offices; while in mine, and that of the world it adds not an iota to his fitness for public service. I have given him a letter to the Secretary at War, in which I have taken care to say nothing but the truth. I have specifically stated the qualities he possesses favorable to his views; but no inference of qualities not specified must be drawn: and that this caveat, which I confide to

---

14. Although he had no instructions to do so, Barlow tried to negotiate a commercial treaty with France; see *ibid.*, pp. 406–9, and Stagg, pp. 104–5.
15. JM disavowed General Mathews's seizure of Amelia Island in East Florida; see Rembert W. Patrick, *Florida Fiasco: Rampant Rebels on the Georgia-Florida Border, 1810–1815* (Athens, Ga., 1954), pp. 120–22. His instructions were to take possession if the Spanish governor decided to relinquish control. If either Great Britain or France tried to take possession, he was to occupy the territory. For a careful analysis of JM's "dilemma," see Abraham D. Sofaer, *War, Foreign Affairs and Constitutional Power: The Origins* (Cambridge, Mass., 1976), pp. 303–26.

yourself alone, may not operate further than would be just, I am bound to say that I know of but two points in his character adverse to his wishes: the one that he is a zealous federalist, and as such may be prone to feel and foster the grievances founded and fancied which keep an army always uneasy; the other that he is quarrelsome and may be troublesome to his companions. The army is indeed the school to correct this last propensity, but the correction may cost us the life of a good man. God bless you and give you a happy issue out of all your trials which I know to be severe.

TH JEFFERSON

Jefferson to Madison

Monticello May 25, 1812

DEAR SIR,

The difference between a communication and solicitation is too obvious to need suggestion. While the latter adds to embarrassments, the former only enlarges the field of choice. The inclosed letters are merely communications. Of Stewart I know nothing. Price who recommends him is I believe a good man, not otherwise known to me than as a partner of B. Morgan of N. O. and as having several times communicated to me useful information, while I was in the government. Timothy Matlack I have known well since the first Congress to which he was an assistant secretary. He has been always a good whig, and being an active one has been abused by his opponents, but I have ever thought him an honest man. I think he must be known to yourself.

Flour, depressed under the first panic of the embargo has been rising by degrees to $8\frac{1}{2}$ D. This enables the upper country to get theirs to a good market. Tobacco (except of favorite qualities) is nothing. It's culture is very much abandoned. In this county what little ground had been destined for it is mostly put into corn. Crops of wheat are become very promising, altho' deluged with rain, of which 10. Inches fell in 10. days, and closed with a very destructive hail. I am just returned from Bedford. I believe every county South of James river, from Buckingham to the Blue ridge (the limits of my information) furnished its quota of volunteers. Your declaration of war is expected with perfect calmness, and if those in the North mean systematically to govern the majority it is as good a time for trying them as we can expect. Affectionately adieu.

TH. JEFFERSON

Madison to Jefferson

Washington May 25, 1812

Dear Sir,

The inclosed letters came under cover to me, by the Hornet. France has done nothing towards adjusting our differences with her. It is understood that the B. and M. Decrees are not in force agst the U. S. and no contravention of them can be established agst her. On the contrary positive cases rebut the allegation. Still the manner of the F. Gov^{t}. betrays the design of leaving G. B. a pretext for enforcing her O. in C. And in all other respects, the grounds of our complaints remain the same. The utmost address has been played off on Mr. Barlow's wishes and hopes; inasmuch that at the Departure of the Hornet which had been so long detained for a final answer, without its being obtained, he looked to the return of the Wasp which had just arrived, without despair of making her the Bearer of some satisfactory arrangement. Our calculations differ widely. In the mean time, the business is become more than ever puzzling. To go to war with Eng^{d} and not with France arms the federalists with new matter, and divides the Republicans some of whom with the Quids make a display of impartiality. To go to war agst both, presents a thousand difficulties, above all, that of shutting all the ports of the Continent of Europe agst our Cruisers who can do little without the use of them. It is pretty certain also, that it would not gain over the Federalists, who w^{d} turn all those difficulties agst the administration. The only consideration of weight in favor of this triangular war as it is called, is that it might hasten thro' a peace with G. B. or F. a termination, for a while at least, of the obstinate questions now depending with both.[16]

But even this advantage is not certain. For a prolongation of such a war might be viewed by both Bellig^{ts} as desirable, with as little reason for the opinion, as has prevailed in the past conduct of both. Affectionate respects

JAMES MADISON

Jefferson to Madison

Monticello May 30, 1812

Dear Sir,

Another *communication* is enclosed, and the letter of the applicant is the only information I have of his qualifications. I barely remember such a person as the secretary of Mr. Adams and messenger to the Senate while I was of that body. It enlarges the sphere of choice by adding to it a strong federalist.

The triangular war must be the idea of the Anglomen and malcontents, in other words the federalists and quids. Yet it would reconcile neither. It would only change the topic of abuse with the former, and not cure the mental

---

16. See Stagg, p. 109, and Brant, V, pp. 465–66.

disease of the latter. It would prevent our eastern capitalists and seamen from emploiment in privateering, thus take away the only chance of conciliating them, and keep them at home idle to swell the discontents; it would compleatly disarm us of the most powerful weapon we can employ against Great Britain, by shutting every port to our prizes, and yet would not add a single vessel to their number; it would shut every market to our agricultural productions, and engender impatience and discontent with that class which in fact composes the nation, it would insulate us in general negotiations for peace, making all the parties our opposers; and very indifferent about peace with us, if they have it with the rest of the world, and would exhibit a solecism worthy of Don Quixot[e] only, that of a choice to fight two enemies at a time, rather than to take them by succession. And the only motive for all this is a sublimated impartiality at which the world will laugh, and our own people will turn upon us in mass as soon as it is explained to them, as it will be by the very persons who now are laying that snare. These are the hasty views of one who rarely thinks on these subjects. Your own will be better, and I pray to them every success and to yourself every felicity.

TH. JEFFERSON

Jefferson to Madison

Monticello June 6, 1812

DEAR SIR,

I have taken the liberty of drawing the attention of the Secretary at War to a small depot of military stores at New London, and leave the letter open for your perusal. Be so good as to seal it before delivery. I really thought that Genl. Dearborne had removed them to Lynchburg, undoubtedly a safer and more convenient deposit.

Our county is the only one I have heard of which has required a draught. This proceeded from a mistake of the colonel, who thought he could not recieve individual offers, but that the whole quota, of 241. must present themselves at once. Every one however manifests the utmost alacrity; of the 241. there having been but 10. absentees at the first muster called. A further proof is that Capt. Carr's company of volunteer cavalry being specifically called for by the Governor, though consisting of but 28 when called on, has got up to 50 by new engagements since their call was known. The only enquiry they make is whether they are to go to Canada or Florida? Not a man as far as I have learnt, entertains any of those doubts which puzzle the lawyers of Congress, and astonish common sense, whether it is lawful for them to pursue a retreating enemy across the boundary line of the Union?

I hope Barlow's correspondence has satisfied all our Quixots who thought we should undertake nothing less than to fight all Europe at once. I inclose you a letter from Dr. Bruff, a mighty good, and very ingenious man. His method of manufacturing bullets and shot, has the merit of increasing their specific gravity greatly (being made by compression) and rendering them as much heavier and better than the common leaden bullet, as that is than an iron one. It is a pity he should not have the benefit of furnishing the public when it would be equally to their benefit also. God bless you.

Madison to Jefferson

[Washington] June 22, 1812

DEAR SIR,

The inclosed letter was sent to me, with a request that I would forward it. The reason assigned was, that the one of which it is a duplicate was presumed to have miscarried, no answer to it having been received. An answer will of course be expected.

I inclose a paper containing the Declaration of war, etc. merely to supply a possible miscarriage of others usually received by you.[17] It is understood that the Federalists in Congress are to put all the strength of their talents into a protest against the war, and that the party at large are to be brought out in all their force.

It is impossible to say what effect will follow the assassination of Perceval. In England, it is doubted whether there will be a successor of the same kidney; whether Wellesley will be the man, with some modifications not affecting the character of the Cabinet; or whether he will be allowed to make one for himself, in which case it is supposed he will bring in the Tax party.[18] All this will depend on the Prince, who, it seems, is ruled at present by Lady Herbert who, at the age of 60 years, has some secret fascination for his vitiated caprice.[19] Yrs. affecly

JAMES MADISON

Jefferson to Madison

Monticello June 29, 1812

DEAR SIR

I duly recieved your favor of the 22d covering the declaration of war. It is entirely popular here, the only opinion being that it should have been issued the moment the season admitted the militia to enter Canada. The federalists

17. The House voted for war on June 4, but the Senate delayed until June 17. JM issued the declaration of war on June 18, 1812; see Stagg, pp. 110–15, and Brant, V, pp. 460–83.

18. Perceval was assassinated on May 11, 1812, in the lobby of the House of Commons. After a month of negotiations with Wellesley and others, the prince regent reconstituted Perceval's ministry under the earl of Liverpool; see Perkins, pp. 333–34.

19. For the prince regent's relations with Lady Fitzherbert, see Christopher Hibbert, *George IV, Regent and King* (London, 1973), and Shane Leslie, *Mrs. Fitzherbert* (New York, 1939).

indeed are open mouthed against the declaration, but they are poor devils here, not worthy of notice. A barrel of tar to each state South of the Potomac will keep all in order, and that will be freely contributed without troubling government. To the North they will give you more trouble. You may there have to apply the rougher drastics of Govr. Wright, hemp and confiscation.

To continue the war popular two things are necessary mainly. 1. to stop Indian barbarities. The conquest of Canada will do this. 2. to furnish markets for our produce, say indeed for our flour, for tobacco is already given up, and seemingly without reluctance. The great profits of the wheat crop have allured every one to it; and never was such a crop on the ground as that which we generally begin to cut this day. It would be mortifying to the farmer to see such an one rot in his barn. It would soon sicken him of war. Nor can this be a matter of wonder or of blame on him. Ours is the only country on earth where war is an instantaneous and total suspension of all the objects of his industry and support. For carrying our produce to foreign markets our own ships, neutral ships, and even enemy ships under neutral flags, which I would wink at, will probably suffice. But the coasting trade is of double importance, because both seller and buyer are disappointed, and both are our own citizens. You will remember that in this trade our greatest distress in the last war was produced by our own pilot boats taken by the British and kept as tenders to their larger vessels. These being the swiftest vessels on the ocean, they took them, and selected the swiftest from the whole mass. Filled with men, they scoured every thing along shore; and compleatly cut up that coasting business which might otherwise have been carried on within the range of vessels of force and draught. Why should not we then line our coast with vessels of pilot boat construction, filled with men, armed with cannonades, and only so much larger as to assure the mastery of the pilot boat? The British cannot counterwork us by building similar ones, because, the fact is, however unaccountable, that our builders alone understand that construction. It is on our own pilot boats the British will depend, which our larger vessels may thus retake. These however are the ideas of a landsman only. Mr. Hamilton's judgment will test their soundness.

Our militia are much afraid of being called to Norfolk at this season. They all declare a preference of a march to Canada. I trust however that Governor Barbour will attend to circumstances, and so apportion the service among the counties, that those acclimated by birth or residence may perform the summer tour, and the winter service be allotted to the upper counties.

I trouble you with a letter for General Kosciuzko. It covers a bill of exchange from Mr. Barnes for him, and is therefore of great importance to him.[20] Hoping you will have the goodness so far to befriend the General as to give it your safest conveyance, I commit it to you, with the assurance of my sincere affections.

---

20. For TJ's financial dealings with Barnes on behalf of Kościuszko, see Malone, VI, pp. 39, 41.

Jefferson to Madison

Monticello Aug. 5, 1812

DEAR SIR

In a letter of May 6. from Foronda is this passage.

'No remito a Vm exemplares de mis papelitos para el ilustrado y sabro Madison, aunque le tributo todos mis respetos: pero es Presidente. y las vilas almas, lexos de conocer que esto seria un acto de Cortesania que no tiene relacion con la presidencia, metacharian talver de poco afecto a la patria, alegando que tenia consideraciones con quien nos la Tomado a Baton rouge.'[21] You will draw the inferences both personal and public from this paragraph which it authorises. He nevertheless sent me duplicates of his publications, and I have no doubt I fulfill his wish in sending you one of them.

The inclosed letter to Kosciusko is important to him as covering a bill of exchange, the proceeds of his funds here. A safe conveyance is more important than a speedy one. If you can have it so disposed of in the office of state as to give it the protection of Barlow's cover, it will serve one of our most genuine foreign friends.

I am glad of the re-establishment of a Percival ministry. The opposition would have recruited our Minority by half-way offers. With Canada in hand we can go to treaty with an off-set for spoliations before the war. Our farmers are cheerful in the expectation of a good price for wheat in autumn. Their pulse will be regulated by this, and not by the successes or disasters of the war. To keep open sufficient markets is the very first object towards maintaining the popularity of the war which is as great at present as could be desired. We have just had a fine rain of 1¼ inches in the most critical time for our corn. The weather during harvest was as advantageous as could be. I am sorry to find you remaining so long at Washington. The effect on your health may lose us a great deal of your time; a couple of months at Montpelier at this season need not lose us an hour. Affectionate salutations to Mrs. Madison and yourself.

Jefferson to Madison

Monticello Aug. 10, 1812

DEAR SIR

The death of my much valued friend and relation George Jefferson will doubtless produce many competitors for the office of Consul at Lisbon.[22]

---

21. "I do not send you examples of my little papers for the enlightened and wise Madison, although I offer him my respects: but he is president, and mean spirits, far from recognizing that this would be an act of courtesy which has no relation to the presidency, would perhaps accuse me of little affection for my native country, alleging that I had regard for him who has robbed us at Baton Rouge." I am indebted to Mary Hackett for this translation.

22. George Jefferson, who had been TJ's factor in Richmond, served as American consul at Lisbon for about a year, then took his life on the return trip home; see Malone, VI, p. 82.

Among these a neighbor of mine, Mr David Higginbotham wishes to be considered. He is a merchant of Milton, of very fair character, steady application to business, sound in his circumstances, and perfectly correct in all his conduct. He is a native of this part of the country, brought up to mercantile business, of a temper and manners entirely conciliatory and obliging and would, I am persuaded execute the duties of the office with all the diligence and zeal in his power. Should no person of better qualifications be proposed his appointment would gratify his many friends here as well,[23] as Dear Sir Your affectionate friend and servt.

         Th Jefferson

Jefferson to Madison

              Monticello Aug. 10, 1812

Dear Sir

The letter within which this is inclosed contains the truth: there is not a word in it that is not so. But while the sollicitations of a friend have obliged me to present his case, duty to yourself and the public oblige me to say it does not contain the whole truth. One single circumstance is to be added: this candidate for the office of Consul at Lisbon, who often has to transact diplomatic business with that government, as we have no minister there, is not qualified by education or understanding for the duties of the office. He is uninformed and unlettered, and so much so as to be entirely insensible of it himself. His understanding is equal to the business he is in, but not to that which would be incumbent on him at that post. His letter now inclosed is a specimen by which you can judge, which after perusal be so good as to return under cover to me, without taking the trouble of saying a word on the subject. My outer letter will probably go on your files; I have written this separately that it may not do so, but remain among your private papers, unwilling to make a public record of it in the case of so good a man.

Constant rains are detracting from the produce of our harvest, by rendering it impossible to thresh; and in the mean time injuring the grain in the stacks. Ever affectionately yours

         Th Jefferson

---

23. Higginbotham was a merchant and neighbor of TJ's at nearby Milton; see TJ's second letter to JM of Aug. 10, 1812, below.

Madison to Jefferson

Washington Aug. 17, 1812

DEAR SIR,

I have rec^d yours of the 10th, and return as you request, the letter of Mr. Higginbotham. He will probably have understood from Col: Monroe that the Consulate of Lisbon is the object of numerous and respectable candidates.

The seditious opposition in Mass and Con^t with the intrigues elsewhere insidiously co-operating with it, have so clogged the wheels of the war that I fear the campaign will not accomplish the object of it. With the most united efforts, in stimulating volunteers, they would have probably fallen much short of the number required by the deficiency of regular enlistments. But under the discouragements substituted, and the little attraction contained in the volunteer Act, the two classes together, leave us dependent for every primary operation, on militia, either as volunteers or draughts for six months.[24] We are nevertheless doing as well as we can, in securing the maritime frontier, and in providing for an effective penetration into Upper Canada. It would probably have been best, if it had been practicable in time, to have concentrated a force which could have seized on Montreal, and thus at one stroke, have secured the upper Province, and cut off the sap that nourished Indian hostilities.[25] But this could not be attempted, without sacrificing the Western and N. W. Frontier, threatened with an inundation of savages under the influence of the British establishment near Detroit. Another reason for the expedition of Hull was that the unanimity and ardor of Kentucky and Ohio, promised the requisite force at once for that service, whilst it was too distant from the other points to be assailed.[26] We just learn, but from what cause remains to be known, that the important post of Machilimackinac has fallen into the hands of the Enemy.[27] If the reinforcement of about 2000 ordered from the Ohio, and on the way to Hull, should not enable him to take Malden, and awe the savages emboldened by the British success, his situation will be very ineligible. It is hoped that he will either be strong eno', as he has cannon and mortars, to reduce that Fort, or to leave a force that will justify him in passing on towards the other end of Lake Erie, and place the British troops there, between him, and those embodied under arrangements of Dearborn and Tomkins at Niagara, for the purpose of occupying the central part of Upper Canada. In the mean time the preparations agst Montreal are going on, and perhaps may furnish a feint towards it, that may conspire with the other plan. I find that Kingston at the East End of

---

24. The Federalist governors of Massachusetts, Connecticut, and Rhode Island refused to furnish militia quotas requested by General Henry Dearborn four days after war was declared; see Stagg, pp. 258–62, and Hickey, pp. 259–64.
25. For JM's plan for a strike at Montreal, see Stagg, pp. 227–31.
26. For the western campaign from Detroit, see *ibid.*, pp. 190–201.
27. For the fall of Michilimackinac, see *ibid.*, p. 201.

L. Ontario is an object with Genl D. The multiplication of these offensive measures has grown out of the defensive precautions for the Frontiers of N. York.[28]

We have no information from England since the war was known there, or even, seriously suspected, by the public. I think it not improbable that the sudden change in relation to the Orders in Council, first in yielding to a qualified suspension, and then a repeal,[29] was the effect of apprehensions in the Cabinet that the deliberations of Cong^s would have that issue, and that the Ministry could not stand ag^st the popular torrent ag^st the Orders in Council, swelled as it would be by the addition of a war with the U. S. to the pressure of the non-importation Act. What course will be taken when the declaration here, shall be known, is uncertain, both in reference to the American shipments instituted under the repeal of the Orders, and to the question between vindictive efforts for pushing the war ag^st us, and early advances for terminating it. A very informal and as it has turned out erroneous communication of the intended change in the Orders, was hurried over, evidently with a view to prevent a declaration of war, if it should arrive in time. And the communication was accompanied by a proposal from the *local* authorities at Halifax sanctioned by Foster, to suspend hostilities both at sea and on land. The late message of Prevost to Dearborn, noticed in the Newspapers has this for its object.[30] The insuperable objections to a concurrence of the Executive in the project are obvious. Without alluding to others, drawn from a limited authority, and from the effect on patriotic ardor, the advantage over us in captures w^d be past, before it could take effect. As we do not apprehend invasion by land, and preparations on each side were to be unrestrained, nothing could be gained by us, whilst arrangements and reinforcements adverse to Hull might be decisive; and on every supposition the Indians w^d continue to be active ag^st our frontiers, the more so in consequence of the fall of Machilimackinac. Nothing but triumphant operations on the Theatre, which forms their connection with the Enemy, will controul their bloody inroads.

I have been indulging my hopes of getting away from this place, in the course of the present week. It is quite possible however that my stay here may be indispensable. As yet I have less of bilious sensations than I could have expected.

Your two letters to Kosciuzco have been duly attended to. Affectionately yours,

JAMES MADISON

---

28. For defensive preparations in upstate New York, see *ibid.*, pp. 233–44.

29. For the repeal of the orders-in-council, see Perkins, pp. 300–41.

30. For Dearborn's acceptance of an armistice with the governor of Lower Canada on Aug. 8, 1812, see Stagg, p. 245, and Hickey, p. 283. JM repudiated the armistice on Aug. 15 and ordered Dearborn to march against Montreal.

Jefferson to Madison

Monticello Aug. 30, 1812

DEAR SIR

The mail of yesterday does not tell us whether you have left Washington. I am this moment setting out for Bedford, and shall be absent 3. or 4. weeks. Should you be at Monpelier when I return I shall certainly have the pleasure of paying my respects to Mrs Madison and yourself. In the mean time accept the assurance of my affectionate esteem and respect

TH JEFFERSON

Jefferson to Madison

Monticello Oct. 2, 1812

DEAR SIR

I take the liberty of inclosing to you a letter from Mr Meigs, heretofore President of the University of Georgia. This has been delayed by the same absence from home which prevented my having the pleasure of delivering it to you personally at Monpelier. I do not know Mr Meigs personally, but have always heard him highly spoken of as a man of science. He was selected for the university of Georgia by our late friend [Abraham] Baldwin, and I remember he was considered as a great acquisition there. Of the state of the place he asks for I am ignorant, but if in that or any other place you can benefit the public by employing him, I am sure you will do it as well on their behalf as from your own disposition to patronise science.

I avail myself of this as of every other occasion to renew to you the assurance of my constant friendship and wishes for your health and success in the awful charge you have on you.

TH JEFFERSON

Madison to Jefferson

Washington Oct. 14, 1812

DEAR SIR

I rec^d your favor of the 2d, inclosing the letter from Mr. Meigs. The place he wishes has been long allotted to Mr. Mansfield, who preferred it to that of the Surveyorship held by him, and who has just obtained the exchange; and a Commission for the place vacated, has just been sent to Mr. Meigs, who was long ago recommended for it; and who it was understood wished it. It is the more probable that it will be acceptable to him, as he has connections in the W. Country, particularly the Govr of Ohio.³¹

I see so little chance of being able to peruse the lucubrations of Foronda you were so good as to send me, that I replace them, for the present at least in your hands.

The last intelligence from the Westward left a military crisis near Fort Defiance.³² Winchester with about half the army, was encamped within 3 miles of the encampment of about 300 British troops with some field pieces and a body of Indians stated at 2000 or 2500. It is probable they were destined agst Fort Wayne, with the general view of finding employment for our forces on their way to Detroit, until the Season should be spent, or Brock could send troops from below. Of our affairs at Niagara and the neighbourhood of Montreal, it is difficult to judge, the force of the Enemy being imperfectly known, and that under General Dearborn, depending so much on circumstances. Our best hopes for the campaign rest on Harrison; and if no disaster, always to be feared from Indian combats, befall him, there is a probability that he will regain Detroit, and perhaps do more.³³ He has a force of 8 or 10,000 men at least, enthusiastically confiding in him, and a prospect of adequate supplies of every sort, unless it be Cannon, which tho' on the way, may possibly encounter fatal delays. This article however he appears not to make a sine qua non; nor will it be wanted for Detroit, if it be true as is reported that every piece has been withdrawn by the British.

The latest acc^{ts} from Europe are in the Newspapers. The ideas of which Foster and Russel are put in possession will soon draw from the B. Gov^t some evidence of their views as to peace. From France we hear nothing; and shall probably meet Cong^s under the perplexity of that situation.

The current Elections bring the popularity of the War or of the Administration, or both, to the Experimentum crucis. In this State³⁴ the issue is not favorable, tho' less otherwise than would appear. In the Congressional Districts the Republicans I believe, have not lost ground at all, notwithstanding the auxiliaries to federalism. In the State Legislature, they will be in a minority on a joint vote. Penn^a, altho' admitted to be shaken, is represented to be safe. New Jersey is doubtful at least. The same is the case with New Hampshire. North Carolina also is reported to be in considerable vibration. The other States remain pretty decided on one hand or on the other.³⁵

31. The governor of Ohio was Return Jonathan Meigs; see Stagg, p. 190.

32. General James Winchester of Tennessee, who headed an army that tried to recapture Detroit after Hull's surrender, reached Fort Defiance on Oct. 2, 1812; see *ibid.*, p. 220.

33. General William Henry Harrison succeeded Hull as commander in the Northwest; see *ibid.*, p. 224, and Hickey, p. 85.

34. Maryland.

35. The best account of the election is by Norman K. Risjord, "Election of 1812," in *History of American Presidential Elections, 1789–1968*, ed. Arthur M. Schlesinger, Jr., and Fred L. Israel, 4 vols. (New York, 1971), I, pp. 249–91.

You will be amused with the little work of the Author of several humorous publications, Irvine[36] of N. York. It sinks occasionally into low and local phrases, and some times forgets Allegorical character; But is in general good painting on substantial Canvas. Affec.^e respects,

Jefferson to Madison

Monticello Oct. 31, 1812

DEAR SIR

This will be handed you by Monsr. de Neufville a person of distinction from France who came over to this country with his family some years ago, and is established as an Agricultural citizen near New Brunswick in Jersey.[37] He brought recommendations from some friends of mine which established his merit, as well as his right to any service I could render him. Since his settlement in Jersey I have heard him spoken of as one of the most amiable and unoffending men on earth. He has asked a letter of introduction to you, as he goes on to Washington to sollicit the reception of his nephew in the military school at West point. The nephew is 15. years old, and so far has recieved an education tres soignée. I have apprised M. de Neufville of the possibility that the number of competitors for places in that school may produce difficulties and delays, that the principles of our government admit little exercise of partialities in it's public functionaries, and have prepared him of course for a possible disappointment proceeding from circumstances unconnected with the dispositions of the Executive, so that should he succeed he will be made the more happy and thankful. In any event he will be very sensible to any kindnesses and attentions which shall manifest a recognition of the personal merit of which he cannot but feel a consciousness. The favor will at the same time be acknoleged by myself on behalf of friends beyond the water who have claims of gratitude on me towards a person recommended by them. Accept always the assurance of my constant friendship and respect.

TH JEFFERSON

Jefferson to Madison

Monticello Nov. 6, 1812

DEAR SIR,

I inclose you a letter from Colo: Gibson Secretary under Governor Harrison. I suppose he has addressed it to me on the footing of a very old acquaint-

---

36. James K. Paulding, not Washington Irving, wrote *The Diverting History of John Bull and Brother Jonathan* (New York, 1812).

37. For de Neufville, see p. 1655, n. 1, above.

ance. He is a very honest man, very old in public service and much esteemed by all who know him. All this I believe however is known to yourself and possibly he may be personally known to you.

The seeing whether our untried Generals will stand proof is a very dear operation. Two of them have cost us a great many men. We can tell by his plumage whether a cock is dunghill or game. But with us cowardice and courage wear the same plume. Hull will of course be shot for cowardice and treachery. And will not Van Renslaer be broke for cowardice and incapacity? To advance such a body of men across a river without securing boats to bring them off in case of disaster, has cost us 700 men: and to have taken no part himself in such an action and against such a general could be nothing but cowardice.[38] These are the reflections of a solitary reader of his own letter. Dearborne and Harrison have both courage and understanding, and having no longer a Brock to encounter, I hope we shall ere long hear something good from them. If we could but get Canada to Trois rivieres in our hands we should have a set off against spoliations to be treated of, and in the mean time separate the Indians from them and set the friendly to attack the hostile part with our aid. Ever affectionately yours.

38. For Stephen Van Rensselaer's surrender at Queenstown Heights, see Stagg, p. 249, and Hickey, pp. 86–87.

40

THE WAR OF 1812: A FEW VICTORIES BUT MORE DEFEATS, 1812–1813

AFTER THE DISASTROUS LOSSES OF 1812, President Madison concluded that the military chaos dictated that he replace William Eustis, secretary of war, a likable incompetent overwhelmed by the work of war, and Paul Hamilton, secretary of the navy, a congenial colleague rendered useless by alcoholism. For the first post, Madison turned to John Armstrong, a Revolutionary War general and, more recently, minister to France. For the second, he appointed William Jones, a Philadelphia sea captain and merchant to whom Jefferson had offered the post in his first term. In a quick note to his predecessor, Madison said "I have not time to explain the late changes in the Executive Department, if I were disposed to trouble you with them."[1]

But Jefferson needed no explanation. "The accession to your Cabinet," he assured Madison, "meets general approbation. This is chiefly at present given to the character most known, but will be equally so to the other when better known. I think you could not have made better appointments."[2] Late in life, Madison praised Jones as "the fittest minister who had ever been charged with the Navy Department."[3]

For three months, Jefferson had stewed in silence about American military losses, giving the president "a long holiday from my intrusions." "I am become so averse to the writing table," he told Madison, "that I do not know

---

1. JM to TJ, Jan. 27, 1813, below. For Armstrong, see C. Edward Skeen, "Mr. Madison's Secretary of War," *PMHB* 100 (1976): 336–55. For a brief biography of Jones, see Edward K. Eckert, "William Jones: Mr. Madison's Secretary of the Navy," *PMHB* 96 (1972): 167–82. Also see Frank L. Owsley, Jr., "Paul Hamilton," in *American Secretaries of the Navy*, ed. Paolo E. Coletta, 2 vols. (Annapolis, 1980), I, pp. 93–98.

2. TJ to JM, Feb. 8, 1813, below.

3. Ketcham, p. 546.

whether I shall muster resolution enough" to send along suggestions that had occurred to him. But when he received a twenty-eight-page indictment of Brigadier General Alexander Smyth's debacle at Niagara from Colonel Isaac Coles, his former private secretary and Dolley Madison's cousin, he sent it to the president as proof of Smyth's "indecision in purpose, inattention to preparation, and imprudence of demeanor . . . a total incompetence for military direction."[4]

Two weeks later, Jefferson deplored the defeat of General James Winchester at Frenchtown, south of Detroit.[5] "Another General it seems has given proof of his military qualifications by the loss of another thousand of men: for there cannot be a surprise but thro' the fault of the Commanders, and especially by an enemy who has given us heretofore so many of these lessons."[6]

But Jefferson was enthusiastic about "the brilliant atchievements of our little navy. They have deeply wounded the pride of our enemy, and been balm to ours, humiliated on the land where our real strength was felt to lie."[7] The president was also heartened "by our little naval triumphs," which aroused "rage and jealousy" in England at the same time that they raised American spirits, despite the dismal land losses.[8]

Madison needed all the little triumphs he could get as he entered his second presidential term. In his inaugural address, he observed that "our national sovereignty" was staked on the outcome of the war, and he concentrated on impressment—"the unlawfulness of the practice by which our mariners are forced at the will of every cruising officer from their own vessels into foreign ones"—as a vital cause of the war. Finally, he praised American naval heroes and played down army losses: "Already have the gallant exploits of our naval heroes proved to the world our inherent capacity to maintain our rights on one element. If the reputation of our arms has been thrown under clouds on the other, presaging flashes of heroic enterprise assure us that nothing is wanting to correspondent triumphs there also, but the discipline and habits which are in daily progress."[9]

When the prince regent informed Parliament that impressment of British seamen found on neutral vessels was an undisputed right, Madison called the speech to Jefferson's attention, writing that "nothing but the difficulty of their affairs will open their ears, and that without opening their hearts to peace." When the astounding news of Napoleon's retreat from Moscow filtered across

---

4. TJ to JM, Feb. 8, 1813, below, and Apr. 10, 1813, below. See also Brant, VI, pp. 89–95, and Malone, VI, pp. 112–13. During his second term, TJ had appointed Smyth as inspector general.

5. The encounter took place on Jan. 22, 1813.

6. TJ to JM, Feb. 21, 1813, below.

7. TJ to JM, May 21, 1813, below.

8. JM to TJ, Mar. 10, 1813, below. One cabinet minister, the earl of Harrowby, admitted that "it is a cruel mortification to be beat by the second-hand Englishmen upon our element"; see Bradford Perkins, *Castlereagh and Adams: England and the United States, 1812–1823* (Berkeley, 1964), p. 18.

9. JM's inaugural address, Mar. 4, 1813, in Richardson, I, pp. 524–26.

the Atlantic, the president conjectured that the effect of the French defeat "on his compulsory allies may once more turn the tables quite around in the case between France and England."[10]

One unexpected by-product of the Russian victory was an offer by Czar Alexander, Great Britain's ally, to mediate the war between England and the United States. Madison promptly informed his predecessor that Russia "is tendering her mediating friendship, with the collateral view, there is reason to believe, of deriving advantage from our *neutral* interference with British monopoly in the trade with her. We shall endeavor," he added, "to turn the good will of Russia to the proper account. Whether England will accede to the mediation, or do so with evasive purposes, remains to be seen. That she has brought it about, I cannot readily suppose, because I think she would not promote our political intercourse with the Baltic, where she apprehends a sympathy with our maritime doctrines, and not with hers." Of one thing he was convinced, however. "The present occasion proves the good policy of having cultivated the favorable dispositions of the Emperor Alexander. We have good reason to believe that Sweden is as well inclined towards us as Russia."[11]

Without waiting to learn if England had accepted the Russian proposal, Madison promptly appointed a bipartisan peace commission. Ex-Federalist John Quincy Adams had been appointed Republican minister to Russia by the president in 1809. His most talented negotiator at home was Secretary of the Treasury Albert Gallatin, who was appointed to head the delegation to Russia. Third place went to James A. Bayard, senator from Delaware, the least objectionable Federalist to the president. Gallatin and Bayard sailed for St. Petersburg in May 1813.

Although Lord Castlereagh informed the czar that Great Britain viewed impressment as a national right not subject to mediation, thus avoiding a coalition between the United States and Russia on neutral rights, the British Foreign Office proposed direct negotiations with the United States in November. The president promptly dispatched Speaker Henry Clay and the former chargé d'affaires in London, Jonathan Russell, to join the three envoys from Russia at the Swedish town of Gothenburg.[12]

"The catastrophe of the French Army" in Russia brought "the usual exultation" in England, Madison informed his friend at Monticello, allowing the ministry to unleash a "gigantic force . . . against us on the water."[13] By the spring, the British navy under Admiral Sir John Warren had established an effective blockade of the East Coast from New York to Georgia. New England, as Jefferson observed, was "treated by the enemy as neutrals."[14] Squadrons

10. JM to TJ, Jan. 27, 1813, below, and Brant, VI, p. 152.
11. JM to TJ, Mar. 10, 1813, below.
12. Brant, VI, pp. 149-63, discusses the Russian mediation offer.
13. JM to TJ, Mar. 10, 1813, below.
14. TJ to JM, June 21, 1813, below.

commanded by Rear Admiral Sir George Cockburn concentrated on raids in the Chesapeake and Delaware bays, ravaging Lynnhaven Bay near Norfolk and destroying military supplies and small vessels before burning the towns of Havre de Grace, Frenchtown, and Georgetown, Maryland. "All their war is concentrated on the Delaware and Chesapeake," Jefferson thought, because the mid-Atlantic states were "the most zealous supporters of the war, and therefore the peculiar objects of the vindictive efforts of the enemy." He was convinced that "the over-proportioned hostilities pointed at" the Chesapeake area accounted for "the harassment of the militia, the burnings of towns and houses, depredations of farms, and the hard trial of the spirit of the middle states."[15]

"When we cast our eyes on the map," Jefferson wrote, "and see the extent of country, from New York to North Carolina inclusive, whose product is raised on the waters of the Chesapeake, (for Albemarle sound is, by the canal of Norfolk become a water of the Chesapeake,) and consider its productiveness, in comparison with the rest of the Atlantic States, probably a full half, and that all this can be shut up by two or three ships of the line lying at the mouth of the bay, we see that an injury so vast to ourselves and so cheap to our enemy, must forever be resorted to by them, and constantly maintained. To defend all of the shores of those waters in detail, is impossible," he conceded. "But is there not a single point where they may be all defended by means to which the magnitude of the object gives a title? I mean at the mouth of the Chesapeake."[16]

Jefferson knew that the United States did not have enough "ships of the line, or frigates" to challenge the world's strongest navy. But he made an impassioned plea for his favorite naval weapon, "the humble, the ridiculed, but the formidable gun boat," which he had favored when he was president. "Would not a sufficient number of gun-boats of *small* draught, stationed in Lynhaven river, render it unsafe for ships of war either to ascend the Chesapeake or to lie at its mouth?" He quickly acknowledged that "the station of Lynhaven river would not be safe against land attacks on the boats" and suggested digging a canal to connect that river with the Elizabeth River as "a channel of retreat," where the gunboats could aid in "the defence of Norfolk, if attacked from the sea. And the Norfolk canal gives them a further passage into Albemarle sound, if necessary for their safety, or in aid of the flotilla of that Sound, or to receive the aid of that flotilla either at Norfolk or in Lynhaven river. For such a flotilla there also will doubtless be thought necessary, that being the only outlet now, as during the last [Revolutionary] war, for the waters of the Chesapeake."[17]

One month later, Jefferson sent the president lengthy "supplementary

15. *Ibid.*
16. TJ to JM, May 21, 1813, below.
17. *Ibid.* On TJ's enthusiasm for gunboats, see Frederick C. Leiner, "The 'Whimsical Phylosophic President' and His Gunboats," *American Neptune* 43 (1983): 245–66, and Dean R. Mayhew, "Jeffersonian Gunboats in the War of 1812," *American Neptune* 42 (1982): 101–17.

observations" on gunboats and canals, including a map of the route of the canal made during the Revolutionary War when he was governor of Virginia. Although he pushed his point of view vigorously, Jefferson was not "pertinacious in the opinion I have formed." Instead, the president alone was "qualified for decision, by the whole view which you can command: and so confident am I in the intentions as well as wisdom of the government that I shall always be satisfied that what is not done, either cannot, or ought not to be done."[18]

Madison was diplomatic in his reply to his predecessor. "Your suggestions for protecting the trade of the Chesapeake by Gun boats at the South end of it, with a safe retreat provided for them, have been taken into consideration, with all the respect due to the importance as well as the motives of them," he wrote. "The present Secretary of the Navy is not unfriendly to gun-boats; and in general, the call for them by the Inhabitants of the Coast proves a diffusive sense of their utility. It seems agreed at the same time that, being too slow in sailing, and too heavy for rowing, they are limited in their use to particular situations, and rarely for other than defensive co-operations." Even when "guarding the interior navigation of the Bay," however, they would be ineffective against British "Cruisers on the outside of the Capes," which could "still blockade the external commerce."[19]

Before Gallatin left for St. Petersburg, he had participated in cabinet discussions about military plans for 1813. After the reverses of 1812, Madison understood that "the command of the [Great] Lakes" was "a fundamental point."[20] He sent Commodore Isaac Chauncey to Lake Ontario and Commander Oliver Hazard Perry to Lake Erie to build fleets to meet British squadrons bent on keeping their supply lines open to the west. Perry won a hard-fought victory on Lake Erie and sent a laconic message that became a snappy wartime slogan: "We have met the enemy and they are ours." As soon as Major General Harrison heard the message, he moved quickly against Fort Malden, below Detroit on Lake Erie, carrying his troops from Ohio on landing craft constructed on the lake, forcing the evacuation of both the fort and Detroit, then defeating British regulars and Indians in the Battle of the Thames, where Tecumseh met a mysterious end.[21]

On Lake Ontario, Chauncey launched an amphibious strike at York (Toronto), the capital of Upper Canada, then took Fort George on the Niagara River. The British retaliated with a raid on Sackett's Harbor, where an incomplete ship was burned, but they were repulsed by American regulars and militia. By the end of the year, the British had retaken Fort George, captured Fort Niagara, and swept into Buffalo, which they burned.

18. TJ to JM, June 21, 1813, below.
19. JM to TJ, June 6, 1813, below.
20. JM to Henry Dearborn, Oct. 7, 1812, in Hunt, VIII, p. 217.
21. See Gerard T. Altoff, "Oliver Hazard Perry and the Battle of Lake Erie," *Michigan Historical Review* 14 (1988): 25–57, and Carl F. Klinck, ed., *Tecumseh: Fact and Fiction in Early Records* (Englewood Cliffs, N.J., 1961), pp. 189–231.

For the Montreal campaign, Secretary Armstrong relieved Dearborn as commanding general in midsummer, replacing him with James Wilkinson of Burrite fame. Wilkinson's invasion of Canada was no more successful than Dearborn's had been, and after an inconclusive battle at Chrysler's Farm, Wilkinson retreated to American soil.

While the Canadian campaign sputtered and the new Congress met in special session, Madison suffered a near-fatal illness that confined him to bed for nearly a month. Monroe informed Jefferson that the president's fever had raged for two weeks, "perhaps never left him, even for an hour, and occasionally symptoms have been unfavorable."[22] Jefferson wrote an apologetic letter for burdening Madison with his advocacy of gunboats when "you were too ill to be troubled with any matter of business. My comfort has been in the confidence that care would of course be taken not to disturb you with letters. My hope in writing the present is of a pleasanter kind, the flattering one that you are entirely recovered. If the prayers of millions have been of avail," he said, "they have been poured forth with the deepest anxiety."[23]

By August, Madison had improved enough for a visit to Virginia, and Jefferson planned on "the pleasure of seeing you at Montpelier, by which time I hope a perfect reestablishment of your health and relief from influenza will render the visit you promise us for Mrs Madison and yourself as recreating to you as welcome to us."[24]

THE LETTERS

Madison to Jefferson

Washington Jan. 27, 1813

DEAR SIR

I snatch a moment to intimate that Dr. J. Ewell is under circumstances which induce him to surround himself with respectable names as he can. Yours has been already brought into point, and he is waiting himself to the utmost of your alledged patronage of him. I think it probable that he will endeavor to draw from you by letter whatever may be yielded by your politeness or benevolence; and I cannot do less than put you on your guard.[1]

---

22. James Monroe to TJ, June 28, 1813, cited in Ketcham, p. 561.

23. TJ to JM, July 13, 1813, below.

24. TJ to JM, Aug. 15, 1813, below. JM's letter promising to visit Monticello is missing; see Brant, VI, pp. 208–19.

1. JM had received allegations that gunpowder manufactured in Dr. James Ewell's mills did not meet navy specifications, rendering it impossible for American warships "to contend with an Enemy's Sloop of war"; see Charles W. Goldsborough to JM, Jan. 21, 1813, Presidential Papers Microfilm, James Madison Papers, reel 14. Goldsborough was chief clerk in the Navy Department; see *PJM* (Pres. ser.), I, p. 157.

Congress proceed with their usual slowness, even on the most essential subjects; and the undercurrent against us is as strong as ever. I have not time to explain the late changes in the Executive Department, if I were disposed to trouble you with them.[2] Bonaparte, according to his own shewing, is in serious danger; and if half the official accounts of the Russians be true, his own escape is barely possible, and that of his army impossible. The effect of such a catastrophe on his compulsory allies may once more turn the tables quite round in the case between France and England.[3] You will have seen the speech of the Regent. The debates on it have not reached us. Wellesley's party attack the Ministry for not prosecuting the war more vigorously against us. Nothing but the difficulty of their affairs will open their ears, and that without opening their hearts to peace.[4] In the Peninsula, the French are driving Wellington back to Lisbon, and there now is no doubt that the late harvest is a very short one, and the quality for the most part bad. Their expenditures, also are enormous, beyond former years; and their Bank paper 35 per cent below specie. I have for you a copy of Cooper's Justinian, which I will forward by next mail. Yours always and affectly

Jefferson to Madison

Monticello Feb. 8, 1813

DEAR SIR,

Your favor of the 27th ult. has been duly recieved. You have had a long holiday from my intrusions. In truth I have had nothing to write about, and your time should not be consumed by letters about nothing. The inclosed paper however makes it a duty to give you the trouble of reading it. You know the handwriting and the faith due to it.[5] Our intimacy with the writer leaves no doubt about his facts, and in his letter to me he pledges himself for their fidelity. He says the Narrative was written at the request of a young friend in Virginia, and a copy made for my perusal on the presumption it would be interesting to me. Whether the word 'Confidential' at the head of the paper was meant only for his young friend or for myself also, nothing in his letter indicates. I must therefore govern myself by considerations of discretion and of duty combined. Discretion dictates that I ought not so to use the paper as

---

2. For the replacement of Secretary of War William Eustis and Secretary of the Navy Paul Hamilton by John Armstrong and William Jones, see Brant, VI, pp. 114-29.

3. For a brief account of Napoleon's failure in Russia, see Georges Lefebvre, *Napoleon: From Tilsit to Waterloo, 1807-1815* (New York, 1969), pp. 311-18.

4. For a discussion of the prince regent's speech, see Perkins, pp. 15-16.

5. The letter was written by Colonel Isaac Coles, Dolley Madison's cousin and TJ's former secretary, who was in charge of a regiment in the army commanded by General Alexander Smyth; see Brant, VI, pp. 94-95, and Malone, VI, p. 112.

to compromit my friend; an effect which would be as fatal to my peace as it might be to his person. But duty tells me that the public interest is so deeply concerned in your perfect knolege of the characters employed in its high stations, that nothing should be withheld which can give you useful information. On these grounds I commit it to yourself and the Secretary at War, to whose functions it relates more immediately. It may have effect on your future designation of those to whom particular enterprizes are to be committed, and this is the object of the communication. If you should think it necessary that the minds of the other members of the Cabinet should be equally apprised of it's contents, altho' not immediately respecting their departments, the same considerations, and an entire confidence in them personally, would dictate it's communication to them also. But beyond this no sense of duty calls on me for it's disclosure, and fidelity to my friend strongly forbids it. The paper presents such a picture of indecision in purpose, inattention to preparation, and imprudence of demeanor, as to fix a total incompetence for military direction. How greatly we were decieved in this character, as is generally the case in appointments not on our own knolege. I remember when we appointed him we rejoiced in the acquisition of an officer of so much understanding and integrity, as we imputed to him; and placed him as near the head of the army as the commands then at our disposal admitted. Perhaps, still, you may possess information giving a different aspect to this case, of which I sincerely wish it may be susceptible. I will ask the return of the paper when no longer useful to you.

The accession to your Cabinet meets general approbation. This is chiefly at present given to the character most known, but will be equally so to the other when better known. I think you could not have made better appointments.

The autumn and winter have been most unfriendly to the wheat in red lands, by continued cold and alternate frosts and thaws. The late snows of about 10.I now disappearing have revived it. That grain is got to two Dollars at Richmond. This is the true barometer of the popularity of the war. Ever affectionately yours.

TH. JEFFERSON

Jefferson to Madison

Monticello Feb. 21, 1813

DEAR SIR,

On the occasion of your separation from Mr. Robert Smith, I recollect your mentioning in one of your letters to me that among the circumstances which afflicted you, was the impression it might make on his connections in this quarter, for whom you entertained so much friendship and esteem. It was soon discernible that on one of them whom I had the most frequent opportunities of seeing, no other impression was made than that which every man of understanding felt: of which I think I informed you at the time: and there has never been one moment of remission on his part in his zealous attachment to yourself and your administration. Of Mr. Nicholas's feelings I have not had as good occasions of judging for myself. I see him seldom, at his own house only, and in the midst of his family, before whom, of course, neither he nor I should think of introducing the subject. Indulgence to the feelings of their families would necessarily, in their presence, impose reserve on both of these gentlemen. I have lately however, thro' a channel which can leave no doubt on the subject, ascertained that on Mr. Nicholas also no impression unfavorable to you was made by that transaction, and that his friendship for you has never felt a moment's abatement. Indeed we might have been sure of this from his integrity, his good sense, and his sound judgment of men and things. Very serious and urgent letters too written by him to both General Smith and Giles on the course pursued by them are proofs of the undeviating character of his own. Knowing your value of him, and that which we both set on the attachment to republican government of a family so estimable, so able, and so strong in its connections, I have believed it would be pleasing to you to be assured of these facts.[6] I am led to the communication too by another motive, the opportunity which I think I see of cementing these dispositions by a measure which will at the same time be useful to the public. He has a son, Robert Carter Nicholas, whom I cannot praise more than by saying he is exactly the father over again. The same strong observation, sound judgment, prudence and honesty of purpose improved by more education and reading. He has been brought up to the bar; but on the insults to his country, he felt the animation they were calculated to inspire more especially in young and ardent minds, and he obtained a captaincy in one of the regiments lately authorised. There can be few such men in our army, and it is highly interesting to us all, that these few should be approached, on all fair occasions, as much as possible towards the higher grades of the army. He is one of those who, in relation, as well as in action, will gratify our national feelings. There being more regiments now to be raised I have supposed he might be advanced a grade, say to a majority, in one of these. I wish his age and experience had been such as to justify more. Such a measure, while promoting the good of the service, would have a cordial effect on the mind of the father; and the more so in proportion as it is unsollicited and unexpected. It would remove all scruples and anxieties on both sides, by manifesting to him the state of your mind, and strengthening your conviction of his dispositions towards you. I will take the liberty of suggesting this transfer to Genl. Armstrong also, whose particular acquaintance with the father will raise more favorable presumptions as to the son, and facilitate the measure should it meet with your own approbation.[7]

6. Wilson Cary Nicholas was married to Margaret Smith of Baltimore, sister of Robert Smith.
7. Robert Carter Nicholas was appointed major in the army; see JM to TJ, Mar. 10, 1813, below.

Another General it seems has given proof of his military qualifications by the loss of another thousand of men: for there cannot be a surprise but thro' the fault of the Commanders, and especially by an enemy who has given us heretofore so many of these lessons.[8] Perhaps we ought to expect such trials after deperdition of all military science consequent on so long a peace: and I am happy to observe the public mind not discouraged, and that it does not associate it's government with these unfortunate agents. These experiments will at least have the good effect of bringing forward those whom nature has qualified for military trust; and whenever we have good commanders, we shall have good souldiers, and good successes. God bless you, and give you that success which wisdom and integrity ought to ensure to you.

TH. JEFFERSON

Madison to Jefferson

Washington Mar. 10, 1813

DEAR SIR,

I have received your two favors of the 8 and 21 ult. The conduct and character of the late Commander at Niagara, as portrayed in the narrative enclosed in the first, had been before sufficiently brought to our knowledge. Some of his disqualifications for *such* a trust were indeed understood when he was appointed *Inspector General*. Gen[l] Dearborn seems not to have been apprised of some of the sides of his character, though he has an apology for what he did in the paucity of General officers provided for the army at that time, and the difficulty of making a satisfactory selection. The narrative is returned, as you desire. It gives me pleasure to receive a confirmation of the unchanged dispositions of those whose sympathies with R[obert] S[mith] could not fail to be most excited. The opportunity of proving to one of them that I have not permitted my belief or my dispositions to be affected by reports or presumptions inconsistent with his penetration, candour, and justice, has been promptly embraced, as you will see by the late military appointments. His son has just received the rank of Major. You will see, also, that I have taken the liberty of naming Mr. Randolph to the Senate for the command of a Regiment, and that it is now within his acceptance.[9] I was aware of all the considerations and embracing those around him, which were mingled with the subject. But knowing his superiority in the talents and military acquirements so much

---

8. For the defeat of General James Winchester at Frenchtown and the surrender of his army to prevent needless loss of life, see J. C. A. Stagg, *Mr. Madison's War: Politics, Diplomacy, and Warfare in the Early American Republic, 1783–1830* (Princeton, 1983), p. 225.

9. For the appointment of Thomas Mann Randolph, TJ's son-in-law, see Malone, VI, p. 118, and William H. Gaines, *Thomas Mann Randolph: Jefferson's Son-in-Law* (Baton Rouge, 1966), pp. 83–89.

needed in our army, and that they had occurred to others of his friends as well as myself, I could not do less than give the public a chance of having the benefit of them. I should indeed have taken the same liberty in the original nominations, but for the less decided state of things than that now existing.

If you do not receive the New York Mercantile Advertiser, the enclosed will give you the Russian account of the catastrophe of the French Army. It is doubtless much exaggerated; but there is no doubt that the losses are beyond example. Whether they can be so replaced as to prevent the defection of Allies, and to present another formidable countenance to the North, is uncertain. It does not appear that any thing like despondence is felt at Paris; and so many interests on the Continent have become associated with the ascendancy of Napoleon, that it will not be surprising, if, with the terrors of his name, he should surmount his difficulties.[10] In England, the usual exultation is indulged on the recent events, and, united with the rage and jealousy produced by our little naval triumphs, account for the gigantic force she is bringing against us on the water.[11] In the meantime, Russia, as you will observe, is tendering her mediating friendship, with the collateral view, there is reason to believe, of deriving advantage from our *neutral* interference with British monopoly in the trade with her. We shall endeavor to turn the good will of Russia to the proper account. Whether England will accede to the mediation, or do so with evasive purposes, remains to be seen.[12] That she has brought it about, I cannot readily suppose, because I think she would not promote our political intercourse with the Baltic, where she apprehends a sympathy with our maritime doctrines, and not with hers. The present occasion proves the good policy of having cultivated the favorable dispositions of the Emperor Alexander. We have good reason to believe that Sweden is as well inclined towards us as Russia. Accept my affectionate respect

JAMES MADISON

Jefferson to Madison

Monticello Apr. 10, 1813

DEAR SIR

The writer of the inclosed letter being as well known to yourself as to me, I forward it merely because he has wished me to mention his sollicitation to you.[13] I should in like manner inclose you a letter from Dr. Barton but that it would take you more time to decypher than you ought to give to it. The object

---

10. For Napoleon's resiliency, see Lefebvre, pp. 326–28.
11. For the diversion of one-seventh of Britain's naval strength to the Chesapeake, see Perkins, pp. 18–19.
12. For England's rejection of mediation by Russia, see *ibid.*, pp. 20–22.
13. Enclosure not found.

of it is to be appointed to the Medical department of the army. His reputation is as well known to yourself as to me, and his qualifications for the office he asks are I suppose unquestionable.[14]

I wish to communicate to you some views formerly taken of the defence of the Chesapeake, because as they respected the departments of the war and navy more immediately, I do not recollect their having then been explained to you but I am become so averse to the writing table that I do not know whether I shall muster resolution enough. This aversion too is encouraged by the presumption that the same views will have occurred to yourself. In all cases be assured of my constant attachment and respect.

Th Jefferson

Jefferson to Madison

Monticello May 21, 1813

Dear Sir,

The enclosed letter from Whit was unquestionably intended for you. The subject, the address, both of title and place, prove it, and the mistake of the name only shows the writer to be a very uninquisitive statesman. Dr. Waterhouse's letter too was intended for your eye; and although the immediate object fails by previous appointment, yet he seems to entertain further wishes. I enclose, too, the newspapers he refers to, as some of their matter may have escaped your notice, and the traitorous designs fostered in Massachusetts, and explained in them, call for attention.

We have never seen so unpromising a crop of wheat as that now growing. The winter killed an unusual proportion of it, and the fly is destroying the remainder. We may estimate the latter loss at one third at present, and fast increasing from the effect of the extraordinary drought. With such a prospect before us, the blockade is acting severely on our past labors. It caught nearly the whole wheat of the middle and upper country in the hands of the farmers and millers, whose interior situation had prevented their getting it to an earlier market. From this neighborhood very little had been sold. When we cast our eyes on the map, and see the extent of country, from New York to North Carolina inclusive, whose product is raised on the waters of the Chesapeake, (for Albemarle sound is, by the canal of Norfolk become a water of the Chesapeake,) and consider its productiveness, in comparison with the rest of the Atlantic States, probably a full half, and that all this can be shut up by two or three ships of the line lying at the mouth of the bay, we see that an injury so vast to ourselves and so cheap to our enemy, must forever be resorted to by

14. For Dr. Benjamin S. Barton, professor of natural history, botany, and materia medica at the University of Pennsylvania and physician at the Pennsylvania Hospital, see John C. Greene, *American Science in the Age of Jefferson* (Ames, Iowa, 1984), pp. 43–45, 193–95, 256–61, 379–96.

them, and constantly maintained. To defend all the shores of those waters in detail, is impossible. But is there not a single point where they may be all defended by means to which the magnitude of the object gives a title? I mean at the mouth of the Chesapeake. Not by ships of the line, or frigates; for I know that with our present enemy we cannot contend in that way. But would not a sufficient number of gun-boats of *small* draught, stationed in Lynhaven river, render it unsafe for ships of war either to ascend the Chesapeake or to lie at its mouth? I am not unaware of the effect of the ridicule cast on this instrument of defence, by those who wished for engines of offence. But resort is had to ridicule only when reason is against us. I know too the prejudices of the gentlemen of the navy and that these are very natural. No one has been more gratified than myself by the brilliant atchievements of our little navy. They have deeply wounded the pride of our enemy, and been balm to ours, humiliated on the land where our real strength was felt to lie. But divesting ourselves of the enthusiasm these brave actions have justly excited, it is impossible not to see that all these vessels must be taken and added to the already overwhelming force of our enemy; that even while we keep them, they contribute nothing to our defence, and that so far as we are to be defended by any thing on the water, it must be by such vessels as can assail under advantageous circumstances, and, under adverse ones, withdraw from the reach of the enemy. This, in shoally waters, is the humble, the ridiculed, but the formidable gun boats. I acknolege that in the case which produces these reflections, the station of Lynhaven river would not be safe against land attacks on the boats, and that a retreat for them is necessary in this event. With a view to this there was a survey made by Colonel Tatham, which was lodged either in the War or Navy office, shewing the depth and length of a canal which would give them a retreat from Lynhaven river into the Eastern branch of Elizabeth river. I think the distance is not over six or eight miles, perhaps not so much, through a country entirely flat, and little above the level of the sea. A cut of ten yards wide and four yards deep, requiring the removal of 40. cubic yards of earth for every yard in length of the canal, at 20. cents the cubic yard, would cost about 15,000 D. a mile. But, even doubling this, to cover all errors of estimate, although in a country offering the cheapest kind of labor, it would be nothing compared with the extent and productions of the country it is to protect. It would, for so great a country, bear no proportion to what has been expended, and justly expended by the Union, to defend the single spot of New York.

While such a channel of retreat secures effectually the safety of the gunboats, it insures also their aid for the defence of Norfolk, if attacked from the sea. And the Norfolk canal gives them a further passage into Albemarle sound, if necessary for their safety, or in aid of the flotilla of that Sound, or to receive the aid of that flotilla either at Norfolk or in Lynhaven river. For such a flotilla there also will doubtless be thought necessary, that being the only outlet now, as during the last war, for the waters of the Chesapeake. Colonel Monroe, I think, is personally intimate with the face of all that country, and no one, I am certain is more able, or more disposed than the present Secretary of the Navy, to place himself above the Navy prejudices, and do justice to the aptitude of these humble and economical vessels to the shallow waters of the South. On the bold Northern shores they would be of less account, and the larger vessels will of course be more employed there. Were they stationed with us, they would rather attract danger than ward it off. The only service they can render us would be to come *in a body*[15] when the occasion offers, of overwhelming a weaker force of the enemy occupying our bay, to oblige them to keep their force in a body, leaving the mass of our coast open.

Although it is probable there may not be an idea here which has not been maturely weighed by yourself, and with a much broader view of the whole field, yet I have frankly hazarded them, because possibly some of the facts or ideas may have escaped in the multiplicity of the objects engaging your notice, and because in every event they will cost you but the trouble of reading. The importance of keeping open a water which covers wholly or considerably, five of the most productive States, containing three-fifths of the population of the Atlantic portion of our union, and of preserving their resources for the support of the war, as far as the state of war and the means of the Confederacy will admit; and especially if it can be done for less than is contributed by the union for more than one single city, will justify our anxieties to have it effected. And should my views of the subject be even wrong, I am sure they will find their apology with you in the purity of the motives of personal and public regard which induce a suggestion of them. In all cases I am satisfied you are doing what is for the best as far as the means put into your hands will enable you; and this thought quiets me under every occurrence, and under every occurrence I am sincerely, affectionately and respectfully your's.

TH. JEFFERSON

Madison to Jefferson

Washington June 6, 1813

DEAR SIR,

I received your favor of the [21st of May], and now return the letter of Doctor Waterhouse, with the newspapers sent with it.[16] He appears to be a man of ability and learning, and to have been rendered interesting to several distinguished friends to the Administration by the persecutions he has suffered from its enemies. Like many others however I see at present no reward for him, but in his own virtues. The Treasury of the Mint was allotted by the general

---

15. TJ's italics.

16. For Dr. Benjamin Waterhouse, see I. Bernard Cohen, *The Life and Scientific and Medical Career of Benjamin Waterhouse: With Some Account of the Introduction of Vaccination in America* (New York, 1980), and Worthington C. Ford, ed., *Statesman and Friend: Correspondence of John Adams and Benjamin Waterhouse, 1784–1822* (Boston, 1927).

sentiment to Doctor J. Rush. And Doctor Tilton has long since been had in view for the superintendence of the Medical Department of the Army.

Your suggestions for protecting the trade of the Chesapeake by Gun boats at the South end of it, with a safe retreat provided for them, have been taken into consideration, with all the respect due to the importance as well as the motives of them. The present Secretary of the Navy is not unfriendly to gunboats; and in general, the call for them by the Inhabitants of the Coast proves a diffusive sense of their utility. It seems agreed at the same time that, being too slow in sailing, and too heavy for rowing, they are limited in their use to particular situations, and rarely for other than defensive co-operations. That an adequate number of them, in Lynhaven Bay, with a safety of retreat, would be useful, cannot be doubtful; but if the enemy chuse to bring such a force as they have applied and with appearances of an intended increase, the number of Gun boats necessary to controul them would be very great, and their effect pretty much restricted to guarding the interior navigation of the Bay. Cruisers on the outside of the Capes, beyond the range of the Gun boats, would still blockade the external commerce.

Commodore Barney has suggested a species of Row Galley, which he considers as better fitted for protecting the interior trade of the Bay than the Gun boat, or rather as an essential auxiliary to the Gun-boats. His plan is to allow them twenty oars and muskets on each side, to be planked up for protection of the oarsmen against small arms in the Enemy's launches, and to have one long and heavy gun; their construction to fit them for speed and for shallow water, and their length and form to be such that at the end of the war they might be easily raised on, and become ordinary coasters. Twenty of these, costing 50 or 60 thousand dollars, he thinks would put an end to the depredations of the smaller vessels, which have been the greatest, and might even attack large ones in the night, or under special circumstances.

I have not ascertained the opinion of the Secretary of the Navy, who adds to a sound judgment a great deal of practical knowledge on such subjects.

You have in the newspapers all the latest news, both foreign and domestic. Be assured of my constant and sincerest affection

JAMES MADISON

Jefferson to Madison
Monticello June 18, 1813

Your kind answer of the 16th[17] entirely satisfies my doubts as to the employment of the navy, if kept within striking distance of our coast; and shows how erroneous views are apt to be with those who have not all in view.

17. TJ meant JM's letter of June 6, 1813.

Yet as I know from experience that profitable suggestions sometimes come from lookers on, they may be usefully tolerated, provided they do not pretend to the right of an answer. They would cost very dear indeed were they to occupy the time of a high officer in writing when he should be acting. I intended no such trouble to you, my dear Sir, and were you to suppose I expected it, I must cease to offer a thought on our public affairs. Although my entire confidence in their direction prevents my reflecting on them but accidentally, yet sometimes facts, and sometimes ideas occur, which I hazard as worth the trouble of reading but not of answering. Of this kind was my suggestion of the facts which I recollected as to the defence of the Chesapeake, and of what had been contemplated at the time between the Secretaries of War and the Navy and myself. If our views were sound, the object might be effected in one year, even of war, and at an expense which is nothing compared to the population and productions it would cover. We are here laboring under the most extreme drought ever remembered at this season. We have had but one rain to lay the dust in two months. That was a good one, but was three weeks ago. Corn is but a few inches high and dying. Oats will not yield their seed. Of wheat, the hard winter and fly leave us about two-thirds of an ordinary crop. So that in the lotteries of human life you see that even farming is but gambling. We have had three days of excessive heat. The thermometer on the 16th was at 92°, on the 17th 92½°, and yesterday at 93°. It had never before exceeded 92½ at this place; at least within the periods of my observations. Ever and affectionately yours.

Jefferson to Madison

Monticello June 21, 1813

Dear Sir,

Your favor of the 6th. has been recieved, and I will beg leave to add a few supplementary observations on the subject of my former letter. I am not a judge of the best forms which may be given to the gunboat; and indeed I suppose they should be of various forms suited to the various circumstances to which they would be applied. Among these no doubt, Commodore Barney's would find their place. While the largest and more expensive are fitted for moving from one seaport to another coast-wise, to aid in a particular emergency, those of smaller draught and expense suit shallower waters; and of these shallow and cheap forms must be those for Lynhaven river. Commodore Preble in his lifetime undertook to build such in the best manner for two or three thousand Dollars. Colo. Monroe, to whose knolege of the face of the country I had referred, approves, in a letter to me of such a plan of defence as was suggested, adding to it a fort on the Middle grounds; but thinks the work too great to be executed during a war. Such a fort certainly could not be built during a war, in the face of an enemy. Its practicability at any time has been doubted, and altho' a good auxiliary, is not a necessary member of this scheme of defence. But the canal of retreat is really a small work, of a few months execution; the laborers would be protected by the military guard on the spot, and many of these would assist in the execution for fatigue, rations and pay. The exact magnitude of the work I would not affirm, nor do I think we should trust for it to Tatham's survey; still less would I call in a Latrobe, who would immediately contemplate a canal of Languedoc. I would sooner trust such a man as Thomas Moore to take the level, measure the distances, and estimate the expense. And if the plan were well matured the ensuing winter, and laborers engaged at the proper season, it might be executed in time to mitigate the blockade of the next summer. On recurring to an actual survey of that part of the country, made in the beginning of the Revolutionary war under the orders of the Governor and Council, by Mr. Andrews I think, a copy of which I took with great care, instead of the half dozen miles I had conjectured in my former letter, the canal would seem to be of not half that length. I send you a copy of that part of the map, which may be useful to you on other occasions, and is more to be depended on for minutiae, probably, than any other existing. I have marked on that the conjectured route of the canal, to wit, from the bridge on Lynhaven river to Kemp's landing on the Eastern branch. The exact draught of water into Lynhaven river you have in the Navy office. I think it is over 4. feet.

When we consider the population and productions of the Chesapeake country, extending from the Génissee to the Saura towns and Albemarle Sound, it's safety and commerce seem entitled even to greater efforts, if greater could secure them. That a defence at the entrance of the bay can be made mainly effective, that it will cost less in money harrass the militia less, place the inhabitants on it's interior waters freer from alarm and depredation, and render provisions and water more difficult to the enemy, is so possible as to render thoro' inquiry certainly expedient. Some of the larger gunboats, or vessels better uniting swiftness with force, would also be necessary to scour the interior, and cut off any pickaroons which might venture up the bay or rivers. The loss on James river alone this year is estimated at 200,000 barrels of flour, now on hand, for which the half price is not to be expected. This then is a million of Dollars levied on a single water of the Chesapeake, and to be levied every year during the war. If a concentration of its defence at the entrance of the Chesapeake should be found inadequate, then we must of necessity submit to the expenses of detailed defence, to the harassment of the militia, the burnings of towns and houses, depredations of farms, and the hard trial of the spirit of the middle states, the most zealous supporters of the war, and therefore the peculiar objects of the vindictive efforts of the enemy. Those north of the Hudson need nothing, because treated by the enemy as neutrals. All their war is concentrated on the Delaware and Chesapeake; and these therefore stand in principal need of the shield of the Union. The Delaware can be defended more easily. But I should not think 100. gunboats (costing less than one frigate) an over-proportioned allotment to the Chesapeake country, against the over-proportioned hostilities pointed at it.

I am too sensible of the partial and defective state of my information to be over-confident, or pertinacious in the opinion I have formed. A thoro' examination of the ground will settle it. We may suggest, perhaps it is a duty to do it. But you alone are qualified for decision, by the whole view which you can command: and so confident am I in the intentions as well as wisdom of the government that I shall always be satisfied that what is not done, either cannot, or ought not to be done. While I trust that no difficulties will dishearten us, I am anxious to lessen the trial as much as possible. Heaven preserve you under yours, and help you thro' all its perplexities and perversities.

TH. JEFFERSON

Jefferson to Madison

Monticello July 13, 1813

DEAR SIR

I was so unlucky as to write you a long letter of business, when, as I learned soon afterwards, you were too ill to be troubled with any matter of business. My comfort has been in the confidence that care would of course be taken not to disturb you with letters. My hope in writing the present is of a pleasanter kind, the flattering one that you are entirely recovered. If the prayers of millions have been of avail, they have been poured forth with the deepest anxiety. The inclosed letter from Mr Fulton will inform you why a similar one did not go to you direct, and that this is forwarded by express desire. Mr Fulton's ingenuity is inexhaustible, and his disinterested devotion of it to his country very laudable. If his present device depended on me I should try it, on the judgment of an officer so well skilled as Decatur. It is one of those experiments which neither the personal interest nor the faculties of a private individual can ever bring into use, while it is highly interesting to the nation. Intersected as we are by many and deep waters, and unable to meet the enemy on them with an equal force, our only hope is in the discovery of the means which ingenuity may devise whereby the weak may defend themselves against the strong. This is done at land by fortifications, and, not being against any law of nature, we may hope that something equivalent may be discovered for the water.[18]

18. As early as 1810, Robert Fulton had persuaded JM and Navy Secretary Hamilton to test his invention of the torpedo for naval warfare; see Brant, V, p. 142. Fulton later invented a steam frigate as a floating battery that was "bomb and shot proof," but he and Decatur agreed that its engine power was too weak for the storms on the Great Lakes; see *ibid.*, VI, p. 346.

You know the present situation of our friend Strode, entirely penniless. How he comes to be left to subsist himself by his labours in subordinate emploiments, while his son is at his ease, I am not informed, nor whether they have had any difference. Yet the fact is that he is in indigence, and anxious to get his living by any services he can render. You know his qualifications. The public iron works, the Armoury, the army or some of the sedentary offices at Washington may perhaps offer some employment analogous to his talents. His wish is to earn a livelihood; and altho' in his letter to me he does not propose to sollicit any thing, yet the expressions of his situation shew that some decent emploiment could not fail to be very acceptable.

We are at the close of the poorest harvest I have ever seen. I shall not carry into my barn more than one third of an ordinary crop. But one rain to wet the ground since April. A remarkable drying wind with great heat the first days of the harvest dryed up the stem of the wheat so that it fell before the scythe instead of being cut. I have seen harvests lost by wet, but never before saw one lost by dry weather. I have suffered more by the drought than my neighbors. Most of them will make half a crop; some two thirds. Much of the evil had been prepared by the winter and the fly. It is not too late yet for the corn to recover should there come rains shortly. It never was seen so low before at this date. Our gardens are totally burnt up: and the river so low that you may almost jump over it in some places. Wishing a speedy and perfect reestablishment of your health, I pray you to accept the assurance of my constant and affectionate esteem and respect

TH JEFFERSON

Jefferson to Madison

Monticello Aug. 15, 1813

DEAR SIR

I congratulate you on your release from the corvée of a session of Congress, and on the pleasure of revisiting your own fields and friends: and I hope your fields have been more fortunate than ours which have been wet but once since the 14th. of April, and present an aspect never seen since the year 1755. when we lost so many people by famine. But the present drought is only partial; that was general. There are now districts of country that have suffered little.

I am obliged to set out for Bedford on Wednesday or Thursday next, to be absent 3. or 4. weeks. On my return I shall have the pleasure of seeing you at Montpelier, by which time I hope a perfect reestablishment of your health and relief from influenza will render the visit you promise us for Mrs Madison and yourself as recreating to you as welcome to us. The paper you were so kind as to inclose me presents me the first copy I have seen of the assessment law.[19] In the appointment of Collector we shall feel little interest; but that of principal Assessor will be awfully important, as he alone is to decide the quantum of tax each man is to pay in 4. counties. If indeed he is to be governed by the state valuations pro ratâ he will need to be only a good arithmetician. Otherwise, he should be just, capable, clear of party and personal biasses beyond all suspicion. I suppose he would best be taken from either Nelson or Albemarle, the two central counties. I am too little acquainted to know whether there now lives in either such a man as Colo. Nicholas Lewis was. I will endeavor to get the best men of our county to consult and enquire and give their opinions, presuming it may be in time to send their recommendation to you. Present me with all affection to Mrs Madison in which Mrs Randolph joins me, and accept for yourself assurances of my constant attachment and respect.

TH JEFFERSON

Jefferson to Madison

Monticello Aug. 23, 1813

DEAR SIR

I have been prevented setting out to Bedford as early as I had counted. I depart tomorrow. In the mean time, I have consulted with as many as I could of the leading men of our county on the subject of the Principal assessor, as I proposed in my letter of the 15th. Of those consulted who are known to yourself were Mr Divers, the Mr Carr's, Mr Randolph, Bankhead etc. One character has struck all of these in the first instance, that of Peter Minor. He is the son of Colo. Garrett Minor of Louisa, married to a daughter of Dr. Gilmer, and settled about 4. miles up the river from Charlottesville. He is a farmer, an excellent one, a man of sound judgment, honest, independant, and well acquainted with the value of the taxable subjects. He was brought up to the law, but declined entering into the practice, clear of any passions which might produce bias and the strict justice of his character so well known that his decisions will satisfy those submitted to them. I observe the quota of our county is something under 10,000 D. This is to be divided among the owners of taxable property first by the sub-assessors, and then to be equalised by the principal assessor. This is what makes him important. The most abominable and barefaced partialities under the former real tax by Congress have excited attention here on the revival of a similar measure. I suppose the appointment will be made in this county or Nelson, as being the middle of the 4. counties

---

19. If the paper was accompanied by a letter from JM, that letter is missing. For the taxes passed at the special session of Congress during the summer of 1813, see Brant, VI, pp. 196–97, and Stagg, pp. 314–16.

lying in a string along James River. I am not acquainted in Nelson: if they offer a better man than Minor we shall be glad to be under his agency. I hope you continue to gain strength and that on my return I shall find you in good health. Affectionate salutations
>TH JEFFERSON

P. S. I shall see Mr Nicholas, Patterson etc. tomorrow. If they suggest a better person than Minor, I will write to you from Warren

THE CRITICAL YEAR: 1814

THE YEAR 1814 was the critical one of the War of 1812, and the pressures of the conflict weighed so heavily on Madison that his correspondence with Jefferson almost lapsed.[1] As the war wore on, it became increasingly clear, as Richard Rush had written at the beginning of the conflict, that "Mr. Madison is not a Mr. Jefferson or a General Washington, either of whom, from their vast ascendancy over Congress and the publick . . . might be gratified in any little executive freak dear to their heart."[2] Nonetheless, the president did his best to rally national unity, telling Congress that the war was "illustrating the capacity and the destiny of the United States to be a great, a flourishing, and a powerful nation."

Madison boldly hailed Captain Oliver H. Perry's defeat of the British fleet on Lake Erie as "a victory never surpassed in luster," adding that it opened the way for Major General William Henry Harrison's recovery of Detroit and the liberation of the Northwest. He paid tribute to Major General Andrew Jackson, "an officer equally distinguished for his patriotism and his military talents," for his victory over the Indians in the Southwest. But he also confessed that the war had brought "increased spoliations on the ocean and . . . predatory incursions on the land," although he said that these adversities stimulated "the national means of retaliating the former and providing protection against the latter."[3]

Early in 1814, the president informed Congress of Britain's proposal to initiate direct negotiations for peace, after rejecting Russia's offer of mediation. Although he recommended negotiations for peace, he also stressed the need for "vigorous preparations for carrying on the war," if the wish for peace failed.[4] To smooth the path to peace, Madison had already proposed, and

1. JM sent no letters to TJ between June 6, 1813, and May 10, 1814, but he did enclose a paper, now missing, with a new assessment law sometime during the summer of 1813, which TJ acknowledged in his letter of Aug. 15, 1813, above.
2. Richard Rush to Charles J. Ingersoll, Sept. 18, 1812, cited in Ketcham, p. 563.
3. JM, Annual Message to Congress, Dec. 7, 1813, in Richardson, I, pp. 534–40.
4. JM, message to Congress, Jan. 6, 1814, *ibid.,* pp. 541–42.

Congress had passed, legislation excluding British seamen from American vessels after the war ended. To meet England's fear of losing seamen through expatriation and naturalization, he also proposed to exclude all foreign-born seamen who had not started naturalization proceedings before peace was concluded.[5] To eliminate peacefully the "degrading practice" of impressment, he now suggested that British seamen deserting in American ports would be surrendered. "The British Government," he told Jefferson, "cannot do less than send negotiators to meet ours; but whether in the spirit of ours, is the important question."[6]

After Congress adjourned, the Madisons made a short visit to Montpellier in the spring, their first trip at that season since Madison had become president. Although they wanted to visit Monticello, the uncertainty of their scheduled return to Washington made that impossible since Madison had "to hold myself in readiness to hasten it, at any moment of notice. We must postpone therefore the pleasure of paying our respects there till the autumn," he explained to his friend, "when I hope we shall be less restricted in time."

By the time the Madisons returned to Washington in June, the president had learned that Napoleon had abdicated in April 1814, opening European markets to the British at the same time that it freed trained troops and the navy for use in America. Madison hoped that peace in Europe would "strengthen the motives to get rid of the war with us." On the domestic front, he thought that Republican election victories in New York would crush "the [disunionist] project of the [Federalist] Junto faction so long fostered by and flattering the expectations of the British Cabinet."[7]

But even stronger than this hope was his fear that the British would continue the war in order "to break down our Government." From his post in Europe, Gallatin concluded that "a well organized and large army is at once liberated from any European employment, and ready, together with a superabundant naval force, to act immediately against us. . . . The English people eagerly wish that their pride may be fully gratified by what they call 'the punishment of America.' They do not even suspect that we had any just cause for war, and ascribe it solely to a premeditated concert with Bonaparte at a time when we thought him triumphant and their cause desperate."[8]

Madison and his cabinet had already approved a campaign against Canada for the spring of 1814. Since the victories of Perry and Harrison had made Lake Erie secure, the Americans concentrated their forces on the Niagara peninsula and Montreal. At the end of March, Wilkinson marched a large force across the border south of Montreal, failed to dislodge a small fortified garrison at Lacolle, and marched back to Lake Champlain, where he was

---

5. Brant, VI, pp. 136–37.
6. JM to TJ, May 10, 1814, below.
7. *Ibid.*
8. Ketcham, p. 571.

relieved of his command. From Niagara, American troops were to move along the north shore of Lake Ontario to York, with the navy providing protection. The army performed well, capturing Fort Erie and sweeping on to the lake. When the navy failed to rendezvous for the move north, the army fought a sharp battle with British troops at Lundy's Lane, then returned to Fort Erie, where a British attack was repulsed. Despite a skillfully fought series of battles by the northern army, the Lake Ontario campaign ended in a stalemate.

On the coast, the British navy continued to launch running raids at will. During the summer, combined forces occupied the northern portion of Maine east of the Penobscot River in order to secure an overland route from Halifax to Quebec. The navy then clamped on a blockade from Maine to the Mississippi, a move that Madison denounced as "destitute of the character of a regular and legal blockade as defined and recognized by the established law of nations."[9]

By August, 10,000 British veterans from Wellington's victorious army in Europe joined Governor General Prevost's forces in Canada for an invasion down Lake Champlain designed to cut off New England. But a brilliant naval victory by Captain Thomas Macdonough near Plattsburgh forced Prevost's army to retreat to Canada, the most decisive American victory during the war.

As a feint to help Prevost, a veteran British army sailed into the Chesapeake to launch diversionary attacks on Washington and Baltimore, setting the stage for the most humiliating episode in American history. The new commander of the British naval forces in American waters, Vice Admiral Sir Alexander Cochrane, had said that he wanted to give the Americans "a drubbing before peace is made." In a bold move, 3,400 British regular troops and 700 Royal Marines brushed aside American regulars and militiamen and swept into the nation's capital, where they burned the President's House, the Capitol (including the library of Congress), and other public buildings as well as the office of the *National Intelligencer,* the administration newspaper. Rear Admiral George Cockburn directed the Royal Marines to destroy the presses and throw away the type, especially "all C's so they can't abuse my name."

Madison, who watched defense preparations as the invading troops approached, stayed on the outskirts of Washington until "it became manifest that the battle was lost." Before returning to the President's House, he told his cabinet officers to meet him at Frederick, Maryland, if the British occupied the city. He then returned to the White House, found that Dolley Madison had escaped into Virginia, and crossed the Potomac to search for his wife. After a worrisome night apart, they met at an inn near Great Falls and decided to return to Washington, though the president confessed to his wife, "I know not where we are in the first instance to hide our heads."[10]

After the debacle in the nation's capital, Jefferson broke a four-month

---

9. JM, Proclamation of June 29, 1814, in Richardson, I, pp. 543–44.
10. Robert Allen Rutland, *The Presidency of James Madison* (Lawrence, Kans., 1990), pp. 157–67.

silence—"I have really had nothing to write which ought to have occupied your time," he explained—to sympathize with his friend. "In the late events at Washington," he commiserated, "I have felt so much for you that I cannot withhold the expression of my sympathies." Nor did he hold the commander in chief responsible for the failure to defend the nation's capital against the invading enemy. "For altho' every reasonable man must be sensible that all you can do is to order, that execution must depend on others, and failures be imputable to them alone, yet I know that when such failures happen they afflict even those who have done everything they could to prevent them. Had General Washington himself been now at the head of our affairs, the same event would probably have happened. We all remember," he recalled, "the disgraces which befel us in his time in a trifling war with one or two petty tribes of Indians, in which two armies were cut off by not half their numbers. Every one knew, and I personally knew, because I was then of his council, that no blame was imputable to him, and that his officers alone were the cause of the disasters. They must now do [you] the same justice," he concluded.[11]

Turning from the Washington fiasco, the nadir of the war from the American point of view, to the Lake Champlain victory, perhaps the zenith, Jefferson congratulated Madison "on the destruction of a second hostile fleet on the lakes by McDonough. . . . While our enemies cannot but feel shame for their barbarous atchievements at Washington, they will be stung to the soul by these repeated victories over them on that element on which they wish the world to think them invincible." One could almost hear him chortle when he proudly proclaimed that "we can beat them gun to gun, ship to ship, and fleet to fleet."[12]

From news accounts, Jefferson also learned of "the loss of the library of Congress," and he promptly offered his personal collection of books, "now of about 9. or 10,000. vols.," as a replacement. To Samuel Harrison Smith, now commissioner of revenue, he sent a copy of the catalogue of his collection.[13] "I believe you are acquainted with the condition of the books," Jefferson wrote the president. "I have long been sensible that my library would be an interesting possession for the public, and the loss Congress has recently sustained, and the difficulty of replacing it, while our intercourse with Europe is so obstructed, renders this the proper moment for placing it at their service."[14]

Madison was immensely pleased with Jefferson's magnificent offer, pre-

---

11. TJ to JM, Sept. 24, 1814, below. For the British sweep into Washington, see James Pack, *The Man Who Burned the White House: Admiral Sir George Cockburn* (Annapolis, 1987).

12. TJ to JM, Sept. 24, 1814, below. See also Allan S. Everett, *The War of 1812 in the Champlain Valley* (Syracuse, 1981).

13. TJ to JM, Sept. 24, 1814, below, and TJ to Samuel Harrison Smith, Sept. 21, 1814, in Ford, IX, pp. 485-88.

14. TJ to JM, Sept. 24, 1814, below. For a fuller account of the transfer, see Malone, VI, pp. 169-84. Congress paid $23,950 for 6,487 volumes. See also E. Millicent Sowerby, *Catalogue of the Library of Thomas Jefferson*, 5 vols. (Washington, 1952-59), and Charles Sanford, *Thomas Jefferson and His Library: A Study of His Literary Interests and of the Religious Attitudes Revealed by Relevant Titles in His Library* (Hamden, Conn., 1977).

dicting "that the Library Com[mitte]e will report favorably on your proposition to supply the loss of books by Cong[res]s. It will prove a gain to them, if they have the wisdom to replace it by such a Collection as yours."[15] Later that day, the Senate unanimously adopted the resolution by the Joint Committee on the Library to acquire Jefferson's library.

The British burned the public buildings in Washington on August 25 and 26, 1814. Madison reentered the smoldering city on August 27 and decided that the national government would carry on there, viewing the British invasion as nothing more than a temporary disruption of "the ordinary public business at the seat of Government."[16] On September 1, the defiant president issued a proclamation denouncing the British for giving the war "a character of extended devastation and barbarism" and calling on the people of the nation to unite "in manful and universal determination to chastise and expel the invader."[17]

For the remainder of his presidency, the Madisons lived in temporary quarters while the White House was being repaired.[18] They moved first to the Octagon House at Eighteenth Street and New York Avenue. To house Congress, the president ordered the conversion of the Post Office and the Patent Office building (which had not been torched because of the plea of Dr. William Thornton that "it was the Museum of the Arts") into temporary meeting rooms for the Senate and the House, scheduled to convene on September 19 in special session.[19]

After the British sacked Washington, Madison sacked Armstrong as secretary of war, putting Monroe in charge of the War Department. He also accepted resignations from Secretary of the Navy William Jones, whose public service led to huge private debts, and Secretary of the Treasury George Washington Campbell, who was ill. They were replaced by Benjamin W. Crowninshield of Massachusetts and Alexander James Dallas of Pennsylvania. In a letter to Jefferson about war finances and peace negotiations, Madison concluded his long discussion by saying, "I intended to have said something on the changes in the Cabinet, involving in one instance [Armstrong], circumstances of which the public can as yet very little judge, but cannot do it now."[20]

By his vigorous persistence in pursuing his duties as commander in chief and chief executive in the most trying situations, Madison steadied his admin-

15. JM to TJ, Oct. 10, 1814, below. For a fascinating novel about TJ's sale of his library to Congress and a suggestion that the original library was not burned, see Charles Goodrum, *The Best Cellar: Murder and Mystery at the Werner Bok Library* (New York, 1987). This book was called to my attention by P. L. Harrison.

16. JM, Sixth Annual Message to Congress, Sept. 20, 1814, in Richardson, I, pp. 547-48.

17. *Ibid.*

18. William Seale, *The President's House: A History,* 2 vols. (Washington, 1986), I, pp. 138-56.

19. Brant, VI, pp. 305, 323, and Richardson, I, p. 546.

20. JM to TJ, Oct. 10, 1814, below. JM fired Armstrong for usurpation of authority and insubordination. After resigning, the secretary launched a newspaper attack on JM's administration; see Brant, VI, pp. 309-15, and J. C. A. Stagg, *Mr. Madison's War: Politics, Diplomacy, and Warfare in the Early American Republic, 1783-1830* (Princeton, 1983), pp. 419-22, 431-35.

istration and kept his eyes on both the conduct of the war and the pursuit of peace through negotiations at Ghent, where the discussions had opened in August. As Congress assembled in the charred capital, news arrived of the unsuccessful British attempt to do unto Baltimore what they had done unto Washington. Watching the bombardment of Fort McHenry in Baltimore harbor "by the dawn's early light" on September 14, Francis Scott Key, a Washington lawyer sent by Madison to negotiate a prisoner-of-war exchange, was inspired to write "The Star-spangled Banner" to commemorate the victory. On September 19, the day that Congress convened, Madison learned of the double defeat of the British on Lake Champlain: Commodore Macdonough's naval triumph and General Macomb's report on the retreat of the British veterans under Prevost.

Madison attributed the British defeats at Baltimore and Lake Champlain to "the progressive discipline of the American soldiery" and to intrepid naval forces, but he warned that the "barbarous" British, who refused to conform to "the usages of civilized warfare," were still powerful and could now aim their "undivided force . . . at our growing prosperity, perhaps at our national existence."[21]

As an example of British perceptions of their own power, Madison cited the "arrogance" of their demands at Ghent. He told Jefferson that the British negotiators had treated the United States as a conquered nation, demanding "a Cession of as much of Maine as w^d remove the obstruction to a *direct* communication between Quebec and Halifax, confirmed to her the Passamaquoddy Islands as always hers of right; included in the pacification the Indian Allies, with a boundary for them (such as that of the Treaty of Greenville) agst the U. S. mutually guaranteed, and the Indians restrained from selling their lands to either party, but free to sell them to a *third* party; prohibited the U. S. from having an armed force on the Lakes or forts on their shores, the British prohibited as to neither; and substituted for the present N. W. limit of the U. S. a line running direct from the W. end of L[ake] Superior to the Mississippi, with a right of G. B. to the navigation of this river." The British also "excluded us from fishing within the sovereignty attached to her shores [in Canada], and from using these in curing fish."[22]

"The arrogance of such demands," Madison concluded, might lead the American envoys—Gallatin, Adams, Clay, Bayard, and Russell—to "an indignant rupture of the negotiation." Indeed, he expected that "they w^d probably leave Ghent shortly" unless the British demands were changed.[23]

After hearing this grim news, Jefferson decided that the British had changed the character of the conflict. "The war undertaken, on both sides, to

21. Richardson, I, pp. 547–51.
22. JM to TJ, Oct. 10, 1814, below. The best analysis of British thinking on these issues is J. Leitch Wright, *Britain and the American Frontier, 1783–1815* (Athens, Ga., 1975), pp. 151–85.
23. JM to TJ, Oct. 10, 1814, below. JM received the diplomatic dispatches by courier on Oct. 8 and laid them before Congress on the day that he wrote TJ.

settle the questions of impressment, and the Orders of council, now that these are done away by events, is declared by Great Britain to have changed its object, and to have become a war of Conquest, to be waged until she conquers from us our fisheries, the province of Maine, the lakes, states and territories north of the Ohio, and the navigation of the Mississippi; in other words till she reduces us to unconditional submission." If that were the case, he told Madison, the United States "ought to propose, as a counterchange of object," and lay down its new demand: "the establishment of the meridian of the mouth of Sorel northwardly as the Western boundary of all her possessions" in North America.[24] To enforce its new demand, the United States needed to "prepare for interminable war" and provide "men and money to indefinite extent."[25] For manpower, Jefferson proposed the federalization of the militia and congressional authorization of its use beyond "imaginary" state lines. To finance this new phase of the war, he also favored the federalization of the monetary system by the issuance of Treasury notes redeemable by taxes instead of the circulation of state bank notes.[26]

Since the charter of the Bank of the United States had not been renewed in 1811, the only banks operating during the War of 1812 were state banks. But wartime experience with these proliferating banks had made Jefferson almost as much an enemy of them as he had been of the federally chartered bank. Linking the state banks with the disastrous paper-money schemes of the Revolutionary era, he blasted "the continual creation of new banks" and denounced their emissions as "trash." Early in 1814, he had predicted that "the whole system must blow up before the year is out."[27]

After the burning of Washington, most of the state banks, except for those in New England, suspended specie payment, precipitating an economic crisis that "marked the lowest ebb in the financial history of the United States."[28] "I am afraid the failure of our banks will occasion embarrasment for a while," Jefferson wrote his successor, "altho' it restores to us a fund which ought never to have been surrendered by the nation, and which now, prudently used, will carry us thro' all the fiscal difficulties of the war." He informed the president that he had written lengthy letters on war finances to Monroe, then doubling as secretary of state and secretary of war. These letters, in which Jefferson sketched his belief that the suspension of specie payments would now allow the federal government to regain control over the nation's money supply, were much too long for the busy president to read, but Jeffer-

24. TJ to JM, Oct. 15, 1814, below. Sorel is located at the confluence of the Richelieu River and the St. Lawrence, due north of Lake Champlain; see Lester J. Cappon, Barbara B. Petchenik, and John H. Long, eds., *Atlas of Early American History: The Revolutionary Era, 1760–1790* (Princeton, 1976), p. 2.
25. TJ to James Monroe, Oct. 16, 1814, in Ford, IX, p. 492.
26. TJ to JM, Oct. 15, 1814, below.
27. TJ to JM, Feb. 16, 1814, below.
28. Harry Coles, *The War of 1812* (Chicago, 1965), p. 238.

son suggested that Monroe could, "in a few sentences, state to you their outline."[29]

After reading Jefferson's first letter to Monroe, Madison rejected his friend's Treasury-bill proposal to create "a circulating medium," one designed "to answer the purpose of a loan, or rather anticipation of a tax." No matter how often the Treasury issued notes and redeemed them with taxes, he argued, "resort must eventually be had to loans of the usual sort, or an augmentation of taxes, according to the public exigencies." Despite his stand in 1791 against the constitutionality of the Bank of the United States, a position that he then had shared with Jefferson, Madison now preferred to reestablish a national bank, from which the Treasury could borrow money to finance the war. Indeed, he cited the Bank of England as an excellent model, arguing that "the paper medium, is a legal tender" for payment of taxes, interest to public creditors, and settlement of private debts, "with little if any depreciation," despite the "mass of paper . . . afloat."[30]

Jefferson responded promptly, trying to clarify "what either I have ill expressed, or you have misapprehended." At the risk of trespassing on the president's busy schedule, he gave a lengthy explanation of his views on finances, distinguishing between the needs of a very short war and long-term needs "which we might safely call indefinite." In both cases, however, he advocated Treasury bills or notes, redeemable by taxes, as the circulating medium and opposed paper money "emitted either by public or private authority" such as banks, a term that he carefully avoided using. "The circulating fund," he concluded, "is the only one we can ever command with certainty. It is sufficient for all our wants; and the impossibility of even defending the country without its aid as a borrowing fund, renders it indispensable that the nation should take and keep it in their own hands, as their exclusive resource," rather than share it with a national bank and with state banks.[31]

The busy president, who had already decided to recharter the Bank of the United States, was patient enough to take time out to explore "the variance in our ideas" about national finances. Writing less than a week after Secretary of the Treasury Dallas had recommended to Congress the establishment of a new national bank in Philadelphia,[32] Madison criticized "the probable quantity of circulating medium" under his friend's plan and "the effect of an annual augmentation of it." Given "the present stagnation of private dealings, and the proposed limitation of taxes" to redeem the Treasury bills, "the two great absorbents of money," he doubted whether "the circulating sum would

---

29. TJ to JM, Sept. 24, 1814, below. TJ proposed that treasury notes, backed by taxes, be made a national circulating medium.

30. JM to TJ, Oct. 10, 1814, below.

31. TJ to JM, Oct. 15, 1814, below.

32. Stagg, p. 440, and Brant, VI, pp. 338–39.

amount even to 20 millions," the theoretical figure cited by Jefferson as the annual loan needed to carry on the war.³³

"But be this amount what it may," the president continued, "every emission beyond it must either enter into circulation, and depreciate the whole mass, or it must be locked up." It could be locked up only to accumulate interest, or, if held during a period of inflation, it could be held as a hedge against depreciation, when its value at a future day might rise. Otherwise, it would circulate and create a depreciation comparable to "the career of the old continental currency" of the American Revolution.

Despite "the gloomy inferences" to be drawn from his analysis, Madison thought "that our case is not altogether without remedy." Without mentioning his proposal to recharter a national bank, he said that "paper, in some form or other, will, as a circulating medium, answer the purpose your plan contemplates," while increased taxes would siphon off enough paper to prevent inflation. Indirectly stating the case for a new national bank, he added that he could not "but think that a domestic capital, existing under various shapes, and disposable to the public, may still be obtained on terms, though hard, not intolerable." Although he made no reference to the recent victories at Baltimore and Lake Champlain, he suggested their international impact, saying "it will not be very long before the money market abroad will not be entirely shut against us; a market, however ineligible in some respects, not to be declined under our circumstances."³⁴

THE LETTERS

Madison to Jefferson

Washington Feb. 13, 1814

DEAR SIR

You will have noticed the propositions in the H. of Reps which tend to lift the veil which has so long covered the operations of the post off. Dept. They grew out of the disposition of Granger to appoint Leib to the vacant post office in Phila. in opposition to the known aversion of the City and of the whole State; and to the recommendation of the Pen: delegation in Congs. Having actually made the appointment, contrary to my sentiments also, which

33. JM did not indicate that Dallas had just estimated the cost of the war for 1815 at $28 million or that the administration's bank proposal, which called for a capital of $50 million, authorized a loan of up to $30 million to the United States at 6 percent interest.

34. JM to TJ, Oct. 23, 1814, below. JM vetoed a watered-down bank bill on Jan. 30, 1815, but approved the second Bank of the United States in Apr. 1816.

he asked and recd, much excitement prevails agst. him, and he is of course sparing no means, to ward the effects of it.[1]

Among other misfeasances charged on him, is his continuance, or probably reappointment, of Tayloe, since his residence in this City, as postmaster of a little office near his seat in Virga., no otherwise of importance than as it gives the postmaster the privilege of franking, which is said to amount to more than the income of the office, and which is exercised by the non-resident officer. The exhibition of this abuse to the public, is anxiously dreaded by G: and as a chance to prevent it, a very extraordinary conversation has been held by him with a particular friend of mine with a view doubtless, that it might be communicated to me and perhaps to others of your friends.

Instead of denying or justifying the abuses he stated that whilst Docr. Jones was a candidate for Congs. a Baptist Preacher, who electioneered for him, enjoyed a contract for carrying the mail; that Tayloe who became an under-bidder for the contract, was about to oust the Preacher; and that the only expedient to save and satisfy the electioneering friend of the Docr. was to buy off Tayloe, by giving him the post office, which was brought about by Docr. Jones *with your sanction;* that the present obnoxious arrangement had that origin; and if the enquiry is pushed on him he must come out with the whole story.

It would be superfluous to make remarks on the turpitude of character here developed. I have thought it proper to hint it to you, as a caution agst. any snare that may be laid for you by artful letters, and that you may recollect any circumstances which have been perverted for so wicked a purpose.

I have nothing to add to the contents of the enclosed Newspaper. Affectionate respects

JAMES MADISON

Jefferson to Madison

Monticello Feb. 16, 1814

DEAR SIR,

A letter from Colo. Earle of S. C. induces me to apprehend that the government is called on to reimburse expences to which I am persuaded it is no wise liable either in justice or liberality. I inclose you a copy of my answer to

---

1. JM had retained TJ's postmaster general, Gideon Granger, who increasingly sided with JM's political enemies, including Senator Michael Leib, leader of the dissident Republicans in Pennsylvania. When Leib was defeated in 1814, Granger appointed him postmaster of Philadelphia. Madison promptly dismissed Granger and appointed Governor Return Jonathan Meigs of Ohio. Granger then appealed to TJ for aid in his public vindication; see Brant, VI, pp. 243–45.

him, as it may induce further enquiry, and particularly of Genl. Dearborn. The Tennessee Senators of that day can also give some information.[2]

We have not yet seen the scheme of the new loan, but the continual creation of new banks cannot fail to facilitate it; for already there is so much of their trash afloat that the great holders of it shew vast anxiety to get rid of it. They perceive that now, as in the revolutionary war, we are engaged in the old game of Robin's alive. They are ravenous after lands, and stick at no price. In the neighborhood of Richmond, the seat of that sort of sensibility, they offer twice as much now as they would give a year ago. 200 Millions in actual circulation and 200 Millions more likely to be legitimated by the legislative sessions of this winter, will give us about 40 times the wholesome circulation for 8. millions of people. When the new emissions get out, our legislatures will see, what they otherwise cannot believe, that it is possible to have too much money. It will insure your loan for this year; but what will you do for the next? For I think it impossible but that the whole system must blow up before the year is out: and thus a tax of 3. or 400 millions will be levied on our citizens who had found it a work of so much time and labour to pay off a debt of 80. millions which had redeemed them from bondage. The new taxes are paid here with great cheerfulness. Those on stills and carriages will be wonderfully productive. A general return to the cultivation of tobo. is taking place, because *it will keep.* This proves that the public mind is made up to a continuance of the war. Ever affectionately yours.

TH. JEFFERSON

Jefferson to Madison

Monticello Feb. 17, 1814

DEAR SIR

In my letter of yesterday I forgot to put the inclosed one from Mr Mill, which I now send merely to inform you of his wishes, and to do on it what you find right. He is an excellent young man, modest, cautious and very manageable. His skill in architecture will be proved by his drawings and he has had a good deal of experience. He married a daughter of Colo. Smith of Winchester formerly (perhaps now) a member of Congress.[3] Affectionately Yours

TH: JEFFERSON

2. Colonel Elias Earle, who proposed to explore the Cherokee lands for a site to locate an ironworks to supply Indian needs, had asked to be allowed by the government to bargain with the Cherokees. TJ recalled that his proposal "was on your own motion altogether, and not on the request or Account of the government" but "at your own expense"; see TJ to Elias Earle, Feb. 16, 1814, Presidential Papers Microfilm, James Madison Papers, reel 16.

3. TJ referred to Robert Mills; see Helen M. P. Gallagher, *Robert Mills: Architect of the Washington Monument, 1781–1855* (New York, 1935).

Jefferson to Madison

Monticello Mar. 10, 1814

DEAR SIR,

Your favor of Feb. 7. was duly recieved. That which it gave me reason to expect from Mr. G[ranger] did not come till the 4th inst. He mentioned in it that a state of things existed which probably would oblige him to make a solemn appeal to the public, and he asked my testimony to certain specific facts which he stated. These related solely to charges against him as a Burrite, and to his agency in dismissing the prosecutions in Connecticut under the Sedition law. The facts alledged as disproving his Burrism were 1. That he thro' Mr. Erving in 1800, put Virginia on her guard against the designs of Burr. 2. That in 1803. 4. at my request he communicated to De Witt Clinton Burr's aspiring to the government of New York. 3. That in 1806. he gave us the first effectual notice of Burr's Western projects, by which we were enabled to take specific measures to meet them. 4. His mission of Mr. Pease on the route to N. Orleans to expedite the mails and remove suspected agents of the Post office. These appeals to my very defective memory are very painful. I have looked over my papers, and answered his enquiries as exactly as I could, under a sense not only of the general duty of bearing testimony to truth, but of justice to him personally for his conduct towards me was ever friendly and faithful, and I on several occasions used his services to the advantage of the public.

He said nothing on the subject of Tayloe's post office, but I remember the substance, altho' not the minutiae of that case. He informed me that Mr Tayloe held a post office near Mount Airy, and exercised it by his steward as a deputy, himself residing at Washington, merely for the purpose of carrying on his plantation correspondence free of postage. I advised his immediate appointment of another, as well on the ground of the abusive use of the office, as to suppress the example of non-residents holding local offices, which would otherwise lead immediately to the most pernicious practices of sinecure.

Of the Baptist preacher, and Mr Tayloe's underbidding him I recollect nothing. I remember that Mr. Granger soon after he came into office, informed me of a devise, practised by the federalists in the Eastern states to favor the circulation of their papers and defeat that of the republicans, which was when ever a republican rider was employed, to underbid to a price below what the business could be done for, submitting to that loss for one year, and the next to demand the full price, the republican being thus removed from the competition, by the disposal of his horses etc. I desired him whenever a bidder should offer below the real worth, and there should be reason to suspect this fraud, to reject him, and I would take on myself the responsibility. If I was consulted on the competition of Tayloe and the baptist preacher, and gave an opinion on it, it must have been stated as a case of this class. As to the compromise alledged of giving up the one case for the other, no such idea was ever presented to me, nor would Mr G. have ventured to present it, and I am certain that not a word ever passed between Doctr Jones and myself on the subject. The true remedy for putting those appointments into a wholesome state would be a law vesting them in the President, but without the intervention of the Senate. That intervention would make the matter worse. Every Senator would expect to dispose of all the post offices in his vicinage, or perhaps in his state. At present the President has some controul over those appointments by his authority over the Postmaster himself. And I should think it well to require him to lay all his appointments previously before the President for his approbation or rejection. An expression in Mr G's letter gave me ground to advise him to confine his vindication to it's important points whatever they might be, and not to let his passions lead him into matter which would degrade himself alone in the public opinion, and I have urged it in such terms as I trust will have effect.[4]

Our agriculture presents little interesting. Wheat looks badly, much having been killed by the late severe weather. Corn is scarce, but it's price kept down to 3. D. by the substitute of wheat as food both for laborers and horses, costing only 3/6 to 4/. They begin to distill the old flour, getting 10. galls of whiskey from the barrel, which produces 5. to 6. D. the barrel and consequently more than we can get at Richmond for the new. Tobacco is high, from it's scarcity, there having been not more than ⅓ of an ordinary crop planted the last year. This year there will probably be ⅔. Ever affectionately yours.

Jefferson to Madison

Monticello Mar. 16, 1814

DEAR SIR

I inclose you two letters from Mr Burrall, postmaster of Baltimore. You will percieve by them that the removal of Mr Granger has spread some dismay in the ranks. I lodged in the same house with him (Francis's) during the sessions of Congress of 97. 98. 99. We breakfasted, dined etc. at the same table. He classed himself with the federalists, but I did not know why, for he scarcely ever uttered a word on the subject, altho' it was in the reign of addresses, of Mcpherson's blues and of terror. He would sometimes make a single observation in support of the administration. He is an honest and a good man, and, as far as I have observed him, has been correct, faithful and obliging in the conduct of his office. Altho' I am sure it is unnecessary, yet I could not when requested refuse this testimony to the truth. Ever and affectionately yours

TH JEFFERSON

4. TJ warned Granger against spreading "gossiping trash"; see Ketcham, pp. 569–70.

Jefferson to Madison

Monticello Mar. 26, 1814

DEAR SIR

The inclosed from Dr. Brown is this moment come to hand, and supposing it may possibly be of some importance I send it off immediately to the post office in the bare possibility it may get there in time for the mail of this morning. If it fails it will have to wait there 4. days longer. Ever affectly. yours

TH: JEFFERSON

Madison to Jefferson

Montpellier May 10, 1814

DEAR SIR,

Having particular occasion, and the state of business at Washington not forbidding, I am on a short visit at my farm. Mrs. M., as well as myself, would gladly extend it to Monticello, but with a certainty that our return to Washington must be very soon. I am obliged moreover to hold myself in readiness to hasten it, at any moment of notice. We must postpone therefore the pleasure of paying our respects there till the autumn, when I hope we shall be less restricted in time.

We have received no information from our Envoys to the Baltic for a very long time. From those last appointed there has not been time to hear after their arrival at Gottenburg. Neither have we any accounts from England, other than the newspaper paragraphs which you have seen. The British Government cannot do less than send negotiators to meet ours; but whether in the spirit of ours, is the important question. The turn of recent events in Europe, if truly represented, must strengthen the motives to get rid of the war with us; and their hopes by a continuance of it, to break down our Government, must be more and more damped by occurrences here as they become known there. The election in New York alone crushes the project of the Junto faction so long fostered by and flattering the expectations of the British Cabinet.[5] Still it is possible that new fallacies may suffice for a willingness to be deceived. Our difficulties in procuring money without heavy taxes, and the supposed odium of these, will probably be made the most of by our internal enemies to [reconsider?] the experiment of prolonged hostilities.[6]

The idea of an armistice so much bandied in the newspapers, rests on no

---

5. The Republicans won 21 seats to the Federalists' 6 in the New York congressional delegation; see David M. Ellis, *Landlords and Farmers in the Hudson-Mohawk Region, 1790–1850* (Ithaca, 1946), pp. 118–20.

6. For the financial difficulties of 1814, see Stagg, pp. 375–80.

very precise foundation. It is not doubted that it is wished for in Canada, and might coincide with the opinions of the Naval Commander; but it is presumable that the latter has no commensurate power, and it is taken for granted that the power in Canada is limited to operations of land forces.[7]

I found my wheat fields uncommonly flourishing with the exception of parts under the depredation of the Hessian fly. The appearance changes for the worse so rapidly, that the crop must be greatly reduced, and may be in a manner destroyed. I know not the extent of the Evil beyond this neighbourhood. I hope yours is exempt from it. Accept assurances of affectionate respect

Jefferson to Madison

Monticello May 17, 1814

DEAR SIR

The inclosed paper came to me for I know not what purpose; as it came just as you see it, without a scrip of a pen: perhaps that I might join in the sollicitation. Augustus Chouteau, the signer, I always considered as the most respectable man of the territory, and the more valuable as he is a native. Of the other signers I know nothing; and I know how easy it is to get signers to such a paper, and that no man possesses that art more perfectly than the one recommended. He must have changed character much if he is worthy of it. I remember we formed a very different opinion of him; and I think he was removed for faction and extortion or champerty from some office he held; either that of Attorney for the U S. or of land Commissioner, or something of that sort. Perhaps you will recollect it better than I do. It is probable you have recieved such a paper; but lest you should not, I send you this.

We learnt your arrival at home about a week ago. I was then, as I am now, on the point of setting out to Bedford, delayed from day to day for a carriage daily promised. My present prospect is to set out in two days. This will prevent my intruding a visit on you during your present stay at Montpelier, and the rather as I am sensible that all visits must be inconveniently intrusive on the objects which bring you home.

I sincerely congratulate you on the success of the loan, and wish that resource may continue good.[8] I have not expected it could be pushed very far, from the unfortunate circumstance of our circulating medium being delivered over to enrich private adventurers at the public expence, when in our own hands it might have been made a competent supplement to our other war resources.

---

7. For a discussion of armistice negotiations in 1814, see *ibid.*, pp. 385–86.

8. For the success of a short-term loan of $10 million to tide the government over while seeking a long-term solution to its financial problems, see *ibid.*, pp. 378–80.

Mrs Randolph joins me in friendly respects to Mrs Madison. Mr Randolph is at Varina. Ever affectionately yours

TH JEFFERSON

I have this moment been called on for Wynne's life of Jenkins [?], and find it not in the library. The last I remember of it was the carrying it to Washington for your use while engaged on the subject of neutral rights. I suspect therefore it may still be in the office of State. Can you recollect, or will you be so good as to enquire after it. I have re-opened my letter to state this.

Jefferson to Madison

Monticello Sept. 24, 1814

DEAR SIR,

It is very long since I troubled you with a letter, which has proceeded from discretion, and not want of inclination; because I have really had nothing to write which ought to have occupied your time. But in the late events at Washington I have felt so much for you that I cannot withhold the expression of my sympathies.[9] For altho' every reasonable man must be sensible that all you can do is to order, that execution must depend on others, and failures be imputable to them alone, yet I know that when such failures happen they afflict even those who have done everything they could to prevent them. Had General Washington himself been now at the head of our affairs, the same event would probably have happened. We all remember the disgraces which befel us in his time in a trifling war with one or two petty tribes of Indians, in which two armies were cut off by not half their numbers. Every one knew, and I personally knew, because I was then of his council, that no blame was imputable to him, and that his officers alone were the cause of the disasters. They must now do the same justice.

I am happy to turn to a countervailing event, and to congratulate you on the destruction of a second hostile fleet on the lakes by McDonough; of which however we have not the details.[10] While our enemies cannot but feel shame for their barbarous atchievements at Washington, they will be stung to the soul by these repeated victories over them on that element on which they wish the world to think them invincible. We have dissipated that error. They must now feel a conviction themselves that we can beat them gun to gun, ship to ship, and fleet to fleet; and that their early successes on the land have been either purchased from traitors, or obtained from raw men entrusted of necessity with commands for which no experience had qualified them, and that every day is adding that experience to unquestioned bravery.

9. TJ referred to the burning of Washington by the British.
10. See Everett, pp. 179-92.

The Critical Year: 1814

I am afraid the failure of our banks will occasion embarrasment for a while, altho' it restores to us a fund which ought never to have been surrendered by the nation, and which now, prudently used, will carry us thro' all the fiscal difficulties of the war. At the request of Mr Eppes, who was chairman of the committee of finance at the preceding session, I had written him some long letters on this subject.[11] Colo. Monroe asked the reading of them some time ago, and I now send him another, written to a member of our legislature, who requested my ideas on the recent bank events. They are too long for your reading, but Colo. Monroe can, in a few sentences, state to you their outline.

Learning by the papers the loss of the library of Congress,[12] I have sent my catalogue to S. H. Smith, to make to their library committee the offer of my collection, now of about 9. or 10,000. vols., which may be delivered to them instantly, on a valuation by persons of their own naming, and be paid for in any way, and at any term they please; in stock, for example, of any loan they have, unissued, or of any one they may institute at this session; or in such annual instalments as are at the disposal of the committee. I believe you are acquainted with the condition of the books, should they wish to be ascertained of this. I have long been sensible that my library would be an interesting possession for the public, and the loss Congress has recently sustained, and the difficulty of replacing it, while our intercourse with Europe is so obstructed, renders this the proper moment for placing it at their service.[13] Accept assurances of my constant and affectionate friendship and respect.

Madison to Jefferson

Washington Oct. 10, 1814

Dear Sir

Your favor of the 24th Ult: came duly to hand. I learn that the Library Com^e will report favorably on your proposition to supply the loss of books by Cong^s It will prove a gain to them, if they have the wisdom to replace it by such a Collection as yours. Mr. Smith will doubtless write you on the subject.

I have not yet read your last communication to Mr. Monroe on the subject of finance.[14] It seems clear, according to your reasoning in the preceding one, that a circulating medium, to take the place of a bank or metallic medium, may be created by law and made to answer the purpose of a loan, or

---

11. For TJ's letter to John Wayles Eppes, Sept. 11, 1813, see Ford, IX, pp. 395–403.
12. For a fascinating detective story that cites historical evidence that the library was carted off before the British burned the congressional building, see Goodrum.
13. For a detailed description of TJ's holdings, see Sowerby. For the recent discovery of TJ's classification system of his books, long believed lost, see James Gilreath and Douglas L. Wilson, eds., *Thomas Jefferson's Library: A Catalog with the Entries in His Own Order* (Washington, 1989).
14. For a discussion of TJ's views, see Malone, VI, pp. 137–50.

rather anticipation of a tax; but as the resource cannot be extended beyond the amount of a *sufficient* medium, and of course cannot be *continued*[15] but by successive re-emissions and redemptions by taxes, resort must eventually be had to loans of the usual sort, or an augmentation of taxes, according to the public exigencies: I say augmentations of taxes, because these absorbing a larger sum into circulation, will admit an enlargement of the medium employed for the purpose. In England where the paper medium, is a legal tender in paying a hundred millions of taxes, thirty millions of interest to the public creditors etc. etc. and in private debts, so as to stay a final recovery, we have seen what a mass of paper has been kept afloat, with little if any depreciation. That the difference in value between the circulating notes and the metals proceeded rather from the rise in the latter than from the depreciation of the former, is now proved by the fact, that the notes are, notwithstanding a late increase of their quantity, rising towards a par with the metals, in consequence of a favorable balance of trade which diminishes the demand of them for foreign markets.

We have just received despatches from Ghent, which I shall lay before Cong^s to-day. The British sine qua non, excluded us from fishing within the sovereignty attached to her shores, and from using these in curing fish; required a Cession of as much of Maine as w^d remove the obstruction to a *direct* communication between Quebec and Halifax, confirmed to her the Passamaquoddy Islands as always hers of right; included in the pacification the Indian Allies, with a boundary for them (such as that of the Treaty of Greenville) agst the U. S. mutually guarantied, and the Indians restrained from selling their lands to either party, but free to sell them to a *third* party; prohibited the U. S. from having an armed force on the Lakes or forts on their shores, the British prohibited as to neither; and substituted for the present N. W. limit of the U. S. a line running direct from the W. end of L. Superior to the Mississippi, with a right of G. B. to the navigation of this river. Our ministers were all present and in perfect harmony of opinion on the arrogance of such demands. They w^d probably leave Ghent shortly after the sailing of the vessel just arrived. Nothing can prevent it, but a sudden change in the B. Cabinet not likely to happen, tho' it might be somewhat favored by an indignant rupture of the negotiation, as well as by the intelligence from this Country, and the fermentations taking place in Europe.[16]

I intended to have said something on the changes in the Cabinet, involving in one instance, circumstances of which the public can as yet very little judge, but cannot do it now.[17]

15. JM's italics here and below.

16. For a brief discussion of the negotiations at Ghent, see Brant, VI, pp. 326–39.

17. For JM's dismissal of Armstrong as secretary of war, see *ibid.*, pp. 309–15, and C. Edward Skeen, *John Armstrong, Jr., 1758–1843: A Biography* (Syracuse, 1981), pp. 200–3.

The situation of Sacketts Harbour is very critical. I hope for the best, but have serious apprehensions. With truest affection always y.rs

JAMES MADISON

Jefferson to Madison

Monticello Oct. 13, 1814

DEAR SIR

It seems as if we should never find men for our public agencies with mind enough to rise above the little motives of pride and jealousy, and to do their duties in harmony, as the good of their country, and their own happiness would require. Poor Warden, I find, has been thought an object of jealousy to Crawford, and the scenes of Dr. Franklin and Mr Adams, Dr. Franklin and Lee, Dr. Franklin and Izard (si magnis componere parva licebit) [if I may be permitted to use the comparison] are to be acted over again in Crawford and Warden.[18] I inclose you a letter from the latter, which seems so simple a narrative as to carry truth on it's face. Warden has science enough, with his modest manners, to have gained the affections and society of the literati, and even those of the high circles of the place. Crawford has sound sense, but no science, speaks not a word of the language, and has not the easy manners which open the doors of the polite circle. His functions are limited by insuperable barriers to a formal correspondence, *by letter,*[19] with the Minister. It is natural that in this situation he should be uneasy and discontented, and easy for him to mistake the objects on which it should be manifested. I have no doubt, from what I learn through other channels, that Warden renders us an essential service, which mere superiority of office does not put in the power of the other, of keeping the public there truly informed of the events of the war here. I have as little doubt that if Crawford could suppress the little pride and jealousy which are beneath him, he might often make Warden the entering wedge for accomplishing with that government, what will be totally beyond his own faculties. I fear his experience has not yet taught him the lesson, indispensable in the practical business of life, to consider men, as other machines, to be used for what they are fitted; that a razor should be employed to shave our beards, and an axe to cut our wood, and that we should not throw away the axe because it will not shave us, nor the razor because it will not cut our wood. It is true that on the subject of the letter inclosed, I have heard not

18. For the controversy between Crawford and Warden, see Chase C. Mooney, *William H. Crawford, 1772–1834* (Lexington, Ky., 1974), p. 56. JM had appointed Crawford as American minister to France after the death of Joel Barlow; see JM to TJ, Oct. 23, 1814, below.
19. TJ's italics.

a tittle from any other source. To you, who have doubtless recieved the doleances of Crawford, I have thought it would be satisfactory audire alteram partem [to listen to what is said on both sides]; and the rather as he has perhaps unbosomed himself to a private individual more unreservedly than he would in a formal defence addressed to yourself. Ever affectionately and respectfully yours.

       TH JEFFERSON

Jefferson to Madison

       Monticello Oct. 15, 1814

DEAR SIR,

 I thank you for the information of your letter of the 10th. It gives at length a fixed character to our prospects. The war undertaken, on both sides, to settle the questions of impressment, and the Orders of council, now that these are done away by events, is declared by Great Britain to have changed its object, and to have become a war of Conquest, to be waged until she conquers from us our fisheries, the province of Maine, the lakes, states and territories north of the Ohio, and the navigation of the Mississippi; in other words till she reduces us to unconditional submission. On our part then we ought to propose, as a counterchange of object, the establishment of the meridian of the mouth of the Sorel northwardly as the Western boundary of all her possessions. Two measures will enable us to effect it, and without these, we cannot even defend ourselves. 1. To organize the militia into classes assigning to each class the duties for which it is fitted, (which, had it been done when proposed years ago, would have prevented all our misfortunes,) abolishing by a Declaratory law the doubts which abstract scruples in some, and cowardice and treachery in others, have conjured up about passing imaginary lines, and limiting at the same time their services to the *contiguous* provinces of the enemy. The 2d is the Ways and Means. You have seen my ideas on this subject, and I shall add nothing but a rectification of what either I have ill expressed, or you have misapprehended. If I have used any expression restraining the emissions of treasury notes to a *sufficient* medium, as your letter seems to imply, I have done it inadvertently, and under the impression then possessing me, that the war would be very short. A *sufficient* medium would not, on the principles of any writer, exceed 30. Millions of Dollars, and on those of some not 10. Millions. Our experience has proved it may be run up to 2. or 300. Millions, without more than doubling what would be the prices of things under a *sufficient* medium, or say a metallic one, which would always keep itself at the *sufficient* point: and, if the rise to this term, and descent from it, be gradual, it would not produce sensible revolutions in private fortunes. I shall be able to explain my views more definitely by the use of numbers. Suppose we require, to carry on the war, an annual loan of 20. millions, then I propose that, in the 1st.

year, you shall lay a tax of 2. millions, and emit 20. Millions of Treasury notes, of a size proper for circulation, and bearing no interest, to the redemption of which the proceeds of that tax shall be inviolably pledged and applied, by recalling annually their amount of the identical bills funded on them. The 2. year lay another tax of 2. millions, and emit 20. millions more. The 3d. year the same, and so on, until you reach the maximum of taxes which ought to be imposed. Let me suppose this maximum to be 1. Dollar a head, or 10. millions of Dollars, merely as an exemplification more familiar than would be the algebraical symbols x or y. You would reach this in 5. years. The 6th. year then still emit 20. millions of treasury notes, and continue all the taxes two years longer. The 7th. year 20. millions more, and continue the whole taxes another 2. years: and so on. Observe, that altho' you emit 20. millions of Dollars a year, you call in 10. millions, and consequently, add but 10. millions annually to the circulation. It would be in 30. years then, *primâ facie,* that you would reach the present circulation of 300. millions, or the ultimate term to which we might adventure. But observe also that in that time we shall have become 30. millions of people, to whom 300. millions of Dollars would be no more than 100. millions to us now; which sum would probably not have raised prices more than 50. per cent. on what may be deemed the standard, or metallic prices. This increased population and consumption, while it would be increasing the proceeds of the redemption tax, and lessening the balance annually thrown into circulation, would also absorb, without saturation, more of the surplus medium, and enable us to push the same process to a much higher term, to one which we might safely call indefinite, because extending so far beyond the limits, either in time or expense, of any supposable war. All we should have to do would be, when the war should be ended, to leave the gradual extinction of these notes to the operation of the taxes pledged for their redemption; not to suffer a dollar of paper to be emitted either by public or private authority, but let the Metallic medium flow back into the channels of circulation, and occupy them until another war should oblige us to recur, for it's support, to the same resource, and the same process, on the circulating medium.

The citizens of a country like ours will never have unemployed capital. Too many enterprises are open, offering high profits, to permit them to lend their capitals on a regular and moderate interest. They are too enterprising and sanguine themselves not to believe they can do better with it. I never did believe you could have gone beyond a 1st. or at most a 2d. loan, not from a want of confidence in the public faith, which is perfectly sound, but from a want of disposable funds in individuals. The circulating fund is the only one we can ever command with certainty. It is sufficient for all our wants; and the impossibility of even defending the country without its aid as a borrowing fund, renders it indispensable that the nation should take and keep it in their own hands, as their exclusive resource.[20]

20. See Malone, VI, pp. 137-46.

I have trespassed on your time so far, for explanation only. I will do it no further than by adding the assurances of my affectionate and respectful attachment.

Years.	Emissions.	Taxes & Redemptions.	Bal. in circulation at end of year.
1815	20 millions	2 millions	18 millions.
1816	20 "	4 "	34 "
1817	20 "	6 "	48 "
1818	20 "	8 "	60 "
1819	20 "	10 "	70 "
1820	20 "	10 "	80 "
1821	20 "	10 "	90 "
	140		

Suppose the war to terminate here, to wit, at the end of 7d. years, then the reduction will proceed as follows:

Years.	Taxes & Redemptions.	Bal. in cir. at end of year.
1822	10 millions	80 millions
1823	10 "	70 "
1824	10 "	60 "
1825	10 "	50 "
1826	10 "	40 "
1827	10 "	30 "
1828	10 "	20 "
1829	10 "	10 "
1830	10 "	0 "
	140	

This is a tabular statement of the amount of emissions, taxes, redemptions, and balances left in circulation every year, on the plan above sketched.

Madison to Jefferson

Washington Oct. 23, 1814

DEAR SIR,

I have received yours of the 15th, and attended to your remarks on "ways and means." I find that the variance in our ideas relates—1. To the probable quantity of circulating medium. 2. To the effect of an annual augmentation of it. I cannot persuade myself that in the present stagnation of private dealings, and the proposed limitation of taxes, the two great absorbents of money, the circulating sum would amount even to 20 millions. But be this amount what it may, every emission beyond it must either enter into circulation, and depreciate the whole mass, or it must be locked up. If it bear an interest, it may be locked up for the sake of the interest; in which case it is a loan, both in substance and in form, and implies a capacity to lend; in other words, a disposable capital in the Country. If it does not bear an interest it could not be locked up, but on the supposition that the terms on which it is received are such as to promise indemnity at least for the intermediate loss of interest, by its value at a future day; but this both involves the substance of a loan, to the amount of the value locked up: and implies a depreciation differing only from the career of the old continental currency by a gradual return from a certain point of depression to its original level. If this view of the subject be in any measure correct, I am aware of the gloomy inferences from it. I trust, however, that our case is not altogether without remedy. To a certain extent, paper, in some form or other, will, as a circulating medium, answer the purpose your plan contemplates. The increase of taxes will have the double operation of widening the channel of circulation, and of pumping the medium out of it. And I cannot but think that a domestic capital, existing under various shapes, and disposable to the public, may still be obtained on terms, though hard, not intolerable; and that it will not be very long before the money market abroad will not be entirely shut against us; a market, however ineligible in some respects, not to be declined under our circumstances.[21]

We hear nothing from our Envoys since the dispatches now in print, nor any thing else of importance from abroad. We continue anxious for the situation of Sackett's Harbour. Izard has joined Brown on the Canada side of the straight; and offered battle to Drummond, which he does not accept, and which it seems cannot be forced on him without risk of reinforcements now transportable to him. The most that can fairly be hoped for by us now is, that the campaign may end where it is. Be assured always of my most affectionate respects

JAMES MADISON

Madison to Jefferson

Washington Oct. 23, 1814

DEAR SIR

I have recd. yours of Ocr [13] with that inclosed from Warden. His tale is plausibly told but entitled to little confidence. Be assured he is not the man he passed for with all of us originally. His apparent modesty and suavity cover ambition vanity avidity (from poverty at least) and intrigue. These traits began to betray themselves before he last left the U. S. On his arrival in Paris with his

21. For a discussion of federal financial problems in 1814, see Stagg, pp. 438–45.

office confirmed by the Senate, they rapidly disclosed themselves. And on the death of Barlow, and the scuffle for the Charge of our affairs, the mask fell off entirely. He behaved badly to Mrs. Barlow, and having made himself acceptable to the French Govt. thro' his intimacy with subalterns, he seized, with their concurrence, the station for which he had as little of qualifications as of pretensions. Crawford carried with him our view of W.s character, and his experience in Paris has greatly strengthened it. He states circumstances convicting W. of equal impudence and mendacity. The friends of the latter there consist of the Irish, and persons of   and science to whom he has paid his court, and passed himself for the favorite of certain individuals here as well as the Govt. Crawford is a man of strong intellect and sound integrity: but of a temper not perhaps sufficiently pliant, or manners sufficiently polished for diplomatic life. These however will improve, whilst he remains abroad. I cannot believe that his high tone of mind would have permitted him to be jealous of a man whom he must justly regard as so infinitely below him. I return you Wardens letter; and that, if you chuse you may present the possibility of future publicity to yours to me, I inclose yours with it, and keep no copy of this.[22] Affecy. yours

22. JM dismissed Warden, who remained in Paris until his death in 1846; see Skeen, p. 245.

42

MR. MADISON'S WAR ENDS: 1815

THE PEACE NEGOTIATIONS with Great Britain, which had been moved from Gothenburg in Sweden to Ghent in the Austrian Netherlands at the initiative of the British government in August 1814, were coordinated with the reconstruction of post-Napoleonic Europe at the Congress of Vienna. After the fall of Bonaparte and the restoration of peace in Europe, Great Britain no longer needed to impress seamen, so questions relating to maritime rights in wartime became academic. Madison, therefore, directed Secretary of State James Monroe in October to instruct the American negotiating team not to make an issue of impressment, but to accept "the *status quo ante bellum* as the basis for negotiation," a return to the prewar territorial arrangement. The altered instructions reflected a realistic decision to drop mandatory demands on an issue that no longer presented a practical problem.

On December 1, 1814, the president sent Congress a set of dispatches relating to the negotiations at Ghent, which contrasted the administration's new instructions with Britain's insistence on the principle of uti possidetis, a recognition of territorial gains made during the war. Madison's move was designed to unify the country, if the war continued, against an aggressor who no longer needed to abduct seamen for combat service but now seemed clearly bent on a war of conquest (John Adams labeled the British territorial claims an attempt "to stunt our growth"[1]) or the destruction of the United States.

While the negotiators debated in Ghent, the British launched a massive amphibious attack on Louisiana, with New Orleans and control of the Mississippi River as the goal. For the invasion, a fleet commanded by Vice Admiral Sir Alexander Cochrane brought 10,000 veterans of the duke of Wellington's army under Lieutenant General Sir Edward Pakenham, Wellington's brother-in-law.

Confident of victory, the combined force also brought a cadre of civilians that included officers for a new British colonial government in Louisiana and perhaps in the Mississippi Valley, since the governor's commission stated that

---

1. Marshall Smelser, *The Democratic Republic, 1801–1815* (New York, 1968), p. 306.

the Louisiana Purchase had been fraudulently obtained from Napoleon.[2] In a spectacular battle fought after the peace treaty had been signed but before the news had arrived in America, American troops and militia under Major General Andrew Jackson massacred the British, killing Pakenham and inflicting more than 2,000 casualties while suffering only 21.[3]

On Christmas Eve 1814, the American and British negotiators signed the Treaty of Ghent ending the War of 1812. On the advice of the duke of Wellington, who thought that British demands for territorial concessions were not justified by the state of their military operations in America,[4] the British ministry abandoned its demands for uti possidetis. The treaty, therefore, restored peace on the basis of the status quo ante bellum and referred unresolved issues to mixed arbitration commissions for future adjustment. The prince regent ratified the treaty on December 28, 1814, glad, as Lord Castlereagh observed, to be "released from the millstone of the American war."

On Saint Valentine's Day 1815, Secretary of State James Monroe presented to the president the official dispatches that announced the end of the Second War for American Independence. Late that evening, after attending a party celebrating the good news, one of Madison's supporters, Senator Jonathan Roberts of Pennsylvania, drove to the president's temporary quarters at the Octagon House to congratulate him:

> On arriving there all was still and dark. I found Mr. Madison sitting solitary in his parlor... in perfect tranquility, not even a servant in waiting. What a contrast from the scene I had just left. I apologiz'd for my intrusion, stating that I had heard a rumor of Peace, but I apprehended it was incorrect. Take a seat, said he, and I will tell you all I know.... I believe there is peace, but we have not as yet the information in such form, as that we can publish it officially.... The self command, and greatness of mind, I wittness'd on this occasion was in entire accordance with what I have before stated of the Pres[iden]t, when to me things looked so dark. I think it to be regretted that these evidences, of the solidity and Sterling worth of his character, will perhaps find no place in the history of his administration, brilliant as it must ever appear.

"The next morning," Senator Roberts concluded, "the news was out." Madison sent the treaty to the Senate on February 15, 1815, and the senators promptly and unanimously ratified the agreement on February 16. On February 17, the president formally proclaimed that the war had ended.[5] On the next day, the *National Intelligencer* ran a bold headline:

---

2. Thomas P. Abernethy, *The South in the New Nation, 1789–1819* (Baton Rouge, 1961), pp. 400–2; Harry Coles, *The War of 1812* (Chicago, 1965), pp. 233–35; and Smelser, pp. 278–84.

3. James A. Carr, "The Battle of New Orleans and the Treaty of Ghent," *Diplomatic History* 3 (1979): 273–82.

4. The duke thought that such demands could be made only if the British established naval control of the Great Lakes; see Henry Adams, *The Life of Albert Gallatin* (Philadelphia, 1879), pp. 538–39. For a fuller discussion, see Dudley Mills, "The Duke of Wellington and the Peace Negotiations at Ghent in 1814," *Canadian Historical Review* 2 (1921): 19–32.

5. Robert Allen Rutland, *The Presidency of James Madison* (Lawrence, Kans., 1990), p. 187.

GLORIOUS NEWS
[New] Orleans saved and peace concluded.
. . .
*Who would not be an American? Long live the republic!
All hail! last asylum of oppressed humanity!*[6]

"I sincerely congratulate you on the peace," Jefferson wrote Madison in March, "and more especially on the eclat with which the war was closed. The affair of New Orleans was fraught with useful lessons to ourselves, our enemies, and our friends, and will powerfully influence our future relations with the nations of Europe. It will shew them we mean to take no part in their wars, and count no odds when engaged in our own. I presume," he added hopefully, "that, having spared to the pride of England her formal acknolegement of the atrocity of impressment in an article of the treaty, she will concur in a convention for relinquishing it. Without this she must understand that the present is but a truce, determinable on the first act of impressment of an American citizen, committed by any officer of hers."[7]

As the retired diplomat pondered the postwar problems, his thoughts turned to the perennial issue of commercial relations with Great Britain. "Would it not be better," the Sage of Monticello suggested, "that this Convention should be a separate act, unconnected with any treaty of commerce, and made an indispensable preliminary to all other treaty? If blended with a treaty of commerce she will make it the price of injurious concessions. Indeed," he continued, getting caught up in thoughts dating to the Revolutionary era, "we are infinitely better [off] without such treaties with any nation. We cannot too distinctly detach ourselves from the European system, which is essentially belligerent, nor too sedulously cultivate an American system, essentially pacific. But if we go into commercial treaties at all, they should be with all at the same time with whom we have important commercial relations. France, Spain, Portugal, Holland, Denmark, Sweden, Russia, all should proceed *pari passu*."

There were several advantages to reviving the diplomacy of the Revolutionary era for the period following America's Second War for Independence. "Our ministers marching in phalanx on the same line, and intercommunicating freely, each will be supported by the weight of the whole mass, and the facility with which the other nations will agree to equal terms of intercourse, will discountenance the selfish higglings of England, or justify our rejection of them. Perhaps," he concluded, "with all of them, it would be best to have but the single article *gentis amicissimae,* leaving everything else to the usages and courtesies of civilized nations. But all these things," he added diplomatically,

---

6. J. C. A. Stagg, *Mr. Madison's War: Politics, Diplomacy, and Warfare in the Early American Republic, 1783–1830* (Princeton, 1983), p. 500, and Thomas A. Bailey, *A Diplomatic History of the American People* (New York, 1969), p. 157.

7. TJ to JM, Mar. 23, 1815, below.

"will occur to yourself, with their counter-considerations."[8]

Madison had also considered postwar relations with Great Britain, especially after "the mischief produced by the Declaration of the Prince Regent and other misstatements" about the causes, character, and conduct of the War of 1812. These comments had so "poisoned the opinion of the world on the subject" that the president had decided, while the conflict was still under way, that it was necessary to set the historical record straight. "It was accordingly determined soon after the meeting of Cong[res]s," he informed Jefferson, "that a correct and full view of the War, should be prepared and made public in the usual Demiofficial form."[9]

The white paper was assigned to Secretary of the Treasury Alexander J. Dallas, but "its contents were as much the work of Madison as they were of Dallas."[10] Undertaken in case the negotiations at Ghent broke down, the report was designed to usher "in a new epoch particularly inviting a new appeal to the neutral public." Although Dallas "hastened it as much as the nature of it, and his other laborious attentions admitted, it was not finished in time for publication before the news of peace arrived," the president confided to Jefferson. Indeed, "the latter pages had not even been struck off at the press."

With the conclusion of peace, Madison had three options in dealing with the white paper: (1) it could be published "with a prefatory notice that it was written before the cessation of hostilities, and thence derived its spirit and language"; (2) it could be suppressed; or (3) it could be rewritten "with a view to preserve the substantial vindication of our Country agst prevailing calumnies, and avoid asperities of every sort unbecoming the change in the relations of the two Countries."

Madison preferred the last option, "but it required a time and labour not to be spared for it." Of the other options, he preferred suppression to an apologetic preface, "which w^d have been liable to misconstructions of an injurious tendency." For the moment, he was holding several hundred printed copies of the pamphlet since it would ultimately "contribute materials for a historical review of the period which the document embraces."

Knowing that his friend would read the report with a critical eye, the president pulled one copy from the stack and mailed it to Monticello. "I have thought a perusal of it might amuse an hour of your leisure," he told Jefferson. But he requested that, "as it is to be guarded agst publication, you will be so good as either to return the Copy, or to place it where it will be in no danger of escaping. You will observe, from the plan and cast of the work, that it was meant for the eye of the British people, and of our own, as well as for that of the Neutral world. This threefold object increased the labor not a little, and

---

8. *Ibid.*
9. JM to TJ, Mar. 12, 1815, below.
10. Stagg, p. 452.

gives the composition some features not otherwise to be explained."[11]

After reading and returning the pamphlet, Jefferson developed an "irresistible desire that it should be published." He cited three solid reasons for publication: it would serve useful purposes in Europe, England, and the United States. On the Continent, "they have totally mistaken our character. Accustomed to rise at a feather themselves, and to be always fighting, they will see in our conduct, fairly stated, that acquiescence under wrong, to a certain degree, is wisdom, and not pusillanimity; and that peace and happiness are preferable to that false honor which, by eternal wars, keeps their people in eternal labor, want and wretchedness."

In Great Britain, it would enlighten those "who have been decieved as to the causes and conduct of the war" and who believed "that it was entirely wanton and wicked on our part, and under the order of Bonaparte. By rectifying their ideas," Jefferson contended, "it will tend to that conciliation which is absolutely necessary to the peace and prosperity of both nations." Finally, he concluded, "it is necessary for our own people, who, altho' they have known the details as they went along, yet have been so plied with false facts and false views by the federalists, that some impression has been left that all has not been right."[12]

Jefferson conceded that the pamphlet would be criticized by some as unfriendly to Britain. But he argued that "truths necessary for our own character must not be suppressed out of tenderness to it's calumniators. Although written generally with great moderation, there may be some things in the pamphlet which may perhaps irritate. The characterizing every act, for example, by it's appropriate epithet is not necessary to show its deformity to an intelligent reader. The naked narrative will present it truly to his mind, and the more strongly, from it's moderation, as he will percieve that no exaggeration is aimed at."

The former president offered three suggestions for editorial consideration before publishing the pamphlet: (1) retain the original date; (2) "rub down" any obvious "roughnesses"; (3) add "a soothing Postscript" to "make it acceptable to both" nations. With an eye to historians, he also recommended the addition of an appendix to some copies, "containing all the documents referred to, to be preserved in libraries, and to facilitate to the present and future writers of history, the acquisition of the materials which test the truth it contains."[13]

Two days after writing his letter urging publication of the pamphlet, Jefferson received his copy of the Philadelphia *Aurora,* which carried the first installment of "The Causes and Conduct of the War." The president had

11. JM to TJ, Mar. 12, 1815, below.
12. TJ to JM, Mar. 23, 1815, below.
13. *Ibid.*

authorized Attorney General Richard Rush to leak the document to Congressman Charles Ingersoll, who handed it to William Duane for publication in his paper.[14] Even so, Jefferson still thought it advisable "for the government to smooth and reprint it. If done instantly," he told Madison, "it will get to Europe before the newspaper details, and at any rate may be declared to be the genuine edition as *published by the government,* and may be with truth so declared in a conciliatory P. S."[15]

The president followed the international proceedings at the Congress of Vienna carefully, but he thought them enveloped "in a fog, which rather thickens than disperses." After Napoleon's exile to Elba, the Bourbon monarchy was restored, with the eldest brother of the hapless Louis XVI assuming the title of Louis XVIII. But Madison believed that "the situation of France also has yet . . . to pass some clearing up shower." The peace between the United States and Great Britain relieved the French "Gov^t and the Nation, from the dilemma, of humiliating submissions to the antineutral measures of G. Britain, or a premature contest with her," he told Jefferson. "In Spain, every thing suffers under the phrenzy of the Throne, and the fanaticism of the People. But for our peace with England, it is not impossible, that a new war from that quarter would have been opened upon us. The affair at New Orleans will perhaps be a better guarantee agst such an event," he concluded.[16]

Jefferson also followed the international news avidly. The restoration of the Bourbon monarchy seemed unpopular in France, according to recent accounts, and he doubted that the triumphant powers at the Congress of Vienna "can force a sovereign on that nation." If not, they might "prefer a compromise." If that were the case, he predicted that the financial difficulties of England would "deter her from the Quixotism of attempting it single-handed."[17]

As much as Jefferson disliked Napoleon—he called him "a political engine only, and a very wicked one," "a restless spirit [who] leaves no hope of peace to the world"[18]—he welcomed the French leader's return from Elba in 1815 as an opportunity to reestablish France as a counterweight to the postwar hegemony of Britain and the Continental coalition of Russia, Prussia, and Austria. "Bonaparte, unprincipled as he is," he wrote Madison, "is at length placed in a situation to claim all our prayers against the enterprises meditated on the independance of his nation."[19]

Madison thought not of prayer, but of national security. If Great Britain

---

14. Brant, VI, pp. 382–83.
15. TJ to JM, Mar. 25, 1815, below. The white paper appeared subsequently under the title *An Exposition of the Causes and Character of the Late War between the United States and Great Britain.*
16. JM to TJ, Mar. 12, 1815, below.
17. TJ to JM, May 12, 1815, below.
18. TJ to Thomas Leiper, June 12, 1815, in Ford, IX, pp. 519–20.
19. TJ to JM, June 15, 1815, below.

and France resumed their conflict, he said, "our great objects will be to save our peace and our rights from the effect of it; and whether war ensue or not, to take advantage of the crisis to adjust our interests with both."[20] He continued to hope, as he had since 1801, that the competition between France and England "in aggressions on us will be succeeded by rival dispositions to court our good will, or at least to cultivate our neutrality."[21]

The president and the former president probably discussed the role of the United States in the postwar world when the Madisons resumed their annual visits to Monticello in April 1815.[22] But they spent most of their time talking about books. Jefferson was preparing thousands of volumes for shipment to Washington, where they would replace the library of Congress burned by the British. "I am now employing as many hours of every day as my strength will permit in arranging the books, and putting every one in its place on the shelves, corresponding with it's order in the Catalogue, and shall have them numbered correspondently," he informed the president. When the Madisons arrived for their visit, the learned librarian was in the midst of "this operation [which] will employ me a considerable time yet."[23]

As the two friends reviewed the books, they also discussed the need for "a competent agent," "a character acquainted with books," to double-check each title against the catalogue in order to verify the count before the lids were nailed on the shipping cases. This procedure, Jefferson thought, was "necessary for my safety and your satisfaction as a just caution for the public. You know that there are persons, both in and out of the public councils, who will seize every occasion of imputation on either of us, the more difficult to be repelled in this case, in which a negative could not be proved."[24]

Later in the year, the friends exchanged summer visits and discussed Napoleon's defeat at Waterloo, hopeful that the Quadruple Alliance "may not advance beyond safe measures of power, [and] that a salutary balance may be ever maintained among the nations." And they agreed that "the less we have to do with the amities or enmities of Europe, the better."[25]

Looking back over the course of the second war with Great Britain, the modest Madison had much to be proud of. He had led a young and second-rate power through its first national war, one that had, as he told Congress, "become a necessary resort, to assert the rights and independence of the nation." The conflict, which began on a disastrous note, was punctuated by naval victories of significance and ended with an unprecedented series of victories

20. JM to James Monroe, May 9, 1815, cited in Brant, VI, p. 385.
21. JM to Alexander J. Dallas, Apr. 25, 1815, May 4, 1815, and May 22, 1815, cited in Ketcham, p. 600.
22. JM mentioned his hope to visit TJ in his letter of Mar. 12, 1815, below. For the visit, see Ketcham, p. 600.
23. TJ to JM, Mar. 23, 1815, below.
24. *Ibid.*
25. JM to Alexander J. Dallas, Sept. 15, 1815, cited in Ketcham, p. 601.

against veteran troops from the Napoleonic Wars, creating a new sense of nationhood. "Peace has come in a most welcome time," wrote Supreme Court Justice Joseph Story of Massachusetts. "Never did a country occupy more lofty ground; we have stood the contest, single-handed, against the conquerer of Europe; and we are at peace, with all out blushing victories thick crowding on us. If I do not much mistake, we shall attain a very high character abroad."

As the war drew to an end, Secretary of State James Monroe had noted that the pressure of war "tends evidently to unite our people, to draw out our resources, to invigorate our means, and to make us more truly an independent nation." In a moment of postwar euphoria, the "republican citizens of Baltimore" reiterated that view in an address to President Madison:

That struggle has revived, with added lustre, the renown which brightened the morning of our independence: it has called forth and organized the dormant resources of the empire: it has tried and vindicated our republican institutions: it has given us that moral strength, which consists in the well earned respect of the world, and in a just respect for ourselves. It has raised up and consolidated a national character, dear to the hearts of the people, as an object of honest pride and a pledge of future union, tranquility, and greatness.

As if to confirm these views, the French minister to the United States observed that the American army had improved in discipline, fought with valor, and "in three great attacks saw Wellington's best corps flee before their militia." On the sea, the naval performance was "a prelude to the lofty destiny to which they are called on that element." More importantly, he concluded, "the war has given the Americans what they so essentially lacked, a national character founded on a glory common to all."[26]

This new national feeling also impressed Albert Gallatin after he returned home following two and a half years abroad. "The war," he wrote, "has been productive of evil and good, but I think the good preponderates. Independent of the loss of lives, and the losses of property by individuals, the war has laid the foundation of permanent taxes and military establishments which the Republicans had deemed unfavorable to the happiness and free institutions of the country. But under our former system we were becoming too selfish, too much attached exclusively to the acquisition of wealth, above all, too much confined in our political feelings to local and state objects. The war has renewed and reinstated the national feelings and character which the Revolution had given, and which were daily lessened. The people have now more general objects of attachment with which their pride and political opinions are connected. They are more American: they feel and act more as a Nation, and I hope that the permanency of the Union is thereby better secured."[27]

26. For Story's quotation, see Rutland, p. 189. For Monroe's quotation and the "republican citizens of Baltimore" address, Apr. 10, 1815, see Steven Watts, *The Republic Reborn: War and the Making of Liberal America, 1790–1820* (Baltimore, 1987), p. 317. For the French minister, Louis Sérurier, to Talleyrand, Feb. 21, 1815, see Brant, VI, pp. 377–78.

27. Adams, p. 560.

Charles Jared Ingersoll, a Republican congressman from Pennsylvania, writing thirty years after the war ended, credited much of the change to Madison, who had conducted the war

> without yielding a principle to his enemies or a point to his adversaries; leaving a United States, which he found embarrassed and discredited, successful, prosperous, glorious and content. A constitution which its opponents pronounced incapable of hostilities, under his administration triumphantly bore their severest brunt. Checkered by the inevitable vissicitudes of war, its trials never disturbed the composure of the commander-in-chief, always calm, consistent and conscientious, never much elated by victory or depressed by defeat, never once by the utmost exigencies of war, betrayed into a breach of the constitution.[28]

Madison had also learned from the mistakes of the Federalists. Despite the unpopularity of the war in New England and continual criticism by the disloyal opposition, the party that had resorted to the Alien and Sedition Laws to suppress Republican criticism during the quasi war with France, Madison quietly guarded the civil liberties of Americans and aliens alike, including those who dissented from national policy, and ended his presidency with more popularity than when he entered it. In a Fourth of July oration in Washington in 1816, Benjamin L. Lear observed that there had not been "one trial for treason, or even one prosecution for libel" during the war.[29] A year later, on Madison's retirement from the presidency, the citizens of Washington hailed his conduct of the war "without the sacrifice of civil or political liberty"—indeed, "without infringing a political, civil, or religious right."[30]

Perhaps the most measured appraisal of President Madison's conduct came from his ancient antagonist, "Honest" John Adams, who had reestablished his friendship with Jefferson during the war.[31] He wrote a typically astringent appraisal of "our good Brother Madison" after the war: "a thousand faults and blunders [aside], his Administration has acquired more glory, and established more Union, than all his three predecessors, Washington Adams and Jefferson, put together."[32] And another president from Massachusetts, John F. Kennedy, called Madison our most underrated president.[33]

As for Madison himself, he was much more modest in his appraisal of the Second War for American Independence:

---

28. Charles Jared Ingersoll, *Historical Sketch of the Second War between the United States... and Great Britain*, cited by Marcus Cunliffe, "Madison," in *The Ultimate Decision: The President As Commander-in-Chief*, ed. Ernest R. May (New York, 1960), pp. 52–53.

29. Brant, VI, p. 407.

30. Resolutions of Mar. 6, 1817, cited *ibid.*, p. 419. Smelser, p. 319, stresses this point. See also Samuel Eliot Morison, Frederick Merk, and Frank Freidel, eds., *Dissent in Three American Wars* (Cambridge, Mass., 1970), pp. 3–31, and Cunliffe, pp. 51–52.

31. See Lyman H. Butterfield, "The Dream of Benjamin Rush: The Reconciliation of John Adams and Thomas Jefferson," *Yale Review* 40 (1950): 297–319.

32. John Adams to TJ, Feb. 2, 1817, in Cappon, II, p. 508.

33. Irving Brant, *The Books of James Madison and Some Comments on the Reading of Franklin D. Roosevelt and John F. Kennedy* (Charlottesville, 1965), p. 10.

Whatever be the light in which any individual actor on the public theatre may appear, the contest exhibited in its true features can not fail to do honor to our country; and in one respect particularly to be auspicious to its solid and lasting interest. If our first struggle was a war of our infancy, this last war was that of our youth; and the issue of both, wisely improved, may long postpone if not forever prevent a necessity for exerting the strength of our manhood.[34]

─────────────── THE LETTERS ───────────────

Madison to Jefferson

Washington Mar. 12, 1815

DEAR SIR

It was long desirable that an Expose of the causes and character of the War between the U. S. and G. B. should remedy the mischief produced by the Declaration of the Prince Regent and other misstatements which had poisoned the opinion of the world on the subject. Since the pacification in Europe and the effect of that and other occurrences in turning the attention of that quarter of the World towards the U. S. the antidote became at once more necessary and more hopeful. It was accordingly determined soon after the meeting of Cong^s that a correct and full view of the War, should be prepared and made public in the usual demiofficial form. The commencement of it was however somewhat delayed by the probability of an early termination of the Negotiations at Ghent, either, in a peace, or in a new epoch particularly inviting a new appeal to the neutral public. The long suspension of intelligence from our Envoys, and the critical state of our affairs at home, as well as abroad, finally overruled this delay, and the execution of the task was committed to Mr. Dallas. Altho' he hastened it as much as the nature of it, and his other laborious attentions admitted, it was not finished in time for publication before the news of peace arrived. The latter pages had not even been struck off at the press. Under these circumstances, it became a question whether it should be published with a prefatory notice that it was written before the cessation of hostilities, and thence derived its spirit and language; or should be suppressed; or written over with a view to preserve the substantial vindication of our Country agst prevailing calumnies, and avoid asperities of every sort unbecoming the change in the relations of the two Countries. This last course, tho' not a little difficult might have been best in itself, but it required a time and labour not to be spared for it. And the suppression was preferred to the first course, which w^d have been liable to misconstructions of an injurious tendency. The printed copies however amounting to several hundred are not

---

34. JM to Charles Ingersoll, Jan. 4, 1818, cited in Brant, VI, p. 380.

destroyed, and will hereafter contribute materials for a historical review of the period which the document embraces. I have thought a perusal of it might amuse an hour of your leisure; requesting only that as it is to be guarded agst publication, you will be so good as either to return the Copy, or to place it where it will be in no danger of escaping. You will observe, from the plan and cast of the work, that it was meant for the eye of the British people, and of our own, as well as for that of the Neutral world. This threefold object increased the labor not a little, and gives the composition some features not otherwise to be explained.

The dispatch vessel with the peace via France, has just arrived. It brings little more than duplicates of what was rec^d via England. The affairs at Vienna remain in a fog, which rather thickens than disperses. The situation of France also has yet it would seem to pass some clearing up shower. The peace between this Country and G. B. gives sincere pleasure there as relieving the Gov^t and the Nation, from the dilemma, of humiliating submissions to the antineutral measures of G. Britain, or a premature contest with her. In Spain, every thing suffers under the phrenzy of the Throne, and the fanaticism of the People. But for our peace with England, it is not impossible, that a new war from that quarter would have been opened upon us. The affair at New Orleans will perhaps be a better guarantee agst such an event.

Mr. Smith will have communicated to you the result of our consultation on the transportation of the Library.

We are indulging hopes of paying a trip soon to our farm; and shall not fail, if it be practicable, to add to it the pleasure of a visit to Monticello. Always and with sincerest affection y^{rs},

JAMES MADISON

Jefferson to Madison

Monticello Mar. 23, 1815

DEAR SIR,

I duly recieved your favor of the 12th, and with it the pamphlet on the causes and conduct of the war, which I now return. I have read it with great pleasure, but with irresistible desire that it should be published. The reasons in favor of this are so strong, and those against it are so easily gotten over, that there appears to me no balance between them. 1. We need it in Europe. They have totally mistaken our character. Accustomed to rise at a feather themselves, and to be always fighting, they will see in our conduct, fairly stated, that acquiescence under wrong, to a certain degree, is wisdom, and not pusillanimity; and that peace and happiness are preferable to that false honor which, by eternal wars, keeps their people in eternal labor, want and wretchedness. 2. It is necessary for the people of England, who have been decieved as to the causes and conduct of the war, and do not entertain a doubt, that it was entirely wanton and wicked on our part, and under the order of Bonaparte. By rectifying their ideas, it will tend to that conciliation which is absolutely necessary to the peace and prosperity of both nations. 3. It is necessary for our own people, who, altho' they have known the details as they went along, yet have been so plied with false facts and false views by the federalists, that some impression has been left that all has not been right. It may be said that it will be thought unfriendly, but truths necessary for our own character must not be suppressed out of tenderness to it's calumniators. Although written generally with great moderation, there may be some things in the pamphlet which may perhaps irritate. The characterizing every act, for example, by it's appropriate epithet is not necessary to show its deformity to an intelligent reader. The naked narrative will present it truly to his mind, and the more strongly, from it's moderation, as he will percieve that no exaggeration is aimed at. Rubbing down these roughnesses, and they are neither many nor prominent, and preserving the original date might I think remove all the offensiveness, and give more effect to the publication. Indeed, I think that a soothing Postscript, addressed to the interests, the prospects and the sober reason of both nations, would make it acceptable to both. The trifling expence of reprinting it ought not to be considered a moment. Mr. Gallatin could have it translated into French, and suffer it to get abroad in Europe without either avowal or disavowal. But it would be useful to print some copies of an Appendix containing all the documents referred to, to be preserved in libraries, and to facilitate to the present and future writers of history, the acquisition of the materials which test the truth it contains.

I sincerely congratulate you on the peace, and more especially on the eclat[1] with which the war was closed. The affair of New Orleans was fraught with useful lessons to ourselves, our enemies, and our friends, and will powerfully influence our future relations with the nations of Europe. It will shew them we mean to take no part in their wars, and count no odds when engaged in our own. I presume that, having spared to the pride of England her formal acknolegement of the atrocity of impressment in an article of the treaty, she will concur in a convention for relinquishing it. Without this she must understand that the present is but a truce, determinable on the first act of impressment of an American citizen, committed by any officer of hers. Would it not be better that this Convention should be a separate act, unconnected with any treaty of commerce, and made an indispensable preliminary to all other treaty? If blended with a treaty of commerce she will make it the price of injurious concessions. Indeed we are infinitely better without such treaties with any nation. We cannot too distinctly detach ourselves from the European system,

1. Malone, VI, p. 125, notes that TJ "used the word 'eclat' in other letters, apparently liking it."

which is essentially belligerent, nor too sedulously cultivate an American system, essentially pacific. But if we go into commercial treaties at all, they should be with all at the same time with whom we have important commercial relations. France, Spain, Portugal, Holland, Denmark, Sweden, Russia, all should proceed *pari passu*. Our ministers marching in phalanx on the same line, and intercommunicating freely, each will be supported by the weight of the whole mass, and the facility with which the other nations will agree to equal terms of intercourse, will discountenance the selfish higglings of England, or justify our rejection of them. Perhaps, with all of them, it would be best to have but the single article *gentis amicissimæ*, leaving everything else to the usages and courtesies of civilized nations. But all these things will occur to yourself, with their counter-considerations.

Mr. Smith wrote to me on the transportation of the library, and particularly that it is submitted to your direction. He mentioned also that Dougherty would be engaged to superintend it. No one will more carefully and faithfully execute all those duties which would belong to a waggon master.[2] But it requires a character acquainted with books to recieve the library. I am now employing as many hours of every day as my strength will permit in arranging the books, and putting every one in its place on the shelves corresponding with it's order in the Catalogue, and shall have them numbered correspondently. This operation will employ me a considerable time yet. Then I should wish a competent agent to attend, and, with the catalogue in his hand, see that every book is on the shelves, and have their lids nailed on, one by one, as he proceeds. This would take such a person about two days, after which Dougherty's business would be the mere mechanical removal at convenience. I inclose you a letter from Mr. Milligan offering his service, which would not cost more than 8. or 10. days' reasonable compensation. This is necessary for my safety and your satisfaction as a just caution for the public.[3] You know that there are persons, both in and out of the public councils, who will seize every occasion of imputation on either of us, the more difficult to be repelled in this case, in which a negative could not be proved. If you approve of it therefore, as soon as I am thro' the review, I will give notice to Mr. Milligan, or any other person whom you will name, to come on immediately. Indeed it would be well worth while to add to his duty that of covering the books with a little paper (the good bindings at least,) and filling the vacancies of the presses with paper parings, to be brought from Washington. This would add little more to the time, as he could carry on both operations at once. Accept the assurance of my constant and affectionate friendship and respect.

TH. JEFFERSON

2. Joseph Dougherty had been TJ's coachman during his presidency; see *ibid.*, p. 5.
3. Joseph Milligan was a Georgetown bookseller who double-checked the accuracy of TJ's catalogue; see *ibid.*, pp. 172, 180–81.

Jefferson to Madison

Monticello Mar. 24, 1815

DEAR SIR

I had written the inclosed letter but had not yet sent it to the post office when Mr Nelson calling, informed me you were to leave Washington on Tuesday last (the 20th.)[4] I have thought it better therefore to inclose it to you at Montpelier. I am laboriously employed in arranging the library, to be ready for it's delivery. And as soon as I can name the day on which I shall have finished I will give notice to the person whom you may appoint to verify the catalogue.

On this subject I shall be glad to hear from you as soon as possible, but this will be retarded by the unlucky arrangement of our mails; for altho' we have two departures in the week for Washington, yet they are on Wednesday and Thursday, leaving inte[r]vals of 24. hours, or of 6. days. This letter therefore will lie 5. days in our office before it's departure. I wish much to see you, and if the arrangement of the library should give me any inte[r]val during your stay, and the roads permit, I will try to pay you a visit. I say, if the roads permit, for increasing feebleness obliges me now to be driven by others, and consequently to the use of heavier carriages. A visit by Mrs Madison and yourself altho' always desired, it would be unreasonable to expect out of the short time you are permitted to stay and after so long an absence. But if you can afford it, I should recieve it as a deodand. Adieu affectionately.

TH JEFFERSON

Jefferson to Madison

Monticello Mar. 25, 1815

DEAR SIR

After I had sent my letters of yesterday and the day before to the post office the return of the messenger brought me a letter from Saml. H. Smith informing me you had directed Milligan to come on whenever I should call for him. I mention this to save you the trouble of further writing on that subject.

The same mail brought me the Aurora, beginning the publication of the Causes and Conduct of the war, which settles the question of publication. I still think however it would be worth while for the government to smooth and reprint it. If done instantly it will get to Europe before the newspaper details,[5]

---

4. Hugh Nelson was the Republican congressman from TJ's district; see *ibid.*, pp. 332–34, and Stagg, pp. 83–84.

5. Besides being printed in the Philadelphia *Aurora,* the white paper was published separately as a pamphlet and was reprinted in London; see Brant, VI, pp. 382–83, and Stagg, pp. 451–52. It was also reprinted in the *Annals of Congress,* 13th Cong., III, 1416 ff. For its reception in England, see Bradford Perkins, *Castlereagh and Adams: England and the United States, 1812–1823* (Berkeley, 1964), pp. 156–57.

and at any rate may be declared to be the genuine edition as *published by the government,* and may be with truth so declared in a conciliatory P. S. Ever and affectionately Your's

TH JEFFERSON

Jefferson to Madison

Monticello May 12, 1815

DEAR SIR

I have totally forgotten the writer of the letter I forward to you, and every circumstance of his case. I leave it therefore on his own letter and that of the Marquis de la Fayette to you, which came inclosed, and is now forwarded with the other. I shall set out for Bedford within three days, and expect to be absent as many weeks. The newspapers have begun the war for the European powers; but if the people of France are as unanimous as they represent, I cannot believe that those powers will imagine they can force a sovereign on that nation, and therefore presume the Continental powers will prefer a compromise, and that the financial difficulties of England will deter her from the Quixotism of attempting it single-handed. Present us all affectionately to Mrs Madison and accept best wishes for your own health, quiet and happiness.

TH JEFFERSON

Jefferson to Madison

Monticello June 15, 1815

DEAR SIR

However firm my resolution has been not to torment the government, nor be harrassed my self with sollicitations for office, cases will now and then arise which cannot be denied. Charles Jouett formerly of this neighborhood, was appointed by Genl Dearborne an Indian agent. This was on the sollicitations of W. C. Nicholas, Mr Carr and every respectable person of this neighborhood, and indeed from my own knolege of him. He is a man of sound good sense, prud[ent and] perfect integrity and a zealous republican. Dearborne I know considered him, on trial to be the honestest and best agent in the Indian department; and he had great influence over the Indians of his department. He thinks he was shuffled by Eustis into a resignation of his office. He is poor, has married some time ago a French girle as poor as himself, and now sollicits to return again to the same or any other employment which will give him bread. I should not fear answering for his execution of any trust with fidelity and ability, were there an opening for him. But if there be not, without injustice to others, he must submit to it, as his misfortune.

Monroe is with us, and his daughter Mrs Hay extremely ill.

Bonaparte, unprincipled as he is, is at length placed in a situation to claim all our prayers against the enterprises meditated on the independance of his nation.[6] Ever and affectionately yours

TH JEFFERSON

Jefferson to Madison

Monticello July 16, 1815

DR. SIR

I recieved yesterday from our friend Govr. Nicholas a letter stating that very advantageous offers had been made to his son in Baltimore (late a colonel in the army) which would induce him to go and fix himself at Leghorn, and that it would add very much to his prospects to be appointed Consul there, and counting on my knolege of the character of his son, he supposed my testimony of it to you might befriend his views. With respect to the character of the son I should certainly bear honorable and ample testimony, as of a high order: but, there is more than that in the case as it respects myself. I suppose the office to be at present full and that there are considerations due to the incumbent from myself. I cannot give you a better view therefore of the footing on which my answer to the governor places it than by transcribing what related to it, as follows. 'Your favor of yesterday is this moment recieved, and furnishes me matter of real regret; because there is nothing just and honorable which I would not cheerfully do for yourself or any member of your family. But the case in question stands thus. While I lived in Paris I became acquainted with Thomas Appleton of Boston then a young man, and recommended him to the Old Congress as consul at Leghorn, and he was appointed. On the commencement of the new government he was confirmed by Genl. Washington on my recommendation also. He has been now about 30. years in possession of the office, has conducted himself with integrity and diligence, and has never done an act to incur blame from the government. Under these circumstances it would be immoral in me to sollicit his removal. He is not a man who could be put into comparison with your son on any original competition; but 30. years of possession and approbation cannot fail to be a weight in his scale. I recieved a letter from him some months ago asking my aid to get him removed to Paris from Leghorn. I did nothing in it upon my general principle of declining these sollicitations. I know that Fulwar Skipwith was appointed to

---

6. For a brief discussion of TJ's views on Napoleon after the latter's return from Elba, see Malone, VI, p. 133.

Paris, and was preparing to go, when the return of Bonaparte suspended it, some former transactions having made it doubtful whether he would recieve him, and perhaps whether our government could with propriety propose him.[7] How this has been settled I know not. But in the event of Appleton's removal to Paris, there would be an opening at Leghorn. On the hypothesis therefore that Leghorn may be now vacant I will cheerfully communicate your wishes to the President by our next mail. Yet I know at the same time that the President's own dispositions to do any thing in his power which would be agreeable to yourself or your family will render my application merely an evidence of my wishes to be useful to you.' This extract placing the case fully before you, I will add nothing more to the trouble of reading it but the assurances of my affectionate attachment and respect.

TH JEFFERSON

Jefferson to Madison

Monticello July 23, 1815

DEAR SIR

One of those cases now occurs which oblige me to relax from my general wish not to add to your troubles in the disposal of offices. I inclose you the papers which produce the occasion, and they will present to you all the grounds of interest which I can possibly feel in the success of the application. They will have with you exactly the weight they intrinsically merit and no m[ore.] Accept the assurance of my constant friendship and respect

TH: JEFFERSON

Madison to Jefferson

[Washington Nov. 15, 1815]

DEAR SIR

Mr. Gray, son of Mr. William Gray so distinguished for his wealth and his patriotism, wishing with his lady to pay their respects at Monticello, I can not do less than favor the opportunity by a line of introduction. I am unacquainted with him, otherwise than by his introduction thro' a friend here, but doubt not that he will be found worthy of your civilities, which will be acceptable to his father as well as himself. They are on a visit to Georgia, where Mrs. Gray's father resides. It may not be amiss to intimate that Mr. G's political

---

7. See Henry Bartholomew Cox, *The Parisian American: Fulwar Skipwith of Virginia* (Washington, 1964).

connections may not altogether correspond with the sentiments of his father. On this point however I am not certain. His view in desiring the purest[8]

Jefferson to Madison

Monticello Dec. 22, 1815

DEAR SIR

Declining in every possible case to harrass you with sollicitations for office, I yet venture to do it in cases of science and of great merit, because in so doing I am sure I consult your partialities as well as my own. Mr Hassler furnishes an occasion of doing this. You will find his character, his situation and claims stated in the inclosed letter from Rob. Patterson, whose integrity and qualifications to judge of Mr Hassler's merit cannot need any additional testimony from me, altho' I conscientiously join my opinions and wishes to his.

The case of Dupont, the grandson I have warmly at heart. The father has merit for his establishments of gun powder and of broadcloth, but no foreigner stands more prominently for us than the grandfather. He has been intimately known to me 30. years, and during that time I can testify that there has been no more zealous American out of America. From 1784. to 1789. while at the head of a bureau of commerce in France I was under infinite obligations to him for patronising in every way in his power our commercial intercourse with France. I considered him as among the ablest and most honest men in France, and in the foremost rank of their science: but all this is so well known to yourself, as he is also personally, that my dwelling on it is merely to gratify my own affections.[9]

I inclose a letter from Mr. Spafford who being personally known to you, and not to myself I forward it merely ut valeat quantum valere debet [take it for what it is worth]. God bless you and aid you in the numerous good things you have brought under the notice of the present legislature.

TH JEFFERSON

---

8. The fragment of this letter ends here.

9. TJ had just missed seeing Pierre-Samuel du Pont de Nemours, who visited Monticello while TJ was at Poplar Forest; see Malone, VI, p. 164.

43

A JOINT RETIREMENT PROJECT: THE ORIGINS OF THE UNIVERSITY OF VIRGINIA, 1816–1817

*I*N THE YEARS following the Peace of Ghent, American interest turned inward towards the development of the nation's resources. "In 1815 for the first time Americans ceased to doubt the path they were to follow," wrote Henry Adams in concluding his nine-volume *History of the United States during the Administrations of Thomas Jefferson and James Madison.* "Not only was the unity of the nation established, but its probable divergence from older societies was also well defined.... As far as politics supplied a test, the national character had already diverged from any foreign type.... The American, in his political character, was a new variety of man.... American character was formed, if not fixed. ... The public seemed obstinate only in believing that all was for the best, as far as the United States were concerned, in the affairs of mankind."[1]

To ensure that the republic was secure at last, Madison, in his annual message to Congress in December 1815, called for the completion of defense works, maintenance of naval armaments, enlargement of the military academy, reorganization of the militia system, and compensation to discharged veterans. Confident finally in his position as national leader, he outlined a positive role for the federal government to play in national economic policy, calling for a new Bank of the United States, a protective tariff, a national university, and internal improvements such as roads and canals, if an authorizing amendment was added to the Constitution.

More Jeffersonian than Hamiltonian, this "Madisonian platform" was the culmination of the Republican experience inaugurated by Jefferson in 1801

---

1. Henry Adams, *History of the United States during the Administrations of Thomas Jefferson and James Madison,* 9 vols. (New York, 1889–91), IX, pp. 220–21, 240–1.

and continued by Madison after 1809. The president concluded with a postwar tribute to "our highly favored and happy country . . . [whose] political institutions [were] founded in human rights and framed for their preservation."[2] From Jefferson came a prompt endorsement: "God bless you and aid you in the numerous good things you have brought under the notice of the present legislature."

By the end of the war, positive, even vigorous, federal activity was accepted by both Madison and Jefferson, though with differing emphases.[3] Congress passed—and Madison signed—bills chartering the second Bank of the United States, establishing tariffs at a protective level, expanding the navy and maintaining the army for national defense, and providing pensions for invalid veterans and war widows. The president also submitted a new commercial treaty with Great Britain, which the Senate quickly ratified.

To John Randolph of Roanoke, who returned to Congress after a two-year absence, it was a new world. Long suspicious that Madison had forsaken "the principles of '98," he now thought that the president "out-Hamilton's Alexander Hamilton," thus raising the question "whether or not we are willing to become one great, consolidated nation, or whether we have still respect enough for the old, respectable institutions to regard their integrity and preservation as part of our policy."[4]

To the duc de Richelieu in Paris, the French chargé d'affairs in Washington reported that the Madison administration "moves with giant strides toward an extension of strength and power which insensibly changes its nature," ushering in a new age characterized by "the advance of civilization, the increase of public revenue, and the development of wealth and industry."[5] Madison agreed that "the nation seems determined to lose nothing of the character it has gained," citing the congressional measures as evidence of the new national mood.[6]

Early in June 1816, the Madisons began their longest summer retreat to Montpellier since 1801. Jefferson, his daughter Martha, and his granddaughter Ellen had counted on "the pleasure of seeing" them in July, but Martha's fever, which confined her to bed for several days, delayed their trip to Montpellier until August.[7] Later that month, the Madison's visited Monticello.[8] Indeed, after the War of 1812 ended, the two friends relied for almost two years on visits rather than correspondence as a means of exchanging views.

2. For JM's message, see Richardson, I, pp. 562–69. For TJ's endorsement, see TJ to JM, Dec. 22, 1815, above. Merrill D. Peterson uses the "Madisonian platform" phrase in his *Olive Branch and Sword: The Compromise of 1833* (Baton Rouge, 1982), p. 4.
3. See Marshall Smelser, *The Democratic Republic, 1801–1815* (New York, 1968), pp. 314–16.
4. Ketcham, p. 603.
5. Brant, VI, p. 404.
6. JM to William Eustis, May 12, 1816, cited in Ketcham, p. 606.
7. TJ to JM, Aug. 2, 1816, below.
8. Ketcham, p. 607.

A Joint Retirement Project: 1816–1817

After his letter of March 12, 1815, describing the pamphlet that he and Secretary of the Treasury Dallas had written about the causes and conduct of the war, Madison wrote only three letters to Jefferson in two years before his second term ended in March 1817. Similarly, Jefferson, who had developed a definite aversion to the writing table,[9] wrote only three letters to the president between July 23, 1815, and February 8, 1817.

When the Madisons made their final trip to Washington in the fall of 1816, the restoration of the White House and the Capitol was approaching completion, although neither was finished before Madison left office.[10] In his final message to Congress, the president stressed the need to complete the program for national development inaugurated at the previous session. Noting his forthcoming retirement, he proudly reflected on the first forty years of the United States as an independent nation, observing that for nearly a generation the American people "have had experience of their present Constitution, the offspring of their undisturbed deliberations and of their free choice; that they have found it . . . to contain in its combination of the federate and elective principles a reconcilement of public strength with individual liberty, of national power for the defense of national rights."

That Constitution, he noted with pride, had expanded over a vast territory and an increased population "without losing its vital energies." The American people were devoted "to true liberty and to the Constitution which is its palladium," living under a government that pursued "the public good as its sole object" and protected the purity of elections, freedom of speech and press, trial by jury, separation of church and state, security of persons and property, and the promotion of the "general diffusion of knowledge," on which public liberty depended.[11]

In his final letter to Jefferson from Washington, Madison lamented that Congress had spent most of its time on a law dealing with congressional compensation. The congressmen were also debating "the Claims law as it is called, relating to horses and houses destroyed by the enemy, which is still undecided in the Senate. They shrink from a struggle for reciprocity in the W. India trade; but the House of Representatives have sent to the Senate a navigation act, reciprocating the great principle of the British act, which, if passed by the Senate, will be felt deeply in Great Britain, in its example, if not by its operation." He also reported that John C. Calhoun's bonus bill to fund internal improvements was "of a very extraordinary character" since "the object of it, is to compass by law only," without a constitutional amendment, "an authority over roads and Canals."[12]

9. See TJ to Joseph C. Cabell, Oct. 24, 1817, cited in Malone, VI, p. 267.
10. See William Seale, *The President's House: A History,* 2 vols. (Washington, 1986), I, pp. 138–56.
11. Richardson, I, pp. 573–80.
12. JM to TJ, Feb. 15, 1817, below. The bill proposed to set aside the "bonus" paid to the federal government by the second Bank of the United States as a fund to underwrite the construction costs of roads and canals. In his last official act as president, JM vetoed Calhoun's bill. For

Jefferson had whetted Madison's appetite for retirement by sending him a weather and crop report, suggesting that "this may serve as a little preparation for your return to these contemplations."[13] Madison acknowledged that he was anxious to "hasten my departure from this place as much as possible; but I fear I shall be detained longer after the 4th of March than I wish. The severe weather"—it was 6½ degrees above zero in mid-February when he wrote—"unites with the winding up of my public business, in retarding the preparations during the session of Congress, and they will from their multiplicity be a little tedious after we can devote ourselves exclusively thereto."[14]

In one of his last official acts as president, Madison met with the painter John Trumbull, whom Jefferson had befriended in Paris, to select four pictures to be painted by Trumbull for the Rotunda of the Capitol, then being restored after being burned by the British. Since both Madison and Jefferson had subscribed to the series of engravings of Trumbull's historical paintings at the turn of the century, the president was familiar with the quality of the painter's work. They quickly agreed on two civil scenes—*The Declaration of Independence,* already completed, and *The Resignation of General Washington,* a long-planned picture not yet composed—and two military scenes—the surrender of huge British armies at Saratoga in 1778 and at Yorktown in 1781. *The Surrender of Lord Cornwallis at Yorktown,* like the *The Declaration of Independence,* had long been finished, but *The Surrender of General Burgoyne at Saratoga* had not yet been composed. What surprised and pleased Trumbull was that Madison decided on large, life-sized pictures, twelve feet by eighteen feet. The president especially liked the creation of a picture showing Washington's transfer of military power to civilian authorities. "It was," he said, "a glorious action," one that he and Jefferson had witnessed in 1783.[15]

Jefferson was also delighted with the project. Recalling his early association with Trumbull in France, he lauded the artist's work: "For his merit as a painter I can . . . assure you that on the continent of Europe . . . he was considered as superior to [Benjamin] West. . . . I pretended not to be a connoisseur in the art myself, but comparing him with others of that day I thought him superior to any historical painter of the time except [Jacques-Louis] David," the great painter of the French Revolution. He considered

---

extensive discussions, see John Lauritz Larson, " 'Bind the Republic Together': The National Union and the Struggle for a System of Internal Improvements," *JAH* 74 (1987): 377-85, and the more probing analysis in Drew R. McCoy, *The Last of the Fathers: James Madison and the Republican Legacy* (New York, 1989), pp. 92-103.

13. TJ to JM, Feb. 8, 1817, below.

14. JM to TJ, Feb. 15, 1817, below.

15. See the sprightly essays by Jules David Prown, "John Trumbull As History Painter," in *John Trumbull: The Hand and Spirit of a Painter,* ed. Helen A. Cooper (New Haven, 1982), pp. 39-41, and Egon Verheyen, "John Trumbull and the U.S. Capitol," *ibid.,* pp. 262-65. For a key that locates TJ, "Member of Congress," and JM, "Spectator," in Trumbull's *The Resignation of General Washington, at Annapolis, Maryland, 3 December 1783,* see Theodore Sizer, *The Works of Colonel John Trumbull* (New Haven, 1967), figs. 203 and 204.

A JOINT RETIREMENT PROJECT: 1816-1817

Trumbull's paintings "as monuments of the taste as well as the great revolutionary scenes of our country."[16] Senator Rufus King agreed. Trumbull's object, he wrote, was "to adorn the Capitol with pictures which shall perpetuate the great events and the glories of the Revolution, as the Ducal Palace of Venice, and the State House at Amsterdam, by the talents of the great painters of the day, have commemorated those of these republics."[17]

In the whirlwind of farewells and preparations for departure, the Madisons took time out to sit for portraits painted by Joseph Wood. Both were good likenesses, but the one of James, according to one of Dolley's friends, "almost breathes, and expresses much of the serenity of his feelings at the moment it was taken. In short, it is, *himself*"—the accomplished statesman at the moment of retirement.[18] Madison's serenity may have reflected his feelings about the qualified praise that he had recently received from his ancient antagonist, John Randolph, who conceded that "he was a great man—for such he unquestionably was in some respects—and he sincerely wished him all happiness in his retirement."[19]

In his inaugural address, President James Monroe praised his predecessor and wished that "he may long enjoy in his retirement the affections of a grateful country, the best reward of exalted talents and the most faithful and meritorious services."[20] Jefferson, impatiently awaiting his friend's return to his neighborhood, congratulated him twice, first "on the riddance of your burthens," then "on your release from incessant labors, corroding anxieties, active enemies and interested friends, and on your return to your books and farm, to tranquility and independence."[21]

The Sage of Monticello was anxious to have the Sage of Montpellier back in the neighborhood because the former had already staked out a significant retirement project for them: the creation of the University of Virginia. Both had recommended to Congress the establishment of a national university, following the examples of Presidents Washington and Adams. But with Madison's most recent request pigeonholed by Congress, the two Virginians, who had labored unsuccessfully to enact Jefferson's Bill for the More General Diffusion of Knowledge, now cooperated on the state level to revive an interest in education and, at long last, win legislative support.

Jefferson had taken the lead shortly after he retired to Monticello. "I have two great measures at heart, without which no republic can maintain itself in

---

16. See John Trumbull, *The Autobiography of Colonel John Trumbull: Patriot-Artist, 1756–1843*, ed. Theodore Sizer (New Haven, 1953), p. 310, and Irma B. Jaffe, *John Trumbull: Patriot-Artist of the American Revolution* (Boston, 1975), pp. 235–36.
17. Rufus King to Christopher Gore, Jan. 17, 1817, cited by Verheyen, p. 265.
18. Eliza Lee to Dolley Madison, Mar. 1817, in *PJM*, I, p. xiii.
19. See Randolph's speeches in Congress, Jan. 30, 1817, and Jan. 31, 1817, quoted in Brant, VI, pp. 415–16.
20. Richardson, II, p. 10.
21. TJ to JM, Mar. 10, 1817, below, and Apr. 15, 1817, below.

strength. 1. That of general education, to enable every man to judge for himself what will secure or endanger his freedom. 2. To divide every county into hundreds, of such size that all the children of each will be within reach of a central school in it." The hundreds, or wards, would be comparable to New England townships, participatory republics involving every citizen at the local level. To the elementary or primary schools, Jefferson added two other levels—general and professional. The general schools contained features of secondary schools and junior colleges, and Jefferson usually called them "colleges." The professional schools would constitute the university level, where "each science is to be taught in the highest degree it has yet attained."[22]

In 1814, Jefferson was appointed to the governing board of Albemarle Academy in Charlottesville, a private secondary school not yet functioning. Seizing this opportunity, he proposed to transform the school into a college, then into a university. Accordingly, he drafted a bill for this purpose but failed to get it introduced in the state legislature at its session in 1814–1815. When the legislature convened in 1816, however, it enacted the bill, converting Albemarle Academy into Central College and authorizing it to raise money from a lottery, subscriptions, and the sale of parish lands formerly owned by the Established Church in Albemarle County. The act of incorporation made the governor, Jefferson's neighbor Wilson Cary Nicholas, an ex officio member of the board and lifted the college from local to state significance by vesting the power to appoint the Board of Visitors with the governor. He soon appointed Jefferson, Madison, and Monroe to the board, along with David Watson of Louisa County, General John H. Cocke of Fluvanna, and Joseph C. Cabell of Nelson.[23]

Jefferson timed the first meeting of the Board of Visitors in 1817 so that Madison could attend, writing him a note "to await your arrival at home" and inviting him to come to Monticello "the day or evening before, that we may have some previous consultation on the subject."[24] But Madison was delayed in his departure from Washington, and President Monroe could not make the meeting either. Nor could Watson, who was sick. "Only Genl. Cocke, Mr Cabell and myself met," the disappointed Jefferson informed his friend. "Altho' not a majority, the urgency of some circumstances obliged us to take some provisional steps, in which we hope the approbation of our colleagues at a future meeting."[25] Jefferson emphasized the need for "a *full meeting* of *all* the visitors*,*" especially of his two successors, Madison and Monroe, for the group would then "decide the location of the State University for this place in opposition to the pretensions of Stanton, which unites the tramontane inter-

22. See Peterson, pp. 961–64, and Malone, VI, pp. 241–44. TJ also called for technical evening schools for artisans and craftsmen.
23. Malone, VI, pp. 241–50. The section of TJ's bill dealing with elementary schools was dropped by the Senate.
24. TJ to JM, Mar. 10, 1817, below.
25. TJ to JM, Apr. 13, 1817, below.

est. The location," he pointed out, "will be decided on at the next session of the legislature."[26]

Madison promised that he and his wife would visit Monticello, and Jefferson urged them to come "a day or two before our meeting [so] that we might have time to talk over the measures we ought to take."[27] Madison, Monroe, and Cocke joined Jefferson at the first official meeting of the Board of Visitors of Central College on May 5, when they ratified the choice of a site for the college west of Charlottesville and approved the purchase of 200 acres of land and the construction of the first building. They also launched a fundraising campaign by subscriptions and pledged $1,000 each. Jefferson then unveiled his plan for an "academical village" that featured "a distinct pavilion or building for each separate professorship, and for arranging these around a square, each pavilion containing a schoolroom and two apartments for the accommodation of the professor, with other reasonable conveniences." As additional pavilions and dormitories were erected, they would be joined by a covered walkway for "dry communications."[28]

The presence of three presidents of the United States in Charlottesville for the May meeting of the Board of Visitors attracted "the eager gaze of their Fellow Citizens," according to the Richmond *Enquirer*. The appearance of Jefferson, Madison, and Monroe "together at a village where the citizens of the county had met to attend their court, is an event, which for its singularity, deserves the notice of a passing paragraph."[29] "From such a noble Tryumviratre," wrote John Adams, "the World will expect something very great and very new," something "quite original, and very excellent."[30]

Jefferson surveyed the building site himself and laid out the grounds on July 18, 1817, picking the spot for the first pavilion. Less than a week later, he expanded his proposed visit to Montpellier into an informal meeting of the board to discuss "some important questions which I had thought might have laid over to our periodical meeting the last of September. Having an opportunity of writing to Genl. Cocke," he informed the unsuspecting host for the meeting, "I invited him to join me in a visit to you on Friday the 25th. I recd his answer last night, that he would do so and would try to bring Mr Cabell with him. Last night also an opportunity was offered me of sending a letter to Mr Watson. I do so; and he probably will be with you also. Thus the visit I had promised for myself singly to you on my return [from Bedford County], is

---

26. *Ibid.*
27. TJ to JM, Apr. 15, 1817, below. JM's letter of Apr. 10, 1817, is missing, but TJ mentions "Mrs. Madison's proposing to join you in the visit."
28. Malone, VI, pp. 255-57. For careful detective work in dating TJ's drawing of his university plan in 1814 instead of 1817, see Patricia C. Sherwood, "The Mystery Solved: New Dates and a New Perspective on Thomas Jefferson's Architectural Plans for Educational Institutions in Virginia," *Arts in Virginia* 30 (1992-93): 10-25.
29. Malone, VI, p. 255.
30. John Adams to TJ, May 26, 1817, in Cappon, II, p. 518.

suddenly manufactured into a meeting of our visitors at Montpelier, te inconsulto."[31]

The Montpellier meeting of the Board of Visitors assigned fund-raising duties to its members, and each wrote letters asking key leaders throughout the state to circulate subscription papers in their neighborhoods. The board also appointed Jefferson a search committee of one to find professors for the fledgling institution. At its October meeting, President Monroe presided at the laying of the cornerstone of the first pavilion, with Jefferson, Madison, and the other members of the board in attendance.[32] The board also authorized the construction of two additional pavilions.[33] Since Jefferson had sent his three editions of Palladio to Washington, he asked the only person in Virginia likely to have a copy to loan it to him for a year. "Nobody in this part of the country," he told Madison, "has one unless you have."[34] Madison mailed his copy promptly so that it would be at Monticello when Jefferson returned from his Bedford home.[35]

On the professorial search, Jefferson had consulted with Thomas Cooper, whom he considered "the greatest man in America in the powers of the mind and acquired information."[36] In November, he told Madison that "Cooper is not able to get us a Professor of languages above the common order" for the first pavilion. Jefferson thought about turning for suggestions to Dugald Stewart, the Scottish philosopher he had met in Paris, but decided to "defer writing till we know whether the legislature will adopt us, because that will greatly add to the inducements of a foreigner to come to us."[37] In the meantime, Cooper himself expressed an interest in joining the college faculty.[38]

During the fall, Jefferson also prepared a double-barreled approach for state funding of Central College. First, he gave Cabell, a state senator whose district included Albemarle, "a sketch of a bill for establishing the ward schools, Colleges, and University at an expence within the funds of the [state] library board," also known as the Literary Fund.[39] At the end of the year, he also submitted "a report of our proceedings and prospects to the Govr. as our patron to be laid before the legislature," hopeful that Central College might be transformed into the University of Virginia with state funding. And, as he

31. TJ to JM, June 22, 1817, below, and July 23, 1817, below.
32. Pavilion No. 7 now houses the Colonnade Club, the faculty club of the University of Virginia.
33. Malone, VI, pp. 261–65.
34. TJ to JM, Nov. 15, 1817, below.
35. JM to TJ, Nov. 29, 1817, below.
36. Peterson, p. 977. For an excellent biography, see Dumas Malone, *The Public Life of Thomas Cooper, 1783–1839* (New Haven, 1926).
37. TJ to JM, Nov. 15, 1817, below.
38. JM to TJ, Nov. 29, 1817, below, and TJ to JM, Dec. 30, 1817, below.
39. TJ to JM, Nov. 15, 1817, below.

had done so often in the past, he asked Madison for advice: "I pray you to correct [it] both in style and matter, to do this freely, and make it what it should be and to return it with your corrections."[40]

─────────────── THE LETTERS ───────────────

Madison to Jefferson
[Washington ca. Aug. 1, 1816]

The translation of the Dey of Algiers letter, after a curious display of Oriental Bombast, presents the alternative of reestablishing the Old Treaty, instead of the late one as annulled by our breach of it, or a withdrawal of our Consul which means a commencement of war by him. The answer concludes with the declaration that as peace is better than war, war is better than tribute. Letters from Shaler as late as June 29, leave things in the suspence connected with the appeal made by the Dey's letter. It is probable that war will be prevented by the presence of our augmented squadron, unless it shd. result from an adjustment between the Dey and G. B. If the article in our Treaty isolating that of the English, be the only obstacle to peace, it will be got over. The serious danger is that G. B. will support Algiers, either from a view to her navigation in the Mediterranean, or from her policy of being well with the Grand Seynor in the event of a variance with Russia. This is probably meant by "the centrality of interests and views" which Ld. Cart. mixes up with the subject in his late speech. The Dey has submitted to the Grand Seynor his dispute with Exmouth and it appears that he has lately recd. solemn confirmation on the throne, from Constantinople. Harris' late communications present a better prospect at St. P. The dispatches by Mr. Coles cannot well fail, to turn the sensibility of the Emperor agst. the quarter wch. excited it agst. the U.S. Our Affairs at Tunis and Tripoli are in a good State. The departure of Consul Jones from the former was transitory and unmeaning[1]

40. TJ to JM, Dec. 30, 1817, below.

1. This fragment of a letter deals with relations between the United States and the dey of Algiers, who had begun "open and direct warfare" against American sailors in 1812 and still held several of them captive at the end of the War of 1812. After that war was concluded, JM asked Congress to declare war against Algiers on Feb. 23, 1815, in order to obtain "peace without tribute." Commodore Stephen Decatur and Consul General William Shaler obtained a treaty "dictated at the mouth of the cannon," one that renounced the tribute system. Subsequently, the dey, upset with slow restitution of a brig captured by Decatur but later promised as a good-will gift, threatened to renew war; see Brant, VI, pp. 381, 387, 390, 395, 398, 407. For JM's reiteration of his view that the United States "wish for War with no nation, [but] will buy peace of none," stating that "as peace is better than War, War is better than tribute," see JM to the dey of Algiers, Aug. 1, 1816 (New-York Historical Society).

Jefferson to Madison

Monticello Aug. 2, 1816

DEAR SIR,
Mrs. Randolph, Ellen and myself intended before this to have had the pleasure of seeing Mrs Madison and yourself at Montpelier as we mentioned to Mr Coles; but three days ago Mrs Randolph was taken with a fever, which has confined her to her bed ever since. It is so moderate that we are in the hourly hope of its leaving her and, after a little time to recruit her strength, of carrying her purpose into execution, which we shall lose no time in doing. In the meantime I salute Mrs Madison and yourself with unceasing affection and respect.

Jefferson to Madison

Monticello Aug. 15, 1816

DEAR SIR
I do not know whether you were acquainted with the late Major Duncanson of Washington, uncle of the writer of the inclosed letter. He was one of the earliest adventurers to the city of Washington. He had made a princely fortune in the E. Indies, the whole of which he employed in the establishments of that city and finally sunk. His political merits were a most persevering republicanism in the worst of times, having been one of the four only republicans in Washington and George town in the time of Mr Adams. When I first went there, a stranger, I found him often useful for information as to characters, and I always believed him an honest and honorable man, altho' the warmth of his temper made him many enemies. These are the merits of the uncle. Of the nephew I know nothing and have therefore informed him I could render him no other service than that of stating to you what I knew of his uncle, considering it as a duty to bear testimony to truth. I salute you with affectionate attachment and respect

TH JEFFERSON

Jefferson to Madison

Monticello Feb. 8, 1817

DEAR SIR
In a late letter from Mr Spafford of Albany I recieved the inclosed with a request that after perusal I would forward it to you, adding a desire that, when

read, you would address it under cover to him, as he sets some value on the possession of it. His object in making the communication to either of us is not explained, but perhaps it may be understood by you. Your frank on a blank cover will let him see that I have complied with his request.

We have at length received commissions for the Visitors of our Central college; but as we may expect the pleasure of your return among us with the returning spring, I defer asking a meeting until it shall be convenient to you to join us.[2]

As you are at the fountain head of political news, I shall give you that only which is agricultural. We have had a most severe spell of cold, which commenced on the 11th. of Jan. On the 19th. of that month the thermometer was at 6°, that is 26° below freezing. On the 5th of this month it was at 9½° has been twice at 13°. and only three mornings of the last 3. weeks above freezing. Within that time it has been 7. days below freezing thro' the day. 6½ I. only of snow have fallen at different times, and I think the winter has been as remarkably dry as the summer was. Apprehensions are entertained for our wheat, which looks wretchedly. But the fine autumn and month of Dec. may have enabled it to push it's roots beyond the reach of frost. The tobacco fever is over and little preparation making for that plant. Corn is at 5. 6. and 7. D. according to it's position, and the apprehension of want continues. This may serve as a little preparation for your return to these contemplations, and especially as furnishing an opportunity of assuring you of my constant and affectionate friendship and respect

TH JEFFERSON

Madison to Jefferson

Washington Feb. 15, 1817

DEAR SIR,

I received yesterday yours covering the letter of Mr. Spafford, which was forwarded to him as you suggested. His object in communicating it I collect only from its contents. He probably exhibited it as a proof of the spirit and views of the Eastern States during the late war.

As with you, the weather here has of late been remarkable both for the degree and continuance of cold, and the winter throughout for its dryness. The Earth has however had the advantage of a cover of snow during the period most needing it. The wheat fields still have a slight protection from it. This morning is the coldest we have yet had. The Thermometer, on the North side

---

2. For the appointment of TJ and JM to Central College's Board of Visitors, see Malone, VI, p. 250.

of the House under an open shed, was at 8 oclock 4° above o. At this moment, half after 9 o'clock, it stands at 6½°. Yesterday morning about the same hour it was at 8°, and at 3 o'clock between 10 and 11°.

Our information from abroad has been very scanty for a long time, and we are without any of late date. From St Petersburg nothing has been received shewing the effect of Mr. Coles' communications on the Emperor.[3] Mr. Pinkney left Naples re infecta. He had to contend with pride, poverty, and want of principle.[4] Mr. Gallatin's demands of indemnity are not received with the same insensibility, but will have a very diminutive success, if any at all.[5] The Government of Spain, with its habitual mean cunning, after drawing the negotiations to Madrid, has now sent them back to Onis, with *powers,* without *instructions.* They foolishly forget that, with respect to the territorial questions at least, we are in possession of that portion of our claims which is immediately wanted, and that delay is our ally, and even guarantee for every thing.[6] The British Cabinet seems as well disposed as is consistent with its jealousies, and the prejudices it has worked up in the nation against us.[7] We are anxious to learn the result of our answer to the Dey of Algiers. It is nearly three months since a line was received from Chauncey or Shaler; nor has even a rumor reached us since their return to Algiers.

All the latest accounts from Europe turn principally on the failure of the harvests, and the prospects of scarcity. If they are not greatly exaggerated, the distress must be severe in many districts, and considerable every where. When the failure in this Country comes to be known, which was not the case at the latest dates, the prospect will doubtless be more gloomy.

You will see that Congress have spent their time chiefly on the Compensation law, which has finally taken the most exceptionable of all turns,[8] and on the Claims law as it is called, relating to horses and houses destroyed by the enemy, which is still undecided in the Senate. They shrink from a struggle for reciprocity in the W. India trade; but the House of Representatives have sent to the Senate a navigation act, reciprocating the great principle of the British act, which, if passed by the Senate, will be felt deeply in Great Britain, in its example, if not in its operation. Another Bill has gone to the Senate which I

3. Edward Coles went to Russia to explain why Consul General Nicholas Kosloff, despite diplomatic immunity, had been arrested on a charge of rape; see Brant, VI, pp. 397-98, 409, 411.

4. William Pinkney, the new minister to Russia, made a side trip to Naples to try to negotiate indemnities for maritime spoliations; see *ibid.,* p. 402.

5. JM appointed Gallatin minister to France after Gallatin had headed the American peace mission at Ghent; see *ibid.,* p. 382.

6. JM's italics. For JM's recognition of Onís as the Spanish minister to the United States even though the president had personal objections to him, see *ibid.,* pp. 393, 414.

7. Bradford Perkins entitles one chapter "The Uneasy Armistice" in *Castlereagh and Adams: England and the United States, 1812-1823* (Berkeley, 1964), pp. 156-72.

8. Congress repealed its salary increase; see Robert A. Rutland, *James Madison: The Founding Father* (New York, 1987), p. 238.

have not seen; and of a very extraordinary character, if it has been rightly stated to me. The object of it, is to compass by law only an authority over roads and Canals. It is said the Senate are not likely to concur in the project; whether from an objection to the principle or the expediency of it, is uncertain.[9]

I shall hasten my departure from this place as much as possible; but I fear I shall be detained longer after the 4th of March than I wish. The severe weather unites with the winding up of my public business, in retarding the preparations during the session of Congress, and they will from their multiplicity be a little tedious after we can devote ourselves exclusively thereto. On my reaching home, I shall recollect your notice of the call which will afford me the pleasure of assuring you in person of my sincere and constant affection.

JAMES MADISON

Jefferson to Madison

Monticello Feb. 16, 1817

DEAR SIR

The bearer hereof, Mr George Flower, is an English gentleman farmer, was the companion of Mr Burkbeck in his jour[ney] through France, and is the person to whom the dedication of that book is addressed. He came over on behalf of his own family and that of Mr Burkbeck, to chuse a settlement for them. Having made the tour of the temperate latitudes of the U S. he has purchased a settlement near Lynchburg. He came recommended to me from M. de la Fayette and M. de Lastayrie, and is indeed worthy of all recommendation. He is well informed of men and things in England, without prejudice in their favor, and communicative. Believing you will find satisfaction and information from his conversation, I ask permission for him to make his bow to you as he passes through Washington where he proposes to rest a day or two in his progress Northwardly to embark for England.[10] Ever affectionately and respectfully yours

TH JEFFERSON

9. For Calhoun's bonus bill and JM's veto, see Brant, VI, p. 416, and Larson, 363-87.

10. TJ owned Birkbeck's *Notes on a Tour in France,* an account of his visit there with Flower, where Lafayette gave them a letter of introduction to TJ. In 1816-17, Flower visited the United States in search of a site for a settlement. Birkbeck came over in 1817, and together they headed for southern Illinois, where they founded the town of Albion; see Morris Birkbeck, *Letters from Illinois* (London, 1818), and George Flower, *History of the English Settlement in Edwards County, Illinois, Founded in 1817 and 1818, by Morris Birkbeck and George Flower* (Chicago, 1882). See Charles Boewe, "The English Settlement," in *Prairie Albion: An English Settlement in Pioneer Illinois,* ed. Charles Boewe (Carbondale, Ill., 1962), for a fascinating anthology of early writings.

Jefferson to Madison

Monticello Mar. 10, 1817

DEAR SIR

Berey calling on me for some seed allows me just time to write a line to await your arrival at home, requesting your attendance as a visitor of our proposed college on Tuesday the 8th. of April, being the day after our election. You will of course, I am in hopes come here the day or evening before, that we may have some previous consultation on the subject. I shall also request Genl. Cocke and Mr Watson to make this their head quarters, as I have done Mr Cabell. Colo. Monroe I suppose will not be in the neighborhood. Congratulating you on the riddance of your burthens, I salute you affectionately and respectfully.

TH JEFFERSON

Madison to Jefferson

Montpellier Apr. 10, 1817

DEAR SIR

Having been detained in Washington untill the 6th. inst. I did not reach home till tuesday night, and of course too late to comply with the arrangement notified in yours of the 10th. March by Bizet. I take for granted that the other Visitors met, and that for the present at least my attendance will not be needed. As it has always been our purpose to pay a visit to Monticello at no distant day after our final return from Washington, I could wish it to coincide with the time that may be fixt for the next meeting for the business of the College, and that this if discretionary may not be required for some time. Besides the effect of a fatiguing journey, our presence will for some time be necessary at home in order to attend to a thousand little preparations and some important ones, which will not admit of delay. Your affectionate friend

JAMES MADISON

Jefferson to Madison

Monticello Apr. 13, 1817

DEAR SIR

Your letter of Feb. 15. having given me the hope you would attend [t]he meeting of the Visitors of the Central college near Charlottesville I lodged one for you at Montpelier notifying that our meeting would be on the day after our

April court. A detention at Washington I presume prevented your attendance. And Mr Watson being sick, only Genl. Cocke, Mr Cabell and myself met. Altho' not a majority, the urgency of some circumstances obliged us to take some provisional steps, in which we hope the approbation of our colleagues at a future meeting, which we agreed to call for on the 6th of May, being the day after our court. Circumstances which will be explained to you make us believe that a *full meeting* of *all* the visitors, on the first occasion at least, will decide a great object in the state system of general education; and I have accordingly so pressed the subject on Colo. Monroe as will I think ensure his attendance, and I hope we shall not fail in yours.

The people of this section of our country, look to a *full meeting* of *all* with unusual anxiety, all believing it will decide the location of the State University for this place in opposition to the pretensions of Stanton, which unites the tramontane interest. The location will be decided on at the next session of the legislature.[11] I set out for Bedford within 2. or 3. days, but shall make a point of returning in time, in the hope of seeing you. Constant and affectionate respect.

TH JEFFERSON

Jefferson to Madison

Monticello Apr. 15, 1817

DEAR SIR

I sincerely congratulate you on your release from incessant labors, corroding anxieties, active enemies and interested friends, and on your return to your books and farm, to tranquility and independance. A day of these is worth ages of the former, but all this you know. Yours of the 10th. was delivered to me yesterday. Mine of the 13th. had been sent off the moment it was written. We are made happy by Mrs Madison's proposing to join you in the visit. I wish you could come a day or two before our meeting that we might have time to talk over the measures we ought to take. The first day of the spring and fall terms of our circuit court is what the law has appointed for our semi-annual meetings. We did not think of that when we appointed the 2d. day. the 1st. being the day of our County as well as District court, there will be a great collection of people, and so far one end of our meeting would be better promoted. And I have no doubt the other gentlemen will be at court, in which case, if you are here, it will be a legal meeting notwithstanding our appointing another day. I hope therefore you will be with us.[12] I set out for Bedford tomorrow morning

---

11. See Malone, VI, p. 253.
12. For an account of the first regular meeting of the Board of Visitors on May 5, 1817, see *ibid.*, pp. 255–56.

and shall be back here the 29th. All join me in affectionate respects to Mrs Madison and yourself.

TH JEFFERSON

Jefferson to Madison

Monticello June 22, 1817

DEAR SIR

In two packages, distinct from this letter, I return you your father's meteorological diaries, which you were so kind as to lend me, and a piece on paper money recieved from you sometime ago. From the former I have made out tables of rain and snow, and a calendar of animal and vegetable matters announcing the advance of seasons. Having now completed 7. years of observations since my return home, I have drawn such general results from them in the form of tables and otherwise, as may be comprehended by the mind, and retained by the memory. They constitute an estimate of our climate, the only useful object to which they can be applied. I inclose you a copy of both.[13]

I have for some time been very anxious to pay you a visit: but Mrs Randolph wishing to join in it, and detained by the daily expectation of the measles appearing among her children, it has been put off until I am now within 2 or 3. days of setting out for my harvest in Bedford to be absent 3. weeks; and as I shall pass the months of Aug. and Sep. there, we must pay our visit in July, after the harvest is over. When here an observation fell from you once or twice which did not strike me at the time, but reflection afterwards led me to hope it had meaning: and that you thought of applying your retirement to the best use possible, to a work which we have both long wished to see well done, and which we thought at one time would have been done. My printed materials are all gone to Washington, but those in letters and Notes and memms. remain with me, are very voluminous, very full, and shall be entirely at your command. But this subject can be fathomed only in conversation, and must therefore await the visit.[14]

We just learn the desperate situation of young Eston Randolph son of T. E. Randolph our neighbor, the two families being in their intercourse and relations almost as one, fills that of Monticello with affliction. He had just

---

13. For a discussion of TJ's interest in meteorology, see *ibid.*, pp. 50–54. His summary of his observations after he retired in 1809 is printed in Edwin M. Betts, ed., *Thomas Jefferson's Garden Book, 1766–1824* (Philadelphia, 1944), pp. 622–28.

14. TJ implied that JM would write a Republican history to offset John Marshall's biography of Washington. Earlier, TJ and JM had tried to persuade Joel Barlow to undertake the task, offering to "open all the public archives to you" and to share their knowledge of things "not on paper, but only within ourselves for verbal communication"; see TJ to Joel Barlow, May 3, 1802, in Ford, VIII, pp. 148–51.

landed at Baltimore from an East India voyage.[15] Ever and affectionately yours.

TH JEFFERSON

Jefferson to Madison

Monticello July 23, 1817

DEAR SIR

The promptitude and success of our subscription paper, now amounting to upwards of 20,000 D. with a prospect much beyond that renders the decision immediately necessary of some important questions which I had thought might have laid over to our periodical meeting the last of September. Having an opportunity of writing to Genl. Cocke, I invited him to join me in a visit to you on Friday the 25th. I recd his answer last night, that he would do so and would try to bring Mr Cabell with him. Last night also an opportunity was offered me of sending a letter to Mr Watson. I do so; and he probably will be with you also. Thus the visit I had promised for myself singly to you on my return, is suddenly manufactured into a meeting of our visitors at Monpelier, te inconsulto. I do not know whether Mr Cabell and Mr Watson will certainly come, but Genl. Cocke and myself will be certainly with you on Friday, to dinner if we can get there by half after two; if not, we will dine at Gordon's and be with you afterwards, therefore do not wait a moment for us.[16] The illness of our principal driver will disappoint Mrs Randolph in the participation in the visit which she had much at heart. Affectionate esteem and respect to Mrs Madison and yourself:

TH JEFFERSON

Jefferson to Madison

Monticello Nov. 15, 1817

DEAR SIR

We are sadly at a loss here for a Palladio. I had three different editions, but they are at Washington, and nobody in this part of the country has one unless you have.[17] If you have you will greatly aid us by letting us have the use of it for

---

15. Thomas Easton Randolph was a brother-in-law of Thomas Mann Randolph; see Malone, VI, p. 390.
16. For the meeting at Montpellier on July 28, 1817, see *ibid.*, pp. 261-62.
17. For descriptions of TJ's copies of Palladio's works in English, French, and Italian, see E. Millicent Sowerby, *Catalogue of the Library of Thomas Jefferson*, 5 vols. (Washington, 1952-59), IV, pp. 359-61, 363-64, 380.

a year to come. It will come safely by the stage, and may be left at the stage office of either Milton or Charlottesville, and either postmaster will pay the postage for me to the driver. We fail in finishing our 1st. pavilion this season by the sloth and discord of our workmen, who have given me much trouble. They have finished the 1st. story, and covered it against the winter. I set out to Bedford tomorrow, on a short visit, and at Lynchbg shall engage undertakers for the whole of next summer's brickwork.[18]

Cooper is not able to get us a Professor of languages above the common order; and is suspended as to coming here. Efforts are on foot in Philadelphia to get from the Medical department permission for their students to attend their own chemical professor or Cooper at the choice of the student. In this case all will quit the former and attend the latter, which will ensure him more than he can get here, and in a more agreeable situation. We shall have to write to Dugald Stewart and Professor Leslie, who I am sure will select for us those of the 1st. order. But we had better defer writing till we know whether the legislature will adopt us, because that will greatly add to the inducements of a foreigner to come to us. I have given to Mr Cabell a sketch of a bill for establishing the ward schools, Colleges, and University at an expence within the funds of the library board now in hand. Their funds could not have met Mercer's bill in a century.[19] I hope they will pass mine. We all join in affectionate respects to Mrs Madison and yourself

TH JEFFERSON

Madison to Jefferson

Montpellier Nov. 29, 1817

DEAR SIR

I recd. some days ago yours of the 15th. and shall send my Palladio by the Stage of tuesday. It will probably arrive by the time you get back from Bedford.

I send you the inclosed from Mr. Cooper, that in case of the supposed miscarriage of his letter to you, it may enable you to give him the answer for which he is so anxious. I shall inform him that I have done so, without undertaking to decide the question whether he can rely on $1500 for the next year. I hope your estimates will justify an affirmative decision. As he is determined to leave Philada. and Williamsburg is no longer a competitor, it will be hard on both him and the College to fail of his employment. I have not recd. a

---

18. For the work on Pavilion VII, see Malone, VI, pp. 265–66. For two early sketches by TJ, with brief notes by Frederick D. Nichols, see William Howard Adams, ed., *The Eye of Thomas Jefferson* (Charlottesville, 1981), pp. 287, 292.

19. For a discussion of these bills, see Malone, VI, pp. 267–71.

single return of subscriptions from the Counties to which the papers were transmitted. Should the Legislature shut its funds agst. us it may be worth while to make renewed efforts. Are you aware that Leslie is unfriendly to the U. S.? Mr. E. Coles who had a personal oppy. of judging found him so. His Philosophy may so far prevail over his politics as to make him a safe resort for the selection of a Teacher, but, the aid of Duguld Stuart may be preferable if as I presume, his political feelings be not at variance with his philosophical dispositions. Affectionate respects

JAMES MADISON

Be so good as to return to Mr. C. the letter to him from the Visitors of W. & M.

Jefferson to Madison

Monticello Dec. 30, 1817

DEAR SIR

I returned from Bedford a week ago, after an absence of 6. weeks, and found here the Palladio, with your two favors of Nov. 29. and Dec. 1 and with 3. from Dr. Cooper, written before he had recieved one from me of Nov. 25. from Poplar Forest.[20]

It was agreed, you know, that we should make a report of our proceedings and prospects to the Govr. as our patron to be laid before the legislature. Being myself chiefly possessed of the materials I have prepared the inclosed draught which I pray you to correct both in style and matter, to do this freely, and make it what it should be and to return it with your corrections by the bearer, who is sent express for this purpose. I think it very material that it should get to the legislature immediately, before they come to any resolutions on the general subject.[21] I think it indispensable that each of us should write a circular to those gentlemen to whom we respectively sent subscription papers, and request the return either of the originals or copies of the subscriptions. I shall do it immediately myself and request the other gentlemen to do the same. On the last page of the inclosed is a particular statement of our affairs, which is not meant however to accompany the report, the general one it contains being deemed sufficient. I defer writing to Edinburg until we can see what are the dispositions of the legislature, and whether they will adopt us, or help us. If neither, we can only write for a Professor of languages, if either, we may then cut our coat according to our cloth. In the mean time, I think it will be best to appoint Doctr. Cooper the Physiological and Law professor as heretofore proposed, but to request him to suspend these functions and exercise those of

20. JM's letter of Dec. 1, 1817, has not been found.
21. For a discussion of the report, see Malone, VI, p. 271.

Languages until a classical Professor is procured. This would allow him the 1000. D. salary of his proper professorship with the tuition fees of the numerous grammar scholars who will be crowding on us from the start. And this will have prepared a nucleus for his Physiological and Law students to be aggregated to, whereas these last lectures, proposed by themselves, would I fear shew very meagrely and discoragingly at first and for some time. Give me your opinion on this question, as I shall withold writing to Cooper until I recieve it.[22]

I have not yet been able to engage our brickwork. The workmen of Lynchburg asked me 15. D. a thousand, which I refused. I wrote to Mr Cabell to see what engagements could be obtained in Richmond. That and Lynchburg are our only resources, and I very much fear we shall have to give 13. if not 14. D. It is this advance of price which has raised my estimate of the pavilions and Dormitories to 7000. D. Be so good as to detain the bearer till you have time to correct and return the report. Ever and affectionately your's

TH JEFFERSON

22. For TJ's negotiations with Thomas Cooper for a professorship at Central College, see *ibid.*, pp. 264, 266.

Founding the University of Virginia, 1818–1819

After retiring to Montpellier, Madison made it clear that he had not retired from the life of the mind. Knowing his friend as he did, Jefferson informed John Adams that "such a mind as his, fraught with information, and with matter for reflection, can never know ennui. Besides, there will always be work enough cut out for him to continue his active usefulness to his country."[1]

Madison quickly established a daily routine, rising early so that Mrs. Madison could do his hair with loving care, then reading and writing before eating breakfast about eight. After visiting with guests, he rode around his farms on his favorite horse, Liberty, opening gates "with a crooked stick, without dismounting, a feat which required no little skill." Returning before two, he joined his wife for their daily visit to his eighty-five-year-old mother, who lived in the right wing of the house and dined separately. He and his wife occasionally walked out to the telescope on the front portico to "spy the road where carriages and large parties were seen almost daily" on their way to Montpellier. About four o'clock, the Madisons had dinner with their company, which usually included a number of relatives and the inevitable stream of visitors.

After dinner, they walked on the portico or in the formal garden laid out by the French gardener in a horseshoe pattern based on the design of the seats in the House of Representatives. Then they retired to the drawing room for coffee and conversation, which usually lasted until ten o'clock. On rainy days, the Madisons often walked back and forth on the front porch for exercise, and guests were sometimes startled to see the sixty-six-year-old Madison break into a foot race with his younger wife, who, one chauvinistic guest reported, could run very well for her age.[2]

1. TJ to John Adams, May 5, 1817, in Cappon, II, p. 513.
2. Ralph L. Ketcham, ed., "An Unpublished Sketch of James Madison by James K. Paulding [1818]," *VMHB* 67 (1959): 432–37. Paulding made no comment about JM's running ability. For JM's routine, see Brant, VI, pp. 421–22, and Ketcham, pp. 619–20.

Like Jefferson, Madison was a passionate collector of art and sculpture. Margaret Bayard Smith reported that the walls of Montpellier "were covered with pictures, some very fine, from the ancient masters, but most of them portraits of our most distinguished men, six or eight by Stewart [Gilbert Stuart]. The mantelpiece," she continued, and "tables in each corner and in fact wherever one could be fixed, were filled with busts, and groups of figures in plaster, so that this apartment had more the appearance of a museum of the arts than of a drawing room." And Mrs. William Thornton observed that the Madisons displayed "a taste for the arts which is rarely . . . found in such remote and retired situations."[3]

Although Madison continued to collect art after retiring to Montpellier, he devoted most of his time to the management of the Montpellier farms. Almost as interested in agriculture as he was in politics, he had been touted by Jefferson a decade earlier as "the best farmer in the world," the person "who united with other sciences the greatest agricultural knowledge of any man he knew." In 1817, Jefferson and his son-in-law, Thomas Mann Randolph, joined other planters in the Piedmont region in organizing the Albemarle Agricultural Society. For president, the members chose Madison, who made the society a vital center for both scientific and practical information about farming.[4]

But the closest collaboration between the two friends in retirement came on the educational front, especially in the founding of the University of Virginia. Every letter they exchanged in 1818 and 1819 discussed that subject—often to the exclusion of any other topic. Jefferson was to be known as the father of the university, but Madison was an enthusiastic supporter from the beginning. When Jefferson circulated his first report on Central College to his colleagues on the Board of Visitors, Madison made several revisions and asked Jefferson to sign his name to the final draft.[5] "I have adopted your amendments," Jefferson replied, but he sent the final draft back to Madison for his personal signature since Jefferson planned to sign for President Monroe and did not want to "take on myself a 3d."[6] The report indicated that the Board of Visitors was prepared to transfer to the state all the property of Central College if the legislature should decide to create a university and choose it as the site. Cabell presented the report to the governor, and the legislature authorized the printing of 250 copies.[7]

---

3. For a fine account of the Madisons at Montpellier, see Conover Hunt-Jones, *Dolley and the "Great Little Madison"* (Washington, 1977), especially the chapter "Art at Montpelier," pp. 75-96.

4. Ketcham, pp. 621-23. For JM's presidential address to the society, see *Letters and Other Writings of James Madison,* [ed. William C. Rives and Philip R. Fendall], 4 vols. (Philadelphia, 1865), III, pp. 63-95.

5. JM to TJ, Jan. 1, 1818, below.

6. TJ to JM, Jan. 2, 1818, below.

7. Malone, VI, p. 273.

Cabell had also presented Jefferson's bill for the establishment of a state system of elementary schools, district colleges, and a university, but it died in the Senate committee. Nor did it win enough votes when offered in the House. Instead of Jefferson's statewide system of schools funded by local tax levies, the House appropriated money from the Literary Fund for "charity schools" in any county that chose to establish them and proposed "to give an annual sum to 4. colleges of which our's is one," Jefferson told Madison. "Mr. Cabell will endeavor to fill the blank with 5000. D[ollars]. This would pay all our annual charges," he assured Madison, "so that we might lay out our whole subscriptions [and pledges] in buildings."[8]

When the House measure came to the Senate, the provisions relating to colleges were dropped, but Cabell amended the bill to provide for the establishment of a state university and tapped the Literary Fund for an annual appropriation of $15,000 after a site had been picked and an educational plan developed. The governor was to appoint a statewide commission of twenty-four members, representing the senatorial districts. This group was to meet on August 1 at Rockfish Gap on the crest of the Blue Ridge to make recommendations to the legislature about the site and the plan of the University.[9]

Jefferson was elated with this partial victory and doubly pleased when the governor appointed him, along with Madison, Cabell, Judge Spencer Roane, and other worthies, to the commission. He had already predicted that any "plan of fixing the site of their university by the vote of an elector from each Senatorial district" would lead to its location at Charlottesville.[10] In April, he informed Madison that they should "confer on our campaign of Rockfish gap."[11] The other locations under consideration were Williamsburg, with the College of William and Mary; Lexington, with Washington College; and Staunton, which aspired not only to the new university, but also to becoming the state's new capital.

At its May meeting, the Board of Visitors of Central College agreed to offer a deed of conveyance to the state if Charlottesville was chosen as the site of the university. Jefferson must also have agreed to develop an educational plan for discussion at the Rockfish Gap meeting in August. Late in June, he informed Madison that he had been "preparing such a report as I can, to be offered there to our colleagues." It was aimed not at "an assembly of philosophers," but at the state legislature, which would have to act on the commission's recommendations. In that body, there were three groups, according to Jefferson: one "decidedly for education," another "decidedly opposed to it," and "a floating body of doubtful and wavering men who not having judgment enough for decisive opinion, can make the majority as they please. I have

---

8. TJ to JM, Feb. 6, 1818, below.
9. Malone, VI, p. 275.
10. TJ to JM, Feb. 6, 1818, below.
11. TJ to JM, Apr. 11, 1818, below.

therefore thrown in some leading ideas on the benefits of education, wherever the subject would admit it, in the hope that some of these might catch on some crotchet in their mind, and bring them over to us." He also stressed the desirability of "the establishment of the general system of primary, and secondary schools preliminary to [admission to] the University. These two objects," he concluded, "will explain to you matters in the report, which do not necessarily belong to it."[12]

Jefferson had done his homework carefully, preparing statistical tables on the population "of every county taken from the last census, estimates of the comparative numbers on each side of the divisional lines which may come into view, and such a report as these grounds may seem to authorise in the opinion of those who consider the Central college as the preferable site."[13] From this material, he had produced a map that spoke louder than words, showing Charlottesville at the exact geographical and population center of the Old Dominion.[14]

At Jefferson's invitation, Madison rode over to Monticello on July 28 and reviewed the report on July 29. For the trip to Rockfish Gap, the seventy-five-year-old Jefferson had already decided that "the roughness of the roads will induce me to go on horseback, as easier than a carriage." Accordingly, he and Madison set out on July 30, riding an easy seven miles to Farmington for "a dinner and bed" before riding the final twenty-three miles on the last day of the month.[15]

On August 1, his fellow commissioners elected Jefferson president and made him chairman of the committee, which included Madison, to prepare a report on all matters of educational policy before the commission other than the location of the university. After reviewing Jefferson's ready-made report over the weekend, the commission adopted it unanimously on Monday. For the separate decision on location, his carefully drawn map carried the vote for Central College, with Charlottesville gaining sixteen votes, Lexington three, Staunton two, and Williamsburg none.

The Rockfish Gap report called for ten divisions of higher learning at the university, each headed by a distinguished professor: ancient languages; modern languages; pure mathematics; physico-mathematics, including astronomy and geography; natural philosophy, including chemistry and geology; botany and zoology; anatomy and medicine; government, including history and political economy; law; and ideology or humanities, including literature and the fine arts. The report omitted a chair of divinity, which was barred by "the

12. TJ to JM, June 28, 1818, below.
13. *Ibid.*
14. Malone, VI, p. 276.
15. TJ had designed Farmington for his friend George Divers; for the elevation and plan, with brief notes by Frederick D. Nichols, see William Howard Adams, ed., *The Eye of Thomas Jefferson* (Charlottesville, 1981), p. 281.

principles of our Constitution, which places all sects of religion on an equal footing" and by "the sentiments of the Legislature in favor of freedom of religion." But Jefferson recognized that religion in its moral, historical, and literary aspects had a claim on the curriculum, which would teach "moral obligations . . . in which all sects agree" but leave "every sect to provide, as they think fittest, the means of further instruction in their own peculiar tenets."[16]

After the meeting at Rockfish Gap, Madison returned home while Jefferson visited Warm Springs, where he developed debilitating boils on his bottom that made sitting uncomfortable and writing so difficult that he penned few letters to anyone and none to Madison for more than seven months. When word got out that he was near death, Madison hurried over in December to check on his condition and found that Jefferson was again able to ride on horseback.[17] But two months later, Madison complained that "I have not been able to learn a tittle of your health since I saw you. It has, I hope, been entirely re-established."[18] "My health," Jefferson grumped, ". . . is tolerably established, leaving me indeed in a state of increased debility, yet no[t] so much as to render" traveling impossible.[19]

When the commission's report was published by the legislature, it was attributed to the "ever-luminous pen" of Thomas Jefferson, and it carried the day, winning legislative approval in January 1819.[20] Madison sent his friend prompt congratulations "on the success of the Report to the Legislature on the subject of the University," but he wondered about "what steps have been taken by the Governor towards giving effect to the law."[21] He did not have to wonder very long. On the next day, the governor appointed the new Board of Visitors for the university, picking Jefferson, Madison, Cabell, and Cocke from the Central College board and adding two from the Valley and one from Tidewater Virginia. He set March 29, 1819, for the first meeting of the Board of Visitors.

Since the new university would rise on the foundations of Central College, Jefferson quickly convened the old board to push plans for construction. "The late day to which the Governor has fixed the 1st. meeting of the Visitors of the University . . . ," he explained to Madison, "renders a meeting of the College visitors immediately necessary, some measures of high importance to the institution not admitting that delay; and the laws having authorised us to continue our functions until the actual meeting of the new appointment."

16. For the Rockfish Gap report, Aug. 4, 1818, see Thomas Jefferson, *Thomas Jefferson: Writings*, ed. Merrill D. Peterson (New York, 1984), pp. 457–73. See also Malone, VI, pp. 276–78.
17. *Ibid.*, pp. 279–81.
18. JM to TJ, Feb. 12, 1819, below.
19. TJ to JM, Feb. 19, 1819, below.
20. Malone, VI, pp. 280–82.
21. JM to TJ, Feb. 12, 1819, below.

Jefferson called the meeting at Montpellier "in order to alternate with you the journeyings to our meetings," and he planned to ride over "on horseback, taking two days."[22] At its final meeting, the Central College Board of Visitors authorized two more pavilions, a hotel or dining room for students, and additional dormitories, then transferred its assets to the new university.[23]

Between the last meeting of the old board and the first meeting of the new, Jefferson learned that "the 'sour grapes' of Wm. and Mary are spreading; but," he told Madison, "certainly not to the 'enlightened part of society.' "[24] Madison also hoped that "the hostility to the University" was exaggerated, but he worried that "if there should be a dearth in the Treasury, there may be danger from the predilection in favor of the popular [charity] schools," which were also financed by the Literary Fund.[25]

Before the Board of Visitors of the university held its first meeting, Jefferson invited the Madisons and the other members of the new board to come to Monticello the day before the meeting so that "by talking matters over at our leisure we may make a short business of it at the University where we shall have no accomodation."[26] Mrs. Madison visited with the Monticello family while the Board of Visitors deliberated.

At its first meeting on March 29, the board elected Jefferson rector of the university, and he also doubled informally as scribe although the board named a secretary.[27] The new board confirmed the action of the old one for adding pavilions and other buildings and confirmed the appointment of Thomas Cooper as the first professor, beginning in April 1820. Jefferson had also been busy at his architectural drawing board and unveiled a plan for four parallel rows of buildings instead of the two approved for Central College.[28]

The inauguration of the University of Virginia was a complete triumph for Jefferson, transforming the emerging Central College based on his designs into the embryonic university. Madison and the Board of Visitors followed his lead, partly out of "unaffected deference . . . for his judgment and experience," according to an observer, "and partly for the reason often urged by Mr. Madison, that as the scheme was originally Mr. Jefferson's, and the chief responsibility for its success or failure would fall on him, it was but fair to let him execute it in his own way."[29]

22. TJ to JM, Feb. 19, 1819, below.
23. Malone, VI, p. 366.
24. TJ to JM, Mar. 3, 1819, below.
25. JM to TJ, Mar. 6, 1819, below.
26. TJ to JM, Mar. 11, 1819, below. See also Malone, VI, p. 369.
27. Malone, VI, p. 369, notes that the minutes were usually in TJ's handwriting.
28. The four-row plan is illustrated in William B. O'Neal, *Pictorial History of the University of Virginia* (Charlottesville, 1970), p. 29.
29. Ketcham, p. 651.

But Jefferson was also flexible, listening to suggestions and changing his plans when convinced by argument. For example, his four-row plan showed the two middle rows of pavilions and dormitories bordered by two outside rows of dormitories and dining rooms or hotels facing the rear of the pavilions, with gardens located behind them. "You may remember," he wrote Madison in July, "that almost in the moment of our separation at the last meeting, one of our Colleagues proposed a change of a part of the plan so as to place the gardens of the Professors adjacent to the rear of their pavilion. The first aspect of the proposition presented to me a difficulty, which I then thought insuperable, to wit, that of the approach of carriages, wood-carts, etc. to the back of the buildings. Mr. Cabell's desire however appeared so strong, and the object itself indeed appearing to merit it, that after separation, I undertook to examine whether it could not be accomplished, and was happy to find it could be, by a change which was approved by Genl. Cocke," who, with Jefferson, served as superintendent of construction for the Board of Visitors.

"I think it a real improvement," he confessed, "and the greater as by throwing the Hotels and additional dormitories on a back street, it forms in fact the commencement of a regular town which is capable of being enlarged to any extent which future circumstances may call for."[30] After placing the gardens between the inner rows and the outer rows, the rector also turned the outer rows around so that they faced the street rather than the backside of the pavilions.

But he could also stick by his plans when he thought that suggestions did not promise improvement. He noted that Cocke had "proposed another change of our plan to wit that the Hotels and Dormitories should be united in massive buildings of 2. or 3. stories high, on the back street." Jefferson's plan called for one-story buildings, with "the separation of the students in different and independant rooms by two's and two's." Even if he had concurred in Cocke's proposition—and he clearly did not—he thought that the committee of superintendence could not undertake such a fundamental change in the original plan. "It was approved by the first Visitors of the Central college, stated by them in their first report to the Governor as their patron and by him laid before the legislature; it was approved and reported by the Commissioners of Rockfish gap to the legislature; of whose opinion indeed we have no other evidence than their acting on it without directing a change."

But Jefferson did not try to veto Cocke's proposal as rector. Instead, he agreed to suspend the building of "any hotel until the Visitors should have an opportunity of considering the subject." That decision required that they switch from constructing hotels on the west range and "begin the Eastern range of Pavilions, which I thought the Visitors would not disapprove, as

30. TJ to JM, July 7, 1819, below.

these can be used for hotels" until needed by professors.

Finally, he and Cocke had taken one step without the sanction of the Board of Visitors "because it accords entirely with the principles expressed and acted on at their meeting, and we are confident they would have adopted it had it then occurred. The principle of our determinations then was to push the buildings to the extent of all the funds we could command. Altho' we had recieved the opinion of the Treasurer and literary board that we might command at any moment the whole donation for this year, yet it seems not to have occurred to any of us that we might do the same next year, and consequently draw it's 15,000 D[ollars] on the 1st. day of January next. The thought occurring afterwards, we have not hesitated to act on it, and we are proceeding to have 3. Pavilions erected on the Eastern range, with their appurtenant dormitories, in addition to the 4 built or to be built on the Western range; so that we may have 7. pavilions with their dormotories in progress this year, to be finished the next."

But plans were running far ahead of construction, Jefferson groaned—"not a brick is yet laid." Nonetheless, two work crews had been lined up, with local craftsmen assigned to the western range and workers imported from Philadelphia to the eastern. Two imported stonecutters—"Italian artists," Jefferson called them—had finally arrived to carve the Ionic and Corinthian capitals. They worked only "on the difficult parts" that local craftsmen could not execute. By the October meeting of the Board of Visitors, Jefferson predicted, "our buildings will begin to shew, and we shall be enabled to judge what is next to be done."

In the meantime, the rector had made plans for training students for university admission by establishing a grammar school in Charlottesville, persuading Gerald Stack, "a teacher of Latin and Greek of high recommendations," to take on the task. "He has done so," Jefferson informed Madison, "and answers my best expectations, by a style of instruction critical and solid beyond any example I have ever known in this state, or indeed in the U S. He received his education at Trinity college, Dublin, and appears to be a correct, modest and estimable man. He teaches French also; and to give an opportunity to the students of acquiring the habit of speaking that, we have got Laporte and his family from the Calfpasture to establish a Boarding house, where nothing but French being permitted to be spoken, his boarders begin already to ask for all their wants in that language and to learn the familiar phrases of conversation."[31]

The energetic septuagenarian took time out for his summer visit to Poplar Forest, where he drafted his first annual report on the University of Virginia. It was addressed to the president and directors of the state Literary Fund, now headed by Jefferson's son-in-law, Governor Thomas Mann Randolph. Writing

31. *Ibid.* TJ also discussed his efforts to recruit faculty members.

to Madison before the October meeting of the Board of Visitors, he observed that "the condition of the University is our part of the Report which I presume should be made at the October session. The season for building is then near it's close, the session of the legislature approaching, and the time proper for determining on the operations of the next year, either with or without the aid and controul of the legislature." He enclosed his draft of the report; "but not being satisfied [with] what should be exactly it's form and matter," he asked for "suggestions of any thing more which you think it should contain, or any thing in it, which you think should be out."[32]

At its meeting in Charlottesville on October 4, the Board of Visitors approved Jefferson's draft, which reported the appointment of Thomas Cooper as the first professor at the university. Cooper's beginning date was still uncertain, however, and the board announced that no other professors would be appointed until housing was available for them and their students. In his letter of transmittal, the rector stated that seven pavilions and thirty-seven dormitories were walled up but not yet roofed.[33]

THE LETTERS

Jefferson to Madison and the Board of Visitors of Central College

Monticello Jan. 2, 1818[1]

A report to the Governor having been agreed on at our last meeting, and it's materials being chiefly in my possession, I have presumed to make a draught and now sent it for your consideration. If approved as it is, be so good as to sign it; if any material alteration be thought necessary, if such as not to deface the paper be so good as to make it and sign. If it deface the paper I must request a return of it, and I will make out another fair copy and send it round again for subscription.

Dr. Cooper accepts the Physiological professorship on the condition we ensure him 1500 D. a year, i.e. his salary of 1000 D and that the tuition fees shall make up 500. more: and he offers further to take care of our classical school until we can get a professor. This I think we should agree to, because it ensures the additional 500. D. and because it gives us time to see what the

---

32. TJ to JM, Sept. 23, 1819, below.

33. Malone, VI, p. 374.

1. Although this letter is dated Jan. 2, 1818, the date on which TJ sent the Board of Visitors' report to the governor, he circulated both the letter and the report to JM on Dec. 31, 1817, as JM's response of Jan. 1, 1818, indicates; see that letter and this.

legislature will do, for on that depends whether we are to ask from Edinburg one, two, or ten professors. But on this I ask you to send me your opinions before I write to Mr Cooper. I think we should each of us write immediately to the gentlemen to whom we addressed subscription papers, pressing their immediate return that we may know how far we may engage for the next season. The bricklayers in Lynchbg asked me 15. D. a thousand for the brickwork, which I refused. I made however a provisional bargain with one of the best of them, to give what shall be given in Lynchbg the ensuing season. The employers there expect to reduce the price to 13. D. I reserved time to consult you, and in the mean time wrote to Mr Cabell to see whether we can get as good workmen and better terms from Richmond. If the workmen will not come to our terms, we must go to theirs I suppose, because the work must be done.

Should the absence of either of you oblige the bearer to leave this letter, I must request it's being immediately returned to me by express that I may get it's signature compleated as I think every day important to have it before the legislature before they take up the general subject of education. I salute you with the most friendly attachment and respect.

TH. JEFFERSON

P.S. The estimate on a separate paper is intended for your own personal satisfaction, not to be sent to the Govr.

Estimate of the objects of application.

		D	C
	Land	1,518.75	
	Hire of laborers for 1818	1,000.	
Professor of languages, his pavilion and Dormitories		7,000	
	Salary Deposit	8,333.33	
Physiological professor, pavilion and Dormitories		7,000.	
	Salary Deposit	16,666.67	
Mathematical . . .	Pavilion	3,000.	
		44,518.75	
	Dormitories	4,000	
	Salary Deposit	16,666.67	
Ideological . . .	pavilion and Dormitories	7,000.	
	Salary Deposit	16,666.67	
Proctor	Salary Deposit	8,333.33	
		97,185.09	
2. boarding houses		6,000.	

		D C
Albemarle	Glebe lands.	3,195.86
	Subscriptions	27,610.
Fluvanna		2,590
Nelson		2,052
Lynchburg		900
Richmond		820
Williamsbg.		200.
Spotsylvania		400.
Charles city		500
Orange		30
amount of papers returnd		38,297.86

the following are by information

Orange and Louise about	3,000.
Cumberland	3,000
Goochland	800
Winchester	1,200
	8,000

Madison to Jefferson

Montpellier Jan. 1, 1818

DEAR SIR

Yours by the bearer of this was safely delivered last evening. I return the letter to the Govr. which is well adapted to its object. The pencilled marks will merely suggest for your consideration, whether the term *monastic,* tho' the most significant that could be chosen, may not give umbrage to the Institutions to which it is applicable, and whether the idea of seeking professors *abroad* may not excite prejudices with some, who entertain them agst. the countries furnishing the professors. The mark at the close of the letter suggests a choice between two words of the minimum sort. A repetition of *dutiful* may possibly be criticized as bordering on flattery. How is the letter to be subscribed[;] if by the visitors seratim, be so good as to put my name to it, for which this will be an authority.

I approve entirely of what you propose as to Cooper. It would be unfortunate if the no. of pupils should not raise his emoluments to $1500. But I think there is scarcely a possibility of such a failure; and as he is determined to leave Phila. and is shut out of W. & M. he can not be unwilling to run that small risk.

I am very sorry for the misconduct of the workmen; and particularly for the trouble thrown upon you. The increase of expence is an evil, but a less one than delay or an inferiority in the materials or workmanship employed in the Buildings.

I shall write to the holders of subscription papers within my precincts. I have neither recd. a return nor heard a word from any of them, since I saw you. If the Legislature do not espouse our cause, it may be well to renew the effort in a varied form. Affecy. yours.

JAMES MADISON

Jefferson to Madison

Monticello Jan. 2, 1818

DEAR SIR

Expecting daily an answer from the President authorising me to sign the within for him I had rather not take on myself a 3d. and therefore send it to you. I have adopted your amendments and made some other small ones. To economise writing I make one letter do for the other g[entlemen], joining you with them, altho' it contains no more than I had before written to you. After signing yourself be so good as to inclose it to Mr Watson by the bearer with a request that he will do the same to Genl. Cocke to whom also the bearer will carry it. I shall send it to Mr Cabell to be signed by him and delivered to the Govr. I will request him also to secure a negociation with the banks if we should need their aid as is probable. Ever and affectionately your's

TH JEFFERSON

Jefferson to Madison

Monticello Feb. 6, 1818

DEAR SIR

I inclose you a letter from Dr. Cooper, considerably important to the first successes of our college. I will request you to return it to me. I inclose also the answer which I think should be given. If you think so likewise be so good as to seal and forward it. If not, return it, as I should be unwilling to take on myself alone so important a relinquishment. Yet I think it right that we should not hold him to a place of 1500. D. a year, if he can get one of 7000. D. and in a society which he would prefer. Indeed the probability is that he will think the case justified a retraction of his engagement with us, and that he would refuse to come.[2]

I observe that the bill on education before the H. of Repr. proposes to

---

2. Cooper eventually resigned in order to accept an appointment at the University of South Carolina; see Malone, VI, pp. 366, 377-80.

give an annual sum to 4. colleges of which our's is one. Mr Cabell will endeavor to fill the blank with 5000. D. This would pay all our annual charges, so that we might lay out our whole subscriptions in buildings. And indeed I have little doubt but on their plan of fixing the site of their university by the vote of an elector from each Senatorial district, Charlottesville will obtain it. The greatest fear is that they will do nothing, and that this immense fund, the interest of which is near 100,000. D. a year will continue to be idle, or be perverted to something else.[3] Affecty. yours.

TH JEFFERSON

Madison to Jefferson

Montpellier Feb. 12, 1818

DEAR SIR

I have recd. yours of the 6th. inclosing the letters to and from Dr. Cooper, and forward the former by this days mail, the first that has offered. The relinquishment of our claim on him was unavoidable, and but reasonable. And it could not have been made known to him in more suitable terms.

Madison to Jefferson

Montpellier Mar. 29, 1818

DEAR SIR

The day on which the first instalment for the Central College becomes due, being near at hand, I think it not amiss, as no conveyance of mine offers, to intimate, that it shall be paid on draft, or if requisite sent by a special hand. Yrs. affectionately

JAMES MADISON

Jefferson to Madison

Monticello Apr. 11, 1818

DEAR SIR

Yours of Mar. 29. came duly to hand, but I put off answering it because I expected to have written sooner by the bearer of the present Mr Coffee. Noth-

---

3. The Literary Fund was supplemented in 1816 by the appropriation of the surplus of the federal debt to the state for expenditures during the War of 1812, estimated to add nearly $1 million to the fund; see *ibid.*, p. 249.

ing presses as to the payment of the instalment which is the subject of your letter. It may either be paid to the Richmd bank of Virginia, or sent to Mr Garret or Mr Barksdale by any body happening to be coming, or brought when you come to our meeting of May 11th. I am in hopes you will then find Correa and Cooper here.[4] Then also we will confer on our campaign of Rockfish gap. The most urging thing at present is to get a return of the subscription papers of your quarter. Not a single one has been recieved from the North Eastern quarter.

Mr. Coffee the bearer of this is a Sculptor lately from England, and really able in his art. He makes busts in plaister or terra cotta. He came from Richmond to take your bust and mine, and gives less trouble than any artist, painter or Sculptor I have ever submitted myself to. I join him therefore in solliciting your indulging him and your friends in setting for him.[5] I set out for Bedford tomorrow to return the 1st. week of May. Ever and affectionately yours.

TH JEFFERSON

Jefferson to Madison

Monticello June 28, 1818

DEAR SIR

Being to set out in a few days for Bdford from whence [I] shall not return till about a week before our Rockfish meeting, I have been preparing such a report as I can, to be offered there to our colleagues. It is not such an one as I should propose to them to make to an assembly of philosophers, who would require nothing but the table of professorships, but I have endeavored to adapt it to our H. of representatives. I learn that in that body the party decidedly for education, and that decidedly opposed to it, are minorities of the whole, of which the former is strongest. That there is a floating body of doubtful and wavering men who not having judgment enough for decisive opinion, can make the majority as they please. I have therefore thrown in some leading ideas on the benefits of education, wherever the subject would admit

---

4. José Francisco Correa de Serra was a Portuguese botanist who served as his government's minister to the United States during Monroe's presidency. For an excellent account, see Richard Beale Davis, "The Abbe Correa in America, 1812–1820," *Transactions* (American Philosophical Society), n.s. 45 (1955): pt. 2, 87–197.

5. See George C. Groce, "John William Coffee, Long-Lost Sculptor," *American Collector* 15 (1946): 14–15, 19–20, Harold E. Dickson, "'TH. J.' Art Collector," in *Jefferson and the Arts: An Extended View*, ed. William Howard Adams (Washington, 1976), p. 126; and Hunt-Jones, p. 84. Coffee's bust of Dolley Madison was illustrated in *Antiques* 118 (Mar. 1988): 617; it is now on public display at Montpellier, which is owned by the National Trust for Historic Preservation.

it, in the hope that some of these might catch on some crotchet in their mind, and bring them over to us. Nor could I, in the report, lose sight of the establishment of the general system of primary, and secondary schools preliminary to the University. These two objects will explain to you matters in the report, which do not necessarily belong to it. I now inclose it, and ask your free revisal of it both as to style and matter, and that you will make it such as yourself can concur in with self-approbation. I would be glad to find it at home on my return, because if the corrections should make a fair copy necessary I should have little time enough to copy it. Observe that what I propose to be offered to the board is only from page 3. to 17. which sheets are stitched together. The detached leaves contain the white population of every county taken from the last census, estimates of the comparative numbers on each side of the divisional lines which may come into view, and such a report as these grounds may seem to authorise in the opinion of those who consider the Central college as the preferable site. I shall this day write to Judge Roane and invite him to come here a day or two beforehand as I hope you will, that we may have a consultation on it. I know of no other member who will probably pass this way whom it would be particularly desirable to consult, without endangering jealousy. The 1st. day of August happens of a Saturday. The roughness of the roads will induce me to go on horseback, as easier than a carriage; but as it is 30. miles from here to the Rockfish gap, which is more than I could advisably try in one day, I would propose that we ask a dinner and bed from Mr Divers on the Thursday evening, which will give us 23. miles for the next day. This of course would require Wednesday for our consultation, and Tuesday at furthest for the arrival of yourself and Judge Roane here.[6]

My liaisons with Tazewell oblige me to ask him to make this a stage, and to propose to him to be here on the Wednesday, to take the road hence together. I am in hopes Mrs Madison will think it more agreeable to come and while away your absence with Mrs Randolph. Judge Stewart is zealous that as soon [as] we meet at the gap, we should adjourn to Staunton, and he invites you and myself to make his house our quarters while there; this I mention to you because he desired it but entirely against any adjournment myself, that we may avoid not only the reality but the suspicion of intrigue; and be urged to short work by less comfortable entertainment. As we shall probably do nothing on Saturday, I shall have no objection to go home with him that evening, and return into place on Monday morning. In the hope of seeing you here in good time for consultation and the journey I salute you with affectionate friendship

       Th Jefferson

---

6. For the meeting of the Rockfish Gap commission, see Malone, VI, pp. 275–78.

Madison to Jefferson

[Montpellier Oct. 1818]

I was much gratified in learning from the President that you were so well recovering from the attack your health suffered beyond the mountains. I wish I could join you at the meeting of the Visitors on Monday, and attend also that of the Agricultural Society. But circumstances do not allow that pleasure.

Madison to Jefferson

Montpellier Feb. 12, 1819

DEAR SIR,

I have not been able to learn a tittle of your health since I saw you. It has, I hope, been entirely re-established. I congratulate you on the success of the Report to the Legislature on the subject of the University. It does not yet appear what steps have been taken by the Governor towards giving effect to the law.[7]

Will you be so good as to have the inclosed forwarded when convenient to Mr. Minor? I leave it open that you may peruse the printed Memoir, which the author, T. Coxe, wishes you may have an opportunity of doing. It is short, and contains facts and remarks which will pay for the trouble.[8] He refers me, also, to an article from his pen in the Amn. Edit. of Rees's Cyclopedia, under the head "United States," which I believe he would be gratified by your looking into. I have not seen it, but understand that it contains not only other remarks on the subject of the Memoir, under the sectional head "Agriculture," but a review of the most important transactions—quorum partes fuimus [in which we participated].

The President intimates to me that there is a prospect of an early and satisfactory close to the negociations with Spain, promoted he doubts not by the course of events of late date and the account to which they have been turned.[9]

7. For the legislature's adoption of the Rockfish Gap report and the granting of the University of Virginia's charter, see *ibid.*, pp. 280–82.

8. Peter Minor was secretary of the first Board of Visitors of the University of Virginia; see Richard Beale Davis, ed., *The Correspondence of Thomas Jefferson and Francis Walker Gilmer, 1814–1826* (Columbia, S.C., 1946), p. 17. Tench Coxe had written *A Memoir . . .* in 1817 on cotton manufactories and the next year wrote *An Addition, of December 1818, to the Memoir . . .*; see Jacob E. Cooke, *Tench Coxe and the Early Republic* (Chapel Hill, 1978), p. 534.

9. President Monroe and Secretary of State John Quincy Adams turned General Andrew Jackson's rambunctious raid into East Florida into the Transcontinental Treaty by which Spain ceded all territory east of the Mississippi to the United States, after the administration demanded that Spain either exercise responsible control over Indians in the area or cede it to the United States. The best accounts are in Samuel Flagg Bemis, *John Quincy Adams and the Foundations of American Foreign*

Jefferson to Madison

Monticello Feb. 19, 1819

DEAR SIR

Yours of the 12th. has been duly recieved, and the pamphlet it covered has been sent to Mr Minor. The late day to which the Governor has fixed the 1st. meeting of the Visitors of the University (the last Monday in March) renders a meeting of the College visitors immediately necessary, some measures of high importance to the institution not admitting that delay; and the laws having authorised us to continue our functions until the actual meeting of the new appointment. General Cocke, who was here about three weeks ago, sensible of the necessity of a meeting agreed to attend on any day I should name, and, in order to alternate with you the journeyings to our meetings I proposed to him to meet at your house, to which he consented. I have now requested his attendance at Montpellier in the forenoon of Friday next (the 26th. inst.) as I have also that of Mr Watson. Mr Cabell cannot attend. The roads being impassable for a carriage, I shall take it on horseback, taking two days. If the weather is good, I may possibly go to Colo. Lindsay's on Wednesday, and be with you the next day. But the weather must govern me in that. My health after which you kindly enquire is tolerably established, leaving me indeed in a state of increased debility, yet no[t] so much as to render me unequal to the journey proposed.[10] My grandson Jefferson, of the accident to whom you have probably heard, was brought home two days ago, his wounds, altho' healing slowly, being in a very satisfactory state.[11] We all join in affectionate salutations to Mrs Madison and yourself

TH JEFFERSON

Jefferson to Madison

Monticello Mar. 3, 1819

DEAR SIR,

I promised your gardener some seeds which I put under a separate cover and address to you by mail. I also inclose you a letter from Mr. Cabell which will shew you that the 'sour grapes' of Wm. and Mary are spreading; but certainly not to the 'enlightened part of society' as the letter supposes. I have sent him a transcript from our journals that he may see how far we are under

---

Policy (New York, 1949), pp. 317–40, and Harry Ammon, *James Monroe: The Quest for National Identity* (New York, 1971), pp. 426–28.

10. TJ rode horseback through a snowstorm to attend the meeting at Montpellier; see Malone, VI, p. 366.

11. Thomas Jefferson Randolph was seriously wounded by his drunken brother-in-law, Charles Bankhead, in Charlottesville on Feb. 1, 1819; see *ibid.*, pp. 299–300.

engagements to Dr. Cooper. I observe Ritchie imputes to you and myself opinions against Jackson's conduct in the Seminole war. I certainly never doubted that the military entrance into Florida, the temporary occupation of their posts, and the execution of Arbuthnot and Ambrister were all justifiable. If I had ever doubted, P. Barber's speech would have brought me to rights. I at first felt regret at the execution; but I have ceased to feel it on mature reflection, and a belief the example will save much blood.[12] Affectionately your's.

P. S. On my return I fell in with Mr. Watson who signed our proceedings.

Madison to Jefferson

Montpellier Mar. 6, 1819

DEAR SIR,

Your favor of March 3d came safe to hand, with the seeds you were so kind as to send with it.

I return Mr. Cabell's letter. I hope his fears exaggerate the hostility to the University; though, if there should be a dearth in the Treasury, there may be danger from the predilection in favor of the popular schools. I begin to be uneasy on the subject of Cooper. It will be a dreadful shock to him if serious difficulties should beset his appointment.[13] A suspicion of them, even, will deeply wound his feelings and may alienate him from his purpose. I understand that a part of his articles are packed up, to be in readiness for his removal.

I had noticed the liberty taken by the press with my opinion as well as yours, as to the conduct of General Jackson. I certainly never said any thing justifying such a publication, or any publication. In truth, I soon perceived that both the legality and the expediency of what was done depended essentially on all the circumstances; and this information I do not even yet fully possess, having not read the documents, and part only of the debates, which give different shades at least to the facts brought into view. As far as I have taken any part in conversations, I have always expressed the fullest confidence in the patriotism of his views, that if he should have erred in any point, the error ought not to be separated from that merit, and that no one could thoroughly appreciate the transactions without putting himself precisely in his situation. I believe I expressed also in a few lines answering a letter from a friend, my regret that the question in Congress could not take some turn that

12. Alexander Arbuthnot and Robert C. Ambrister were British traders in East Florida accused by General Andrew Jackson of fomenting Indian raids into American territory. Jackson court-martialed both men, executing Arbuthnot by hanging and Ambrister by rifle fire. Castlereagh's ministry did not press the issue; see Bemis, I, p. 315, and Bradford Perkins, *Castlereagh and Adams: England and the United States, 1812–1823* (Berkeley, 1964), pp. 288–90.

13. Thomas Cooper had been elected to a professorship in Central College, which TJ considered binding on the university. Cabell and Cocke opposed the appointment; see Malone, VI, pp. 366–67.

would satisfy the feelings of the General and the scruples of his friends and admirers.

The paper from Detroit which you will see is from Woodward, came to me by mistake, with one directed to me. I inclose it, as a more certain conveyance than the newspaper mail. Truly and affecty. yours

JAMES MADISON

Jefferson to Madison

Monticello Mar. 8, 1819

DEAR SIR

I now return you the letter from Mr Watson whom I met with on the road as mentioned in mine of the 3d. In consequence of the doubts discovered on the subject of Cooper, I wrote to Mr Cabell, to Correa, and to Cooper himself, and inclose you copies of my letters for perusal that you may see on what ground I place the matter with each. To Cooper I barely hold up the possibility of new views from a new majority, altho' I do not apprehend any change. I have no doubt that Cabell will acquiesce.[14] I must pray you to return me his letter, and the copies of mine now inclosed and salute you affectionately and respectfully

TH JEFFERSON

Madison to Jefferson

Montpellier Mar. 11, 1819

DEAR SIR

I recd. yesterday morning yours of the 8th. and return the several copies of letters inclosed in it. The letter to you from Mr. Cabell was returned by the mail before the last. I know not any course better to be taken in relation to Dr. Cooper, than your letter to him and Correa. I have not a particle of doubt that the answer of the latter will compleatly remove the objection brought forward agst. the former; and I hope if there are others not disclosed, that they will evaporate before the moment for decision. Cooper under- . . .[15]

I presume that he will not be precluded from Law-Lectures, at least untill a professor for that Branch shall be in his functions. He will probably receive a

---

14. See *ibid.*, pp. 367-68.

15. The top fragment of this letter is from the JM Papers in the Library of Congress, and the bottom portion is from the Brown University Library. I am indebted to the Papers of James Madison project for the bottom portion.

greater emolument from the Law, than of Classical Students, and for some time both together may not exceed a quant: sufficit. I am very glad to see that the additional appropriation of $20,000, had fallen through   Health and all other happiness.

JAMES MADISON

Jefferson to Madison

Monticello Mar. 11, 1819

DEAR SIR

I inclose you a letter recieved last night from Mr Cabell containing inter[e]sting information as to our University as well as something further with respect to Dr. Cooper. Be so good as to return it with those formerly sent you. I recieved by the same mai[l] a commision as visitor, and an authentic appointment of the last Monday of this month for our first meeting at the University.[16] I have written to the new members to request them to come here the day before that by talking matters over at our leisure we may make a short business of it at the University where we shall have no accomodation. Ever and affectionately your's

TH JEFFERSON

Madison to Jefferson

Montpellier Mar. 16, 1819

DEAR SIR

I recd. yesterday yours of the 11th. The letter from Mr. Cabell which I return is of very agreeable import. His other letter was returned several days ago, and probably reached Monticello soon after the date of yours. Health and all other happiness

JAMES MADISON

Jefferson to Madison

Monticello July 7, 1819

DEAR SIR

Proposing within 4. or 5. days to set out for Bedford, where I shall continue two months, I have thought it would be acceptable to you to learn

---

16. At the meeting of the Board of Visitors on Mar. 29, 1819, Cooper was elected to a professorship; see Malone, VI, p. 369.

the present state of things at the University, and the prospect for the year. You may remember that almost in the moment of our separation at the last meeting, one of our Colleagues proposed a change of a part of the plan so as to place the gardens of the Professors adjacent to the rear of their pavilion. The first aspect of the proposition presented to me a difficulty, which I then thought insuperable, to wit, that of the approach of carriages, wood-carts etc. to the back of the buildings. Mr Cabell's desire however appeared so strong, and the object itself indeed appearing to merit it, that after separation, I undertook to examine whether it could not be accomplished, and was happy to find it could be, by a change which was approved by Genl. Cocke, and since by Mr Cabell, who has been lately with me. I think it a real improvement, and the greater as by throwing the Hotels and additional dormitories on a back street, it forms in fact the commencement of a regular town which is capable of being enlarged to any extent which future circumstances may call for.

My colleague of the Committee of superintendance proposed another change of our plan to wit that the Hotels and Dormitories should be united in massive buildings of 2. or 3. stories high, on the back street. Had my judgment concurred in this proposition, I should not have thought ourselves competent to it, as a committee of superintendance. The separation of the students in different and independant rooms by two's and two's seems a fundamental of the plan. It was approved by the first Visitors of the Central college, stated by them in their first report to the Governor as their patron and by him laid before the legislature; it was approved and reported by the Commissioners of Rockfish gap to the legislature; of whose opinion indeed we have no other evidence than their acting on it without directing a change. Not thinking therefore that the committee was competent to this change, I so far concurred as to suspend the building any hotel until the Visitors should have an opportunity of considering the subject: and instead of building one or two hotels as the Visitors had directed we concluded to begin the Eastern range of Pavilions, which I thought the Visitors would not disapprove, as these can be used for hotels until wanting for the Professors.

We have adopted one measure however, without their sanction, because it accords entirely with the principles expressed and acted on at their meeting, and we are confident they would have adopted it had it then occurred. The principle of our determinations then was to push the buildings to the extent of all the funds we could command. Altho' we had recieved the opinion of the Treasurer and literary board that we might command at any moment the whole donation for this year, yet it seems not to have occurred to any of us that we might do the same the next year, and consequently draw it's 15,000. D. on the 1st. day of January next. The thought occurring afterwards, we have not hesitated to act on it, and we are proceding to have 3. Pavilions erected on the Eastern range, with their appurtenant dormitories, in addition to the 4 built or to be built on the Western range; so that we may have 7. pavilions with their dormotories in progress this year, to be finished the next.

Our works have gone on miserably slow. Not a brick is yet laid. They are now however prepared to begin laying the Western pavilion No. 1. Our advertisement for workmen could not be put into the paper until after the meeting of the visitors at the close of March. The offers from the undertakers of our own state were from 25. to 40. per cent on the Philadelphia printed prices. We at length got an offer from Philadelphia at 15. p.c. below the printed prices, and learnt the fact that when work abounds there the workmen are able to raise prices 10. or 15. p.c. above the printed ones, and when work is scarce the employers are able to beat them down 10. or 15. p.c. below the printed prices; which however, if continued, soon breaks them. We did not think it either our duty or interest to break our workmen, and considering the printed, as the fair living prices, we undertook to give them the printed prices. A workman came on to see the extent of the work we had to do. This brought our own people down to the same prices, so we assigned to them the completion of the Western range, and to the Philadelphians the Eastern. The undertaker went back, and I recieved a letter of June 17. from him, informing me that their workmen would sail on the 20th. in the packet for Richmond, and that himself the master brickmaker and master bricklayer would meet them by the stage at Richmond, and I expect hourly to hear of their arrival there, where Mr Brockenbrough will recieve and forward them.[17]

I had begun to despair of our two Italian artists, and enquired therefore of Mr Cardelli, whether such as could cut an Ionic or Corinthian capital could be had at Washington. He informed me they could; at 3. Dollars a day. Luckily the two Italians arrived a week ago. They will cost us, passage and board included about 2. D. a day, and are men of quite superior character. I was just setting off for my other home in Bedford to stay there two months, but have deferred my departure till Mr Brockenbrough can arrive here, in order to see them fixed and put under way, that the stone might be quarried and roughed out for them, so that they should be employed on the difficult parts only.

Our principle being to employ the whole of our funds on the building I thought it so important to be preparing subjects for the University by the time that should open, that I invited a Mr Stack, a teacher of Latin and Greek of high recommendations, to come and set up a school in Charlottesville. He has done so, and answers my best expectations, by a style of instruction critical and solid beyond any example I have ever known in this state, or indeed in the U S. He received his education at Trinity college, Dublin, and appears to be a correct, modest and estimable man. He teaches French also; and to give an opportunity to the students of acquiring the habit of speaking that, we have got Laporte and his family from the Calfpasture to establish a Boarding house, where nothing but French being permitted to be spoken, his boarders begin already to ask for all their wants in that language and to learn the familiar phrases of conversation. Mr Stack has as yet but 14. pupils and Laporte 9.

---

17. See *ibid.*, pp. 370–71.

boarders;[18] but as soon as the present sessions in the schools of the state generally are over, and the youths freed from their present engagements, we have reason to believe more will be offered than can be recieved, and in this way I think we shall have from 50. to 100. subjects fully prepared to attend the scientific proprietors the moment the University opens. I have recieved from London the offer of a Professor of modern languages, of qualification literary and moral, so high as to merit our suffrage, if we can get over the difficulty that, French being the most important of the modern languages, Mr Blattermann is not a native of France. Mr Ticknor declines coming to us. I shall again try Mr Bowditch, with some additional, but with not much hope. We have the offer of a botanist of distinguished science, a Mr Nuttal, but whether a native or not, is not said. Doctor Cooper, his wife and family have certainly set their minds strongly to us. His collection of minerals have been selected, valued, and packed to come on at the time prescribed.[19]

I hope we shall see you at the October visitation, by which time our buildings will begin to shew, and we shall be enabled to judge what is next to be done. In the mean time, and at all times, be assured of my constant and affectionate friendship and respect.

TH JEFFERSON

Jefferson to Madison

Monticello Sept. 23, 1819

DEAR SIR

The law establishing the University requires the Visitors to make a report annually embracing a full account of the disbursements, the funds on hand, and a general statement of the condition of the said University. The account of disbursements and funds belongs to the Bursar and Proctor, who are accordingly instructed to have them made up to the last day of this month. The condition of the University is our part of the Report which I presume should be made at the October session. The season for building is then near it's close, the session of the legislature approaching, and the time proper for determining on the operations of the next year, either with or without the aid and controul of the legislature. As this is the first occasion of forming such a report, I have sketched one according to existing facts, but not being satisfied what should be exactly it's form and matter, I inclose it to you and request your suggestions of any thing more which you think it should contain, or any thing in it, which you think should be out, and to return it by mail.[20]

18. For the Stack-Laporte school, see *ibid.*, pp. 371–73.
19. For the complications with Professor Cooper, see *ibid.*, pp. 374, 376–79.
20. TJ drafted the first annual report of the University of Virginia Board of Visitors at Poplar Forest in the summer. This letter, which was originally dated Sept. 4, 1819, when TJ was at Poplar

On my return from Bedford I found here a volume from the colonisation society for you under the same cover with one addressed to myself which I forward you by this mail.[21] In the mass of my letters too was one for you, the seal of which I had broken before I observed that it was addressed to you. With a request for pardon for this inadvertence I now inclose it, unread. I hope you will be with us at least a day before our meeting on Monday the 4th. of October, as the other gentlemen are requested to be, that we may talk over our business at our leisure before the meeting in form at the University and that Mrs Madison will do us the favor of accompanying you. Ever and affectionately yours

TH JEFFERSON

Madison to Jefferson

Montpellier Sept. 28, 1819

DEAR SIR

I received yesterday yours of the 23d. inclosing the draft of a report from the Visitors, in which I see no occasion for addition or alteration, but much for regret at the deficiency of our resources. The subject is presented however to the Legislature, with the most inviting aspect for their attention and assistance. I shall endeavour to be with you about Saturday, and Mrs. Madison will have the pleasure of joining in the opportunity of seeing you all as she does in offering now affectionate salutations and respects.

JAMES MADISON

Jefferson to Madison

Monticello Oct. 18, 1819

DEAR SIR

By this day's mail I forward you ⅓ of a parcel of seeds of the Sea-Kale sent here by Genl. Cock for you, Mr Divers and myself. I feared to await a private conveyance because they lose their vegetative power if not planted soon.

Forest, was later endorsed as written on Sept. 23, 1819, from Monticello and was so entered by TJ in his Epistolary Ledger. The board adopted the report on Oct. 4, 1819, and TJ sent it to Richmond on Dec. 1; see *ibid.*, pp. 374-75.

21. The American Colonization Society was organized in 1816 to promote the settlement of freed slaves in an African country to be called Liberia. JM was a life member, becoming president in 1833. See P. J. Staudenraus, *The African Colonization Movement, 1816-1865* (New York, 1961); Drew R. McCoy, *The Last of the Fathers: James Madison and the Republican Legacy* (New York, 1989), pp. 297, 301; and Malone, VI, p. 325.

The day after you left us I was taken with a cholic which attended with a stricture of the upper bowels brought me into great pain and immediate danger. The obstacle was at length overcome and I am recovering, but have not yet left my room. A salivation brought on by a dose of 8. or 9 grs. of calomel with Jalap occasions my present confinement. I can swallow only fluids, which keep me very weak. I thought it due to your friendship to free it from the uncertainty of floating rumors and I salute you with affection and respect.

Madison to Jefferson

Montpellier Oct. 23, 1819

DEAR SIR

Your favor of the 18th. which authenticates your convalescence was most welcome, and I thank you much for your kindness in relieving me from the anxieties which preceded it. Fortunately the first account we had of your illness was accompanied with some encouragement to hope that the crisis had been passed favorably; and this hope was fostered by the information of Col: P. Barbour on his return from the Court at Charlottesville. But our apprehensions were not entirely removed till the receipt of your letter, and that of Miss Ellen to Mrs. M. Whilst I indulge the pleasure these have afforded, I must intreat that your health may be more a primary object than you have hitherto allowed it to be. Your constitution has been well tested, and you owe it to many considerations, to bestow on it the care which its remaining strength justly merits.[22]

The Sea-Kale seed from Gen: Cocke came safe to hand; for which I thank you both. Accept my thanks also for the French pamphlets. I wish you most fervently a speedy re-establishment of your health, and every other blessing.

JAMES MADISON

Madison to Jefferson

Montpellier Oct. 25, 1819

DEAR SIR,

I received a few days ago the two inclosed letters, one from Mr. Hackley, the other from the Botanical professor at Madrid; the latter accompanied by the three little pamphlets also inclosed, and by thirty specimens of wheat, with four of barley, and between 2 and 300 papers of the seeds referred to as "rarion

---

22. For a reference to TJ's brief but dangerous illness—a "violent and obstinate cholic"—see Malone, VI, p. 373.

Horti Botan., Matritaises." The Wheats and Barleys, notwithstanding the numerous varieties, I will endeavor to have sowed. The Garden seeds which probably include many which would be very acceptable to a Botanical professor at the University, if we had one, I am at a loss what to do with. I know not that I can do better with them than to give you an opportunity of inspecting their names, and with the aid of Mr. Randolph, judging how far any of them ought to be kept for the University, and into what hands the others can best be disposed of. They are therefore herewith also inclosed. Be so good as to return the two letters. Mr. Randolph perhaps may be willing to look into the pamphlets, which he will best understand and appreciate. Affectionate respects

JAMES MADISON

Jefferson to Madison

[Monticello] Nov. 30, 1819

DEAR SIR

A visit of the ladies of our family to Mrs Madison gives me an opportunity of sending you our correspondence with Dr. Cooper and of recieving it back again safely. It is necessary to observe that our first letter and his first crossed each other on the road, so that each party had expressed their mind before knowing that of the other. On the whole this embarrassed transaction ends well enough, except as we have been led by it to ensure 7000. D. in two years, when 4000. would have satisfied him. Ever and affectionately Yours

TH. JEFFERSON

Madison to Jefferson

[Montpellier] Dec. 6, 1819

DEAR SIR

By the return of the ladies who have favored Mrs Madison with so agreable a visit, I send back the correspondence with Cooper. It has ended better than I expected.

I learn with the greatest pleasure that your health is so well restored. I hope you will be careful of it. Above all avoid the fatigues of the pen.

I do not say with the Spaniards I kiss your hands, but I say with all my heart God preserve you. Most affectionately

JAMES MADISON

45

LIBERTY AND LEARNING, 1820–1822

THE CREATION of the University of Virginia had been an incredible performance. From Albemarle Academy in 1814 to Central College in 1816, neither of which had ever enrolled a student, had emerged the University of Virginia in 1819, located where Jefferson wanted it, laid out according to his innovative plan, with the academical village going up according to his designs. Jefferson was, indeed, as Madison later observed, "the great projector and the mainspring" of the University of Virginia.[1]

From the beginning, the parsimonious legislature became the object of Jefferson's "campaign" for the university. The act creating the state school coincided with the Panic of 1819, the first great depression in the nation's history. Even though Jefferson's son-in-law, a devoted friend of the university, served as governor of the Commonwealth for the next three years, the Board of Visitors received only reluctant support from the legislature. Early in 1820, Jefferson confessed to Madison that "the finances of the University are in a most painful state." The $15,000 annual allotment from the Literary Fund for that year had been spent by the middle of February, "and we still owe 15,000 for work already done." Private subscriptions were running behind pledges, and the continuing depression meant that "little is expected to be recieved."[2]

Moreover, the septuagenarian, whose astonishing burst of energy must have astounded his colleagues during his campaign to charter the university, came down with a long spell of illness that kept him "low, weak, able to walk little, and venturing to ride little on account of suspicious symptoms in my legs which Dr. Watkins flatters himself will disappear in the spring."[3] Three

---

1. JM to Frederick Beasley, Dec. 22, 1824, in Hunt, IX, p. 212.
2. TJ to JM, Feb. 16, 1820, below.
3. *Ibid.*

months later, he noted that his health had mended somewhat, "altho' I do not gain strength." Moreover, "the stiffening of my wrist" made writing "slow and painful."[4] Not until January 1821 did he report the complete "restoration of my health."[5]

Healthy or not, the rector rejoiced when the legislature authorized the Board of Visitors to borrow $60,000 from the Literary Fund. A special meeting of the board in April 1820 agreed to use the money to complete buildings under construction and approved three more pavilions with adjoining dormitories, steps that Jefferson thought were "of a very leading character," committing the state to the completion of the Rockfish Gap plan.[6]

At the same time, the rector lamented an intellectual setback for the university: the loss of the only faculty member yet named. Thomas Cooper, scheduled to begin his duties in 1820, was marking time with a one-year position at South Carolina College. His appointment at Virginia had been greeted with a rising tide of clerical criticism. Fearful of the controversial Cooper's Unitarianism, the Presbyterians were especially vociferous in their complaints. Jefferson labeled them "the most intolerant of all sects, the most tyrannical, and ambitious; ready at the word of the lawgiver, if such a word could be obtained, to put the torch to the pile, and to rekindle in this virgin hemisphere the flames in which their oracle Calvin consumed the poor Servetus."[7]

Madison agreed with his friend that Cooper was a powerful intellect but had confessed early on that he was "uneasy on the subject" of Cooper's appointment.[8] When Cabell and other members of the board argued that a democratic state university could not afford to alienate its constituency, Jefferson fought a rear-guard action, regretting the hailstorm of criticism but insisting on honoring the appointment at the contractual stipend of $1,500 for the year. If necessary, the four Visitors from the Central College board, which had made the appointment, should pay it by private subscriptions for they stood "so engaged on our personal honor that Dr. Cooper's draught . . . shall be paid." "This is our only security," he told Madison, "for keeping faith and honor with Cooper."[9] They were rescued from their dilemma when Cooper was offered a permanent position at South Carolina and agreed to resign at Virginia. The rector and board took the graceful way out and accepted his resignation in October.[10]

By midsummer, Jefferson was his optimistic self again. "Our buildings at

4. TJ to JM, May 17, 1820, below.

5. TJ to JM, Jan. 28, 1821, below.

6. TJ to JM, May 17, 1820, below; see also Malone, VI, pp. 375–76.

7. Peterson, p. 979.

8. JM to TJ, Mar. 6, 1819, above.

9. TJ to JM, Feb. 16, 1820, below.

10. Malone, VI, pp. 376–80, and Dumas Malone, *The Public Life of Thomas Cooper, 1783–1839* (New Haven, 1922), pp. 234–46.

the University go on so rapidly," he reported to Madison gleefully, "and will exhibit such a state and prospect by the meeting of the legislature that no one seems to think it possible they should fail to enable us to open the institution the ensuing year."[11] But in his annual review to the governor and the directors of the Literary Fund, he pointed out that the university could not be opened for another eight years if the $60,000 loan had to be paid off from the annual allotment from the fund.[12] He, therefore, urged remission of the loan, an appropriation of $40,000 for the Rotunda to house the library and other offices, and an increase in the annual allotment to fund the faculty.[13]

The Board of Visitors had to settle for a second loan bill in 1821, and at their spring meeting they ordered a tally of outstanding obligations. By the fall, the rector had a report on "the cost of the buildings finished at the University, that we might obtain a more correct view of the state of our funds, and see whether a competency will remain for the Library." Basing his figures on "actual experience" in building costs, the proctor concluded "that our actual reciepts heretofore, with what is still to be recieved of the loan of this year, after paying for the lands and all incidental and current expences, will exactly compleat the 4 rows of buildings for the accomodation of the Professors and students, amounting in the whole to 195,000. Dollars, and leave us without either debt or contract."[14]

The new figures exceeded the previous estimate by $18,000 for the buildings in the academical village, a "not over-considerable" overrun, according to Jefferson. That could be offset by collecting "the *unpaid subscriptions*" by private donors, leaving "the 3. annuities of 1822. 23. and 24." from the Literary Fund for "the Library and current charges." But the rector left "that undertaking entirely open and undecided, for the opinion of the Visitors at their meeting in November."[15]

During his visit to Poplar Forest in October 1821, Jefferson refined his figures and drafted the board's annual report. He listed seven pavilions, sixty-five dormitories, and three hotels completed and paid for, "leaving in the estimate class 3. Pavilions, 3. Hotels, and 22. dormitories, and these estimated from experience." As for the library, he was "decidedly of opinion we should undertake it," throwing its charges "on the 3. ensuing years of the annuity which had always been included in our estimates."[16]

Jefferson had consistently argued that the university should not be opened until the academical village was complete, and he always maintained that the Rotunda, modeled on the Pantheon, was necessary "to give it unity

---

11. TJ to JM, Aug. 13, 1820, below.
12. The annual interest on the loan had to be paid before the costs of construction could be met.
13. Malone, VI, p. 382.
14. TJ to JM, Sept. 30, 1821, below.
15. *Ibid.*
16. TJ to JM, Oct. 30, 1821, below.

and consolidation as a single object."17 "If we stop short of the compleat establishment," the rector told Madison, "it will never be compleated. On the other hand, the stronger we make the mass, the more certainly will it force itself into action. The world will never bear to see the doors of such an establishment locked up, and if the legislature shall become disposed to remit the debt, they will swallow a pill of 165,000. D[ollars] with the same effort as one of 120,000. D[ollars]."18

Madison sharpened some of the figures in the annual report, and he suggested adding "the objects, other than the library, to be provided for in the Pantheon. It will aid in accounting for the estimated cost, and may otherwise mitigate difficulties." He also assured Jefferson that "the view you take of the question of commencing the library and trusting to the alternative with the Legislature will claim for it a fair consideration with the visitors."19

At its November meeting, the members of the board agreed that an engraving of the ground plan of the buildings should be made for promotional purposes. Jefferson was sure that "it will be a splendid establishment, would be thought so in Europe, and for the chastity of its architecture and classical taste leaves everything in America far behind it."20

Despite Jefferson's high hopes for support from the legislature of 1821–1822, it did "absolutely nothing at all for the institution." The Rotunda was the stumbling block, being viewed by many as an extravagant expense, if not an architectural folly. Jefferson told Madison that "one of the zealous friends to the University, in a Philippic against the Rotunda declared he would never vote another Dollar to the University but on condition that it should not be applied to that building." Indeed, Chapman Johnson, a member of the Board of Visitors from Staunton, had consistently opposed "every proposition . . . to begin that building, and moved himself in the late session [of the legislature] to suspend interest with an express Proviso that no money should be applied to that building."21

Madison replied that "one of the most popular objections to the Institution . . . is the expence added by what is called the ornamental style of the Architecture." He doubted that the additional expense was "as great as is supposed," but even if it were, he thought "the objection ought the less to be regarded as it is short of the sum saved to the public by the private subscribers who approve of such an application of their subscriptions."22

At the spring meeting of the Board of Visitors, which Madison missed,

17. TJ to William Short, Nov. 24, 1824, cited in Malone, VI, p. 386.
18. TJ to JM, Oct. 30, 1821, below.
19. JM to TJ, Nov. 10, 1821, below.
20. TJ to William Short, Nov. 24, 1821, cited in Malone, VI, pp. 386–87.
21. TJ to JM, Apr. 7, 1822, below.
22. JM to TJ, Jan. 15, 1823, below.

"there was not a single thing requisite to act on," Jefferson reported. "We have to finish the 4. rows and appendages this summer [1822] which will be done and then to rest on our oars," waiting for the public to "come right and approve us in the end." Although he did not alter his strategy for completing the university's physical plant before admitting students, he did adjust his timetable. Jefferson, Madison, and the majority of the board members had always been of the opinion "never to open the institution until the buildings shall be compleat; because as soon as opened, all the funds will be absorbed by salaries etc. and the buildings remain for ever incompleat. We have thought it better to open it fully, altho' a few years later, than let it go on for ever in an imperfect state." He, therefore, counseled patience, observing that "the establishment is now at that stage at which it will force itself on." Nor should the board forsake Johnson. "We must manage our dissenting brother softly," the elderly statesman recommended; "he is of too much weight to be given up."[23]

Madison also remained committed to public support of education consistent with "the genius of Republican Government." In a letter to a friend in Kentucky, he observed that "a popular Government without popular information, or the means of acquiring it, is but a Prologue to a Farce or a Tragedy; or, perhaps both." He argued that "Learned Institutions ought to be favorite objects with every free people" and cited the Virginia Bill for the More General Diffusion of Knowledge as a model "favorable to the intellectual and moral improvement of Man" since it was "conformable to his individual and social Rights. What spectacle can be more edifying or more seasonable," he concluded, "than that of Liberty and Learning, each leaning on the other for their mutual and surest support."[24]

Although Jefferson seldom strayed very far from university affairs in his later letters to Madison, there was an undercurrent of apprehension and bewilderment after the Panic of 1819 caused his financial problems to multiply. The Missouri crisis of 1819–1820 was to Jefferson "a fire bell in the night" that compounded his fear that the federal government might become a consolidated Leviathan threatening the American experiment in republicanism. The proposed restriction on the right of Missouri citizens to own slaves not only violated the Constitution, according to the Sage of Monticello, but it also threatened self-government unless Congress yielded "to Missouri her entrance on the same footing with other states, that is to say with the right to admit or exclude slaves at her own discretion."[25] Indeed, his growing zeal for states' rights, as his biographer Dumas Malone concluded, "bordered on fanaticism."[26]

23. TJ to JM, Apr. 7, 1822, below.
24. JM to W. T. Barry, Aug. 4, 1822, in Hunt, IX, pp. 103–8.
25. TJ to JM, Jan. 13, 1821, below.
26. Malone, VI, p. 356.

THE LETTERS

Jefferson to Madison

Monticello Feb. 16, 1820

DEAR SIR

With this letter I commit for you to the mail a bundle of seeds, one parcel of which was sent by you to Mr Randolph for inspection. The other is seakale seed lodged here for you by Genl Cocke. Have I returned your Vitruvius to you? I am in great tribulation about it. I keep my borrowed books on a particular shelf that they may neither be forgotten nor confounded with my own. It is not on that shelf, nor can I find it. I know that I meant to return it to you on reciept of a copy of it among some books which came to hand from Paris 3. weeks ago:[1] but not recollecting the act of returning I am uneasy and wish to know from you. The finances of the University are in a most painful state. The donation of 1820. is recieved and paid away, and we still owe 15,000 for work already done. In our reports we have always calculated on a punctual payment of the subscriptions, and were they so paid we should be perfectly at ease. But 8000. D. are in arrear on the instalments of 1819. and of that of 11,000 for [18]20. payable Apr. 1. little is expected to be recieved.[2] To us, visitors, who stand so engaged on our personal honor that Dr. Cooper's draught in Apr. or May shall be paid, it is important to give a preference to that draught, and there is no chance of doing it from the general collection. I have notified the Proctor therefore to appropriate to that the instalments of half a dozen by name whose punctuality can be counted on, to wit, the 4. visitors subscribers, Mr Divers and Colo. Lindsay. This is our only security for keeping faith and honor with Cooper.[3]

My health is as usual: no pain, but low, weak, able to walk little, and venturing to ride little on account of suspicious symptoms in my legs which Dr. Watkins flatters himself will disappear in the spring. I salute you with constant affection and respect.

TH JEFFERSON

---

1. For TJ's efforts to build a new book collection after selling his library to Congress in 1815, see Malone, VI, pp. 185-89.
2. On Feb. 20, 1820, the legislature passed the University Loan Act authorizing the Board of Visitors to borrow up to $60,000; see *ibid.*, pp. 375-76.
3. For negotiations with Cooper, then at South Carolina College, see *ibid.*, pp. 376-80.

Madison to Jefferson

[Montpellier ca. Feb. 26, 1820]

I congratulate you on the loan, scanty as it is, for the University, in the confidence that it is a gift masked under that name and in the hope that it is a pledge for any remnant of aid the Establishment may need in order to be totus teres atque rotundus [every way round and smooth, so as to roll through the world unbiased by any asperity].

Can you not have the hands set to work without the formality of a previous meeting of the Visito[rs?] I have re[cd.] no notice from Richmond on the subject   Health and every other happiness

JAMES MADISON

Madison to Jefferson

[Montpellier] Mar. 31, 1820[4]

DEAR SIR

Judge Todd accompanied by one of his sons being on his return thro' this your neighbourhood will call to pay his respects to you. His great worth justly entitles him to this introduction to your recollections.

I propose to be with you tomorrow evening. Mrs. M. will not lose the opportunity of making a visit to the ladies of Monticello. Yours always and affectly.

JAMES MADISON

Jefferson to Madison

Monticello Apr. 11, 1820

DEAR SIR

Our brewing for the use of the present year has been some time over. About the last of Oct. or beginning of Nov. we begin for the ensuing year, and malt and brew 3. 60 gallon casks *successively,* which will give so many successive lessons to the person you send. On his return he can try his hand with you in order to discover what parts of the processes he will have learnt imperfectly, and come again to our spring brewing of a single cask in order to perfect himself, and go back to you to try his hand again in as much as you will want.

---

4. This letter, which is in the Andre De Coppet Collection at the Princeton University Library, was called to my attention by Eugene Sheridan.

You will want a house for malting, which is quickest made by digging into the steep side of a hill, so as to need a roof only, and you will want a haircloth also of the size of your loft to lay the grain on. This can only be had from Phila or N. Y.[5]

I set out for Bedford the first of next week to be absent till the 1st. week in May. I will give you notice in the fall when we are to commence malting and our malter and brewer is uncommonly intelligent and capable of giving instruction if your pupil is as ready at comprehending it. Ever and affectionately yours

TH JEFFERSON

Jefferson to Madison

Monticello May 17, 1820

DEAR SIR

As the measures which were adopted at the last meeting of our visitors were of a very leading character I have thought it proper to inform our absent colleagues of them; and have delayed the communication only until I could add what has been done under the resolutions of the board. As this latter information has not been recieved by you, I inclose you my letter to General Taylor for perusal and pray you, when read, to stick a wafer in it and put it into the post office.[6] You will excuse this economy of labor, as from the stiffening of my wrist, writing is become slow and painful. I have moreover such another letter to write to Mr Johnson, and a good part of it to Genl. Breckenridge.

My general health is mended, altho' I do not gain strength. I am obliged to continue bandages, altho' under their pressure the swelling is kept down, yet it returns on omitting them. I salute you with constant and unchangeable friendship.

TH JEFFERSON

Jefferson to Madison

Monticello Aug. 13, 1820

DEAR SIR

I recieved yesterday the inclosed letter proposing to me an interposition which my situation renders impracticable. The gentlemen of my family have

---

5. For TJ's brewing activities, see Edwin M. Betts, ed., *Thomas Jefferson's Farm Book* . . . (Princeton, 1953), pp. 413–21.

6. At a special meeting on Apr. 3, 1820, the Board of Visitors decided to complete the buildings under construction and add three more pavilions with adjoining dormitories; see Malone, VI, p. 376.

manifested at times some opposition to Mr Nelson's elections: which has produced an intermission of intercourse between the families: and altho' I never took the smallest part in it, and nothing but what is respectful has ever passed between Mr Nelson and myself, yet I cannot but feel the ground too suspicious to venture on the experiment proposed, and indeed the thing is so delicate that I know not whether any ground, however cordial, could render it safe. But of this you will be the best judge as to yourself, for which purpose I inclose you the letter. I suppose myself it is impossible that a Virginian can be elected and that Mr N's competition would only defeat Genl. Smiths election and ensure a Northern and unfriendly choice.[7]

Our buildings at the University go on so rapidly, and will exhibit such a state and prospect by the meeting of the legislature that no one seems to think it possible they should fail to enable us to open the institution the ensuing year. I salute Mrs Madison and yourself with constant affection and respect.

Th Jefferson

Jefferson to Madison

Poplar Forest Nov. 29, 1820

Dear Sir,

The inclosed letter from our antient friend Tenche Coxe came unfortunately to Monticello after I had left it and has had a dilatory passage to this place where I recieved it yesterday and obey it's injunction of immediate transmission to you. We should have recognized the stile even without a signature, and altho so written as to be much of it indecypherable. This is a sample of the effects we may expect from the late mischievous law vacating every 4. years nearly all the executive offices of the government. It saps the constitutional and salutary functions of the President, and introduces a principle of intrigue and corruption, which will soon leaven the mass, not only of Senators, but of citizens. It is more baneful than the attempt which failed in the beginning of the government to make all officers irremovable but with the consent of the Senate. This places, every 4. years, all appointments under their power, and even obliges them to act on every one nomination. It will keep in constant excitement all the hungry cormorants for office, render them, as well as those in place sycophants to their Senators, engage these in eternal intrigue to turn out one and put in another, in cabals to swap work; and make of them, what all executive directories become, mere sinks of corruption and faction. This must have been one of the midnight signatures of the President, when he had not

---

7. Hugh Nelson of Albemarle County served as a Republican congressman from 1811 until 1823; see Daniel P. Jordan, *Political Leadership in Jefferson's Virginia* (Charlottesville, 1983), pp. 192, 228.

time to consider, or even to read the law; and the more fatal as being irrepealable but with the consent of the Senate, which will never be obtained.[8]

F. Gilmer has communicated to me Mr. Correa's letter to him of adieux to his friends here, among whom he names most affectionately Mrs. Madison and yourself. No foreigner I believe has ever carried with him more friendly regrets. He was to sail the next day (Nov. 10.) in the British packet for England, and thence take his passage in Jan. for Brazil. His present views are of course liable to be affected by the events of Portugal, and the possible effects of their example on Brazil.[9] I expect to return to Monticello about the middle of the ensuing month and salute you with constant affection and respect.

Madison to Jefferson

Montpellier Dec. 10, 1820

DEAR SIR,

Yours of November 29 came to hand a few days ago. The letter from T. Coxe   is returned. I had one from him lately on the same subject, and, in consequence, reminded the President of his political career; dropping at the same time a few lines in his favour to our Senator, Mr. Barbour. I sincerely wish something proper in itself could be done for him. He needs it and deserves it.

The law terminating appointments at periods of four years is pregnant with mischiefs such as you describe. It overlooks the important distinction between repealing or modifying the office, and displacing the officer. The former is a Legislative, the latter an Executive function; and even the former, if done with a view of re-establishing the office and letting in a new appointment, would be an indirect violation of the Theory and policy of the Constitution. If the principle of the late statute be a sound one, nothing is necessary but to limit appointments held during pleasure, to a single year, or the next meeting of Congress, in order to make the pleasure of the Senate a tenure of office, instead of that of the President alone. If the error be not soon corrected, the task will be very difficult; for it is of a nature to take a deep root.[10]

8. The Tenure of Office Act of 1820 established a four-year term for federal officeholders whose duties involved financial responsibility; see Harry Ammon, *James Monroe: The Quest for National Identity* (New York, 1971), pp. 494–95.

9. For the Abbe Correa, see TJ to JM, Apr. 11, 1818, above.

10. For the congressional drive to exert greater influence over executive appointments by enacting the so-called Tenure of Office Act of 1820, see Ammon, pp. 495–96, and Drew R. McCoy, *The Last of the Fathers: James Madison and the Republican Legacy* (New York, 1989), pp. 103–4. For JM's support of executive autonomy, see Ralph Ketcham, *Presidents above Party: The First American Presidency* (Chapel Hill, 1984), pp. 114–17.

On application, through Mr. Stephenson, I have obtained from the Legislative files at Richmond a copy of Col. Bland's letter to you, for which I gave you the trouble of a search last fall. The letter being a public, not a private one, was sent to the Legislature, according to the intention of the writer. It contains what I expected to find in it; a proof that I differed from him on the question of ceding the Mississippi to Spain in 1780.[11]

This will wait for your return from Poplar forest, accompanied I hope with evidence of the good effects of the trip on your health. Affectionately and truly yours

Madison to Jefferson

Montpellier Jan. 7, 1821

DEAR SIR,

In the inclosed you will see the ground on which I forward it for your perusal.

In the late views taken by us of the act of Congress vacating periodically the Executive offices, it was not recollected, in justice to the President, that the measure was not without precedents. I suspect however that these are confined to the Territorial establishments, where they were introduced by the old Congress in whom all powers of Government were confounded; and continued by the new Congress, who have exercised a like confusion of powers within the same limits. Whether the Congressional code contains any precedent of a like sort, more particularly misleading the President, I have not fully examined. If it does, it must have blindly followed the territorial examples.[12]

We have had for several months a typhus fever in the family, which does not yield in the least to the progress of the season. Out of twenty odd cases, there have been six deaths, and there are several depending cases threatening a like issue. The fever has not yet reached any part of our White family; but in the overseer's, there have been five cases of it including himself. None of them, however, has been mortal. Health and every other blessing

JAMES MADISON

---

11. For the difference of opinion between JM and Bland in 1780 over navigation of the Mississippi, see JM and the Virginia congressional delegation to Jefferson, Nov. 22, 1780, above.

12. TJ was closer to the mark when he suggested that Monroe's approval of the Tenure of Office Act "must have been one of the midnight signatures of the President, when he had not time to consider, or even to read the law"; see TJ to JM, Nov. 29, 1820, above. Ammon, p. 494, agrees that "Monroe signed the bill without knowing its contents."

Jefferson to Madison

Monticello Jan. 13, 1821

DEAR SIR,

I return you Mr. Coxe's letter without saying I have read it. I made out enough to see that it was about the Missouri question, and the printed papers told me on which side he was. Could I have devoted a day to it, by interlining the words as I could pick them out, I might have got at more. The lost books of Livy or Tacitus might be worth this. Our friend would do well to write less and write plainer.

I am sorry to hear of the situation of your family, and the more so as that species of fever is dangerous in the hands of our medical boys. I am not a physician and still less a quack but I may relate a fact. While I was at Paris, both my daughters were taken with what we formerly called a nervous fever, now a typhus, distinguished very certainly by a thread-like pulse, low, quick and every now and then fluttering. Dr. Gem, an English physician, old, and of great experience, and certainly the ablest I ever met with, attended them. The one was about 5. or 6. weeks ill, the other 10. years old was 8. or ten weeks. He never gave them a single dose of physic. He told me it was a disease which tended with certainty to wear itself off, but so slowly that the strength of the patient might first fail if not kept up. That this alone was the object to be attended to by nourishment and stimulus. He forced them to eat a cup of rice, or panada, or gruel, or of some of the farinaceous substances of easy digestion every 2. hours and to drink a glass of Madeira. The youngest took a pint of Madeira a day without feeling it and that for many weeks. For costiveness, injections were used; and he observed that a single dose of medicine taken into the stomach and consuming any of the strength of the patient was often fatal. He was attending a grandson of Mde. Helvetius, of 10. years old, at the same time, and under the same disease. The boy got so low that the old lady became alarmed and wished to call in another physician for consultation. Gem consented. That physician gave a gentle purgative, but it exhausted what remained of strength, and the patient expired in a few hours.

I have had this fever in my family 3. or 4. times since I have lived at home, and have carried between 20. and 30. patients thro' it without losing a single one, by a rigorous observance of Dr. Gem's plan and principle. Instead of Madeira I have used toddy of French brandy about as strong as Madeira. Brown preferred this stimulus to Madeira. I rarely had a case, if taken in hand early, to last above 1. 2. or 3. weeks, except a single one of 7. weeks, in whom when I thought him near his last, I discovered a change in his pulse to regularity, and in 12. hours he was out of danger. I vouch for these facts only, not for their theory. You may, on their authority, think it expedient to try a single case before it has shewn signs of danger.

On the portentous question before Congress I think our Holy Alliance will find themselves so embarrassed with the difficulties presented to them as to find their solution only in yielding to Missouri her entrance on the same footing with the other states, that is to say with the right to admit or exclude slaves at her own discretion.[13] Ever and affectionately yours.

P. S. I should have observed that the same typhus fever prevailed in my neighborhood at the same times as in my family, and that it was very fatal in the hands of our Philadelphia Tyros.

Jefferson to Madison

Monticello Jan. 28, 1821

DEAR SIR

My neighbor, friend and physician, Doctr. Watkins, being called to Philadelphia, is desirous to pay his respects to you en passant, and asks me, by a line to you, to lessen his scruples on doing so. You will find my justification in his character when known to you. His understanding is excellent, well informed, of pleasant conversation, and of great worth. As a Physician I should put myself in his hands with more confidence than any one I have ever known in this state, and am indebted to his experience and cautious practice for the restoration of my health.[14] Recieve him therefore with your wonted kindness and accept the assurance of my affectionate respect.

TH JEFFERSON

Jefferson to Madison

Monticello Jan. 30, 1821

DEAR SIR

The inclosed letter to Mr. Cabell so fully explains its object, and the grounds on which your signature to the paper is proposed if approved, that I will spare my stiffening and aching wrist the pain of adding more than the assurance of my constant and affectionate friendship.

TH. JEFFERSON

13. For TJ's reaction to the slavery question in the Missouri Compromise, see Don E. Fehrenbacher, "The Missouri Controversy and the Sources of Southern Separatism," *Southern Review* 14 (1978): 653–67; Malone, VI, pp. 328–44; John Chester Miller, *The Wolf by the Ears: Thomas Jefferson and Slavery* (New York, 1977), pp. 221–52.

14. For Dr. T. G. Watkins, see Malone, VI, pp. 448, 455.

Jefferson to Madison and the Board of Visitors of the University of Virginia

Monticello Aug. 15, 1821

Dear Sir,

In obedience to the resolution of the visitors of the University at their last session, the Proctor has been constantly employed in ascertaining the state of accounts under contracts already made, and the expence of compleating the buildings begun and contemplated, and we have consequently suspended, according to instructions, the entering into any contracts for the Library until we see that it may be done without interfering with the finishing of all the pavilions, hotels and dormitories begun and to be begun. The Proctor will require yet considerable time to compleat his settlements, insomuch that it is very doubtful whether there will be any thing ready for us to act on at our stated meeting in October, should that take place. But by deferring our meeting to the approach of that of the Genl. Assembly, it is believed we shall be able to report to them that nearly the whole of the buildings of accommodation are finished, and the sum they will have cost, that the few remaining will be finished by the spring, and what this probable cost will be, as ascertained by experience, and further to show the balance of the funds still at our command, and how far they will be competent to the erection of the library. On this view of the unreadiness of matter for our next stated meeting, and of the prospect that a deferred one will enable us to make a clear and satisfactory report, I venture to propose the omission of our October meeting, and the special call of an occasional one on the Thursday preceding the meeting of the legislature. That day is fixed on for the convenience of the gentlemen who are members of the legislature; as it brings them so far on their way to Richmond, with time to get to the 1st. day of the session. Not having an opportunity of personal consultation with my colleague of the Committee of advice, I pass the letters thro' his hands, if he approved the proposition he will subjoin his approbation and forward them to their several addresses; otherwise, not. If approved, it will be proper you should subscribe the enclosed notice and return it to me to be placed among our records.

I have just received an order of the Literary board for 29,100 D. in part of the loan of 60,000 D. lately authorised; and following the practice of the Legislature, I have thought it just and safest to have the deposit made by moieties in the Virginia and Farmer's banks. I salute you with great friendship and respect.

Jefferson to Madison

Monticello Sept. 16, 1821

DEAR SIR,

I have no doubt you have occasionally been led to reflect on the character of the duty imposed by Congress on the importation of books. Some few years ago, when the tariff was before Congress, I engaged some of our members of Congress to endeavor to get the duty repealed and wrote on the subject to some other acquaintances in Congress, and pressingly to the Secretary of the treasury. The effort was made by some members with zeal and earnestness, but it failed. The Northern colleges are now proposing to make a combined effort for that purpose, as you will see by the inclosed extract of a letter from Mr. Ticknor asking the cooperation of the Southern and Western institutions, and of our university particularly.[15] Mr. Ticknor goes so ably into all the considerations justifying this step, that nothing need be added here, and especially to you; and we have only to answer his questions, whether we think with them on the subject of the tax? What should be the extent of the relaxation sollicited? What mode of proceeding we think best? And whether we will co-operate in our visitatorial character? I must earnestly request your thoughts on these questions, fearful of answering them unadvisedly, and on my own opinions alone.

I think that another measure, auxiliary to that of petitioning might be employed with great effect. That is for the several institutions, in their corporate capacities, to address letters to their representatives in both houses of Congress, recommending the proposition to their advocation. Such a recommendation would certainly be respected, and might excite to activity those who might otherwise be indifferent and inactive and in this way a great vote, perhaps a majority might be obtained. There is a consideration going to the injustice of the tax which might be added to those noticed by Mr. Ticknor. Books constitute capital. A library book lasts as long as a house, for hundreds of years. It is not then an article of mere consumption but fairly of capital, and often in the case of professional men, setting out in life it is their only capital. Now there is no other form of capital which is first taxed 18. per cent on the gross, and the proprietor then left to pay the same taxes in detail with others whose capital has paid no tax on the gross. Nor is there a description of men less proper to be singled out for extra taxation. Mr. Ticknor, you observe asks a prompt answer, and I must ask it from you for the additional reason that within about a week, I set out for Bedford to remain there till the approach of winter. Be so good as to return me also the inclosed extract and to be assured of my constant and affectionate friendship.

---

15. For the relationship between Ticknor and TJ, see O. W. Long, *Thomas Jefferson and George Ticknor* (Williamstown, Mass., 1933).

Madison to Jefferson

Montpellier Sept. 20, 1821

DEAR SIR,

I received yesterday yours of the 16th, inclosing the paper from Mr. Ticknor on the tax imposed on books imported. He has taken a very comprehensive and judicious view of the subject. The remark you add to it is a proper one also; that books, being a permanent property, ought not to be taxed whilst other permanent property is exempt, both in the acquisition and possession.

I have always considered the tax in question as an impolitic and disreputable measure; as of little account in point of revenue, and as a sacrifice of intellectual improvement to mechanical profits. These two considerations however produced the tax and will be the obstacles to its removal. Of the precise amount it yields to the revenue, I have no knowledge. It cannot I presume be such as to weigh, even in the present difficulties of the Treasury, against the arguments for its discontinuance. If the fiscal consideration is to prevail, a better course would be to substitute an equivalent advance on some other articles imported. As to the encouragement of the book printers, their interest might be saved in the mode suggested by Mr. Ticknor, by a continuance of the tax on books republished within a specified time. And perhaps the encouragement is recommended by the interests of literature as well as by the advantage of conciliating an active and valuable profession; reprinted books being likely to obtain a greater number of purchasers and readers, especially when founded on previous subscriptions, than would seek for or purchase imported originals. As I approve, therefore, the general object of the Northern Literati, I should prefer at the same time a modification of it in favor of republishers. I see no adequate reason for distinguishing between English and other books whether in modern or ancient languages. If it were possible to define such as would fall under the head of luxurious or demoralizing amusements, there might be a specious plea for their exception from the repeal; but besides the impracticability of the discrimination, it would invoke a principle of censorship which puts at once a veto on it.

The proposed concert among the Learned Institutions in presenting the grievance to Congress, would seem to afford the best hope of success in drawing their favorable attention to it. A captious or fastidious adversary may perhaps insinuate that the proper petitioners for redress are those who feel the grievance, not those who are exempt from it; that the latter assume the office of Counsellors, under the name of petitioners; and that from Corporate bodies, above all a combination of them, the precedent ought to be regarded with a jealous eye. The motives of modesty which would doubtless be stamped on the face of the interposition in this case will be the best answer to such objections; or if there should be any serious apprehension of danger from them, the auxiliary expedient you suggest, of addressing the respective representatives instead of Congress, might be made a substitute, instead of an auxiliary. I should suppose that our University would not withhold their concurrence in either or both modes. In that of addressing the particular representatives in Congress, there could be no room for hesitation. Mr. Ticknor's wishes for information as to the other Institutions in Virginia, and to the South and West, proper to be invited into the plan, you can satisfy as well without as with my attempt to enumerate them. The members of Congress most proper to be engaged in the cause could be best selected on the spot, where I presume some well chosen agent or agents, none better than Mr. Ticknor himself, will be provided in the quarter giving birth to the experiment.

These are hasty thoughts, but I send them in compliance with your request of an immediate answer. Take them for what they are worth only. Affectionately yours

JAMES MADISON

Jefferson to Madison

Monticello Sept. 30, 1821

DEAR SIR

Mr. Brockenbrough has been closely engaged, since our last meeting in settling the cost of the buildings finished at the University, that we might obtain a more correct view of the state of our funds, and see whether a competency will remain for the Library.[16] He has settled for 6. pavilions, 1. hotel, and 35. dormitories, and will proceed with the rest; so that I hope, by our next meeting, the whole of the 4. rows will be nearly settled. From what is done he has formed an estimate of the cost of what is yet to be done; and guided in it by actual experience, it is probably nearly correct. The result is that our actual reciepts heretofore, with what is still to be recieved of the loan of this year, after paying for the lands and all incidental and current expences, will exactly compleat the 4 rows of buildings for the accomodation of the Professors and students, amounting in the whole to 195,000. Dollars, and leave us without either debt or contract.

In the conjectural estimate laid before the Visitors at their last meeting it was supposed that the 3. annuities of 1822. 23. and 24. would suffice for the Library and current charges, without the aid of the *unpaid subscriptions,* which were reserved therefore as a contingent fund. By this more actual estimate it appears that the unpaid subscriptions, valued at 18,000. D. will be *necessary* to compleat that building. So that that conjectural estimate fell short by 18,000.

---

16. Arthur S. Brockenbrough was provost of the university who oversaw the construction of the buildings; see Malone, VI, p. 370.

D. of the real cost of the 4. rows; which in a total of 195,000. D. is perhaps not over-considerable. I call it the *real* cost because that of the unfinished buildings is reckoned by the real cost of those finished. The season being now too far advanced to begin the Library, and the afflicting sickness in Genl. Cocke's family having deprived me of the benefit of consultation with him, I think it a duty to leave that undertaking entirely open and undecided, for the opinion of the Visitors at their meeting in November, when it is believed the actual settlements will have reached every thing, except 1. pavilion and 3. hotels, which alone will be unfinished until the spring.[17]

The considerations which urge the building the hull, at least, of the Library, seemed to impress the board strongly at their last meeting; and it is put in our power to undertake it with perfect safety, by the indefinite suspension by the Legislature, of the commencement of our instalments. This leaves us free to take another year's annuity, to wit, that of 25. before we begin instalments, should the funds fall short which are here counted on for that building. The Undertakers are disposed to accept and collect themselves the outstanding subscriptions in part of payment.

You will distinguish in this statement by their enormous cost the pavilions No 3. and 7. and 16. Dormitories, contracted for in 1817. and 18. at the inflated prices prevailing then while we acted as a Central College only. In 1819. and the following years, prices were reduced from 25. to 50. per cent. The enlarged cost of the latter dormitories has been occasioned by the unevenness of the ground, which required cellars under many of them.

I shall hope to have the pleasure of recieving you at Monticello a day, at least, before that of our meeting, as we can prepare our business here so much more at leisure than at the University. I salute you with great Friendship and respect.

Th Jefferson

A view of the whole expences and of the Funds of the University	Actual Cost D.	Estimated D.	Averages D.
Pavilions No. 3 and 7 undertaken in 1817.18	19,149.81	—	9,574.90
No. 2. 4. 5. 9.	33,563.15		8,390.78
(18)17. marble capitals for No. 2. 3. 5. 8. from Italy	1,784.		
No. 1. 6. 8. 10. not finished		33,563.15	
Hotel B. B.	4,609.58		
5. other Hotels not finished			
6		20,000.	4,000.

---

17. For the estimates, see *ibid.*, pp. 385–86.

Dormitories. 16. undertaken in 1817.	13,898.34		868.64
19.	11,083.63		583.34
74. not finished, but contracted for		38,462.60	519.76
— 109.			
Lands, wages, and contingencies (suppose for round numbers)		18,885.74	
	84,088.51	110,911.49	
		195,000	

Funds. Glebe lands	3,104.09
Annuities of 1819.20.21.	45,000.
Loan of 1820.	60,000.
Loan of 1821.	60,000.
Subscriptions recieved to Sep. 1821. about	25,000.
Balance to be carried forward	1,895.91
	195,000

	Actual	*Estimated*	*Average*
Expences still to be incurred			
Walls of backyards, gardens, etc. about 100,000 bricks		1,500.	
Wages and contingencies for 1822.23.		6,000.	
Library Hull 30,200 D. + Interior 13,476 D.		43,675.	
Interest for 1821.22.23.		13,700.	
		64,875	

Funds. Balance brought forward	1,895.91
Subscriptions. 19,133.33 of which are sperale (?)	18,000.
Annuities of 1822.23.24.	45,000.
	64,895.91

A more summary view of the cost of the 4. rows of buildings and Library

10.	Pavilions	88,060.11
6.	Hotels	24,609.58
109.	Dormitories	63,445.57
	Library	43,675.
		219,790.26

Jefferson to Madison

Monticello Oct. 30, 1821

DEAR SIR

I heard in Bedford that you were attacked with the prevailing fever, and with great joy on my return that you were recovered from it. In the strange state of the health of our country every fever gives alarm.

I got home from Bedford on the 27th. and am obliged to return there within 3. or 4. days, having an appointment at the Natural bridge on the 11th. prox. As our proposed petition to Congress will of course be in collation with those from other seminaries, I availed myself of my leisure at Poplar Forest to sketch it, and I now inclose it to you to be made what it should be which I pray you to do with severity.

Knowing my time would be crouded thro' the month of November, I took the same opportunity to sketch our November report on the basis of Mr Brockenbrough's settlement as far as he has gone,[18] which I had communicated to you, with some subsequent corrections. His further advance in the settlements, will by the time of our meeting enable us to put into the class of settled accounts 7. pavilions, instead of 6. 3 hotels instead of 1. 65. dormitories instead of 30. leaving in the estimate class 3. Pavilions, 3. Hotels, and 22. dormitories, and these estimated from experience. He has corrected too the article of the cost of lands, hire of laborers etc. The cost of the Library must be thrown on the 3. ensuing years of the annuity which had always been included in our estimates: and I am decidedly of opinion we should undertake it on that ground. If we stop short of the compleat establishment, it will never be compleated. On the other hand, the stronger we make the mass, the more certainly will it force itself into action. The world will never bear to see the doors of such an establishment locked up, and if the legislature shall become disposed to remit the debt, they will swallow a pill of 165,000. D. with the same effort as one of 120,000. D. Be so good as to return me these papers with your amendments by the middle of November. With my respectful souvenirs to Mrs Madison accept assurances of my constant affection and respect.

TH JEFFERSON

Madison to Jefferson

Montpellier Nov. 10, 1821

DEAR SIR,

I return the several papers which accompanied yours of the 30th ult. I have interlined with a pencil for your consideration a very slight change in the

---

18. For TJ's annual report of Nov. 30, 1821, see *ibid.,* pp. 386–87.

petition to Congress,[19] and another in the Report to the President and Directors of the Literary Fund. The first is intended to parry objections from the reprinters of foreign books, by a phraseology not precluding exceptions in their favour. The exceptions can be made without injury to the main object; and although not necessary for the protection of the American Editions, the greater cheapness here being a sufficient one, will probably be called for by the patrons of domestic industry. I find that, besides the few classics for schools, and popular works others of solid value continue to be republished in the Northern Cities. The other interlineation suggests the objects, other than the library, to be provided for in the Pantheon. It will aid in accounting for the estimated cost, and may otherwise mitigate difficulties.

The view you take of the question of commencing the library and trusting to the alternative with the Legislature will claim for it a fair consideration with the visitors. I shall endeavour to be with you at [the] time you have fixed for their meeting. Yours always and affectionately

JAMES MADISON

Jefferson to Madison

Monticello Feb. 25, 1822

DEAR SIR

I have no doubt you have recieved, as I have done, a letter from Dr. Morse with a printed pamphlet, proposing to us a place in a self constituted society for the civilisation of the Indians etc.[20] I am anxious to know your thoughts on the subject because they would affect my confidence in my own. I disapprove the proposition altogether. I acknolege the right of voluntary associations for laudable purposes and in moderate numbers. I acknolege too the expediency, for revolutionary purposes, of general associations, coextensive with the nation. But where as in our case, no abuses call for revolution, voluntary associations so extensive as to grapple with and controul the government, should such be or become their purpose, are dangerous machines, and should be frowned down in every regulated government. Here is one proposed to comprehend all the functionaries of the government executive, legislative and

---

19. In the Petition of the Rector and Visitors of the University of Virginia to the Senate and House of Representatives of the United States in Congress assembled, Nov. 30, 1821, TJ asked for the removal of duties imposed on the importation of books as "an unfair impediment to the American student"; see the Jefferson Papers of the University of Virginia, 1732–1828 (microfilm, reel 9). In a letter to President John T. Kirkland of Harvard, Dec. 26, 1821, he noted that Virginia was cooperating in the petitioning campaign with universities in Massachusetts, North Carolina, South Carolina, Georgia, and Kentucky; see *ibid*.

20. For Morse's American Society for Promoting the Civilization and General Improvement of the Indian Tribes in the United States, see the concise study by Joseph W. Phillips, *Jedidiah Morse and New England Congregationalism* (New Brunswick, N.J., 1983), pp. 199–213.

Judiciary, all officers of the army or navy, governors of the states, learned institutions, the whole body of the clergy who will be 19/20 of the whole association, and as many other individuals as can be enlisted for 5. D. apiece. For what object? One which the government is pursuing with superior means, superior wisdom, and under limits of legal prescription. And by whom? A half dozen or dozen private individuals, of whom we know neither the number nor names, except of Elias B. Caldwell their foreman, Jedidiah Morse of Ocean memory their present Secretary and in petto their future Agent, etc. These clubbists of Washington, who from their residence there will be the real society, have undertaken to embody even the government itself into an instrument to be wielded by themselves and for purposes directed by themselves. Observe that they omit the President's name, and for reasons too flimsy to be the true ones. No doubt they have proposed it to him, and his prudence has refused his name. And shall we suffer ourselves to be constituted into tools by such an authority? Who, after this example, may not impress us into their purposes? Feeling that the association is unnecessary, presumptuous and of dangerous example, my present impression is to decline membership, to give my reasons for it, in terms of respect, but with frankness. But as the answer is not pressing, I suspend it until I can hear from you in the hope you will exchange thoughts with me, that I may shape my answer as much in conformity with yours as coincidence in our views of the subject may admit: and I will pray to hear from you by the first mail. Ever and affectionately your's

Th Jefferson

Madison to Jefferson

Montpellier Mar. 5, 1822

Dear Sir,

This is the first mail since I received yours of the 25 ult., which did not come to hand in time for an earlier answer, having lain a day or two at Orange Court House.

Regarding the New Society for the benefit of the Indians as limited to their civilization, an object laudable in itself, and taking for granted, perhaps too hastily, that the plan had not been formed and published without the sanction of the most respectable names on the spot; finding moreover that no act of incorporation from the Government was contemplated, I thought it not amiss to give the inclosed answer to Mr. Morse. In its principle, the association, though a great amplification, is analogous to that of the Academy of Languages and Belles-lettres.

The project appears to me to be rather ostentatious than dangerous. Those embraced by it are too numerous, too heterogeneous, and too much dispersed to concentrate their views in any covert or illicit object; nor is the immediate object a sufficient cement to hold them long together for active purposes. The clergy who may prove a great majority of the whole, and might be most naturally distrusted are themselves made up of such repulsive sects that they are not likely to form a noxious confederacy, especially with ecclesiastical views.

On a closer attention than I had given to the matter before I received your letter, I perceive that the organization of the Board of Directors is a just subject of animadversion. The powers vested in it may devolve on too few to be charged with the collection and application of the funds. As the proceedings however will be at the seat of Government, and under the eye of so many of every description of observers there will be no little controul against abuses. It is pretty remarkable that Doctor Morse and one of his own name may be two-thirds of a majority of a Board. This person has I believe lately returned from some agency under the Government, along with Governor Cass, among the Northern tribes of Indians; which makes it the more probable that his present plans are in accord with the ideas of the War Department at least.

Had I not written my answer, I should be led by my present view of the subject to suspend it till more should be known of this project, and particularly how far the high characters named, on the spot or elsewhere had embarked in it. I find by a Gazette just received, that a member of the Senate has denounced the project in very harsh terms. He is from a State however not distant from the Indians, and may have opinions and feelings on topics relating to them not common to the members of the Body. Always and affecy. yours

JAMES MADISON

Jefferson to Madison

Monticello Apr. 7, 1822
DEAR SIR
Your favor of Mar. 29.[21] did not come to hand until the 4th. instant. Only Mr Cabell, Genl. Cocke and myself attended. Messrs. Johnson and Taylor were retained in Richmond on Lithgow's case, and Genl. Breckinridge hindered by business. It was not material as there was not a single thing requisite to act on. We have to finish the 4. rows and appendages this summer which will be done and then to rest on our oars. The question of the removal of the seat of government has unhappily come athwart us, and is the real thing now entangling us. Staunton and Richmond are both friendly to us as an University, but the latter fears that our Rotunda will induce the legislature to

21. Letter not found.

quit them, and Staunton fears it will stop them here. You will recollect that our brother Johnson has opposed constantly every proposition in the board to begin that building, and moved himself in the late session to suspend interest with an express Proviso that no money should be applied to that building; and Mr Harvie, one of the zealous friends to the University, in a Philippic against the Rotunda declared he would never vote another Dollar to the University but on condition that it should not be applied to that building. Our opinion, and a very sound one, has been from the beginning never to open the institution until the buildings shall be compleat; because as soon as opened, all the funds will be absorbed by salaries etc. and the buildings remain for ever incompleat. We have thought it better to open it fully, altho' a few years later, than let it go on for ever in an imperfect state. I learn from those who were present at the last proceedings of the legislature, that there was a general regret even with the opposition itself, when they found that they had done absolutely nothing at all for the institution. Our course is a plain one, to pursue what is best, and the public will come right and approve us in the end. This bugbear of the seat of government will be understood at the next session, and we shall be enabled to proceed. The establishment is now at that stage at which it will force itself on. We must manage our dissenting brother softly; he is of too much weight to be given up.[22] I inclose you his letter and two from Mr Cabell which will inform you more particularly of the state of things. Be so good as to return them when perused. Ever and affectionately your's

TH JEFFERSON

Jefferson to Madison

Monticello May 12, 1822

DEAR SIR

I thank you for the communication of Mr Rush's letter which I now return.[23] Mr Benthan's character of Alexander is I believe unjust and that worse traits might still be added to it equally just. He is now certainly become the watchman of tyranny for Europe, as dear to it's oppressors as detestable to the oppressed.[24] If however he should engage in war with the Turks, as I expect, his employment there may give opportunities for the friends of liberty to proceed in their work. I set out for Bedford tomorrow to be absent three weeks. I salute you with constant and affectionate friendship and respect.

TH JEFFERSON

22. For the failure of the legislature to act on university issues in 1822, see Malone, VI, p. 388.
23. JM's letter transmitting Richard Rush's has not been found.
24. For TJ's disappointment with Czar Alexander, see Malone, VI, p. 427.

Jefferson to Madison

Monticello Nov. 22, 1822

DEAR SIR

The person who hands you this letter is an interesting subject of curiosity. He was taken prisoner by the Kickapoos when he supposes he must have been about 3. or 4. years of age, knows not whence taken, nor who were his parents. He escaped from the Indians at about 19. as he supposes, and about 7. years ago. He has applied himself to education, is a student of Medicine, and has assumed the name of Hunter as the translation of that given him by the Indians. To a good degree of genius he adds great observation and correct character. He has been recieved with great courtesy at N. York and Philada by the literati especially and also by the gens du monde. He has been long enough in this neighborhood to be much esteemed. He is setting out for the Medical lectures of Philada and asked me to give him a letter to you which I do, satisfied that the enquiries you will make of him, and to which he will answer with great willingness will gratify you to the full worth of the intrusion. He has prepared a very interesting book for publication.

Ten days ago I incurred the accident of breaking the small bone of the left fore-arm, and some disturbance of the small bones of the wrist. Dr. Watkins attended promptly, set them well and all is doing well.[25] He tells me I must submit to confinement till Christmas day. I had intended a visit to you shortly, but this disappoints it. Dawson has finished the account books very ably. Genl. Cocke has been 3. days examining them. The vouchers wanting are reduced to about 4000. D. which can be got immediately, the persons being in the neighborhood. He thinks there will be scarcely a dollar unvouched. I salute Mrs Madison and yourself with constant affection and respect.

TH: JEFFERSON

25. Despite this optimistic progress report, TJ's arm remained in a sling for several months; see *ibid.*, p. 390.

46

REMINISCING ABOUT THE REVOLUTION AND THE REPUBLIC, 1823

*D*URING THE SUMMER OF 1822, the engraving of the ground plan of the University of Virginia was approved by Jefferson and was distributed among the legislators when they convened for their session of 1822–1823. It showed the four rows of completed buildings and depicted the proposed Rotunda as a circular building bridging the two rows of pavilions and dormitories, the capstone of the academical village. In his annual report for 1822, Jefferson stated that all the pavilions, dormitories, and hotels were complete except for a bit of plastering and a few capitals ordered from Italy to top off some incomplete columns. As for the "remaining building" (he carefully avoided the use of the words *Rotunda* and *Pantheon*), construction had not begun because of lack of funds. But he and the Board of Visitors argued for the completion of the total physical plant before opening the doors of the university.

In a politically astute move, the board also proposed a step to conciliate the sectarian opponents of the university. The several denominations were invited to establish theologial schools near the university where divinity students might have access to its courses and facilities. The proposal had more influence with legislators than it did with religious groups, as Cabell reported from Richmond: "It is the Franklin that had drawn the lightning from the cloud of opposition."[1]

Nevertheless, "the friends of the University in the Assembly," Madison conceded, "seem to have a delicate task on their hands." The big stumbling block remained the Rotunda. If the request for funding was successful, he was sure that it would be applied "to the new Edifice," thus completing the academical village and allowing the board to "close the business handsomely."[2]

---

1. Malone, VI, pp. 392–93. None of the denominations decided to locate a theological school in Charlottesville.
2. JM to TJ, Jan. 15, 1823, below.

Late in the session, the legislature authorized a third loan of $60,000 from the Literary Fund, assuring the construction of the Rotunda.[3]

Jefferson already had contractors' estimates, and he quickly polled the board in February for approval of the loan and the letting of contracts so "we may engage our workmen before they enter into other undertakings for the season." After receiving approval, Jefferson and Cocke authorized "the engagement of the workmen . . . to begin their work immediately and to provide materials for the Library,"[4] a project that might take as long as three years to construct. The terms with the contractor "will make our money go the farthest possible, for good work," Jefferson assured Madison and the other Visitors, "and his engagement is only for the hull compleat. That done, we can pay for it, see the state of our funds and engage a portion of the inside work so as to stop where our funds may fail, should they fail before it's entire completion. There it may rest ever so long, be used, and not delay the opening of the institution."[5]

Six days before Jefferson's eightieth birthday, the Visitors confirmed the policy outlined by the rector, who then pressed the Literary Board for an advance to pay workmen, some of whom "are distressed, the discharged ones especially."[6] That board, he reported in June, "have advanced 40,000 D[ollars] and will retain the balance for us as requested until the end of the year." And, he added happily, "the building is going on rapidly."[7]

By the fall, the walls of the Rotunda were up, but the building could not be roofed until the next year. Then the recruitment of the faculty could begin, but only if the university's debt were forgiven by the legislature. Otherwise, the rector estimated that it would take more than two decades to pay back the state loans from the annual annuity of $15,000 from the Literary Fund.[8]

In the meantime, Jefferson fretted about "1. the size of the lecturing rooms. 2. depositories for the [scientific] Apparatuses. 3. the arrangement of the seats for the Students," and 4. the potential use of the oval rooms in the Rotunda as large lecture halls.[9] Towards the end of the year, the board began making provisional preparations for appointing a search committee of one "to procure Professors" abroad in case "the ensuing legislature will dispose in some way of the University debt, and liberate our funds." Cabell, who had made the

---

3. Malone, VI, p. 394. See William B. O'Neal, *Jefferson's Buildings at the University of Virginia: The Rotunda* (Charlottesville, 1960), and Joseph Lee Vaughn and Omer Allen Grunning, Jr., *Thomas Jefferson's Rotunda Restored, 1973–1976: A Pictorial Review with Commentary* (Charlottesville, 1981).
4. TJ to JM and James Breckinridge, Feb. 16, 1823, below. JM sent his approval on Feb. 19.
5. TJ to JM and the Board of Visitors of the University of Virginia, Mar. 12, 1823, below.
6. TJ to JM, Apr. 30, 1823, below, and Malone, VI, p. 394.
7. TJ to JM, June 13, 1823, below.
8. Malone, VI, pp. 394–95.
9. TJ to JM, Apr. 30, 1823, below.

grand tour twenty years earlier, visiting British and Continental universities, "was disposed to undertake the business," but illness forced him to decline.

Jefferson then proposed Francis Walker Gilmer, whom he considered the best-educated Virginian of his generation. Gilmer was also Madison's first choice for the law professorship. Jefferson and Madison explored the possibility of combining the search mission with the law post in an attempt to persuade Gilmer since "our Professor of law must be a native.... The offer of this with the mission," the rector hoped, "would probably be accepted." If Madison approved, Jefferson would undertake negotiations with Gilmer, which would remain "inviolably secret, but to us three" until approved by the Board of Visitors.[10]

For the first time in several years, the two retired presidents lifted their eyes in 1823 from the University of Virginia, which continued to dominate their correspondence, to a wide range of political topics, both foreign and domestic. When George Canning, the British foreign secretary, proposed that the United States join with Great Britain in a joint declaration designed to prevent intervention in the New World by the Holy Alliance, headed by Czar Alexander I of Russia, President Monroe quickly consulted both of his predecessors. After a series of revolutions erupted in Spain, Portugal, Naples, and Greece in 1820 and 1821, the restored monarchs of Europe attempted to suppress the uprisings, leading Jefferson to label Alexander "the watchman of tyranny for Europe, as dear to it's oppressors as detestable to the oppressed."[11] When a French army invaded Spain in 1823 and restored the ousted monarch, Madison protested that "the people of Spain as well as of Portugal need still further light and heat too from the American example before they will be a Match for the armies, the intrigues and the bribes of their Enemies, the treachery of their leaders, and what is most of all to be dreaded, their priests and their prejudices. Still," he added, "their cause is so just, that whilst there is life in it, hope ought not to be abandoned."[12]

When rumors spread that a combined French and Spanish force might be dispatched to South America to suppress the revolutionary republics that had been established during the upheaval in Spain, both Jefferson and Madison advised Monroe to welcome "the advances of the B. Govt. having an eye to the forms of our Constitution in every step in the road to war. With the British power and navy combined with our own," Madison wrote Jefferson, "we have nothing to fear from the rest of the world; and in the great struggle of the Epoch between liberty and despotism, we owe it to ourselves to sustain the former, in this hemisphere at least." Jefferson replied that "your opinion and

10. TJ to JM, Nov. 6, 1823, below, and JM to TJ, Nov. 11, 1823, below. The negotiations are discussed in Richard Beale Davis, *Francis Walker Gilmer: Life and Learning in Jefferson's Virginia* (Richmond, 1939).

11. TJ to JM, May 12, 1822, above.

12. JM to TJ, Sept. 6, 1823, below.

mine on Canning's proposition, I have no doubt have been mainly the same."[13]

Ultimately, Monroe chose to announce his doctrine unilaterally rather than "come in as a cock-boat in the wake of the British man-of-war," as his secretary of state, John Quincy Adams, phrased it.[14] But the Monroe Doctrine, his famous pronouncement, built upon the views of his predecessors on nonentanglement, nonintervention, no transfer of territory, and the closing of the Western Hemisphere to European powers.[15]

On the domestic front, Jefferson's reputation as author of the Declaration of Independence was caught in a cross fire of latter-day Federalist attempts to denigrate it in Massachusetts and Virginia. Relying on a letter from John Adams, who had fired him as secretary of state, Timothy Pickering, an ancient enemy of Jefferson, suggested in a Fourth of July address in Salem, Massachusetts, that the ideas in the Declaration were "hackneyed" by 1776, having been adumbrated by James Otis of Massachusetts in his pamphlet *The Rights of the British Colonies Asserted and Proved,* published in 1764.

Jefferson quickly absolved his old friend Adams of any animosity and instead attributed the attack to Pickering's "principles and prejudices personal and political." On the charge that the Declaration was overrated, that it "contained no new ideas, that it is a commonplace compilation, it's sentiments hackneyed in Congress for two years before, and its essence contained in Otis's pamphlet," all this, Jefferson said, "may . . . be true. Of that I am not to be the judge. Richard Henry Lee charged it as copied from Locke's treatise on government," he told Madison.[16]

But he denied ever having seen Otis's pamphlet and added:

Whether I had gathered my ideas from reading or reflection I do not know. I know only that I turned to neither book or pamphlet while writing it. I did not consider it as any part of my charge to invent new ideas altogether and to offer no sentiment which had ever been expressed before. Had Mr. Adams been so restrained, Congress would have lost the benefit of his bold and impressive advocations of the rights of revolution. For no man's confident and fervid addresses, more than Mr. Adams's encouraged and supported us thro' the difficulties surrounding us, which, like the ceaseless action of gravity, weighed on us by night and by day. Yet, on the same ground, we may ask what of these elevated thoughts was new, or can be affirmed never before to have entered the conceptions of man?

On Adams's recollection that he served on a subcommittee with Jefferson to draft the Declaration, the Virginian thought his friend's memory a bit faulty

13. JM to TJ, Nov. 1, 1823, below, and TJ to JM, Nov. 6, 1823, below.
14. John Quincy Adams, *Memoirs of John Quincy Adams, Comprising Portions of His Diary from 1795 to 1848,* ed. Charles Francis Adams, 12 vols. (Philadelphia, 1874–77), VI, p. 179 (Nov. 7, 1823).
15. The standard study is still Dexter Perkins, *A History of the Monroe Doctrine* (Cambridge, 1927).
16. TJ to JM, Aug. 30, 1823, below.

"in some of the particulars." "At the age of 88., and 47. years after the transactions of Independence," Jefferson wrote Madison with the lightheartedness of an octogenarian, "this is not wonderful. Nor should I, at the age of 80., on the small advantage of that difference only, venture to oppose my memory to his, were it not supported by written notes, taken by myself at the moment and on the spot."

Jefferson then set the record straight, correcting Adams's recollection that he had served on a subcommittee "to make the draught" of the Declaration. Instead, "no such thing as a subcommittee was proposed, but they unanimously pressed on myself alone to undertake the draught. I consented; I drew it; but before I reported it to the committee, I communicated it *separately* to Dr. Franklin and Mr. Adams, requesting their corrections . . . and you have seen the original paper now in my hands," he reminded Madison, "with the corrections of Doctor Franklin and Mr. Adams interlined in their own handwritings. Their alterations were two or three only, and merely verbal. I then wrote a fair copy, reported it to the Committee, and from them, unaltered to Congress. This personal communication and consultation with Mr. Adams, he has misremembered into the actings of a sub-committee."[17]

Turning again to his purpose in drafting the Declaration, Jefferson continued: "Whether also the sentiments of independence, and the reasons for declaring it which make so great a portion of the instrument, had been hackneyed in Congress for two years before the 4th. of July '76, or this dictum also of Mr. Adams be another slip of memory, let history say. This however I will say for Mr. Adams, that he supported the Declaration with zeal and ability, fighting fearlessly for every word of it."

Jefferson recalled "the acrimonious criticisms on some of its parts" during the debates in the Continental Congress. Like any anxious author whose work is being cut and altered, he remembered "writhing a little," and he noted that Pickering (he playfully called him Timothy) thought "the instrument the better for having a fourth of it expunged." Then he turned to take a dig at his critic and his Anglophilism:

He would have thought it still better had the other three-fourths gone out also, all but the single sentiment (the only one he approves), which recommends friendship to his dear England, whenever she is willing to be at peace with us. His insinuations are that altho' 'the high tone of the instrument was in unison with the warm feelings of the times, this sentiment of habitual friendship to England should never be forgotten, and that the duties it enjoins should *especially* be borne in mind on every celebration of this anniversary.' In other words, that the Declaration, as being a libel on the government of England, composed in times of passion, should now be buried in utter oblivion to spare the feelings of our English friends and Angloman fellow citizens.[18]

17. *Ibid.*
18. *Ibid.* See also Gerard H. Clarfield, *Timothy Pickering and the American Republic* (Pittsburgh, 1980).

This was too much for the author of the Declaration of Independence, who denied that the annual celebration of the Fourth of July was designed to wound the feelings of Englishmen or anyone else. The day should be kept in mind in order "to cherish the principles of the instrument in the bosoms of our own citizens: and it is a heavenly comfort to see that these principles are yet so strongly felt, as to render a circumstance so trifling as this little lapse of memory of Mr. Adams worthy of being solemnly announced and supported at an anniversary assemblage of the nation on its birthday. In opposition however to Mr. Pickering," he assured Madison, "I pray God that these principles may be eternal."[19]

A sympathetic Madison agreed with his friend fully, calling his letter "a correction of the apocryphal tradition, furnished by Pickering" and "derived ... from the misrecollections of Mr. Adams" and "the fallibility of his aged memory. Nothing can be more absurd than the cavil that the Declaration contains known and not new truths. The object was to assert not to discover truths, and to make them the basis for the Revolutionary Act. The merit of the Draught," he concluded, "could consist only in a lucid communication of human rights, a condensed enumeration of the reasons for such an exercise of them, and in a style and tone appropriate to the great occasion, and to the spirit of the American people."[20]

Madison also reviewed the efforts of the friends of Richard Henry Lee to downgrade Jefferson's draft of the Declaration and upgrade Lee's role in the move for independence. Lee had submitted the resolution of June 7, 1776, calling for a declaration. But he had acted on orders from the Virginia convention, in which Madison served. It "gave a positive instruction to her Deputies [in Congress] to make the Motion [for independence]. It was made by him as next in the list to P[eyton] Randolph then deceased. Had Mr. Lee been absent the task would have devolved on you," Madison reminded his friend. "As this measure of Virg^a makes a link in the history of our National birth, it is but right that every circumstance attending it, should be ascertained and preserved." Indeed, Madison thought that Jefferson could probably "best tell where the instruction had its origin and by whose pen it was prepared. The impression at the time," he recalled, "was, that it was communicated in a letter from you to [Mr. Wythe] a member of the Convention."[21]

The two friends also reviewed the authorship of Washington's Farewell Address, citing "a dispute between Genl. Washington's friends and Mr. Hamilton."[22] Madison recalled that Washington never "valued himself on his

---

19. TJ to JM, Aug. 30, 1823, below.

20. JM to TJ, Sept. 6, 1823, below.

21. *Ibid.* JM seems to have added George Wythe's name at a later date.

22. For TJ's recollections, see TJ to William Johnson, June 12, 1823, which he enclosed in TJ to JM, June 13, 1823, below. For an analysis of JM's and Hamilton's contributions to Washington's Farewell Address, see Felix Gilbert, *To the Farewell Address: Ideas of Early American Foreign Policy* (Princeton, 1961), pp. 115–47.

writing talent" and sometimes called on colleagues "whom he supposed more practised than himself in studied composition." Indeed, the president had asked him to draft a "farewell Address" at the end of Washington's first term, after setting forth his general ideas. Madison, therefore, took it for granted that Hamilton had drafted the Farewell Address, and he presumed that Washington had "put into his hands his own letter to me suggesting his general ideas, with the paper prepared by me in conformity with them." Nonetheless, the Farewell Address should be viewed as "the pure legacy of the Father of his Country," containing the principles of Washington and carrying "the weight given to it by his sanction."

Madison regretted the controversy because the address might be viewed "as the performance of another held in different estimation. It will not only lose the charm of the name subscribed to it; but it will not be surprising if particular passages be understood in new senses, and with applications derived from the political doctrines and party feelings of the discovered Author." As for his own role in the composition of the address, Madison thought that the confidence that existed between him and Washington in 1792 forbade publicity, although he conceded that "the lapse of time should wear out the seal on it, and the truth of history should put in a fair claim to such disclosures."[23]

Inevitably, a review of the era between the Declaration of Independence and Washington's Farewell Address drew Madison and Jefferson into a broader discussion of the emergence of the Federalist and Republican parties and of "the line dividing the jurisdiction of the general and state governments." These questions had been posed by William Johnson, who had been appointed to the Supreme Court by Jefferson, as a preliminary to a history of political parties Johnson was preparing.[24] When Jefferson sent Madison a copy of his response, the latter wrote that the judge "is much indebted to you for your remarks on the definition of parties. The radical distinction between them," he declared, "has always been a confidence of one, and distrust of the other, as to the capacity of Mankind for self Government."

But on the second question, the drawing of "a precise demarkation of the boundary between the Federal and the State Authorities," Madison took sharp issue with Jefferson, telling him politely but firmly that he was wrong on two basic points: where the line was drawn and who should decide in case of a boundary dispute. Long alarmed by a series of controversial decisions of the Supreme Court under Chief Justice John Marshall that stressed federal power and asserted that the Court itself was the ultimate arbiter, Jefferson consistently attacked the "consolidationist" tendency of the Court and denied its right to resolve such constitutional disputes. Although he conceded the difficulty of laying down "any general formula of words which shall decide at

23. JM to TJ, June 27, 1823, below.

24. TJ to JM, June 13, 1823, below. See Donald G. Morgan, *Justice William Johnson, the First Dissenter: The Career and Constitutional Philosophy of a Jeffersonian Judge* (Columbia, S.C., 1954), chs. IX, X.

once, and with precision, in every case, this limit of jurisdiction," he cited two canons as guides in such cases. The first asserted that the Constitution left with the states "all authorities which respected their own citizens only" and transferred to the federal government "those which respected citizens of foreign or other States," making "us several as to ourselves, but one as to all others. In the latter case, then, constructions should lean to the general jurisdiction, if the words will bear it; and in favor of the States in the former, if possible to be so construed." "I believe," he added, "the States can best govern our home concerns, and the General Government our foreign ones." The second canon urged constant recurrence to the debates at the time the Constitution was ratified for the probable meaning in which it was passed.

Instead of Marshall's emphasis on federal power, Jefferson preferred the Virginia views of Judge Spencer Roane and John Taylor of Caroline, who argued that the Marshall Court "had usurped on the State jurisdictions." Indeed, he confessed that Roane's arguments "appeared to me to pulverize every word which had been delivered by Judge Marshall" on the "constitutional limits between the General and State jurisdictions."[25]

About the only thing on which Jefferson agreed with Marshall was the chief justice's statement that "there must be an ultimate arbiter somewhere." His response was, "True, there must." But it was in neither party to the dispute, the federal or the state governments. "The ultimate arbiter" in constitutional controversies, according to the Sage of Monticello, "is the people of the Union, assembled by their deputies in convention, at the call of Congress, or of two-thirds of the States. Let them decide to which they mean to give an authority claimed by two of their organs."[26] Thus, the amending process, which had been utilized to add the ten amendments in the Bill of Rights and two other amendments to the Constitution, became the constitutional mechanism by which Jefferson would resolve controversies about the meaning of the Constitution.

Madison eased into the discussion of his disagreement with Jefferson. The issues were complex, he conceded, and a complete answer would require "a critical commentary on the whole text of the Constitution. The two general Canons you lay down would be of much use in such a task; particularly that which refers to the sense of the State Conventions, whose ratifications alone made the Constitution what it is." But the other canon was too simplistic since the Constitution had extended federal jurisdiction to more controversies between citizens of the same state than the single case cited by Jefferson. "To mention one only," he wrote: "In cases arising under a Bankrupt law, there is

---

25. JM to TJ, June 27, 1823, below, and TJ to William Johnson, June 12, 1823, enclosed in TJ to JM, June 13, 1823, below.

26. See TJ to William Johnson, June 12, 1823, enclosed in TJ to JM, June 13, 1823, below. TJ referred specifically to Chief Justice Marshall's decision in *Cohens* v. *Virginia* in 1821. For a summary of the case, see G. Edward White, *The Marshall Court and Cultural Change, 1815–1835* (New York, 1988), pp. 504–24.

no distinction between those to which Citizens of the same and of different States are parties."

Indeed, Madison told his friend, indirectly but firmly, that his interpretation of the Constitution was doubly wrong, both historically and in principle. To refute the views of Judge Roane, which Jefferson favored, Madison enclosed copies of two letters that he had sent to the Virginia judge denying that jurist's insistence on the right of state courts in their individual capacity to decide disagreements between the federal and state governments about their respective spheres of authority. "The Gordian Knot of the Constitution," Madison told Roane, "seems to lie in the problem of collision between the federal and State powers, especially as eventually exercised by their respective Tribunals. . . . I have always thought that a construction of the instrument ought to be favoured, as far as the text would warrant, which would obviate the dilemma of a Judicial rencounter or a mutual paralysis; and that on the abstract question whether the federal or the State decisions ought to prevail, the sounder policy would yield to the claims of the former."[27]

Unless that were the case, he told Jefferson, the Constitution and laws of the United States would soon be interpreted differently in different states, thus destroying "that equality and uniformity of rights and duties which form the essence of the Compact, to say nothing of the opportunity given to the States individually of involving by their decisions the whole Union in foreign Contests. To leave conflicting decisions to be settled between the Judicial parties could not promise a happy result," he concluded. "The end must be a trial between the [federal] Posse headed by the Marshal and the [state] Posse headed by the Sheriff."[28]

Nor could the disputed issues be safely entrusted "to a compromise between the two Gov^{ts}; the case of a disagreement between different Gov^{ts} being essentially different from a disagreement between branches of the same Gov^t. In the latter case," he observed, "neither party being able to consummate its will without the concurrence of the other, there is a necessity on both to consult and to accommodate. Not so, with different Gov^{ts}[,] each possessing every branch of power necessary to carry its purpose into compleat effect. It here becomes a question between Independent Nations, with no other *dernier* resort than physical force," resulting in civil war. "Negotiation might indeed in some instances avoid this extremity; but how often would it happen, among

27. See JM to Spencer Roane, May 6, 1821, and June 29, 1821, enclosed in JM to TJ, June 27, 1823, below.

28. JM to TJ, June 27, 1823, below. In the Dolley Madison Papers at the Library of Congress is the following statement about TJ and JM on the Constitution, which she filed sometime after JM's death in 1836: "Thomas Jefferson was not in America pending the framing of the Constitution, whose information in all that occurred in the Convention, and of the motives and intents of the framers was derived from Mr. Madison whose opinions guided him in the construction of that instrument, is looked up to by many as its father and almost unanimously as its only true repositor."

so many States, that an unaccommodating spirit in some would render that resource unavailing."

That brought Madison face to face with the question of who had the ultimate authority under the Constitution to decide disputed questions relating to state and federal authority. As he put it, "We arrive at the agitated question whether the Judicial Authority of the U. S. be the constitutional resort for determining the line between the federal and State jurisdictions. Believing as I do that the General [Philadelphia] Convention regarded a provision within the Constitution for deciding in a peaceable and regular mode all cases arising in the course of its operation, as essential to an adequate System of Gov^t: that it intended the Authority vested in the Judicial Department as a final resort in relation to the States, for cases resulting to it in the exercise of its functions, (the concurrence of the Senate chosen by the State Legislatures, in appointing the Judges, and the oaths and official tenures of these, with the surveillance of public Opinion, being relied on as guarantying their impartiality); and that this intention is expressed by the articles declaring that the federal Constitution and laws shall be the supreme law of the land, and that the Judicial Power of the U. S. shall extend to all cases arising under them: Believing moreover that this was the prevailing view of the subject when the Constitution was adopted and put into execution; that it has so continued thro' the long period which has elapsed [since ratification]; and that even at this time an appeal to a national decision would prove that no general change has taken place: thus believing," he concluded his overly long sentence, "I have never yielded my original opinion indicated in the 'Federalist' N° 39 to the ingenious reasonings of Col: [John] Taylor"—or, he might have added, Judge Spencer Roane—"agst this construction of the Constitution."[29]

After coming down squarely on the side of judicial review, Madison conceded "that the Judiciary career has not corresponded with what was anticipated." He acknowledged that at the time of the Alien and Sedition Laws, "the Judges perverted the Bench of Justice into a rostrum for partizan harangues." And both he and Jefferson agreed that the Marshall Court, "by some of its decisions, still more by extrajudicial reasonings and dicta, has manifested a propensity to enlarge the general authority in derogation of the local, and to amplify its own jurisdiction, which has justly incurred the public censure. But," he concluded with epigrammatic emphasis, "the abuse of a trust does not disprove its existence."

If there were no remedy under the Constitution for such abuse, he preferred to amend the Supreme Court clause itself instead of following Jefferson's proposal of making "continual appeals from its controverted decisions to that

---

29. JM to TJ, June 27, 1823, below. TJ had endorsed the states' rights views of Taylor as set forth in Taylor's *Construction Construed and Constitutions Vindicated* (1820), a slashing attack on the Supreme Court's authority to decide constitutional questions for the states or for the other branches of the federal government.

Ultimate Arbiter." He thought this legitimate use of the amending process superior to Jefferson's suggested use of state conventions of the sovereign people as the ultimate arbiter. "To refer every point of disagreement to the people in Conventions would be a process too tardy, too troublesome, and too expensive." Moreover, such frequent appeals would have a "tendency to lessen a salutary veneration for an Instrument so often calling for such explanatory interpositions," thus undermining stable, orderly, and responsible government.[30]

After this lecture by the Father of the Constitution to the Author of the Declaration of Independence, one of their sharpest disagreements in retirement, Madison agreed with Jefferson that the Supreme Court justices should deliver seriatim opinions in order to curb Chief Justice Marshall's power, each judge setting forth his opinion. Otherwise, opinions would continue to be, as Jefferson said, "huddled up in conclave, perhaps by a majority of one, delivered as if unanimous, and with the silent acquiescence of lazy or timid associates, by a crafty chief judge who sophisticates the law of his mind, by the turn of his own reasoning."[31]

——————————— THE LETTERS ———————————

Jefferson to Madison

Monticello Jan. 6, 1823

DEAR SIR,

I send you a mass of reading, and so rapidly does my hand fail me in writing that I can give but very briefly the necessary explanations.

1. Mr. Cabell's letter to me and mine to him which passed each other on the road will give you the state of things respecting the University, and I am happy to add that letters recieved from Appleton give us reason to expect our capitals by the first vessel from Leghorn, done of superior marble and in superior style.

2. Young E. Gerry informed me some time ago that he had engaged a person to write the life of his father, and asked for any materials I could furnish. I sent him some letters, but in searching for them, I found two, too precious to be trusted by mail, of the date of 1801. Jan. 15. and 20. in answer

---

30. JM to TJ, June 27, 1823, below. For a fascinating analysis of JM's renewal in the 1820s of his debate with TJ during the 1780s, see Drew R. McCoy, *The Last of the Fathers: James Madison and the Republican Legacy* (New York, 1989), pp. 64–73.

31. TJ to Thomas Ritchie, Dec. 26, 1820, in Ford, X, p. 171.

to one I had written him Jan. 26. 99. two years before.[1] It furnishes authentic proof that in the X. Y. Z. mission to France, it was the wish of Pickering, Marshall, Pinckney and the Federalists of that stamp, to avoid a treaty with France and to bring on war, a fact we charged on them at the time and this letter proves, and that their X. Y. Z. report was cooked up to dispose the people to war. Gerry their colleague was not of their sentiment, and this is his statement of that transaction. During the 2. years between my letter and his answer, he was wavering between Mr. Adams and myself, between his attachment to Mr. Adams personally on the one hand, and to republicanism on the other; for he was republican, but timid and indecisive. The event of the election of 1800-1. put an end to his hesitations.

3. A letter of mine to Judge Johnson and his answer. This conveys his views of things, and they are so serious and sound, that they are worth your reading. I am sure that in communicating it to you, I commit no breach of trust to him; for he and every one knows that I have no political secrets for you; and from the tenor of his letter with respect to yourself, it is evident he would as willingly have them known to you as myself.

You will observe that Mr. Cabell, if the loan bill should pass, proposes to come up with Mr. Loyall, probably Mr. Johnson, and Genl. Cocke to have a special meeting.[2] This is necessary to engage our workmen before they undertake other work for the ensuing season. I shall desire him, as soon as the loan bill passes the lower house (as we know it will pass the Senate) to name a day by mail to yourself to meet us, as reasonable notice *to all the members* is necessary to make the meeting legal. I hope you will attend, as the important decision as to the Rotunda may depend on it.

Our family is all well and joins in affections to Mrs. Madison and yourself. My arm goes on slowly, still in a sling and incapable of any use, and will so continue some time yet. Be so good as to return the inclosed when read and to be assured of my constant and affectionate friendship.

Madison to Jefferson

Montpellier Jan. 15, 1823

Dear Sir

I have duly received yours of the 6th, with the letters of Mr. Cabell, Mr. Gerry, and Judge Johnson. The letter from Mr. C. proposing an Extra Meet-

---

1. TJ's letter to Gerry has been called the Republican platform for the election of 1800; see Noble E. Cunningham, *In Pursuit of Reason: The Life of Thomas Jefferson* (Baton Rouge, 1987), p. 223. See also George A. Billias, *Elbridge Gerry: Founding Father and Republican Statesman* (New York, 1976), pp. 300-1.

2. In lieu of a special meeting, TJ polled the Board of Visitors, who confirmed their decision at their Apr. meeting; see TJ to JM, Feb. 16, 1823, below.

ing of the Visitors, and referred to in yours was not sent, and of course is not among those returned.

The friends of the University in the Assembly seem to have a delicate task on their hands. They have the best means of knowing what is best to be done, and I have entire confidence in their judgment as well as their good intentions. The idea of Mr. Cabell, if successful will close the business handsomely. One of the most popular objections to the Institution, I find is the expence added by what is called the ornamental style of the Architecture. Were this additional expence as great as is supposed, the objection ought the less to be regarded as it is short of the sum saved to the public by the private subscribers who approve of such an application of their subscriptions. I shall not fail to join you on receiving the expected notice from Mr. Cabell, if the weather and my health will permit; but I am persuaded it will be a supernumerary attendance, if the money be obtained, and the sole question be on its application to the new Edifice.

The two letters from Mr. Gerry are valuable documents on a subject that will fill some interesting pages in our history. The disposition of a party among us to find a cause of rupture with France, and to kindle a popular flame for the occasion, will go to posterity with too many proofs to leave a doubt with them. I have not looked over Mr. Gerry's letters to me which are very numerous, but may be of dates not connected with the period in question. No resort has been had to them for materials for his biography, perhaps from the idea that his correspondence with me may contain nothing of importance or possibly from a displeasure in the family at my disappointing the expectations of two of them. Mr. Austen the son in law, was anxious to be made Comptroller instead of Anderson, who had been a Revolutionary officer, a Judge in Tennessee, and a Senator from that State in Congress; and with equal pretentions only had in his scale the turning weight of being from the West, which considers itself without a fair proportion of National appointments. Mr. Austin I believe a man of very respectable talents, and had erroneously inferred from Mr. Gerry's communications, that I was under a pledge to name him for the vacancy when it should happen. Thinking himself thus doubly entitled to the office, his alienation has been the more decided. With every predisposition in favor of young Gerry, he was represented to me from the most friendly quarters as such a dolt, that if his youth could have been got over, it was impossible to prefer him to the place (in the Customs) to which he aspired. I believe that some peculiarities in his manner led to an exaggeration of his deficiencies and that he acquits himself well eno' in the subordinate place he now holds.

Judge Johnson's letter was well entitled to the perusal you recommended. I am glad you have put him in possession of such just views of the course that ought to be pursued by the Court in delivering its opinions.[3] I have taken frequent occasions to impress the necessity of the seriatim mode; but the

---

3. For TJ to William Johnson, Dec. 10, 1822, see Ford, XII, p. 274.

contrary practice is too deeply rooted to be changed without the injunction of a law, or some very cogent manifestation of the public discontent. I have long thought with the Judge also that the Supreme Court ought to be relieved from its circuit duties, by some such organization as he suggests. The necessity of it is now rendered obvious by the impossibility, in the same individual, of being a circuit Judge in Missouri etc., and a Judge of the supreme Court at the seat of Government. He is under a mistake in charging, on the Executive at least, an inattention to this point. Before I left Washington I recommended to Congress the importance of establishing the Supreme Court at the seat of Gov^t, which would at once enable the Judges to go thro' the business, and to qualify themselves by the necessary studies for doing so, with justice to themselves and credit to the Nation. The reduction of the number of Judges would also be an improvement and might be conveniently effected in the way pointed out. It cannot be denied that there are advantages in uniting the local and general functions in the same persons if permitted by the extent of the Country. But if this were ever the case, our expanding settlements put an end to it. The organization of the Judiciary Department over the extent which a Federal system can reach involves peculiar difficulties. There is scarcely a limit to the distance which Turnpikes and steamboats may, at the public expence, convey the members of the Gov^t and distribute the laws. But the delays and expence of suits brought from the extremities of the Empire, must be a severe burden on individuals. And in proportion as this is diminished by giving to local Tribunals a final jurisdiction, the evil is incurred of destroying the uniformity of the law.

I hope you will find an occasion for correcting the error of the Judge in supposing that I am at work on the same ground as will be occupied by his historical view of parties, and for *animating* him to the completion of what he has begun on that subject.[4] Nothing less than full-length likenesses of the two great parties which have figured in the National politics will sufficiently expose the deceptive colours under which they have been painted. It appears that he has already collected materials, and I infer from your acc^t of his biography of Green[5] which I have not yet seen, that he is capable of making the proper use of them. A good work on the side of truth, from his pen will be an apt and effective antidote to that of his Colleague which has been poisoning the Public mind, and gaining a passport to posterity.[6]

I was afraid the Doc^r was too sanguine in promising so early a cure of the fracture in your arm. The milder weather soon to be looked for, will doubtless favor the vis medicatrix which nature employs in repairing the injuries done her. Health and every other happiness.

4. JM's italics. For the rumor that JM planned to write a political history of the early Republic, see TJ to JM, June 22, 1817, above.
5. Johnson had published *Sketches of the Life and Correspondence of Nathaniel Greene* . . . , 2 vols. (Charleston, S.C., 1822); see Morgan, pp. 148–51.
6. JM referred to John Marshall's biography of Washington.

Jefferson to Madison and James Breckinridge

Monticello Feb. 16, 1823

DEAR SIR

You already know that the legislature has authorised the Literary board to lend us another 60,000. D. It is necessary we should act on this immediately so far as to accept the loan, that we may engage our workmen before they enter into other undertakings for the season. But the badness of the roads, the uncertainty of the weather and the personal inconvenience of a journey to the members of our board, render a speedy meeting desperate. Mr Cabell and Mr Loyall have by letters to me expressed their approbation of the loan and that they will confirm it regularly at our April meeting. If you think proper to do the same, Genl. Cocke and myself will authorise the engagement of the workmen and they will be satisfied to begin their work immediately and to provide materials for the Library. The sooner you can conveniently give me your answer, the sooner the operations may be commenced. Accept my affectionate esteem and respect.

TH. JEFFERSON

Madison to Jefferson

[Montpellier Feb. 19, 1823]

I congratulate you on the loan, scanty as it is, for the University; in the confidence that it is a gift masked under that name; and in the hope that it is a pledge for any remnant of aid the Establishment may need in order to be totus teres atque rotundus [in the clear].

Can you not have the hands set to work without the formality of a previous meeting of the Visitors? I have recd no notice from Richmond on the subject. Health and every other happiness

JAMES MADISON

Madison to Jefferson

Montpellier Feb. 19, 1823

DEAR SIR

The inclosed letters and papers being addressed to you as well as me I am not at liberty to withold them, tho' I know the disrelish you will feel for such appeals. I shall give an answer, in a manner for us both, intimating the propriety of our abstaining from any participation in the electioneering measures on foot.

Jefferson to Madison

Monticello Feb. 24, 1823

DEAR SIR

I have read Mr Cox's letters and some of his papers which I now return you. It is impossible for me to write to him. With two crippled hands I abandon writing but from the most urgent necessities; and above all things I should not meddle in a Presidential election, never even express a sentiment on the subject of the Candidates. As you propose to write to him, will you be so good as to add a line for me of the above purport? It will be a great relief to me; as it hurts me much to take no notice of the letter of an old friend.[7]

The acceptance of the loan being now approved by five of us I shall proceed immediately to have the workmen engaged. As there are some very important points to be decided on previously to embarking in such a building, I sent to request Genl. Cocke to join me in setting the thing agoing. But he had engagements which prevented his leaving home; and as the case admits no delay I shall proceed according to the best of my judgment, with the aid of Mr Brokenbrough, and with all the caution the case admits. Ever and Affectly. yours

TH. JEFFERSON

Jefferson to Madison and the Board of Visitors of the University of Virginia

Monticello Mar. 12, 1823

DEAR SIR

Having recieved from all our brethren approbations of the loan, I authorised Mr Brockenbrough to engage the work of the Rotunda, and have it commenced immediately. We had only two bricklayers and two carpenters capable of executing it with solidity, and correctness, [and] these had not capital sufficient for so great an undertaking, nor would they have risked their little all but for a great advance on the estimated cost, probably 50. per cent.

---

7. On Mar. 1, 1823, JM wrote to Tench Coxe saying that both he and TJ thought it "best to abstain strictly from the Presidential election"; see James Madison, *Letters and Other Writings of James Madison,* [ed. William C. Rives and Philip R. Fendall], 4 vols. (Philadelphia, 1865), III, pp. 304–5. For a brief discussion of Coxe at this time, see Jacob E. Cooke, *Tench Coxe and the Early Republic* (Chapel Hill, 1978), pp. 517–18.

For this reason and others very decisive Mr Brockenbrough declined that mode of engagement, and on consideration of his reasons I approved of them. He has engaged Thorn and Chamberlain for the brickwork, and Dinsmore and Nelson for the roof and carpenter's work on terms which I think will make our money go the farthest possible, for good work; and his engagement is only for the hull compleat. That done, we can pay for it, see the state of our funds and engage a portion of the inside work so as to stop where our funds may fail, should they fail before it's entire completion. There it may rest ever so long, be used, and not delay the opening of the institution. The work will occupy three years. All this will be more fully explained at our meeting and will I hope recieve your approbation. I shall hope to see you at Monticello the day before at least. Accept the assurance of my friendly esteem and respect.

TH. JEFFERSON

Jefferson to Madison

Monticello Mar. 14, 1823

DEAR SIR

The inclosed lre in Gr. Lat. Fr. and Eng. with it's accompaniments being intended for your inspection as much as mine, is now forwarded for your perusal. You will be so good as to reinclose them that I may return them to the writer. The answer I propose to give is, what I have given on all similar applications, that until the debt of the University is discharged, and it's funds liberated, the board has thot it wd be premature to act at all on the subject of Professors. But however qualified Mr O'Flaherty may be, a character taken from an ordinary grammar school, whose measure is of course exactly known, would not be so likely to fulfill our views of eclat, and to fill the public imagination with so much expectation as one selected for us by distinguished men from an institution of the First celebrity in the world, as Oxford; and from which we may justly expect a person of the highest qualifications. Ever and affectly. yours

TH J

Jefferson to Madison

Monticello Mar. 20, 1823

DEAR SIR

Mr. Dodge, our Consul at Marseilles, wishing to pay his respects to you on his way to Richmd. and apprehending that altho presented to you some half dozen years ago, you may not now recollect him, requests me to give him a line of re-introduction. You will find him a person of very general information and good sense, and particularly familiar with the affairs of Southern Europe.

We shall hope to see Mrs Madison and yourself some time before the 7th. prox. I hope you recieved mine of the 14th. inclosing the recommendatory papers of a Mr. O'Flaherty to be returned at your convenience that I may restore them to him. Ever and affectionately yours

TH: JEFFERSON

Madison to Jefferson

Montpellier Mar. 21, 1823

DEAR SIR

I have recd. your two letters of the 12th and 14th Inst. You will have inferred my approbation of the course taken in order to avoid the loss of time in executing the Rotunda. I shall be with you at the Meeting of the Visitors if possible.

The letter from O. Flaherty with its companions, are herewith inclosed. It is quite presumable that he possesses the technical qualifications for the professorship he aims at, but there are adventitious recommendations also which must be attended to, in filling it. Your proposed answer to him is doubtless the proper one.

I have been lately led into a transient correspondence with Professor Everett of Boston. From some of his enquiries on the subject of our University and the embarrassments of which he speaks as incident to the Sectarian monopoly of his own, I am not sure that a translation may not be within his speculations. There is nothing however in his letter, inconsistent with his disclaiming such a thought. He is unquestionably a man of superior talents, of valuable acquirements, and is said, as he appears, to be of fine temper and manners. He says he has relinquished, and shall never re-enter the Pulpit. He is, I perceive, tho' a heretic in the general creed of N. England, not entirely weaned from its mixture of ecclesiastical and civil polity. But I suspect he has taken le premier pas qui coute [the difficult first step] towards some revolution in his local notions. I have named him on this occasion because Ticknor, who is understood to be of inferior grade, was at one time undergoing consideration. Yours with all my best wishes

Madison to Jefferson

[Montpellier Apr. 29?, 1823]

What is the proper quetus [quietus] for the solicitudes within expressed?
J. M.

Jefferson to Madison

Monticello Apr. 30, 1823

DEAR SIR
    The anxieties expressed in the inclosed letter are pointed to 3. articles. 1. the size of the lecturing rooms. 2. depositories for the Apparatuses. 3. the arrangement of the seats for the Students. 1. If we could have foretold what number of students would come to our University, and what proportion of them would be in attendance on any one Professor at one time, lecturing rooms might have been constructed exactly to hold them. But having no data on which we could act with precision, we were obliged to assume some numbers conjecturally. The ordinary lecturing rooms were therefore adapted to an audience of about 150 students. I question if there ever were more than 25 at any one school of Wm. and Mary, at one time, except the Grammar school. I doubt if in Harvard even they have 100. in attendance, in any one school. At the great Medical schools of Philadelphia, N. York, Etc. there are doubtless more. If any school should go with us beyond the content of the ordinary lecturing rooms, the rooms in the Rotunda will accomodate double the number. But no human voice can be habitually exerted to the extent of such an audience. We cannot expect our Professors to bawl daily to multitudes and do what actors do once a year. They must break the numbers into two parts accomodated to voice and hearing and repeat the lecture to them separately
    2. The Apparatus for Natural philosophy, even the fullest, does not occupy much space, not more than may be arranged on shelves along the walls of the lecturing rooms. If more space however should be wanting, a door of communication with the adjacent dormitories will supply it to any extent. An Astronomical apparatus must have more room. My expectation has always been that the houses now occupied by Mr. Brockenbrough must, in the beginning, be taken, and perhaps improved for Astronomical purposes. Their insulated situation, and the elevation of the ground fit the room for that purpose. But if the Professor prefers having his apparatus annexed to his lecturing room, the adjacent dormitories offer an abundant recource. For the Professor of Chemistry, such experiments as require the use of furnace, cannot be exhibited in his ordinary lecturing room. We therefore prepare the rooms under the

oval rooms of the ground floor of the Rotunda for furnaces, stoves, etc. These rooms are of 1100 square feet area each.

3. As to the arrangement of the seats, some schools require them to be by steps one above another, others not. Natural philosophy, Chemistry, Anatomy will be the better with rising seats; but such are not at all necessary for lectures in languages, history, ethics, metaphysics, belles lettres, Law, Politics, Etc. Whenever it shall be known what particular Pavilions will be allotted to the Professors of the former schools, the rising benches for them can be readily set up. No doubt that where the numbers to be prepared for are so totally uncertain, their conjectural accomodations will be found to have been miscalculated in some instances, and will require modifications to actual facts when they shall become known. In the mean time our plan is such as to admit much facility of adaptation to varying circumstances.

Immediately after our last meeting I made to the literary board the proposition of letting us recieve our money by suitable installments, but have no answer as yet. In the mean time our workmen are distressed, the discharged ones especially, and, not to prolong their sufferings by my absence, I put off my visit of Bedford till after our next court. Ever affectionately and respectfully yours

TH: JEFFERSON

Jefferson to Madison

Monticello June 13, 1823

DEAR SIR

I communicated to you a former part of a correspondence between Judge Johnson of Charleston and myself, chiefly on the practice of caucusing opinions which is that of the Supreme Court of the US. but on some other matters also particularly his *history of parties.* In a late letter he asks me to give my idea of the precise principles and views of the Republicans in their oppositions to the Federalists, when that opposition was highest, also my opinion of the line dividing the jurisdiction of the general and state governments, mentions a dispute between Genl. Washington's friends and Mr. Hamilton as to the authorship of their Valedictory, and expresses his concurrence with me on the subject of seriatim opinions.[8] This last being of primary importance I inclose you a copy of my answer to the judge, because if you think of it as I do, I suppose your connection with Judge Todd and your antient intimacy with Judge Duval might give you an opening to say something to them on the subject. If Johnson could be backed by them in the practice, the others would be obliged to follow suit and this dangerous engine of consolidation would

---

8. For TJ's correspondence with Johnson, see Morgan, pp. 151–64.

feel a proper restraint by their being compelled to explain publicly the grounds of their opinions.

What I have stated as the Valedictory, is according to my recollection; if you find any error it shall be corrected in another letter.

When you shall have read the inclosed to be so good as to return it, as I have no other copy.

The literary board have advanced 40,000 D. and will retain the balance for us as requested until the end of the year, and the building is going on rapidly. Ever and affectionately yours

ENCLOSURE
[Jefferson to William Johnson]

DEAR SIR,   Monticello June 12, 1823

Our correspondence is of that accommodating character, which admits of suspension at the convenience of either party, without inconvenience to the other. Hence this tardy acknowledgment of your favor of April the 11th. I learn from that with great pleasure, that you have resolved on continuing your history of parties. Our opponents are far ahead of us in preparations for placing their cause favorably before posterity. Yet I hope even from some of them the escape of precious truths, in angry explosions or effusions of vanity, which will betray the genuine monarchism of their principles. They do not themselves believe what they endeavor to inculcate, that we were an opposition party, not on principle, but merely seeking for office. The fact is, that at the formation of our government, many had formed their political opinions on European writings and practices, believing the experience of old countries, and especially of England, abusive as it was, to be a safer guide than mere theory. The doctrines of Europe were, that men in numerous associations cannot be restrained within the limits of order and justice, but by forces physical and moral, wielded over them by authorities independent of their will. Hence their organization of kings, hereditary nobles, and priests. Still further to constrain the brute force of the people, they deem it necessary to keep them down by hard labor, poverty and ignorance, and to take from them, as from bees, so much of their earnings, as that unremitting labor shall be necessary to obtain a sufficient surplus barely to sustain a scanty and miserable life. And these earnings they apply to maintain their privileged orders in splendor and idleness, to fascinate the eyes of the people, and excite in them an humble adoration and submission, as to an order of superior beings. Although few among us had gone all these lengths of opinion, yet many had advanced, some more, some less, on the way. And in the convention which formed our government, they endeavored to draw the cords of power as tight as they could obtain them, to lessen the dependence of the general functionaries on their constituents, to subject to them those of the States, and to weaken their means of maintaining the steady equilibrium which the majority of the convention had deemed salutary for both branches, general and local. To recover, therefore, in practice the powers which the nation had refused, and to warp to their own wishes those actually given, was the steady object of the federal party. Ours, on the contrary, was to maintain the will of the majority of the convention, and of the people themselves. We believed, with them, that man was a rational animal, endowed by nature with rights, and with an innate sense of justice; and that he could be restrained from wrong and protected in right, by moderate powers, confided to persons of his own choice, and held to their duties by dependence on his own will. We believed that the complicated organization of kings, nobles, and priests, was not the wisest nor best to effect the happiness of associated man; that wisdom and virtue were not hereditary; that the trappings of such a machinery, consumed by their expense, those earnings of industry, they were meant to protect, and, by the inequalities they produced, exposed liberty to sufferance. We believed that men, enjoying in ease and security the full fruits of their own industry, enlisted by all their interests on the side of law and order, habituated to think for themselves, and to follow their reason as their guide, would be more easily and safely governed, than with minds nourished in error, and vitiated and debased, as in Europe, by ignorance, indigence and oppression. The cherishment of the people then was our principle, the fear and distrust of them, that of the other party. Composed, as we were, of the landed and laboring interests of the country, we could not be less anxious for a government of law and order than were the inhabitants of the cities, the strongholds of federalism. And whether our efforts to save the principles and form of our Constitution have not been salutary, let the present republican freedom, order and prosperity of our country determine. History may distort truth, and will distort it for a time, by the superior efforts at justification of those who are conscious of needing it most. Nor will the opening scenes of our present government be seen in their true aspect, until the letters of the day, now held in private hoards, shall be broken up and laid open to public view. What a treasure will be found in General Washington's cabinet, when it shall pass into the hands of as candid a friend to truth as he was himself! When no longer, like Cæsar's notes and memorandums in the hands of Antony, it shall be open to the high priests of federalism only, and garbled to say so much, and no more, as suits their views!

With respect to his farewell address, to the authorship of which, it seems, there are conflicting claims, I can state to you some facts. He had determined to decline a re-election at the end of his first term, and so far determined, that he had requested Mr. Madison to prepare for him something valedictory, to be addressed to his constituents on his retirement. This was done, but he was finally persuaded to acquiesce in a second election, to which no one more strenuously pressed him than myself, from a conviction of the importance of strengthening, by longer habit, the respect necessary for that office, which the weight of his character only could effect. When, at the end of this second term, his Valedictory came out, Mr. Madison recognized in it several passages of his draught; several others, we were both satisfied, were from the pen of Hamilton, and others from that of the President himself. These he probably put into the hands of Hamilton to form into a whole, and hence it may all appear in Hamilton's handwriting, as if it were all of his composition.

I have stated above, that the original objects of the federalists were, 1st, to warp our government more to the form and principles of monarchy, and, 2d, to weaken the barriers of the State governments as coördinate powers. In the first they have been so completely foiled by the universal spirit of the nation, that they have abandoned the enterprise, shrunk from the odium of their old appellation, taken to themselves a participation of ours, and under the pseudo-republican mask, are now aiming at their second object, and strengthened by unsuspecting or apostate recruits from our ranks, are advancing fast towards an ascendency. I have been blamed for saying, that a prevalence of the doctrines of consolidation would one day call for reformation or *revolution*. I answer by asking if a single State of the Union would have agreed to the Constitution, had it given all powers to the General Government? If the whole opposition to it did not proceed from the jealousy and fear of every State, of being subjected to the other States in matters merely its own? And if there is any reason to believe the States more disposed now than then, to acquiesce in this general surrender of all their rights and powers to a consolidated government, one and undivided?

You request me confidentially, to examine the question, whether the Supreme Court has advanced beyond its constitutional limits, and trespassed on those of the State authorities? I do not undertake it, my dear Sir, because I am unable. Age and the wane of mind consequent on it, have disqualified me from investigations so severe, and researches so laborious. And it is the less necessary in this case, as having been already done by others with a logic and learning to which I could add nothing. On the decision of the case of Cohens *vs.* The State of Virginia, in the Supreme Court of the United States, in March, 1821, Judge Roane, under the signature of Algernon Sidney, wrote for the Enquirer a series of papers on the law of that case. I considered these papers maturely as they came out, and confess that they appeared to me to pulverize every word which had been delivered by Judge Marshall, of the extra-judicial part of his opinion; and all was extra-judicial, except the decision that the act of Congress had not purported to give to the corporation of Washington the authority claimed by their lottery law, of controlling the laws of the States within the States themselves. But unable to claim that case, he could not let it go entirely, but went on gratuitously to prove, that notwithstanding the eleventh amendment of the Constitution, a State *could* be brought as a defendant, to the bar of his court; and again, that Congress might authorize a corporation of its territory to exercise legislation within a State, and paramount to the laws of that State. I cite the sum and result only of his doctrines, according to the impression made on my mind at the time, and still remaining. If not strictly accurate in circumstance, it is so in substance. This doctrine was so completely refuted by Roane, that if he can be answered, I surrender human reason as a vain and useless faculty, given to bewilder, and not to guide us. And I mention this particular case as one only of several, because it gave occasion to that thorough examination of the constitutional limits between the General and State jurisdictions, which you have asked for. There were two other writers in the same paper, under the signatures of Fletcher of Saltoun, and Somers, who, in a few essays, presented some very luminous and striking views of the question. And there was a particular paper which recapitulated all the cases in which it was thought the federal court had usurped on the State jurisdictions. These essays will be found in the Enquirers of 1821, from May the 10th to July the 13th. It is not in my present power to send them to you, but if Ritchie can furnish them, I will procure and forward them. If they had been read in the other States, as they were here, I think they would have left, there as here, no dissentients from their doctrine. The subject was taken up by our legislature of 1821-'22, and two draughts of remonstrances were prepared and discussed. As well as I remember, there was no difference of opinion as to the matter of right; but there was as to the expediency of a remonstrance at that time, the general mind of the States being then under extraordinary excitement by the Missouri question; and it was dropped on that consideration. But this case is not dead, it only sleepeth. The Indian chief said he did not go to war for every petty injury by itself, but put it into his pouch, and when that was full, he then made war. Thank Heaven, we have provided a more peaceable and rational mode of redress.

This practice of Judge Marshall, of travelling out of his case to prescribe what the law would be in a moot case not before the court, is very irregular and very censurable. I recollect another instance, and the more particularly, perhaps, because it in some measure bore on myself. Among the midnight appointments of Mr. Adams, were commissions to some federal justices of the peace for Alexandria. These were signed and sealed by him, but not delivered. I found them on the table of the Department of State, on my entrance into office, and I forbade their delivery. Marbury, named in one of them, applied to the Supreme Court for a mandamus to the Secretary of State, (Mr. Madison) to deliver the commission intended for him. The Court determined at once, that being an original process, they had no cognizance of it; and therefore the question before them was ended. But the Chief Justice went on to lay down what the law would be, had they jurisdiction of the case, to wit: that they should command the delivery. The object was clearly to instruct any other court having the jurisdiction, what they should do if Marbury should apply to them. Besides the impropriety of this gratuitous interference, could anything exceed the perversion of law? For if there is any principle of law never yet contradicted, it is that delivery is one of the essentials to the validity of a deed. Although signed and sealed, yet as long as it remains in the hands of the party himself, it is *in fieri* only, it is not a deed, and can be made so only by its delivery. In the hands of a third person it may be made an escrow. But whatever is in the executive offices is certainly deemed to be in the hands of the President; and in this case, was actually in my hands, because, when I countermanded them, there was as yet no Secretary of State. Yet this case of Marbury and Madison is continually cited by bench and bar, as if it were settled law, without any animadversion on its being merely an *obiter* dissertation of the Chief Justice.

It may be impracticable to lay down any general formula of words which shall decide at once, and with precision, in every case, this limit of jurisdiction. But there are two canons which will guide us safely in most of the cases. 1st. The capital and leading object of the Constitution was to leave with the States all authorities which respected their own citizens only, and to transfer to the United States those which respected citizens of foreign or other States: to make us several as to ourselves, but one as to all others. In the latter case, then, constructions should lean to the general jurisdiction, if the words will bear it; and in favor of the States in the former, if possible to be so construed. And indeed, between citizens and citizens of the same State, and under their own laws, I know but a single case in which a jurisdiction is given to the General Government. That is, where anything but gold or silver is made a lawful tender, or the obligation of contracts is any otherwise impaired. The separate legislatures had so often abused that power, that the citizens themselves chose to trust it to the general, rather than to their own special authorities. 2d. On every question of construction, carry ourselves back to the time when the Constitution was adopted, recollect the spirit manifested in the debates, and instead of trying what meaning may be squeezed out of the text, or invented against it, conform to the probable one in which it was passed. Let us try Cohen's case by these canons only, referring always, however, for full argument, to the essays before cited.

1. It was between a citizen and his own State, and under a law of his State. It was a domestic case, therefore, and not a foreign one.

2. Can it be believed, that under the jealousies prevailing against the General Government, at the adoption of the Constitution, the States meant to surrender the authority of preserving order, of enforcing moral duties and restraining vice, within their own territory? And this is the present case, that of Cohen being under the ancient and general law of gaming. Can any good be effected by taking from the States the moral rule of their citizens, and subordinating it to the general authority, or to one of

their corporations, which may justify forcing the meaning of words, hunting after possible constructions, and hanging inference on inference, from heaven to earth, like Jacob's ladder? Such an intention was impossible, and such a licentiousness of construction and inference, if exercised by both governments, as may be done with equal right, would equally authorize both to claim all power, general and particular, and break up the foundations of the Union. Laws are made for men of ordinary understanding, and should, therefore, be construed by the ordinary rules of common sense. Their meaning is not to be sought for in metaphysical subtleties, which may make anything mean everything or nothing, at pleasure. It should be left to the sophisms of advocates, whose trade it is, to prove that a defendant is a plaintiff, though dragged into court, *torto collo,* like Bonaparte's volunteers, into the field in chains, or that a power has been given, because it ought to have been given, *et alia talia.* The States supposed that by their tenth amendment, they had secured themselves against constructive powers. They were not lessoned yet by Cohen's case, nor aware of the slipperiness of the eels of the law. I ask for no straining of words against the General Government, nor yet against the States. I believe the States can best govern our home concerns, and the General Government our foreign ones. I wish, therefore, to see maintained that wholesome distribution of powers established by the Constitution for the limitation of both; and never to see all offices transferred to Washington, where, further withdrawn from the eyes of the people, they may more secretly be bought and sold as at market.

But the Chief Justice says, "there must be an ultimate arbiter somewhere." True, there must; but does that prove it is either party? The ultimate arbiter is the people of the Union, assembled by their deputies in convention, at the call of Congress, or of two-thirds of the States. Let them decide to which they mean to give an authority claimed by two of their organs. And it has been the peculiar wisdom and felicity of our Constitution, to have provided this peaceable appeal, where that of other nations is at once to force.

I rejoice in the example you set of *seriatim* opinions. I have heard it often noticed, and always with high approbation. Some of your brethren will be encouraged to follow it occasionally, and in time, it may be felt by all as a duty, and the sound practice of the primitive court be again restored. Why should not every judge be asked his opinion, and give it from the bench, if only by yea or nay? Besides ascertaining the fact of his opinion, which the public have a right to know, in order to judge whether it is impeachable or not, it would show whether the opinions were unanimous or not, and thus settle more exactly the weight of their authority.

The close of my second sheet warns me that it is time now to relieve you from this letter of unmerciful length. Indeed, I wonder how I have accomplished it, with two crippled wrists, the one scarcely able to move my pen, the other to hold my paper. But I am hurried sometimes beyond the sense of pain, when unbosoming myself to friends who harmonize with me in principle. You and I may differ occasionally in details of minor consequence, as no two minds, more than two faces, are the same in every feature. But our general objects are the same; to preserve the republican form and principles of our Constitution, and cleave to the salutary distribution of powers which that has established. These are the two sheet anchors of our Union. If driven from either, we shall be in danger of foundering. To my prayers for its safety and perpetuity, I add those for the continuation of your health, happiness, and usefulness to your country.

Madison to Jefferson

Montpellier June 27, 1823

DEAR SIR

I return the copy of your letter to Judge Johnson inclosed in your favor of the [13 June] instant. Your statement relating to the farewell Address of Gen! Washington is substantially correct. If there be any circumstantial inaccuracy, it is in imputing to him more agency in composing the document than he probably had. Taking for granted that it was drawn up by Hamilton, the best conjecture is that the General put into his hands his own letter to me suggesting his general ideas, with the paper prepared by me in conformity with them; and if he varied the draught of Hamilton at all, it was by a few verbal or qualifying amendments only. It is very inconsiderate in the friends of Gen! Washington to make the merit of the Address a question between him and Col: Hamilton, and somewhat extraordinary, if countenanced by those who possess the files of the General where it is presumed the truth might be traced. They ought to claim for him the merit only of cherishing the principles and views addressed to his Country, and for the Address itself the weight given to it by his sanction; leaving the literary merit whatever it be to the friendly pen employed on the occasion, the rather as it was never understood that Washington valued himself on his writing talent, and no secret to some that he occasionally availed himself of the friendship of others whom he supposed more practised than himself in studied composition. In a general view it is to be regretted that the Address is likely to be presented to the public not as the pure legacy of the Father of his Country, as has been all along believed, but as the performance of another held in different estimation. It will not only lose the charm of the name subscribed to it; but it will not be surprizing if particular passages be understood in new senses, and with applications derived from the political doctrines and party feelings of the discovered Author.

At some future day it may be an object with the curious to compare the two draughts made at different epochs with each other, and the letter of Gen! W. with both. The comparison will shew a greater conformity in the first with the tenor and tone of the letter, than in the other; and the difference will be more remarkable perhaps in what is omitted, than in what is added in the Address as it stands.[9]

If the solicitude of Gen! Washington's connexions be such as is represented, I foresee that I shall share their displeasure, if public use be made of what passed between him and me at the approaching expiration of his first term. Altho' it be impossible to question the facts, I may be charged with indelicacy, if not breach of confidence, in making them known; and the irritation will be the greater, if the Authorship of the Address continue to be

---

9. For an analysis, see Gilbert, pp. 115–36. For the various drafts by Washington, Hamilton, and JM, see Victor Hugo Palsits, *Washington's Farewell Address* (New York, 1935).

claimed for the signer of it; since the call on me on one occasion, will favor the allegation of a call on another on another occasion. I hope therefore that the Judge will not understand your communication as intended for the new work he has in hand. I do not know that your statement would justify all the complaint its public appearance might bring on me; but there certainly was a species of confidence at the time in what passed, forbidding publicity, at least till the lapse of time should wear out the seal on it, and the truth of history should put in a fair claim to such disclosures.[10]

    I wish the rather that the Judge may be put on his guard, because with all his good qualities, he has been betrayed into errors which shew that his discretion is not always awake. A remarkable instance is his ascribing to Gouverneur Morris the Newburg letters written by Armstrong, which has drawn from the latter a corrosive attack which must pain his feelings, if it should not affect his standing with the Public. Another appears in a stroke at Judge Cooper in a letter to the Education Committee in Kentucky, which has plunged him into an envenomed dispute with an antagonist, the force of whose mind and pen you well know. And what is worse than all, I perceive from one of Cooper's publications casually falling within my notice, that among the effects of Judge Johnson's excitement, he has stooped to invoke the religious prejudices circulated agst Cooper.[11]

    Johnson is much indebted to you for your remarks on the definition of parties. The radical distinction between them has always been a confidence of one, and distrust of the other, as to the capacity of Mankind for self Government. He expected far too much, in requesting a precise demarkation of the boundary between the Federal and the State Authorities. The answer would have required a critical commentary on the whole text of the Constitution. The two general Canons you lay down would be of much use in such a task; particularly that which refers to the sense of the State Conventions, whose ratifications alone made the Constitution what it is. In exemplifying the other Canon, there are more exceptions than occurred to you, of cases in which the federal jurisdiction is extended to controversies between Citizens of the same State. To mention one only: In cases arising under a Bankrupt law, there is no distinction between those to which Citizens of the same and of different States are parties.

    But after surmounting the difficulty in tracing the boundary between the General and State Gov^{ts} the problem remains for maintaining it in practice; particularly in cases of Judicial cognizance. To refer every point of disagreement to the people in Conventions would be a process too tardy, too troublesome, and too expensive; besides its tendency to lessen a salutary veneration for an Instrument so often calling for such explanatory interpositions. A para-

---

10. For JM's response to Washington's request in 1792, see Brant, III, pp. 355–56; Robert A. Rutland, *James Madison: The Founding Father* (New York, 1987), p. 115; and *PJM,* XIV, pp. 319–24.

11. For Johnson's controversy with Cooper, see Morgan, pp. 144–45.

mount or even a definitive Authority in the individual States, would soon make the Constitution and laws different in different States, and thus destroy that equality and uniformity of rights and duties which form the essence of the Compact, to say nothing of the opportunity given to the States individually of involving by their decisions the whole Union in foreign Contests. To leave conflicting decisions to be settled between the Judicial parties could not promise a happy result. The end must be a trial of strength between the Posse headed by the Marshal and the Posse headed by the Sheriff. Nor would the issue be safe if left to a compromise between the two Gov^{ts}; the case of a disagreement between different Gov^{ts} being essentially different from a disagreement between branches of the same Gov^t. In the latter case neither party being able to consummate its will without the concurrence of the other, there is a necessity on both to consult and to accommodate. Not so, with different Gov^{ts} each possessing every branch of power necessary to carry its purpose into compleat effect. It here becomes a question between Independent Nations, with no other *dernier* resort than physical force. Negotiation might indeed in some instances avoid this extremity; but how often would it happen, among so many States, that an unaccommodating spirit in some would render that resource unavailing.

We arrive at the agitated question whether the Judicial Authority of the U. S. be the constitutional resort for determining the line between the federal and State jurisdictions. Believing as I do that the General Convention regarded a provision within the Constitution for deciding in a peaceable and regular mode all cases arising in the course of its operation, as essential to an adequate System of Gov^t: that it intended the Authority vested in the Judicial Department as a final resort in relation to the States, for cases resulting to it in the exercise of its functions, (the concurrence of the Senate chosen by the State Legislatures, in appointing the Judges, and the oaths and official tenures of these, with the surveillance of public Opinion, being relied on as guarantying their impartiality); and that this intention is expressed by the articles declaring that the federal Constitution and laws shall be the supreme law of the land, and that the Judicial Power of the U. S. shall extend to all cases arising under them: Believing moreover that this was the prevailing view of the subject when the Constitution was adopted and put into execution; that it has so continued thro' the long period which has elapsed; and that even at this time an appeal to a national decision would prove that no general change has taken place: thus believing I have never yielded my original opinion indicated in the "Federalist" N° 39 to the ingenious reasonings of Col: Taylor agst this construction of the Constitution.[12]

I am not unaware that the Judiciary career has not corresponded with what was anticipated. At one period the Judges perverted the Bench of Justice

---

12. TJ endorsed Taylor's views in general; see Malone, VI, pp. 354-60. JM denied them; see Brant, VI, pp. 432-34.

into a rostrum for partizan harangues. And latterly the Court, by some of its decisions, still more by extrajudicial reasonings and dicta, has manifested a propensity to enlarge the general authority in derogation of the local, and to amplify its own jurisdiction, which has justly incurred the public censure. But the abuse of a trust does not disprove its existence. And if no remedy for the abuse be practicable under the forms of the Constitution, I should prefer a resort to the Nation for an amendment of the Tribunal itself, to continual appeals from its controverted decisions to that Ultimate Arbiter.

In the year 1821, I was engaged in a correspondence with Judge Roane, which grew out of the proceedings of the Supreme Court of the U. S. Having said so much here I will send you a copy of my letters to him as soon as I can have a legible one made, that a fuller view of my ideas with respect to them may be before you.[13]

I agree entirely with you on the subject of seriatim opinions by the Judges, which you have placed in so strong a light in your letter to Judge Johnson, whose example it seems is in favor of the practice. An argument addressed to others, all of whose dislikes to it are not known, may be a delicate experiment. My particular connexion with Judge Todd, whom I expect to see, may tempt me to touch on the subject; and, if encouraged, to present views of it wch thro' him may find the way to his intimates.

In turning over some bundles of Pamphlets, I met with several Copies of a very small one which at the desire of my political associates I threw out in 1795. As it relates to the state of parties I inclose a Copy. It had the advantage of being written with the subject full and fresh in my mind, and the disadvantage of being hurried, at the close of a fatiguing session of Cong^s by an impatience to return home, from which I was detained by that Job only. The temper of the pamphlet is explained if not excused by the excitements of the period. Always and Affectionately yours.

JAMES MADISON

ENCLOSURE
[Madison to Spencer Roane]

DEAR SIR,   Montpellier May 6, 1821
I rec^d more than two weeks ago, your letter of Ap^l 17. A visit to a sick friend at a distance, with a series of unavoidable attentions have prevented an earlier acknowledgment of it.

Under any circumstances I should be disposed rather to put such a subject as that to which it relates into your hands than to take it out of them. Apart from this consideration, a variety of demands on my time would restrain me from the task of unravelling the arguments applied by the Supreme Court of the U. S. to their late decision. I am

---

13. See the enclosures JM to Spencer Roane, May 6, 1821, and June 29, 1821, in JM to TJ, June 27, 1823, below, which were stimulated by Judge Roane's slashing attack on Chief Justice John Marshall's decision in *Cohens* v. *Virginia,* published in a series of articles in the *Richmond Enquirer* in May and June 1821.

particularly aware moreover that they are made to rest not a little on technical points of law, which are as foreign to my studies as they are familiar to yours.

It is to be regretted that the Court is so much in the practice of mingling with their judgments pronounced, comments and reasonings of a scope beyond them; and that there is often an apparent disposition to amplify the authorities of the Union at the expence of those of the States. It is of great importance as well as of indispensable obligation, that the constitutional boundary between them should be impartially maintained. Every deviation from it in practice detracts from the superiority of a Chartered over a traditional Gov^t and mars the experiment which is to determine the interesting Problem whether the organization of the Political system of the U. S. establishes a just equilibrium; or tends to a preponderance of the National or the local powers, and in the latter case, whether of the national or of the local.

A candid review of the vicissitudes which have marked the progress of the General Gov^t does not preclude doubts as to the ultimate and fixed character of a Political Establishment distinguished by so novel and complex a mechanism. On some occasions the advantage taken of favorable circumstances gave an impetus and direction to it which seemed to threaten subversive encroachments on the rights and authorities of the States. At a certain period we witnessed a spirit of usurpation by some of these on the necessary and legitimate functions of the former. At the present date, theoretic innovations at least are putting new weights into the scale of federal sovereignty which make it highly proper to bring them to the Bar of the Constitution.

In looking to the probable course and eventual bearing of the compound Gov^t of our Country, I cannot but think that much will depend not only on the moral changes incident to the progress of society; but on the increasing number of the members of the Union. Were the members very few, and each very powerful, a feeling of self-sufficiency would have a relaxing effect on the bands holding them together. Were they numerous and weak, the Gov. over the whole would find less difficulty in maintaining and increasing subordination. It happens that whilst the power of some is swelling to a great size, the entire number is swelling also. In this respect a corresponding increase of centripetal and centrifugal forces, may be equivalent to no increase of either.

In the existing posture of things, my reflections lead me to infer that whatever may be the latitude of Jurisdiction assumed by the Judicial Power of the U. S. it is less formidable to the reserved sovereignty of the States than the latitude of power which it has assigned to the National Legislature; and that encroachments of the latter are more to be apprehended from impulses given to it by a majority of the States seduced by expected advantages, than from the love of Power in the Body itself, controuled as it *now* is by its responsibility to the Constituent Body.

Such is the plastic faculty of Legislation, that notwithstanding the firm tenure which judges have on their offices, they can by various regulations be kept or reduced within the paths of duty; more especially with the aid of their amenability to the Legislative tribunal in the form of impeachment. It is not probable that the Supreme Court would long be indulged in a career of usurpation opposed to the decided opinions and policy of the Legislature.

Nor do I think that Congress, even seconded by the Judicial Power, can, without some change in the character of the nation, succeed in *durable* violations of the rights and authorities of the States. The responsibility of one branch to the people, and of the other branch to the Legislatures, of the States, seem to be, in the present stage at least of our political history, an adequate barrier. In the case of the alien and sedition laws, which violated the general *sense* as well as the *rights* of the States, the usurping experiment was crushed at once, notwithstanding the co-operation of the federal Judges with the federal laws.

But what is to controul Congress when backed and even pushed on by a majority of their Constituents, as was the case in the late contest relative to Missouri, and as may again happen in the constructive power relating to Roads and Canals? Nothing within the pale of the Constitution but sound arguments and conciliatory expostulations addressed both to Congress and to their Constituents.

On the questions brought before the Public by the late doctrines of the Supreme Court of the U. S. concerning the extent of their own powers, and that of the exclusive jurisdiction of Congress over the ten miles square and other specified places, there is as yet no evidence that they express either the opinions of Congress or those of their Constituents. There is nothing therefore to discourage a development of whatever flaws the doctrines may contain, or tendencies they may threaten. Congress if convinced of these may not only abstain from the exercise of Powers claimed for them by the Court, but find the means of controuling those claimed by the Court for itself. And should Congress not be convinced, their Constituents, if so, can certainly under the forms of the Constitution effectuate a compliance with their deliberate judgment and settled determination.

In expounding the Constitution the Court seems not insensible that the intention of the parties to it ought to be kept in view; and that as far as the language of the instrument will permit, this intention ought to be traced in the contemporaneous expositions. But is the Court as prompt and as careful in citing and following this evidence, when agst the federal Authority as when agst that of the States? (See the partial reference of the Court to "The Federalist.")[14]

The exclusive jurisdiction over the ten miles square is itself an anomaly in our Representative System. And its object being manifest, and attested by the views taken of it, at its date, there seems a peculiar impropriety in making it the fulcrum for a lever stretching into the most distant parts of the Union, and overruling the municipal policy of the States. The remark is still more striking when applied to the smaller places over which an exclusive jurisdiction was suggested by a regard to the defence and the property of the Nation.

Some difficulty, it must be admitted may result in particular cases from the impossibility of executing some of these powers within the defined spaces, according to the principles and rules enjoined by the Constitution; and from the want of a constitutional provision for the surrender of malefactors whose escape must be so easy, on the demand of the U. States as well as of the Individual States. It is true also that these exclusive jurisdictions are in the class of enumerated powers, to wch is subjoined the "power in Congress to pass all laws necessary and proper for their execution." All however that could be exacted by these considerations would be that the means of execution should be of the most obvious and essential kind; and exerted in the ways as little intrusive as possible on the powers and police of the States. And, after all, the

---

14. In *Cohens* v. *Virginia*, Chief Justice Marshall noted that "the opinion of the *Federalist* has always been considered as of great authority. It is a complete commentary on our constitution, and is appealed to by all parties in the questions to which that instrument has given birth. Its intrinsic merit entitles it to this high rank; and the part two of its authors performed in framing the constitution, put it very much in their power to explain the views with which it was framed"; see 6 *Wheaton* 294.

question would remain whether the better course would not be to regard the case as an omitted one, to be provided for by an amendment of the Constitution. In resorting to legal precedents as sanctions to power, the distinctions should ever be strictly attended to, between such as take place under transitory impressions, or without full examination and deliberation, and such as pass with solemnities and repetitions sufficient to imply a concurrence of the judgment and the will of those, who having granted the power, have the ultimate right to explain the grant. Altho' I cannot join in the protest of some against the validity of all precedents, however uniform and multiplied, in expounding the Constitution, yet I am persuaded that Legislative precedents are frequently of a character entitled to little respect, and that those of Congress are sometimes liable to peculiar distrust. They not only follow the example of other Legislative assemblies in first procrastinating and then precipitating their acts; but, owing to the termination of their session every other year at a fixed day and hour, a mass of business is struck off, as it were at shorthand, and in a moment. These midnight precedents of every sort ought to have little weight in any case.

On the question relating to involuntary submissions of the States to the Tribunal of the Supreme Court, the Court seems not to have adverted at all to the expository language when the Constitution was adopted; nor to that of the Eleventh Amendment, which may as well import that it was declaratory, as that it was restrictive of the meaning of the original text. It seems to be a strange reasoning also that would imply that a State in controversies with its own Citizens might have less of sovereignty, than in controversies with foreign individuals, by which the national relations might be affected. Nor is it less to be wondered that it should have appeared to the Court that the dignity of a State was not more compromitted by being made a party agst a private person than agst a co-ordinate Party.

The Judicial power of the U. S. over cases arising under the Constitution, must be admitted to be a vital part of the System. But that there are limitations and exceptions to its efficient character, is among the admissions of the Court itself. The Eleventh Amendment introduces exceptions if there were none before. A liberal and steady course of practice can alone reconcile the several provisions of the Constitution literally at variance with each other; of which there is an example in the Treaty Power and the Legislative Power on subjects to which both are extended by the words of the Constitution. It is particularly incumbent, in taking cognizance of cases arising under the Constitution, and in which the laws and rights of the States may be involved, to let the proceedings touch individuals only. Prudence enjoins this if there were no other motive, in consideration of the impracticability of applying coercion to States.

I am sensible Sir, that these ideas are too vague to be of value, and that they may not even hint for consideration anything not occurring to yourself. Be so good as to see in them at least an unwillingness to disregard altogether your request. Should any of the ideas be erroneous as well as vague, I have the satisfaction to know that they will be viewed by a friendly as well as a candid eye.

ENCLOSURE
[Madison to Spencer Roane]

Dear Sir,   Montpellier June 29, 1821

I have rec^d, and return my thanks for your obliging communication of the 20th instant. The papers of "Algernon Sidney" have given their full lustre to the arguments agst the suability of States by individuals, and agst the projectile capacity of the power of Congress within the "ten miles square." The publication is well worthy of a Pamphlet form, but must attract Public attention in any form.

The Gordian Knot of the Constitution seems to lie in the problem of collision between the federal and State powers, especially as eventually exercised by their respective Tribunals. If the knot cannot be untied by the text of the Constitution it ought not, certainly, to be cut by any Political Alexander.

I have always thought that a construction of the instrument ought to be favoured, as far as the text would warrant, which would obviate the dilemma of a Judicial rencounter or a mutual paralysis; and that on the abstract question whether the federal or the State decisions ought to prevail, the sounder policy would yield to the claims of the former.

Our Governmental System is established by a compact, not between the Government of the U. States, and the State Governments; but between the States, as sovereign communities, stipulating each with the others, a surrender of certain portions, of their respective authorities, to be exercised by a Common Gov^t and a reservation, for their own exercise, of all their other Authorities. The possibility of disagreements concerning the line of division between these portions could not escape attention; and the existence of some Provision for terminating regularly and authoritatively such disagreements, not but be regarded as a material desideratum.

Were this trust to be vested in the States in their individual characters, the Constitution of the U. S. might become different in every State, and would be pretty sure to do so in some; the State Gov^{ts} would not stand all in the same relation to the General Gov^t, some retaining more, others less of sovereignty; and the vital principle of equality, which cements their Union thus gradually be deprived of its virtue. Such a trust vested in the Gov^t representing the whole and exercised by its tribunals, would not be exposed to these consequences; whilst the trust itself would be controulable by the States who directly or indirectly appoint the Trustees: whereas in the hands of the States no federal controul direct or indirect would exist the functionaries holding their appointments by tenures altogether independent of the General Gov^t.

Is it not a reasonable calculation also that the room for jarring opinions between the National and State tribunals will be narrowed by successive decisions sanctioned by the Public concurrence; and that the weight of the State tribunals will be increased by improved organizations, by selections of abler Judges, and consequently by more enlightened proceedings? Much of the distrust of these departments in the States, which prevailed when the National Constitution was formed has already been removed. Were they filled everywhere, as they are in some of the States, one of which I need not name, their decisions at once indicating and influencing the sense of their Constituents, and founded on united interpretations of constitutional points, could scarcely fail to frustrate an assumption of unconstitutional powers by the federal tribunals.

Is it too much to anticipate even that the federal and State Judges, as they become more and more co-ordinate in talents, with equal integrity, and feeling alike the impartiality enjoined by their oaths, will vary less and less also in their reasonings and opinions on all Judicial subjects; and thereby mutually contribute to the clearer and firmer establishment of the true boundaries of power, on which must depend the success and permanency of the federal republic, the best Guardian, as we believe, of the liberty, the safety, and the happiness of men. In these hypothetical views I may permit my wishes to sway too much my hopes. I submit the whole nevertheless to your perusal, well assured that you will approve the former, if you cannot join fully in the latter.

Under all circumstances I beg you to be assured of my distinguished esteem and sincere regard.

Jefferson to Madison

Monticello Aug. 30, 1823

DEAR SIR,

I received the enclosed letters from the President, with a request, that after perusal I would forward them to you, for perusal by yourself also and to be returned then to him.

You have doubtless seen Timothy Pickering's 4th. of July observations on the Declaration of Independence. If his principles and prejudices personal and political, gave us no reason to doubt whether he had truly quoted the information he alledges to have recieved from Mr. Adams, I should then say that, in some of the particulars, Mr. Adams' memory has led him into unquestionable error. At the age of 88., and 47. years after the transactions of Independence, this is not wonderful. Nor should I, at the age of 80., on the small advantage of that difference only, venture to oppose my memory to his, were it not supported by written notes, taken by myself at the moment and on the spot. He says, 'the committee (of 5. to wit, Dr. Franklin, Sherman, Livingston, and ourselves) met, discussed the subject, and then appointed him and myself to make the draught; that we, as a subcommittee, met, and after the urgencies of each on the other, I consented to undertake the task; that the draught being made, we, the subcommittee, met, and conned the paper over, and he does not remember that he made or suggested a single alteration.' Now these details are quite incorrect. The committee of 5. met, no such thing as as a subcommittee was proposed, but they unanimously pressed on myself alone to undertake the draught. I consented; I drew it; but before I reported it to the committee, I communicated it *separately* to Dr. Franklin and Mr. Adams, requesting their corrections, because they were the two members of whose judgments and amendments I wished most to have the benefit, before presenting it to the Committee; and you have seen the original paper now in my hands, with the corrections of Doctor Franklin and Mr. Adams interlined in their own handwritings. Their alterations were two or three only, and merely verbal. I then wrote a fair copy, reported it to the Committee, and from them, unaltered to Congress. This personal communication and consultation with Mr. Adams, he has misremembered into the actings of a sub-committee. Pickering's observations, and Mr. Adams' in addition, 'that it contained no new ideas, that it is a commonplace compilation, it's sentiments hackneyed in Congress for two years before, and its essence contained in Otis's pamphlet,' may all be true. Of that I am not to be the judge. Richard Henry Lee charged it as copied from Locke's treatise on government. Otis's pamphlet I never saw, and whether I had gathered my ideas from reading or reflection I do not know. I know only that I turned to neither book or pamphlet while writing it. I did not consider it as any part of my charge to invent new ideas altogether and to offer no sentiment which had ever been expressed before. Had Mr. Adams been so restrained, Congress would have lost the benefit of his bold and impressive advocations of the rights of revolution. For no man's confident and fervid addresses, more than Mr. Adams's encouraged and supported us thro' the difficulties surrounding us, which, like the ceaseless action of gravity, weighed on us by night and by day. Yet, on the same ground, we may ask what of these elevated thoughts was new, or can be affirmed never before to have entered the conceptions of man?

Whether also the sentiments of independence, and the reasons for declaring it which make so great a portion of the instrument, had been hackneyed in Congress for two years before the 4th. of July '76, or this dictum also of Mr. Adams be another slip of memory, let history say. This however I will say for Mr. Adams, that he supported the Declaration with zeal and ability, fighting fearlessly for every word of it. As to myself, I thought it a duty to be, on that occasion, a passive auditor of the opinions of others, more impartial judges than I could be, of its merits or demerits. During the debate I was sitting by Dr Franklin, and he observed that I was writhing a little under the acrimonious criticisms on some of its parts; and it was on that occasion that, by way of comfort, he told me the story of John Thompson, the Hatter, and his new sign.[15]

Timothy thinks the instrument the better for having a fourth of it expunged. He would have thought it still better had the other three-fourths gone out also, all but the single sentiment (the only one he approves), which recommends friendship to his dear England, whenever she is willing to be at peace with us. His insinuations are that altho' 'the high tone of the instrument was in unison with the warm feelings of the times, this sentiment of habitual friendship to England should never be forgotten, and that the duties it enjoins should *especially* be borne in mind on every celebration of this anniversary.' In other words, that the Declaration, as being a libel on the government of England, composed in times of passion, should now be buried in utter oblivion to spare the feelings of our English friends and Angloman fellow citizens. But it is not to wound them that we wish to keep it in mind; but to cherish the

---

15. Franklin commiserated with anyone who drafted papers to be reviewed by a public body, citing the case of an apprentice hatter who, about to go into business for himself, designed a signboard "John Thompson, Hatter, makes and sells hats for ready money," with the figure of a hat outlined. But his friends, acting as critics, persuaded him to omit some words as tautologous and others as unnecessary. "So his inscription," Franklin told TJ, "was reduced ultimately to 'John Thompson' with the figure of a hat subjoined"; see Paul M. Zall, *Ben Franklin Laughing: Anecdotes from Original Sources by and about Benjamin Franklin* (Berkeley, 1980), pp. 137–38.

principles of the instrument in the bosoms of our own citizens: and it is a heavenly comfort to see that these principles are yet so strongly felt, as to render a circumstance so trifling as this little lapse of memory of Mr. Adams worthy of being solemnly announced and supported at an anniversary assemblage of the nation on its birthday. In opposition however to Mr. Pickering, I pray God that these principles may be eternal and close the prayer with my affectionate wishes for yourself of long life, health and happiness.

Madison to Jefferson

Montpellier Sept. 6, 1823

DEAR SIR,

I return the two communications from the President inclosed in your letter of Aug. 30.

I am afraid the people of Spain as well as of Portugal need still further light and heat too from the American example before they will be a Match for the armies, the intrigues and the bribes of their Enemies, the treachery of their leaders, and what is most of all to be dreaded, their priests and their prejudices. Still their cause is so just, that whilst there is life in it, hope ought not to be abandoned.[16]

I am glad you have put on paper a correction of the apocryphal tradition furnished by Pickering, of the "Draught" of the Declaration of Independence. If he derived it from the misrecollections of Mr. Adams, it is well that the alterations of the original paper proposed by the latter in his own handwriting attest the fallibility of his aged memory. Nothing can be more absurd than the cavil that the Declaration contains known and not new truths. The object was to assert not to discover truths, and to make them the basis of the Revolutionary Act. The merit of the Draught could consist only in a lucid communication of human rights, a condensed enumeration of the reasons for such an exercise of them, and in a style and tone appropriate to the great occasion, and to the spirit of the American people.

The friends of R. H. Lee have shewn not only injustice in underrating the Draught, but much weakness in overrating the Motion in Cong^s preceding it; all the merit of which belongs to the Convention of Virg^a which gave a positive instruction to her Deputies to make the Motion. It was made by him as next in the list to P. Randolph then deceased. Had Mr. Lee been absent the task would have devolved on you. As this measure of Virg^a makes a link in the history of our National birth, it is but right that every circumstance attending it, should be ascertained and preserved. You probably can best tell where the

---

16. For a brief discussion of the independence movement in Latin America, see Samuel Flagg Bemis, *John Quincy Adams and the Foundations of American Foreign Policy* (New York, 1949), pp. 341–62.

instruction had its origin and by whose pen it was prepared. The impression at the time was, that it was communicated in a letter from you to [Mr. Wythe] a member of the Convention.[17]

J.M.

Jefferson to Madison

Monticello Oct. 18, 1823

DEAR SIR,

I return you Mr. Coxe's letter which has cost me much time at two or three different attempts to decypher it. Had I such a correspondent I should certainly admonish him that if he would not so far respect my time as to write to me legibly, I should so far respect it myself as not to waste it in decomposing and recomposing his hieroglyphics.

The jarrings between the friends of Hamilton and Pickering will be of advantage to the cause of truth. It will denudate the monarchism of the former and justify our opposition to him, and the malignity of the latter which nullifies his testimony in all cases which his passion can discolor. God bless you, and preserve you many years.

Jefferson to Madison

Monticello Oct. 24, 1823

TH: J. TO J. MADISON

I forward you two most important letters sent to me by the President and add his letter to me by which you will percieve his *prima facie* views. This you will be so good as to return to me and forward the others to him.[18]

I have recieved Trumbull's print of the Decln of Independance, and turning to his letter am able to inform you more certainly than I could by memory that the print costs 20. D. and the frame and glass 12. D. say 32. D. in all.[19]

To answer your question[20] Pythagoras has the reputation of having first

---

17. JM seems to have added Wythe's name at a later date.

18. Writing on Oct. 16, 1823, President Monroe sought advice from TJ and JM on Canning's proposal of a joint British-American statement condemning any attempt by European powers to restore Spain's authority in Latin America; see Harry Ammon, *James Monroe: The Quest for National Identity* (New York, 1971), pp. 478–79.

19. When John Trumbull, at JM's request, prepared an enlarged painting of *The Declaration of Independence* in 1818 for installation in the rebuilt Capitol, he chose Asher B. Durand to engrave a print of it; see Jules B. Prown, "John Trumbull As History Painter," in *John Trumbull: The Hand and Spirit of a Painter,* ed. Helen A. Cooper (New Haven, 1982), p. 40.

20. JM's letter raising this question has not been found.

taught the true position of the sun in the center of our system and the revolutions of the planets around it. His doctrine, after a long eclipse was restored by Copernicus, and hence it is called either the Pythagorean or Copernican system. Health and affectionate salutns to Mrs M. and yourself

Madison to Jefferson

Montpellier Nov. 1, 1823

D^R S<small>IR</small>,

I return the letter of the President. The correspondence from abroad has gone back to him, as you desired. I have expressed to him my concurrence in the policy of meeting the advances of the B. Govt. having an eye to the forms of our Constitution in every step in the road to war. With the British power and navy combined with our own we have nothing to fear from the rest of the world; and in the great struggle of the Epoch between liberty and despotism, we owe it to ourselves to sustain the former, in this hemisphere at least.[21] I have even suggested an invitation to the B. Govt to join in applying the "small effort for so much good" to the French invasion of Spain, and to make Greece an object of some such favorable attention. Why Mr. Canning and his colleagues did not sooner interpose agst. the calamity wch. could not have escaped foresight cannot be otherwise explained but by the different aspect of the question when it related to liberty in Spain, and to the extension of British commerce to her former Colonies.[22] Health and every other blessing

J<small>AMES</small> M<small>ADISON</small>

Jefferson to Madison

Monticello Nov. 6, 1823

D<small>EAR</small> S<small>IR</small>

The belief is so universal that the ensuing legislature will dispose in some way of the University debt, and liberate our funds, as that we ought to save what time we can by provisional preparations. We have all, I believe, agreed that an Agent to Gr. Britain will be necessary to procure Professors; and I have therefore mentioned to you that Mr Cabell was disposed to undertake the

---

21. For JM's exchange of views with Monroe, see Ammon, pp. 479–80.
22. The best study of the Monroe Doctrine remains Dexter Perkins's *The Monroe Doctrine, 1823–1826* (Cambridge, Mass., 1927), but for Canning's proposal, see also Bradford Perkins, *Castlereagh and Adams: England and the United States, 1812–1823* (Berkeley, 1964), pp. 305–47, and Bemis, pp. 363–408.

business. But the inclosed letter informs me he must decline it.[23] We ought then to lose no time in having a substitute ready to be proposed to our colleagues at the next meeting. Whom shall we appoint? No one occurs to me so competent as F. Gilmer. Yet certainly he would not displace himself at the bar for this occasional mission. Our Professor of law must be a native, and you seemed to think with me that no fitter one than him could be found for that chair. The offer of this with the mission would probably be accepted. If you would approve of him for both offices, I could venture to say to him that I have no doubt our Colleagues will concur with us, and ask from him as prompt a decision as he can give; requiring that the proposition and answer shall be inviolably secret, but to us three, as well out of respect to our colleagues, as to prevent the cabals and plots which might attack and mar it. What might I say to him hypothetically as to salary? For altho' we have talked of 2000. Dollars we have not fixed it. Shall I say that we believe that our colleagues as well as ourselves contemplate that sum? What allowance for the mission? Shall we propose to him his choice 1. to let his salary begin on the day of his departure? or 2. a fixed sum of 1. or 2000. Dollars for the trip? or his expences, to be governed by his discretion? all however to be finally submitted to our board. Or would you prefer offering one of these singly, or any thing else?[24]

Your opinion and mine on Canning's proposition, I have no doubt have been mainly the same.[25] I inclose you my answer to the President, which you will be so good as to return with Mr Cabell's. Pray subjoin to your answer the state and prospect of Mr Crawford's health. 21. bleedings and a course of mercury give me, when the present danger is over, serious apprehensions for the future. Ever and affectionately yours'

TH: JEFFERSON

Madison to Jefferson

Montpellier Nov. 11, 1823

DEAR SIR,

I have received yours of the 6th. My preference for F. Gilmer for the law professorship, to any other name brought into view, has not changed; and I know of no one better suited for the mission now declined by Mr. Cabell. It will be well, I think, to hold out, in the first instance at least, not more than $1,500 for the salary, as the reduction of the number of professors from 10 to

---

23. For the search for professors, see Malone, VI, pp. 397–410.
24. *The Correspondence of Thomas Jefferson and Francis Walker Gilmer, 1814–1826* (Columbia, S.C., 1946) has been edited by Richard Beale Davis.
25. For TJ's exchange of views with Monroe, see Malone, VI, pp. 428–30.

7 may not be finally settled; and if settled in the negative, the annuity would fall short. It is true that a professor of law, if taken from the Bar, may be expected to make a greater pecuniary sacrifice than might be made by the others; but on the other hand, his class and his fees will probably be more numerous. I should prefer a fixed sum for the service abroad to defraying actual expenses. You can better estimate these than I can. Supposing that he will be absent not more than 6, 7, or 8 months, I suggest $1,500 for the allowance; but shall acquiesce in any sum you may prefer, not exceeding $2,000. The gratification of such a trip to Europe, will doubtless be felt as an item in the compensation. I incline to making the allowance a special provision for the service rather than a salary for professional services not performed. The distinction however is more nominal than material.

I return Mr. Cabell's letter, with the copy of your answer to the President. You will see by mine inclosed that they substantially agree, and you will see by Mr. Rush's letter, which I also inclose, and which is of later date than his correspondence sent us by the President, how skittish the British Cabinet is on the very business into which it has invited us. It is not impossible that Canning, looking more ahead than his colleagues, and more to the *vox populi* at the moment may be drawn back occasionally from his own advances.

Mr. Crawford proceeded hence on his way to Washington this afternoon. He came from Governor Barbour's on Sunday, and was detained here yesterday and part of today by the State of the Weather. He seems equal to the Journey; but his Constitution seems a good deal shaken and will require care as well as time for a thorough repair.[26]

With Mr. Rush's letter you will be kind enough to return my answer to the President. Adieu with every good wish

JAMES MADISON

Jefferson to Madison

Monticello Nov. 15, 1823

DEAR SIR,

I return your letter to the President and that of Mr. Rush to you with thanks for the communication. The* matters which Mr. Rush states as under considn with the British govmt are verily interesting. But that about the navigation of the St. Lawrence and Misspi. I would rather they would let alone. The navign. of the former, since the N. Y. canal is of too little interest to be cared about, that of the latter too serious on account of the inlet it would give

---

26. William H. Crawford was secretary of the treasury in Monroe's administration. The standard study is Chase C. Mooney, *William H. Crawford, 1772–1834* (Lexington, Ky., 1974), p. 241, who discusses Crawford's visit to Virginia in 1823 but does not mention his stopover with TJ.

to British smuggling and British tampering with the Indians. It would be an entering wedge to incalculable mischief, a powerful agent towds. separating the states.

I send you the rough draught of the letter I propose to write to F. Gilmer for your considn. and correction and salute you affectly.

*"to wit. 1. Our commercial intercourse embracing navign of St. Lawrence and Missipi.
2. Suppression of slave trade.
3. Northern boundary.
4. Fisheries on W. coast of N. F-land.
5. Points of Maritime law.
6. Russian Ukase as to N. W. coast of America."[27]

Madison to Jefferson

Montpellier Dec. 18, 1823

DEAR SIR,

I return the letter from Mr. Gilmer. It would have been more agreeable if he had not suspended his decision as to the ulterior object offered him; but he cannot be blamed for yielding to the reasons he gives for it.[28] There is weight in what he suggests as to an extension of his research into Germany; and there may be some advantage in the attraction which a professor from that quarter might have for students from the German regions of the United States. But there will be time for consideration before a final instruction on the subject will be given. If the Continent of Europe however be opened at all, it may be well not to shut out some other parts of it. I hope if the Assembly fulfils our wishes at an early period of the Session, that the Envoy will be able to embark before the end of it if it be a long one.

27. For Rush's instructions on these issues, see Ammon, pp. 515–25.
28. For TJ's negotiations with Gilmer, see Malone, VI, pp. 397–402.

Recruiting a Faculty, 1824

Early in 1824, the Virginia General Assembly agreed to relieve the university from its pledge to repay the loans from the Literary Fund, although the assembly maintained the right to reimpose this debt, if necessary. At the same time, however, it promised $50,000 for books and equipment, to be paid by the state from its claim against the federal government for interest on expenditures during the War of 1812. It was, therefore, time to assemble a faculty.

At its meeting in April, the Board of Visitors reported their opinion "that to obtain professors of the first order of science in their respective lines, they must resort principally to Europe."[1] Except for the premature appointment of Thomas Cooper, the board's attempts to attract professors in the United States had failed. When Cooper came under fire from "his clerical persecutors" in South Carolina, however, Jefferson was willing to reopen negotiations with him, although he did not want "to seduce him from that college, nor to force him on our colleagues by a bare majority."[2]

Madison regretted that Cooper, "at his stage of life and in the midst of his valuable labours, . . . should experience the persecutions which torment and depress him." But he opposed any efforts to entice Cooper to come to Virginia. On the other hand, "should he finally wish to exchange his present berth for one in our University, and make the proposition without any advances on our part, there could be no indelicacy in our receiving him. What I should dread," he added, "would be that notwithstanding his pre-eminent qualifications, there might be difficulties to be overcome among ourselves in the first instance; and what is worse that the spirit which persecutes him where he is, would find a co-partner here not less active in poisoning his happiness and impairing the popularity of the Institution."[3]

As early as 1818, shortly after Cooper's appointment to the faculty, Jef-

---

1. Malone, VI, p. 397.
2. TJ to JM, Jan. 7, 1824, below.
3. JM to TJ, Jan. 14, 1824, below. Cooper did not reapply to Virginia.

ferson had invited George Ticknor, later professor of modern languages at Harvard, and Nathaniel Bowditch, an eminent mathematician from Massachusetts, to join the faculty, but both declined. Thereafter, the rector and the Board of Visitors concentrated their search for "supereminent professors" in Europe, Jefferson arguing that "with scientists and men of letters, the globe itself is one great commonwealth, in which no geographical divisions are acknowledged; but all compose one fraternity of fellow citizens."[4] He reserved only the appointments in law and moral philosophy for Americans.

In an effort to persuade Gilmer to undertake the task of recruiting professors in Europe, the board offered him the law and government chair. "The offer of this," Jefferson told Madison, "with the mission [abroad] would probably be accepted."[5] Madison had always preferred Gilmer for the law professorship, and he agreed that there was "no one better suited for the mission." Moreover, "the gratification of such a trip to Europe, will doubtless be felt as an item in the compensation."[6]

Gilmer quickly accepted the recruiting tour but delayed a decision on the faculty appointment. At its spring meeting in 1824, the board decided that its budget could not cover the expenses of ten professors, for whom the pavilions had been built. Instead, they decided on seven professorships, with an eighth one in anatomy being conditional upon funding. If Gilmer's search was successful, the board hoped to open the university in February 1825.[7]

Two days after the board meeting, the rector recalculated the budget and found that the surplus would allow the Visitors to "safely engage 8. professors. . . . The opportunity of procuring the anatomical professor is so advantageous, that I propose to make the *provisional* instruction for his engagement *absolute*. On this subject," he wrote Madison, "I ask your opinion, to be given to me without delay that it may be in time to be acted on."[8] Madison promptly acceded "to the [p]rovision of an Anatomical as an 8th. pro[f]essor" if Gilmer could find "a foreigner of very high distinction . . . for that Chair." Otherwise, "it may be well to take the chance of filling it a[t] home."[9]

Ten days later, the rector officially appointed Gilmer as a search committee of one to proceed to Europe to engage professors for the different schools of the University of Virginia. Gilmer sailed from New York in May with letters of introduction to Richard Rush, the American minister to Great Britain; Samuel Parr, whom Jefferson called the "purest classic" in the world; and Dugald Stewart of Edinburgh, the leading proponent of Scotish "common

---

4. Peterson, p. 977.
5. TJ to JM, Nov. 6, 1823, above.
6. JM to TJ, Nov. 11, 1823, above.
7. Malone, VI, p. 398.
8. TJ to JM and the Board of Visitors of the University of Virginia, Apr. 9, 1824, below.
9. JM to TJ, Apr. 16, 1824, below. Only Chapman Johnson voted against the appointment; see TJ to JM, May 16, 1824, below.

sense" philosophy, whom Jefferson had met in Paris. He also carried copies of the engraving of the university's ground plan in case anyone doubted the existence of a university in the middle of rural Virginia. The Board of Visitors had already agreed to appoint George Blaetterman, a German living in London who had been recommended by Ticknor, as professor of modern languages, if Gilmer approved after a personal interview. He signed on with Gilmer quickly.

For the other positions, Gilmer encountered difficulties in England that ran the gamut from ignorance to indifference. Madison hoped that "Scotland will do more for him than Engd. is likely to do. Germany may open a field of choice better in some respects than either," he advised. "But the alien language, and less affinity of manners are grounds of unfavorable comparison. It wd. seem," he concluded, "that we must at last be obliged to resort to the domestic fund for filling most of the Chairs," if Gilmer failed to find "foreigners of the first rate only."[10]

In the fall, shortly after their regular meeting, the board received a crushing letter from Gilmer that seemed to confirm Madison's prediction. "Within 6. hours after we had all dispersed yesterday to our several homes," Jefferson informed Madison, "the inclosed most unwelcome letter came to hand. I have never recieved a greater damper on my hopes and spirits." Gilmer had failed to persuade any first-rate professor to leave his ancient and honorable position at Oxford or Cambridge for the relatively low stipend and heavy teaching load at a new and untried university in the wilds of America.

Jefferson was distraught. "I consider that his return without any professors will compleatly quash every hope of the institution. The legislature will consider the undertaking as abortive, and the public also, considering the thing as having failed. We can no longer hope to recieve the number of students, which their expectations hitherto flattered us with." But the eternally optimistic Jefferson thought that there might be a way out, much as he might dislike it. "I think therefore he had better bring the best he can get. They will be preferable to secondaries of our country because the stature of these is known," he concluded, wringing a favorable result out of unfavorable facts, "whereas those he would bring would be unknown, and would be readily imagined to be of the high grade we have calculated on."[11]

Madison conceded that "the foreign prospect for the University is very gloomy, and the domestic far from bright." But he assumed Jefferson's usually optimistic role and counseled his colleague: "We must not however despond. What occurs to me as best on the occasion, is that Mr. Gilmer pro[ceed] to exhaust the experiment in G. B. and if necessary then extend it to Ireland. . . . If he could obtain good professors of the anticent languages. and of

---

10. JM to TJ, Sept. 17, 1824, below. For TJ's briefing of Gilmer, see Malone, VI, pp. 399-401. For references to progress reports from Gilmer, see TJ to JM, Aug. 8, 1824, below, and JM to TJ, Aug. 16, 1824, and Sept. 17, 1824, below.

11. TJ to JM, Oct. 6, 1824, below.

Mathematics, and astronomy, these with the accomplished professor of Modern Languages, would blunt the edge of the disappointment and abridge essentially the task of filling vacancies from our own Stock."

Moreover, Madison preferred native secondary professors to those from abroad, especially if they were "of good dispositions better ascertained; and the two be in the same degree of secondaries." To buttress his preference, he observed that "the Medical class in our Country is so numerous that a competent choice may be hoped for. Natural History has been a good deal studied of late in the North[er]n States, but I rather recollect [n]ames, than know characters." Nonetheless, he knowledgeably listed leading figures in chemistry, natural history, and law.[12]

Then, almost miraculously, a glorious letter from Gilmer quickly "dispelled the gloom which that from Edinb[ur]g had produced," Jefferson confessed, his optimism returning, "and gives me hopes that all will end well."[13] A sick and exhausted Gilmer soon arrived in New York with news that he had found five of the six professors he had searched for abroad: George Blaetterman, modern languages; Thomas H. Key of Cambridge, mathematics; George Long of Cambridge, classics; Charles Bonnycastle, "son of the Mathematician," according to Jefferson, who had been educated at the Royal Military Academy, natural philosophy; and Robley Dunglison, who had been educated in medicine in London and Erlangen, Germany, anatomy.[14] In New York, Gilmer signed the sixth, John Patton Emmet, an Irish-born mathematician and physician, for the chair of natural history.[15]

Madison found Gilmer's appointments "very encouraging." He especially liked their youthful ages, which ran from twenty-five to twenty-nine, except for Blaetterman. "They will be the less inflexible in their habits," he thought, "the more improveable in their qualifications, and will last the longer." Both he and Jefferson still hoped to persuade Gilmer to accept the law professorship, leaving the moral philosophy or ethics chair as the other post for an American.[16]

"This subject," the rector wrote, "has been so exclusively confined to the

---

12. JM to TJ, Oct. 9, 1824, below.

13. TJ to JM, Oct. 11, 1824, below.

14. TJ to JM, Nov. 20, 1824, below. The first faculty is discussed in William B. O'Neal, *Pictorial History of the University of Virginia* (Charlottesville, 1970), pp. 44-46, and Malone, VI, p. 409. The appointment of Bonnycastle threatened to create a minor diplomatic incident since he had received a free education at the Royal Military Academy by signing a bond not to enter foreign service without the government's consent. TJ asked Rufus King, the American minister to the Court of St. James's, to stop prosecution on the bond and for remission of any penalty that might be imposed on the Virginia professor. The British government refused to relent officially but eventually dropped legal proceedings against the delinquent professor as a personal favor to the American ambassador; see Robert Ernst, *Rufus King, American Federalist* (Chapel Hill, 1968), pp. 398-99.

15. TJ to JM, Dec. 10, 1824, below, and JM to TJ, Dec. 15, 1824, below.

16. JM to TJ, Dec. 3, 1824, below.

RECRUITING A FACULTY, 1824

clergy, that when forced to seek one, not of that body, it becomes difficult." Even so, he was optimistic about overcoming the difficulty since the literature "for the general science of mind" was abundant "and that of Ethics is still more trite." "Any ingenious man" with a solid education, "otherwise worthy of a place among his scientific brethren might soon qualify himself."[17]

It was Madison who came up with the best candidate for the post, which was expanded to include belles lettres. "What are the collateral aptitudes of George Tucker the member of Congress. I have never seen him, and can only judge of him by a volume of miscellaneous Essays published not very long ago. They are written with acuteness and elegance," said the retired president as critic, "and indicate a capacity and taste for Philosophical literature."[18]

Jefferson jumped at the suggestion and fired off inquiries that resulted "in a highly fav[ora]ble acct of his character and temper." Like Madison, he judged Tucker's talents "from his Essay on Taste, Morals and National politics." And he had learned in the tangled web of Virginia relationships that Tucker was a relative of Cabell's by marriage, which might incline that board member in Tucker's favor. "Altho' not a native" (Tucker was born in Bermuda but had studied law at William and Mary), "he is considered as thoroughly a Virginian and of high standing," Jefferson noted.[19] Jefferson's inquiries strengthened Madison's "favorable view of his fitness for the Ethical Chair," and Tucker was subsequently appointed. At the age of fifty, he was by far the senior member of the teaching staff, and he became chairman of the faculty in 1825.[20]

By the end of the year, the faculty began trickling in. "Long and Blaettermann are here located in their pavilions as drawn by lot," Jefferson reported. Long, who drew Pavilion V, which had the most impressive portico of all, "is a fine young man and well qualified." Blaetterman, who drew Pavilion IV across the lawn, was "rather a rough looking German, speaking English roughly, but of an excellent mind and high qualifications." Key, Bonnycastle, and Dunglison were en route from London, but the rector thought that "it is time they should be here now."[21]

While the faculty was being recruited, Jefferson had begun "to make out a catalogue of books for our library, being encouraged to it by the possession of a collection of excellent [booksellers'] catalogues, and knowing no one, capable, to whom we could refer the task. It has been laborious far beyond my expectation," he groused about his self-assigned job, "having already devoted 4. hours a day to it for upwards of two months, and the whole day for some

---

17. TJ to JM, Nov. 30, 1824, below.
18. JM to TJ, Dec. 3, 1824, below.
19. TJ to JM, Dec. 10, 1824, below.
20. JM to TJ, Dec. 15, 1824, below. See also O'Neal, p. 46, and Robert C. McLean, *George Tucker: Moral Philosopher and Man of Letters* (Chapel Hill, 1961).
21. TJ to JM, Dec. 26, 1824, below.

time past and not yet in sight of the end. It will enable us to judge what the object will cost," he told Madison. Recalling that his friend had explored the study of divinity "in your early days," he asked Madison to suggest "any works really worthy of place in the catalogue. The good moral writers," he added, "Christian as well as Pagan I have set down; but there are writers of celebrity in religious metaphysics, such as Duns Scotus, etc. . . . whom you can suggest."[22]

Madison agreed "to make out a list of Theological Works," but he protested that he was "less qualified for the task than you seem to think." Moreover, "there is a difficulty in marking the proper limit to so inexhaustible a chapter, whether with a view to the library in its infant or more mature state."[23] But he began a "very leisurely [search] in noting such Authors as seemed proper for the collection," working his way through the "five first Centuries" of Christianity, when Jefferson prodded him two weeks later for his list.

Since he had found the task tedious, "especially considering the intermixture of the doctrinal and controversial part of Divinity with the moral and metaphysical part," Madison quickly incorporated "the list I had made out, with an addition on the same paper, of such Books as a hasty glance of a few catalogues and my recollection suggested."[24] Two weeks later, Jefferson sent Madison his completed catalogue of 6,860 volumes, costing $24,076 "or 3 ½ D[ollars] a vol. on an average of all sizes." If the board could invest $16,000 in stock, it would establish an endowment yielding $1,000 "a year forever which beginning with such a nucleus as this would make and keep our library what it should be."[25]

In the midst of their preparations to open the University of Virginia, Madison and Jefferson learned of Lafayette's dramatic and triumphant return to the United States as the "nation's guest." His visit to America, Madison predicted, "will make an annus mirabilis in the history of Liberty."[26] For Jefferson, the visit was equally important for its effect on the Union. "Every occasion which rallies us to a single object," he wrote, "rekindles our union in mutual affection and strengthens the habit of considering our country as one and indivisible."[27]

22. TJ to JM, Aug. 8, 1824, below.
23. JM to TJ, Aug. 16, 1824, below.
24. TJ to JM, Sept. 3, 1824, below, and JM to TJ, Sept. 10, 1824, below. See the enclosure to the latter letter, entitled "A Theological Catalogue for the Library of the University of Virginia."
25. TJ to JM, Sept. 24, 1824, below.
26. JM to TJ, Sept. 10, 1824, below. For an illustrated account of Lafayette's tour of all twenty-four American states, see Stanley J. Idzerda, Anne C. Loveland, and Marc H. Miller, *Lafayette, Hero of Two Worlds: The Art and Pageantry of His Farewell Tour of America, 1824–1825* (Hanover, N.H., 1989).
27. TJ to Francis W. Gilmer, Oct. 12, 1824, in the Jefferson Papers of the University of Virginia, 1732–1828, microfilm, reel 9.

Jefferson informed his friend that "Charlottesville is preparing for La Fayette. As he will see you at your own house," he observed, "we shall hope you will come here with him."[28] But Lafayette's plans changed, and he visited Monticello before stopping at Montpellier. "He will be here on Thursday," the Sage of Monticello told Madison, "and expresses his hope to meet you here.... If Mrs Madison will accompany you it will be the more welcome to us all. There is a scarcity of carriages," he added. "Yours will be a convenience if you can come in it."[29]

On November 4, 1824, General Lafayette arrived at Monticello, escorted by the Albemarle County Lafayette Guards and a long procession of citizens. The eighty-one-year-old Jefferson, who was recovering from an illness of almost a month, tottered unsteadily to greet his friend, whom he had not seen since the early months of the French Revolution. His feeble steps quickened as he approached Lafayette for a fraternal embrace, a dramatic and emotional moment that brought tears to the eyes of both men.

"God bless you, General," said the host.

"Bless you my dear Jefferson," replied the guest of the nation.[30]

Madison arrived about sunset, just as the company began dessert. "My old friend embraced me with great warmth," he wrote Dolley the next morning. "He is in fine health and spirits but so much increased in bulk and changed in aspect that I should not have known him."[31]

The next day, the "Hero of the Revolution with two of its Sages" initiated the Rotunda with the first public dinner at the academical village, with Lafayette as "its first guest." Lafayette sat next to Jefferson and Madison.[32] The general thought Jefferson was "much aged" after a third of a century but "marvelously well" and "in full possession of all the vigor of his mind and heart." Lafayette's secretary observed that Madison on this occasion was the sharpest of the guests "for the originality of his mind and the delicacy of his illusions."[33]

After ten days with Jefferson, Lafayette set out for Montpellier for a week's visit with the Madisons. "I would have accompanied the General today," the octogenarian wrote his friend, "but for two reasons, I have not strength, and it would only have added to your embarrassment."[34]

28. TJ to JM, Sept. 24, 1824, below.
29. TJ to JM, Nov. 1, 1824, below.
30. Malone, VI, p. 404, gives a brief account. The quotations are from the *Central Gazette of Albemarle* (Nov. 10, 1824), cited in *Lafayette in America, Day by Day*, ed. J. Bennett Nolan (Baltimore, 1934), p. 257.
31. Ketcham, p. 664.
32. TJ to the marquis de Lafayette, Oct. 9, 1824, in Thomas Jefferson, *Thomas Jefferson: Writings*, ed. Merrill D. Peterson (New York, 1984), p. 1496, and Malone, VI, p. 408.
33. Malone, VI, p. 405, and Ketcham, p. 664.
34. TJ to JM, Nov. 15, 1824, below.

─────────── THE LETTERS ───────────

Jefferson to Madison

Monticello Jan. 7, 1824

DEAR SIR

I send you two letters of Dr. Cooper for perusal. Altho' the trustees of that College and the Legislature have supported him most triumphantly against his clerical persecutors, yet it is evident he does not feel himself secure. I think you will see from these letters that he keeps us in his eye. And altho' I doubt, were he now offered a place here, whether he would think he could accept it with honor, when so much has been done for him there, yet I suspect he wishes it. Something from him, in a former letter, gave me a favorable opening for hazarding an intimation from which he might infer that his engagements there would in honor preclude all views of ours on him, as well on principle, as that we should be open, beyond all others, to loss, by an example of pyrating on a sister institution. But these letters are written since that intimation. Knowing you concur with me in friendship for him, as well as in high opinion of his qualifications, I wished you to know exactly the state of his mind, and the ground on which we may be placed. I have no hesitation in saying I should be willing myself to accept him, but not to seduce him from that college, nor to force him on our colleagues by a bare majority. Probably however there might not be more than one dissentient among us; but the former objection would be a sufficient bar. Affectly. yours.

TH. JEFFERSON

Madison to Jefferson

Montpellier Jan. 14, 1824

D̲ᴿ SIR

I return the letters from Doc.ʳ Cooper inclosed in yours of the 7th. It is truly to be lamented that at his stage of life and in the midst of his valuable labours, he should experience the persecutions which torment and depress him. Should he finally wish to exchange his present berth for one in our University, and make the proposition without any advances on our part, there could be no indelicacy in our receiving him. What I should dread would be that notwithstanding his pre-eminent qualifications, there might be difficulties to be overcome among ourselves in the first instance; and what is worse that the spirit which persecutes him where he is, would find a co-partner here not less active in poisoning his happiness and impairing the popularity of the Institution. We must await the contingency and act for the best.

You have probably noticed that the manner in which the Constitution as it stands may operate in the approaching election of President, is multiplying projects for amending it. If electoral Districts, and an eventual decision by joint ballot of the two Houses of Congress could be established, it would I think be a real improvement; and as the smaller States would approve the one, and the larger the other, a spirit of compromise might adopt both.

An appeal from an abortive ballot in the first meeting of the Electors, to a reassemblage of them, a part of the several plans, has something plausible, and in comparison with the existing arrangement, might not be inadmissible. But it is not free from material objections. It relinquishes, particularly, the policy of the Constitution in allowing as little time as possible for the Electors to be known and tampered with. And beside the opportunities for intrigue furnished by the interval between the first and second meeting, the danger of having one electoral Body played off against another, by artful misrepresentations rapidly transmitted, a danger not to be avoided, would be at least doubled. It is a fact within my own knowledge, that the equality of votes which threatened such mischief in 1801 was the result of false assurances despatched at the critical moment to the Electors of one State, that the votes of another would be different from what they proved to be.

Having received letters from certain quarters on the subject of the proposed amendments, which I could not decline answering, I have suggested for consideration, "that each Elector should give two votes, one naming his first choice, the other naming his next choice. If there be a majority for the first, he to be elected; if not, and a majority for the next, he to be elected: If there be not a majority for either, then the names having the two highest number of votes on the two lists taken together, to be referred to a joint ballot of the Legislature."[1] It is not probable that this modification will be relished by either of those to whom it has been suggested; both of them having in hand projects of their own. Nor am I sure that there may not be objections to it which have been overlooked. It was recommended to my reflections by its avoiding the inconveniċes of a second meeting of Electors, and at the same time doubling the chance of avoiding a final resort to Congress. I have intimated to my correspondents my disinclination to be brought in any way into the public discussion of the subject; the rather as every thing having a future relation only to a Presidential Election may be misconstrued into some bearing on that now depending. Affectionately yours

JAMES MADISON

---

1. Five candidates vied for the presidency in 1824, three of them in Monroe's cabinet: John Quincy Adams, secretary of state; William H. Crawford, secretary of the treasury; and John C. Calhoun, secretary of war. The other contenders were Henry Clay, Speaker of the House, and General Andrew Jackson, senator from Tennessee.

Jefferson to Madison and the Board of Visitors of the University of Virginia

Monticello Apr. 9, 1824

Dear Sir

Notwithstanding the reduction which was made in the rents proposed, it appears that that on the salaries will so much enlarge our surplus, that we may very safely engage 8. professors, and still have a surplus this year of 6000. d. and annually after of 5024. D. The opportunity of procuring the anatomical professor is so advantageous, that I propose to make the *provisional* instruction for his engagement *absolute*. On this subject I ask your opinion, to be given to me without delay that it may be in time to be acted on. The statements below will enable you to form your opinion. Accept assurances of my esteem and respect.

Th: Jefferson

Estimated account for 1824———

Current expences of the institution for this year	4,500	
expence of procuring Professors	1,500	
Salaries of 8. Professors for Oct. Nov. Dec.	3,000	
Surplus for apparatus, book, contingencies	6,000	
To be paid by the annuity of 1824	15,000	

Annual account after 1824. as may be now estimated.

		D
Income. Annuity	15,000	
Rent of 6. Hotels @ 150.D	900	
100 Dormitories @ 16.D	1600	
9. smaller ds. @ 12.D	108	
University rent on 218. students @ 12. D	2,616	20,224
Expenditure. Current expences of the Institution	3,000	
8. Professors @ 1500 . D. each	12,000	
a military Instructor	200	
Surplus for apparatus, books, contingencies	5,024	20,224

this year's surplus of 6000. D. will afford for text books 1000. apparatus
    Chemical 1000. Anatomical 1000
    Astronomical, physical, mathematical 3000.

Madison to Jefferson

[Montpellier] Apr. 10, 1824

Dr. Sir

I inclose the letter dated Jany. 24. 1796. referred to in your memorandum.[2] You will observe that it acknowledges two of mine, one of Decr. 27. 1795 the other of Jany. 10. 1796. As these are not among the letters from me to you, which you were so good as to transfer from your files to mine, and as it may be proper for me to examine them, for the reasons you wished a return of the one inclosed, I must request the favor of you to see whether they may not have been left behind and if so to forward them. It is possible that others may also have been overlooked. Health and all other happiness

JAMES MADISON

Madison to Jefferson

[Montpellier] Apr. 16, 1824

Dr. Sir

Yours of the 9th. was not recd. till the evening before the last, and could not be sooner answered than by the mail which [p]asses[3] our Court House today. As it is pro[p]er to give as wide an opening to the Uni[v]ersity as we can, I readily accede to the [p]rovision of an Anatomical as an 8th. pro[f]essor, which you propose as within a [f]air estimate of its resources. I think however that unless a foreigner of very high distinction can be obtained for that Chair, it may be well to take the chance of filling it a[t] home. Our Medical School more than any other seems to have risen towards a level with those of Europe; and in none of the learned classes, is there perhaps so much danger of jealousies and antipathies which might obstruct the popularity and success of a Professor from abroad.

J M.

Jefferson to Madison

Monticello May 16, 1824

Dear Sir

You will see by the inclosed letter from Mr Cabell that a project is in agitation respecting Wm. and Mary Coll. which gives him much alarm. I

2. TJ's memorandum to JM has not been found. Nor has his letter of Jan. 24, 1796, been found, but the enclosures in that letter (TJ to George Wythe, Jan. 12, 1796, and Jan. 16, 1796) are printed in ch. 20, above, as are JM's letters of Dec. 27, 1795, and Jan. 10, 1796.

3. Because of the frayed left margin of this letter, it has been necessary to supply the bracketed letters throughout this letter.

communicate to you the letter as he requests, and with it my answer, as shewing the point in which I view it. I will ask their return when read, that I may be enabled to lodge my answer in Richmd. before his arrival there.[4]

On the question of engaging a Medical professor, yourself, Mr Cabell, Genl. Cocke and myself concurred in the affirmative, Mr Johnson was in the negative. 4. being a majority of the whole board, I considered it as so decided, and gave the instruction accdly. Our agent sailed from N. Y. on the 8th. inst. I did not consult Genl. Breckenridge and Mr Loyall, because neither were acqd. with the previous proceedings on the subject, and their distance also, and the promptness of decision necessary did not give time. Ever and affectly. your's

TH:J.

Madison to Jefferson

Montpellier May 20, 1824

DEAR SIR,

I return the letter from Mr. Cabell with your answer to it, inclosed in yours of the 16th, just come to hand.

It is not probable that a removal of the College from Williamsburg will be espoused by a majority of the Visitors, controuled as they will be by the popular voice in that quarter. If it should, Richmond will not be without competitors. The pretensions of Petersburg have already been brought forward. And if, in its new position, it is to be co-ordinate with the present University, there will be a bold claim by the Ultramontane Country. After all, is the climate of Richmond so different in the public eye from that of Williamsburg as to make it a satisfactory substitute? Is not Richmond also becoming too much of a city to be an eligible site for such an Institution? The most extensive and flourishing of our learned Institutions are not in the most populous towns. That in Philadelphia is eclipsed by rising seminaries in other parts of the State. In New York the case is not dissimilar. Be all this as it may be, I concur entirely in your opinion, that the best counsel for us is to be passive during the experiment, and turn the result to the best account we can for the interest of Science and of the State.[5]

I wish Mr. Cabell may comply with your invitation to a conversation interview on his way to Warminster; with an understanding that mine is included, and that we should be much gratified in welcoming him and his lady over our threshhold. Yours with affection and esteem.

JAMES MADISON

---

4. For the petition to remove the College of William and Mary from Williamsburg to Richmond, see Malone, VI, pp. 411–13.

5. The petition to move the college was defeated in the Virginia House of Delegates in 1825; see *ibid.*, p. 413.

Madison to Jefferson

Montpellier July 12, 1824

Dr. Sir

I have recd. from Mr. H. Wheaton who is engaged in a Biography of the late W. Pinkney a letter wch. I inclose with my answer. If your recollection or memoranda can confirm or enlarge the information I have given with respect to the origin of the Embargo, be so good as to return my answer that it may be improved: If otherwise, it may be sealed and forwarded: The letter from Mr. Wheaton to be returned in either case. I infer from a former letter from Mr. W. that his work will probably embrace somewhat of a historical review of the Biographical period.

Jefferson to Madison

Monticello July 14, 1824

Dear Sir,

I have attentively read your letter to Mr Wheaton on the question whether at the date of the message to Congress recommending the embargo of 1807 we had knolege of the order of council of Nov. 11.; and according to your request I have resorted to my papers, as well as my memory for the testimony these might afford additional to your's. There is no fact in the course of my life which I recollect more strongly than that of my being at the date of the message in possession of an English newspaper containing a copy of the proclamation. I am almost certain too that it was under the ordinary authentication of the government and between Nov. 11. and Dec. 17. there was time enough, 35. days to admit the reciept of such a paper, which I think came to me through a private channel, probably put on board some vessel about sailing, the moment it appeared.[6]

Turning to my papers I find that I had prepared a first draught of a message in which was this paragraph: 'The British regulations had before reduced us to a direct voyage to a single port of their enemies, and it is now believed they will interdict all commerce whatever with them. A proclamation too of that government of —— (not officially indeed communicated to us, yet so given out to the public as to become a rule of action with them) seems to have shut the door on all negociation with us except as to the single aggression on the Chesapeak.' You however suggested a substitute (which I have now

---

6. Although TJ did not transmit the orders-in-council of Nov. 11, 1807, to Congress until Feb. 14, 1808, news of their promulgation reached New York on Dec. 12, 1807, and appeared in the Philadelphia *Aurora* on Dec. 17, 1807, and the *National Intelligencer* on Dec. 18, 1807. For TJ's draft of the embargo message, Dec. 17, 1807, and JM's revision, Dec. 17, 1807, see ch. 34, above. On the next day, TJ sent his embargo message to Congress. See Malone, V, p. 481; Brant, IV, p. 394, and Richardson, I, p. 433.

before me written with a pencil and) which, with some unimportant amendments I preferred to my own, and was the one I sent to Congress. It was in these words 'the *communications* now made, shewing the great and increasing dangers with which seamen etc., —— ports of the United States.'⁷ This shews that we communicated to them papers of information on the subject; and as it was our interest, and our duty to give them the strongest information we possessed to justify our opinion and their action on it, there can be no doubt we sent them this identical paper. For what stronger could we send them? I am the more strengthened in the belief that we did send it from the fact, which the newspapers of the day will prove, that in the reprobations of the measure published in them by it's enemies, they indulged themselves in severe criticisms on our having considered a newspaper as a proper document to lay before Congress and a sufficient foundation for so serious a measure, and considering this as no sufficient information of the fact, they continued perseveringly to deny that we had knolege of the order of council when we recommended the embargo, admitting because they could not deny the existence of the order, they insisted only on our supposed ignorance of it as furnishing them a ground of crimination. But I had no idea that this gratuitous charge was believed by any one at this day. In addition to our testimony, I am sure Mr. Gallatin, General Dearborn and Mr. Smith will recollect that we possessed the newspaper and acted on a view of the proclamation it contained. If you think this statement can add anything in corroboration of your's, make what use you please of it, and accept assurances of my constant affection and respect.

Jefferson to Madison

Monticello Aug. 8, 1824

DEAR SIR

I recd. yesterday a letter from Mr Gilmer which I now inclose, as also a former one, which had only communicated his arrival at Liverpool. I add also a letter from Mr Rush. So far his trust is going on well. I wish the suggestion from Mr Brougham respecting Ivory may be found groundless.⁸ There is no mathematician in Gr. Br. who can rival him but Woodhouse professor of Mathematics at Cambridge, who is following the track and close treading on the heels of the first members of the French school. The Ed[inburgh] Reviewers place Ivory in the first rank, and his very name would set our institution

---

7. For the full paragraph, see Brant, IV, p. 395. Also see ch. 34, above.

8. Gilmer reported that Henry Brougham, a founder of the *Edinburgh Review*, had recommended James Ivory for the mathematics post but added that the professor "had recently been a good deal disordered in his mind"; see Francis Walker Gilmer to TJ, June 21, 1824, in *Correspondence of Thomas Jefferson and Francis Walker Gilmer, 1814–1826*, ed. Richard Beale Davis (Columbia, S.C., 1946), pp. 86–87.

above all rivalship. I had long ago cast my eye on him, but was told that his birth [berth] at the head of the Mathematical school at Woolwich was too good to expect him.

I have undertaken to make out a catalogue of books for our library, being encouraged to it by the possession of a collection of excellent catalogues, and knowing no one, capable, to whom we could refer the task. It has been laborious far beyond my expectation, having already devoted 4. hours a day to it for upwards of two months, and the whole day for some time past and not yet in sight of the end. It will enable us to judge what the object will cost. The chapter in which I am most at a loss is that of divinity; and knowing that in your early days you bestowed attention on this subject, I wish you could suggest to me any works really worthy of place in the catalogue. The good moral writers, Christian as well as Pagan I have set down; but there are writers of celebrity in religious metaphysics, such as Duns Scotus etc. alii tales [and others of such kind] whom you can suggest. Pray think of it and help me.

Our library must of course possess such a standard book as the Polyglott bible. Lackington the cheapest bookseller in England by far, states it's price in his catalogue at 50. Guineas or 333. D. There is a good copy now to be had in Boston for 85. D. I should not hesitate to take on myself the responsibility of the purchase but for the scantiness of our building funds, and the slow progress in the collection of subscriptions. Yet with your encouragement, I might perhaps do it.[9] Affectionately yours.

Th: J.

Madison to Jefferson

[Montpellier] Aug. 12, 1824

Dear Sir

The bearer Mr. E. Tayloe, son of Col. Tayloe of Washington is desirous of making a respectful call at Monticello, and I can not refuse to his motive the gratification of a line presenting him to you. He is at present a resident of Fredericksburg reading Law with his kinsman Mr. Lomax; and appears to be quite estimable and amiable.

Mr. T. is so good as to take charge of the 4 last volumes of Las Casas, which have been waiting for some such oppy. to get back to you. With every allowance for the painting talent and partial pencil of the Author, the picture of Napoleon, exhibits a most gigantic mind, and with some better features than the world had seen in his character. Affectionate respects

James Madison

P.S. I have just rec'd your letter enclosing Mr. Gs and Rs.

9. See Malone, VI, pp. 401-2.

Madison to Jefferson

Montpellier Aug. 16, 1824

D^R SIR,

I acknowledged in my last yours of the 8th, and now return the letters of Mr. Gilmer and Mr. Rush inclosed in it. It would be a matter of much regret if insanity should befall such a man as Ivory; but it is to be hoped his condition will be fixed before he leaves England or rather before any engagement of him. I hope Mr. Gilmer will be able to avoid, also, men much advanced in life. After a certain age they will be less flexible to our manners, and the sooner lost by death or debility. A limitation to a suitable age furnishes a convenient reply to domestic applicants beyond it.

The cheapness of the Polyglot in Boston is very tempting; but considering the ticklish footing on which we are with the Assembly and the chance that the article may remain unsold, it may be best to suspend the purchase till we can decide more understandingly. I observe in the London Catalogue of Longman & Co., in 1816, there are several copies of Walton's Polyglot, one of which, in 6 volumes, fol. is at £42 sterling, noted as the "Republican" copy because patronised by Cromwell and his Council. You have I presume this catalogue. If not, I will send it.

I will endeavour to make out a list of Theological Works, but am less qualified for the task than you seem to think; and fear also that my Catalogues are less copious than might be wished. There is a difficulty in marking the proper limit to so inexhaustible a chapter, whether with a view to the Library in its infant or more mature state. Health and all other happiness

Jefferson to Madison

Monticello Sept. 3, 1824

TH:J. TO J. M.

I am near closing my catalogue, and it is important I should recieve the kindness of your Theological supplement, by the 1st. or 2d. mail, or it's insertion will be impracticable. Be so good as to expedite it as much as possible. Affectionate salutations.

Madison to Jefferson

Montpellier Sept. 10, 1824

DEAR SIR

On the rec.^t of yours of Aug. 8, I turned my thoughts to its request on the subject of a Theological Catalogue for the Library of the University; and not being aware that so early an answer was wished, as I now find was the case, I had proceeded very leisurely in noting such Authors as seemed proper for the collection. Supposing also, that altho' Theology was not to be taught in the University, its Library ought to contain pretty full information for such as might voluntarily seek it in that branch of Learning, I had contemplated as much of a comprehensive and systematic selection as my scanty materials admitted; and had gone thro' the five first Centuries of Xnity when yours of the 3d instant came to hand which was the evening before the last. This conveyed to me more distinctly the limited object your letter had in view, and relieved me from a task which I found extremely tedious; especially considering the intermixture of the doctrinal and controversial part of Divinity with the moral and metaphysical part, and the immense extent of the whole. I send you the list I had made out, with an addition on the same paper, of such Books as a hasty glance of a few catalogues and my recollection suggested. Perhaps some of them may not have occurred to you and may suit the blank you have not filled. I am sorry I could not make a fair copy without failing to comply with the time pointed out.

I find by a letter from Fayette, in answer to a few lines I wrote him on his arrival at N. Y. that he means to see us before the 19th of Oc^r, as you have probably learned from himself. His visit to the United States will make an annus mirabilis in the history of Liberty. Affectionately yours

JAMES MADISON

ENCLOSURE
A Theological Catalogue for the Library of the University of Virginia

Cent^y. I. ———Clemens Epist^e. to the Corinthians—published at Cambridge 1788.
Ignatius Epist^s————Amsterdam 1607.
Cotelier—Recuiel de Monumens des pères dans les tems apostoliques edit par le Cleve Amsterdam 1774, 2 v. fol.
Flavius Josephus [in English by Whiston] Amsterdam 1726, 2v. fol.
Philo Judaeus [Greek & Latin] English Ed^n. 1742, 2 v. fol.
Lucian's Works———Amsterdam 1743, 3 v. 4°
Fabricius Biblio Græc:
———Delectus &c. See Mosh^m. v. 1, p. 106

Cent: II. Justin Martyrs apolos, &c. [Edited by Prudent Maraud Benedictine] 1742, 1 v. fol.
Hermias———Oxford 1700—8°.
Athenagoras———Oxford 1706—8°.
Clemens Alexandrinus [Ed. by Potter] Oxford 1715 2 vol. fol.
Tertullian————Venice 1746, 1 v. fol.,
Theophilus of Antioch [first adopted the term Trinity]—1742 1 v. fol.
Irenaeus [Ed. by Grabe] 1702, 1 v. fol.
Tatian———agst. the Gentiles———Oxford, 1700, 8°.
Ammonius Saccas's Harmony of the Evangelists—

	Celsus [translated par Bouhereau] Amsterdam 1700 4°.
Cent. III.	Minutius Felix [translated by Reeves] Leiden 1672, 8°.

Origen———4 vol. fol. Greek & Latin.
Cyprian———[translated into French by Lombert] 1 v. fol.
Gregory Thaumaturgus———Grec. & Lat. 1626, 1 v. fol.
Arnobius Africanus. Amsterdam 1651, 1 v. 4°.
Anatolius———Antwerp, 1634, 1 v. fol.
Methodius Eubulius———Rome 1656, 8°.
Philostratus' life of Apollonius Tyanaeus [Grec & Lat. with notes by Godefroy Olearius, Leipsic, 1709, 1 v. fol: Frenched by De Vigenere, Englished in part by Chs. Blount.]

Cent: IV. Lactantius.———Edit by Lenglet Paris 1748, 2 v. 4°.
Eusebius of Cæsarea———
Athanasius, par Montfauçon 1698, 3 v. fol.
Antonius' [founder of the Monastic order] seven letters &c. Latin.
S^r. Cyril (of Jerusalem) Gr. & Lat. Paris 1720, 1 v. fol.
S . Hilary. Ed. by Massci Verona 1730.

Cent: IV. Lucifer, Bishop of Cagliari. Paris 1586 1 v. 8°.
Epiphanius. Gr. & Lat. Edit Pere Petau, 1622, 2 v. fol.
Optatus. Ed. by Dupin. 1700. fol.
Pacianus. Paris, 1538. 4°.
Basil (B. of Cæsarea) Gr. & Lat. 1721. 3 v. fol.
Gregory (of Nazianzi) G. & L. Paris 1609-11 2 v. fol.
———(of Nyssa) 1615 2 v. fol.
Ambrosius———Paris 1600 2 v. fol.
Jerome.———Paris 1693-1706. 5 v. fol.
Ruffinus———Paris 1580———1 v. fol.
Augustin———1679-1700 8 v. fol.
Chrysostom John Gr. & L.———10 v. fol.
Ammianus Marcellinus
Julian's works

Cent: V. Sulpicius Severus. Verona 1754, 2 v. 4°.
Isidorus (of Pelusium) Paris 1638. Gr. & L. 1 v. fol.
Cyril (of Alex^a.) Gr. & L. 6 v. fol.
Orosius———Leyden. 1738. 4°.
Theodoret. Edit by Pere Simond. G. & L. 1642. 4 v. fol. in 1684. vol. V. by Garnier.
Philostorgius, by Godefroi. G. & L. 1642, 1 v. 4°.
Vincentius Lyrinensis. Rome. 4°.
Socrates' Eccles. History
Sozomen. d°. d°.
Leo (the great) by Quesnel Lyons. 1700. fol.
Æneas (of Gaza) Gr. with Latin version, by Barthius &c. 1655. 4°.

Miscellaneous Thomas Aquinas [Do^r, Angelicus] Head of the Thomists. 12 v. fol.
The Koran, Duns Scotus [Doctor Subtilis] Head of the Scotists, 12 v. fol.
Caves Lives of the Fathers. Dailles Use & abuse of them.
Erasmus, Luther, Calvin, Socinus, Bellarmin, Chillingworth.

Council of Trent by F. Paul; by Palavicini; by Basnaze.
Grotius on the truth of Xn Religion. Sherlock's [Bishop] Sermons.
Tillotsons &c. Tillemont, Baronius, Lardner,[10] Hookers Ecclesiastical Polity. Pierson on the Creed. Bossuet on 39 Articles. Pascal's lettres Provenciales. do Penseès. Fenelon Bossuet Bourdelon Sauvin Fletcher Manillon. Warburton's Divine Legation. Hannah Adams—View of all Religions
Stackhouses———Hist. of the Bible
S^r. Isaac Newtons works on Religious subjects.
Locke's do. Stillingfleets controversy with him on the possibility of endowing matter with thought.
Clarke on the Being & Attributes of God
———Sermons.
Butler's Analogy. Eight Sermons at Boyles. Lectures by Bentley
Whitby on the 5 points.
Whiston's Theological Works.
Taylor (Jeremiah) Sermons.
John Taylor [of Norwich] agst original Sin Edward's in answer. Edward's on free will———on virtue.
Soame Jenyn's Enquiry into the nature & origin of evil
Liturgy for King's Chapel Boston.
Matheis Essays to do good. Price on Morals.
Wallaston's Religion of Nature delineated
Barclay's apology for Quakers. Wm Penn's works
King's Enquiry into the Constitution discipline & worship of the Church, within 3 first cent.
King [W^m] Essay on Origin of Evil; notes by Law. Wesley on Original Sin.
Priestley's & Horesley's controversies
Historical view of the Controversy on the intermediate state of the Soul by Dean Blackburne.
The Confessional by same.
Jone's method of settling the canonical Scripture of N. Test^t.
Leibnitz on Goodness of God, liberty of man & origin of evil.
Paley's Works. Warburton's principles of Nat. & Rev^d. Religion
Blairs Sermons. Buckmeisters (of Boston) do.
Necker's importance of Religion.
Latrobe's (Benjamin) Doctrine of the Moravians
Ray's wisdom of God in the Creation
Durham's Astrotheology.
Bibliotheca fratrum Polonorum 9 vol. fol.

The Catalogue of Eastburn & Co. New York, particularly the Theological part at the end, deserves attention. Some rare books are found in it, and might probably be bought at cheap prices.—

---

10. JM added the following note to this entry: "With life by Kippis 1788."

Madison to Jefferson

[Montpellier] Sept. 17, 1824

I return Mr. Gilmer's letter.[11] The uncertainty of his sickness, and the increase of his expence, give an unwelcome aspect to his Mission. It is to be hoped that Scotland will do more for him than Engd. is likely to do. Germany may open a field of choice better in some respects than either: But the alien language, and less affinity of manners are grounds of unfavorable comparison. It wd. seem that we must at last be obliged to resort to the domestic fund for filling most of the Chairs.

Foreigners of the first rate only would be relished by the public.

Jefferson to Madison

Monticello Sept. 24, 1824

DEAR SIR

I have got thro' my catalogue except the Alphabet and send you the result. The inclosed table shews the number, size, and cost of the whole and it's parts. 6860. vols will cost 24,076 D. or 3½ D. a vol. on an average of all sizes. If we get our 50. M D [$50,000] and also if 10,000 would do for apparatus, there would remain 16,000. to invest in stock. This would give us 1000 D. a year forever which beginning with such a nucleus as this would make and keep our library what it should be.[12]

Charlottesville is preparing for La Fayette. As he will see you at your own house we shall hope you will come here with him. But in the mean time you will be with us as a Visitor a day or two before the 4th. Affectionately yours

TH: J.

Madison to Jefferson

Montpellier Sept. 28, 1824

DEAR SIR

The list of books you have made out will do very well as a nest Egg for the Library. May not the high prices of some of them have been occasioned by a scarcity since removed by Editions both better and cheaper. I know nothing of

---

11. TJ's letter transmitting Gilmer's of July 20, 1824, has not been found. TJ received the letter on Sept. 9, 1824; see Malone, VI, p. 401.
12. See *ibid.*, p. 402.

Fayette's movements but through the Newspapers, from which it appears that he cannot leave Philada before the 1st of October. It becomes questionable I think whether he will be able to visit this quarter before the day on which he must be at Yorktown. I shall endeavor to be with you on friday or saturday evening. Always and affectionately yours

JAMES MADISON

Jefferson to Madison

Monticello Oct. 6, 1824

DEAR SIR

Within 6. hours after we had all dispersed yesterday to our several homes the inclosed most unwelcome letter came to hand.[13] I have never recieved a greater damper on my hopes and spirits. It is so contrary to the state of things as given us by Ticknor, a state which I cannot still but respect because he staid many months at each of these places. Gilmer says there are Professors who recieve 4000. Guineas a year. Certainly those do whose names are known and high. Cullen, whose salary was 50. Guineas a year, recieved 7. or 8000. G. a year. He says the Greek Professor recieves 1500. G. a year. This supposes that 250. of their 2. or 3000 students attend the lectures of that school. Russel says that in that school each student pays 3. Guin. for Gr. and 3. G. for Latin. But can we suppose that there are not young men, unprovided, who can be had on much more moderate terms? Were the literary branch of industry of such high profits generally, so many would flock into it of preference as soon to reduce it to the common level. We know too that there are fellows at those universities, of a high degree of learning, whose fellowships are, some of them, as low as 50 £ sterl. In speaking too of our having united branches never combined in the same person in Europe, he seems to have forgotten the qualification of that union, with a copy of which he was furnished, to wit 'that occasional exchanges of particular branches, in accomodation of the particular qualifications of the different Professors, were to be admitted.' Besides in their seminaries of 20. or 30. professors they must subdivide on a very different scale from our 8. professors.

However, these reflections are useless, and our only question now is, What is to be done. For he must be written to immediately or he will be come away. There being no time therefore to consult our colleagues I must ask your advice and act on such modifications of my own opinion as you may favor me with, stating what occurs to myself on first thought. I consider that his return without any professors will compleatly quash every hope of the institution. The legislature will consider the undertaking as abortive, and the public also, considering the thing as having failed. We can no longer hope to recieve the

13. Gilmer's letter of Aug. 13, 1824, from Scotland reached TJ on Oct. 5; see *ibid*.

number of students, which their expectations hitherto flattered us with. I think therefore he had better bring the best he can get. They will be preferable to secondaries of our country because the stature of these is known, whereas those he would bring would be unknown, and would be readily imagined to be of the high grade we have calculated on.

As to Leslie's proposition we cannot look at it. We have no money for an Apparatus; and I wonder much at the idea of going for it to Germany or France. If he would come here to stay his name alone would set us up. But a mere visit of two months would be perhaps worse than nothing.

I do not clearly understand Gilmer's declining *the election* we had given him. If he means the professorship of law, I should consider it a serious misfortune. Pray answer me as promptly and as fully as you can as not a day should be lost in writing to Gilmer which can be avoided. Do you not think also we had better suspend advertising the hotels, at a fixed day, under our present prospects. I will immediately desire Brockenbro' to stay that measure till I can hear from you. Absolute silence must be our motto. Ever and affectly. yours.

TH. JEFFERSON

Madison to Jefferson

Montpellier Oct. 9, 1824

DR. SIR

Yours of the 6th. inclosing the letter of Mr. Gilmer did not reach me till this evening. The foreign prospect for the University is very gloomy, and the domestic far from bright. We must not however despond. What occurs to me as best on the occasion, is that Mr. Gilmer pro[ceed] to exhaust the experiment in G. B. and if necessary then extend it to Ireland. On the question how long he should be allowed to pospone his return, I think he ought to be so limited that he may arrive with his recruits by the month of April; unless indeed a longer stay would insure some important success. If he could obtain good professors of the anticent languages. and of Mathematics, and astronomy, these with the accomplished professor of Modern Languages, would blunt the edge of the disappointment and abridge essentially the task of filling vacancies from our own Stock. I am sensible of the disadvantage and mortification of taking secondary characters, whether native or foreign; but I am not sure that the objections to the former are stronger than to the latter, especially if the former should be of good dispositions better ascertained; and the two be in the same degree of secondaries. Be this as it may it seems inc[um]bent on us to prepare for the worst by provisional enquiries in every direction for the blanks which may not be filled by Mr. Gilmer. For the Chemical chair, Vaneuxeur may claim attention. He was strongly recommended by Cooper, and If

I am no[t] mistaken, has been handsomely spoken of some where in print. It is possible he may have been put beyond our reach. The Medical class in our Country is so numerous that a competent choice may be hoped for. Natural History has been a good deal studied of late in the Northn. States, but I rather recollect [n]ames, than know characters. Say, Barton and Bigelow are among the most prominent; but I can say nothing of their collateral fitnesses; nor whether either of them wd. be attainable. Mr Elliot of S. Carolina, enjoys a very high reputation, but is he not either a wealthy Amateur or already in a professional niche? I understand Mr. Gilmer to decline the professorship of law; unless satisfactory associates should be obtained. In filling that department, we are restricted to the U. S. or rather our own State, and the difficulty will be very great. I doubt much whether my neighbour whom I mentioned for consideration in the event now communicated would leave his pursuits and *his home* for such a birth. A judgship which would not separate him altogether from the latter, and leave him a larger portion of his time, is probably in his contemplation.

Leslie would be a prize, but his terms seem to forbid the thought of him. If he could be brought over at an admissible expence, the chance of keeping him might balance other objections.[14]

There were so many candidates for the Hotels at our late meeting who have and will spread the knowledge of the time agreed on for letting them, that a change of it might beget inferences worse than the inconveniency to those appointed from a premature letting them. It may be proper for Mr. Brockenbough to impress on these the possibility that they might pay dead rent longer than they suppose.

As you wish an early answer to your letter I give you these hurried[?] ideas by Mr. Harris[15] who leaves us this afternoon or tomorrow and will be at Monticellos before you wd. receive this by the mail.

Jefferson to Madison

Monticello Oct. 11, 1824

DEAR SIR

The reciept of the inclosed letter did not give me more pleasure than I feel in communicating it to you.[16] It has dispelled the gloom which that from

---

14. JM had mentioned Judge Philip Pendelton Barbour for the law post. Neither TJ's "great persuasive power in a conversation of two hours at Monticello" nor a visit from Madison could persuade him to join the faculty; see *ibid.,* pp. 422–23. Sir John Leslie, mathematician and natural philosopher, had been a tutor in the Randolph family as a young man; see Davis, pp. 95–97.

15. Levett Harris had been consul general at St. Petersburg; see *ibid.,* V, p. 442.

16. For Gilmer's letter of Aug. 27, 1824, from London announcing the faculty appointments, see *ibid.,* VI, p. 402. TJ received it on Oct. 9, 1824.

Edinbg had produced, and gives me hopes that all will end well. With a good Professor of modern languages assured, a good one of antient languages in view, a prime Mathematician engaged, we want really nothing essential but an able Natl. Philosopher, and that he cannot fail to find. As to a Medical professor it is the one we can best do without. Nat. history we can supply here. We may therefore let him go on and hope well. I shall still however write and communicate our sentiments to him in which we differ nothing except in admitting the idea of one of our Sangrados. Better nothing than bad. It is the school we are least prepared for. Let it lie therefore, unless he should have already filled it up.

I direct the advertisement to be issued this day, as decided by the Visitors. I shall give notice to Gilmer that the Professors books will be duty free.

I have been glad to learn from Mr Harris that Alexander has not entirely abandoned all concern as to the opinions of the world. Affectly. yours

TH: J.

Jefferson to Madison

Monticello Oct. 15, 1824

DEAR SIR

I wished to have communicated to you my letter to Gilmer before I sent it off.[17] But the danger of it's not getting there before his departure induced me to send it off as soon as written. My rough draught being illegible I have taken time to make a legible copy, now inclosed, for your perusal. I think there is nothing in it which does not accord with the sentiments of your last letter. Affectionately yours

TH: J.

Madison to Jefferson

Montpellier Oct. 22, 1824

DEAR SIR

I return your letter to Gilmer as fairly copied. Will he understand that he is not to return without a Nat: Philosopher, tho' bringing the other Professors

---

17. The standard biography of Gilmer is Richard Beale Davis, *Francis Walker Gilmer: Life and Learning in Jefferson's Virginia* (Richmond, 1939).

named and despairing of that one? There will however be time for final instructions on this point after hearing further from him. Yrs. affectly

JAMES MADISON

Jefferson to Madison

Monticello Nov. 1, 1824

MY DEAR SIR

I recd yesterday from La Fayette a letter confirming his movements as stated in the Enquirer of Friday last; he says he will be here on Thursday, and expressed his hope to meet you here. I presume you also have heard from him, but hope at any rate this will reach you in time to be with us on Wednesday. If Mrs Madison will accompany you it will be the more welcome to us all. There is a scarcity of carriages. Yours will be a convenience if you can come in it.[18] I know nothing of his subsequent movements, but the understanding is that he goes hence to Montpellier and thence to Fredrbg.

Nothing more from Gilmer. Yours affectionately

TH: J.

Jefferson to Madison

Monticello Nov. 15, 1824

TH: J. TO J. M.

I would have accompanied the General to-day but for two reasons, I have not strength, and it would only have added to your embarrasment.[19] He leaves you Friday morning to partake of a dinner and ball at Fredsbg on Saturday. The miss Wrights are detained here by the sickness of one of them.[20] They go hence to the Natural bridge and return to Washington by Staunton, Winchester and Harper's ferry.

No letter yet from Gilmer. His last was Aug. 27. Affectly. yours.

---

18. JM joined TJ and Lafayette at Monticello on Nov. 4, 1824; see Malone, VI, p. 404.
19. For Lafayette's visit with TJ, see *ibid.*, pp. 405–8.
20. For the visit of Fanny and Camilla Wright, see *ibid.*, pp. 403, 405, and Celia Morris Eckhardt, *Fanny Wright: Rebel in America* (Cambridge, 1984), pp. 81, 84–85.

Jefferson to Madison

Monticello Nov. 20, 1824

TH: J. TO J. MADISON

Gilmer is arrived in N. Y. sick of a fever which he has had thro' the whole passage of 35. days and likely to remain there some time in the hands of the Doctors. He has engaged 5. professors to wit

> George Long, Antient languages.
> Geo. Blaetterman. Modern ditto.
> Thos. H. Key. Mathematics.
> Chas. Bonnycastle (son of the Mathematician) Nat. Philos.
> Robley Dunglison. Anatomy etc.[21]

This last wishes to add Chemistry to his lectures which we may well agree to as we are not well prepared for Anatomy.

Gilmer expected them to arrive 10. days after him but does not say where. We shall advertise the Dormitories as soon as they arrive. The Hotels are all engaged. There were numerous applications for them. Affecte. salutations.

Jefferson to Madison

Monticello Nov. 30, 1824

DEAR SIR

I detained the inclosed letters awhile to enable me to write my letter of information additional to our Report to the Governor, and then in expectn some of the Visitors might call on their way to the legislature and wish to read them. None have called however, and I now inclose them for your perusal. On the reciept of Gilmer's letter of Sep. 15 from London which came to hand 3. days after those from New York, I wrote to him conjuring him not to think of declining his professorship of law, and I rather think he will not. I write to him to-day to know whether Torrey will accept that of Nat. history. He will be a great acquisition, being highly qualified in Botany. Say also is highly worthy of the appointment.

It will occur to you that we must have a meeting of the Visitors as soon as practicable to appoint Professors of Nat. hist. and Ethics. As soon as I hear from Gilmer as to Torrey and himself I shall write to our Colleagues in the legislature to appoint a day convenient to themselves, and notify yourself and Genl. Cocke of it by mail.

---

21. For brief biographical sketches, see O'Neal, pp. 44–46.

I am quite at a loss for a Professor of Ethics. This subject has been so exclusively confined to the clergy, that when forced to seek one, not of that body, it becomes difficult. But it is a branch of science of little difficulty to any ingenious man. Locke, Stewart, Brown, Tracy for the general science of mind furnish material abundant, and that of Ethics is still more trite. I should think any person, with a general education rendering them otherwise worthy of a place among his scientific brethren might soon qualify himself. Wm. Campbell Preston, son of Francis, who returned from his travels in Europe about 5. years ago has occurred to me. He is a fine young man in point of intelligence, much improved by his travels, considered at Edinbg as among the most distinguished of our countrymen who visited that place, a Native and educated at Wm. and M. He is practising law, I believe, in S. Carolina, and I suspect would prefer a quiet birth here to that contentious life. You may know him as writer of the defense of his gr. father Colo. Wm. Campbell against the attack of Govr. Shelby. Dabney Terril, a native of Virga now of Kentucky, educated at Geneva, and particularly esteemed and recommended by Pictet, prepared lately for the law, but not yet engaged in it, is a fine character also; but not perhaps equal to Preston. Yourself and the other gentlemen will think of others. Affecty. yours

Th:J.

P. S. a letter from Mr Gilmer of Nov. 21. to Colo. T. M. Randolph informs him he is still in bed.

Madison to Jefferson

Montpellier Dec. 3, 1824

Dr. Sir

I return the letters from Mr Gilmer inclosed in yours of Novr. 30. His account of the engaged professors is very encouraging. It is a happy circumstance that none of them are beyond the ages he mentions. They will be the less inflexible in their habits, the more improveable in their qualifications, and will last the longer. It wd. seem that Mr. Gilmer's mind leans now to the Station he declined; and that the immediate call on us is limited to the Botanical and Ethical chairs. All that I have heard of Torrey is favorable. So also of Say. Of their comparative ages and incidental fitnesses, I know nothing. The greatest difficulty is in finding a good tenant for the other vacancy and for the reason you mention. Of Mr. Terrill, I know nothing but the slight hints from yourself. Mr. Preston I have not seen since his return from Europe whither he went quite a youth. He is well spoken of as a promising Genius, adorned with noble sentiments, but of the precise character of his mind and its acquirements, I am uninformed. He is indeed young eno' to learn. But is he not too young to meet the public expectation unless marked out by a more appropriate and better known fitness. Cooper's opinion would be valuable. How far have Judge Carr's studies prepared or disposed him for the place in question.[22] It could be scarcely hoped however that he would give up his present office. What are the collateral aptitudes of George Tucker the member of Congress. I have never seen him, and can only judge of him by a volume of miscellaneous Essays published not very long ago. They are written with acuteness and elegance: and indicate a capacity and taste for Philosophical literature. No other name occurs even for consideration.

Jefferson to Madison

Monticello Dec. 10, 1824

DEAR SIR

I send you the sequel of Gilmer's letters recd since my last to you. Torrey you will see does not accept. I had before recd. from the Secy. at War the inclosed letter to him from Mr Emmet the father recommending his son Doctr. John Patton Emmet, for Professor of Chemistry.[23] Considering that branch as expected by Doctr. Dunglison I had given an answer that the place was filled. But learning now that we are free and observing that our group of articles for that Professorship are exactly of botany, zoology, mineralogy, geology, chemistry and rural economy, and Gilmer's acct. of his qualificns in all these except the last which however is involved in chemistry partly I doubt if we can make a better choice, and if you approve it I will write to him that subseq. informn (his age and being a foreigner are objections, but overweighed by higher considns) enables me to say that that Professorship is still open to our appmt and that I will propose him to the Visitors, but that being but 1. of 7, I can engage only for myself. This may prevent his engaging elsewhere

Jefferson to Madison;

[Monticello Dec. 10, 1824]

of the 8. Professors[24]

I like your suggestion of George Tucker for the Ethical chair better than either of my own, and my enquiries since it's reciept, result in a highly favble

22. TJ sounded out Judge Dabney Carr about the law professorship, but his nephew declined; see Malone, VI, p. 423. John Torrey was professor of chemistry at West Point, and Jean Baptiste Say taught natural history in Paris; see Davis, pp. 114, 18, 97.

23. Emmet became professor of natural history; see *ibid.,* p. 410.

24. This fragment of a letter, like the preceding fragment, also dated Dec. 10, 1824, may have been a part of the same letter. They are labeled fragments in the *Guide* to the Presidential Papers Microfilm, Thomas Jefferson Papers, p. 94.

acct of his character and temper. Of his talents I judge from his Essay on Taste, Morals and National politics. I imagine Mr Cabell's connection and knolege of him will have impressed him favbly also, and if you are satisfied and will say so, I will write to him, *in my own name only,* to know if he would accept, should our colleagues concur. Altho' not a native he is considered as thoroughly a Virginian and of high standing.²⁵ We must soon have a meeting to make these appmts. and I presume that within the week after I write, we may hear from him but I shall not write either to him or Emmit until I hear from you. B. M. Carter (of the Shirley family) now in London has made us a donation of 341. vols. the half at least of which are acceptable, and many of them were already placed in our own catalogue. Affectionately yours.

Th:J.

Madison to Jefferson

[Montpellier] Dec. 15, 1824

Dr. Sir

I return Mr. Gilmers two letters to you and that of Mr. Emmet to Mr Calhoun, inclosed in yours of the 10th.

I have so much confidence in the opinion of Mr. Gilmer, and respect for the testimony of the father, with every abatement for partia[lity] that I can not doubt the chemical and other merits ascribed to young Emmet. As a letter however such as you propose, would be viewed by him as equivalent nearly to an appointment and preclude the Visitors from the freedom of decision, some of them might [conclude] there might be some hazard in this step. For myself I should allow but little weight to the circumstance of foreign nativity agst. superior qualifications in the other scale, especially where naturalization and a fixture in the Country had taken place. But [so]me of our Colleagues, to say nothing of the public [illegible] may vary from our way of thinking, and prefer [an] arrangement giving Chemistry to Dunglison [w]ith Natural History and rural Economy, in the hands [of] a Native, to a change which would leave but a single professorship for a native, in case the Ethical professor should be of foreign birth.²⁶

Something may depend on the comparative Science fitness for the Chemical Chair of the two [cand]idates, and the probable effect of a disappoint[ment] on Dunglison, who tho' having no Stipulation or pledge, may feel it in his profits, as well a[s i]n his wishes and hopes: and it may be well as he appears to be a great acquisition that he enter on his career with all the satisfaction that can be secured without a sensible sacrifice of the interests of the

---

25. Tucker was born in Bermuda; see Malone, VI, p. 410.
26. For the opposition to the importation of foreign professors, see *ibid.,* pp. 409–10.

University. Suppose instead of writing to Emmet, or otherwise making a commitment, you were to drop a line to Gilmer, who may not have left N. Y. with a view [to] prevent Young Emmet from disposing of himself, should there be any immediate danger of it. This may probably be done for a very short but sufficient time in a way not even commiting Mr. G. himself. [If] you, after all, think it best to take the step you sugg[ested] I am very willing to take my share of the responsibility.

I am glad to learn that the result of your inquiries concerning Mr. Tucker strengthens my favorable view of his fitness for the Ethical Chair. I wish Mr. Cabel, who doubtless knows every feature of his character, could have be[en] consulted on the subject. Would it not be better to request L.W.C.[?] if concurring with us to sound him, than to write directly yourself. The delay will be trifling; Mr. T. being now at Washington.

Jefferson to Madison

Monticello Dec. 26, 1824

Th:J. to J. M.

I inclose you a long letter from Mr. Cabell and a long answer from myself, not much worth reading, but that it is well you should know every thing.[27] No letter since my last from Gilmer, but he is believed to be now in Richmond. Long and Blaettermann are here located in their pavilions as drawn by lot. The former is a fine young man and well qualified, the latter rather a rough looking German, speaking English roughly, but of an excellent mind and high qualifications. He thinks the Competitor bound to Norfolk with the other three would not sail till about the 10th. of November. It is time they should be here now. You will see what I wrote Cabell about a meeting on their arrival. I wrote him a private letter also as to Tucker, and I have written *privately*[28] to Genl. Breckenridge, enquiring concerning Wm. C. Preston in case Gilmer should absolutely decline. I have done nothing as to Dr. Emmet, because I supposed Gilmer would have left N. Y. before my letter could reach there. You will see what I have recommended as to the last donation. I write this day to Govr. Barber to press a decision through Congress without loss of time.[29] I wish you would do the same that he might be sensible of it's urgency. Affectly. Adieu.

---

27. TJ's letter to Cabell dealt with a plan to move the College of William and Mary from Williamsburg to Richmond; see *ibid.*, pp. 411–12.

28. TJ's italics.

29. Near the end of its session in Mar. 1824, the state legislature had pledged $50,000 to the university from Virginia's claim against the federal government for interest on expenditures during the War of 1812. Congress passed the bill at the end of Feb. 1825; see Malone, VI, pp. 395, 411.

Madison to Jefferson

Montpellier Dec. 31, 1824

DEAR SIR

I have received yours without date inclosing the letter of Mr. Cabell and your answer. I approve entirely the course you recommend to the friends of the University at Richmond, on the proposed removal of the College at Williamsburg.[30] It would be fortunate if the occasion could be improved for the purpose of filling up the general Plan of Education, by the introduction of the grade of Seminaries between the Primary Schools and the University. I have little hope however that the College will accede to any arrangement which is to take from it a part of its funds, and subject it to the Legislative Authority. And in resisting this latter innovation, it will probably be supported by all the Sectarian Seminaries, tho' to be adopted as legal establishments of the intermediate grade. It is questionable also whether the sectarian Seminaries would not take side with William and Mary in combating the right of the Public to interfere in any manner with the property it holds. The perpetual inviolability of Charters, and of donations both Public and private, for pious and charitable uses, seems to have been too deeply imprinted on the Public mind to be readily given up. But the time surely cannot be distant when it must be seen by all that what is granted by the public authority for the public good, not for that of individuals, may be withdrawn and otherwise applied, when the public good so requires; with an equitable saving or indemnity only in behalf of the individuals actually enjoying vested emoluments.[31] Nor can it long be believed that altho' the owner of property cannot secure its descent but for a short period even to those who inherit his blood, he may entail it irrevocably and forever on those succeeding to his creed however absurd or contrary to that of a more enlightened Age. According to such doctrines, the Great Reformation of Ecclesiastical abuses in the 16th Century was itself the greatest of abuses; and entails or other fetters attached to the descent of property by legal acts of its owners, must be as lasting as the Society suffering from them.

It may well be supposed, Should William and Mary be transplanted to Richmond, that those interested in the City will unite with those partial to the College, and both be reinforced by the enemies of the University, in efforts to aggrandize the former into a Rival of the latter; and that their hopes of success will rest a good deal on the advantage presented at Richmond to Medical

---

30. TJ proposed that the endowment of William and Mary be used to establish a system of ten intermediate institutions between lower-level schools and the university in conformity with the plan recommended by the Rockfish Gap commission. For that purpose he drafted "A bill for the discontinuance of the College of William and Mary, and the establishment of other colleges in convenient distribution over the state"; see *ibid.*, p. 412.

31. Both TJ and JM disagreed with John Marshall's decision to the contrary in the *Dartmouth College* case.

Students in the better chance of Anatomic subjects;[32] and in the opportunity of Clinical Lectures; and to Law Students in the presence of the Upper Courts. It will not surprize if some of the most distinguished of the Bar and Bench should take the Lecturing Chair either for profit, or to give an attractive eclât to the regenerated Institution. As the Medical and Law Departments may invite the greatest number of Pupils, and of course be the most profitable to Professors, the obligation on us is the greater to engage for the University, conspicuous qualifications for those Chairs. I trust this has been done in the Medical appointment actually made, and hope we shall not be unsuccessful in making the other. In opening the door a little wider for the admission of students of the Ancient Languages, it will be found, I think, that we did well: considering the competition for students that may be encountered, and the importance of filling our Dormitories at an early period.

I return the letter of Mr. Cabell, and as your answer may be a fair Copy for your files I return that also.

Yours always and affectionately

I write a few lines to Govr Barbour, on the Virg.^{a} claim in which the University is interested; tho' it is I believe only applying the spur to a willing Steed.

32. The proposal to move William and Mary to Richmond included a plan to add a medical school, thus making it a second university in the state; see Malone, VI, pp. 411-12.

48

THE UNIVERSITY OPENS, 1825

BY THE END OF 1824, Jefferson's impressive academical village stood ready for faculty and students, although the interior of the Rotunda was still unfinished. Professor George Ticknor of Harvard described it to a colleague as "more beautiful than anything architectural in New England, and more appropriate to an university than can be found, perhaps, in the world,"[1] a claim confirmed in 1976, when it was voted by the American Institute of Architects as "the proudest achievement of American architecture in the past 200 years."[2]

During the winter of 1824–1825, Jefferson and Madison alternately fumed and fretted about "the non arrival of the foreign Professors [which] begins to be alarming."[3] They had left London in October but had been delayed by gales in the English Channel for more than six weeks. When Jefferson learned that they would sail in December 1824, he scheduled a special meeting of the Board of Visitors "as soon as the arrival of the Professors at Norfolk is credibly announced."[4] After their arrival in February, the rector proclaimed that the university would open on March 7, following a meeting of the board on March 4, 1825.

The professors lingered in Richmond for several days, and Cabell informed Jefferson that he and his colleagues in the legislature "were much pleased with them." From the capital, they rode by stagecoach to Charlottesville, met with the members of the board, and began teaching classes on March 7 with about thirty students in attendance. Another twenty or thirty had dribbled in by the end of the month, Jefferson reported, "and are coming in 2. or 3. every day. We hear of many on the road who cannot come on, the

1. George Ticknor to W. H. Prescott, Dec. 16, 1824, in Malone, VI, p. 423.
2. American Institute of Architects, *Journal* 65 (1976): 91, cited *ibid.*, p. xvii. For an excellent illustrated guide to the University of Virginia, see Pendleton Hogan and Bill Sublette, *The Lawn: A Guide to Jefferson's University* (Charlottesville, 1987).
3. JM to TJ, Jan. 28, 1825, below.
4. TJ to JM, Feb. 1, 1825, below, and Feb. 15, 1825, below.

Richmond and Fredsbg stages having ceased to run" because of spring floods. But many eager students found other means of transportation, Jefferson added: "Some of them hire horses and get on."[5]

The university opened without ceremony and without a law professor. "The schools of antient and modern languages, and Mathematics," the rector informed Madison, "have a little over or under 30 [students] each. Nat. Philosophy [has] fewer, because few come yet well enough prepared in Mathematics to enter that school to any adv[anta]ge." Their lack of preparation was compounded by the lack of textbooks, the order from Boston "being not yet arrived."[6] But the chief concern of Jefferson and Madison was the absence of a law professor. In a circular letter to the Board of Visitors, the rector discussed "the anxieties we have all had on this subject," citing "the public impatience for some appointment to this school."[7] Privately, Jefferson confessed that "for the professorship of law I am almost in despair," and Madison agreed that "our situation is distressing."[8]

After Gilmer's "ultimate and peremptory refusal," Jefferson asked Madison plaintively, "What are we to do? I abhor the idea of a mere Gothic lawyer who has no ideas beyond his [Sir Edward] Coke [upon] Littleton[,] who could not associate in conversation with his Colleagues, nor utter a single Academical idea to an enquiring stranger."[9] Together they ticked off names of learned lawyers in Virginia who were not tainted by Federalist conceptions of broad construction and consolidation.[10] Both agreed that they needed an able professor worthy of the rank of the university, who could "compete sucessfully with the [other] Law Schools now bidding for Students."[11] Jefferson listed William C. Preston and Henry St. George Tucker, while Madison recommended Philip Pendelton Barbour, Dabney Carr, Judge Dade, and John Tayloe Lomax, who finally accepted the appointment in April 1826.[12]

Much of the difficulty in filling the law post sprang from Jefferson and

---

5. TJ to JM, Feb. 22, 1825, below, and Mar. 22, 1825, below. By May 13, there were seventy-nine students enrolled.

6. TJ to JM, Mar. 22, 1825, below.

7. TJ to JM and the Board of Visitors of the University of Virginia, May 13, 1825, below.

8. TJ to JM, Feb. 22, 1825, below, and JM to TJ, Apr. 12, 1825, below.

9. TJ to JM, Jan. 23, 1825, below.

10. For excellent descriptions of TJ's morbid fear of the federal judiciary and its "consolidationist" tendencies, which led to the revival of his states' rights politics, see Malone, VI, pp. 328–61, 437–43, and Peterson, pp. 992–1004. See also TJ to JM, Dec. 24, 1825, below, and JM to TJ, Dec. 28, 1825, below.

11. JM to TJ, Mar. 26, 1825, below.

12. Seventeen of the twenty-eight letters in this chapter discuss candidates for the law professorship. For Lomax, see E. Lee Shepard's sketch in *Legal Education in Virginia, 1779–1979: A Biographical Approach*, ed. W. Hamilton Bryson (Charlottesville, 1982), pp. 359–66. For Henry St. George Tucker, see the sketch by J. Randolph Tucker, *ibid.*, pp. 601–12.

Madison's concern for the political purity of both the professor and the law school, where "the general principles of liberty and the rights of man, in nature and in society," as well as those in government and political economy were to be taught.[13] It was the one area where they fell below the high expectations marked out for the university by Jefferson when he wrote that "this institution will be based on the illimitable freedom of the human mind. For here we are not afraid to follow truth wherever it may lead, nor to tolerate any error so long as reason is left free to combat it."[14]

Jefferson thought that the politics of law professors as well as textbooks on government should pass tests for Republican orthodoxy. "In the selection of our Law Professor," he told Madison, "we must be rigorously attentive to his political principles."[15] In one of his recommendations, Madison backed a candidate despite the fact that he was a "convert to the constitutionality of canals," citing him as one of "several instances of distinguished politicians who reject the general heresies of federalism, most decidedly the amalgamating magic of the terms 'General Welfare,' who yet admit the authority of Congress as to roads and canals, which they squeeze out of the enumerated articles." But on other issues of Republican orthodoxy, the candidate "adhered, *I believe* to the Virginia Creed of which he had been a warm advocate. What his political sentiments are at the moment I know not."[16]

While flirting with the proscription of ideas antithetical to his strict-constructionist view of the federal system, Jefferson also suggested the prescription of basic textbooks in the field of government, an exception to his general rule of leaving the choice of texts to professors. "In most public seminaries," he told Madison, "a text-book is prescribed to the several schools as the Norma docendi in them, and this is frequently done by the Trustees. I should not propose this generally in our University because I believe none of us are so much at the heights of science in the several branches, as to undertake this, and therefore that it will be best left to the Professors, until occasion of interference shall be given. But there is one branch in which I think we are the best judges, and the branch itself is of that interesting character to our state, and the U. S. as to make it a duty in us to lay down the principles which are to be taught. It is that of gov[ern]m[en]t."[17]

Jefferson kept his ears pricked up for any hint of unorthodox political views and quickly denied a rumor that Gilmer was "too much infected with the principles of the Richmond lawyers, who are rank Federalists as formerly denominated, and now consolidationists." But after Gilmer withdrew his

---

13. Board of Visitors meeting, Mar. 4, 1825, in L. and B., XIX, p. 460.
14. TJ to William Roscoe, Dec. 27, 1820, *ibid.,* XV, p. 303.
15. TJ to JM, Feb. 17, 1826, below.
16. JM to TJ, Feb. 17, 1825, below.
17. TJ to JM, Feb. 1, 1825, below.

name for the law post, Jefferson redoubled his guard against "some one of that school." Even so, the possibility that they might have to take a Richmond lawyer made it all the more necessary "to guard against [that] danger by a previous prescription of the texts to be adopted."[18]

But this was too much for Madison. Even though he agreed that it was "very material that the true doctrines of liberty, as exemplified in our Political System, should be inculcated on those who are to sustain and may administer it," he obviously thought that it would be difficult to find books that would be "both guides and guards for the purpose." Algernon Sidney and John Locke, whom Jefferson had listed as required reading, might inspire a love of free government, but neither afforded any "aid in guarding our Republican Charters against constructive violations." Similarly, the Declaration of Independence, "tho' rich in fundamental principles," and *The Federalist*, "regarded as the most authentic exposition of the text of the federal Constitution," were subject to "misconstructions," and "neither of the great rival Parties have acquiesced" in all the comments in the latter. Harvard and Brown required students to read *The Federalist*, "but probably at the choice of the Professors, without any injunction from the superior authority."[19]

Finally, on Jefferson's suggestion of "the Virginia Document of 1799," its author modestly suggested that there might be "more room for hesitation" on the eighty-page report that he had written at white heat to protest the Alien and Sedition Laws of 1798. He thought that its basic arguments corresponded "with the predominant sense of the Nation," but he also pointed out that it was "of local origin," referred "to a state of Parties not yet extinct," and thus "might excite prejudices against the University as under Party Banners." To lay down an absolute prescription of it in the school of law might "induce the more bigoted to withhold from it their sons, even when destined for other than the studies of the Law School." Indeed, he doubted that his report was "on every point satisfactory to all who belong to the same Party." It might even include "our brethren of the Board" of Visitors, among whom was the moderate Federalist James Breckinridge.

Resorting to argument by analogy, the author of the First Amendment suggested that trying to establish political orthodoxy by prescription raised the same sort of issues involved in trying to impose religious orthodoxy, "tho' the public right be very different in the two cases. If the Articles be in very general terms, they do not answer the purpose; if in very particular terms, they divide and exclude where meant to unite and fortify." He thought it best to avoid extremes, preferring to suggest "Standards without requiring an unqualified conformity to them." Whether the selections were made by the Board of

---

18. *Ibid.* He attached a resolution and a list of books, which have now been lost but which can be reconstructed in part from JM's reply of Feb. 8, 1825, below.

19. JM to TJ, Feb. 8, 1825, below.

Visitors or by the professor, however, "the most effectual safeguard against heretical intrusions into the School of Politics, will be an Able and Orthodox Professor."

After demolishing Jefferson's proposal for prescribed texts, Madison amended the rector's resolution "to relax the absoluteness of its injunction, and added to your list of Documents the Inaugural Speech and the Farewell Address of President Washington." The sentiments of the first president would "help down what might be less readily swallowed, and [they] contain nothing which is not good; unless it be the laudatory reference in the Address to the [Jay] Treaty of 1795 with G. B. which ought not to weigh against the sound sentiments characterizing it."[20] Jefferson seemed doubly pleased with Madison's modifications, expressing "entire satisfaction in your amendment of my resolution." He was also "peculiarly pleased with your insertion of Genl. Washington's addresses, which had not occurred to me or I should have referred to them also."[21]

A month later, the board adopted the rector's resolution as amended by Madison. It opened with an expression of opinion that the best guides on "the distinctive principles of the Government of our own State, and that of the United States" were to be found in the listed texts, but it concluded by treating the guides as guards: "these shall be used as the texts and documents of the [Law] School," "where the principles of government . . . shall be inculcated."[22]

Although the rector was pleased with the professors, he thought that the students were not as well prepared as they should be. Moreover, "they are half idle, all, for want of books,"[23] a condition that led shortly to "some incipient irregularities of the students."[24] Jefferson divided the student body into three parts: one-third were hard workers, one-third fairly diligent, and one-third "idle ramblers incapable of application."[25] A month later, he concluded that two-thirds of the students, the older ones, not only required no government, but by their example would control the younger group.[26] Indeed, he reported

---

20. *Ibid*.
21. TJ to JM, Feb. 12, 1825, below.
22. JM's amendment is attached to his letter to TJ of Feb. 12, 1825, below. For the board's action of Mar. 4, 1825, see L. and B., XIX, pp. 460–61. The fullest discussion is in Arthur Bestor, "Thomas Jefferson and the Freedom of Books," in *Three Presidents and Their Books* (Urbana, Ill., 1955), pp. 24–35. A harsher judgment is in Leonard W. Levy, *Jefferson and Civil Liberties: The Darker Side* (Cambridge, Mass., 1963), pp. 148–57; softer ones are in Adrienne Koch, *Jefferson and Madison: The Great Collaboration* (New York, 1950), pp. 275–79, and Malone, VI, pp. 417–18.
23. TJ to JM, Mar. 22, 1825, below.
24. TJ to JM, Apr. 15, 1825, below.
25. TJ to Robert Greenhow, July 24, 1825, cited in Malone, VI, p. 463.
26. Peterson, p. 987.

the university to be as quiet as a convent.[27] But it was the calm before the storm.

Within a month, a series of riots by drunken and rowdy students rumbled across the Lawn, "a rich fool" smashing Professor Long's pavilion window and fourteen masked students forcibly defying the faculty's efforts to restore order. Professors Long and Key promptly resigned, a move rejected by the members of the board, who expelled three students, including Jefferson's great-great-nephew, and disciplined eleven others. Jefferson, whose health was "very low, not having been able to leave the house for three months," rallied enough to ride down the hill from Monticello, where he, Madison, President Monroe, and the board met the entire student body and faculty to restore order. One of the students, Henry Tutwiler, who later became a professor at the university, described the dramatic meeting, which was held in the Rotunda: "At a long table near the center of the room sat the most august body of men I had ever seen—Jefferson, Madison and Monroe. . . . Chapman Johnson . . . Cabell . . . Cocke. . . . Jefferson arose to address the students. He began by declaring that it was one of the most painful events of his life, but he had not gone far before his feelings overcame him, and he sat down, saying that he would leave to abler hands the task of saying what he wished to say." Jeferson, Madison, and the Visitors then established a stricter code for student conduct.[28]

After returning to Montpellier, Madison told the rector that he had "heard nothing as to the University since I parted from you. I hope things continue well there; and that Key and Long will have seen their error in the course so hastily taken by them." Putting the best face on things, he anticipated "permanent good to the Institution from the incidents which threw a transient cloud over it."[29]

The rector replied that "every thing is going on smoothly at the University. The students are attending their schools with more assiduity, and looking to their Professors with more respect. The authority of the latter is visibly strengthened, as is the confidence of those who visit the place, and the effect, on the whole, has been salutary. The Professors are all lecturing," he concluded, although he pointed out that Professors Long and Key, "the Cantabs [were] somewhat in the pouts as yet."[30] But he was sure that "the vigilance of the faculty and energy of the civil power" would prevent the recurrence of such a "serious incident" in the future.[31]

27. TJ to William Short, Aug. 9, 1825, cited in Malone, VI, p. 464.
28. Malone, VI, pp. 463–68; Brant, VI, p. 455; TJ to Fanny Wright, Aug. 7, 1825, in Ford, X, p. 344.
29. JM to TJ, Oct. 14, 1825, below.
30. TJ to JM, Oct. 18, 1825, below.
31. TJ to Joseph Coolidge, Jr., Oct. 13, 1825, cited in Malone, VI, p. 467. The Board of Visitors made the provost responsible for enforcing the laws of the state and for cooperating with the civil authorities.

The Letters

Madison to Jefferson

Montpellier Jan. 15, 1825[1]

Dear Sir

I am sorry Mr. Tucker requires time for deliberation. It shows the difficulty in our country of withdrawing talents from rival pursuits into the service of Education. I do not think he will have chosen the best of literary careers, if he devotes himself to Novel writing. The public taste is nearly satiated with the fashionable, perhaps the best species, in which the success of Walter Scott has kindled so extensive an emulation. I wish the plea of Mr. T. may not cover or be combined with political aspirations more to be dreaded by us than the muse he is courting, to whom his occasional addresses would not be prevented and might even be improved by the atmosphere in which his professorship would place him. The time he asks must of course be limited to the moment when an option presents itself.

Mr. Cabell's letter makes it probable that the projected removal of William and Mary will be stifled by the covering put by its friends on the arcana of its affairs. I hope the occasion will bring into view the sound principles on which the claims of corporations ought to be decided. It would be well also, if it should lead to a standing law limiting all incorporating acts to a certain period, and to the practice of specifying in every case the amount of property tenable by those artificial beings. Always yours,

James Madison

Jefferson to Madison

Monticello Jan. 23, 1825

Th: J. to J. Madison

I inclose you a letter from Mr Cabell and a copy of the bill which I prepared and sent him as he requested.[2]

I send you also a letter from Mr. Gilmer by which he seems determined not to undertake our professorship. What are we to do? I abhor the idea of a

---

1. For a discussion of this letter, see Koch, p. 274. Major portions of the text were omitted without being indicated in James Madison, *Letters and Other Writings of James Madison,* [ed. William C. Rives and Philip R. Fendall], 4 vols. (Philadelphia, 1865), III, p. 480.

2. The bill proposed the discontinuance of the College of William and Mary and the establishment of other colleges in ten districts around the state; see Philip Alexander Bruce, *History of the University of Virginia, 1819–1919,* 5 vols. (New York, 1920), I, pp. 308–21.

mere Gothic lawyer who has no ideas beyond his [Sir Edward] Coke [upon] Littleton who could not associate in conversation with his Colleagues, nor utter a single Academical idea to an enquiring stranger. The only substitute for Gilmer I can think of is Wm. C. Preston, who wrote the answer to Shelby on the charge agt. his gr. fath. Col. Wm. Campbell of King's mountain.[3] He is a fine young man, has travelled to great advantage, and left behind him the most respectable recollections. I wrote to Genl. Breckinridge to enquire concerning him but have no answer. I hear nothing further from Tucker, nor of our three Professors from London. Gilmer seems to have made a considble purchase of books. They are at the University, but cannot be opened for want of the Catalogue, for which I have written to him. I desired him to give expectns to Dr. Emmet. Affectly. yours,

Th:J.

Madison to Jefferson

Montpellier Jan. 28, 1825

Dear Sir

I have recd. yours of the 23d. inclosing a copy of the Bill sent to Mr. Cabell; but omitting the letter from him. Without that I cannot estimate the reception such a measure will have in the Assembly. The grounds on which the Bill dissolves the Charter of the College, and disposes of its funds are captivating. But there will probably be a powerful opposition to it. The uncertain and scanty provision for the Ex Professors,[4] the repugnance of the existing Seminaries, for the most part Presbyterian, to a legal superintendence, and perhaps that of the other Sects as having little chance at present of predominating in the new ones, seem to discourage expectation. Mr. Cabell however is a much better judge of the physiognomy of the Legislature than I can be. The Bill may have a good effect at least, in leading the public attention to better views of the subject than have hitherto been taken. The enemies of the University will at the same time endeavor to trace the Bill to that source, and to turn whatever of unpopularity it may have agst. the Institution.

I am sorry Mr Gilmer will not accept the allotted place. All that I learn of Mr. Preston is favorable to him: But the more qualified he may be, the less is my hope, that he will devote himself to such a service. He is very rich in patrimonial prospects, and likely to yield to political temptations, with which

---

3. For TJ's appraisal of Preston, see TJ to JM, Nov. 30, 1824, above, where he recommended Preston as a candidate for professor of ethics.

4. TJ had suggested that the endowment of William and Mary be used to establish other colleges, including one at Williamsburg and one in Richmond, thus providing positions for the professors at William and Mary who would be displaced by the discontinuance of the college; see Malone, VI, p. 412.

his forensic pursuits will co-incide. If wealth be passion with him, it is at the Bar also that he can augment it, not in the University. These calculations may however be agreeably superceded by the expected information from Mr. Breckinridge. Should we be obliged to look elsewhere no one occurs but my neighbour P. P. Barbour His mind is a strong one, and very capable of expanding itself beyond the limits of technical law. He has also of late turned his attention with good effect to political Economy, of which a proof was given in a very able speech on the Tariff. In purity of character and habits of severe application he is surpassed by no one. He may not be without deficiencies in some of the more external accomplishments, but not in a forbidding degree, especially as his temper is amiable, and his deportment consiliating. I give this portrait however without a hope, should the likeness be in no point objected to, that he would enter into the service of the University, or any other indeed that would remove him from his Domestic Establishment which he has made very attractive. If a Judgship w[d.] not require that sacrifice he would probably exchange for it his practice at the Bar.

The silence of Mr. Tucker admits a favorable construction. The non arrival of the foreign Professors begins to be alarming

Jefferson to Madison

Monticello Feb. 1, 1825

DEAR SIR

I concur with you in the favorable opinion of Mr Barber; and altho' I should prefer Preston, as rather of a more academical cast, yet I could readily give a first vote to Barber. His reputation in Congress would be of service.

In most public seminaries a text-book is prescribed to the several schools as the Norma docendi in them, and this is frequently done by the Trustees. I should not propose this generally in our University because I believe none of us are so much at the heights of science in the several branches, as to undertake this, and therefore that it will be best left to the Professors, until occasion of interference shall be given. But there is one branch in which I think we are the best judges, and the branch itself is of that interesting character to our state, and the U. S. as to make it a duty in us to lay down the principles which are to be taught. It is that of govmt. Even while Mr Gilmer was considered as our choice, I recieved from many persons expressions of great uneasiness lest the doctrines of that school should have an improper bias. He was believed by some, and strongly believed, to be too much infected with the principles of the Richmond lawyers, who are rank Federalists as formerly denominated, and now consolidationists. I do not believe this myself. I never heard an unsound opinion on govmt uttered by him. But now that he is withdrawn, and the successor uncertain, and a possibility has arisen that a Richmond lawyer or some one of that school may be proposed, I think it a duty to guard against danger by a previous prescription of the texts to be adopted. I inclose you a resoln which I think of proposing at our next meeting, for your considn, with a prayer that you will correct it freely, and make it what you think it ought to be. I inclose for your perusal a letter of the 28th from Mr Cabell. Affectly yours

Th:J.

P. S. I this moment recieved another letter of the 30th from Mr Cabell which I inclose also. By a N. Y. paper giving Lloyd's list to Dec. 2. we learn that the Competitor was at Portsmouth the 27th. Nov. and by a Norfolk paper of Jan. 28. that She was at Plymouth Dec. 5th. to sail soon.[5] This is reviving.

Madison to Jefferson

Montpellier Feb. 8, 1825

DEAR SIR

The letters from Mr Cabell are herein returned. I just see that he has succeeded in defeating the project for removing the College from Williamsburg.

I hope your concurrence in what I said of Mr Barbour will not divert your thoughts from others. It is possible that the drudgery of his profession, the uncertainty of Judicial appointment acceptable to him, and some other attractions at the University for his young family, might reconcile him to a removal thither; but I think the chance very slender.

I have looked with attention over your intended proposal of a text book for the Law School. It is certainly very material that the true doctrines of liberty, as exemplified in our Political System, should be inculcated on those who are to sustain and may administer it. It is, at the same time, not easy to find standard books that will be both guides and guards for the purpose. Sidney and Locke are admirably calculated to impress on young minds the right of Nations to establish their own Governments, and to inspire a love of free ones; but afford no aid in guarding our Republican Charters against constructive violations. The Declaration of Independence, tho' rich in fundamental principles, and saying every thing that could be said in the same number of words, falls nearly under a like observation. The "Federalist" may fairly enough be regarded as the most authentic exposition of the text of the federal Constitution, as understood by the Body which prepared and the Authority which accepted it. Yet it did not foresee all the misconstructions which have occurred; nor prevent some that it did foresee. And what equally deserves re-

---

5. The *Competitor* was the vessel carrying Professors Bonnycastle, Dunglison, and Key; see *ibid.*, p. 413.

mark, neither of the great rival Parties have acquiesced in all its comments. It may nevertheless be admissible as a School book, if any will be that goes so much into detail. It has been actually admitted into two Universities, if not more—those of Harvard and Rh: Island; but probably at the choice of the Professors, without any injunction from the superior authority. With respect to the Virginia Document of 1799, there may be more room for hesitation. Tho' corresponding with the predominant sense of the Nation; being of local origin and having reference to a state of Parties not yet extinct, an absolute prescription of it, might excite prejudices against the University as under Party Banners, and induce the more bigoted to withhold from it their sons, even when destined for other than the studies of the Law School. It may be added that the Document is not on every point satisfactory to all who belong to the same Party. Are we sure that to our brethren of the Board it is so? In framing a political creed, a like difficulty occurs as in the case of religion tho' the public right be very different in the two cases. If the Articles be in very general terms, they do not answer the purpose; if in very particular terms, they divide and exclude where meant to unite and fortify. The best that can be done in our case seems to be, to avoid the two extremes, by referring to selected Standards without requiring an unqualified conformity to them, which indeed might not in every instance be possible. The selection would give them authority with the Students, and might controul or counteract deviations of the Professor. I have, for your consideration, sketched a modification of the operative passage in your draught, with a view to relax the absoluteness of its injunction, and added to your list of Documents the Inaugural Speech and the Farewell Address of President Washington. They may help down what might be less readily swallowed, and contain nothing which is not good; unless it be the laudatory reference in the Address to the Treaty of 1795 with G. B. which ought not to weigh against the sound sentiments characterizing it.

After all, the most effectual safeguard against heretical intrusions into the School of Politics, will be an Able and Orthodox Professor, whose course of instruction will be an example to his successors, and may carry with it a sanction from the Visitors. Affectionately yours.

Sketch.

And on the distinctive principles of the Government of our own State, and of that of the U. States, the best guides are to be found in—1. The Declaration of Independence, as the fundamental act of Union of these States. 2. the book known by the title of the 'Federalist,' being an authority to which appeal is habitually made by all and rarely declined or denied by any, as evidence of the general opinion of those who framed and those who accepted the Constitution of the U. States on questions as to its genuine meaning. 3. the Resolutions of the General Assembly of Virg^a in 1799, on the subject of the Alien and Sedition laws, which appeared to accord with the predominant sense of the people of the U. S. 4. The Inaugural Speech and Farewell Address of

President Washington, as conveying political lessons of peculiar value; and that in the branch of the School of law which is to treat on the subject of Gov^t, these shall be used as the text and documents of the School.

Jefferson to Madison

Monticello Feb. 12, 1825

TH:J. TO J. M.

I concur with entire satisfaction in your amendment of my resolution, and am peculiarly pleased with your insertion of Genl. Washington's addresses, which had not occurred to me or I should have referred to them also.

I send you another letter of Mr Cabell which I think you will read with pleasure.[6] Affectte. salutns.

Jefferson to Madison

Monticello Feb. 15, 1825

TH:J. TO J. M.

Mr. Cabell's last letter to me of Feb. 11 says that if the Professors do not arrive before the assembly rises, they (the Visitors there) shall disperse, and a regular call will be necessary; but if they arrive, he and Mr Loyall will come up from that place by way of New Canton, and probably in Friday's stage. Should the former be the case, I should propose, if you approve it, that as soon as the arrival of the Professors at Norfolk is credibly announced, a special meeting of the visitors shall be called, to meet on the day fortnight of the summonses leaving our Post office, and, to save time I will direct a distinct summons to each at the same time, as their signature to separate papers will be as effective as if to a single one running the rounds, and so consuming more time.

I hear nothing from Breckenridge, on the subject of Preston, and I presume my lre has miscarried. Barber's late appointment as Judge may perhaps add another chance against his acceptance. Mr Cabell suggests Henry St. George Tucker, son of the judge, and himself a Chancellor of the Winchester district. I believe him entirely qualified for the professorship of Law, but as little likely to accept as either of the others. And here ends my catalogue. Affectly. Adieu.

6. Cabell's letter to TJ of Feb. 7, 1825, reported the defeat of the William and Mary petition to relocate in Richmond; see *ibid.*

Madison to Jefferson

Montpellier Feb. 17, 1825[7]

DEAR SIR

I received yesterday your letters of the 12th and 15th, and enclose the letter from Mr. Cabell enclosed in one of them. I approve the course you have in view for obtaining an eventual meeting of the Visitors.

The Judicial appointment of Mr. Barbour will, I understand, be accepted and as it is in the road to the court of appeals, lessens the chance of him for the university. I am sorry you hear nothing of Mr. Preston, especially as information is immediately wanted, and the channel for obtaining it so circuitous. If Mr. Breckenridge should attend the called meeting of the Visitors and have the personal knowledge requisite the miscarriage of your letter to him may be unimportant but his attendance is very uncertain.

Chancellor Tucker had occurred to me. But finding that he was adding to his legal salary the profits of a Law School I took for granted that he was out of our reach. I recollected also that he had become a convert to the constitutionality of canals etc. in favor of which he drew up the Report of a Committee of Congress, some years ago, a copy of which he sent me, but which I can not now find. In other respects he adhered, *I believe* to the Virginia Creed of which he had been a warm advocate. What his political sentiments are at the moment I know not.

It seems a strange, but it is a certain fact, that there are several instances of distinguished politicians who reject the general heresies of federalism, most decidedly the amalgamating magic of the terms "General Welfare," who yet admit the authority of Congress as to roads and canals, which they squeeze out of the enumerated articles. In truth, the great temptation of "utility," brought home to local feelings, is the most dangerous snare for Constitutional orthodoxy; and I am not sure that the Judiciary branch of the Government is not a safer expositor of the power of Congress than Congress will be when backed and even pushed on by their constituents, as in the canal and the Missouri cases. Were the unauthorized schemes of internal improvement as disagreeable to a majority of the people and of the States as they are deemed aadvantageous, who can doubt the different reasonings and result that would be observed within the walls of Congress? The will of the nation being omnipotent for right, is so for wrong also; and the will of the nation being in the majority, the minority must submit to that danger of oppression as an evil infinitely less than the danger to the whole nation from a will independent of it. I consider the question as to canals, etc., as decided, therefore, because sanctioned by the nation under the permanent influence of benefit to the major part of it; and if not carried into practice, will owe its failure to other than Constitutional obstacles.

---

7. For a discussion of this letter, see Koch, p. 275. In Rives and Fendall, III, p. 483, portions of the text were omitted without being indicated.

I have thought it proper that you should be apprized of what is here communicated with respect to Mr. Tucker. It will be for consideration how far, with that flaw, if there be no other material one, it may not be better to avail the University of his talents and reputation to which may be added, as I believe, great amiableness of temper, than to run the risk of being driven to an appointment less satisfactory either on the score of talent or of fitness in other respects. The chance I fear is bad of making one unexceptionable in every respect. Affectionately yours,

JAMES MADISON

Jefferson to Madison

Monticello Feb. 22, 1825

DEAR SIR

Our Colleagues on the legislature have called a meeting of the Visitors for the 4th. of March. I presume they have notified you of it by mail, but lest they should not have done so I have thot it safe to inform you.

Our newly arrived Professors will come up in the stage of the day after tomorrow. Mr Cabell writes me that they were much pleased with them in Richmd. We are much so with the two here. I hope we can depend on getting Emmet and Tucker of Bedford.[8] For the professorship of law I am almost in despair. Your's affectly.

TH:J.

Jefferson to Madison

Monticello Mar. 10, 1825

DEAR SIR

Considering Chancellor Tucker's acceptance as absolutely desperate, the reasons he assigned being of an immovable character,[9] and the hopeless state in which we should be if Barber also declined I took advge of his being at our court to ask him to call on me. He did so. I entered with him on the subject of his undertaking our chair of Law. He stiffly maintained at first the preference of his present office in his situation. I went minutely thro all the items of comparison between the two places, we were two hours on the subject. On a minute comparison, he evidently began to relax, and I really think he became

---

8. George Tucker lived in Lynchburg in Bedford County; see William B. O'Neal, *Pictorial History of the University of Virginia* (Charlottesville, 1970), p. 46.

9. Henry St. George Tucker was chancellor of the Winchester district; see TJ to JM, Feb. 15, 1825, above.

The University Opens, 1825

sensible that there was not a single point in which the situation here wd not be preferable; profit greatly superior, convenience to the managemt of his estate, and the ease of drawing all his supplies from it, constant residence with his family, it's educn at little expence, favble situan for his daurs, fine society, a stationary residce for himself instead of eternal travelling, equal firmness of tenure only 2 hours of service every other day required, his being still equally in the road to preferment, and the greater public good he would render by instructing our youth in sound principles of civil polity, he became manifestly shaken. He suggested the holding both, giving the summer to his present office and winter to our's. I told him at once that that was inadmissable and against a rule we had expressly laid down and must maintain, but observed we could defer the opening that school until he had gone thro' his first circuit. He said that would be indispensable, because there was not time enough left for the engagement of a successor. He asked a week or ten days to consider and consult his family. He was evidently and seriously impressed, and in this state of suspence your pressure on him would have great and decisive effects If therefore you could see him and press[?] him in like manner, and perhaps use persuasives to his wife, I am satisfied he will yield. I did not say any thing of the offer to Tucker, as that wd have added another difficulty to those already in our way and on so nice a balance might have turned the scale and if contrary almost to possibility Tucker were to retire from all his objections, a sound apology to Barber would be easily found. I hope you will take a ride there and secure his acceptance. We are desperate without it. I saw clearly that a mere letter to him would have had no effect and that it was the viva voce representation alone which would have succeeded   Affectly yours

Th: J.

P. S. Mr G. Tucker is here and accepts. The acquisn of Barber will crown all our wishes.

Jefferson to Madison

Monticello Mar. 22, 1825

Dear Sir

George Tucker accepts, as you know, and will be in place early in April. Emmet accepts and will be here about the same time. Henry St. George Tucker declines, expressly on the grounds of the local attachments of his family, with abundance of thanks etc. to the Visitors. Barber throws a greedy grapple at both places. I inclose you his letter and my answer. I still have some hope that when he sees that he can have a choice of the one or the other, his clear head will see the great superiority of our offer. If he refuses I must exercise the power you gave me of calling a meeting. But what then? I have been able to think of no new subject have you? Preston and Robertson alone occur to me. I would prefer the former, but have scarcely a ray of hope of his acceptance. I wish you would enquire into the character of Robertson. I have done so from many, who know him well. They agree in characterising him as able, amiable, probe, and soundly orthodox in his politics, remarkably clear and ready in developing his ideas, and closely logical at the same time. His educn has been a common classical one. Mr Loyal who said he was acquainted with him, did not think him equal to Tucker or Barbour, and indeed did not consider him as of high qualificns.

Our students are at present between 50. and 60. and are coming in 2. or 3. every day. We hear of many on the road who cannot come on, the Richmond and Fredsbg stages having ceased to run. Some of them hire horses and get on. The schools of antient and modern languages, and Mathematics have a little over or under 30 each. Nat. Philosophy fewer, because few come yet well enough prepared in Mathematics to enter that school to any advge. They are half idle, all, for want of books, Hilliard's supply shipped from Boston the 2d. inst. being not yet arrived. Charlottesville has not had the offer of a single boarder, and I think will not have one as long as a dormitory is unoccupied.[10]

Madison to Jefferson

Montpellier Mar. 26, 1825

DEAR SIR

I recd some days ago yours of Mar. 10. The last mail brought me that of Mar. 22. inclosing the letter of Col. Barbour and your answer, both of which I return. If you have not satisfied him of the value of your proposition, he must at least be convinced of the unreasonableness of his own. I have not yet seen him since I recd. your letter requesting me to do so having been confined by a very bad cold attended with continual fever. I am so far recovered now that if tomorrow be a good day I will ride over to his house. It appeared of the less consequence to add my efforts to yours, as it was known that he had *publickly* spoken of the offer made him, and of his determination not to accept it but as an adjunct to the office he holds. It is possible that your letter may produce a favorable reconsideration of the subject: but I suspect he is secretly influenced by a belief that a professorship does not lead so directly to the Judicial goal to which he has an eye, as the path he is now in. Should it be impossible to obtain him I am as much at a non plus as you are. Of Preston I have no hope. Of

---

10. The following sentence appears in TJ's draft copy but was omitted in the recipient's copy: "Our code of rules is in press, and are moreover in a course of publication in the Central Gazette."

Robertson I have no knowledge: nor have I an opportunity of consulting with any competent Judge of his qualifications and public standing. Mr. Loyal's opinion is a bad omen of the result if he should be named for the decision of the Board. I shall not fail however to sound for his character wherever information may be hoped for. We must not forget that an Able professor only will comport with the rank of the University, or compete sucessfully with the Law Schools now bidding for Students.

I do not think you ought to consider the refusal of Barbour as calling for a meeting of the Visitors before there be some chance of an efficient one. An abortive Meeting would make everything worse. And rather than be forced into a bad appointment, it might be better to wait the return of Barbour from his spring Circuit, which will be very early in June, if not within May, and let him take the Law chair till September. / This he would probably do: and whilst giving us time for an appointment might [possibly become converted?] to an acceptance of it himself. I suggest this alternative however merely because nothing free from difficulty occurs. I wish you may have found relief in something better.[11]

Madison to Jefferson

Montpellier Mar. 28, 1825

Dr. Sir

I saw Col. Barbour yesterday as I intended. He remains decided agst. relinquishing his Judgship, without a previous experiment of the Chair in the University. He feels evidently a strong attraction towards it: and I think a growing one. It is quite possible that the experiment he is making of his Judicial duties, carrying him as they will beyond the Mountains, will diminish his preference of the plan he holds. I did not allude to the idea mentioned in mine of yesterday. viz that of his taking the Law Chair between his Spring and Fall Circuits, because I did not consider myself warranted to do so: and I may add, because it occurred that he would have an interferring call to the Genl. Court at Richmd. It is much to be regretted that we are likely to lose him, with so little prospect of an acc/eptable substitute.[12] I am persuaded he would be able indefatigable and successful in his station if appointed; and that his reputation for talents and Law arguments spreading from Washington, would invite Students from other States.

J M.

11. The recipient's copy ends at the slash mark above, except for TJ's notation at the end. The remainder of the letter is from JM's retained draft.

12. The recipient's copy ends at the slash mark in this sentence, except for TJ's notation at the end. The remainder of the letter is from JM's retained draft.

I cd. not ascertain the bias of his family; but discovered nothing of aversion to the University.

Jefferson to Madison

Monticello Mar. 29, [1825]

DEAR SIR

Not knowing whether you may have obtained Mr Barber's acceptance in the visit you proposed, I have thot of a proposn, which it has been suggested to me would reconcile him to our offer. If therefore he has not accepted that of joining us at the end of his first circuit, and you would approve of giving him a year on his assurance that he would then accept, forward to him if you please the inclosed letter. But retain it if he has already accepted or if you would disapprove of it. Affectionately yours

TH:J.

Madison to Jefferson

Montpellier Apr. 12, 1825

DEAR SIR

The letter for Judge Barbour inclosed in your last to me did not reach him till his return on saturday evening from his visit to Culpeper. Yesterday he called on me on his way to his Court in this County. I found that he adhered to his purpose last communicated, and that such would be his answer to you. There can be no chance therefore of obtaining him for the University, unless the vacancy should be very inconveniently prolonged, and his mind should, in the time, undergo an improbable change. For the present our situation is distressing. Do you know any thing of Judge [W.A.C.] Da/de?[13] It is said that he is not a little distinguished among his brethren of the Superior Courts, not only for Law but other intellectual acquirements. He was a Commissioner with us at Rockfish Gap, when the Site of the Central College was fixed. The outside of his character at least appeared to advantage. I am told that he lost somewhat of his popularity with the Assembly some years ago, by some unreasonable item in his acct. with the public; but without more knowlege of the case than I have, no judgment can be formed of it. Mr. Cabell is probably well

13. A fragment of the recipient's copy, which is in the Presidential Papers Microfilm, James Madison Papers, ends at the slash mark in this sentence. I discovered the remainder of this copy in the Jefferson Papers of the University of Virginia, 1732–1828, microfilm, reel 9, mistakenly filed under Apr. 30, 1825, with this note: "or Feb. 17, 1825." I then checked the complete letter by reading it against JM's retained draft of Apr. 12, which is in the Presidential Papers Microfilm.

acquainted with that and every thing else necessary to an appreciation of both the Judge and the Man. Affecly yours

Madison to Jefferson

Montpellier Apr. 13, 1825

DEAR SIR

When I suggested some time ago, Judge Carr for the Law Chair in the University, I did not know that he had been taken into view by any other member of our Board; and inferring from the silent reception given to my letter, and the attractions of the place he now holds, that I ought not to persist in the idea of his appointment. My thoughts were turned altogether to other chances. By a letter just recd. I find that the Judge had occurred to two of our Colleagues long before my suggestion of him; and from their anxiety for his appointment I presume that they do not despair of his consent to exchange his seat in the Court of Appeals and residence in Richmond for the location proposed for him. With this encouragement I must renew my wish that he may be named for the Law Chair, and that no feelings of delicacy may be permitted to interfere with a measure of such obvious propriety, and such critical importance to the University.[14] Altho' I cannot decide from personal acquaintance on the merits of Mr. C. there is abundant evidence of his legal qualifications for the Professorship, and that he is unrivalled in every other recommendatory trait of character I am entirely persuaded that his name will be welcomed by every Visitor as well as by the Public; and hope that you will at once obtain the separate sanctions of the former in such terms as may introduce the Professor, without the necessity of a Meeting of the Board before the Autumnal period./[15]

Not knowing where Mr. Cabell will be found I must ask the favor of you to add what is wanting in the address of the inclosed letter and then have it forwarded.

Jefferson to Madison

Monticello Apr. 15, 1825

DEAR SIR

I have received a proposition from Mr Perry the owner of the lands which separate the two tracts of the University which I think of so much importance

---

14. TJ sounded out Carr, who declined; see Malone, VI, p. 423.

15. The recipient's copy ends at the slash mark in this sentence, except for TJ's notation at the end. The remainder of the letter is from JM's retained draft.

to that institution as to communicate to the visitors by letter in their separate situations. The University tract of 100 acres is ¼ of a mile distant from that of the Observatory of 153 acres. The water which supplies the cisterns of the University by pipes arises in the mountain a little without this last tract, and the pipes pass on Perry's side of the line and thro' his interjacent lands till they enter the University tract. On his side of the line also is a very bold spring, which might be brought by a small ditch so near the buildings of the University as to be of common use. It is in his power at any time to cut off our pipes and deprive us of that indispensable supply of water. We have always been anxious to purchase this interjacent parcel not only to consolidate our two tracts but to secure the supply of water; but we have never more than intimated a willingness to purchase without pressing him, lest it might induce him to ask an unreasonable price. He is under (as I believe) some pressure which obliges him now to sell it. He gives us the refusal, which if we do not accept, he will sell in lots as he can readily do. We gave him about four years ago 45.D. an acre for the 50 acres adjacent to it. Since that, lands around the University have got to 100. and 130. D. the acre. He offered the parcel in question to the University for 60. D. I refused to treat with him at that, and told him that at 50. D. I would lay it before the Visitors for consideration. He at length agreed, stipulating for 3000. D. in hand, one half the balance at the end of one year, and the other half at the end of the second, with interest from the date. On these terms I cannot but strongly recommend its purchase. If once it is sold out in lots we shall never be able to buy again but at exorbitant rates if at all, and our supply of water will assuredly be cut off from us. What passes thro' our present pipes with the additional spring will give us the most abundant supply of that element for ever. That you may judge of our means of paying for it, I send you a statement of our income and expenditure for the present and the two next years, drawn up on consultation with Mr Brockenbrough.[16] You will perceive that I propose to borrow the first payment of 3000. D. from the library fund, which can be repaid from our general funds the next year, in addition to our second payment of 2067. D. to Perry, and still leaving a surplus of 2,679 D. for contingencies that year; and that the same funds will make our third and last payment of 2184. D. in 1827, leaving a contingent surplus for that year of 3094. D. The library fund can well spare the money for awhile as we need not use of it for a year or two more than 40,000. D. leaving 10,000 for mineralogical and geological collections which may be deferred without inconvenience. My own opinion therefore is that we can make the purchase without any danger of embarrassment, and that if not made now it will be forever lost. The part which I think indispensable contains about 110 acres, but it would be better to take in also the 37 acres as it squares our lines, and the Timber on it is worth the price.

---

16. See the enclosure "State of Income and Expenditures . . . ," below.

Although the subject is of great and permanent interest to the University I have not thought of proposing a meeting on it, of the great inconvenience of which to the gentlemen I am sensible, and the rather as the sketch of the ground, which I send you, and the prospect of payment can be considered as well separately as together. The only article in the statement of our finances which does not rest on certainty is the number of students calculated on for the next year. For this year I have calculated only on the number now entered 68, and they are coming in nearly every day, and at the summer vacation of the other schools, when they will be disengaged we know that a large number will come, and that in the course of the year we shall be over 100. That we shall have as many the next year as our Dormitories will lodge, all information assures us, and probably as many additional to that as Charlottesville can accommodate, which is expected to be about 100. and would add 1500. D. more to our income. As far as we can judge not one will go to Charlottesville as long as a Dormitory is to be had. As yet there has not been a single application to that place, altho' several house keepers there had prepared themselves to take in boarders. If this purchase is approved by your separate letters, I will undertake to act on them as if regularly ordered by the board, as you can pass a vote of confirmation at our first meeting. Perry is pressing (as I believe he is pressed) for an immediate answer.[17]

All our professors are in place except Mr Tucker daily expected, and the professor [of] law whom we have yet to name. We await Mr Tucker's arrival to form a board of faculty[18] that the Professors may enter on their functions of order and discipline which some incipient irregularities of the students begin to call for. From a view which I took of their ages when the whole number was 61. I found 6. of 21. and upwards, 9. of 20, 23. of 19, 10. of 18, 10. of 17, and 3. of 16. Two thirds therefore being of 19. and upwards we may hope are of sufficient discretion to govern themselves, and that the younger 3d. by their example as well as by moderate coercion will not be very difficult to keep in order.

I enclose you a printed copy of our regulations which appear to give satisfaction to both Professors and Students.[19] Affectionately and respectfully your's

TH: JEFFERSON[20]

---

17. For the acquisition of the Perry property, see Malone, VI, p. 469.

18. The faculty elected George Tucker chairman for a one-year term. There was no president or other administrative officer; see *ibid.*, pp. 422, 484.

19. For the regulations, see *ibid.*, pp. 419, 425.

20. Only the complimentary close and the signature are in TJ's hand. The copy of the map of the property is missing.

ENCLOSURE

State of Income and Expenditures for the University of Virginia, 1825–1827

Estimate of Income	Dollars	Estimate of Expenditures	Dollars
1825			
Due from Literary board of annuity of 1823	800	Proctor's debts to individuals	6,144
Annuity of 1825	15,000	Remitted to Italy for Capitals, bases, pavement	3,000
Debt from Library fund, advance for books, etc.	6,000	Ordinary expences of the establishment	3,500
Bank loan on credit of Subscription arrears	5,000	Salaries of 5. Professors from Jan. 1	7,500
Subscription arrears, separate (7,468 of which) ½ this year	3,734	2 Professors from Apr. 15	2,145
		1 Professor (Law) suppose May 1	1,011
Rent of 6. Hotels from Mar. 7	993	Anatomical theatre	4,000
Rent of 34 dormitories, ⅛ off	476	Payment to bank in part of loan (½ subscriptions collected)	3,734
Rent of 20. dormitories half of year	160		
University rent from 68. students ⅛ off	893	Surplus for Contingencies of this year	2,322
University rent from 40. students half of year	330		33,356
	33,356		
1826			
Annuity for 1826	15,000	Salaries of 8. Professors	12,000
Subscription arrears, the other half	3,734	Military Instructor	200
Rent of 6. Hotels	1,200	Librarian 150 Dollars Secretary of Faculty 50 Dollars	200
100 Dormitories @ 16 Dollars each	1,600	Ordinary expences of establishment	3,500
9 Dormitories @ 12 Dollars each	108	Repayment to bank balance of loan (5000 − 3734)	1,266
University rent from 218 Students @ 15 Dollars	3,270	Repayment to library fund of loan for Perry	2,067
	24,912	Second payment to Perry, with interest	2,067
		Surplus for Contingencies of the year	2,679
			24,912

1827

Annuity for 1827	15,000	Salaries of 8. Professors	12,000
Rent of 6. Hotels	1,200	Military Instructor, Librarian, Secretary of Faculty	400
109 Dormitories	1,708	Ordinary expences of establishment	3,500
University rent from 218 students	3,270	3rd payment to Perry with interest	2,184
	21,178	Surplus for Contingencies of the year	3,094
			21,178

After 1827. (when Perry's purchase shall have been discharged) the annual surplus will be 5,278 Dollars and as much more as the increased number of Students over 218 @ 15 Dollars each may amount to.

Madison to Jefferson

[Montpellier] Apr. 21, 1825

DR. SIR

I have recd yours of the 15th. relating to a purchase of the parcels of land offered for sale by Mr. Perry and very cheerfully concur in your proposition for making it. The advantage of thus connecting the separate parcels of the University, and securing the sources and ducts which are to supply it with water, seems well to justify the measure on the terms and in the mode explained by you. Even in a pecuniary view, the situation of the property wd. be a guaranty agst. loss.

Will you have 2 or 3 copies of the "Enactments etc." inclosed to me. I find I shall need them to comply with friendly requests out of the State.

Jefferson to Madison and the Board of Visitors of the University of Virginia

Monticello May 13, 1825

DEAR SIR

Every offer of our Law chair has been declined, and a late renewal of pressure on Mr Gilmer has proved him inflexibly decided against undertaking it. What are we to do? The clamor is high for some appointment, we are informed too of many students who do not come because that school is not opened, and some now with us think of leaving us for the same reason. You may remember that among those who were the subjects of conversation at our last meeting Judge Dade was one. But the minds of the Board were so much turned to two particular characters, that little was said of any others. An idea has got abroad, I know not from what source, that we have appointed Judge Dade, and that he has accepted. This has spread extensively, perhaps from a general sense of his fitness, and I learn that it has been recieved with much favor, and particularly among the students of the University. I know no more myself of Judge Dade than what I saw of him at our Rockfish meeting, and a short visit he made me in returning from that place. As far as that opportunity enabled me to form an opinion, I certainly thought very highly of the strength of his mind, and soundness of his judgement. I happened to recieve Mr Gilmer's ultimate and peremptory refusal, while Judge Stuart and Mr Howe Peyton of Staunton were with me. The former, you know, is his colleague on the bench of the Genl. court, the latter has been more particularly intimate with him, as having been brought up with him at the same school. I asked from them information respecting Mr Dade, and they spoke of him in terms of high commendation. They state him to be an excellent Latin and Greek scholar, of clear and sound ideas, lucid in communicating them, equal as a lawyer to any one of the judiciary corps, and superior to all as a writer, that his character is perfectly correct, his mind liberal and accomodating, yet firm, of sound republican principles, and in their judgement entirely superior to the person for whose acceptance we had so much negociation. This is the substance, and these, I may say, the terms in which they spoke of him; and when I considered the characters of these two gentlemen, and their opportunities of knowing what they attested, I could not but be strongly imprest. It happened, very much to my gratification, that Genl. Cocke was here at the same time, recieved the same information and impression, and authorises me to add his concurrence in proposing this appointment to our Colleagues, and to say moreover, that if on such further enquiry as they may make, they should approve the choice, and express it by letter in preference to a meeting for conference on the subject, I might write to Judge Dade, and, on his acceptance, issue his commission. I should add that the gentlemen above named were confident he would accept, as well from other circumstances, as from his having three sons to educate. Of course this would put an end to the anxieties we have all had on this subject. The public impatience for some appointment to this school renders desirable as early an answer as Your convenience admits. Accept the assurance of my great esteem and respect

Th: Jefferson

P. S. Our numbers are now 79.

Madison to Jefferson

[Montpellier] May 19, 1825

Dr Sir

I did not receive yours of the 12.th in time to be answered by the last mail. My thoughts, as heretofore intimated, had been turned to Judge Dade for the

Law Chair; and with the recommendatory opinions which you enumerate, I can not hesitate to concur in the offer of it, as is proposed. I concur also in the issuing of a Commission on the written sanction of the Visitors without the formality of a Special Meeting. With affc. respects

J. M.

Madison to Jefferson

[Montpellier] Aug. 4, 1825

DEAR SIR

Having but little hope that Judge Dade will accept the place offered to him, and having occasionally heard Mr. Lomax of Fredg. spoken of favorably, I sought an occasion yesterday of learning more of him from Judge Barbour (without disclosing my object) who has long been at the same Bar with him, and is otherwise well acquainted with his character. The Judge considers him as a man of solid talents and a well informed Lawyer, with an advantageous elocution. I asked whether Mr Lomax had extended his studies beyond the ordinary municipal law, to the law of nations and to a more philosophical view of the general subject of law. The judge said he could not answer that question, but thought his mind very capable of this task, and knew him to be habitually laborious in his application to the duties of his profession. Nothing was said on the subject of political Economy; nor did the Judge know the extent of Mr. L's classical attainments.

From the same and from other sources, I have understood that Mr. Lomax is of amiable disposition, polished manners, and of the best habits of every sort; and that he has been a uniform and sound patriot. He is at the age of about forty.

I have thought it proper to make this communication as the basis of further enquiries which you may have opportunities of making.

We had the pleasure of hearing a few days ago that your health is improving. Affecy. yours

J. M.

Jefferson to Madison and the Board of Visitors of the University of Virginia

Monticello Aug. 4, 1825

DEAR SIR

Chancellor Tucker, Mr. Barbour, Judge Carr, as you know had declined accepting the law chair of the University, and yesterday I received a letter from

Judge Dade finally declining also. Mr. Gilmer, our first choice had declined on account of his health, very much deranged by his voyage to Europe. That is now in a good degree reestablished, and he is writing to accept. What shall we do? Shall we return to our first choice, and be done with the difficulty? or have a meeting and look out for some other? or do nothing till October? The vacancy of this chair is very disadvantageous, being thought by many more wanting than all the others. If you agree to the appointment of Mr. Gilmer, perhaps you will signify it by letter as in pressing cases, as discussion can promise nothing new on his subject.

Our last 50,000 Dollars were placed by the treasurer in the Virginia bank and have been disposed of as follows

- 7,626 to replace so much advanced for books and apparatus by the general fund
- 6,000 to finish library room
- 18,000 advanced to Hilland (?) to complete the library
- 6,000 committed to Mr. King our Minister in London for Philosophical apparatus
- 3,000 for Anatomical apparatus
- 700 paid to Dr. Emmet for Chemical Apparatus
- 8,674 balance remaining

50,000

Accept the assurance of my high respect and esteem.

TH JEFFERSON

Madison to Jefferson

Montpellier Aug. 10, 1825

DEAR SIR

Your Circular of the 4th. instant did not come to hand till yesterday. In the present attitude of things the reappointment of Mr. Gilmer to the Law professorship seems a matter of course; though I am sorry to learn that there is some ground to apprehend that his qualifications are not as well understood and as highly estimated as they deserve to [be][21]

---

21. Gilmer was elected by the Board of Visitors in Oct. 1825 but died before he could join the faculty; see Malone, VI, pp. 469, 482.

Jefferson to Madison and the Board of Visitors of the University of Virginia

Monticello Sept. 10, 1825

DEAR SIR

The state of my health renders it perfectly certain that I shall not be able to attend the next meeting of the visitors (Oct. 3) *at the University*.[22] Yet I think there is no one but myself to whom the matters to be acted on are sufficiently known for communication to them. This adds a reason the more for inducing the members to meet at Monticello the day before, which has been heretofore found to facilitate and shorten our business. If you could be here then on the sunday to dinner, that afternoon and evening and the morning of the Monday will suffice for all our business and the board will only have to ride to the University pro forma for attesting the proceedings. Permit me therefore to expect you to dinner on that day (Oct. 2) which as it is ever grateful to me, seems on this occasion to be peculiarly urgent. Accept I pray you the assurance of my high esteem and respect.

TH. JEFFERSON

P. S. The above is circular, but I hope you will be able to come a day before that proposed for the other gentlemen, that you may have time to go over the papers at leisure.

Madison to Jefferson

Montpellier Oct. 14, 1825

DR SIR.

Mr. Browere (pronounced Brower) is so anxious to pay his respects to you that I can not refuse him a line of introduction His object is to take your likeness in plaster, much desired it appears by patrons of a Public Gallery. His success as an Artist is very highly attested. His bust of Genl Lafayette is pronounced by other imitative artists a conspicuous proof of his talent. The little specimen he has given here accords with his reputation. Being apprized that you will not submit to the tedious operation for a Bust, he limits his hopes to a Mask of the face only, which can be quickly taken with but little fatigue to the patient and to which he can add the other parts from a mere outline on paper.[23]

---

22. TJ's italics.

23. John H. I. Browere made a life mask of TJ in Oct.; see Malone, VI, pp. 469–70. It is illustrated in Alfred L. Bush, "The Life Portraits of Thomas Jefferson," in *Jefferson and the Arts: An Extended View*, ed. William Howard Adams (Washington, 1976), p. 96.

I have heard nothing as to the University since I parted from you.[24] I hope things continue well there; and that Key and Long will have seen their error in the course so hastily taken by them. I find all I meet with anticipating permanent good to the Institution from the incidents which threw a transient cloud over it.

Jefferson to Madison

Monticello Oct. 18, 1825

TH:J TO J. MADISON

Every thing is going on smoothly at the University. The students are attending their schools with more assiduity, and looking to their Professors with more respect. The authority of the latter is visibly strengthened, as is the confidence of those who visit the place, and the effect, on the whole, has been salutary. The Professors are all lecturing, the Cantabs somewhat in the pouts as yet. I sent a copy of the new enactments the other day, with a request they might be read to the schools, at their lectures, for promulgation. The other Professors did it, these did not, nor said why.

My rides to the University have brought on me great sufferings, reducing my intervals of ease from 45. to 20. minutes. This is a good index of the changes occurring.

I was taken in by Mr Browere. He said his operation would be of about 20. minutes and less unpleasant than Houdon's method. I submitted therefore without enquiry but it was a bold experiment on his part on the health of an Octogenary, worn down by sickness as well as age. Successive coats of thin grout plaistered on the naked head, and kept there an hour, would have been a severe trial of a young and hale person. He suffered the plaister also to get so dry that separation became difficult and even dangerous. He was obliged to use freely the mallet and chissel to break it into pieces and cut off a piece at a time. These thumps of the mallet would have been sensible almost to a loggerhead. The family became alarmed, and he confused, till I was quite exhausted, and there became real danger that the ears would separate from the head sooner than from the plaister. I now bid adieu for ever to busts and even portraits.[25]

I do not know whether you are acquainted with Colo Bernard Peyton, commission merchant of Richmond.[26] As honest and worthy a man as lives,

24. JM attended the Board of Visitors meeting, Oct. 3-7, 1825, which dealt with the student riots and supported the expulsion of three offenders and the reprimanding of eleven others; see Malone, VI, p. 466.

25. When word circulated of TJ's displeasure, Browere requested a testimonial from TJ, which TJ promptly furnished; see *ibid.*, p. 470. See also Bush, pp. 95-98, and Charles Henry Hart, *Browere's Life Masks of Great Americans* (New York, 1899), pp. 36-49 for TJ, and pp. 56-59 for JM and Mrs. Madison.

26. For Bernard Peyton's service as TJ's agent in Richmond, see Malone, VI, pp. 314-15.

and the most punctual in business I ever knew, he understands that Lay, your correspondent there is become bankrupt, and he would gladly serve you there. He has been my homme d'affaires there 10. or 12. years, and I never had one who in the smallest as well as great matters was so kind and zealous. He has the business of this neighborhood generally and that of the Staunton country. I know that these connections are dictated often by very special and personal considerations, and my mention of his is only ut valeat quantum valere debet [take it for what it is worth]. Ever and affectly. yours,

TH. JEFFERSON

Jefferson to Madison

Monticello Dec. 24, 1825

DEAR SIR,

I have for some time considered the question of Internal improvement as desperate. The torrent of general opinion sets so strongly in favor of it as to be irresistible. And I suppose that even the opposition in Congress will hereafter be feeble and formal, unless something can be done which may give a gleam of encouragement to our friends, or alarm their opponents in their fancied security. I learn from Richmond that those who think with us there are in a state of perfect dismay, not knowing what to do or what to propose. Mr. Gordon, our representative, particularly, has written to me in very desponding terms, not disposed to yield indeed, but pressing for opinions and advice on the subject.[27] I have no doubt you are pressed in the same way, and I hope you have devised and recommended something to them. If you have, stop here and read no more, but consider all that follows as *non-avenue*. I shall be better satisfied to adopt implicitly anything which you may have advised, than anything occurring to myself. For I have long ceased to think on subjects of this kind, and pay little attention to public proceedings. But if you have done nothing in it, then I risk for your consideration what has occurred to me, and is expressed in the enclosed paper.[28] Bailey's propositions, which came to hand since I wrote the paper, and which I suppose to have come from the President himself, show a little hesitation in the purposes of his party;[29] and in that state of mind, a bolt shot critically may decide the contest by its effect on the less bold. The olive branch held out to them at this moment may be accepted and the constitution thus saved at a moderate sacrifice. I say nothing of the paper, which will

---

27. For the proposals of President John Quincy Adams on internal improvements in his first annual message to Congress in Dec. 1825, see *ibid.,* p. 437.

28. See the enclosure "The solemn Declaration and Protest . . . ," below.

29. Congressman John Bailey of Massachusetts proposed a constitutional amendment authorizing the use of federal funds for internal improvements; see Malone, VI, p. 438.

explain itself. The following heads of consideration, or some of them, may weigh in its favor:

It may intimidate the wavering.

It may break the western coalition, by offering the same thing in a different form.

It will be viewed with favor in contrast with the Georgia opposition and fear of strengthening it.

It will be an example of a temperate mode of opposition in future and similar cases.

It will delay the measure a year at least.

It will give us the chance of better times and of intervening accidents; and in no way place us in a worse than our present situation.

I do not dwell on these topics; your mind will develop them.

The first question is, whether you approve of doing anything of the kind. If not, send it back to me, and it shall be suppressed; for I would not hazard so important a measure against your opinion, nor even without its support. If you think it may be a canvass on which to put something good, make what alterations you please, and I will forward it to Gordon, under the most sacred injunctions that it shall be so used as that not a shadow of suspicion shall fall on you or myself, that it has come from either of us. But what you do, do as promptly as your convenience will admit, lest it shall be anticipated by something worse.[30] Ever and affectionately yours

TH. JEFFERSON

ENCLOSURE
The solemn Declaration and Protest of the commonwealth of Virginia on the principles of the constitution of the US. of America and of the violations of them.

We the General Assembly of Virginia, on behalf, and in the name of the people thereof do declare as follows.

The states in N. America which confederated to establish their independance of the government of Great Britain, of which Virginia was one, became, on that acquisition, free and independant states, and as such authorised to constitute governments, each for itself, in such form as it thought best.

They entered into a compact (which is called the Constitution of the US. of America) by which they agreed to unite in a single government as to their relations with each other, and with foreign nations, and as to certain other articles particularly specified. They retained at the same time, each to itself the other rights of independant government comprehending mainly their domestic interests.

For the administration of their Federal branch they agreed to appoint, in conjunction, a distinct set of functionaries, legislative, executive and judiciary, in the manner

---

30. For a discussion of TJ's position, see *ibid.,* pp. 438–39. See also Gordon S. Wood, "The Trials and Tribulations of Thomas Jefferson," in *Jeffersonian Legacies,* ed. Peter S. Onuf (Charlottesville, 1993), pp. 409–15.

settled in that compact: while to each severally and of course, remained it's original right of appointing, each for itself, a separate set of functionaries, legislative, executive and judiciary also, for administering the Domestic branch of their respective governments.

Those two sets of officers, each independant of the other, constitute thus a *whole* of government, for each state separately the powers ascribed to the one, as specifically made federal, exercisable over the whole, the residuary powers, retained to the other, exercisable exclusively over it's particular state, foreign herein, each to the others, as they were before their original compact.

To this construction of government and distribution of it's powers, the Commonwealth of Virginia does religiously and affectionately adhere, opposing with equal fidelity and firmness, the usurpation of either set of functionaries on the rightful powers of the other.

But the federal branch has assumed in some cases and claimed in others, a right of enlarging it's own powers by constructions, inferences, and indefinite deductions, from those directly given, which this assembly does declare to be usurpations of the powers retained to the independant branches, mere interpolations into the compact, and direct infractions of it.

They claim, for example, and have commenced the exercise of a right to construct roads, open canals, and effect other internal improvements within the territories and jurisdictions exclusively belonging to the several states, which this assembly does declare has not been given to that branch by the constitutional compact, but remain to each state among it's domestic and unalienated powers exercisable within itself, and by it's domestic authorities alone.

This assembly does further disavow, and declare to be most false and unfounded, the doctrine, that the compact, in authorising it's federal branch to lay and collect taxes, duties, imposts and excises to pay the debts and provide for the common defence and general welfare of the U S. has given them thereby a power to do whatever *they* may think, or pretend, would promote the general welfare, which construction would make that, of itself, a complete government, without limitation of powers; but that the plain sense and obvious meaning was that they might levy the taxes necessary to provide for the general welfare by the various acts of power therein specified and delegated to them, and by no others.

Nor is it admitted, as has been said, that the people of these states, by not investing their federal branch with all means of bettering their condition, have denied to themselves any which may effect that purpose since, in the distribution of these means, they have given to that branch those which belong to it's department, and to the states have reserved separately the residue which belong to them separately. And thus by the organization of the two branches taken together, have completely secured the first object of human association, the full improvement of their condition, and reserved to themselves all the faculties of multiplying their own blessings.

Whilst the General assembly thus declares the rights retained by the states, rights which they have never yielded, and which this state will never voluntarily yield, they do not mean to raise the banner of disaffection, or of separation from their sister-states, co-parties with themselves to this compact. They know and value too highly the blessings of their union as to foreign nations and questions arising among themselves, to consider every infraction as to be met by actual resistance; they respect too affectionately the opinions of those possessing the same rights under the same instrument, to make every difference of construction a ground of immediate rupture. They would indeed consider such a rupture as among the greatest calamities which could befall them; but not the greatest. There is yet one greater, submission to a government of unlimited powers. It is only when the hope of avoiding this shall become absolutely desperate that further forbearance could not be indulged. Should a majority of the Co-parties therefore contrary to the expectation and hope of this assembly, prefer at this time, acquiescence in these assumptions of power by the federal member of the government, we will be patient and suffer much, under the confidence that time, ere it be too late, will prove to them also the bitter consequences in which this usurpation will involve us all. In the meanwhile we will breast with them, rather than separate from them, every misfortune save that only of living under a government of unlimited powers. We owe every other sacrifice to ourselves, to our federal brethren, and to the world at large, to pursue with temper and perseverance the great experiment which shall prove that man is capable of living in society, governing itself by laws self-imposed, and securing to its' members the enjoyment of life, liberty, property and peace; and further to shew that even when the government of it's choice shall shew a tendency to degeneracy, we are not at once to despair but that the will and the watchfulness of it's sounder parts will reform it's aberrations, recall it to original and legitimate principles and restrain it within the rightful limits of self-government. And these are the objects of this Declaration and Protest.

Supposing then that it might be for the good of the whole, as some of it's Co-states seem to think, that this power of making roads and canals should be added to those directly given to the federal branch, as more likely to be systematically and beneficially directed, than by the independant action of the several states, this Commonwealth, from respect to these opinions, and a desire of conciliation with it's Co-states, will consent, in concurrence with them, to make this addition, provided it be done regularly by an amendment of the compact, in the way established by that instrument, and provided also it be sufficiently guarded against abuses, compromises, and corrupt practices, not only of possible, but of probable occurrence. And as a further pledge of the sincere and cordial attachment of this commonwealth to the Union of the whole so far as has been consented to by the compact called 'the Constitution of the US. of America' (construed according to the plain and ordinary meaning of it's language, to the common intendment of the time, and of those who framed it) to give also to all parties and authorities time for reflection, and for consideration whether, under a temperate view of the possible consequences, and especially of the constant obstructions which an equivocal majority must ever expect to meet, they will still prefer the assumption of this power rather than it's acceptance from the free will of their constituents, and to preserve peace in the meanwhile, we proceed to make it the duty of our citizens, until the legislature shall otherwise and ultimately decide, to acquiesce under those acts of the federal branch of our government which we have declared to be usurpations, and against which, in point of right, we do protest as null and void, and never to be quoted as precedents of right.

We therefore do enact, and be it enacted by the General assembly of Virginia that all citizens of this commonwealth, and persons and authorities within the same, shall pay full obedience at all times to the Acts which may be past by the Congress of the US. the object of which shall be the construction of postroads, making canals of navigation, and maintaining the same in any part of the US. in like manner as if the said acts were, totidem verbis past by the legislature of this commonwealth.

Madison to Jefferson

Montpellier Dec. 28, 1825

Dear Sir

I rec^d yesterday evening yours of the 24th inst: inclosing a paper drawn up with a view to the question of "Roads & Canals," and to the course of proceeding most expedient for the Legislature of Virg^a, now in session.

In my retired position it is difficult to scan the precise tendency of measures addressed to the opinions and feelings of the States and of their Representatives; these being imperfectly understood, and continually undergoing also more or less of modifications. In general, I have doubted the policy of any attempt by Virginia to take the lead, or the appearance of it, in opposing the obnoxious career of Congress, or, rather of their Constituents; considering the prejudices which seem to have been excited of late agst her. And the doubt is now strengthened, by the diversity of opinion apparently taking place among her opponents, which if not checked by interpositions on her part, may break the Phalanx with which she has to deal. Hitherto the encroachments of Congress have not proceeded far enough to rouse the full attention of some of the States; who tho' not opposing the limited expence of Surveying Engineers, or the productive subscriptions to projected improvements by particular States, will unite with Virginia in combating the exercise of powers which must not only interfere with their local jurisdictions, but expend vast sums of money, from which their share of benefit, would not be proportioned to their share of the burden. To this consideration I refer the recent proposition of Mr. Bailey. It may have had in part, the motives you allude to. But it can be explained by the local calculations under its surface. The members of Cong^s from N. England have never been entirely united on the subject of National Canals etc. and altho' sundry projects of that sort have lately appeared in that quarter as elsewhere, it is probable that most of them will be found either impracticable, or threatening changes in the channels of trade causing them to be abandoned. It is pretty certain that the progress made by N. England in her internal improvements reduces her interest in the prosecution of them with the national revenue, below her contributions to it, or her portion of a dividend from it. The remark is applicable to the weighty State of N. York, where the power assumed by Congress has always been viewed with a degree of jealousy, and where I believe a decided opposition would be made agst a claim that w^d touch her soil or introduce a jurisdiction over it, without the express consent of the State. Her Senator Van Buren, it appears, has already taken up the subject, and no doubt with a purpose of controuling the assumed power.[31] The progress made by other States in like improvements

---

31. Van Buren's views on internal improvements emphasized state-funded projects instead of national development; see John Niven, *Martin Van Buren: The Romantic Age of American Politics* (New York, 1983), p. 164.

under their own authority, may be expected to enlist some of them on the same side of the question. Were Congress indeed possessed of the undisputed power in the case, it would be a problem, whether it would not be paralysed by the difficulty of adapting a system of Roads and Canals to the diversified situations of the States, and of making a satisfactory apportionment of the benefits and burdens among them. As this is a view of the subject however not likely to quiet the apprehensions which prevail, and might yield to fuller information with regard to it, I should suppose Virginia would find an eligible compromise in Mr. Bailey's project; notwithstanding the bearing it may have in favor of a prolonged tariff, as the nurse of the manufacturing system. It may be well at least to know the weakness of the proposition in and out of Congress, before any irrevocable decision be had at Richmond.

Should any strong interposition there be ultimately required, your paper will be a valuable resort. But I must submit to your consideration whether the expedient with which it closes of enacting statutes of Congress into Virginia Statutes, would not be an anomaly without any operative character, besides the objection to a lumping and anticipating enactment. As the Acts in question would not be executed by the ordinary functionaries of Virg^a, and she could not convert the federal into State functionaries, the whole proceeding would be as exclusively under the federal authority as if the legislative interference of Virg^a had not taken place; her interference amounting to nothing more than *a recommendation* to her Citizens to acquiesce in the exercise of the power assumed by Congress, for which there is no apparent necessity or obligation.

Previous to the rec^t of your communication, a letter from Mr. Ritchie, marked with all his warm feelings, on the occasion, made a pressing call for my opinions and advice. I inclose it with my answer, in which you will see the course which occurred to me as most eligible or least questionable;[32] Bailey's proposition being at the time unknown. I was apprehensive that encouragement to a stronger course, in the present stage of the business and temper of the Assembly might lead to a stile and tone irritating rather than subduing prejudices, instead of the true policy as well as dignity of mingling as much of molliter in modo [gentleness in manner], as would be consistent with the fortiter in re [firmness in acting]. Whilst Congress feel themselves backed by a Majority of their Constituents, menace or defiance, will never deter them from their purposes; particularly when such language proceeds from the section of the Union, to which there is a habit of alluding as distinguished by causes of internal weakness.

You asked an early answer and I have hurried one, at the risk of crudeness in some of its views of the subject. If there be errors, they can do no harm when under your controul. Health and all other good wishes

JAMES MADISON

Return if you please the letter of Ritchie and the answer.

32. See the enclosure [JM to Thomas Ritchie], Dec. 18, 1825, below.

ENCLOSURE
[Madison to Thomas Ritchie]

Dear Sir   Montpellier Dec. 18, 1825

Yours of the 10th inst: was rec^d a few days ago and I give it the earliest answer which circumstances have permitted.

It has been impossible not to observe the license of construction applied to the Constitution of the U. States; and that the premises from which powers are inferred, often cover more ground than inferences themselves.

In seeking a remedy for these aberrations, we must not lose sight of the essential distinction, too little heeded, between assumptions of power by the General Government, in opposition to the Will of the Constituent Body, and assumptions by the Constituent Body through the Government as the Organ of its will. In the first case, nothing is necessary but to rouse the attention of the people, and a remedy ensues thro' the forms of the Constitution. This was seen when the Constitution was violated by the Alien and Sedition Acts. In the second case, the appeal can only be made to the recollections, the reason, and the conciliatory spirit of the Majority of the people agst their own errors; with a persevering hope of success, and an eventual acquiescence in disappointment unless indeed oppression should reach an extremity overruling all other considerations. This second case is illustrated by the apparent call of a majority of the States and of the people for national Roads and Canals; with respect to the latter of which, it is remarkable that Mr. Hamilton, himself on an occasion when he was giving to the text of the Constitution its utmost ductility, (see his Report on the Bank) was constrained to admit that they exceeded the authority of Congress.

All power in human hands is liable to be abused. In Governm^{ts} independent of the people, the rights and interests of the whole may be sacrificed to the views of the Governm^t. In Republics, where the people govern themselves, and where of course the majority Govern, a danger to the minority, arises from opportunities tempting a sacrifice of their rights to the interests real or supposed of the Majority. No form of Gov^t therefore can be a perfect guard agst the abuse of Power. The recommendation of the Republican form is that the danger of abuse is less than in any other; and the superior recommendation of the federo-Republican system is, that whilst it provides more effectually against external danger, it involves a greater security to the minority against the hasty formation of oppressive majorities.

These general observations lead to the several questions you ask as to the course which, in the present state of things, it becomes Virginia to pursue.

1. "Ought an amendment of the Constitution, giving to Congress a Power as to Roads and Canals, to be proposed on her part; and what part taken by her if proposed from any other quarter?"

Those who think the power a proper one, and that it does not exist, must espouse such an amendment; and those who think the power neither existing nor proper, may prefer a specific grant forming a restrictive precedent, to a moral certainty of an exercise of the power, furnishing a contrary precedent. Of the individual ways of thinking on this point, you can probably make a better estimate than I can.

2. "Ought a proposed amendment to comprize a particular guard agst the sweeping misconstruction of the terms, 'common defence and general welfare.'"

The wish for such a guard is natural. But the fallacious inferences from a failure however happening, would seem to require for the experiment a very flattering prospect of success. As yet the unlimited power expressed by the terms, if disjoined from the explanatory specifications, seems to have been claimed for Congress rather incidentally and unimpressively, than under circumstances indicating a dangerous prevalence of the heresy. Gov. Van Ness alone appears to have officially adopted it; and possibly with some unexpressed qualification. Has not the Supreme Court of the U. S. on some occasion disclaimed the import of the naked terms as the measure of Congressional authority? In general the advocates of the Road and Canal powers, have rested the claim on deductions from some one or more of the enumerated grants.

The doctrine presenting the most serious aspect is that which limits the claim to the mere "appropriation of money" for the General Welfare. However untenable or artificial the distinction may be, its seducing tendencies and the progress made in giving it a practical sanction, render it pretty certain that a Constitutional prohibition is not at present attainable; whilst an abortive attempt would but give to the innovation a greater stability. Should a specific amendment take place on the subject of roads and canals, the zeal for this appropriating power would be cooled by the provision for the primary and popular object of it; at the same time that the implied necessity of the amendment would have a salutary influence on other points of Construction.

3. "Ought Virg^a to protest agst the Power of internal improvement by Roads and Canals; with an avowal of readiness to acquiesce in a decision agst her by ¾ of her Sister States?"

By such a decision is understood a mere expression of concurrent opinions by ¾ of the State Legislatures. However conciliatory the motives to such a proposition might be, it could not fail to be criticised as requiring a surrender of the Constitutional rights of the majority in expounding the Constitution, to an extra Constitutional project of a protesting State. May it not be added that such a test, if acceded to, would, in the present state of Public Opinion, end in a riveting decision against Virginia?

Virginia has doubtless a right to manifest her sense of the Constitution, and of proceedings under it, either by protest or other equivalent modes. Perhaps the mode as well suited as any to the present occasion, if the occasion itself be a suitable one, would be that of instructions to her Representatives in Cong^s to oppose measures violating her constructions of the Instrument; with a preamble appealing, for the truth of her constructions to the contemporary expositions by those best acquainted with the intentions of the Convention which framed the Constitution; to the Debates and proceedings of the State Conventions which ratified it; to the universal understanding that the Gov^t of the Union was a limited not an unlimited one; to the inevitable tendency of the latitude of construction in behalf of internal improvements, to break down the barriers against unlimited power; it being obvious that the ingenuity which deduces the authority for such measures, could readily find it for any others whatever; and particularly to the inconclusiveness of the reasoning from the sovereign character of the powers invested in Cong^s, and the great utility of particular measures, to the rightful exercise of the powers required for such measures; a reasoning which however applicable to the case of a single Gov^t charged with the whole powers of Gov^t loses its force in the case of a compound Gov^t like that of the U. S., where the delegated sovereignty is divided between the General and the State Gov^{ts}; where one sovereignty loses what the other gains; and where particular powers and duties may have been withheld from one, because deemed more proper to be left with the other.

I have thrown out these hasty remarks more in compliance with your request than from a belief that they offer anything new on the beaten subject. Should the topics touched on be thought worthy on any account of being publicly developed, they will be in hands very competent to the task. My views of the Constitutional questions before the public are already known as far as they can be entitled to notice, and I find myself every day more indisposed, and, as may be presumed, less fit, for reappearance on the political Arena.

49

JEFFERSON'S LAST YEAR, 1826

ON NEW YEAR'S DAY 1826, Jefferson, "now far gone in my 83d year," cast an uncharacteristic glance backward. "Yesterday," he wrote, "the last of the year closed on the 61st of my continued services to the public. I came into it as soon as of age which was in 1764." Beginning with his election as justice of the Albemarle County court, he then listed his election by his neighbors to the Virginia colonial assembly as "their Representative" before going to the Continental Congress. Thereafter, he returned to the Virginia legislature in 1776, was employed for two years on the revision of the law code, then served as governor, congressman again, minister plenipotentiary to France, secretary of state, vice president, president, and board member and rector of the University of Virginia.[1]

He was beginning to feel the toll taken by the years. At the age of eighty-two, he had complained facetiously that he had "one foot in the grave, and the other uplifted to follow it."[2] As the new year opened, he reported that he was "weakened in body by infirmities and in mind by age . . . reading one newspaper only and forgetting immediately what I read in that."[3] But after a three-week confinement to his couch, he was able to leave the house and walk outdoors, a welcome relief from the "disease, debility, age, and embarrassed affairs" that depressed him when he occasionally lost sight of having lived "a long life with fewer circumstances of affliction than are the lot of most men."[4]

Yet there was a certain sadness about Jefferson's last years, when he occasionally felt that he had lived too long and had been bypassed by the postwar democratic forces that he and Madison had helped create. "All, all dead!" he

1. TJ to William F. Gordon, Jan. 1, 1826, in Ford, X, pp. 358–59. Portions of this letter are illegible, but TJ repeated this information in his "Thoughts on Lotteries," Feb. 1826, *ibid.*, p. 368.
2. TJ to Fanny Wright, Aug. 7, 1825, *ibid.*, p. 344.
3. TJ to William F. Gordon, Jan. 1, 1826, *ibid.*, p. 358.
4. TJ to Thomas Jefferson Randolph, Feb. 8, 1826, *ibid.*, pp. 374–75.

moaned to an old friend in 1825, "and ourselves left alone midst a new gener-[atio]n whom we know not, and who know not us."[5] Although he remained optimistic about "the future fame, fortune and prosperity" of the University of Virginia,[6] he was gloomy about its present prospects when he learned that the legislature in 1826 had decided by an overwhelming vote "against giving us another Dollar" for the university.

At the same time, his burden of debt "had become considerable," something of an understatement after Wilson Cary Nicholas defaulted during the Panic of 1819 on $20,000 in promissory notes that Jefferson had endorsed and for which he then became liable. Indeed, he called the Nicholas debt "the *coup de grace*. Ever since that," he confessed in one of his few letters of complaint to Madison, "I have been paying 1200 dollars a year interest on his debt, which, with my own, was absorbing so much of my annual income, as that the Maintenance of my family was making deep and rapid inroads on my capital."

"Reflecting on these things," he continued, "the practice occurred to me, of selling [property], on fair valuation, and by way of lottery, often resorted to before the Revolution to effect large sales, and still in constant usage in every State for individual as well as corporation purposes. If it is permitted in my case"—he had petitioned the legislature for approval—"my lands here alone, with the mills, etc., will pay every thing, and leave me Monticello and a farm free. If refused, I must sell everything here, perhaps considerably in Bedford [County], move thither with my family, where I have not even a log hut to put my head into, and whether ground for burial, will depend on the depredations which, under the form of sales, shall have been committed on my property. The question then with me was *ultrum horum* [take which ever of those you prefer]?"[7]

The sympathetic Madison sent a prompt reply, confessing that he had suspected "that the causes you enumerate were undermining your estate." But his fears "did not reach the extent of the evil. Some of these causes were indeed forced on my attention by my own experience," he lamented like any forlorn farmer who operates at the risk of weather. "Since my return to private life (and the case was worse during my absence in Public) such have been the unkind seasons, and the ravages of insects, that I have made but one tolerable crop of Tobacco, and but one of Wheat, the proceeds of both of which were greatly curtailed by mishaps in the sale of them. And having no resources but in the earth I cultivate, I have been living very much throughout on borrowed means. As a necessary consequence, my debts have swelled to an amount, which if called for at the present conjuncture, would give to my situation a degree of analogy to yours. Fortunately I am not threatened with any rigid

5. TJ to Francis Adrian van der Kemp, Jan. 11, 1825, *ibid.*, pp. 336–38.
6. TJ used this phrase in his "Thoughts on Lotteries," Feb. 1826, *ibid.*, p. 370.
7. TJ to JM, Feb. 17, 1826, below.

pressure, and have the chance of better crops and prices, with the prospect of a more leisurely disposal of the property which must be a final resort."[8]

The gloom generated by Jefferson's financial problems merged with his growing fears of "consolidation," pushing him in the direction of a rabid defense of states' rights and cooperation with the Old Republicans, including his ancient enemy, John Randolph of Roanoke, as well as William B. Giles and John Taylor.[9] When the new president, John Quincy Adams, sent his first annual message to Congress in 1825, he advocated adoption of "the American System," a series of measures varying from a protective tariff for the support of manufactures to a national program of internal improvements such as the federal construction of roads and canals to promote the general welfare.

Although Adams viewed his proposals as updated versions of Jefferson's and Madison's mature politics, Jefferson was persuaded that "the question of internal improvement [w]as desperate. The torrent of general opinion sets so strongly in favor of it as to be irresistible. And I suppose," he informed Madison, "that even the opposition in Congress will hereafter be feeble and formal, unless something can be done which may give a gleam of encouragement to our friends, or alarm their opponents in their fancied security."[10]

Accordingly, the agitated and impulsive octogenarian wrote out in detail his closet ruminations about the evils of consolidation, which seemed to him to threaten a constitutional crisis. He entitled it "The solemn Declaration and Protest of the commonwealth of Virginia on the principles of the constitution of the US. of America and of the violations of them." A sharp indictment of the federal government for "usurpations of the powers retained" by the states, the protest charged that by "mere interpolations into the compact, and direct infractions of it" the "federal branch has assumed in some cases and claimed in others, a right of enlarging it's own powers by constructions, inferences, and indefinite deductions, from those directly given" and specifically mentioned in the Constitution. "They claim . . . and have commenced the exercise of a right to construct roads, open canals, and effect other internal improvements within the territories and jurisdictions exclusively belonging to the several states." Such claims, he argued with the vigor he had had in 1798, amounted to a usurpation of power, and he declared them "null and void." Although he proclaimed a rupture of the Union "as among the greatest calamities" that could befall the people of his state, it was not the greatest since "submission to a government of unlimited powers" would be worse.

8. JM to TJ, Feb. 24, 1826, below.

9. On TJ's disillusionment, see Malone, VI, pp. 302–14, 328–37; Peterson, pp. 980–1009; Gordon S. Wood, *The Radicalism of the American Revolution* (New York, 1992), pp. 367–68; and Joseph J. Ellis, *Passionate Sage: The Character and Legacy of John Adams* (New York, 1993), pp. 141–42. For extended treatments, see Robert E. Shalhope, "Thomas Jefferson's Republicanism and Antebellum Southern Thought," *J. So. Hist.* 42 (1976): 529–56, and Joseph H. Harrison, Jr., "*Sic et non:* Thomas Jefferson and Internal Improvement," *JER* 7 (1987): 335–49.

10. TJ to JM, Dec. 24, 1825, above.

Having moved that far towards his language in his draft of the Kentucky resolutions, the disillusioned Jefferson backed off to avoid raising "the banner of disaffection, or of separation from their sister-states." Virginia's attachment to the Union would bar resistance until it was the last resort. If a majority of the states endorsed President Adams's program, "we will be patient and suffer much, under the confidence that time, ere it be too late, will prove to them also the bitter consequences in which this usurpation will involve us all." The way out of the constitutional dilemma, Jefferson suggested, was the adoption of an amendment to add the "power of making roads and canals . . . to those directly given to the federal branch," provided that it was "sufficiently guarded against abuses, compromises, and corrupt practices, not only of possible, but of probable occurrence."

During the amending process, Virginians should acquiesce in the federal usurpations, recognizing under protest "the assumption of this power rather than it's acceptance from the free will of their constituents, and [thus] to preserve peace in the meanwhile." Finally, he proposed that the Virginia assembly enact legislation obligating all citizens of the Old Dominion to obey federal legislation on internal improvements "as if the said acts were . . . past by the legislature of this commonwealth."[11]

Before sending his protest to Richmond for consideration by the Virginia assembly, however, Jefferson followed his usual practice of asking Madison's advice. On Christmas Eve, 1825, Jefferson sent his paper to Montpellier, confessing that he "would not hazard so important a measure against your opinion, nor even without its support." He hoped that Madison had already prepared a position paper, saying that he would "be better satisfied to adopt implicitly anything which you may have advised, than anything occurring to myself." If Madison had not yet acted, however, Jefferson submitted "what has occurred to me" for his friend's consideration and ran through the reasons for favoring a protest:

It may intimidate the wavering. . . .
It will be an example of a temperate mode of opposition in future and similar cases.
It will delay the measure a year at least.
It will give us the chance of better times and of intervening accidents; and in no way place us in a worse than our present situation.

Almost as an afterthought, Jefferson added: "The first question is, whether you approve of doing anything of the kind. If not, send it back to me, and it shall be suppressed."[12]

Madison moved quickly to squelch Jefferson's proposal to protest on the one hand and to promise compliance on the other. Earlier in the year, Madison had told his disillusioned colleague that he considered the question of canals already decided, even without the amendment that they both preferred,

11. For "The solemn Declaration and Protest . . . ," see TJ to JM, Dec. 24, 1825, above.
12. *Ibid.*

"because sanctioned by the nation under the permanent influence of benefit to the major part of it." "The will of the nation being omnipotent for right, is so for wrong also; and the will of the nation being in the majority, the minority must submit to that danger of oppression as an evil infinitely less than the danger to the whole nation from a will independent of it."[13]

It was predictable, therefore, that Madison would oppose Jefferson's proposed course of state action. Most of his counterarguments dealt with issues of practical politics and the difficulty from his retired position "to scan the precise tendency of measures addressed to the opinions and feelings of the States and of their Representatives." Madison also doubted the policy of Virginia's taking the lead in any protest movement, "considering the prejudices which seem to have been excited of late agst her" as a chronic complainer. He thought that both New England and New York had made state-financed improvements that would reduce their interest "in the prosecution of them with the national revenue" and would lead them and other states that had made similar improvement under their own authority to oppose such federal measures. On the whole, he preferred a constitutional amendment, which had just been introduced by Congressman John Bailey of Massachusetts, as an "eligible compromise" for Virginia, "notwithstanding the bearing it may have in favor of a prolonged tariff, as the nurse of the manufacturing system. It may be well," he concluded, "at least to know the weakness of the proposition in and out of Congress, before any irrevocable decision be had at Richmond."[14]

But Madison's ultimate argument against Jefferson's proposal rested on federal-state relations under the Constitution. He thought that the suggestion that Virginia enact federal statutes into state laws would be "an anomaly without any operative character" as well as "a lumping and anticipating enactment. As the Acts in question would not be executed by the ordinary functionaries of Virg[ini]a and she could not convert the federal into State functionaries, the whole proceeding would be as exclusively under the federal authority as if the legislative interference of Virg[ini]a had not taken place; her interference amounting to nothing more than *a recommendation* to her Citizens to acquiesce in the exercise of the power assumed by Congress, for which there is no apparent necessity or obligation."

In addition to backing Bailey's amendment, Madison argued that the "most eligible or least questionable" action by the Virginia legislature would be adoption of a set "of instructions to her Representatives in Cong^s to oppose measures violating her constructions of the Instrument." He admitted that he "was apprehensive that encouragement to a stronger course, in the present stage of the business and temper of the Assembly might lead to a stile and tone irritating rather than subduing prejudices, instead of the true policy as well as

---

13. JM to TJ, Feb. 17, 1825, above. For a careful analysis of this exchange, see Drew R. McCoy, *The Last of the Fathers: James Madison and the Republican Legacy* (New York, 1989), pp. 113–18.
14. JM to TJ, Dec. 28, 1825, above.

dignity of mingling as much of molliter in modo, as would be consistent with the fortiter in re.[15] Whilst Congress feel themselves backed by a Majority of their Constituents, menace or defiance, will never deter them from their purposes; particularly when such language proceeds from the section of the Union, to which there is a habit of alluding as distinguished by causes of internal weakness."[16]

To underscore his argument, Madison enclosed a copy of his recent letter to the Old Republican editor of the *Richmond Enquirer*. Neither in this letter to Thomas Ritchie nor in his response to Jefferson did he call the internal-improvement proposals "usurpations"; instead, he used such words as "aberrations" and "abuses." "All power in human hands," he observed, "is liable to be abused," although the danger of abuse in a republican form of government is less than in any other, offering "a greater security to the minority against the hasty formation of oppressive majorities." How should abuses, such as "the apparent call of a majority of the States and of the people for national Roads and Canals," be opposed constitutionally? "The appeal," Madison counseled, "can only be made to the recollections, the reason, and the conciliatory spirit of the Majority of the people agst their own errors; with a persevering hope of success, and an eventual acquiescence in disappointment unless indeed oppression should reach an extremity overruling all other considerations."[17]

That clearly was not the case with the young advocates of internal improvements, according to Madison. Instead of appeals to unlimited power, they had, "in general . . . rested the claim on deductions from some one or more of the enumerated grants." If there had been abuses, there had been no usurpations. Instead of declaring federal enactments null and void, a move that he had opposed at the time of the Alien and Sedition Laws a quarter of a century earlier, Madison suggested an appeal to public opinion, "either by protest or other equivalent modes. Perhaps the mode as well suited as any to the present occasion . . . would be that of instructions to her Representatives in Cong^s to oppose measures violating her constructions of the Instrument." If that failed, he thought the disappointed minority should acquiesce in the majority decision.[18]

Jefferson quickly acquiesced in Madison's arguments and suppressed "The solemn Declaration and Protest." He endorsed Madison's views "with entire approbation," confessing that when he wrote his paper on Christmas Eve, "all was gloom, and the question of roads and canals was thought desperate at Washington after the President's message." In light of quick action by South Carolina, Senator Martin Van Buren of New York, and Congressman Bailey— Jefferson said that this "propos[itio]n of Am[en]dm[en]t, [was] believed to

15. *Molliter in modo* means "gentleness in manner"; *fortiter in re* means "firmness in acting."
16. JM to TJ, Dec. 28, 1825, above.
17. JM to Thomas Ritchie, Dec. 18, 1825, enclosed in JM to TJ, Dec. 28, 1825, above.
18. *Ibid.*

come from the President himself"—he was now convinced that his proposition "would certainly be premature."[19] Accordingly, he told his state representative that "we had better . . . rest awhile on our oars and see which way the tide will set, in Congress and in the state legislatures."[20]

In his last year, Jefferson kept his eye firmly fixed on the University of Virginia. Like Madison, he deplored the tightfistedness and "the hardheartedness of the Legislature towards what ought to be the favorite offspring of the State."[21] But as soon as he learned that funding had been cut off in February, the old Sachem braved the winter blasts and rode to the university to issue orders "to engage in nothing new, to stop everything on hand which could be done without," and to utilize the remaining funds "in finishing the Circular room [in the Rotunda] for the books, and the Anatomical theatre" for the medical school. As he told Madison, he thought it prudent "to clear the decks thoroughly, to see how we shall stand, and what we may accomplish further."[22]

Jefferson lived long enough to see the completion of the faculty with the appointment of a law professor. The Board of Visitors had finally persuaded Gilmer to acquiesce in the appointment, but when he fell ill, the search began again. In selecting a replacement, Jefferson continued to stress the need to scrutinize the political principles of any candidate. "You will recollect," he told Madison, "that before the revolution, Coke [on] Littleton was the Universal elementary book of Law students, and a sounder whig never wrote, nor of profounder learning in the orthodox doctrines of the British constitution, or in what were called English liberties. You remember also that our lawyers were then all Whigs. But when his black-letter text, and uncouth but cunning learning got out of fashion, and the honied Mansfieldism of Blackstone became the Student's Hornbook, from that moment, that profession (the nursery of our Congress) began to slide into toryism, and nearly all the young brood of lawyers now are of that hue. They suppose themselves, indeed, to be whigs, because they no longer know what whigism or republicanism means."[23]

But the University of Virginia could redress this shortcoming. "It is in our Seminary that that Vestal flame is to be kept alive; it is thence it is to spread anew over our own and the sister states. If we are true and vigilant in our trust, within a dozen or 20. years a majority of our own legislature will be from our school, and many disciples will have carried it's doctrines home with them to their several States, and will have leavened thus the whole mass." Referring to the controversy over internal improvements, he cited the actions of New York

---

19. TJ to JM, Jan. 2, 1826, below.
20. TJ to William F. Gordon, Jan. 1, 1826, in Ford, X, pp. 358–59.
21. JM to TJ, Feb. 24, 1826, below.
22. TJ to JM, Feb. 17, 1826, below.
23. On TJ's dislike of William Blackstone's "Mansfieldism," see Julian S. Waterman, "Thomas Jefferson and Blackstone's *Commentaries*," *Illinois Law Review* 27 (1933): 629–59.

and South Carolina "in vindication of the constitution" but again backed off about Virginia's taking the lead, deferring instead to Madison's views, as he had done at the beginning of the year.[24]

For the law professorship, Madison recommended John Tayloe Lomax of Fredericksburg, although he did not know Lomax personally "and have otherwise a very slight knowledge of."[25] The Visitors first choice was William Wirt, attorney general of the United States, to whom they offered the post along with the newly created office of president of the university. Jefferson favored Wirt's appointment to the professorship but filed his only dissenting opinion as rector in opposition to the resolution creating the president's office. When Wirt turned down the joint offer, invalidating the resolution on the presidential office, the board appointed Lomax, completing the faculty three months before Jefferson's death.[26]

Madison and Jefferson met for the last time on April 3 and 4, 1826, at the Board of Visitors sessions in Charlottesville. In their final exchange of letters, they discussed the enlargement of the professors' teaching duties by "entering on the branches of science with which they are charged additionally to their principal one." Jefferson especially wanted Professor Emmet, who held the chair of natural history, to establish a botanical garden, and he sent all of the correspondence to Madison because implementation "must ere long devolve on you."[27] Professorlike, Emmet protested the expansion of his teaching load. His reluctance, Madison observed, "is neither to be wondered at nor yielded to."[28] Jefferson selected a site for the botanical garden in May, but after the rector's death Emmet was relieved of his botany assignment.[29]

Fortunately, Jefferson did not put off till his last illness his final expression of affection for Madison. In March, he made out his last will and testament, leaving his gold-headed walking stick to his friend of fifty years. A month earlier, he had left him a more important legacy: the care and supervision of the University of Virginia. "The friendship which has subsisted between us, now half a century," he wrote in his customary strong and clear handwriting, "and the harmony of our political principles and pursuits, have been sources of constant happiness to me through that long period. And if I move beyond the reach of attentions to the University, or beyond the bourne of life itself, as I soon must, it is a comfort to leave that institution under your care, and an assurance that they will neither be spared, nor ineffectual."

But he also left a continuing charge with Madison: protecting his—or,

---

24. TJ to JM, Feb. 17, 1826, below.

25. JM to TJ, Jan. 25, 1826, below.

26. The board had approved the combined offer only for Wirt. Lomax joined the faculty on July 5, 1825, the day after TJ died; see Malone, VI, pp. 484–85, and JM to TJ, Apr. 25, 1826, below.

27. TJ to JM, May 3, 1826, below.

28. JM to TJ, May 6, 1826, below.

29. Malone, VI, pp. 485–86.

rather, their—reputation. "It has also been a great solace to me," he confided, "to believe that you are engaged in vindicating to posterity the course we have pursued for preserving to them, *in all their purity,* the blessings of self-government, which we had assisted too in acquiring for them. If ever the earth has beheld a system of administration conducted with a single and steadfast eye to the general interest and happiness of those committed to it, one which, protected by truth, can never know reproach, it is that to which our lives have been devoted."

In a final salute to their joint efforts, he concluded: "To myself you have been a pillar of support through life. Take care of me when dead, and be assured that I shall leave with you my last affections."[30]

The ever-modest Madison, who was seldom as demonstrative as his friend, was clearly touched by the passing of the university torch to him. "You do not overrate the interest I feel in the University, as the Temple thro' which alone lies the road to that of Liberty. But you entirely do my aptitude to be your successor in watching over its prosperity. It would be the pretension of a mere worshipper," he protested, " 'remplacer' the Tutelary Genius of the Sanctuary. The best hope is, in the continuance of your cares, till they can be replaced by the stability and self-growth of the Institution. Little reliance can be put even on the fellowship of my services. The past year," he confessed, "has given me sufficient intimation of the infirmities in wait for me. In calculating the probabilities of survivorship, the inferiority of my constitution forms an equation at least with the seniority of yours."[31]

On the matter of their friendship, though, he said that his views coincided with that of his neighbor. "You cannot look back to the long period of our private friendship and political harmony," he replied, "with more affecting recollections than I do. If they are a source of pleasure to you, what ought they not to be to me? We cannot be deprived of the happy consciousness of the pure devotion to the public good with which we discharged the trusts committed to us. And I indulge a confidence that sufficient evidence will find its way to another generation, to ensure, after we are gone, whatever of justice may be withheld whilst we are here. The political horizon is already yielding in your case at least, the surest auguries of it. Wishing and hoping that you may yet live to increase the debt which our Country owes you, and to witness the increasing gratitude, which alone can pay it, I offer you the fullest return of affectionate assurances."[32]

The final exchange between the aged Sages added a footnote to their friendship. After complaining about the "unceasing drudgery of writing [which] keeps me in unceasing pain and peevishness," Jefferson mellowed and added: "The correspondence of my bosom-friends is still very dear, and wel-

30. TJ to JM, Feb. 17, 1826, below.
31. JM to TJ, Feb. 24, 1826, below.
32. *Ibid.*

come and consolatory. Yours among the most."³³ Madison promptly suggested that his friend cut down on "the epistolary taxation with which you are still persecuted" by adopting "a formula, to be copied by one of the family, ... acknowledging the communication. ... Nothing short of some positive check will relieve you from the afflicting burden, and no check short of that will probably suffice."³⁴

But Jefferson's scribbling did not end until his final illness. On June 24, 1826, he summoned Dr. Dunglison, professor of anatomy and medicine at the university, after writing his final letter. Appropriately enough, it was a commentary on the fiftieth anniversary of the Declaration of Independence, written in response to an invitation from the citizens of Washington:

> May it be to the world, what I believe it will be, (to some parts sooner, to others later, but finally to all,) the signal of arousing men to burst the chains under which monkish ignorance and superstition had persuaded them to bind themselves, and to assume the blessings and security of self-government. That form which we have substituted, restores the free right to the unbounded exercise of reason and freedom of opinion. All eyes are opened, or opening, to the rights of man. The general spread of the light of science has already laid open to every view the palpable truth, that the mass of mankind has not been born with saddles on their backs, nor a favored few booted and spurred, ready to ride them legitimately, by the grace of God. These are grounds of hope for others. For ourselves, let the annual return of this day forever refresh our recollections of these rights, and an undiminished devotion to them.³⁵

THE LETTERS

Jefferson to Madison

Monticello Jan. 2, 1826

DEAR SIR,

I now return you Ritchie's letter and your answer. I have read the last with entire approbation and adoption of it's views. When my paper was written all was gloom, and the question of roads and canals was thought desperate at Washington after the President's message. Since that however have appeared the S. C. resolns, Van Buren's motion, and above all Baylie's proposn of Amdmt, believed to come from the President himself, who may have motives

---

33. TJ to JM, May 3, 1826, below.
34. JM to TJ, May 6, 1826, below.
35. TJ to Roger Weightman, June 24, 1826, in Ford, X, pp. 390–92. For the source of TJ's metaphor about the mass of mankind, see Douglass Adair, "Rumbold's Dying Speech, 1685, and Jefferson's Last Words on Democracy, 1826," in Douglass Adair, *Fame and the Founding Fathers: Essays by Douglass Adair,* ed. H. Trevor Colbourn (New York, 1974), pp. 192–201.

for it. After these, before we can see their issue my proposn would certainly be premature. I think with you too that any measures of opposition would come with more hope from any other state than from Virginia, and S. C. N. York and Massachusetts being willing to take the lead, we had better follow. I have therefore suppressed my paper, and recommend to Gordon to do nothing until we see the course Bailey's proposn will take, which I think a desirable one in itself.[1]

I have been quite anxious to get a good drawing master in the Military or landscape line for the University. It is a branch of male educn most highly and justly valued on the continent of Europe. One, most highly recommended as a landscape painter and as a personal character offered himself under a mistaken expectn as to the emoluments. I authorized Dr. Emmet to speak with him on the subject, and inclose you his letter. Rembrandt Peale, whose opinion I asked is as high in his praises as Emmet. I fear his present birth is too good to leave it for ours under it's present uncertainties. His predilection to come to us might have some weight. Whether the offer to pay the expenses of his removal might be sufficient for him and approvable by us is a question. There is a more advantageous offer we might make him. You know we have 2. pavilions not yet occupied, nor likely soon to be so. A rent of 8. p. c. would be 600 D. a year. We could let him have the occupn gratis until an addition to our Professors might call for a resumption of it. I shall suggest this offer to Emmet but to avoid all engagement till the sanction of the Visitors should be obtained. Be so good as to return me the letter. Ever and affectly yours.

Madison to Jefferson

Montpellier Jan. 7, 1826

DEAR SIR

I return Dr. Emmets letter as requested. Wall's qualifications as a Drawing Master, are sufficiently authenticated to make his connection with the University very desirable. But there seems little ground for hope that he will exchange for it his present advantages in N Y. The only material attraction beyond the fees, is that of a Pavilion rent free, of which his tenure wd. be

---

1. For South Carolina's support of the principle of strict construction and opposition to internal improvements and protective tariffs, see William W. Freehling, *Prelude to Civil War: The Nullification Controversy in South Carolina, 1816–1836* (New York, 1965), pp. 117–18. As a senator from New York, where the Erie Canal had been completed in 1825, Martin Van Buren opposed federally financed internal improvements; see Richard E. Ellis, *The Union at Risk: Jacksonian Democracy, States' Rights, and the Nullification Crisis* (New York, 1987), p. 52. Congressman John Bailey of Massachusetts proposed an amendment to the Constitution to validate federal expenditures for internal improvements; see Malone, VI, p. 438.

uncertain perhaps of short continuance; and at most leaving his pecuniary prospects here, inferior to those where he is. Your suggestions to Emmet however are of the happy sort that may do good, and can not do harm.

Jefferson to Madison and the Board of Visitors of the University of Virginia

Monticello Jan. 20, 1826

DEAR SIR

It is with the utmost regret I inform you that we are likely to be again at default for our professor of law. Mr. Gilmer's situation is become decidedly pulmonary and hopeless. He has not yet been made sensible of the real character of his case and therefore only notifies me in a letter that it is certain he shall not be in health for the commencement of the term and suggests the idea of an appointment protem. Before however we shall have made up our minds on a successor, he will probably know better the hopelessness of his situation. What are we to do? If we meet and agree on one, a refusal of acceptance will probably call immediately for a 2nd meeting and so for a 3rd. 4th. etc. to what extent we know not. The following expedient has therefore occurred to me, which however I shall readily relinquish for any other which may be proposed by my brethern. Each of us to form a list of those to whom we may be wishing to offer the chair, stating their names in the order of preference we would give them respectively. Collating these together we may form a first list in the order in which the number of votes may place each. In submitting this to each other again we may approximate still nearer to a choice, till we reduce the competition to two alone, between whom we may decide by a plurality of votes. The above may then be consulted and if he declines we may resume and repeat the operation, until we can obtain an acceptance. To save time I will begin, only praying that if you can propose any better expedient, you will consider my list as if never written. Promptness in our interchange of letters is very necessary.

After writing so far, a 2nd. expedient occurs; i.e. to meet and form a list of *successive* applications chose as you please. Accept my salutations of esteem and respect.

TH JEFFERSON

P.S. Mr. Terrell being unknown to yourself as well as our colleagues I enclose you one of Professor Pictet's letters to me respecting him and pray you after perusal to inclose it to any one of our three colleagues in the legislature, with a request that when they shall have read it, they will return it to me. They will recieve their Circular on Monday and I wish them to get this letter of Pictet's as soon after as possible.

Madison to Jefferson

Montpellier Jan. 25, 1826

Dr. Sir

Your Circular of the 20h. postmarked 23rd. was recd. last evening, and the letter from Mr. Pictet is forwarded as desired to our Colleagues at Richd.

I concur in your mode of providing for the foreseen vacancy which I sincerely lament, on every account; as I should in any admissible mode that would avoid the necessity for an Extra meeting of the Visitors.[2]

I am acquiescent also in your order of preferences among the names you propose for the vacancy; without being prepared to add a single one to them, unless indeed Mr. Lomax whom I do not personally know and have otherwise a very slight knowledge of should be thought proper for the list. Perhaps a like concurrence of our Colleages may render not only a Meeting of the Board, but further consultations by letter unnecessary.

I consider the chance so desperate as to both Barbour and Dade, that it is scarcely justifiable to submit to the delay of a renewed offer to them. The remark is in some degree applicable to Mr. Rives, whose state of health as well as the considerations you notice forbids a hope of his acceptance. I understand his rank in Congress, corresponds with the view you have formed of his talents and acquirements. The great distance of Mr. Preston, with the bare possibility of his acceptance, seem to require us to lose sight of him also on the occasion. Of Mr. Robertson, I know not but from Report, which ascribes to him good talents and good principles. The Visitors at Richmond must be able to judge so much better of his qualifications than I can, that I am ready to subscribe to their estimate of them. Of Mr. Terrell I am personally altogether ignorant; but your portrait of him to say nothing of the testimony of Pictet, makes me willing to concur in a selection of him at once, if there be nothing in the answers from Richd. inconsistent with such a course.

Jefferson to Madison

Monticello Feb. 17, 1826

Dear Sir—

My Circular was answered by General Breckinridge, approving, as we had done, of the immediate appointment of Terril to the chair of Law, but our 4. colleagues who were together in Richmond concluded not to appoint until our meeting in April. In the meantime the term of the present lamented incumbent draws near to a close. About 150. students have already entered, many of those who engaged for a 2nd year are yet to come. What I think we may count [on is] that our dormitories will be filled. Whether there will be any

---

2. Gilmer's death left the law post open.

overflowing for the accommodations provided in the vicinage, which are quite considerable is not yet known. None will enter there while a dormitory remains vacant. Were the law chair filled, it would add 50. at least to the number.

Immediately on seeing the overwhelming vote of the House of Representatives against giving us another Dollar, I rode to the University and desired Mr. Brockenbrough to engage in nothing new, to stop everything on hand which could be done without, and to employ all his force and funds in finishing the Circular room for the books, and the Anatomical theatre. These cannot be done without; and for these and all our debts we have funds enough. But I think it prudent then to clear the decks thoroughly, to see how we shall stand, and what we may accomplish further. In the meanwhile, there are arrived for us, in different ports of the United States, 10. boxes of books from Paris, 7 from London, and from Germany I know not how many; in all, perhaps, about 25. boxes. Not one of these can be opened until the book-room is completely finished, and all the shelves ready to receive their charge directly from the boxes as they shall be opened. This cannot be till May. I hear nothing definitive of the 2000. dollars duty of which we are asking the remission from Congress.

In the selection of our Law Professor, we must be rigorously attentive to his political principles. You will recollect that before the revolution, Coke Littleton was the Universal elementary book of Law students, and a sounder whig never wrote, nor of profounder learning in the orthodox doctrines of the British constitution, or in what were called English liberties. You remember also that our lawyers were then all Whigs. But when his black-letter text, and uncouth but cunning learning got out of fashion, and the honied Mansfield-ism of Blackstone became the Student's Hornbook, from that moment, that profession (the nursery of our Congress) began to slide into toryism, and nearly all the young brood of lawyers now are of that hue. They suppose themselves, indeed, to be whigs, because they no longer know what whigism or republicanism means. It is in our Seminary that that Vestal flame is to be kept alive; it is thence it is to spread anew over our own and the sister states. If we are true and vigilant in our trust, within a dozen or 20. years a majority of our own legislature will be from our school, and many disciples will have carried it's doctrines home with them to their several States, and will have leavened thus the whole mass. New York has taken strong ground in vindication of the constitution; South Carolina had already done the same. Although I was against our leading, I am equally against omitting to follow in the same line, and backing them firmly; and I hope that yourself or some other will mark out the track to be pursued by us.

You will have seen in the newspapers some proceedings in the legislature, which have cost me much mortification.[3] My own debts had become consider-

---

3. For TJ's request for a lottery to relieve him of debt, see Malone, VI, pp. 473-82.

able, but not beyond the effect of some lopping of property, which would have been little felt, when our friend W.C.N. gave me the *coup de grace*.[4] Ever since that I have been paying 1200 dollars a year interest on his debt, which, with my own, was absorbing so much of my annual income, as that the Maintenance of my family was making deep and rapid inroads on my capital. Still, sales at a fair price would leave me competently provided. Had crops and prices for several years been such as to maintain a steady competition of substantial bidders at market, all would have been safe. But the long succession of years of stunted crops, of reduced prices, the general prostration of the farming business, under levies for supporting manufactures, etc., with the calamitous fluctuations of value in our paper medium, have kept agriculture in a state of abject depression, which has peopled the Western States, by silently breaking up those on the Atlantic, and glutted the land market, while it drew off its bidders. In such a state of things, property has lost its character of being a resource for debts. Highland in Bedford, which, in the days of our plethory, sold readily for from 50. to 100. dollars the acre, (and such sales were many there,) would not now sell for more than from 10. to 20. dollars, or ¼ or ⅕ of their former price. Reflecting on these things, the practice occurred to me, of selling, on fair valuation, and by way of lottery, often resorted to before the Revolution to effect large sales, and still in constant usage in every State for individual as well as corporation purposes. If it is permitted in my case, my lands here alone, with the mills, etc., will pay every thing, and leave me Monticello and a farm free. If refused, I must sell everything here, perhaps considerably in Bedford, move thither with my family, where I have not even a log hut to put my head into, and whether ground for burial, will depend on the depredations which, under the form of sales, shall have been committed on my property. The question then with me was *ultrum horum* [take which ever of those you prefer]? But why afflict you with these details? I cannot tell, indeed, unless pains are lessened by communication with a friend. The friendship which has subsisted between us, now half a century, and the harmony of our political principles and pursuits, have been sources of constant happiness to me through that long period. And if I remove beyond the reach of attentions to the University, or beyond the bourne of life itself, as I soon must, it is a comfort to leave that institution under your care, and an assurance that they will neither be spared, nor ineffectual. It has also been a great solace to me, to believe that you are engaged in vindicating to posterity the course we have pursued for preserving to them, *in all their purity,* the blessings of self-government, which we had assisted too in acquiring for them. If ever the earth has beheld a system of administration conducted with a single and steadfast eye to the general interest and happiness of those committed to it, one which, protected by truth, can never know reproach, it is that to which our lives have

---

4. TJ's italics here and below. For the impact of Wilson Cary Nicholas's default on TJ, who had endorsed notes on his behalf, see *ibid.,* pp. 309–14, 448.

been devoted. To myself you have been a pillar of support through life. Take care of me when dead, and be assured that I shall leave with you my last affections.[5]

Madison to Jefferson

Montpellier Feb. 24, 1826

DEAR SIR,

Yours of the 17th was duly rec^d. The awkward state of the Law professorship is truly distressing, but seems to be without immediate remedy. Considering the hopeless condition of Mr. Gilmour, a temporary appointment, if an acceptable successor were at hand, whilst not indelicate towards the worthy moribond incumbent, might be regarded as equivalent to a permanent one. And if the hesitation of our colleagues at Richmond has no reference to Mr. Terril, but is merely tenderness towards Mr. Gilmour, I see no objection to a communication to Mr. T. that would bring him to Virg^a at once, and thus abridge the loss of time. The hardheartedness of the Legislature towards what ought to be the favorite offspring of the State, is as reproachful as deplorable. Let us hope that the reflections of another year, will produce a more parental sensibility.

I had noticed the disclosures at Richmond with feelings which I am sure I need not express; any more than the alleviation of them by the sequel. I had not been without fears, that the causes you enumerate were undermining your estate. But they did not reach the extent of the evil. Some of these causes were indeed forced on my attention by my own experience. Since my return to private life (and the case was worse during my absence in Public) such have been the unkind seasons, and the ravages of insects, that I have made but one tolerable crop of Tobacco, and but one of Wheat, the proceeds of both of which were greatly curtailed by mishaps in the sale of them. And having no resources but in the earth I cultivate, I have been living very much throughout on borrowed means. As a necessary consequence, my debts have swelled to an amount, which if called for at the present conjuncture, would give to my situation a degree of analogy to yours. Fortunately I am not threatened with any rigid pressure, and have the chance of better crops and prices, with the prospect of a more leisurely disposal of the property which must be a final resort.

You do not overrate the interest I feel in the University, as the Temple thro' which alone lies the road to that of Liberty. But you entirely do my aptitude to be your successor in watching over its prosperity. It would be the

---

5. For a discussion of TJ's charge to JM, see Adrienne Koch, *Jefferson and Madison: The Great Collaboration* (New York, 1950), pp. 283-90.

pretension of a mere worshipper "remplacer" the Tutelary Genius of the Sanctuary. The best hope is, in the continuance of your cares, till they can be replaced by the stability and self-growth of the Institution. Little reliance can be put even on the fellowship of my services. The past year has given me sufficient intimation of the infirmities in wait for me. In calculating the probabilities of survivorship, the inferiority of my constitution forms an equation at least with the seniority of yours.

It would seem that some interposition is meditated at Richmond against the assumed powers of Internal Improvement; and in the mode recommended by Govr Pleasants, in which my letter to Mr. Ritchie concurred, of instructions to the Senators in Congress. No better mode, can perhaps be taken, if an interposition be likely to do good; a point on which the opinion of the Virginia members at Washington ought to have much weight. They can best judge of the tendency of such a measure at the present moment. The public mind is certainly more divided on the subject than it lately was, and it is not improbable that the question, whether the powers exist, will more and more give way to the question, how far they ought to be granted.[6]

You cannot look back to the long period of our private friendship and political harmony, with more affecting recollections than I do. If they are a source of pleasure to you, what ought they not to be to me? We cannot be deprived of the happy consciousness of the pure devotion to the public good with which we discharged the trusts committed to us. And I indulge a confidence that sufficient evidence will find its way to another generation, to ensure, after we are gone, whatever of justice may be withheld whilst we are here. The political horizon is already yielding in your case at least, the surest auguries of it. Wishing and hoping that you may yet live to increase the debt which our Country owes you, and to witness the increasing gratitude, which alone can pay it, I offer you the fullest return of affectionate assurances.

Jefferson to Madison and the Board of Visitors of the University of Virginia

Charlottesville, Apr. 3-4, 1826

The subscriber, rector of the University, fully and expressly concurring in the appointment of William Wirt to the professor of the school of law, dissents from, and protests against, so much of these enactments as go to the establishment of the office of president of the University, for these reasons:

---

6. In the "Virginia Resolutions Concerning the Powers of the Federal Government," passed early in 1826, the legislature denied the authority of Congress over internal improvements and protective tariffs; see Malone, VI, p. 439.

1. Because the law establishing the University, delineating the organization of the authorities by which it should be directed and governed, and placing at its head a Board of rector and Visitors, has enumerated with great precision the special powers it meant to give to that Board, in which enumeration is not to be found that of creating a president, making him a member of the faculty of professors, and with controlling powers over that faculty; and it is not conceivable that, while descending, in their enumeration to give specially the power of appointing officers of the minutest grade, they should have omitted to name him of the highest, who was to govern and preside over the whole. If this is not among the enumerated powers, it is believed it cannot be legitimately inferred, by construction, from the words giving a general authority to do all things expedient for promoting the purposes of the institution; for, so construed, it would render nugatory the whole enumeration, and confer on the Board powers unrestrained within any limits.

2. Because he is of opinion that every function ascribed to the president by this enactment, can be performed, and is now as well performed by the faculty, as now established by law.

3. Because we owe debts at this time of at least 11,000 dollars beyond what can be paid by any means we have in possession, or may command within any definite period of time; and fixes on us permanently an additional expense of 15,000 dollars a year.

4. Because he thinks that so fundamental a change in the organization of the institution ought not to be made by a thin Board, two of the seven constituting it, being now absent.

For these reasons the subscriber protests against both the expedience and the validity of the establishment of this office.[7]

TH. JEFFERSON

Jefferson to Madison and the Board of Visitors of the University of Virginia

Monticello Apr. 21, 1826

DEAR SIR

Mr. Wirt declined the offices proposed to him.[8] Mr. Lomax has accepted the Professorship of Law, and will open his school on the 1st. day of July. He has paid us a visit, and his appointment appears to have given the highest

---

7. For a brief discussion of TJ's opposition to creating the office of president of the university, see *ibid.*, p. 484. JM did not concur in TJ's dissenting opinion.

8. When Wirt declined the dual offer of president and professor of law, the resolution creating the office of president became invalid. TJ's "favorite system" continued until 1904, when Edwin A. Alderman became the first president of the university; see *ibid.*

degree of satisfaction to every body, Professors Students, Neighbors, and to none more than to myself. We have now 166 students, and on the opening of the Law school, we expect to have all our Dormitories filled, order and industry nearly complete and sensibly improving every day. Affectionately yours

TH: JEFFERSON

Madison to Jefferson

[Montpellier] Apr. 25, 1826

I have recd yours of the 21st. The refusal of the offer to Mr. Wirt, inviting as it was, does not surprise me. It is very gratifying to learn that Mr. Lomax takes so well with every body. I hope his success will make some amends for the delay in filling the Chair which is to receive him.

I have made a beginning with Capt. Peyton as the consignee of my business at Richmond, as recommended in yrs. of the 8th.

J M

Jefferson to Madison

Monticello May 3, 1826

DEAR SIR

I have percieved in some of our Professors a disinclination to the preparing themselves for entering on the branches of science with which they are charged additionally to their principal one. I took occasion therefore lately to urge one of them (Dr. Emmet) to begin preparations for his Botanical school, for which the previous works necessary furnished unoffensive ground.[9] His answer confirming my doubts, gave me a favorable opportunity of going into explanations which might be communicated to the others also without particular umbrage to them. The case being fundamentally interesting to our institution, and lest any thing further should grow out of it, I pray you to read and return me the letters inclosed and if you can suggest any thing either corrective or additional, to do so. I am anxious you should be intimately possessed of whatever material passes here, as a more peculiar attention to it must ere long devolve on you.[10]

In comparison with my sufferings of the last year, my health, altho not restored, is greatly better. Could I be permitted to employ myself in what

9. For TJ's exchanges with Emmet about teaching botany and laying out a botanical garden, see *ibid.*, pp. 485–86.
10. This was TJ's last letter to JM.

would be most agreeable to myself, which would be the passive occupation of reading I should probably wear on in tolerable ease and tranquility. But the unceasing drudgery of writing keeps me in unceasing pain and peevishness. I must still however rest on the hitherto illusive hope that the discretion of those who have no claims upon me, will at length advert to the circumstances of my age and ill health, and feel the duty of sparing both. The correspondence of my bosom-friends is still very dear, and welcome and consolatory. Yours among the most, being ever and the most affectionately yours.

TH:JEFFERSON

Madison to Jefferson

Montpellier May 6, 1826

DR SIR.

I return the correspondence inclosed in yours of the 3d. inst. The reluctance of Mr. Emmett, and probably of his colleagues, to the enlargement of their duties, is neither to be wondered at nor yielded to. You have put the matter on a ground to which I can suggest no improvement. It may be well perhaps that what has passed, should not be generally known. With some, it might produce reflections on the professors, with others an idea that in the present condition of the University, the education was, in some branches at least, to be more superficial than comports with the pretensions of the Institution. The truth however ought to be felt by the Legislature, as a powerful impulse to a more beneficent patronage.

You appear not to be aware of the death of Thoüin.[11] But it need not affect the object in view. I find that his successor continues to forward large parcels of seeds to our Agricult: Society, on the supposition that it has a botanical garden. I lately recd. a letter from N. York informing me that the annual box has just arrived there. I sent the letter of course to my successor, Secretary Barbour. The Society will doubtless readily make over its interest in this correspondence to the University to which its botanical garden will in fact give it the better title.

The epistolary taxation with which you are still persecuted is a cruelty not to be borne; and which I fear will never cease of itself. Why not adopt a formula, to be copied by one of the family, nicely [merely?] acknowledging the communication, and referring to the general rule imposed by necessity, of limiting the answer to that, and an expression of thanks. Nothing short of some positive check will relieve you from the afflicting burden, and no check short of that will probably suffice.

11. For brief references to Professor André Thouin, director of the Jardin des Plantes in Paris, see Edwin M. Betts, ed., *Thomas Jefferson's Farm Book* . . . (Princeton, 1953), pp. 57–58, and Malone, VI, pp. 47, 163.

50

"Take Care of Me When Dead": Madison's Final Years, 1826–1836

As DEATH STALKED the Sage of Monticello in June of 1826, Jefferson wrote out in his still-bold handwriting an overly modest but characteristically precise instruction for preparing his tombstone, prescribing this brief inscription "and not a word more":

> Here was buried
> Thomas Jefferson
> Author of the Declaration of American Independence
> of the Statute of Virginia's for religious freedom
> and Father of the University of Virginia

Jefferson seems never to have explained his choice of these accomplishments nor why he ignored the long list of public services he had compiled on New Year's Day 1826, beginning with his election as justice of the Albemarle County court and culminating with his two terms as president of the United States. But the list on the obelisk at Monticello clearly and simply singled out what he had done for the people, while the elective offices reflected what the people had done for him.

Dr. Dunglison stayed at Monticello with Jefferson during his fatal crisis, remaining at his bedside from June 24 until July 4. On July 1, Dunglison warned Madison of Jefferson's "serious indisposition" and expressed his fear of "the result of the struggle." "Until the 2nd and 3rd of July," the doctor recalled, "he spoke freely of his approaching death; made all his arrangements with his grandson, Mr. Randolph, in regard to his private affairs, and expressed his anxiety for the prosperity of the University; and his confidence in the exertion in its behalf of Mr. Madison and the other visitors. . . . In the course of the day and night of the 2nd of July, he was affected with stupor, with intervals of wakefulness and consciousness; but on the 3rd, the stupor became permanent. About seven o'clock in the evening of that day, he awoke, and seeing me standing at his bedside, exclaimed 'Ah Doctor are you still there?' in a voice, however, that was husky and indistinct. He then asked, 'Is it the 4th?' to which I replied, 'It soon will be.' These were the last words I heard him utter." Jefferson was ready for his last great adventure—"untried by the living, unreported by the dead."[1]

Jefferson died on the Fourth of July 1826. Later on the same day, the Golden Jubilee of the Declaration of Independence, John Adams roused himself from his deathbed and said, "Thomas Jefferson still survives." Nicholas P. Trist, Jefferson's grandson-in-law, was with the attending physician when the Sage of Monticello died, and Trist immediately notified Madison, who had been prepared for the sad news by "a few lines from Dr. Dunglison." "I never doubted that the last Scene of our illustrious friend would be worthy of the life which it closed," he wrote Trist. But now his friend belonged to the ages. "We are more than consoled for the loss . . . by the assurance that he lives and will live in the memory and gratitude of the wise and good, as a luminary of Science, as a votary of liberty, as a model of patriotism, and as a benefactor of human kind. In these characters, I have known him, and not less in the virtues and charms of social life, for a period of fifty years, during which there has not been an interruption or diminution of mutual confidence and cordial friendship, for a single moment in a single instance. What I feel therefore now, need not, I should say, cannot, be expressed."[2]

When President John Quincy Adams learned that his father, John Adams, the patriarch of Massachusetts, and Thomas Jefferson, the patriarch of Virginia, had died on the memorable day marking the fiftieth anniversary of the signing of the Declaration of Independence, he saw the "visible and palpable mark of Divine favor," a remark echoed across the country.[3] As postriders set out from Massachusetts carrying news of Adams's death, couriers from Virginia were riding north with news of Jefferson's demise. The messengers met in Philadelphia, a coincidence that Horace Greeley, then a young man in Vermont, remembered vividly years later: "When we learned . . . that Thomas Jefferson and John Adams, the author and the great champion, respectively, of the Declaration, had both died on that day, and that the messengers bearing

---

1. Robley Dunglison to JM, July 1, 1826, Presidential Papers Microfilm, James Madison Papers, reel 21; Robley Dunglison, *The Autobiographical Ana of Robley Dunglison, M. D.,* ed. Samuel X. Radbill, *Transactions* (American Philosophical Society) n.s., 53 (1963): pt. 8, p. 32. See also Peterson, pp. 1007–8, and John M. Dorsey, ed., *The Jefferson-Dunglison Letters* (Charlottesville, 1968), pp. 68–69. The final quotation in the paragraph is from Wendell Garrett's editorial in *Antiques* 106 (1974): 83, on the bicentennial of the American Revolution.
2. JM to Nicholas P. Trist, July 6, 1826, in Hunt, IX, pp. 247–48.
3. See the superb accounts by Lyman H. Butterfield, "The Jubilee of Independence, July 4, 1826," *VMHB* 61 (1953): 119–40, and Merrill D. Peterson, *The Jefferson Image in the American Mind* (New York, 1960), pp. 3–8.

South and North, respectively, the tidings of their decease, had met in Philadelphia, under the shadow of that Hall in which our independence was declared, it seemed that a Divine attestation had solemnly hallowed and sanctified the great anniversary by the impressive ministration of Death."[4]

The providential coincidence of their deaths seemed also to mark the close of the Age of Revolution, "a period glorious for our country," as Madison observed, "and, more than any preceding one, likely to improve the social condition of man. The lights and lessons afforded by our Revolution, on all the subjects most interesting to that condition, are already diffusing themselves in every direction, and form a source of peculiar gratification to those who had any part in the great event. Fortunately," he told a Revolutionary friend, "we are not excluded from the number. If we cannot associate with the two luminaries who have just sunk below the horizon, leaving inextinguishable traces behind, we have at least a place in the galaxy of faithful citizens who did their best for their country when it needed their services." He expressed pleasure at being "one who laboured with you in the worst of times, and has lived to rejoice with you in the best that have fallen to the lot of any nation."[5]

When Dr. Dunglison delivered Jefferson's bequest of his favorite gold-mounted walking stick to Madison, Madison accepted it as "a token of the place I held in the friendship of one whom I so much revered and loved when living, and whose memory can never cease to be dear to me."[6] As Jefferson had wished, Madison succeeded him as rector of the University of Virginia, which, he said, bore the stamp of Jefferson's genius "and will be a noble monument of his fame. His general view," one that Madison shared, "was to make it a nursery of Republican patriots as well as genuine scholars."[7] For eight of the ten years left to him, Madison devoted his attention as rector to the rearing of the university that he had helped found, never missing a meeting of the Board of Visitors or a public examination session unless he was ill. He and Dolley stayed in Charlottesville on those occasions, and students could see the aging couple walking on the university Lawn, representatives of the beginning of the Republic and of the university, which Madison called "a temple dedicated to science and Liberty."[8]

Madison was seventy-five when Jefferson died, and Dolley a mere fifty-eight, "young enough for Mr. Madison's daughter." Instead of "a little old dried-up woman," wrote a surprised observer, Mrs. Madison was "tall, young, active and elegant," captivating "by her artless though warm affability." Madison was "in tolerably good health, thin of flesh, rather under the common

---

4. Theodore H. White, "The American Idea," *New York Times Magazine* (July 6, 1986), 13.
5. JM to Richard Peters, Sept. 8, 1826, in James Madison, *Letters and Other Writing of James Madison,* [ed. William C. Rives and Philip R. Fendall], 4 vols. (Philadelphia, 1865), III, p. 527.
6. JM to Thomas Jefferson Randolph, July 8, 1826, cited in Brant, VI, pp. 456–57.
7. JM to Samuel Harrison Smith, Nov. 4, 1826, in Hunt, IX, pp. 256–61.
8. *Ibid.* See also Ketcham, p. 657.

size, and dressed in his customary black, old-fashioned clothes. His form [was] erect, his step firm but somewhat slow," although he walked "without a staff."

Three years after Jefferson's death, Professor Tucker found Madison "rejuvenated . . . his cheerfulness and amenity and abundant stock of racy anecdotes were the delight of every social board."[9] Another visitor agreed that Madison "looks scarcely as old as he is . . . and seems very hale and hearty—the expression of his face is full of good humour." Mrs. Madison was still "quite stylish in a turban and fine gown—she has a great deal of dignity blended with good humour and knowledge of the world."[10]

Madison's charm continued to captivate his intimate friends. When Margaret Bayard Smith and her husband, Samuel Harrison Smith, visited Montpellier in 1828, she described her host's conversation as a "stream of history . . . so rich in sentiments and facts, so enlivened by anecdotes and epigrammatic remarks, so frank and confidential as to opinions on men and measures, that it had an interest and charm, which the conversation of few men now living, could have. He spoke of scenes in which he himself had acted a conspicuous part and of great men, who had been actors in the same theatre. . . . Every sentence he spoke was worthy of being written down. The formation and adoption of the Constitution. The Convention and first congress, the character of their members and the secret debates. Franklin, Washington, Hamilton, John Adams, Jefferson, Jay, Patrick Henry and a host of other great men were spoken of and characteristic anecdotes of all related. It was living History!"[11]

Madison served as a trustworthy guardian of Jefferson's reputation, which was linked so inextricably to his own. To biographers, historians, and eulogists, he outlined the highlights of Jefferson's career and urged the use of Jefferson's grandson's edition of his grandfather's writings, published in 1829, always stressing the revised code of Virginia and the creation of the university as key contributions. The code was "perhaps the most severe of his public labours. It consisted of 126 Bills, comprizing and recasting the whole statutory code, British and Colonial, then admitted to be in force, or proper to be adopted, and some of the most important articles of the unwritten law, with original laws on particular subjects; the whole adapted to the Independent and Republican form of Government." After his "retirement from the political sphere, the object nearest his heart" was the University of Virginia. "His devotion to it was intense, and his exertions unceasing."[12]

By the time Madison met him in 1776, Jefferson "was certainly one of the

---

9. Ketcham, pp. 636-37, quotes Anne Royall on Mrs. Madison and cites George Tucker and Robert Scott on Madison in 1829.

10. Henry D. Gilpin to Joshua Gilpin, Sept. 16, 1827, cited *ibid.*, p. 620.

11. Margaret Bayard Smith, *The First Forty Years of Washington Society, Portrayed by the Family Letters of Mrs. Samuel Harrison Smith . . .*, ed. Gaillard Hunt (New York, 1906), p. 235.

12. JM to Samuel Harrison Smith, Nov. 4, 1826, in Hunt, IX, pp. 256-61.

most learned men of the age," a "walking Library"—indeed, a prodigy with whom "the Genius of Philosophy ever walked hand in hand." He could read French, Italian, Spanish, and Anglo-Saxon; he was a knowledgeable lawyer, architect, and connoisseur of the fine arts. In addition to these achievements, Madison was most impressed by the remarkable range of Jefferson's miscellaneous readings, "for which he derived leisure from a methodical and indefatigable application of the time required for indispensable objects, and particularly from his rule of never letting the sun rise before him. His relish for Books never forsook him, not even in his infirm years and in his devoted attention to the rearing of the University, which led him often to express his regret that he was so much deprived of that luxury, by the epistolary tasks, which fell upon him, and which consumed his health as well as his time."[13]

When Jefferson's first biographer, Henry Gilpin, sent a copy of his book to Madison, the latter complimented the author on "its historical materials as well as . . . its biographical portrait of the highly distinguished individual." But he added two corrections based on personal observation: Jefferson's hair was "not *red,* but between *yellow and red*"; and his nose was "rather under, certainly not above, common size."[14]

Those were the last of Madison's minor corrections on Jefferson's behalf, for larger matters of constitutional importance soon occupied a major portion of his time in taking care of his friend's reputation and, as it turned out, his own. It all began in the year following Jefferson's death, when Madison learned that the Virginia legislature had "pronounced the opinion that Duties for the protection of domestic manufactures are unconstitutional," with William B. Giles citing a private letter from Jefferson as authority for this stance.[15]

Madison, who had recommended the protective tariff of 1816 to Congress, promptly denounced the legislature for taking "a ground which cannot be maintained, on which the State will probably stand alone, and which by lessening the confidence of other States in the wisdom of its Councils, must impede the progress of sounder doctrines." Reviewing forty years of history, which he hoped would settle the question, he noted that one of the reasons for replacing the Articles of Confederation with the federal Constitution was to transfer the power to regulate trade "from the States to the Gov[ernmen]t of the U[nited] S[tates]." From the first Congress on, "the power over commerce has been exercised or admitted, so as to bear on internal objects of utility or policy, without a reference to revenue." Indeed, every president from Washington to John Quincy Adams, including Jefferson and Madison, "has recog-

---

13. *Ibid.*
14. JM to Henry D. Gilpin, Oct. 25, 1827, in Rives and Fendall, III, p. 593.
15. Joseph C. Cabell to JM, Mar. 12, 1827, in Hunt, IX, p. 284, and Drew R. McCoy, *The Last of the Fathers: James Madison and the Republican Legacy* (New York, 1989), p. 124. The legislature also cited Madison's Virginia resolutions of 1798 as well as his report of 1799-1800. For Giles's role, see Dice R. Anderson, *William Branch Giles: A Study in the Politics of Virginia and the Nation from 1790 to 1830* (Menasha, Wis., 1914).

nised the power of a tariff in favor of Manufactures, without indicating a doubt, or that a doubt existed anywhere."[16]

Thus, the constitutionality of protective tariffs had been given "a national sanction not to be reversed, but by an evidence at least equivalent to the National will" through a constitutional amendment withdrawing the delegated power. Otherwise, every new Congress might disregard "a meaning of the instrument uniformly sustained by their predecessors, for such a period," shattering constitutional government as he and the other Founders had conceived of it.

"In expounding the Constitution," Madison pointed out, "it is as essential as it is obvious, that the distinction should be kept in view, between the usurpation, and the abuse of a power." Congress's power to pass tariff laws might fall in the latter category, but "mere *inequality*, in imposing taxes" could not be made "synonymous with *unconstitutionality*." Indeed, the abuse of a legitimate power "cannot be regarded as a breach of the fundamental compact, till it reaches a degree of oppression, so iniquitous and intolerable as to justify civil war, or disunion pregnant with wars, then to be foreign ones. This distinction," he suggested, "may be a key to the language of Mr. J[efferso]n," whose letter Madison had not yet seen.[17]

Although Madison had persuaded Jefferson in December 1825 to suppress his proposed "Declaration and Protest" against federal internal improvements, his impulsive friend had written at the same time a similar blast, in a private letter, to William B. Giles—carefully labeling it "not intended for the public eye"—denouncing consolidation. He argued that federal functionaries, acting "under the power to regulate commerce," had assumed "indefinitely that also over agriculture and manufactures, and call it regulation to take the earnings of one of these branches of industry, and that too the most depressed, and put them into the pockets of the other, the most flourishing of all." The new breed of Republicans, Jefferson had complained, had "nothing in them of the principles of '76" and were running the risk of "a single and splendid government of an aristocracy, founded on banking institutions, and moneyed incorporations . . . riding and ruling over the plundered ploughman and beggared yeomanry." Using the language privately that Madison was to persuade him two days later not to use publicly, Jefferson plunged on recklessly towards the fatal conclusion that if it should finally become a question of "dissolution of our Union . . . or submission to a government without limitation of powers," he would choose liberty.[18]

---

16. JM to Joseph C. Cabell, Mar. 22, 1827, in Hunt, IX, pp. 284-87.

17. *Ibid.* JM did not discuss the Virginia resolutions since Cabell had not mentioned them in his report of March 12.

18. TJ to William Branch Giles, Dec. 26, 1825, in Ford, X, pp. 354-57, was written two days after TJ sent JM his "solemn Declaration and Protest" and two days before JM wrote his letter persuading TJ to suppress his proposal. For discussions of TJ's letter to Giles, see Malone, VI, pp. 440-41; Brant, VI, pp. 468-70; and McCoy, pp. 124-30.

When Giles, who had become governor on the strength of his opposition to the tariff, published Jefferson's private letter, Madison concluded that the governor and those denying Congress's power to enact protective tariffs had "in some respects misunderstood" Jefferson's sentence.[19] "It would seem," he suggested, that Jefferson, in "writing confidentially, and probably in haste, ... did not discriminate with the care he otherwise might have done, between an assumption of power and an abuse of power; relying on the term '*indefinitely*' to indicate an excess of the latter; and [thus] to imply an admission of a *definite* or reasonable use of the power to regulate trade for the encouragement of manufacturing and agricultural products. This view of the subject," he continued, "is recommended by its avoiding a variance with Mr. Jefferson's known sanctions, in official acts and private correspondence, to a power in Congress to encourage manufactures by commercial regulations. It is not easy to believe that he could have intended to reject *altogether* such a power."[20]

Although Madison admitted privately that his friend had used "unstudied and unguarded language" in his letter to Giles,[21] he thought that his public explanation "obviates any collision between the opinion of Mr. Jefferson and that I have espoused on the constitutional branch of the Tariff question." Indeed, he pointed out that the power to protect and foster manufactures by regulations of trade had received "uniform and practical sanction . . . by the Gen[era]l Gov[ernmen]t for nearly 40 years with a concurrence and acquiescence of every State Gov[ernmen]t throughout the same period. . . . No novel construction however ingeniously devised, or however respectable and patriotic its Patrons, can withstand the weight of such authorities, or the unbroken current of so prolonged and universal a practice."[22]

Privately, Madison was outraged with Governor Giles's manipulation of Jefferson's ambiguities for local political advantage—for playing the lowest form of politics with the memory of the Sage of Monticello while proclaiming the highest reverence for it. "The inconsistency," he insisted, "is monstrous between the professed veneration for his name and the anxiety to make him avow opinions in the most pointed opposition to those maintained by him in his more deliberate correspondence with others, and acted on through his whole official life."[23] Jefferson's true view had never denied the constitutionality of the tariff, Madison insisted, and the letter to Giles had been meant only

---

19. On the publication of the letter, see Peterson, *Jefferson Image*, pp. 27–28, and Malone, VI, p. 441.
20. JM to Joseph C. Cabell, Dec. 5, 1828, in Hunt, IX, pp. 326–27. JM also suggested that TJ's heated remarks might have been based on "a latent reference . . . to the reports of Mr. Hamilton and Executive recommendations to Congress favorable to indefinite power over both agriculture and manufactures."
21. JM to William Cabell Rives, Jan. 23, 1829, in Rives and Fendall, IV, pp. 7–8.
22. JM to Joseph C. Cabell, Sept. 18, 1828, in Hunt, IX, pp. 316–40 at 333. See also JM to Joseph C. Cabell, Oct. 30, 1828, *ibid.*, pp. 317–26.
23. JM to William Cabell Rives, Jan. 23, 1829, in Rives and Fendall, IV, pp. 7–9.

as a denunciation of the abuse of a delegated power.[24]

When Madison's letters on the constitutionality of protective tariffs were published in Richmond and Washington in December 1828, *Niles' Register* reported that they had "nearly silenced the *constitutional* croakers—they are as 'frogs frozen up in a pond.' "[25] When the croaking persisted, however, Madison returned to the defense of his friend against "the strange misconstructions which continue to be put" on his letter to Giles. He took the time to search through Jefferson's "elaborate report in 1793, when Secretary of State, on the foreign commerce of the United States, and all his messages when President." This careful scrutiny revealed that in all of them Jefferson gave "the most explicit and reiterated sanctions . . . to the power to regulate *trade* or commerce in favour of manufactures." Against this overwhelming evidence, Giles had set up a letter whose "unstudied and unguarded language incident to a hasty and confidential correspondence" was displayed as "a self-contradiction" since it seemed to turn "the letter against those opinions."

But Madison again cited Jefferson's use of the word "indefinitely," which would explain away the seeming contradiction if interpreted "to imply that a *definite* or limited use of the power might not be unconstitutional." Otherwise, it would appear that Jefferson in power had consciously violated "the Great Charter which he had bound himself by oath not to violate," that "he had been all his life inhaling despotism, and had then [in 1825], for the first time 'scented the tainted breeze.' " Such a conclusion, Madison argued, was inconsistent with "every rule of fair construction, as well as every motive of friendly respect" for Jefferson.[26]

Madison's latter-day career as caretaker of Jefferson's memory soon merged with his role as interpreter of his own record. The transition came in 1828–1829, when he had to turn from interpreting the meaning of Jefferson's views to defending himself from critics among the passionate new generation of Republicans who had the effrontery to reinterpret for him the true meaning of his own views expressed in the distant past and now seen by him, according to his critics, through the haze of age, confusion, and a faulty memory.

While Madison was defending Jefferson by combating "the gross misstatements, the strange misconstructions, and the sophisticated comments" on the tariff issue in Virginia, Congress in 1828 passed the so-called "tariff of abominations," which radicalized the antitariff movement and made South Carolina, not the Old Dominion, the new hotbed for the even more dangerous innovation: the doctrine of nullification.[27] At the request of a special

---

24. JM to Joseph C. Cabell, Dec. 5, 1828, in Hunt, IX, pp. 326–27; JM to William Cabell Rives, Jan. 23, 1829, in Rives and Fendall, IV, pp. 7–8; and JM to Joseph C. Cabell, Feb. 2, 1829, *ibid.*, pp. 10–11.

25. Brant, VI, p. 474.

26. JM to William Cabell Rives, Jan. 23, 1829, in Rives and Fendall, IV, pp. 7–9.

27. For JM's earliest concern about South Carolina, see the draft of his letter to Thomas Lehre, Aug. 2, 1828 (not sent), *ibid.*, III, pp. 635–36.

committee of the South Carolina legislature, Vice President John C. Calhoun, whose nationalist bonus bill Madison had vetoed as his last official act as president, now turned extreme states' righter and secretly wrote *The South Carolina Exposition and Protest* proclaiming the constitutional right of a single state to nullify federal enactments that it deemed in violation of the Constitution. And instead of citing Jefferson, as Giles had done, Calhoun cited Madison, the author of the Virginia resolutions of 1798, as the patriotic patron of the doctrine of nullification.[28]

Calhoun's theory rested on two basic propositions: the Constitution was a compact between sovereign states; and sovereignty, being indivisible, remained with each state. As the agency of the states, the federal government could not be the ultimate arbiter of its own powers. Every state, therefore, had a constitutional right to "interpose" its authority and declare null and void any federal law that it deemed to be a violation of the original compact. The state veto of federal law, exercised by the state through a convention elected by the people, was to be presumed valid and in force unless three-fourths of the states, meeting in popularly elected conventions, overruled the nullifying state and amended the Constitution to specifically grant the powers in question. The protesting state could then acquiesce or secede from the Union.[29]

In defending state sovereignty, Calhoun rejected the section of the Judiciary Act of 1789 that provided for an appeal from state courts to the Supreme Court of the United States.[30] "A position more false and fatal," he wrote, "cannot be conceived. Fortunately, it has been so ably refuted by Mr. Madison, in his Report to the Virginia Legislature in 1800, on the Alien and Sedition Acts, as to supercede the necessity of further comments." Calhoun, who preferred to call his doctrine state interposition instead of nullification,[31] then quoted Madison's statement about the right and duty of the state to interpose to arrest the evil, should the federal judiciary sanction powers beyond those delegated by the Constitution. But he skipped over Madison's definition of interposition as a solemn appeal to public opinion and asserted instead the

---

28. For three recent appraisals of JM's role in the nullification controversy, each superb in special ways, see McCoy, pp. 132–59, 171–72, 336–37; Merrill D. Peterson, *Olive Branch and Sword: The Compromise of 1833* (Baton Rouge, 1982); and Richard E. Ellis, *The Union at Risk: Jacksonian Democracy, States' Rights, and the Nullification Crisis* (New York, 1987).

29. See William W. Freehling, *Prelude to Civil War: The Nullification Controversy in South Carolina, 1816–1836* (New York, 1965), pp. 134–76, and Peterson, *Jefferson Image,* pp. 51–66.

30. In the House of Representatives's debates on the Judiciary Act of 1789, JM had argued that state courts "cannot be trusted with the execution of the federal laws. . . . On the whole, he said, he did not see how it could be made compatible with the constitution, or safe to the federal interests to make a transfer of the federal jurisdiction to the state courts"; see JM's comments on the judiciary bill, Aug. 29, 1789, in *PJM,* XII, pp. 367–68. Federal judges, he emphasized, "are the guardians of the laws and of the constitution of the United States, and, I trust, of the individual states also"; see *ibid.,* p. 411.

31. See Ellis, p. 7. See also Brant, VI, p. 475, and Charles Warren, "Legislative and Judicial Attacks on the Supreme Court of the United States: A History of the Twenty-fifth Section of the Judiciary Act," *American Law Review* 47 (1913): 1–34, 161–89.

right of a state to nullify federal law, if the state followed the formal constitutional procedure of having the people act through a state convention and not through the legislature. The state government could then prevent enforcement of the contested measure within its limits.

Except for the tariff controversy in Virginia, the venerable Madison had carefully avoided taking a public stand on political issues since leaving office in 1817. But the "preposterous and anarchical pretension"[32] set forth in the anonymous *South Carolina Exposition* pushed him into the center of the seething nullification controversy and kept him there, defending himself—and Jefferson—for the rest of his life. For almost at this precise moment, Governor Giles, having scanned the three-volume edition of Jefferson's *Writings* published in 1829, now cited Jefferson's "Solemn Protest" of 1825, which Jefferson had suppressed on Madison's advice, as supporting the antitariff cause.[33]

Madison quickly decided that nullification and its twin evil, secession, were greater threats to the Union than the "Tariff heresy, which is understood to be tottering in the public opinion." For tactical reasons, however, he concentrated on "the disorganizing doctrine which asserts a right in every State to withdraw itself from the Union" and on Calhoun's gratuitous rejection of the section of the Judiciary Act of 1789, which provided for an appeal from state courts to the Supreme Court of the United States, as an infringement of state sovereignty. He vehemently denied "both the Judicial and the anti-union heresies" of Calhoun and Giles.

Their fundamental error, the president-as-historian patiently pointed out, "lies in supposing the State Governments to be parties to the Constitutional compact from which the Gov[ernmen]t of the U. S. results." Facts, not theories, were important, and "the plain fact of the case is," he observed, "that the Constitution of the U. S. was created by the people composing the respective States, who alone had the right." In that sense, "the real parties to the const[itutiona]l compact of the U. S. are the *States*—that is, the people thereof respectively in their sovereign character, and they *alone,* so declared in the Resolutions of 98, and so explained in the Report of 99."[34]

"Nothing can be more clear," he wrote in 1830, "than that the Constitution of the U. S. has created a Government, in as strict a sense of the term, as the Governments of the States created by their respective Constitutions. . . . And the operation is to be directly on persons and things in the one Gov[ernmen]t as in the others. If in some cases, the jurisdiction is concurrent as it is in

---

32. JM uses this phrase in his letter to Nicholas P. Trist, Dec. 1831, in Hunt, IX, p. 472.

33. Giles erroneously claimed that TJ's paper had been written "with the aid or concurrence of Mr. Madison"; see Brant, VI, p. 475.

34. JM to Joseph C. Cabell, Sept. 7, 1829, in Hunt, IX, pp. 347-48; JM, "Outline [on the Nullification Doctrine]," Sept. 1829, *ibid.,* pp. 351-57. JM noted that in his original draft of the Virginia resolutions of 1798, "the word *alone,* wch. guarded agst. error on this point, was struck out . . . and led to misconceptions and misreasonings concerning the true character of the pol[itical] system."

others exclusive, this is one of the features constituting the peculiarity of the system."35

As "a compact among the States in their highest sovereign capacity," the Constitution formed the people of all the states into "one people for certain purposes," and the laws passed under its authority could not "be altered or annulled," as Calhoun claimed, "at the will of the States individually, as the Constitution of a State may be at its individual will." Instead, the Constitution had provided for "a peaceable and authoritative termination" of controversies about boundaries of jurisdiction between the federal and state governments.36 Such disputes were to be "decided by the Supreme Court of the U. S. so constituted as to be as impartial as it could be made by the mode of appointment and responsibility for the Judges."37

In an essay on nullification written in 1829, Madison elaborated on several safeguards available if the Supreme Court should concur in usurpations, listing "constitutional remedies such as have been found effectual; particularly in the case of [the] alien and sedition laws, and such as will in all cases be effectual, whilst the responsibility of the G[enera]l Gov[ermen]t to its constituents continues:—Remonstrances and instructions—recurring elections and impeachments; amend[men]t of [the] Const[itution] as provided by itself and exemplified in the 11th article limiting the suability of the States."38

Madison confessed his "surprize and sorrow at the proceedings of S[outh] Carolina," calling them "unhappy aberrations"39 that rejected the fundamental maxim of republican government that the will of the majority must ultimately rule. South Carolina had shifted from majority action by the people of the states to minority action by each state government to "interpose," then had redefined that action not in terms of an appeal to public opinion to protest a usurpation of authority, but in terms of an assertion of the right to "finally decide, by virtue of her sovereignty, that the Constitution has been violated; and that if not yielded to by the Federal Government, tho' supported by all the other States, she may rightfully resist it and withdraw itself from the Union."40 Madison flatly rejected a theory that claimed that a single state could institute a process that would lead to the ascendancy of a minority over a large majority in a republican system.

Moreover, the doctrine of nullification "would convert the Federal Gov-

35. JM to Nicholas P. Trist, Feb. 15, 1830, *ibid.*, p. 354.

36. JM to Edward Everett, Aug. 1830, in Rives and Fendall, IV, pp. 95-97.

37. JM, "Outline." JM also cited the supreme authority of the Supreme Court in several letters, and in one he mentioned his defense of the Court as ultimate arbiter in *The Federalist* Number 39, as he had done in his letter to TJ in 1823; see JM to Joseph C. Cabell, Aug. 16, 1829, and Sept. 7, 1829, in Hunt, IX, pp. 341-44, 346-51, and JM to Nicholas P. Trist, Feb. 15, 1830, *ibid.*, pp. 354-58.

38. JM, "Outline."

39. JM to Nicholas P. Trist, Feb. 15, 1830, in Hunt, IX, pp. 357-58.

40. JM to Joseph C. Cabell, Aug. 16, 1829, *ibid.*, pp. 341-44.

ernment into a mere league, which would quickly throw the States back into a chaos, out of which, not order a second time, but lasting disorders of the worst kind, could not fail to come."[41] But the Constitution was not "a mere Treaty between independent nations, without any resort for terminating disputes but negotiation, and that failing, the sword" of civil war.

Madison countered with the argument that "the Union of the States is, according to the Virg[ini]a doctrine in 98-99, a *Constitutional Union*" that established a political system providing for "a peaceable and effectual decision of all controversies among the parties."[42] Finally, if all constitutional remedies failed against usurpations of power, Madison concluded, there still remained two other fundamental rights: the natural right of revolution, which the people could exercise "if deprived of rights absolutely essential" to safety and happiness; and the right of expatriation, which individuals could invoke through voluntary exile.[43]

Madison consistently appealed to history for "evidence that ought of itself to settle" questions relating to the constitutionality of tariffs or of nullification.[44] The only way one could understand the "novel and complex" nature of the American political system was to study "the process of its formation."[45] In addition to the text of the Constitution, one must also understand the historical context, especially of "the evils which were to be cured" and "the benefits to be obtained" by ratification.[46] The most rudimentary knowledge of the period would show that the Constitution had not been formed, as had the Articles of Confederation, by the sovereign state governments. Instead, "the people in each of the States, acting in their highest sovereign capacity," had established it through popularly elected ratifying conventions. The doctrine of nullification threatened to dissolve the Union created in 1787-1788, giving a belated victory to Antifederalist dogma disguised as nullification theory.[47]

In one of his more pessimistic moments, the elderly statesman warned about "the awful consequences of a final rupture and dissolution of the Union," which he had labored so long and so diligently to establish. "Such a prospect," which nullification seemed to threaten, "must be deprecated, must be shuddered at by every friend to his country, to liberty, to the happiness of man. For, in the event of a dissolution of the Union, an impossibility of ever renewing it is brought home to every mind by the difficulties encountered in establishing it.... The happy Union of these States is a wonder; their Const-

---

41. JM to Richard Rush, Jan. 17, 1829, in Rives and Fendall, IV, pp. 5-6.

42. JM to Joseph C. Cabell, Sept. 7, 1829, in Hunt, IX, pp. 346-51.

43. JM, "Outline," p. 353. JM appended a note stressing "the distinction between an expatriating individual withdrawing only his person and moveable effects, and the withdrawal of a State mutilating the domain of the Union."

44. See JM to Joseph C. Cabell, Sept. 18, 1828, in Hunt, IX, p. 333.

45. JM to James Robertson, Apr. 20, 1831, in Rives and Fendall, IV, p. 171.

46. JM, "Notes," appended to JM to Joseph C. Cabell, Oct. 30, 1828, in Hunt, IX, p. 323.

47. JM to Edward Everett, Aug. 1830, in Rives and Fendall, IV, pp. 95-97.

[itutio]n a miracle; their example the hope of Liberty throughout the World. Woe to the ambition that would meditate the destruction of either!"[48]

Being a historian is never an easy assignment, as Madison was to learn in the last years of his life. And protecting his own reputation—and Jefferson's—proved to be an especially difficult task since he was dealing with a younger generation eager to make the older generation worthy of its descendants by reinterpreting for the elders the meaning of past events in which they had participated. He respected the intelligence and the desire of the new generation to sort things out for themselves, but he was appalled by their myopic view of the recent past, finding it a bizarre compound of ignorance and arrogance that created a situation in which old orators, like Giles, and new statesmen, like Calhoun, seemed at their best—and, to their local audiences, most appealing—when they were unhampered by the facts, particularly when they invoked the names of the two ancient leaders of the Republicans, Jefferson and Madison.[49]

In retirement, Madison was destined to witness what George Dangerfield has labeled "the agonized passing of the Jeffersonian world" and the inauguration of the passionate age of Jackson that ushered in what John Higham has described as "an age of boundlessness."[50] In this new phase of American republicanism, Madison was impressed by what he considered striking similarities between the events and issues of the 1820s and 1830s and the Confederation period prior to the adoption of the Constitution.

He must have found it especially galling, therefore, to be told, as one of his defenders observed sarcastically in 1833, that "those who live in the present day, although unborn when the Constitution was formed, understand the views and objects of the framers of that instrument, better than they who formed it!" Madison rejected the sarcasm but agreed on the need for serious research by historically minded investigators. "I wish your example in tracing our constitutional history through its earlier periods could be followed by our public men of the present generation," he told William Cabell Rives, who later became his first biographer. "The few surveyors of the past seem to have forgotten what they once knew, and those of the present to shrink from such researches."[51]

Early in 1830, as the age of Jackson dawned, the debate by public men of the younger generation moved from Virginia and South Carolina to Congress, where Senator Daniel Webster of Massachusetts and Senator Robert Y.

---

48. JM, "Outline," pp. 353–57. See also Paul C. Nagel, *One Nation Indivisible: The Union in American Thought* (New York, 1964).

49. McCoy, pp. 130–53, gives a brilliant analysis of JM as historian.

50. See George Dangerfield, *The Awakening of American Nationalism, 1815–1828* (New York, 1965), p. 300, and John Higham, *From Boundlessness to Consolidation: The Transformation of American Culture* (Ann Arbor, 1969).

51. McCoy, p. 157, quotes the views of "Germanicus," who defended JM against the attacks by "Mutius." See also JM to William Cabell Rives, Dec. 20, 1828, cited *ibid.*, p. 132.

Hayne of South Carolina each claimed Madison's support for diametrically opposed views, while Vice President Calhoun watched and listened as presiding officer of the Senate. Although Madison's letter on the constitutionality of the tariff had been published, his views on nullification had not yet been made public since the octogenarian thought that "the task of combating such unhappy aberrations belongs to other hands."[52]

Hayne could, therefore, claim, as Calhoun had done, that the South Carolina doctrine was "the good old Republican doctrine of '98; the doctrine of . . . that celebrated report which is familiarly known as 'Madison's Report.'" Quoting from it selectively, he asserted that the Virginia doctrine of interposition validated the constitutional right to resist and nullify acts of Congress and decisions of the Supreme Court. The federal Constitution, Hayne declared, "is (in the language of Mr. Madison) 'a compact to which the States are parties,'" the federal government exercising certain delegated powers and the state governments retaining all other aspects of sovereignty. "All sovereigns are of necessity equal," he argued, and in case of disputes between them, the states and the federal government must be their own judges.[53]

As Giles and Calhoun had done, Hayne eliminated any reference to Madison's statements in the report that declarations by a state in such cases were "expressions of opinion, unaccompanied with any other effect than what they may produce on opinion by exciting reflection." Madison flatly denied that his report or the debates on it in the Virginia House of Delegates contained "any reference to a constitutional right in an individual State to arrest by force the operation of a law of the U. S." Instead, the Virginia resolutions were "an invitation to the other States 'to *concur* in declaring the [Alien and Sedition] acts to be unconstitutional, and to *co-operate*'" in taking majority action through "measures known to the Constitution" against them. Such concurrence and cooperation, he argued, should be based on the collective force of public opinion.[54]

Like Hayne, Webster did not know Madison's views on nullification, but he cited Madison's opinion on the constitutionality of protective tariffs—the subject of the Webster-Hayne debates—as "impregnable." "Mr. Madison himself," he pointed out, "deems this same tariff law quite constitutional. Instead of a clear and palpable violation, it is, in his judgment, no violation at all. So that, while they use his authority for a hypothetical case, they reject it in the very case before them." Moreover, interposition might have a meaning other than the one given by Hayne. It might merely mean protest or remonstrance or some other measure known to the Constitution, such as amendment through the procedures outlined in the instrument. Webster professed "much respect for the constitutional opinions of Mr. Madison," but he doubted that

---

52. Brant, VI, p. 476.
53. *Ibid.*, p. 478.
54. *Ibid.*, p. 477; JM to Robert Y. Hayne, Apr. [3 or 4?], 1830, in Hunt, IX, p. 388.

Madison had ever approved of the right of a single state to nullify an act of Congress.[55]

Both Hayne and Webster sent copies of their speeches to Madison. To Hayne, Madison wrote a 4,000-word reply, about 50 in acknowledgment and praise for the author's "ability and eloquence" and 3,950 in a detailed dissent from, and rebuttal of, the South Carolina doctrine that a single state government had "a constitutional right to resist and by force annul within itself acts of the Government of the U. S. which it deems unauthorized by the Constitution of the U. S.; although such acts be not within the extreme cases of oppression, which justly absolve the State from the Constitutional compact to which it is a party." On the contrary, Madison argued, the government created by the Constitution "must be its own interpreter according to its text and *the facts of the case*"—text and context. History demonstrated that "a political system that does not provide for a peaceable and authoritative termination of occurring controversies, can be but the name and shadow of a Gov[ernmen]t[,] the very object and end of a real Gov[ernmen]t being the substitution of law and order for uncertainty[,] confusion and violence."

What would be the consequences of the South Carolina contention? Madison had a ready answer: "That a final decision of such controversies, if left to each of the 13 States[,] now 24 with a prospective increase, would make the Constitution and laws of the U. S. different in different States, was obvious; and equally obvious that this diversity of independent decisions must disorganize the Government of the Union, and even decompose the Union itself."[56]

As for the Virginia resolutions of 1798, he cited his role in writing them and the report, explaining their meaning, and said that both the resolutions and the report were inconsistent with the South Carolina doctrine. In the Virginia denunciation of the Alien and Sedition Laws, an attempt had been made to insert the following words after the word "unconstitutional," *"and not law, but utterly null void and of no power or effect,"* but they had been "stricken out by common consent. It appears that the words had been regarded as only surplusage by the friends of the Resolution; but lest they should be misconstrued into a nullifying import instead of a declaration of opinion, the word unconstitutional alone was retained, as more safe agst. that error. The term *nullification* to which such an important meaning is now attached," he added in an attempt to clear Jefferson as well as himself of the charge, "was never a part of the [Virginia] Resolutions and appears not to have been contained in the Kentucky Resolutions as *originally* passed, but to have been introduced at an after date." Madison could not remember whether the italicized words that were stricken out "were in the draft from my pen or added before the Resolutions were introduced by a member who withdrew them" since Madison had not retained a copy of his draft and his "memory [was] not

---

55. Brant, VI, p. 477.
56. JM to Robert Y. Hayne, Apr. [3 or 4?], 1830, in Hunt, IX, pp. 383–94.

to be trusted after such a lapse of time." But he was certain that he had "never disapproved the erasure of them."[57]

As a clinching argument, Madison cited the answers given by the state legislatures, mostly controlled by the Federalist party, which rejected the Virginia and Kentucky resolutions. "Their great objection, with a few undefined complaints of the spirit and character of the Resolutions, was directed agst. the assumed authority of a State Legislature to declare a law of the U. S. to be unconstitutional[,] which they considered an unwarrantable interference with the exclusive jurisdiction of the Supreme Court of the U. S. Had the Resolutions been regarded as avowing and maintaining a right in an individual State to arrest by force the execution of a law of the U. S. it must be presumed that it would have been a pointed and conspicuous object of their denunciation."[58]

To Congressman Edward Everett of Massachusetts, who also doubled as editor of the influential *North American Review,* Madison sent an unidentified copy of his letter to Hayne. And in a personal letter to Webster on the overwhelming effect of the senator's speeches, the venerable Virginian referred Webster to Everett's copy of his views, praising Webster for combating so effectively the South Carolina "champion of the new doctrine" while explaining how Webster's views on "We the people" differed from his own. Both Madison and Webster rejected Hayne's theory of state sovereignty and stressed the concept that a sovereign people could divide sovereignty and allocate powers between the federal and state governments. Both emphasized the power of the Supreme Court of the United States to decide boundary disputes between state and federal authority. Both agreed that it was "We, the people of the United States," who established the Constitution, thus making them one people. But Webster interpreted the phrase to mean "the people of the United States in the aggregate," an extreme nationalist position, while Madison argued that it meant the people of the United States constituted as "the people of the several states," making them "one people for certain purposes, with a government competent to the effectuation of them."[59] The Constitution had created a governmental system "so unexampled in its origin, so complex in its structure, and so peculiar in some of its features" that the traditional political vocabulary did not "furnish terms sufficiently distinctive and appropriate, without a detailed resort to the facts of the case."[60]

To other congressmen, including Edward Livingston of Louisiana and Andrew Stevenson of Virginia, Speaker of the House of Representatives, Madison claimed a halfway house between the extreme nullifiers, led by Hayne and Calhoun, and the extreme nationalists, led by Webster, offering a historical

57. *Ibid.,* p. 388. For TJ's role in having the words inserted, see ch. 24, above.

58. *Ibid.,* p. 389.

59. Brant, VI, pp. 479-80. For the similarities and differences between JM and Webster, see McCoy, pp. 147-51; for the similarities and differences between JM and the Hayne-Calhoun states' righters, see Ellis.

60. JM to Daniel Webster, May 27, 1830, in Rives and Fendall, IV, p. 85.

alternative to both. Livingston came closest to his views, arguing that in all the "attributes of sovereignty, which, by the federal compact, were transferred to the General Government, that government is sovereign and supreme; the States have abandoned, and can never reclaim them." By the Constitution, they had "unequivocally surrendered every constitutional right of impeding or resisting the execution of any decree or judgment of the Supreme Court." He agreed that a state might elect in an extreme case to attempt secession. Such action, however, "is not a right derived from the constitution," but an extra-legal or revolutionary right, and "whenever resorted to, it must be at the risk of all the penalties attached to an unsuccessful resistance to established authority."[61]

When Livingston told Madison that he had based his speech on a close reading of Madison's writings in *The Federalist* and the Virginia report of 1800 as well as his personal knowledge of Madison's views, he received a note from Montpellier endorsing his disavowal of the nullification doctrine. It was "as new to me as it was to you," Madison confessed, and the nullifiers' error arose "from a failure to distinguish between what is declaratory of opinion and what is *ipso facto* executory; [and] between the rights of *the parties* to the Constitution and of a single party." He agreed that Webster had defined federal powers too broadly in arguing for unitary national sovereignty while Hayne had defined them too narrowly in arguing for state sovereignty.[62] Both were wrong, Madison said, since the true theory was that of divided sovereignty. To Stevenson, he said that his view rested "on a middle ground between a form wholly national and one merely federal" or confederationist.[63]

As the constitutional crisis deepened, pressure built on Madison to make his private views public. Everett hoped to publish Madison's letter to Hayne as an essay by an unnamed correspondent. But when Hayne and his coterie continued their misrepresentations of his views, Madison rewrote his letter and sent it to the editor of the *North American Review*, who published it as Madison's essay in October 1830.[64] After rehearsing his views on the divisibility of sovereignty and the role of the people in the formation of the Constitution, he turned to nullification, noting that "the distinguished names and high authorities which appear to have asserted" the doctrine entitled it "to a respect which it might be difficult otherwise to feel for it."

First, he listed the steps in the procedure outlined by Calhoun: election of delegates to a state convention; the interposition of state authority by the convention in declaring a federal act null and void, if it were deemed unconsti-

---

61. Kenneth M. Stampp, "The Concept of a Perpetual Union," *JAH* 65 (1978): 29. See William B. Hatcher, "Edward Livingston's View of the Nature of the Union," *Louisiana Historical Quarterly* 24 (1941): 698–728, for an excellent discussion. See also Francis Fay Wayland, *Andrew Stevenson: Democrat and Diplomat, 1785–1857* (Philadelphia, 1949), pp. 74–102.

62. JM to Edward Livingston, May 8, 1830, in Rives and Fendall, IV, p. 80. See also Brant, VI, pp. 479–80.

63. JM to Andrew Stevenson, Nov. 27, 1830, in Rives and Fendall, IV, p. 131.

64. See JM to Edward Everett, Aug. 28, 1830, in Hunt, IX, pp. 383–403.

tutional; and the blocking of enforcement of the tainted law within the state. Congress might then acquiesce in nullification of the condemned statute, or it might propose a constitutional amendment conferring on the federal government the challenged authority, if it were ratified by three-fourths of the states. "If the doctrine were to be understood as requiring the three-fourths of the States to sustain, instead of that proportion to reverse, the decision of the appealing State," Madison observed, "the decision to be without effect during the appeal, it wd. be sufficient to remark, that this extra const[itutiona]l course might well give way to that marked out by the Const[itution] which authorizes ⅔ of the States to institute and ¾ to effectuate, an amendment to the Const[itutio]n establishing a permanent rule of the highest auth[orit]y in place of an irregular precedent of construction only."

Instead, the nullifying doctrine presumed that the decision of the state was valid, "and that it overrules the law of the U. S. unless overruled by ¾ of the States. Can more be necessary to demonstrate the inadmissibility of such a doctrine," Madison queried, "than that it puts it in the power of the smallest fraction over ¼ of the U. S.—that is, of 7 States out of 24—to give the law and even the Const[itutio]n to 17 States, each of the 17 having as parties to the Const[itutio]n an equal right with each of the 7 to expound it and to insist on the exposition. That the 7 might, in particular instances be right and the 17 wrong, is," he conceded, "more than possible. But to establish a positive and permanent rule giving such a power to such a minority over such a majority, would overturn the firt principle of free Gov[ernmen]t and in practice necessarily overturn the Gov[ernmen]t itself."[65]

Madison again cited his *Federalist* Number 39 on the Supreme Court as the authority to decide "the boundary of jurisdiction between the Federal and State Gov[ernmen]ts." Chief Justice John Marshall happily proclaimed his "peculiar pleasure" that Madison was "himself again, [avowing] the opinion of his best days."[66]

After Madison's stern public disapproval of Calhoun's doctrine, the nullifiers adopted one of two tactics: they dropped him and rallied to Jefferson's Kentucky resolutions as the true "principles of '98"; or they swept aside "Mr. Madison's opinions at seventy-nine years of age," pitting his faded memories against "his opinions of fifty, and the incontestable argument which support them, whatever may be Mr. Madison's own opinions at the present moment."[67]

As Drew McCoy has observed, "Unlike Madison, Jefferson was no longer around to refute their claims, and in his case there was much less to refute."[68] In 1830, while he was searching through his papers for material relating to his

---

65. *Ibid.*, p. 399.

66. *Ibid.*, p. 397. See also Ketcham, p. 643.

67. Brant, VI, pp. 475, 487–88. McCoy, pp. 153–54, has a perceptive account of "this relentless age-baiting."

68. *Ibid.*, p. 143.

preparation of the Virginia resolutions of 1798, Madison had concluded that Jefferson had had nothing to do with the preparation of the Kentucky resolutions of 1799, in which the word "nullification" first appeared in public print.[69] But a few months later, he ran across a copy of Jefferson's draft of the Kentucky resolutions of 1798 "containing the term just noticed," and he had to change his tune. "Not a word of explanation is mentioned," he told Nicholas P. Trist, who had married one of Jefferson's granddaughters and was soon to become a White House aide to President Andrew Jackson. "It was probably sent," he conjectured, "and possibly at my request, in consequence of my being a member elect of the Virg[ini]a Legislature of 1799, which would have to vindicate its contemporary Resol[utio]ns of -98. It is remarkable that the paper differs both from the Kentucky Resolutions of -98 [as adopted], and from those of -99. It agrees with the former in the main and must have been the pattern of the Resol[ution]s of that year, but certain passages omitted in them, which employ the terms nullification and nullifying; and it differs in the quantity of matter from the Resolutions of -99, but agrees with them in a passage which employs that language, and would seem to have been the origin of it." Madison presumed that Jefferson's correspondent in Kentucky had left out the questionable terms in 1798 but that the legislature had used them in 1799, including "the phraseology containing the term 'nullification.'"[70]

But Madison, the concerned custodian of his friend's reputation, was not ready to admit that Jefferson was a nullifier in the Calhoun-Hayne sense. Since Jefferson had used the dread term, however, Madison counseled Everett and Trist not to publish denials that he had any "connection with or responsibility for the use of such [a] term on such an occasion. Still," he concluded, searching desperately for a way to separate his old friend from his new foes, "I believe that he did not attach to it the idea of a constitutional right in the sense of S[outh] Carolina, but that of a natural right in cases justly appealing to it."[71] When Senator Henry Clay of Kentucky gave a speech in Cincinnati that, according to Madison, rescued "the Resolutions of Kentucky of -98 and -99, from the misconstructions of them . . . as an *aegis* to the nullifying doctrine," with its "hideous aspect and fatal tendency," Madison sent him a congratulatory note, calling attention to his own views recently published in the *North American Review*.[72]

Throughout 1831 and 1832, the increasingly disillusioned Madison continued to scribble long and learned letters, essays, and memoranda deploring "the strange doctrines and misconceptions" of the nullifiers and their formula

---

69. JM to Nicholas P. Trist, June 3, 1830, in Rives and Fendall, IV, p. 87, and JM to Edward Everett, Aug. 20, 1830, in Hunt, IX, pp. 394–95.

70. JM to Edward Everett, Sept. 10, 1830, *ibid.*, pp. 395–96 and JM to Nicholas P. Trist, Sept. 23, 1830, *ibid.*

71. *Ibid.*

72. JM to Henry Clay, Oct. 9, 1830, *ibid.*, pp. 410–11. For an indictment of TJ for "intellectual sloppiness and irresponsibility" in drafting the Kentucky resolutions, see McCoy, p. 144.

for anarchy, increasingly worried that "the tendency of them [was] the more to be dreaded, as they are patronized by Statesmen of shining talents, and patriotic reputations." He feared that "the obvious, inevitable and disastrous consequences of a separation of the States, whether into alien confederacies or individual nations," would be "rivalships collisions and animosities" that would "quickly kindle the passions which are the forerunners of war."[73]

Throughout the latter part of 1831 and the first part of 1832, Madison was often depressed, usually bedridden, and occasionally silenced.[74] He was both heartened and saddened in 1831 when he learned that he was the lone survivor of the signers of the Constitution, the "members of the Revol[u-tionar]y Con[gres]s prior to the close of the war," and "the members of the Convention of 1776 which formed the first Const[itutio]n for Virg[ini]a." But he retained enough of his perky sense of humor to observe that "having outlived so many of my co[n]temporaries, I ought not to forget that I may be thought to have outlived myself."[75] To James Monroe, he wrote that "my stiffening fingers make smaller letters, as my feet take shorter steps."[76]

But his mind was sharp and clear, and he quickly reentered the political arena when the nullifiers, whom he considered slow learners, persisted in invoking Jefferson's name, an action that he thought could be explained only by "an impenetrable stupidity . . . [or] an incurable prejudice," given the national record of his closest friend. "What might or would have been the meaning attached to the term 'nullify' by Mr. Jefferson," Madison wrote in October 1831, "is to be gathered from his language in the resolutions of 1798 and elsewhere, as in his letter to Mr. Giles, December 25, 1825, viz, to extreme cases, as alone justifying a resort to any forcible relief."[77]

As the caretaker of Jefferson's legacy, Madison constantly recurred to his friend's emphasis on democratic majority rule. "That he ever asserted a right in a single State to arrest the execution of an act of Congress, the arrest to be valid and permanent unless reversed by three-fourths of the States, is contenanced by nothing known to have been said or done by him. In his letter to Major Cartwright,[78] he refers to a Convention as a peaceable remedy for conflicting claims of power in our compound Government; but whether he alluded to a convention as prescribed by the Constitution, or brought about by any other mode, his respect for the will of majorities, as the vital principle of Republican Government, makes it certain that he could not have meant a convention in which a minority of seven States was to prevail over seventeen,

---

73. JM to Matthew Carey, July 27, 1831, in Hunt, IX, pp. 462–63.
74. See McCoy, pp. 151–62.
75. JM to Jared Sparks, June 1, 1831, in Hunt, IX, p. 460.
76. JM to James Monroe, Apr. 21, 1831, *ibid.*, p. 459.
77. JM to Nicholas P. Trist, Sept. 23, 1831, in McCoy, p. 152, and JM to John Townsend, Oct. 18, 1831, in Rives and Fendall, IV, p. 199.
78. See TJ to John Cartwright, June 5, 1824, in L. and B., XVI, pp. 42–52.

either in amending or expounding the Constitution," a contention that Madison later labeled "an inversion of the Repub[lica]n order of things."[79]

As the nullification controversy built to a crisis in 1832, pitting President Andrew Jackson against Vice President John C. Calhoun, Madison maintained a steady correspondence with Nicholas P. Trist, who became a clerk in the State Department in 1829 before being promoted to private secretary to the president in 1831.[80] As commander in chief, Madison had promoted Jackson to major general during the War of 1812, and he remained on friendly terms with "Old Hickory," who visited Montpellier in July 1832 while he was running for reelection.[81] Moreover, President Jackson, shortly after the Webster-Hayne debate in 1830, had given his famous toast at a public banquet, looking squarely at Vice President Calhoun: "Our Federal Union—it must be preserved." That stance put him squarely in the camp with Madison.

For two years after that dinner, the doctrine of nullification was debated intermittently but was not put to the test until 1832, when Henry Clay pushed through a new tariff, which Jackson signed in July. Madison had appealed to Clay to reduce tariffs enough to separate the moderate from "the more violent opponents," hoping that "some accomodating arrangements" might avoid "the disastrous consequences of disunion."[82] And the new tariff did remove some of the "abominations" from the law of 1828. But it also retained high tariffs on textiles and iron, and it began to look like protective tariffs would be permanent. Instead of accommodation, therefore, Calhoun and "the more violent opponents" invoked their nullification procedures, which Madison thought could only lead to disunion. In an effort "to arrest the headlong course of South Carolina," Madison fired off two quick letters to Trist, which were obviously meant for President Jackson since Madison declared that "they may be suggested where it is most likely they will be well received," noting that "the wisdom that meets the crisis with the due effect will greatly signalize itself."

The letters were written while the Father of the Constitution was "reflecting in my sick bed . . . on the dangers hovering over our Constitution and even the Union itself." He was appalled by the "monstrous" alternative backed by Calhoun. "The idea that a Constitution which has been so fruitful of blessings, and a Union admitted to be the only guardian of the peace, liberty and happiness of the people of the States comprizing it should be broken up and scattered to the winds without greater than any existing causes is more painful than words can express."

Although confined to his bed "with my malady, my debility, and my age

---

79. JM to John Townsend, Oct. 18, 1831, in Rives and Fendall, IV, p. 199, and JM to Nicholas P. Trist, Dec. 1831, in Hunt, IX, p. 472.
80. For Nicholas P. Trist, see McCoy, pp. 152–53, 207–21, 325–28.
81. Brant, VI, pp. 485–92.
82. JM to Henry Clay, Mar. 22, 1832, in Hunt, IX, pp. 477–78.

in triple alliance against me," Madison dictated another defense of Jefferson, whose draft of the Kentucky resolutions was still being used by the nullifiers as a justification for their doctrine. He thought that "the charges against Mr. Jefferson can be duly refuted," adding that "allowances also ought to be made for a habit in Mr. Jefferson as in others of great genius[,] of expressing in strong and round terms, impressions of the moment."[83]

After Jackson signed the tariff of 1832, South Carolina's congressional delegation informed their constituents that "all hope for relief from Congress is irrevocably gone." In the Palmetto State, the nullifiers, spurred on by Hayne and Calhoun, swept the fall elections, setting the stage for the implementation of the nullification procedures outlined four years earlier by Calhoun. The nullifiers dominated almost four-fifths of the House and nearly three-fourths of the Senate.

The new legislature quickly summoned a state convention, which promptly put theory into practice on November 24, adopting by an overwhelming majority an ordinance declaring the tariff "unauthorized by the Constitution, null, void, and no law, nor binding upon this State, its officers or citizens." The nullification ordinance also forbade federal officials from collecting duties under the Tariff Act after February 1, 1833, prohibited appeals to federal courts, and threatened secession the moment the federal government attempted to enforce the law, blockade Charleston, or coerce the state.

In an address to the people of South Carolina, the convention boldly based its action on Madison's Virginia resolutions of 1798, which it claimed made nullification a constitutional right, a view that Madison had consistently opposed. Aware of the old man's recent distinction between the natural right of revolution, which he accepted, and a constitutional right of nullification, which he rejected, the convention conceded that "Mr. Madison himself has been brought forward to give a construction to this Resolution contrary to the most obvious import of the terms." Nonetheless, the convention then used Madison's language of 1798, with one exception, announcing that the federal compact derived its existence from the states that were parties to it, and "in the case of a deliberate, palpable, and dangerous exercise of powers not granted by the said compact, the States . . . have the right . . . to interpose for arresting the progress of the evil and for maintaining within their respective limits, the authorities, rights and liberties appertaining to them." Since the Virginia legislature of 1799-1800 had declared the resolutions consonant with the Constitution, the South Carolina convention contended, the proposed remedy of nullification must be a constitutional right.[84]

The one exception made by the nullifiers changed two words used by

---

83. JM to Nicholas P. Trist, May —, 1832, and May 29, 1832, *ibid.*, pp. 478-82.

84. For a brief summary, see Brant, VI, pp. 493-94. For an extensive account, see Freehling, pp. 219-59.

Madison in 1798, substituting for "the States . . . have" the singular "the State has." Madison pounced on this tampering, denouncing it as "the fallacy" that allowed South Carolina to draw "a different conclusion from them" than the one drawn by Virginia a third of a century earlier. "In the Virginia Resolutions and Report," he told Trist, "the *plural* number, *States*, is in *every* instance used where reference is made to the authority which presided over the Government. As I am now known to have drawn those documents, I may say as I do with a distinct recollection, that the distinction was intentional. It was in fact required by the course of reasoning employed on the occasion."

"The essential difference between a free Government and Governments not free," Madison continued, "is that the former is founded in compact, the parties to which are mutually and equally bound by it. Neither of them therefore can have a greater right to break off from the bargain, than the other or others have to hold them to it. And certainly there is nothing in the Virginia resolutions of -98, adverse to this principle, which is that of common sense and common justice." The nullifiers' error, he reiterated, "lies in confounding a *single* party, with the *parties* to the Constitutional compact of the United States. The latter having made the compact may do with it what they will with it. The former as one only of the parties, owes fidelity to it, till released by consent, or absolved by an intolerable abuse of the power created."

Indeed, he pinpointed the "pretext for the liberty taken" with the Virginia resolutions, citing "the word *respective,* prefixed to the 'rights' etc. to be secured within the States. Could the abuse of the expression [in 1832] have been foreseen or suspected [in 1798]," he confessed, "the form of it would doubtless have been varied. But what can be more consistent with common sense," he concluded, "than that all having the same rights etc., should unite in contending for the security of them to each."[85]

Having fended off the attempt to hang the nullification tag around his neck, Madison turned to beat off the attempt to implicate Jefferson—a more difficult assignment. He conceded that "the Kentucky Resolutions being less guarded have been more easily perverted." But he thought that "it is remarkable how closely the nullifiers who make the name of Mr. Jefferson the pedestal for their colossal heresy, shut their eyes and lips, whenever his authority is ever so clearly and emphatically against them."

Madison reminded Trist of Jefferson's advocacy during the Confederation government of the use of force "to coerce delinquent States" that had not met their financial requisition to Congress "and his reasons for preferring for the purpose a naval to a military force." Moreover, Jefferson had claimed that "it was not necessary to find a right to coerce" in the Articles of Confederation, arguing that it "was inherent in the nature of a compact," which was far weaker than the Union created by the Constitution. "It is high time," Madison concluded, "that the claim to secede at will should be put down by the

---

85. JM to Nicholas P. Trist, Dec. 23, 1832, in Hunt, IX, pp. 489-91. JM elaborated on this theme in his letter to Alexander Rives, [Jan. 1833], *ibid.,* pp. 495-98.

public opinion; and I shall be glad to see the task commenced by one who understands the subject."[86]

Following the nullification convention in South Carolina, a political game of musical chairs rotated the state's two leading advocates of nullification into new positions of power. After Hayne resigned as United States senator, he was elected governor of the Palmetto State. Calhoun then resigned as vice president of the United States and was elected as Hayne's successor in the United States Senate, where the anonymous author of the *South Carolina Exposition and Protest* now came out openly for his doctrine of nullification. After listening to Hayne's belligerent inaugural address as governor, a spectator predicted that "civil war must *soon* come."[87]

That President Jackson's understanding of the subject was closer to Madison's than to Calhoun's and to South Carolina's became clear on December 10, 1832, when the president issued a proclamation denouncing both nullification and secession. This document was prepared for Jackson by Secretary of State Edward Livingston,[88] whose views on nullification were closest to those of Madison. The nullification doctrine, Jackson said, was founded on the peculiar proposition that a state might retain its constitutional place in the Union and yet be bound only by those laws that it chose to obey. The power of a single state to nullify a law of the United States, the president declared, was *"incompatible with the existence of the Union, contradicted expressly by the letter of the Constitution, unauthorized by its spirit, inconsistent with every principle on which it was founded, and destructive of the great object for which it was formed."*

As for the right of secession, which Calhoun had inferred from the compact method utilized to create the Union, the president proclaimed that "the Constitution of the United States . . . forms a *government,* not a league; and whether it be formed by compact between the States or in any other manner, its character is the same. It is a Government in which all the people are represented, which operates directly on the people individually, not upon the States; they retained all the power they did not grant. But each State, having expressly parted with so many powers as to constitute, jointly with the other States, a single nation, can not, from that period, possess any right to secede, because such secession does not break a league, but destroys the unity of a nation. . . . To say that any State may at pleasure secede from the Union is to say that the United States are not a nation. . . . Secession, like any other revolutionary act, may be morally justified by the extremity of oppression; but to call it a constitutional right is confounding the meaning of terms." The object of the nullifiers, Jackson concluded, "is disunion. But be not deceived by names. Disunion by armed force is *treason*."[89]

86. *Ibid.,* p. 491. For JM's draft of the Virginia resolutions of 1798, see *PJM,* XVII, pp. 185-91.
87. For the remark at Hayne's inaugural address, see Freehling, p. 264; Hatcher, p. 721; and Stampp, 31.
88. For Livingston's role in preparing Jackson's proclamation, see Hatcher, p. 721, and Stampp, 31.
89. Richardson, II, pp. 640-56.

President Jackson's stance, the opposition of the Virginia legislature to the nullification doctrine,[90] and powerful speeches by Senator Daniel Webster of Massachusetts and Senator William Cabell Rives of Virginia gave Madison hope for the Union in 1833. "Your late very powerful Speech in the Senate," Madison wrote Webster, ". . . crushes 'nullification,' and must hasten the abandonment of 'Secession.' "[91] He told Rives that the nullifiers' "endeavor to shelter themselves under a distinction between a delegation and a surrender of powers. But if the powers be attributes of sovereignty and nationality and the grant of them be perpetual, as is necessarily implied, where not otherwise expressed, sovereignty and nationality according to the extent of the grant are effectually transferred by it, and a dispute about the name, is but a battle of words." But the practical result was the same in both cases: "The words of the Constitution are explicit that the Constitution and laws of the U. S. shall be supreme over the Constitution and laws of the several States; supreme in their exposition and execution as well as in their authority."[92]

In the bitter battle of words, he told Webster, "Secession" had too often been given two meanings, allowing the nullifiers to confound "the claim to secede at will, with the right of seceding from intolerable oppression." Examined separately, the claim to secede at will "answers itself, being a violation, without cause, of a faith solemnly pledged. The latter is another name only for revolution, about which there is no theoretic controversy." Madison thought that the double meaning used by the nullifiers had also become mixed "with the question whether the Constitution of the U. S. was formed by the people or by the States, now under a theoretic discussion by animated partizans."

Fortunately, the last of the Founding Fathers continued, "disputed theories, can be decided by undisputed facts. And here the undisputed fact is, that the Constitution was made by the people, but as embodied into the several States, who were parties to it and therefore made by the States in their highest authoritative capacity." Shifting from the theoretical basis of the Union to the practical results of a government resting on the people, he observed that while the Constitution remained in force, "*its operation,* in *every respect* must be precisely the *same,* whether its authority be derived from that of the *people,* in the one or the other of the modes, in question; the authority being Competent in both; and that, without an annulment of the Constitution itself its supremacy must be submitted to."[93]

Madison was also impressed by the maiden speech given by Senator William Cabell Rives, a young protégé of his and Jefferson's from Albemarle

---

90. JM noted that the General Assembly of Virginia had announced "that the resolutions of 98-99, gave no support to the nullifying doctrine of South Carolina"; see JM, "Notes on Nullification," in Hunt, IX, p. 589. Hunt attributes this essay to 1835-1836, but Brant, VI, p. 577, states that it was written in "January 1833, plus later insertions." See also McCoy, p. 155.
91. JM to Daniel Webster, Mar. 15, 1833, in Hunt, IX, p. 604.
92. JM to William Cabell Rives, Mar. 12, 1833, *ibid.,* p. 512.
93. JM to Daniel Webster, Mar. 15, 1833, *ibid.,* p. 605.

County who had recently been elected by the Virginia legislature to fill a vacancy in the United States Senate.[94] According to a Philadelphia newspaper, the new senator "met Mr. Calhoun on his own ground, and . . . demolished the doctrine of nullification, root and branch."[95] Madison called the speech "a very able and enlightening view of its subject," rejecting the contention "that the States have never parted with an atom of their sovereignty." To him it seemed "strange that it should be necessary to disprove this novel and nullifying doctrine." It was preposterous "to say that the States as united are in no respect or degree, a Nation, which implies sovereignty; altho' acknowledged to be such by all other Nations and Sovereigns, and maintaining with them, all the international relations, of war and peace, treaties, commerce, etc., and, on the other hand and at the same time, to say that the States separately are compleatly nations and sovereigns; although they can separately neither speak nor harken to any other nation, nor maintain with it any of the international relations whatever and would be disowned as Nations if presenting themselves in that character."[96]

Following Andrew Jackson's ringing presidential proclamation against nullification and secession, the South Carolina legislature rejected his views as both "erroneous and dangerous" and vowed to meet force with force. On January 16, 1833, fifteen days before the deadline set by the nullification ordinance for withdrawal from the Union if necessary, Jackson recommended the passage of a force bill, authorizing the use of the army and navy to enforce federal laws in South Carolina. Before its enactment, Henry Clay, claiming that he "adhered to the doctrines of the ablest, wisest and purest of American statesmen, James Madison," introduced his compromise tariff bill and began negotiations with Calhoun, and thereafter compulsion and conciliation moved together through Congress.[97]

On March 1, 1833, Congress passed the force bill and Clay's tariff, which provided for a gradual scaling down of duties over the next ten years, "a compromise to which South Carolina could accede with dignity," said Calhoun, who voted for it. On March 15, the South Carolina convention reassembled, accepted the compromise tariff, repealed its nullification ordinance, and, in a final defiant gesture, nullified the force bill.[98]

Thus, the nullification crisis ended peaceably, and a relieved Madison

---

94. There is no biography of Rives, but for an excellent account of his relations with TJ and JM, see McCoy, pp. 321-69 and *passim*.

95. Brant, VI, pp. 497-98.

96. JM to William Cabell Rives, Mar. 12, 1833, in Hunt, IX, ppp. 511-12.

97. Brant, VI, pp. 498-500. For a careful analysis of President Jackson's use of conciliation and coercion, see Richard B. Latner, "The Nullification Crisis and Republican Subversion," *J. So. Hist.* 43 (1971): 19-38. The fullest account is in Peterson, *Olive Branch and Sword*.

98. For a sympathetic account, see Pauline Maier, "The Road Not Taken: Nullification, John C. Calhoun, and the Revolutionary Tradition in South Carolina," *South Carolina Historical Magazine* 82 (1981): 1-19.

promptly congratulated Clay on his "compromizing tariff," which he hoped would "have a course and effect [of] avoiding a renewal of the contest between the S[outh] and the North."[99] But he worried about the double legacy left by South Carolina, "the torch of discord" and her "contagious zeal in vindicating and varnishing the doctrines of nullification and secession," which tended to create "a disgust with the Union, and then open the way out of it."

The only hope for the nation, he told Clay, was "that, as the gulf is approached the deluded will recoil from its horrors, and that the deluders, if not themselves sufficiently startled, will be abandoned and overwhelmed by their followers."[100] "What *madness* in the South," he moaned, "to look for greater safety in disunion. It would be worse than jumping out of the Frying-pan into the fire: it wd. be jumping into the fire for fear of the Frying-pan."[101]

For the rest of his life, Madison worried about the rising popularity of nullification in the South, fearing, as President Jackson did, that the "next pretext will be the Negro, or slavery question,"[102] which might bring on civil war. "Nullification has the effect of putting powder under the Constitution and Union," he told Edward Coles, his private secretary while he was president, "and a match in the hand of every party, to blow them up at pleasure. And for its progress, hearken to the tone in which it is now preached; cast your eye on its increasing minorities in most of the S[outhern] States without a decrease in any one of them." He doubted that the "anarchical principle" would ever win support in a majority of the states, but he suspected that the southern states were susceptible and feared that "popular leaders aspiring to the highest stations, and despairing of success on the Federal theatre, [would attempt] to unite the South, on some critical occasion, in a course that will end in creating a new theatre of great tho' inferior extent. In pursuing this course, the first and most obvious step is nullification; the next secession; and the last, a farewell separation"—a fatal threat "of breaking a more beautiful China vase than the British Empire ever was, into parts which a miracle only could reunite."[103]

During the nullification crisis, Madison wrote three important unpublished essays defending the role that he and Jefferson had played in creating and administering the government of the United States and rejecting the

---

99. JM to Henry Clay, June 1833, in Hunt, IX, p. 516.

100. JM to Henry Clay, Apr. 2, 1833, in Rives and Fendall, IV, p. 567.

101. JM to Henry Clay, June 1833, in Hunt, IX, p. 517.

102. Andrew Jackson to Andrew J. Crawford, May 1, 1833, in Andrew Jackson, *The Correspondence of Andrew Jackson*, ed. John S. Bassett, 7 vols. (Washington, 1926–35), IV, p. 504.

103. JM to Edward Coles, Aug. 29, 1834, in Hunt, IX, pp. 536–42. Madison appended a note citing Benjamin Franklin's use of the China-vase metaphor. In a letter to Lord Howe on July 20, 1776, Franklin noted his unsuccessful efforts "to preserve from breaking, that fine and noble China Vase the British Empire: for I knew that being once broken . . . a perfect Re-Union . . . could scarce ever be hoped for"; see Benjamin Franklin, *Benjamin Franklin: Writings*, ed. J. A. Leo Lemay (New York, 1987), p. 993. See also Esmond Wright, "'The fine and noble china vase, the British Empire': Benjamin Franklin's 'Love-Hate' View of England," *PMHB* 111 (1987): 435–64.

"anomalous conceit," the "naked and suicidal form," the "novel notion," and the "spurious doctrine of nullification," that "fatal inlet to anarchy." Two were short pieces, "Majority Governments" and "Sovereignty," and the third was a longer piece entitled "Notes on Nullification."[104]

The first concentrated on Calhoun's "sweeping denunciation of majority Gov[ernmen]ts as the most tyrannical and intolerable of all Gov[ernmen]ts" and the South Carolinian's claim "that repub[lica]n Gov[ernmen]ts could only exist within a small compas[s]" such as a single state. Both views, the author of *The Federalist* Number 10 explained patiently, had been exploded by "experience and reflection" on the federal experiment in republicanism, which, "by enlarging the practicable sphere of popular governments, promises a consummation of all the reasonable hopes of the patrons of free Gov[ernmen]t." The Constitution had restrained the risk of majority abuse while preserving the principle of representative government by establishing, as his famous essay of 1787 phrased it, "a republican remedy for the diseases most incident to republican government." In his essay of 1833, he declared that "the people of the U. S., by combining a federal with a republican organization, [voted] to enlarge still more the sphere of representative Gov[ernmen]t and by convenient partitions and distributions of power, to provide the better for internal justice and order, whilst it afforded the best protection against external dangers."

The leading architect of the "extended republic" seemed to view "the Patrons of this new heresy" of nullification as latter-day Antifederalists who attempted "in vain to mask its anti-republicanism." The problem to be solved, Madison declared, "is, not what form of Government is perfect, but which of the forms is least imperfect; and here the general question must be between a republican Gov[ernmen]t in which the majority rule the minority, and a Gov[ernmen]t in which a lesser number or the least number rule the majority. If the republican form is, as all of us agree, to be preferred, the final question must be, what is the structure of it that will best guard ag[ainst] precipitate counsels and factious combinations for unjust purposes, without a sacrifice of the fundamental principle of Republicanism. Those who denounce majority Gov[ernmen]ts altogether because they may have an interest in abusing their power," he concluded, "denounce at the same time all Republican Gov[ernmen]t and must maintain that minority governments would feel less of the bias of interest or the seductions of power."

Appealing to the historical circumstances that led to the Philadelphia convention, Madison reminded the states' rights nullifiers that "the abuses committed within the individual States previous to the present Constitution, by interested or misguided majorities, were among the prominent causes of its adoption." And "whatever may have been the just complaints of unequal laws and sectional partialities under the majority Gov[ernmen]t of the United

---

104. The quotations are taken from JM's "Notes on Nullification," pp. 573–607 at 575, 588, 595, 601, and 606.

States . . . ," he declared in 1833, "the abuses have been less frequent and less palpable than those which disfigured the administrations of the State Gov[ernmen]ts while all the effective powers of sovereignty were separately exercised by them." Indeed, the attempt to return "the effective powers of sovereignty" to the individual states was not only antirepublican, it was a counterrevolutionary attempt to undo what the Founding Fathers had done in 1787–1788.[105]

Like his essay "Majority Governments," which stressed the role of the people in creating governments, Madison's views in "Sovereignty" suggested that "the *majority* of the people in each State [acting] in their highest sovereign capacity" had divided sovereignty, allotting "the supreme power of Gov[ernmen]t partly to the United States by special grants, partly to the individual States by general reservations." In the creation of new states, he emphasized, the majority of people within a state had "divided the sovereignty of the society by actually dividing the society itself into distinct societies equally sovereign," as in the case of Kentucky separating from Virginia and Maine from Massachusetts. Conversely, majorities within the states could make "a partial surrender of sovereignty," a division that was "in fact illustrated by . . . the several confederacies which have existed, and particularly in that which preceded the present Constitution of the United States."

Madison concluded that "it is fortunate that the powers of Gov[ernmen]t[,] supreme as well as subordinate[,] can be so moulded and distributed, so compounded and divided by those on whom they are to operate as will be most suitable to their conditions, will best guard their freedom, and best provide for their safety." In the case of the federal Constitution, the powers of government expressly assigned by the people who ratified it constituted "the attributes of sovereig[n]ty of the U. S.," and the charter itself "declares a practical supremacy of them over the powers reserved to the States; a supremacy essentially involving that of exposition as well as of execution; for a law could not be supreme in one depository of power if the final exposition of it belonged to another."[106]

Madison's essay entitled "Notes on Nullification" contrasted the action taken by Virginia and Kentucky against the Alien and Sedition Acts in 1798, which called for cooperative action to repeal the obnoxious laws, with South Carolina's action against the tariff in 1828 and 1832, which relied upon action by a single state. He rejected the nullifiers' theory that any state "may arrest the operation of a law of the United States, and institute a process which is to terminate in the ascendency of a minority over a large majority, in a Republican System, the characteristic rule of which is that the major will is the ruling will."

In the waning years of his life, Madison consistently worked to clear Jefferson's name as much as he fought to defend his own. Writing for the

---

105. JM, "Majority Governments," 1833, in Hunt, IX, pp. 520–28.
106. JM, "Sovereignty," [1835?], *ibid.*, pp. 568–73.

historical record, he went to great lengths in his "Notes on Nullification" to defend "Mr. Jefferson the apostle of republicanism" from "this newfangled theory [which] is attempted to be fathered" on him, citing his words in his inaugural address of 1801 which "declare that 'acquiescence in the decision of the majority is the vital principle'" of republicanism. "And well may the friends of Mr. J[efferson] disclaim any sanction . . . to any *constitutional* right of nullification from his opinions. His memory is fortunately rescued from such imputations, by the very Document procured from his files and so triumphantly appealed to by the nullifying partisans of every description. In this Document, the remedial right of nullification is expressly called a *natural* right, and, consequently, not a right derived from the Constitution, but from abuses or usurpations, releasing the parties to it from their obligation."[107]

"It cannot be supposed for a moment," Madison concluded his defense of his oldest friend, "that Mr. Jefferson would not revolt at the doctrine of South Carolina, that a single state could constitutionally resist a law of the Union while remaining within it, and that with the accession of a small minority of the others, overrule the will of a great majority of the whole, and constitutionally annul the law everywhere. . . . The authority of Mr. Jefferson, therefore, belongs not, but is directly opposed to, the nullifying party who have so unwarrantably availed themselves of it."[108]

It seems altogether fitting and proper that the last letter written by Madison, composed only "thirteen hours before his decease,"[109] gave him an opportunity to make a final summing-up of his friendship with Jefferson. On June 27, 1836, he spent much of his remaining energy dictating a response to Professor George Tucker, who had dedicated his biography of Jefferson to the Sage of Montpellier. Madison accepted the dedication because of "my confidence in your capacity to do justice to a character so interesting to his country and to the world; and, I may be permitted to add, with whose principles of liberty and political career mine have been so extensively congenial." He added a summary view about his own career that was equally applicable to his collaboration with Jefferson: their public services and private friendship had been marked by "a sincere and steadfast co-operation in promoting such a reconstruction of our political system as would provide for the permanent liberty and happiness of the United States."[110]

But Madison's final thoughts were of the American people and of the perpetual Union that they had created. Indeed, the flood of "writings of his last years," as Kenneth M. Stampp has observed, "constitute something approaching a revised version of his contributions to *The Federalist*, with the new

---

107. JM, "Notes on Nullification," Jan. 1833, plus insertions in 1835-1836, *ibid.*, pp. 573-607 at 588-89, and Brant, VI, p. 577.
108. JM appended this view as a footnote to his "Notes on Nullification," pp. 589-90.
109. George Tucker, "Memoir of James Madison," cited in Ketcham p. 669.
110. JM to George Tucker, June 27, 1836, in Rives and Fendall, IV, p. 435.

emphasis decidedly more on the national features of the Constitution and less on the surviving aspects of state sovereignty."[111] To the end of his life, he retained a stoic faith that the Union of the Founding Fathers could, should, and, he hoped, would withstand the upheavals of a new age and a passionate new generation.

Just a year after the nullification crisis, created by the "preposterous and anarchical pretension" advanced by Calhoun, Madison had prepared his final message to his fellow citizens. Entitled "Advice to My Country," it was meant to be the final political testament of the last Founding Father:

As this advice, if it ever see the light will not do so till I am no more, it may be considered as issuing from the tomb, where truth alone can be respected, and the happiness of man alone consulted. It will be entitled, therefore, to whatever weight can be derived from good intentions, and from the experience of one who has served his country in various stations through a period of forty years; who espoused in his youth, and adhered through his life, to the cause of its liberty, and who has borne a part in most of the great transactions which will constitute epochs of its destiny.

The advice nearest my heart and deepest in my convictions is, that the Union of the States be cherished and perpetuated. Let the open enemy to it be regarded as a Pandora with her box opened, and the disguised one as the Serpent creeping with his deadly wiles into Paradise.[112]

Had James Madison written an inscription for his tombstone at Montpelier, as Jefferson had done at Monticello a decade earlier, singling out his role on behalf of the American people in the "great transactions" of the period, he could have listed himself as

Author of the Memorial and Remonstrance
for Religious Freedom
Father of the Constitution of the United States
and of the Federal Bill of Rights
and Defender of the Union

111. Stampp, 31.
112. Rives and Fendall, IV, p. 439. Brant, VI, pp. 530–31, dates JM's original draft Oct. 1834, stating that it was written "apparently, with the pen to which he shifted during his warnings to [Edward] Coles" against nullification on Aug. 29, 1834. For an elaborate analysis, see Adrienne Koch, *Madison's "Advice to My Country"* (Princeton, 1966).

BIBLIOGRAPHICAL ESSAY

THIS SELECTIVE BIBLIOGRAPHY includes the basic books and essays that have been most useful in shaping my analysis of the people and events during the fifty-year friendship between Jefferson and Madison.

Writings

"It has been remarked," Madison wrote late in life, "that the biography of an author must be a history of his writings. So must that of one whose whole life has in a manner been a public life be gathered from his . . . manuscript papers on public subjects, including letters to as well as from him." Jefferson agreed emphatically. "The letters of a person," he observed, "especially of one whose business has been transacted by letters, form the only full and genuine journal of his life."

Both Madison and Jefferson spent an incredible amount of time each day at the writing desk, consciously aware that they were central participants in creating the first new nation in world history conceived in liberty and dedicated to the proposition that all men are created equal. Jefferson was a meticulous recordkeeper as a young man, and by the time of the Revolution he had already accumulated a sizable archive. The youthful Madison was an indifferent preserver of letters until he began to recognize the significance of the revolutionary movement that swept him and Jefferson into prominence. Once he was exposed to Jefferson's tidy files of records and accounts in 1779, he seems to have imitated his friend's example.

Both men compiled immense collections of letters sent and received, notes for speeches and public papers, memoranda, drafts of important documents, and other archival material, such as Jefferson's incomparable corpus of the laws of colonial Virginia, which he labeled "precious monuments of our . . . history." That comment can be applied with equal force to the personal letters of the two men and to the other records that they preserved such as Madison's irreplaceable "Notes of the Debates in the Federal Convention of 1787," which Jefferson later praised as "the ablest work of this kind ever executed," done with "a labor and exactness beyond comprehension."

The Papers of James Madison in the Library of Congress and other depositories contain more than 30,000 letters and documents; and those of Thomas Jefferson number more than 60,000 items, a collection so vast that Gilbert Chinard called it "the richest treasure house of historical information ever left by a single man." Both collections have been published in microfilm form by the Library of Congress in its Presidential Papers series. Other collections of Jefferson manuscript material have also been published on microfilm by the Massachusetts Historical Society, the University of Virginia, the Missouri Historical Society, and the Henry E. Huntington Library.

The first edition of Jefferson's papers, edited by his grandson, appeared only three years after the death of the Sage of Monticello (Thomas Jefferson Randolph, *Memoir, Correspondence, and Miscellanies from the Papers of Thomas Jefferson* [Charlottesville, 1829]). It was replaced by the nine-volume edition of *The Writings of Thomas Jefferson* (Washington, 1853–54), edited by Henry A. Washington. Four decades later, Paul Leicester Ford presented a more carefully edited compilation with the same title: *The Writings of Thomas Jefferson*, 10 vols. (New York, 1892–99); it was reissued, with a new title *(The Works of Thomas Jefferson)*, in 12 volumes in 1904 as the "Federal Edition." At about the same time, a more comprehensive but less reliable edition was prepared by A. A. Lipscomb and A. E. Bergh (*The Writings of Thomas Jefferson*, 20 vols. [New York, 1903]).

But the definitive edition of *The Papers of Thomas Jefferson* was initiated by Julian P. Boyd at Princeton University in 1950 and has been continued under the editorship of Charles Cullen and then of John Catanzariti, Eugene R. Sheridan, and an unsung but able staff, superseding all earlier editions as far as it goes. This continuing project currently numbers 25 volumes in the chronological series, which ends on May 10, 1793. Series 2 includes Dickinson W. Adams, ed., *Jefferson's Extracts from the Gospels: "The Philosophy of Jesus" and "The Life and Morals of Jesus"* (Princeton, 1983); Wilbur Samuel Howell, ed., *Jefferson's Parliamentary Writings: "Parliamentary Pocket-Book" and A Manual of Parliamentary Practice* (Princeton, 1988); Douglas L. Wilson, ed., *Jefferson's Literary Commonplace Book* (Princeton, 1989); and the forthcoming volume by James A. Bear, Jr., and Lucia C. Stanton, eds., *Jefferson's Memorandum Books: Accounts, with Legal Records and Miscellany, 1767–1826,* a superlative record for keeping track of Jefferson that did not appear in time to be used in preparing this book. For a rare glimpse of the sort of mail that Jefferson received from his constituents, see Jack McLaughlin, *To His Excellency Thomas Jefferson: Letters to a President* (New York, 1991). John Catanzariti analyzes "Thomas Jefferson, Correspondent," in *Proceedings* (Massachusetts Historical Society) 104 (forthcoming).

The first edition of Madison's papers appeared in 1840, four years after his death; it was edited by Henry D. Gilpin: *The Papers of James Madison*, 3 vols. (Washington). The "Congressional Edition" followed in 1865; it was edited by William C. Rives and Philip R. Fendall, *Letters and Other Writings of James Madison*, 4 vols. (Philadelphia). That edition was replaced by Gaillard Hunt, ed., *The Writings of James Madison*, 9 vols. (New York, 1900–10).

But the definitive edition of *The Papers of James Madison,* which was jointly sponsored by the University of Chicago and the University of Virginia, was initiated by William T. Hutchinson and William M. E. Rachal in 1962 and has been continued under the editorship of Robert A. Rutland and then of J. C. A. Stagg and a superb staff at the University of Virginia. This continuing project currently numbers 17 volumes in the chronological series, which comes down to March 3, 1801. There are also three volumes in the Secretary of State series (March 4–July 31, 1801; August 1, 1801–February 28, 1802; March 1 – October 31, 1802) plus two volumes in the Presidential series (March 1 – September 30, 1809, October 1, 1809 – November 2, 1810).

The best one-volume edition of Jefferson's letters and writings is Merrill D. Peterson, ed., *Thomas Jefferson: Writings* (New York: Library of America, 1984), although Peterson has also edited a less-inclusive but useful collection (*The Portable Thomas Jefferson* [New York, 1975]). Peterson has also edited *The Political Writings of Thomas Jefferson* (Charlottesville, 1993).

The best one-volume edition of selections from Madison's writings is Marvin Meyers, ed., *The Mind of the Founder: Sources of the Political Thought of James Madison*, rev. ed. (Hanover, N.H., 1981). Saul K. Padover has a briefer collection, entitled (somewhat misleadingly) *The Complete Madison* (New York, 1953); the paperback version has been retitled *The Forging of American Federalism: Selected Writings of James Madison* (New York, 1965). Too often overlooked are two volumes edited by Merrill D. Peterson: *Thomas Jefferson: A Biography in His Own Words* (New York, 1974) and *James Madison: A Biography in His Own Words* (New York, 1974).

For the best edition of Jefferson's only book, see William Peden, ed., *Notes on the State of Virginia by Thomas Jefferson* (Chapel Hill, 1955; rpt. New York, 1982). For the best edition of Madison's only book, see Jacob E. Cooke, ed., *The Federalist* (Cleveland, 1961).

Biographies of Jefferson and Madison

The most detailed—indeed, the definitive—biography of Jefferson is the superlative study by Dumas Malone, *Jefferson and His Time*, 6 vols. (Boston, 1948–81): I, *Jefferson the Virginian* (1948); II, *Jefferson and the Rights of Man* (1951); III, *Jefferson and the Ordeal of Liberty* (1962); IV, *Jefferson the President: First Term, 1801–1805* (1970); V, *Jefferson the President: Second Term, 1805–1809* (1974); and VI, *The Sage of Monticello* (1981).

An enormously useful and monumental biography of Madison was written by Irving Brant, *The Life of James Madison*, 6 vols. (Indianapolis, 1941–61): I, *James Madison: The Virginia Revolutionist* (1941); II, *James Madison: The Nationalist* (1948); III, *James Madison: Father of the Constitution* (1950); IV, *James Madison: Secretary of State* (1953); V, *James Madison: The President* (1956); VI, *James Madison: Commander in Chief* (1961).

The best one-volume biography of Jefferson is Merrill D. Peterson, *Thomas Jefferson and the New Nation: A Biography* (New York, 1970), and the best one-volume biography of Madison is Ralph Ketcham, *James Madison: A Biography* (New York, 1971). Brant also condensed his multivolume work into a large one-volume study, *The Fourth President: A Life of James Madison* (Indianapolis, 1970). Noble E. Cunningham, *In Pursuit of Reason: The Life of Thomas Jefferson* (Baton Rouge, 1987), is the best short study of Jefferson. For a briefer but solid account, see Norman K. Risjord, *Thomas Jefferson* (Madison, Wis., 1993). Also useful is Merrill D. Peterson, ed., *Thomas Jefferson: A Reference Biography* (New York, 1986).

The best brief biography of Madison is Robert A. Rutland, *James Madison: The Founding Father* (New York, 1987), but the even briefer study by Jack Rakove, *James Madison and the Creation of the American Republic* (Glenview, Ill., 1990), is excellent. William Lee Miller's book, *The Business of May Next: James Madison and the Founding*

(Charlottesville, 1992), is useful. For Madison in retirement, see the stimulating portrait drawn by Drew R. McCoy, *The Last of the Fathers: James Madison and the Republican Legacy* (New York, 1989). For a brief but brilliant comparison of the two leaders, see Merrill D. Peterson, *Jefferson and Madison and the Making of Constitutions* (Charlottesville, 1987).

The pioneering account of the friendship and partnership between Jefferson and Madison is Adrienne Koch, *Jefferson and Madison: The Great Collaboration* (New York, 1950), although she tends to make Madison a junior Jefferson. She followed up this study with *Madison's "Advice to My Country"* (Princeton, 1966), a brilliant appraisal that parallels her earlier *The Philosophy of Thomas Jefferson* (New York, 1943). Garrett Ward Sheldon's *The Political Philosophy of Thomas Jefferson* (Baltimore, 1991) is the latest appraisal. See also David Mayer, *The Constitutional Thought of Thomas Jefferson* (forthcoming).

Republicanism

Recent works that have examined the ideology of republicanism include Lance Banning, *The Jeffersonian Persuasion: Evolution of Party Ideology* (Ithaca, 1978). Banning has also written several penetrating articles on Madison as a prelude to a full-scale study tentatively entitled *The Sacred Fire of Liberty: James Madison and the Creation of the Federal Republic, 1780–1792* (Ithaca, forthcoming). He also has in press his Merrill Jensen Lectures on Madison and Jefferson (Madison, Wis., forthcoming). For an example of his essays, see "The Practicable Sphere of a Republic: James Madison, the Constitutional Convention, and the Emergence of a Revolutionary Federalism," in *Beyond Confederation: Origins of the Constitution and American National Identity*, ed. Richard Beeman, Stephen Botein, and Edward C. Carter II (Chapel Hill, 1987), pp. 162–87.

Other important studies of republicanism are Drew R. McCoy, *The Elusive Republic: Political Economy in Jeffersonian America* (Chapel Hill, 1980; rpt. New York, 1982); Richard Buel, Jr., *Securing the Revolution: Ideology in American Politics, 1789–1815* (Ithaca, 1972); and Joyce Appleby, *Capitalism and a New Social Order: The Republican Vision of the 1790s* (New York, 1984). For an introduction to the scholarly debate about the meaning of republicanism and Jeffersonian ideology, see Lance Banning, "Jeffersonian Ideology Revisited: Liberal and Classical Ideas in the New American Republic," *William and Mary Quarterly* 43 (1986): 3–19, and Joyce Appleby, "Republicanism in Old and New Contexts," *William and Mary Quarterly* 43 (1986): 20–34. Appleby has since expanded her arguments in *Liberalism and Republicanism in the Historical Imagination* (Cambridge, Mass., 1992), a collection of her essays on these central themes.

Three extremely useful review articles on republicanism are by Robert E. Shalhope: "Toward a Republican Synthesis: The Emergence of an Understanding of Republicanism in American Historiography," *William and Mary Quarterly* 29 (1972): 49–80; "Republicanism and Early American Historiography," *William and Mary Quarterly* 39 (1982): 334–56; and "Republicanism, Liberalism, and Democracy: Political Culture in the New Nation," *Proceedings* (American Antiquarian Society) 102 (1992): 99–152. The most recent summary of scholarship, one that includes Shalhope's 1992 article, is in a symposium entitled "The Republican Synthesis Revisited: Essays in Honor of George Athan Billias," *Proceedings* (American Antiquarian Society) 102 (1992): 69–224; it includes essays by Drew R. McCoy, Isaac Kramnick, Lance Banning, Peter S. Onuf and Cathy Matson, and Gordon S. Wood. For a premature obituary of "Republicanism: The Career of a Concept," see that article, by Daniel T. Rodgers, in *Journal of American History* 79 (1992): 11-38.

Party Politics

The emergence of Madison and Jefferson as party leaders can best be followed in two significant monographs by Noble E. Cunningham, Jr., published by the University of North Carolina Press for the Institute of Early American History and Culture, a research, teaching, and publication center in Williamsburg, Virginia, where the two friends first met. *The Jeffersonian Republicans: The Formation of Party Organization, 1789–1801* (1957) includes a chapter on the emergence of "Madison's Party" between 1793 and 1796 and another on "Jefferson in Command" after the election of 1796, when he was elected vice president. The second volume is entitled *The Jeffersonian Republicans in Power: Party Operations, 1801–1809* (1963).

Cunningham completed his study of Jeffersonian leadership with a trailblazing analysis of the mechanisms through which the executive and legislative branches of government operated during his presidency; see *The Process of Government under Jefferson* (Princeton, 1978). By coincidence, another significant study of the Jefferson presidency appeared the same year; see Robert M. Johnstone, Jr., *Jefferson and the Presidency: Leadership in the Young Republic* (Ithaca, 1978).

But the most extensive study of the presidencies of Jefferson and Madison remains Henry Adams's monumental nine-volume *History of the United States of America during the Administrations of Thomas Jefferson and James Madison* (New York, 1889-91), generally acknowledged to be a literary masterpiece. The continuing popularity of Adams's work is indicated by its inclusion in the Library of America series in a two-volume edition in 1986; it went into a second printing shortly after being published.

In the original version of Adams's study, the first four volumes dealt with Jefferson's presidency and the last five with Madison's. Together they portray both men as ineffective and inconsistent presidents, the defects and defeats of Jefferson's statesmanship leading the nation to the brink of disaster, the weakness and timidity of Madison pushing it over the side and dropping it to the depths of democratic degradation. "The wreck of Mr. Jefferson's administration," Adams wrote, was succeeded by Madison's, when "the government of the United States reached . . . the lowest point of its long decline."

This account, written by the great-grandson of John Adams, whom Jefferson defeated for the presidency in 1800, has come in for its share of criticism in the last forty years. In 1952, Irving Brant concluded that Adams, who did not understand their policies at all, was "a solid mass of conditioned reflexes . . . against Jefferson and Madison." No one else has gone that far, although Merrill D. Peterson agreed in 1963 that Adams "ultimately . . . was unable to solve the enigma of Jefferson" and Robert Allen Rutland concluded in 1990 that Adams "was far too harsh on Madison as chief executive." In 1988, Noble E. Cunningham, Jr., wrote a revisionist critique of Adams's highly praised introductory chapters on "the United States in 1800," calling them "brilliant but flawed," presenting an analysis that badly "misjudged the state of the nation in 1800." Despite his prejudices, however, Adams's account remains useful because of its thoroughness and readability. See Brant, "James Madison and His Time," *American Historical Review* 57 (1952): 853-70; Peterson, "Henry Adams on Jefferson, the President," *Virginia Quarterly Review* 39 (1963): 187-201; Rutland, *The*

Presidency of James Madison (Lawrence, Kans., 1990), p. 221; and Cunningham, *The United States in 1800: Henry Adams Revisited* (Charlottesville, 1988), pp. 63, 68.

One of the most balanced appraisals of the presidencies of Jefferson and Madison, which moves beyond the shadow of Adams's great history, is the sprightly reinterpretation in Marshall Smelser, *The Democratic Republic, 1801–1815* (New York, 1968). On the other hand, Forrest McDonald almost out-Adamses Adams in his interpretation of *The Presidency of Thomas Jefferson* (Lawrence, Kans., 1976), an idiosyncratic mixture of perceptive insights and wildly improbable statements by an author who has labeled Jefferson in another context a "wild-eyed political quack." By way of contrast, Robert Allen Rutland, *The Presidency of James Madison* (Lawrence, Kans., 1990), is a carefully considered evaluation of Madison's administration. And for a detailed appraisal of Madison as president, one that embraces a larger time scale than that adopted by Adams, see J. C. A. Stagg, *Mr. Madison's War: Politics, Diplomacy, and Warfare in the Early American Republic, 1783–1830* (Princeton, 1983), which moves back to the Peace of Paris in 1783 to locate the problems that dominated the history of the nation for the next three decades.

The lack of adequate records has handicapped biographers of Dolley Madison, but the following accounts are useful: Conover Hunt-Jones, *Dolley and the "Great Little Madison"* (Washington, 1977); Ethel S. Arnett, *Mrs. James Madison: The Incomparable Dolley* (Greensboro, N.C., 1972); Katherine Anthony, *Dolly Madison, Her Life and Times* (Garden City, N.Y., 1949); and Virginia Moore, *The Madisons: A Biography* (New York, 1979). For sparkling details based on the observations of Margaret Bayard Smith, see her *The First Forty Years of Washington Society, Portrayed by the Family Letters of Mrs. Samuel Harrison Smith . . .*, ed. Gaillard Hunt (New York, 1906).

Specialized Studies

There are tons of specialized studies on Jefferson and very few on Madison. There are, for example, two extensive bibliographies about Jefferson (Eugene L. Huddleston, *Thomas Jefferson: A Reference Guide* [Boston, 1982], and Frank Shuffelton, *Thomas Jefferson: A Comprehensive Annotated Bibliography of Writings about Him, 1826–1980* [New York, 1983]) plus Shuffelton's supplement, *Thomas Jefferson, 1981–1990: An Annotated Bibliography* (New York, 1990), and none about Madison.

The gap widened in 1993 when the Jefferson bibliography got a big boost during the commemoration of the two-hundred-fiftieth anniversary of Jefferson's birth. Two of the outstanding books from that recent outpouring are Peter S. Onuf, ed., *Jeffersonian Legacies* (Charlottesville, 1993), and Susan R. Stein, *The Worlds of Thomas Jefferson at Monticello* (New York, 1993). The second assembles more than 150 objects acquired by Jefferson and brought together in an exhibition at Monticello for the first time since they were dispersed after Jefferson's death in 1826. The former features more than a dozen essays by such luminaries as Joyce Appleby, Jack P. Greene, Walter LaFeber, and Gordon S. Wood, knowledgeable scholars all but none of the them Jeffersonian specialists. Notably absent were all of the leading Jefferson scholars such as Merrill D. Peterson, Noble E. Cunningham, Jr., Jack McLaughlin, William Howard Adams, and Garrett Ward Sheldon. For a brilliant summary of recent appraisals of Jefferson, see Peter S. Onuf, "The Scholars' Jefferson," *William and Mary Quarterly* 50 (1993): 671–99.

The most useful specialized studies for the correspondence between Jefferson and Madison include two books edited by Edwin M. Betts: *Thomas Jefferson's Garden Book,*

1766-1824, ... (Philadelphia, 1944) and *Thomas Jefferson's Farm Book* ... (Princeton, 1953). Two others deal with Jefferson's perpetual project of constructing Monticello: William Howard Adams, *Jefferson's Monticello* (New York, 1983), and Jack McLaughlin, *Jefferson and Monticello: The Biography of a Builder* (New York, 1988). Adams has also edited *Jefferson and the Arts: An Extended View* (Washington, 1976) and *The Eye of Thomas Jefferson* (Charlottesville, 1981). On Jefferson's library, the definitive work is E. Millicent Sowerby, *Catalogue of the Library of Thomas Jefferson*, 5 vols. (Washington, 1952-59), but see also the recent book based on the discovery of Jefferson's classification scheme, in which he attempted to categorize all knowledge: James Gilreath and Douglas L. Wilson, eds., *Thomas Jefferson's Library: A Catalog with the Entries in His Own Order* (Washington, 1989).

There are two good accounts of Montpellier as James and Dolley Madison knew it: Conover Hunt-Jones, *Dolley and the "Great Little Madison* (Washington, 1977), and William Seale, *Of Houses and Time: Personal Histories of America's National Trust Properties* (New York, 1992). Marion du Pont Scott, *Montpelier: Recollections of Marion du Pont Scott* (New York, 1976), tells more about Mrs. Scott's interest in horses than it does about the Madisons, but she later donated the property to the National Trust to be preserved as "an historic shrine . . . to James Madison and his times." For a brief account of Jefferson's cooperation with Madison in remodeling Montpellier, see Garry Wills, "Jefferson's Other Buildings," *Atlantic* 271 (1993): 80-87, which also discusses Poplar Forest.

For the first complete account of Poplar Forest, see the carefully researched book by S. Allen Chambers, Jr., *Poplar Forest and Thomas Jefferson* (Forest, Va., 1993). Shorter accounts include Norma Cuthbert, "Poplar Forest: Jefferson's Legacy to His Grandson," *Huntington Library Quarterly* 6 (1943): 333-56; C. Allan Brown, "Thomas Jefferson's Poplar Forest: The Mathematics of an Ideal Villa," *Journal of Garden History* 10 (1990): 117-39; Travis C. McDonald, Jr., "Poplar Forest: A Masterpiece Rediscovered," *Virginia Cavalcade* 42 (1993): 112-21; and Wayne Fields, "Jefferson's Second Home," *American Heritage* 44 (Apr. 1993): 104-13.

For "The Life Portraits of James Madison," see the article by Theodore Bolton in the *William and Mary Quarterly* 8 (1951): 25-45. For portraits of Dolley Madison, see Allen C. Clark, *The Life and Letters of Dolley Madison* (Washington, 1914). For portraits of Jefferson, see Alfred L. Bush, *The Life Portraits of Thomas Jefferson* (Charlottesville, 1962), which has been reprinted with revisions in William Howard Adams, ed., *Jefferson and the Arts: An Extended View* (Washington, 1976); and Noble E. Cunningham, Jr., *The Image of Thomas Jefferson in the Public Eye: Portraits for the People, 1800-1809* (Charlottesville, 1981).

Other specialized studies include Leonard W. Levy, *Jefferson and Civil Liberties: The Darker Side* (Cambridge, Mass., 1963); Howard C. Rice, Jr., *Thomas Jefferson's Paris* (Princeton, 1976); Pendleton Hogan and Bill Sublette, *The Lawn: A Guide to Jefferson's University* (Charlottesville, 1987); R. de Treville Lawrence III, ed., *Jefferson and Wine: Model of Moderation*, 2d ed. (The Plains, Va., 1989); and Bernard W. Sheehan, *Seeds of Extinction: Jeffersonian Philanthropy and the American Indian* (Chapel Hill, 1973; rpt. New York, 1974).

Biographies of Contemporaries

Ralph Waldo Emerson once said that "there is properly no history, only biography." At the other end of the literary spectrum is Janet Malcolm, herself a biographer, who claims that biography is a spurious art characterized by an orderly narrative that is "stale, hashed over, told and retold, dubious, unauthentic, suspect." Although most historians and biographers disagree with these generalizations, most also agree that biography is an acceptable way to write history, and I have utilized a wide variety of biographies to document the fifty years between 1776 and 1826. One of the most important is John Alexander Carroll and Mary Wells Ashworth, *George Washington: First in Peace* (New York, 1957), which is volume 7 in Douglas Southall Freeman, *George Washington: A Biography*, 7 vols. (New York, 1948–57). For Patrick Henry, see Richard Beeman, *Patrick Henry: A Biography* (New York, 1974); Robert Douthat Meade, *Patrick Henry*, 2 vols. (Philadelphia, 1957, 1969); and Henry Mayer, *A Son of Thunder: Patrick Henry and the American Republic* (Charlottesville, 1991). For Jefferson's law mentor, see Imogene M. Brown, *American Aristides: A Biography of George Wythe* (Rutherford, N.J., 1981); Alonzo Thomas Dill, *George Wythe: Teacher of Liberty* (Williamsburg, 1979); and Joyce Blackburn, *George Wythe of Williamsburg* (New York, 1975). For Jefferson's and Madison's mutual friend, see Harry Ammon, *James Monroe: The Quest for National Identity* (New York, 1971), the standard study. Also useful are Robert E. Shalhope, *John Taylor of Caroline: Pastoral Republican* (Columbia, S.C., 1980), and John J. Reardon, *Edmund Randolph: A Biography* (New York, 1974).

Biographies of other Republican leaders include Aleine Austin, *Matthew Lyon: "New Man" of the Democratic Revolution, 1749–1822* (University Park, Pa., 1981); John S. Pancake, *Samuel Smith and the Politics of Business, 1752–1839* (University, Ala., 1972); Frank Cassell, *Merchant Congressman in the Young Republic: Samuel Smith of Maryland, 1752–1839* (Madison, 1971); Frederick B. Tolles, *George Logan of Philadelphia* (New York, 1953), a model biography; William B. Hatcher, *Edward Livingston: Jeffersonian Republican and Jacksonian Democrat* (Baton Rouge, 1940); and Dice R. Anderson, *William Branch Giles: A Study in the Politics of Virginia and the Nation from 1790 to 1830* (Menasha, Wis., 1914), which leaves room for a modern biography of this opportunistic politician.

Raymond Walters, Jr., *Albert Gallatin: Jeffersonian Financier and Diplomat* (New York, 1957), is an excellent study of Jefferson's and Madison's secretary of the treasury. John P. Kaminski, *George Clinton: Yeoman Politician of the New Republic* (Madison, 1990), is a solid study of the man who served as vice president under both Jefferson and Madison. For Jefferson's first vice president, see Milton Lomask, *Aaron Burr: The Years from Princeton to Vice President, 1756–1805* (New York, 1979). For Madison's second vice president, see George A. Billias, *Elbridge Gerry: Founding Father and Republican Statesman* (New York, 1976). Also useful is Richard A. Erney's account of the secretary of war under both men: *The Public Life of Henry Dearborn* (New York, 1979). For Jefferson's attorney general, see Lowell Harrison, *John Breckinridge, Jeffersonian Republican* (Louisville, 1969). For Madison's secretary of war, see C. Edward Skeen, *John Armstrong, Jr., 1758–1843: A Biography* (Syracuse, 1981).

Of the many biographies of other Republicans, these stand out: Milton E. Flower, *John Dickinson: Conservative Revolutionary* (Charlottesville, 1983), the only biography of this enigmatic leader; George Dangerfield, *Chancellor Robert R. Livingston of New York, 1746–1813* (New York, 1960), a model biography; Donald G. Johnson, *Justice William Johnson, the First Dissenter: The Career and Constitutional Philosophy of a Jeffersonian Judge* (Columbia, S.C., 1954), a study of Jefferson's only appointee to the Supreme Court; R. Kent Newmyer, *Supreme Court Justice Joseph Story: Statesman of the Old Republic* (Chapel Hill, 1983), the definitive analysis of Madison's only appointee to the high Court; William H. Gaines, *Thomas Mann Randolph: Jefferson's Son-in-Law* (Baton Rouge, 1966); Jacob E. Cooke, *Tench Coxe and the Early Republic* (Chapel Hill, 1978); and Stanley J. Idzerda, Anne C. Loveland, and Marc H. Miller, *Lafayette, Hero of Two Worlds: The Art and Pageantry of His Farewell Tour of America, 1824-1825* (Hanover, N.H., 1989). Lesser figures include Michael Durey, *"With the Hammer of Truth": James Thomson Callender and America's Early National Heroes* (Charlottesville, 1990); James Tagg, *Benjamin Franklin Bache and the Philadelphia Aurora* (Philadelphia, 1990); James R. Jacobs, *Tarnished Warrior: Major General James Wilkinson* (New York, 1938); and Chase C. Mooney, *William H. Crawford, 1772-1834* (Lexington, Ky., 1974). Daniel P. Jordan, *Political Leadership in Jefferson's Virginia* (Charlottesville, 1983), is extremely useful. George Green Shackelford, *Jefferson's Adoptive Son: The Life of William Short, 1759-1848* (Lexington, Ky., 1993), appeared too late to be of use in this book.

For the Federalists, I have relied on David Hackett Fischer, *The Revolution of American Conservatism: The Federalist Party in the Era of Jeffersonian Democracy* (New York, 1965), which has an appendix of 186 pages containing 462 brief biographies of Federalist leaders. Page Smith, *John Adams,* 2 vols. (Garden City, N.Y., 1963), is the standard study. John Ferling, *John Adams: A Life* (Knoxville, 1992), is a solid, brief account, and Joseph J. Ellis, *Passionate Sage: The Character and Legacy of John Adams* (New York, 1993), is a sympathetic analysis of this extraordinary man whom Jefferson loved and Madison loathed. Of the many studies of Hamilton, I found John C. Miller, *Alexander Hamilton: Portrait in Paradox* (New York, 1959), most useful.

Other important biographies include Winfred E. A. Bernhard, *Fisher Ames: Federalist and Statesman* (Chapel Hill, 1965); Morton Borden, *The Federalism of James A. Bayard* (New York, 1955); Robert Ernst, *Rufus King, American Federalist* (Chapel Hill, 1968); Gerard H. Clarfield, *Timothy Pickering and American Diplomacy, 1795-1800* (Columbia, Mo., 1969), and *Timothy Pickering and the American Republic* (Pittsburgh, 1980); Marvin R. Zahniser, *Charles Cotesworth Pinckney, Founding Father* (Chapel Hill, 1967); George C. Rogers, junior, *Evolution of a Federalist: William Loughton Smith of South Carolina, 1758-1812* (Columbia, S.C., 1962); and Richard E. Welch, Jr., *Theodore Sedgwick: Federalist* (Middletown, Conn., 1965). Albert J. Beveridge, *The Life of John Marshall,* 4 vols. (Boston, 1916-19), is still useful, but the best study of the judiciary in the new nation is Richard E. Ellis, *The Jeffersonian Crisis: Courts and Politics in the Young Republic* (New York, 1971; rpt. New York, 1974).

General Histories

For the sweep through the first fifty years of the new nation's history, I relied on two sterling studies about the Revolution: Robert Middlekauf, *The Glorious Cause: The American Revolution, 1763-1789* (New York, 1982), and John R. Alden, *A History of the American Revolution* (New York, 1969); two basic books about Virginia: Rhys Isaac, *The Transformation of Virginia, 1740-1790* (Chapel Hill, 1982; rpt. New York, 1988), and John E. Selby, *The Revolution in Virginia, 1775-1783* (Williamsburg, 1988); four imposing accounts of the Confederation period: Richard B. Morris, *The Forging of the Union, 1781-1789* (New York, 1987), Jack Rakove, *The Beginnings of National Politics: An Interpretive History of the Continental Congress* (Cambridge, Mass., 1979), a superlative study, Merrill Jensen, *The New Nation: A History of the United States during the Confederation, 1781-1789* (New York, 1950), the standard study, and Edmund Cody Burnett, *The Continental Congress* (New York, 1941); and three essential accounts of the framing of the Constitution: Forrest McDonald, *Novus Ordo Seclorum: The Intellectual Origins of the Constitution* (Lawrence, Kans., 1985), Gordon S. Wood, *The Creation of the American Republic, 1776–1787* (Chapel Hill, 1969; rpt. New York, 1972), a magisterial study, and Clinton Rossiter, *1787: The Grand Convention* (New York, 1966; rpt. New York, 1987). The best accounts of the state ratification conventions are Michael Allen Gillespie and Michael Lienesch, eds., *Ratifying the Constitution* (Lawrence, Kans., 1989), which is well documented, and Patrick T. Conley and John P. Kaminski, eds., *The Constitution and the States: The Role of the Original Thirteen in the Framing and Adoption of the Federal Constitution* (Madison, 1988), which is not footnoted.

Robert A. Rutland, *The Birth of the Bill of Rights* (Chapel Hill, 1955), is the standard study, but Bernard Schwartz, *The Great Rights of Mankind: A History of the American Bill of Rights* (New York, 1977), is useful. For recent reappraisals, see the essays in Patrick T. Conley and John P. Kaminski, eds., *The Bill of Rights and the States: The Colonial and Revolutionary Origins of American Liberties* (Madison, 1990). See also Michael J. Lacey and Knud Haakonssen, eds., *A Culture of Rights: The Bill of Rights in Philosophy, Politics, and Law, 1791 and 1991* (New York, 1991), especially Jack N. Rakove, "Parchment Barriers and the Politics of Rights," pp. 95–143, and James H. Hutson, "The Bill of Rights and the American Revolutionary Experience," pp. 62–97. Other essays of significance are Paul Finkelman, "James Madison and the Bill of Rights: A Reluctant Paternity," in *The Supreme Court Review for 1990*, ed. Gerhard Casper, Dennis J. Hutchinson, and David A. Strauss (Chicago, 1991), pp. 301–47, and Gordon S. Wood, "The Origins of the Bill of Rights," *Proceedings* (American Antiquarian Society) 101 (1992): 254–74. There are two helpful documentary studies: Bernard Schwartz, ed., *The Bill of Rights: A Documentary History* (New York, 1971), and Helen E. Veit, Kenneth Bowling, and Charlene Bickford, eds., *Creating the Bill of Rights: The Documentary Record from the First Federal Congress* (Baltimore, 1991).

The best one-volume account of the Revolutionary and early national period is Norman K. Risjord, *Jefferson's America, 1760–1815* (Madison, 1991). For the early national period, I have relied on John C. Miller, *The Federalist Era, 1789–1801* (New York, 1960), and Marshall Smelser, *The Democratic Republic, 1801–1815* (New York, 1968). Also important are Stephen G. Kurtz, *The Presidency of John Adams: The Collapse of Federalism, 1795–1800* (Philadelphia, 1957); Manning J. Dauer, *The Adams Federalists* (Baltimore, 1953); and Daniel Sisson, *The American Revolution of 1800* (New York, 1974).

Four important books that were published in 1993 appeared too late to be of use in this book: Roger H. Brown, *Redeeming the Republic: Federalists, Taxation, and the Origins of the Constitution* (Baltimore, 1993); Stanley Elkins and Eric McKitrick, *The Age of Federalism* (New York, 1993); Peter S. Onuf and Nicholas G. Onuf, *Federal Union, Modern World: The Law of Nations in an Age of Revolutions, 1776–1814* (Madison, 1993); and James Roger Sharp, *American Politics in the Early Republic: The New Nation in Crisis* (New Haven, 1993).

Selected Topics

Specialized studies on sundry topics include E. James Ferguson, *The Power of the Purse: A History of American Public Finance, 1776–1790* (Chapel Hill, 1961), which unravels a tangled story; John R. Nelson, Jr., *Liberty and Property: Political Economy and*

Policymaking in the New Nation, 1789–1812 (Baltimore, 1987); Richard Beale Davis, Intellectual Life in Jefferson's Virginia (Chapel Hill, 1954); John C. Greene, American Science in the Age of Jefferson (Ames, Iowa, 1984); Charles M. Thomas, American Neutrality in 1793: A Study in Cabinet Government (New York, 1931); Harry Ammon, The Genet Mission (New York, 1973); Julian P. Boyd, Number 7: Alexander Hamilton's Secret Attempts to Control American Foreign Policy... (Princeton, 1964); Thomas P. Slaughter, The Whiskey Rebellion (New York, 1986); Steven R. Boyd, ed., The Whiskey Rebellion: Past and Present Perspectives (Westport, Conn., 1985); Leland D. Baldwin, Whiskey Rebels: The Story of a Frontier Uprising (Pittsburgh, 1939); Philip S. Foner, ed., The Democratic-Republican Societies, 1790–1800: A Documentary Sourcebook of Constitutions, Declarations, Addresses, Resolutions, and Toasts (Westport, Conn., 1976); Donald H. Stewart, The Opposition Press of the Federalist Period (Albany, N.Y., 1969); James Morton Smith, Freedom's Fetters: The Alien and Sedition Laws and American Civil Liberties (Ithaca, 1956); John C. Miller, Crisis in Freedom: The Alien and Sedition Acts (Boston, 1951); Leonard W. Levy, Emergence of a Free Press (New York, 1985); Norman K. Risjord, Cheasapeake Politics, 1781–1800 (New York, 1978), and The Old Republicans: Southern Conservatism in the Age of Jefferson (New York, 1965); Richard Beeman, The Old Dominion and the New Nation, 1788–1801 (Lexington, Ky., 1972); Richard E. Ellis, The Jeffersonian Crisis: Courts and Politics in the Young Republic (New York, 1971; New York, 1974); Linda Kerber, Federalists in Dissent: Imagery and Ideology in Jeffersonian America (Ithaca, 1970); James M. Banner, Jr., To the Hartford Convention: The Federalists and the Origins of Party Politics in Massachusetts, 1789–1815 (New York, 1970); Everett Somerville Brown, The Constitutional History of the Louisiana Purchase, 1803–1812 (Berkeley, 1920); Thomas P. Abernethy, The Burr Conspiracy (New York, 1954); Theodore J. Crackel, Mr. Jefferson's Army: Political and Social Reform of the Military Establishment, 1801–1809 (New York, 1987); and C. Peter Magrath, Yazoo: Law and Politics in the New Republic, the Case of Fletcher v. Peck (Providence, 1966).

Diplomatic Histories

American historians of early American diplomacy have made major contributions to the understanding of foreign policy from the first American Revolution through the War of 1812—the Second War for American Independence—to the formulation of the Monroe Doctrine in 1823. Samuel Flagg Bemis has written four superb studies covering the fifty years between 1775 and 1825: *The Diplomacy of the American Revolution* (Bloomington, Ind., 1957); *Jay's Treaty: A Study in Commerce and Diplomacy*, 2d ed. (New Haven, 1962); *Pinckney's Treaty: America's Advantage from European Distresses, 1783–1800*, rev. ed. (New Haven, 1960); and *John Quincy Adams and the Foundations of American Foreign Policy* (New York, 1949). Richard B. Morris, *The Peacemakers: The Great Powers and American Independence* (New York, 1965), is also a work of fundamental importance, and Charles R. Ritcheson, *Aftermath of Revolution: British Policy toward the United States, 1783–1795* (Dallas, 1969), is useful. For the domestic repercussions of Jay's treaty, see Jerald A. Combs, *The Jay Treaty: Political Battleground of the Founding Fathers* (Berkeley, 1970).

Bradford Perkins has published a trilogy of well-written books that are landmark studies of Anglo-American diplomacy: *The First Rapprochement: England and the United States, 1795–1805* (Philadelphia, 1955); *Prologue to War: England and the United States, 1805–1812* (Berkeley, 1963); and *Castlereagh and Adams: England and the United

States, 1812–1823 (Berkeley, 1964). Perkins's overview of early American foreign relations, *The Creation of a Republican Empire, 1776–1865* (New York, 1993), appeared too late to be of use in this volume.

Alexander De Conde has also written a trio of significant studies dealing with the presidencies of Washington, Adams, and Jefferson: *Entangling Alliance: Politics and Diplomacy under George Washington* (Durham, N.C., 1958); *The Quasi-War: The Politics and Diplomacy of the Undeclared War with France, 1797–1801* (New York, 1966); and *This Affair of Louisiana* (New York, 1976). Two books by Paul A. Varg give an overview of early American foreign policy: *Foreign Policies of the Founding Fathers* (East Lansing, 1963), which covers the period between 1774 and 1815, and *New England and Foreign Relations, 1789–1850* (Hanover, N.H., 1983).

For the undeclared war with the Barbary pirates, the most useful studies are Ray W. Irwin, *The Diplomatic Relations of the United States with the Barbary Powers* (Chapel Hill, 1931); Louis B. Wright and Julia H. Macleod, *The First Americans in North Africa: William Eaton's Struggle for a Vigorous Policy against the Barbary Pirates, 1799–1805* (Princeton, 1945); Gardner W. Allen, *Our Navy and the Barbary Corsairs* (Boston, 1905); William M. Fowler, Jr., *Jack Tars and Commodores: The American Navy, 1783–1815* (Boston, 1984); and A. B. C. Whipple, *To the Shores of Tripoli: The Birth of the United States Navy and Marines* (New York, 1991).

For Franco-American diplomacy during the early national period, there are two detailed studies, each well done: Albert H. Bowman, *The Struggle for Neutrality: A History of the Diplomatic Relations between the United States and France, 1790–1801* (Knoxville, 1974), and Clifford L. Egan, *Neither Peace nor War: Franco-American Relations, 1803–1812* (Baton Rouge, 1983). William Stinchcombe, *The XYZ Affair* (Westport, Conn., 1980), traces that fascinating episode in detail.

Two important studies concentrate on the relationship between commerce and diplomacy. Arthur P. Whitaker, *The Mississippi Question, 1795–1803: A Study in Trade, Politics, and Diplomacy* (New York, 1934), is a superior monograph, and Burton Spivak, *Jefferson's English Crisis: Commerce, Embargo, and the Republican Revolution* (Charlottesville, 1979), is a valuable study of Republican efforts to avoid war.

Jefferson and Madison's policy towards the Floridas is examined critically in three studies: Isaac Joslin Cox, *The West Florida Controversy, 1798–1813* (Baltimore, 1918), the most scholarly appraisal; Rembert W. Patrick, *Florida Fiasco: Rampant Rebels on the Georgia-Florida Border, 1810–1815* (Athens, Ga., 1954), the most fun to read; and Joseph Burkholder Smith's melodramatically entitled book *The Plot to Steal Florida: James Madison's Phony War* (New York, 1983), a slashing attack on Madison as "the father of covert-action operations." Too often overlooked is a carefully researched and balanced book, *War, Foreign Affairs and Constitutional Power: The Origins* (Cambridge, Mass., 1976), by Abraham D. Sofaer.

For two powerful indictments of Jefferson and Madison's foreign policy, see Robert W. Tucker and David C. Hendrickson, *Empire of Liberty: The Statecraft of Thomas Jefferson* (New York, 1990), and Doron S. Ben-Atar, *The Origins of Jeffersonian Commercial Policy and Diplomacy* (London, 1992).

The War of 1812

The best brief account remains Harry L. Coles, *The War of 1812* (Chicago, 1965). For more detailed histories, see Donald R. Hickey, *The War of 1812: A Forgotten*

Conflict (Urbana, 1989); John K. Mahon, *The War of 1812* (Gainesville, Fla., 1972); and Reginald Horsman, *The War of 1812* (New York, 1969). But the most comprehensive account, a sweeping interpretation of military, diplomatic, and domestic history, is J. C. A. Stagg, *Mr. Madison's War: Politics, Diplomacy, and Warfare in the Early American Republic, 1783–1830* (Princeton, 1983). For an excellent appraisal of Madison as commander in chief during the War of 1812, see Marcus Cunliffe's essay "Madison (1812–1815)," in *The Ultimate Decision: The President As Commander-in-Chief,* ed. Ernest R. May (New York, 1960), pp. 21–53.

Two special studies of fundamental importance are Roger Brown, *The Republic in Peril: 1812* (New York, 1964), and Steven Watts, *The Republic Reborn: War and the Making of Liberal America, 1790–1820* (Baltimore, 1987), a bold and provocative interpretation. The best account of *The Monroe Doctrine, 1823–1826* remains the early study by Dexter Perkins (Cambridge, Mass., 1927).

European History

Two books by R. R. Palmer are indispensable for an understanding of the international ferment generated by the American Revolution and the creation of the American Republic. The first volume of *The Age of the Democratic Revolution: A Political History of Europe and America, 1760–1800* (Princeton, 1959) is subtitled *The Challenge* and covers the period from 1760 to 1789. It is a brilliant work in comparative constitutional history at the time of the French and American Revolutions that sets the stage for the second volume, subtitled *The Struggle* (Princeton, 1964), which covers the period from 1789 to 1800, focusing on the causes of the French Revolution and its consequences in Europe and America. Together the volumes are classic history—or history classics—at its best. For the diplomatic history of Europe, which Jefferson and Madison followed closely as secretaries of state and presidents, I have relied on the concise account in Steven T. Ross, *European Diplomatic History, 1789–1815: France against Europe* (New York, 1969).

Other books that are extremely useful include John F. Bosher, *French Finances, 1770–1795: From Business to Bureaucracy* (Cambridge, Eng., 1970); Georges Lefebvre's detailed histories of the French Revolution and the Napoleonic era: *The Coming of the French Revolution* (Princeton, 1947), *The French Revolution from 1793 to 1799* (New York, 1964), *Napoleon: From 18 Brumaire to Tilsit, 1799–1807* (New York, 1969), and *Napoleon: From Tilsit to Waterloo, 1807–1815* (New York, 1969); and Simon Schama, *Citizens: A Chronicle of the French Revolution* (New York, 1989). Schama's *Patriots and Liberators: Revolution in the Netherlands, 1780–1813* (New York, 1977), is a fine work, and Pieter J. van Winter, *American Finance and Dutch Investment, 1780–1805,* 2 vols. (New York, 1977), is also helpful.

Slavery

In the past quarter of a century, there has been a revolution in the interpretation of the Founding Fathers and slavery, which is now dominated by revisionists who have been labeled by David Brion Davis, one of the leading scholars in the group, as "debunkers" of what used to be called "Jeffersonian antislavery." In a perceptive lecture at Oxford University in 1970, Davis posed the question, *Was Thomas Jefferson an Authentic Enemy of Slavery?,* and answered it in the negative, a view that he elaborated in his magisterial study, *The Problem of Slavery in the Age of Revolution, 1770–1823* (Ithaca, N.Y., 1975), the best book about slavery in the early Republic. The pioneering study by "the disillusionists," as Davis has also called the revisionists, was by Robert McColley in his *Slavery and Jeffersonian Virginia* (Urbana, Ill., 1964). The most elaborate analysis of Jefferson's anti-Negro views is in the brilliant book by Winthrop D. Jordan. *White over Black: American Attitudes toward the Negro, 1550–1812* (Chapel Hill, 1968; rpt. New York, 1977). The most thorough treatment of Jefferson's views on slavery over his entire career is the excellent account in John Chester Miller, *The Wolf by the Ears: Thomas Jefferson and Slavery* (New York, 1977). For the most recent interpretive survey of the new scholarship on slavery in America, see the sweeping narrative by Peter Kolchin, *American Slavery, 1619–1877* (New York, 1993).

The most recent appraisals of Jefferson's views on race and slavery are in Peter S. Onuf, ed., *Jeffersonian Legacies* (Charlottesville, 1993). Scot A. French and Edward L. Ayers survey the changing attitudes of scholars over the past half century on Jefferson, race, and slavery, including the hotly debated question of Sally Hemings (pp. 418–56); Paul Finkelman presents a prosecuter's case against Jefferson as a slaveholder (pp. 181–221); and Lucia C. Stanton assesses Jefferson's relationship with the slaves he owned at Monticello for more than sixty years (pp. 147–80). Each author stresses the grinding irony that America's chief spokesman for liberty and equality was a leading slaveowner throughout his adult life, despite his lifelong objections to slavery.

For the allegation that Sally Hemings was Jefferson's mistress, see the psychobiography by Fawn M. Brodie, *Thomas Jefferson: An Intimate History* (New York, 1974). For a rebuttal, see Clifford Dowdey, *The Jefferson Scandals: A Rebuttal* (New York, 1981). For a thoughtful appraisal, see the essay "The Jefferson Scandals" that Douglass Adair wrote in 1960 but did not publish until 1974 in his *Fame and the Founding Fathers: Essays by Douglass Adair*, ed. H. Trevor Colbourn (New York, 1974). For another rebuttal, see Dumas Malone, "The Miscegenation Legend," in *Jefferson the President: First Term, 1801–1805* (Boston, 1970), pp. 494–98, and Malone, "The Hemings Family," in *The Sage of Monticello* (Boston, 1981), pp. 513–14. For the racial context, see Winthrop D. Jordan, *White over Black: American Attitudes toward the Negro, 1550–1812* (Chapel Hill, 1968; rpt. New York, 1977), pp. 429–81. For a balanced, scholarly appraisal of Sally Hemings, see Joel Williamson, *New People: Miscegenation and Mulattoes in the United States* (New York, 1980), pp. 42–48. For the most careful analysis of Jefferson's relations with the Hemings family, see Douglas R. Egerton, "A Matter of Blood: Thomas Jefferson and the Hemings Family," a paper read at the 1993 conference of the Society for the History of the Early American Republic.

Other important works include Edmund S. Morgan, "Slavery and Freedom: The American Paradox," *Journal of American History* 59 (1972): 5–29; Edmund S. Morgan, *American Slavery—American Freedom: The Ordeal of Colonial Virginia* (New York, 1975); William Cohen, "Thomas Jefferson and the Problem of Slavery," *Journal of American History* 56 (1969): 503–26; Staughton Lynd, *Class Conflict, Slavery, and the United States Constitution* (Indianapolis, 1968); Donald L. Robinson, *Slavery in the Structure of American Politics, 1765–1820* (New York, 1971); John T. Noonan, Jr., *Persons and Masks of the Law: Cardozo, Holmes, Jefferson, and Wythe As Makers of the Masks* (New York, 1976); Ira Berlin and Ronald Hoffman, eds., *Slavery and Freedom in the Age of the American Revolution* (Charlottesville, 1983); Paul Finkelman, "Slavery and the Constitutional Convention: Making a Covenant with Death," in *Beyond Confederation: Origins of the Constitution and American National Identity*, ed. Richard Beeman, Stephen

Botein, and Edward C. Carter II (Chapel Hill, 1987), pp. 188–225; Gary B. Nash, *Race and Revolution* (Madison, 1990); and Charles L. Griswold, Jr., "Rights and Wrongs: Jefferson, Slavery, and Philosophical Quandaries," in *A Culture of Rights: The Bill of Rights in Philosophy, Politics, and Law, 1791 and 1991*, ed. Michael J. Lacey and Knud Haakonssen (New York, 1991).

For a critique of the revisionists, which has influenced my treatment of Jefferson's and Madison's views on slavery, see William W. Freehling, "The Founding Fathers and Slavery," *American Historical Review* 77 (1972): 81–93, and his reformulation of his thesis in *The Road to Disunion: Secessionists at Bay, 1776–1854* (New York, 1990). For the most thorough—indeed, the first systematic—appraisal of Madison's views on slavery, see Drew R. McCoy, *The Last of the Fathers: James Madison and the Republican Legacy* (New York, 1989). Also useful is P. J. Straudenraus, *The African Colonization Movement, 1816–1865* (New York, 1961).

The Nullification Crisis

For the most extensive and perceptive account of Madison's efforts to protect Jefferson's and his own reputation against the distortions of the nullifiers, see Drew R. McCoy, *The Last of the Fathers: James Madison and the Republican Legacy* (New York, 1989). William W. Freehling's books, *Prelude to Civil War: The Nullification Controversy in South Carolina, 1816–1836* (New York, 1965) and *The Road to Disunion: Secessionists at Bay, 1776–1854* (New York, 1990), are expert analyses of the nullification crisis, as are Richard E. Ellis, *The Union at Risk: Jacksonian Democracy, States' Rights, and the Nullification Crisis* (New York, 1987), and Merrill D. Peterson, *Olive Branch and Sword: The Compromise of 1833* (Baton Rouge, 1982). And one of the most thoughtful and balanced evaluations of "The Concept of a Perpetual Union" is Kenneth M. Stampp's article in the *Journal of American History* 65 (1978): 5–33.

INDEX

Entries for pages 1 through 661 appear in Volume One.
Entries for pages 662 through 1351 appear in Volume Two.
Entries following page 1351 appear in Volume Three.

A., Miss: and William L. Smith, 766
Abbedin, M., 1305
Abbess of Pentemont, 486, 512
Abell, Francis: quoted, 63
Abernethy, Thomas P.: quoted, 1664
Acacia trees, three thorned, 511
Achæan League, 498
Act Concerning Aliens. *See* Alien Friends Act
Acton, John Francis Edward, Chevalier, 1278
Adair, Douglass: quoted, 441
Adams, Abigail: TJ and, 325, 398, 439, 540, 737, 1171, 1407; on XYZ affair, 1002–3; on second peace mission to France, 1074
Adams, Charles Francis: quoted, 4–5
Adams, Henry: quoted, 1256, 1505, 1771

ADAMS, JOHN
on JM's presidency, 1, 894, 895, 947–48, 1761; on American Revolution, 2; death of, 2, 1973; confrontational style of, 7; on TJ, 45, 49, 325–26, 445, 946, 977; mission to Netherlands, 166, 306, 453, 482, 486, 506; negotiates Dutch loan, 525–26, 536, 537–38, 767; and Norfolk merchants, 180; JM critical of, 208, 221, 244, 250, 943, 1032, 1048–49, 1157, 1162; TJ on, 223, 446, 462–63, 626, 648, 668, 688, 1791; on need for common revenue, 272–73; in commission with Franklin and Jay, 293–94; and foreign commercial negotiations, 301, 315; appointed minister to Great Britain, 326, 398, 399, 417–18, 505; and Philip Mazzei, 307; and William Stephens Smith, 439, 1407; writes *A Defence of the Constitutions of Government of the United States of America,* 478–79, 688; expenses as minister in Europe, 540; candidate for vice president, 554, 563, 579, 590, 605, 606; favors titles for president, 592, 612; as vice president, 737, 744–45, 813, 827, 848, 890; writes "Discourses on Davila," 668–70, 688; contrasted with George Wythe, 691; Beckley on criticism of, 697; on French Revolution, 746, 1051; JM urges reconciliation between TJ and, 944, 945; and election of 1796, 948, 950, 951–52, 955, 964

AS PRESIDENT
continues Washington's appointees in cabinet, 964–65, 1168; takes oath as president, 966–67; calls for preparedness measures against France, 969, 999, 1029, 1085, 1187; appoints peace mission to France, 970–71; condemns efforts to separate people from government, 969, 970; drafts war message, 999; answers addresses, 1004, 1044; proclaims day of prayer, 1005; diplomatic relations with France end, 1007, 1059; quasi war with France begins, 1008; appoints Washington as commander in chief, 1008; and postponement of meeting of Congress, 1011, 1012; on necessity of Senate, 1023; opposes removal of government to Washington, 1031; and XYZ affair, 1052, 1853; on British constitution, 1053; lacks faith in France, 1053, 1054; refuses exequatur to Victor du Pont, 1055; and administration of Sedition Act, 1067, 1074, 1087, 1137; and retaliation bill, 1095; Desforneaux denies French enmity against United States, 1097; appoints second peace mission to France, 1074–75, 1097, 1098–99, 1110, 1200; calls for Logan Act, 1086; dismisses Pickering and McHenry, 1117–18; and election of 1800, 1117, 1140, 1141, 1142, 1154, 1157; and Robbins affair, 1128; nominates Marshall as chief justice, 1142; appoints Bayard as minister to France, 1142; valedictory message to Congress, 1152; nominates Jay as chief justice, 1154; midnight appointments of, 1155, 1161, 1170–71, 1865; leaves Washington before TJ's inaugural, 1164; personnel policy of, 1171; administrative procedures under, 1202; relations with Santo Domingo, 1311; and Pickering, 1614; recommends national university, 1775

IN RETIREMENT
and Franklin, 1747; on British demands at Ghent, 1753; on Central College, 1777; and Declaration of Independence, 1845–46, 1847, 1875, 1876, 1877; mentioned, 14, 137, 179, 246, 398, 469, 962, 1780, 1975

Adams, John Quincy: on friendship between TJ and JM, 1–2, 7, 12; and internal improvements, 35, 1943; writes as "Publicola," 691, 697; on Holland's attitude towards French pressure, 977; nominated minister to Berlin, 978; nominated commissioner plenipotentiary to Sweden, 1028; negotiates treaty with Prussia, 1190; mission to London, 1214, 1314;

Adams (*continued*)
  praises JM's *Examination of the British Doctrine
    . . .*, 1408; on JM's inaugural ball, 1563; appointed
    minister to Russia, 1594, 1597; rejects Supreme
    Court appointment, 1621, 1647, 1659, 1663;
    supports War of 1812, 1681; appointed peace
    commissioner, 1710, 1734; and Transcontinental
    Treaty, 1806; and Monroe Doctrine, 1845; as
    president, 1891, 1954, 1957; on death of TJ and
    John Adams, 1973; mentioned, 1958, 1961
Adams, Louisa Catherine (Mrs. John Quincy), 1563
Adams, Mr.: and British prisoners, 120
Adams, Samuel, 563, 917, 1152
Adams, William Howard: quoted, 848
"Adams and Liberty" (song), 1002
Addington, Henry, Viscount Sidmouth, 1294–95
"Address to the States" (JM), 230, 232
Adet, Pierre A. (French minister to United States):
  interferes in election of 1796, 941–42, 948–49;
  appraisal of TJ, 942; mission suspended, 946;
  recalled, 968; mentioned, 907, 1006, 1051
"Advice to My Country" (JM), 2002
Aesop's fables, 854, 868
Agee, James, 5
Agrarian Justice (Thomas Paine), 982
Airth, Mr., 1430
Aitken, Robert, 319
Aix-en-Provence, 464, 480
Albany, N.Y., 1242, 1251, 1464
Albemarle Academy, 1776
Albemarle Agricultural Society, 1792, 1806, 1971
Albemarle County, Va.: committee welcomes TJ
  from France, 639; institutes draft, 1697; Lafayette
  Guards of, 1889; mentioned, 1189, 1475, 1727,
  1952, 1972, 1996–97
Albemarle County court, 675
Albemarle Sound, 1711, 1719, 1720
Albion, Ill., 1783
Alcove bedrooms, 774
Alexander, Amos, 1465
Alexander, Charles, Jr., 1465
Alexander, Governor (of North Carolina), 1483
Alexander, Robert, 1465
Alexander, William, Lord Stirling, 117, 364
Alexander I (of Russia): education by La Harpe,
  1311; and *Philadelphia* case, 1324; JM on, 1345;
  TJ on, 1419, 1840; and visit of Russian ships to
  Philadelphia, 1436; and neutral rights, 1510; and
  Short's appointment to Russia, 1526, 1528;
  appoints Daschkoff to United States, 1594; offers
  mediation in War of 1812, 1710, 1718; and Holy
  Alliance, 1844; mentioned, 1296, 1906
Alexandria, Va.: races at, 265, 267; and Virginia port
  bill, 279–80, 322, 349; and Genet, 777; and Jay's
  treaty, 885, 896; mail schedule from, 1284;
  mentioned, 504, 663, 673, 1252, 1432
Alexandria County (District of Columbia), 1465
Algeciras, Spain, 1402
Algerines: in Virginia, 403
"Algernon Sidney" (pseudonym: Spencer Roane),
  1864, 1873–74
Algiers: reputed capture of Virginians, 554–55;
  treaty with, 916, 918, 921–22, 924, 933, 1170,
  1314; American captives in, 583, 639, 932–33,
  956; dey of, 1191, 1494; annual remittance to,
  1231, 1232, 1264, 1266; threatens war, 1264;
  Tobias Lear as consul to, 1267; mentioned, 1194,
  1213, 1301, 1340
Alien and Sedition Acts: TJ opposes, 1066; petitions
  against, 1072–73, 1091, 1106–7; House endorses,
  1075; and North Carolina legislature, 1090;
  defended as internal security system, 1104–6; and
  federal judiciary, 1851; JM on, 1871–72, 1949;
  and public opinion, 1957; and Virginia resolutions,
  1986, 2000; and Kentucky resolutions, 2000;
  mentioned, 31–32, 1980, 1982

Alien bill. *See* Alien Friends Act
Alien enemies: during Revolution, 86–87
Alien Enemies Act, 1066
Alien friends, 1183
Alien Friends Act: House bill, 1003, 1042; scares off
  French visitors, 1045; in Senate, 1047, 1048, 1049,
  1052, 1054, 1056; TJ on, 1081–82, 1083
Allen, Ethan, 91
Allen, John, 1065
Alliances, entangling, 1165
Allison, Mr., 91
Allston, Joseph, 1139, 1151, 1152
Alt, John, 1465
Ambler, Jacquelin, 187
Amboy, N.J., 1225
Ambrister, Robert C., 1808
Amelia County, Va., 886
Amelia Island, 1692, 1694
Amelot, M. *See* Amyot, Joseph Marie
Amendments to Constitution: for emancipation and
  colonization of freed slaves, 22, 23, 25–26;
  Massachusetts recommends, 519, 520, 524; New
  York proposes second convention for, 521,
  548–49; discussed in ratification conventions,
  563–64; Bill of Rights as subsequent to, 579, 614,
  615; adoption of Twenty-seventh in 1992, 599;
  adoption of Twelfth, 1331, 1334; TJ on need of, for
  internal improvements, 1365. *See also* Bill of
  Rights, federal
America (British warship), 164
"American, An" (Alexander Hamilton), 714
American Colonization Society, 22, 1814
American Institute of Architects, 1915
American Museum (magazine), 506
American Philosophical Society: JM's membership
  in, 273; *Transactions* of, 530, 543; committee on
  Hessian fly, 690; TJ and, 824, 947; mentioned, 146,
  285
American Revolution: JM on, 2, 429; early progress
  of, 58; financing of, 125–27; British successes, in
  1780, 127, 131–32; European reaction to, 380–81;
  French officers in, 436, 486; Constitution designed
  to implement principles of, 595, 600; Bill of Rights
  as culmination of, 600; historic sites of, 670
American Society for Promoting the Civilization of
  and General Improvement of the Indian Tribes in
  the United States, 1837, 1838
"American System," 1954
Ames, Fisher: appraisal of JM, 592; on French
  Revolution, 746; burned in effigy, 838; reelected in
  1794, 859, 866; denounces Virginia amendments of
  1795, 888; on election of 1796, 940; and
  Washington's final address, 949; succeeded by
  Harrison Gray Otis, 978; on XYZ affair, 1000–1;
  praises John Adams, 1006; mentioned, 813
Amherst, Jeffrey Baron, 164
Amherst County, Va., 1014
Amiability: TJ on, 7
Amphitrite (British frigate), 160
Amphyction Confederacy, 498
Ampthill (plantation), 216
Amsterdam: TJ and John Adams negotiate loan in,
  525–26, 536; State House of, 1775
Amyot, Jean-Joseph-Marie, 485
Anderson, Garland, Jr., 1134
Anderson, George, 152, 158, 162
Anderson, Howard, 7
Anderson, John, 777
Anderson, Joseph, 1053, 1129, 1472, 1854
Anderson, Olive: quoted, 93
André, John, 147
Andrews, Mr., 1724
Andrews, Robert, 534, 896, 1122
Anglican Church in Virginia, 55
Anglo-Russian treaty of 1801, 1409
Animal magnetism, 332, 351, 367

Index

Annapolis, Md.: Lafayette's troops at, 181, 186; and location of national capital, 269, 271; mentioned, 233, 261, 663
Annapolis Convention: and commercial regulation, 395; calls for constitutional convention, 396, 454; Virginia delegates to, 404, 405; JM on purpose of, 415–16, 420; states choose delegates to, 430; TJ on, 458; mentioned, 281, 414
Annual Register, 1305–6
Anonymous letters, 1529–30
Anthony, Joseph, Jr., 1135
Antifederalists: oppose ratification of Constitution, 29, 519, 520; JM on southern, 552; and Bill of Rights, 524, 564, 600, 618; Federalists conciliatory towards, after ratification, 591; in elections of 1788, 605; in Congress, 606; JM views nullifiers as latter-day, 1999; mentioned, 531, 578–79
Anti-Publicolas, 697
Antirepublican party, 710
Antislavery thought: historiography of, 15–26
Appleby, Joyce: quoted, 8
Apples, 391, 424, 508, 511, 529. *See also specific varieties*
Appleton, Thomas, 1281, 1344, 1522, 1768, 1852
Arata, Mr., 1686
Arbitration commissions: and British debts, 882, 889, 977, 1040
Arbuthnot, Alexander, 1808
Arbuthnot, Marriot, 189
Archer, Thomas, 1251
Architecture: TJ on, 37, 848; JM requests TJ's help on, 849
Argand cylinder lamp, 332, 351, 368
Ariel (American warship), 152, 165
"Aristides" (attributed to Noah Webster), 1156
Aristocracy: JM on, 709, 937
Aristotle, 448
Arkansas River, 1270, 1282, 1493
Armstrong, John: appointed minister to France, 1334; and Bonaparte's title, 1338, 1344; and negotiations with Spain, 1357, 1358, 1367, 1385, 1389; JM on, 1366, 1388; TJ's appraisal of, 1369; and claims under Convention of 1800, 1376–77, 1378, 1391, 1392–93; on western boundary of Louisiana, 1386–87; and Floridas, 1405, 1423–24, 1541, 1542, 1544; teamed with Bowdoin, 1419, 1425; goes to The Hague, 1422; letters from, 1425, 1474, 1513, 1519, 1577, 1608; and d'Yrujo, 1427; on Miranda expedition, 1428; on Burr's propositions overseas, 1472–73; relationship with Warden, 1489, 1660, 1662–63, 1663–64, 1665; proceeds to French camp, 1496; and Short, 1526; and Guillaume's plow, 1593; and disavowal of Erskine Agreement, 1607; and French decrees, 1516, 1594–95, 1619, 1637, 1648; as presidential possibility, 1667; appointed secretary of war, 1708, 1714; and Alexander Smyth, 1715; and Wilson Cary Nicholas, 1716; JM dismisses, 1733, 1746; writes Newburgh letters, 1868; mentioned, 1337, 1541, 1610, 1624, 1627
Army: expansion of, 1074, 1086, 1088, 1091, 1092, 1094; additional, 1074, 1086, 1091, 1092, 1096; eventual, 1074, 1091, 1092, 1096; volunteer, 1074, 1091, 1092; provisional, 1042, 1045, 1047, 1049, 1050, 1091, 1092; reorganization of, 1095; Congress begins to dismantle, 1113
Arnold, Benedict: destroys Virginia records, 60, 198–99; treason of, 131–32, 147, 160, 165; invades Virginia, 8, 132–33, 156, 159, 172–73, 181; burned in effigy, 838
Arnold, Margaret Shippen (Mrs. Benedict), 147
Articles of Confederation: ratification of, 9, 129, 130–31, 171, 446; TJ on, 27, 445; and land companies, 151; JM researches history of, 300–1; movement to amend, 395, 396–97, 431; Virginia Plan proposes replacement of, 443; replaced by Constitution, 446; inadequacy of, 500; expiration of government under, 590, 606; and nullifiers, 1983, 1984, 1994
Artois, Charles-Phillipe, comte d', 625
Ashworth, Mary Wells: quoted, 951
Asparagus, 840
Assembly of Notables, 452, 567
Assumption of state debts, 643–45, 655, 715, 768, 850
Atlacapis (Orleans), 1343
Atticism, 3, 9
Atwater, Reuben, 1250
Auckland, William Eden, Baron, 1410
Augusta, Ga., 1263
Augusta County, Va., 213
Aurora (newspaper). *See* Philadelphia *Aurora*
Austin, James Trecothick, 1854
Austria: and Naples, 460; and Prussia, 460; and surrender at Leoben, 965; signs alliance with Great Britain, 1358
Autobiography: JM's, 4; TJ's, 4, 13, 19, 25, 124–25
Aviso (U.S. ship), 1543
Azalea, 670, 690
Azzara, Mr., 1324

Bache, Benjamin Franklin: and Jay's treaty, 927, 931; attacks Washington, 991; Abigail Adams on, 1003; critical of John Adams, 1003; Sedition Act aimed at, 1003, 1004, 1042, 1045; publishes Talleyrand's letter, 1008–9, 1061; receives pamphlets from France, 1010; prints letter addressed to TJ, 1033; indicted for seditious libel, 1064; TJ's relations with, 1065–66; death of, 1192
Bache, Catharine Wistar (Mrs. William), 1145
Bache, William, 1145, 1161, 1192, 1193, 1249, 1284
Backus, Azel, 1479–80, 1491, 1497–98
Backus, Elijah, 1347
Bacon, Ezekiel, 1614, 1647, 1648
Bacon, Francis, 2, 6
Baer, George, Jr., 1140, 1154
Bailén, Spain, 1546
Bailey, John, 1943, 1947–48, 1956, 1957–58, 1961, 1962
Bailey, Mr., 1531
Bailey, Theodorus, 1010–11, 1012, 1018, 1039, 1041
Bailly, Jean-Sylvain, 617, 618
Bainbridge, William, 1194, 1303, 1685
Bailyn, Bernard: quoted, 449, 450
Baker, John Martin, 1542, 1544
Baker, Mr., 1238–39, 1522
Baker, Russell, 6
Bald Friar's, Md., 217
Baldwin, Abraham: delegate to Constitutional Convention, 478, 660, 949, 1093, 1224, 1368, 1704
Ballendine, John, 99–102
Ballooning, 332, 351, 369
Balsam poplar, 690
Baltic Sea, 1159, 1497, 1536, 1710, 1718
Baltimore, George Calvert, Lord, 302
Baltimore, Md.: proposed as national capital, 548, 552; Republican Society of, 865; and Jay's treaty, 934; foreign consuls at, 1307; French frigate at, 1343; *North American* (Federalist newspaper), 1614; attack on Fort McHenry, 1734, 1737; mentioned, 664, 1263, 1266, 1311, 1323, 1369, 1371, 1587
Bancroft, Edward, 413, 419
Bancroft, George, 50
Banister, John, Jr., 465, 483, 529, 530
Bankhead, Charles Lewis, 1727, 1807
Bank of England, 969, 976, 977, 1277
Bank of Pennsylvania, 141
Bank of the United States: first, 31; and speculators, 685; subscriptions to, 694–95, 695–96, 697–98; and TJ, 759, 803, 1588, 1589; law to punish frauds on, 1080; and state bank in New Orleans, 1310;

Bank of the United States (*continued*)
  recharter of, 1651, 1736–37, 1771, 1772; and bonus bill, 1773; mentioned, 1059, 1236
Bankruptcies: in England, 789
Bankruptcy, 1012, 1017, 1237
Bankruptcy bill, 745, 760–61, 1088
Bankruptcy law, 1131, 1849–50
Banks, Henry, 1430
Banks, state: during War of 1812, 1735–36
Banning, Lance: quoted, 518–19
Bapstropp, Mr. *See* Bastrop, Felipe Neri
Barbary States: and Mediterranean commerce, 314; TJ's dealings with in 1780s, 1170; TJ on, 1193–94, 1296; hostilities toward United States, 1209–10; expenses for relations with, 1216; possibility of war with, 1234; and law of nations, 1281; consuls to, 1315; JM on, 1459; mentioned, 1208, 1447. *See also* Algiers; Morocco; Tripoli; Tunis
Barbé-Marbois, François, marquis de: and TJ's *Notes on the State of Virginia,* 206, 214, 372; on terms of peace treaty, 246; becomes French chargé d'affaires, 311; attacked by Longchamps, 320, 324; and western trip with JM and Lafayette, 345; and Louisiana Purchase, 1255; mentioned, 580
Barbetrac, Jean, 297
Barbour, James: on JM's sense of humor, 9; mentioned, 1134, 1148, 1149, 1699, 1826, 1881, 1912, 1914, 1971
Barbour, Philip Pendleton: and Andrew Jackson's raid into East Florida, 1808; reports on TJ's illness, 1815; considered for law professorship, 1905, 1916, 1923, 1924, 1926, 1927, 1928–29, 1930; declines law post, 1931–32, 1939; mentioned, 720, 1964
Barcelona, Spain, 1301
Barclay, Charles, 482
Barclay, John, 819
Barclay, Thomas, 1246, 1302
Barclay, Vice Admiral, 1488
Barksdale, Mr., 1804
Barley, 1385
Barlow, Joel: and Barbary negotiations, 1214; and Mellimelli, 1421; visits Montpellier, 1546; appointed minister to France, 1658; answers Robert Smith's attack on JM, 1671; and commercial treaty with France, 1679, 1694, 1696; TJ on, 1697; death of, 1752; discusses writing history of early republic, 1786; mentioned, 1544, 1655, 1700, 1747
Barlow, Ruth (Mrs. Joel), 1533, 1752
Barnes, David Leonard, 1186
Barnes, John: Monroe writes draft on, 1018; agent for JM, 1048, 1056, 1085, 1094, 1126, 1130, 1135, 1145, 1146, 1147, 1148; and French wine, 1377, 1382; signs bank loan for TJ, 1588, 1589–90; agent for Kościuszko, 1699; mentioned, 1047
Barnes, Joseph, 1278–79, 1283, 1308, 1309, 1311, 1366–67
Barnet, Isaac Cox, 1301, 1437
Barnett, James, 81
Barney, Joshua: in French navy, 1345; mentioned, 1195, 1197, 1339, 1341, 1722, 1723
Barnwell, George, 1363
Barnwell, John, 860
Barras, Jacques-Melchior Saint-Laurent, comte de, 200
Barrets Ford, Va., 1519
Barrington, Daines, 319
Barron, Samuel, 1340, 1376
Barry, John, 1132
Barry, Richard, 1640
Barthélemy, Jean-Jacques, Abbé, 583, 607
Bartlett, Josiah, 579
Barton, Benjamin Smith, 1719
Barton, Professor, 1905

Bartram, John, Jr., 780
Bartram, William, 780, 784
Bartram House, 780
Bartram's Garden, 780
Bashaw of Tripoli, 1301, 1311, 1423, 1510–11
Bassett, Burrell, 216
Bassett, Richard, 478, 579
Bassette, John, 1639, 1641
Bastille, fall of, 528, 602, 625
Bastrop, Felipe Neri, baron de, 1329
Batavian Republic: declares war on Great Britain, 935; offers to mediate quasi war, 1086; mentioned, 1501. *See also* Holland; Netherlands, the
Bates, Frederick, 1347
Baton Rouge, West Florida, 1648, 1700
Battle of Bennington, 670, 671
Battle of Bunker Hill, 45
Battle of Bunker Hill, The (print), 1127
Battle of Chrysler's Farm, 1713
Battle of Fallen Timbers, 863–64
Battle of Tippecanoe, 1676
Battle of Yorktown, 411
Batture: Livingston's claim to, 1518–19, 1521; Rodney's ruling on, 1521; and Moreau's memoir, 1641; and TJ's legal brief, 1690, 1693; mentioned, 1619, 1633, 1640, 1642
Bayard, James A.: and Robbins's affair, 1128, 1129; and election of 1800, 1144; appointed minister to France, 1161, 1200; on War of 1812 peace commission, 1710, 1734; on war taxes, 1677; mentioned, 1142
Bayard, Samuel, 1220
Baylor, George, 103, 117
Baynham, William, 1375
Baynton, Peter, 688
Bay of St. Bernard, 1329, 1387, 1402
Bayonne: Bonaparte forces abdication of Ferdinand of Spain at, 1527; Decree of, 1509; mentioned, 1609, 1666
Bayou Pierre, 1402, 1455, 1456, 1457, 1473
Beard, Jonas, 304–5
Beatty, John, 309
Beaufort, N.C., 1300
Beaujoin, M., 1472
Beaumarchais, Pierre-Augustin Caron de, 486
Becker, Carl, 5
Beckley, John: clerk of Virginia House of Delegates, 409; and Paine's *Rights of Man,* 668, 687; and trip with JM, 689; reports on trip to Boston, 697; clerk of House of Representatives, 720, 971, 976, 1224; and Monroe, 742; writes pamphlet on Hamilton, 766; and Mazzei, 879; and Jay's treaty, 897; mentioned, 70
Becks, Will, 1246
Beckwith, George: secret agent for Lord Dorchester, 646–47, 682; and Nootka Sound incident, 658; relations with Hamilton, 667, 710; at JM's boardinghouse, 681–83; critical of TJ, 668, 688; JM critical of, 689; mentioned, 698
Bedford, Gunning, 478
Bedford County, Va.: TJ visits in 1805, 1372; in 1807, 1492, 1493; in 1809, 1602, 1607; in 1810, 1624, 1625, 1640, 1645; in 1812, 1689, 1704; in 1813, 1726; in 1814, 1743; in 1815, 1767; in 1817, 1778, 1785, 1786, 1789; in 1818, 1804; in 1819, 1810, 1814; in 1820, 1824; in 1821, 1831, 1836; in 1822, 1840; land prices in, 1966; mentioned, 878, 1432, 1434, 1435, 1540, 1593, 1595, 1599. *See also* Poplar Forest
Bed of justice, 490
Belette. *See* Weasel
Bell, Robert, 319
Bell, Thomas, 1011
Bellachasse, J. D., 1336, 1337, 1343
Belle Grove, Va., 857

INDEX   2023

Bellini, Charles, 1108
Belt, Joseph Sprigg, 1465
Bemis, Samuel Flagg: quoted, 712, 722
Bennet, Jeremiah, Jr., 1268, 1300
Bennington, Vt., 1277
Benson, Mr., 1604
Bentham, Jeremy, 1840
Benton, Lemuel, 978
Berceau (French corvette), 1215
Berciau (ship), 1262
Berckel, Pieter Johan van, 251, 472–73
Beresford, Richard, 289
Berey, Mr., 1784
Berkeley, George Cranfield, 1449, 1453, 1499
Berkeley (plantation), 159
Berkeley Springs, Va., 84, 1240
Berlin Decree, 1446, 1448, 1503–4, 1593, 1618, 1657
Berman, Eleanor, 3
Bermuda, 82–83, 134, 152, 158, 182, 1470
Bermuda Hundred, Va., 280, 322
Bernadotte, Jean Baptiste Jules, 1273
Bernard's Ford, Va., 1524
Bernis, Council of, 692
Berry & Rogers, 690
Bethlehem, Conn., 1480
Bertling, Capt. (British prisoner), 83
Betsy (American brig), 380
Beverly, Mass., 1231, 1250, 1300
Bey of Tunis: demands frigate from United States, 1267; and Lear, 1342; possibility of war with, 1349; and mission of Mellimelli, 1411, 1431; vessel presented to, 1426; presents for, 1428, 1432; mentioned, 1236, 1265, 1340, 1341, 1403
Bibb, George M., 1464
Biddle, Samuel, 789
Bidwell, Barnabas, 1646
Bigelow, Jacob, 1905
"Bill Establishing a Provision for Teachers of the Christian Religion, 1784" (Patrick Henry), 331
Billey (JM's slave). *See* Gardner, William
Bill for Proportioning Capital Crimes and Punishments, 437, 466, 483
Bill for the More General Diffusion of Knowledge (TJ), 437, 455, 466, 1775
Bill of Rights, federal: JM supports subsequent to ratification, 28–29, 522–24, 564–66, 591; TJ deplores lack of, in Constitution, 450–51; 522, 524, 545–46, 580; omitted from Constitution, 503; TJ on necessity of, 512–13, 567, 580, 587–88; James Wilson defends Constitution without, 513; as supplemental safeguards to liberty, 552; JM introduces, 594–98; as complementary to Constitution, 595, 1164; TJ announces ratification of, 599; JM as father of, 600, 2002; as culmination of American Revolution, 600; postponed, 614; JM sends draft of, to TJ, 622–24; TJ lists additional provisions to JM's, 629–30. *See also* Declaration of the Rights of Man and Citizen
Bingham, Anne Willing (Mrs. William), 463
Bingham, William: TJ's appraisal of, 436, 463; and JM interview Gardoqui, 471; on move to replace Adams as vice president, 728; opposes commercial discrimination, 834; and Whiskey Rebellion, 866; and arming merchant vessels, 980; as director of Bank of United States, 1062; amends Ross bill, 1127; case of, 1189, 1191, 1194; mentioned, 139, 781, 766, 869
Birch bark, 694, 695
Birkbeck, Morris, 1783
Bishop, Abraham, 1301
Bishop, Samuel, 1185, 1186
Bissent, Abraham, 1464
Bizet, Mr., 1784
Blackburn, Thomas, 357
Blackledge, William, 1625

Black's Law Dictionary: quoted, 1180
Blackstone, Sir William, 1958, 1965
Blaettermann, George, 1813, 1886, 1887, 1908, 1912
Blagden, Mrs., 1533
Blair, Archibald, 76, 82
Blair, Hugh, 290, 292
Blair, James, 796
Blair, John: and supplemental revision of Virginia code, 455, 466; delegate to Constitutional Convention, 468, 470, 476, 477, 478; favors ratification, 534; mentioned, 587, 919
Blake, George, 1647, 1649
Blake, James, 840, 844, 845, 846
Blakeley, Josiah, 1468
Bland, Richard, 908
Bland, Theodorick: and Saratoga troops, 71, 83, 90, 103, 113, 117, 120; and western land claims, 130; on navigation of Mississippi, 131, 150–52; on British invasion of Virginia, 133; in Continental and Confederation Congress, 152, 153, 154, 156, 161, 163, 164, 165, 169, 180; expedites military supplies to Virginia, 174; elected to Virginia assembly, 420, 456; opposes ratification, 509, 534; favors second convention, 594; elected to first Congress, 605; mentioned, 157, 189, 191, 193, 201, 216
Blennerhassett, Harman, 1471
Blennerhassett Island, 1443
Blicher Olsen, Peder, 1191, 1193, 1283
Blockade: TJ on definition of, 1465; France on England's definition of, 1607, 1618; as established by Fox, 1674; effect on farmers, 1719; British establish, from Maine to Mississippi River, 1731; JM denounces, 1731; mentioned, 1413–14
Blockran, Charles, 1250
Blockran, Robert, 1250
Bloodgood, Abraham, 1242, 1244, 1251
Bloodworth, Samuel, 965
Bloodworth, Timothy, 965
Blount, Thomas, 893
Blount, William: delegate to Constitutional Convention, 478; expelled from Senate, 992; and Liston's plot, 1011; impeachment of, discussed, 1013, 1016, 1017; conspiracy of, 1326; mentioned, 226
Blue Run (Orange County), Va., 1484, 1485
Board of Treasury, 436
Boardley, John Beale. *See* Bordley, John Beale
Bob (TJ's servant), 337
Bockius Tavern (Germantown, Pa.), 829
Bogert, John J., 321
Boinod, Daniel, 297, 303, 319
Bollman, Justus Erich, 1545
Bonaparte, Jerome, 1275, 1276, 1344, 1383
Bonaparte, Joseph, 1527, 1530, 1544, 1546, 1581, 1606
Bonaparte, Napoléon: puts down Paris resistance, 903; defeats Austrian army, 965, 969, 980; and Treaty of Leoben, 981; in Egypt, 1089, 1091; overthrows French Republic, 1112, 1117, 1123, 1126–27; JM on, 1113, 1567, 1630; Hamilton compares TJ to, 1138; and negotiation of Convention of 1800, 1151; as first consul, 1199, 1275; and secret treaty with Spain regarding Louisiana, 1208; Lear on ambitions of, 1225; Livingston's appraisal of, 1254; renounces Louisiana, 1255, 1256, 1257, 1264, 1285, 1289, 1297; resumes war with Great Britain, 1255; intercedes with Tripoli, 1308, 1324; as emperor, 1334, 1338, 1344, 1374; relations with Spain, 1355, 1376, 1406; proposes invasion of England, 1358; moves army to Bavaria, 1358; TJ on, 1371, 1382, 1475, 1567–68, 1586, 1638, 1662, 1675, 1689, 1897; banishes Moreau, 1381; Armstrong and Monroe on, 1387; victory at Austerlitz, 1404; and Mr. Haumont, 1441; proclaims blockade of

Bonaparte (*continued*)
  Britain, 1446; use of militia by, 1451; victories on Continent, 1452; and duke of Portland ministry, 1470; attitude towards United States, 1500; expands decrees, 1509, 1626; issues Milan Decree, 1515; installs Joseph Bonaparte as king of Spain, 1527, 1530; transfers army to Spain, 1534; confiscates American ships, 1617; reputation for chicanery, 1619; policy after Cadore letter, 1653, 1657, 1670; retreat from Moscow, 1709, 1714, 1718; abdicates, 1730; exile of, 1758; returns from Elba, 1758, 1768; defeat at Waterloo, 1759; mentioned, 1384, 1388, 1866
Bond, Mr.: builds Belle Grove, 857
Bond, Phineas, 729
Bonhomme Richard (American warship), 171
Bonnycastle, Charles, 1886, 1887, 1908
Bonus bill, 1783
Books: for Confederation Congress, 14
Books: JM requests TJ to order, 332, 367–68, 401, 419, 487–89, 529, 631, 649; TJ buys for JM in France, 350–51, 352, 381, 382–83, 384, 386, 409, 410, 459, 485, 487, 610, 636; TJ loans, 858, 876; JM retrieves for TJ, 861; TJ sends, to JM, 1132; tariff duty on, 1831, 1832–33, 1837; Gilmer buys for university, 1922, 1965
Bordeaux wine, 391, 1373
Bordley, John Beale, 876
Boré, Jean Étienne (Stephan), 1336, 1343
Boston (U.S. frigate), 1195, 1196, 1197, 1199, 1228, 1234, 1240, 1276
Boston, Mass.: evacuation of, 411; and Constitution, 504; Democratic-Republican Society in, 865; and Jay's treaty, 885, 895, 896, 933–34, 937; and representation in state legislature, 1628; mentioned, 1187, 1378, 1432
Boston Tea Party, 39, 40
Bosutti, Salvatore, 1431
Boswell, James, 10
Boudinot, Elias, 244, 245, 870, 1236
Boufflers, Louis-François, duc de, 94
Bouillé, François-Claude-Amour de, Marquis, 463
Bourbon, Louis-Henri-Joseph de Condé, duc de, 625
Bourbon monarchy: rumored restoration of, 1758
Bourgain, François-Joseph, 512
Bourne, Sylvanus, 1052, 1055, 1332
Bournonville, Charles François, 1015
Bowditch, Nathaniel, 1813, 1884
Bowdoin, James: governor of Massachusetts, 474; appointed minister to Spain, 1357–58, 1374, 1375, 1377, 1380, 1384; delays going to Madrid, 1387, 1389, 1391, 1392; on war with Great Britain, 1419; letter from, 1423; teamed with Armstrong, 1425
Bowman, John, 78–79, 104
Boyd, Joseph, 1262
Boyd, Julian P.: on correspondence between TJ and JM, 3; on TJ, 53; and TJ's letters as governor, 61; and TJ's original appraisal of Lafayette, 348; quoted, 364, 604
Bradford, John, 163, 1268, 1366
Bradford, Mr. (Philadelphia bookseller), 288
Bradford, Thomas, 982
Bradford, William, 38, 39, 40, 42, 43, 47
Bradley, Stephen Row, 860, 1240, 1425
Bran, Mr. (bookbinder), 908
Brant, Irving: on friendship between JM and TJ, 60; quoted, 267, 664, 1383, 1398, 1492
Brant, Joseph, 732–33, 735, 1199
Brawner, Mr., 1176
Braxton, Carter: opposes regulation of commerce, 405; favors postponing taxes, 406; on Virginia Executive Council, 408; mentioned, 149–50
Brazil, 1826
Brearly, David, 478
Breck, Samuel, 766

Breckinridge, James: and Virginia Board of Visitors, 1824, 1839, 1856, 1894; and faculty recruitment, 1912, 1918, 1922, 1923, 1926, 1927, 1961
Breckinridge, John: moves to Kentucky, 769; and Kentucky resolutions, 1068, 1070; and Louisiana Purchase, 1288; illness of, 1454; JM substitutes for, as attorney general, 1460–61
Breckinridge, Robert, 729
Brehan, Marquise de, 494, 580, 612, 614
Brent, Daniel: State Department clerk, 1213, 1228, 1239, 1241; and war with Morocco, 1235–36; and commissioners of bankruptcy, 1240; and Guadaloupe negroes, 1248; recommends Wallace, 1284; collects session laws for TJ, 1467; and Algiers, 1494; mentioned, 1244, 1245, 1246, 1247, 1492
Brent, Robert, 1465, 1522
Bretagny, France. *See* Brittany, France
Breteuil, Louis-Charles-Auguste le Tonnelier, baron de, 625
Bridgetown, N.J., 1269, 1300
Brienne, Étienne-Charles de Loménie de, 543
Briggs, Isaac, 1301
Bright, Michael, 1589
Bringhurst, John: Philadelphia merchant, 871, 874, 916, 919; and TJ's nailery, 920, 922, 924, 929, 930, 935; visits JM and TJ, 984, 985, 992; calls on TJ in Philadelphia, 1047; letter to Dolley Madison, 1136; mentioned, 992, 1044
Briscoe, Mr., 1427
Brissot de Warville, Jacques-Pierre: and land speculation, 535–36, 538; delivers items from TJ to JM, 539, 547; guillotined, 833
British constitution, 1965
British debts: provisions of Treaty of Paris about, 250, 542; JM on, 337; payment of, 361–62; Virginia legislature debates, 361–62, 405, 432, 456, 532; TJ and Adams discuss, with British merchants, 398–99; TJ on, 417–18, 459, 724; sequestration of, 840; arbitration commission for, 882, 977, 1088; mentioned, 711, 712, 725, 727, 785
British fleet: mutiny in, 969, 981
British Museum, 284, 291
British Parliament: and royal negative, 498
British West Indies, 1496
Brittany, France, 412, 527–28, 789
Broadbent, John, 1421, 1422
Broadie, David, 1347
Broadway, Va., 159
Brock, Isaac, 1683, 1684, 1705, 1707
Brockenbrough, Arthur S.: and cost estimates for University of Virginia, 1833, 1834–35, 1836; and Rotunda, 1858; mentioned, 1860, 1904, 1905
Brodeau, Mrs., 1249
Broglio, Victor François, 625
"Broken voyage": principle of, 1360
Bronatd, Mr., 1520
Brooke, Robert, 961
Brookes, John, 1133
Broom, Jacob, 478
Broome, John, 486, 493, 506, 508
Brougham, Henry, 1896
Browere, John Henri Isaac, 1941, 1942
Brown, Andrew, 693, 1035
Brown, Benjamin, 1134
Brown, Catherine, 1153, 1156, 1160
Brown, David, 1172
Brown, Dr., 1742, 1828
Brown, Jacob, 1751
Brown, James (Richmond merchant), 694
Brown, James (secretary of Orleans territory), 1336
Brown, James (U.S. attorney for Orleans), 1365, 1366
Brown, John: and Gardoqui, 551; elected to Congress, 605; and Kentucky statehood, 614; and Kentucky offices, 729; Kentucky senator, 739; mentioned, 555, 1244

Brown, Mr., 1434, 1578
Brown, Mr.: and the mind, 1909
Brown, Ralph Adams: quoted, 1085
Brown, William, 1609
Browne, Joseph, 1365
Browne, William S.: and Burke case, 493, 507–8, 532–33, 543, 555
Browne, Mrs. William S., 532
Brown University, 1918
Brudenhem, Mr., 1425
Bruff, Dr., 1697–98
Brunswick, Ga., 1300
Brunswick, Karl Wilhelm Ferdinand, duke of, 772, 776
Brunswick, N.J., 228, 243
Bry, Theodor de, 1639
Buchanan, James, 242, 319
Buchanan and Hay: and Virginia Capitol, 384, 412
Buckingham, Va., 99
Buck Island, 1434
Buck Tavern, Pa., 1385
Buell, Joseph, 1475
Buenos Aires, 1236, 1237, 1243, 1385
Buffalo, N.Y., 1279, 1712
Buffalo Creek, N.Y., 1300
Buffon, Georges-Louis Leclerc, comte de: theory of central heat of earth, 284; JM on, 286–87, 291–92, 368, 421–22; and Catherine the Great, 308; TJ rebuts, in *Notes,* 333; on weasels, 425–28; colored plates from, 423, 460; mentioned, 292, 303
Buford, Abraham, 80, 81, 82
Bull, John, 660
Bull Run Hill, Va., 1176–77
Burges, Dempsey, 978
Burgos, 1133
Burgoyne, John, 58, 63, 94, 670
Burgundy wine, 391
Burk, John Daly, 1068
Burke, Edmund: writes *Reflections on the Revolution in France,* 667–68, 684–85, 689, 691
Burke, James: *see* Burke, John
Burke, John, 486, 492–93
Burke, Thomas: case of, 486, 493, 506, 512, 532, 555
Burke, Mrs. Thomas, 493, 555, 583
Burlington, Richard Boyle, third earl of, 1136
Burnley, Garland, 97
Burnley, Mr., 1523
Burr, Aaron: and northern excursion by TJ and JM, 670; introduces JM to Dolley Payne Todd, 847; and Franco-American affairs, 969; welcomes Monroe from France, 977; Abigail Adams critical of, 1003; listed as member of American Executive Directory, 1010; on elections of 1798, 1047; nominated for vice president, 1117; and New York election of 1800, 1129, 1131, 1138; and party solidarity, 1139; and tie vote in 1800, 1141, 1142, 1143, 1144, 1149, 1154; Monroe warns JM of ambitions of, 1153; not renominated for vice president, 1352; and Swartout, 1408, 1423; kills Hamilton, 1442; conspiracy, 1442, 1443, 1444, 1454, 1461; offers assistance to British, 1443; indicted for treason, 1444, 1620; acquitted, 1445; escapes to England, 1445; and compulsory process in different courts, 1491; and James Wilkinson, 1665; and Granger, 1740; mentioned, 1151, 1198, 1204
Burr, Theodosia, 1151
Burrall, Charles (assistant postmaster general), 1011
Burrall, Mr., 1741
Burton, James, 97
Burwell, William A., 1423, 1615
Burwell's Ferry, Va., 154
Bush Hill, Pa., 1385

Butler, Pierce: delegate to Constitutional Convention, 469, 478; and French wine, 1361, 1377, 1391; mentioned, 933, 936, 1149, 1150
Butler, Richard, 157, 347–48
Bynkershoek, Cornelius van, 297, 304, 319, 723, 1262
Byrd, William, 908

Cabaret, M. (bookbinder), 487
Cabell, Colonel Joseph, 117
Cabell, Joseph Carrington: and Central College, 1776, 1777, 1784, 1785, 1787, 1792, 1800, 1802, 1807; and TJ's education bill, 1788, 1793; on Rockfish Gap commission, 1793; on university Board of Visitors, 1795; and architectural plan for University of Virginia, 1797; and state funding for Central College, 1803; on hostility to university, 1808; opposes Cooper's appointment, 1808, 1809, 1810, 1818; and theological schools, 1842; and faculty recruitment, 1843–44, 1879–80, 1894, 1933; letters from, 1852, 1880; and Rotunda, 1853, 1854, 1856; opposes move of William and Mary to Richmond, 1893–94, 1913, 1921, 1922, 1924, 1926; and George Tucker, 1912; and European professors, 1915, 1928; and student discipline, 1920; mentioned, 1829, 1839, 1840, 1911
Cabell, Samuel Jordan: elected to Congress, 871, 875; grand jury presentment of, 973–74, 975, 1014; TJ writes petition against presentment of, 986–90, 1076–78; JM advises TJ on petition, 991–92; leaves Congress early, 1039, 1042, 1052; and Kentucky resolutions, 1067
Cabell, William H. (governor of Virginia), 1450, 1481, 1482, 1483, 1484, 1488, 1506
Cabell family, 507, 534
Cabinet, Washington convenes, 710
Cabin Point, Va., 160
Cabot, George, 718, 1045
Cabot, Samuel, 1219, 1226, 1672
Cadiz, 1377, 1441, 1579, 1582
Cadore, duc de. *See* Champagny, Jean-Baptiste Nompère de
Cadore letter: revokes French decrees, 1658, 1674, 1675
Caesar, Caius, 384
Cahokia, 63
Caldwell, Elias B., 1838
Calhoun, John Caldwell: proposes bonus bill, 1773, 1783, 1980; JM vetoes bonus bill, 1773; secretary of war, 1891; writes *South Carolina Exposition and Protest,* 1980; and nullification doctrine, 1984, 1985, 1988–89, 2002; invokes nullification procedures, 1992, 1993; succeeds Hayne in Senate, 1995; votes for Clay's compromise tariff, 1997; mentioned, 1676
Callender, James Thomson: TJ and, 953, 1163, 1172; accuses Hamilton, 973, 984; indicted for seditious libels, 1116, 1137, 1138; and JM, 1053, 1152, 1160, 1163; and Leiper, 1242
Callis, William Overton, 342
Calonne, Charles-Alexandre de, 457, 467, 530, 692
Calonton, Stephen P., 1213
Calvin, John, 1818
Cambrian (British warship), 1334, 1410, 1462, 1463
Cambridge University, 1885
"Camillus" (pseudonym: Fisher Ames), 813
"Camillus" (pseudonym: Alexander Hamilton), 896, 901
Campbell, Alexander, 921, 925
Campbell, Arthur, 214, 245, 363–64, 407
Campbell, Captain, 1234
Campbell, George Washington, 1550, 1733
Campbell, Hugh, 1303
Campbell, John, 729
Campbell, Lieutenant (British prisoner), 83

Campbell, Mr., 1436
Campbell, William, 1909, 1922
Canada: TJ on acquisition of, 1568, 1586
Canals: in Virginia, 280–81; TJ on need for, 295–96, 354; JM on need for, 302; Virginia legislature establishes companies for, 331; between Virginia and North Carolina, 358; Tatham suggests, 1560; mentioned, 1917, 1927
"Candid State of Parties, A" (JM), 709–10
Candleberry myrtle trees, 511
Canning, George: disavows right to search U.S. ships of war, 1453; and *Chesapeake* affair, 1496, 1499, 1503; takes hard line with Pinkney, 1508, 1539, 1559; disavows Erskine Agreement, 1569, 1597, 1599; and Portland ministry, 1573; and orders-in-council, 1581; TJ critical of, 1509, 1570, 1571, 1573, 1591; JM wary of, 1534, 1572, 1601, 1607; claims ocean as British conquest, 1602; and European intervention in Americas, 1878, 1880; mentioned, 1470
Cano y Olmedilla, Juan de la Cruz, 692
Cantavelle, Mr., 1343
Cape François, 1260
Capellen, J. D., baron van der, 533
Cape of Good Hope, 1447
Cape Trafalgar, 1404
Cappon, Lester J.: quoted, 10
Caracas, 1648
Cardelli, Peter, 1812
Carey, James, 1042, 1046, 1049
Carey, Matthew, 701
Carey, William, 1248
Carleton, Sir Guy, 74, 91, 247, 680. *See also* Dorchester, Lord
Carleton Island, 1434
Carmichael, William: TJ's appraisal of, 436, 463; in Madrid, 489, 840; mentioned, 163, 200, 779
Caroline County, Va., 759, 816, 886
Carondelet canal, 1369
Carr, Dabney (TJ's friend and brother-in-law), 285, 316
Carr, Dabney, Jr.: and educational oversight by JM, 285, 316, 323, 351, 364; tutored by Peter Carr, 370; at Hampden-Sydney Academy, 370–71, 392, 421, 468, 479; TJ supplies funds to educate, 489; mentioned, 434, 1727, 1910, 1916, 1933, 1939
Carr, Martha Jefferson (Mrs. Dabney): TJ supplies funds to educate sons of, 323, 342, 414, 468, 487, 489, 581; mentioned, 207, 285, 316, 407, 433, 454
Carr, Peter: and educational oversight by JM, 273–74, 285, 288, 290, 316, 323, 342, 351; goes to Walker Maury's school, 323, 342, 364, 370, 392, 407; TJ supplies funds for education of, 381, 468, 489; at William and Mary, 433, 479; visits New York, 614, 615; sells property, 868; in Philadelphia, 907; circulates petition against Cabell's presentment, 975, 986; son dies, 1148; and Samuel Smith, 1495; captain in cavalry, 1697; and Charles Jouett, 1767; mentioned, 931, 1121, 1161, 1604, 1666, 1727
Carr, Sam, 1486
Carr, Samuel, 1727
Carriage tax: TJ on, 872; mentioned, 841, 842, 845, 921, 925
Carrington, Edward: in Confederation Congress, 408, 456; TJ writes, 519, 520; sends *The Federalist* to TJ, 524, 548, 567; and John Paul Jones's bust, 610, 636; on excise law, 689; federal collector of revenue in Virginia, 743; and Jay's treaty, 896; mentioned, 495, 506, 542, 1366
Carrington, Paul, 507
Carroll, Charles, 223, 478, 508
Carroll, Daniel: in Confederation Congress, 246; opposes Annapolis Convention, 420; delegate to Constitutional Convention, 478, 508; and District of Columbia, 673–74; mentioned, 223, 742, 764
Carroll, Bishop John, 1495, 1575
Carroll, John A.: quoted, 951
Carter, B. M., 1911
Carter, Edward, 369, 420
Cartwright, John, 1991
Cary, Archibald, 70, 84, 216, 473, 477, 492
Cary, Mr., 1249
Casa Calvo, marquis de: and post roads to New Orleans, 1339, 1341–42; TJ proposes expulsion of, 1391, 1392; and status quo in disputed areas, 1415–16; mentioned, 1358, 1389, 1522
Casinove, Mr., 1381
Cass, Lewis, 1839
Castlereagh, Robert Stewart, second viscount: TJ on, 1570, 1591; and War of 1812, 1710; and Andrew Jackson's courtmartial of British traders, 1808; mentioned, 1607, 1681, 1691
Castor, 685–87
Castries, Charles-Eugène-Gabriel de la Croix, marquis de, 346
Caswell, Richard, 85–86, 109–10, 510
Catanzariti, John, 317
Caterpillar, 1425
Cathalan, Étienne, 1244
Cathalan, Stephen, Jr., 1263, 1340, 1366, 1368
Cathalan, Stephen, Sr. (father), 1244
Cathcart, James Leander: consul at Tripoli, 1194, 1315, 1390; and treaty with Tunis, 1214; flees Tripoli for Italy, 1228; JM's instructions to, 1240; and Eaton, 1267; and factorship among Indians, 1390; and Mellimelli, 1428, 1429, 1432, 1435; mentioned, 1265, 1301, 1434, 1437, 1440, 1522
Catherine the Great, 262, 284, 290, 308, 536, 630
"Catullus" (pseudonym: Alexander Hamilton), 766
"Causes and Conduct of the War [of 1812], The": white paper on, 1757–58, 1763–64, 1766
Celia (slave), 161
Census: Senate rejects bill for, 654; in Virginia, 689; of 1790, 707; second, 1204–5
Centerville, Va., 1177
Central College: Board of Visitors meets, 1776–77, 1785; selects site near Charlottesville, 1777; TJ and, 1778–79, 1781, 1789, 1799–1800; first pavilion at, 1788; fund raising for, 1787, 1789, 1802, 1804; agrees to deed property to university, 1793, 1796; final board meeting of, 1795–96; mentioned, 1807, 1818, 1932
Ceracchi, Mrs. Giuseppe, 1381
Ceres (American ship): TJ sails aboard, 321, 325
Cerfs (deer), 391
Cevallos, Pedro de, 1323, 1347, 1355, 1522
Chalmers, George, 861, 866
Chamberlain, Mr. (brickmason), 1858
Champagne, 391
Champagny, Jean-Baptiste Nompère de, duc de Cadore, 1513, 1544, 1618
Champion, Richard, 679
Channing, Edward: quoted, 1256
Charles (archduke of Austria), 1595
Charles II (king of England), 783, 1279
Charles III (king of Spain), 250
Charles IV (king of Spain), 1323, 1527, 1608
Charles Carter (American ship), 1276
Charles City County, Va., 159, 908
Charleston, S.C.: British capture of, 127, 135–36, 139, 140; French citizens in, outfit privateers, 778–79; favors commercial discrimination, 838; mentioned, 1139, 1307, 1332
Charlestown (British frigate), 160
Charlestown, Mississippi Territory, 1475
Charlestown, S.C. *See* Charleston, S.C.
Charlottesville, Va.: Lafayette visits, 1902, 1903; mentioned, 176–77, 199, 816, 1429, 1442

INDEX

2027

Charlottesville *Central Gazette,* 1930
Charters, 1922
Chase, Samuel, 369, 504, 508, 531, 919
Chastellux, Alfred de, 922
Chastellux, François-Jean, marquis de, 206, 207, 216, 297
Chastellux, Marie-Josephine-Charlotte-Brigette Plunkett, marquise de, 902, 920
Chatham, Va., 817
Chatham, William Pitt, first earl of, 800, 808
Chauncey, Isaac, 1712, 1782
Chauvelin, François Bernard, marquis de, 767
Chauvigny, Bertier de, 626
Cheatham, James. *See* Cheetham, James
Checks and balances, 669, 709
Cheetham, James, 1156, 1541
Chemistry: JM's interest in, 425, 465, 487
Cherokee Indians: in Revolution, 67, 78; intruders on land of, 1574–75; mentioned, 80, 104, 109–10, 1426
Cherries: French and American compared, 391
Cherry, William, 96
Chesapeake (U.S. frigate), 1234, 1421, 1512
Chesapeake affair: British impress sailors from U.S. warship, 1445; crisis following attack on, 1449–50, 1452; TJ condemns attack, 1476–79, 1488; British execute impressed sailors, 1499; negotiations over, break down of, 1504;
· mentioned, 1675
Chesapeake Bay, 154, 1711, 1719–20
Chester, Pa., 664
Chesterfield County, Va., 1133
Chestertown, Md., 146
Chevalier, M., 454
Chewning, Reuben, 1084
Chichester (British frigate), 1439, 1488
Chickamauga Indians, 78
Chickasaw Bluffs, Tenn., 964, 1606, 1609
Chickasaw Indians, 1426, 1574–75
Chihuahua, Mexico, 1493
Childs, Francis, 685, 698, 700
China, 1447
Chinard, Gilbert: quoted, 584–85, 603, 631
Chinch bug, 338
Chipman, Darius, 1250
Chipman, Nathaniel, 1013
Chisholm, Hugh, 1540, 1546, 1570
Chisholm, John, 1326
Chisman, Mount Edward, 1347
Cholera morbus: and JM, 14, 992
Chote, Mr., 1329
Chouteau, René Auguste, 1743
Christian, William (of Kentucky), 421
Christian, William (of Virginia), 96, 363
Christie, Gabriel, 874, 875
Chuning, Mr. *See* Chewning, Reuben
Church, Angelica, 995
Church, Edward, 1197
Ciphers: used by TJ and JM, 6, 217; JM's use of, 347; TJ revises, 372; TJ makes new one, 387; TJ and JM resume use of, 750; mentioned, 248–49, 260, 469, 608
Ciracchi, Mrs. *See* Ceracchi, Mrs. Giuseppe
Cissi Mohammed, Bashaw. *See* Karamanli, Hamet
Citizen Genet (French privateer), 805
"Citizen of N. York, a" (James Cheetham writes as), 1156
"Citizen of the United States, A" (JM writes as), 1073, 1094
City Point, Va., 159
Civil liberties: Kentucky and Virginia resolutions and, 1067, 1069, 1072
Civil rights, 448
Civil war: JM fears, 1983, 1986, 1989, 1992, 1995, 1998

Claiborne, William Charles Coles: governor of Mississippi Territory, 1236, 1299; governor of Orleans Territory, 1304, 1333, 1336; cannot find Treaty of 1762, 1306; charters bank in New Orleans, 1310; and bank failure, 1323; and St. Julien, 1328; and West Florida, 1329, 1358; and Indian trade, 1329–30; and post roads, 1339; orders departure of former authorities, 1341; and legislative council, 1343; political adversaries of, 1366; TJ on, 1367; and Casa Calvo, 1389, 1392, 1402; and status quo in disputed areas, 1415–16; and Wilkinson, 1456; and Folch, 1498; on public property in New Orleans, 1513–14; and navigation of Mississippi, 1517; and prize sloop *Guadaloupe,* 1526; claims batture for United States, 1619; and merino sheep, 1649; mentioned, 1337, 1340, 1434, 1528, 1531
Claims law, 1773, 1782
Clairfayt, General, 772
Clark, Abraham, 478, 843, 859
Clark, Christopher, 1423
Clark, Daniel: appointed to legislative council of Orleans territory, 1336, 1337, 1343; mentioned, 1040, 1242, 1244, 1280, 1281, 1286, 1299, 1663, 1664
Clark, George Rogers: and Henry Hamilton, 63, 77, 78, 80, 90; and Oliver Pollock, 105, 107; western campaign of, 134; and Simon Nathan, 135; mentioned, 67, 71, 103, 159, 168
Clark, William, 1257, 1480, 1608
Clarke, Dr., 1522, 1526
Clarke, Mr., 1512
Clarke, Mr.: and Emden, 1278
Classes, social: JM on, 501
Clavière, Étienne, 735–36
Clay, Henry: Speaker of the House, 1891; and Kentucky resolutions, 1990; and tariff of 1832, 1992; and JM, 1997; mentioned, 1676, 1710, 1734
Clay, Joseph, 1190, 1191, 1666
Clay, Matthew, 769, 979, 980, 1042, 1052
Claypoole, David, 982
Clergy: order in Estates General, 616, 617, 624, 625
Clérisseau, Charles-Louis, 335, 384–85
Clermont (estate), 1160
Cleveland, William, 1241, 1251
Clinton, Cornelia Tappen, 758, 829
Clinton, DeWitt: and Mellimelli, 1411; and rebellious Tunisians, 1427, 1428, 1429, 1430, 1432, 1435, 1436; runs against JM in 1812, 1685; mentioned, 1198, 1440
Clinton, George: as Antifederalist, 579, 605; and New York gubernatorial election of 1792, 728; TJ doubts republicanism of, 731–32; runs for vice president in 1792, 744–45; and election of 1800, 1129, 1131; and Guadaloupe negroes, 1240; nominated for vice presidency, 1352, 1548; presidential ambitions of, 1548; turns against embargo, 1552; ignored by JM, 1650; defeats recharter of Bank of the United States, 1651; death of, 1685; mentioned, 179, 873, 1199, 1337, 1521
Clinton, Sir Henry: succeeds Howe as British commander, 58; captures Charleston, 127, 136, 141; raids Chesapeake, 129; and mutiny of Pennsylvania Line, 157; mentioned, 160, 164, 193, 198
Clock, pendulum, 494
Clopton, John, 1039, 1042
Cloture, 1677
Cloupet, Captain, 1275, 1284
Clymer, George, 478
Coaster, 685–87
Cobb, Gideon D., 1476
Cobbett, William, 907, 973, 1415, 1504. *See also Porcupine's Gazette*
Cobham, Va., 159

Coburn, Mr., 1368
Cochran, Robert, 1464
Cochrane, Sir Alexander, 1731, 1753
Cockburn, Sir George, 1711, 1731
Cocke, John Hartwell: and Central College, 1776, 1777, 1784, 1787, 1802, 1807; joins university Board of Visitors, 1795; and architectural plan, 1797–98; opposes Cooper's appointment, 1808; and sea kale, 1822; illness of, 1834; and Rotunda, 1843, 1853, 1856; and faculty appointments, 1894, 1908, 1938; and student discipline, 1920; mentioned, 1785, 1814, 1815, 1839, 1841
Cocke, Mr. (at Martinique), 1484, 1485
Code d'humanité, 367
Codman, Richard, 1088
Coffee, John William, 1803–4
Cohen, William, 15
Cohens v. *Virginia,* 1849, 1864, 1865, 1866, 1870
Coit, Joshua, 996, 1003, 1042
Coke, Sir Edward, 278, 304, 319, 1916, 1922, 1958, 1965
Colchester, Va., 765
Colchis, 737
Colden, Alexander, 612, 613
Colden, Cadwallader, 612
Colden, Henrietta Bethune, 612
Coleman, Samuel, 87
Coles, Catherine Thompson (Mrs. Isaac), 847
Coles, Edward, 8, 1776, 1782, 1789, 1998
Coles, Captain Isaac: TJ's private secretary, 1577; mission to France, 1594, 1597, 1599; and papers of Meriwether Lewis, 1609; on Smyth's debacle at Niagara, 1709, 1714–15, 1717; mentioned, 1602, 1603, 1605, 1649
Coles, Colonel Isaac: elected to Congress, 605, 769; and Patrick Henry, 903; mentioned, 847
College of New Jersey: JM attends, 38.
College of Philadelphia (University of Pennsylvania), 487
College of William and Mary. *See* William and Mary, College of
Collins, Thomas, 1263
Collot, Victor, 1003, 1042
Colonial Williamsburg Foundation, 648
Colonization: of emancipated slaves, 20, 22
Colorado River, 1327, 1329, 1396
Columbia, Va., 1475
Columbian Magazine, 506
Columbine (British ship), 1488
Comité, Le: carries military supplies for Virginia, 134, 155, 160, 166, 173, 179, 183, 185, 188
Commager, Henry Steele: quoted, 92
Commercial depression of 1784–1785, 393
Commercial discrimination: Great Britain imposes, on American trade, 435; JM on need for, 593, 608, 711, 834, 835–36, 837; Senate opposes, 593, 613, 619–20; TJ on need for, 629
Commercial regulation: efforts to empower Confederation for, 313, 327–28, 380–81, 388, 394–95; and call for Annapolis Convention, 404; TJ on necessity for, 410; JM on necessity for, 414–15; under Constitution, 491, 503, 711–12, 1409, 1448, 1976–77
Commercial report: by TJ, 831–32
Commercial treaties: Confederation and, 314; TJ drafts instructions for negotiating, 326–28; TJ and John Adams's efforts to negotiate, 417; with France, 593; proposed, with Great Britain, 593
Committee of the States: proposed, 309, 458; acts as executive during recess of Confederation Congress, 329, 480; ineffectiveness of, 343–44; TJ inquires about, 365; dissolution of, 374; mentioned, 294, 301, 316, 349
Committee on "the natural history of Hessian fly," 690
Committee on Ways and Means: creation of, 838, 890; and Hamilton, 838; proposes new taxes, 841, 842; and land tax, 963–64; mentioned, 845, 916–17
Common law, federal: Federalists claim jurisdiction under, 1064; Bache and Burk indicted under, 1068; TJ denies existence of, 1068; Republicans reject, 1112; JM denies existence of, 1124, 1125, 1126; and Duane's indictment, 1183–84
Common law, state, 1121
Commons: order in Estates General, 616–17. *See also* Third Estate
Common Sense (Thomas Paine), 687
Compact Maritime (Thomas Paine), 1161
Compact theory: TJ on, 1069–70, 1082–83; JM disagrees with TJ on, 1109; Calhoun's definition of, 1980; JM's definition of, 1981, 1982
Compensation Law, 1782
Competitor (ship), 1912, 1924
Compromise of 1790: and location of national capital, 643–45, 768
Comptes rendus au Roi, 537
Condé-sur-l'Escaut, France, 794
Conditional termination of slavery, 16
Condorcet, Marie-Jean-Antoine-Nicolas de Caritat, marquis de, 544, 562, 583, 607
Condy, Jonathan Williams, 976
Congress *Continental*: rejects parliamentary authority over colonies, 42; recommends that Virginia establish provincial government, 48; votes for independence, 49, 50; protests Virginia's retention of Continental arms, 65–66; adopts Virginia's plan for western land cessions, 130; recommends mid-Atlantic states supply southern army, 167; mentioned, 45, 1287 *Confederation*: and JM's proposal for Library of Congress, 14; finances of, 192; ratifies Treaty of Paris, 209; criticism of itinerant moves of, 271; TJ favors strengthening of, 321; JM favors strengthening of, 387–88; and commercial regulations, 388; defaults on Dutch loan, 453; expires, 590 *Federal*: adopts thirty-day embargo against Great Britain, 826; debates nonimportation bill, 827; considers change of meeting place, 828; amends excise tax in 1792, 850; votes to implement Jay's treaty, 894; special session in 1797, 968, 982, 983; enacts defense and internal security program in 1798, 1003–4; funds Louisiana negotiations, 1255; funds Lewis and Clark expedition, 1257; enacts retaliatory measures against British impressment officers, 1359; requires armed U.S. merchant ships to post bond, 1363–64; funds Florida negotiations, 1400; passes Nonimportation Act, 1409; passes Embargo Act, 1504, 1551; enacts defense measures, 1506–7; JM on "unhinged state" of, 1626; dominated by war hawks, 1676, 1677, 1727; declares war, 1680; excludes British seamen from American vessels, 1730; Virginia Board of Visitors petitions, 1836–37; passes "Tariff of Abominations," 1979
Congressional Register, 607
Congress of Vienna, 1753, 1758, 1763
Connecticut: and Revolutionary finances, 138; western land claims of, 210; and revenue system of 1783, 237; TJ visits, 285, 321; rejects paper money, 430; ratifies Constitution, 504, 508, 519, 531; federal lawsuits in, 1217; in election of 1804, 1352; opposes Embargo Act, 1551
Connecticut Historical Society, 1010
Connecticut River, 670, 687
Conrad's Hotel, 1161
Constable, William, 697
Constantine (prince of Russia), 134
Constantinople, 1095, 1308
Constellation (U.S. frigate), 1128

INDEX

Constitutional construction, 31, 32–35
Construction Construed and Constitutions Vindicated (John Taylor), 1851
Constitution, federal: JM sends copy to TJ, 445; relation of, to American Revolution and Declaration of Independence, 595; as functional Bill of Rights, 596; as culmination of American Revolution, 600; TJ on, 1164; JM praises forty years under, 1773
Constitution (U.S. warship), 1234, 1685, 1689
Constitutional Convention: call for, issued by Annapolis Convention, 396; JM's preparation for, 439–42; JM's "Notes of Debates" of, 444, 681, 1640; TJ on need for, 458; meets in secret sessions, 478, 490, 892; JM outlines provisions of, 490–91; JM describes work of, 496–504, 1851; movement for second, 520, 521, 551–52, 554, 580; JM on danger of second, 550; opposition to second, 567, 579; federal elections thwart calling of, 582; Theodorick Bland favors, 594; unpublished journal of, 681; and Hamilton's plan, 1640–41; mentioned, 281
Continental army, 139, 140
Continental Association, 42, 48
Continental Board of War, 174
Continental currency: depreciation of, 125–26, 174, 181, 196; exchange rate in Virginia, 149–50; and state redemption of, 156; TJ on lack of, 175–76, 184; collapse of, 176, 195, 196; Congress reports on, 314–15, 316–17; mentioned, 310–11
Continental finances: and state requisitions, 142–43, 144–45
Continuous voyage: doctrine of, 1360, 1413–14
Convention army. *See* Saratoga prisoners
Convention of 1800: ends quasi war, 1142, 1180, 1200, 1207; arrives in United States, 1154; TJ on, 1156, 1170; JM on, 1158, 1159, 1198; and British snow *Windsor,* 1185; ratification of, 1190, 1196; expenses to implement, 1215; mentioned, 1151, 1169
Cook, Orchard, 1553–54
Cooper, Richard, 1219
Cooper, Thomas: represents Duane, 1115; indicted for seditious libel, 1116; political pamphlet by, 1131; on admiralty courts, 1637, 1638; TJ's appraisal of, 1638; and Central College, 1788, 1789–90, 1799–1800, 1801, 1802, 1803, 1807; visits Monticello, 1804; appointed professor at Virginia, 1799, 1808, 1809, 1810, 1816; resigns teaching post, 1818; payment of, 1822; does not reapply at Virginia, 1883; and controversy with William Johnson, 1868; at South Carolina College, 1890–91; mentioned, 1813, 1904, 1910
Cooper, Mrs. Thomas, 1813
Cooper's Town, N.Y., 1219
Copenhagen, 1600, 1601
Copernicus, 1879
Copper mines, 1219
Copying press, 381, 412, 414, 465, 474, 487
Corbin, Francis, 404, 509, 534, 743
Corcoran, Thomas, 1465
Cork acorns, 529, 542
Cork, Ireland, 1278
Corn: crop in 1784, 338; price in 1785, 371, 375; price in 1786, 408, 416, 420–21, 457; crop in 1787, 484, 491; crop in 1788, 553; guinea, from Jamaica, 693, 694; crop in 1792, 738; crop in 1793, 794, 798, 799, 800, 810; price in 1794, 858, 860, 865; price in 1796, 918, 928, 932; proposed embargo on, 931; price in 1805, 1379; crop in 1806, 1425, 1428–29, 1430, 1438; crop of 1809, 1604; crop of 1810, 1638; crop of 1812, 1695; crop of 1813, 1723; crop of 1814, 1741; crop of 1817, 1781; supplied to West Indies by evasion of embargo, 1534
Cornell, Ezekiel, 196

Cornwallis, Charles, first marquis and second earl: captures Charleston, 127; commands British troops in South, 141, 172–73, 176, 177; surrenders at Yorktown, 202, 204; exchanged for Laurens, 224; mentioned, 218
Corporations, 1921
Correa de Serra, Abbe José Francisco, 1804, 1809, 1826
Corruption, 727
Cortés, Hernando, 840, 841
Corunna (La Coruña), Spain, 1133
Cosway, Maria, 13, 400, 602
Coulaux la Vigne (Vigna), J., 185
Council of State. *See* Virginia Executive Council
Courier (London paper), 1665–66
Courier d'Europe (French merchant ship), 163
Courts of assize: established in Virginia, 330–31, 355–56, 374; suspended, 394, 404; repealed, 438, 456
Cowper, William, 3
Cox, James M., 4
Coxe, Charles D., 1191, 1192
Coxe, Tench: assistant secretary of treasury, 679, 700; writes *A Brief Examination of Lord Sheffield's Observations...,* 701, 703, 704; Federalists dismiss, 1012, 1157; TJ appoints, as supervisor, 1231; letter from, 1425, 1878; writes memoir on cotton manufactures, 1806, 1807; and Tenure of Office Act, 1825, 1826; on Missouri crisis, 1828; mentioned, 702, 766, 869, 897, 1191, 1251, 1272, 1301, 1857
Craig, Sir James Henry, 1690
Cramond, John, 186
Cranberries, 493, 508, 529
Cranmer, Mr. *See* Cramond, John
Cranz, David, 734
Craunch, Mr., 1274
Craven, John, 1148
Crawford, William H.: and recharter of Bank of United States, 1651; mentioned, 1213, 1747–48, 1752, 1880, 1881, 1891
Credit: TJ on national need for, 536–37
Creek Indians, 507, 779, 787
Crèvecoeur, Michel-Guillaume St. Jean de, 532, 562
Crockett, Joseph, 96, 105
Cromwell, Oliver, 1898
Crop rotation: TJ on, 789–91, 848; Logan on, 961
Cross, Jeanne, 1270
Cross, Ralph, 1251
Crowninshield, Benjamin Williams, 1733
Crowninshield, Jacob, 1492, 1496
Cuba: TJ on acquisition of, 1452, 1568, 1583, 1586; Turreau's reaction to TJ's interest in, 1587
Cuisagues, Mr., 1336
Cullen, Professor, 1903
Culpeper, Va., 148, 708, 1524, 1932
Cumberland, Richard, 200
Cumberland, Va., 155
Cumberland Road, 1427
Cummings, Alexander, 81
Cunningham, Noble E., Jr.: quoted, 1364
Curaçao, 169, 1472
"Curtius" (pseudonym: Noah Webster and James Kent), 897
Curwen, Samuel, 58
Cushing, William, 919, 1620, 1646
Custis, George Washington Parke, 701
Custom duties: and Hamiltonian system, 710–11
Cutts, Anna Payne, 1362
Cutts, Richard, 1362

Dade, Mr., 1527
Dade, W. A. C.: considered for law professorship at university, 1916, 1932, 1937–39, 1940, 1964

Dalbarton, M.: alias for Jerome Bonaparte, 1275
D'Albon, Claude Camille François, comte, 485
Dale, Richard, 1170, 1197, 1259
Dallas, Alexander James: and Genet, 775, 813; and Duane case, 1115, 1182, 1183, 1184, 1190, 1191; on Jackson's case, 1228; and *New Jersey,* 1393; and recharter of Bank of the United States, 1736; and white paper on War of 1812, 1756, 1762, 1773; mentioned, 1363, 1733, 1737
Dalton, Tristram, 579, 1373, 1375
Damen, John, 1340
Dana, Francis: minister to Russia, 262; delegate to Constitutional Convention, 469; nominated envoy to France, 978, 983; mentioned, 250, 374, 1099
Danbury, Conn., 1128
Dandridge, Bartholemew, 371
Dane, Nathan, 505
Dangerfield, George: quoted, 1984
Danish West Indies, 1261, 1488
D'Anmours, Charles François, chevalier, 67, 108, 116
D'Arendt, Henri Léonard Philip, Baron, 135, 155, 161, 163
Dartmouth College case, 1913
Daschkoff, Andre de, 1594, 1595, 1596–97, 1602
D'Aubenton, Louis-Jean-Marie, 421, 425
Dauer, Manning J.: quoted, 1114
Daugherty, Joseph, 1627, 1637, 1638, 1765
David, Jacques-Louis, 1774
Davie, William R., 478, 1154, 1155, 1158
Davis, Augustine, 831
Davis, David Brion: quoted, 15, 16
Davis, George: and treaty with Tunis, 1214; and Mellimelli, 1403; consul in Tripoli, 1511; mentioned, 1281, 1340, 1341
Davis, Isaac, Jr., 1134
Davis, John, 1495
Davis, Jonathan, 1476
Davis, Judge, 1236
Davis, Matthew Livingston, 1197–98, 1199
Davis, Mr.: and La Plata provinces, 1243
Davis, Thomas T., 1197
Davis, William, 178, 185, 188
Dawidoff, Robert: quoted, 3–4
Dawson, John: opposes tariff, 534; and JM, 890, 1019, 1123, 1125, 1150; and "Liston's plot," 992; on election in 1800, 1147; and Convention of 1800, 1190, 1214, 1278; and Jerome Bonaparte, 1276; allowance for, 1282; mentioned, 984, 1046, 1089, 1275
Dawson, Mr., 1841
Dayton, Jonathan: and sequestration of British debts, 826, 838; reelected, 870; Speaker of the House, 906; joins Federalists, 1020; and Burr conspiracy, 1444, 1445; mentioned, 902, 978, 1486
Dean, Joseph, 1465
Deane, Silas: and alliance with France, 53; returns to United States, 630; mentioned, 203, 304, 319, 321, 337
Dearborn, Henry: appointed secretary of war, 1167, 1174, 1175; recommends Gilman, 1179; health of, 1241; goes to Philadelphia, 1225; and Santo Domingo blacks, 1248; and intruders on public lands, 1303; and TJ, 1376, 1387, 1416, 1540, 1707; and Miranda case, 1407, 1425; orders expulsion of Spanish forces, 1416; remains in Washington, 1422; investigates British fort on isthmus, 1434; and Bayou Pierre, 1473; and Burr conspiracy, 1475; and flags of truce, 1482; and enlistment of foreign deserters, 1489, 1523; and Pike's expenses, 1493; and Bishop Carroll, 1495; and Judge Woodward, 1498; posts troops near Floridas and Texas, 1508, 1533; in Maine, 1527; orders intruders off Indian lands, 1574; and Indian school, 1575, 1612–13; and son's military commission, 1578; on Bidwell, 1646; as general in War of 1812, 1682, 1683, 1684, 1702, 1703, 1717, 1739; on De la Croix, 1686; and military stores in Virginia, 1697; relieved of command, 1713; and Charles Jouett, 1767; and embargo, 1896; mentioned, 1244, 1259, 1484, 1514, 1522, 1523, 1705
Debnam, Mr., 908
Debtors, 415, 429
Decatur, Stephen: commander of Norfolk navy yard, 1449–50; and interdicted British vessels, 1482, 1492, 1497; and treaty with Algiers, 1779; mentioned, 1725
"Decius" (pseudonym: John Randolph), 1423
Declaration of Independence: TJ on, 2, 1164–65; antislavery views in draft of, 18; political principles in, 49–50; adoption of, 51; TJ sends copy to JM, 234, 249; principles of, implemented by Constitution, 595; amount of time to compose, 1164; TJ's reputation as author of, 1845–47; TJ on fiftieth anniversary of, 1961, 1973; mentioned, 1918, 1924
Declaration of Independence, The (painting), 1774, 1878
"Declaration of the Causes and Necessity for Taking Up Arms" (TJ), 46–47, 50
Declaration of the Rights of Man and the Citizen: TJ and Lafayette collaborate on, 528, 603, 627, 631
Deer, 391, 421
Deer park, 857
Defence of the Constitutions of Government of the United States of America, A (John Adams), 478–79, 688
Deference: John Adams on, 669
Defiance (British warship), 136
Definition of Parties, A (John Taylor), 844
Degen, Charles Frederic, 1522
De Grasse, François-Joseph-Paul, comte, 200
Dejean, Philip, 74, 75, 95, 118
De la Croix, Jacques Vincent, 1686
De la Forest, Antoine-René-Charles-Mathurin, 515, 833
Delaware: JM denounces, 187; favors impost, 232, 263; and revenue system of 1783, 238; ratifies Constitution, 451, 508, 515, 519, 530; election of 1795 in, 899; federal lawsuits in, 1217; election of 1804 in, 1352
Delaware Bay, 190
Delaware River, 429, 1188, 1253, 1308, 1666
Delvahar, Mr., 1336
Demobilization: after Revolution, 233, 235
Democratic-Republican party. *See* Republican party
Democratic societies: oppose Jay as envoy to England, 843; and Whiskey Rebellion, 852, 853–54; JM on, 861–64; Washington denounces, 892
Democratic Society of Philadelphia, 756–57, 804
Democracy: JM on simple, 500–1; Edmund Burke denounces, 668
Denmark, 1600
De Peyster, Mr., 1474
De Ponceau, Mr., 1437
Derbigny, Pierre Auguste Charles Bourguignon, 1343
Derieux, Justin Pierre Plumard, 1278, 1280, 1281, 1282, 1283, 1306
Descamps, Jacob, 1475
Desforneaux, Edmé-Etienne Borne, 1096
Despinville, Count, 1686
Dessalines, Jean-Jacques, 1348
Destouches, Charles-René-Dominique Gochet, Chevalier, 133, 154, 165, 166, 167, 179
Destréhan, Jean Noël, 1343
Detourt, Mr., 1485
Detrahan, Mr. *See* Destréhan, Jean Noël

INDEX

Detroit: speculation in lands near, 905–6; Father Richard's school at, 1575, 1611; Hull surrenders, 1683, 1705; recapture of, 1712; mentioned, 1347, 1524, 1702
Dexter, Samuel: and elections of 1794, 859, 866; and Naturalization Act of 1795, 869; and election of 1795, 870–71, 872–73; continues temporarily in Treasury Department under TJ, 1174
Dey of Algiers, 1263, 1265, 1779, 1782
Dick, Elisha Cullen, 1465
Dickerson, Mahlon, 1331, 1334, 1336
Dickinson, John: collaborates with TJ on "Causes and Necessity for Taking Up Arms," 46–47; president of Supreme Executive Council of Pennsylvania, 320; delegate to Constitutional Convention, 478; writes as "Fabius," 982; mentioned, 1287
Dickson, Harold E.: quoted, 648
Dictionnaire historique et bibliographie portarif (Ladvocat), 647
Diderot, Denis, 13
Diffusion of slavery: TJ and JM advocate, 24–25
Digges, Dudley, 60
Dinmore, Richard, 1465
Dinsmore, James, 1540, 1546, 1570, 1583, 1858
Directory, French, 1052, 1057
Direct taxes, 917
"Discourses on Davila" (John Adams), 688, 691
Dismal Swamp, 407, 429
District courts in Virginia, 467, 532
District of Columbia: as location of national capital, 659–61, 662, 764–65
Disunion: Patrick Henry and, 534
Divers, George, 1727, 1794, 1805, 1814, 1822
Divers, Mr., 1148
Diverting History of John Bull and Brother Jonathan, The (Paulding), 1686, 1706
Division of powers: between federal and state governments, 446, 496; TJ on, 458; debates in Constitutional Convention on, 498–502
Dixon, John, 687
Dobbyns, Mr., 546–47
Dobell, Peter, 1301
Dobson, Thomas, 871
Dodge, John, 74
Dodge, Mr. (consul at Marsailles), 1858
Dogs, shepherd, 1640, 1641, 1642
Dogwood trees, 511
Dohrman, Arnold Henry: U.S. agent in Lisbon, 479–50; and debt to Mazzei, 548, 676, 684, 700, 702, 858, 859, 879, 918; pays debt, 928, 933; mentioned, 484, 492
Dohrman, Mr. (brother of Arnold), 684
Donald, Alexander, 492, 507, 532, 542
Donath, Joseph, 1047
Donath, Josiah, 871, 874
Don Quixote, 1680, 1697
Doradour, Comte, 372, 387
Dorchester, Guy Carlton, Lord: and Nootka Sound incident, 646–47; governor-general of Canada, 680; Beckwith as agent for, 681–83; predicts war between Indians and United States, 845. *See also* Carleton, Sir Guy
Doublehead (chief of Chickasaws), 1575
Dougherty, Joseph. *See* Daugherty, Joseph
Douglas, Captain, 1276
Douglas, Mr., 722
Doury, Mr., 1520
Dow, Robert, 1336, 1337, 1343
Draft, military, 67
Drayton, William, 529
Drew, Elizabeth, 7
Driver (British frigate), 1463, 1488
Drought, 730
Drummond, Captain, 1378

Drummond, Sir Gordon, 1684, 1751
Duane, James, 542
Duane, William: condemned by Senate, 1115, 1116, 1128–29, 1190, 1191; indicted under Sedition Law, 1172, 1182–83, 1184, 1190, 1654; indicted for stealing Liston's dispatches, 1182–83; on acquisition of Louisiana, 1276, 1280; TJ's appraisal of, 1283–84; attacks Gallatin, 1650, 1652, 1654; and Robert Smith, 1655; TJ tries to raise money for, 1666; breaks with JM, 1668; publishes white paper on War of 1812, 1758; mentioned, 1277, 1278
Dublin, Ireland, 353
Dubuys, Mr., 1336, 1343
Dudley, Benjamin, 304, 313, 318
Dudley, Thomas, 1300
Duer, William, 737, 766, 768
Duffield, George, 1365
Dugan, Mr., 1324
Dumas, Charles William Frederic: U.S. agent at The Hague, 250, 453, 482, 491
Dumfries, Va., 1332
Dumouriez, Charles-François du Périer: defects to Austrians, 782–83, 785, 788, 838; mentioned, 736, 776, 779, 819
Dunbar, Mr., 1524
Dunbar, Robert, 1044
Duncansern, Mr., 1425
Duncanson, Major, 1780
Duncanson, Mr. (nephew of Major Duncanson), 1780
Dundas, Henry, Lord Melville, 1472
Dunglison, Robley: on TJ and JM's relationship, 12, 26–27; attends TJ during final illness, 1961, 1972–73; mentioned, 1886, 1908, 1910, 1911
Dunkirk, France, 829
Dunlap, John, 143–44, 166, 766, 768, 802
Dunmore, Lord. *See* Murray, John, fourth earl of
Duplaine, Antoine Charbonnet, 812–13
Duplantier, Armand, 1425, 1631
Dupont, François, 819
Du Pont, Victor, 1055, 1057
Du Pont de l'Étang, Pierre-Antoine, Comte 1546
Du Pont de Nemours, Eleuthère Irenée, 1770
Du Pont de Nemours, Marie Françoise Robin Poivre (Mrs. Pierre-Samuel), 1133
Du Pont de Nemours, Pierre-Samuel: negotiates commercial treaty between France and England, 544; sends pamphlet to JM, 562; JM's appraisal of, 1134; intermediary in Louisiana negotiations, 1253, 1262; to come to United States, 1369; on claims under Convention of 1800, 1376–77; and national plan of education, 1603, 1604; on government finances, 1659; visits Monticello, 1770; mentioned, 1133, 1225, 1228, 1247, 1554
Durand, Asher Brown, 1878
Durfes, Thomas, 1300
Dutch East Indies, 1447
Dutch loan (of 1793), 798
Dutch Luthern Church (Philadelphia), 205
Duties, import: in first Congress, 612, 613, 618–19
Duvall, Gabriel, 1153, 1363, 1861
Duvall, John Pierce, 96
Dynamometer, 1625

Earle, Elias, 1738–39
Early, Passhall, 1134
Earthquakes: near New Madrid, Mo., 1687
Eastburn & Co., 1901
Eastern Junto. *See* Essex Junto
Eastern Shore, 190, 662–63
East Florida: fugitive slaves in, 507; negotiations to acquire, 1327–28, 1354–55, 1396; plans for temporary possession of, 1661; TJ on, 1689; Amelia Island seized, 1692, 1694; Spain cedes to

East Florida (*continued*)
 United States, 1806; Andrew Jackson invades, 1808
Easton, Md., 1300
Easton, Rufus, 1365, 1471
Eastwoode v. Vinke, 722
Eaton, William: consul at Tunis, 1191; TJ's appraisal of, 1193; and treaty with Tunis, 1214; and Cathcart, 1228, 1267; JM's instructions to, 1240; and Tunisian demand for frigate, 1265; critical of naval commanders, 1267; accounts of, 1430–31; Burr offers military command to, 1443; mentioned, 1194, 1213, 1244, 1301
Edinburgh, Scotland, 1789, 1886, 1906, 1909
Edinburgh Review, 1896
Education: and preservation of liberty, 514, 1821
Edwards, Brian, 321
Edwards, H. W., 1480
Edwards, John, 739
Edwards, Jonathan, 552
Edwards, Pierpont: and Miranda trial, 1432; mentioned, 1179, 1423, 1424, 1434
Egglestone, Joseph, 517
Ehrenpreis, Irvin, 7
Eilbeck, Jonathan, 199
Elections: of 1792, 745; of 1793, 768–69; of 1796, 940, 942–48; of 1800, 1112, 1117, 1125, 1129, 1134, 1137–44, 1165; of 1804, 1294; of 1812, 1654–55, 1667, 1685, 1705
Electoral college, 605, 1891
Eleventh Amendment, 1873, 1982
Elizabeth River, 1492, 1493, 1711, 1720
Elizabethtown, N.J., 1469
Elk Hill (TJ's plantation), 177
Elk Run Church, Va., 737, 1226
Elkton, Md., 144, 190, 200, 664, 789, 831
Ellicott, Andrew, 660, 737
Elliot, James, 1250
Elliot, Mr., 1318
Elliot, Robert, 81
Elliott, Professor, 1905
Ellis, Richard: quoted, 1218
Ellsworth, Dorothy (Mrs. Verdine), 689, 690, 691
Ellsworth, Oliver: delegate to Constitutional Convention, 478; Connecticut senator, 579; and election of 1796, 952; envoy to France, 1099; and disputed elections, 1114; resigns as chief justice, 1141, 1154; and Convention of 1800, 1158
Ellsworth, Verdine, 694
Elluots Mills, 1519
Elmer, Jonathan, 579
Elzey, Dr., 1372
Emancipation of slaves, 21
Embargo: in Virginia (1779), 118–19; in Pennsylvania (1781), 189; TJ's early views on, 366; Resolutions of 1794, 834, 836–37, 841, 843, 845; JM endorses idea of (1796), 918–19; JM on efficacy of (1805), 1385; as prelude to war (1812), 1678, 1691, 1692, 1693
Embargo Act: passed by Congress (1807), 1504; enforcement of, 1506–8; TJ's draft of embargo message, 1512–13; JM's draft, 1513; smuggling to avoid, 1532; as issue in election of 1808, 1548–49; debates over continuance, 1550–52; repeal of, 1552; effect in England, 1581; JM laments repeal of, 1616, 1627; spurs domestic manufacturing, 1621; TJ laments repeal of, 1638; secret mission of John Henry during, 1690; TJ on origin of, 1895–96
Embden. *See* Emden, Germany
Emden, Germany, 1278
Emmet, John Patton: appointed at Virginia, 1929; and botanical school, 1970; and enlargement of duties, 1971; mentioned, 1886, 1910, 1911, 1912, 1922, 1928, 1940, 1959, 1962, 1963
Emmius, Ubbo, 495

Emperor of Morocco: seizes American ship, 380; treaty with, 463; and Simpson, 1267; JM on aggressions of, 1302; confirms treaty of 1786, 1303; mentioned, 1210, 1231, 1232, 1233
Encyclopédie méthodique: sketch of JM in, 13, 437–38; prints Virginia Statute for Religious Freedom, 394, 458–59; JM on, 413–14, 419; mentioned, 15, 332, 353, 410–11, 460, 495–96, 610
England: declares war on Netherlands, 169; insurrections in, 514; credit rating of, 536. *See also* Great Britain
Enquiry into the Principles and Tendency of Certain Public Measures, An (John Taylor), 760
Entail, abolition of law of, 54
Enterprise (U.S. schooner), 1228
Envoys to France: John Adams appoints, 978; Gerry replaces Dana, 983; Talleyrand ends discussions with, 1009; Gerry stays after others leave, 1009, 1057, 1062; in Paris, 1014, 1022; JM on difficulties facing negotiators, 1018–19; dispatches published, 1035; JM on XYZ affair, 1051, 1056; instructions to, 1061; Adams declares negotiations ended, 1062; Gerry's dispatches published, 1094, 1096; Adams appoints second mission, 1075, 1097, 1098–99, 1132–33, 1149, 1200; TJ on, 1112, 1123, 1133–34, 1150
Epilepsy, 14
Eppes, Francis, 355, 562, 589, 649
Eppes, John Wayles: marries Maria Jefferson, 994; TJ visits, 1137; visits Monticello, 1145; mentioned, 1145, 1160, 1636, 1745
Eppes, Lucy, 1636
Eppes, Maria Jefferson (TJ's daughter): has accident, 995, 1120; visits Monticello, 1133, 1138, 1145; TJ visits, 1137; TJ contrasts family with political life for, 1143; death of, 1296–97, 1323; illness of, 1304, 1307, 1309, 1310; mentioned, 1143. *See also* Jefferson, Maria
Eppington (plantation), 1607
Erfurt, 1534
Erie Canal, 1881
Ernest, Mathew, 1611
Erskine, David Montagu: quoted, 1074; British minister to United States, and *Chesapeake* affair, 1450, 1482, 1499; and *Cambrian* affair, 1462–63; demands reparations for water casks, 1488; and alleged enlistment of British deserters, 1489, 1490; letter to, 1498; and Clarke's claim, 1512; and British claims in Mississippi Territory, 1517; and prize sloop *Guadaloupe,* 1526–27; and Bailey's letter, 1531; and Rose mission, 1534; TJ on style of, 1545; negotiates Erskine Agreement, 1566, 1569–70, 1571; agreement disavowed by Canning, 1571, 1587, 1591, 1597; and Oakley, 1581; JM on agreement, 1584–85, 1662; TJ on, 1585–86; recalled, 1599; mentioned, 1446
Erskine, Thomas, 982
Erving, George William: TJ's appraisal of, 1152; consul at London, 1179; as claims agent under Jay's treaty, 1220–21, 1670–72; letter from, 1371, 1373, 1520; on Monroe's arrival in London, 1384, 1385; as chargé d'affaires in Madrid, 1385, 1389, 1392; and expulsion of Yrujo, 1426–27; on Bonaparte's attitude towards United States, 1500; and Mobile area, 1522; and Joseph Bonaparte, 1579, 1581; and Hackley, 1582; visits TJ and JM, 1645; Robert Smith's charges against, 1670; mentioned, 1153, 1213, 1226, 1314, 1341, 1544
Erwin, Mr. *See* Erving, George William
Escheat law, 406
Esopus spitzenburg apples, 511
Essex (U.S. frigate), 1428, 1429, 1657, 1665, 1670
Essex case: in British admiralty court, 1359–60, 1389, 1398, 1409, 1410
Essex Junto, 1590, 1690, 1730

Estaing, Charles-Hector, comte d', 165, 411, 658
Estates General: to be convened in Paris, 453, 486, 527, 528, 567, 589; maneuvering in, 600–1; and Louis XVI, 602, 625; three orders in, 610, 616; mentioned, 440
Etruria, 1208
European diplomacy: TJ reports on, from France, 460
Eustis, William: secretary of war, 1688; replaced by Armstrong, 1708, 1714; mentioned, 1559, 1694, 1697, 1767
Evans, Emory G.: quoted, 725
Evans, Thomas, 979, 999, 1029
Eve, George, 591
Everett, Edward, 1859, 1987
Everlasting apples, 511
Ewell, James, 1713
Ewing, Nathaniel, 1348
Examination of the British Doctrine..., An... (JM), 1408
Examination... Respecting the Official Conduct of the Secretary of the Treasury, An (John Beckley), 766
Excise tax: unpopularity of, 729, 850, 867, 869, 873, 917
Expatriation, 723, 1983
Extended republic: JM's theory of, 448–49, 500–2
Extradition, 721

"Fabius" (pseudonym: John Dickinson), 982
Faction: Hamilton calls Republicans a, 714, 735
Fairfax, Thomas, sixth lord, 406
Fairfax County, Va., 504
Fairfax Courthouse, Va., 1176, 1177, 1226
Fairfax Purchase, 817
Falkland Islands, 800
Falls of Delaware: and location of national capital, 268
Falls of Potomac: and location of national capital, 268
Falmouth, England, 1544
Falmouth, Me., 1300
Fame, 2, 3
Farley, Joseph, 1250
Farmers General: and Virginia tobacco, 364; and tobacco monopoly in France, 458, 515; debts owed to, 486
Farmington: designed by TJ, 1794
Farrand, Max: quoted, 518
Fauchet, Jean Antoine Joseph: replaces Genet, 833; JM on, 835, 837; requests recall of Gouverneur Morris, 841; and French loan, 846; publishes pamphlet, 1013
Fauquier County, Va., 708
Fauquier's Courthouse, Va., 1524
Favré, Simon, 1336, 1337
Fayette County, Ky., 553
Febiger, Christian, 183, 188, 193–94
Federal city: loan for, 929. *See also* District of Columbia; Washington, D.C.
Federal common law. *See* Common law, federal
Federal district. *See* District of Columbia
Federal government: inauguration of, 552
Federalist, The: No. 38, 2; JM's contributions to, 4, 519, 548, 1918; No. 10, 29, 448–49, 501, 1353, 1999; No. 49, 29–30; No. 39, 34, 1851, 1869, 1989; JM on legislative sovereignty in, 441; No. 37, 496; No. 45, 499–500; JM sends, to TJ, 524, 551; No. 62, 652; published in France, 747; Marshall on authority of, 1872; Edward Livingston cites, 1988; mentioned, 808, 809, 1924–25
Federalists: TJ labels, as Monocrats, 746, 747, 766, 789, 839, 996; TJ on distinctions between, and Republicans, 747, 774; JM labels, as Anglican party, 758; oppose JM's discriminatory duties, 824–25; denounce Democratic societies, 852; JM calls, "a British party," 884, 890, 969, 982, 996, 1599; support Jay's treaty, 885, 893–94; Marshall as one, 888; JM equates, with "Aristocracy, Anglicanism, and mercantilism," 937; JM calls, British faction, 943, 952, 962; choose John Adams in 1796, 940; TJ calls, "Antirepublicans," 970, 976, 1013, 1017; TJ calls, "Anglican, monarchical, and aristocratical party," 971, 1122, 1862, 1863; TJ on, as advocates of executive power, 996; and XYZ affair, 1002–3, 1006; split on celebration of Washington's birthday, 1024; split into Adams Federalists and High Federalists, 1097, 1099, 1100, 1110, 1118; and constitutional defense of Alien and Sedition laws, 1100–7, 1987; legislative attempt to retain power, 1113–14; TJ calls, "Consolidationers," 1118, 1917; attempt to manipulate election returns in 1800, 1140, 1141, 1142, 1143–44, 1154, 1157; Adams dismisses Hamiltonians in cabinet, 1141; vote for Burr over TJ, 1142, 1143–44, 1156, 1161; TJ appeals to, in inaugural address, 1165; satiric attack on, by TJ, 1364; critical of embargo system, 1507, 1509, 1531, 1538–39; nominate C. C. Pinckney and Rufus King in 1808, 1548; and Erskine Agreement, 1571, 1590; gain seats in 1809, 1585; and *Olmstead* case, 1598; oppose War of 1812, 1682, 1696, 1698, 1700, 1702
Federal negative: JM proposes, 442, 444, 445–49, 470, 498–502; TJ opposes, 442–43, 480–81
Federal-state relations: JM on, 1848–51, 1868–69, 1874–75, 1956–57; TJ on, 1863–64, 1865–66; Marshall on, 1864; Roane on, 1864; mentioned, 1980–82, 1985–87, 1989, 1991–92, 1993–94, 1995–96, 1997–98
Federal supremacy: JM on, 1996, 2000
Federal veto: JM inserts in draft Bill of Rights, 597
Félice, Fortune Barthélemy de, 352
Fenner, Arthur, 1152
Fenno, John: TJ's appraisal of, 699, 878; attacks Edmund Randolph, 904; denounces Monroe's vindication, 1013; prints Adams's answers to addresses, 1039, 1044; denies speculation by congressmen, 1726; mentioned, 672, 735, 791, 802, 807, 1004, 1049, 1065
Fenwick, Thomas, 1465
Ferdinand VII (king of Spain), 1527, 1530, 1579, 1606, 1608
Ferns, 391
Ferrand, Marie-Louis: decree of, 1369, 1370–71; TJ on, 1371; mentioned, 1414, 1468
Feudal constitutions, 499–500
Few, William, 478, 1326
Findley, William, 1052
Fine arts: TJ's interest in, 37
Finnie, William, 72, 82, 184, 188
Firearms, 65–66, 73
First Amendment: TJ on, 1080–81; Federalists' views on, 1104; mentioned, 1918. *See also* Bill of Rights, federal; Freedom of the press; Freedom of religion
Fisher, Daniel, 705
Fisher, Mr., 637
Fisheries, 608, 1882
Fitzherbert, Alleyne, 219
Fitzherbert, Maria Anne, Lady, 1698
Fitzhugh, Daniel and Theodorick, TJ's loan to, 381, 414, 460, 468, 482, 485–86, 487, 1226; mentioned, 384, 413
Fitzhugh, Daniel McCarty, 434
Fitzhugh, Theodorick, 434
Fitzhugh, William, 605, 660
Fitzpatrick, Thomas, 1347
Fitzsimmons, Thomas: delegate to Constitutional Convention, 478; and Proclamation of Neutrality, 775; opposes commercial discrimination, 834; and Democratic societies, 851, 861; defeated by

Fitzsimmons (*continued*)
  Swanwick, 860; mentioned, 230, 694, 1236, 1326, 1340
FitzSimons, Thomas. *See* Fitzsimmons, Thomas
Flags of truce: for TJ's trip to France in 1782, 220; mentioned, 83, 120, 224
Flanagans, Messrs., 1402
Fleming, Mr.: TJ's merchant neighbor, 861
Fleming, William, 62, 70, 96
"Fletcher of Saltoun," 1864
Floridablanca, José Moñino y Redondo, count de, 463
Floridas: in Louisiana negotiations, 1255, 1270, 1282; JM on right to acquire, 1289, 1290; TJ on right to acquire, 1290, 1586; and "Blount conspiracy," 1326; proposed treaty to acquire, 1358, 1359, 1406, 1416–17, 1452, 1508; Talleyrand suggests price for, 1359; and Bonaparte, 1583; mentioned, 1254, 1305
Flower, George, 1783
Floyd, Catherine ("Kitty"): JM's engagement to, 218, 228–30, 242, 246; TJ on, 245; ends engagement, 262, 270
Floyd, Davis, 1471
Floyd, Polly, 223, 226, 227, 244, 249, 260
Floyd, William, 218, 228, 243, 873
Floyd, Mrs. William, 228
Flushing, Netherlands, 1604
Flushing, N.Y., 694, 695
Folch, Vincente: governor of Pensacola, 1329, 1342, 1498
Fontainebleau, France, 389
Fontana, Felice, 319
Food shortages, 67–68
Forbes, John Murray, 1423, 1425
Forbes, Mr., 1285
Force bill, 1997
Foreign Affairs Department: created under Constitution, 613, 622
Foreign debt: TJ proposes transfer of, from France to Dutch, 453; TJ on payment of, 526, 537, 568, 569–76, 607; vote to fund, 653
"Foreign Influence" (JM), 1073, 1087, 1090, 1093
Foreign officers: congressional pledge to pay, 505
Foronda, Valentin de: and money advanced for Pike's expedition, 1493; on navigation of Mississippi and Mobile rivers, 1517–18; and JM, 1700, 1705; mentioned, 1531, 1533, 1688
Fort Adams, 1260, 1300, 1455
Fort Defiance, 1705
Fort Erie, 1731
Fort George, 1712
Fort Malden, 1712
Fort Massac, 1260
Fort Pickering, 1609
Fort Randolph, 96, 97
Fort Schuyler, 139, 328, 344, 345–46
Fort Stanwix: treaty of, 344, 345
Fort Stoddert, 1327, 1347
Fort Wayne, 1684, 1705
Foster, Sir Augustus John: compares TJ and JM, 11; threatens retaliation against United States, 1657; discusses Fox's blockade, 1674; and early armistice (1812), 1703; mentioned, 1492, 1656, 1658, 1665, 1668, 1672, 1705
Foster, Dwight, 1057
Foulon, Joseph François, 626
Founding Fathers: and slavery, 15–26
Four freedoms: TJ's, 1165
Fowey (British frigate), 160
Fowler, John, 1366
Fox (American merchantman), 1378
Fox, Charles James: Laurens on, 249–50; and Prince of Wales, 311; and *Leander* incident, 1410, 1428; and regularization of trade with United States, 1424; mentioned, 306, 1409, 1653, 1661

France: TJ on desirability of attachment to, 436; and Holland, 460; insurrections in, 514; and most-favored-nation status, 613, 979–80; and American salt provisions in, 639; and Nootka Sound incident, 645–47, 658; and tobacco monopoly, 690–91; Jacobins in power in, 779; seizes American ships, 963; breaks diplomatic relations with United States, 947, 968–69; confiscates American vessels, 968, 1027; peace mission to, 998, 1011; abandons plan to invade England, 1024; and XYZ affair, 1034–35; and Convention of 1800, 1142, 1158; reclaims Louisiana, 1253–54; resumes war with England, 1257; and U.S. spoliation claims, 1309–10; and rumored restoration of monarchy, 1333; privateers from, in American ports, 1344; TJ sends instructions to Armstrong on, 1357; supports Spain's claim to West Florida, 1367–68; on boundaries of Louisiana, 1386–87; and U.S.-Spanish negotiations, 1395; on privateers as pirates, 1413; treats foreigners as prisoners of war, 1414; and Santo Domingo, 1433; refuses to repeal decrees, 1554; and Erskine Agreement, 1567; and Macon's Bill No. 2, 1617, 1631; revocation of decrees of, 1646. *See also* Envoys to France; Franco-American alliance
Francis' Hotel, 971, 1110
Franco-American alliance: ratified by Virginia, 62, 69–70; JM on, 677, 772; and American neutrality, 749; and Jay's treaty, 938; Pickering's pamphlet on, 941, 961; Congress abrogates, 1008, 1054, 1057, 1062, 1112, 1158; JM on, 1150; mentioned, 58, 127–28, 797, 883
Francophilism: Hamilton accuses TJ of, 710
Franklin (American merchantman), 1239
"Franklin" (pseudonym: John Taylor), 800, 808, 813, 814, 818
Franklin (U.S. ship), 1428, 1432
Franklin, Benjamin: and Declaration of Independence, 49, 1846, 1875, 1876; and alliance with France, 53; and Izard, 208, 217; and John Adams, 221, 293–94, 325, 593, 626, 1058; Mazzei's charges against, 307; and commercial negotiations, 315; TJ joins, in France, 325; recalled in 1785, 326; president of Pennsylvania Supreme Executive Council, 388; bust of, 412, 419; and Constitution, 449, 476, 478; TJ ships books to, 485, 495; recommends Bourgain, 512; expenses as minister, 540; founds American Philosophical Society, 947; TJ's appraisal of, 1065; and story of John Thompson, 1876; mentioned, 14, 147, 300, 583, 1192, 1686, 1747, 1975
Franklin, J. (Georgia senator), 1224
Franklin, Temple, 388
Franklin, W. T., 692
Franks, David S.: TJ on, 223, 463; JM on, 227; and negotiations with Morocco, 463; returns from England, 464; mentioned, 217, 465, 474
Franzoni, Giuseppe, 1579, 1581
Frederick, Md., 1731
Fredericksburg, Va.: armament factory in, 65; reception of Genet, 777; postal schedule of, 1493; mentioned, 76–77, 769, 1237, 1485, 1959
Frederick the Great (king of Prussia), 583–84, 607, 776
Freedom of opinion, 1165–66
Freedom of religion: in Virginia, 55–56; in Bill of Rights, 451; TJ on, 545; limitation on state's power over, 597–98; TJ and JM on, 1364; JM on, 1562; mentioned, 1069
Freedom of the press: in Bill of Rights, 451; TJ on, 545, 853, 867, 974–75, 1069, 1080–81, 1353–54; limitation on state's power over, 597, 598; JM on, 768, 852–53, 861, 1111, 1562; and Sedition Act, 1056–57, 1103–4.
Freedom of the seas, 883

Freehling, William W., 15, 16, 24
Freeman, John, 1584
Freeman, Jonathan, 976, 1052
Freeman, Lewis, 1179
French brandy, 670, 1828
French Constitution of 1795, 899, 903, 905, 907
French East Indies, 1447
French furniture: TJ's, 675; JM's, 967
French officers in American Revolution: congressional pledge to pay, 453–54, 486, 538
French Revolution: beginning of, 486; king exiles Parlement, 490; TJ on early reforms, 526–28, 600–3; king's role in, 545; riots in, 609–10; violence in, 624–26; National Assembly debates constitution, 627–28; scarcity of food during, 649–50; Republic proclaimed, 746; execution of Louis XVI during, 746
Frenchtown, 1717
Frenchtown, Md., 1709, 1711
French West Indies, 797, 833–34, 839
French wines, 467, 472
Freneau, Philip: TJ and JM recruit, as newspaper editor, 671–72, 684, 698–99, 700; founds *National Gazette,* 709; Hamilton criticizes, 714; critical of Washington, 752; wrongly identified as Jonathan Pinder, 792; JM sends information to, 800; publishes John Taylor's essays, 806–8; defends Genet, 813; mentioned, 687, 696, 730, 771
Fresco painters, 870, 874
Friend of the People (newspaper), 1155
Friendship: Francis Bacon on, 6; role of letter writing in, 7–8, 13, 315, 318, 495; JM's for TJ, 9–10, 228, 305, 371, 879, 1816, 1960–61, 1968, 1973, 1974, 2001; between JM and TJ, 10–11, 124, 126; TJ's for JM, 10, 242, 355, 855, 1021, 1023, 1043, 1045, 1055, 1058, 1061, 1121, 1160, 1247, 1591, 1815, 1834, 1959–60, 1960–61, 1966–67, 1971; John Quincy Adams on, between TJ and JM, 12; Otto on, between TJ and JM, 444; TJ anticipates reunion with, 568; TJ invites JM to share house, 664–65; JM on pleasure of conversation with TJ, 681;·TJ longs to see JM, 878; TJ on, with all nations, 1165; Margaret Bayard Smith on, between TJ and JM, 1562; TJ on "character of a friend," 1564; TJ's circular letter on, with JM, 1574; between Dolley Madison and Martha Randolph, 1816
Fries's Rebellion, 1454
Frigates: construction of, 146–47, 833, 835
Frontier. *See* Northwest posts
Frontignac wine, 391
Frost, Robert: quoted, 1
Frousant, Mr., 1393
Fruit, 371, 670
Fry, Joshua, 369, 492
Fulton, Robert, 1623, 1625, 1665, 1725
Funding Act of 1790, 642–43, 705
Furquahar, Mr., 1332
Fur trade, 346, 724, 883

Gabriel's Rebellion, 1204
Gadsden, Christopher, 838
Gadsden, Philip, 838
Gaillard, Alexander, 297
Gaines, M., 1176
Gales, Joseph, 982, 1146
Galicia, Spain, 1385
Gallatin, Albert: and Whiskey Rebellion, 866; and Jay's treaty, 891; writes *A Sketch of the Finances of the United States,* 922, 950, 956; JM on, 891, 917; and TJ, 927–28, 996; welcomes Monroe from France, 977; replaces JM as House leader, 995; and Alien and Sedition Laws, 1003, 1042, 1100; on Federalist majority, 1013; on Robbins's affair, 1128; as TJ's Treasury secretary, 1140, 1154, 1167, 1174; on political extremism, 1141; stays in Washington in summer, 1172, 1225, 1249, 1274, 1372, 1439; and passports for vessels, 1178; and *Windsor,* 1189; and political appointments, 1199, 1331, 1434; TJ consults, 1203, 1376, 1398, 1493; and Yazoo compromise, 1221–22, 1405; and Barbary affairs, 1210, 1231, 1232, 1240; health of, 1241; and Guadaloupe negroes, 1242; and Capt. Cloupet, 1284; and the *John Adams,* 1249; and Louisiana, 1279, 1280, 1281, 1310, 1323, 1416; on Stevens case, 1312, 1314; and Florida negotiations, 1329, 1384; on western trip, 1422; letter from, 1424, 1439, 1521; and Santo Domingo trade, 1430; and Sanford, 1434–35; and visit of Russian ships, 1436; and Miranda case, 1407, 1408; on employing British seamen, 1446, 1466, 1467–68, 1469–70, 1473–74; and Monroe-Pinkney Treaty, 1448; on Turreau's request, 1472; and Burr conspiracy, 1475; and Embargo Act, 1505, 1525, 1536, 1537, 1896; and batture case, 1518, 1640, 1642, 1645; urges TJ not to abdicate leadership, 1549–50, 1557–58; as JM's Treasury secretary, 1566, 1615, 1650, 1651, 1652, 1659; and Erskine Agreement, 1571, 1587; visits Montpellier and Monticello, 1572, 1599, 1601; and Father Richard, 1612–13; and Lafayette's lands in Louisiana, 1623; visits farm in Pennsylvania, 1634; denounced by Duane, 1650, 1666–67, 1668, 1669; and Erving's claims, 1672; heads peace commission, 1710, 1712, 1730, 1734; on sense of nationhood, 1760; and white paper, 1764; appointed minister to France, 1782; mentioned, 1179, 1232, 1281, 1283, 1423, 1513, 1522, 1528, 1540, 1545
Gallatin, Hannah Nicholson (Mrs. Albert), 1572, 1599, 1601
Galley, row, 1722
Gallop, Oliver, 1250
Gálvez, Bernardo de, 61, 65, 106–8, 140, 190
Gamble, Mr., 1488
Ganges (American sloop), 1054
Gantt, Edward, 1187, 1688
Garde des sceaux, 544
Gardenier, Barent, 1598–99
Gardens: TJ tours, in England, 417
Gardens: at Woodlands (estate), 1136
Gardner, William, 18–19, 777, 786, 794, 811
Gardoqui, Don Diego de, 396, 431, 467, 471, 475–76, 481, 551, 607
Garland, Edward, 1134
Garland, William G., 1326
Garnett, James Mercer, 1655
Garrard, James, 1070
Garrard, William, 1639
Garrett, Alexander, 1804
Gates, Horatio: defeated at Camden, 131; and navigation of Potomac, 357; TJ proposes bust of, 412, 419; favors ratification, 534; and election of 1800, 1129, 1131; mentioned, 296, 321, 1198, 1415
Gavino, John, 1240, 1284, 1337
Gazette of the United States (newspaper), 692, 791, 801, 807, 962, 1064–65
Gelston, David, 1151–52, 1155, 1348, 1393, 1438
Gelston, Maltby, 1587, 1597–98
Gem, Richard, 528, 583, 603, 1828
General Greene (U.S. warship), 1231, 1232, 1236
General tax assessment: for teachers of Christian religion, 56, 322–23, 331, 361, 369; opposition to, 374; JM's remonstrance against, 375–80, 410
Generational theory: TJ's, 603–4, 631–36, 640–42, 648; JM disagrees with, 650–53; Edmund Burke on, 684–85; mentioned, 654
Genessee County, N.Y., 692
Genet, Cornelia Tappen Clinton (Mrs. Edmond), 829
Genet, Edmond-Charles-Édouard: French minister to United States, 746; recognition of, 748, 749, 750; reception of, 751–52, 772, 774, 775, 777; TJ on, 752–53, 782, 792, 793, 802, 813, 819; recall of,

Genet (*continued*)
    755–56, 757–58, 798, 799, 803, 808, 827; Republican disillusionment with, 758; JM on, 777, 794; urges war with Great Britain, 805; appeals over Washington's head, 811, 813, 830, 1293; interferes with federal marshals, 818; Washington sends correspondence to Congress, 822; proposes new commercial treaty, 823; replaced by Fauchet, 833; mentioned, 700, 766, 767, 812, 871, 1009, 1015
Geneva, 1909
Genoa, 1301, 1381
Geographer of the United States: *see* Hutchins, Thomas
George III (king of England): and Declaration of Independence, 18, 50; JM on, 40; TJ recommends petition to, 41–42; supports suppression of colonial opposition, 43; and end of American Revolution, 222, 225; snubs TJ, 399; opposes commercial treaty with United States, 417; madness of, 589, 609, 616, 1653, 1661, 1686; and orders-in-council, 813, 826; and Jay's treaty, 881; desire for peace, 969; and Ministry of All-the-Talents, 1409, 1424; and impressment, 1446, 1504; and conciliation with United States, 1572, 1600; and regency government, 1663; convalescence of, 1665, 1672; erroneous announcement of death of, 1673; mentioned, 746
George IV (as prince regent): retains Perceval's ministry, 1665, 1678, 1691; TJ's appraisal of, 1689; reconstitutes Perceval's party under Liverpool, 1698; on right of impressment, 1709; on War of 1812, 1762; mentioned, 589, 1653, 1656, 1660, 1672, 1688–89, 1714, 1756
Georgetown, Md.: as location of capital, 315, 663, 673; TJ and JM inspect federal district, 708; and Genet, 777
Georgetown, Md. (on Chesapeake), 1711
George Washington (U.S. frigate), 1194
Georgia: and revenue system of 1783, 239; and slave trade, 503; and Creek Indians, 507; ratifies Constitution, 507, 519, 531; western land claims of, 1211, 1221–22, 1222–24; federal lawsuits in, 1218; ratifies Twelfth Amendment, 1341, 1352
Gérard, Conrad Alexandre, 62, 69, 71, 464, 825, 832
Gerlach, Heinrich, 198
Germain, George Lord, Viscount Sackville, 200
German linens, 846
German Empire, 498–99
Germantown, Pa., 822, 828
Gerna, Anthony, 1686
Gerry, Elbridge: delegate to Constitutional Convention, 469, 477; refuses to sign Constitution, 503; refuses election in 1794, 866; appointed envoy to France, 970–71, 983; and XYZ affair, 1000–1; remains in France, 1009, 1057, 1060, 1062; correspondence as envoy published, 1086, 1088, 1091, 1094, 1096; JM's vice presidential candidate (1812), 1685; TJ on, 1852–53; letter from, 1854
Gerry, Elbridge, Jr., 1852
Gerry, Samuel R., 1230
Ghent: JM on arrogance of British demands at, 1734; peace negotiations at, 1746, 1748, 1753; TJ on British demands, 1748; Treaty of, 1754
Gheretti (Ottoman ketch), 1432
Gholson, Thomas, Jr., 1616
Gibaut, John, 1250
Gibraltar, 137, 164, 165, 1170, 1197, 1281
Gibson, Charles, 1300
Gibson, George, 103
Gibson, Colonel John (in Revolution), 117
Gibson, Colonel John (secretary of Indiana Territory) 1309, 1706
Giles, William Branch: attempts to discredit Hamilton, 745–46, 767; critical of Washington,
951; leaves Congress early, 1039, 1042, 1052; against Alien and Sedition laws, 1112, 1122, 1124, 1125; on JM's cabinet, 1566; praises JM's handling of Erskine and Jackson, 1615; critic of Gallatin, 1650; and recharter of Bank of the United States, 1651; and Wilson Cary Nicholas, 1716; opposes protective tariffs, 1976, 1977; uses TJ's letter to become governor, 1978, 1981; as states' righter, 1984; mentioned, 742, 830, 901, 906, 923, 950, 1018, 1019, 1954
Gill, Samuel, 96
Gillon, Alexander, 736, 860
Gilman, Nicholas, 1179
Gilmer, Francis, 1826
Gilmer, Francis Walker: and search for professors, 1844, 1880, 1882, 1884–86, 1894, 1898, 1903, 1912; offered law chair at Virginia, 1884; returns with European professors, 1908; declines law chair, 1904, 1905, 1908, 1916, 1917–18, 1921, 1922, 1937–38, 1940; illness of, 1909, 1963; criticism of, 1923; death of, 1940, 1958, 1964; accepts law chair, 1958, 1963; mentioned, 1902, 1906, 1967
Gilmer, George, 1727
Gilmer, George, Jr., 730, 902
Gilmer, Walker, 687
Gilpin, George, 1214, 1252, 1465
Gilpin, Henry Dilworth, 1975, 1976
Gimbrede, Thomas, 1689
Girod, Nicholas F., 1329
Gist, Mordecai, 117
Glanville, Ranulf de, 858
Glasgow merchants, 362
Glass cutter, 1095
Glebe lands, 467
Gloucester, Mass., 1250
Gmelin, Johann Georg, 735
Godwin, Money, 161
Goetschius, John M., 1301
Goforth, William, 1233
Goldsborough, Charles W., 1713
Gooch, Gideon, 1640, 1641, 1642, 1649
Goochland County, Va., 886
Goodhue, Benjamin, 866, 998, 1024, 1031
Goodrich, Elizur, 1185, 1186
Gooseberries, 391
Gordon, William, 581, 1087
Gordon, William Fitzhugh, 1943–44, 1962
Gordon's Tavern, Va., 1175, 1176, 1492, 1502, 1787
Gordonsville, Va., 1175
Gore, Christopher, 1213
Gorham, Nathaniel, 469, 477, 660, 692
Gorham and Phelps, land purchase of, 692
Gossip, 7–8
Gothenburg, Sweden, 1710, 1742, 1753
Government Printing Office, 916
Governor-in-Council. *See* Virginia Executive Council
Governor's Palace (Williamsburg, Va.), 59
Græcorum Respublicæ ab Ubbone Emmio descriptæ, 432
Graham, John: JM's appraisal of, 1199; requests leave, 1282; recommends paymaster, 1522; State Department clerk, 1541; and merino sheep, 1636; and batture case, 1642; mentioned, 1185, 1198, 1213, 1280, 1281, 1443, 1525, 1543, 1545
Grand, Ferdinand, 352–53, 368, 459
Grand Duchy of Warsaw, 1469
Grand Seigneur at Constantinople: presents sent to, 1311; and case of *Philadelphia*, 1324; mentioned, 1306, 1308, 1309, 1779
Granger, Gideon: on election of 1800, 1149; and post road to New Orleans, 1339, 1341, 1342; on trespasses on public land, 1372; reports Burr conspiracy, 1443; and Backus case, 1491, 1498;

INDEX

and Yazoo land deal, 1648; seeks Supreme Court appointment, 1659; appoints Leib, 1737; JM dismisses, 1738, 1740–41; mentioned, 1047, 1049, 1212, 1228, 1332, 1363, 1647, 1694
Grant, Mr., 1246
Grant, Sir William, 1360
Grapes, 391
Grasse, François-Joseph-Paul, comte de, 920, 922
Gravier, Mr., 1521
Gray, Mr. (son of William), 1769
Gray, Mrs. (wife of Mr.), 1769
Gray, William, 1769
Grays Ferry, Pa., 767, 775, 780
Grayson, William: on Virginia credit, 176; in Confederation Congress, 388, 408, 456; and navigation of Mississippi, 472; opposes ratification, 534; as Antifederalist senator, 579, 591; opposes commercial discrimination, 613; and most favored nation, 621
Great Britain: peace treaty ends American Revolution, 209; refuses commercial treaty with United States, 235, 246, 265–66; and trade with United States, 272–73; JM on commercial retaliation against, 373, 608; and most-favored-nation status, 613, 619–21; and Nootka Sound incident, 645–47, 657–59; sends ambassador, 647; TJ's table on, based on wars in Europe, 678–80; and French Revolutionary wars, 746, 748, 751, 767, 770, 771, 842, 1105, 1293; and orders-in-council and seizure of American ships, 821, 823, 825, 826, 834–35, 963, 1060; and Jay's treaty, 882; regulates neutral trade, 1020–21; France abandons plans to invade, 1024; and Convention of 1800, 1158–59; on Louisiana Purchase, 1276; resumes war with France, 1257; renews impressments, 1294, 1504; renews seizing American ships, 1360; proposed alliance with, 1362; forms Third Coalition against Bonaparte, 1404; and Maine border, 1480–81; and *Chesapeake* affair, 1494; renounces right to search U.S. warships for deserters, 1499; JM on trade policy of, 1536–37; refuses to repeal orders-in-council, 1554, 1674, 1675; and Macon's Bill No. 2, 1616–17; suspends orders-in-council, 1681; repeals orders-in-council, 1703; blockades East Coast, 1710, 1718; sends naval fleet to Chesapeake, 1718; initiates direct negotiations for peace, 1729; JM submits commercial treaty with, 1772. *See also* England
Great Falls of Potomac, 515, 1731
Great Island, Va. *See* Long Island, Va.
Great Lakes: in War of 1812, 1683–84, 1712
Greece, 1844, 1879
Greeley, Horace, 1973
Green, Moses, 1134
Green, Timothy, 1012, 1018
Green Briar County, Va., 491–92
Greene, Catherine (Mrs. Nathanael), 653
Greene, George Washington (son of Nathanael), 653
Greene, Griffin, 1331
Greene, Nathanael: on need for lead, 186; TJ proposes bust of, 411, 419; mentioned, 133, 478, 653, 1855
Greene, Philip, 1331
Greenleaf, Thomas, 697, 813
Green Spring, Va., 1482
Greenup, Christopher, 729, 769
Greenville, Tenn., 1365
Greenville, Treaty of, 933, 1734, 1746
Greetham, William, 1178
Gregg, Andrew, 1406, 1424
Grenville, William Wyndham, Baron and Lord: and western posts, 832; on Jay's treaty, 884; mentioned, 712, 713, 842, 1653, 1661, 1692
Grieve, George, 19

2037

Griffin, Cyrus: president of Confederation Congress, 534, 581; TJ's appraisal of, 1620; mentioned, 139, 457, 535, 1631, 1632
Griffin, Samuel, 605, 765, 769
Griffith, Robert E., 1378
Griswold, Roger, 976, 997, 1073–74
Grotius, Hugo, 360, 1262, 1360, 1408
Grundy, Felix, 1676
Grymes, Ludwell, 303, 308
Grymes, Mr., 1525
Guadaloupe: black leaders of, shipped to France, 1240, 1242; mentioned, 1261, 1302, 1484
Guadaloupe (French warship), 218, 220, 224
Guadaloupe (prize sloop), 1526
Guadaloupe River, 1395
Guardian of Freedom (Lexington, Ky., newspaper), 1268
Guardoqui, Don Diego de. *See* Gardoqui, Don Diego de
Guarrant, Mr. *See* Garrard, William
Guillaumes, Mr., 1593
Gum Spring, Va., 1499
Gunboats, 1532, 1711, 1712, 1720, 1723–25
Gunn, James, 860, 978
Gunston Hall, Va., 663, 673, 740
Gurley, John W., 1366

Habeas corpus: TJ on, 528, 545, 567; in Bill of Rights, 451; mentioned, 566, 598
Habersham, Joseph, 1197, 1198
Hackley, Richard, 1441, 1526, 1546, 1582, 1583, 1815–16
Hagerstown, Md., 1147
Hague, The, 525
"Hail, Columbia" (song), 1002
Haiti, 1348
Haley, Nathan, 1541
Halifax, Nova Scotia, 1361, 1703, 1731, 1734, 1746
Hall, Dominick Augustin, 1336, 1337, 1434
Hall, Edward, 1347
Hamburg, Germany, 1260
Hamet Caramalli (former pasha of Tripoli), 1431
Hamilton, Alexander: JM and and TJ oppose, 31; and revenue system of Confederation, 230; opposes assumption of state debts (1783), 236, 242–43; compared with JM, 444; delegate to Constitutional Convention, 469, 478, 1640–41, 1641–42; coauthor of *Federalist*, 524, 548, 850; supports ratification, 542; JM on qualifications for Treasury Department, 594, 613, 622; writes "Report on Public Credit," 642, 649, 653, 665; and Compromise of 1790, 643–44; and foreign policy, 646–47; and Bank of United States, 665, 666, 696; on political parties, 667; critical of TJ, 668, 688, 710, 715–16, 766, 1117; TJ opposes, 668, 954; critical of TJ and JM's northern excursion, 670–71; JM critical of, 689, 700, 704, 706, 709, 817; relations with Beckwith, 710; and TJ's negotiations with Hammond, 711, 712, 721, 726; relations with Hammond, 712, 713, 714, 715; condemns Republican party as faction, 714, 1006; on differences with JM, 715, 744; and Marshall, 735, 1060; and national debt, 739; and Washington's second term, 744; Republican move to discredit, 745; French citizenship conferred on, 747; opposes recognition of Genet, 748–49, 770, 803; and neutrality, 749, 771, 773, 791; writes as "Pacificus," 754, 792, 795, 799; denounces Democratic societies, 757, 804, 851; resignation of, 757, 759, 805, 856, 866, 873, 890, 917, 922; in Philadelphia, 767, 789; proposes Dutch loan, 781; views in Virginia on, 794; objects to "war of liberty on herself," 809; illness of, 818–19; condemns British seizure of noncontraband goods, 823; mentioned as special envoy, 826–27, 840, 841; and

Hamilton (*continued*)
  enlarged army, 836; requests investigation to clear name, 837, 841; and Whiskey Rebellion, 850–51, 859, 953; succeeded by Wolcott, 869, 886; final report of, 870, 873–74; and Jay's treaty, 885, 893, 896; as "Camillus," 892, 896, 897, 898, 929; supports carriage tax, 921, 925, 926; and John Adams, 941, 942, 945, 948, 1156, 1157; and Adams's cabinet, 969, 1085, 1086; confesses to adultery, 973, 984, 993; writes *Observations...* denying speculation, 993; as general in quasi war, 1008, 1086; and Thomas Pinckney interest, 1033; declines appointment as senator, 1042, 1045, 1049–50; writes as "Titus Manlius," 1045; proposes use of army against Virginia, 1073, 1113; as leader of High Federalists, 1099; proposes tampering with election returns, 1138; prefers TJ to Burr, 1142, 1144, 1161; argues treaty with France unnecessary, 1152; views on administration, 1169; and general appropriations, 1207; killed by Burr, 1442; and authorship of Washington's Farewell Address, 1847–48, 1861, 1863, 1867, 1878; on constitutionality of roads and canals, 1949; mentioned, 687, 802, 819, 828–29, 1158, 1975, 1978
Hamilton, Elizabeth Schuyler (Mrs. Alexander), 819
Hamilton, Henry: captured by George Rogers Clark, 63, 64; use of Indians by, 72; placed in irons, 74–76, 89–90; treatment reported to Congress, 79, 80; mentioned, 78, 118
Hamilton, Paul, 1699, 1708, 1714, 1725
Hamilton, William, 1136
Hamiltonian system, 710–11, 728
Hammond, George: appointed minister to United States, 711; negotiations with TJ, 712–13, 721, 722–25, 726–27, 822, 823, 840, 876; dines with Joseph Brant, 733; on French privateers, 779; TJ on views of, 792; and Edmund Randolph, 832–33; and Dorchester's speech to Indians, 845; in Vienna, 981; mentioned, 733, 871
Hampden-Sydney Academy, 371, 392, 468
Hampton, Va., 154, 155, 1347
Hampton, Wade, 1155, 1240, 1611
Hancock, George, 304–5, 769
Hancock, John, 439, 474, 563, 564, 580, 828
Hanover County, Va., 44, 55, 1346, 1577
Harbor defenses, 1515–16
Hardy, Samuel, 309, 388
Hares, 391, 726
Harewood, Jefferson County, Va., 847
Harmar, Josiah, 293
Harper, Robert Goodloe: elected to Congress, 860; on arming merchant ships, 980; criticizes TJ in House, 996–97, 1074; charges treasonable correspondence between Republicans and France, 1009, 1061; and Stamp Act, 1024; and Lyon-Griswold affair, 1026; opposes Sprigg resolutions, 1030; prefers borrowing to taxing, 1059; and Logan Act, 1088; mentioned, 979
Harpers Ferry, Va., 428, 967, 1907
Harris, James, first earl of Malmesbury, 956
Harris, Levitt: and Russian intervention in case of *Philadelphia*, 1325; letter from, 1468, 1472, 1541; mentioned, 1301, 1311, 1345, 1471, 1519, 1779, 1805, 1906
Harrison, Anna Mercer (Mrs. Benjamin), 492
Harrison, Benjamin: Speaker of Virginia House, 73; seeks military assistance for Virginia, 133–34, 162, 165; and payment of Virginia congressional delegation, 148–49, 153; as governor of Virginia, 272, 275, 363; and navigation of Potomac, 356; and general assessment for religious teaching, 361; and residency requirement, 369; elected to Virginia legislature, 375; elected Speaker, 401; opposes revised code, 402; opposes Confederation regulation of commerce, 404; runs for House, 420, 456, 477; opposes ratification, 534; mentioned, 70, 98, 103, 116, 149, 163, 182
Harrison, Colonel Benjamin (of Barclay), 687
Harrison, Charles, 117
Harrison, Mr., 321
Harrison, P. L., 848, 1733
Harrison, Richard, 1151, 1197, 1241
Harrison, William Henry: defeats Tecumseh, 1676; appointed commanding general in West, 1684, 1705; TJ on, 1707; victor in Battle of the Thames, 1712; liberates Northwest, 1729; mentioned, 1368, 1581, 1730
Harrowby, Lord, 1709
Hartford, Conn., 1480, 1498
Hartley, David, 250
Harvard College, 1860, 1915, 1918, 1925
Harvey, John. *See* Harvie, John
Harvie, John, 350, 509, 605, 868
Harvie, Mr., 1840
Harwood, B., 1347
Hassler, Ferdinand Rudolph, 1770
Haumont, Mr., 1441
Havana, Cuba, 1430
Havre de Grace, France, 1301
Havre de Grace, Md., 217, 1711
Hawkesbury, Charles Jenkinson, first Baron, 723
Hawkesbury, Robert Banks Jenkinson, second Baron, 1276, 1681
Hawkins, Benjamin: opposes permanent foreign establishments, 717, 718; on vetch, 872; mentioned, 678, 900, 1197
Hawthorne, Nathaniel, 5
Hay, George, 1445, 1633, 1640, 1654, 1664
Hay, Mrs. George, 1768
Hay, John, 118
Hay, Samuel, 1301
Hay, William, 459, 485, 495
Hayes, James, 166, 170
Hayne, Robert Young, 1984–85, 1986, 1993–94, 1995
Hays, William, 408
Head of Elk. *See* Elkton, Md.
Heath, Captain, 103
Heath, Colonel, 117
Helmbold, George, Jr., 1184
Helvetic Confederacy, 498
Helvétius, Mme. Claude-Adrien, 1828
"Helvidius" (pseudonym; JM), 754–55, 758, 795, 799, 800, 817, 820; TJ relays essays to press, 809, 813–14; mentioned, 1408
Hemings, James, 285, 321
Hemings, Sally, 1480
Hemmings, James. *See* Hemings, James
Hemp, 338
Henderson, Alexander, 323, 369
Henfield, Gideon, 805
Hening, W. W., 908
Hennin, Pierre-Michel, 464
Henrich (Danish brigantine), 1260–61, 1262
Henry, James M., 1366
Henry, John, 860, 978, 1690
Henry, Patrick: TJ on 13, 245, 353–54; opposes parliamentary authority over colonies, 43; and Dunmore's seizure of gunpowder, 44; first governor of Virginia, 51, 88; and Virginia Executive Council, 57, 60; on Washington's need for supplies, 58; requests Spanish aid, 61, 106; and Bland's expense account, 120; and Confederation impost, 232, 248, 252; favors strengthening Confederation, 278, 281–82, 318; opposes revision of Virginia Constitution, 282, 302, 322, 878; supports moratorium on tax collection, 282; favors

INDEX 2039

tax assessment for religious teaching, 282, 323, 361; and Mazzei, 307; reelected governor, 330, 355, 363; opposes TJ's bill for religious freedom, 331; and law of nations, 360; opposes revised code, 437, 467; rejects election to Constitutional Convention, 454, 468, 470, 476; and navigation of Mississippi, 471–72; favors paper money, 473, 476; opposes ratification, 479, 505, 507, 509, 515, 520, 534, 542; and fulfillment of Treaty of Paris, 516; and rejection of Constitution by North Carolina, 550; supports call for second convention, 552; as Antifederalist leader, 579; opposes JM's election, 581, 590; as presidential elector, 605; Washington offers secretary of state post to, 903; nominated envoy to France, 1099; mentioned, 71, 119, 1975
Hermine. *See* Weasel
Hermitage wine, 1361, 1391, 1393
Herndon, Edward, 97
Heron's Tavern (Culpeper County), Va., 1174
Hessian fly, 543, 670, 690, 1151, 1525, 1639, 1669, 1670, 1672, 1719, 1743
Hessians, 411
Hester (slave), 161
Heth, Mr., 1242
Heth, William, 517, 1203, 1231
Hewes, Captain, 1500, 1501
Hickey, Donald R.: quoted, 1448, 1466
Hickman, R., 908
Higginson, Stephen, 1144, 1161, 1243, 1246
Higham, John: quoted, 1984
High Federalists, 947–48
Highwassee, 1575
Hill, Henry, 1134
Hill, Henry, Jr., 1366
Hill, Mr., 1520, 1522, 1525
Hilland, Mr., 1940
Hiller, Joseph, 1231
Hillhouse, James, 1003, 1033, 1042, 1049, 1670
Hilliard, Mr., 1930
Hislop, Governor, 1521
History: JM appeals to, 1981; 1983–84, 1986, 1987, 1988, 1996, 1999, 2000
Hite, Abraham, 96
Hite, Isaac, 857
Hobart, John Sloss, 1042, 1369
Hobbes, Thomas, 954
Hobbs' Hole, Va., 349
Hobday, John, 77
Hoffman, Jacob, 1465
Holland: and France, 460; transfer of Revolutionary debt to, 505; Dutch bankers make loan to United States, 525–26; shelters C. C. Pinckney, 976–77; excludes British trade, 1601; mentioned, 1298. *See also* Batavian Republic; Netherlands, the
Holland, Henry Richard Vassall Fox, third Baron, 1410, 1599, 1653, 1657, 1661
Hollins, John, 1145
Hollins, Mrs. John, 1145
Holt, Charles, 1149
Holy Alliance, 1844
Honeysuckles, standing American, 1511
Honor, 2
Hoods, Va., 154, 159
Hooe, J. H., 1635–36, 1638–39, 1649
Hoops, Adam, 1040
Hope (U.S. ship), 1536, 1547, 1554
Hopkins, John, Jr., 896
Hopkinson, Francis, 285, 492, 512, 687, 688
Hornet (U.S. dispatch ship): delay in return of (1812), 1692; returns from Europe, 1696; mentioned, 1536, 1678, 1679, 1694
Horse stealers, 466
Hoskins, Richard Q., 1529
Houard, David, 858, 876

Houdeton, countess d'. *See* Houdetot, Elizabeth Françoise Sophie
Houdetot, Elisabeth Françoise Sophie, countess d', 1686
Houdon, Jean-Antoine, 329, 411, 419
House, George, 1269
House, Mary (Mrs. Samuel): TJ and, 271, 320, 349, 389, 433, 655, 662, 664; JM and, 290, 291, 292, 311, 662, 664; death of, 779; mentioned, 217, 218, 228, 246, 251, 264, 267, 287, 344, 347, 769
House, Samuel, 291, 321
House Committee on Commerce and Manufactures, 1483
House of Representatives: debates defense measures against France, 980, 981; debates taxes, 983, 1042, 1045, 1047, 1049, 1054, 1057, 1059; and naturalization bill, 1003, 1042, 1044, 1057; and XYZ affair, 1033, 1034; and alien friends bill, 1042, 1045, 1048, 1052; and sedition bill, 1042, 1056–57; creates Navy Department, 1042, 1043, 1095; and provisional army bill, 1042, 1045, 1047, 1049, 1050; and bill for capturing French cruisers, 1052, 1054; suspends commercial intercourse with France, 1054, 1091, 1095; and abrogation of Franco-American alliance, 1054, 1057; adopts report supporting Alien and Sedition Laws, 1075, 1100–7; acts on presidential tie vote in election of 1800, 1140, 1141, 1142, 1157, 1160, 1161, 1162; and navigation of Mississippi, 1254
Houston, William Churchill, 478
Howe, Robert, 261
Howe, Sir William, 58
Howe, William: case of, 717
Howell, David, 276, 314, 1185, 1186
Howell, Samuel, Sr., 920, 923, 929, 935, 937
Howell, Wilbur Samuel: quoted, 1139
Howland, John, 495
Hubbard, Nicholas, 935
Hudson River, 432, 670, 883, 1253
Hughes, Mr., 1283
Hughes, Victor, 1096
Hulings, William E., 1252, 1266
Hull, Isaac, 1685
Hull, Mr., 1336
Hull, William: as governor of Michigan Territory, 1523; surrenders Detroit, 1683, 1684, 1702, 1707; court-martialed, 1685; mentioned, 1372, 1474, 1526, 1703
Human rights, 1772, 1877
Humboldt, Alexander von, 1691
Hume, David, 125, 448
Humor: TJ's, 8, 671, 1488; JM's 8–9
Humphreys, David, 933, 1204, 1214
Humphries, David. *See* Humphreys, David
Hundreds (wards), and education, 1776
Hunt, Mr., 1526
Hunter, John, 860
Hunter, Mr., 1841
Hunter, William, 291, 292
Huntington, Samuel, 113, 121, 167, 173
Huntress (American merchant vessel), 1402
Hurt, Dr. John (translator), 586, 618
Hurt, John, 1135, 1145
Huskanoyed, 544
Hutchins, Thomas, 194, 473
Hutchinson, James, 775, 813, 819
Hydrophobia, 730
Hypochrondria: TJ and JM's symptoms of, 14

Iberville River, 1328
Icehouse: JM's 1570
Illinois Company, 151
Illinois nut. *See* Pecans
Illinois River, 475
Ilsley, Isaac, 1300

Immortality: JM on, 2
Impeachment: and jury trials, 1016, 1020, 1023, 1025; process of, 1017, 1021; universality of, 1023
Impost: and revenue system of 1783, 231; proposed, 314; authorized in Virginia, 331; attempt to enact without unanimity, 363; status in 1786, 421–31; New York rejects, 468; debated by first Congress, 607–8; mentioned, 232, 517
Impressment: Jay's treaty silent on, 883; House debate on (1796), 894; King attempts to negotiate ban on, 1257; JM on, 1257–58, 1259, 1283; TJ on, 1274, 1294, 1509, 1583; by British, 1257, 1258; by French, 1258; Thornton on, 1280; JM's remonstrance against, 1285; JM reports on, 1302; JM on number of Americans under, 1409; Monroe-Pinkney efforts to restrain, 1409, 1446; TJ demands abolition of, 1445, 1449, 1464, 1465; and *Chesapeake* affair, 1445–46; JM proposes new negotiations on, 1448, 1473–74, 1569, 1587, 1730; and Nonimportation Act, 1496; and War of 1812, 1795; mentioned, 1086, 1128, 1177, 1278, 1413, 1656
Incognitum, 284, 291, 292, 408
Indefatigable (ship), 1438, 1501
India, 882, 1447
Indiana Company, 210, 215
Indian affairs: Jay's treaty silent on 883; TJ on commerce with tribes, 1350; TJ and JM on, 1364; on Missouri River, 1497
Indiana Territory: Indian warfare in, 1676
Indian pottery, 408
Indians: cooperation with British during Revolution, 63, 74–75, 139, 346; British military supplies to, in American territory, 681–83; want Ohio River as boundary, 819; in Louisiana Purchase territory, 1257, 1289, 1290, 1456–57; removal of, beyond Mississippi, 1574; school for, 1575, 1611–13; in War of 1812, 1702, 1703; British demands on, at Ghent, 1734, 1746
Indian treaty of 1795. *See* Greenville, Treaty of
Indian vocabularies, 1625
Individual liberties: JM on, 27–28; protected in an extended republic, 448–49; mentioned, 1164–65
Individual rights: state encroachments on, 447; and federal negative, 500–2; and majority rule, 523, 1164; property of, 709
Indostan (U.S. ship), 1436
Inflation, 125–26, 134–35
Ingenhousz, Jan, 319
Ingersoll, Charles, 1758
Ingersoll, Jared, 478, 921, 925
Ingles, Mr., 242
Innes, James, 457, 504–5, 509, 534, 1040, 1057–58, 1060
Inoculation, 216
Insurance Company of North America, 1095
Insurrections: in southwestern Virginia, 135, 148, 1454, 1458–59
Internal improvements: TJ's states' rights attitude on, 1943; J. Q. Adams advocates, 1959; JM on constitutionality of, 1956; Virginia denies constitutionality of, 1968; mentioned 35–36, 1927
International law. *See* Law of nations
Interposition, 31, 1071, 1980–81. *See also* State interposition
Invalides, 602, 625
Iredell, James, 934, 974
Ireland, 290, 366, 1089, 1092
Iris (British frigate), 160
Irish, Nathaniel, 159, 210, 211
Iroquois Indians, 71, 347–48
Irvine, Callender, 1300
Irvine, Mr., 1279
Irvine, William, 319, 728, 733, 791
Irving, Washington, 1686, 1706

Isaac, Rhys: quoted, 394
Ishomel, Mr., 1531
Isley, David, Jr.; *see* Ilsley, Isaac
Israel, Israel, 1023
Isthmus, 1434
Ivory, James, 1896, 1898
Izard, George, 1751
Izard, Ralph, 217, 492, 718, 860, 933, 1747

Jackson, Andrew ("Old Hickory"): on Louisiana Purchase, 1288; defeats Indians in Southwest, 1729; and Battle of New Orleans, 1754; and Seminole war, 1808–9; Trist as aide to, 1990; toasts federal Union, 1992; signs tariff of 1832, 1993; denounces nullification and secession, 1995; mentioned, 1891, 1984
Jackson, Francis James ("Copenhagen"): British minister to United States, 1572–73, 1601, 1656, 1665; JM on, 1603; TJ on, 1604; and Onís, 1606; and Canning, 1607; JM demands recall of, 1608
Jackson, Henry, 1086
Jackson, James, 1224
Jackson, John George, 1623–24
Jackson, Mr., 1530
Jackson, Major William, 477
Jackson, William: and Yrujo, 1346
Jacobinism: term used by Federalists for Republican party, 1093
Jacobin party, in France, 736
Jacobins, establish revolutionary government in France, 779
Jamaica, 1213
James Madison Annex, at Library of Congress, 15
Jameson, David, 60, 222
James River: canal at falls of, 99, 101, 429, 516; navigation of, 357–58; mentioned, 1724
James River Company, 375
Jamestown, Va., 154, 159
Jamieson, Neill, 350, 365
Jardin des Plantes (Paris), 1971
Jarvis, William: consul at Lisbon, 1582; sends merino sheep to TJ and JM, 1621, 1624, 1625, 1627, 1635–36, 1638; mentioned, 1267, 1368, 1370, 1526, 1649
Jay, Sir J., 1522
Jay, John: appointed minister to Spain, 113, 131, 163, 197, 539–40; TJ congratulates, on peace treaty with Great Britain, 209; secretary of foreign affairs, 235, 285, 315, 471, 473; John Adams on, 244; in commission with Adams and Franklin, 293–94; at Bath, 306; negotiations for navigation of Mississippi, 395–96, 431, 467, 475–76, 481, 551; TJ sends *Notes* to, 492; co-author of *Federalist,* 524, 548; TJ's dispatches to, 526; on expenses of ministers to European nations, 553; supports ratification, 542; candidate for vice president, 554; candidate for secretary of state, 594, 613; and TJ's leave of absence, 606; and New York gubernatorial election of 1792, 728, 737; critical of French Revolution, 785; Washington on, 806; and Genet's appeal to people, 811; as special envoy to Great Britain, 827, 841, 843, 869, 885; runs for governor of New York, 876, 1013, 1037, 1045; rejects Hamilton's proposal to tamper with election results, 1138; and tie vote in 1800, 1156; appointed chief justice by Adams, 1141, 1142; names Hamilton senator, 1042, 1046; mentioned, 79, 146, 225, 536, 538, 539, 543, 583, 584, 588, 618, 870, 873, 897, 1975
Jay's treaty: JM's expectations of, 872, 876; kept secret, 879; TJ receives copy of, 880; Washington predicts "hot Session" over, 881; provisions of, 881–83; reaction to, 885–94; as capstone of Hamiltonian system, 894–95; House attitude towards, 904–5, 926, 929; British ratification of

INDEX 2041

916, 925; JM's resolutions on, 930–31, 933; mercantile party launches petitions for, 934; French denounce, 941–42; John Adams promises to implement, 966; and envoys' mission to France, 1015; JM on, 1026, 1046, 1569; and Convention of 1800, 1158, 1159; and British snow *Windsor,* 1185; and Spanish armed merchantman, 1188; abandons "free ships make free goods," 1190; expiration of, 1196; arbitration commission awards, 1219–20; incorporates TJ's letter to Hammond, 1260; compared with Monroe-Pinkney Treaty, 1447; TJ denounces in retirement, 1567; Erving as claims agent under, 1670–72; mentioned, 921, 922, 923, 1032, 1408, 1465, 1919, 1925
Jefferson, George, 1583, 1647, 1649, 1700
Jefferson, Maria (Polly, TJ's daughter): with Mrs. Carr while TJ in France, 407; at Pentemont, 512; returns to United States, 630; travels to Philadelphia with President and Mrs. Washington, 708; marries John Wayles Eppes, 994; mentioned, 821; *See also* Eppes, Maria Jefferson
Jefferson, Martha (Patsy, TJ's daughter): corresponds with Polly Floyd, 227; schooling for, 265, 267, 271; accompanies TJ to France, 285, 325 364; Mrs. Trist writes, 389; attends school at abbey of Pentemont, 486; returns to United States, 568, 630; mentioned, 207, 221, 222–23, 226, 243, 244, 248, 249, 251, 272, 344, 433, 814. *See also* Randolph, Martha "Patsy" Jefferson
Jefferson, Martha Wayles Skelton (TJ's wife) 51, 52, 83, 206, 207
Jefferson, Peter, 492

JEFFERSON, THOMAS
PERSONAL LIFE
Characteristics of: archives and letters of, 3, 125; and gossip, 7–8; impulsiveness of, 12–13; description of, in 1776, 53–54; sense of humor of, 172, 184, 671, 1488; family life of, 206, 216; and education of daughters and nephews, 270, 350–51, 512; death of daughter, 1296–97; suspicious of Federalist Post Offices, 788, 792, 793, 796, 802–3; great coat of, 1428, 1434 *Slavery:* antislavery views of, 16–18, 19–20, 26; anti-Negro views of, 16, 20–21; leaves antislavery movement to younger generation, 23; recommends prohibition of slave trade, 24; on diffusion of slavery, 25; as slaveholder, 26 *Farming:* and Scotch threshing machine, 776; outlines crop rotation, 789–91; establishes nailery, 848, 1148; grist mill of, 1429; reports on crops, 1564; and plows, 1622–3, 1625–26; and merino sheep, 1621–22, 1628–29, 1639–40, 1642, 1649; on brewing, 1823–24 *Health:* inoculation of family of, 216; breaks wrist, 400, 457, 464; health of, 905, 1807, 1822, 1824, 1970; feebleness of, 1766; illness of, 1815, 1817–18; dies on Fourth of July, 1973 *Personal relations:* on George Mason, 52; on John Adams, 208, 223; at Mrs. House's boardinghouse, 228; critical of Patrick Henry, 252, 353–54; appraises Lafayette, 329, 365, 411; and Maria Cosway, 400; and Dohrman's debt to Mazzei, 676; sends greeting to the Monroes, 844; writes Deborah Logan, 1008, 1009; confesses to attempt to seduce Betsey Walker, 1491 *Scientific and intellectual interests:* generational theory of, 30–31, 603–4, 631–36; buys map by Thomas Hutchins, 194; on Buffon's theory of central heat, 288–89; and Maison Carrée, 335–36; linguistic interests of, 552–53, 582; as chairman of committee on "the natural history of the Hessian fly," 690; retrieves books loaned out in Philadelphia, 858; on international status of scientific explorers, 1520 *Money problems:* as congressman, 275, 296; as president, 1588, 1591–92; as farmer, 1953, 1965; plans lottery to meet debts, 1953, 1965–66 *Miscellaneous:* on laboring poor in France, 390–91; French furniture of, 662; disillusioned with newspapers, 840, 1576; painted by Polk, 1120; leaves Philadelphia for last time, 1137; as wine connoisseur, 1361; on summers at Monticello, 1373; writes tombstone inscription, 1972

FRIENDSHIP WITH MADISON
On friendship with JM, 10–11, 13, 57, 60, 68, 1815 *On abilities of JM:* calls JM "greatest man in the world," 13, 648; on regard for JM's judgment, 26–27, 68, 273–74; and first impressions of JM, 37–38, 52–53; on "powers and polish of his pen," 68; shares common interests with JM, 124–25; on correspondence with JM, 206, 1729, 1893; acquires portrait of JM, 648; and request by JM for TJ's aid as architect, 774, 791, 849, 1546; has no secrets from JM, 1068; gives JM his portrait by Kościuszko, 1225 *Purchasing agent for JM:* ships books from Paris, 15, 332, 350, 492, 1351; statement of account with JM, 385–86, 487–89, 493, 1584; makes purchases for JM in Philadelphia, 1043–44, 1047, 1050–51, 1052, 1058, 1060, 1061; ships nails to JM, 1080, 1118 *Camaraderie:* reunited with JM in Philadelphia (1782), 207–98; reunited with JM in Philadelphia (1783), 271; and JM's romance with Kitty Floyd, 228–29, 264; urges JM to settle near Monticello, 283–84, 293, 336, 354–55; sends JM draft constitution for Virginia (1783), 252–60; asks JM to keep weather information, 306; asks JM's advise on distribution of *Notes,* 334–35; invites JM to France, 336, 354–55, 671; praises JM for work on revisal of Virginia laws, 437; praises JM's contributions to *Federalist,* 524, 567; takes northern excursion with JM, 670–71, 687; invites JM to share house, 680; buys horse from JM, 663, 675–76, 677; and death of horse, 663, 664, 678; sends journal of European travels to JM, 671, 702; acquires bust and portrait of JM, 648; on conferring of French citizenship on JM, 782; congratulates Madisons on their marriage, 848; sends greetings to Dolley, 983; on JM's health, 1176, 1197, 1713, 1725, 1726; regrets Mrs. Madison's knee operation, 1362, 1375 *Visits to Montpellier:* visits JM, 633, 822, 1067, 1140, 1167, 1502, 1525, 1596, 1640, 1658; calls off visit to JM at Monroe's suggestion, 1109–10, 1120, 1121 *Madisons at Monticello:* invites JM to Monticello, 898, 984, 985, 986, 1133, 1145–46, 1184, 1246, 1248–49, 1333, 1596, 1599, 1646 *Political collaboration:* congratulates JM on election to federal Congress, 610; accompanies JM on trip to Philadelphia, 662–64, 708; asks JM to report on Beckwith, 681–83; urges JM to reply to "Pacificus," 754; revises JM's "Helvidius" essays, 818; consults with JM and Monroe on party strategy, 821; urges JM to run for president in 1796, 854–56, 868, 877, 943, 949; asks JM to send copy of correspondence with Genet and Hammond, 871; on JM's campaign against Jay's treaty, 902; urges JM to write newspaper articles, 1034, 1035–36, 1073; urges JM to publish "Notes on Debates," 1089; praises JM's articles, 1098; consults JM on renewing Kentucky and Virginia resolutions, 1109; discusses cabinet appointments with JM, 1140; invites JM to Washington for inaugural, 1154; invites Madisons to dinner at President's House, 1216; asks JM to revise message to Congress, 1218, 1251, 1396–97; asks JM to tally federal lawsuits, 1242; praises JM's pamphlet on Rule of 1756, 1408; attends Madison's inauguration, 1561, 1562; writes from retirement to JM, 1564; writes circular letter about relations with

FRIENDSHIP WITH MADISON (*continued*)
President Madison, 1574; congratulates JM on retirement, 1785; asks JM to revise annual report of University of Virginia, 1799, 1813; asks JM to revise letter on botanical school, 1970; final request to JM, 1960–61

CONTINENTAL CONGRESS AND VIRGINIA LEGISLATURE
Member of Continental Congress: Declaration of Independence and, 2, 234, 274–75; on tyranny of state legislatures, 27, 588; advocates periodic constitutional revision, 29–30; reaction to British colonial policy, 40–41; writes *Summary View of the Rights of British America,* 41–42; reaction of to Battle of Lexington, 44; rejects Lord North's conciliatory proposal, 44–45, 46; as delegate to second Continental Congress, 45; cooperates with John Dickinson in writing "Declaration of Causes and Necessity for Taking Up Arms," 46–47; chairs committee to draft Declaration of Independence, 49; resigns from Continental Congress, 51 *Member of Virginia legislature:* drafts plan for military defense of Virginia, 43; appointed commander in chief of Albemarle County militia, 47; elected to Virginia convention, 48; constitutional proposals of adopted in Virginia, 51; on constitution making, 51; drafts law to abolish entail, 54; heads committee to revise Virginia laws, 54, 330, 364, 393–94; and Virginia Statute for Religious Freedom, 55, 56, 458–59

GOVERNOR OF VIRGINIA
Elected as governor, 58, 59; entertains British prisoners of war, 63, 197; revises curriculum of William and Mary, 128; military recruitment of in 1780, 128; and Revolutionary campaigns in the South, 132–34; recommends anchorages for French fleet, 132, 154–55; offers reward for capture of Arnold, 133; on Arnolds's invasion of Virginia, 172; last days as governor of, 176–77; legislature calls for inquiry into conduct of as governor, 178, 204, 205; on need for military supplies in Virginia, 183–84; congratulates Washington on Yorktown victory, 205; on peace treaty with Great Britain, 209; on western land claims of Virginia, 213–14

CONFEDERATION CONGRESS
First proposal for Library of Congress, 14; appointed to peace commission, 207, 216; and suspension of peace commission, 209, 226; elected to Virginia legislature in 1782 but resigns, 215; drafts constitution for Virginia, 235–36; favors strengthening Confederation, 229, 232, 233, 285, 326–27, 395, 396–97, 440; supports assumption of state debts (1783), 243, 244; replaces JM in Congress, 234, 270; lobbies for revenue system of 1783, 245; on federal courts under Confederation, 275; and Land Ordinance of 1784, 276–77, 308–9, 311–13; supports Potomac canal, 281, 337; and ratification of peace treaty, 298–99; and western land speculation, 350; on East-West tensions during Confederation, 462

MINISTER TO FRANCE
Appointed minister plenipotentiary for foreign commercial negotiations, 285, 315, 325; succeeds Franklin as minister to France, 326; reports on diplomatic affairs in Europe, 352, 355, 380, 588–89, 609, 615–16; reports on anti-American aspect of British politics, 366; visits London to negotiate trade treaty, 398, 399, 417; on French political reforms (1787), 452, 526–28; tours southern France and northern Italy, 480; on renewal of appointment to France, 482–83, 505, 511–12; urges transfer of debt from France to Holland, 486; on impost duties, 517; joins John Adams to negotiate Dutch loan, 525–26, 536, 767; and plan for funding foreign debt of United States, 538, 569–75; submits accounts as minister to France, 539–41, 553, 562–63; requests permission to return to United States, 567–68, 603, 606, 609, 613, 614–15, 618, 630; negotiates commercial treaty with France, 593; collaborates with Lafayette on French Declaration of the Rights of Man and the Citizen, 631; smuggles rice out of Italy, 512, 1244; recalls Trumbull in Paris, 1774

SECRETARY OF STATE
Early reactions to Constitution of, 27, 443, 445, 450–51, 458, 512–14, 542; on Shays's Rebellion, 438, 461; on judiciary as protector of individual rights, 447, 587; has second thoughts about Constitution, 519–20; praises Constitution, 520, 522, 529–30, 545; on need for Bill of Rights, 587–88, 598; opposes titles for president, 592; appointed secretary of state, 613, 631, 637, 640, 654; role of in location of national capital, 643–45, 659, 663, 707; and Nootka Sound incident, 645–47, 657–59; "Report on Weights and Measures," 647, 656–57; on conveying communications from states to Congress, 655, 656; visits Rhode Island with Washington, 662; denies constitutionality of Bank of United States, 666, 716, 740–41; and preface to Paine's *Rights of Man,* 667, 687–88; publicly critical of Hamilton, 667–68, 710, 745, 761–63, 763–64; champions French Revolution, 669, 749; writes "Report on the American Fisheries," 678–80; critical of John Adams's "Discourses on Davila," 688; discusses European diplomatic tensions, 693, 699; and commercial reciprocity, 711; negotiates with Hammond on treaty violations, 712–13, 726–27, 1260; and Howe's case, 717; on alloy of dollar, 718–19; submits report on proposed convention with Spain, 720, 721; urges Washington not to retire, 726, 744; on contested election between Clinton and Jay, 731–32; on national debt of United States compared with European countries, 732; on Hamilton and Marshall, 735; on Jacobin party in France, 736; labeled "Generalissimo" of Republican party, 744; retires from Washington's cabinet, 745, 753, 780–81, 799, 803, 805–6, 807, 811, 820, 821, 881; argues for recognition of French Republic, 747–48; advocates "fair neutrality," 749, 751, 765–66, 787, 798–99; and Genet, 752, 755–56, 775, 776, 802, 803, 822; and Edmund Randolph, 752, 801–2; outlines party strategy in 1793, 756–57; praises Taylor's pamphlet on bank, 759–60, 808; on federal commissioners' compensation, 764–65; moves to Grays Ferry, 767, 768; letter to Monroe, 771–72; on popular support for France, 782; predicts war with Spain, 787; plans new party strategy (1793), 803; protests British seizure of noncontraband goods, 823; commercial report of, 823, 831–32; and commercial reciprocity, 823–24; on place of meeting of Congress, 828; on diplomatic contests in Europe, 829; ascribes William Loughton Smith's speech to Hamilton, 839; helps enforce excise tax, 850

RETIREMENT INTERLUDE
Denounces denunciation of Democratic societies, 853; denounces excise law and Washington's handling of Whiskey Rebellion, 854, 858, 864; on Hamilton's resignation, 856; identifies southern interest with Republican, 877–78; opposes Jay's treaty, 883, 885–86, 887–88, 889, 891–92, 900–1, 906, 927, 928, 931, 940, 1586; prefers retirement over running for president in 1796,

INDEX 2043

855–56; on Hamilton as "a colossus," 897–98; mistakenly identifies Hamilton as "Curtius," 897; and collection of laws of Virginia, 907–15; reconciled to vice presidency, 944, 949–50, 955, 963, 966, 967; relations with John Adams after election of 1796, 944–45, 946, 947, 953, 954–55, 956–58, 960, 962–63; critical of Washington, 955; appointed Virginia commissioner on Potomac boundary, 960–61

VICE PRESIDENT
Attends special session of Congress in 1797, 968; succeeds JM as Republican leader, 971, 995; writes petition against Cabell presentment, 974–75, 986–90; welcomes Monroe after recall from France, 977; letter to Mazzei, 985–86; lambasted as traitor by Federalists, 996–97, 1000, 1003, 1005, 1010, 1050; on Lyon-Griswold affair, 997; glosses over XYZ affair, 999, 1001–2; on linkage between foreign policy and domestic repression, 1003; deplores Adams's replies to addresses, 1004, 1044; appraises alien bills, 1006, 1052, 1054, 1056, 1059, 1063; on Marshall's return from France, 1007; on Logan's mission, 1008, 1009; on Federalist charge of treasonable correspondence between Republicans and France, 1009; on Monroe's vindication, 1013; on jury trial for impeachments, 1016, 1023, 1025; on Republican strategy during quasi war with France, 1029; suspicious of postal tampering, 1033, 1089, 1108, 1116–17, 1118, 1121, 1139, 1142, 1143, 1145, 1153, 1161; on XYZ dispatches, 1034–35, 1957; interprets Constitution mistakenly, 1040; on elections of 1798, 1047; on battle of cockades, 1048, 1049; on absenteeism of Republicans, 1052; hopes for French invasion of England, 1057; sends petition for reform of British Parliament to Callender, 1058; leaves Congress before adjournment (1798), 1063–64; on his relations with Bache, 1065–66; interprets Constitution, 1069–70, 1080–84; and Virginia resolutions, 1071; on Lyon's conviction, 1071, 1079; fears use of force against Virginia, 1072–73, 1091; linking of by Harper to Logan's peace mission to France, 1074; on Adams's second peace mission, 1075, 1099; on reform of jury system in Virginia, 1075–78, 1079, 1121; sends Kentucky resolutions to JM, 1079–84; on moderation of Adams's speech (Dec. 1798), 1086; outlines party strategy for election of 1800, 1110; rejects federal common-law jurisdiction, 1112; on Bonaparte's overthrow of French Republic, 1112; compares Hamilton to Bonaparte, 1113; counsels with JM on renewing Kentucky and Virginia resolutions, 1118–19; on spoils system, 1121–22; supports defense of Callender, 1138; writes *Manual of Parliamentary Practice,* 1139; nominated for presidency in 1800, 1113, 1117, 1138, 1139; outlines party strategy for 1800, 1122; on tie vote with Burr, 1140, 1142, 1143–44, 1154, 1156; on Adams's midnight appointees, 1143; seeks understanding with Adams, 1155

PRESIDENT
Remits Callender's fine, 1163; inaugural address, 1164–65; selects cabinet, 1167; operates as chief executive officer, 1168–69; opposes paying tribute to Barbary States, 1170, 1210; personnel policy of, 1170, 1185; rejects "midnight appointments" of Adams, 1171; pardons Freeman, 1179; interprets Constitution, 1180, 1181–82; and policy towards belligerents, 1188; on case of the *Windsor,* 1189; and circular letter to heads of departments, 1201; administrative procedures of, 1202–3, 1211–12; and condemnation of Sedition Act, 1203; and Gabriel's Rebellion, 1204; on revolution of 1800, 1206, 1646–47; submits annual message to Congress in writing, 1206; on Hamiltonian system, 1207; domestic policies of, 1207–8; on Bonaparte and French control of Louisiana, 1209; requests tabular roll of federal employees, 1212; on number of federal lawsuits since 1789, 1218; on negotiations for Louisiana, 1253, 1256, 1269–71, 1271–72, 1273, 1278, 1286, 1287, 1288–90, 1291, 1327–28; on case of the *Henrich,* 1262; on negotiations for the Floridas, 1272–73, 1291; proposes armed batteries in every port, 1277; on rumored restoration of Bourbon dynasty, 1293, 1335; on French violations of neutral rights, 1295; on foreign intervention after *Philadelphia* capture, 1295–96, 1308, 1324–25; consults cabinet collectively and individually, 1303–4; on location of consuls, 1307–8; on Stevens case, 1314; on religious freedom and church discipline, 1328; on admiralty cases and prizes, 1350; second inaugural of, 1353; on freedom and licentiousness of press, 1353–54; formulates foreign-policy priorities, 1354; considers alliance with Great Britain, 1355–56, 1357, 1358, 1359, 1360, 1375, 1376, 1382, 1391, 1394; on civilizing process for Indians, 1364; on reception of Moreau, 1381; suspects France of treacherous intentions, 1381; and negotiations with Spain, 1387, 1400–1, 1402, 1405; dual system of diplomatic correspondence, 1397; and reorganization of militia, 1397, 1400; warlike message of 1805, 1404; teams Monroe and Pinkney for London negotiations, 1408; bans *Leander* from American ports, 1410; messge on neutral rights, 1414; plan for defense of New Orleans, 1416; Burr conspiracy, 1443, 1444, 1445, 1489; critical of Monroe-Pinkney Treaty, 1446, 1447, 1448, 1465, 1471; authorizes military preparations after attack on *Chesapeake,* 1449, 1451, 1487–88, 1492, 1493, 1494; hopes French pressure makes Britain conciliatory, 1452, 1489–90; proposes convention of American and Spanish troops, 1456–57; deletes condemnation of standing armies, 1459–60; on defense expenditures, 1460; proposes constitutional amendment to support education and internal improvements, 1460; on agreement not to employ British seamen, 1465; and Backus case, 1479–80, 1486, 1490–92; sets goals for Floridas, 1486; denies participation in Miranda expedition, 1486; on reciprocity of river navigation, 1498; urges preparedness measures, 1503; on breakdown of *Chesapeake* negotiations, 1504; on embargo or war, 1504, 1506, 1512–13, 1514–15, 1540, 1549, 1552–53; and secret mission to Russia, 1510; sends message on fortifying harbors, 1515–16; on British policy towards United States, 1516–17, 1540; on Spanish right to navigate Mississippi, 1518; Edward Livingston's lawsuit over batture, 1521, 1620, 1633, 1640, 1642, 1690, 1693; on army appointments, 1523; discusses seizing disputed Spanish territory, 1533; urged to seek third term, 1548; retires after second term, 1548; abdicates leadership, 1549; signs bill repealing Embargo Act, 1554; retires to Monticello, 1554, 1563, 1576; lists final correspondence with Washington, 1558; defends embargo as temporary restriction of commerce, 1559; offers library to university if one is established, 1604

RETIREMENT
Daily routine in retirement of, 1563; on Latrobe's expensive tastes, 1565–66; on Erskine Agreement, 1567, 1585, 1591, 1600; on "empire for liberty," 1568; blasts British ministry, 1571, 1573; critical of Congress, 1576; on Monroe's break with John Randolph, 1580; on Bonaparte and Floridas, 1583, 1586; and Short's letter of credence, 1595;

RETIREMENT *(continued)*
advocates seizing Floridas in case of war, 1600; on dismissal of "Copenhagen" Jackson, 1614; wishes a pox on both Great Britain and France, 1617; on England's claim to exclusive right to the sea, 1618, 1638; on revocation of French decrees, 1618, 1646; on reconciliation between JM and Monroe, 1610–11, 1654; on Duane's apostasy, 1655, 1669; critical of Robert Smith's antiadministration pamphlet, 1670; on war or submission, 1674, 1678, 1679, 1690; on embargo of 1812, 1678; recommendations of, on conduct of War of 1812, 1682, 1684, 1685, 1699, 1700, 1708–9, 1711, 1712, 1719–21, 1723–25; on handling of wartime dissidents, 1699; praises naval victories, 1709, 1720; on Treaty of Ghent, 1734, 1748, 1755, 1764; offers books for Library of Congress, 1745, 1759, 1766; on wartime monetary policy, 1734–35, 1739, 1745, 1748–50; commiserates with JM after British torch Washington, 1732, 1744; proposes federalization of militia, 1735; on postwar commercial diplomacy, 1755–56; on white paper on War of 1812, 1756–57, 1763; and postwar lapse in correspondence with JM, 1772–73; welcomes JM's retirement, 1775, 1791; and Albemarle Academy, 1776; and search committee for professors, 1778, 1894, 1958; and Central College, 1789, 1800–1; organizes Albemarle Agricultural Society, 1792; drafts educational plan for Rockfish Gap meeting, 1793–94, 1804–5; and founding of University of Virginia, 1794–95, 1796, 1797, 1798, 1799, 1810, 1813; establishes grammar school, 1798; on Andrew Jackson's invasion of East Florida, 1808; on Missouri crisis, 1821, 1829; builds new book collection, 1822; and Monroe Doctrine, 1844–45; and Rotunda, 1856, 1860–61; and authorship of Washington's Farewell Address, 1863; favors seriatim opinions by Supreme Court, 32–35, 1852, 1864–65, 1866; and reputation as author of Declaration of Independence, 1875–77; and Trumbull's print of *Declaration of Independence*, 1878; Lafayette visits, 1889; and states' rights, 1916; and student discipline, 1920; favors discontinuance of William and Mary, 1921; writes "Solemn Declaration and Protest," 35, 36, 1944–46, 1954, 1955, 1957, 1961–62, 1977; views internal improvements as consolidationist, 32, 1944–46, 1954, 1977; reviews public services, 1952; on new generation, 1952–53; makes last will and testament, 1959; and final meeting with JM, 1959; dissents on appointing president of university, 1969; uses term "nullification," 1990; and Rives, 1996.
Jenkins, Captain Charles: master of *Juno,* 529
Jenkins, Charles Jones, 1301
Jennifer, Daniel, of St. Thomas, 369, 478
Jersey greening apples, 511
Jockey Club, of Alexandria, 265, 267
John Adams (U.S. frigate): carries U.S. remittance to Holland, 1623; brings dispatches from Great Britain and France, 1631, 1634, 1636, 1637; mentioned, 1234, 1240, 1242, 1245, 1311
Johnson, Chapman, 1820, 1824, 1839, 1840, 1853, 1920
Johnson, Sir John, 345
Johnson, Samuel, 6
Johnson, Thomas, 478, 508, 764, 806, 816, 828
Johnson, William: and seriatim opinions, 1861; TJ's letter to, 1862–66; and controversy with Cooper, 1868; mentioned, 1848, 1853, 1854
Johnson, William Samuel, 477, 579
Johnson, Zachary, 509, 534, 605
Johnston, Francis, 156–57
Johnstown, N.Y., 203
Jones, Evan, 1336, 1337, 1343

Jones, Gabriel, 509, 532, 542
Jones, John, 737
Jones, John Paul: delivers gunpower from France, 165; and ratification of Articles of Confederation, 171; and Catherine the Great, 630; sends his bust to TM, 610, 636, 649; mentioned, 152, 490, 495, 506
Jones, Joseph: in Continental Congress, 129; on British invasion of Virginia, 133; confers with Luzerne, 163, 164, 165, 166, 167; and western land claims of Virginia, 211; at Princeton, 234, 266; replaced in Congress, 261; favors strengthening Confederation, 278; and British debts, 361–62; and Colonel Le Maire, 367; collects information for TJ, 408; declines reelection to Confederation Congress, 456; critical of Edmund Randolph, 817; and Jay's treaty, 887; mentioned, 145, 167, 201, 222, 243, 265, 363, 897, 956
Jones, Meriwether, 1435
Jones, Michael, 1475
Jones, Mr. (clerk), 1179
Jones, Mr. (consul at Tunis), 1779
Jones, Mr. (at Guadaloupe), 1232, 1233
Jones, Mr. (petition for pardon), 1434
Jones, Robert H., 1525
Jones, W., 1273
Jones, Dr. Walter, 404–5, 509, 534, 730, 1195, 1738
Jones, Wiley, 510
Jones, William: appointed secretary of navy, 1708, 1712, 1714, 1721, 1722, 1733; mentioned, 1175
Jones, Willie, 153–54
Jordan, Richard, 1347
Jordan, Winthrop D., 13, 15, 16, 19–20, 21
Joseph II (Holy Roman emperor), 262, 290, 365, 536
Jouett, Charles, 1767
Jouett, John, 177
Jouett, Robert, 928
Journals of the Continental Congress, 9
Joy, George, 615, 866, 1341, 1531
Judicial review: TJ advocates, under Confederation, 480–81; TJ favors, to protect individual rights, 525; JM on, 1868–69, 1873, 1982; mentioned, 1069, 1849–52, 1989
Judicial supremacy, 500, 1851–52
Judiciary Act of 1789: JM on, 1980, 1981; Calhoun on, 1980
Judiciary Act of 1801, 1143, 1154–55, 1156, 1161, 1207, 1218, 1245
Judiciary Department, establishment of, 622
Jury selection: TJ proposes reform of, in Virginia, 1067, 1121
Justice, and majority rule, 448, 502

Kammen, Michael: quoted, 518
Karamanli, Hamet, 1228
Kaskaskia, 63, 78, 1347
Kaskaskia Indians, 78, 1298
Kaskaskia River, 1426
Keeper of the seals, 544
Kello, Samuel, 605
Kelty, Mr., 1274
Kemble, Mr.: *see* Kimball, Hazen
Kemble, Peter, 555
Kemp, John, 696
Kemper, Reuben, 1402
Kemper, Samuel, 1402
Kempers, the: case of, 1402
Kemp's Landing, Va., 1724
Kennedy, David, 76
Kennedy, John F.: on TJ, 1; on JM, 1, 1761
Kenner, William, 1343
Kent, James, 897
Kentucky: statehood for, 295, 406, 566, 614; petitions Virginia legislature, 369; skirmishes with Indians in, 421; and ratification of Constitution,

535; and navigation of Mississippi, 607; Constitution of 1792, 729; coffee trees, 780, 784; Kentucky resolutions, 1067, 1068–69, 1070, 1079–84, 1096, 1989; federal lawsuits in, 1217; war spirit in (1812), 1683
Kermelin, Baron de, 251
Kerr, George, 179, 180
Kerr, James, 1148
Kerr, Joseph, 1427
Kerr, Mr., 166
Ketcham, Ralph: quoted, 1796
Key, Ann Bibb, 1145
Key, Edmund, 1347
Key, Francis Scott, 1734
Key, John, 286, 297, 316, 342
Key, Thomas H., 1886, 1887, 1908, 1920, 1942
Kickapoo Indians, 1841
Killam, Mr., 1241, 1251
Kimball, Hazen, 1200, 1201
King, Cyrus, 1030
King, Rufus: as delegate to Constitutional Convention, 469, 477, 932; and JM, 685, 816, 1211; on "Publicola," 691; Jay on, 806; and Genet's appeal to people, 811; as New York senator, 860; Republican toast against, 885; appointed minister to Great Britain, 939; advocates peace with France, 981, 982; and retaliation bill, 1095; and arbitration commission, 1214; and impressments, 1257, 1258, 1281; and return of Maryland bank stock, 1277; compares sale of Louisiana with sale of Dunkirk, 1279; on sale of Louisiana, 1283; accounts of as minister, 1329; resigns as minister to Great Britain, 1354; as vice presidential candidate, 1352, 1548; on instructions to Erskine, 1569; on Trumbull's paintings, 1775; and Bonnycastle, 1886; and University of Virginia, 1940; mentioned, 1010, 1213, 1226, 1247, 1274, 1276, 1332
King and Queen Courthouse, Va., 155
King, William, 1326
King of Württemberg, 1430, 1435, 1436
King's Mountain, Battle of, 1922
Kingston, N.Y., 267, 1463, 1703
Kinlock, Francis, 530
Kirby, Ephraim, 1272, 1336, 1337
Kirby, John B., 1465
Kirkland, John T., 1837
Kirkland, Samuel, 347
Kirkpatrick, William, 1265
Kittera, John Wilkes, 976
Knapp, John, 993
Knox, Henry: heads War Department, 594, 613; and plan for militia, 649; dines with Joseph Brant, 733; and neutrality, 749; on Democratic society of Philadelphia, 756–57; and Genet's recall, 803; resignation of, 856, 866; succeeded by Pickering, 869, 886; bankruptcy of, 1086; and fortifications at Newport, 1187; mentioned, 196, 554, 802, 818, 828
Knox, James, 96, 104, 111
Knyphausen, Wilhelm Baron von, 141
Koch, Adrienne, 10, 11, 524, 1068
Kościuszko, Tadeusz, 1225, 1469, 1699, 1700, 1703
Kosloff, Nicholas, 1782
Kuhn, Peter, Jr., 1381
Kurtz, Stephen G.: quoted, 948, 980, 1042, 1085

Lafayette, Marie-Joseph-Paul-Yves-Roch-Gilbert du Motier, marquis de: and Arnold's treason, 132, 147; and Arnold's invasion of Virginia, 169, 172–73, 181; pledges personal credit for military supplies, 174; and General Phillips, 198; and Spain's policy on Mississippi River, 328, 370; first postwar visit to United States, 328, 381; JM's appraisal of, 328–29, 343, 374; at Indian treaty negotiations, 344–45, 345–46, 347–49; made citizen of Virginia, 346, 394, 403; TJ's appraisal of, 365, 436; as auxiliary to TJ in France, 400, 401, 457, 463; busts of, commissioned, 329, 411, 465, 1941; TJ proposes gift of land to, 419, 1369; collaborates with TJ on Declaration of the Rights of Man and the Citizen, 528, 631; during French Revolution, 527–28, 543, 582–83, 584–85, 603, 625, 696; and James Swan, 899; JM writes, 554; and George Washington Greene, 653; Louisiana lands of, 1350, 1608, 1623, 1659; debts of, 1631; visits America as nation's guest, 1888–89, 1899, 1902; visits Montpellier, 1907; visits Monticello, 1907; mentioned, 189, 772, 903, 1545, 1546, 1767, 1783
La Harpe, Jean-François, 1311
Lake Champlain: American victories on, 1731, 1732, 1734, 1737; mentioned, 670, 1507, 1730
Lake Erie, 1372, 1712, 1729
Lake George, N.Y., 670
Lake Ontario, 1703, 1712, 1731
Lake Superior, 1219
Lambert, Claude Guillaume, II, 544
Lambert, William, 897
Lamothe, William, 74, 75, 94, 118
Lancaster, Pa., 548, 552, 1184
Land Act of 1796, 920–21, 925
Land bounty, 120
Landless poor: in France, 333–34, 390; in America, 334, 390–91
Land Ordinance of 1784, 18, 277, 309, 311–13
Land tax (1798), 1042, 1049, 1054
Langdon, John: refuses to vote on naturalization bill, 1059; rejects Navy Department; 1167, 1174; mentioned 579, 860, 945, 962–63, 976, 1031
Languedoc, France, 464, 1724
Lansing, Abraham, 469, 478
La Plata provinces, 1243
Laporte, Mr., 1798, 1812–13
La Rochefoucauld-Liancourt, François-Alexandre-Frédéric, duc de, 902, 903, 927
Lastayrie, M. de, 1783
Latimer, George, 1231
Latimer, Henry, 873
Latouche, Captain de: see Destouches, Charles-René-Dominique Gochet, Chevalier
Latrobe, Benjamin Henry: compares TJ and JM, 12; sues Thornton for libel, 1436; refurnishes President's House, 1565; and remodeling of Montpellier, 1570; claims additional compensation, 1577, 1579–80, 1581; mentioned, 1135, 1435, 1547, 1724
Lattimore, David, 1368, 1370
Laurance, John, 976, 1062
Laurens, Henry: imprisoned in the Tower of London, 152, 208; exchanged for Lord Cornwallis; 224; on earl of Shelburne 249; mentioned, 306, 469, 478
Laussat, Pierre-Clément de, 1306, 1308, 1328, 1387
La Vallette, Charles François Chandéon, Chevalier de, 225
La Vauguyon, Paul François de Quélen de Stuer de Caussade, duc de, 625
La Villebrance, Jacques Aimé Le Sarge, chevalier de. See Villebrune, Jacques Aimé Le Sarge, chevalier de la
La Villebrune, Jacques Aimé Le Sarge, Chevalier de. See Villebrune, Jacques Aimé Le Sarge, chevalier de la
Law, Judge, 1248
Law, Richard, 1234, 1236
Law of nations, 360, 1196, 1281, 1338, 1356, 1384, 1398, 1408, 1412–14
Lawson, Mr., 534
Lay, Mr., 1943
Lead, 173, 184, 190, 295
League of Armed Neutrality, 153, 250

Leander (British warship), 1410, 1415, 1428, 1462, 1463
Leander (U.S. ship), 1436, 1437
Lear, Benjamin L., 1761
Lear, Tobias: secretary to President Washington, 655, 656, 701, 702; TJ considers for Navy Department, 1174; TJ appoints, as commercial agent to Santo Domingo, 1190, 1208, 1225; consul general to Algiers, 1265, 1266, 1267, 1494; and peace treaty with Tripoli, 1296, 1315, 1325, 1510–11; JM on, 1302–3; and Mellimelli, 1438; mentioned, 1277, 1301, 1340, 1342, 1421, 1428, 1429
Leavenworth, Henry, 1664
Le Blanc, Georges-Pierre, 833
Leblanc, Régis, 1096, 1097
Leclerc, Charles-Victor-Emmanuel, 1208, 1225, 1227, 1240, 1255
Lee, Arthur: elected to Confederation Congress, 261; and peace treaty, 293; TJ on, 294; as Indian commissioner, 309, 347–48; in Virginia legislature, 370, 401; opposes ratification, 505; member of Treasury board, 563; and Bank of United States, 696; mentioned, 245, 251, 283, 743, 1747
Lee, Charles: and Jay's treaty, 902; supports carriage tax, 925; attends Washington ball, 998, 1024; TJ attributes "Scipio's" essays to, 1013, 1017; on Duane's indictment, 1183; mentioned, 921, 971, 978, 979, 1024, 1161
Lee, General Charles, 49
Lee, Eliza, 1775
Lee, Francis Lightfoot, 534
Lee, Henry ("Light Horse Harry"): on excise tax, 689; and Freneau, 700; TJ sends greetings to, 703; on Coxe and Hamilton, 704; and state banks, 740, 742; and Proclamation of Neutrality, 830; commands troops against Whiskey Rebellion, 851, 859; and Backus case, 1480; mentioned, 614, 630, 694, 704, 705, 1490, 1491
Lee, Henry, Jr., 534
Lee, Ludwell, 476, 961
Lee, Mr., 91
Lee, R. B., 765
Lee, Richard Bland, 605, 768
Lee, Richard Henry: writes address to citizens of Great Britain, 47; and Declaration of Independence, 49, 1845, 1847, 1876, 1877; in Virginia legislature, 278; favors revision of Virginia Constitution, 282, 318, 322; president of Confederation Congress, 388, 408, 456; and citizenship for Lafayette, 403; opposes ratification, 505, 515; as Antifederalist senator from Virginia, 579, 590–91, 612, 613, 621, 718, 743; and secession, 643; mentioned, 51, 88, 186, 245, 476
Lee, Robert, 1279, 1301
Lee, Thomas Ludwell, 54
Lee, Thomas Sim, 168, 508–9
Lee, William, 155, 161
Lee, William: consul at Bordeaux, 1367, 1373, 1423, 1425, 1474, 1647, 1649; replies to Robert Smith's attack on JM, 1655, 1671
Lee, William, Jr., 1332
Lee, William R., 1231, 1250
Lee family, 896–97
Lefebvre, Georges: quoted, 603, 631
Leghorn, Italy, 1228, 1852
Legislative sovereignty: JM critical of, 441, 442, 470
Legislature: TJ and JM's use of term, in Kentucky and Virginia resolutions, 1072
Leib, Michael, 1206, 1650, 1651, 1738
Leiper, Thomas: handles TJ and JM's tobacco sales, 693, 1241, 1242; mentioned, 689, 733, 819, 1244, 1666
Le Maire, Étienne, 1428, 1467, 1583

Le Maire, Jacques: Virginia's commercial agent, 66, 98, 351–52; TJ makes loan to, 381, 414, 416; returns to France, 407–8; mentioned, 487, 489
L'Enfant, Pierre Charles, 708
Lenox, David, 1213, 1326
Lenthall, John, 1547, 1577, 1579–80
Lenud's Ferry, S.C., 143
Leoben, Treaty of, 981, 983
Leonard, John, 1301
Leonidas (ship), 1526, 1529
Leopard (British warship), 1445
Leslie, Alexander, 197
Leslie, Sir John, 1904, 1905
Leslie, Professor, 1788, 1789
Letombe, Philippe-André-Joseph de, 1014, 1055, 1190
Letters: TJ and JM on, 4, 6, 1863; James Agee on, 5; Carl Becker on, 5; Nathaniel Hawthorne on, 5; as intimate conversation, 6; in eighteenth century, 7; formality of TJ and JM's, 9; and intimate friendship, 13; as autobiography, 125
Letters from an American Farmer (Michel-Guillaume St. Jean de Crèvecoeur), 532
Letters of marque, 166
L'Eveille (French warship), 182
Le Veillard, Louis-Guillaume, 400
Levi, Mr., 242
Levy, Leonard: quoted, 1111
Levy, Mr., 1363
Lexington, Battle of, 44
Leyden Gazette, 410, 1306
Lewis, Andrew, 96
Lewis, Meriwether, 1167, 1257, 1268, 1434, 1606, 1608, 1609, 1623
Lewis, Mr., 1087
Lewis, Mr., 1134, 1135, 1145
Lewis, Nicholas, handles TJ's financial affairs, 364; mentioned, 355, 494, 562, 589, 649, 1160–61, 1673, 1727
Lewis, Mrs. Nicholas, 1673
Lewis, Nicholas, Jr., 1673
Lewis, St., 1272
Lewis, Thomas, 534, 1436, 1437, 1438
Lewis, Warner, 605
Lewis, William, 828, 921
Lewis and Clark expedition, 1257, 1459, 1608
L'Hommedieu, Ezra, 878
Liancourt, duc de. *See* La Rochefoucauld-Liancourt, François-Alexandre-Frédéric, duc de
Libby, Richard, 1465
Liberty: and republican government, 448; and education, 514, 1821; JM discusses power and, 522, 523–24; and power, 565; and Bill of Rights, 595–98; Washington on, 600; and order, 669–70; TJ on French Republic and, 749, 757–58; JM on, and French Revolution, 784; and university, 1960, 1967; and Lafayette's 1824 visit, 1899
Liberty (JM's horse), 1791
Library Company of Philadelphia, 146
Library of Congress: 14, 15, 208, 1360, 1731, 1732, 1745
Lilac, 840
Limestone, Mississippi district, 1476
Limozin, André: U.S. agent at Havre, 385, 460, 485–87, 488, 493, 508, 568
Lincoln, Benjamin, 473, 1086
Lincoln, Levi: TJ's appraisal of, 1149; appointed attorney general, 1167; as acting secretary of state, 1174, 1175; and Duane's indictments, 1183; and Bingham's case, 1194; and Yazoo land compromise, 1221–22, 1405; rejects Supreme Court appointment, 1621, 1647, 1648, 1659; mentioned, 1173, 1219, 1227, 1260, 1311, 1324
Lindemann, Mr. (governor of Danish West Indies), 1261
Lindsay, Joseph (of New Orleans), 106–7

INDEX *2047*

Lindsey, Reuben (TJ's neighbor), 1381, 1645, 1807, 1822
Linn, James, 1140, 1154
Linnaeus, Carolus, 690
Lisbon, Portugal, 1128, 1130, 1132, 1190, 1197
Liston, Robert: and Blount conspiracy, 992, 1011, 1019, 1326; and Duane's indictment for libeling, 1183. *See also* "Liston's plot"
"Liston's plot," 992, 1011. *See also* Blount, William
Literary Fund: Virginia legislature and, 1793, 1796, 1803; and University of Virginia, 1817, 1818, 1819, 1837, 1843, 1861, 1862
Lithgow's case, 1839
Little Belt (British sloop of war), 1656, 1669, 1675
Littlepage, Lewis, 544
Little's Lane, Virginia, 1167, 1176
Livermore, Edward St. Loe, 1185
Livermore, Samuel, 976, 1086, 1090, 1093
Liverpool, Lord, 1688, 1690, 1691, 1698. *See also* Hawkesbury, Robert Banks Jenkinson, second Baron
Livingston, Edward: election of, 854, 865, 872; and documents relating to Jay's treaty, 890–91, 925, 926; leaves Congress early, 1052; rides with Marshall from New York, 1060; drowned out in debate, 1100; and Robbins's affair, 1128; and election of 1800, 1129; shortage in his office as district attorney, 1274, 1620; and Laussat, 1308; and Baron de Bastrop, 1330; and Lafayette, 1369; sues Jefferson over batture, 1518–19, 1521, 1619–20, 1633, 1634, 1640, 1644; moves to New Orleans, 1620; and nullification doctrine, 1987–88, 1995; mentioned, 1198, 1301
Livingston, Henry Brockholst, 1334, 1363
Livingston, Robert R.: on committee to draft Declaration of Independence, 47, 1875; as secretary of foreign affairs, 221, 222, 234–35, 250–51; candidate for secretary of the treasury, 613; TJ and JM visit on northern excursion, 670; Washington on, 806; opposes Jay's treaty, 884, 896, 897; runs for governor of New York, 1013; rejects TJ's offer of Navy Department, 1140, 1154, 1156, 1160, 1167, 1174; minister to France, 1169–70, 1190, 1195, 1196, 1197, 1198, 1199, 1200, 1283; and negotiations for Louisiana, 1253, 1256, 1272, 1279, 1289, 1290; forces Sumter's resignation, 1238, 1246, 1247; TJ critical of, 1255, 1265–66, 1278, 1338; JM critical of 1255, 1264; and captured crew of *Philadelphia,* 1305; letter from, 1323, 1332, 1342; reduces Skipwith's salary, 1334; and American claims for spoliations against France, 1310, 1331, 1337, 1345; visits London, 1334; mentioned, 172, 828, 1213, 1225, 1227, 1234, 1235, 1246, 1281, 1311, 1366
Livingston, William, 478
Livingston v. Jefferson, 1620
Llewellensburg, 1347
Lloyd, Edward, IV, 660
Lloyd, James, 1013, 1064, 1065, 1196
Lloyd, Thomas, 607, 982
Locke, John, 6, 808, 1845, 1876, 1909, 1918, 1924
Logan, Deborah Norris (Mrs. George), 1008, 1009
Logan, George: and JM's plows, 769, 770, 793–94, 797, 1624; sends pamphlet to JM, 787; writes book on crop rotation, 961; unofficial peace mission to France of, 1008, 1061; and Logan Act, 1073, 1074, 1086, 1088, 1090–91, 1103, 1193; elected to Pennsylvania legislature, 1074, 1086; pretended memorial of, 1088; on trade with Santo Domingo, 1371; role in negotiations for Florida, 1406; mentioned, 871, 1086
Lomax, John Tayloe, 1897, 1916, 1939, 1959, 1964, 1969, 1970
Loménie de Brienne, Étienne-Charles de, 543
London (British warship), 164
London, England, 1192, 1213, 1324, 1915

London *Times,* 1255
Long, George, 1886, 1887, 1908, 1912, 1920, 1942
Longchamps, Charles Julien, 320, 349
Long Island, N.Y., 543, 687
Long Island, Va., 110
Longman and Company, 1898
Lookout boats, 115
Looming, 734
Lorient, France, 1132, 1246
Lorton's Tavern, Charles City County, Va., 908
Lottery. *See* Jefferson, Thomas: Personal life
Louis XIV (king of France), 384, 1186, 1521
Louis XVI (king of France): confers military honor on John Paul Jones, 171; promises financial assistance to United States, 200, 486; TJ's appraisal of, 481–82; abrogates power of provincial parlements, 527; and constitutional reforms, 600, 601–2; capitulation of, 602; and taxation, 617, 618; and National Assembly, 624–25; arrested, 747; mentioned, 250, 769
Louis XVIII (king of France), 1758
Louisa County, Va., 1776
Louisiana: and Bonaparte, 1208, 1254, 1255; purchase of, 1253, 1254–55, 1256, 1297, 1299; TJ researches boundaries of, 1282; TJ proposes constitutional amendment dealing with, 1282, 1288; TJ on significance of, 1287, 1288, 1290; and Anglo-American reconciliation, 1294; delivery of, to Spain (1762), 1305–6; and spoliation claims, 1331–32; TJ proposes citizenship for residents of, 1335; boundaries of, 1356, 1396; commissioners of, 1417, 1418; and West Florida, 1651
Louisville, Ky., 1251, 1263
Loune, Messrs., 1522
Lownes, Caleb, 920, 923, 929, 935
Loyalists, 59, 711, 712
Loyall, George, 1853, 1856, 1894, 1926, 1930, 1931
Lucas, John Baptiste Charles, 1365
Lucas, Nathaniel, 81
Lucius Caesar, 384
Ludlow, Charles, 1262
Lumsden, William, 1118
Lundy's Lane, Battle of, 1731
Luzerne, Anne-César, chevalier de la: and ratification of Articles of Confederation, 129, 171; and Benedict Arnold, 132, 147; and *Romulus,* 199; and TJ's appointment to peace mission, 216, 224, 226; and Peace of Paris, 274; tours United States, 311; as French ambassador to Great Britain, 544, 698; mentioned, 154, 155, 167, 182, 195, 200, 203, 294, 462
Luzerne, César-Henri, comte de la, TJ's appraisal of, 544, 626
Luzerne, marquise de la (Mrs. Anne-César), 544
Lycian Confederacy, 498
Lycurgus: JM on, 2
Lyman, Mr., 1666
Lyman, William, 824, 1230
Lynch, Anthony, 1096
Lynch, Marcus, Jr., 1332
Lynch, Mr., 1246
Lynchburg, Va., 1697, 1783, 1800, 1928
Lynd, Staughton, 15
Lynhaven Bay, 1560, 1722
Lynnhaven River, 1711, 1720, 1723, 1724
Lyon, James, 1155, 1156
Lyon, Matthew: attempt to expel from House, 997, 1020, 1087; convicted of sedition, 1071, 1079; reelected while in jail, 1074, 1086; and tie vote in 1800, 1144, 1161; mentioned, 1155
Lyon-Griswold affair, 1021–22, 1026, 1030

Mably, Gabriel Bonnot de, 485, 488, 858, 876
MacAllister, Archibald T., 676
Macarty, William, 581
McCally, Hugh, 1581

McClay, William, 554, 563, 579, 1031
McClurg, James: is delegate to Constitutional Convention, 476, 477, 478, 503; supports ratification, 509; Washington on, 806–7; mentioned, 696, 828
McColley, Robert, 15, 16
McCoy, Drew R., 23, 1989
McDonald, Forrest: quoted, 519
Macdonough, Thomas, 1731, 1732, 1734, 1744
McDougal, Alexander, 179, 188
McDougall, George, 1523
McDowall, General. *See* McDougal, Alexander
McFarland, George, 1347
McGee, Mr.: buys nails for JM, 1118; mentioned, 1085, 1087, 1089–90, 1147, 1148
McGehee, William, 1644–45
Macgruder's grist mill, 1429, 1486
McHenry, James: is delegate to Constitutional Convention, 478; appointed secretary of war, 919; attends Washington ball, 998, 1024; Adams dismisses, 1117; mentioned, 1020, 1028, 1039
Machias, Maine, 1464
Machir, James, 979
MacIntosh, Lachlan, 71
McIlwaine, H. R., 60–61
McKean, Thomas, 1013, 1129, 1227, 1241, 1292, 1380, 1472
McKinley, Mr., 1530
McKinney, John, 1465
McLanachan, Blair, 1053
McLean, Archibald, 691
McNeill, Daniel, 1228, 1235, 1236
Macomb, Alexander, 1734
Macon, Nathaniel, 1055, 1150, 1615, 1616, 1618
McPherson, Charles, 1132
McPherson, Christopher, 1132, 1133, 1134
McPherson, Clarinda, 1132
McPherson's Blues, 1741
Mcradie, Mr., 1427
Madeira, 1192
Madeira wine, 1828
Madison, Dolley Payne Todd: marries JM, 847–48; TJ sends respects to, 858, 1050, 1121, 1146, 1176, 1177, 1704; TJ sends greetings to, 860, 872, 923, 928, 932, 982, 1014, 1017, 1018, 1021, 1023, 1028, 1036, 1726; TJ urges, not let JM retire, 868; TJ invites, to visit Monticello with JM, 986, 1481, 1486, 1492, 1533, 1537, 1658, 1805, 1814; enjoys visits to Monticello, 992, 1489; TJ sends salutations to, 1040, 1045, 1058, 1060, 1061, 1080, 1089, 1092, 1093, 1098, 1130, 1131, 1133, 1146, 1148, 1160, 1161, 1174, 1175, 1191, 1284, 1371, 1375, 1434, 1589, 1604, 1640, 1700, 1767, 1780, 1786, 1788, 1807, 1825, 1841; visits Monticello, 1118, 1139, 1730, 1772, 1777, 1785, 1796; TJ carries purchases for, from Philadelphia, 1136, 1145; on account with TJ's nailery, 1147; and TJ's family, 1185; TJ thanks, 1273; and Mrs. Pichon, 1341; expects company, 1342; in Philadelphia for knee operation, 1354, 1360, 1361–62, 1372–73, 1374; slow recovery of, 1357, 1362, 1377, 1379, 1380, 1384, 1385–86, 1388, 1391, 1394; TJ wishes speedy recovery for, 1362, 1373, 1375, 1376, 1381, 1383, 1391, 1395; buys wig for Martha Randolph, 1362; returns to Washington, 1362; TJ on surgery of, 1387; and Dr. Park, 1393; described by Margaret Bayard Smith, 1562; described by Louisa Catherine Adams, 1563; and JM move into President's House, 1565; and Latrobe refurnish President's House, 1565; on TJ's list of final correspondence with Washington, 1558; TJ recommends gardener to, 1583–84; TJ's affection for, 1727, 1853; reunited with JM after British burn Washington, 1731; and regard for Martha Randolph, 1744, 1823; painted by Wood, 1775; retirement routine of, 1791; sculpted by Coffee, 1804; and friendship for Randolph children, 1815, 1816; Correa's regard for, 1826; on TJ's views of Constitution, 1850; Anne Newport Royall on, 1974–75
Madison, Francis Taylor (JM's sister), 967, 984. *See also* Rose, Frances Taylor Madison

MADISON, JAMES
PERSONAL LIFE
Characteristics: archives and letters of, 3, 125; and gossip, 7–8; sense of humor of, 8–9, 171, 671, 1686; love of books of, 14; TJ purchases books for, in Paris, 15; studies government and law, 38, 277–78, 286; description of, in 1776, 53–54; suspicions of postal tampering of, 1036; painted by Wood, 1775; art collection of, 1792 *Family life:* at Mrs. House's boardinghouse, 228; marries Dolley Payne Todd, 847, 848; buys French furniture, 849; TJ congratulates, on marriage, 858; nurses wife after her knee operation, 1354, 1361–62, 1373, 1388, 1389; and retirement from Congress, 947, 967; and retirement from presidency, 1776, 1799–1800 *Slavery:* antislavery views of, 17, 18–19, 23–24, 26; on white prejudice against blacks, 21–22; and colonization of emancipated slaves, 22; on manumission, 23; slavery and aristocratic government, 24; on diffusion of slavery, 25; as slaveholder, 26 *Farming:* and plows, 785, 1622–23, 1625, 1626; adds portico to Montpellier, 787; on rotation farming, 820; visits Montpellier, 1256–57, 1570, 1572, 1637, 1658, 1713, 1726, 1742; and merino sheep, 1621–22, 1627, 1630, 1634, 1635, 1636–37, 1638, 1638–39, 1641, 1649; interest in agriculture of, 1792; as president of Albemarle Agricultural Society, 1792 *Health:* fear of epilepsy of, 14; and cholera morbus, 14; illness of, 693, 697, 1122, 1204, 1713; health of, 708, 1156, 1159, 1160, 1167, 1172, 1175, 1195, 1197, 1204, 1641, 1703, 1836 *Intellectual interests:* on periodic constitutional revision, 29–30; on TJ's generational theory, 30–31, 604, 640–42, 650–53; on Buffon's theories, 284, 288–89; on Incognitum, 284; on monax and marmotte, 421–23; observations on TJ's draft constitution, 555–62 *Personal relations:* critical of John Adams, 7, 479, 563, 668–69, 689–90; visits George Mason, 286; joins Lafayette on western trip, 328–29, 343, 344–45, 348–49; visits Washington, 388–89; Mazzei gives power of attorney to, 676; and Monroe, 830, 831, 849, 1010, 1012; Lafayette visits, 1889 *Finances:* purchases land on Mohawk River, 400, 432–33, 538; western lands of, 428; indebtedness of, 1953–54, 1967 *Miscellaneous:* John Adams on presidency of, 1, 1761; John F. Kennedy on, 1, 1761; Luzerne's appraisal of, 273; on laboring poor, 397–98, 423–24; as historian, 1981, 1983–84, 1986, 1987, 1988, 1996, 1999–2000, 2001; George Tucker and Robert Scott on, 1974–75

FRIENDSHIP WITH JEFFERSON
On friendship with TJ, 10–11, 57, 60, 68, 228; compared with TJ, 11–12; described by TJ, 13, 52; on TJ's rhetorical excess, 13, 1978; regard for TJ's judgment, 26–27; shares interests with TJ, 14–15, 124–25; and first impressions of TJ, 37–38, 52–53; deplores TJ's retirement as governor, 180, 205, 209–10; asks Congress to reinstate TJ as peace commissioner, 207; asks TJ to research Virginia's western land claims, 210, 211; briefs TJ on revenue system of 1783, 231; briefs TJ on congressional issues, 231–35; briefs TJ on location of national capital, 267–69; and revision of Virginia laws, 283, 323, 393–94, 401–3; keeps TJ

INDEX 2049

informed in France, 326; defends TJ against charge of land speculation, 331, 342; intrigued by gadgets shipped from France, 332; TJ sends *Notes* to, 334–35, 392, 401, 419; briefs TJ on Virginia legislation (1784), 355–63; thanks TJ for "literary cargo," 413; pushes TJ's plan for Virginia capitol, 413; sends TJ statement of accounts, 416, 1604; briefs TJ on Constitutional Convention, 442, 467–68; briefs TJ on ratification campaign in Virginia, 520, 541–42; sends *Federalist* to TJ, 524; acquires portrait of TJ, 648; urges TJ not to retire as secretary of state, 745, 777, 816; orders nails from TJ, 1146, 1147; Dolley and, move into White House temporarily with TJ, 1167; TJ on, as auxiliary, 1353; brings TJ's great coat, 1433; retrieves session laws for TJ, 1467; pays tribute to TJ, 1561; on TJ's contributions, 1975–76; as custodian of TJ's reputation, 1978–79, 1989–90, 1991–93, 1994–95, 2000–1 *Camaraderie:* is reunited with TJ in Philadelphia (1782), 207–8; is reunited with TJ in 1783, 271; and education of TJ's nephews, 285; accompanies TJ on trip to Virginia (1790), 662–64; accompanies TJ on trip to Philadelphia (1790), 664; takes northern excursion with TJ, 670–71, 689; thanks TJ for invitation to share house, 680–81; TJ sends journal and map of European travels to, 703, 704; travels to and from Virginia with TJ (1791), 708 *Consultant:* advises TJ about letter to Mazzei, 972; asked by TJ for revision of message to Congress, 1203; sends revisions, 1216–18, 1297, 1349, 1364, 1395, 1401, 1458–60, 1559; visits TJ to counsel on renewal of Kentucky and Virginia resolutions, 1119 *Visits to Monticello:* first visit of, 639; visits in 1790, 664; visits in 1795, 857; visits in 1800, 1139; TJ invites, 1187; visits with Thorntons, 1246; visits in 1803, 1282, 1290; TJ invites, 1435; visits in 1806, 1437, 1442; visits in 1807, 1489; visits in 1808, 1535; visits in 1809, 1572, 1597; visits in 1811, 1658; resumes annual visits in 1815, 1759; visits in 1816, 1772; visits in 1819, 1814; visits in 1820, 1823; visits in 1825, 1941

REACTION TO BRITISH COLONIAL POLICY
Reaction of, to Boston Tea Party, 38; supports action by first Continental Congress, 42; elected to Orange County Committee of Safety, 43; reaction to Battle of Lexington, 44; as marksman, 45; praises authors of "Declaration of Causes and Necessity for Taking Up Arms," 47; appointed colonel of Orange County militia, 47

VIRGINIA LEGISLATURE
Elected to Virginia convention, 48: votes for independence, 49; and religious freedom, 50; on Virginia Constitution of 1776, 51; and revision of Virginia laws, 55; serves on Committee on Religion, 55; loses bid for reelection in 1777, 57

VIRGINIA EXECUTIVE COUNCIL
Elected to: serves with Governor Patrick Henry, 57, 58; on TJ's council, 59; writes letter for TJ's signature as governor, 61, 84

CONTINENTAL AND CONFEDERATION CONGRESS
Elected to Continental Congress, 61, 68; on paper money, 125; on state control of Revolutionary financing, 126–27, 137, 138; and cession of western land claims, 130–31; and navigation of Mississippi River, 131, 151, 343, 370, 395–96, 396, 431, 538, 720; on Arnold's treason, 132; on British invasion of Virginia, 133; on Continental finance, 136; celebrates ratification of Articles, 171; expedites military supplies to Virginia, 173–74, 180–81; proposes coercing states to meet Confederation needs, 175, 186–87, 194, 211, 330, 387–88; on collapse of Continental currency, 176; on victory at Yorktown, 205; and first proposal for Library of Congress, 14, 208; on peace treaty with Great Britain, 209, 299–300; on Virginia's western land claims, 210, 215, 247–48; favors strengthening Confederation, 229–32; proposes revenue system of 1783, 230–31; supports assumption of state debts (1783), 243; and end of first term in Congress, 273; on constitutional issues under Confederation, 276

VIRGINIA LEGISLATURE REVISITED
Reelected to Virginia House, 270, 278, 279, 308; and Virginia port bill, 279–80; and revision of Virginia Constitution, 282; on postwar economic conditions in Virginia, 286, 420; interprets Articles of Confederation, 301–2; critical of Virginia Executive Council, 302; appointed Potomac commissioner, 323; chairs Virginia Committee for Courts of Justice, 330; rumored as minister to Spain, 336, 367; writes "Memorial and Remonstrance" against religious assessments, 336, 375–80; appointed delegate to Annapolis Convention, 395, 396, 404–5; and British debts, 398–99; writes "Resolution on Uniform Commercial Regulations," 408–9; writes inscription for Houdon's statue of Washington, 411, 419

CONFEDERATION AND CONSTITUTIONAL CONVENTION
Defends national negative on state laws, 27–28, 446–47, 498–502; on advantages of extended republic, 27–28, 448–49, 502; on majority rule and minority rights, 27–28, 448–49, 500–2; reelected to Confederation Congress, 435, 456; condemns Shays's Rebellion, 438–39; preparation of, for Constitutional Convention, 439–42; William Pierce's appraisal of, 444; preserves "Notes on Debates," 444; role of, at convention, 449; as delegate to convention, 468, 478; briefs TJ on state delegations to convention, 469–70; briefs TJ on proposed reforms at convention, 470–71; briefs TJ on Jay-Gardoqui negotiations, 471–72; on secrecy of convention, 483; calls agreement on Constitution a miracle, 496; describes work of convention, 496–504; as Father of Constitution, 518–19; carries Virginia's ratification to Congress, 521; on adding Bill of Rights after ratification, 522–24, 524–25, 564–66; decides to run for House, 581

FEDERAL CONGRESS
Elected to first House, 591, 605; as leader in House, 592; opposes titles for president, 592; proposes executive departments for foreign affairs, war, and finance, 594; proposes Bill of Rights, 594–98, 622–24; as Father of Bill of Rights, 600; and first revenue law under Constitution, 603; and bust of John Paul Jones, 636; on funding and assumption, 642–45; and Nootka Sound incident, 645, 657–59; on TJ's "Report on Weights and Measures," 647, 656–57; on Hamilton's "Report on Public Credit," 649; and residence act for national capital, 659–61; on constitutionality of bill to locate capital, 659; opposes Bank of the United States, 665–66; heads opposition to Hamiltonian system, 667, 744; and Paine's *Rights of Man,* 670, 687, 689; discusses northwest posts with Beckwith, 681–83; on speculative spirit, 685, 705–6; on Burke's *Reflections,* 689; attempts to recruit Freneau, 700; denies interference in Treasury Department, 700, 704; contributes essays to *National Gazette,* 709–10; on political parties,

FEDERAL CONGRESS (*continued*)
709–10; and commercial reciprocity, 711; TJ consults, on negotiations with Hammond, 712, 722–25, 729; defends TJ against Hamilton's newspaper attack, 715; and Howe's case, 717; on contested election between Clinton and Jay, 734; and Washington's second term, 744; on differences with Hamilton, 744; and election of 1792, 744; French citizenship conferred on, 747, 750, 778, 782; on Proclamation of Neutrality, 749, 750–51, 783, 786, 788, 810; writes as "Helvidius," 754, 793, 795–96, 797, 799, 800, 809–10; discusses party strategy with TJ, 756–57; Washington considers for cabinet, 757; labels Federalists as Anglican party, 758, 815; organizes county meetings, 758–59; on federal commissioner's compensation, 764–65; on affection to France, 777–78; equates liberty with French Republic, 784; interprets Constitution, 783–84; on Franco-American treaty provisions, 799; on Genet, 799, 815; accused of apostacy, 804; Washington on, 806; and Monroe plan county protests, 812, 815–16; on British orders-in-council, 821; consults with TJ and Monroe on party strategy, 821; and Navigation Act of 1791, 823; introduces commercial resolutions, 824–25, 834, 835–36, 837; Federalist papers attack, 825, 832; sees Monroes off to France, 827; TJ finds lodging for, 829; supports TJ's commercial report, 831–32; portrays Federalists as aristocratic faction, 833; on Washington's influence over Congress, 845; on excise taxes, 850; on Washington's denunciation of Democratic societies, 851, 861–64, 865; and Madisonian societies, 852; prevents House censure of Democratic societies, 853–54; and Whiskey Rebellion, 854, 862–64; urged by TJ to run for president in 1796, 854–55, 855, 868; on Hamilton's resignation, 856–57; on elections of 1794, 859–60; on Jay's memorial to George III, 860; discusses diplomatic contests in Europe, 869, 870, 929–30; rejects presidential race, 875–76; writes *Political Observations,* 879–80; heads Republican party, 881; expectations for Jay's treaty, 881–82, 884–86, 887–88, 889, 891, 892–93, 929, 930–31; returns to Philadelphia in November 1795, 888; calls Federalists tories, 890; condemns Washington's use of secret journal of Constitutional Convention, 892, 930; decides to retire from Congress, 895, 936; proposes survey of national post road, 32, 923; proposes renegotiation of Jay's treaty, 933; on Washington's popularity carrying Jay's treaty, 937, 938; depressed over Federalist victory on treaty, 940; disowns Adet's interference in election of 1796, 942; reports election results to TJ, 942–48, 948–49, 950–52, 955–56; mentioned as special envoy to France, 947–48, 961, 971, 978; on Franco-American affairs, 963; and Washington's final address to Congress, 949; squelches TJ's letter to John Adams, 962

RETIREMENT INTERLUDE AND VIRGINIA LEGISLATURE
On Hamilton's pamphlet defending his financial probity, 973, 993; TJ discusses Cabell's presentment with, 974, 975, 991–92; advises TJ on Mazzei letter, 990–91; on Lyon-Griswold affair, 997, 998; compares John Adams with Washington, 1021, 1058; urges House to call for XYZ dispatches, 1000, 1032; glosses over XYZ affair, 1001, 1043, 1046, 1051; Abigail Adams critical of, 1003; on linkage between foreign policy and domestic repression, 1003, 1048; critical of Adams's responses to addresses, 1005–6, 1040–41, 1051, 1058; appraisal of Alien Friends Act, 1006, 1051; listed as member of American Directory, 1010; on Monroe's vindication, 1014; on difficulties facing envoys, 1018–19; and jury trials for impeachments, 1021, 1025; on Talleyrand, 1036–37; on Adams's dislike for Washington, D.C., 1038; refuses to write newspaper articles, 1038; on freedom of press, 1046, 1049; on XYZ dispatches, 1046, 1051; critical of Adams, 1048–49, 1058; on direct tax bill, 1053; and parliamentary reform, 1053; and Callender, 1053–54; on trade policy, 1058; on law for capturing French cruisers, 1058; TJ wants, consulted on Kentucky resolutions, 1068, 1070; writes Virginia resolutions, 1070–71; differs with TJ on meaning of "state," 1071–72, 1085, 1124; alters TJ's petition on selection of jurors, 1078; on Gerry's letters as envoy, 1090, 1094; publishes articles in *Aurora,* 1094, 1098; discusses possible publication of "Notes on Debates," 1094; suspects mail tampering, 1094, 1108; elected to Virginia legislature, 1108, 1121; drafts legislative report vindicating Virginia resolutions, 1110–11, 1122, 1123, 1124, 1125; on Bonaparte's overthrow of French Republic, 1113; on elections of 1800, 1117, 1139; and Christopher McPherson, 1132; remodels Montpellier, 1139; informs TJ of election as president, 1140; TJ offers secretary of state position to, 1140; accepts position, 1159, 1166–67, 1172–73; TJ urges, to attend inaugural, 1141, 1159; on tie vote in 1800, 1141, 1144, 1155, 1157; on second peace mission to France, 1150; interprets Constitution, 1157–58

SECRETARY OF STATE
Moves into house near State Department, 1168; on new policy towards Barbary powers, 1170; on passports for vessels, 1178; on postal contracts, 1178–79; and the *Windsor,* 1188–89; hires free Negro, 1194; writes Naturalization Act of 1795, 1207; instructions of, to Lear, 1208; and naval force in Mediterranean, 1210; lists State Department employees, 1212–13; on special diplomatic emissaries, 1213–14; lists lawsuits in federal courts, 1216–17, 1244; as federal commissioner on Georgia's western land claims, 1221–22, 1405; on charges against St. Clair, 1229–30; suggests purchasing New Orleans, 1254; on significance of Louisiana Purchase, 1256; and Lewis and Clark expedition, 1257; reports on *Henrich,* 1260–61; on constitutionality of acquiring Louisiana, 1270, 1288–89; instructions of, to Monroe regarding Spanish negotiations, 1274; and Maryland stock in Bank of England, 1279; on the Floridas, 1291; Yrujo's break with, 1292; on rumored restoration of Bourbon dynasty, 1293; on French violations of neutral rights, 1295; interprets Constitution, 1297; and transfer of Louisiana from France to Spain (1762), 1305; report on Stevens case, 1312–22; disagrees with TJ on alliance with Great Britain, 1355–56, 1357, 1358, 1380, 1384, 1388, 1392; and Spain's termination of negotiations, 1357–58, 1374; calls British seizures insults, 1360; and liberation of French wine, 1361; returns to Washington after Dolley's operation, 1362, 1395; on rules for armed merchantmen, 1363; on factional politics in Pennsylvania, 1380; on reorganization of militia, 1397; subpoenaed in Miranda case, 1407, 1424; writes *Examination of the British Doctrine....* 1408; on Fox's conciliatory moves, 1410; on interpolations on neutral rights, 1412–14, 1415; on scope of appropriations to foreign intercourse, 1441; on Burr conspiracy, 1444, 1489, 1460–61; and impressment issue, 1446–47; critical of Monroe-Pinkney Treaty, 1447, 1473; on

INDEX   2051

conciliation with Great Britain, 1453; proposes revision of TJ's convention between American and Spanish troops, 1457; and use of British seamen on American ships, 1467–68, 1469; subpoenaed in Backus case, 1479–80, 1490, 1492; defends embargo policy, 1505–6; urges naval force to enforce embargo system, 1507–8, 1532; denounces French decrees, 1509; rewrites TJ's embargo message, 1513; on sites for forts, 1515–16; and batture, 1518–19, 1521; and Short's appointment to Russia, 1528; on Turreau's request for transport, 1533–34; and antiembargo forces, 1538, 1542, 1552–53; and supporters of embargo, 1541; urges TJ not to abdicate leadership, 1549–50, 1557–58; outlines policy priorities, 1550; and repeal of Embargo Act, 1551–52; proposes Nonintercourse Act, 1553; and suspension of Embargo Act and revocation of belligerents' edicts, 1554–57

PRESIDENT
Nominated for president in 1808, 1548; inauguration of, 1561–62; cabinet appointments of, 1566; and Erskine Agreement, 1566, 1570, 1584–85, 1598; asks for recall of "Copenhagen" Jackson, 1573, 1614; on Perceval ministry, 1573; on Bonaparte and Floridas, 1585; signs bank loan for TJ, 1588, 1589–90, 1592; puzzled by order-in-council following Erskine Agreement, 1591, 1592–93; on Canning's disavowal of Erskine Agreement, 1597; sends weather journal to TJ, 1602; and reconciliation with Monroe, 1609, 1623; defends Erskine Agreement, 1614; on Macon's Bill No. 2, 1616–17, 1618; accepts Cadore letter and reimposes Nonintercourse Act against Great Britain, 1619, 1651; on Livingston's batture case, 1621, 1634, 1640, 1642, 1643–44, 1691; on separation of powers, 1634; annexes West Florida, 1648, 1651; and failure to recharter Bank of United States, 1651; replaces Robert Smith with Monroe, 1652; on French policy after Cadore letter, 1656; recommends national defense measures, 1658, 1675–76, 1677; and break with Duane, 1669; on Indian warfare in 1811, 1676; on embargo of 1812, 1678, 1693; weighs war options, 1679–80, 1696; sends war message to Congress, 1680; reports earthquake felt in Washington, 1687; and House vote for taxes, 1688; repudiates armistice, 1703; praises naval victories, 1709; second inaugural address of, 1709; accepts Russia's offer of mediation, 1710; and TJ's suggestions on conduct of War of 1812, 1712; on Smyth's debacle at Niagara, 1717; on use of gunboats, 1722; postwar lapse in correspondence with TJ, 1729, 1772–73; praises Perry and Jackson, 1729; on continuation of war after Bonaparte's abdication, 1730; and burning of Washington, 1731; and Library of Congress, 1732–33, 1745, 1759; reenters Washington, 1733; on arrogance of British peace demands, 1734, 1746; disagrees with TJ on monetary policy, 1746, 1750–51; reaction to Treaty of Ghent, 1754; on white paper on War of 1812, 1756, 1762–63; and civil liberties during wartime, 1761; Ingersoll on conduct of war by, 1761; on Second War of American Independence, 1762; postwar policy recommendations, 1771–72; on sense of nationhood, 1772; on forty years under Constitution, 1773; recommends national university, 1775

RETIREMENT
On Board of Visitors of Central College, 1776, 1777, 1784–85, 1792, 1801; considers writing history of early Republic, 1786; retirement routine, 1791; on Rockfish Gap commission, 1793; on Board of Visitors of University of Virginia, 1795; on TJ's health, 1795, 1806; and construction of Rotunda, 1820, 1856, 1859; on public support of education, 1821; differs from Bland on Mississippi, 1827; on revolutions in Spain and Portugal, 1844, 1877; and Monroe Doctrine, 1844–45, 1879; on Virginia resolution to declare independence, 1847; and authorship of Washington's Farewell Address, 1848, 1863, 1867; on seriatim opinions in the Supreme Court, 1852, 1854–55; recommends George Tucker for faculty, 1886; disagrees with TJ about textbooks, 1918–19; and student discipline, 1920; dissuades TJ from transmitting "Solemn Declaration and Protest," 1947–48, 1955–57; interprets Constitution, 1947–48, 1948–51; final meeting with TJ, 1959; TJ leaves walking stick to, 1959; on aging, 1960; commiserates with TJ on indebtedness, 1967; and TJ's final illness, 1972; notified of TJ's death, 1973; becomes rector of university, 1974; and the close of the Age of Revolution, 1974; on TJ's learning, 1976; denounces Virginia legislature's opposition to protective tariffs, 1976; defends constitutionality of protective tariffs, 1976–77; interprets Constitution, 1976–77, 1981–83, 2000; blasts Giles's use of TJ's letter, 1978; researches TJ's writings on protective tariffs, 1979; Calhoun cites his report of 1800, 1980; publishes views on nullification, 1988; last of the signers, 1991; promotes Andrew Jackson, 1992; denounces nullifiers for misquoting him, 1994; congratulates Clay on "compromizing tariff," 1997–98

Madison, Bishop James (JM's cousin): JM rooms at President's House at William and Mary with, 59; exchanges weather information with TJ, 293; TJ buys books for, 410; denounces Jay's treaty, 883–84, 896; TJ sends JM's nailery account by, 1149; visits Montpellier, 1195; visits Monticello, 1248, 1249; and Mr. Mansfield, 1335; mentioned, 52, 740, 743, 1249, 1337

Madison, James, Sr. (JM's father): spectacles for, 304, 311, 313, 318; JM coaches, on sincerity of retirement, 967; TJ sends respects to, 1080; painted by Polk, 1120; TJ sends gold to, 1135; makes nails, 1147; health of, 1159, 1160; death of, 1162, 1167, 1173, 1174; will of, 1173; JM settles estate of, 1201; meteorological diaries of, 1786; mentioned, 248, 252, 899

Madison, Nelly Conway (Mrs. James, Sr., JM's mother): painted by Polk, 1120; mentioned, 1791

Madison, William (JM's brother), 774, 787, 1045, 1049

Madrid, Spain: American consuls general at, 1307; negotiations at, 1402; mentioned, 1213, 1292, 1310, 1498

Madrid *Gazette*, 1515

Magadore, 1485

Magee, Mr. *See* McGehee, William

Maine: attitude of, towards Constitution, 531; arbitration commission to settle boundary of, 882–83; federal lawsuits in, 1217; British occupy northern portion of, 1731; British demand portion of, 1734, 1746; mentioned, 1586

Mainz, Germany, 1013

Maire, Jacques le, 367

Maison Carrée, 335, 384–85, 412, 791

Maitland, Thomas, 1092

Majoritarian democracy: and individual rights, 447

Majority rule: JM on, 451, 514; and individual rights, 447–48, 564–65; and minority rights, 501, 1164–65; and religious freedom, 522–23; and individual liberty, 600; and natural law, 641, 652; threatened by nullification, 1989; Calhoun denounces, 1999

Malden, 1702

Malesherbes, Chrétien-Guillaume de Lamoignon de, 391, 481
Malmesbury, Lord. *See* Harris, James, first earl of Malmesbury
Malone, Dumas: on TJ's rhetorical excess, 13; on TJ glossing over XYZ affair, 1002; quoted, 887, 941, 1270, 1504, 1507, 1508, 1821
Malta, 1228, 1421
Maly, Captain, 1260
Mann's Inn, 663
Mansfield, Jared, 1301
Mansfield, Mr., 1335, 1340, 1704
Mansfield, William Murray, first earl of, 1183, 1647
Mantua, 1013
Manual of Parliamentary Practice, A (TJ), 1139
Manumissions, 23, 405
Maple sugar, 694, 695, 702, 703
Marat, Jean-Paul, 1066
Marat, M. (1808), 1544
Maratists, 1066
Marblehead, Mass., 1230, 1250, 1326
Marbois. *See* Barbé-Marbois, François, marquis de
Marbury v. *Madison,* 1620
"Marcellus": TJ attributes, to Hamilton, 1034; JM doubts attribution, 1038; mentioned, 1045
Marchant's case, 1179
Marie-Antionette, Josèphe-Jeanne, de Lorraine (queen of France), 481, 486, 624
Marietta, Mississippi district, 1475
Marietta, Ohio, 1251, 1331
Marks, John, 1608, 1609
Marmotte, 421–23
Marque and reprisal, 1693
"Marseilles cargo": French wine for TJ and JM, 1361, 1377, 1382
Marshall, Humphrey, 1016, 1017, 1055, 1058, 1129, 1135
Marshall, James Markham, 785
Marshall, John: as chief justice, 32–35; on JM's eloquence, 124; opposes paper money, 476; favors ratification, 504–5, 509, 534; and Hamilton, 735; and Fairfax purchase, 817; and Jay's treaty, 887–88; TJ's appraisal of, 888, 900–1; and *Ware* v. *Hylton,* 921; appointed commissioner on Potomac boundary, 961; nominated envoy to France, 970–71, 978; and XYZ affair, 1000–1, 1007, 1008, 1052, 1060–61, 1853; runs for Congress, 1090; appointed secretary of state, 1118, 1141; and nonintercourse bill, 1128; on Robbins's affair, 1129; and amendments to Ross bill, 1135; nominated as chief justice, 1142; and tie vote in 1800, 1156; administers oath to TJ as president, 1164; on federal commission relating to western land claims of Georgia, 1211; and Backus case, 1479–80; and *Olmstead* case, 1589; TJ on "twistifications" of, 1620; rules against Livingston in batture case, 1620; TJ critical of, 1631, 1848–49; writes biography of Washington, 1786, 1855; JM supports views of, on Constitution, 1849–56; TJ and JM criticize dicta by, 1851; and seriatim opinions, 1852; in *Marbury* v. *Madison* case, 1865; on judicial review, 1866; in *Cohens* v. *Virginia,* 1870; on JM, 1989; mentioned, 457, 1057, 1060–61
Martel, Mr., 1308
Martin, Alexander, 478
Martin, Francis Xavier, 1625
Martin, Joseph, 104, 110
Martin, Luther, 478, 1546
Martin, Thomas Bryan, 406
Martin, Thomas C., 1049
Martineau, Harriet, 26
Martinez d'Yrujo, Don Carlos. *See* Yrujo, Don Carlos Martinez d'
Martinique, 842, 1302, 1378, 1393, 1484, 1485

Martin v. *Hunter's Lessee,* 406
Maryland: delays ratification of Articles of Confederation, 129–31; and Confederation impost, 232, 263; and revenue system of 1783, 238; and navigation of Potomac, 356–57; paper money in, 430; ratifies Constitution, 504, 508, 531; federal lawsuits in, 1217; and stock in Bank of England, 1277; in election of 1804, 1352; election of 1812 in, 1685, 1705
Maryland (American public vessel), 1190
Mason, George: TJ on, 13, 52, 288; and Virginia Declaration of Rights, 18; on committee to revise Virginia laws, 54; and western land claims, 211; JM visits, 274, 286; and revision of Virginia Constitution, 302, 318; and jurisdiction over Potomac River, 323, 369; as delegate to Annapolis Convention, 404–5; elected to Virginia House, 420; opposes paper money, 430, 476; as delegate to Constitutional Convention, 468, 476, 477, 478; in Virginia ratification convention, 542; opposes ratification, 503, 505, 509, 515, 520–21, 534, 542; TJ and JM visit, 663; and location of national capital, 673; death of, 740, 742; on laws regulating commerce, 1128; mentioned, 669
Mason, John (of Bordeaux), 615
Mason, John Thomson, 1331, 1363
Mason, Stevens Thomson: and Jay's treaty, 882, 887, 888, 902; on Senate debate on sedition bill, 1065; TJ predicts to, state protests against Alien and Sedition Laws, 1069; mentioned, 245, 1148, 1149, 1274
Mason, Thomson, 371
Massac, Mississippi district, 1250, 1476
Massachusetts: and revenue system of 1783, 237; and impost, 263; TJ visits, 285, 321; rejects paper money, 430; ratifies Constitution, 506–7, 508, 519, 531; recommends amendments to Constitution, 531; federal lawsuits in, 1217; and boundary of Maine district, 1480–81; defies embargo system, 1507, 1551; elections in 1809, 1590; elections in 1810, 1627
Massey, Lee, 660
Matagorda, 1357, 1387
Mathews, Thomas, 402, 1488
Matlack, Timothy, 1695
Matthew (JM's servant), 706
Matthews, George, 1040, 1692, 1694
Matthews, Sampson, 96, 105, 113, 118, 517
Maurice, Mr., 1468, 1471
Maury, Captain, 1527
Maury, Fontaine: as agent for JM, 291, 292, 304, 305, 739, 796, 857, 1132, 1240, 1381
Maury, Walker: as schoolmaster, 288; moves school to Williamsburg, 290; borrows books from TJ, 303; tutors Peter Carr, 316, 323, 379, 392; mentioned, 308
Mazzei, Philip: as Virginia's financial agent, 64; reports subterranean city in Siberia, 284, 308; in Richmond, 292; as enemy of Franklin, 306; JM and, 307, 373, 380, 479–80, 492, 523, 548, 676; agent for king of Poland, 544; and debt owed by Dohrman, 684, 699, 700, 702, 859; TJ writes, 702; Dohrman pays debt to, 931, 933, 935; writes *Recherches historiques,* 1025, 1027; and government of Naples, 1278; and *Philadelphia* case, 1323–24; TJ's letter to, creates furor, 971–73, 985–86, 990–91, 1558; mentioned, 194, 484, 928, 1578, 1581
Mead, Clarke. *See* Mead, Cowles
Mead, Cowles, 1263, 1467, 1471
Meade, Richard Worsam, 1436, 1489, 1583
Mease, James, 730
Mecklen, Mr., 1520
Medals, 636, 649
Mediterranean fund, 1419

INDEX 2053

Mediterranean Sea: American policy in, 1170, 1281, 1284
Meigs, Mr., 1704
Meigs, Return Jonathan, 1365, 1574, 1705, 1738
Meilhan sur l'esprit et les moeurs, 539
Mellimelli, Sidi Suliman: as Tunisian minister to United States, 9, 1402–3; plans to visit Montpellier and Monticello, 1411, 1438; entourage rebels against, 1411, 1427, 1428, 1429, 1430, 1432, 1439; returns to Tunis, 1411, 1433; JM seeks transportation for, 1412, 1421, 1427, 1432; proposes naval supplies in exchange for peace, 1419; requests concubines, 9, 1441; mentioned, 1434
Melville, Lord. *See* Dundas, Henry, Lord Melville
"Memorial and Remonstrance . . ., A," against religious assessments (JM), 336, 374, 375–80
Mentor (U.S. ship), 1575, 1586, 1593
Mentz. *See* Mainz, Germany
Mercer, Charles F., 1788
Mercer, James, 505
Mercer, John Francis: TJ's appraisal of, 310, 313; opposes revised code, 402; and escheat law, 406; loses election in 1786, 420; delegate to Constitutional Convention, 478, 508; TJ sends *Notes* to, 492; election of, 742; and Committee on Ways and Means, 838; as governor of Maryland, 1277; and Maryland stock in Bank of England, 1279; mentioned, 261, 287, 291, 309, 741
Mercure de France, 483, 529, 530
Meredith, Samuel, 766, 1197, 1212
Merino sheep: gift of, to TJ and JM, 1621, 1624, 1626, 1627, 1634, 1637, 1649
Merry, Anthony: as British minister to United States, 1258; JM denounces British impressments to, 1294, 1439; corrects an injustice, 1322; and Pitt administration, 1342; JM labels, "pettifogger," 1343; frees TJ and JM's French wine, 1361; protests action of U.S. armed merchantmen, 1363–64; and Yrujo, 1385; recalled by Fox, 1409; on Nonimportation Act, 1410; apologizes for *Leander* incident, 1410, 1428; on British blockade, 1424; complains of American certificates of citizenship to British sailors, 1437, 1438; and murder committed by British subject, 1440–41; and Burr, 1442–43; mentioned, 1273, 1309, 1337, 1345, 1425
Merry, Mrs. Anthony, 1385
Mesmerism, 332
Messina, Italy, 1421
Methodists, 405
Mexico, 1359
Michaux, François-André, 1520, 1531, 1535
Michigan, 1514
Michilimackinac, 346, 1702
Midnight appointments, 1143
Mifflin, Thomas, 478, 946, 963
Migraine headaches, 14
Milan Decree, 1515, 1618
Military supplies in Virginia, 161, 173, 183–84
Militia: in Virginia, 406; TJ and JM propose reform of, 1451–52; uses of, 1454; and success of French arms, 1471; TJ discusses dispatching, to Canada, 1499
Milledge, John, 1224, 1340
Miller, Arthur, 1040
Miller, John Chester, 15, 21, 710–11, 1213
Miller, Mr. (Gallatin's clerk), 1240
Miller, Mr. (pardon for), 1275
Miller, Philip, 871
Miller, Samuel, 1274, 1275
Milligan, Joseph, 1765, 1766
Mills, Robert, 1739
Milner, Mr., 1425
Milton, John, 841

Milton, Va.: postal schedule of, 1330, 1493; mentioned, 1184, 1243, 1246, 1429, 1438, 1539, 1701
Ministry of All-the-Talents, 1409
Minor, Garrett, 1727
Minor, Peter, 1727, 1806, 1807
Minorca, 203, 1238
Mint bill, 718, 1236
Mirabeau, Constantin-François Chasebouef, comte de, 539
Mirabeau, Honoré-Gabriel Riqueti, comte de, 628
Miranda, Francisco de, 1406, 1425, 1436, 1485, 1522
Mississippi River: navigation of, 131, 151–52, 158, 162, 350, 431, 435, 553, 639; JM on navigation of, 147, 153, 328, 338–42; and Jay-Gardoqui negotiations on, 454–55, 467, 471, 475–76; East/West tensions over, 458, 481, 550–51; TJ on navigation of, 461–62, 582; Confederation Congress on navigation of, 551; and Kentucky connection with Spain, 607; British claim right to navigate, 713, 1734, 1746, 1881–82; Monroe discusses, 718; Pinckney's treaty secures navigation of, 893, 921; and Jay's treaty, 977; JM on, 1209, 1253; Spain levies duty on American cargoes transported on, 1252; threat created by French possession of, 1253, 1254; and exploration of headwaters of, 1257, 1278, 1459; TJ reports hostile party to descend, 1259; and right of deposit, 1263; and Louisiana Purchase, 1288; military expulsion of intrusion west of, 1312; neutral zone between, and Rio Bravo, 1357; mentioned, 1396, 1456, 1457, 1643, 1645
Mississippi Territory, 1171, 1192, 1222, 1272, 1516–17
Missouri: Indian affairs in, 1497; and Lewis and Clark expedition, 1459; mentioned, 1396
Missouri Compromise: TJ on, 26; JM on, 1872; mentioned, 24, 1821, 1828–29, 1864, 1927
Missouri River: TJ proposes exploration of headwaters of, 1276
Mobile Act: and Yrujo, 1346; TJ on, 1349; mentioned, 1292, 1342, 1355
Mobile River: navigation of, 1367, 1368, 1370; mentioned, 1292, 1328, 1402
Mohawk River, 432–33
Mohawk Valley, 203
Mohegan language, 552–53
Moira, Francis Rawdon-Hastings, earl of, 1661
Molasses, 608, 619
Mole, 425. *See also* Monax
Monarchy: TJ fears drift towards, 668; JM on, 709, 710
Monax, 421–23
Moncks Corner, S.C., 143
Moñino y Redondo, José. *See* Floridablanca, José Moñino y Redondo, Count de
Moniteur (Paris newspaper), 1428
Monkey bread, 249
Monopolies: restrictioin against, in Bill of Rights, 451; TJ on, 545; regulation of, 566; mentioned, 598
Monroe, Elizabeth Kortright (Mrs. James): at Monticello during husband's absence, 730; accompanies husband to France, 827; mentioned, 772, 831, 840
Monroe, James: urges TJ to reenter public life, 206; buys farm near TJ, 284, 297, 336, 354, 849, 1148, 1248–49, 1564; and vote on slavery (1784), 309; begins correspondence with JM, 316; TJ sends *Notes* to, 334, 372; tours western New York with JM, 346, 375; and Indian treaty, 386–87; in Confederation Congress, 388, 408; informed about Constitutional Convention, 396; purchases land on Mohawk River, 400, 428, 432–33, 538; loses election in 1786, 420; and navigation of Mississippi, 431; TJ's appraisal of, 464–65;

Monroe (*continued*)
opposes paper money, 476; opposes ratification, 534; runs against JM for House, 591, 605; welcomes TJ home from France, 639; TJ explains Compromise of 1790 to, 645; defends TJ against Hamilton's newspaper attack, 715; on Short's nomination as minister to The Hague, 718; appointed to Virginia committee on revised code, 730; visits JM, 742; and election of 1792, 744; organizes county meetings, 758–59; TJ writes to, 773, 776, 793; cooperates with John Taylor's attack on banking system, 800; relations with TJ and JM, 809; JM visits, 810, 811, 812, 815; and county meetings on Franco-American relations, 812, 816; on Genet, 816–17; consults with TJ and JM on party strategy, 821; appointed minister to France, 827, 846; TJ finds lodging for, 829; leases house in Philadelphia, 830; JM lodges with, 831; TJ's letter to, 840, 1420; letters from, 842, 1323, 1366, 1370, 1422, 1440, 1472, 1875, 1877; on nonimportation bill of 1794, 843; buys French furniture for Madison, 849; reception of, in France, 860, 870, 879; on Jacobin clubs in France, 876; as spokesman for TJ, 878; JM admits authorship of *Political Observations* to, 879; and Jay's treaty, 891, 927, 938; on Americans resident in France, 898–99; writes JM on French affairs, 905, 907; on European affairs, 929; recalled from France, 946, 956, 961, 964, 965, 981, 992; replaced by C. C. Pinckney, 968; and TJ's Mazzei letter, 972, 985, 986, 990–91; welcomed by Republicans after recall, 972–73, 977, 983; TJ sends his protest against Cabell's presentment, 975; sends JM Hamilton's pamphlet denying speculation, 993; TJ writes, about federal accusations against himself, 1000; calls XYZ demands "a swindling experiment," 1002, 1043; listed as member of American Directory, 1010; JM draws draft on, 1010; writes *View of the Conduct...*, 1011, 1013, 1019, 1023; and draft on Barnes, 1018; called "disgraced minister" by Adams, 1050, 1052, 1058; suggests TJ cancel trip to Montpellier, 1109, 1120, 1121; elected governor of Virginia, 1111, 1152, 1153, 1187, 1189, 1245; on need to defend Callender, 1137–38; on vote in 1800, 1143, 1155; warns TJ of Burr's ambitions, 1153; and Gabriel's Rebellion, 1204; and Barbary negotiations, 1214; and Louisiana Purchase, 1254, 1255, 1256, 1262, 1272, 1283, 1290, 1306, 1338; on rumored restoration of Bourbon monarchy, 1293, 1333; and recall of Yrujo, 1293, 1347; on Livingston's visit to London, 1334; letter from, 1337; and Monroe-Pinkney Treaty, 1342, 1384, 1392, 1409, 1424, 1446, 1496, 1582; special mission to Spain, 1354–55, 1357, 1358, 1359, 1367, 1373; claims Rio Grande as western boundary of Louisiana Purchase, 1368; on policy towards France, 1387; runs for president in 1808, 1548; and reconciliation with JM, 1564, 1565, 1610–11, 1650, 1664; breaks with John Randolph, 1580, 1611; visits Kentucky, 1609; elected governor of Virginia (1810), 1632; JM appoints, as secretary of state, 1652, 1653–54, 1655, 1663, 1677; on Foster's threat of retaliation, 1657, 1672; visits Montpellier (1811), 1658; on Fox's blockade, 1674; on JM's illness, 1713; and gunboats, 1723; TJ writes to, about monetary policy, 1736, 1745; on *status quo ante bellum*, 1753; on sense of nationhood, 1760; visits Monticello, 1768; praises JM as president, 1775; and Central College Board of Visitors, 1776, 1777, 1778, 1784, 1785; and Transcontinental Treaty, 1806; and Coxe, 1826; and Tenure of Office Act, 1827; and Monroe Doctrine, 1844–45, 1878, 1881; and student discipline at university, 1920; JM writes, 1991; mentioned, 205, 248, 739, 803, 862, 921, 1132, 1160, 1246, 1280, 1281, 1311, 1337, 1702, 1721

Monroe, John, 1605
Monroe, Joseph Jones, 928
Monroes, Thomas, 1251
Montesquieu, Charles-Louis de Secondat, baron de la Brède et de, 125, 448, 514, 808
Montgomery, Robert, 1526
Montgomery, Mr., 1544
Montgomery County, Virginia, 148, 173
Monticello: TJ's obelisk at, 2–3; TJ returns to, in 1776, 52; TJ returns to, from France, 638; remodeling of, 774, 849, 984, 986; TJ's love for, 849; roofing of, 1108; rebuilding of, 1138–39; TJ visits, 1256; Maria at, during illness, 1304; JM visits, 1334, 1344; Madisons to visit, 1496, 1497, 1601; cemetary at, 1972; mentioned, 246, 568, 1953
Montmorin de Saint-Herem, Armand-Marc, comte de, 451–52, 481, 543–44, 625
Montpellier: JM's obelisk at, 3; TJ visits, 663, 995, 1140, 1289; JM remodels, 967, 968, 1011, 1570, 1583; portico of, 1132, 1135–36, 1147; garden at, 1791; art collection at, 1792; TJ's first use of name, 1523; JM's first use of name, 1528; mentioned, 1704
Montreal: in War of 1812, 1683, 1702
Moor, Peter, 96
Moore, Alexander, 1475
Moore, Andrew, 605, 769
Moore, John, 728, 733
Moore, John Hamilton, 689, 692
Moore, Thomas, 1427, 1724
Moralès, Juan Ventura: departure from New Orleans, 1341; sells lands in West Florida, 1358; expulsion of, 1389, 1391, 1392; mentioned, 1263, 1264, 1437, 1438
Moreau, Jean-Victor-Marie, 1381, 1384
Moreau de Lislet, Louis Casimir Elizabeth, 1633, 1634, 1640, 1641, 1642
Morellet, André, Abbé, 410
Moreri, Louis, 367
Morgan, Benjamin, 1023, 1337, 1343, 1695
Morgan, Daniel, 979
Morgan, Edmund S.: quoted, 518
Morgan, George, 607
Morocco: treaty with, 932–33, 1170; declares war on United States, 1209–10, 1235, 1239, 1240; TJ debates gifts to or war with, 1210; gun carriages sent to, 1265; shipment of supplies to, 1266; end of war with, 1302–3; mentioned, 1213, 1284
Morocco, emperor of. See Emperor of Morocco
Morris, Captain (of *Franklin*), 1239
Morris, Gouverneur: delegate to Constitutional Convention, 478; JM introduces, to TJ, 578; and trip to Europe, 580; plan of, on American finances, 610–11; in London, 698; appointed minister to France, 718, 726, 736, 801; and recall of Genet, 757, 809; JM on, 817; recall of, 827, 841; London mission of, 1213–14; mentioned, 605, 1131, 1541, 1868
Morris, Lewis R., 1144, 1154, 1161
Morris, Richard B.: quoted, 92
Morris, Richard V.: commodore of Mediterranean fleet, 1234, 1235, 1240, 1265; replaces Dale, 1259; to consult Eaton, 1267; replaced by Preble, 1295; and Tunisian property, 1341
Morris, Robert: superintendent of finance, 235, 266, 268–69; obtains tobacco monopoly in France, 458, 515; delegate to Constitutional Convention, 478; senator from Pennsylvania, 554, 563, 579; financial affairs of, 580; purchases New York land from Gorham and Phelps, 692; and Bank of United States subscriptions, 694; on move to replace

INDEX 2055

Adams as vice president, 728; plans of, to retire, 781; in debtor's prison, 1174; mentioned, 172, 203, 222, 225, 226, 269, 860
Morristown, New Jersey, 157
Morse, Jedidiah, 1837, 1838, 1839
Morton, Perez, 1647, 1648
Moss, James W., 1476
Moss, John, 117
Most-favored-nation status: Jay's treaty provisions on, 884
Moultrie, William, 828–29
Mountain cress, 676
Mount Airy, Va., 1740
Mt. Vernon, TJ and JM visit, 708; TJ visits, 716, 740; mentioned, 388, 663, 664, 689, 748, 787
Mt. Vernon Conference (1785), 281
Moustier, Eléonore François Élie, comte de: suceeds Luzerne as French minister to United States, 462; TJ's appraisal of 462, 494–95; carries watch to JM, 493–94, 529, 530; JM's appraisal of, 580, 612, 614; mentioned, 51
Moutier, count de. *See* Moustier, Eléonore François Élie
Moylan, Stephen, 1010, 1048, 1084, 1135, 1145
Muhlenburg, Frederick Augustus Conrad: as Speaker of the House, 862; and Jay's treaty, 894, 936; defeated by Logan, 1074, 1086; mentioned, 828, 902, 1036, 1041
Muhlenburg, Peter, 1231, 1250, 1436
Mulgrave, Henry Phipps, Baron, 1393
Murray, Alexander, 1234, 1268
Murray, John, fourth earl of Dunmore: as governor of Virginia, 41, 43–44; flees to British warship, 44, 48; JM critical of, 45; mentioned, 80, 199
Murray, William Vans: denounces Republican newspapers, 852; and Jay's treaty, 929; appointed minister to France, 1075, 1097, 1098–99; on conciliatory attitude of France, 1086; in Paris, 1133; returns to The Hague, 1154; and Convention of 1800, 1158, 1169, 1195, 1196, 1197, 1199, 1200; mentioned, 1185, 1195
Muscavado, 695
Muskingum, Ohio, 553
Musschenbroek, Pieter van: and *cours de physique*, 297
Mussey, John, 1262
Muter, George, 128, 729, 739
Mutiny: in Continental army in 1780, 127; of Pennsylvania Line, 135; of Connecticut regiments, 139; of troops, which force Congress to leave Philadelphia, 233, 261, 266, 288

Nacogdoches: Spain sends troops to, 1387, 1402; mentioned, 1357, 1455, 1456, 1457
Nailery: TJ establishes, 848; JM orders from, 967–68, 1012, 1014, 1025, 1118, 1148; JM visits, 1019, 1109; JM's account with, 1084, 1126, 1130, 1147, 1148–49; TJ's chief occupation, 1148; mentioned, 920, 923, 1023, 1146
Namur, castle of, 94, 695
Nanjemoy, 1347
Nantes, France, 1246
Naples, 460, 1278, 1844
Napoleon. *See* Bonaparte, Napoléon
Narrow seas, 1258
Nash, Abner, 225–26, 242
Nash, Thomas, 1128
Nashville, 1606
Natchez: post road to New Orleans, 1339; mentioned, 1016, 1019, 1022, 1266, 1299, 1307, 1347, 1476
Natchitoches: Indian affairs at, 1497; mentioned, 1455, 1456, 1457
Nathan, Simon: and George Rogers Clark, 135; mentioned, 168, 179, 182–83, 185, 248

National Assembly: and Declaration of Rights of Man, 603: establishment of, 616; proceeding of, 617–18; and French constitution, 627–28; follows American constitutional examples, 628–29; cancels trade concessions negotiated by TJ, 691; and constitution for French colonies, 699; confers citizenship on foreigners, 747; mentioned, 602, 747, 772
National capital: debate on location of 233, 234, 261, 265, 294; and inauguration of new government under Constitution, 547–48; and sectional bargain to locate on Potomac, 644, 659; and District of Columbia, 674, 1033, 1137
National character: TJ on, 410
National debt: and income from western land sales, 454; and Gouverneur Morris's plan to finance, 610–11; and excise taxes, 850. *See also* Public debts; "Report on Public Credit"
National Gazette: Freneau establishes, 672, 709; Hamilton denounces, 714; popularity of, in Virginia, 730: mentioned, 731, 1547. *See also* Freneau, Philip
National Intelligencer (edited by Samuel Harrison Smith), 1155; as unofficial organ for government communications, 1276; on Louisiana Purchase, 1287; on militia reform, 1451; quotes British disavowal of right to search U.S. warships, 1453; and Bonaparte's militia system, 1475; publishes Canning's promise, 1500, 1501; carries JM's defense of Embargo Act, 1506; reports on British and French policies, 1630, 1636; carries rebuttal to Robert Smith's charges against JM, 1671; takes hard line towards Great Britain, 1675; reports on Congress's declaration of war in 1812, 1680; burned by British, 1731; on Battle of New Orleans, 1754–55; mentioned, 1412, 1577, 1689
National negative of state laws: JM advocates, 27–28; TJ rejects, 28
National Trust for Historic Preservation: owns Montpellier, 967
Natural Bridge, Virginia, 1836, 1907
Natural history, 459
Naturalization Act: of 1795, 868–69, 870, 1207; of 1798, 1003, 1042, 1044, 1059, 1066, 1207; of 1802, 1207
Natural right: TJ appeals to, 1...   ...; JM refuses to appeal to, 1072; and neutral rights, 1186; mentioned, 1181
Navigation Acts, 517
Navoni, Mr., 1522
Navy Department: JM on need for, 187; creation of (1798), 1042, 1043; expansion of, 1086 1088, 1091, 1095, 1105–6; enlistments stopped, 1127; gunboats of, 1294; victories in 1812, 1685; and Perry's victory on Lake Erie, 1729
Necker, Jacques: dismissed by king, 602, 624, 625; and financial plan for France, 627, 631; mentioned, 539
Neelly, James, 1608, 1609, 1623, 1624
Negro cotton, 844, 846
Negroes: removal of, by British, 459
Neilson, John, 1570
Nelson, Horatio, Admiral Lord, 1084, 1295, 1404
Nelson, Hugh, 1122, 1766, 1825
Nelson, John, 1570, 1583, 1858
Nelson, Mr., 1490, 1491
Nelson, Mr. *See* Neilson, John
Nelson, Thomas: succeeds TJ as Virginia governor, 178; rejects election to Philadelphia convention, 476; mentioned, 51, 160, 245, 420, 507, 509, 1476
Nelson, William, 245, 507
Nelson County, Virginia, 1474, 1727, 1776
Nepean, S. E., 1309
Netherlands, the: England declares war on, 152, 191; John Adams mission to, 180; and patriot

Netherlands (*continued*)
  movement against stadtholder, 290, 365–66; treaty with, 883; British order excludes neutral ships from, 1591. *See also* Batavian Republic; Holland
Nettels, Curtis P.: quoted, 420
Neue Philadelphia Correspondenz, 1184
Neufville, Jean de, 1655, 1686, 1706
Neutrality: discussed at time of Nootka Sound incident, 645–47; debate over method of declaring, 748. *See also* Proclamation of Neutrality
Neutral rights: Jay's treaty makes concessions on, 883; Pinckney's treaty and, 925; Schlegel's pamphlet on, 1186; TJ on, 1195, 1237–38, 1281–82, 1349; and case of the *Henrich,* 1261; violations by Britain, 1294–95, 1359–60; violations by France, 1294, 1295; and unneutral acts, 1298; and Rule of 1756, 1360; JM writes defense of, 1360–61, 1390, 1398, 1412–14, 1558, 1637; and General Ferrand's decree, 1369–70; TJ's warlike message on, 1404; and *Chesapeake* crisis, 1588; mentioned, 1257, 1274
New, Anthony, 765
New, Robert Anderson, 1251
Newark, N.J.: Republican Society of, 65
New Brunswick, N.J., 1706
Newburgh, N.Y., 196
Newburgh letters, 1868
Newburyport, Mass., 1230, 1251
New Canton, Va., 1926
Newcastle, Del., 190
New Colony on the Ohio, 215
New England, 1685, 1690
New Hampshire: and revenue system of 1783, 236–37; TJ visits, 285, 321; paper money in, 430; and federal Constitution, 504, 508, 521, 531, 542; federal lawsuits in, 1217; in election of 1809, 1590; in election of 1812, 1685, 1705
New Haven, Conn., 687, 1185, 1301, 1480, 1543, 1670
New Jersey: and collapse of Continental currency, 195; and Confederation impost, 232, 263; and revenue system of 1783, 238; paper money in, 429; ratifies Constitution, 504, 515, 519; Hessian fly in, 543; and elections to first Congress, 607; federal lawsuits in, 1217; in election of 1812, 1685, 1705
New Jersey (U.S. merchantman), 1376–77, 1378, 1393
New Jersey Line: mutiny of, 135, 162–63
New London, Conn., 1234, 1262
New London, Va., 1697
New Madrid, Mo., 1687
New Orleans: and navigation of the Mississippi, 339–42, 657; British merchants in, 720; right of deposit at, suspended, 1252, 1254, 1266; strategic importance of, 1253–54; transfer to American authorities, 1291; and foreign consuls, 1308; and Louisiana Bank, 1323; French privateer in, 1328–29; post road from Natchez, 1339, 1340; delays in Spanish evacuation of, 1402; TJ on force to defend, 1416, 1456, 1458; JM on public property in, 1513–14; prize ship in, 1526; Battle of, 1753–54, 1758, 1763, 1764; mentioned, 105, 106, 107, 776, 779, 785, 1226, 1326, 1525, 1695
New Orleans (American merchantman), 1361
Newport, Del., 217
Newport, R.I.: French fleet at, 154, 189; fortifications at, 1187
Newport News, Va., 159
Newspapers: TJ on, 848, 1582, 1952
Newton, Sir Isaac, 20
Newton, Mr., 1281
Newton, Thomas, Jr., 161, 1439, 1483, 1492
Newtown pippin apples, 391, 493, 508, 511

Newtown Spitzenburg apples, 511
New Windsor, N.Y., 196
New York, N.Y.: Democratic Society of, 865; and Jay's treaty, 885, 896, 933–34; British ships in harbor of, 1338; defense of, 1720; mentioned, 1262, 1268, 1300, 1326, 1361
New York (U.S. frigate), 1239, 1245
New York *Evening Post,* 1673
New York Magazine, 678
New York *Mercantile Advertiser,* 1718
New York *Minerva,* 939
New York State: cedes western land claims, 129, 202, 210; and revenue system of 1783, 238; paper money in, 429–30; and Constitution, 504, 508, 521, 530, 531, 542, 543, 547, 549; elections in, 607, 662, 872, 1131, 1132, 1587, 1590, 1627, 1685, 1742; and Vermont statehood, 614; federal lawsuits in, 1217; and embargo, 1521
New York *Time Piece,* 1068
Niagara: British retain troops at, 346; Smyth's debacle at, 1684, 1709; mentioned, 1279, 1301, 1702
Niagara River, 1712
Nicholas, Elizabeth. *See* Randolph, Elizabeth Nicholas
Nicholas, George, 245, 420, 509, 534, 729, 1096
Nicholas, John: on Whiskey Rebellion, 862, 863; leaves Congress early, 1042, 1052; attacks Sedition Law, 1100; on Robbins's affair, 1128; reports on fires in government offices, 1162; mentioned, 420, 765, 795, 797, 978
Nicholas, John, Jr. (Charlottesville Federalist), 1121
Nicholas, Margaret Smith (Mrs. Wilson Cary), 1716
Nicholas, Philip Norborne, 1160
Nicholas, Robert Carter, 55, 56, 1272, 1326, 1716, 1717, 1768
Nicholas, Wilson Cary: favors ratification, 534; on French Revolution, 785, 795; JM on views of, 817; buys land near Charlottesville, 868; and speculation, 871–72; reelected to Virginia House, 928; and TJ's petition on Cabell's presentment, 986; middleman for TJ and Kentucky resolutions 1068; middleman for JM and Virginia resolutions, 1071; and renewal of Kentucky and Virginia resolutions, 1109, 1118; and Ross bill, 1131; carries letter to Dolley Madison, 1136; carries TJ's money from Philadelphia, 1145; and Louisiana, 1209, 1283, 1290; and policy towards Spain, 1359; and repeal of Embargo Act, 1551–52; reaction of, to Robert Smith's dismissal, 1716; and Charles Jouett, 1767; as governor of Virginia, 1768, 1776, 1792, 1802; and Rockfish Gap commission, 1793; appoints Virginia Board of Visitors, 1795; and TJ's indebtedness, 1953, 1966; mentioned, 779, 784, 797, 800, 812, 1121, 1128, 1135
Nicholson, George, 193, 200
Nicholson, John, 767–68
Nicklin, Philip: and *New Jersey,* 1378
Niemcewicz, Julian U., 1469, 1471
Neimcewicz, Susan Livingston Kean (Mrs. Julian U.), 1469
Nile River, 1643, 1645
Niles' Register, 1979
Nimes, France, 335
Nimms, James, 1251
Noailles, Louis-Marie, vicomte de, 772, 903
Nobles: order in Estates General, 616–17, 624, 625
"No Jacobin" (pseudonym: Alexander Hamilton), 802
Nonimportation bill of 1794, 840, 841, 843
Nonimportation Act of 1806; enactment of, 1409; postponed, 1410, 1446, 1462; goes into effect, 1504; and debate on extension to France, 1551; New England petitions against, 1670; mentioned, 1703

INDEX

Nonintercourse Act: replaces Embargo Act, 1553; applied to France, 1593; applied to England and France, 1597; JM's interpretation of, 1598; expiration of, 1615; reimposed on Great Britain, 1619; mentioned, 1590
Noonan, John T., Jr., 15
Nootka Sound incident, 645–47, 657–59
Norfolk, Va.: and Virginia port bill of 1784, 279–80, 322, 349; British use navy yard at, 1411, 1439, 1440; and canal to Albemarle Sound, 1711; defense of, 1720; professors arrive at, 1915, 1926; mentioned, 1281, 1307, 1483
Norman's Ford, Va., 1226, 1519
North, Frederick, second earl of Guilford: 44–45, 306
North, William, 166, 180, 1050
North American: newspaper essays by, 267
North American Review: publishes JM's views on nullification, 1987, 1988, 1990
Northampton County, Pa., 1454
North Carolina: and revenue system of 1783, 238–39; paper money in, 429; and Constitution, 505, 531, 542, 550, 595; resolutions, 1067; and Alien and Sedition Laws, 1090; federal lawsuits in, 1218; in election of 1812, 1685, 1705
Northern Confederacy of Neutrals, 1159
Northern Neck of Virginia, 403–4, 407, 535
North River. *See* Rio Grande
Northwest Ordinance of 1787, 436
Northwest posts: retained by British, 435, 681–83, 711, 712–13, 722, 724, 727; Jay's treaty on, 872, 882, 893
Northwest Territory: TJ on, 294–95; British demand slice of, 1734, 1746; mentioned, 244
"Notes on Ancient and Modern Confederacies" (JM), 440–41
"Notes on the Debates of the Constitutional Convention": JM preserves, 444, 681; TJ praises, 525; JM lends, to TJ, 887, 899–900, 930, 931, 932; mentioned, 936, 1094
Notes on the State of Virginia (TJ), 4, 206; TJ's antislavery views in, 19–20; TJ's anti-Negro views in, 20–21; John Chester Miller on, 21; and TJ's draft constitution for Virginia, 29, 235–36; TJ publishes, 285, 319, 332–35, 372; JM and, 381, 387, 392, 401, 419, 492; distribution of, 410, 530; Jefferson-Fry map of Virginia in, 492; mentioned, 23, 27, 155
Nova Scotia, 212, 717
Nullification: term used in Kentucky resolutions of 1799, 1082, 1109; South Carolina doctrine of, 1979–80; JM attacks South Carolina doctrine of, 1981, 1982, 1988, 1999; Hayne defends doctrine of, 1985; and minority rule, 1989; Andrew Jackson denounces, 1995; crisis ends peaceably, 1997–98; JM on popularity of, in South, 1998; mentioned, 31–32, 1989
Nullifiers: switch from JM to TJ as patron saint, 1989–90; JM rebuts, 1990–91; invoke JM's Virginia resolutions, 1993–94; adopt Nullification Ordinance in South Carolina, 1993–94; JM labels, counterrevolutionaries, 2000. *See also* Calhoun, John Caldwell; Giles, William Branch; Hayne, Robert Young; Nullification
Nuttal, Thomas, 1813

Oakley, Charles, 1581, 1583
Oak trees: live, 511
O'Brien, Richard: as consul at Algiers, 583, 1194, 1213; and treaty with Tunis, 1214; mentioned, 1240, 1263, 1264, 1265, 1266
Observations on Modern Gardening (Thomas Whately), 399
"Observator" (Alexander Hamilton), 1152
Octagon House, 1733

Odometer, 708
Oeller's Hotel, 973
Office of Discount and Deposit, 1330, 1589
O'Flaherty, Mr., 1858, 1859
Ogden, Samuel G., 1407, 1432, 1436, 1437
O'Hara, Colonel, 117
O'Hara, James, 103, 105
Ohio: Territory, 1197; war spirit in (1812), 1683
Ohms, Mr., 1438
Old Republicans, 32, 1954, 1957
Olmstead case, 1589
Oneida Indians, 348
Olson, Mr. *See* Blicher Olsen, Peder
Onís, Don Luis (Chevalier de Onís), 1606, 1608, 1782
Opelousas, La., 1343, 1638
Opossum, 421, 493, 508, 529
Orange County, Va., 43, 44, 737, 774
Order: and liberty, 669
Orders-in-council: spoliation payments for, of 1793 and 1794, 882; mentioned, 1735
Ordinance of 1787: antislavery provisions of, 25
O'Reily, Henry, 1465
Orléans, Louis-Philippe-Joseph, duc d', 628
Orleans Territory, 1332, 1336, 1341
Orr, Benjamin Grayson, 637, 1185
Ortega, Mr., 1526
Osage (U.S. ship), 1536
Osgood, Samuel, 697, 1268, 1300
Oster, Martin, 363
Oswald, Eleazer, 982
Oswald, Richard, 219, 250
Oswego, N.Y., 346
Otis, Harrison Gray, 978, 1061, 1088, 1161, 1185
Otis, James, 1845, 1876
Otis, Samuel Allyn, 590, 1224
Otsego County, N.Y., 731, 734
Otto, Louis: appraisal of JM of, 444, 472, 677, 1247
Overton, John, 687
Owings, David, 720
Oxford University, 1858, 1885
Oznabrigs, 844

Paca, William, 504
Pacific (U.S. ship), 1590, 1591
"Pacificus" (Alexander Hamilton), 754, 791, 792, 795, 801; JM on, 810, 817; Edmund Randolph on, 817
Page, Francis, 1577
Page, John: TJ's oldest friend, 11, 59; acts as lieutenant governor of Virginia, 65–66; reportedly opposes ratification, 509; favors ratification, 534; elected to first Congress, 605; and Mazzei, 651; gives TJ grandfather's manuscript, 909; TJ appoints, as collector, 1231; visits Monticello, 1284; appointed to loan office, 1435; mentioned, 123, 923, 950, 1160, 1163, 1282, 1577
Page, Mann, 245, 420, 505, 534, 785, 901, 1160
Page, Matthew, 909
Pain de singe, 249
Paine, Elijah, 860
Paine, Ephraim, 310
Paine, Thomas: writes *Public Good,* 215; proposed remuneration for, 283, 323; presented farm in New York, 319; TJ on services of, 319, 354; TJ writes preface to *Rights of Man* of, 667, 685; *Rights of Man* of, JM on, 688–89; mentioned for postmaster general, 697, 698, 699, 700; attacked by *Plain Truth,* 771; on luxury taxes, 843; confined by Robespierre, 907; attacks Washington for supporting Jay's treaty, 950, 956; writes *Agrarian Justice,* 982; letter of, to the French, 1031; TJ offers passage to, on American vessel, 1190; writes *Compact Maritime,* 1161; mentioned, 981, 1276, 1277

Pakenham, Sir Edward, 1753
Palladio, Andrea, 1136, 1778, 1787, 1788, 1789
Palmer, Aaron Haight, 1601–2
Palmer, Jonathan, 1464
Pamunkey River, Va., 155
Panic of 1819, 1817, 1821, 1953
Pantheon: and Rotunda, 1819; mentioned, 1820, 1842
Paoli (U.S. ship), 1260
"Paper blockade": JM on, 1424
Paper money: Virginia redeems Continental currency, 142; JM on, 397, 405, 415, 429, 470; Constitution restricts states' power over, 445; Virginia assembly rejects, 455, 491; Patrick Henry favors, 473, 479; debated in Virginia (1787), 476; ceases to circulate in Philadelphia, 484; federal restriction on state emission of, 491, 500; faction in Rhode Island, 504; opposed in Kentucky, 553; mentioned, 125–27, 725
Paradise, John: JM on claims of, 419, 432; mentioned, 412–13, 418, 534, 535
Paradise, Lucy Ludwell, 418
Pardon: power of Virginia governor to, 403
Park, Dr., 1393, 1394
Park, Miss, 1393, 1394
Parker, Josiah, 80, 81, 605, 742, 1042
Parker, Richard, 532
Paris, France: and French Revolution, 602; troops dispatched to, 625; American consul general at, 1307; and loss of *Philadelphia*, 1324; mentioned, 1213
Paris Society of Agriculture, 1622
Parlement of Paris, 452, 486, 490
Parliamentary authority: JM rejects, 39–40; TJ rejects, 40–42
Parr, Samuel, 1884
Parrott, Richard, 1465
Parsons, Theophilus, 1161
Parton, James, 53
Pasha of Tripoli, 1296, 1431–32
Passamaquoddy, 1500, 1734, 1746
Passports: for Mediterranean, 1178
Patent Office building, 1733
Paterson, William: as New Jersey's senator, 579; presides at Lyon's trial, 1079; Miranda case, 1407; death of, 1440; and mentioned, 478, 579
Patten, John, 860
Patterson, Edgar, 1541
Patterson, Elizabeth, 1383
Patterson, Mr., 1728
Patterson, Robert, 1770
Patterson, William: as vice consul at L'Orient, 1246
Paul, Mr., 1179
Paulding, James Kirke: on Dolley Madison's ability as a runner, 1791; mentioned, 1686, 1706
Paulet, Jesse, 97
Paulett, Richard, 97
Payne, Anna, 967, 1187, 1191, 1195. *See also* Cutts, Anna Payne
Payne, John C., 1021
Peace of Amiens, 1255, 1257, 1409
Peaches, 391
Peale, Charles Willson: invents polygraph, 1367; mentioned, 726, 1120
Peale, Rembrandt, 1962
Peale's Museum, 726
Pearl River, 1272, 1301, 1456
Peas, 391, 542
Pecans: JM sends, to TJ, 474, 477; TJ receives, in France, 483, 493; mentioned, 412, 421, 469, 479, 485
Peckham, Howard H.: quoted, 91
Pederson, Peder, 1283
Pedometer, 411, 419, 487, 494, 529, 538

Pendleton, Edmund: on committee to revise Virginia laws, 54, 330; opposes disestablishment of Anglican Church, 55; and Simon Nathan, 168; and western land claims of Virginia, 210; appointed to supplemental revision committee, 455, 466; favors ratification, 504, 509, 534; sends recommendation for Supreme Court justice, 701, 702; on Franco-American relations, 812, 816; and election of 1800, 1112; mentioned, 243, 587, 745
Pendleton, Nathaniel, Jr., 478, 701
Penet, Peter, 64–65, 88
Penet Company (of France), 155, 163
Penet Wendel and Company, 65, 98–103, 106
Pennsylvania: legislature authorizes commandeering supplies for Continental army, 140; and collapse of Continental currency, 195; and revenue plan of 1783, 238; paper money in, 429; ratifies Constitution, 451, 504, 508, 515, 519, 530; move for second convention in, 552; elections to first Congress, 582; assembly expels members from Whiskey Rebellion counties, 869; elections in 1795, 899; federal lawsuits in, 1217; defies federal authority, 1588–89; in election of 1812, 1685, 1705
Pennsylvania Line of Continental troops: assigned to southern army, 134; mutiny of, 135, 156–57, 162–63; assigned to Virginia, 173, 181, 189, 193
Penobscot River, 1731
Pensacola, 1342
Pentemont, Abbeye Royale de, 486
Perceval, Spencer: ministry of, 1573, 1665; JM on "quackeries" of, 1607, 1676, 1688; Prince of Wales and ministry of, 1661; strengthens British order-in-council, 1672; assassination of, 1681, 1698; TJ on, 1689, 1700; mentioned, 1470, 1534, 1692
Perdido River: TJ discusses right to, 1327; as disputed boundary of Louisiana, 1518; mentioned, 1282, 1328, 1452, 1494
Pernier, John, 1609
Perry, Mr., 1933–35, 1936, 1937
Perry, Oliver Hazard, 1712, 1729, 1730
Perryman, Mr., 1434
Peru, 1359
Pervis, Mr., 908, 909
Peters, Richard, 267, 766, 871, 1465, 1974
Petersburg, Va., 630, 886, 1231, 1241, 1251, 1529
Peterson, Merrill D.: quoted, 10, 1002, 1505
Petry, Jean Baptiste, 833, 1393, 1472
Pettus, Samuel O., 97
Peyton, Bernard, 1942–43, 1970
Peyton, Howe, 1938
Peyton, John, 108
Phlegon, 647
Phelps, Mr., 1434
Phelps, Oliver, 692
Philadelphia: celebrates ratification of Articles of Confederation, 171; and location of national capital, 268–69, 547–48, 552, 662; and Jay's treaty, 885, 896, 933; TJ returns to (1797), 995; fracas in, during war crisis of 1798, 1004–5; foreign consuls at, 1308; Russian ships visit, 1436; shipmasters petition TJ, 1537, 1538; mentioned, 1375
Philadelphia (U.S. frigate), captured, 1295; Decatur destroys, 1295; crew ransomed, 1296; and request for foreign intervention, 1311, 1324
Philadelphia *Aurora:* prints Gallatin's speech on Jay's treaty, 927; predicts election of 1796 will be decided by House, 959; reprints letters forged by British to discredit Washington, 991; "Pliny" critical of, 1064–65; publishes JM's articles, 1073, 1087, 1094; publishes Ross bill, 1115; TJ subscribes to, for Captain Winston, 1136; and libel on Liston, 1183; and Duane, 1129, 1172, 1280–81;

INDEX

on Louisiana Purchase, 1287; on yellow fever (1805), 1380; publishes white paper on War of 1812, 1766; mentioned, 1149, 1155
Philadelphia *Gazette of the United States,* 692, 791, 801, 807, 962, 1008, 1064–65
"Philadelphia Junto," 1650
Phillips, William: intercedes on behalf of Henry Hamilton, 63–64, 90, 91–95, 118; captured at Saratoga, 72, 82–84, 119; commands in Virginia, 197; dies, 197–98
Phosphorous matches, 332, 333, 351, 367
Physick, Philip Syng, 1354, 1361, 1373, 1375, 1385
Piankesha Indians, 1426
Pichon, Louis André: as French chargé d'affairs to United States, 1189; and Leclerc's seizures of American cargoes, 1225; cancels visit to Monticello and Montpellier, 1240, 1342, 1344–45; and French Negroes from Guadaloupe, 1240, 1248; on right of deposit at New Orleans, 1263–64, 1265; and case of Cloupet, 1275; JM discusses Jerome Bonaparte with, 1276; and Spanish protest of sale of Louisiana, 1285; on French consul in Kentucky, 1306, 1307–8; at Baltimore, 1311; complains of British ships in American waters, 1338; returns to France, 1344; protests actions of U.S. armed merchantmen, 1363–64; mentioned, 1097, 1099, 1232, 1233, 1241, 1340
Pickens, Andrew, 838, 1197, 1199
Pickering (U.S. public vessel), 1260
Pickering, Timothy: appointed secretary of war, 869; succeeds Randolph as secretary of state, 886, 890, 899; and Jay's treaty, 906; receives journal of federal convention, 930; writes pamphlet on Franco-American affairs, 961; on XYZ affair, 962, 1001, 1006, 1060, 1853; attends Washington ball, 998, 1024; Federalist attitudes towards, 1028; instructions of, to envoys, 1061, 1094; on impressment, 1086; and retaliation bill, 1095; Adams dismisses, 1117–18, 1141; on federal commission relating to western land claims of Georgia, 1211; ousted as senator, 1669–70; disunion sentiments of, 1682; on Declaration of Independence, 1845, 1846, 1875–77, 1878; mentioned, 898, 1321, 1578, 1614
Pickett, Martin, 696
Pictet, Professor, 1909, 1963, 1964
Pierce, John, 1428, 1462, 1476
Pierce, William, 444, 478
Pike, Zebulon Montgomery, 1493, 1522
Pinckney, Charles: delegate to Constitutional Convention, 469, 478; and navigation of Mississippi, 506; introduces jury bill, 1126; introduces amendment to bar federal judges from holding other federal appointments, 1127, 1131, 1133; heads Republican committee in South Carolina, 1139–40; as minister to Spain, 1198, 1199, 1200; on complaints of American merchants, 1236; and Algeciras depredations, 1238; and Spanish protest against sale of Louisiana, 1285; and the Floridas, 1292; letter from, 1293, 1327, 1368, 1370, 1374; JM critical of, 1305; and Mobile Act, 1342, 1346; and Yrujo, 1345, 1347; teamed with Monroe, 1354–55; and collapse of negotiations with Spain, 1354, 1373, 1375, 1379; returns from Spain, 1385, 1387, 1392; mentioned, 1185, 1213, 1242, 1243, 1279, 1280, 1281, 1306, 1311, 1363
Pinckney, Charles Cotesworth: delegate to Constitutional Convention, 469, 478; appointed minister to France, 956, 958, 961, 964, 965; rejected as American ambassador by France, 946–47, 968, 975; nominated to three-man mission to France, 970–71, 978; and Jay's treaty, 979; and XYZ affair, 1000–1, 1057, 1853; as general in provisional army, 1086; nominated for vice presidency in 1800, 1117, 1118, 1140, 1154; as presidential candidate in 1804, 1352; as presidential candidate in 1808, 1548; mentioned, 1139, 1148
Pinckney, Thomas: appointed minister to Great Britain, 718, 813; denies hereditary wisdom, 728; and TJ's threshing machine, 770, 776, 814; and British seizure of noncontraband goods, 823; Republicans prefer, to special envoy, 827; corresponds with Grenville about neutral rights, 832; negotiates favorable treaty with Spain, 893, 925; retires as minister to Great Britain, 939; as Federalist vice presidential candidate in 1796, 941, 942, 948, 951, 952, 955; TJ writes to, about political dissension, 970; and Jay's treaty, 979; opposes Sprigg resolutions, 1030; and Hamilton party, 1033; Adams impugns character of, 1157; mentioned, 825, 874, 875
Pinckney's treaty: grants free navigation of Mississippi, 893, 924–25; fate linked with Jay's treaty, 921, 933, 934, 964; TJ on, 923; and Spanish armed merchantman, 1188; JM on, 1252; and right of deposit at New Orleans, 1254; mentioned, 916, 918, 921, 1260
Pine, Robert Edge, 648
Pinkney, Judge (of Orleans territory), 1336
Pinkney, William: and joint mission with Monroe to Great Britain, 1420, 1422; negotiates with Canning, 1508–9, 1533, 1539, 1559, 1597, 1601; letter from, 1519, 1541, 1581, 1590, 1658; JM on error of, 1534; on "Copenhagen" Jackson, 1572; and Cadore letter, 1619, 1648; and Wellesley, 1631; resigns as minister to Great Britain, 1656, 1657, 1663, 1668, 1672; appointed minister to Russia, 1782; mentioned, 1213, 1277, 1408, 1514, 1521, 1525, 1528, 1531, 1548, 1601, 1637, 1895
Pintard, John Marsden, 1191
Pinus Strobus, 690
Piper, George, 1183
Pippin apples, 508
Piracy, 116
Pirkman, John, 321
Pitt, T., 723
Pitt, William (the Younger): as British prime minister, 311, 698, 739; and impressments, 1342–43; death of, 1409; mentioned, 306, 935, 1294
Pittsburgh, Pa., 850, 1529
Pittsburgh *Tree of Liberty,* 1530
Pittsylvania County, Va., 148
Plain Facts (Samuel Wharton), 215
Plain Truth (James Chalmers), 771
Plattsburgh, N.Y., 1731
Pleasanton, Stephen, 1501
Pleasants, James, 1968
Plenary Court (France), 527
"Pliny": critical of TJ, 1064
Plows: JM buys, from Logan, 769, 777, 785, 794, 1623; Tull's, 782; JM on, 820; TJ designs mould board of, 1623; TJ and, 1624; TJ and JM on, 1622–23
Plumer, William, 1290–91
Plums, 391, 511
Plymouth, Mass., 1300
Pocket compass, 332, 368
Pocket telescope, 368
Poinsett, Joel R., 1190
Pt. Coupeé (Orleans), 1343, 1631
Polanen, R. G., 1233
Polignac family, 625
Political Arithmetic (Thomas Cooper), 1116
Political intolerance: TJ on, 1165

Political Observations (JM), 856, 879
Political parties: origins of, 667; and newspapers, 672; JM on, 709, 910
"Political Reflections" (JM), 1073, 1094
Polk, Charles Peale, 1120
Pollock, George, 1336, 1337, 1343
Pollock, Mr., 477
Pollock, Oliver, 248
Polly case, 1360
Polybius, 498
Polyglot Bible, 1897, 1898
Polygraph, 1367
Polytype. *See* Copying press
Pond, Peter, 678
Popham, Sir H., 1471
Poplar Forest: TJ visits (1805), 1372; TJ visits (1807), 1492, 1493; TJ visits (1809), 1602, 1607; TJ visits (1810), 1624, 1625, 1640, 1645; TJ visits (1812), 1689, 1704; TJ visits (1813), 1726; TJ visits (1814), 1743; TJ visits (1815), 1767; TJ visits (1817), 1778, 1785, 1786, 1789; TJ visits (1818), 1804; TJ visits (1819), 1810, 1814; TJ visits (1820), 1824; TJ visits (1821), 1831, 1836; TJ visits (1822), 1840; mentioned, 1344, 1595–96, 1789, 1813–14
Popular elections, 1353
Popular government. *See* Representative government
Popular sovereignty: contrasted with legislative sovereignty, 447
Population: JM on political economy and distribution of, 423–24
"Porcupine, Peter." *See* Cobbett, William
Porcupine's Gazette: quoted, 973; blasts Logan's mission to France, 1008; calls Bache "organ of the French," 1009; on TJ's role in "treasonable correspondence," 1009, 1061; denounces TJ as head of French faction, 1010; links TJ, Bache, and treasonable conspiracy, 1065
Pork, 408
Port Deposit, Md., 217
Porte, 460, 1309, 1311
Porter, Charles, 278, 308
Porter, Captain Thomas, 97
Portland, Me., 1262, 1300
Portland, William Henry Cavendish Bentinck, third duke of: Laurens on, 249–50; forms Tory ministry, 1448, 1470, 1472, 1473, 1474, 1475; repudiates Erskine Agreement, 1570; collapse of ministry of, 1607
Portopotank, Va., 154
Potomac Company, 374
Potomac River: jurisdiction over, 281, 302–3, 307–8, 323, 369, 960; navigation of, 356–57; canal, 428–29, 459–60, 516; mentioned, 1253
Potomac River Company, 389
Portsmouth (U.S. frigate), 1133
Portsmouth, N.H., 885, 896, 1250
Portugal, 152–53, 1013, 1826, 1844
Posse comitatus: TJ on use of, 1351
Postal system: TJ and JM suspicious of, 750
Post office: and contracts for carrying mail, 1177–78, 1179; and schedule between Washington and Milton, Virginia, 1330
Post Office building: as temporary home of Congress, 1733
Post road, national: TJ and JM differ over, 32, 923–24, 929
Potter, James, 156
Potter, Judge, 1522–23
Potts, Richard, 860
Poulson's American Daily Advertiser (Philadelphia), 1665
Powell, Cuthbert, 1465
Powell, Robert, 96
Powell's Valley, Va., 104, 110
Power: and liberty, 565

Poydras, Julien de Lalande, 1336, 1337, 1343, 1418, 1419, 1633, 1634
Practical Navigator and Seaman's New Daily Assistant, The, 689, 690
Preble, Edward: negotiates end of war with Morocco, 1303; captures Tripoline vessel, 1306, 1308–9; and Grand Seignor, 1311; and Navy Department, 1337; purchases vessel as gift to Tunis, 1426; and gunboats, 1723; mentioned, 1259, 1368
Prentis, Joseph, 59–60, 456, 532
Prentis, Joshua, 1326
Prentiss, Samuel, 1250
Presbyterians, 1818, 1922
President (U.S. frigate), 1656, 1669
President, office of: constitutional provisions for, 496–97
President's House: burned by British, 1731
Preston, Francis, 769, 1197, 1199, 1909
Preston, William, 148
Preston, William Campbell, 1909–10, 1912, 1916, 1922, 1926, 1930, 1964
Prevost, Sir George, 1683, 1703, 1731
Prevost, J. B., 1331, 1336, 1337, 1419
Price, Mr., 1695
Pride, Mr., 605
Priestley, Joseph, 319, 684–85, 1124, 1287, 1311, 1604
Primogeniture, 334
Prince, William, 508, 529, 694, 695, 697
Prince Edward County, Va., 55, 479
Princeton, N.J.: and Pennsylvania Line mutiny, 157; Congress moves to, 233, 261, 268; TJ arrives at, 271–72; JM visits, 684
Princeton University. *See* College of New Jersey
Printing: TJ describes plates for, 412
Printing press: needed in Richmond, 134, 143–44, 166
Prisoners of war: British, 63, 74–76, 91–95, 113, 114, 118; American, 63, 64, 91–92, 93, 118, 120
Pritchard, Mr., 319
Privateers, 883, 898
Private rights, 448. *See also* Individual liberties
Prizes: restitution of, 1180–82
"Probationary Odes of Jonathan Pindar, The" (St. George Tucker), 792
Proceedings of the Government of the United States . . . Against the Intrusion of Edward Livingston, The (TJ), 1690
Proclamation of Neutrality, 749, 751, 765–66, 787, 798–99, 801–2, 803, 822
Proclamation of 1763, 215
Property: and factions, 501
Property rights: TJ's generational theory of, 641, 651–52; JM on, 709
Prophet (Indian leader), 1676
Prophetstown, 1676
Prospect before Us, The (James T. Callender), 1137, 1152
Protective tariffs, 1976
Protestant Episcopal Church, 331, 360–61, 466
Prussia: and Baron D'Arendt, 161–62; and Austria, 460; and Holland, 460; treaty with, 883, 1190; mentioned, 1150, 1309
Public accounts: settlement of Revolutionary, 475
Public credit: JM's efforts to establish, 593; Congress levies taxes to pay, 613; and national defense, 645
Public debts: and TJ's generational theory, 640–42, 651; and mint bill, 719. *See also* National debt; "Report on Public Credit"
Public Good (Thomas Paine), 215
Public lands: sale of, 491. *See also* Western lands
"Publicola" (John Quincy Adams), 695, 691, 693, 697. *See also* Adams, John Quincy
Public opinion: JM on, 502; TJ on, 1165, 1166, 1294, 1322–23, 1353

INDEX

"Publius," 1408
Pufendorf, Samuel, Freiherr von, 360, 1360
Purchas, Samuel: edits *Purchas His Pilgrimes,* 212
Purviance, Mr., 1438, 1896
Purvis, Captain James, 97
Putnam, P., 1301
Pyrenees, 1531
Pythagoras, 1878

Quadruple Alliance, 1759
Quakers, 1031
Queenston, 1684
Quasi war with France, 1008, 1029–30, 1086, 1142, 1169
Quebec, 1490, 1687, 1731, 1746
Queen Anne's, Md., 663
Queenstown Heights, 1707
Quids, 1405, 1696
Quitrents: abolished in Northern Neck, 403–4

Rabbits, 391
Racial prejudice: TJ's views on, 16, 20–21
Rademaker, Mr., 1520, 1522
Rakove, Jack: quoted, 518
Raleigh, N.C., 1139, 1146
Ralston, Mr., 1471
Ramage, Mr., 1537
Rambouillet Decree, 1617–18
Rampart arms, 191–92, 193, 196, 197
Ramsay, David, 539, 581, 838, 1130
Randall family, 1529
Randolph, Anne Cary, 739
Randolph, Archibald C., 1694
Randolph, B. R., 1529, 1530
Randolph, Benjamin Franklin, 1630
Randolph, Beverley, 509
Randolph, David Meade, 801, 802, 808, 810, 812, 815, 816
Randolph, Edmund: on JM, 53–54; and western land claims of Virginia, 212–13, 215; as attorney general of Virginia, 221; TJ urges, to go into Virginia legislature, 223, 270; JM discusses national debt with, 247; on JM's reputation, 278; referred to as the attorney, 304–5; tutors JM in law, 364; and Virginia capitol, 385, 413, 424–25; as delegate to Annapolis Convention, 396, 404, 405; TJ buys books for, 410; as delegate to Constitutional Convention, 454, 468, 469–70, 476, 477, 478, 497; elected governor of Virginia, 456; and bust of Lafayette, 465, 474; on office of president, 497; opposes ratification, 503, 509, 515, 534; supports call for second convention, 552; and navigation of Mississippi, 538; and instructions to American peace commissioners, 567; denies constitutionality of Bank of the United States, 666; TJ consults, on negotiations with Hammond, 712, 721; defends TJ against Hamilton's newspaper attack, 715; drafts Proclamation of Neutrality, 749, 751, 774–75, 787, 791, 817; TJ increasingly critical of, 752, 773–74, 804–5; on federal commissioners' compensation, 764–65; on John Nicholson, 767–68; marries Elizabeth Nicholas, 779; sounds public opinion in Virginia, 794, 795, 797; and Dutch loan, 798; and Democratic Society of Philadelphia, 804; and advisory board on foreign affairs, 805; Washington mentions, 806, 807; and recall of Genet, 809; on place of meeting of Congress, 828; as secretary of state, negotiates with Hammond, 832–33; on meeting between Washington and Fauchet, 833; borrows books from TJ, 840, 841, 858, 861, 876; on Lord Dorchester's speech to Indians, 845; on Dohrman's debt to Mazzei, 859; TJ writes, about University of Geneva, 874, 875; Monroe writes, about his reception in France, 879; forced to resign by Washington, 886, 887, 899; succeeded by Pickering, 890; publishes *Vindication,* 900, 901, 903, 904, 907; *Vindication* attacked by "Peter Porcupine," 907; appointed Virginia commissioner on Potomac boundary, 961; attends Albemarle court, 1176; mentioned, 70, 245, 324, 689, 705, 707, 726, 784, 802, 840
Randolph, Elizabeth Nicholas (Mrs. Edmund), 779
Randolph, Ellen, 1772, 1780, 1815
Randolph, Eston, 1786
Randolph, James Madison: born in President's House, 1412
Randolph, John: breaks with TJ, 1400, 1405, 1667; animosity of, for JM, 1405–6; ridicules JM's *Examination of the British Doctrine,* 1408–9; and neutral rights, 1414; writes as "Decius," 1423; attempts to "assassinate" Two Million Dollar Act, 1424; supports Monroe in 1808, 1548; and repeal of Embargo Act, 1552; breaks with Monroe, 1564, 1580, 1611, 1647, 1654, 1664; on Erskine Agreement, 1566; opposes economic coercion, 1650–51; on conflict in JM's cabinet, 1652; and Yazoo land case, 1647; critical of JM in postwar years, 1772; on JM as a great man, 1775; mentioned, 1954
Randolph, Sir John, 908
Randolph, Martha "Patsy" Jefferson: first son born to, 739; and illness of husband, 880, 898; TJ tells, of party hatreds, 1063; in residence at Monticello, 1146; TJ buys wig for, 1362; stays with TJ at President's House, 1412; illness of, 1371, 1780; illness of child of, 1602, 1603, 1786; affection for Dolley Madison, 1727, 1744, 1772, 1787, 1805; visits Madisons (1816), 1772
Randolph, Peter (of Chatsworth, Va.), 687
Randolph, Peyton (died 1775), 45, 908, 1847, 1877
Randolph, Peyton (1738–1784), 391
Randolph, Ryland, 371, 1425
Randolph, Thomas Easton, 1786
Randolph, Thomas Jefferson: birth of, 739; wounded by Bankhead, 1807; and TJ's final illness, 1972; edits TJ's writings, 1975; mentioned, 1563
Randolph, Thomas Mann: marries Martha Jefferson, 654; TJ writes, about Freneau, 672; seeks horse for TJ, 675, 707; on crops (1791) 699; illness of, 880, 898; and Jay's treaty, 887; letter to TJ from, 900, 901–2, 1063–64; TJ writes, about Adams's cabinet firings, 1117–18; in residence at Monticello, 1146; TJ writes to, about daily schedules, 1210; and family stay with TJ in President's House, 1412; and illness of family, 1429; farm of, 1438; and Hackley, 1441; and merino sheep, 1640; and McGehee, 1644–45; JM appoints, to army command, 1717; organizes Albemarle Agriculture Society, 1792, 1822; as governor of Virginia, 1798; and TJ, 1816; and university, 1817; mentioned, 737, 739, 800–1, 862, 1019, 1160, 1582, 1727, 1744, 1909
Rape, 459
Rapine, Daniel, 1465
Raskin, Mr., 1373
Ratford, Jenkin, 1499
Ratification, popular: of U.S. Constitution, 445
Ratification conventions. *See individual states*
Ravensworth, Fairfax County, Va., 1176, 1226
Rawle, William, 828
Ray, Mr., 1577
Raynal, Guillaume-Thomas-François, Abbé de, 333
Read, George, 293, 478, 579
Read, Jacob, 310, 313, 1023, 1062
Read, James, 1203
Read, John, 1186
Reade, Captain Edmund, 186
Reading, Pa., 1184
Rebellion: TJ on need for, 514

Record of the Federal Convention of 1787, The, 518
Recruiting, military: in Virginia, 67, 128
Red birds, 493, 508, 529
Red clover, 878
Redman, Vincent, 81
Red River, 1456, 1457, 1459, 1493
Reed, George. *See* Read, George
Reed, Joseph, 371
Reed, Mr.: and Burr conspiracy, 1471
Rees's *Cyclopedia,* 1806
Reeve, Tapping, 1526, 1528
Reflections on the Revolution in France (Edmund Burke), 667–68, 685, 689
Reign of Terror: in France, 752, 779
Religion: JM's interest in freedom of, 38, 40, 50; general tax assessment to support, 282–83; TJ on enactment of Virginia Statute on Religious Freedom, 458–59; and individual rights, 448, 502. *See also* Freedom of religion
Religious intolerance: TJ on, 1165
Removal power of president, 31, 621–22
"Report concerning Continental Bills of Credit," 316–17
"Report of the Committee of Revisors on the Revision of the Laws," 331. *See also* Virginia revised code of laws
"Report on Public Credit" (Alexander Hamilton): provisions of, 642; TJ critical of, 642–43; JM's views on, 653–54
"Report on Restoring Public Credit" (JM), 230–31, 239–41
"Report on the American Fisheries" (TJ), 678–80
"Report on the [Virginia] Resolutions" (JM), 1111, 1123, 1124, 1125, 1918, 1925, 1988
"Report on Weights and Measures" (TJ), 647, 677, 696, 719
Representation: JM on, 442; and delegated powers, 447; based on population, 470–71, 496; in Congress, 503
Representative government: and American Revolution, 2, 6; TJ on, 3; JM on, 28; founded on the people, 443; and ratification of Constitution by the people, 446
Republican government: and representation of the people, 446; JM on, 448–49, 496
Republicanism: and slavery, 15–26; and individual rights, 500–2; distinguished from royalism, 588; and titles, 609; JM on, 614, 709, 710; and Freneau, 672; TJ links American and French, 751; and Democratic societies, 861; TJ on, 1165–66; and majority rule, 1982, 1991–92; new phase of, 1984; rejected by nullification, 1989; mentioned, 668, 669
Republican party: JM's use of the term, 710; Hamilton calls, a faction, 714, 1006; labeled "Mr. Madison's party," 744, 881; in election of 1792, 745; TJ on distinctions between, and Federalists, 747, 774; TJ outlines party strategy of, 756–57; and discriminatory duties, 825–26; JM on weakness of (1794), 827; and Democratic societies, 862; in New York, 866; in New Jersey, 866; doubles representation in New York (1795), 872; TJ and JM plan strategy of, after Jay's treaty, 886–87; caucuses in House for first time, 892; calls for treaty to replace Jay's, 893; shrivels after opposing Jay's treaty, 895; nominates TJ for presidency (1796), 940; TJ succeeds JM as leader of, 971, 995, 996; as advocate of legislative power, 996; TJ on names for, 996, 1047, 1093; representatives attend Washington ball, 998; labeled faction by Sedgwick, 999; labeled French partisans, 1000; JM calls, "the Constitutional party," 1032; TJ on strategy for (1798–99), 1073; upsets Federalists in New York (1800), 1138; New England wing revolts against embargo, 1552; collapse of leadership of (1809), 1553–54;

nominates JM in 1808, 1548; loses seats in House (1809), 1585; JM on disorientation of (1809), 1623; schisms in, 1589, 1650, 1696; election victories of, in New York (1814), 1730; JM on origins of, 1848; TJ on principles of, 1862–63; mentioned, 31, 672
Republic of letters: TJ on, 3
Republics: size of, 448
Reputation: Francis Bacon on, 2
Residence Act: rumor of repeal attempt, 735
Resignation of General Washington, The (painting), 1774
Retaliation (U.S. armed vessel), 1086, 1096
Retaliation bill, 1096
Reveley, John, 99
Revenue cutters, 731, 733
Revenue system of 1783: JM briefs TJ on, 236–39; JM's efforts to establish, 593; mentioned, 221, 230–31, 420, 435
Revised code of Virginia. *See* Virginia revised code of laws
Revisionist historians: of slavery, 15–26
Revolution: right of, 1983, 1996
"Revolution of 1800": TJ on, 1166, 1620–21
Reyneval, Joseph Matthais Gérard de, TJ's appraisal of, 436, 464
Reynolds, James, 984
Reynolds, Maria (Mrs. James), 984
Reynolds, William, 1248, 1249
Rhea, John, 1337, 1552
Rhode Island: opposes Confederation impost, 230–31, 363; and revenue system of 1783, 237; TJ visits, 285, 321; vetoes efforts to strengthen Confederation, 387; paper money in, 430; referred to as Rogue's Island, 443; refuses to send delegates to Constitutional Convention, 476; and federal Constitution, 504; refuses to call ratification convention for Constitution, 504, 508, 547; favors Bill of Rights, 595; ratifies Constitution, 662; federal lawsuits in, 1217
Rhode Island: college in. *See* Brown University
Rhode Island greening apples, 511
Rhododendrons, 511, 694
Rice: TJ ships to South Carolina, 495, 512; African upland, 694
Richard, Father Gabriel, 1575, 1611–13, 1665
Richards, John, 1465
Richards, Mark, 1250
Richardson, Richard: and TJ's nailery, 1146, 1148; mentioned, 1076, 1078, 1079, 1084
Richardson, Samuel, 6
Richelieu, Armand-Emmanuel du Plessis, duc de: on JM and postwar America, 1772
Richelieu River, 1735
Richmond Enquirer, 36, 1137, 1530, 1669, 1864, 1870, 1957
Richmond, Va.: state capitol moves to, 66–67, 71, 84, 128; and printing press, 166; British force state government to flee, 176–77; public buildings in, 323; branch of Bank of United States to be established in, 737; and Genet, 816; and Jay's treaty, 885, 886, 896, 902; Burr's trial in, 1444; JM visits as elector for TJ, 1155; mentioned, 973–74, 1139, 1141, 1187, 1189, 1604, 1839, 1979
Riddle, William, 1529, 1530
Ridgeley, Mr., 1522
Ridgely, Charles, 741
Ridgeway, Mr., 1341
Riedesel, Baron Friedrich von, 83, 84, 119
Riedesel, Baroness Frederika von, 83, 84
Rigaud, André, 1092
Rights of Man, The (Thomas Paine): TJ endorses, 667, 687
Rights of the British Colonies Asserted and Proved, The (James Otis), 1845, 1876
Rio Bravo del Norte. *See* Rio Grande

Rio de Janeiro, 1583
Rio Grande, 1292, 1327, 1329, 1354, 1359, 1387, 1493, 1522
Ritcheson, Charles R.: quoted, 722
Ritchie, Thomas: on Andrew Jackson, 1807-8; JM writes, 1948-51, 1957; mentioned, 36, 1669, 1864, 1961, 1968
Rittenhouse, David: TJ ships books to, 492; travels to New York with TJ, 688; welcomes Genet, 775; and kitchen stoves, 922, 926; mentioned, 146, 687, 947
Rittenhouse, Hannah Jacobs (Mrs. David), 926
Rittenhouse, Miss, 581
Rivanna River, 1429
Rives, William Cabell, 1964, 1978, 1984, 1996, 1997
Rivington, James, 139, 689, 690, 1027
Roach, Isaac, 736
Roads: joint efforts by Virginia, Maryland, and Pennsylvania to build, beyond Potomac, 358; discussed in TJ's *Notes,* 425; from Potomac to Ohio River, 429
Roane, Spencer: opposes John Marshall's decisions, 34, 1870; and Virginia Executive Council, 363, 456; as presidential elector, 605; on Rockfish Gap commission, 1793; states' rights views of, 1850, 1851; on federal-state relations, 1864; JM's letters to, 1870-75; mentioned, 1805
Robbins, Jonathan, 1128
Roberts, Anne Jean: and ballooning, 332, 351, 367
Roberts, John, 1134
Roberts, Jonathan, 1754
Robertson, David, 916
Robertson, Mr., 1930, 1931, 1964
Robertson, Thomas Bolling, 1481, 1490, 1498
Robespierre, Maximilien-François-Marie-Isadore de, 758, 907, 998, 1004, 1021, 1046
Robinson, Donald L., 15
Robinson, Moses, 671, 690
Robinson, Mr., 1486
Rochambeau, Jean-Baptiste-Donatien de Vimeur, comte de: plans campaign of 1781, 167, 174, 200; sails for France, 225; TJ proposes gift of land to, 412, 419
Rochambeau, Donatien-Marie-Joseph de Vimeur, vicomte de, 200
Rockfish Gap, Va., 1793, 1794-95, 1804, 1818, 1932
Rock Hall, Md., 663
Rodgers, John: TJ praises, 1303; on Mediterranean affairs, 1429; mentioned, 1432, 1656, 1669, 1685
Rodney, Caesar A.: and Burr conspiracy, 1475, 1487; and Judge Davis, 1495; rules that batture is property of United States, 1521, 1642; and Hull, 1523; mentioned, 1363, 1466, 1467, 1471, 1474, 1512, 1523, 1604, 1607, 1634
Rodney, Admiral Sir George, 169, 190
Rodney, Thomas, 1272, 1301, 1336
Rogers, David, 106
Rogers, Richard, 1199, 1300
Roland, Jean-Marie, 782
Roman, James, 1336, 1343
Romanzoff, Count Nicholas de, 1608
Rome, N.Y., 344
Romulus (French warship), 188, 199, 1190; as ship assigned to carry TJ to France (1782), 217, 218, 222, 224
Ronald, William, 405, 534
Rose, Francis Taylor Madison (JM's sister), 1184
Rose, George H.: special envoy to United States, 1496, 1503; failure of mission of, 1508, 1534, 1656, 1665
Rose, Robert H., 1184, 1185
Roses, 694
Ross, David: Virginia commercial agent, 119, 172, 174, 184, 189, 404-5, 1132
Ross, James: runs for governor of Pennsylvania, 1013; introduces partisan electoral count bill in Senate, 1111-14, 1115, 1130, 1135; mentioned, 978
Ross, John, 636, 707, 828
Rossiter, Clinton: quoted, 518
Rotation in office, 450, 513, 546, 552
Rotation of crops, 866
Rotunda (University of Virginia): criticism of, 1820; funding for, approved, 1842-43, 1853; JM on, 1854; work on, begins, 1857; classrooms in, 1860, 1861; first public dinner in, 1889; mentioned, 1819, 1834, 1839
Rowley, Mass., 1542, 1543
Royal absolutism: in France, 452
Royall, Anne Newport, 1975
Royal Military Academy, 1886
Royster, Charles: quoted, 64
Ruby, Mr., 1303
Rufini, Mr., 1340
Rule of 1756: JM on illegality of, 1360-61, 1386; TJ on, 1398; Stephen defends, 1471; mentioned, 883, 1359-60, 1408, 1412-14, 1537, 1569
Rum, 608, 619
Rumsey, James, 359-60, 369, 389
Rush, Benjamin: records TJ's appraisal of JM, 648; on election of 1800, 1149; mentioned, 730, 957, 1522, 1722
Rush, Richard: compares JM with TJ and Washington, 1729; minister to Great Britain, 1884, 1896; mentioned, 1528, 1681, 1758, 1840, 1881, 1898
Russel, Professor, 1903
Russel, William, 408
Russell, Gilbert C., 1609
Russell, Jonathan: U.S. chargé in London, 1705; appointed to peace commission, 1710, 1734; mentioned, 1672
Russell, Mr., 1306, 1311, 1324
Russia: and the Porte, 460; JM warns against United States being drawn into politics of, 1345; signs alliance with Great Britain, 1358; Short appointed as minister to, 1576; and French Continental policy, 1585; excludes British trade, 1601; Robert Smith offered post as minister to, 1652, 1663; offers to mediate war of 1812, 1710, 1718; ukase on northwest coast of America, 1882
Rutherford, Robert, 765, 768
Rutland, Robert A.: quoted, 444, 528, 1687
Rutledge, Edward: TJ sends *Notes* to, 492; JM on, 816; mentioned, 828, 838, 860, 970
Rutledge, John: delegate to Constitutional Convention, 469, 478; mentioned, 109, 110, 222, 563, 919
Rutledge, John, Jr., 860, 976, 979, 1187
Rutter, Thomas, 1326
Rye: JM on price of (1786), 428

Sabine River: Spanish forces cross, 1402, 1416; as dividing line between American and Spanish troops, 1455, 1456, 1457, 1458; mentioned, 1327
Sackett's Harbor, 1712, 1747, 1751
St. Bernard Bay, 1282
St. Christopher, British West Indies, 1260
St. Clair, Arthur, 636, 710, 1224, 1230
St. Croix River, 1338
St. Eustatius, 169
St. Fond, Faujas de, 308
St. John, Mr. *See* Crèvecoeur, Michel-Guillaume St. Jean de
St. Julien, Lewis, 1328
St. Lawrence River, 1735, 1881
St. Louis: transfer from Spanish to French to American authorities, 1291; mentioned, 1471, 1684
St. Lucia, 165

St. Martin, French West Indies, 166, 699
St. Mary River, 1338
St. Mary's, Ga., 1464
St. Michael (U.S. dispatch ship), 1528, 1534, 1536, 1544, 1547
St. Petersburg, Russia, 1171, 1192, 1301, 1311, 1536, 1710, 1712, 1905
Saint-Priest, Emmanuel Guignard, comte de, 625
St. Thomas, Danish West Indies, 1406, 1433
St. Trise, Mr. *See* St. Trys, chevalier de
St. Trys, chevalier de, 582, 637
Salcedo, Nemesio de, 1493
Salem, Mass., 1231, 1250, 1251, 1268, 1300
Salt tax (1798), 1042
San Antonio, 1357, 1387, 1457
Sandusky, 1684
Sanford, Nathan, 1301, 1432, 1434–35
Sanlúcar, 1441, 1582
Santa Fe, 1493
Santander, 1377, 1441
Santiago, Cuba, 1221
Santo Domingo: French campaign in 1255; mission to, by Dr. Stevens, 1312–22; trade with, 1406, 1433, 1520; and Bonaparte, 1585; mentioned, 829, 1311, 1335
Saratoga prisoners: quartered near Charlottesville, 63, 134; provisions for, 162; mentioned, 72, 113–14, 117, 120, 152, 198
Saunders, Captain (British army), 1488, 1489
Saunders, Parson. *See* Saunderson, Nicholas
Saunders, Robert, 1122
Saunderson, Nicholas, 854, 868
Savage, William, 1213, 1344
Savannah, Ga., 507
Saxe-Coburg, Friedrich Josias, duke of, 772, 779, 783
Say, Jean Baptiste, 1908, 1909
Sayre, Stephen, 1227
Schaedler, Louis C., 4
Scheele, Carl Wilhelm, 319
Scheele, Peter, 1260–61
Scheld River, 339, 352, 365–66
Schlegel, Johan Frederik Wilhelm, 1186
Schoepf, Johann David, 49
Schultz, Harold S.: quoted, 519
Schuyler, Philip, 671, 696, 728, 978, 1327
Schuylkill River, 767, 780
"Scipio." *See* Tracy, Uriah
Scott, Charles: captured at Charleston, 197; campaign against Indians in Kentucky, 699, 701, 703; mentioned, 80, 103, 117, 696
Scott, Marion du Pont, 967
Scott, Mr., 1233
Scott, Robert, 1975
Scott, Thomas, 851, 861
Scott, Walter, 1921
Scott, William, Baron Stowell: and *Essex* decision, 1350, 1360, 1361, 1390
Sea kale, 1814, 1815, 1822
Secession (scission): TJ on, 1119; JM attacks doctrine of, 1977, 1981, 1994–95; South Carolina doctrine of, 1980; Andrew Jackson denounces, 1995; dual definition of, 1996; mentioned, 1109, 1982
Seckel, David, 830
Secretary's Ford (Albemarle County), Va., 984
Secret service, 1327
Sedgwick, Theodore: proposes enlargement of army, 836; and election of 1794, 859, 866; and denunciation of Democratic societies, 851, 861; and Jay's treaty, 889, 903; on Gallatin as Republican leader, 995; critical of TJ, 997, 1010; refuses to attend Washington ball, 998, 1024; views Republicans as faction, 999; opposes funding federal building in District of Columbia, 1033; on banishment, 1087; on retaliation bill, 1095; as Speaker of the House, 1117

Sedition Act: aimed at Republican newspapers, 1003; foreshadowed by Adams's replies to addresses, 1004; TJ's appraisal of, 1007, 1080, 1083; aimed at Bache, 1045; Lloyd's bill, 1064, 1065; TJ receives text of, 1068; amended by Logan Act, 1073–74; enforcement pattern in 1800, 1116; expiration of, 1172; mentioned, 1042, 1056–57, 1067
Sedition bill: in England, 925, 926
Seditious libel: TJ dismisses Backus case, 1497
Selden, Miles, 363, 517
"Self-created" societies, 861–64
Selman, John, 1213, 1251
Seminole war, 1808
Senate: debates in federal convention on, 497–98; endorses Washington's denunciation of Democratic societies, 861; opens door to public, 903; and alienation of affections of citizens from federal government, 970; debates defense measures against France, 980, 981–82, 983; Alien Friends Act in, 1003, 1042, 1044, 1045, 1047, 1049, 1051, 1052, 1054, 1056, 1063; votes to publish envoys' dispatches, 1034; bill from, for capturing French cruisers, 1052; and suspension of intercourse with France, 1057, 1092; levies tax on lands, houses, and slaves, 1059; debates loan of armed ships during quasi war, 1059; passes nautralization bill, 1057, 1059; agrees to adjourn in July 1798, 1061; debates treason and sedition bill, 1064, 1065; passes retaliation bill against France, 1095; passes army reorganization bill, 1095, 1096; and volunteer army bill, 1096; passes eventual army bill, 1096; divided on peace mission to France, 1097; condemns Duane, 1115, 1116, 1133, 1190; requests indictment of Duane, 1116; and TJ's *Manual of Parliamentary Practice,* 1139; TJ presides over, 1142; passes Judiciary Act of 1801, 1143; and ratification of Convention of 1800, 1158; and Duane case, 1190; ratifies Louisiana Purchase Treaty, 1290, 1297; and *New Jersey,* 1378; mentioned, 1061, 1062, 1140, 1378
Separation of powers: in Constitution, 445, 491, 500; JM and TJ on, 442, 458, 471, 480
Sequestration, 883
Serapis (British frigate), 165, 171
Sergeant, Jonathan Dickinson, 168, 775
Sergeant, Winthrop, 1045
Sérurier, Louis, 1760
Servetus, Michael, 1818
Sevier, John, 1337
Sewall, Samuel, 1026
Sewell, Clement, 1465
Shadwell, Va., 1184, 1438
Shadwell Ford (Albemarle County), Va., 984
Shaler, William, 1779, 1782
Sharp, James Roger: quoted, 878
Sharpless, Jonathan, 920, 922, 929, 935
Shawnee Indians, 78–79
Shays's Rebellion: JM condemns, 436, 438–39, 473, 474; TJ on, 450–51, 461, 514; Virginia raises taxes for troops to suppress, 467; mentioned, 441, 531
Shee, Mr., 1533
Sheffield, John Baker Holroyd, first earl of, 279, 679, 701
Shelburne, William Petty, second earl of: Henry Laurens on, 249–50
Shelby, Evan, 78, 80
Shelby, Isaac, 733, 1909, 1922
Shepherd, David, 78, 111
Sheridan, Eugene R., 317
Sherman, Roger, 49, 477, 599, 796, 1875
Shippen, Alice Lee (Mrs. William, Jr.), 249, 663
Shippen, Thomas Lee, 567, 663, 766
Shippen, William, Jr., 249, 663
Shirley Plantation, 1911
Shore, John, 1242, 1244, 1251

INDEX 2065

Short, William: and JM, 201–2, 279, 322, 337, 364, 371, 437–38, 487; TJ on qualifications of, 245, 296; urged by TJ to enter Virginia legislature, 270; favors strengthening Confederation, 278; on Virginia Executive Council, 279, 363; as TJ's secretary in France, 285, 316, 318, 343, 347, 349, 353; buys land near Monticello, 284, 297, 336, 354; as candidate for Confederation Congress, 309; carries Isaac Zane's letter to TJ, 324; trip of, to London, 381; and Nootka Sound incident, 646; nominated minister to The Hague, 718; appraises Girondist cabinet, 735–36; in Madrid, 779, 840, 939; writes TJ, 1233; visits Monticello, 1240, 1248, 1249; appointed minister to Russia, 1510, 1526, 1535, 1536, 1542, 1543, 1576, 1577, 1578, 1594, 1596, 1658; on political factions in Pennsylvania, 1540; in Paris, 1594; mentioned, 248, 344, 482, 484, 630, 1541, 1607
Shorter, Mr., 1578
Shrader, Mr., 1425
Siberia, 284, 308, 371
Sibley, John, 1473
Sicily, 1421
Sidi Suliman Mellimelli. *See* Mellimelli, Sidi Suliman
"Sidney" (writer in *National Gazette*), 729
"Sidney" (writer in Bache's *Aurora*), 1046
Sidney, Algernon, 1918, 1924
"Sidney, Algernon" (pseudonym: Spencer Roane), 34
Simms, Captain, 691, 694
Simpson, James: as consul at Morocco, 1213, 1231, 1234, 1235, 1240, 1242; and presents for Morocco, 1266, 1267, 1280, 1281; as consul at Algiers, 1303; and ransoming, 1436; mentioned, 1277, 1485
Simson, James. *See* Simpson, James
Sitgreaves, Samuel, 889, 903, 949, 1052, 1053, 1211, 1214
Six Nations: and western land titles, 215
Sketches on Rotations of Crops (John Beale Bordley), 871, 876
Sketch of the Finances of the United States, A (Albert Gallatin), 922
Skinner, Thomson G., 1326
Skinner, Thomson Joseph, 1052
Skinner, Richard, 1250
Skipwith, Fulwar: in London, 418, 432; letter of, to TJ confiscated, 1010; as agent at Paris for prize cases, 1213, 1309–10; as consul in France, 1314, 1660; Livingston quarrels with, 1334, 1338; and Barney's claims, 1345; and Milan Decree, 1515; mentioned, 542, 1337, 1769
Slacum, George, 1465
Slaughter, Ensign, 97
Slaughter, George, 104
Slaughter, John, 97
Slavery: and slave trade, 17; in Northwest Territory, 277; and Land Ordinance of 1784, 309; and slave tax in Virginia, 324; Lafayette's views on, 348; petitions against, in Virginia, 405; and emigrants, 869; and nullification, 1998
Slavery and Jeffersonian Virginia (Robert McColley), 16
Slaves: use of, in wartime manufactories, 65, 119; Lafayette favors manumission of, 328; importation of, 503; carried off after Revolution, 711, 722, 883; smuggling of, 1241
Slave tax, 315
Slave trade: prohibited after 1808, 23, 24, 1882; mentioned, 17, 388
Smallpox: in Richmond, 831, 838, 839, 840, 1187
Smallwood, Samuel N., 1465
Smallwood, William, 159
Smelser, Marshall: quoted, 1564, 1680
Smith, Adam, 368
Smith, Alexander, 1465

Smith, Charles Page: quoted, 141
Smith, Colonel, 1739
Smith, Granville, 199
Smith, Israel, 1240
Smith, James Morton: quoted, 1153
Smith, John (Frederick County, Va.,), 76, 77
Smith, John (Virginia congressman), 768
Smith, John (clerk in War Department), 1578
Smith, John Blair, 421, 468, 479, 687, 688
Smith, Joseph: and Benedict Arnold, 147
Smith, Joseph Allen, 1193
Smith, Logan Pearsall, 3
Smith, Margaret Bayard (Mrs. Samuel Harrison): on TJ's inauguration, 1166; on TJ with grandchildren, 1412; on friendship between TJ and JM, 1562; on JM's story-telling ability, 1975
Smith, Meriwether, 180, 189, 192, 193, 197; on Virginia congressional delegation (1781), 201; to Annapolis Convention, 404–5; opposes ratification, 534; mentioned, 363
Smith, Mr. (son of Meriwether Smith), 637
Smith, Robert: heads Navy Department, 1174, 1264; and death of son, 1199; TJ consults, 1203, 1376, 1379–80; and naval force in Mediterranean, 1210, 1239, 1268, 1423; and Barbary powers, 1239–40, 1423; and the *John Adams*, 1249; and supplies to Algiers, 1263; and shipments to Morocco, 1266, 1280, 1281; praises naval officers, 1302–3; and case of *Philadelphia*, 1325; and Preble, 1368; and Miranda case, 1407, 1425; and Mellimelli, 1421; and bashaw of Tripoli, 1423; and Cumberland Road, 1427; and navy agents, 1436; and flags of truce to interdicted vessels, 1483, 1497; and gunboats stationed near Floridas, 1508, 1533; and letter from Boston tories, 1531; and Meade, 1583; and "Copenhagen" Jackson, 1601; and batture case, 1640, 1642; JM appoints, as secretary of state, 1566; and Erskine Agreement, 1581, 1585; JM dismisses, 1652, 1662, 1663, 1664; writes pamphlet attacking JM, 1655; and Duane, 1668, 1669; and W. C. Nicholas, 1716, 1717; and embargo, 1896; mentioned, 1225, 1231, 1245, 1281, 1422, 1650
Smith, Samuel: TJ offers Navy Department to, 1140, 1160, 1167, 1174, 1175; asks TJ about Federalist accusations, 1065; and Moreau incident, 1383; and British violations, 1424; on Monroe-Pinkney Treaty, 1447, 1466, 1468, 1471, 1473; and East India commerce, 1495–96; brother of Robert Smith, 1566; critical of Gallatin, 1650; and recharter of Bank of the United States, 1651; opposes Macon's Bill No. 1, 1652; and W. C. Nicholas, 1716; mentioned, 741, 917, 1052, 1195, 1197, 1339, 1519, 1825
Smith, Samuel Harrison: prints TJ's preface to Paine's *Rights*, 687, 688; as editor of *National Intelligencer*, 1155; prints TJ's inaugural address, 1166; at President's House, 1412; publishes Bonaparte's militia system, 1475; publishes Canning's promise, 1500, 1501; and TJ's books for Library of Congress, 1732, 1745, 1763, 1765, 1766; visits Montpellier, 1975; mentioned 982, 1276, 1465
Smith, Samuel Stanhope, 684
Smith, William: TJ requests map from, 145–46; mentioned, 128, 180, 212
Smith, William, Jr.,: and history of New York, 288, 290, 292
Smith, William, Jr. (of Canada), 685
Smith, William, Sr. (of Canada), 685
Smith, William Loughton: on "Mr. Madison's party," 744; Hamilton writes speech for, 824, 839; burned in effigy, 838; favors embargo of 1794, 843; reelected in 1794, 860; supports Jay's treaty, 901; and answer to Washington's final address, 949; on

Smith (*continued*)
    transfer of power from Washington to Adams, 966; on arming merchant vessels, 980; appointed minister to Constantinople, 1095; mentioned, 736, 737, 766, 806, 828, 831, 979
Smith, William Stephens: TJ and, 439, 464–65, 1408; returns from London, 692; sends JM pamphlet on Genessee Country, 683, 694, 696; and Miranda expedition, 1407–8, 1423, 1425, 1429, 1432–33, 1437; mentioned, 691, 766
Smith and Buchanan, 1519, 1520
Smithsonian magazine, 14
Smuggling, 608
Smyrna, 1447
Smyth, Alexander, 1709, 1717
Society of Agriculture of Paris, 1624
Society of the Cincinnati, 853, 867
Söderström, Richard, 1191, 1522, 1545, 1546
Sofaer, Abraham D.: quoted, 1397
Solicitations for office: TJ on, 546
"Somers," 1864
Songster's, Va., 1226
Sophia (American brig), 1055, 1057
Sorel, 1735
Southall, Turner, 687
South America, 692, 693, 1844
South Carolina: and revenue system of 1783, 239; paper money in, 429; and slave trade, 503; ratifies Constitution, 505, 531, 542; in election of 1800, 1139, 1140, 1154, 1155; federal lawsuits in, 1218; and internal improvements, 1957, 1959, 1961, 1962; and nullification theory, 1979, 1982; adopts nullification ordinance, 1993; repeals nullification ordinance, 1997
South Carolina College, 1818, 1822
South Carolina Exposition (by John C. Calhoun): 1980, 1981; JM denounces, 1980, 1981, 1995
Southside, Va., 535
Souvé, Mr., 1343
Soverign states: and Articles of Confederation, 446
Sovereignty: JM on divisibility of, 1980, 1982, 1983; Calhoun on indivisibility of, 1980: JM on dual meanings of, 2000
Spafford, Mr. (of Albany), 1770, 1780, 1781
Spaight, Richard Dobbs, 310, 478
Spain: and American Revolution, 62, 131; and navigation of Mississippi, 153; JM on need for treaty with, 328; and Jay-Guardoqui negotiations, 431; and Nootka Sound incident, 645, 657–59; and Proclamation of Neutrality, 787; TJ expects war with (1793), 788; Pinckney's treaty with, 924–25, 977; declares war on Great Britain, 956, 958; U.S. relations with, at Natchez, 1016, 1019; evacuates posts, 1022; cedes Louisiana to France, 1208, 1253–54, 1541; suspends right of deposit, 1254; spoliations committed by, 1221, 1260, 1374, 1396; detains American vessels in Buenos Aires, 1236; protests sale of Louisiana, 1285, 1286; relinquishes opposition to transfer of Louisiana, 1323, 1349; and the Floridas, 1291, 1305, 1358–59, 1373–74; demands revocation of Mobile Act, 1342, 1346, 1354–55; suspends Convention of 1802, 1345, 1349; defaults on subsidy to France, 1359; TJ proposes new negotiations, 1378–79, 1394–95, 1396; sends troops to Nacogdoches, 1387; and reciprocal extradition of fugitives, 1433–34; TJ on probability of war with, 1452, 1458, 1494; revolt in, 1508; and uprising against Joseph Bonaparte, 1531; Bonaparte's campaign in, 1595; cedes East Florida to United States, 1806; monarchy restored in, 1844, 1879
Spanish East Indies, 1447
Spanish treaty. *See* Pinckney's treaty
Speculation, spirit of: JM on, 709
Spinning wheel, 1593

Spirit of '76 (Richmond newspaper), 1580
Spoliation claims: against Great Britain, 883; against France, 1256, 1309–10; against Spain, 1354–55, 1356, 1357, 1359, 1417, 1494
Spence, Dr., 554, 555, 583
Spence, Mrs., 554
Sprigg, Richard, Jr., 1030
Sprigg, Sophia (Mrs. John Francis Mercer), 294
Sprigg resolutions, 1030, 1033, 1036, 1037
Springfield, Mass., 196
Squatters Act of 1807, 1619
Squirrel (British vessel of war), 1177
Stack, Gerald, 1798, 1812–13
Stadtholder, 460
Stagg, J. C. A.: quoted, 878, 1658
Stamp Act: of 1794, 845; of 1798, 1024–25, 1027
Stampp, Kenneth M.: quoted, 2001–2
Standing armies, 451, 545, 566, 598, 873
Stanisław II (king of Poland), 699
Staphorst, house of (Jacob and Nicholas van): and Dohrman, 676; and Mazzei, 858; mentioned, 928, 931, 935
Staphorst, Jacob van: plan for funding foreign debt, 576–78; mentioned, 526, 538
Staphorst, Nicholas van, 937
Stark, Bolling, 457
Stark, Theodore, 1192, 1193
"Star-Spangled Banner, The" (song), 1734
State: TJ and JM's use of term, 1072
State interposition: Calhoun's name for nullification, 1980; South Carolina version of, 1982, 1985, 1988
State sovereignty, 447; TJ and JM's use of term, 1072; JM on meaning of, 1981
States' rights: TJ's use of, 1069–70, 1821, 1848–51, 1954, 1965; Roane's views of, 1850
Staunton, Va.: magazine at, 112–13; contender for site of state university, 1785, 1793, 1805; and the Rotunda, 1839, 1840; mentioned, 177, 178, 213, 816, 1907, 1938, 1943
Stebbins, Edward, 1215
Steele, General, 1533
Steele, John, 1045
Steele, Mr., 1156, 1244
Stephen, Adam, 534
Stephen, James, 1451, 1471
Stephen, John, 1263
Stephens, Edward, 605
Stephenson, Mr., 1827
Sterett, Andrew, 128
Steuben, Friedrich Wilhelm Ludolf Gerhard Augustin, Baron von, 159, 160, 169, 186, 190, 198, 1050
Stevens, Edward, 1097, 1307, 1311–22
Stevenson, Andrew, 1987–88
Stewart. *See also* Stuart
Stewart, Dr. *See* Stuart, David
Stewart, Dugald, 1778, 1788, 1789, 1884, 1909
Stewart, Mr., 1695
Stewart, Mr.: and postmaster general, 132
Stewart, Walter, 157, 766
Stirling, Lord. *See* Alexander, William, Lord Stirling
Stock Exchange, 737
Stockton, Richard, 1053, 1095
Stoddard, Amos, 1291
Stodder, David, 166, 179, 180
Stoddert, Benjamin, 1045, 1169, 1174
Stokes, Anson Phelps: quoted, 336
Stone, Thomas, 281, 310, 478, 509
Stonington, Conn., 1464
Stopfield, Captain, 1488
Story, Joseph: JM appoints, to Supreme Court, 1621; on sense of nationhood, 1760; mentioned, 1251, 1330, 1647, 1648
Strawberries, 391
Strode, John, 737
Strode, Mr., 1726

Index

Strong, Caleb, 469, 477, 579, 1310
Strother, French, 785
Stuart, Archibald: favors ratification, 507, 534; on James River canal, 516; on Franco-American relations, 816; mentioned, 245, 1161, 1805, 1938
Stuart, David, 530, 534, 563, 605, 737, 764, 896–97
Stuart, Gilbert, 648, 1792
Stuart, John, 1122
Sugar maple tree, 412, 421, 469, 508, 511, 555, 694
Sulla (from Malta), 529, 542
Sullivan, James, 1310, 1522, 1531–32, 1535
Sullivan, John, 71, 139
Sullivan, Mr., 1437
Summary View of the Rights of British America, A (TJ), 17, 41–42, 50
Sumptuary law, 366, 416
Sumter, General Thomas, 1091
Sumter, Thomas, Jr., 1213, 1233, 1238, 1246, 1274, 1338
Supreme Court: TJ rejects supremacy of, 32–33; JM defends supremacy of, 33–35; refuses to rule on political questions, 799, 804
Surinam, 1375
Surrender of General Burgoyne at Saratoga, The (painting), 1774
Surrender of Lord Cornwallis at Yorktown, The (painting), 1774
Susquehanna River, 217, 429
Suter, Mr., 1543
Swan, James, 899, 1337, 1339
Swansboro, N.C., 1300
Swanwick, John, 834, 860, 1052
Swartout, John, 1408, 1423
Sweden: U.S. treaty with, 234, 262, 263, 883; cooperates with United States in Mediterranean, 1234, 1239; mentioned, 1210, 1710
Swift, Dean, 1225
Symmes land claims, 1233, 1251
Symmonds, Commodore Thomas, 159–60
Syren (U.S. sloop), 1587
Syrett, Harold: quoted, 714

Talavera, Spain, 1604
Talleyrand-Périgord, Charles-Maurice de: and XYZ affair, 1000–1, 1009, 1014, 1034, 1036–37; dismisses Pinkney and Marshall but not Gerry, 1060, 1061; promises reception of American minister (1798–99), 1097, 1098–99; letter to second peace mission, 1133; calls Louisiana a bargain, 1291; and Laussat, 1308; and Armstrong, 1338; and Bonaparte as emperor, 1344; and proposed sale of Florida, 1359, 1405; and western boundary of Louisiana, 1368, 1370; and Miranda episode, 1428
Tangier, 1234
Tappahannock, Va., 280, 322
Target, Guy-Jean-Baptiste, 616, 617, 618
"Tariff of Abominations," 1979
Tariffs: JM signs protective, 1772; Virginia denies constitutionality of protective, 1968; of 1832, 1992; and Clay compromise bill of 1833, 1997; mentioned, 1923, 1954
Tarleton, Banastre, 177
Tatham, William, 1560, 1720, 1724
Tattnall, Josiah, 978, 1093
Taw, Abraham, 1465
Taxation: TJ on, 353; and postponement of Virginia Confederation requisition, 359, 394, 397, 405–6, 415, 416; JM on, 368–69; and Virginia's empty treasury, 456; Virginia levies, 467; under Constitution, 491; and Ways and Means Committee, 838
Tayloe, Benjamin, 1738, 1740
Tayloe, Col., 1897
Tayloe, E., 1897

Taylor, Francis, 97, 103, 114, 117
Taylor, G., 1433
Taylor, Hubbard, 729, 739
Taylor, John: opposes John Marshall's rulings, 34; opposes ratification of Constitution, 507; and "United States of the Bank," 716; elected Virginia senator, 743; writes pamphlet against Bank of the United States, 759, 800, 821, 844; writes JM, 760; writes pamphlet on parties, 844; appointed Virginia commissioner on Potomac boundary, 961; introduces Virginia resolutions, 1071; TJ supports views of, 1869; mentioned, 245, 1527, 1851, 1954
Taylor, Lieutenant John, 97
Taylor, Keith, 1161
Taylor, Mr. (Board of Visitors), 1839
Taylor, Mr. (friend of George Wythe), 909
Taylor, Robert, 1824
Tazewell, Henry: on peace negotiations, 62; and Jay's treaty, 887, 888; TJ writes, about reception as vice president, 959, 962; illness of, 1019; on jury trials in impeachments, 1023, 1025; opposes extension of foreign ministries, 1028; and Sedition Act, 1065, 1068; death of, 1135; mentioned, 245, 323, 958, 978, 1053
Tazewell, Littleton Waller, 1640, 1805, 1912
Tecumseh, 1676, 1712
Telescope, 332, 465
Telfair, Edward, 860
Temple, George Nugent-Temple-Grenville, second earl of, 306
Temple, Sir William, 1360
Tennessee, 1218, 1287, 1331, 1352
Tennis Court Oath, 601
Tenth Amendment, 1080, 1866
Tenure of Office Act, 1825–26
Ternant, Jean Baptiste de, 766, 772, 775
Terrill, Dabney, 1909, 1963, 1964, 1967
Terror, the: in French Revolution, 1066
Texas, 1292, 1357, 1358–59, 1416
Texel, the, 169–70
Textbooks, 1917–19, 1923–26
Thacher, James, 91
Thames (British frigate), 160
Theological Catalogue for the Library of the University of Virginia, A (JM), 1899–1901
Theological schools, 1842
Thierry, J. B. S., 1643
Third Estate: becomes National Assembly, 601, 610, 624–25
Thom, Christopher S., 1213
Thomas, Daniel, 1183
Thomas, Jesse Burgess, 1368–69, 1581
Thomas, John, 741
Thomas, Joseph, 1183
Thomas, Simeon, 1262
Thomas, William (of British navy), 186
Thomas Jefferson Building: at Library of Congress, 15
Thompson, Claud, 1300
Thompson, John, 1366
Thompson, John (father), 1177
Thompson, John (son), 1177
Thompson, John (the Hatter), 1876
Thompson, Jonah, 1465
Thompson, Melissa Jane Smith, 1361
Thomson, Charles, 166, 220, 300, 330, 335, 492, 581, 1284
Thorn, Mr., 1858
Thornton, Anna Maria Brodeau (Mrs. William), 968, 1246, 1440, 1792
Thornton, Edward (British chargé): and the *Windsor,* 1185, 1186, 1188, 1244; and Jay's treaty, 1192; on significance of Louisiana Purchase, 1256; on impressments, 1276, 1280, 1281, 1283; mentioned, 1030, 1204
Thornton, John, 857

Thornton, William: visits Montpellier and Monticello, 1249; and complaint against Latrobe, 1436; designs one-story wings for Montpellier, 1570; and merino sheep, 1621; TJ gives dogs to, 1640, 1641; saves Patent Office building, 1733; mentioned, 1174, 1197, 1246, 1425, 1435, 1440, 1465
Thou, Jacques August de, 352, 367
Thouin, André, 1971
Three-fifths clause, 231
Threilkidd, John, 1465
Threshing machine: TJ's model of, 776, 782, 814, 820; JM on model of, 778; mentioned, 1642
Thruston, Charles Mynn, 245, 402, 404–5
Thumb, Tom, 868
Thweatt, Archibald, 1636
Tichenor, Isaac, 1013
Ticknor, George: declines appointment at Virginia, 1884; recommends Blaettermann, 1885; on architecture of university, 1915; mentioned, 1813, 1831, 1832–33, 1859, 1903
Ticonderoga: battle at, 670
Tilghman, Edward, 921
Tilly, Arnaud de Gardeur de, 181, 182, 195
Tilton, Daniel, 1040, 1045
Tilton, Dr., 1722
Titles: debate over, for president, 592, 608–9, 612, 626, 629
"Titus Manlius" (pseudonym: Alexander Hamilton), 1045
Tiverton, R.I., 1300
Tobacco: price of, in 1784, 338; TJ on international trade in, 366; price of, in 1785, 371, 375; accepted in payment of taxes, 397, 429, 456; in France, 400, 457–58, 690–91, 693; price of, in 1786, 408, 416, 420, 424, 457; Virginia tax on, 439, 467; price of, in 1788, 535, 553; smuggled into Canada, 670; price of, in 1791, 699; price of, in 1794, 831; price of, in 1796, 932; TJ enemy of, 955; price of, in 1797, 979; price of, in 1798, 1012, 1016, 1025, 1050; price of, in 1799, 1089, 1092; price of, in 1800, 1123, 1128; low prices force burning of, 1241; caterpillar attacks, 1425; crop in Maryland, 1430; crop in 1806, 1438; crop in 1809, 1576, 1592; crop in 1812, 1695; crop in 1814, 1739, 1741; crop in 1817, 1781; mentioned, 484, 1027. See also Farmers General
Todd, Dolley Payne: marries "the great little Madison," 847. See also Madison, Dolley Payne Todd
Todd, John, 106
Todd, John Payne (Dolley's son), 967
Todd, Thomas, 1823, 1861
Tom (slave), 161
Tombigbee River, 1416
Tompkins, Daniel D., 1369, 1702
Tomson, Mr., 1341
Tom Thumb. See Thumb, Tom
Tonnage tax: Virginia imposes, on British vessels, 394, 407
Tories: JM uses, as label for Federalists, 890
Toronto. See York (Toronto), Canada
Torrey, John, 1908, 1909
Toulman, Mr. See Toulmin, Harry
Toulmin, Harry, 1277, 1278, 1336, 1337, 1347, 1440
Toulon, 829, 835, 842
Tousard, Lewis, 1187
Toussaint l'Ouverture, François-Dominique: leads slave revolt in Santo Domingo, 1208; and Stevens's case, 1311, 1312–22; succeeded by Dessalines, 1348; mentioned, 1091, 1093, 1096, 1183, 1190
"Toussaint's clause," 1092, 1095
Tower of London: Laurens incarcerated in, 208
Townsend, Secretary Thomas, first Viscount Sydney, 227
Townships: and education, 1776

Tracy, Destutt de, 1690–91, 1909
Tracy, Uriah, 976, 1013, 1019, 1024, 1031, 1053, 1061, 1115
Transcontinental Treaty: and cession of East Florida, 1806
Treadwell, John, 1049
Treason: TJ on Bank of the United States and, 716, 740–41; Whiskey rebels charged with, 851; Lloyd introduces peacetime bill on, 1064; *Porcupine's Gazette* accuses TJ of, 1065; Burr indicted for, 1444; Andrew Jackson on, 1995
Treasury Board (Confederation): insolvency of, 516; and payment to French officers, 538
Treasury Department: provisions establishing, 622; fire in, 1162
Treaty of Amiens, 1207
Treaty of Campo Formio, 1013–14, 1359
Treaty of Fort Stanwix, 215
Treaty of Lancaster, 215
Treaty of Logstown, 215
Treaty of Paris (1783): arrives in Philadelphia, 272; recognizes American independence, 274–75; definitive version of, reaches Congress, 288; ratification of, 293; and British debts, 398–99; and removal of Negroes by British, 459; enforcement of provisions of, 471; obstructions to fulfillment of, 516; unresolved issues of, 711, 712; infractions of, 722–25; mentioned, 209
Treaty of Tilsit, 1452
Treaty of Westminster (1674), 215
Trees: 511, 529
Tremble, James, 1366
Trenton, N.J., 233, 268, 311, 552
Trescott, Samuel, 1418, 1464
Trial by jury: in Bill of Rights, 451, 597, 598
Trinidad, 1361
Trinity River, 1416
Trois Rivières, 1685, 1707
Tripoli: pasha of, declares war on United States, 1170, 1209–10, 1228, 1259; bashaw of, 1193; American campaign against, 1234, 1265, 1284, 1295; and *Philadelphia* case, 1295, 1308, 1325; and Grand Seignor, 1311; negotiations of peace with, 1315; TJ on "barbarians" of and peace with, 1350; treaty with, 1419; ruling family in, 1431–32; mentioned, 1170, 1213
Trist, Elizabeth House (Mrs. Nicholas): and schooling for TJ's daughter, 264, 267; plans reunion with husband, 288; leaves Philadelphia, 290, 344; JM's concern about, 311; at Fort Pitt, 311; death of husband of, 320, 349; corresponds with TJ, 321, 433; returns home after husband's death, 389; mentioned, 244, 251, 325, 780, 1348, 1578, 1580
Trist, Hore Browse, 344, 780, 1128, 1131, 1148, 1151, 1300, 1348
Trist, Mary Brown (Mrs. Hore), 1153
Trist, Nicholas, 349
Trist, Nicholas P.: quoted, 470; mentioned, 1973, 1990, 1992, 1994
Trott, Perient, 152, 158, 162
Troup, Robert, 670, 1042
Troyes, France, 453, 490
Trudeau, Mr., 1521
Trumbull, John: JM subscribes to prints by, 1127, 1135; paints pictures for Rotunda of Capitol, 1774; TJ recalls, in Paris, 1774; and engravings of his historical paintings, 1774; paints *Declaration of Independence* for Capitol, 1878
Trumbull, Jonathan, 849–50, 1213
Trumbull & Co., 149
Truxton, Thomas, 1128, 1131, 1149, 1393
Tucker, George: on JM's sense of humor, 8–9; JM recommends, 1910; TJ on, 1910–11; as professor at Virginia, 1929; writes biography of TJ, 2001;

INDEX   2069

mentioned, 1912, 1921, 1922, 1923, 1928, 1935, 1975
Tucker, Henry St. George: declines appointment at Virginia, 1929; mentioned, 1916, 1926, 1927–28, 1928–29, 1930, 1939
Tucker, St. George: on powers of Virginia Executive Council, 59; as delegate to Annapolis Convention, 404–5; opposes ratification, 507; appointed judge, 532; writes as Jonathan Pindar, 792; drafts bill for reforming Virginia jury system, 1126; mentioned, 82–83
Tucker, Thomas Tudor, 660, 860, 1163, 1197
Tudor, Delia Jarvis (Mrs. William), 1187
Tudor, William, 1187
Tudor, William, Jr., 1187
Tuft, Mr., 1533
Tull, Jethro, 782, 786
Tunis: treaty with, 1170, 1193; bey of, 1192, 1195; sends Mellimelli to United States, 1411; state of affairs with, 1419; mentioned, 1213, 1236, 1301, 1459
Turberville, George Lee, 554, 555
Turgot, Anne-Robert-Jacques, 1603, 1604
Turkey, 290, 514
Turner, Edward, 1266, 1301
Turner, Edward D., 1347
Turner, Joseph, 1300
Turreau, Louis Marie: appointed minister to United States, 1344; protests actions of U.S. armed merchantmen, 1363–64; and General Ferrand's decree, 1369–70, 1371; letter from, 1379, 1381, 1446; and Moreau's visit, 1381, 1383; on Louisiana claims, 1387; and American consul at Martinique, 1393; and trade with Santo Domingo, 1433; complaints of, must be supported by affidavits, 1436; JM rejects request for loan, 1439, 1440, 1441; on violations of jurisdiction and indemnification, 1469; asks for advance against account on Beaujoin, 1472, 1474; requests transportation for French stranded by embargo, 1519, 1520, 1533, 1535–36, 1537; complains of enlistment of French deserters, 1523, 1524; TJ and JM on lack of writing skills of, 1542; JM complains about complaints of, 1543, 1545; on TJ's ambitions for Cuba, 1568, 1587; on Erskine Agreement and repeal of French edicts, 1587; mentioned, 1434, 1546, 1609
Tuscany, 217
Tutwiler, Henry, 1920
Twelfth Amendment, 1340, 1352
Twenty-seventh Amendment, 599
Two Million Dollar Act, 1405, 1408
Tyler, Comfort, 1471
Tyler, John: as Speaker of Virginia House, 278, 369–70; and law of nations, 360; loses to Harrison for Speaker, 401; appointed to Virginia Court of Admiralty, 408; opposes ratification, 534; TJ recommends, for Supreme Court, 1620; TJ's appraisal of, 1631–32; JM appoints, as federal district judge, 1632; applies for federal office, 1632–33; mentioned, 245, 1631, 1632–33
Tyng, Dudley A., 1230
Typhus fever, 1827, 1828, 1829

Ubbo. *See* Emmius, Ubbo
Umbrella cane, 487
Underwood, Reuben, 364, 369
Unemployed, 334
Union (U.S. ship), 1547
Union: JM views, as perpetual, 36, 1986, 2001–2
United Netherlands: and stadtholder, 498
United States (U.S. warship): takes *Macedonian*, 1685
United States: suspends payment on debt to France, 747; resumes payment of debt to France, 748; and French seizure of neutral ships, 1027–28, 1028–29; envoys from, refused official recognition as American negotiators, 1015, 1025, 1029; defense measures of, in 1798, 1019–20, 1028, 1031; Capitol of, burned by British, 1731, 1773
University of Geneva, 874
University of Virginia: and Rockfish Gap commission, 1794–95; wins legislative approval, 1795; first meeting of Board of Visitors, 1796; appoints Cooper as first professor, 1796; annual reports of, 1798–99, 1813, 1819, 1836; fund raising for, 1800, 1817, 1819, 1833; and Panic of 1819, 1806, 1817; plan of, for buildings and gardens, 1811–12, 1820, 1842, 1855; and Rotunda, 1819; TJ on finances of, 1822, 1834–35, 1892; pavilions and dormitories of, completed (1822), 1842; library of, 1887–88, 1898–1901, 1902, 1922; professors arrive at, 1915; classes begin at, 1915, 1916; law professorship at, 1916; student riots at, 1920, 1942; George Tucker appointed at, 1929; budgets for 1825, 1826, and 1827, 1936–37; funding cut off, 1953, 1958, 1965, 1967; TJ transfers care of, to JM, 1959, 1974; JM on, and liberty, 1960; Wirt appointed at, 1968; TJ dissents on appointing president of, 1969; Lomax appointed professor of law at, 1969; JM on TJ's devotion to, 1975
Upper Canada, 1490
Urqhart, Thomas, 1336, 1337
Utrum Horum? (Irish pamphlet), 982

Vail, Mr., 1246, 1337
Valmy, France, 779
Van Berckel, Pieter Johan: Dutch minister to United States, 251, 472–73
Van Buren, Martin, 1947, 1957, 1961
Van Cortlandt, Philip, 1012, 1041
Vancouver Island, 645
Vandalia Company, 151, 215
Vanderburgh, Henry, 1523
Van der Kemp, Francis Adrian, 533
Vaneuxeur, Professor, 1904
Van Ness, William Peter, 1950
Van Rensselaer, Stephen, 873, 1684, 1685, 1707
Van Staphorsts. *See* Staphorst, house of
Varina: plantation of Thomas Mann and Martha Jefferson Randolph, 872
Varnum, James Mitchell, 164, 194, 873
Varnum, Joseph Bradley, 1670
Van Staphorsts. *See* Staphorst, house of
Vattel, Emmerich von, 360, 749, 770, 772–73
Vaudreuil, Louis-Philippe de Rigaud, marquis de, 224, 625
Vaughan, John, 477, 479
Vauguyon, M. *See* La Vauguyon, Paul François de Quélon de Stuer de Caussade, duc de
Venable, Abraham B., 742, 830, 950, 976, 1530
Vengeance, La (French frigate), 1128
Venice: ducal palace of, 1775
Vergennes, Charles Gravier, comte de: Lafayette writes to, on navigation of Mississippi, 343, 344, 345, 346; TJ's appraisal of, 436, 463–64; death of, 451, 482
Vermond, Matthieu Jacques, abbé de, 625
Vermont: and negotiations with New York for statehood, 311, 473, 614; TJ and JM visit, 670, 687; and election of 1796, 958–59; federal lawsuits in, 1217; in election of 1812, 1685
Vermont, Abbé. *See* Vermond, Matthieu Jacques, abbé de
Vernon, John, 1464
Versailles, France, 602, 625
Vetch, 871, 875
Vettenhort, Mr., 1425
"Vices of the Political System of the United States" (JM), 441, 448

Vidua, Count Carlo, 11
Vildeiul, M. *See* Villedeiul, Pierre-Charles-Laurent de
Villandry, Mr., 1332
Villebrune, Jacques Aimé Le Sarge, chavalier de la, 217, 218–19, 223–24
Villedeuil, Pierre-Charles-Laurent de, 544, 625
Villeneuve, Admiral Pierre-Charles-Jean-Baptiste-Silvestre de, 1413–14
Vincennes, 63, 78, 80, 1348
Vincennes River, 1426
Vining, John, 736
Virginia: and Constitution of 1776, 18, 29, 51, 1991; and proposed revision of state Constitution, 18, 235, 245, 322, 353–54, 420; House of Burgesses of, opposes closing Boston port, 40–41; convention of 1775 in, 43; and convention of 1776 and resolution for independence, 48, 49, 1877; House of Delegates of, praises TJ's service in Congress, 53; committee on religion of, 55; state financial system of, 64, 88, 324; Board of War of, 65–66, 67, 73, 97–98, 108, 111, 114–15; state navy of, 66, 80, 85–86, 88–89, 103, 119; Board of Trade of, 104; assembly requests Continental troops, 140; abandons Continental currency as legal tender, 195; western land claims of, 202–3, 204, 210, 214–15, 247–48, 264, 294; and revenue system of 1783, 238; postwar economic conditions in, 279, 280; and navigation of Potomac, 356–57; Maison Carrée as model for Capitol of, 381, 413, 420; and paper money, 430; Jefferson-Fry map of, 492; ratifies Constitution, 504–5, 507, 508, 509, 521, 532, 541–42, 553; and bill on crimes and punishments, 506; and amendments of 1795, 887, 888, 917, 1016; TJ's collection of laws of, 908–15; legislature adopts resolution condemning Cabell's presentment, 975, 986–90; TJ fears efforts to coerce, 1091; election of 1800 in, 1111–12, 1125, 1126, 1130, 1134, 1139, 1153; legislature votes pay increase, 1126; federal lawsuits in, 1218; Gabriel's Rebellion in, 1204; election results in (1809), 1585; legislature opposes protective tariffs, 1976; legislature opposes South Carolina's nullification doctrine, 1996
Virginia and Farmers Bank, 1830
Virginia Creed, 1917, 1927
Virginia Declaration of Rights: and George Mason, 18, 50; JM and, 50, 522; and freedom of religion, 50; cited by JM in "A Memorial and Remonstrance," 376, 377, 378, 379; serves as model for French Declaration of the Rights of Man, 528, 603; serves as model for federal Bill of Rights, 597; mentioned, 448
Virginia Document of 1799. *See* "Report on the [Virginia] Resolutions"
Virginia Executive Council: JM elected to, 57; constitutional authority of, 59; requests Spanish aid, 61; critical of Congress, 62, 70–71; and British prisoners of war, 63–64, 78–79, 84, 113–14; and state finances, 64–65, 71, 88; and quest for firearms, 65–66, 73; and state navy, 66, 85–86, 88–89; and military recruitment, 67, 78, 79, 81, 103, 104, 105, 117, 142–43; and relocation of state capital, 66–67; and range of issues dealt with, 61–62, 68; proclaims embargo, 68, 118–19, 179; and Henry Hamilton's case, 72, 74–76, 89–90, 91–95; advises TJ to act without council's consent, if no quorum, 68, 112; and Conrad Alexandre Gérard, 69; and Benjamin Harrison, 73, 98, 103; and Continental Board of War, 76–77; and Charles Scott, 80; authorizes trade with Bermuda, 82–83; and flags of truce, 83; and public buildings in Richmond, 84; and alien enemies, 86–87, 403; appoints Peter Penet as commercial agent, 88; and frontier defense, 95; and state Board of War, 97–98, 108, 111, 112–13, 114–15, 178–79; and military supplies, 98–103, 148, 161; and state Board of Trade, 104, 105–6, 119; requests Spanish aid, 106–8; and Cherokee Indians, 109–10; and French consul, 116; and George Washington, 116–18; authorizes slaves to conduct foundry, 119; and American prisoners of war, 119–20; and Bland's expense account, 120; and retention of Continental arms, 121–23; TJ on duties of, 296; JM critical of, 302
Virginia Federalist, 1137
Virginia Plan: JM outlines, 441–42; approved by Virginia delegation to Philadelphia convention, 443; provisions of, 443–44
Virginia port bill (1784): enacted, 279–80; European reaction to, 327; JM on, 337–38; TJ on, 349; and trade within state, 373–74; effort to amend, defeated, 405; Eastern Shore ports added, 456; George Mason opposes, 510; mentioned, 322, 420
Virginia resolutions: JM writes, 1067, 1070–71; distinguishes between state and legislature, 1085; North Carolina legislative action on, 1123; JM interprets, 1983, 1986
Virginia revised code of laws: committee appointed to revise laws, 54–55; revision of laws, 283, 291, 292, 310, 416, 507; report on revisal of state laws printed, 323, 364; final phase of, 436–37; supplemental revision committee appointed, 455, 466–67; TJ on, 459; Patrick Henry opposes further consideration of, 510; JM on TJ's work on, 1975
Virginia Statute for Religious Freedom: JM on importance of, 402–3; inserted in *Encyclopédie méthodique,* 458–59; and majority rule, 522; mentioned, 29, 56, 393–94
Vitruvius, Pollio, 1822
Volney, Constantin-François Chassebouef, comte de; doubts France will make peace with England, 981; target of Alien Friends Act, 1003, 1042, 1045; sails for France, 1055, 1057; mentioned, 950
Volney sur la guerre des Turcs, 539
Vonnegut, Kurt, 15
Vowles, Mr., 1524

Wabash River, 475
Wadsworth, Colonel Jeremiah, 636
Wafford's settlement, 1575
Wagner, Jacob (JM's chief clerk): and printing of laws, 1184, 1226; edits Federalist paper, 1185; sends commissions for JM's signature, 1187; and "Danish Resident," 1189; and William Eaton, 1191; and Barbary powers, 1193; and instructions to Livingston, 1195, 1280; illness of, 1221; considered for commissioner of bankruptcy, 1231; and handling of pardons, 1273, 1274, 1275; and Armstrong's appointment to France, 1334; and commissions for Louisiana, 1336; and TJ, 1341; and JM's letter to Pichon, 1344; and Mobile Act, 1346; and Yrujo, 1347; on black convicts from Surinam, 1375; TJ on skills of, 1392; and extradition of fugitives, 1434; sends commission to John Page, 1435; transmits letters for TJ, 1436; and Thomas Lewis, 1437; and Mellimelli, 1438; becomes harsh critic of JM, 1614; mentioned, 1213, 1279, 1345, 1393, 1440
Walcheren Island, 1604, 1607
Waldoboro, Me., 1250
Walk, Mr., 605
Walker, Brian, 1300
Walker, Elizabeth (Betsey) Moore (Mrs. John): TJ admits impropriety of conduct towards, 1480, 1645
Walker, Francis (Frank), 8, 769, 871, 875, 1134, 1381

Walker, John, 145, 150–51, 897, 1018, 1480, 1491
Walker, Robert, 1263
Walker, Thomas, 60, 350
Walking stick, 465
Wall, Mr., 1962–63
Wallace, Dr., 1284
Waller, Benjamin, 60, 408
Walls, George, 96
Walls, Thomas, 96
Walpole, Horace, 3
Walpole Company, 215
Walter, Thomas: author of *Flora Caroliniana,* 584
Walton, George, 478
Walton's Polyglot, 1898
Ward, Samuel, 1268, 1300
Warden, Davis Bailie: visits Monticello, 1660; controversy with Crawford, 1747; JM dismisses, 1751–52; mentioned, 1489, 1595, 1596, 1662, 1663–64, 1690
War Department, 613, 622, 1162
Wards: and education, 1776
Ware v. *Hylton,* 921
War for American Independence, *See* American Revolution
War in Disguise (James Stephen), 1451, 1471, 1474, 1475
Warminster, Va., 1894
Warm Springs, Va., 1795
War of 1812: British destroy Library of Congress, 15; grievances causing, 1680; as Second War for American Independence, 1681, 1754; TJ recommends harsh treatment for Federalist opponents of, 1682; campaign against Canada, 1683–85; declaration of, 1698; Montreal campaign (1813), 1713; campaign of 1814, 1730–32, 1734–35
Warren, Henry, 1230, 1300
Warren, Sir John, 1710
Warrenton, N.C., 1525
Warville, Brissot de. *See* Brissot de Warville, Jacques-Pierre
Washington, Bushrod, 534, 961
Washington, George: JM sends *Federalist* essays to, 29; appointed to command colonial troops, 45; appoints Charles Lee as commanding general in Southern Department, 49; victories at Trenton and Princeton, 58; at Valley Forge, 58; on treatment of prisoners of war, 64, 78–79, 89–90, 114; urges best men to serve in Congress, 68; and Virginia troops, 116–17; supports Bland's expense account, 120; on lack of food for army, 136; and financing of the Revolution, 138; suppresses mutiny, 139; and Arnold's treason, 132, 147; warns of invasion of Virginia in 1781, 156; TJ requests military assistance from, 173; and campaign of 1781, 174, 181–82, 200; TJ congratulates, on Yorktown victory, 205; and demobilization, 233, 263; confers with Sir Guy Carleton, 247; on peacetime army, 266; TJ reviews Virginia land cession with, 272; interest in canals, 331; and navigation of Potomac, 296, 356–57, 389, 403, 459, 516; JM visits, 388–89; JM writes inscription for Houdon's statue of, 411; supports George Mason, 420; on lands on Mohawk, 432; delegate to Constitutional Convention, 454, 468, 470, 476, 477, 932; supports ratification, 504, 509, 521–22; writes to TJ, 554; elected president, 554, 579, 590, 605, 606; recommends Bill of Rights, 594; illness of, 622, 623, 701, 702–3, 781, 787; appoints TJ secretary of state, 637, 638, 639, 654; and Nootka Sound incident, 645–47, 657–59; and communications from states to Congress, 647, 655, 656; visits Rhode Island with TJ, 662; and TJ and JM (1790), 663, 664; and Bank of the United States, 666; and District of Columbia, 673, 707; TJ informs, of JM's discussion with Beckwith, 681–83; first convenes cabinet, 710; and Mt. Vernon, 689, 736, 737, 738, 767, 811, 818, 967; relations of, with JM, 708; and commercial reciprocity, 711; and negotiations with Hammond, 712, 726; and Jefferson-Hamilton animosity, 713–14, 715–16; signs mint bill, 718; and discussion of hereditary descent versus election, 728; dines with Joseph Brant, 733; and second term, 715–16, 730, 740, 744; recognizes French Republic, 747–48; and neutrality, 748, 749–50, 752, 774; and Democratic Society of Philadelphia, 756–57, 804; and TJ's retirement from cabinet, 757, 805–7; and federal commissioners' compensation, 764–65; thin skinned about criticism, 781–82; and Proclamation of Neutrality, 786–87, 799, 801, 805; and Genet, 803; TJ visits, 821; at Germantown, 822, 828, 829–30; JM on influence of (1794), 827; and Jay's treaty, 827, 840, 882, 886, 887, 889–90, 892, 895, 925, 929; on place of meeting of Congress, 828; visits Reading, Pa., 829; meets Fauchet, 833; authorizes sale of French prizes, 846; denounces Democratic societies, 851, 861–62, 862–64, 867; and Whiskey Rebellion, 850, 851, 854, 859; TJ writes to, about University of Geneva, 874, 875; forces resignation of Edmund Randolph, 886; birthday celebrated in 1796, 889, 922; TJ critical of, 892, 928, 944; Paine breaks with, 907; and treaty with Algiers, 921; sends Pinckney's treaty to Senate, 921; delivers journal of Constitutional Convention to secretary of state, 930; signs appropriation bills to implement Jay's, Pinckney's, Greenville, and Algiers treaties, 936; Farewell Address of, 940, 1847–48, 1861, 1919, 1925, 1926; and relations with France, 951, 956, 961; and TJ's letter to Mazzei, 972, 985–86; disavows forged letters, 991; birthday ball for, in 1798, 997–98, 1020, 1024, 1027; John Adams appoints, as commander in chief during quasi war, 1008, 1056, 1086; death of, 1113; Adams's "oblique stroke" at, 1157; TJ on administrative procedures under, 1168, 1171, 1202; and passports for Mediterranean, 1178; and policy towards belligerents, 1188; TJ invokes name of, 1446; TJ lists final correspondence with, 1558; and Indian wars, 1732, 1744; recommends national university, 1775; inaugural address of, 1919, 1925, 1926; mentioned, 23, 129, 189, 193, 495, 553, 802, 1975, 1979
Washington, George Steptoe, 847, 857
Washington, John Augustine, 477
Washington, Lucy Payne (Mrs. George Steptoe), 847
Washington, Martha (Mrs. George), 664, 708, 821
Washington, William Augustine, 143
Washington (American packet), 209
Washington College (Chestertown, Md.), 146
Washington College (Lexington, Va.), 1793
Washington County (D.C.), 1465
Washington, D.C.: TJ visits as vice president, 1140; British burn, 1731; JM reenters, 1733; mentioned, 1151, 1330, 1519, 1523, 1524
Wasp (U.S. frigate), 1470, 1473, 1536, 1607, 1610, 1696
Watch, pocket: TJ orders for JM, 411, 419, 459, 487, 493–94, 529
Waterhouse, Benjamin; 1719, 1721
Watkins, George, 1263
Watkins, Dr. John, 1343
Watkins, T. G., 1817, 1822, 1829, 1841
Watson, David: and Central College, 1776, 1777, 1784, 1785, 1787, 1802, 1807, 1808, 1809
Watson, James, 1131
Watson, William, 1300
Watts, John, 865, 872
Way, Nicholas, 993

Wayles, John (father-in-law of TJ), 908
Wayne, Anthony: commands Pennsylvania Line, 156, 173, 189, 201; and western campaign against Indians, 830, 863–64, 873; mentioned, 819
Ways and Means Committee. *See* House of Representatives
Weasel, 425–28
Weather observations: TJ begins, 293, 307, 371
Webb, Foster, 548
Webster, Daniel: cites JM on tariffs, 1984–85, 1987, 1996
Webster, Noah: on TJ's "Report on Weights and Measures," 677; writes as "Curtius," 897, 898; attacks Edmund Randolph, 904; and TJ's Mazzei letter, 973; predicts French invasion will install TJ and JM as American Directory, 1010; on TJ's removal of Goodrich, 1185; TJ's appraisal of, 1186; mentioned, 1156
Weedon, George, 160
Wellesley, Sir Arthur. *See* Wellington, Arthur Wellesley, first duke of
Wellesley, Richard Colley, first marquis of: and anti-American colleagues, 1626; and Pinkney, 1627, 1663; JM says views of, tied to American elections, 1631; and Foster's mission, 1665; and War of 1812, 1714; mentioned, 1617, 1637, 1656, 1691, 1698
Wellington, Arthur Wellesley, first duke of, 1604, 1678, 1714, 1754
Welscher, Joseph, 1215
Wentworth, George, 1250
Wentworth, John (lieutenant governor of Nova Scotia), 1377
West, Benjamin, 819, 1774
West, John S., 1418, 1483
Western lands: and ratification of Articles of Confederation, 129–31; state cessions of, 202–3, 247–48, 473, 475, 506, 512, 530; TJ on state claims of, 294–95; survey and sale of, 473, 475, 506, 512, 530; and payment of national debt, 454, 461, 481; foreign investments in, 460; mentioned, 204
Western settlements: government for, 475
Western states: TJ favors small ones, 458
West Florida: boundary of, 1022; as part of Louisiana Purchase, 1291; Folch protests American claims to, 1329; R. R. Livingston on, 1331; negotiations with Spain for, 1354–55; sale of land in, 1358; Spain rejects American claims to, 1367–68; cabinet proposes cession of, to United States, 1396; revolt in, 1648; annexed to Orleans Territory, 1648; mentioned, 1256
Westham, Va.: site of armament factory, 65, 99, 100, 119; canal at, 516
West Indies: U.S. trade with, 235, 246, 620–21, 883; mentioned, 824, 1447
Weston, Mr., 1425
Westover (plantation), 159
West Point, N.Y., 131–32
West Point, Va., 154
Wethersfield, Conn., 174, 200
Wetmore, William, 1040
Wharton, Samuel, 215
Whately, Thomas, 399
Wheat: crop in 1784, 338; crop in 1785, 371; crop in 1786, 408, 424, 428; crop in 1787, 484; crop in 1790, 654; crop in 1791, 687; crop in 1792, 730, 733, 738; crop in 1793, 778, 785, 788, 794, 798; crop in 1794, 831, 844, 858, 860, 865, 900; price in 1795, 905; crop in 1796, 918, 926, 932; crop in 1797, 955; crop in 1798, 1012, 1015, 1016, 1025, 1058, 1060; samples of, from Buenos Aires and Chile, 1385; crop in 1806, 1429; crop in 1808, 1524–25, 1529; crop in 1809, 1576, 1580, 1585, 1586; crop in 1810, 1624, 1639; crop in 1811, 1686;
crop in 1812, 1693, 1694, 1695, 1699, 1700; crop in 1813, 1715, 1719, 1723; crop in 1814, 1741, 1743; crop in 1817, 1781; crop in 1819, 1815–16; mentioned, 1022, 1027, 1038, 1050
Wheaton, Henry, 1895
Wheeler, Isaac, 1301
Wheeler, Mr., 1272
Whippoorwill, 840
Whiskey Rebellion: excise officer forced to resign, 775; in western Pennsylvania, 850–54; mopping-up operations following, 854; TJ critical of suppression of, 864, 867–68; and Edmund Randolph, 886
Whit, Mr., 1719
Whitcomb, Samuel, 11
White, Alexander, 245, 534, 605, 768, 1031
White, Anthony Walton, 143
White, Mr.: and Burr conspiracy, 1444, 1467
White, Richard, 97
White House: restoration of, 1773
Whitehurst, John, 459
White over Black (Winthrop D. Jordan), 16
White pine, 690
Whiting, Thomas, 84
Whitten, L., 1084
Whitten, W., 1084
Wiatt, William, 1012
Wickelhausen, Frederick Jacob, 1337
Wickham, John, 1633
Wicquefort, Abraham van, 319, 352
Wigginton, Mr., 1340–41
Wikoff, William, 1336, 1337, 1343
Wilberforce, William, 723
Wilkes, John, 1087
Wilkinson, James: compensation to, 1304–5; appointed governor of Louisiana Territory, 1365; and Burr conspiracy, 1443, 1471, 1487, 1663, 1664; and Neutral Ground Agreement, 1455, 1458; Monroe on, 1565, 1611; TJ's appraisal of, 1664–65; court martial of, 1687; invades Canada, 1713, 1730; relieved of command, 1731; mentioned, 1197, 1440, 1474
Willett, Marinus, 203
William III (king of England), 94
William and Mary, College of: Continental troops quartered in, 49; Reverend James Madison at, 52; President's House at, 59; law school established at, 128, 143; TJ revises curriculum of, 128; and distribution of TJ's *Notes*, 334–35, 372, 401; TJ sends books to, 487; as contender for designation as state university, 1793, 1796, 1807; and proposed move to Richmond, 1893–94, 1912, 1913, 1926; TJ favors discontinuance of, 1913; mentioned, 1788, 1789, 1860, 1887, 1909
Williamos, Charles, 410
Williams, David Rogerson, 1552
Williams, Eli, 1427
Williams, Jonathan, 152
Williams, Mr., 1441
Williams, Robert, 1272, 1336, 1337, 1471
Williams, Samuel, 1220
Williams, Thomas H., 1471, 1475
Williamsburg, Va.: Dunmore seizes colonial gunpower in, 43–44; Dunmore abandons, 48; Continental troops in, 48–49; description of, 52; state capital moves from, 66; efforts to return Virginia capital to, 413
Williamson, Hugh, 293, 478
Williamson, John Postal, 1215
Willing, Thomas, 819, 828
Willis, William, 1301
Willocks, Alexander, 921
Willow oak trees, 529, 542
Wilmington, Del., 552
Wilmington, N.C., 1464

INDEX

Wilson, James: represents Simon Nathan, 168; delegate to Constitutional Convention, 478, 932; and Bill of Rights, 513, 564; and Whiskey Rebellion, 858; TJ loans books to, 858, 859, 861, 876; mentioned, 222
Wilson, Joseph, 1250
Wilson, Mr., 1341, 1525
Wimpffen, Baron Félix de, 794
Winchester, James, 1705, 1709, 1717
Winchester, Virginia, 1907, 1926
Winder, William, Jr., 1013
Windsor (British snow), 1185, 1186, 1188, 1189, 1244, 1245
Wine: castor for, 685–87
Winn, Dr., 1372
Winston, Captain, 1518
Winston, Dr., 1346
Winston, Isaac, Sr., 1136, 1149, 1175, 1332
Winston, John, 97
Wirt, William: elected clerk of Virginia House, 1121–22; represents TJ in batture case, 1633, 1640, 1642, 1645; and Duane, 1667; rejects appointment at University of Virginia, 1959, 1968, 1969, 1970; mentioned, 1605, 1666
Wirth, Mr., 1337
Witherall, Judge, 1523
Witherspoon, John, 684
Wolcott, Alexander, 1647
Wolcott, Oliver, Jr., appointed comptroller of treasury, 700; TJ on, 807; JM on, 816; succeeds Hamilton, 869, 890; role of, in resignation of Edmund Randolph, 886; attends Washington ball, 998, 1024; lists Republican leadership triumvirate, 995; attempts to tie TJ to treasonable plot, 1009–10; to be retained in case of war, 1028; on federal commission relating to western lands of Georgia, 1211; mentioned, 660, 766
Wolcott, Oliver, Sr., 347–48
Wolf by the Ears, The: Thomas Jefferson and Slavery (John Chester Miller), 21
Wolfius, Christianus, 304, 319
Wolleston, Frederick H., 1301
Wood, Captain, 675
Wood, James, 114
Wood, General James, 605
Wood, Joseph, 1251
Wood, Mr., 1673
Woodbery Forest School, Va., 774
Woodhouse, Professor, 1896
Woodlands (estate), 1136
Woods, David, 720
Woods, William, 1134
Wood's grist mill, 1429, 1486
Woodward, Augustus Brevoort, 1498, 1523, 1524, 1809
Woodward, Mr., 1469
Wool: and merino sheep, 1621
Wormley, Ralph, Jr., 534
Worthington, Thomas, 1224, 1229–30
Wren, Colonel, 1176, 1177
Wright, Camilla, 1907
Wright, Fanny, 1907
Wright, Governor, 1699
Wright, Joseph, 819
Wright, Mrs. Joseph, 819
Wyatt, Mr. *See* Wiatt, William
Wykoff, Mr. *See* Wikoff, William

Wythe, Elizabeth Taliafarro (Mrs. George), 478, 492, 503
Wythe, George: on Virginia Constitution of 1776, 51; TJ on, 52; on committee to revise Virginia laws, 54, 330; heads law school at William and Mary, 128, 143; and Simon Nathan, 168; and Confederation, 234; on distribution of TJ's *Notes*, 335, 401; monitors Peter Carr's education, 342, 433, 479; on Maury's school, 370; JM visits, 392; and supplemental revision of Virginia code, 455, 466; as delegate to Constitutional Convention, 468, 470, 476, 477, 478, 492; TJ ships books to, 492, 507; and federal Constitution, 509, 534; TJ sends information to, 647; and Genet, 811; TJ writes to, 848; opposes Jay's treaty, 886, 896; TJ sends volumes of laws to, 907–15; TJ sends JM copies of letters to, 918; and Dr. Wallace, 1284; and election of 1800, 1112; and Declaration of Independence, 1878; mentioned, 245, 532, 587, 1847

Xebeck (ship), 1421
XYZ affair: and repressive legislation, 1063; Gerry's correspondence on, 1091; and Talleyrand, 1359; Gerry's role in, 1853; JM on, 1854; mentioned, 1000–1, 1034–35, 1072, 1142

Yancey, Robert, 1134
Yard, James, 1090, 1093, 1241, 1321, 1620
Yates, Robert, 469, 478, 873, 876
Yazoo land compromise, 1221–24, 1405
Yellow fever: in Philadelphia (1793), 760, 814, 818, 819, 829, 830, 874; in Santo Domingo, 1209; in Philadelphia (1805), 1362, 1380, 1384, 1385, 1386, 1388, 1394; in New York (1805), 1393; mentioned, 1086–87, 1192, 1231, 1399
York, James Stuart, duke of, 215
York, Pa., 181, 189
York (Toronto), Canada, 1731
York River, Va., 154
Yorktown, Va.: and Virginia Port Bill of 1784, 279–80, 322, 349; mentioned, 154, 155, 1251, 1476, 1577
Young, Alfred F.: quoted, 731
Young, Moses, 1310
Young, Mr., 1392
Young, Nicholas, 1465
Young, Robert, 1465
Yrujo, Don Carlos Martínez d': protests insult to Spanish flag, 1227; on right of deposit at New Orleans, 1263, 1265, 1266; protests sale of Louisiana, 1285, 1342; denounces Mobile Act, 1292; visits Monticello (1804), 1293, 1345, 1346; recalled, 1293, 1347; breaks with JM, 1324; attempts to bribe editor, 1346; JM on maneuvers of, in Philadelphia, 1379; sends JM samples of wheat, 1385; expulsion of, 1385, 1391, 1392; exchanges insults with JM, 1415; ordered to leave United States, 1426–27; at Cadiz, 1579; mentioned, 1381, 1469, 1522, 1606
Yrujo, Sarah McKean (Mrs. Carlos) d', 1087, 1292, 1293, 1324, 1346
Yusuf (pasha of Tripoli), 1431
Yznardi, Josef M., 1436, 1440, 1489, 1582, 1583

Zane, Isaac, 77, 273, 319, 324
Zeigler, Mr., 1368
Zimmerman, Eberhard A. W. von, 732

ABOUT THE EDITOR

James Morton Smith is Director Emeritus of The Henry Francis du Pont Winterthur Museum and a past Director of the Wisconsin State Historical Society. In addition to his many books, he is general editor of the bicentennial series The States and the Nation, published by W. W. Norton & Company.